80591

The Clinical Psychology Handbook
(PGPS-120)

Pergamon Titles of Related Interest

Anchin/Kiesler HANDBOOK OF INTERPERSONAL
PSYCHOTHERAPY
Hersen/Bellack BEHAVIORAL ASSESSMENT: A Practical Handbook,
Second Edition
Karoly/Kanfer SELF-MANAGEMENT AND BEHAVIOR CHANGE:
From Theory to Practice
Matson/Mulick HANDBOOK OF MENTAL RETARDATION
Walker CLINICAL PRACTICE OF BEHAVIOR THERAPY, Third Edition

Related Journals*

ADVANCES IN BEHAVIOUR RESEARCH AND THERAPY
BEHAVIORAL ASSESSMENT
BEHAVIOUR RESEARCH AND THERAPY
CLINICAL PSYCHOLOGY REVIEW
PERSONALITY AND INDIVIDUAL DIFFERENCES

*Free specimen copies available upon request.

PERGAMON GENERAL PSYCHOLOGY SERIES
EDITORS
Arnold P. Goldstein, *Syracuse University*
Leonard Krasner, *SUNY at Stony Brook*

The Clinical Psychology Handbook

edited by
Michel Hersen
University of Pittsburgh School of Medicine

Alan E. Kazdin
University of Pittsburgh School of Medicine

Alan S. Bellack
*Medical College of Pennsylvania at
Eastern Pennsylvania Psychiatric Institute*

PERGAMON PRESS
New York   Oxford   Toronto   Sydney   Paris   Frankfurt

Pergamon Press Offices:

U.S.A.   Pergamon Press Inc., Maxwell House, Fairview Park,
                     Elmsford, New York 10523, U.S.A.

U.K.   Pergamon Press Ltd., Headington Hill Hall,
                     Oxford OX3 0BW, England

CANADA   Pergamon Press Canada Ltd., Suite 104, 150 Consumers Road,
                     Willowdale, Ontario M2J 1P9, Canada

AUSTRALIA   Pergamon Press (Aust.) Pty. Ltd., P.O. Box 544,
                     Potts Point, NSW 2011, Australia

FRANCE   Pergamon Press SARL, 24 rue des Ecoles,
                     75240 Paris, Cedex 05, France

FEDERAL REPUBLIC Pergamon Press GmbH, Hammerweg 6,
OF GERMANY   D-6242 Kronberg-Taunus, Federal Republic of Germany

Copyright © 1983 Pergamon Press Inc.

Library of Congress Cataloging in Publication Data

Main entry under title:

The Clinical psychology handbook.

    (Pergamon general psychology series ; 120)
    Includes indexes.
    1. Clinical psychology. 2. Psychotherapy.
3. Personality assessment. I. Hersen, Michel.
II. Kazdin, Alan E. III. Bellack, Alan S. [DNLM:
1. Psychology, Clinical. WM 105 C636]
RC467.C586   1983   616.89   82-24567
ISBN 0-08-028058-7

Printed in the United States of America

CONTENTS

PREFACE

To state that the field of clinical psychology has expanded greatly in the last two decades is probably something of an understatement. Indeed, one should say that the area has exploded geometrically. Surprising as it may seem, though, no attempt has been made to compact this accumulation of data in one sourcebook since Benjamin B. Wolman's massive tome was published in 1965. Those of us who were in graduate school in those days appreciated that effort, since even at that time the data base for our field was massive. But today a computer search would be required to help us keep abreast of the exciting developments that have taken place.

When we first undertook the task of outlining the contents for *The Clinical Psychology Handbook* in 1981, we were struck most by how the number of activities clinical psychologists now pursue has increased since the 1960s. This, of course, is something that we have attempted to underscore in our endeavor. Consider the following areas of interest today that were only nascent in the 1960s: mental health policy; community psychology; single-case experimental research; behavioral assessment; a multitude of behavior therapy strategies; behavioral medicine; concern with pharmacological treatments; psychopathology in minorities; primary prevention; and experimental designs calling for multivariate statistics.

In considering marked changes in these two decades, we present the reader with a review of contemporary theory, research, and practice. But we also have done our best to preserve the important and classic contributions of the past. It is safe to say that each of our authors was fully aware of the rich legacy left us by our eminent predecessors in clinical psychology. And, the historic basis for present-day thinking has been fully acknowledged.

Our handbook is divided into six major sections. The first, "General Issues," deals with history, theoretical foundations, clinical training, roles, and mental health policy. The second is concerned with the spectrum of "Personality Theories and Models." The third part involves an examination of "Research Issues and Problems" facing the field. This is followed by chapters on "Assessment and Diagnosis" that cover diagnosis, interviewing, personality assessment, intellectual evaluation, neuropsychological evaluation, behavioral assessment, psychophysiological assessment, and medical assessment. The next section, "Treatment," encompasses the major approaches that are carried out today. Finally, the section on "Community Approaches" addresses issues ranging from primary prevention to actual consultation in the community setting.

As editors, we each carried our fair share of the editorial burden. But we definitely must acknowledge the contribution of numerous individuals who eagerly participated in the development and completion of this project. First and foremost are our eminent contributors who cheerfully agreed to carry out the dictates of their tasks. We are most grateful to them for sharing with us and with you their thinking about their respective areas of expertise. Next, we sincerely thank our secretaries (Mary Newell, Susan Capozzoli, and Claudia Wolfson) who typed and retyped many parts of the manuscript. We thank the good people at Pergamon Press for their herculean effort to put this large manuscript into readable form. Finally, but hardly least of all, we appreciate the tireless efforts of Jerome B. Frank, our editor, who was sufficiently patient to wait to see the proverbial light at the end of the tunnel. His consistent encouragement and good cheer were a constant source of motivation for us.

Michel Hersen
Alan E. Kazdin
Alan S. Bellack

PART I
GENERAL ISSUES

INTRODUCTION

Contrasted to most of the other helping professions, the history of clinical psychology has been relatively brief. Indeed, most of the important findings in the field appeared after World War I, and the real bulk after World War II. Despite the brevity of its existence, clinical psychology has a very rich heritage, with various roots in philosophy, psychophysics, the early testing movement, early behaviorism, and psychoanalysis. But despite these multifaceted influences, clinical psychology, as a unique discipline, has developed its own character. The area is consistently increasing in scope, with its practitioners carrying out a multitude of tasks and functions on a daily basis. Its popularity within the general field of psychology is still extending, as evidenced by the very large enrollments in all programs focusing on this specialty. Thus, the field is alive and healthy. But as a result of its exponential growth it has become more complex. Such complexity is amply documented in this handbook.

In this part of the handbook we provide the reader with an overview of clinical psychology in addition to outlining important issues that affect the discipline at this time. In Chapter 1, Sheldon Korchin presents a thoughtful review of the history of clinical psychology. A major portion of this chapter is personalized, given the fact that the author has been privileged to witness himself many of the developments that have transpired. In Chapter 2, Irving B. Weiner considers the theoretical foundations of clinical psychology, with emphasis on psychoanalytic, learning, and humanistic theory. He evaluates the trend toward eclecticism, expressing some reservation where the lack of a cohesive frame of reference is apparent. Barry A. Edelstein and William S. Brasted, in Chapter 3, examine in detail the clinical training of psychologists from the historical perspective and in terms of current issues. Future perspectives are considered as well with attention directed to funding, computerization, and the role in prevention. Theodore H. Blau, in Chapter 4, outlines the issues that underscore the roles and professional practice of the clinical psychologist. Emphasis is placed on education and training, supervision, credentialling, and actual practice. In Chapter 5, Charles A. Kiesler tackles the importance of psychology as it relates to overall mental health policy. He argues for a more empirical evaluation of this area, describing it as one that could benefit from systematic inquiry.

1 THE HISTORY OF CLINICAL PSYCHOLOGY: A PERSONAL VIEW

Sheldon J. Korchin

If we take 1896—the year of Witmer's founding of the first Psychological Clinic at the University of Pennsylvania—as the birthday of clinical psychology, then my career in the field spans precisely half of its history. In 1939, although still an undergraduate, I obtained my first job in psychology; I was hired as a laboratory assistant at the New York State Psychiatric Institute. Although the field changed greatly between Witmer's time and 1939, it was in the latter 43 years that the growth rate really accelerated and clinical psychology emerged in its current form(s). In this chapter, I will talk about clinical psychology as I have seen it evolve, and I will call attention to some new and some persistent problems in the future of the field. But first, let us look briefly at the earliest days of clinical psychology.

The Origins of Clinical Psychology

Clinical psychology is heir to both the psychometric and the dynamic traditions of psychology (Korchin, 1976; Watson, 1953). In its first phase, the psychometric tradition, with its empha-sis on measurement and individual differences in mental functioning, dominated. The earliest clinicians were mental testers. The dynamic tradition, focusing on motivation, adaptation, and personality change, came into greater prominence in the more recent history of the field, as clinicians' interests have shifted toward personality dynamics, development, and psychotherapy.

Both the psychometric and the dynamic orientations were anchored in 19th-century European psychology, but they transplanted readily and flourished in the intellectual climate of America in the 1890s. The functionalist and pragmatic themes in American psychology provided a particularly receptive soil for clinical and other applied psychologies. Americans had little patience for either a psychology that dissects into minute detail the structures of the mind (which, said the great William James, intrigues him as much as counting the rocks on his Vermont farm) or for a psychology that speculates grandly about the ultimate nature of the human mind. Concerned with what could be measured and studied empirically, American psychology had an early and continuing concern with altering and improving human functioning.

*An earlier version of this chapter was presented as an invited "Distinguished Lecture on the History of Clinical Psychology," American Psychological Association, Washington, D.C., August 24, 1982.

The Psychometric Tradition

Not long after the pioneers of experimental psychology had developed techniques for measuring psychological processes, in the hope of discovering general psychological laws, such techniques were being used to compare individuals. Sir Francis Galton's studies of differences among people laid the groundwork of differential psychology. By 1890, James McKeen Cattell had coined the term "mental tests." Within short order, statistical procedures evolved for the development and standardization of tests of psychological functions, in many realms. An event of considerable importance in this story occurred in 1904 when the Minister of Public Instruction of Paris sought the help of Alfred Binet in order to distinguish mentally defective children who should be taught in special rather than regular classes. The resulting Binet-Simon scale included tests of attention, memory, imagination, motor skills, comprehension, and other psychological functions. Some years later, the German psychologist William Stern suggested that Binet's "mental-age" scores be evaluated in terms of a child's chronological age in order to achieve a stable "intelligence quotient" (IQ). Through successive revisions, notably by Lewis Terman in the United States, the present Stanford-Binet evolved. For many years, a major function of clinical psychologists was to test children and report a Stanford-Binet IQ. By the 1920s and continuing through to the present, arguments raged over the nature of intelligence, the constancy of the IQ, racial and ethnic differences in IQ scores, culture-bias in test items and standardization, and kindred issues.

Lightner Witmer might be thought of as the father of clinical psychology (Reisman, 1981). He was a student of James McKeen Cattell and took his doctorate with Cattell's own teacher, the great Wilhelm Wundt of Leipzig. Using the test and laboratory procedures of his time, Witmer studied children with school and learning problems. He was the first to use the term "clinical psychology" and to describe the "clinical method in psychology." According to his friend Joseph Collins, in a 1896 talk before the American Psychological Association, Witmer pointed out that "clinical psychology is derived from the results of an examination of many human beings, one at a time, and the analytic method of discriminating mental abilities and defects develops an ordered classification of observed behavior, by means of postanalytic generalization." He put forth the claim that the psy-

chological clinic is an institution for social and public service, for original research, and for the instruction of students in "psychological orthogenics which includes vocational, educational, correctional, hygienic, industrial, and social guidance." And, Witmer's friend continued, "The only reaction he got from the audience was slight elevation of the eyebrows on the part of a few of the older members" (Collins, quoted by Brotemarkle, 1947). Even to the eyebrows, the ideas and situation seem remarkably fresh to those of us who have tried to explain the ideas of clinical psychology to academic audiences in more recent years.

The Dynamic Tradition

In the same era that Cattell, Binet, and Witmer were adapting procedures of the experimental laboratories for clinical testing and studies of individual differences, students of abnormal behavior were developing core ideas about motivation, psychopathology, and psychotherapy; their ideas were to have a profound effect on clinical psychology and psychiatry. Charcot, Janet, and other French psychopathologists were studying hypnosis, dissociation, and hysteria, and laying the groundwork for the investigation of conflict in the unconsious as well as the conscious mind. Influenced by them, Freud moved on to what still remains the most extensive and coherent theory of motivation and personality disturbance. Freud's thoroughgoing psychic determinism, attention to early childhood, and conceptualization of unconscious processes profoundly altered psychology. In 1909, William James was to say: "The future of psychology belongs to your work." Although he gained a loyal, if small, group of followers, Freud's writings did not greatly affect the mainstream of European psychology and psychiatry for some years to come.

Freud's influence on American psychology was greatly facilitated by two giants of American academic psychology: G. Stanley Hall and William James. James was a man of broad and rich interests, touching both the scientific and humanistic aspects of psychology. His *Principles of Psychology* (1890) and *Varieties of Religious Experience* (1902) explored the nature of the self and ego, the stream of consciousness, human values, and psychopathology, compared to which the interests of his contemporary structural psychologists seem barren and irrelevant to the emerging clinical psychology. His philosophy of pragmatism encouraged concern with the utility of ideas, which were to be tested in actual experiences. James' own commitment to advancing human well-being later emerged in his support of Clifford Beers' crusade for better conditions for psychiatric inpatients, which he knew well through first-hand experience.

G. Stanley Hall was similarly influential in the early decades of American psychology. He wrote about developmental processes, sexuality, and adolescence. He encouraged clinical practice and research, stimulated the development of psychological tests, and founded journals that would provide outlets for students of abnormal behavior, social processes, and developmental psychology. In 1909, to celebrate the anniversary of Clark University, he assembled many of the finest minds in contemporary psychology, including Freud, Jung, and a number of their psychoanalytic colleagues. This famous meeting left an indelible mark, although clinical psychology was to continue for many years more in the model of Witmer than of Freud. It is noteworthy that it was a psychology department rather than a medical setting that first brought psychoanalysis to the United States. Indeed, until 1913 the only outlet for psychoanalytic publications in the United States was the *Journal of Abnormal Psychology*, founded and edited by Morton Prince (who later founded the Harvard Psychological Clinic). At the 1909 Clark meetings, Carl Jung gave a research report on his studies using word association as a method of discovering unconscious complexes. Along with Freud's analysis of dreams, this was an important forerunner of projective testing. The use of projective techniques in personality and clinical assessment represents a major confluence of the dynamic and psychometric traditions in American clinical psychology, although it was not to emerge for almost 30 years.

From Witmer to World War II

By 1914, there were 20 psychological clinics on university campuses (Watson, 1953). Psychologists moved into mental hospitals and clinics and into special settings for the mentally retarded and physically handicapped. Considerable research was done in hospitals on the psychological functioning of psychotics, using laboratory techniques. Developing, standardizing, and using psychological tests were the major occupation of psychologists. In clinical centers, some became "mental testers," reporting test findings to medical superiors. Few held doctorates in psychology.

The First World War accelerated the growth of clinical psychology. The military faced the difficult task of evaluating the abilities of large numbers of men so that they could be placed in the most suitable jobs. A number of psychologists, including leaders of experimental psychology, took on the challenge and developed group intelligence tests. The Army Alpha was a verbal test, sampling such abilities as vocabulary, arithmetic, and judgment. Paralleling it was the Army Beta, which was nonverbal and intended for illiterate or non-English-speaking soldiers. Robert S. Woodworth's Psychoneurotic Inventory (more delicately labeled "Personal Data Sheet" on the form given to the men) screened soldiers with emotional problems. It is the prototype of the numerous paper-and-pencil personality inventories developed since 1917. Indeed, items tend to be carried over from one inventory to another; traces of original Woodworth are still to be found in scales in current use. By the end of the war, it was estimated that 1,726,000 men had been group-tested and another 83,000 tested individually (Reisman, 1976). Published findings showing racial differences, a high order of illiteracy, and an average "mental age" of the American soldier to be 13.5 years led to widespread and understandable consternation.

During the 1920s and 1930s, clinicians were in the main assessing the intellectual and educational functioning of children, although increasing numbers worked in adult psychiatric settings. Under the impetus of the Child Guidance Movement, new clinics were formed and the "team approach" evolved. The team was led by the medically trained psychiatrist, who was responsible for doing psychotherapy and for major clinical decisions. Psychologists were primarily involved in psychological testing and in applying educational and remedial therapies. Unlike in earlier years, however, psychologists used a wider range of tests, including the new-fangled projective techniques, as part of a test battery. Ideally, the psychologist's task was that of a consultant assembling all revelant information into an assessment report, which would include not only a description and interpretation of the person's character and problems but also suggestions as to the best strategies of treatment. The psychologist was no longer a technician, a mental tester reporting test findings to a superior. The third member of the team was a social worker, who took care of intake and social history interviews, did casework with parents, and maintained liaison with other helping agencies. This pattern was maintained up to and through the Second World War. However, clinical psychology was to become a more autonomous profession. Along with Rogers (1942), psychologists were increasingly looking to psychotherapy as their primary function. Discontent with the treatment they received at the hands of academic colleagues led many to resign from the American Psychological Association and to form an American Association for Applied Psychology. The AAAP, eventually rejoined the APA in the postwar honeymoon between applied and academic psychology.

Thus far, I have been discussing history, (events that happened before I was born or at least before I knew that they would matter to me). But from here on, over the past 40 + years the evolving story is part of my personal memory, and I will discuss it from a personal vantage. These were years of great growth and diversification for clinical psychology, which became evident to me in terms of a strange little experience that happened to me in Rome in the fall of 1976.

Modern Clinical Psychology — Then and Now

Modern Clinical Psychology (Korchin, 1976) was published in the spring of 1976. After so many years of hard work, I was overwhelmed with feelings of relief and accomplishment. Prepublication copies had been sent to a number of respected senior psychologists, and their reviews were gratifyingly laudatory. I had wanted to describe the field as fully and fairly as possible and to affirm my faith in clinical psychology. It appeared that I had succeeded in both regards.

The spring was made even happier by the fact that my wife and I were about to leave for another sabbatical year of living and working in Italy. In fact, the book had been started during the preceding sabbatical, in Rome in 1970. To return to Rome was an appropriate celebration of a significant life phase.

Shortly after we arrived in Rome, the church that serves the American community had a bazaar celebrating the U.S. Bicentennial. Along with hot dogs and cokes, there were tables full of wonderful old things contributed by church members from their attics and basements. Browsing through a table of books, uniformly priced at 500 lire (then about 60¢), I happened on something that immediately changed the mood of the day. There was a

copy of *Modern Clinical Psychology* but authored by T. W. Richards and published in 1946. Humbled, all I could do was mutter: "*Sic transit gloria mundi.*" (It's always helpful in Rome to have a bit of Latin handy!)

Now, with two identically titled volumes in hand, published 30 years apart but joined by this mystic bond, we can properly ask how the "modern" of 1946 differs from the "modern" of 1976.

At the first level, the books differ in sheer size: MCP-46 consists of 331 pages; MCP-76 has 672, and they are more densely printed. Similarly, there are 145 references in MCP-46; well over 1,200 in MCP-76. These figures, of course, might only reveal differences in the verbosity or scholarly obsessiveness of the two authors, but it is more likely that they reflect the state of the field in the two eras. This emerges more vividly as we examine the contents of the books.

About two-thirds of the pages in Richards' MCP are devoted to discussion of "psychological appraisal," ingeniously grouped under three headings: (1) *Motivation* (goals, interests, values), (2) *Capacity* (intellectual resources to cope with environment), and (3) *Control* (processes for utilizing capacities and curbing impulse in the direction of socially acceptable adjustment). In each domain, malfunctions are discussed (e.g., homosexuality, retardation, and anxiety) and methods of appraisal (mainly psychological tests) presented and illustrated. Although more issues and techniques are discussed by Korchin, less than one-quarter of MCP-76 is concerned with "clinical assessment."

By contrast, about 30 percent of MCP-76 is concerned with psychotherapy — individual, group, and family; the first of these is barely mentioned by Richards, the latter two not at all. Although his section on "Readjustment" contains a thoughtful analysis of the processes of individual change (insight, abreaction, etc.), psychotherapy as such is not discussed. Korchin's attention to community and social interventions (about one-fifth of MCP-76) is clearly beyond the ken of MCP-46. Nor does Richards devote much space to discussion of professional roles and functions, the history of the field, training, emergent directions, and related issues, which figure rather importantly in MCP-76.

Richards is firmly in the dynamic tradition. In his preface he acknowledges being influenced by Freud and Jung, Murray, Rorschach, and Klopfer. I too am committed to a dynamic perspective and share respect for these notables. In *MCP*-76, however, clinical psychology is necessarily presented in a broader and more eclectic framework. Over the years since 1946 the field has become increasingly diversified. Added to the psychometric and dynamic orientations of the forties have been behavioral, humanistic/existential, and social/community approaches, each in several subforms. At the same time, the variety of professional roles and functions of clinicians has expanded enormously. The prototypic clinician at the time of *MCP*-46 was a psychodiagnostician who tested patients, interpreted, and reported assessment findings, toward the end of advising colleagues who carried responsibility for psychotherapy or other interventions. Today's clinician may be primarily a psychological assessor, psychotherapist, social-change agent, or behavioral engineer, working with individuals, groups, organizations, or communities toward the end of understanding, treating, or preventing human problems.

A 1946 Ph.D.

For the world, for clinical psychology, and for me personally, 1946 was a fine year. The Second World War had just ended, with the resounding defeat of fascism. A Pax Americana reigned, and the United States was cooperating with other nations toward building a United Nations to guarantee enduring peace. Millions of men left the military services, many to enter colleges and universities who never would have made it save for the generous GI Bill. On their parts, colleges and universities expanded to meet the demand. The Veterans Administration underwrote graduate training in clinical psychology. The newly formed National Institute of Mental Health made its first training grants in clinical psychology in 1946. With relatively few Ph.D.s granted during the war, choice jobs were available for almost anyone with a new degree and a modicum of experience and talent. And in 1946, I received a Ph.D. in Psychology from Harvard University.

Edwin G. Boring, consummate historian of psychology, impressed on me that mine was the last degree to be awarded by the department that gave its first Ph.D. to G. Stanley Hall. That fall, a new Department of Social Relations, composed of Social and Clinical Psychology, Sociology, and Cultural Anthropology, was to be launched, while the remainder of Psychology (Paleopsychology in Boring's bitter phase) was to continue in different

quarters. In my fantasy at least, I had inherited responsibility for maintaining the unity and integrity of psychology, to protect it from fragmentation and hyperspecialization — one discipline, indivisible, under God — rather a heavy load for shoulders not yet 25 years old.

Student days: Brooklyn College (1938–1942).

As a student, indeed throughout my career, I have had the singularly good fortune to observe and in some measure participate in major events in the modern history of psychology. Before moving forward from 1946 to the present, let me go back to the beginnings of my career in psychology.

As an undergraduate in Brooklyn College (1938–1942), I never had any doubt about wanting a career in psychology, although it seemed a highly improbable goal in those Depression years. Still, two cousins had completed Ph.D.s at Cornell and were working together on a psychophysiological research project at the New York State Psychiatric Institute (part of Columbia University's Department of Psychiatry), which was to provide me with my first job in psychology, a bottom-level research assistantship. Cousins or no, for months I worked as a volunteer, until — entirely on merit — I was elevated to a $4/day salary. I felt that I had arrived professionally. Between chores in the lab, I could browse in the Institute's fine library, even get to handle some of the books in the Freud library recently ransomed from the Nazis, or sit in on clinical conferences.

Brooklyn College in those years had a vital and exciting Psychology Department, including Solomon E. Asch, H. A. Witkin, Abraham Maslow, Helen Block Lewis, Rosalind Gould, along with a number of lesser known but fine psychologists. The dominant orientation was Gestalt Psychology, and we were visited by the greats of the Gestalt movement: Max Wertheimer, Wolfgang Köhler, Kurt Koffka, and Kurt Goldstein. As I recall, the only one I didn't hear talk on campus was Kurt Lewin, who was off in the exotic reaches of Iowa. Along with the Gestalt influence was a contrapuntal interest in psychoanalysis and dynamic psychology, taught mainly by Maslow who had not yet become spokesman for "third-force" psychology. Derided was behaviorism, despite its dominant place elsewhere in American psychology.

Brooklyn College at that time had, I believe, the largest undergraduate enrollment of any American institution, and hundreds majored in psychology. Yet, with no graduate students, the handful of students sincerely committed to a career in psychology, likely to make it into and through graduate school, were given very special attention by the faculty. We were little Rockys being groomed to become champions in the great arena outside the ghetto. When I graduated, I was awarded the department's highest prize—two books of my very own choosing. One was Goldstein's (1939) classic *The Organism*; the other Klopfer and Kelley's (1942) newly published *The Rorschach Technique*. Thus, I was provided with both theory and method to go on to a career in clinical psychology. With my job at the Psychiatric Institute, I felt quite the young professional, no longer simply a student. Getting married on graduation day made definite the transition into adulthood, although neither Sylvia nor I would be able to vote or to drink in a bar for some months to come.

Clark University (1942–1943)

In good part, choosing a graduate school depended on the amount of support available, and Clark Univeristy won out with an offer of tuition, one meal a day, and a room in a men's dormitory. In those days, graduate students were not supposed to be married. However, a sympathetic dean helped by allowing us to rent the dorm room and apply the money toward an off-campus room.

In its own right, however, Clark was a good choice. By Brooklyn standards, it was a tiny place. There were then 50 graduate students in the entire university, five of whom were in psychology. With its library, laboratories, and the great G. Stanley Hall seminar room, the history of psychology lived on at Clark. Nearby was the historic Worcester State Hospital with its excellent medical staff and psychologists such as David Shakow, Saul Rosenzweig, and Eliot Rodnick. Rosenzweig and Rodnik taught at the university at that time. I studied abnormal psychology with Rosenzweig and did my masters thesis with him. From Rodnick, newly out of a Yale Ph.D., I took the one course in learning I have had in my entire life. Rodnick, who was to go on to direct the clinical program at Duke and later at UCLA, conveyed the substance and logic of Hull's approach sufficiently well to impress if not convince a Gestalt skeptic. These men were all exemplars of what would soon be called the "scientist-professional" clinician, for they were equally at home in research, scholarship, and clinical practice. I will never forget the excitement I felt being allowed to browse in Shakow's and Rosenzweig's personal libraries, which were of a size and variety I thought existed only in public institutions. Over the years, I was to know Shakow (and his books) better during our common years in Chicago and Bethesda.

At the university, I also took courses in statistics and experimental psychology, an excellent course in child development from Charlotte Bühler, and Hudson Hoagland's year-long physiology course. Hoagland, originally trained in psychology, emphasized general adaptation, stress physiology, and endocrine and metabolic processes of a sort more relevant, I believe, to students of personality and clinical psychology than the more usual courses in physiological psychology that emphasize sensory and CNS processes. Hoagland invited me to be a voluntary research assistant in his lab. In part, this consisted of serving as a subject in experiments on the effects of cold pressor stress on adrenal functioning. I also was taught to do 17-ketosteroid extractions. Smelling constantly of urine and ether dampened my enthusiasm for laboratory work. The research, however, furthered my interest in the psychological and physiological effects of stress and anxiety, which started with my work at the Psychiatric Institute and my honors' thesis at Brooklyn College, and matured in Philadelphia, Chicago, and Bethesda, which I will talk about shortly. Looking back, it is hard to believe that so much could be packed into one academic year.

A Student at Harvard (1943–1946)

A visit to Harvard and a talk with Gordon Allport recalled how much I had really wanted to go to Harvard the year before. This time, a respectable fellowship could be offered to be followed for the next two years by appointments as a Teaching Fellow and Tutor. Because I had taken so many courses at Clark, I was free to wander through the Harvard course offerings, sampling seminars in philosophy, political science, and sociology; in psychology, taking only the Psychology Proseminar, taught that year by Carroll Pratt and George W. Hartmann rather than Boring, and individual reading/research courses with Robert White and Gordon Allport.

Most of my time was spent in the lovely old Harvard Psychological Clinic on Plympton Street, where the spirit of the *Explorations in Personality* (Murray, 1938) was still very much in the air, although Murray himself, along with a number of Clinic people of earlier years, was in uniform commanding the Office of Strategic Services assessment program. Shortly after I arrived in 1943, there was a party for Murray at which he passed out copies of the TAT cards just published by the Harvard University Press. I cherish a set numbered 007. But during my years at Harvard, Bob White was the central figure in the Clinic. It was from him, Silvan Tomkins, Eugenia Hanfmann, and the small but vigorous group of fellow graduate students, often over lunch in the Clinic library, sometimes with a visiting clinician, that I absorbed a great deal about personality theory, psychopathology, personality assessment, and psychotherapy. Another important learning experience was assisting in the teaching of undergraduates. On one or more occasions, I taught sections or otherwise assisted Allport, Boring, White, Tomkins, James Miller, and, during a visiting appointment, Hoagland in his physiological course. About the same time, I worked with Allport and Talcott Parsons in their joint course on racial prejudice and intergroup conflict. I would like to think that I was truly a universal scholar, knowledgeable in all these areas. In fact, however, during the war years there was such a shortage of teaching staff that we were all pressed into teaching over the widest possible range, and learned in the process. I also had a chance to watch master teachers at work.

"Clinical experience," on the other hand, was limited largely to some supervised work with White in the Clinic and to a part-time summer spent with James G. Miller at the Massachussetts General Hospital. By today's standards, there was precious little practicum experience, but somehow in the Clinic with people profoundly concerned to understand how people function, why they misfunction, and how they can be changed, I seem to have learned a good deal.

Surprisingly, I did not do a thesis project along clinical or personological lines, working with White or perhaps with Allport, but instead decided on a survey research study of voting behavior. In part, this reflected a longstanding and continuing interest in social issues, but actually it resulted more from a rare opportunity becoming available. The National Opinion Research Center, on whose board of directors Gordon Allport sat, was trying to encourage social research in the areas of their survey interests. Thus, it was possible for me to have resources of NORC for a panel study of a representative sample of American adults before and after the 1944 presidential election. I created an interview schedule, and three thousand people were interviewed for me on two occasions! That's heady stuff for a graduate student.

The study focused on the psychological and social determinants of partisanship and participation (voting versus not voting), and—of greatest interest—the question of how attitudes change from before to after an election or, as I named it, "the *fait accompli* effect." And so my Ph.D. in Psychology notes that I worked in the special field of the "Psychology of community mores," rather an elegant version of social psychology. To my knowledge, I was the first American psychologist to get a Ph.D. based on survey research data.

In those days, of course, personality, clinical, abnormal, and social psychology were more closely related than they are today. The single *Journal of Abnormal and Social Psychology* amply served my interests. However, the fields have grown apart; with the emergence of experimental social psychology in the 1950s, even personality and social psychology have separated. In the more recent past, it seems to me, as there is a resurgence of interest in phenomena and experience and less concern with constructs and methods, these areas are converging again. There is also a healthy return of interest in a personological perspective (Maddi, in press). Still, I have to fight off copy editors intent on changing the middle o to an a.

Cambridge (1946–1947)

I was appointed an Instructor in Social Psychology, then the first step on the tenure ladder, in Harvard's new Department of Social Relations. That year, I taught what had been Murray's popular course in Dynamic Psychology and a graduate seminar on the History of Social Psychology, normally taught by Gordon Allport. Many of the students were older and more mature than I. They had returned from military service, in some cases with extensive experience in clinical settings or social research units. But for the grace of polio in infancy and a 4-F classification, I should have been the student and they my teachers: a problem that stayed with me for many years. I felt like David Rapaport's Hungarian who enters a revolving door behind you and leaves ahead of you. My graduate seminar, which included a number of people destined to be today's leaders in social psychology, was most democratically organized, not out of ideology but for necessity.

In the Psychological Clinic that year (1946–1947), a group of us led by Brewster Smith, Jerome Bruner, and Robert White collaborated in a study of the relation between social attitudes and personality dynamics; the focus of the study was on attitudes toward the Soviet Union and communism (Smith, Bruner, & White, 1956). The heart of the study involved in-depth assessment of a small group of people on which each of the collaborators had gathered information in a particular realm (e.g., sexual history, Rorschach, attitudes toward communism) which was combined into a conceptualization of a real, in-the-round, vital human being through the collective consideration of the "Diagnostic Council." It was an exciting adventure in personological research, where the focus is on gaining knowledge through the study of persons rather than the study of variables.

By the end of 1946–1947, I decided to resign from Harvard, though my appointment still had two more years to run, to take a position in the Philadelphia Mental Hygiene Clinic. There were a number of reasons for this decision, but central among them was a sincere desire for clinical training and experience.

In an important sense, I bridged between the prewar and postwar generations of clinicians, between those whose clinical training was catch-as-catch-can and those who went through formal graduate programs in clinical psychology, with their prescribed curricula and internships. When I entered graduate work, these barely existed; by 1947, the Shakow Committee had issued its report describing an ideal model of clinical training (APA, Committee on Training in Clinical Psychology, 1947) which was affirmed by leaders of the field in the famous Boulder Conference of 1949 (Raimy, 1950). The new clinical psychologist was to be a "scientist-professional," with a Ph.D. from a university psychology department and an internship in a clinical setting. First a psychologist and only then a clinician, the clinical student was expected to be broadly grounded in the major areas of psychological theory, knowledge, and research, particularly in personality, social, and abnormal psychology, and to learn the competencies needed for clinical intervention. The fully trained clinician was expected to function autonomously in psychological assessment, psychotherapy, and research. Whatever the professional role, it was

hoped that the clinician would be a scholar and researcher, in order to increase knowledge about the nature of human distress and its treatment. Procedures were developed for the evaluation and accreditation of both university graduate programs and internship programs in clinical centers, so-called "APA-approved" programs.

The move from Harvard to the Veterans Administration began a 16-year period—of exile in the minds of academic friends, of personal development to my mind—during which I worked mainly in clinical centers, though often with part-time teaching at a local university as well. I take it as a mark of distinction that I have never held appointments as an Assistant Professor or an Associate Professor. Hence, I never had to fight my way up the tenure ladder. I had time and support for developing clinical knowledge, skills, and attitudes in settings that valued them. I am firmly convinced that clinical psychology is best represented on university faculties by people who have matured outside of academia.

Before leaving Cambridge, however, I had the unique opportunity to share in the birth, during the summer of 1947, of the National Training Laboratory summer workshop in Bethel, Maine, which was to influence the course of group therapy and, conceived as "group therapy for normals," to be a root source of the encounter movement of the 1960s. Kurt Lewin, along with his talented coterie of colleagues and graduate students, had come to the Massachusetts Institute of Technology the year before, and I was able to participate in his seminar, unfortunately the last he was to teach.

A program was developed at Bethel for people from industry, education, and government intended to increase productivity and morale through more effective group functioning; the T-group was born. To evaluate this program, John R. P. French organized a research unit, with me heading the "personality section," to discover the elements of group effectiveness, the relation between personality and group dynamics, and the nature of the changes in both personal and social functioning that occurred as a result of the Bethel training experiences. Our unit studied a small number of group leaders and group participants, in the Diagnositic Council spirit, to discover how leader personality affected leadership behaviors and how leader-member personality pairings shaped the process of group functioning.

There was great excitement in Bethel that summer, with many convinced that a new technique was evolving that could lead people to happier, more democratic, and more productive lives. Those of us who were more person oriented wondered how much change could be expected from any intervention during a month period. We were also frightened by the almost religious fervor and cult like conviction of many of the participants and the group leaders. Years later, when NTL groups in the Lewinian tradition were to be the conservative end of the encounter movement (Back, 1972), I reexperienced similar but more intense concerns along with many other psychologists (Koch, 1971; Korchin, 1976; Leiberman, Yalom, & Miles, 1973; Strupp, 1976). A powerful bias among those who were reared in the dynamic tradition is that personality growth and change are both processes requiring time. We remain suspicious of claims for quick, simple, and painless change agents.

Philadelphia (1947–1950)

The VA in 1947 was bustling with enthusiasm and vitality. With the exception of a few prewar administrators, everyone was young and hopeful; burnout had not yet been invented. I went into the VA to learn to be a proper clinician, but in short order I found myself Assistant Chief Psychologist in charge of training and responsible for 18 talented and energetic University of Pennsylvania students, many with considerable wartime clinical experience (the revolving door again!). Although, in the Boulder spirit, graduate training was supposed to be a partnership between the university, which taught theory and research, and the clinic, which gave practicum experience, in fact, we ran a rather complete "graduate program" in the VA Clinic. There were seminars on theory and methods, colloquia, case conferences, and the like, as well as many hours spent in direct services with patients and in clinical supervision. All the while, a number of research studies were being done, some as students' theses at the university, others generated simply out of curiosity. Among the studies I did at the time, collaborating with student-interns, were ones on the effect of psychological stress on cognition, tests of Werner's sensory-tonic theory, and race differences in TAT performance.

The VA job descriptions of the time described the clinical psychologist in terms of diagnosis, psychotherapy, and research — the holy trinity of the time. In actuality, however, we were mainly expected to be psychodiagnosticians. We tested, using a battery in the Rapaport-Menninger style, as members of a psychiatric team. Research was tolerated and actually supported in fair degree, but it was not viewed as central. Of necessity, psychologists were increasingly involved in psychotherapy — group as well as individual — of a psychoanalytically oriented or Rogerian sort. There were so many of them and so few of us that everyone had to pitch in, and we learned as we worked as much from talented supervisees as from supervisors. By the end of my three years in Philadelphia, I felt myself to be a reasonably seasoned clinician, although I preserved my identity as a social psychologist by teaching one year part-time at Princeton University and doing survey research for the next two years in a Philadelphia institute. A particularly exciting study explored the changes in values and attitudes of the first German exchange students to come to the United States after the war.

Chicago (1950–1959)

In 1950 I was invited to be Director of the Psychology Laboratory of the Michael Reese Hospital in Chicago and simultaneously, Lecturer in Psychology at the University of Chicago. At the hospital, I replaced Samuel J. Beck, whose pioneer work had established the Rorschach as a major tool of clinical practice and research, in what was surely one of the nation's finest centers of psychiatric training, research, and practice, under the leadership of Roy R. Grinker. During nine years there, I collaborated with a number of fine psychoanalytic and psychosomatic scholars (Grinker, Spiegel, Hamburg, Sabshin, Kepecs, and others) as well as a number of people in the vital Psychoanalytic Institute (e.g., Alexander, French, Piers, Benedek, Kohut, Szasz, among others). The community of psychology at the University of Chicago included many talented people as diverse as Carl Rogers, L. L. Thurstone, Ward Halstead, and Bruno Bettleheim, although I interacted more closely with the younger faculty, particularly Morris Stein, Don Friske, Don Campbell, Hedda Bolgar, Erika Fromm, Bill Henry, Bernice Neugarten, Jack Butler, and Howard Hunt. Chicago was an exciting center for psychology in those years. In the ferment of the 1950s, many of us were very much involved in trying to make the South Side a racially integrated neighborhood. In no other time or place would I have agreed to be president of a home owners association and president of a PTA. As it happened, these experiences became relevant again as my interests turned some 25 years later to issues of minority mental health (Jones & Korchin, 1982; Korchin, 1980).

At Michael Reese Hospital, the Psychology Laboratory epitomized the scientist-professional concept of clinical psychology. We had practicing, teaching, and research clinicians (in every combination), neuropsychologists, psychophysiologists, social psychologists, cognitive psychologists, and animal behavior researchers. There was a steady flow of predoctoral interns and postdoctoral fellows. We had one of the first three NIMH-supported postdoctoral programs in the country.

A major focus of research was on issues of stress and anxiety, which involved the collaboration of psychologists, psychiatrists, biochemists, and physiologists. (Once again, I was involved in studies of steroids, but happily there were others to do the extractions!) A basic tenet of this research program was that one had to study stress and anxiety at many levels simultaneously and over sufficient time in response to real and intense stimuli rather than in contrived situations. We did some experimental and clinical studies of one or a few variables, but we argued that the ideal investigation should include multidisciplinary, multivariable, over-time measurement during real-life stress, although preferably of a known and controllable sort, as exemplified in our studies of soldiers in paratrooper training (Basowitz, Persky, Korchin, & Grinker, 1955). Today, almost everyone is critical of contrived, if not downright unethical, psychological experiments (Korchin & Cowan, 1982), but 30 years ago they were in full fashion.

The University of Chicago, then one of the nation's greatest centers of pure intellectuality, provided a nice balance during our years in Chicago. Most years I taught one seminar, either in personality theory or research, but mainly I worked with individual students who came to the Michael Reese laboratory to do theses or other research. By being part-time, I could remain aloof from the politics of the department. This was not at all an unhappy state during a time when the name of the clinical program was changed to "personality and psychopathology." As James Bryant Conant said

about coeducation at Harvard during the war, it existed "in fact only." And so it was with clinical psychology at Chicago.

Bethesda, Rome, Bethesda (1959–1963)

During a sabbatical in 1959–1960, I went to NIMH as a guest of David Hamburg's Adult Psychiatry Branch as a "Visiting Scientist," a prestigious title usually reserved for foreign scientists. For the first time in years, I was free of all administrative, teaching, and if I wished, research obligations; at my command were all the rich resources of the National Institutes of Health in their halcyon days. It was a marvelous time out from reality. During the year, I happily accepted an offer to stay on to develop and direct a new "laboratory of stress." But first I had one more fantasy to realize: to live and work in Italy. So I agreed to come to NIMH provided I could accept a Fulbright Professorship in Italy during 1960–1961. I had been invited the previous year to teach psychotherapy in the Psychiatry Department of the University of Genoa where, incidentally, Cerletti and Bini developed electroshock in 1937. Needless to say, the year abroad was a beautiful experience, the beginning of a continuing love affair with Italy, to which we have returned many times since. Still, difficult as it was, we returned to Bethesda and NIMH, now part of John Kennedy's Camelot.

Before going abroad, George Ruff and I had started a multidisciplinary, multilevel, longitudinal study of stress responses among the Mercury Astronauts during training exercises and flights (Korchin & Ruff, 1964; Ruff & Korchin, 1964), conducted in collaboration with a number of university and government scientists with NASA support. Hardly surprising was the fact that physical stresses such as high g, isolation, or even danger were minor compared to social stress resulting from the rapid change from competent but anonymous test pilots to lauded public heroes. After NASA gained assurance that space flight did no medical or psychological damage, their interest in having outside scientists involved in the project waned considerably. But while it lasted, it provided a fascinating change — new people, new activities, and new settings — from my usual research activities. It also provided a unique opportunity to study personality competence and coping mechanisms, the obverse side of the defensive and regressive behaviors usually the focus of stress research, in an unusual population.

Berkeley (1963–present)

The new laboratory was barely launched when, in 1963, I was invited to Berkeley as Professor and Head of the new Psychology Clinic and Director of the Graduate Clinical Program. It was a true challenge. Berkeley was a complex setting, an elite university with great commitment to pure scholarship and misgiving about applied fields. After the postwar honeymoon ended, some comparable universities — Stanford, Harvard, Chicago — were giving up clinical programs; would Berkeley reverse the trend? Good sense dictated remaining in the stress-free world of NIMH doing research on stress. But, to tell the truth, I realized that I missed contact with people — notably student-people and patient-people — in the singular and monastic devotion to research and scholarship at NIMH. Then too, I felt the pull of an incompleted task tension, dating back 16 years to Harvard in 1947. I accepted the Berkeley offer, with a sense of returning home, although now with a surer sense of identity, competencies, values, and goals than I had when I left it. I directed the clinic and graduate program through 1972, at which point Philip A. Cowan took over the task. However, both before and since that date we two, along with other colleagues of the clinical program, have collaborated on policy making in terms of shared values.

We have tried to make the clinical program truly express the scientist-professional ideal, valuing ideas and the discovery of knowledge along with, and as part of, interventions intended to help distressed persons (groups, or communities, as well) solve human problems. We shared Lewin's faith in action research, that a phenomenon can best be understood in the context of trying to change it. Central were ideals carried over from the Harvard Psychological Clinic (White, 1981) — the importance of a personological perspective, readiness to use empathic and subjective as well as objective measures, importance of understanding personality in depth, concern with hidden as well as manifest motives, respecting the proactive and prosocial trends in human functioning as well as the more pathological, among others. Although it was decided early on that the central activity of the clinic would be individual psychotherapy, personality and clinical assessment is still valued for its

contributions to understanding the patient, sharpening the clinician's perception, and as a tool for clinical research (Korchin & Schuldberg, 1981). Students, we would hope, would avoid the illusion that there were what Allport caricatured as "simple and sovereign" concepts or solutions to human issues. Above all, they should respect people in psychological distress.

As time has gone by we have become increasingly involved in social and community interventions, shorter-term therapies, couple and family therapies, as well as individual psychotherapy. We have tried to visualize the possible roles we could take, as a "clinic without walls," in helping schools and other social entities through consultation. My own research from the late sixties to the present has also veered more in a social direction, including (1) working with Bill Soskin (Soskin, Ross, & Korchin, 1971) in developing a quasi-therapeutic program for alienated youth; (2) developing a research program bearing on issues of minority mental health (Jones & Korchin, 1982), which went along with an effort to train greater numbers of minority students (Korchin, 1980); and (3) in the more recent past, research on the psychosocial problems of disabled university students.

During the past 19 years at Berkeley, psychology and the world in general have changed greatly. But clinical psychology continues to be a vigorous and exciting field, attracting many talented young people who, we hope, will go on to become scholarly clinicians or clinical scholars, not simply technicians practicing a craft. That we have islands of knowledge drifting in a sea of ignorance is evident, and we have an obligation to reduce ignorance if we are to help people in psychological distress more effectively. Particularly as the field continues to grow and diversify, established knowledge is needed to guide its growth (Garmezy, 1982; Shakow, 1965). But the kind of knowledge needed to improve clinical interventions is best obtained by clinicians working within the clinical context rather than by outsiders who do not share the clinician's vantage or concerns.

This is the paradox and the challenge of the clinical field. At Berkeley as elsewhere, in our time as in Witmer's, the blending of understanding and helping that defines the clinical field is not easily appreciated by academic colleagues who view scientific and applied concerns as necessarily opposed rather than complementary, as I believe they are. The boundary between pure and applied, between science and helping profession, is at best tenuous even in the classic comparisons between physiology and medicine. However, in our field, I would argue further, the polarization of science and application can be distinctly harmful to both clinical and general psychology. Each needs the other.

Clinical psychology is best defined by the conjunction of understanding and helping, as Witmer viewed the field and as I have seen it evolve during my career. It will, I believe, continue to give our science-profession its unique character in the future. Thus, my book, *Modern Clinical Psychology*, concluded with the statement:

> What most distinguishes the psychological clinician . . . is a way of thinking, an orientation toward human beings, rather than a particular subject matter, special techniques or a professional role. The clinician wants to study and understand the individual in psychological distress in order to help him. Relevant information is gained, in the clinical process itself, in the transactions between the clinician and the patient. Central to the work of the clinician is the need "to do something about it," to facilitate the adaptation of the patient. However fascinating knowledge is in its own right, it is sought by the clinician in order to help better the lot of the patient. Furthermore, the clinical approach is necessarily personological, for the clinician must deal with individual lives in their complexities as patients struggle to adapt and grow. Processes in the person or in the environment, of his physiological nature or his social situation, are most relevant as they come to focus in, and have meaning for, the particular person.
>
> Can such a definition continue to describe and guide our work as clinical psychology becomes more diverse? As some move toward biological and others toward social factors in the quest for the sources of human distress? As interventions center as much on the functioning of biological and social systems as on the experiences of the individual? I believe it can and should. Ultimately, many sciences and professions will have to contribute if human well-being is to be advanced. But the particular contribution of psychological clinicians rests, most critically, on their unique perceptive—participating with unique indi-

viduals in their adaptive struggles in order to understand and to help them. [Korchin, 1976, p. 612]

The Future of Clinical Psychology: Some Trends and Some Concerns

In the mid-1940s, Boring observed that if the growth curves of APA membership and of the American population should keep their slopes, then by the year 2000 all Americans would be psychologists. Fortunately, trends shifted, but still a much larger fraction of Americans are psychologists, want to become psychologists, believe in psychologists, and are being treated by psychologists than anyone could have reasonably predicted in the 1930s. Correspondingly, the field has broadened continuously. Sarason in 1954 opened his book on *The Clinical Interaction* with the statement: "Clinical psychology is no longer an area of specialization which can be described within the confines of a book. . . . When one remembers that clinical psychology as we know it today is largely a phenomenon of the last decade, one can only be amazed by the rate of its growth and the problems it has come to encompass" (p. 1). How much truer is this today.

In looking back over the history of clinical psychology, it is well to realize that most of the change is to be accounted for by the impact of social history rather than simply by the evolution of ideas or the cumulation of findings within the profession. The Stanford-Binet was developed in response to the needs of Paris educators; World War I accelerated psychometric testing; World War II brought forth the present conception of the clinician; and postwar concerns for veterans spurred the unprecedented growth of the field; the War on Poverty, the fight for Civil Rights, and the recognition of the rights and needs of underserved groups fostered the community mental health movement. No history could be written, of course, without due attention to the contributions of Freud, Witmer, Cattell, Murray, Rorschach, Rogers, Rapaport, Watson, Skinner, among others, but in the last analysis it may be the social, legislative, and legal events of the time that determine the rate and direction of growth of the profession (Levine, 1981). It surely is true that the social climate that supported vigorous postwar growth of psychology has shifted in a conservative direction likely to slow future progress in psychology.

Over the past 40 years, clinical psychology has

gained in stature while at the same time diversifying and differentiating in numerous ways. On the whole, these are healthy trends—some are inevitable parts of professional growth—but they contain some dangers as well. In concluding this chapter, I would like to comment on some of these issues.

Psychology as an Autonomous Profession

Psychology has become, in fair measure, an autonomous, self-regulating profession. There are standards and accreditation procedures for graduate education and internships, licensing laws in all states, diplomatic examinations, and ethical codes for clinical practice and research, all of which should contribute to higher standards of training and practice to the ultimate benefit of the public. However, danger lies in such regulation becoming bureaucratized and serving, ultimately, the guild interests of already established psychologists. The doctorate has been established as the appropriate degree for fully independent professional functioning, but this leaves uncertain how subdoctoral clinicians and nonprofessional workers can make their contribution. While legislated standards, licenses, accreditation, and the like can contribute to better practice, they can also lead to the rigidification of a profession.

New Models of Clinical Training

At Boulder in 1949, the scientist-professional model of the clinician, with a Ph.D. from a university, was established. The "Boulder model" was reaffirmed at conferences in Miami in 1958 and in Chicago in 1965, although there was growing pressure for legitimizing more purely professional training, perhaps leading to a professional degree (e.g., Doctor of Psychology), either in new settings within traditional universities or in free-standing professional schools. At the Vail Conference of 1973, the concept of a "professional" in addition to "scientist-professional" clinician was approved. In that era, a number of new programs and alternative institutions evolved. As of now, in California at least, far more clinicians are being trained in professional schools than in traditional university programs. Many defenders of the Boulder idea (e.g., Garmezy, 1982) are deeply concerned that the professional school movement will lead to a kind of Gresham's Law in clinical psychology. Since

the professional schools (even those that award Ph.D.s) tend to value research less than Boulder programs, there is particular fear that a large part of the new generation of clinicians will lack the interest and skills to contribute to new knowledge or even to be self-critical in evaluating their own practice.

Serving a More Diverse Clientele in More Diverse Ways

The human problems with which clinicians now deal range from the enduring and grossly disabling to the minor problems of life. Some reflect medical conditions, others distortions of psychological development and personal experience, and still others relate directly to the stresses of social life. Correspondingly, but not in any one-to-one way, interventions range from drugs to the many forms of individual therapy, family therapy, group therapy, to social and community interventions. The range of patients served includes children, students, adults, the aged, workers, and executives, the poor and racial minorities as well as the affluent and educated, the physically disabled, mentally retarded, brain-damaged, and medically ill, as well as those with more strictly psychological problems. Not least, the setttings in which clinicians work include schools and universities, community agencies and organizations, and streets and homes as well as clinics and hospitals. The opportunity to serve has greatly increased, but also the need to understand more diverse people, suffering more diverse problems, in more varied settings.

Conceptual Frameworks for Clinical Intervention

Another face of the growing complexity of the clinician's world is revealed by the range of conceptual frameworks within which interventions are done, including those of biological psychiatry (neuropsychology, medical psychology, etc.), psychoanalytic, behavioral, and humanistic/existential psychologies, and social, organizational, and community psychology. Herink (1980) has recently estimated that one can chose from among 250 different psychotherapies, each of which is endorsed enthusiastically by at least its founder, a loyal band of followers, and a number of satisfied customers. Although there has been a gratifying increase in well-designed research studies evaluating therapeutic outcome, there is yet little conclusive evidence of the value of one therapeutic system over another (e.g., Luborsky, Singer, & Luborsky, 1975). Moreover, serious question is being raised as to whether all or most therapies are effective in terms of properties they have in common rather than in terms of those qualities that distinguish them (Frank, 1973; Goldfried, 1982; Korchin & Sands, 1982). With this recognition, there has been a serious movement toward rapprochement among contending therapeutic systems, with the possibility that the overall effectiveness of therapy can be increased by including elements from different systems. This trend is also reflected in the greater willingness of clinicians to call themselves "eclectic" rather than affiliated from any school (Garfield & Kurtz, 1976).

Specialization

These many trends support the simple proposition that clinicians will function in many modes in the future; instead of one speciality, there will be a family of clinical psychologies. The new clinician will be more of a specialist and less of a generalist, although I would hope, with enough breadth and wisdom not to deserve the jibe that "a specialist is one who knows everything about his field except its relative unimportance." Traditionally, as we have seen, the work of the clinician consisted of assessment, therapy, and research in either academic or psychiatric settings. There is no end of possible jobs, including: (1) medical psychologist working with patients in hospitals; (2) health psychologist, working in such areas as stress management or smoking control; (3) child clinician; (4) gerontological clinician, working with problems of the aged; (5) private practice psychotherapist; (6) community psychologist; (7) research clinical psychologist; (8) evaluation researcher; (9) consultant to school or industry, among others. The development of new specialties presents challenging new opportunities for service and for gratifying careers. At the same time, there is the danger of fragmentation of the broader field. Obviously, to do each of these jobs requires special knowledge and training, but is there a core of the parent field of clinical psychology that should be incorporated in the training of all these (sub)specialists? Curiously, this is a rephrasing of a question of 1947: Is there a core of general psychology that should be included in the education of all clinical psychologists? There was no simple answer then, nor is there one now.

From a personal standpoint, all of these trends highlight the exciting state of clinical psychology today and the challenges in its future. With so many choices, so much diversity, and change so rapid, my own inclination is to argue for the traditional virtues embodied in the scientist-professional concept with the blend of understanding and helping that has made clinical psychology unique. There is room and need for competent practitioners of course, but even as Shakow noted in 1965, the greater need is for research that can guide future clinical practice.

Summary

I have tried to sketch the history of clinical psychology as it has evolved since 1896. For the first part of the story, I describe history, events that occurred before they were of any importance to me. The second half, however, is autobiographical since my career corresponds to the period of most vigorous and exciting growth. During this period, clinical psychology emerged as an autonomous profession, grew and diversified greatly, in terms of the variety of people served, roles and functions of clinicians, types of interventions, and patterns of training. Clinical psychology is more a family of fields than a single speciality, and there are dangers of fragmentation, overspecialization, and professionalism. Such problems can best be averted if clinical psychology continues to be committed to the values that gave it definition and distinction. Central among these is the unique blend of understanding and helping that distinguishes clinical psychology from other areas of psychology.

References

American Psychological Association, Committee on Training in Clinical Psychology. Recommended graduate training programs in clinical psychology. *American Psychologist*, 1947, **2**, 539–558.

Back, K. W. *Beyond words: The story of sensitivity training and the encounter movement.* New York: Russell Sage Foundation, 1972.

Basowitz, H., Persky, H., Korchin, S. J., & Grinker, R. R. *Anxiety and stress.* New York: McGraw-Hill, 1955.

Brotemarkle, R. A. Fifty years of clinical psychology: Clinical psychology, 1896–1946. *Journal of Consulting Psychology*, 1947, **11**, 1–4.

Frank, J. D. *Persuasion and healing.* (Rev. ed.) Baltimore, Md.: The Johns Hopkins University Press, 1973.

Garfield, S. L., & Kurtz, R. Clinical psychologists in the 1970's. *American Psychologist*, 1976, **31**, 1–9.

Garmezy, N. Research in clinical psychology: Serving the future hour. In P. C. Kendall & J. N. Butcher (Eds.), *Handbook of research methods in clinical psychology.* New York: Wiley, 1982.

Goldfried, M. R. (Ed.). *Converging themes in the practice of psychotherapy*. New York: Springer, 1982.

Goldstein, K. *The organism*. New York: American Book Company, 1939.

Herink, R. (Ed.). *The psychotherapy handbook: The A to Z guide to more than 250 different therapies in use today*. New York: New American Library (Meridian), 1980.

James, W. *Principles of psychology*. New York: Holt, 1890.

James, W. *Varieties of religious experiencing: A study in human nature*. New York: Longmans Green, 1902.

Jones, E. E., & Krochin, S. J. (Eds.). *Minority mental health*. New York: Praeger, 1982.

Klopfer, B., & Davidson, H. H. *The Rorschach technique: An introductory manual*. New York: Harcourt, Brace & World, 1942.

Koch, S. The image of man implicit in encounter group theory. *Journal of Humanistic Psychology*, 1971, **11**, 109–128.

Korchin, S. J. *Modern clinical psychology*. New York: Basic Books, 1976.

Korchin, S. J. Clinical psychology and minority problems. *American Psychologist*, 1980, **35**, 262–269.

Korchin, S. J., & Cowan, P. A. Ethical perspectives in clinical research. In P. C. Kendall & J. H. Butcher (Eds.), *Handbook of research methods in clinical research*. New York: Wiley, 1982.

Korchin, S. J., & Ruff, G. E. Personality characteristics of the Mercury astronauts. In G. H. Grosser, H. Wechsler, & M. Greenblatt (Eds.), *The threat of impending disaster: Contributions to the psychology of stress*. Cambridge, Mass.: The M.I.T. Press, 1964.

Korchin, S. J., & Sands, S. H. Principles common to all psychotherapies. In C. E. Walker (Ed.), *Handbook of clinical psychology*. Homewood, Ill.: Dow Jones-Irwin, 1982.

Korchin, S. J., & Schuldberg, D. The future of clinical assessment. *American Psychologist*, 1981, **36**, 1,147–1,158.

Levine, M. *The history and politics of community mental health*. New York: Oxford, 1981.

Lieberman, M. A., Yalom, I. D., & Miles, M. B. *Encounter groups: First facts*. New York: Basic Books, 1973.

Luborsky, L., Singer, B., & Luborsky, L. Comparative studies of psychotherapies: Is it true that "Everyone has won and all must have prizes"? *Archives of General Psychiatry*, 1975, **32**, 995–1,008.

Maddi, S. R. Personology for the 1980s. Opening address in the Michigan State University H. A. Murray Lectures in Personality, April 16–17, 1982.

Murray, H. A. *Explorations in personality*. New York: Oxford University Press, 1938.

Raimy, V. C. (Ed.). *Training in clinical psychology*. Englewood Cliffs, N. J.: Prentice-Hall, 1950.

Reisman, J. M. *A history of clinical psychology*. New York: Irvington Publishers, 1976.

Reisman, J. M. History and current trends in clinical psychology. In C. E. Walker (Ed.), *Clinical practice of psychology: A guide for mental health professionals*. New York: Pergamon, 1981.

Richards, T. W. *Modern clinical psychology*. New York: McGraw-Hill, 1946.

Rogers, C. R. *Counseling and psychotherapy*. Boston: Houghton-Mifflin, 1942.

Ruff, G. E., & Korchin, S. J. Psychological responses of the Mercury astronauts to stress. In G. H. Grosser, H. Wechsler, & M. Greenblatt (Eds.), *The threat of impending disaster: Contributions to the psychology of stress*. Cambridge, Mass.: The M.I.T. Press, 1964.

Sarason, S. B. *The clinical interaction*. New York: Harper, 1954.

Shakow, D. Seventeen years later: Clinical psychology in the light of the 1947 Committee on Training in Clinical Psychology in the light of the 1947 Committee on Training in Clinical Psychology report. *American Psychologist*, 1965, **20**, 353–362.

Smith, M. B., Bruner, J. S., & White, R. W. *Opinions and personality*. New York: Wiley, 1956.

Soskin, W. F., Ross, N., & Korchin, S. J. The origin of Project Community: Innovating a social institution for adolescents. *Seminars in Psychiatry*, 1971, **3**, 271–287.

Strupp, H. H. Clinical psychology, irrationalism, and the erosion of excellence. *American Psychologist*, 1976, **31**, 561–571.

Watson, R. I. A brief history of clinical psychology. *Psychological Bulletin*, 1953, **50** 321–346.

White, R. W. Exploring personality the long way: The study of lives. In A. I. Rabin, J. Aronoff, A. H. Barclay, & R. A. Zucker (Eds.). *Further explorations in personality*. New York: Wiley, 1981.

2 THEORETICAL FOUNDATIONS OF CLINICAL PSYCHOLOGY

Irving B. Weiner

Contemporary thinking and practice in clinical psychology primarily have been shaped by three lines of theory: psychoanalytic theory, learning theory, and humanistic theory. As elaborated in Part II of this handbook, each of these seminal frames of reference is comprised of diverse schools of thought and shades of emphasis; in fact, groups of psychoanalytic, learning, and humanistic theorists sometimes differ as much among themselves as from each other (Bandura, 1977; Feldman & Broadhurst, 1976; Mahrer, 1978; Munroe, 1955; Shaffer, 1978; Wyss, 1973). Nevertheless, these broad lines of theory have influenced clinical psychology through fostering three distinctive approaches to conceptualizing, assessing, and attempting to ameliorate abnormal behavior. Psychoanalytic theories have generated various *dynamic* approaches in clinical practice and research; learning theories have provided the basis for numerous *behavioral* approaches; and humanistic theories are reflected in certain *experiential* approaches.

The present chapter summarizes the basic postulates of these three approaches and identifies their distinctive emphases and abiding influences on clinical psychology. The discussion, then, turns to some lines of convergence among these approaches, especially in relation to common threads of cognitive emphasis, and comments on alternative ways in which clinicians have attempted to accommodate such commonalities. The chapter concludes by calling attention to a substantial extent of theoretical eclecticism among clinical psychologists.

Dynamic Approaches

Dynamic approaches in clinical psychology revolve around the belief that human behavior is determined by the interplay of psychological forces. As formulated by Freud (1923, 1926, 1933) in his structural model of personality functioning, these forces include (a) basic needs, wishes, and impulses, many of which lie outside of conscious awareness (*id*); (b) capacities for thinking, feeling, and acting in ways that express or gratify needs, wishes, and impulses (*ego*); (c) a sense of propriety or conscience concerning whether particular needs, wishes, and impulses should be expressed or gratified (*superego*); and (d) the opportunities for self-expression or gratification that exist in the external environment (*reality*).

From this perspective, the balance that is struck among the frequently contradictory demands and constraints of id, ego, superego, and reality shapes an individual's personality style and preferred action patterns. Failure or inability to resolve conflicts among these four agencies generates anxiety, which is a painful affect that people seek to reduce or eliminate. Maladaptive efforts to minimize anxiety produce various forms of psychopathology, which are regarded as inadequate or immature defensive reactions to distress stemming from unresolved psychological conflicts (Cameron, 1963; Fenichel, 1945; Holzman, 1970).

The dynamic formulation of psychopathology leads to an emphasis in personality assessment on two questions. First, with respect to personality dynamics, what are the conflicting thoughts and feelings that are causing an individual to experience anxiety? Second, with respect to personality structure, what are the preferred coping styles that account for why the individual is dealing with anxiety in certain adaptive or maladaptive ways (Allison, Blatt, & Zimet, 1968; Pope, 1979; Rapaport, Gill, & Schafer, 1968; Shafer, 1954; Spitzer & Endicott, 1973; Weiner, 1966; Weins, 1976)?

In treatment, dynamic approaches seek to help people gain increased understanding of why they are anxious and how they are coping ineffectively with their anxiety. Interpretations are used to expand client awareness of underlying concerns and maladaptive response styles. This expanded awareness allows troubled people to reflect more rationally than before on their unresolved conflicts and to opt for more effective coping behaviors (Chessick, 1973; Dewald, 1971; Greenson, 1967; Langs, 1973; Weiner, 1975).

Distinctive Emphases

Dynamic approaches to assessment and treatment involve three distinctive emphases. First, dynamic approaches are based on *inferred processes*. Behavior is explained in terms of underlying aspects of personality structure and dynamics that are considered to account for it. The answer to why a disturbed person shows a particular symptom, gives a particular test response, or develops a particular reaction in psychotherapy is to be found in some type of personality process that exists independently of whatever behavior is manifest.

Second, dynamic approaches stress *intellectual processes* as the highest order of human functioning. To be sure, psychoanalytic formulations address the part that inappropriate, excessive, or ambivalent affects play in psychological maladjustment. In the end, however, success in dynami-

cally oriented psychotherapy is expected to depend on how extensively a person can gain understanding and impose reason on emotion. The more that reason prevails, the more effectively people will be able to overcome psychological stress and find satisfaction in their work and pleasure in their interpersonal relationships. Freud's (1933) words on the importance of mastering the irrational were, "Where id was, there shall ego be" (p. 80).

Third, dynamic approaches emphasize *historical processes*. Psychological difficulties are believed to originate in prior life experiences that have burdened a person with unresolved conflicts and maladaptive coping styles. Assessment and therapy in this framework are exploratory efforts to unearth clues to the nature of these prior experiences, so that they can be reexperienced or reevaluated in the critical light of current perspectives. The following illustrative interpretive observation to a client captures this emphasis on inferred, intellectual, and historical processes in the dynamic approach: "From what we have learned about you, we can see that now, as an adult with children of your own, you still tend to respond to women as you did to your mother when you were a child."

Abiding Influences

The abiding influences of dynamic approaches in clinical psychology are closely entwined with the historical influence of the psychoanalytic movement. As elaborated by Shakow and Rapaport (1964), Freud's formulations have left their stamp on virtually all of psychology, and especially on the areas of abnormal, developmental, personality, and social psychology. Probably most significant in each of these areas is the lasting impact of Freud's insistence that all behavior—no matter how strange, irrational, self-defeating, or seemingly incomprehensible—can be *understood* in psychological terms.

Some of Freud's specific proposals for understanding behavior have stood the test of time better than others, and substantial revisions of his notions have been recommended even by theorists committed to a traditional psychoanalytic point of view (Arlow & Brenner, 1964; Blanck & Blanck, 1974; Fairbairn, 1954; Fisher & Greenberg, 1977; Hartmann, 1958). Nevertheless, two of Freud's early works—a chapter on psychotherapy that he wrote for *Studies on Hysteria* (Breuer & Freud, 1893-1895) and his *Psychopathology of Everyday Life* (1901)—remain as influential today as they were originally in establishing: (a) that potentially understandable psychological factors determine human behavior, and (b) that this psychological determination provides avenues for alleviating emotional disorder through psychological interventions.

Behavioral Approaches

Behavioral approaches in clinical psychology are based on the conviction that all behavior, normal and abnormal, is learned. Various patterns of psychopathology result when people learn maladaptive ways of coping with their experience, and poor psychological adjustment thus consists of bad habits (Eysenck, 1959; Kanfer & Phillips, 1970; Wolpe, 1958; Yates, 1970). In this frame of reference the manifest symptoms of psychological disorder constitute the disorder and their removal constitutes its cure: "There is no neurosis underlying the symptom, but merely the symptom itself. Get rid of the symptom . . . and you have eliminated the neurosis" (Eysenck & Rachman, 1965, p. 10).

Whereas dynamic approaches to assessment seek to account for *why* people behave as they do, assessment from the behavioral perspective focuses on *how* people actually behave in particular situations or in response to various reinforcement contingencies. Assessment data are derived as much as possible from observations of behavior in natural settings, with special attention to antecedent and consequent events that elicit and sustain overt response patterns. When naturalistic observations cannot be made and assessment situations must be contrived, every effort is made to use methods that will yield a representative sample of what the actual behavior would be (Barlow, 1981; Ciminero, Calhoun, & Adams, 1977; Cone & Hawkins, 1977; Goldfried & Kent, 1972; Hersen & Bellack, 1976; Mash & Terdal, 1981).

The central treatment strategy in behavioral approaches consists of exposing people to new learning situations that will modify their maladaptive response patterns. The therapist's task is to implement reinforcement contingencies that will inhibit pathological habits and expand a person's repertoire of adaptive coping behaviors — sometimes through pairing pleasant experience with previously painful situations (systematic desensitization), sometimes through pairing painful experience with undesirable behavior (aversion therapy), sometimes through fostering and re-

warding specific types of constructive action patterns (operant conditioning), and sometimes through education in more effective ways of dealing with experience (modeling). If the therapist can provide a corrective set of reinforcements, the client's abnormal behavior can be expected to change for the better (Bandura, 1969; Goldfried & Davison, 1976; Goldstein & Foa, 1980; Rosenthal & Bandura, 1978; Turner, Calhoun, & Adams, 1981; Wolpe, 1969).

Distinctive Emphases

In contrast to the emphasis in dynamic approaches on inferred, intellectual, and historical processes, behavioral approaches are first of all concerned with *observable processes*. The appropriate subject of the clinician's attention is what people can actually be observed to do, not possible explanations of their actions in terms of underlying personality processes.

Second, the central focus in this approach is on *behavioral processes*, not thoughts or feelings. What is real about people is how they act. The behavioral tradition recognizes that disturbed people may experience troubling thoughts and painful affects. If, however, they can be helped to act differently, their progress toward more effective behavior patterns will be accompanied by a corresponding reduction in their distressing thoughts and feelings (Weiner, 1967).

Third, behaviorally oriented clinicians concentrate on *ahistorical processes*. To be sure, learning theorists believe that a person's preferred behavior patterns are shaped by prior experiences that have produced a hierarchy of habits of various strengths. However, clinical work from the behavioral perspective consists not of uncovering such prior experiences, but instead of establishing a present set of reinforcement contingencies that will alter the existing habit-strength hierarchy. This traditional emphasis on observable behavioral and ahistorical processes in the behavioral approach is summarized as follows by Eysenck and Rachman (1965, p. 12):

All treatment of neurotic disorders is concerned with habits existing at present; the historical development is largely irrelevant. Cures are achieved by treating the symptom itself. . . . Interpretation, even if not completely subjective and erroneous, is irrelevant. Symptomatic treatment leads to permanent recovery.

Abiding Influences

Whereas psychoanalytic theorists have had their major impact on clinical psychology by establishing that psychopathology can be *understood*, learning theorists have had their most abiding influence by insisting that psychopathology must be *objectified*. The inferred processes inherent in dynamic approaches are difficult to translate into reliably measurable variables for research purposes. Although increasingly sophisticated designs are being utilized to meet this challenge, relatively little definitive research has been done to demonstrate the validity of psychoanalytic theories. Moreover, many dynamically oriented clinicians write and teach as if their point of view is fully supportable by clinical impressions and above reproach from research workers (Fisher & Greenberg, 1977; Luborsky & Spence, 1978).

The impressionistic, self-validating tack often taken by psychoanalytic theories has alienated many psychologists who define their discipline as a behavioral science. The impact of learning theorists on clinical psychology has had the positive infuence of reducing this alienation. By objectifying the content of clinical psychology for research purposes, behavioral approaches have fostered the accumulation of verifiable knowledge. By increasing the interest of experimentally oriented psychologists in clinical problems and also encouraging dynamically oriented clinicians to think in more objective terms, behaviorally oriented clinicians have brought clinical pursuits increasingly into the mainstream of psychology and enriched the field with new ideas, new methods, and a new generation of teachers, scholars, and practitioners.

As a second abiding influence, behavioral approaches have expanded the range of problems that clinical psychologists have felt they could address effectively. In the dynamic approach, successful treatment requires clients to participate in an intellectual process of gaining insight into their problems. Depending on how well they can participate in such a process, some people will profit more from psychotherapy than others, and people with some kinds of disorder have traditionally been considered unlikely to profit at all.

By contrast, the behavioral focus on manifest symptoms instead of underlying disorder creates the potential for any problem to be ameliorated through psychological interventions. If the clinician can present reinforcement contingencies that will shape more desirable behavior, the client's adjustment will be improved—even if he or she happens to be autistic, retarded, brain-damaged, psychopathic, addicted, elderly, physically ill, or nonverbal, to pick some of the characteristics that have often been regarded as contraindicating psychotherapy or any major treatment role for clinical psychologists. The work of behaviorally oriented therapists with people who have such characteristics has substantially broadened the scope of substantive concerns, professional activities, and work settings that compose contemporary clinical psychology (Kazdin, 1978, 1979a; Leitenberg, 1976; Sloane et al., 1975).

Experiential Approaches

Experiential approaches in clinical psychology depart from dynamic and behavioral approaches in two significant respects. First, people are not regarded as passive products either of the balance that is struck between competing forces or of reinforcements that shape habit hierarchies. Instead, people are seen as inherently active, self-affirming organisms who forge their own destiny and have enormous capacity for positive personal growth. Progress toward improved adjustment is conceived not as an effort to throw off the shackles of previously determined psychological handicaps, but as a future-oriented exercise of free will in the pursuit of self-fulfillment (Allport, 1937, 1961; Kelly, 1955, 1980; Maslow, 1962; May, Angel, & Ellenberger, 1958).

Second, the humanistic tradition from which experiential approaches emerge is an *idiographic* psychology. There is no place in this orientation for prinicples of behavior that presume to account for prevalent or recurrent action patterns among groups of people. Rather, humanism is concerned with the uniqueness of each individual person, with how people differ from each other instead of with how they are alike (Mahrer, 1978; Shaffer, 1978). Maslow (1966) summarizes this stress on human individuality as follows: "I must approach a person as an individual unique and peculiar, the sole member of his class" (p. 10).

From this perspective, the natural tendencies of men and women are to develop into kind, friendly, self-accepting, socialized human beings. Maladjustment occurs only when people live in an atmosphere that interferes with such personal growth. Psychopathology consists of the reduced expression of human potential and a loss of congruence with one's internal self-experience. To be precise, however, it is not "psychopathology" of which experientially oriented clinicians speak, but "problems in living"—difficulties in experiencing oneself, inability to find pleasure and fulfillment in one's activities, and failure to make meaningful contact with others (Jourard, 1964; Rogers, 1961).

Consistent with an idiographic emphasis, experiential assessment seeks to identify the unique and individual meanings that people attach to their experience. Experientially oriented clinicians are not concerned with assessing personality structures or habit systems, nor do they endorse attempts to classify people according to diagnostic labels, shared personality traits, or quantitative positions along various dimensions of behavior. Such classification is rejected as a dehumanizing procedure that strips people of their dignity and self-respect. The proper focus in assessment is a *qualitative* study of the individual case, with special attention to the ways in which a person is interacting with and feeling about his or her environment (Brown, 1972; Dana & Leech, 1974; Kelly, 1955, chapters 5 & 6; Jourard, 1968, 1971).

The treatment aim in experiential approaches is to promote positive personal growth, maximal self-awareness, and increased understanding of how one is relating to one's world. Heightening consciousness in these respects is expected to expand the client's possibilities for richer and more meaningful living and greater realization of his or her human potential. By being helped to come into closer contact with what they are experiencing, clients gain greater freedom to choose rewarding commitments to other people and to creative endeavors.

The specific techniques employed by experientially oriented therapists vary across four major types of experiential therapy: client-centered therapy, existential therapy, gestalt therapy, and personal construct therapy. These varieties of experiential therapy share two common themes. First, the essence of the therapists' role is not *what they should do*, as in providing interpretations or reinforcements, but *how they should be*, in order to provide an atmosphere in which clients can grow and seek their own solutions to their problems in living. Second, psychotherapy is regarded less as a *treatment* conducted by the therapist than as a *personal encounter* used by clients to increase their capacity to relate to themselves, to others, and to their own needs, talents, and future prospects (Bannister, 1975; Boss, 1963; Bugental, 1978; Landfield & Leitner, 1980; Perls, Hefferline, &

Goodman, 1951; Polster & Polster, 1973; Rogers, 1951, 1961; Yalom, 1980).

Distinctive Emphases

In experiential approaches to working with troubled people, neither the inferred processes formulated by dynamically oriented clinicians nor the observable processes stressed by behaviorally oriented clinicians are particularly relevant, primarily because both reflect the *clinician's* perspective on the client. In the humanistic tradition, behavior can be understood only from the client's perspective. Accordingly, *subjective processes*, as experienced and reported by the client, hold the key to what a person is like and whether he or she can be helped to change.

For similar reasons, experiential approaches stress *emotional processes* instead of intellectual or behavioral processes. It is not what people think or do that is important, but how they feel. How individuals experience their life is a function of how they feel about it, and the personal growth by which people overcome problems in living while in psychotherapy requires an interaction in which meanings are intensely felt.

Finally, experiential approaches emphasize *ahistorical processes* in both the origin and the treatment of problems in living. Psychological maladjustment consists of current difficulties in finding self-fulfillment and a comfortable way of being in the world, and therapy succeeds to the extent that present encounters with a clinician can help people construct for themselves new and more rewarding ways of being.

Abiding Influences

Humanistic theorists have influenced clinical psychology most by insisting that difficulties in living should be *personalized*. Instead of asking what causes or constitutes certain kinds of psychopathology, experientially oriented clinicians ask how individual people are failing to come to terms with themselves or their environment. This frame of reference has heightened psychologists' sensitivity to unique feelings and attitudes of clients that differ from or even run counter to how most people usually think and feel.

Instead of asking how psychopathy, schizophrenia, motivation, intelligence, social class, and other client characteristics might affect the outcome of psychotherapy, experiential clinicians ask how the therapy environment can liberate each client's inherent potential for personal growth. This humanistic perspective has encouraged researchers and practitioners to look closely at therapist as well as client variables in psychotherapy. Of special importance in this regard is the attention that experiential clinicians have called to how therapists help their clients not by their skills as interpreters or reinforcers of behavior, but by their qualities as human beings, their sharing of their own experience, and their skill in sustaining a personal encounter.

In addition, the optimistic and person-centered tone of experiential approaches has attracted to clinical work psychologists for whom dynamic and behavioral approaches have little appeal. Dynamic psychology, its diversity notwithstanding, has a legacy of pessimism in which neurotic conflicts are believed to persist or recur despite extensive increments in self-understanding. In one of his last major works, Freud (1937) concluded that "A normal ego . . . is, like normality in general, an ideal fiction" (p. 235). Analysis, he continued, may thus be "the third of those 'impossible' professions in which one can be sure beforehand of achieving unsatisfying results. The other two, which have been known much longer, are education and government" (p. 248).

Behavioral approaches, their evolution over the years also notwithstanding, share a legacy in which techniques are administered by therapists to clients independently of any relevant personal relationship between them. The therapist operates mechanically, as a "reinforcement machine," and "Personal relations are not essential for cures of neurotic disorders, although they may be useful in certain circumstances" (Eysenck & Rachman, 1965, p. 12). Many psychologists who would find the dynamic tradition too pessimistic and the behavioral tradition too impersonal have been drawn by the experiential perspective into making valuable contributions to theory and practice in clinical psychology.

Lines of Convergence Among Approaches

Table 2.1 summarizes the central differences among dynamic, behavioral, and experiential approaches in clinical psychology. Although these differences reflect contrasting theoretical positions, they are not as discrete as they may appear or are sometimes believed to be. Diverse schools of thought within each approach blur many boundaries among them, as noted earlier, and certain common threads run through the practice of psychological assessment and intervention in all approaches. For example, despite differences in whether they are most concerned with intellectual, behavioral, or emotional processes, clinicians of all persuasions address the totality of how people think, feel, and act. As elaborated next, numerous other aspects of each approach can be identified in the other two.

TABLE 2.1. CENTRAL DIFFERENCES AMONG APPROACHES IN CLINICAL PSYCHOLOGY.

	Dynamic Approaches	Behavioral Approaches	Experiential Approaches
Nature of psychopathology	Maladaptive efforts to minimize anxiety stemming from unresolved psychological conflicts	Learned maladaptive habits	Difficulties in finding pleasure and fulfillment in relating to oneself and one's environment
Assessment question	Why do people behave as they do?	How do people behave in particular situations?	What unique and individual meanings do people attach to their experience?
Treatment aim	Promote increased self-understanding through interpretation	Modify maladaptive response patterns through corrective reinforcement contingencies	Facilitate positive personal growth through providing an atmosphere that expands self-awareness
Distinctive emphases	Inferred processes Intellectual processes Historical processes	Observable processes Behavioral processes Ahistorical processes	Subjective processes Emotional processes Ahistorical processes
Focal influence	Psychopathology can be understood	Psychopathology must be objectified	Psychopathology should be personalized

Behavioral and Experiential Aspects of the Dynamic Approach

Personality assessment as currently practiced within the dynamic tradition attends to many of the concerns of behaviorally and experientially oriented clinicians. Contemporary developments with respect to the Rorschach test, for example, conceive of the ink blots as a perceptual-cognitive task and stress the importance of minimizing levels of inference by sampling representative behavior. Clients are given a problem to solve ("What might this be?"), and the manner in which they configure their responses is taken as an indication of how they cope with other situations that call for perceptual-cognitive structuring (Exner & Weiner, 1982, chapter 1; Goldfried, Stricker, & Weiner, 1971, chapter 13; Weiner, 1977).

In experiential terms, adequate assessment within a dynamic frame of reference pays just as much attention to how people are different from each other as to how they are alike. Traditional psychodiagnosticians regard idiographic and nomothetic approaches to working with people as complementary, not mutually exclusive, and they consistently emphasize humanistic considerations in applying their findings (Applebaum, 1976; Shevrin & Shectman, 1973; Sugarman, 1978; Weiner, 1972).

Historically, in fact, attention to assessing the unique meanings people attach to their experience has characterized psychoanalytic theory since Freud (1900) wrote in *The Interpretation of Dreams*, "I . . . am prepared to find that the same piece of content may conceal a different meaning when it occurs in various people or in various contexts" (p. 105). Bonime (1962) has more recently affirmed this idiographic emphasis in psychoanalytic work as follows: "Dream symbols arise out of the specific life history of each individual, and it is only from the individual's life history that we can derive the meaning of his dream symbols" (p. 32).

In treatment, dynamically oriented clinicians strive to promote self-understanding, but this strategy does not constitute the goal of the treatment. As in behavioral approaches, the goal of dynamic psychotherapy is positive behavior change, including relief from emotional distress and modification of maladaptive personality characteristics. Self-understanding is considered to be the most effective means to this end, but it is not regarded as the end itself (Weiner, 1975, chapter 1).

In common with experiential approaches, dynamic psychotherapy addresses how people can achieve a greater sense of personal freedom, human relatedness, and self-fulfillment (Strupp, 1980; Sugarman, 1976). As viewed by Strupp (1975), "Analytic therapy is an education for optimal personal freedom in the context of social living" (p. 135). The experiential concern with the client-therapist relationship also has a prominent place in dynamic formulations of the treatment process. Many dynamically oriented clinicians regard analysis of the here-and-now treatment relationship, in which the therapist serves as a "participant observer," as the most powerful tool for identifying and correcting maladaptive ways of thinking and feeling (Bordin, 1979; Freud, 1912; Greenson, 1967, chapter 3; Sullivan, 1954; Weiner, 1957, chapter 10).

Dynamic and Experiential Aspects of the Behavioral Approach

In behavioral as in traditional assessment, good clinical practice attends to distinctive as well as shared features of how people respond to their experience. Along with this humanistic component, behavioral assessment has in common with dynamic approaches an inescapable need to make inferential interpretations. Only rare circumstances allow a meaningful assessment question to be answered fully by sampling behavior in a perfectly representative situation. Behavioral and traditional assessors alike must constantly consider how representative their data are, how sizable an inferential leap must be made to derive useful conclusions from these data, and how reliable their conclusions are consequently likely to be (Bellack, Hersen, & Lamparski, 1979; Kazdin, 1979b; Kendall & Hollon, 1981).

In therapy, many behaviorally oriented clinicians have begun in recent years to recognize the role of client attitudes and the treatment relationship in fostering and sustaining desired behavior change. As perceived by these clinicians, maximally effective treatment occurs only when clients understand the manner in which reinforcement contingencies have determined and can modify their behavior; when they develop improved internal capacities for self-control and self-determination; and when they hold a positive view of the helping potential of the treatment relationship (Ford, 1978; Goldfried & Merbaum, 1973; Kazdin, 1979b; Lazarus, 1971; Mahoney & Arnkoff, 1978; Wilson & Evans, 1977).

These trends in contemporary behavior therapy reflect a cognitive-behavioral orientation that includes a traditionally dynamic focus on internal, covert processes, such as what clients think, imagine, expect, and believe (Kendall & Hollon, 1979; Meichenbaum, 1977). From this perspective, the original formulations of behavior therapy placed too much emphasis on observable events and too little emphasis on how people perceive and evaluate these events. "Environmental events *per se*, although important, are not of *primary* importance; rather what the client says to himself about those events influences his behavior" (Meichenbaum, 1977, p. 108).

Dynamic and Behavioral Aspects of the Experiential Approach

In common with the traditional dynamic emphasis and recent trends within the behavioral approach, experientially oriented clinicians have been attaching increasing importance to the role of cognitive processes in promoting personal growth. Many client-centered theorists have supplemented their traditional stress on personal growth through openness to experience with the conviction that clients must understand as well as experience life situations. From this perspective, the ability to achieve and sustain a richer existence is measured by how adequately people can acquire and organize information about themselves and their world (Anderson, 1974; Wexler, 1974; Zimring, 1974). As Greenwald (1973) puts it, "There is need for both the experiential approach . . . and for the cognitive approach, if therapy is to be anything but kicks" (p. 27).

This cognitive-experiential trend is especially clear in the rational-emotive therapy developed by Ellis (Ellis, 1962; Ellis & Grieger, 1977). The basic assumption in rational-emotive therapy is that emotional distress and self-defeating behavior result from misperceptions and mistaken beliefs, and the treatment consists of directives and exercises intended to modify what people think and say to themselves. Although Ellis' formulations can be seen as contributing to the emergence of contemporary cognitive-behavior therapy, he regards his approach as a humanistic psychotherapy that aims at helping clients become maximally self-accepting (Ellis, 1974, 1980). Ellis' work thus has added a cognitive component to experiential approaches while also linking learning theory and humanistic influences on the practice of clinical psychology.

The cognitive emphasis that has traditionally characterized dynamic approaches and has more recently emerged in behavioral and experiential approaches as well has been suggested by some theorists to constitute a distinct approach to clinical psychology in its own right. From this perspective, psychological adjustment can be fully understood and described in terms of cognitive-representational processes: maladjustment or problems in living derive from irrational fears, beliefs, or expectations, and clinical work consists of a cognitive process of identifying thoughts, wishes, and feelings and making psychological connections among them (Beck, 1976; Bieber, 1980; Mahoney, 1977; Raimy, 1975). Time will tell whether such cognitive formulations continue to be refined as a bridge among dynamic, behavioral, and experiential approaches or instead, supported by theoretical and research developments in cognitive psychology, become established as a fourth major approach in clinical psychology.

Accommodating Lines of Convergence

Clinicians have responded in several different ways to the lines of convergence among dynamic, behavioral, and experiential approaches. Some have chosen simply to ignore or deny their existence. Clinicians who adopt this "stonewalling" stance adhere strictly to a single point of view, as if it were the revealed truth, and decline to consider that other frames of reference might add something useful to the understanding and treatment of psychological disorder. Typically, they reinforce their convictions by listening only to colleagues who share their narrow outlook. In accounting for this reluctance to recognize lines of convergence, Frank (1976) observes that "little glory derives from showing that the particular method one has mastered with so much effort may be indistinguishable from other methods in its effects" (p. 74).

Fortunately, most clinicians combine some theoretical preference with a supportive or at least tolerant attitude toward other approaches. Setting a good example in this regard, Freud (1904) made no bones about his view that "the analytic method of psychotherapy is the one that penetrates most deeply and carries furthest" (p. 260).

He preceded this remark, however, with the following observation: "There are many ways and means of practicing psychotherapy. All that lead to recovery are good" (p. 259).

Although Freud's followers and disciplines of other theorists have not always heeded this wise counsel, there is reason to believe that parochial dogmatism is on the wane. Experienced clinicians are becoming increasingly open to each other's views and prepared to utilize treatment strategies of demonstrated effectiveness, whatever their theoretical origin (Goldfried, 1980). Despite the influence of stonewallers in some quarters, then, clinical psychology appears to be reaching a point of agreement with the present author that "effective psychotherapy is defined not by its brand name, but by how well it meets the needs of the patient" (Weiner, 1975, p. 44).

A second response to lines of convergence has been an effort to accomodate them through *reformulation*, which consists of translating the concepts of other theoretical formulations into the language of some preferred frame of reference. As cases in point, both psychoanalytic and client-centered methods have been presented in the conceptual language of social learning theory (Dollard & Miller, 1950; Martin, 1972). The problem with such reformulations is that they can easily end up as sterile exercises. The robustness of one approach may be demonstrated by its capacity to absorb the concepts of other approaches, but the ensuing result does little to enrich the scope of clinical methods.

Another accommodation of the lines of convergence among approaches in clinical psychology has consisted of efforts at *amalgamation*. From an amalgamation perspective, the distinctive theoretical formulations associated with different schools of thought are little more than window dressing. Although they may provide a professionally supportive sense of identity with some theoretical tradition, they have less bearing on how clinical psychology is actually practiced than do lessons learned from experience. In this frame of reference, all roads lead to Rome. Talented and experienced clinicians will end up working with their clients in pretty much the same ways, regardless of the theories they espouse. Advances in knowledge in clinical psychology will accordingly come not from comparative theoretical analyses, but instead from identifying common principles of behavior change that transcend all variations in theoretical language.

In discussing the possible amalgamation of theories that have influenced clinical practice, numerous writers have called attention to *general* factors that promote positive behavior change in any psychotherapy relationship. These general factors include the opportunity for catharsis that all forms of psychotherapy provide the client; the expectations of change that clients bring into psychotherapy or develop from their therapist's willingness to work with them; regular occasions for clients to talk with another person who respects their dignity and is trying to understand and be helpful; and reinforcing effects of how and when therapists respond to positive aspects of what their clients say and do. These general factors foster increments in well-being independently of *specific* treatment techniques prescribed by one or another theoretical stance, such as interpretation, modeling, and self-disclosure (Frank, 1971; Kazdin, 1979c; Strupp, 1970, 1973; Weiner, 1976).

Support for the argument that different approaches in clinical psychology should be amalgamated requires evidence that general factors account fully for behavior change in psychotherapy, while specific theory-driven procedures produce neither enhanced nor distinctive results. In addition, it should be demonstrable that experienced therapists of all persuasions do in fact conduct therapy in essentially the same way.

With respect to the first kind of evidence, adequate research has not yet been done to clearly separate the contribution of general and specific factors to psychotherapy outcome. Whatever the results of such research may be, however, many psychologists would caution against exclusive attention to general change agents in psychotherapy. An emphasis on general change aspects can have the unintended consequence of engendering antiscientific, antiprofessional attitudes toward psychotherapy—especially the belief that anyone can conduct successful psychotherapy with a willing client simply by being pleasant, attentive, and nonjudgmental, without having to undergo extensive training to learn complex technical procedures. Regardless of how much evidence emerges for the impact of general factors in psychotherapy, then, psychologists should continue to seek, learn, and teach specific treatment techniques that can enhance and accelerate the therapy process (Lazarus, 1980; Strupp, 1976a; Weiner, 1976).

Regarding distinctive results, available evidence indicates that various schools of therapy are about equally effective when a broad spectrum of clients is considered in general. When particular kinds of disorders are examined, however, some differences appear in how likely they are to respond to particular treatment methods. Although much definitive research remains to be done concerning distinctive outcomes, there is growing empirical support for applying certain specific therapies to certain specific problems (Bergin & Lambert, 1978; Frank et al., 1978; Lazarus, 1980; Strupp & Hadley, 1979).

As for actual practice, several earlier research reports suggested that therapists of all persuasions: (a) endorse many of the same basic treatment strategies, such as providing a warm and accepting atmosphere and having their clients engage in new, corrective experiences; and (b) display more similarities than differences in the tactics of what they actually say to their clients (Fiedler, 1950; Marmor, 1976, Strupp, 1976b; Wrenn, 1960). More recently, however, accumulating evidence on tactics points in the other direction, namely, that therapists with different orientations provide distinctive kinds of treatment and differ in many technical aspects of how they conduct psychotherapy sessions, especially in the amount of direct guidance they provide and how close or distant a personal relationship they maintain with their clients (Bruinink & Schroeder, 1979; Gomes-Schwartz, 1978; Messer & Winokur, 1980; Staples et al., 1975).

On balance, then, efforts to amalgamate approaches in clinical psychology cannot be supported by empirical data. Numerous commonalities among approaches can be identified at the level of clinical strategies, such as providing a warm relationship in psychotherapy. At the level of clinical tactics, however, differences in theory are much more than window dressing. The evidence indicates that the theoretical orientations to which psychologists subscribe influence them to employ many clearly distinctive methods and techniques in their clinical work.

In light of these facts, an increasingly popular fourth approach to dealing with lines of convergence among approaches stresses *complementarity*. From this point of view, the dynamic, behavioral, and experiential perspectives on assessment and intervention complement each other and enrich the ability of clinicians to understand and work effectively with their clients. The complete clinician is one who appreciates the lessons taught by various theories and can draw on the concepts and methods of many different approaches in delivering psychological services (Appelbaum, 1979; Feather & Rhoads, 1972; Hersen, 1970; Lazarus, 1976; Marmor, 1971; Murray, 1976; Murray & Jacobson, 1978; Wachtel, 1977).

Conclusions

The complementarity perspective on lines of convergence among approaches in clinical psychology is reflected in widespread eclecticism among clinicians. In a survey of the theoretical preferences of a representative sample of 479 members of the APA Division of Clinical Psychology, Norcross and Prochaska (1982) found that over 30 percent considered themselves to have an eclectic orientation (see Table 2.2). Of these eclectic psychologists, approximately half were committed to primarily dynamic eclecticism, about one-quarter to behavioral eclecticism, and 10 percent to an experientially based eclecticism.

Some concluding comments on eclecticism are in order. There is a persistent danger in clinical psychology that being "eclectic" will justify a superficial, chaotic approach to assessment and intervention in which practitioners fly by the seat of their pants, their "open-mindedness" and lack of commitment to any single point of view concealing ignorance of any of the theoretical formulations that provide a necessary guide to clinical work. When eclecticism masks the absence of a cohesive frame of reference, clients rarely reap the benefits of cumulative clinical wisdom, and knowl-

TABLE 2.2. THEORETICAL ORIENTATIONS OF CLINICAL PSYCHOLOGISTS.*

Theoretical Orientations	Percentage
Dynamic (Psychoanalytic, Neo-Freudian, Sullivanian)	32.3
Eclectic	30.9
Behavioral	14.4
Experiential (Rogerian, Existentialist, Humanistic)	6.3
Cognitive	6.3
Other	9.8
	100.0

*Based on the Norcross and Prochaska (1982) survey of 479 members of the APA Division of Clinical Psychology.

edge seldom advances through definitive research designs.

Accordingly, eclecticism should not be defined or embraced as an intuitive, nonconceptual approach to clinical work. Instead, following Garfield (1980), it should represent the willingness and capacity of clinicians with some preferred conceptual frame of reference to acknowledge, understand, and utilize in their work the postulates of theorists with other preferences and the empirical data generated by theorists of all preferences. At a time of imperfect knowledge, when each of the traditional theoretical foundations of clinical psychology offers some answers but none holds them all, it would seem professionally irresponsible for clinicians to do otherwise.

References

Allison, J., Blatt, S. J., & Zimet, C. N. *The interpretation of psychological tests.* New York: Harper & Row, 1968.

Allport, G. W. *Personality: A psychological interpretation.* Holt, Rinehart & Winston, 1937.

Allport, G. W. *Pattern and growth in personality.* New York: Holt, Rinehart & Winston, 1961.

Anderson, W. Personal growth and client-centered therapy: An information processing view. In D.A. Wexler & L. N. Rice (Eds.), *Innovations in client-centered therapy.* New York: Wiley, 1974.

Applebaum, S. A. Objections to diagnosis and diagnostic psychological testing diagnosed. *Bulletin of the Menninger Clinic,* 1976, **40**, 559–564.

Appelbaum, S. A. *Out in inner space: A psychoanalyst explores the new therapies.* Garden City, N.Y.: Anchor Books, 1979.

Arlow, J. A., & Brenner, C. *Psychoanalytic concepts and the structural theory.* New York: International Universities Press, 1964.

Bandura, A. *Principles of behavior modification.* New York: Holt, 1969.

Bandura, A. *Social learning theory.* Englewood Cliffs, N.J.: Prentice-Hall, 1977.

Bannister, D. Personal construct theory psychotherapy. In D. Bannister (Ed.), *Issues and approaches in the psychological therapies.* New York: Wiley, 1975.

Barlow, D. H. (Ed.) *Behavioral assessment of adult disorders.* New York: Guilford, 1981.

Beck. A. T. *Cognitive therapy and the emotional disorders.* New York: International Universities Press, 1976.

Bellack, A. S., Hersen, M., & Lamparski, D. Role-playing tests for assessing social skills: Are they valid? Are they useful? *Journal of Consulting and Clinical Psychology,* 1979, **47**, 335–342.

Bergin, A. E., & Lambert, M. J. The evaluation of therapeutic outcomes. In S. L. Garfield & A. E. Bergin (Eds.), *Handbook of psychotherapy and behavior change.* (2nd ed.) New York: Wiley, 1978.

Bieber, I. *Cognitive psychoanalysis.* New York: Aronson, 1980.

Blanck, G., & Blanck, R. *Ego psychology: Theory and practice.* New York: Columbia University Press, 1974.

Bonime, W. *The clinical use of dreams.* New York: Basic Books, 1962.

Bordin, E. S. The generalizability of the psychoanalytic concept of the working alliance. *Psychotherapy: Theory, Research and Practice,* 1979, **16**, 252–259.

Boss, M. *Psychoanalysis and daseinanalysis.* New York: Basic Books, 1963.

Breuer, J. & Freud, S. (1893–1895) Studies on hysteria. *Standard Edition,* Vol. II. London: Hogarth, 1955.

Brown, E. C. Assessment from a humanistic perspective. *Psychotherapy: Theory, Research and Practice,* 1972, **9**, 103–106.

Bruinink, S. A., & Schroeder, H. E. Verbal therapeutic behavior of expert psychoanalytically oriented, Gestalt, and behavior therapists. *Journal of Consulting and Clinical Psychology,* 1979, **47**, 567–574.

Bugental, J. T. F. *Psychotherapy and process: The fundamentals of an existential humanistic approach.* Reading, Mass.: Addison-Wesley, 1978.

Cameron, N. *Personality development and psychopathology: A dynamic approach.* Boston: Houghton-Mifflin, 1963.

Chessick, R. D. *Technique and practice of intensive psychotherapy.* New York: Aronson, 1973.

Ciminero, A. R., Calhoun, K. S., & Adams, H. E. (Eds.). *Handbook of behavioral assessment.* New York: Wiley, 1977.

Cone, J. D., & Hawkins, R. P. (Eds.). *Behavioral assessment: New directions in clinical psychology.* New York: Brunner/Mazel, 1977.

Dana, R. H., & Leech, S. Existential assessment. *Journal of Personality Assessment,* 1974, **38**, 428–435.

Dewald, P. A. *Psychotherapy: A dynamic approach.* (2nd ed.) New York: Basic Books, 1971.

Dollard, J., & Miller, N. E. *Personality and psychotherapy.* New York: McGraw-Hill, 1950.

Ellis, A. *Reason and emotion in psychotherapy.* New York: Lyle Stuart, 1962.

Ellis, A. *Humanistic psychotherapy.* New York: McGraw-Hill, 1974.

Ellis, A. Rational-emotive therapy and cognitive behavior therapy: Similarities and differences. *Cognitive Therapy & Research,* 1980, **4**, 325–340.

Ellis, A., & Grieger, R. (Eds.). *Handbook of rational-emotive therapy.* New York: Springer, 1977.

Exner, J. E., & Weiner, I. B. *The Rorschach: A comprehensive system,* Vol. 3. *Assessment of children and adolescents.* New York: Wiley, 1982.

Eysenck, H. J. Learning theory and behaviour therapy. *Journal of Mental Science,* 1959, **105**, 61–75.

Eysenck, H. J., & Rachman, S. *The causes and cures of neurosis.* San Diego: Knapp, 1965.

Fairbairn, W. R. D. *Object-relations theory of the personality.* New York: Basic Books, 1954.

Feather, B. W., & Rhoads, J. M. Psychodynamic behavior therapy. *Archives of General Psychiatry,* 1972, **26**, 496–511.

Feldman, M. L. & Broadhurst, A. (Eds.). *Theoretical and experimental bases of the behaviour therapies.* New York: Wiley, 1976.

Fenichel, O. *The psychoanalytic theory of neurosis.* New York: Norton, 1945.

Fiedler, F. E. A comparison of therapeutic relationship

in psychoanalytic, nondirective, and Adlerian therapy. *Journal of Consulting Psychology*, 950, **14**, 436–445.

Fisher, S., & Greenberg, R. P. *The scientific credibility of Freud's theories and therapy*. New York: Basic Books, 1977.

Ford, J. D. Therapeutic relationship in behavior therapy: An empirical analysis. *Journal of Consulting and Clinical Psychology*, 1978, **46**, 1302–1314.

Frank, J. D. Therapeutic factors in psychotherapy. *American Journal of Psychotherapy*, 1971, **25**, 350–361.

Frank, J. D. Restoration of morale and behavior change. In A. Burton (Ed.), *What makes behavior change possible?* New York: Brunner/Mazel, 1976.

Frank, J. D., Hoehn-Saric, R., Imber, S. D., Liberman, B. L., & Stone, A. R. *Effective ingredients of successul psychotherapy*. New York: Brunner/Mazel, 1978.

Freud, S. (1900) The interpretation of dreams. *Standard Edition*, Vols. IV and V. London: Hogarth, 1953.

Freud, S. (1900) The psychopathology of everyday life. *Standard Edition*, Vol. VI. London: Hogarth, 1960.

Freud, S. (1904) On psychotherapy. *Standard Edition*, Vol. VII. London: Hogarth, 1953.

Freud, S. (1912) The dynamics of transference. *Standard Edition*, Vol. XII. London: Hogarth, 1958.

Freud, S. (1923) The ego and the id. *Standard Edition*, Vol. XIX. London, Hogarth Press, 1961.

Freud, S. (1926) Inhibitions, symptoms, and anxiety. *Standard Edition*, Vol. XX. London: Hogarth Press, 1959.

Freud, S. (1933) New introductory lectures on psychoanalysis. *Standard Edition*, Vol. XXII. London: Hogarth Press, 1964.

Freud, S. (1937) Analysis terminable and interminable. *Standard Edition*, Vol. XXIII. London: Hogarth, 1964.

Garfield, S. L. *Psychotherapy: An eclectic approach*. New York: Wiley, 1980.

Goldfried, M. R. Toward the delineation of therapeutic change principles. *American Psychologist*, 1980, **35**, 991–999.

Goldfried, M. R., & Davison, G. C. *Clinical behavior therapy*. New York: Holt, Rinehart & Winston, 1976.

Goldfried, M. R. & Kent, R. N. Traditional vs. behavioral personality assessment: A comparison of methodological and theoretical assumptions. *Psychological Bulletin*, 1972, **77**, 409–420.

Goldfried, M. R., & Merbaum, M. (Eds.). *Behavior change through self-control*. New York: Holt, Rinehart & Winston, 1973.

Goldfried, M. R., Stricker, G., & Weiner, I. B. *Rorschach handbook of clinical and research applications*. Englewood Cliffs, N.J.: Prentice-Hall, 1971.

Goldstein, A., & Foa, E. B. (Eds.). *Handbook of behavioral interventions*. New York: Wiley, 1980.

Gomes-Schwartz, B. Effective ingredients in psychotherapy: Prediction of outcome from process variables. *Journal of Consulting and Clinical Psychology*, 1978, **46**, 1,023–1,035.

Greenson, R. R. *The technique and practice of psychoanalysis*. New York: International Universities Press, 1967.

Greenwald, H. From client-centered to therapist-centered. *Contemporary Psychology*, 1973, **18**, 26–27.

Hartmann, H. *Ego psychology and the problem of adaptation*. New York: International Universities Press, 1958.

Hersen, M. The use of behavior modification techniques within a traditional psychotherapeutic context. *American Journal of Psychotherapy*, 1970, **24**, 308–313.

Hersen, M. & Bellack, A. S. (Eds.). *Behavioral assessment: A practical handbook*. New York: Pergamon, 1976.

Holzman, P. S. *Psychoanalysis and psychopathology*. New York: McGraw-Hill, 1970.

Jourard, S. M. *The transparent self: Self-disclosure and well-being*. Princeton, N.J.: Van Nostrand, 1964.

Jourard, S. M. *Disclosing man to himself*. New York: Van Nostrand Reinhold, 1968.

Jourard, S. M. *Self-disclosure: An experimental analysis of the transparent self*. New York: Wiley, 1971.

Kanfer, F., & Phillips, J. *Learning foundations of behavior therapy*. New York: Wiley, 1970.

Kazdin, A. E. The application of operant techniques in treatment, rehabilitation and education. In S. L. Garfield & A. E. Bergin (Eds.). *Handbook of psychotherapy and behavior change*. (2nd ed.) New York: Wiley, 1978.

Kazdin, A. E. Fictions, factions, and functions of behavior therapy. *Behavior Therapy*, 1979, **10**, 629–654. (a)

Kazdin, A. E. Situational specificity: The two-edged sword of behavioral assessment. *Behavioral Assessment*, 1979, **1**, 57–76. (b)

Kazdin, A. E. Nonspecific treatment factors in psychotherapy outcome research. *Journal of Consulting and Clinical Psychology*, 1979, **47**, 846–851. (c)

Kendall, P. C., & Hollon, S. D. (Eds.). *Cognitive-behavioral intervention: Theory, research and procedures*. New York: Academic, 1979.

Kendall, P. C., & Hollon, S. D. (Ed.). *Assessment strategies for cognitive-behavioral interventions*. New York: Academic, 1981.

Kelly, G. A. *The psychology of personal constructs*. New York: Norton, 1955.

Kelly, G. A. A psychology of the optimal man. In A. W. Landfield & L. M. Leitner (Eds.), *Personal construct psychology: Psychotherapy and personality*. New York: Wiley, 1980.

Lanfield, A. W., & Leitner, L. M. (Eds.). *Personal construct psychology: Psychotherapy and personality*. New York: Wiley, 1980.

Langs, R. *The technique of psychoanalytic psychotherapy*. New York: Aronson, 1973.

Lazarus, A. A. *Behavior therapy and beyond*. New York: McGraw-Hill, 1971.

Lazarus, A. A. *Multi-modal behavior therapy*. New York: Springer, 1976.

Lazarus, A. A. Toward delineating some causes of change in psychotherapy. *Professional Psychology*, 1980, **11**, 863–870.

Leitenberg, H. (Ed.). *Handbook of behavior modification and behavior therapy*. Englewood Cliffs, N.J.: Prentice-Hall, 1976.

Luborsky, L., & Spence, D. P. Quantitative research on psychoanalytic therapy. In S. L. Garfield & A. E.

Bergin (Eds.), *Handbook of psychotherapy and behavior change*. (2nd ed.) New York: Wiley, 1978.

Mahoney, M. J. Reflections on the cognitive-learning trend in psychotherapy. *American Psychologist*, 1977, **32**, 5–13.

Mahoney, M. J., & Arnkoff, D. Cognitive and self-control therapies. In S. L. Garfield & A. E. Bergin (Eds.), *Handbook of psychotherapy and behavior change*. (2nd ed.) New York: Wiley, 1978.

Mahrer, A. R. *Experiencing: A humanistic theory of psychology and psychiatry*. New York: Brunner/Mazel, 1978.

Marmor, J. Dynamic psychotherapy and behavior therapy: Are they irreconcilable? *Archives of General Psychiatry*, 1971, **24**, 22–28.

Marmor, J. Common operational factors in diverse approaches to behavior change. In A. Burton (Ed.), *What makes behavior change possible?* New York: Brunner/Mazel, 1976.

Mash, E. J., & Terdal, L. G. (Eds.). *Behavioral asessment of childhood disorders*. New York: Guilford, 1981.

Maslow, A. H. *Toward a psychology of being*. Princeton, N.J.: Van Nostrand, 1962.

Maslow, A. H. *The psychology of science: A reconnaissance*. New York: Harper & Row, 1966.

Martin, D. G. *Learning-based client-centered therapy*. Monterey, Calif.: Brooks/Cole, 1972.

May, R., Angel, E., & Ellenberger, H. F. (Eds.). *Existence: A new dimension in psychiatry and psychology*. New York: Basic Books, 1958.

Meichenbaum, D. *Cognitive-behavior modification*. New York: Plenum, 1977.

Messer, S. B., & Winokur, M. Some limits to the integration of psychoanalytic and behavior therapy. *American Psychologist*, 1980, **35**, 818, 827.

Munroe, R. L. *Schools of psychoanalytic thought*. New York: Dryden Press, 1955.

Murray, E. J., & Jacobson, L. I. Cognition and learning in traditional and behavioral therapy. In S. L. Garfield & A. E. Bergin (Eds.), *Handbook of psychotherapy and behavior change*. (2nd ed.) New York: Wiley, 1978.

Murray, M. E. A dynamic synthesis of analytic and behavioral approaches to symptoms. *American Journal of Psychotherapy*, 1976, **30**, 561–569.

Norcross, J. C., & Prochaska, J. O. A national survey of clinical psychologists: Affiliations and orientations. *Clinical Psychologist*, 1982, **35**, 16.

Perls, F., Hefferline, R., & Goodman, P. *Gestalt therapy*. New York: Julian Press, 1951.

Polster, E., & Polster, M. *Gestalt therapy integrated*. New York, Brunner/Mazel, 1973.

Pope, B. *The mental health interview*. New York: Pergamon, 1979.

Raimy, V. *Misunderstandings of the self: Cognitive psychotherapy and the misconception hypothesis*. San Francisco: Jossey-Bass, 1975.

Rapaport, D., Gill, M. M., & Schafer, R. *Diagnostic psychological testing*. (Rev. ed.) New York: International Universities Press, 1968.

Rogers, C. R. *Client-centered therapy*. Boston: Houghton-Mifflin, 1951.

Rogers, C. R. *On becoming a person: A therapist's view of psychotherapy*. Boston: Houghton-Mifflin, 1961.

Rosenthal, T. & Bandura, A. Psychological modeling: Theory and practice. In S. L. Garfield & A. E. Bergin (Eds.), *Handbook of psychotherapy and behavior change*. (2nd ed.) New York: Wiley, 1978.

Schafer, R. *Psychoanalytic interpretation in Rorschach testing*. New York: Grune & Stratton, 1954.

Shaffer, J. B. P. *Humanistic psychology*. Englewood Cliffs, N.J.: Prentice-Hall, 1978.

Shakow, D., & Rapaport, D. *The influence of Freud on American psychology*. New York: World Publishing Co., 1964.

Shevrin, H., & Shectman, F. The diagnostic process in psychiatric evaluations. *Bulletin of the Menninger Clinic*, 1973, **37**, 451–494.

Sloane, R. B., & Staples, F. R., Cristol, A. H., Yorkston, N. J., & Whipple, K. *Psychotherapy versus behavior therapy*. Cambridge, Mass.: Harvard University Press, 1975.

Spitzer, R. L., & Endicott, J. The value of the interview for the evaluation of psychopathology. In M. Hammer, K. Salzinger, & S. Sutton (Eds.), *Psychopathology: Contributions from social, behavioral, and biological sciences*. New York: Wiley, 1973.

Staples, F. R., Sloane, R. B., Whipple, K., Cristol, A. H., & Yorkston, N. J. Differences between behavior therapists and psychotherapists. *Archives of General Psychiatry*, 1975, **32**, 1,517–1,522.

Strupp, H. H. Specific vs. nonspecific factors in psychotherapy and the problem of control. *Archives of General Psychiatry*, 1970, **23**, 393–401.

Strupp, H. H. On the basic ingredients of psychotherapy. *Journal of Consulting and Clinical Psychology*, 1973, **41**, 1–8.

Strupp, H. H. Psychoanalysis, "focal psychotherapy," and the nature of the therapeutic influence. *Archives of General Psychiatry*, 1975, **32**, 127–135.

Strupp, H. H. Clinical psychology, irrationalism, and the erosion of excellence. *American Psychologist*, 1976, **31**, 561–571. (a)

Strupp, H. H. The nature of the therapeutic influence and its basic ingredients. In A. Burton (Ed.), *What makes behavior change possible?* New York: Brunner/Mazel, 1976. (b)

Strupp, H. H. Humanism and psychotherapy: A personal statement of the therapist's essential values. *Psychotherapy: Theory, Research and Practice*, 1980, **17**, 396–400.

Strupp, H. H., & Hadley, S. W. Specific vs. nonspecific factors in psychotherapy: A controlled study of outcome. *Archives of General Psychiatry*, 1979, **36**, 1,125–1,136.

Sugarman, A. Psychoanalysis as a humanistic psychology. *Psychotherapy: Theory, Research and Practice*, 1976, **14**, 204–211.

Sugarman, A. Is psychodiagnostic assessment humanistic? *Journal of Personality Assessment*, 1978, **42**, 11–21.

Sullivan, H. S. *The psychiatric interview*. New York: Norton, 1954.

Turner, S. M., Calhoun, K. S., & Adams, H. E. (Eds.). *Handbook of clinical behavior therapy*. New York: Wiley, 1981.

Wachtel, P. L. *Psychoanalysis and behavior therapy: Toward an integration*. New York: Basic Books, 1977.

Weiner, I. B. *Psychodiagnosis in schizophrenia*. New York: Wiley, 1966.

Weiner, I. B. Behavior therapy in obsessive-compulsive neurosis: Treatment of an adolescent boy. *Psychotherapy: Theory, Research and Practice*, 1967, **4**, 27–29.

Weiner, I. B. Does psychodiagnosis have a future? *Journal of Personality Assessment*, 1972, **36**, 534–546.

Weiner, I. B. *Principles of psychotherapy*. New York: Wiley, 1975.

Weiner, I. B. Individual psychotherapy. In I. B. Weiner (Ed.), *Clinical methods in psychology*. New York: Wiley, 1976.

Weiner, I. B. Approaches to Rorschach validation. In M. A. Rickers-Ovsiankina (Ed.), *Rorschach psychology*. (2nd ed.) Huntington, N.Y.: Krieger, 1977.

Wexler, D. A. A cognitive theory of experiencing, self-actualization, and therapeutic process. In D. A. Wexler & L. N. Rice (Eds.), *Innovations in client-centered therapy*. New York: Wiley, 1974.

Weins, A. N. The assessment interview. In I. B. Weiner (Ed.), *Clinical methods in psychology*. New York: Wiley, 1976.

Wilson, G. T., & Evans, I. M. The therapist-client relationship in behavior therapy. In A. S. Gurman & A. M. Razin (Eds.), *Effective psychotherapy: A handbook of research*. New York: Pergamon, 1977.

Wolpe, J. *Psychotherapy by reciprocal inhibition*. Stanford, Calif.: Stanford University Press, 1958.

Wolpe, J. *The practice of behavior therapy*. New York: Pergamon, 1969.

Wrenn, R. L. Counselor orientation: Theoretical or situational. *Journal of Counseling Psychology*, 1960, **7**, 40–45.

Wyss, D. *Psychoanalytic schools from the beginning to the present*. New York: Aronson, 1973.

Yalom, I. D. *Existential psychotherapy*. New York: Basic Books, 1980.

Yates, A. J. *Behavior therapy*. New York: Wiley, 1970.

Zimring, F. Theory and practice of client-centered therapy: A cognitive view. In A. D. Wexler & L. N. Rice (Eds.), *Innovations in client-centered therapy*. New York: Wiley, 1974.

3 CLINICAL TRAINING

Barry A. Edelstein
William S. Brasted

History and Introduction

In 1896, Lightner Witmer established the first psychological clinic to offer professional services (Korchin, 1976). Within 15 years, five additional clinics were established, four of which were associated with a department of psychology. During the early 1900s, clinical practicum and internship training occurred in clinics and such clinical settings as the Vineland New Jersey Training School, Boston Psychopathic Hospital, and the Worcester State Hospital (Pottharst, 1976). Clinical training appeared to vary across psychology programs, and many individuals who were to become identified as clinical psychologists received general psychology training followed by an internship. As the need for psychologists expanded, so did the number of psychologists who identified themselves as clinical psychologists.

In 1919, clinical psychologists persuaded the American Psychological Association to form a clinical section. In 1924, the Clinical Section of the APA recommended that clinical psychologists have a Ph.D. degree in psychology, four years of experience, one of which was to be under supervision. (Kendall & Norton-Ford, 1982; Reisman, 1981). This recommendation also supported a sci-entist-practitioner model of training, in which a balance of research and clinical training was suggested. Later, in 1931, the APA committee on Standards of Training for Clinical Psychologists was formed. Their report was published in 1935. Though recommendations were beginning to come forth, there seemed to be little or no attempt to insure adherence to any of the recommendations. In 1938, the first volume of the *Journal of Consulting Psychology* carried articles discussing the training of clinical psychologists as well as the recommendation of a one-year internship (Derner, 1965). In the same year, Shakow (1938) presented his recommendations for an internship year in a psychiatric hospital.

Poffenberger (1938) also published an article that suggested that the doctoral degree be a prerequisite for membership in the newly formed American Association of Applied Psychology (Derner, 1965). The doctorate described by Poffenberger was the Doctor of Psychology (Psy. D.) degree, which emphasized preparation for clinic service and, to a lesser extent, academic research. In the third volume of the *Journal of Consulting Psychology*, Rogers (1939) also described an approach for clinical training and supported the need for an internship.

Though the foregoing events helped to shape early notions of the nature of clinical training, or what it should be, it was World War II that brought about the first apparent attempts to arrive at some consensus regarding the nature of acceptable clinical psychology training. The United States was filled with returning veterans whose needs for psychological intervention far exceeded the mental health manpower of the time. It was estimated that 4,700 new clinical psychologists were needed to provide psychological assessment and therapy in Veterans Administration facilities (Darley & Wolfe, 1946; Kendall & Norton-Ford, 1982). The Veterans Administration and the United States Publish Health Service approached the American Psychological Association with the task of specifying the nature of adequate clinical psychology training and eventually identifying programs that met these criteria. Carl Rogers, then president of the APA, asked David Shakow to chair a Committee on Training in Clinical Psychology. The committee report, presented in September of 1947, was entitled "Recommended Graduate Training Program in Clinical Psychology," and became known as the Shakow Report. The report stated 14 general principles in three major areas: diagnostics, research, and therapy. Most important, the report emphasized both the scientific and the professional aspects of clinical psychology. Programs were encouraged to graduate well-balanced clinical psychologists who could provide clinical services and continue to contribute to the field of psychology in their research efforts. By 1947, 22 universities had training programs in clinical psychology (Reisman, 1981).

Two years after the publication of the Shakow report, 71 representatives of the profession met in Boulder, Colorado, to discuss training (Raimy, 1950). The scientist-professional model was again endorsed and approximately 70 propositions were voted upon. It is important to note that the Boulder Conference was supported financially by the Veterans Administration and the U.S. Public Health Service, a fact that could have clearly affected the general outcome of the meeting (Sarason, 1981). The importance of funding for clinical training and its influence on the directions of the field began here and has continued to the present, when federal funds for training have been all but eliminated. Based upon the recommendations of the Boulder Conference and the stated needs of the Veterans Administration and U.S. Public Health Service, the APA formed an Education and Training Board to monitor the training of clinical psychologists and accredit graduate and internship training through its Committee on Accreditation.

The next major conference to follow the Boulder Conference was entitled the Institute on Education and Training for Psychological Contributions to Mental Health. The conference was held over a four-day period at Stanford University and is sometimes referred to as the Stanford Conference (Strother, 1956). "Three factors which led to this conference were: (a) the trend toward specialization manifested in the Boulder, Northwestern, and Thayer Conferences and its implications for graduate training, (b) the recommendation of the Boulder Conference to review the policies and procedures which it developed, and (c) the rapid growth of the mental hygiene movement" (Lloyd & Newbrough, 1966, p. 127). The major contribution of this conference was the attention to the training needs of psychologists in community mental health programs, who would adopt broader roles than those addressed at the Boulder Conference.

In December 1958, a training conference was held in Miami Beach (Roe et al., 1959). The conference addressed five major issues that pertained to graduate education in psychology in general. Among many issues, the conference addressed fieldwork experiences, alternative degrees in place of the Ph.D., standards for internship and postdoctoral programs, subdoctoral training programs, and accreditation (Lloyd & Newbrough, 1966). Lloyd and Newbrough note that there was a strong consensus that doctoral education in psychology "should continue to educate doctoral psychologists as broadly as possible, limited only by the major aspects of the type of position to which the student is initially oriented" (Roe et al., 1959). There was also considerable agreement that the Ph.D. should remain a research degree and that a nonresearch degree did not demand attention at that time (Lloyd & Newbrough, 1966).

In August 1965, the Chicago Conference on the Professional Preparation of Clinical Psychologists was held (Hoch, Ross, & Winder, 1966). Bernstein and Nietzel (1980) noted that this conference broke two traditions: "It was held in a city with a less than thrilling climate, and it was the first conference to seriously consider some alternative models of clinical training" (p. 474). In their summary of the conference, the conferees agreed that:

Clinical psychology includes the following broad functions: Psychological analysis and assessment for decision-making purposes; psychotherapy and other forms of behavior modification; psychological investigation (research and evaluation); training and education; consultation; administration. It was understood that any individual clinical psychologist need not be equally competent in all these functions, but that a comprehensive training program should introduce him to each of them and prepare him well for several of them. [Hoch, Ross, & Winder, 1966, p. 92]

The conferees also strongly recommended diversification of training opportunities with the objective of providing the opportunity for different students to stress different knowledge and methods in their professional preparation (Roe et al., 1959). Therefore, programs could experiment with different models as long as their primary emphasis was on the training of scientist-professionals. They were free to explore the potential value of greater emphasis on the professional model of training.

The Miami Conference was followed by the Vail Conference, held in Vail, Colorado, in the summer of 1973. The plans for this conference originated in 1969 with the joint appointment by the APA Board of Professional Affairs and the Education and Training Board of an Ad Hoc Committee on Professional Training (Darley, 1973). The Vail Conference was entitled the "National Conference on Levels and Patterns of Professional Training in Psychology." After five days the conferees passed approximately 150 resolutions. The resolutions could be summarized in the context of the following major themes (Korman, 1976): Professional training model; multilevel training; desirable characteristics of professional training; doctoral training; Master's level training; training at Bachelor's level and below; continuing professional training and minority groups; professional training and women and service delivery systems and the social context.

According to Korman (1976, p. 19), "The conference explicitly endorsed professional training programs as one type of heuristic model to guide those programs defining themselves by a basic service orientation." At the same time, the conferees reaffirmed the need to emphasize basic psychological content and methodology as the root of

training and education. They continued to reaffirm empiricism and scientific endeavors. The conferees noted that some programs might decide to adopt primarily professional training programs and that they would support such enterprises as long as the roots in basic psychological content and methodology were retained. The conferees also recognized the acceptability of the Psy.D. degree when the primary emphasis of training was on the direct delivery of professional services and the evaluation and improvement of those services (Korman, 1976).

A most important result of the Vail Conference was attention to the professional trained at the Master's level. The conference stated that: "Many of the psychological services currently performed by Ph.D., and Ed.D. or Psy.D. degree holders could be performed equally well by personnel trained at the master's or lower levels. The real cost of such services to the public could be appreciably lowered by training such personnel to provide them directly" (Korman, 1976, p. 25). It was also suggested that a psychologist trained at the Master's level be given full APA membership and be called a psychologist.

Another major theme of the conference—continuing professional development—was an important feature of this conference relative to previous conferences. It is clear that as the emphasis on professional training increased, the apparent need for continuing professional development and education was becoming a greater issue. The strong emphasis on professional training at the Vail Conference yielded a concomitant emphasis on continuing education.

Accreditation

All of the conferences discussed above have influenced the nature of clinical training since the 1940s, when criteria for acceptable programs were sought by the APA following prompts and financial support from the Veteran's Administration and the U.S. Public Service. The accreditation of doctoral programs has occurred since the Education and Training Board of the APA adopted the report of the Boulder Conference as a basis for their initial accreditation criteria. Over the following years the Education and Training Board has continued to revise its policies and procedures for accreditation as the field of clinical psychology has evolved.

The Education and Training Board of the

American Psychological Association consists at present of at least nine members of the APA and has four continuing committees reporting to it. The Committee on Undergraduate Education is charged with collecting, analyzing, and reporting information concerning undergraduate students, teachers, and programs. The Continuing Education Committee is concerned with the development of continuing education programs, quality criteria for continuing education in psychology, and the APA Continuing Education Sponsor Approval System (*APA Monitor*, 1982). The committee on Graduate Education and Training, which was formed in January 1981, is concerned with graduate education and training in both academic-scientific and professional psychology (*APA Monitor*, 1981). And finally, "The Committee on Accreditation exercises professional judgment in making decisions on programs being considered for accreditation by APA under the current *Accreditation Criteria and Procedures*. It also develops guidance documents and data gathering instruments necessary to carry out this function, institutes programs for the training of site visitors and provides a consultation to programs" (APA, 1982, p. 8).

In 1973, the Committee on Accreditation published the Accreditation Procedures and Criteria. These were revised between 1978 and 1980, resulting in the publication of the *Accreditation Handbook* in 1980. The handbook represents a tremendous step. It contains detailed descriptions of the accreditation process for graduate programs and internships, the current accreditation criteria, instructions for the site visitors who evaluate the training programs, and various suggestions for guiding the accreditation process from the perspectives of both the training program and the site visitors. It was a much needed document for training programs which previously had to guess about some of the information, obtain it second-hand from programs that had recently been site-visited, or obtain the information from professionals who had served as site visitors for other programs.

The second of the accreditation criteria, dealing with training models and curricula, includes statements of principles that are considered basic to sound training in professionals psychology. A portion of that section reads as follows:

A. It is the responsibility of the faculty to integrate practice with theory and research early in the program.

B. Students should form an early identification with their profession. Faculty should be available to demonstrate and model the behaviors that students are expected to learn. A close working relationship between faculty and students is essential.

C. The foundation of professional practice in psychology is the evolving body of knowledge in the discipline of psychology. While programs will vary in emphasis and in available resources, sound graduate education in general psychology is therefore essential in any program. The curriculum shall encompass the equivalent of a minimum of three academic years of full-time resident graduate study. Instruction in scientific and professional ethics and standards, research design and methodology, statistics, psychological measurement, and history, and systems of psychology must be included in every doctoral program in professional psychology. The program shall, further, require each student to demonstrate competence in each of the following substantive content areas:

(1) biological bases of behavior (e.g., physiological psychology, comparative psychology, neuropsychology, sensation, psychopharmacology),

(2) cognitive-affective bases of behavior (e.g., learning, memory, perception, cognition, thinking, motivation, emotion),

(3) social bases of behavior (e.g., social psychology, cultural, ethnic, and group processes; sex roles, organizational and systems theory), and

(4) individual behavior (e.g., personality theory, human development, individual differences, abnormal psychology).

Competence may be demonstrated in a number of ways: by passing suitable comprehensive examinations in each of the four areas, successful completion of at least three or more graduate semester hours (or equivalent quarter hours) in each of the four areas, or by other suitable means. These curriculum requirements represent the necessary core but not a sufficient number of graduate hours for a degree in professional psychology. All professional training programs in psychology will, in addition, include course requirements in specialty areas. [APA, 1980, p. 5]

The section goes on to elaborate training in specific skills, APA policies, ethical standards, APA Standards for Providers of Psychological Services, and APA Standards for Educational and Psychological Tests, among others. Access to training in related fields is emphasized, as are research training, the canons of science, and scholarship. Further, programs are required to develop comprehensive evaluation systems.

These accreditation criteria provide standards for training while permitting considerable flexibility for program innovation and specialization. Thus, training programs offer a variety of didactic courses and seminars on approaches to intervention, assessment, and program evaluation. Other courses frequently deal with various psychological disorders and current research relating to their etiology and treatment. Clinical practica also vary considerably across training programs. Students may see clients in a psychology department or university-based clinic and/or in community agencies. Clinical practica with a greater emphasis on the community and social systems are also offered in some programs, which afford the student opportunities to evaluate and influence large systems.

Internship Training

The vast majority of doctoral programs require students to be enrolled for four years of full-time education. Most programs require the Ph.D. candidate to fulfill either a full-time one-year or two years of half-time internship. Curiously, the history of the internship is longer than that of the other predoctoral curricula, because prior to the Boulder Conference, all clinical training occurred in internshiplike settings. (Korchin, 1976, p. 72). Perhaps for this reason, Shakow (1938) placed significant emphasis on the internship as an integral part of clinical training. Therefore, among Shakow's recommendations was the suggested requirement of a full-year internship experience as part of the overall training. The internship was to provide four basic functions: (1) to develop further "facility with already acquired techniques"; (2) to "saturate the student with experience in the practical aspects of psychopathology"; (3) "further develop the students' experimental-objective attitude"; and (4) "get the student acquainted with the types of thinking and attitudes of his colleagues in other disciplines" (Shakow, 1938, pp. 74–76).

In order to satisfy these functions, the APA developed accreditation standards for internships which have remained virtually unchanged for the subsequent 30 years. The current standards still mirror Shakow's recommendations and involve such criteria as a one-year full-time or two-year half-time requirement, access to numerous role models, and the development of several abilities such as research, therapeutic, and interpersonal skills.

Though the establishment of accreditation guidelines was somewhat effective in standardizing internship training experiences, there remained concern for several years that this was an insufficient solution to the problem of internship regulation. Subsequently, because of the increasing numbers of internship settings and the somewhat vague guidelines determining their functions and structure, the APA established a committee that evolved in 1968 into the Association of Psychology Internship Centers (APIC). The purpose of the APIC was to provide a clearinghouse for internship information and centralization for issues related to APA. Among the various functions that APIC has fulfilled are the establishment of uniform procedures for tendering internship offers, the annual publication of a directory of internship centers, and the provision of a formal liaison between internship centers and the Education and Training Board of the APA (Burstein, 1981b).

Since its inception, APIC also has moved gradually toward greater control of the structure and evaluation of internship training. For example, in 1977, a committee was appointed to determine standards for internship matriculation, such that a minimum competency level could be required prior to both entrance and completion of the internship experience. Unfortunately, the committee has been unable to resolve this issue completely because of the high degree of variation in evaluation methodology evidenced across internship. APIC has, however, succeeded in providing suggestions for both entrance and exit requirements for internships, as well as methods for evaluating intern performance in relation to these criteria.

The diversity and the occasional complete lack of specific evaluative criteria for intern performance found by the APIC committee is suggestive of the current scarcity of experienced data on internship training. In general, the available research has taken the form of surveys targeted either at internship directors' attitudes toward preinternship preparation of students (e.g., Petzel

& Berndt, 1980; Shemberg & Kelley, 1974; Shemberg & Leventhal, 1981), or at the intern's satisfaction with their internship experience (e.g., Khol, Matefy, & Turner, 1972; Rosenkrantz & Holmes, 1974). Surprisingly, there is a dearth of research directed toward the systematic evaluation of either the specific learning experiences occurring at internship relative to APA recommendation (e.g., Kirk, 1970; Tucker, 1970), or intern performance relative to minimum competency standards. Actually, the latter issue is somewhat less surprising considering Miller's (1977) recent finding that less than 30 percent of surveyed internship sites use any form of quantitative data in the evaluation process.

Although the existing literature is inadequate in some respects, it has pointed out some important issues that are likely to affect future trends in training. For example, several studies have indicated that although interns view their experiences as beneficial in areas such as assessment, research, and therapy, there is less satisfaction with training in such areas as administrative and consultative skills (e.g., Miller, 1977; Stout, Holmes, & Rothstein, 1977). Thus, we might see a trend toward the integration of skill training in these areas into the internship experience.

Recent Trends

In the above sections we have considered the historical development of graduate training and internships in addition to some of the issues relevant to the APA's impact on such training. In the following section, we consider some of the more recent changes that have occurred.

Perhaps the most notable change in the field of clinical psychology in the past two decades has been the shift toward increased specialization. Numerous areas now boast their own distinctive sets of problems and problem-solving techniques, in terms of both research and clinical practice. This has resulted in the fractionalization of training programs such that increasing numbers of graduates are being trained in one specific area of clinical psychology rather than in general clinical practice. The following section briefly reviews some of the major new areas and the issues related to graduate training in these areas.

Behavioral Medicine

The most dramatic transition toward a distinctive specialty area has occurred in the field of behavioral medicine and health psychology (Gentry et al., 1981). The continually expanding job market for medical psychologists (Gentry & Matarazzo, 1981; Lubin, Nathan, & Matarazzo, 1978) has ultimately triggered formal recognition of the area as evidenced by the establishment of the Behavioral Medicine special-interest group within the Association for Advancement of Behavior Therapy in 1977, and the APA's Division 38 of Health Psychology in 1978. In addition, 1978 marked the birth of both the Society of Behavioral Medicine and *The Journal of Behavioral Medicine*.

The rather rapid establishment of this area has raised several issues pertaining to graduate education, not the least of which is how to define the area. Numerous definitions have been proposed, such as the Schwartz and Weiss (1978) definition which emanated from the Yale Conference on Behavioral Medicine: "The interdisciplinary field concerned with the development and integration of behavioral and biomedical science, knowledge and techniques relevant to health diagnosis, treatment, and rehabilitations" (p. 250). Their definition stresses the interdisciplinary nature of the field and subsequently deemphasizes the role of the experimental analysis of behavior in directing the development of techniques for practice and research. Subsequent definitions (e.g., Pomerleau, 1978) have attempted to reemphasize the integral force of behavior analysis in defining the field. It should also be noted that some professionals are choosing to define behavioral medicine as a separate entity from medical psychology. Specifically why this is the case is not clear, as definitions for the latter area appear to be conspiciously similar to those for the former. For example, Gentry et al. (1981) have defined medical psychology as "The application of the concepts and methods of normal and abnormal psychology to medical problems. It refers to the cooperative effort between behavioral scientists and medical practitioners in the diagnosis, treatment, and prevention of physical illness and reflects an acceptance of the importance of psychosocial factors in part or in whole to aspects of physical illness" (p. 224). The similarity between this and Schwartz and Weiss's definition for behavioral medicine should be self-evident. Yet, regardless of one's preference for definitions, it is obvious that the particular definition chosen will impact the structure of training programs (Swan, Piccione, & Anderson, 1980). For example, Swan et al. (1980) state that their program is based upon the Pomerleau definition and subsequently stresses data-based behavioral therapy techniques for addressing medical problems.

Other approaches have emphasized self-management techniques (e.g., Stuart, 1977), owing to a preference to view the health psychology input in terms of prevention and maintenance.

A second major issue pertaining to training involves the determination of what elements of clinical psychology training should be transferred to the study of behavioral medicine and what courses need to be added. For example, research skills typically taught in clinical programs may be unadaptable to medical settings or insufficient at best (e.g., Sechrest, 1974). Subsequently, Belar (1980) has recommended that students interested in behavioral medicine take courses in time-series analysis, multivariate statistics, and contingency table analysis among other strategies typically more relevant to epidemiologic research. In terms of clinical training, Belar (1980) suggests that the basic repertoire of clinical skills can and should be transferred to the behavioral medicine curriculum. She states, however, that there should be greater emphasis on time efficiency, succinctness in written reports, and clarification of referral questions, as well as on skills in staff training, crisis management, supportive therapy, and anxiety reduction.

The question of which content areas are to be added leads to a third issue. Students in behavioral medicine are faced with a rather perplexing problem of having to learn the language and techniques of two fields. If one is to function as a psychologist, then one must learn the theory and practice of psychology. Yet, in the case of behavioral medicine, the successful psychologist must also have at least a cursory knowledge of the medical jargon and issues. As this is the case, students of behavioral medicine may inadvertently be subjected to the prospect of being "jacks of all trades and masters of none." Thus, as Belar (1980), has noted, it is perhaps best that students in this area be trained first and foremost as psychologists, and secondly as experts within one specific area in the health field.

A further relevant issue for behavioral medicine training involves precisely where such training will occur. Olbrisch and Sechrest (1979) note that at present there are extremely limited opportunities for training in programs specifically designed for health psychology (e.g., Stone, 1977). Thus, most training in behavioral medicine or health psychology occurs within traditional psychology graduate training programs (Olbrisch & Sechrest, 1979). These authors therefore suggest that students make use of resources available within their own departments, universities, and communities. Considering the vastly increasing numbers of academic psychologists interested in the area, it should not be difficult to adapt ongoing research and clinical experiences so that they are relevant to health issues. Moreover, many internship sites have begun to add medical rotations to their internship programs.

In general, however, considering the field's continued integration into settings, in addition to the continually growing empirical base, it is likely that health psychology will experience greater structure in the training curriculum. Thus, it is probable that the currently limited number of programs offering a behavioral medicine specialty will increase perhaps to the point where programs will offer subspecialties within the general area of health psychology.

Child Clinical and Pediatric Psychology

A second area that has recently experienced a period of rapid expansion is clinical child psychology. Over the past 15 years the number of doctoral-level programs offering specialties in clinical child psychology has steadily risen from fewer than 10 in 1968 (Ross, 1972) to the current number of 34 formal programs. In addition, 52 others offer informal child training experiences (Fischer, 1978). Although the increase has been dramatic, professionals have estimated that the number of trained psychologists will still be 80 percent less than the projected demand for child specialists over the next decade (VandenBos, 1979).

Though the demand for training programs in child psychology is evident and the number of such programs is increasing, several issues remain to be resolved. For example, Erickson (1978) has indicated that there are currently no criteria or models established to guide the design of clinical child psychology programs. Because of the absence of such criteria, it is somewhat difficult at this point to determine minimal requirements or accreditation standards. In fact, in a recent survey, Mannarino and Fisher (1981) found that the majority of programs reporting the establishment of clinical child specialties also indicated that they were still in the process of determing appropriate curricula for the specialty. Thus, because of the current lack of consensus regarding an appropriate curriculum, it is likely that most programs follow essentially the same format as programs that are oriented to adult clinical psychology. Of course, most child therapy appears to be conducted through the parents or caretakers (e.g., Kazdin, 1979), and as such it is probably appropriate to provide training that is oriented to work with adults. Yet, such training is obviously insufficient. Child programs are therefore likely to begin addressing such issues as specific childhood disorders as well as developmental factors (e.g., Hoffman, 1979; Yarrow, 1979). Fortunately, in response to the need for specification of relevant topic areas for the field, attempts are currently being made to assemble a national conference to evaluate potential models for curriculum development for child psychology (Tuma, 1980, 1981).

A further issue facing professionals involved in clinical child psychology involves the definitions for already emerging subareas. For example, a question frequently raised is what is the difference between child and pediatric psychology (Stabler & Whitt, 1980; Tuma, 1975)? Answers to this question have ranged from considering the two terms as synonymous (see Tuma, 1976), to considering pediatric psychology as a distinct subset of child psychology (Tuma, 1981). In a recent article, one author suggested that pediatric psychology refers to "the application of medical psychology skills and methods to children" (Tuma, 1981, p. 519). Thus, it appears that for some the relationship of pediatric psychology to clinical child psychology is analogous to that of behavioral medicine to adult clinical psychology.

Because of the burgeoning nature of this area, it is probable that the next decade will see the development of specific criteria for curriculum design in order to ensure competence in the increasing numbers of graduates trained to meet the demand for child specialists. Thus, this area, like several others (e.g., behavioral medicine, geropsychology, etc.) that are emanating from within a general *zeitgeist* of increased specialization, is currently at a stage of self-definition and regulation.

Community Psychology

Community psychology is yet another area that is frequently considered within the field of clinical psychology and that has developed into a distinct specialty area. Though numerous definitions have been proposed for the area (e.g., Bennett et al., 1966; Bloom, 1973; Rappaport, 1977; Zax & Specter, 1974), the consensus is that community psychology is an approach emphasizing social-system-level interventions designed to alleviate societal problems as opposed to emphasizing indi-

vidual solutions for "individual troubles" (Bloom, 1973, p. 8.).

The specific structure of this area and the training for practice began to be delineated in 1965 at the Boston Conference (Bennett et al., 1966) and continued to be further distinguished and organized at subsequent conferences, such as the Austin Conference in 1967 (Iscoe & Spielberger, 1970), the Vail Conference in 1973 (Korman, 1974), and the National Training Conference on Community Psychology in 1975 (Iscoe, Bloom, & Spielberger, 1977). Throughout this period, community psychology has moved continually closer to becoming a distinctive entity, in addition to moving further away from the more tradition emphasis on the individual. For example, at the Boston Conference, areas such as: (1) the individual's interaction with the physical and social environment; (2) the individual's reaction to community change; and (3) the relationship between social, cultural conditions and individual personality functioning, were among the areas discussed as essential research concerns for community psychology (Bennett et al., 1966). Yet, ten years later at the National Training Conference in 1975, the emphasis had clearly moved toward the understanding of social issues, theory, and research methodology devoted to intervention at the community level (Reiff, 1977), and a general social-system orientation for the field (Kelly, 1977). Further, Sarason (1977) called for the establishment of community psychology as a distinct and separate field from clinical psychology with its own training opportunities and curricula.

Although these conferences have failed to provide a final definitive statement concerning the identity of the field (Barton et al., 1976), they have engendered a significant increase in the training opportunities available in community psychology. For example, Meyer and Gerrard (1977) note that in 1962, Golann, Wurm, and Magoon (1964) found only one program reporting a distinguishable community psychology curriculum; by 1977 the number had increased to 62. It is interesting to note, though, that a current concern in the field is that the content areas of the offered curricula have not evidenced a similar response to the pleas of the last conference. Though the reported emphasis of the field is in broad-based community intervention and analysis, recent surveys have indicated that most coursework is still related to topics such as crisis intervention, group process, and other direct service skills (Barton et al., 1976). This type of finding was also noted by Zolik, Sirbu, and Hopkinson (1975, cited in Barton et al., 1976), who found that topics such as primary prevention and planning, development, and management skills were taught in community psychology programs less frequently than were direct service skills. This appears somewhat surprising considering that the most recent conference called for a deemphasis on community mental-health-related skills (i.e., direct service) and greater emphasis on community psychology skills. Consequently, Bloom (1977) has stated that "the emerging field of community psychology has not made a qualitative break with community mental health, with which it is still very strongly identified" (p. 242).

Bloom's statement appears extremely salient for the field of community psychology. At present, the majority of training and professional experiences occur within the community mental health centers (e.g., Meyer & Gerrard, 1977). Thus, in order to ensure that students and graduates provide useful services for these settings, training must emphasize "traditional" applied skills. Therefore, community psychology is caught in an unfortunate Catch 22. Until funding sources become available to enable students to obtain training experiences and subsequent jobs in community planning organizations, or until community mental health centers become more involved in large-scale operations, it is likely that the field will not close the gap between its rhetoric and reality (Bloom, 1977).

In terms of prevention research, Cowen (1977) has indicated that many people talk about it, but it is rarely done. More specifically, Cowen states, "Measured by what we as psychologists have achieved, the concept is all aura and no substance" (1977, p. 48). Albee (1979) has suggested that the development of prevention programs in general is being prevented by the health bureaucracy within the Department of Health, Education and Welfare and by the mental health establishment. Albee pessimistically concludes that "Unless someone with effective power intervenes to force the bureaucracy to follow the recommendations of the President's Commission, prevention will be an idea whose time has come and gone" (p. 2). This state of affairs is particularly sad because training and work in prevention have such tremendous potential for the field of psychology. The Task Force on Prevention of the President's Commission on Mental Health saw the move toward preventive mental health as "the

fourth revolutionary change in society's approach to the mentally ill" (Murphy & Frank, 1979, p. 182).

Although prevention has been identified as a desirable approach to health and mental health problems, there is much more discussion of the topic than there is substantive research work (Cowen, 1977). The paucity of research literature on prevention yields concomitant problems in determining what should be taught to students who wish to embrace this orientation. New journals, such as the *Journal of Primary Prevention*, collate the available work; but a functional curriculum will not be forthcoming until more content is available on the validity and costs of various prevention interventions. This is unfortunately entangled in the politics of prevention.

Primary prevention has been listed as a priority area for training by the National Institute of Mental Health, which has had an office dedicated to this area for a few years. However, though training funds were made available shortly after the report of the President's Commission on Mental Health, only two clinical training programs were being financially supported for training in prevention by 1981. The future of training in prevention is unclear, muddled primarily by the political realities of this orientation and the lack of research. The need for training in this area is clear, but the opportunities are severely limited.

Thus, in general, community psychology appears to be moving toward becoming a definitive entity, but is still too strongly tied to the community mental health tradition. Until more models for large-scale intervention and analysis become available, as well as funding sources for work, it is likely that the structure of training will retain its current emphasis on direct service skills, and not on the social orientation that is evident in the field's definition.

Clinical Gerontology

A fourth area of specialization that has been receiving considerable attention is clinical gerontology. The training of clinical psychologists to work with the elderly is unfortunately not progressing at the rate at which individuals over the age of 65 are accumulating in the United States. Indeed, there are not enough clinical gerontologists available today to deal with the geriatric population in need of mental health services. In spite of the great need for specialists in clinical gerontology, "training is woefully lacking" (Reveron, 1982,

p. 82). According to a recent survey (Siegler, Gentry, & Edwards, 1979), only two doctoral programs offer a formal program or subspecialty in this area. Only 22 of 97 clinical internship programs surveyed offered formal training with elderly clients.

Two relatively recent events have increased the optimism for training in clinical gerontology. The White House Conference on Aging, held in 1981, raised many issues and heightened the awareness of professionals and the general public regarding the needs and problems of the elderly. Second, the American Psychological Association sponsored a Conference on Training Psychologists for Work in Aging in June 1981, in Boulder, Colorado. This conference, sometimes referred to as the "Older Boulder Conference," was intended to formulate recommendations regarding training for gerontology. It is hoped that these recommendations will soon be forthcoming and will serve as a guide for the development of training programs in clinical gerontology.

Clinical Neuropsychology

An area of training that is rapidly gaining popularity is clinical neuropsychology. Indeed, several clinical training programs are offering specializations in neuropsychology. The development of neuropsychological batteries (e.g., Halstead-Reitan) has led to their use in the diagnosis of neurological disorders, psychiatric disorders, and the localization of brain lesions. Moreover, these batteries have permitted the further development of rehabilitation programs for traumatically brain-injured individuals (see Edelstein & Couture, in press). The increased interest in this area can in part be attributed to the recent publication of books in the area (e.g., Filskov & Boll, 1981; Golden, 1978; Hecaen & Albert, 1978; Heilman & Valenstein, 1979; Lezak, 1976), the popularity of workshops offered on the Halstead-Reitan and Nebraska-Luria Neuropsychological batteries, and the increased accuracy with which one can assess neuropsychological functioning.

Training in clinical neuropsychology is quite varied. Sheer and Lubin (1980) conducted a survey of 627 members of the International Neuropsychological Society and received 178 responses. The survey was conducted to obtain information about the training activities, areas of concentration, course work, research training, clinical training, faculty, students, etc. The respondents expressed a need for more organized and extensive

training in the area. According to the survey, students receive training in neuropsychology through one of four general avenues: (1) minimal training associated with primary service functions on practica or internships; (2) internship programs specifically designed for training in clinical neuropsychology; and (3) standard Ph.D. programs, usually in clinical psychology (some programs are also offering specializations in clinical neuropsychology for students entering predoctoral programs other than clinical); (4) separate formal training in clinical neuropsychology.

A survey by Golden and Kuperman (1980) of 65 APA-approved clinical programs indicated that 32 offered neuropsychology courses and encouraged students interested in neuropsychology to apply to their program. Twenty-eight of the programs offered neuropsychology but did not systematically encourage students to apply if they were specifically interested in that area. Eighteen of the 32 programs that encouraged applications from students offered specializations in clinical neuropsychology. These data clearly indicate a strong trend toward increased training in neuropsychology. The opportunities for merging neuropsychology evaluation and behavioral approaches to rehabilitation offer an exciting future for those who work with traumatically brain-damaged individuals (Goldstein, 1979) and a burgeoning area of training for the clinical psychologist.

Legal/Forensic Psychology

Over the past several years, the legal system has evidenced a growing recognition of the potential roles for psychologists within such areas as the correctional system (e.g., Nietzel & Moss, 1972; Twain, McGee, & Bennett, 1973), the criminal justice system (e.g., Brodsky, 1973; Fowler & Brodsky, 1978; Twain et al., 1973), and the field of civil law (e.g., Levine, Wilson, & Sales, 1980). Subsequently, there has been a dramatic increase in service-oriented and research activities involving the roles for psychology in Law (Tapp, 1977). Though interest is rapidly increasing, Poythress (1979) has noted that training programs have been somewhat slow to integrate forensic issues into program curricula. More specifically, he states: "Since the Jenkins case in 1962 the movement has been snowballing, but 17 years later few graduate programs offer extensive (if any) coursework in forensic psychology, and as yet there is no division of the APA that recognizes this speciality coursework in forensic psychology, and as yet there is no division of the APA that recognizes this speciality area" (p. 613).

In response to this concern, several training models have been elucidated by professionals interested in legal/forensic psychology. For example, a few universities (such as the University of Nebraska and the University of Maryland) have begun offering joint J.D.-Ph.D. programs that enable graduates to practice in either field. However, as Poythress (1979) has noted, such programs may discourage students who would have to meet admission and completion requirements for two fields rather than one, or who may find much of the material irrelevant for their needs.

Another approach has been to design specific legal/forensic course sequences to be provided within psychology programs. Examples of such courses have been presented by Poythress (1979) and Fernster, Litwach, and Symonds (1975). Taking this concept several steps further, some programs offer training specifically within the legal/forensic field. For example, Fowler and Brodsky (1978) describe a new program at the University of Alabama that prepares psychology students to work within any area of the legal system, although in this particular program the most intensive training takes place in the correctional system.

One factor that has enhanced the development of such programs has been the rapid expansion of literature in the area. For example, journals such as *The Law and Psychology Review, Criminal Justice and Behavior, An International Journal of Correctional Psychology*, and *Criminal Justice and Behavior* have become sources for relevant information, along with several books on legal/forensic psychology (e.g., Brodsky, 1973; Sales, 1977). Thus, considering the rapid expansion in both interest and literature, it is likely that legal/forensic psychology will soon become a distinct area of specialization.

Rehabilitation Psychology

The recognition rehabilitation psychology as a distinct specialty area has been much slower in coming, compared to other fields (Shontz & Wright, 1980). Some reasons for this have been suggested in the rehabilitation literature, and include the apparent belief that there are few jobs for psychologists with this specialization (Vineberg, 1971), the fact that much of the literature is published in nonmainstream journals (Shontz & Wright, 1980),

and the belief that the field is only a subset of medical psychology (Vineberg, 1971).

Rehabilitation psychology, however, is a distinct field for which a definitive body of literature concerning theory, research, and methods exists, (e.g., Barker et al., 1953, Garrett, 1953; Meyerson, 1971; Vineberg & Williams, 1971). Furthermore, there have been to date three APA-sponsored conferences on issues and training in rehabilitation psychology (Lofquist, 1960; Neff, 1971; Wright, 1959), in addition to the development of a division of Rehabilitation Psychology within the American Psychological Association. Thus, it is apparent that rehabilitation psychology is actually well advanced in its development. In fact, it may be considered beyond the stage of a subspecialty and may be considered as a separate field altogether. Training in this area has become specialized to the point where numerous universities (e.g., West Virginia University and the University of Kansas) have distinct rehabilitation programs that are functionally separate from the clinical psychology program.

Marriage and Family

The final area to be mentioned briefly is on the opposite end of the continuum toward specialization from rehabilitation psychology; this is the emerging area of family and marital therapy. Over the past several years the number of family therapy training programs in the United States has increased from approximately 14 before 1961 to 154 today (Block & Weiss, 1981). Obviously, all of these programs are not specifically related to clinical psychology programs, nor do they all offer degrees (Block & Weiss, 1981), yet the current number is indicative of the increasing interest in the training of family and marital therapists.

Perhaps because of the relative infancy of training programs in this field, there is a large degree of heterogeneity of course sequences and content areas available across programs. Various professionals have described specific skill areas taught within particular program (e.g., Allred & Kersy, 1977; Cleghorn & Levin, 1973; Garrigan & Bembrick, 1977; Tomm & Wright, 1979), although there remains no consensus on the identity of the field.

Compared to other areas in clinical psychology, family and marital threapy is more quickly evidencing an interest in the evaluation of training sequences. For example, Kniskern and Gurman (1979), who have previously been involved in evaluation of the efficacy of family therapy as a treatment modality (e.g., Gurman & Kniskern, 1978), are now beginning to evaluate the training process itself. If this trend in evaluation continues, it will be interesting to determine if it will enable the field to move more quickly toward increased data-based specification of curriculum sequences and training experiences. If so, family and marital therapy programs may provide useful models for the rest of the field, which is certainly lagging in the area of training evaluation.

Training Models

No issue has sparked more controversy with respect to clinical training than that of the relative weight given to research and professional practice. Ever since the Boulder Conference (Raimy, 1950), this controversy has grown in intensity. Critics have argued that current programs that attempt to implement the Boulder model of training ignore the mental health manpower needs of the nation (Adler, 1972), are disparaging of clinical psychology as a profession, are using relatively inexperienced and untrained individuals to provide clinical training, are not providing an adequate theoretical background for integrating theory, research, and practice, and are not providing many of the vital courses for clinical practice (Matulef & Rothenberg, 1968).

An act that further fired the controversy over professional training was the endorsement by the Vail conferees (Korman, 1974) of professional programs that would train students primarily as service deliverers. The conferees distinguished between the Psy.D. degree for service training and the Ph.D. degree for training in the development of new knowledge. No reason was presented in the report why the Psy.D. degree was needed (Stricker, 1975). In contrast, Peterson (1968, 1976), who began the first Psy.D. program while at the University of Illinois, has argued very strongly for it. Peterson argues that the current need for professional psychologists is not being met by the Ph.D. programs, that "there is no way to train professional psychologists thoroughly except through explicitly professional programs" (1976, p. 795), that current Ph.D. programs do not support the value of professional work, that there is no way to restructure the current Ph.D. programs so that a student could receive adequate professional training

in the four or five years we have allotted for training, and that there is an issue of professional identity raised for practitioners receiving the Ph.D. degree, which he views as a research degree.

Stricker (1975) has argued that we must not consider the issues of the development of professional schools and the awarding of the Psy.D. degree simultaneously. He noted that it is entirely possible to adopt one and not the other. In spite of the admonishments of Stricker (1975) and others, there still seems to be some confusion of the Psy.D. degree programs and the professional schools of psychology. A present, there are 43 schools of professional psychology. Twenty-four of these programs offer the Psy.D. degree and 22 offer the Ph.D. degree. Three programs offer both (McNett, 1982). There are 21 free-standing professional schools of psychology, the first of which was the California School of Professional Psychology which was founded under the auspices of the California Psychological Association in 1969. Of the 21 free-standing professionals schools, only seven offer the Psy.D. degree (McNett, 1982).

The degree requirements of the various professional psychology programs differ considerably. The Psy.D. degree program at Rutgers, for example, requires a dissertation. The Psy.D. degree program at the Denver School of Professional Psychology requires a "doctoral paper," which is usually something less that a traditional dissertation document. The professional program at Wright State University has no dissertation requirement. Instead, students "take two comprehensive examinations to demonstrate and defend their clinical competence and scientific proficiency" (McNett, 1982, p. 11). One might argue that there is as much variety in curriculum and doctoral requirements between programs offering the Psy.D. degree as there is between many of the Psy.D. and Ph.D. programs. In fact, several of the earliest concerns regarding the relatively poor professional preparation of clinical Ph.D. students have been addressed by the new APA accreditation criteria. For example, a minimum number of hours of practicum experience and direct supervision are specified. Whether these new criteria will bring the professional training in the Ph.D. programs up to a level that is adequate for the demands of the profession is perhaps largely dependent on the quality of the supervision, instruction, and breadth of experiences provided on each practicum and in the classroom. At the present time there are, unfortunately, no formal criteria for quality assurance for students practicing their skills as clinical psychologists (Bent, 1982). It is therefore difficult to determine the nature and amount of training necessary to produce a competent professional clinical psychologist. In the absence of suitable criteria and evaluation methods, we are merely guessing about what and how much is needed.

Master's Degree Level Training

The role of M.A.-level training in clinical psychology has been an issue for more than 30 years. Several general issues continue to fuel the debate. The first involves the question of whether M.A.-level training is sufficient to ensure competent provision of psychological services by graduates. Though the APA has set fairly rigorous criteria for the evaluation of doctoral-level training, it has as yet failed to determine or adopt such criteria for M.A.-level programs (Havens, 1979; Periman & Lane, 1981). Therefore, the terminal Master's programs have been forced to determine their own standards for training, with one consequence being a rather large degree of variation across programs (Jones, 1979). Adding to this problem is the fact that M.A. degrees are frequently awarded as "consolation prizes" to students who fail to complete their doctorates (Havens, 1979). This has resulted in a bimodal population including those who are specifically and intensively trained as Master's-level practitioners, and those who receive only the initial training; it is indeed difficult to assure competence in the general case.

In response to this issue, several authors have proposed specific models for the training of M.A.-level psychologist (e.g., Havens & Dimond, 1978; Kelly, 1957) that would ensure a minimum standard of competence. The first guidelines were prepared by Kelly (1957), and included suggestions for a minimum of two years for training and the combination of core coursework including psychopathology, research design, and diagnostics, and supervised practicum experiences. Though these guidelines have failed to be formally recognized (Woods, 1971), later authors are still attempting to develop criteria acceptable to the APA (e.g., Dimond, 1979; Jones, 1979). For example, recent models involve a curriculum sequence of core courses providing a background in psychopathology and treatment, a practicum sequence, and an internship (Jones, 1979). Upon completion of such training, the trainee would be designated

as a "psychological specialist" and would be considered to be at a level somewhat analogous to a physician's assistant or nurse practitioner in the medical field.

The integration of such guidelines would appear to resolve two basic issues in M.A.-level training: competency and labeling. The labeling issue stems from the problem of who can call themselves psychologists. As Periman and Lane (1981) have indicated, it is somewhat confusing from the consumer's standpoint that both Ph.D.s and M.A.s are entitled to the same professional title. Currently, M.A. psychologists have been entitled with different professionals labels across the country. Such labels range from psychometrist to mental health specialist to psychological assistant, depending on which state one practices in (Periman & Lane, 1981). Such variety in labeling can only increase consumer confusion. It would therefore appear beneficial for the APA to determine, along with standardized accreditation criteria, a specific title for graduates of M.A.-level programs.

To date, however, the various recommendations for Master's-level training have not been adopted by the APA. Perhaps one reason for this is the more recent issue of the proposed National Health Insurance Program. Clinical psychologists fear that the inclusion of M.A.-level practitioners in the group of psychologists eligible for third-party reimbursement will seriously threaten the likelihood that even Ph.D.-level clinicians will fully obtain the status of independent and reimbursable practitioners. Simply stated, if M.A.s are included, psychologists must subsequently vie for a large piece of the economic pie, and may not get any of it (Havens, 1979). This has led to a recent surge of statements from various sources (e.g., APA Division 12; American Board of Professional Psychology; and the APA Board of Professional Affairs, cited in Havens, 1979) calling for the eventual elimination of both the training and the independent practice of M.A. psychologists. Thus, at least at this point, it would appear somewhat antithetical for the APA concurrently to develop criteria for M.A. training.

In view of these issues, the future of M.A.-level training may be considered questionable at best. Yet, considering that M.A. psychologists are significantly more plentiful than Ph.D.s (Asher, 1974), and that the number of terminal Master's programs continues to increase (Periman & Lane, 1981), it is unlikely that M.A.s will be totally eliminated from clinical practice. A more probable resolution will involve the APA's provision of standardized criteria for the evaluation and accreditation of Master's programs. With the adoption of such criteria, the issue of competence should be resolved to the extent that within-group variance across Master's-level psychologists will be reduced. A second step designed to reduce heterogeneity has been suggested by Havens (1979) and Jones (1979): it would involve eliminating the Master's degree as a step toward the Ph.D. This will undoubtedly require extensive debate before becoming accepted practice, and may in fact be so unpopular a concept that it will never be integrated into training practice. Finally, the determination of a title other than psychologist for M.A. practitioners may be necessary to allay the problem of consumer confusion.

Training in Assessment Techniques

For the past three decades, psychologists have debated the importance of training clinicians in the use of traditional psychodiagnostic techniques. The ongoing dialogue has involved numerous issues ranging from the scientific credibility of both objective and projective techniques, to legal and institutional demands for the continued use of these devices, to the determination of which particular tests should be taught in the Ph.D. programs. In this section, we will briefly review some of the relevant issues that have affected and will continue to influence the structure of training in clinical psychology. It should be noted that this section will focus on issues involving training in personality assessment as opposed to intelligence, achievement, or vocationally oriented forms of testing, because the former type of assessment appears to be a more highly contested issue in current training practices. (For a thorough review and discussion of issues concerning the latter forms of assessment, the reader is referred to *American Psychologist*, 1981, 36[10], whole issue.)

Perhaps the most important issue involving traditional assessment is the utility of objective and projective tests. Numerous evaluations of these tests have continued to demonstrate their inadequacy in terms of reliability and validity (e.g., Bem, 1972; Meehl, 1954; Mischel, 1968) and yet advocates of traditional assessment continue to suggest that such studies fail to evaluate the intricacies in personality structure that are illuminated by testing (e.g., McCully, 1965; Sarason, 1966).

Though strong arguments have been presented for both sides of this issue, in general it appears that psychologists' attitudes toward the utility of traditional tests are becoming more negative (e.g., Thelan, Varble, & Johnson, 1968).

Contributing to the negative trend in attitudes toward traditional forms of assessment is the increasing dissatisfaction with the medical model role for psychologists as diagnosticians (Mischel, 1968). As psychological therapeutic techniques have gained a continually sounder empirical base, psychologists have vied for increasing independence from traditional roles. Thus, it is somewhat antithetical for psychologists to continue to emphasize a set of skills they would prefer not to use (e.g., Kass, 1958; McCully, 1965). Furthermore, the original function of testing was to assist in the diagnosis of psychological disorders. Since the publication of the DSM-III, however, the utility of testing for diagnosis has diminished because of the greater specificity of behavioral criteria available in the manual. Thus, the recent greater emphasis on behavioral components of disorders, too, appears to have affected practitioners' attitudes toward the utility of personality tests.

This shift in attitude is also becoming evident in university settings. For example, surveys by Shemburg and Kelly (1970), Thelan and Erving (1970), and Jackson and Wohl (1966) have found a decreasing trend in the emphasis placed on testing, especially with projectives, by training programs. More specifically, the surveys have indicated that in established university programs, the emphasis on projectives has declined significantly while emphasis on objective assessment techniques has increased. Further, in newer, less established programs, there is a marked decrease in the emphasis on both forms of testing as compared to older programs (Shemberg & Kelly, 1970). Yet, the authors state that in general, there remains a significant emphasis on testing.

The obvious question raised by these issues is to what degree can testing be deemphasized? A partial answer stems from the psychology marketplace. In a recent survey, Wade and Baker (1977) found that clinical psychologists reported that approximately 35 percent of their professional time was spent administering and evaluating tests. Further, among the most common reasons provided for engaging in these activities were satisfaction of institutional demands and legal requirements, provision of psychologists with a specialty, and the enhancement of employability. Thus, it may be unethical not to provide sufficient training in testing skills if it is likely to reduce a student's subsequent survival in the marketplace.

Since institutional and economic pressures currently (and presumably will continue to) demand testing skills from psychologists, it is apparent that training in testing will retain its significance in the curricula of graduate programs, at least in the foreseeable future. But this too raises several questions. If the psychometric properties of most traditional devices are questionable at best (e.g., Goldfried & Kent, 1972; Kanfer & Saslow, 1965), then what specific tests are to be taught? Surveys have indicated that practicing clinicians report that students should learn at least one test (Wade & Baker, 1977). Futher, the four most commonly suggested tests recommended in this survey were, respectively: the Rorschach Inkblot Test, Thematic Apperception Test, the Wechler Adult Intelligence Scale, and the Minnesota Multiphasic Personality Inventory. It is interesting that the two frequently suggested tests are among the least sound in terms of psychometric properties (Anastasi, 1968; Mischel, 1968). Moreover, only 18.5 percent of the very professionals who recommended training in these devices stated that they used standardized procedures for administering and scoring the tests. The remaining 81.5 percent stated that they used personalized procedures developed through personal clinical experience! This latter group intimated that the use of such individualized procedures alleviated the problems associated with the poor psychometric properties associated with the testing devices. Unfortunately, research has suggested that such clinically determined criteria are even less predictive than the mechanical standardized procedures provided for testing (Sawyer, 1966).

Training institutions are therefore faced with something of a dilemma. The economic marketplace currently requires that graduates in psychology be skilled in testing, and yet the tests that are available and frequently recommended are replete with inadequacies. In the light of this problem, Wade and Baker (1977) suggest that graduate training be directed toward assessment theory and evaluation of psychometric properties, in lieu of specific testing skills. It is unlikely, however, that training programs will stop training in specific test devices. It is more probable that there will be a continuation of the current trend in the direction of objective diagnostic procedures and away from projectives devices (Shemburg & Keeley, 1970).

Continuing Education

It was previously noted that continuing professional development and education have become more significant issues as clinical psychology as a profession has developed. Various reasons for the need for continuing education have been advanced. These include the increasing knowledge base of clinical psychology, the maintenance of high standards of practice, the maintenance of public confidence in the profession (Vitulano & Copeland, 1980; Welch, 1976), the obsolescence of skills (Jensen, 1979), and the emergence of service needs for which psychologists were not trained (Jensen, 1979; Webster, 1971). It has been estimated that 50 percent of a psychologist's knowledge is outmoded within 10 to 12 years (Dublin, 1972). That is quite a startling notion, even if one allows for some inaccuracy in the estimate.

In recent years, the APA has become involved in continuing education. The APA Council of Representatives endorsed the current continuing education sponsor approval system in January 1979. National standards for continuing education in psychology have been articulated and sponsors identified who meet their standards for continuing education. The APA maintains a continuing education registry of credits obtained by individuals under the sponsorship of the APA continuing education approval system. In addition, the APA provides a calendar and clearinghouse for continuing education information and events. As the sponsor approval system has developed, so have private enterprises that provide continuing education approved by the APA.

There are currently ten states that require continuing education for relicensure or recertification. The first state to require continuing education for relicensure was Maryland in July 1957; however, 18 years elapsed before the next state, New Mexico, began to require continuing education. At present, six states require continuing education through both the licensing or certification board and state legislature. One state requires it through legislation only, and three states require it only through licensing or certification board regulations. Nine states have enabling legislation and implementation dates ranging from 1981 to 1984. Three additional states have legislation under consideration, three have regulations through a board, and two have both legislative and board regulations under consideration at this time. Thus, there are 23 states without continuing education requirements for relicensure or recertification. The amount of continuing education required varies from state to state. Credit-hour requirements range from 5 credit-hours per 2 years to 50 credit-hours per year. These data are based upon a survey sent to state Psychology Examining Boards in October of 1980.

The current issues in continuing education center on the amount of credit-hours that should be required, the nature of the training and credit determination, training methods, evaluation methods, who should be permitted to offer the training, and the criteria for satisfactory performance. Training opportunities range from convention institutes and workshops to home education programs developed by private enterprises and sponsored by educational institutions. There appears to be no consensus regarding what kinds of educational experiences are most desirable or acceptable, the method of determining credits, how one should be evaluated (if at all), or whether anyone should be permitted to offer continuing education credits. At the present time, each state that requires continuing education determines the guidelines that pertain to the foregoing issues. It would seem, however, that the ultimate criterion of all this professional development and continuing education should at least be a positive change in professional behavior and in the care of mental health clients (Brown & Uhl, 1970). It is unclear how long it will take the field to get its educational house in order.

Evaluation of Clinical Training

Perhaps the most important and most overlooked issue in clinical training is program evaluation. It is ironic that psychologists whose job is primarily that of training have paid so little attention to the valid evaluation of clinical training. In a review of research on the training of counselors and clinicians, Ford (1979) concluded that "research investigating the effects of different training curricula, curriculum content sequences, and curricular materials, is, unfortunately, non-existent in the counselor/clinician training literature" (p. 87). There is ample evidence that one can train specific clinical skills (see Ford, 1979; and Matarazzo, 1978 for reviews); however, we still do not know what constitutes the effective ingredients of clinical practice in general and psychotherapy in particular (e.g., Matarazzo, 1978). Recent work by Edelstein and his colleagues (e.g., Edelstein et al., 1982) has begun to evaluate the impact of training

on both the behavior of student-clinical interviewers and the outcome of the interviews. In other words, the effectiveness of the interviewer is evaluated against relatively objective outcome measures. Nevertheless, little research exists that points the way to effective clinical skills.

In a recent survey, most clinical directors indicated that clinical practicum training was evaluated (Edelstein, 1982). The evaluation instruments typically consisted of rating scales directed at various skills that were felt to be important for clinical practice. Evaluations of other aspects of professional behavior were also evaluated, though less consistently across clinical programs. None of the evaluation instruments employed appeared to be validated. This is not surprising, however, in light of the difficulty of deciding upon what one would want to predict. The consequences for not having valid indices of training effectiveness are legion. Training programs should be accountable to their students, the school or university, the field of psychology, the future employees of the students, and the individuals or agencies who will receive graduates' professional services. In fact, the consequences of not documenting the effectiveness of training practices may have contributed to the recent withdrawal of funds for clinical psychology training from the federal government.

Though few would dispute the need for adequate evaluation of training, little is being done. The American Psychological Association has apparently discovered this fact and recently created a Task Force on Evaluation of Education, Training, and Service in Clinical Psychology. The topic of the empirical evaluation of clinical training was also a major topic of a presentation at a recent Working Conference on Behavioral Clinical Training held at West Virginia University.

A handful of articles have appeared that suggest a small trend toward the empirical evaluation of clinical training. Hill, Charles, and Reed (1981), for example, have conducted a longitudinal study of changes in counseling skills among graduate students being trained in counseling psychology. The authors analyzed brief counseling sessions of students for each of the three years of training. The results revealed that "students increased their use of minimal encouragers and decreased use of questions and maintained acceptable levels of activity, anxiety, and quality" (p. 428). From a consumer perspective, Walfish, Kaufman, and Kinder (1980) surveyed 316 graduates from APA-approved doctoral programs in clinical psychology and asked them to rate the adequacy of their training in a variety of skill areas. The authors concluded that "For the most part, respondents were relatively satisfied with their training and were most satisfied with traditional skills in therapy and assessment" (p. 1,040). These data were consistent with the results of a survey by Garfield and Kurtz (1976), who found that 77 percent of those surveyed indicated "some degree of satisfaction" with their graduate training.

There are several possible reasons for the paucity of research on the evaluation of clinical training. There is little agreement about what skills a clinical graduate student should be taught, what should form the knowledge base for learning these skills, the level of skills that should be expected, and the criteria that should be used for judging skills. The problem is similar to that of establishing outcome criteria for psychotherapy research (see Kazdin, 1981; Strupp, 1981). The sheer diversity of training approaches and orientations makes the development of commonly acceptable outcome measures a formidable task at best. The fact that we are moderately ignorant of the most effective ingredients of our many approaches to intervention further complicates the issue of what is to be taught and evaluated.

In spite of the rather pessimistic note of the preceding section, evaluation must be done. As research points the way toward effective skills and relevant information, clinical training programs may incorporate the newly acquired information into their training. It is clear that our data base for building effective training programs and evaluating them is sadly limited at this time. In many cases, clinical training programs can graduate very skilled clinical psychologists; one can, however, rarely articulate how it was accomplished. Though the field is safe because of the former, its future is still in question because of the latter.

Future Directions

Formal training in clinical psychology has been with us but a few decades and yet we have witnessed tremendous changes in the role of clinical psychologists and concomitant changes in the nature of their training. One might even argue that the training has not kept pace with the changing roles of clinical psychologists. Indeed, this is part of the argument made by advocates of more professional training for clinicians in lieu of the extensive research training. The gap between training and practice extends well beyond this more general criticism. Clinical psychologists are becoming involved in anything and everything that involves human behavior in its normal and abnormal forms. It is this fact that makes it particularly difficult to predict the future directions of clinical training. They have no bounds.

Although the distant future of clinical training is difficult to predict, the more immediate future is amenable to intelligent guesses. First, we would predict further specialization within the field. It appears that clinical psychology is following in the footsteps of allied health fields by becoming more specialized as the knowledge base and sheer number of skills required increases. Some specializations have already demonstrated exceptional growth in just a matter of years. The area of health psychology, for example, is growing by leaps and bounds and will probably continue to do so as more and more of our health and illness is shown to be related to our behavior and vice versa. Moreover, it would not be surprising to see specializations developing within health psychology (e.g., prevention of cardiovascular disease).

The manner in which clinical training programs obtain funds for training will certainly contribute to the shape of training. The eventual termination of generic training grants will leave programs in a situation many of them have not faced since the beginning of formal clinical training. As students are faced with the prospect of poverty, they will acquire loans when possible and part-time jobs when classes and practica permit. It is our fear that, over time, training programs will be shaped away from the provision of sound scientific and clinical training as they chase financial support that is tied to services that are only tangentially related to acceptable clinical practice. It is the clinical researcher who will probably suffer the most, since the repayment of loans will be much more difficult for those who will hold poorer paying academic and/or research positions. Those who will seek clinical practice, particularly in the private sector, will be most able to weather the hardships of three to four years of full-time clinical training without financial support. The possible effects this could have on the future contributions to the field of clinical psychology should be of considerable concern to directors of clinical training as well as others who are in a position to influence its direction.

The future of clinical training will undoubtedly include a place for the computer. It will be used not only as a tool for controlling elaborate experiments and analyzing data, but also as a means for providing analogue training experiences that test and teach. Competency-based criterion-referenced training will become commonplace as we identify effective clinical behaviors or practices. Computers are already being used to simulate client problems for evaluating professional competence of counseling psychology students (e.g., Berven & Scofield, 1980). The computer will be used for self-assessment, both by students and by professionals who are engaged in graduate or continuing education. This is already being done on a limited basis at meetings of the Association for Advancement of Behavior Therapy.

The clinical psychologist of the future will probably have a broader knowledge base in the biological sciences. As evidence of biological contributions to psychological disorders mounts, the need to take such factors into consideration in training and practice will surely increase. Future clinical psychologists will also receive more training in the use of information derived from sophisticated electronic diagnostic devices. As our technology for measuring brain and nervous system functions continues to develop, it will become necessary for graduate students to understand and utilize information obtained from measures of cerebral blood flow, CAT scans, and tests of event-related cortical potentials.

Finally, we hope that the future holds more promise for research and training in primary prevention. The potential impact on mental and physical health through prevention is, in our estimation, almost unlimited. Though our current knowledge base is limited, the existing evidence for the efficacy of this approach is quite compelling. Training in primary prevention could begin now as an approach that is unencumbered by the disease model: our professional behavior could be controlled by health rather than by disease.

References

Adler, P. T. Will the Ph.D. be the death of professional psychology? *Professional Psychology*, 1972, **3**, 69–72.

Albee, G. Preventing prevention. *APA Monitor*, 1979, **10**, 2.

Allred, F. H., & Kersey, F. L. The AIAE: A design for systematically analyzing marriage and family counseling: A progress report. *Journal of Marriage and Family Counseling*, 1977, **2**, 131–137.

American Psychological Association, *APA Monitor*, 1981, **2**, 11.

American Psychological Association. *Accreditation handbook*, Washington, D.C.: APA, 1980.

Anastasi, A. *Psychological testing*. New York: Macmillan, 1968.

Asher, J. Are MA's undermining professional psychology? *APA Monitor*, 1974.

Barker, R. G., Wright, B. A., Meyerson, L., & Gonich, M. R. *Adjustments to physical handicap and illness: A survey of the social psychology of physique and disability*. (Bulletin 55, Revised.) New York: Social Science Research Council, 1953.

Barton, A. K., Andrulis, D. P., Grove, W. P., & Aponte, J. G. A look at community psychology in the seventies. *American Journal of Community Psychology*, 1976, **4**, 1–11.

Belar, C. Training the clinical psychology student in behavioral medicine. *Professional Psychology*, 1980, **11**, 620–627.

Bem, D. Constructing cross-situation consistencies in behavior: Some thoughts of Alken's critique of Mischel. *Journal of Personality*, 1972, **210**, 17–26.

Bennett, C. C., Anderson, L. S., Hassol, L., Klein, D., & Rosenblum, B. (Eds.). *Community psychology: A report of the Boston conference on the education of psychologists for community mental health*. Boston: Boston University and South Shore Mental Health Center, 1966.

Bent, R. J. The quality assurance process as a management method for psychology training programs. *Professional Psychology*, 1982, **13**, 98–104.

Bernstein, D. A., & Nietzel, M. T. *Introduction to clinical psychology*. New York: McGraw-Hill, 1980.

Berven, N. L., & Scofield, M. E. Evaluation of professional competence through standardized simulations: A review. *Rehabilitation Counseling Bulletin*, 1980, **23**, 178–202.

Bloch, D. A., & Weiss, H. M. Training facilities in marital and family therapy. *Family Process*, 1980, **20**, 133–146.

Bloom, B. L. The domain of community psychology. *American Journal of Community Psychology*, 1973, **1**, 8–11.

Bloom, B. The rhetoric and some views of reality. In I. Isco, B. L. Bloom, & C. D. Spielberger (Eds.), *Community psychology in transition: Proceedings of the national conference on training in community psychology*. Washington, D.C.: Hemisphere, 1977.

Brodsky, S. L. (Ed.) *Psychologists in the criminal justice system*. Chicago: University of Illinois Press, 1973.

Brown, C. R., & Uhl, H. S. Mandatory continuing education: Sense or nonsense? *Journal of the American Medical Association*, 1970, **213**, 1,660–1,668.

Burstein, A. G. Standards for evaluation and training. *APIC Newsletter*, 1981, 7, 20–24. (a)

Burstein, A. G. Personal communication, 1981 (b)

Cleghorn, J., & Levin, S. Training family therapists by setting learning objectives. *American Journal of Orthopsychiatry*, 1973, **43**, 439–446.

Couture, E., & Edelstein, B. A. (Eds.). *Behavioral assessment and rehabilitation of brain damaged individuals*. New York: Plenum, in press.

Cowen, E. L. Baby steps primary prevention. *American Journal of Community Psychology*, 1977, **5**, 1–22.

Darley, J. G. Opening address: Psychology: Science? Profession? In M. Korman (Ed.), *Levels and patterns of professional training in psychology.* Washington, D.C.: APA, 1973.

Derner, G. F. Graduate education in clinical psychology. In B. B. Wolman (Ed.), *Handbook of clinical psychology.* New York: McGraw-Hill, 1965.

Dubin, S. S. Obsolescence of lifelong education: A choice for the professional. *American Psychologist,* 1972, **27,** 486–498.

Edelstein, B. A. Empirical evaluation of clinical training. Paper presented at the Working Conference on Behavioral Clinical Training Morgantown, West Virginia, April 1982.

Edelstein, B. A., Brasted, W., Detrich, R., DiLorenzo, T., Knight, J., Rapp, S., Scott, O., & Sims, C. Sequential dependencies among clinical interviewer and interviewee behaviors. Paper presented at a meeting of the American Psychological Association, Washington, D.C., August 1982.

Erickson, M. D. Letter to the office of APA Educational Affairs on training. *Journal of Clinical Child Psychology,* 1978, **9,** 91.

Fernster, A. C., Litwach, T. R., & Seymonds, M. The making of a forensic psychologist: Needs and goals for doctoral training. *Professional Psychology,* 1975, **6,** 457–467.

Filskov, S., & Boll, T. (Eds.). *Handbook of clinical neuropsychology.* New York: Wiley, 1981.

Fischer, C. T. Graduate programs in clinical child psychology and related fields. *Journal of Clinical Child Psychology,* 1978, **9,** 91.

Ford, J. D. Research on training counselors and clinicians. *Review of Educational Research,* 1979, **49,** 87–130.

Fowler, R. D., & Brodsky, S. L. Development of a correctional-clinical psychology program. *Professional Psychology,* 1978, **9,** 440–447.

Garfield, S. L., & Kurtz, R. Clinical psychologists in the 1970s. *American Psychologist,* 1976, **31,** 1–9.

Garrett, J. F. (Ed.), Psychological aspects of physical disability. *Rehabilitation Services Series Number 210,* Washington, D.C.: U.S. Government Printing Office, 1953.

Garrigan, J. G., & Barnbrick, A. F. Introducing novice therapists to "go-between" techniques of family therapy. *Family Process,* 1977, **16,** 237–246.

Gentry, W. D. (Ed.) *Geropsychology: A model of training and clinical service.* Cambridge, Mass.: Ballinger, 1977.

Gentry, W. D., & Matarazzo, J. D. Medical psychology: Three decades of growth and development. In C. K. Prokop & L. A. Bradley (Eds.), *Medical psychology: Contributions of behavioral medicine.* New York: Academic Press, 1981.

Gentry, W. D., Street, W. J., Masur III, F. T., & Asken, M. J. Training in medical psychology: A survey of graduate and internship training programs. *Professional Psychology,* 1981, **12,** 224–228.

Golann, S. E., Wurm, L. A., & Magoon, T. M. Community mental health content of graduate programs in departments of psychology. *Journal of Clinical Psychology,* 1964, **20,** 518–522.

Golden, C. J. *Diagnosis and rehabilitation in clinical neuropsychology.* Springfield, Il: C. C. Thomas, 1978.

Golden, C. J., & Kuperman, S. K. Graduate training in clinical neuropsychology. *Professional Psychology,* 1980, **11,** 55–63.

Goldfried, M. R., & Kent, R. N. Traditional versus behavioral personality assessment: A comparison of methodological and theoretical assumptions. *Psychological Bulletin,* 1972, **77,** 409–420.

Goldstein, G. Methodological and theoretical issues in neuropsychological assessment. *Journal of Behavioral Assessment,* 1979, **1,** 23–41.

Gottesman, L. E. Clinical psychology and aging: A role model. In W. D. Gentry (Ed.), *Geropsychology: A model of training and clinical service.* Cambridge, Mass.: Ballinger, 1977.

Gurman, A. S., & Kniskern, D. P. Research on marital and family therapy: Progress, perspective and prospect. In S. L. Garfield & A. E. Bergin (Eds.), *Handbook of psychotherapy and behavior change.* (2nd ed.) New York: Wiley, 1978.

Havens, R. A. A brief review of the current M. A. controversy. *Professional Psychology,* 1979, **10,** 185–188.

Havens, R. A., & Dimond, R. E. A proposed education and training model for clinical psychologists. *Teaching of Psychology,* 1978, **5,** 3–6.

Hecaen, H., & Albert, M. L. *Human neuropsychology.* New York: Wiley, 1978.

Heilman, K. M., & Valenstein, E. (Eds.). *Clinical neuropsychology.* New York: Oxford University Press, 1979.

Hill, C. E., Charles, D., & Reed, K. G. A longitudinal analysis of changes in counseling skills during doctoral training in counseling psychology. *Journal of Counseling Psychology,* 1981, **28,** 428–436.

Hoch, E. L., Ross, A. O., & Winder, C. L. (Eds.) *Professional preparation of clinical psychologists.* Washington, D.C.: APA, 1966.

Hoffman, M. L. Development of moral thought, feeling, and behavior. *American Psychologist,* 1979, **34,** 958–966.

Iscoe, I., Bloom, B. L., & Spielberger, C. D. (Eds.). *Community psychology in transition: Proceedings of the national conference on training in community psychology.* Washington, D.C.: Hemisphere, 1977.

Iscoe, I., & Spielberger, D. C. (Eds.). *Community psychology: Perspectives in training and research.* New York: Appleton-Century-Crofts, 1970.

Jackson, C. W., Jr. & Wohl, J. A survey of Rorschach teaching in the university. *Journal of Projective Techniques and Personality Assessment,* 1966, **30,** 115–134.

Jensen, R. E. Competent professional service in psychology: The real issue behind continuing education. *Professional Psychology,* 1979, **10,** 381–389.

Johnson, W., & Stribbe, J. The selection of a psychiatric curriculum for medical students. *American Journal of Psychiatry,* 1975, **132,** 512–516.

Jones, A. C. Model for psychological practice for Ph.D. and M.A. professionals. *Professional Psychology,* 1979, **10,** 189–194.

Kanfer, F. H., & Saslow, G. Behavioral analysis: An alternative to diagnostic classification. *Archives of General Psychiatry,* 1965, **12,** 529–538.

Kass, W. Community on training report. *Journal of Projective Techniques,* 1958, **22,** 120–212.

Kazdin, A. E. Advances in child behavior therapy: Applications and implications. *American Psychologist,* 1979, **34**, 981–987.

Kazdin, A. E. Methodology of psychotherapy outcome research: Recent developments and remaining limitations. In *Psychotherapy research and behavior change: The Master Lecture Series,* Vol. 1. Washington, D.C.: APA, 1981.

Kelly, J. Varied educational settings for community psychology. In I. Iscoe, B. L. Bloom, & C. D. Spielberger (Eds.), *Community psychology in transition: Proceedings of the national conference on training in community psychology.* Washington, D.C.: Hemisphere, 1977.

Kelly, N. (Chair). *A current look at issues in subdoctoral education in psychology.* Task Committee on Subdoctoral Education, American Psychological Association, 1957.

Kendall, P. C., & Norton-Ford, J. D. *Clinical psychology: Scientific and professional dimensions.* New York: Wiley, 1982.

Khol, T., Matefy, R., & Turner, J. Evaluation of APA internship programs: A survey of clinical psychology interns. *Journal of Clinical Psychology,* 1972, **28**, 562–569.

Kirk, B. A. Internship in counseling psychology: Goals and issues. *Journal of Counseling Psychology,* 1970, **17**, 88–90.

Kniskern, D. P., & Gurman, A. S. Research on training in marriage and family therapy: Status, issues and directions. *Journal of Marriage and Family Therapy,* 1979, **5**, 83–94.

Korchin, S. J. *Modern clinical psychology: Principles of intervention in the clinic and community.* New York: Basic Books, 1976.

Korman, M. National conference on levels and patterns of professional training of psychology: The major themes. *American Psychologist,* 1974, **29**, 441–449.

Lawton, M. P. Gerontology in clinical psychology, and vice-versa. *Aging and Human Development,* 1970, **1**, 147–159.

Lawton, M. P., & Gottesman, L. E. Psychological services to the elderly. *American Psychologist,* 1974, **29**, 689–693.

Levine, D., Wilson, K., & Sales, B. D. An exploratory assessment of APA internship with legal/forensic experiences. *Professional Psychology,* 1980, **11**, 64–71.

Lezak, M. *Neuropsychological assessment.* New York: Oxford University Press, 1976.

Lloyd, D. N., & Newbrough, J. R. Previous conferences on graduate education in psychology: A summary and review. In E. L. Hoch, A. O. Ross, & C. L. Winder (Eds.), *Professional preparation of clinical psychologists.* Washington, D.C.: APA, 1966.

Lofquist, L. H. (Ed.). *Psychological research and rehabilitation.* Washington, D.C.: APA, 1960.

Lubin, B., Nathan, R. G., & Matarazzo, J. D. Psychologists in medical education. *American Psychologist,* 1978, **33**, 339–343.

Matarazzo, R. G. Research on the teaching and learning of psychotherapeutic skills. In S. L. Garfield & A. E. Bergin (Eds.), *Handbook of Psychotherapy and Behavior Change: An empirical analysis.* New York: Wiley, 1978.

Matulef, N. J., & Rothenberg, P. J. The crisis in clinical

training: Apathy and action. *Special Bulletin, National Council on Graduate Education in Psychology,* 1968, **2**(1).

McCully, R. S. Current attitudes about projective techniques in APA-approved internship training centers. *Journal of Projective Techniques and Personality Assessment,* 1965, **27**, 271–280.

McNett, I. Psy.D. fills demand for practitioners. *APA Monitor,* 1982, **13**, 10–11.

Meehl, P. E. Wanted—A good cookbook. *American Psychologist,* **11**, 263–272.

Meyer, M. L., & Gerrard, M. Graduate training in community psychology. *American Journal of Community Psychology,* 1977, **5**, 155–162.

Meyerson, L. Somatopsychology of physical disability. In W. M. Gruickshank (Ed.), *Psychology of exceptional children and youth.* (3rd ed.) Englewood Cliffs, N.J.: Prentice-Hall, 1971.

Miller, P. M. Evaluation of trainee performance in psychology internship programs. *The Clinical Psychologist,* 1977, **30**, 2–5.

Mischel, W. *Personality and assessment.* New York: Wiley, 1968.

Murphy, L. B., & Frank, C. Prevention: The clinical psychologist. In M. R. Rosenweign & L. W. Porter (Eds.), *Annual Review of Psychology* (Vol. 30). Palo Alto, Calif.: Annual Reviews, 1979.

Neff, W. S. (Ed.) *Rehabilitation psychology.* Washington, D.C.: American Psychological Association, 1971.

Nietzel, M. T., & Moss, C. S. The psychologist in the criminal justice system. *Professional Psychology,* 1972, **3**, 259–270.

Olbrisch, M. E., & Sechrest, L. Educating health psychologists in traditional graduate training programs. *Professional Psychology,* 1979, **10**, 589–595.

Periman, B., & Lane, R. The clinical master's degree. *Teaching of psychology,* 1981, **8**, 72–77.

Peterson, D. R. The doctor of psychology program at the University of Illinois. *American Psychologist,* 1968, **23**, 511–516.

Peterson, D. R. Need for the doctor of psychology degree in professional psychology. *American Psychologist,* 1976, **31**, 792–798.

Petzel, T. P., & Berndt, D. J. APA internship selection criteria: Relative importance of academic and clinical preparation. *Professional Psychology,* 1980, **11**, 792–796.

Poffenberger, A. T. The training of a clinical psychologist. *Journal of Consulting Psychology,* 1938, **1**, 1–6.

Pomerleau, O. F. On behaviorism in behavioral medicine. *Behavioral Medicine Newsletter,* 1978, **1**, 2.

Pottharst, K. E. A brief history of the professional model of training. In M. Korman (Ed.), *Levels and patterns of professional training in psychology.* Washington, D.C.: American Psychological Association, 1976.

Poythress, N. G., Jr. A proposal for training in forensic psychology. *American Psychology,* 1979, **34**, 612–621.

Raimy, V. C. (Ed.), *Training in clinical psychology.* Englewood Cliffs, N.J.: Prentice-Hall, 1950.

Rappaport, J. *Community psychology: Values, research, and action.* New York: Holt, Rinehart & Winston, 1977.

Reiff, R. Ya gotta believe. In I. Iscoe, B. L. Bloom, & C. D. Spielberger (Eds.), *Community psychology in transition: Proceedings of the national conference on training in community psychology.* Washington, D.C.: Hemisphere, 1977.

Reisman, J. History and current trends in clinical psychology. In C. E. Walker (Ed.), *Clinical practice of psychology.* New York: Pergamon Press, 1981.

Reveron, D. Aged are a mystery to most psychologists. *APA Monitor,* February 1982, 9.

Roe, A., Gustad, J. W., Moore, B. V., Ross, S., & Skodak, M. (Eds.), *Graduate education in psychology.* Washinton, D.C.: APA, 1959.

Rogers, C. R. Needed emphasis in the training of clinical psychologists. *Journal of Consulting Psychology,* 1939, **3,** 141–143.

Rosenkrantz, A. L., & Holmes G. R. A pilot study of clinical internship at the William S. Hall Psychiatric Institute. *Journal of Clinical Psychology,* 1974, **25,** 417–419.

Ross, A. O. The clinical child psychologist. In B. B. Wolman (Ed.), *Manual of child psychopathology.* New York: McGraw-Hill, 1972.

Rothenberg, P. J., & Matulef, N. J. Toward professional training: A special report from the national council on graduate education in psychology. *Professional Psychology,* 1969, **1,** 33–37.

Sarason, I. G. *Personality: An objective approach.* New York: Wiley, 1966.

Sarason, S. B. Community psychology, network, and Mr. Everyman. In I. Iscoe, B. L. Bloom, & C. D. Spielberger (Eds.), *Community psychology in transition: Proceedings of the national conference on training in community psychology.* Washington, D.C.: Hemisphere, 1977.

Sarason, S. B. An asocial psychology and misdirected clinical psychology. *American Psychologist,* 1981, **36,** 827–836.

Sawyer, J. Measurement and prediction, clinical and statistical. *Psychological Bulletin,* 1966, **66,** 178–200.

Schwartz, G. E., & Weiss, S. M. Behavioral medicine revisited: An amended definition. *Journal of Behavioral Medicine,* 1978, **1,** 249–251.

Sechrest, L. Training psychologists for health research. *Task Force on Health Research Newsletter #1.* Washington, D.C.: APA, 1974.

Shakow, D. An internship year for psychologists (with special reference to psychiatric hospitals). *Journal of Consulting Psychology,* 1938, **2,** 73–76.

Sheer, D. E., & Lubin, B. Survey of training programs in clinical neuropsychology. *Journal of Clinical Psychology,* 1980, **36,** 1,035–1,039.

Shemberg, K., & Keeley, S. Psychodiagnostic training in the academic setting: Past and present. *Journal of Consulting and Clinical Psychology,* 1970, **34,** 205–211.

Shemberg, K. M., & Keeley, S. M. Internship training: Training practices and satisfaction with preinternship preparation. *Professional Psychology,* 1974, **5,** 98–105.

Shemberg, K. M., Keeley, S. M., & Leventhal, D. B. University practices and attitudes of clinical directors. *Professional Psychology,* 1976, 16–21.

Shemberg, K. M., & Leventhal, D. B. Attitudes of internship directors toward preinternship training and clinical training models. *Professional Psychology,* 1981, **12,** 639–646.

Shontz, F. C., & Wright, B. A. The distinctiveness of rehabilitation psychology. *Professional Psychology,* 1980, **11,** 919–924.

Siegler, I. C., Gentry, W. D., & Edwards, C. D. Training in geropsychology: A survey of graduate and internship programs. *Professional Psychology,* 1979, **10,** 390–395.

Stabler, B., & Whitt, J. K. Pediatric psychology: Perspectives and training implications. *Journal of Pediatric Psychology,* 1980, **5,** 245–251.

Stone, G. *Health and behavior.* Paper presented at the meeting of the American Psychological Association, San Francisco, August 1977.

Stout, A. L., Holmes, G. R., & Rothstein, W. Responses by graduates to memory of their internship in clinical psychology. *Perceptual and Motor Skills,* 1977, **45,** 863–870.

Stricker, G. On professional schools and professional degrees. *American Psychologist,* 1975, **30,** 1,062–1,066.

Strother, C. R. (Ed.) *Psychology and mental health.* Washington, D.C.: APA, 1956.

Strupp, H. H. The outcome problem in psychotherapy: Contemporary perspectives. In *Psychotherapy research and behavior change. The master lecture series,* Vol. 1. Washington, D.C.: APA, 1981.

Stuart, R. B. (Ed.) *Behavioral self-management: Strategies, techniques, and outcome.* New York: Brunner/Mazel, 1977.

Swan, G. E., Piccione, A., & Anderson, D. C. Internship training in behavioral medicine: Program description, issues, and guidelines. *Professional Psychology,* 1980, **11,** 339–346.

Tapp, J. L. Psychology and law: Look at interface. In B. D. Sales (Ed.) *Psychology and the legal process.* New York: Spectrum, 1977.

Thelan, M. H., & Ewing, D. R. Attitudes of applied clinicians toward roles, functions, and training in clinical psychology: A comparative survey. *Professional Psychology,* 1973, **4,** 28–34.

Thelan, M. H., Varble, D. L., & Johnson, J. Attitudes of academic clinical psychologists toward projective techniques. *American Psychologist,* 1968, **23,** 517–521.

Tomm, K. M., & Wright, L. M. Training in family therapy: Perceptual, conceptual, and executive skills. *Family Process,* 1979, **18,** 227–250.

Tucker, R. L. Strangers in paradise. *Journal of Clinical Psychology,* 1970, **34,** 140–143.

Tuma, J. M. Pediatric psychology? Do you mean child psychology? *Journal of Clinical Child Psychology,* 1975, **4,** 9–12.

Tuma, J. M. *Directory: Practicum and internship training resources in pediatric psychology.* Galveston, Texas: Society of Pediatric Psychology, 1976.

Tuma, J. M. *Proposal for a conference on professional training for clinical child psychologists.* A grant proposal presented to the National Institute of Mental Health, February 1, 1980.

Tuma, J. M. Crisis in training pediatric psychologists. *Professional Psychology,* 1981, **12,** 516–522.

Twain, D., McGree, R., & Bennett, L. A. Functional areas of psychological activity. In S. L. Brodsky (Ed.), *Psychologists in the criminal justice system.* Chicago:

University of Illinois Press, 1973.

VandenBos, G. R. APA input to NIMH regarding planning for mental health personnel development. Washington, D.C.: American Psychological Association, 1979.

Vineberg, S. Psychologists in rehabilitation—Manpower and training. In W. S. Neff (Ed.), *Rehabilitation psychology*. Washington, D.C.: APA, 1971.

Vineberg, S. E., & Willems, E. P. Observation and analysis of patient behavior in the rehabilitation hospital. *Archives of Physical Medicine and Rehabilitation*, 1971, **52**, 8–14.

Vitulano, L., & Copeland, B. Trends in continuing education and competency demonstration. *Professional Psychology*, 1980, **11**, 891–897.

Wade, T. C., & Baker, T. B. Opinions and use of psychological tests: A survey of clinical psychologists. *American Psychologist*, 1977, **32**, 874–882.

Walfish, S., Kaufman, K., & Kinder, B. N. Graduate training in clinical psychology: A view from the consumer. *Journal of Clinical Psychology*, 1980, **36**, 1,040–1,045.

Walker, E. E. Continuing professional development: The future for clinical psychology. *The Clinical Psychologists*, 1977, **30**, 6–7.

Webster, T. F. National priorities for the continuing education of psychologists. *American Psychologist*, 1971, **26**, 1,016–1,019.

Welch, C. E. Professional licensure and hospital delineation of clinical privileges: Relationship to quality assurance. In R. H. Egdahl & P. M. Gertman (Eds.), *Quality assurance in health care*. Germantown, Md.: Aspen Systems, 1976.

Wexler, M. The behavioral sciences in medical education: A view from psychology. *American Psychologist*, 1976, **31**, 275–283.

Woods, P. J. A history of APA's concern with the master's degree: Or "discharged with thanks." *American Psychologist*, 1971, **26**, 696–707.

Wright, B. A. (Ed.) *Psychology and rehabilitation*. Washington, D.C.: APA, 1959.

Yarrow, L. J. Emotional development. *American Psychologist*, 1979, **34**, 951–957.

Zax, M., & Specter, G. A. *An introduction to community psychology*. New York: Wiley, 1974.

Zolik E., Sirbu, W., & Hopkinson, D. Graduate student perspectives on training in community mental health-community psychology. Unpublished manuscript cited in Barton, A. K., Andrulis, D. P., Grove, W. P. & Aponte, J. F. A look at community psychology in the seventies. *American Journal of Community Psychology*, 1976, **4**, 1–11.

4 ROLES AND PROFESSIONAL PRACTICE

Theodore H. Blau

It has been over three-quarters of a century since Lightner Witmer opened his psychological clinic for dealing with children's problems in Philadelphia. At the turn of the century, psychologists such as Witmer and others were offering direct services to those in need, using primitive and elementary psychological methods. These services, however, were directly offered by psychologists without intermediaries or apologies.

Today we see professional psychology benefiting from an enormous amount of research and practice that has occurred since that time. Rather than emerging as an independent profession, however, the larger number of practicing professional psychologists are under the direction or limitation of other professionals in settings that restrict rather than enhance the delivery of psychological services to the consumer. Only in the independent practice setting does the consumer meet directly with the psychologist from the beginning to the end of the clinical process (Blau, 1959). Thus, we find that although the psychologist is the best-trained and best-educated of all of the professionals in the delivery of behavioral and mental health services to the consumer, he or she infrequently practices in a direct and independent manner.

Clinical psychologists offer a wide range of assessment, intervention, and consultation skills. The extent of a clinical psychologist's skills depends on his or her education, training, postdoctoral experience, and specialty training. Psychologists conduct a wide variety of psychotherapeutic interventions, assess intellect, aptitude, personality, neuropsychological functioning, and marital adjustment. Clinical psychologists serve as expert witnesses in a wide range of judicial situations. Clinical psychologists design, direct, and monitor various prevention and intervention programs relating to substance abuse, self-destructive behavior, and the criminal justice system. Clinical psychologists work in many diverse medical settings utilizing uniquely psychological methods and tools that are required in health service. Clinical psychologists rarely work autonomously. They ordinarily function in psychology departments or psychology services in university clinics, hospitals, prisons, community mental health centers, agencies, courts, and treatment centers. Policy is rarely formulated by psychologists in such institutions, and there is very little that is equivalent to academic freedom to allow clinicians to decide on what is the best utilization of their skills and tools. The clinical psychologist generally is an interim professional, receiving consultations or service requests and filling these within the constraints and expectations of a host institution. The skills of clinical psychologists are discussed in detail in other sections of this handbook. This chapter focuses on role development, status issues in the clinical psychologist's professional role, and the growth of autonomy in the practice of clinical psychology.

Background

Throughout the first half of the 20th century, psychology developed as an academic discipline in close association with philosophy and education. Offering direct services to the consumer was apparently rare, and certainly descriptions or discussion of this utilization of psychological knowledge made no appearance in the general psychological literature.

After World War II, interest in the delivery of such services burgeoned considerably. Between 1950 and 1960 a respectable number of psychologists entered into what was then known as "private practice" (Blau, 1959). This move was accepted slowly by organized psychology. Working through the American Psychological Association, a small group of "young turks" established a political baseline to explore the why psychologists should not practice independently. The scope of interests and activities within the APA began to include such matters as independent practice, the eligibility of psychologists for third-party payments, licensure for fully qualified psychologists, hospital privileges for psychologists, and, in general, encouragement for psychologists to become part of the community and deliver direct services without the supervision and constraints of the medical profession, particularly psychiatry.

Clinical psychology has had a mixed heritage. Although a relatively solid data base has been developed over the past 100 years, clinical psychology has taken the medical and psychiatric professions as a partial model. The medical profession, with its tradition of helpfulness, concern, and responsibility, is a respectable model. The issue arises in psychology's imitating or following psychiatry. Psychiatry has generally supported a disease model of disturbance which at some point has classified such things as adolescent rebellion, reading difficulties, and aggressiveness as "diseases" (American Psychiatric Association, 1980). As Albee and Loeffler (1971) have pointed out, psychology must find its own house. Those respon-

sible for designing and implementing education and training in clinical psychology have been unfamiliar with the realities of practice in the community, and so an ignorance gap developed between the quality and style of clinical psychologists' preparation to offer service to those in need, and the realities of the consumer's desires and opportunities for effective practice.

History of Training for Professional Roles

There has been a consistent, though not always open, resistance to the growth of clinical psychology practice among academic colleagues. The first clear acknlowledgment by organized psychology that something beyond academic excellence was required for practice was gently suggested in 1965 during the third (Chicago) APA conference on training in clinical psychology. The conference summary recommended production of a corps of well-trained, rigorous, professionally skillful, science-valuing clinical psychologists whose responsiveness to social needs would rest on careful, systematic observations of meaningful, often complicated, problems, (Hoch, Ross, & Winder, 1966). Earlier efforts at the Boulder Conference focused on the "scientist-professional model with little real emphasis on professional practice" (Raimy, 1950). APA publications describing professional psychology to prospective students continued to deemphasize independent practice with such statements as: "You should decide (a) what specialization (e.g., social, physiological, counseling) in psychology you would like to prepare for" (Fretz & Stang, 1980, p. 9). Reading this recent publication aimed at those preparing for graduate training in psychology, one would be surprised to know that psychology produces clinical practitioners and that this program is the most frequent one chosen by entering students.

In spite of in-house resistance, practice in clinical psychology continues to grow. Norcross and Prochaska (1982) surveyed 479 members of the Division of Clinical Psychology and compared their findings with a similar survey conducted and reported by Garfield and Kurtz (1974). The results are suggestive of trends in professional self-view and affiliation of clinical psychologists between the early 70s and the early 80s.

In the 70s, approximately 59 percent viewed themselves as clinical practitioners and 20 percent as academicians. Almost a decade later, 63 percent saw themselves as practitioners and 17 percent as academicians. Secondary roles chosen in the surveys show that 12 percent doing some practice as a secondary role in the 70s has become 20 percent in the early 80s, suggesting that more clinical psychologists in nonpractitioner roles had begun to see themselves as "ancillary practitioners." Comparison of primary institutional affiliation showed decreases in mental hospitals, community mental health centers, and university departments. The most significant increase was in private practice (23 to 31 percent). The more experienced respondents were more likely to be in private practice settings. Thus, the statement by Fretz and Stang (1980) in APA's definitive description of graduate study in psychology, inaccurately states: "Nearly ½ of all clinical psychologists that have Ph.D.'s work in educational settings such as universities; the remainder work in direct-service settings such as hospitals and clinics" (p. 10). No mention is made of private practice, even though approximately one-third of all those surveyed by Norcross and Prochaska previous to the APA booklet functioned in this role. As a professional and scientific organization, the APA, through its governance structure, has tended to view independent practice as a less than desirable role for clinical psychologists. The body politic of psychology has been reluctant to recognize the long-known failure of institutional mental health delivery systems patterned after the psychiatric model (*Behavior Today*, 1972).

Although clinical psychology has been acknowledged for two decades by APA as the largest category of specialization among psychologists, it is almost always mentioned last, and described begrudgingly (APA, 1968). The most recent model of a clinical psychologist described in *Careers in Psychology* is: "Professor, clinical psychology, at a southwestern university," and goes on to describe a man who received a Ph.D. in clinical psychology, served one year of postdoctoral internship at a school of medicine, and then nine years as a faculty member and director of clinical training for two years. He is described as doing one day of practice a week (APA, 1975).

In the 1970s, a small group of clinical practitioners formed the *Council for the Advancement of the Psychological Professions and Sciences*. They vigorously pursued the concept of full professional roles for clinical psychologists and, without much help from APA, engineered Public Law 93–363 to provide access without prior referral in the federal employee health benefits program (Donahue, 1974). Academic and research colleagues were appalled by the idea of psychologists lobbying in the corridors of power in Washington. Ten years later, these same colleagues have not only acknowledged the wisdom and success of CAPPS group but have now begun to emulate their approach (Cunningham, 1982).

The last major, public effort to define professional psychology by the American Psychological Association took place at a conference at Vail, Colorado, in 1973. Though hopes were high, only a few recommendations were actually implemented. Organized psychology, particularly in the university setting, consistently avoided a definitive analysis of the *training/competencey/task/delivery* model for professional services. The strong plea that university graduate departments of psychology recognize, through selection, education, training, and evaluation that professional practice and research on professional issues may require contrasting skills has largely gone unheeded (Korman, 1976).

Although efforts continue to define the journeyman level of professional practice via various credentialing procedures at the state and national levels, the lag between delineation of implementation and problems, process, and outcomes is much too long to be either explained or justified by concepts such as "public policy concern," "due caution," or, least acceptable in this context "academic freedom" (Albee & Loeffler, 1971; Blau, 1959, 1973).

Since psychologists are rarely trained for independent, applied professional roles, they are less likely to be in a position to deliver their services and make their value known (Kiesler, Cummings, & VandenBos, 1979; Reiff, 1970).

The Current Situation

Although the professional school movement represents an important and considerable effort to resolve traditional role conflicts in psychology, forward movement has slowed. Free-standing schools are having difficulty in matters of funding, facilities, and APA accreditation. The professionally oriented, non-university-affiliated schools find that they have to meet fairly rigid, traditional APA accreditation criteria, that in some respects tend to be inappropriate for doctoral programs that are specifically designed to graduate competent journeymen-level clinicians.

Most doctoral-level graduates of APA-approved programs in clinical psychology are taught, trained, and molded toward research, teaching, or agency practice. Such graduates face the possibility of bland or limited professional careers in respect to their potential skills in service delivery. The most promising clinical graduates often start out strongly influenced by their professors. These academic clinical psychologists, rarely full-time practitioners, tend to advise their best students to model after their mentors: teachers, researchers, and part-time narrow-spectrum practitioners. Those who enter agency or institutional practice are first constrained to narrow their very broad education and skills into the relatively parochial and restricted requirements of the agency or institution. The creative modification of policy and procedures that young enthusiastic graduates can bring to an institution are rarely welcomed or even tolerated. Broadening neuropsychological assessment and neurotraining facilities, establishing divisions of behavioral medicine, designing down-the-road consumer evaluation and revision systems, instituting conflict-resolution opportunities within the agency, establishing professional ties with the Bar and the Bench are too frequently seen as threats to the tranquillity of the institutional mandate and process.

Should young clinicians work well with consumers at an agency, raises in salary and status usually demand that they give up the special professional roles for which they have been trained and become middle managers struggling with budgets, program planning, personnel procedures, and other tasks that could be done better and more cost-effectively by a chief clerk or a graduate of a management program. Such senior staff must then defensively insist that they maintain their clinical skills by having a day a week of practice. Would any thoughtful person want to receive services from a one-fifth-time neurosurgeon, internist, dentist, attorney, or other professional from whom we expect highly skilled services? How many of these part-time professionals would sacrifice a lucrative job offer to move to another city in order to stay at their agency and give their clients continuity and availability? Do we really want the full professor of clinical psychology who in 20 years has had six to seven thousand hours of practice to represent the "best in professional psychology?" Many well-trained clinical psychologists owe much of their early awareness of a proper

health-delivery model to psychiatrists. In medicine, a clinician of limited skill or experience is soon found out. Supervisors of training are more likely to be seasoned clinicians with substantial independent practice background. It is unfortunate that clinical psychology cannot acknowledge its debt to training psychiatrists, realize the limitations of the disease model, and provide more experienced full-time psychological practitioners as supervisors.

A Proposed Preparation and Implementation Model

In spite of various clamorings, the institutional, community, or team model of mental health delivery has largely failed (*Behavior Today*, 1972; Blau, 1981). If psychology is to fulfill its promise, certain conditions for the delivery of services are likely to increase the probability that clinical psychologists will serve consumer needs effectively. Such conditions include:

A. *Education and Training.* The doctorate is the basic academic requirement for the fully professional clinical psychologist. The Psy.D. as it is currently conceived is likely to be a more solid preparation for practice than the Ph.D. Early exposure to real consumers in a setting that is primarily psychological with supervisors who are very experienced and skillful is mandatory. Exposure on a regular basis to skillful, full-time practitioner role models throughout graduate training should be considered essential. Administrative and guild constraints to making such models available in doctoral programs must be resolved if educational institutions are to produce graduates who are able to take psychological services directly to the consumer in competent, ethical, realistic styles. Such education must be standardized in measureable behavioral terms if our programs are to become credible.

B. *Supervision.* Psychology must evaluate, standardize, and mandate postdoctoral experiences for clinical psychologists. These should include broad exposure to a wide assortment of generally accepted procedures and techniques in assessment, therapeutic intervention, crisis consultation, and consultation involving consumer-generated help-requests. Clinical work involves clients along the entire developmental range. Self-evaluate techniques as well as systems of external audit should be intrinsic to such a program to ensure growing competence. This should be based on skill and outcome assessment. At present, two years of postdoctoral experience in a supervised setting seems necessary. Counting predoctoral experience hours, the current licensing requirement style is archaic and counterproductive.

C. *Credentialing.* A strong credentialing program is necessary. This should include licensing at the journeyman level of skill, identification of specialty skills with concomitant training and performance criteria, and board certification of excellent professional practice skills. Continuing education should be mandatory and reevaluation of clinical skills required at regular intervals. Such evaluative systems should be practical, consumer oriented, and reasonable.

D. *Practice.* It is proposed that the ideal model for the delivery of clinical services is the independent practice model. Advantages far outweigh disadvantages and traditional criticism of "private practice." If psychology is of sufficient substance to justify doctoral-level practitioners, it cannot justify constraining its practitioners to practice under the supervision or restrictions of other professions as a primary and recommended style of practice. Independent practice offers the most flexible setting whether the practice is group or individual. Advantages include:

1. The opportunity to offer a broad spectrum of psychological services.
2. The opportunity to develop services that the practitioner knows best, enjoys most, and delivers most effectively.
3. The free choice and opportunity to avoid rendering partial services, long-delayed services, or inappropriate services.
4. Relative freedom from political and bureaucratic constraints and demands.
5. Fair compensation for extra skill, effort, or commitment.
6. The opportunity to become a very experienced practicing clinician without loss of status or income.
7. The opportunity to pursue a broadening of skills and training without the constraints of institutional budgets.
8. The option of offering services to anyone without regard to eligibility by status, income, residence, citizenship, service connection, or other administrative limitation.
9. The opportunity to make oneself available as a trainer of skill and experience.
10. The option of selecting surroundings, equipment, supporting staff, and the style of service delivery. Excellence and its pursuit is limited only by the practitioner's education, training, ethical constraints, and goodwill.
11. Success and failure can be more clearly attributed to the practitioner than in the diffuseness of institutional and agency settings. Accountability is direct and attributable.
12. The psychologist can be the first and last person to see the consumer. Direct access increases the probability of delivery of competent service, more personal involvement, early resolution of misunderstandings, and better evaluation of benefit.
13. The independent practice setting allows psychologists to adjust their fees to the consumer's income.
14. Independent practice removes institutional constraints — real or symbolic — that suggest psychologists may be second-level practitioners.
15. The variety of activity and scheduling opportunity in independent practice is likely to increase the quality of life of practicing professionals.

Conclusions

As dark as the future for salaried professional psychologists may be with tightening governmental budgets, opportunities for independent professional practice abound. In communities where psychologists have committed themselves to the full-time independent practice model, the saturation ratio has been found to be between one full-time practitioner for 2,500 population to one in 135,000 (Blau, 1973b). If we accept a conservative figure of 1:10,000, the population of the United States could probably now support over 22,000 full-time independent clinical practitioners. At this writing there are between 7,000 and 9,000 psychologists in full-time independent practice. It seems apparent that opportunities for practice using the independent model abound.

Until graduate teaching and training institutions recognize the value of independent practice and the opportunities that exist for clinical psychologists to serve the needy and the needful in the community more directly, clinicians will continue to be self-limiting in pursuit of the mandate of psychology to promote human welfare.

References

Albee, G. W., & Loeffler, E. Role conflicts in psychology and their implications for a re-evaluation of training models. *The Canadian Psychologist.* 1971, **12**, 465–481.

American Psychiatric Association. *Diagnostic and statistical manual of mental disorders, III.* Washington, D.C.: Author, 1980.

American Psychological Association. *Psychology as a profession.* Washington, D.C.: Author, 1968.

American Psychological Association. *Careers in psychology.* Washington, D.C.: APA, 1975.

American Psychological Association. *Standards for providers of psychological services.* Washington, D.C.: Author, 1977.

Behavior Today staff. Nader report: Community mental health centers. *Behavior Today,* July 31, 1972.

Blau, T. H. *Private practice in clinical psychology.* New York: Appleton-Century-Crofts, 1959.

Blau, T. H. Exposure to Competence: A simple standard for graduate training in professional psychology. *Professional Psychology,* 1973, **2**, 133–136.(a)

Blau, T. H. A study of saturation of independent practitioners in 51 communities. *Report to the committee on human resources,* APA, 1973.(b)

Blau, T. H. Psychology and national health policy, *Contemporary Psychology,* 1981, **26**, 88–89.

Division of School Psychology. *The school psychologist.* Washington, D.C.: APA, 1975.

Cunningham, S. The politics of psychology. *APA Monitor,* 1982, **13**, 1.

Donahue, J. U.S. freedom-of-choice law to stimulate state action. *Cappsule,* 1974, **3**, 6.

Fretz, B. R., & Stang, D. J. *Preparing for graduate study in Psychology.* Washington, D.C.: APA, 1980, p. 9.

Garfield, S. L., & Kurtz, R. A. A survey of clinical psychologists: Characteristics, activities, and orientations. *The Clinical Psychologist,* 1974, **28**, 7–10.

Hoch, E. L., Ross, A. O., & Winder, C. L. *Professional preparation of clinical psychologists.* Washington, D.C.: APA, 1966.

Kiesler, C. A., Cummings, N. A., & VandenBos, G. R. (Eds.), *Psychology and national health insurance.* Washington, D.C.: APA, 1979.

Korman, M. (Ed.), *Levels and patterns of professional training in psychology.* Washington, D.C.: APA, 1976.

Norcross, J. C., & Prochaska, J. O. A national survey of clinical psychologists: affiliations and orientations. *The Clinical Psychologist,* 1982, **35**, 1–6.

Raimy, V. C. (Ed.), *Training in clinical psychology.* New York: Prentice-Hall, 1950.

Reiff, R. Psychology and public policy. *Professional Psychology,* 1970, **3**, 315–330.

Roe, A., Gustard, J. W., Moore, B. V., Ross, S., & Skodak, M. *Graduate education in psychology.* Washington, D.C.: APA, 1959.

Schofield, W. The role of psychology in the delivery of health services. *American Psychologist,* 1969, **24**, 565–584.

5 PSYCHOLOGY AND MENTAL HEALTH POLICY

Charles A. Kiesler

M ost psychological research and practice is relevant to national mental health policy. However, psychologists have not been very involved in either the development of national mental health policy or its evaluation. The Task Panel on Planning and Review of the President's Commission on Mental Health (PCMH) says more generally, "that mental health professionals, except for public employees in de-livery management systems, play almost no role in developing the policy other than protection of their turf" (Allerton et al., 1978, p. 270). More to the point of this chapter, psychology has not played a strong role in research in mental health policy. I distinguish here between research that is in some way relevant to national policy and policy research per se. Let us define what we mean by mental health policy and allied research before delving more deeply into these issues.

I am defining mental health policy as:

the de facto or de jure aggregate of laws, practices, social structures, or actions occur-ring within our society, the intent of which is improved mental health of individuals and groups. The study of such policy includes, the descriptive parameters of the aggregate,

the comparative assessment of particular techniques, evaluation of a system and its subparts, human resources available and needed, cost-benefit analyses of practices or actions, and the cause and effect relationship of one set of policies, such as mental health, to others, such as welfare and health, as well as the study of institutions or groups seeking to affect such policy [Kiesler, 1980, p. 1,066].

This definition has both de facto and de jure com-ponents. In essence, I am advocating a "top-down" approach to policy analysis. We inquire first what is done in the name of mental health in the United States, at what cost, and with what effects or out-comes?

Policy research can be descriptive, evaluative, or theoretical in nature; all are needed. Descrip-tive research is needed to ascertain what we are now doing in the name of mental health, to assess agency practices and customs, to compute system costs, to inspect statutes that affect professional practice or access to services, to assess the imple-mentation of particular legislative ideals — such as community mental health centers (CMHCs) — and to weigh the potential conflicts among agen-cies — such as between the Alcohol, Drug Abuse,

Mental Health Administration (ADAMHA) and the Social Security Administration (SSA).

Evaluative research is needed to assess both current practices and potential policy alternatives. One aspect of our current national mental health policy is deinstitutionalization, to put fewer people in mental hospitals, and to shorten their stay once there. Evaluative research could assess the implementation of this policy. Are we putting fewer people in mental hospitals? Do they indeed stay a shorter period of time? Are they more likely to return (the revolving-door phenomenon)? Are the outcomes of such treatment more effective for the patient in returning them to more normal lives? This brand of research evaluates the effectiveness and/or the implementation of current national policy. Evaluation research could as well be used to assess potential alternatives, public strategies, or decisions. Such research could focus on the effectiveness and cost-benefit of treatment alternatives to hospitalization.

Theoretical research can be used both to assess à priori current national practices and to pose alternative national strategies. This approach should ask, what do we know about human behavior and how can that knowledge be applied to the construction of national policy alternatives? What, for example, are the cogent theoretically justifiable alternative methods of treating people instead of mental hospitalization?

One can distinguish between policy research and policy-relevant research as a pedagogical aid in understanding the level of the problem we wish to discuss. It surely is not wise, however, to push this distinction very far, or to imply that one brand of research is more needed than another. As an example of the ambiguity in this distinction, consider the work of Azrin (1977), who developed intervention techniques for training the unemployed to become more effective job applicants/occupants. Using behavior modification techniques, Azrin teaches people specific behaviors that raise the probability of an employer hiring them and makes it easier for a person to keep a job once obtained. This applied research is clearly relevant to national policy in the welfare sector. Is it policy research? That may not be a worthwhile question, but policy research does remain to be done before this concept can be implemented at a national level. That research would address the question of the problems of adopting a national policy based on such techniques. We would ask

questions related to the ease of national implementation, including the need for qualified personnel to handle the teaching, the expense of training the teachers, the applicability of the techniques on a broad scale, and the cost-benefits associated with decreasing welfare payments and the like. In short, even though the research of Azrin in this area is clearly relevant to national policy, other research remains to be carried out before the intervention technique could be seriously considered as a national policy alternative. The latter research is clearly policy research. Whether the former is also policy research is moot. Research relevant to policy is important, even though other data may be needed before implementation as national policy. Whether one wishes to attach a particular brand to that type of research is surely of secondary importance. Such fine distinctions are less important than the fact that there is a great dearth of policy research in mental health.

Background Reading

Space limitations prohibit a detailed review of all the research that is relevant to national mental health policy. For those who wish to begin to become educated in this important area, the following preliminary bibliography is recommended:

1. *Mental Health and Social Policy* is an excellent review by David Mechanic (1980), a noted medical sociologist, of a variety of research from the several disciplines related to mental health policy.
2. Kiesler (1980a) describes current national mental health policy and some of the more critical, but uninvestigated, research issues.
3. *Financing Psychotherapy* is a reanalysis of an existing survey of psychiatric practice by Thomas McGuire (1980), a mental health economist, which both addresses the question of how to finance mental health services as well as illustrating techniques used by economists in such an assessment.
4. *The Benefits of Psychotherapy*, by Smith, Glass, and Miller (1980), uses metaanalysis to assess both the effects of psychotherapy and of drugs.
5. *Mental Illness in the United States,* by Dohrenwend et al. (1980), illustrates issues and problems in the epidemiology of mental health problems.

6. *Psychology and National Health Insurance: A Source Book* is a collection of articles edited by Kiesler, Cummings, and VandenBos (1979), that illustrates the rapidly changing nature of political and scientific issues in the delivery of mental health services nationally.

7. *Economics, Mental Health and the Law*, by the economist Jeffrey Rubin (1978), discusses the implications of recent court cases for mental health policy and treatment.

8. *A Primer of Policy Analysis*, by Stokey and Zeckhauser (1978), is an introduction to the general mathematical methods of Policy Analysis.

9. *The President's Commission on Mental Health*, Volumes 2, 3 and 4 (1978), contain not the recommendations of the commission, but rather the reports of the task panels assessing the empirical data that are related to national policy issues; over 2,000 pages, but *essential* reading for a budding policy analyst in mental health.

10. *Experimental Methods for Social Policy Research*, by Fairweather and Tornatzky (1977).

11. *Linking Health and Mental Health*, edited by Broskowski, Marks, and Budman (1981), is an excellent collection of articles on policy issues overlapping health and mental health.

One can see from this set of recommendations, that the field of mental health policy research is extremely broad and certainly interdisciplinary in nature. In addition to the obvious fields of psychiatry and clinical psychology, it includes epidemiology, psychiatric statistics, mental health economics (in the context of health economics), medical sociology, demography, some aspects of political science, and law. Important research that is directly relevant to the study of mental health policy exists in each of these fields.

Obviously, this chapter can only scratch the surface of mental health policy research. The chapter is more conceptually oriented than it is an exhaustive literature review. The general approach will be to describe briefly de facto and de jure mental health policy, and outline some important research issues that are relevant, in particular those issues of greater concern to psychologists. We end by discussing some of the current major theoretical, empirical, and methodological issues as well as some alternative futures for mental health policy research in psychology.

De Facto and De Jure National Mental Health Policy

As with most national policies, mental health policy is not a carefully planned and coordinated set of laws resting on the best of scientific knowledge. A good deal of what we do in the name of mental health rests on historical accident, political pressures, and unintended consequences of well-meaning acts. In particular, we might distinguish between de jure and de facto mental health policy. I have described in some detail elsewhere (Kiesler, 1980a) our national mental health policy and some of the obvious research questions related to it. What follows is more or less a synopsis of that description.

The terms de facto and de jure are used because we intuitively understand them from previous discussions of school desegregation. Our de jure mental health policy is what we intend to accomplish through appropriate legislation and agency practices. Our de facto policy is the whole system of what is done in the name of mental health, whether it is intended or not. In mental health, there are some unintended consequences of our de facto policy that undercut our de jure policy.

The main elements of our de jure policy are those contained in public statements by high officials, in testimony of appropriate federal agencies such as NIMH in the Congress, and the details of laws that are specifically related to mental health (for example, see Klerman, 1979; or Vischi et al., 1980). The two major threads of our national de jure policy currently are: deinstitutionalization of patients from mental hospitals, and the development of outpatient care, particularly through the community mental health center system. The policy regarding deinstitutionalization often includes development of appropriate alternative care mechanisms for patients who would formerly have been institutionalized, the development of after-care mechanisms for those who have already been institutionalized, and the development of community support systems (Bachrach, 1976). Community support systems both link up with other attempts to help those two populations, and serve as a national mechanism for the prevention of serious mental disorders (Piasecki, Leary, & Rutman, 1980). We will inspect some of the data relevant to these various aspects of the de jure mental health policy later in this chapter.

Our de facto policy is dominated, to a considerable extent, by insurance mechanisms that undercut the de jure policy of nonhospitalization and outpatient care. At least 70 percent of the national mental health dollar goes for hospitalization. The largest such program is Medicaid which spends more federal dollars in hospitalizing patients than the community mental health center system does in prevention and treatment of mental disorders on an outpatient basis. The Medicaid program is oriented toward the categorically poor: the aging, the blind, the disabled, and families with dependent children with only one parent capable of providing support. One out of three poor people does not meet that categorical definition. The impact of the Medicaid program on mental health is to provide incentives for hospitalization, or more specifically, disincentives for outpatient care. As the Task Panel on the Cost and Financing of Mental Health of the PCMH says in its report:

> Many mental health services are not reimbursed under Medicaid, including many outreach support services. The program focuses on institutional services, and the proportion of Medicaid patients receiving ambulatory services is far less than among wealthier patients. [Newman et al., 1978]

As we shall discuss later, other private insurance plans also provide such disincentives for outpatient care. The general issue of incentives, alternative insurance plans, their cost, the potential patient usage as a function of alternative plans, are all important policy research questions. We bring them up as appropriate during the chapter.

With this sketchy introduction, let us move to a variety of policy research issues in mental health.

Research Issues

The Scope of the Problem

The field of psychiatric epidemiology focuses on both the incidence and prevalence of mental disorders (Dohrenwend et al., 1980). Prevalence refers to the number of cases existing in the population at a particular time. Incidence refers to the number of new cases during a specified period of time. Some early attempts at psychiatric epidemiology included professional interviews by psychiatrists of entire communities, (e.g., Hagnell, 1966). More recent research has centered around the use of various psychiatric screening devices

(see Mechanic, 1980). A good deal of the evidence and issues related to psychiatric epidemiology are well known to clinical psychologists and need not be extensively reviewed here.

Most professionals agree that about 15 percent of the population is in need of mental health services at any one time. Both the Task Panel on the Scope of the Problem of the PCMH and a related report by senior staff at NIMH independently report this percentage (Mechanic et al., 1978; Regier, Goldberg, & Taube, 1978). An epidemiological study of patients in the National Health Service in Great Britain found that 14 percent of the females and 7 percent of the males consulted general practitioners for some form of "mental illness." A special white paper by the Secretary of State for Social Services (Castle, 1975) concluded that these percentages were low because general practitioners have difficulty detecting psychiatric symptoms.

A separate report conducted under the auspices of the PCMH concludes that a much larger percentage of the population has mental problems. Momentarily disregarding rather sharp differences among social class, sex, and race categories, they conclude that, "the true prevalence of clinical maladaptation among school children is unlikely to average less than 12 percent" (p. 150), the large majority of whom are not receiving treatment; that among adults below the age of 60, between 16 and 25 percent have one of the functional disorders (schizophrenia, affective psychosis, neurosis, or personality disorder); for those above age 60, between 18 and 25 percent of the population have either a functional or organic disorder (the above, plus organic psychosis). In addition, Dohrenwend et al. (1980) find a substantial proportion of the population not fitting established clinical categories, but nonetheless showing severe psychological and somatic distress. They find that 13 percent of the population is in this category, with severe distress but without a diagnosable psychiatric disorder. They apply Frank's (1973) concept of demoralization to this population.

Dohrenwend et al. (1980) thoroughly review the evidence related to the current state of psychiatric epidemiology. They find that the true prevalence of psychiatric disorders varies sharply as a function of age, sex, community and region of the country, socioeconomic class, and race. These important variables aside, Dohrenwend et al. find a substantially larger fraction of the population with serious psychiatric disorders than do others. They further raise the issue of people who do not fit into the psychiatric categories, but who none-theless have severe psychological distress.

There are a number of important research is-sues in this field. Estimates of prevalence of men-tal disorders fluctuate wildly. Some of this fluc-tuation is due to demographic characteristics. However, an unknown, but apparently substan-tial, amount is due to differences in methods and measurement (see Dohrenwend et al.). The preva-lence of mental disorders in the United States is a critical national question, and substantial ad-vances are needed in method and measuring in-struments. In addition, demographic variations are also of importance. The concept of the demor-alized, and the parameters of that population, needs thorough investigation. Part of the issue un-derlying demoralization is the degree to which psychiatric categories (which these people do not fit) adequately describe the population in need or are functionally related to categories of potentially effective treatment (Schact & Nathan, 1977). To the extent that identical treatment is effective for two psychiatric categories, the categories them-selves lessen in diagnostic importance. The con-cept of demoralization also needs to be dovetailed with issues of effective treatment. Who are these people? What specific problems do they have? What sorts of treatment are available for them? Are known treatment methods effective in reliev-ing their psychological distress? Does the distress have outcomes relevant to other social policies, such as education, employment, welfare, child abuse, and the like?

Further complicating epidemiological esti-mates of mental disorders is the clear inter-relationship of physical and mental disorders. Goplerud (1981) provides a comprehensive discus-sion of these issues. For example, in one stratified sample of a Florida community, Schwab et al. (1979) found that 28 percent of the population had emotional problems, 39 percent had one or more physical illnesses, and 26 percent reported psycho-somatic disorders such as nervous stomach, hyper-tension, and colitis. Ten percent of the sample re-ported all three categories of disorder and another 11 percent reported two of the three.

The bilateral linkages between physical and emotional disorders are increasingly recognized by researchers (Eastwood, 1975; Goplerud, 1981), but apparently not by physician practitioners. Hoeper (1980) found that general practitioners de-

tect only 3 percent of psychiatric cases, when the diagnoses were independently assessed.

Psychiatric epidemiology as a field is worthy of considerable investigation and support. In addi-tion to the mining of the field itself, much needs to be done in relating epidemiological categories to known methods of effective treatment. The matrix of diagnostic categories by population and demographic breakdowns should be a plausible starting point for the development of mental health policy to promote professional training, the development of alternative treatment methods, and evaluation strategies.

Match between Services Needed and Number of Providers Available

Whatever estimate of prevalence and incidence one accepts for mental disorders, all agree that few people needing services actually receive them. Regier, Goldberg, and Taube (1978) estimate that only about 15 percent of people needing services actually receive them from the mental health spe-cialty sector. Since they also estimate that 15 per-cent of the population is in need of such services, we can conclude that only about 2 percent of the population receives services of specially trained personnel. Part of the problem, but not all, is due to a mismatch between services needed and num-ber of providers available (Kiesler, 1980a, 1980b).

There are approximately 25,000 trained psychia-trists in the United States (Marmor, Scheidemandel, & Kanns, 1975). Mills, Wellner, and VandenBos (1979) found approximately 25,000 licensed-cer-tified psychologists in the country. Consequently, there are about 50,000 doctoral-level mental health service providers available.

As I point out elsewhere (Kiesler, 1980a, 1980b), this seemingly large number of service providers does not match up well with services needed. Let us accept, for the sake of argument, the 15 percent figure of prevalence of psychiatric disorders. Fif-teen percent of 220 million is 33 million; that is, 33 million people are in need of some sort of mental health service at any given time. (Of course the Dohrenwend et al. estimate of prevalence would result in a much higher figure.) The ratio of people in need and doctoral-level service providers means that there is one provider for every 660 people in need.

Of course, not all psychiatrists and licensed psychologists provide mental health services.

Many of them are engaged in administrative or similar sorts of positions. Further, those who do provide services cannot provide them 40 hours a week. Let us suppose, for the sake of argument, that we have 45,000 licensed/certified psychologists and psychiatrists available to deliver services. Le us also suppose that each could deliver roughly 30 hours of services per week. This would leave some time for conferences, continuing education, research, and other professional commitments. Calculated in this way, our 45,000 service providers have at least a potential service capacity of 67,500,000 person hours of mental health service per year. This is only a potential. Psychiatrists and psychologists together now only deliver somewhere between 35 and 45 million service hours a year (Gottfredson & Dyer, 1978; Kiesler, 1980a).

The potential matchup is distressing. We have 33 million potential patients and 67 million potential service hours. That is, each person needing service could conceivably obtain, at the maximum, two hours of service for his problem during a year.

Policy research questions become clearer in this view. Traditional psychotherapy could only handle a small proportion of patients in need given the current number of service providers. Therefore, research is needed to: consider alternative modes of treatment, rather than traditional psychotherapy; develop the expansion of potential service by doctoral service providers through the use of other providers and paraprofessionals; investigate closely the relative efficacy of various treatment modalities so that effectiveness is enhanced; investigate the potential of voluntary organizations, alternative helping groups, self-help techniques, and social networks relating to the family and friends.

This is a good example of the difference between top-down and bottom-up policy approaches. From the bottom-up, we need to continue to refine therapeutic techniques, increase the number of service providers, develop our capacity for outpatient services, support a network of community mental health health centers, and so forth. From the bottom-up, it looks like we are continuing to make good progress against a serious national problem. The view from the top-down is quite different. The top-down view says that despite a steady track record of continued improvement in the delivery of services, the overall national policy situation is an impossible one. We can never hope to have a sufficient number of doctoral-level mental health service providers to provide traditional mental health services to the number of people who actually need them. This top-down view should induce us to put greater attention on alternative service providers, preventive techniques, and the like.[1]

Alternative Services and Volunteer Groups

Elsewhere (Kiesler, 1980a), I have described three types of other services in mental health: the most formally organized is the community support system; then alternative services; finally, the least-organized and least-researched, the volunteer programs.

The community support system includes rather formal and funded mechanisms to expand upon traditional services, to provide connections between different types of services (e.g., health and social services), and to lessen the impact of deinstitutionalization on individual patients. The major aspects of this program are to expand the impact of existing services and to provide linkups among existing systems of care (Christmas et al., 1978).

Alternative services are substitutes for other services that might otherwise be expected or delivered. One example is the various methods of alternative care as a substitute for mental hospitalization (e.g., Fairweather, Sanders, & Maynard, 1969). Care after hospitalization, depending exactly on how it is conducted, could fit the definition of either alternative services or community support systems (e.g., Budson, 1978). Careful scientific investigation of either group of services is sparse (but see Rose, 1979; Taber, 1980, for reviews). There are evaluations of particular sets of services, but they tend to be demonstrations rather than fulfillments of careful scientific criteria. Evaluation research in this area has been under-

[1]NIMH has had a recent policy of expanding the psychiatric training of general physicians. However, this policy was not developed because of the system mismatch described above; rather, that general physicians were already treating more mental disorders than the specialty mental health sector (Brown & Regier, 1977; Regier, Goldberg, & Taube, 1978; Regier & Taube, 1981).

funded and most evaluations do not meet minimal scientific criteria for either: (1) assessing the absolute impact of a particular service (compared to no treatment), or (2) comparing one instance of service delivery with other ones (a comparative assessment rather than an absolute assessment).

Community support systems and alternative care are two primary mechanisms for expanding the potential of service delivery to large populations. As such, they need to be investigated very carefully, not only with an eye to their absolute efficacy, but also to compare alternative strategies of delivering such services. In particular, cost-benefit analyses of these services are needed, and specifically addressing the question of the ease of developing such services for a national system of delivery (Schulberg, 1979).

Volunteer groups providing services of some sort to people with mental problems are a potentially great national resource, but relatively uninvestigated (but see Christmas et al., 1978; Lieberman & Borman, 1976; Silverman, 1978). These volunteer groups are often composed of ex-patients and, for a variety of reasons, are unsympathetic to more traditional modes of care. We include here both self-help groups and volunteers who devote time to helping others. Some of the groups include what might be called mutual aid, that is, people with the same problem attempting to help each other. Others might be called sequential aid; a person who had a particular mental problem, but who is much improved, now attempts to help others with the same problem.

The PCMH estimates that there are 500,000 self-help groups in the U.S. The groups are often very uncooperative and view outsiders in general as being unsympathetic to their goals. Their cooperation in research is therefore difficult to obtain. Observational research is one obvious method to use. Such research, however, is highly technical in nature, and not at all easy to carry out. Psychologists are often not well prepared to carry out such research in a careful and systematic way. We need to know more about the demographic and sociological characteristics of such groups, even as a preliminary step. On the other hand, our ultimate interest is in learning about the effectiveness of such groups in ameliorating mental health problems. Consequently, outcome research is needed, but the careful detail needed in such research is typically difficult to obtain when the organization being studied is loosely organized. Such groups

need to be evaluated both as a substitute for other services and as a potential expansion of such services. For example, one would like to know whether psychotherapeutic intervention interferes with or facilitates the impact of such groups (and if it facilitates, whether the effect is additive or multiplicative). This implies a detailed personal history of people involved in the group, which frequently would be near impossible to obtain. Further, these groups are indeed volunteer groups, which raises some basic scientific problems in studying them. Typically, an individual who is a member of a voluntary self-help group is a person who admits having the problem, is seeking help from others, and views him or herself as being helped. Of course, acknowledging that one has a particular mental disturbance is often a significant step in ameliorating the problem. However, a particular scientific issue in studying such groups is the last point, self-selection. A person who joins a self-help group and feels that the group is not effective will drop out. There are few barriers to dropping out of such groups, surely less than the barriers against dropping out of psychotherapy, for example, or a mental institution. Knowledge of the degree of such self-selection is an important ingredient in assessing the effectiveness of a voluntary self-help group. At minimum, this means studying the group over a considerable length of time so that the dropout rate could be estimated, and its potential impact on outcome data assessed.

Aside from self-help groups, there is enormous potential in volunteer groups. Sainer (1976) has described RSVP (retired senior volunteer program), begun 20 years ago by a private social agency. Today more than 700 RSVPs exist, with 165,000 volunteers. A similar program, the federally funded foster grandparents program, included at last estimate 16,000 older people, each of whom was willing to spend 20 hours a week working with de-institutionalized younger patients. The potential of such programs is enormous, although relatively unexplored. Evaluation research oriented toward outcome effectiveness in these programs would be very valuable. In addition, the potential of such individuals for further practical training and handling of mental health problems is relatively unexplored. That is, one must distinguish between the current effectiveness of such groups (which surely must be substantial), and the potential effectiveness of such groups were public policy to place emphasis on them as potential service providers.

The Effectiveness of Psychotherapy

Recently there have been at least two major reviews of the effectiveness of psychotherapy. One is the paper on efficacy and cost effectiveness of psychotherapy prepared by Leonard Saxe (1980) for the Office of Technology Assessment (see also, Yates & Newman, 1981). This paper is recommended to the reader, and includes a bibliography of over 300 entries. It concludes that, "in summary, OTA finds that psychotherapy is a complex—yet scientifically assessable—set of technologies. It also finds good evidence of psychotherapy's positive effects. Although therapy may not be generalizable to the wide range of problems for which therapy is employed, it suggests that additional research may provide data useful for the development of mental health policy. Given the potential net benefits of psychotherapy, this effort would seem to be justified" (p. 5).

The other major review of psychotherapy outcomes is the meta-analysis provided by Smith and Glass (1977), and later expanded in book form by Smith, Glass, and Miller (1980). Meta-analysis is an extremely useful technique for psychological studies related to public policy.[2] It derives quantitative measures in a manner that can be aggregated across studies. Specific measures are referred to as effect sizes, which are derived by looking at the mean of an experimental group and the mean of a control group for each measure in a given study, divided by the standard deviation of the control group. In this manner, the effect of the experimental manipulation for a specific study is represented as the number of standard deviations separating the means of the two groups. Their meta-analysis of 475 controlled studies of psychotherapy (with 766 effect-size measures) led to an average finding of effect size of 0.85. This means that in the typical experimental study comparing psychotherapy with no treatment, after therapy the average patient had responses sufficiently positive to be at the 80th percentile of the control group. Thus, a consistent, clear effect of psychotherapy was noted. Exactly what this means for public policy is unclear, since it is difficult to state clearly how desirable it is to be at the 80th percentile of the control group (Kiesler, 1981a). I note that the effect sizes themselves are considered as if they were independent in this analysis. However, when each study is considered to have only one effect size, similar and slightly stronger results were found (Landman & Dawes, 1982; see also, Glass, McGuire, & Smith, 1981).

There are major policy questions regarding psychotherapy, even if acknowledged to be effective as demonstrated by Smith et al. or cost-effective as discussed by Saxe. These include the marginal utility of psychotherapy, when added to a system of existing services (Kiesler, 1980a), comparative or summative effects of psychotherapy compared to drug therapy (Smith et al., 1980), the effects of adding psychotherapy to the existing system of health care (Jones & Vischi, 1980), the cost-effectiveness of psychotherapy when compared to such concerns as prevention (Albee & Joffe, 1980), the moral hazard of insuring psychotherapy, when many fear that if it is insured, almost everyone will undertake therapy (McGuire, 1980), and the question of how best to integrate psychotherapy into an organized system of mental health care (Albee & Kessler, 1977; Budman, 1981; Cummings & VandenBos, 1979). Each of these issues will be raised at appropriate points later in this chapter.

The Effectiveness of Drugs

The specific scientific evidence regarding the effectiveness of drugs is reviewed elsewhere in this handbook. We concentrate here on the policy aspects of ameliorative drug use in mental health services. In policy considerations, drugs as an integral component of mental health services are a tantalizing alternative. When considering potential public policy in mental health, it is conceptually easier to consider giving millions of drug dosages than to consider either, say, a community mental health center within the reach of everyone needing the service or 16 hours of traditional psychotherapy per patient. Given the number of general physicians in the country, there are more people trained to give drugs than there are people to give therapy, and it does not require the consideration of the training of a great new cadre of service providers. As one hears this policy alternative discussed at a national level, one only has to train physicians to recognize symptoms specific to diagnostic catagories with instructions of which drugs to use for which categories. To some extent this describes what we do now nationally. Indeed, one

---

[2]Meta-analysis as a technique is not without its critics and there are some lively controversies; see Bandura, 1978; Cook & Leviton, 1980; Paul & Licht, 1978.

national survey found 31 percent of Americans admitted using a psychotherapeutic drug in the previous year (Hingson, Matthews, & Scotch, 1979; Mellinger et al., 1974).

The average general practitioner in the United States sees more patients with mental disorders than does the average psychiatrist, although the time spent with each patient is dramatically different (Vischi et al., 1980). Nonpsychiatric physicians are four times as likely as psychiatrists to use drugs in treatment. There is considerable variation among general physicians with respect to prescribing drugs. Some use it on almost everybody with a mental disorder, while others are very sparing in their usage (Gilis & Moran, 1981). In a recent study of antipsychotic-drug use in nursing homes, the size of the physician's nursing home practice had a powerful effect on prescriptive practices. The 14 percent of physicians with the largest practices prescribed 81 percent of the antipsychotic medication, and a disproportionate number of them were family practitioners (Ray, Federspiel, & Schaffner, 1980).

Effectiveness equal, the policy advantages of drugs in the treatment of mental disorders are: simplicity of the policy itself and the ease with which it can be communicated to decision makers and the public; the ease of access of people needing treatment to service providers, since potentially the whole network of nonpsychiatric physicians could be utilized; training of service providers is simplified since diagnosis could be emphasized rather than detailed treatment methods; more people could be treated, since the time necessary to treat each one would be sharply reduced if other treatment were not necessary; the cyclical valleys in the long-term progression of a mental disorder could presumably be reduced by occasional reinstatement of a drug regimen; and patients do not have to be monitored as closely, perhaps, as with more traditional psychotherapeutic treatment.

One can see why policy makers are so enthusiastic about the potential for drugs and why federal agencies often tout them. Policy questions directly relate to whether the advantages listed above are in fact empirically valid. Further, in the implementation of such a policy, one would have to be very concerned about typical conditions under which the drug may be used rather than the optimal conditions. Indeed, there is a lively controversy in the literature in reviews of outcome studies of drugs in mental health services, about which

studies should be included in the review and which should not. People can review essentially the same literature but have quite different arrays of studies from which conclusions are drawn. An interesting exception to this is the meta-analysis carried out by Smith et al. (1980) on drug research, which includes studies of drugs versus controls or comparison treatments, and a separate group of studies in which both drug therapy and psychotherapy were included in the experimental design. In all, they included 151 papers in their meta-analysis. Overall, they found the effect size for studies of drugs-only was approximately equal to that for the separate analyses they have done on psychotherapy-only. Considerable caution must be applied since the studies may be qualitatively different, particularly with respect to the use of placebos in the drug studies (as Smith, et al. point out).

Also of specific interest to us are the studies that include both drug therapy and psychotherapy separately or in combinations, with a proper experimental design. These results are really quite startling. In looking only at studies that include such conditions, the effects of drugs alone are approximately equal to the effects of psychotherapy alone. The two treatments, moreover, do not interact. That is, the effects of drugs and psychotherapy used in combination are equal to the additive effects of each used in isolation. The notion, for example, that drugs can be used for psychotics in order to get them to the point where psychotherapy would be more effective is not supported by these data. If that were the case, then a clear interaction would be obtained: the effects of drugs plus psychotherapy would be more than the sum of their effects alone. Smith et al. do a very detailed and convincing analysis that demonstrates, at least for these studies, that such an interaction simply does not exist.

Smith et al. further analyze their data with respect to individual drugs within the categories of antipsychotics, antidepressants, and antianxiety agents. Within categories, there is not great variation among the types of drugs, although there is some considerable variation within types. Take antipsychotic drugs for example. On the basis of these data, one could not say that Chlorpromazine was more effective in the studies in which it was used than, say, Reserpine or Lithium.

The Smith et al. meta-analysis of drug studies and drug-plus-psychotherapy studies is probably the best evidence regarding the policy implications of drug use with mental disorders. The results suggest that more caution should be used about drug therapy in general, and about some drugs in particular, than has been the case. For example, there is no evidence in these studies that Lithium is anything like the magic cure it is often touted to be (although the number of effect sizes in this study for Lithium is very small).

On the other hand, although Smith et al. provide a fairly comprehensive review of the studies in which drugs and psychotherapy were used alone and/or in combination, their analysis of the drug-alone studies is but a sampling of the existing literature (or at least that part which includes both the control conditions and random assignment). What is needed is an exhaustive review of the literature of those studies, even though such an effort might be almost beyond the capacity of individual investigators to carry out. Meta-analysis of studies with particular drugs appears to be less promising than one might otherwise think. Judging by the results of the effect sizes across drugs here, there is some considerable danger in looking only at a specific drug used in a specific condition. It appears that one must look at all of the conditions in which a drug is used plus all of the other drugs that are used in those conditions as well. Further, the larger number of studies is needed partly to get a more stable number of effect sizes studies with particular drugs in specific situations than the results of the Smith et al. allow. Needed are detailed breakdowns of patient populations, including demographic characteristics that control a good deal of the variance in specific mental disorders, as well as institutions versus outpatient care, the institutional site, and the characteristics of the service provider (psychiatrist versus nonpsychiatric physician, and the like). Use of meta-analysis has opened a new door to the assessment of drug effectiveness for mental disorders. Further, there is considerable evidence regarding relatively permanent negative side-effects of prolonged antipsychotic medication (e.g., American Psychiatric Association, 1980; Berger, 1978). Measures of such improvement need to be included in evaluative studies of drug therapy.

Mental Hospitalization

Inpatient care has changed dramatically in the United States over the last two or three decades. For example, the traditional sites of inpatient care of the state/county mental hospitals and private mental hospitals together now account for only 25 percent of the total inpatient episodes in the country (Kiesler & Sibulkin, 1983a). The hospital site where the most inpatient episodes occur now is the general hospital without a psychiatric unit (Kiesler & Sibulkin, 1983a). Further, the general sense that deinstitutionalization has been successful and that inpatient care has either stabilized or decreased is inaccurate. The number of clinical episodes of inpatient care has continued to rise, well in excess of the population increase (Kiesler & Sibulkin, 1983b). Indeed, it is not clear that mental hospitalization is terribly effective. Recently, I reviewed ten studies that included random assignment of seriously disturbed patients to either inpatient care or some alternative outpatient care (Kiesler, 1982a). Inpatient care was less effective than any of the alternative modes of care employed in the individual studies (See also Braun et al., 1981). Further, there was clear evidence of the self-perpetuation of hospitalization. That is, people randomly assigned to a mental hospital were more likely to be readmitted after their initial discharge than were people treated by alternative modes of care ever to be admitted. I have argued elsewhere that most of the assumptions that we make regarding our policy for inpatient care are either untested or empirically disconfirmed (Kiesler, 1982b).

Space prohibits detailed discussion of this complicated issue. However, policy research is clearly needed regarding the efficacy and cost-effectiveness of inpatient care, compared to alternative modes of care. Particularly, research in the demographic characteristics as they interact with inpatient care is needed (Clausen, 1979). Detailed analyses of treatment by site interactions are important, particularly in tracking the relatively uninvestigated, but most frequently used, site of general hospitals without psychiatric units. It seems clear from the data that we are putting people in mental hospitals who could be more effectively and less expensively treated elsewhere. But who should be treated in the mental hospitals? No therapist I have ever met suggested that mental hospitals or inpatient care were unnecessary.

In future research, one must distinguish between psychological variables affecting the decision to hospitalize and the patient variables that make hospitalization effective. There is good reason to expect from the research literature of decisions under uncertainty that mental health professionals would overhospitalize (partly because it seems to be the "safe" thing to do). These decision processes themselves seem well worthy of investigation.

The general notion of how inpatient care fits under our national policy on mental health deserves more investitation then it has received. About 70 percent of the mental health dollar now goes for inpatient care, although there is good resson to believe even that number is an underestimate. In that sense, hospitalization dominates our public policy, without detailed consideration of its efficacy and cost-effectiveness. In a sense, since this practice dominates the policy, it should also dominate policy research.

Medical Utilization

An important policy question for planning is the effect of mental health services on medical utilization. Jones and Vischi (1980) recently reviewed 13 studies in which mental health services were introduced into an organized system of medical care. In 12 of the 13 studies, there was a fairly sharp reduction in the use of medical resources, for those patients who utilized the mental health services. Across the thousands of patients in the studies the median reduction was 20 percent. As one of the more dramatic examples, the Kaiser-Permanente plan (Cummings & Follette, 1976) found that those patients engaged in short-term psychotherapy of eight hours or less reduced their use of medical resources as much as 70 percent for the following five years. Interestingly, they found a similar reduction in absenteeism from the work place in the same time period.

We now spend over 200 billion dollars per year on medical care in the United States, with the number increasing yearly well in excess of the inflation rate. Productivity is a national problem as well and absenteeism at work is a costly national expense. If it is generally true that psychotherapy decreases medical utilization and absenteeism, then it is a tool of considerable national importance.

The effect of psychotherapy on medical utilization recently has played a central role in policy discussions of various national insurance plans. However, it is a point that needs to be accepted with some caution. For example, we still do now know why the effect occurs, at any reasonable level of theoretical understanding. We don't know if it generalizes across practitioners and sites. The studies reviewed by Jones and Vischi (1980) were all conducted in health maintenance organizations (HMOs) or other organized systems of care.

There are several reasons why such an effect might occur at an HMO, but not in CMHCs, or in private practice (Kiesler, 1981a). However, Schlesinger and Mumford (1982) have recently reported a simlar medical offset in a large national fee-for-service plan. Differences in medical offset as a function of patient characteristics, service setting, and the like remain to be investigated (Mumford, Schlesinger, & Glass, 1981).

At one level, we do not know whether the effect is more due to the success of the mental health services than to the failure of the physical health services system. That is, we need to consider which changes in current medical practice could also reduce medical utilization, and whether such changes overlap with or are distinct from the reductions produced by psychotherapy or other mental health services. As we pointed out, there are not many doctoral-level service providers in this country. It would be important to ascertain whether other mental health professionals, such as psychiatric social workers and psychiatric nurses, could produce a similar effect. We have no sense of whether these effects are general across people or specific to particular types of patients with specific sorts of problems. In general, the sorts of patients who are seeking out psychotherapy in an organized system of care tend already to have been very high utilizers of the medical system (Tessler, Mechanic, & Diamond, 1976). Whether specific intervention techniques or changes in medical practice could reduce medical utilization even more when applied earlier in the sequence of behavior is unknown. In sum, this is a critical national area with a generally robust empirical finding. Why medical utilization decreases following psychotherapy is not now well understood, however (see Kiesler, 1981a, for further discussion).

Insuring Mental Health Care

In discussions of insurance in mental health, the following questions typically come up (Califano, 1978; Davis, 1975; McGuire & Weisbrod, 1981). Does psychotherapy work, and can it be insured by the typical methods? If insured, will everyone use psychotherapy and thereby "break the bank"? If one adds mental health services to an existing system of insured medical care, will medical utilization drop? What factors might enhance or reduce the effect on medical utilization? What is the moral hazard in insuring mental health services? That is, how many more people (and with which problems) would use mental health services if they were free under an insurance plan? Specifically, what is the "income-price cross-elasticity of demand," a term economists use to refer to the changes in use patterns among groups of different income as a function of cost of the services? Insurance companies are also worried about adverse selection: that only people who need the services elect that insurance plan, which, as described later, starts a cycle that guarantees the ultimate failure of the plan.

Another important question is the system of care induced by a specific plan. Most insurance plans now offer incentives for hospitilization and disincentives for outpatient care (Kiesler, 1981a, 1981b). People who seek mental health care are typically offered free inpatient care, but outpatient care has fairly substantial co-payments. Even a small increase in the cost of a service can lead to rather substantial shifts in service utilization (Zook, Moore, & Zeckhauser, 1981). One would expect more patients to choose inpatient care because the personal cost is less. As a result of the price differential, the family and the attending professional may see no alternative other than to use the free inpatient care rather than the more personally costly outpatient care. There is also an unintended message delivered to the patient about the quality of services delivered. If an insurance plan offers one service free and an alternative service at a 50 percent cost to the patient, the patient might conclude that free service must be more effective.

Insurance companies are very reluctant to offer a total plan for mental health care. In particular, the concepts of moral hazard, adverse selection, and price elasticity dominate their thinking. There is little evidence to suggest that such fears are justified. For example, Dorken (1977) studied the civilian health and medical program of the uniform services (CHAMPUS), with a total insured population of over six million across the country. He found that less than 2 percent of the beneficiaries used mental health services when they were insured and that the average cost per person covered was approximately $1.75 a month. NIMH has found similar data for the federal employees health benefit plan (FEHBA), with an average cost per covered person of approximately $1.00 per month (NIMH, 1976). Utilization rates in other plans have been fairly similar to these. Liptzin, Regier, and Goldberg (1980) analyzed the 1975 data for the 2.3 million people covered by Michigan Blue Cross/Blue Shield. They found

2.6 percent of the covered population used psychiatric services for a specific disorder, 4.6 percent including those with an unspecified diagnosis. The cost per person covered was $1.75 a month.

The plans that work best are those that do not offer a choice to the beneficiary. McGuire (1980) describes this issue very effectively. If the election of mental health benefits is voluntary to each participant in a insurance plan, the following sequence of adverse selection is not at all unusual. People who initially elect to have the benefits are those who think they need them soon. Thus, in the initial experiences of the plan, an "unexpectedly" large number of people will seek mental health care. As a result of the large cost of such care, the following year the actuaries will increase the cost of that set of services in the insurance plan. As a result of the increased premium, people who have already been treated or who are less sure of the need will drop the optional plan. The remaining insurees must be confident that they will need the care, since they are willing to pay an increased amount for it. This leaves a smaller number, but an even greater density of people electing the plan who need care, thus increasing the rate of utilization, and increasing the cost of the plan the following year. The sequences across years is one of increased density of utilization and rapidly escalating costs per person covered. Under these conditions, the plan will ultimately either break the bank or prove so costly that nobody will choose it.

Mental health is not the only area in which adverse selection occurs, of course, Dental plans have much the same sorts of problems. People have some sense of how much they need dental treatment, and those who need the service disproportionately join the plans. Insurance companies understand this, and typically refuse to insure an organization without all employees being part of the plan. Further, to avoid some of the density of initial use, people often must demonstrate no immediate need. Thus, patients must pay for any needed dental care prior to entering the plan. The plan is then composed of people with little need, it insures only future occurrences of need, and the fiscal underpinnings are quite different.

McGuire emphasizes that utilization rates are only part of the total picture, particularly regarding mental health services. Increased rates of utilization may be seriously misleading. That is, one must inspect the alternative costs when such benefits are not part of a plan. If people are using inappropriate services, such as general physicians and nursing homes when mental health benefits are not available, then those costs should decrease when they are. Further, lack of mental health benefits has other costs, such as medical utilization and general physical costs of stress, which mental health care could reduce. When mental health services are insured, and such services thereby increase, then it does not necessarily follow that the services are being overly utilized. Indeed, the increased services may reflect more adequate and needed utilization, which could provide substantial savings elsewhere — such savings perhaps even exceeding the increased direct charges. The various contingencies affecting utilization and outcome of insured mental health services are in great need of investigation (see Broskowski, Marks, & Budman, 1981).

Sites of Mental Health Service Delivery

Whether analyzing current policy, developing alternative policies for the future, or considering the potential research questions in mental health policy, one must consider the total system and the elements within it. One aspect of the overall system that has not received sufficient attention concerns the sites or places where services are actually delivered. There have been insufficient attempts to analyze each of these, as well as inappropriate application of data obtained at one site to a different site. Consider briefly four general sites in which services are delivered: community mental health centers; HMOs; private practice; and the various sites of hospitalization.

Most research of CMHCs is not evaluative (Cook, 1981). It describes the number of CMHCs, the practitioners, patients, funding, and so on. This descriptive research is oriented toward ascertaining whether national policies regarding CMHCs have been successfully implemented. While this is a reasonable form of research, it does not assess the effectiveness of CMHCs, nor does it often assess the interrelationship of CMHCs with other sites of service delivery. There is some controversy about the cost-effectiveness of CMHCs, as well as some question about whether they simply replaced existing outpatient clinics (Buck, 1982). Most professionals feel very positive about CMHCs and do not think there is a reasonable alternative for the kinds of services they are supposed to deliver. The original Joint Commission on Mental Illness and Health (Action for Mental Health, 1961), when proposing what eventually turned out to be the CMHC system, thought

them to be a critical element in the treatment and transition of patients deinstitutionalized from state and county mental hospitals. This is made less clear in the subsequent enabling legislation, and certainly has not been a central component of the history of the CMHC system. CMHCs have been more effective as alternatives to hospitalization, and most have active day care services. What is less well known are the increasing inpatient services utilized by CMHCs. At last report, the CMHC system had 250,000 clinical inpatient episodes across the country, with a total of four million inpatient days (Kiesler & Sibulkin, 1983a). Thus, CMHCs now have more inpatient episodes and days than either private for-profit or not-for-profit mental hospitals. One research policy issue worth attending to is the effect of the changes in funding CMHCs by President Reagan. NIMH has been the funder and initiator of the CMHC system, even though it provided only about 20 percent of the total funds for the system just prior to Reagan's election. Reagan has eliminated NIMH as a funder of the system, cut the total federal dollars by 25 percent, and given the remainder as block grants to the individual states. Even if the states pass all of these dollars on to the CMHCs within their borders, the budgets for individual centers will be reduced. Some of them will not survive (survival was a frequent issue before the budget cuts). One policy issue is how the others can survive. The press of the system is that the CMHCs must look for other funds to ensure their future. One possibility is to increase funds from third-party payers. However, third-party payment plans favor inpatient care. Although research remains to be done to investigate this alternative, it seems very likely that CMHCs will increase their inpatient care both in frequency of inpatient episodes and perhaps even length of stay. It would be ironic if the system designed to be the national centerpiece in developing easily accessible outpatient care became a central component of inpatient care in order to survive.

The popularity of adding mental health services to HMOs is a relatively recent phenomenon even though examples of it go back at least 20 years (e.g., Kaiser-Permanente). Descriptive research is needed indicating more clearly the problems handled in HMOs, at what cost (particularly related to other services offered), and with what outcome. Comparative research is also needed, contrasting HMOs with other sites, regarding array of patients, diagnoses, costs, and outcomes. Most of the data on HMOs are aggregate data in which it is difficult to track individual patients. Although it is possible to look at outcome effectiveness in aggregate data, it is difficult to inspect the theoretical underpinnings of that effectiveness (patient by patient), and to theorize how the effectiveness might be enhanced. Particularly with the financial crippling of CMHCs, the inclusion of mental health services in HMOs could well be the wave of the future. On the other hand, a good deal of the data on the effectiveness of mental health services in an organized system of care have been accumulated in HMOs. Data on the effect of psychotherapy on the utilization of medical services have been disproportionately gathered in HMOs. We literally do not know whether such services in other sites will produce the same effect (cf. Mumford et al., 1981). There is at least some reason to suspect that the specific organization of an HMO to some degree enhances the effect on medical utilization (Kiesler, 1981a; Mechanic, 1979). Whether this is true or not remains to be investigated. In short, we need outcome data specific to HMOs, but also data comparing outcomes to other methods and sites of delivering services.

The details of private practice as a site of mental health service delivery are least known. There have been some surveys of private psychiatric practitioners (Marmor et al., 1975) and private practice psychologists (Gottfredson & Dyer, 1978) but these barely scratch the surface. Some state and country psychiatric registers attempt to track the patients who are treated in private practice settings, but they depend on the cooperation of the private practitioner, and in all cases are limited to psychiatrists. They do not attempt to track other mental health professionals such as psychologists and clinical social workers. The large-scale study of private practice psychiatrists was methodologically flawed (Albee, 1976), although McGuire (1980) has demonstrated that regression techniques as used by economists can overcome most of the survey flaws. There are some data on utilization of services when private practice is insured (Liptzin et al., 1980), but there are very few data on the outcomes of such services. Note also that in Liptzin et al.'s study of the Michigan experience, almost 50 percent "of those individuals who submitted a claim for physician services for a specific mental disorder received at least some of those services from nonpsychiatric physicians" (p. 556). Outcome data could be extremely informative. One also needs to ask such policy questions as what is the relative cost-effectiveness of insuring services from private practitioners as compared to insuring services within the HMO concept.

The changing sites of mental hospitalization have been relatively uninvestigated. The traditional sites — at least from the public's point of view — now account for a rather small percentage of the total clinical episodes. We know very little indeed about what occurs in the site where most clinical episodes occur — the general hospital that has no psychiatric unit.

We can outline some basic policy questions regarding alternative sites of service delivery. Where shall we put our public money for the greatest effectiveness and cost-benefit? Does each site play a unique role, and therefore deserve public support? Where should we put the most money so as to have the greatest overall effect? If all are uniquely worthwhile and to be supported, what mix of services nationally would make the best public policy? If we design insurance schemes or quasi-insurance schemes, how should we array the incentives and disincentives? Should we have a system in which it is easier and cheaper for the patient to be treated in a CMHC or an HMO, with disincentives for being treated in private practice? Should we erect insurance barriers against mental hospitalization, and incentives favoring outpatient care? If so, should the system be intentionally biased toward a particular form of outpatient care? Which national mix of service delivery systems and sites would have the largest effect on outcomes such as medical utilization and absenteeism? These questions deal very basically with the overall design of a national mental health system. As such, they are central to any discussion of our public policy, as well as consideration of alternative policies for the future. As a whole, however, these policy questions have been relatively uninvestigated.

Prevention

I commend to the reader the report of the Task Panel on Prevention of PCMH (Albee et al., 1978). Both the quantity and quality of research in prevention have been undervalued. The support among professionals and the funding from federal agencies for research in prevention have never been strong — a topic worthy of investigation itself. There is a developing body of literature regarding prevention of mental disorders in populations at risk (see Albee, 1980). Partly interfering with the development of this field has been the analogy of prevention in medical care: innoculation delivered with great effectiveness to millions of people.

There is another aspect of psychological techniques in prevention. Bandura (1978) and others (e.g., Fuchs, 1974) believe that we have essentially reached a limit in the cost-effectiveness of the marginal utility of adding increased medical services on the physical health of the nation. The biggest advances, he believes, are to be made in techniques that change habits of large populations (also see Stachnik, 1980). Such health-threatening habits include diets, smoking, drinking, sleeping partterns, job stress, and social interactions. The recent work of Maccoby and his colleagues (Maccoby & Farquhar, 1975) on changing habits to reduce cardiovascular risks in total communities has demonstrated that such techniques could be broadly applied to other issues as well. Their techniques seem to be not only effective, but cost-effective. The potential of mass communication techniques to change the public's risk incurring habits seems substantial.

Methodological Issues in Mental Health Policy Research

Mental health policy is relatively unique among national policies. The national data base that is policy-relevant is very small compared to other national policy areas. The interaction of public programs in their effect on service delivery, such as Medicare-Medicaid, social security supplemental income, nursing home legislation, and the like have been insufficiently investigated. In addition, mental health policy can be seen as dominated both by health policy and by the perspectives that underlie health policy. The domination includes professional, financial, and metaphorical aspects of policy. There is great resistance to a detached view that considers the potential independence of mental health policy and the ways in which mental health policy might affect health policy to its benefit. There are considerable barriers to effective knowledge use in mental health policy, and often considerable dispute about what it is we know that is relevant to policy (Kiesler, 1981b). In spite of these more basic issues, there still are a number of methodological and training issues that will help determine the quality of future policy research in mental health. A sampling follows.

Computer simulation holds considerable promise to enhance the study of mental health policy. Ultimately, if we understand our policy and the interworkings of its various components,

we should be able to demónstrate our understanding by simulating the national policy in a computer model. The simulation of such a policy would force us first to consider the total policy at a given time, which is now only rarely accomplished. It would also allow us, however, to consider the implementation or change of various policy alternatives. If we could successfully simulate the policy, then we could look at the potential direct and indirect implications of various policy alternatives. For example, we could inspect the impact on the system as a whole resulting from increased insurance incentives for services delivered in HMOs. One subgoal of computer simulation is that it clearly demonstrates that we do indeed understand our national policy as a whole.

The computer simulation of judgmental and decision processes could also be helpful. A good deal of the practice of delivering mental health services is analogous to judgments and decisions under uncertainty, an area in which computer simulation has been utilized very effectively. These studies demonstrate that human beings often inadequately conceptualize their own decision making and judgmental processes (Tversky & Kahneman, 1974). The various weights given to variables entering into a decision are frequently misconstrued by the individuals making the decision. Thus, decisions relating to diagnosis, treatment regimens, and the choice between inpatient and outpatient care could all be simulated to considerable benefit.

Both of these uses of computer simulation relate to the fact that there has been little direct study of overall mental health policy. There are considerable methodological, statistical, and empirical problems in attempting to deal with the system as a whole, partly because of the informal nature of a good deal of the implicit system (e.g., volunteer groups).

A good deal of the research in mental health policy should be oriented toward the evaluation of the outcomes of specific aspects of policy. Meta-analysis in particular, and secondary analysis and evaluation research in general, are extremely useful in attempting to ascertain what we already know about specific aspects of the treatment of mental disorders. Increased methodological sophistication and further refinement of these techniques for use in mental health issues are desirable. Closely related are the techniques of cost-benefit and cost-effectiveness analysis, more typically used in economics. These techniques are more difficult to apply to such processes as psychotherapy than would seem apparent at first blush, with rather questionable assumptions often being made on both the cost and the benefit side of the formula (cf. Saxe, 1980). Research regarding the effects of psychotherapy on medical utilization and absenteeism suggests that one has to be very careful about casting a broad enough net in order to capture benefits of mental health services, including some that are far removed from the immediate service setting. The marginal utility of psychological services is closely related to cost-benefit analysis. Typically, we should not consider the effects of psychological services in isolation, but rather their marginal utility when added to an existing system. We do have well-developed and well-organized systems of welfare and health, and psychological services often must be considered as additions to these systems. Whether the services reduce the cost of the total given system is a reasonable policy question. The marginal utility of such services is often the principal public policy question, even though it might be a secondary or a tertiary scientific question.

We need to develop better methods to approximate answers to existing policy questions. This could be done in various ways. For example, consider my review of ten studies in which people were randomly assigned to hospitals or alternative care. There are several preferred next steps that could be usefully combined in an analysis. It would be useful to do a meta-analysis of those studies that would allow for both the direct aggregation of results across studies, breaking down particular subgroups of patients within studies. For example, across those ten studies some patients were being hospitalized for the first time; others were experienced inpatients. We could ascertain the direct effects of hospitalization and alternative care for patients, as a function of prior hospitalization. In addition, each of these ten studies involved random assignment to a hospital or alternative care. However, there are many other studies without this central scientific feature of random assignment. One could attempt to aggregate studies in conjunction with these ten, by categorizing them as to the type and degree of methodological flaws. Such meta-analysis could allow us to see whether studies very similar to these but without random assignment produced results like those with random assignment. By aggregating and disaggregating studies as a function of type of methodological flaw, we could rule out specific

kinds of competing explanations for the consistency of the results. That is, if studies varied in the degree to which the professional staff felt positive about the alternative care, but the results were consistent across the studies, then the issue of staff attitudes would not explain the consistency of the results. Both meta-analysis across studies and the aggregation of precisely categorized but flawed studies into a multistudy, quasi-experimental design might allow us more fruitfully to utilize the data that currently exist. There are some rather difficult methodological and statistical issues, but this set of ideas is worth serious consideration.

Survey research on public attitudes toward the mentally disabled, and epidemiological research on the incidence and prevalence of mental disorders both have methodological and substantive problems worthy of further investigation. In the former, it is unclear whether increasingly positive attitudes toward the mentally disabled are related either to overt behavior toward the disabled or toward legislation that could improve their lot (Rabkin, Gelb, & Lazar, 1980). On the epidemiological side, the meaning of epidemiological instruments used with large populations is still open to question (Mechanic, 1980). There is a disturbingly large range in the outcomes of epidemiological studies that is not due to sampling problems. If between 15 and 25 percent of the population is in need of mental health services, then the range of estimate is still 10 percent. It can be startling to realize that we are speaking of 10 percent of the population (or 22 million people), about whom we are apparently uncertain whether they need mental health services or not. Surely we have to be more precise than that. On the other hand, there is an implicit assumption that service need is functional; that the services, if used, would be effective. One could as well look at this question from the opposite point of view: carefully inspect which services are effective for which populations, and then calculate the ranges of people in those categories who could be effectively helped. For instance, if nothing we now know about mental health allows us effectively to assist the demoralized, then the number of them cannot affect immediate policy (although it should affect research priorities and planning). Statements of need should carefully consider questions of outcome and effectiveness of mental health services.

The use by economists of multiple regression techniques and dummy variables to study mental health policy issues seems very promising. In particular, these techniques enhance the use of extensively flawed designs. McGuire's (1980) elegant cleaning up of the Marmor et al. (1975) survey of psychiatric private practice provides an excellent example of the potential of this method. Frank's (1982) application of the same method to the effect of freedom of choice laws on psychiatric fees provides another good example.

Other Issues

Space requirement led us to review only a selected subset of the potential issues worthy of study in mental health policy. Issues we have not discussed here, but that are certainly worthy of consideration and research include the following: the clash of public policy needs (regarding services, their organization, and the like), and "citizen" needs (regarding privacy, confidentiality, and commitment proceedings). Data are badly needed in mental health regarding the outcomes of services delivered, and these data often entail looking at other services a citizen might use such as welfare or medical assistance. There is great need for such data, but at the same time available methods of obtaining them raise very serious problems with issues of privacy and confidentiality.

We also have not described research regarding the public's attitudes toward mental illness. Such discussion should include the increasing acceptance of psychotherapy among the public; problems of the public's implicit acceptance of some methods (for example, use of behavior modification in smoking reduction and weight loss), while not accepting the same methods used in other circumstances (e.g., the reduction of aggressive behavior in school settings). Further, the public apparently accepts mental hospitalization and supports it in various ways, suggesting perhaps that the perceived dangerousness and unpredictability of the mentally disabled are still playing a prominent role in the public's attitudes toward public policy alternatives.

We have not discussed at any length the very critical issue of knowledge use and knowledge utilization. Mental health policy appears to be an area in which fairly traditional policies have existed for decades, without due regard for the rapid increase in knowledge about human behavior and the treatment of mental disorders.

We also have not discussed at any length how research issues in mental health policy can or

should affect how psychologists are trained. Clearly, very little of traditional training in psychology, whether clinical or otherwise, is related either to the analysis of existing policy or to techniques of research in public policy. This is a complicated area but one that is worthy of serious debate.

Conclusions

Mental health policy has been implicitly with us for at least 150 years. Research related to mental health policy is at least as old as the history of scientific psychology and psychiatry. However, research that is openly directed toward the assessment of policy and the consideration of public policy alternatives is a relatively recent phenomenon. It involves looking at the overall policy, both explicit and implicit, a perspective we are unaccustomed to. It also involves research techniques and the accumulation of data that are not traditional. It appears to this writer that the time is ripe for very rapid growth in the study of mental health policy. I hope that this chapter has captured for readers some of the flavor of how such policy study might be conducted, as well as some of the intellectual excitement that is inherent in mental health policy research.

References

Action for Mental Health. *Joint commission on mental illness and health.* New York: Basic Books, 1961.

Albee, G. Into the valley of therapy rode the six thousand. *Contemporary Psychology,* 1976, **21,** 525–527.

Albee, G. W. A competency model to replace the defect model. In L. A. Bond & J. C. Rosen (Eds.), *Competence and coping during adulthood.* Hanover, N.H.: University Press of New England, 1980.

Albee, G. W., & Joffe, J. W. (Eds) *The issues: An overview of primary prevention.* Hanover, N.H.: University Press of New England, 1980.

Albee, G. W., & Kessler, M. Evaluating individual deliverers: Private practice and professional standards review organizations. *Professional Psychology,* 1977, **8,** 502–515.

Allerton, W. (Coordinator) Report of the task panel on planning and review. President's Commission on Mental Health, Vol. 2. Washington, D.C.: U.S. Government Printing Office, 1978.

American Psychiatric Association. *Tardive dyskinesia.* Washington, D.C.: Author, 1980.

Azrin, N. H. A strategy tor applied research: Learning based but outcome oriented. *American Psychologist,* 1977, **32,** 140–149.

Bachrach, L. *Deinstitutionalization: An analytical review and sociological perspective.* Washington, D.C.: U.S. Government Printing Office, 1976. Mental Health Statistics Series D, No. 4. DHEW No. (ADM) 79–351.

Bandura, A. On paradigms and recycled ideologies. *Cognitive Therapy and Research,* 1978, **2,** 79–103.

Berger, P. A. The medical treatment of mental illness. *Science,* 1978, **200,** 974–981.

Braun, P., Kochansky, G., Shapiro, R., Greenberg, S., Gudeman, J. E., Johnson, S., & Shore, M. F. Overview: Deinstitutionalization of psychiatric patients, A critical review of outcome studies. *American Journal of Psychiatry,* 1981, **138**(6), 736–749.

Broskowski, A., Marks, E., & Budman, S. H. *Linking health and mental health.* Beverly Hills, Calif.: Sage Publications, 1981.

Brown, B., & Regier, D. How NIMH now views the primary care physician. *Practical Psychology for Physicians,* 1977, **5,** 12–14.

Buck, J. A. Outpatient psychiatric clinics in the state and federal role in mental health, 1946–1965. Unpublished manuscript, 1982.

Budman, S. H. Mental health services in the health maintenance organization. In A. Broskowski, E. Marks, & S. H. Budman (Eds.), *Linking health and mental health,* Beverly Hills, Calif.: Sage Publications, 1981.

Budson, R. D. *The psychiatric half-way house: A handbook of theory and practice.* Pittsburgh: University of Pittsburgh Press, 1978.

Califano, J. Memorandum for the president on the basic decision on developing the national health insurance plan. May 22, 1978. In C. A. Kiesler, N. A. Cummings, & G. R. VandenBos (Eds.), *Psychology and national health insurance: A sourcebook.* Washington, D.C.: APA, 1979.

Castle, B. *Better service for the mentally ill.* London: Her Majesty's Stationery Office, 1975.

Christmas, J. J. (Coordinator). *Report of the Task Panel of Community Support Systems. President's Commission on Mental Health, Vol. 2.* Washington, D.C.: U.S. Government Printing Office, 1978. (President's Commission on Mental Health).

Clausen, J. A. Mental disorder. In H. E. Freeman, S. Levine, & L. G. Reeder (Eds.), *Handbook of Medical Sociology.* (3rd ed.) Englewood Cliffs, NJ: Prentice-Hall, 1979.

Cook, T., & Leviton, L. Reviewing the literature: A comparison of traditional methods with meta-analysis. *Journal of Personality,* 1980, **48,** 449–472.

Cook, T. D., & Shadish, W. R. Meta-evaluation: An evaluation of the CMHC congressionally-mandated evaluation system. In W. R. Tash & G. Stahler (Eds.), *Innovative approaches to mental health evaluation.* New York: Academic Press, 1981.

Cummings, N. A., & Follette, W. T. Brief psychotherapy and medical utilization. In H. Dorken & Associates (Eds.), *Professional psychologists today.* San Francisco: Jossey-Bass, 1976.

Cummings, N. A., & VandenBos, G. R. The general practice of psychology. *Professional Psychology,* 1979, **10,** 430–440.

Davis, K. *National health insurance: Benefits.* Washington, D.C.: Brookings Institution, 1975.

Dohrenwend, B. P., Dohrenwend, B. S., Gould, M. S., Link, B., Neugebaur, R., & Wunsch-Hitzig, R. *Mental illness United States: Epidemiological estimates.* New York: Praeger, 1980.

Dorken, H. CHAMPUS ten-state claim experience for mental disorder: Fiscal year 1975. *American Psychologist,* 1977, **32,** 697–710.

Eastwood, M. R. *The relation between physical and mental illness.* Toronto: University of Toronto Press, 1975.

Fairweather, G. W., Sanders, D. H., & Maynard, H. *Community life for the mentally ill: An alternative to institutional care.* Chicago: Aldine, 1969.

Fairweather, G. W., & Tornatzsky, L. G. *Experimental methods for social policy research.* Beverly Hills, Calif.: Pergamon, 1977.

Frank, J. D. *Persuasion and Healing.* Baltimore, Md.: Johns Hopkins University Press, 1973.

Fuchs, B. R., *Who shall live? Health economics and social choice.* New York: Basic Books, 1974.

Gilis, J. S., & Moran, T. J. An analysis of drug decisions in a state psychiatric hospital. *Journal of Clinical Psychology,* 1981, **37,** 32–42.

Glass, G. V., McGaw, B., & Smith, M. L. *Meta-analysis and social research.* Beverly Hills, Calif.: Sage Publications, 1981.

Goplerud, E. N. The tangled web of clinical and epidemiological evidence. In A. Broskowski, E. Marks, & S. H. Budman, (Eds.), *Linking health and mental health.* Beverly Hills, Calif.: Sage Publications, 1981.

Gottfredson, G. D., & Dyer, S. E. Health service providers in psychology. *American Psychologist,* 1978, **33,** 314–338.

Hagnell, O. A prospective study of the incidence of mental disorder. Stockholm: Svenska Bokforlaget Norstedts-Bonniers, 1966.

Hingson, R. W., Matthews, D., & Scotch, N. A. The use and abuse of psychoactive substances. In H. E. Freeman, S. Levine, & L. G. Reeder (Eds.), *Handbook of medical sociology.* (3rd ed.) Englewood Cliffs, N.J.: Prentice-Hall, 1979.

Hoeper, E. W. Observations on the impact of psychiatric disorders upon primary medical care. In D. L. Parron & F. Solomon (Eds.), *Mental health services in primary care settings.* Washington, D.C.: U.S. Government Printing Office, 1980. DHHS Publication No. (ADM) 80–995.

Jones, K., & Vischi, T. Impact of alcohol, drug abuse, and mental health treatment on medical care utilization: Review of the research literature. *Medical Care,* 1980, (*Supplement 17, 12*).

Kiesler, C. A. Mental health policy as a field of inquiry for psychology. *American Psychologist,* 1980, **35,** 1,066–1,080. (a)

Kiesler, C. A. Psychology and public policy. In L. Bickman (Ed.), *Applied social psychology annual, Vol. 1.* Beverly Hills, Calif.: Sage Publications, 1980. (b)

Kiesler, C. A. Mental health policy: Research site for social psychology. In L. Wheeler (Ed.), *Review of personality and social psychology, Vol. 2.* Beverly Hills, Calif.: Sage Publications, 1981. (a)

Kiesler, C. A. Barriers to effective knowledge use in national mental health policy. *Health Policy Quarterly,* 1981, **1,** 201–215. (b)

Kiesler, C. A. Mental hospitals and alternative care: Non-institutionalization as potential public policy for mental patients. *American Psychologist,* 1982, **37,** 349–360. (a)

Kiesler, C. A. Public and professional myths about mental hospitalization: An empirical reassessment of policy—related beliefs. *American Psychologist*, 1982, **37**, 1323–1339. (b)

Kiesler, C. A., Cummings, N. A., & VandenBos, G. R. *Psychology and national health insurance: A sourcebook.* Washington, D.C.: APA, 1979.

Kiesler, C. A., & Sibulkin, A. E. People, clinical episodes, and mental hospitalization: A multiple-source method of estimation. In R. F. Kidd, & M. J. Saks (Eds.), *Advances in applied social psychology.* In press, 1983. (a)

Kiesler, C. A., & Sibulkin, A. E. Episodic rate of mental hospitalization: Stable or increasing? unpublished manuscript, 1983. (b)

Klerman, G. National trends in hospitalization. *Hospital and Community Psychiatry*, 1979, **30**, 110–113.

Landman, J. T., & Dawes, R. M. Psychotherapy outcome: Smith and Glass' conclusions stand up under scrutiny. *American Psychologist*, 1982, **37**, 504–516.

Lieberman, M. A., & Borman, L. D. (Eds.), A special issue on self help groups. *Journal of Applied Behavioral Science*, 1976, **12**, 3.

Liptsin, B., Regier, D. A., & Goldberg, I. D. Utilization of health and mental health services in a large insured population. *American Journal of Psychiatry*, 1980, **137**, 553–558.

Maccoby, N., & Farquhar, J. W. Communication for health: Unselling heart disease. *Journal of Communication*, 1975, **25**, 114–126.

Marmor, J., Scheidemandel, P. L., & Kanns, C. K. *Psychiatrists and their patients.* Washington, D.C.: American Psychiatric Association, 1975.

McGuire, T. *Financing psychotherapy: Costs, effects, public policy.* Cambridge, Mass.: Ballinger, 1980.

McGuire, T. G., & Weisbrod, B. A. *Economics and Mental Health.* Washington, D.C.: U.S. Government Printing Office, 1981. DHHS Publication No. (ADM) 81–1114.

Mechanic, D. *Mental health and social policy.* Englewood Cliffs, N.J.: Prentice-Hall, 1980.

Mechanic, D. Physicians. In H. E. Freeman, S. Levine, & L. G. Reeder (Eds.), *Handbook of medical sociology.* (3rd ed.) Englewood Cliffs, N.J.: Prentice-Hall, 1979.

Mechanic, D. (Coordinator). Report of the task panel on the nature and scope of the problem. *President's Commission on Mental Health*, Vol. 2. Washington, D.C.: U.S. Government Printing Office, 1978.

Mellinger, G., Balter, M., Parry, H., Manhimer, D., & Cisin, I. An overview of psychotherapeutic drug use in the United States. In E. Josephson & E. Carrol (Eds.), *Drug use: Epidemiologic and social approaches.* Washington, D.C.: Hemisphere, 1974.

Mills, D. H., Wellner, A. M., & VandenBos, G. R. The National Register Survey: The first comprehensive study of all licensed/certified psychologists. In C. A. Kiesler, N. A. Cummings, & G. R. VandenBos (Eds.), *Psychology and national health insurance: A sourcebook.* Washington, D.C.: APA, 1979.

Mumford, E., Schlesinger, H. J., & Glass, G. V. Reducing medical costs through mental health treatment: Research problems and recommendations. In A. Broskowski, E. Marks, & S. H. Budman, (Eds.), *Linking health and mental health*, 1981.

National Institute of Mental Health. The financing, utilization, and quality of mental health care in the United States. [Draft report]. Rockville, Md.: NIMH, 1976.

Newman, H. N. (Coordinator). Report of the Task Panel on Cost and Financing of Mental Health. (President's Commission on Mental Health, Vol. 2, pp. 497–544.) Washington, D.C.: U.S. Government Printing Office.

Paul, G. L., & Licht, M. H. Resurrection of uniformity assumption myths and the fallacy of statistical absolutes in psychotherapy research. *Journal of Consulting and Clinical Psychology*, 1978, **46**, 1,531–1,534.

Piasecki, J. R., Leary, J. E., & Rutman, I. D. Halfway houses and long term community residences for the mentally ill, United States, 1980. National Institute of Mental Health, Series CN No. 1, DHHS publication No. (ADM) 80–1004. Washington, D.C.: U.S. Government Printing Office.

President's Commission on Mental Health. Vol. 2, 3, 4. Washington, D.C.: U.S. Government Printing Office, 1978.

Rabkin, J. G., Gelb, L., & Lazar, J. B. *Attitudes towards the mentally ill: Research perspectives.* Washington, D.C.: U.S. Government Printing Office, 1980. DHHS Publication No. (ADM) 80–1031.

Ray, W. A., Federspiel, C. F., & Schaffner, W. A study of antipsychotic use in nursing homes: Epidemiologic evidence suggesting misuse. *American Journal of Public Health*, 1980, **70**, 485–491.

Regier, D. A., Goldberg, I. D., & Taube, C. A. The de facto U.S. mental health services system: A public health perspective. *Archives of General Psychiatry*, 1978, **35**, 685–693.

Regier, D. A., & Taube, C. A. The delivery of mental health services. In S. Arietti & H. K. H. Brodie (Eds.), *American handbook of psychiatry.* New York: Basic Books, 1981.

Rose, S. M. Deciphering deinstitutionalization: Complexities in policy and program analysis. *Milbank Memorial Fund Quarterly Health and Society*, 1979, **57** (4), 429–460.

Rubin, J. *Economics, mental health and the law.* Lexington, Mass.: D.C. Heath, 1978.

Sainer, J. S. The community cares: Older volunteers. *Social Policy*, 1976, **7** (3), 73–75.

Saxe, L. *The efficacy and cost-effectiveness of psychotherapy.* Technical Report, Office of Technology Assessment, Congress of the U.S. (GPO stock #052-003-00783-5), 1980.

Schact, T., & Nathan, P. E. But is it good for the psychologist? Appraisal and status of DSM-III. *American Psychologist*, 1977, **32**, 1,017–1,025.

Schlesinger, H. J., & Mumford, E. Mental health services and medical care utilization in the fee for service system. Invited paper at Mental Health Policy Symposium Series, Carnegie-Mellon University, Pittsburgh, 1982.

Schulberg, H. C. Community support programs: Program evaluation and public policy. *American Journal of Psychiatry*, 1979, **136**, 1,433–1,437.

Schwab, J. J., Bell, R. A., Warheit, G., & Schwab, R. B. *Social order and mental health.* New York: Brunner/Mazel, 1979.

Silverman, P. R. *Mutual help groups: A guide for mental health workers.* Rockville, Md.: National Institute of Mental Health, 1978.

Smith, M. L., & Glass, G. V. Meta-analysis of psycho-therapy outcome studies. *American Psychologist*, 1977, **32**, 752–760.

Smith, M. L., Glass, G. V., & Miller, T. I. *The benefits of psychotherapy*. Baltimore, Md.: Johns Hopkins University Press, 1980.

Stachnik, T. J. Priorities for psychology in medical education in health care delivery. *American Psycholoist*, 1980, **35**, 8–15.

Stokey, E., & Zeckhauser, R. *A primer for policy analysis*. New York: Norton, 1978.

Taber, M. A. The social context of helping: A review of the literature on alternative care for the physically and mentally handicapped. Washington, D.C.: NIMH, 1980.

Tessler, R., Mechanic, D., & Diamond, M. The effect of psychological distress on physician utilization: A prospective study. *Journal of Health and Social Behavior*, 1976, **17**, 353–364.

Tversky, A., & Kahneman, D. Judgement under uncertainty: Huristics and biases. *Science*, 1974, **185**, 1,121–1,124.

Vischi, T. R., Jones, K. R., Shank, E. L., & Lima, L. H. *The alcohol, drug abuse, and mental health national data book*. Washington, D.C.: U.S. Department of HEW, 1980.

Yates, E. T., & Newman, F. L. Findings of cost-effectiveness and cost-benefit analysis of psychotherapy. In G. R. VandenBos (Ed.), *Psychotherapy: From practice to research to policy*. Beverly Hills, Calif.: Sage, 1981.

Zook, C. T., Moore, F. D., & Zeckhouser, R. J. "Catastrophic" health insurance—A misguided prescription? *The Public Interest*, 1981, **62**, 66–81.

PART II
PERSONALITY THEORIES AND MODELS

INTRODUCTION

The will of the wisp called "personality" lies at the core of clinical psychology. In many respects, it is the focus of almost all research and clinical activity. It therefore should not be surprising that it is one of the most controversial issues as well. There is substantial disagreement over the utility of the entire concept, how it should be defined and assessed, and the laws governing its function. Early efforts at understanding and explaining personality often involved macro theories, such as psychoanalytic theory, which attempted to cover all aspects of behavior. More recently, emphasis has been on micro theories, which deal with only one or a few particular issues. However, while the global theories have not and cannot be validated in toto, several remain powerful influences on the field. They serve as guiding perspectives, shaping peoples' values and approaches to clinical or research activity. The chapters in this part provide an overview of current thinking in the most influential perspectives.

Sidney J. Blatt and Howard Lerner (Chapter 6) discuss the psychodynamic perspective. They exam-

ine the evolution of psychoanalytic theory and describe the most significant current issues, including object relations and the phenomenological perspective. Rachlin and Logue (Chapter 7) present an overview of current issues and controversies in learning theory. Their chapter underscores the biological substrate of learning and behavior. Next, Leon H. Levy (Chapter 8) covers trait approaches. He examines definitional and conceptual issues, and reviews recent evidence on the stability and consistency of traits and the role of idiographic assessment. Robert C. Carson (Chapter 9) discusses the social-interactional viewpoint. He emphasizes the evolving nature of this perspective, which has only recently begun to coalesce into a distinctive orientation. In the final chapter of this part, Hugh B. Urban (Chapter 10) writes on the phenomenological and humanistic approaches. In addition to describing these perspectives, he contrasts the phenomenological way of thinking about the subject matter with the traditional scientific approach.

6   PSYCHODYNAMIC PERSPECTIVES ON PERSONALITY THEORY

Sidney J. Blatt
Howard Lerner

It is important to consider the development of psychoanalytic theory and dynamic psychology over the past century in a broad theoretical context. In 1978 Blatt discussed psychoanalysis as part of a major scientific revolution that began around the middle of the 19th century. He pointed out that around 1850, mathematicians (Gauss, Riemann, Lobachevski, & Bolyai) realized that the conception of the universe based on Euclidean geometry and rectilinear Cartesian coordinates was only one particular way among a number of alternatives to conceptualize the universe. With the development of non-Euclidean geometries and concepts of curvilinearity, it became possible to conceptualize the universe in a number of equally valid ways. These discoveries led, in part, to the realization that the experience and conception of reality is influenced by the relative position and assumptions of the observer. As reflected in the formulations of Kant and Cassirer, there was increasing awareness that nature was not simply observed, but rather was a construction based upon the nature of a particular vantage point. Thus, it was no longer possible simply to accept the manifest, surface appearance of phenomena as valid, since there were multiple ways of describing manifest characteristics. It was recognized that in order to understand phenomena, one had to identify the structure and the organizational principles that underlie surface appearances. This emphasis on internal structure became, in Foucault's term, a major "cultural episteme" of our time. This emphasis on structuralism has been a central focus in multiple fields of endeavor. There has been a search in numerous fields for the identification of the inherent principles of organization that define the relationships among elements and their potential transformations in hierarchically organized systems. This interest in underlying structural principles of organization has been a major emphasis in the physical and biological sciences, as well as in the humanities (e.g., literature, linguistics, anthropology, and the history of art) (Blatt & Blatt, 1983). In all these disciplines there has been increasing emphasis on the need to identify and understand the principles of structural organization that define the interrelationships and potential transformations of elements that determine variations of surface phenomena. Despite this emphasis on internal structure in many fields throughout the 20th century, a large segment of American psychology and psychiatry still maintains an exclusive interest in manifest behavior and overt symptomatology.

There have been notable exceptions, of course, and these exceptions have made major contributions to the understanding of some of the structural principles inherent in human behavior. These include the Gestalt analyses of perception, contemporary approaches to cognitive processes (including the work of Piaget, Werner, Barlett, and others), and psychoanalytic theory (Blatt, 1978).

Attempts in the human sciences to identify principles of structural organization that underlie manifest behavior have emphasized two primary dimensions that are fundamental to the human condition: (1) man's capacity for complex symbolic activity, and (2) a recognition of the importance of the complex interpersonal matrix within which we evolve and exist. These two factors are unique to the human condition and must be accounted for in any understanding of the structural principles that underlie and serve to integrate manifest behavior (Blatt, 1978).

Theoretical Review

Since its inception as a field of scientific inquiry at the threshold of the 20th century, psychoanalytic theory has gone through a number of important revisions, elaborations, and extensions. Freud's monumental discoveries in *The Interpretation of Dreams* (1899–1900) established the importance of the unconscious as a system of the mind and stressed illogical, drive-laden, primary process thinking as an important form of mentation. In this work, Freud laid the basis for his metapsychology and his clinical theory, which he was to revise and elaborate through the next 40 years. Initially, he was interested in understanding the impact of the drives, especially infantile sexuality, upon the development of the psychic apparatus, and their role in the onset of psychopathology. Freud explicated his concepts of infantile sexuality in his *Three Essays on the Theory of Sexuality* (1905), as he discovered the importance of the oedipal complex in normal development and its role in the onset of neurosis. Subsequent focus in psychoanalysis was upon the modulating or control functions of the ego—the defenses—and their interaction with the drives. This interest in the defensive functions of the ego was later broadened to include the ego's external, reality-oriented adaptive functions. Freud established a basis for an ego psychology, a psychology concerned with the defensive and adaptive functions, and the relationship established with reality. These formulations of a

structural theory were articulated in *The Ego and the Id* (Freud, 1923), and in the reformulation of the theory of anxiety in *Inhibitions, Symptoms and Anxiety* (Freud, 1926).

Up to this point, psychoanalysis had a primary focus on innate biological forces: how these predispositions toward discharge and control unfolded in normal personality development, and how disruptions of their interactions could result in personality disturbances. The concepts of ego psychology were consolidated and expanded by Anna Freud in *Ego and the Mechanisms of Defense* (1936), by Hartmann in *Ego Psychology and the Problem of Adaptation* (1939), and by Rapaport in *Organization and Pathology of Thought* (1940). The psychoanalytic ego psychologists, from 1940 to 1960, were interested in the metatheory of psychoanalysis—its economic, topographic, and structural models of the mind—and in the study of ego functions such as impulse-defense configurations, affect modulation and regulation, and the organization of thought processes and other adaptive ego functions.

In the past 20 years there have been further significant revisions and extensions of psychoanalytic theory, which have taken place primarily through integrating the traditional concepts of psychoanalysis with concepts of object relations theory (Blatt, 1974; Blatt, Wild, & Ritzler, 1975; Fairbairn, 1954; Guntrip, 1969; Winnicott, 1965a), with a broadened, psychodynamically based, developmental theory (Blatt & Wild, 1976; Fraiberg, 1969; A. Freud, 1956; Jacobson, 1964; Mahler, 1968, 1975), and a systematic psychology of the self (Balint, 1952; Kohut, 1971, 1977; Winnicott, 1971). These recent developments within psychoanalytic theory are an integral part of an attempt to extend the "experience-distant" metapsychology, which uses concepts of structures, forces, and energies to describe the functioning of the mind— concepts based primarily on a model related to the natural sciences, to a more "experience-near" clinical theory (Klein, 1976). This clinical theory is primarily concerned with concepts of the self and others in a representational world (Jacobson, 1964; Sandler & Rosenblatt, 1962) seen as a central psychological process within a model based primarily on hermeneutics (Home, 1966; Klein, 1976; Steele, 1979), which emphasizes meaning and interpretation rather than forces and counterforces. In psychoanalytic theory there have been attempts to extend beyond an exclusive focus on ego structures, such as impulse-defense configurations and cognitive styles, to include a fuller consideration of the experiences of an individual in an interpersonal matrix as expressed in representations of the self and the object world (Blatt & Lerner, 1983a).

This interest in the study of object relations and in self and object representations evolved as Freud's interest extended beyond basic biological predispositions to include factors of the cultural context and their influence on psychological development. Freud began to discuss issues of object relations and the superego in his papers *On Narcissism* (1914) and *Mourning and Melancholia* (1917), and he later extended these concepts in *The Ego and the Id* (1923) and *Civilization and its Discontents* (1938). Freud's interests in the superego as the internalization of cultural prohibitions and values led to a fuller appreciation of the family as a major mediating force in the transmission of cultural values. There was an increasing interest in the role of parents in shaping psychological development. Psychological growth and development were viewed as a consequence of the caregiving patterns of significant people in the child's early environment. These patterns interact with the child's evolving libidinal and aggressive drives and the modulating and adaptive functions of his ego. The interpersonal interactions with significant, consistent, care-giving figures were now seen as major factors in the formation of cognitive-affective structures, defined primarily in terms of evolving concepts of the self and of others in the object world (Jacobson, 1964). These structures were seen as the result of the complex interaction between the child's biological endowment and predispositions and the interpersonal matrix of the family and culture. Knowledge gained from psychoanalytic work with children and the observation of the normal and disrupted development of infants and children contributed to the further appreciation and understanding of early development sequences, their role in normal personality development, and the occurrence of psychopathology throughout the life cycle.

Freud (1923, 1938), in his formulations about the development of the superego, discussed the process of internalization and how "a portion of the external world, has, at least partially, been abandoned as an object and has instead, by identification, been taken into the ego and thus become an integral part of the internal world. This new psychical agency continues to carry on the functions which have hitherto been performed by the people (the abandoned objects) in the external

world" (Freud, 1938, p. 205). This conceptualization of internalization was subsequently extended beyond superego formation to include all processes in which interactions with the environment are transformed into inner regulators and are assimilated as characteristics of the self (Hartmann, 1958, Hartmann & Lowenstein, 1962; Schafer, 1968, 1970). The internalization of object relations provides one of the primary bases for the development of intrapsychic structures (Blatt, 1974; Blatt, Wild & Ritzler, 1975; Govin-Decarie, 1965; Fenichel, 1945; A. Freud, 1952; Glover, 1950; Hartmann, 1958; Hartmann, Kris, & Loewenstein, 1949; Hoffer, 1952; Jacobson, 1964; Kernberg, 1966, 1972; Loewald, 1951, 1960, 1973; Mahler, 1968; Parens, 1971; Schafer, 1968; Stierlin, 1970). Object relations, through the processes of internalization, result in the formation of intrapsychic structures (ego functions and cognitive structures such as object and self-representations) that regulate and direct behavior. Psychoanalytic theory and research have progressively focused upon the complex interactions among early formative interpersonal relationships and how these transactions result in the formation of intrapsychic structures that are best understood in terms of the quality of the representational world. These concepts or representations of self and others in turn shape and direct subsequent interpersonal relationships.

An understanding of the development of the concept of the object (of the self and others) can be greatly facilitated by an integration of psychoanalytic theory with the contribution of cognitive developmental psychology, particularly the formulations of Jean Piaget and Heiz Werner. Piaget and Werner trace the development of cognitive schemata through several major developmental phases of the life cycle. They identified four major levels or types of cognitive schemata (sensorimotor, preoperational, and concrete and formal operations) through which the child comes to know and think about his world in increasingly sophisticated and symbolic form. Development, for Piaget (1954) and Werner (1948), consists of a progressive unfolding of cognitive structures according to innate principles of functioning in which the construction of new cognitive schemata evolve out of earlier cognitive structures. The child's relationships to his reality become increasingly integrated. The child comes to know the world as a product of his actions upon objects, and through the relationship of his actions to his symbolic representation of actual and potential actions and interactions.

The formulations of the cognitive developmental psychologists about the child's development of cognitive schemata have been based primarily on the study of the child in states of relative quiescence and as the child responds primarily to inanimate objects. In contrast, psychoanalytic theorists offer formulations of the child's development of cognitive structures based on the study of the child in states of relative comfort and discomfort within an interpersonal relationship (Wolff, 1967). According to Jacobson (1964), Mahler (1975), A. Freud (1964), Fraiberg (1969), and others, the representations of self and of others are initially vague and variable, and only develop gradually to become consistent, relatively realistic representations. Based initially on pleasurable and unpleasurable experiences of frustration-gratification, the child begins to build stable representations of the self and of others and to establish enduring investments and affective commitments. At the earliest stage, the self, the object, and interpersonal experiences are all one, undifferentiated, affective, sensorimotor experience of pleasure or unpleasure. As discussed by Mahler, in early autistic and symbiotic stages the infant is in a state of undifferentiated fusion and attachment to the mother. The infant slowly begins to perceive need satisfaction as coming from the mother, and there is a corresponding shift from the internal experience of pleasure to an awareness of a need-satisfying object. The object is recognized at first primarily in terms of its need-gratifying functions and actions. Slowly, the child becomes able to differentiate representations of himself and of others. With development, these representations become more stable and constant, and begin to coalesce into an increasing sense of identity.

These mental schemata or structures are transmitted to the child in an interpersonal matrix — in the relationship between the child and its caring agents and in the child's relationship to the culture at large (see also Parsons & Bales, 1955; Vygotsky, 1962). The child initially internalizes the orderly, predictable regularity of the mother-child, caretaking relationship. These basic differentiations of reality are subsequently extended and elaborated in further interpersonal relationships and experiences within the culture. But it is the basic caring relationship that provides the primary differentiations in reality that are internalized as the earliest and most fundamental principles of cognitive organi-

zation. The relatively predictable sequences of frustration and gratification in the caring relationship provide the child with the foundations for a sense of order and coherence. The infant's experiences of the mother's love and care are essential for the development of a capacity for reality adaptation (Winnicott, 1945). The mother's consistent and reliable care provides the infant with a sense of reality that is predictable and structured. The internalization of the mother's predictability and organization enables the child to tolerate delay that is externally imposed. This eventually develops into the capacity for internal delay, the establishment of psychological structures that permit the postponement of discharge, and the development of the capacity for anticipation, planning, and transformation. It must be stressed, however, that the amount of structure and organization that the environment must provide for these processes to develop will vary from child to child, depending on the child's biological constitution and temperament (Thomas, Chess, & Birch, 1968). What may be an appropriate degree and form of organization for one child may be insufficient or excessive for another. And even further, the degree and nature of the organization and structure provided by the environment must change in response to the child's development. But it is the internalization of the caring agents organized and structured responses that provide the basis for the establishment of the cognitive-affective structures of the representational world (Blatt, 1978).

Broadly defined, object representation refers to the conscious and unconscious mental schemata — including cognitive, affective, and experiential components — significant interpersonal encounters. Beginning as vague, diffuse, variable, sensorimotor experiences of pleasures and unpleasure, schemata gradually develop into differentiated, consistent, relatively realistic representations of the self and the object world. Earlier forms of representations are based on action sequences associated with need gratification, intermediate forms are based on specific perceptual and functional features, and the higher forms are more symbolic and conceptual (Blatt, 1974). There is a constant and reciprocal interaction between past and present interpersonal relations and the development of representations. Schemata evolve from the internalization of object relations, and new levels of object and self representation provide a revised organization for subsequent interpersonal relationships (Blatt, 1974).

This conceptualization of the development of object representation is based on a broadened definition of psychoanalytic theory that integrates the concepts of drive, defense, and adaptation in a developmental model that focuses primarily upon the child's evolving interactions with his caregiving agents. In particular, this expanded theory has implications for clinical practice and research, and has facilitated the study of psychotic, borderline, and narcissistic disorders. It has also resulted in formulations about the mutative forces in psychoanalysis. There is increased emphasis upon directly relevant experiential dimensions in both theory and practice (Mayman, 1976; Schafer, 1968), and a renewed interest in the psychoanalytic context, the role of interpretation, and analytic relationship as important factors in the therapeutic action of psychoanalysis (Loewald, 1960). The expanded conceptualization of psychoanalytic theory has also led to new approaches to research, such as the microanalysis of infant-parent interaction, the study of the development of language and concepts of the self and objects, and the differential impairment of these processes in various forms of psychopathology. Research has also begun to focus on the processes within the psychoanalytic context that facilitate the development of concepts of the self and the capacity to establish meaningful, effective, personally satisfying interpersonal relationships (Blatt & Shichman, 1983). Thus, one of the primary currents in contemporary psychoanalytic thought is the emphasis upon the quality of interpersonal interactions (object relationships) throughout the life cycle, their role in normal development, and their impairments in psychopathology. The ground work for this approach was established by the ego psychologists, such as Heinz Hartmann and David Rapaport, and developmental psychoanalysts, such as Anna Freud, Edith Jacobson, and Margaret Mahler. Important statements in object relations theory include the work of Klein, Winnicott, Fairbairn, Balint, and Guntrip, who provided understanding of the processes of internalization and the establishment of the representational structures — the concepts of the self and the object world. These contributions have led to the work of Kohut and Kernberg, and to current interest in very early childhood experiences and severe forms of psychopathology, the psychosis, borderline conditions and narcissistic disorders. In this chapter, we will review the development of object-relations theory evolving from the early work of Freud, Ferenczi, and Abraham, articulated more fully by Melanie Klein, given further shape and definition by the "British Object Relations Theorists," and culminating in the contemporary theoretical and clinical efforts of Kohut and Kernberg.

Current Issues

The pioneering work of Freud, Ferenczi, and Abraham led to the development of an object-relations theory in psychoanalysis, as seen primarily in the work of Klein, Fairbairn, Balint, Winnicott, and Guntrip. In this approach, the focus is upon the quality of interpersonal relationships and the internalization of these experiences resulting in the construction of an "internal world." Central are the care-taking experiences of the early mother-child relationship and the quality of the interaction with other significant caring figures. These care-taking interactions result in the construction of cognitive and affective structures, which in turn shape and direct the nature of subsequent interpersonal experiences. Thus, interpersonal relations and the establishment of cognitive and affective structures proceed in complex interaction.

The historical antecedents of the "British Object Relations Theorists" (Sutherland, 1980) can be seen in Karl Abraham's (1924, 1927) discussion of the differences in object relationships in melancholia and obsessional neuroses. Abraham (1924) described the different qualities of interpersonal relatedness in the oral, anal, and phallic stages of psychosexual development, and their implications for the nature of psychopathology.

One of the central figures in the development of object relations theory was Melanie Klein, who was particularly attentive to the influence of drives, especially aggression, and anxiety in children. Klein discussed the differences between "paranoid persecutory anxieties" and the "depressive anxieties" of guilt that result from the child's fantasized destruction of significant care-giving objects. Inborn aggression in the "paranoid-schizoid" and "depressive" positions lead to the development of fragmented internal objects. But this internal world also provides the basis for the child's subsequent perceptions and interpersonal relations.

Internal objects develop, according to Klein, from extreme experiences of good and bad that are attributed to fragmented part properties of the maternal object, such as the mother's breast. These representations become increasingly differentiated, integrated, and realistic. Internal objects are not exact replicas of real external objects and experiences, but are always embellished by the infant's drives and fantasies, which are externalized (projected) and reinternalized (introjected). This process of successive projections and introjections enables internal objects to become increasingly integrated and realistic. Good and bad fragmented part properties eventually become integrated into realistic representations, as drive-dominated part objects gradually become more accurate images of realistic, integrated figures.

Klein's formulations of the paranoid-schizoid and depressive positions extended and enriched Freud's structural theory of the mind—id, ego, and superego. In the developmentally earlier "paranoid-schizoid" position, anxiety is primarily experienced around preserving a sense of intactness in a hostile, persecutory world, while anxiety in the latter "depressive" position is aimed at the preservation of a sense of an integrated good object with which the individual is identified. In the paranoid-schizoid position, the child's inner world is filled with split-off, overstated, fragmented part objects. Anxiety and fear are focused on extremely menacing, persecutory external part objects that can invade and destroy the individual. There is an attempt to preserve and protect the overstated, fragmented, all-good part objects that have been tentatively internalized. The aim of the paranoid phase is ruthlessly to possess an ideal object and to project and ward off bad persecutory objects and destructive impulses.

The depressive position begins when objects are no longer experienced as exaggerated, split-off, and fragmented, but rather part properties of the object are integrated into a conception of a whole person with both good and bad properties. The persecutory anxiety of the paranoid position is replaced by feelings of guilt, remorse, and more modulated feelings of sadness about object loss. The resolution of the depressive position is a developmental achievement that ushers in a number of other developmental advances, including the capacity to experience and tolerate ambivalent feelings, the development of symbol formation, the capacity to identify with an integrated, realistic object, and a shift in anxiety from concerns about primitive aggression and destruction to concerns about fears of losing the love and respect of a good object.

Klein's interest in the child's building of internal objects stresses the symbolizing activity of the child. There is an inextricable link between the experiences of love and hate in object relations and the development of cognitive process. According to Melanie Klein (1975, pp. 52–53):

> The analysis of very young children has taught me that there is no individual urge, no anxiety situation, no mental process which does not include object, external or internal, in other words, object relations are at the center of emotional life. Furthermore, love and hatred, fantasies, anxieties, and defenses are also operative from the beginning and are *ab initio* indivisibly linked with object relations. This insight showed the many phenomena in a new light.

Klein's distinctions between the paranoid-schizoid and the depressive position provide another basis for differentiating between psychotic and neurotic processes. The transition between these two positions also describes aspects of borderline phenomena. Klein's formulations have contributed to the widening scope of psychoanalysis by extending the range of understanding to patients often considered unsuitable for psychoanalysis—psychotic, borderline, and narcissistic individuals. The understanding of paranoid-schizoid mechanisms—the primitive defenses, unconscious fantasies, and the quality of internal objects—have provided the basis for a psychoanalytic approach to these more disturbed patients. Klein's articulation of the resolution of the depressive position has also provided a conceptual model for assessing progress toward achieving an integrated sense of one's self and of others.

Klein reminds us that we live in two worlds, including an internal world that is as real and as central as the external world (Meltzer, 1981). This internal world is a *place*, a life space, in which meaning is generated. The reality of this internal world is the origin of personal meaning, which is then expressed in the quality of interpersonal relationships established in the external world.

Michael Balint (1952) stressed that psychological growth and development do not proceed from an initial, objectless, primary narcissism and autoeroticism; rather, at birth the infant has an intense, dependent relatedness to his environment. Balint (1968) discusses severe psychopathology as related to a "basic fault," to "something missing" inside that is universal and that impacts upon the entire functioning of an individual. This sense of fault or of something missing originates from a fundamental "failure of fit" (Sutherland, 1980, p. 832) between the infant's needs and the mother's responses.

Balint considers all psychological processes as originating in a basic two-person structure of the individual (subject) and the primary care-giving person (object). The individual struggles to cling to the object for security while at the same time seeking autonomy from such vulnerability. These two tendencies define two types of object relations that can serve as a defense against the effects of environmental failures. Balint's formulations of these two tendencies are similar to Mahler's emphasis on separation-individuation (Mahler, Pine, & Bergman, 1975), and the importance of the "need-fear dilemma" (Burnham, Gladstone, & Gibson, 1969) in severe psychopathology.

Balint's observations of a "basic fault" describes a developmental arrest that is fundamental to severe psychopathology. Verbal interpretations fail to alter this fundamental fault; what is needed in the treatment of regressed states is "the opportunity to make good a deficiency" (Sutherland, 1980, p. 833) or to establish a "new beginning" (Balint, 1952, 1968). The analyst, in his neutrality, becomes an object in a new environment around which the patient can discover his or her way in the object world. The quality of the therapeutic relationship and the analyst's understanding of the patient's inner world provide the basis for mending a primary developmental deficiency so that the individual can begin to relate to others in more effective and satisfying ways.

Balint contrasts a "benign regression," which has the potential for a "new beginning," with a "malignant regression," in which failures of empathy re-create in the treatment the lack of fit between infant and mother and lead to expressions of insatiable demands for instinctual gratification. Balint's emphasis upon the primacy of object relatedness in psychological development and his articulation of the importance of a failure of fit in the maternal experience has had an important influence in the development of an object-relations theory. Balint's formulations are consistent with Winnicott's conceptions of the "true" and "false" self and the importance of a "holding environment," as well as Kohut's emphasis upon the importance of empathy in the therapeutic process.

Donald Winnicott, because of his dual interests in pediatrics and psychoanalysis, made a distinctive contribution to object-relations theory based on this appreciation of both child development and the experiences of the mother. His interests in the earliest stages of development enabled him to explore, in a poetic and evocative way, preverbal experiences (Dare, 1976). His theoretical formulations remained close to the phenomenological and the experiential, and he eschewed jargon and technical language. Terms such as "ordinary devoted mother" or "good-enough mother," "holding environment," "true and false self," and "transitional object" and "transitional space" capture important personal experiences. Winnicott was especially interested in the momentum toward growth, maturity, and creativity. Instincts and impulses are seen as not just destructive and dangerous, but also as the source of spontaneity, creativity, and productivity. Winnicott maintained a positive view of the person and was interested in the "facilitating environment" that encouraged emotional growth. He was interested in the individual as well as the environment, and especially the interaction between child and mother in facilitating growth and development. "One half of the theory of the parent-infant relationship," according to Winnicott (1960), concerns the infant and the infant's journey from absolute dependence, through relative dependence, to independence. The other half of the parent-infant relationship concerns the qualities and changes in the mother that are responsive to specific developing needs of her infant. For Winnicott (1965), there was no such thing as the baby alone, the infant always existed as an essential part of a relationship. Winnicott focused on the experiencing individual within an interpersonal matrix. But eventually, "the experience of being alone while someone else is present" leads to the capacity to be alone (Winnicott, 1965b). Because Winnicott's concepts remain close to phenomenological experiences, his contributions appear somewhat unsystematic, but they are not without an underlying structure. His formulations are equally applicable to child development, to an understanding of adult psychopathology, and of the psychotherapeutic process.

Winnicott (1960) noted that the complete physical helplessness of the infant indicates the importance of attending to the "facilitating environment" and "the maternal care which together with the infant forms a unit." The infant's innate potential for growth is manifested in numerous spontaneous gestures. "If the inherited potential is to have a choice to become actual in the sense of manifesting itself in the individual person, then the environmental provision must be adequate. It is convenient to use a phrase like 'good-enough mothering' to convey an unidealized view of the maternal function" (Winnicott, 1965b, p. 44). The mother responds to the infant's spontaneous gestures through the development of a "primary maternal preoccupation"—a special psychological condition of the mother in the weeks before and after birth, a particular kind of identification or empathy that "gives the mother her special ability to do the right thing" (Winnicott, 1960, p. 585).

The "fit" between the infant's gesture and the mother's "good-enough" response to the infant's spontaneous gestures, facilitates the development of an infantile omnipotence. Empathy, responsiveness, and "holding" provide a predictable "continuity of being" (Winnicott, 1960); excessive frustration stunts development and impedes the inherent capacity of the true self for relatedness. Excessive and repeated frustration at the hands of a not-good-enough mother impinges upon the infant's omnipotence, creating a negative experience of compliance that subsequently becomes organized to form a false self. In its extreme and malignant form, severe failures in mothering give rise to what Winnicott (1960) terms the "unthinkable anxieties" of going to pieces and losing orientation to oneself and others. Consistent with Balint's (1968) "basic fault," Winnicott considers that experiences assimilated into the true and false self are not based on instinctual gratification, but rather on the quality of the relationship between infant and mother. For Winnicott, the study of psychological development of the infant is inextricably related to the study of maternal relationships.

With experiences of "ordinary good-enough mothering," the infant establishes a sense of wholeness, a conviction about the goodness of reality, and a fundamental "belief in" the world as a secure place. This sensorimotor integration provides the foundation for the emergence of the "true self," initially in the form of an increased repertoire of activity and subsequently in the actualization of "joyful" relations with others. Confidence in the mother allows the infant to relinquish the infantile omnipotence. This process of "disillusionment" is accompanied by intense affects of love and hate. But the "me" of the infant becomes separate from the "not-me" of the mother, and the infant begins a lifelong journey from absolute dependence, to relative dependence, to what Winnicott (1960) refers to as "interdependence" or "mature dependence."

Winnicott (1960) describes psychological growth as a series of overlapping maturational achievements of integration, personalization, and object relations proceeding from absolute to relative dependence. Early experiences of adequate "holding" facilitate the infant's development of an integrated sense of "I am"—a sense of subjective continuity that persists despite temporary experiences of disintegration. This sense of "I am" eventually develops into the "capacity to be alone," "one of the most important signs of maturity in emotional development" (Winnicott, 1965b, p. 29).

Winnicott (1960) also discusses the process of "personalization" through which the infant develops a sense of "me" and "not me" based on sensorimotor experiences of an inner-outer body boundary between oneself and others. Personalization creates the sense of a whole body and of an inner world and a psychic reality. As discussed by Winnicott (1960) and others (e.g., Blatt & Wild, 1976; Federn, 1952; Freud, 1930; Lidz & Lidz, 1952; Tausk, 1919), disruption of boundaries is most apparent in the impaired reality testing and distorted object relations of psychosis. The establishment of the first sense of the other ("object presenting") emerges out of the symbiotic fusion of "subject-object" (Winnicott, 1965c). It is important to note that Winnicott stresss that the infant's initiation of action is crucial to psychological development. "Too much" or "not enough" maternal response can interfere with the emergence of the self and the object out of the fusion of the symbiotic "subject-object."

Winnicott has an essentially positive view of human nature. He discusses the natural unfolding of the infant's potential for growth and how maternal care within a facilitating environment leads to the development of cognitive and affective structures. There is a gradual awareness of a "me" and a "not me," and the development of the capacity for objectivity and for active participation in a world experienced as relatively stable and permanent in time and space. Winnicott (1958) is particularly attentive to the transitional phases in this developmental process, as the child attempts to bridge the gap between fantasy and reality:

> part of the life of the human being . . . is an intermediate area of experiencing, to which inner reality and external life both contribute. . . . I am here staking a claim for an intermediate state between a baby's inability and his growing ability to recognize and ac-

cept reality. I am therefore studying the substance of illusion, that which is allowed to the infant, and which in adult life is inherent in art and religion, and yet becomes the hallmark of madness when an adult puts too powerful a claim on the credulity of others [p. 230–231].

The illusion to which Winnicott refers is the illusion of omnipotence. Without it, "it is not possible for the infant to begin to develop a capacity to experience a relationship to external reality or even form a conception of external reality" (Winnicott, 1958, p. 239). From earliest infancy and within the confines of a "subject object" relationship, there is "something, some activity or sensation in between the infant and the mother." It is in this in-between area or "space" that fantasy and reality join and omnipotence is experienced. In this space the inner and outer worlds overlap in such a way that the infant discovers his or her creation of an outer, "not-me" world. The retaining of an illusion of omnipotence to some degree allows reality to be experienced with a potential sense of joy. This sense of illusion or "potential space" (Winnicott, 1958) occurs through the child's "first 'not-me' possession"—a "transitional object" such as a toy or blanket or a piece of wool (Winnicott, 1958). The child's relationship to the transitional object is marked by a decrease in omnipotence. The relationship established with the transitional object takes on a reality of its own, combining the qualities of being paradoxically created and discovered (Winnicott, 1951, p. 233):

Its fate is to be gradually allowed to be decathected, so that in the course of years it becomes not so much forgotten as relegated to limbo. . . . It is forgotten and it is not mourned. It loses meaning, and this is because the transitional phenomena have become diffused, have become spread out over the whole intermediate territory between "inner psychic reality" and "the external world as perceived by two persons in common," that is to say, over the whole cultural field.

Winnicott (1971) stresses the importance of play in establishing the illusion and the creation of the transitional object in the "potential space" between infant and mother. Play is a facilitator of growth, separation-individuation, symbol formation, and communication. For Winnicott (1971), playing is a creative activity in normal develop-

ment and even in psychotherapy—it is only through play that one can creatively discover the self (Sutherland, 1980).

W. R. D. Fairbairn developed a consistent and systematic object-relations theory of personality based on a developmental model of internalization. Fairbairn, like Klein, was especially influenced by experiences with seriously disturbed, schizoid patients. He stressed the primacy of the paranoid-schizoid position and how a profound detachment and withdrawal evolves from the failure of the infant to experience a sense of "being loved for himself." For Fairbairn (1954), personality development evolves not from instinctual gratification, but from experiences of being a person, valued and enjoyed "for his own sake, as a person in his own right." "Libido is not primarily pleasure-seeking, but object seeking" (Fairbairn, 1954, p. 137). Fairbairn was interested in the "personal" rather than the biological dimensions of Freud's formulations. As Jones (1954) noted in his forward to Fairbairn's (1954) book, *Object Relations Theory of Personality*:

Instead of starting as Freud did, from stimulation of the nervous system proceeding from excitation of various erotogenous zones and internal tension arising from gonadic activity, Dr. Fairbairn starts at the centre of the personality, the ego, and depicts its strivings and difficulties in its endeavour to reach an object where it may find support. . . . This constitutes a fresh approach in psychoanalysis. [p. v]

At birth, the infant begins a libidinal search to establish an infantile dependence with a need-gratifying object. The erogenous zones are the channels through which objects are sought. Libido, in contrast to Freud's concepts of discharge and pleasure seeking through the erogenous zones, is reality oriented and directed toward establishing an attachment to the maternal object. Freud's concepts of psychosexual development are supplemented by concepts of the quality of dependence in object relations. The earliest stage of infantile dependence is characterized by primary identification (fusion) and an incorporative attitude. The gradual separation from the primary object constitutes a transitional stage from which the individual emerges with a capacity for mature dependence; the object and self are fully differentiated as separate individuals with independent identities. In his search for security, the individual must deal with frustrating experiences and malevolent interactions, and try to maintain relations with benevolent figures. Without a secure sense of self, the innate longings for object relations are blunted. It is too frightening to approach others because of fears of rejection. Instead, the individual develops a compensatory inner world of fantasized relationships.

The representations of figures in the environment provide the intrapsychic structures that are expressed in relatively stable and enduring patterns of experiencing and behaving. The representation of objects becomes the enduring features and patterns of personality organization. The quality of these object representations are expressed in dreams, symptoms, and interpersonal relationships. Personality development is a function of the quality of the caring environment. Loving and supportive interactions with a maternal figure facilitate growth, as the individual evolves in a process of differentiation. For Fairbairn, good object relations promote good development (Guntrip, 1973, p. 837). The infant attempts to cope with an unpredictable reality by internalizing external experiences and objects. Frustrating experiences and objects are internalized as an attempt to master and contain those negative experiences that cannot be tolerated in reality.

The earliest internalization of frustrating experiences develop around separation anxiety. According to Fairbairn, the nucleus of psychopathology rests on the extent to which there is a split in the ego. "Two aspects of the internalized object, viz. its exciting and its frustrating aspects, are split off from the main core of the object and repressed by the ego" (Fairbairn, 1963, p. 224). The exciting, gratifying aspects are termed the "libidinal object" and the frustrating, rejecting, prohibiting aspects are called the "antilibidinal object." Fairbairn (1963) continues: "there comes to be constituted two repressed internal objects, viz. the exciting (libidinal) and the rejecting (antilibidinal) object." This fundamental internal situation represents the schizoid position. Fairbairn notes that "the original ego is split into three egos — a central (conscious) ego attached to the ideal object (ego-ideal), a repressed libidinal ego attached to the exciting (or libidinal) object, and a repressed antilibidinal ego attached to the rejecting (or antilibidinal) object" (1963, p. 224).

The vicissitudes of object relations account for normal development, and deviations from the normal internalization of object relations account for the development of psychopathology. Fair-

bairn discussed four neurotic conditions: hysteric, phobic, obsessive, and nonpsychotic paranoid states. These four neurotic conditions correspond to four groups of good and bad, external and internal objects. Hysteria is the prototype of all neurotic psychopathology. In hysteria, good objects are projected into the outer world where the libidinal ego appears to them for help against its bad objects, which are experienced as internal persecutors. Obsessional states represent an attempt to maintain internal control over all good and all bad internalized objects. In phobic states the libidinal ego takes flight from bad objects to safe good ones, all of which are projected and seen as part of outer reality. In nonpsychotic paranoid states, the good object is internal while bad objects are projected into the outer world and hated. These four psychoneurotic conditions are regarded by Fairbairn as psychological modes of relating, and particular patterns of internalized object relations.

Harry Guntrip was influenced by Fairbairn and Winnicott. Guntrip's contributions to object-relations theory stem directly from Fairbairn's formulations and from Guntrip's clinical experience with schizoid patients (Guntrip, 1961, 1969). Guntrip has contributed to object-relations theory by emphasizing the epistemological significance of subjective phenomena and the necessity of conceptualizing clinical phenomena as psychological, dynamic, and personal, rather than as biological, neurological, or sociological. For Guntrip, clinical experience must provide the data for theoretical formulations.

Guntrip's (1961, 1969) emphasis is on the quality of personal life. He discusses the schizoid patient's need to regress, not in search of satisfactions, but rather in search of "recognition as a person." The experience of being accepted and understood enables the patient to feel hopeful and to be "born again" (Guntrip, 1969). The regressed states of schizoid patients feature a massive withdrawal from relationships and a morbid sense of inner deadness. Guntrip discusses how the patient takes flight from all object relations in an attempt to recapture the safety of the intrauterine milieu. The regressive flight toward ultimate security is juxtaposed by the experience of terrifying anxiety involving a loss of self, total isolation, and an apathetic abyss that is equated with death. Guntrip views most forms of psychopathology as defensive attempts to hold the self together against this terror of annihilation. The ultimate therapeutic problem is aiding the patient to cope with these primal anxieties. Rather than emphasizing the vicissitudes of libidinal instincts and primitive aggression, Guntrip focuses on the profound fears of intolerable helplessness and weakness that characterize the infant, especially in an experience of deprivation.

Guntrip (1969) discusses how the schizoid individual "hovers between two opposite fears, the fear of isolation in independence with loss of his ego in a vacuum of experience, and the fear of bondage to, of imprisonment or absorption in the personality of whomsoever he rushes to for protection" (1969, p. 274). The schizoid patient perpetually oscillates between nearness and distance, dependence and independence, trust and mistrust, and the maintenance and fear of the therapeutic relationship. A permanent compromise midway between the extremes of absorption and isolation constitute the nature of treatment stalemates with disturbed patients. Guntrip notes that this schizoid compromise is an essential intermediate phase through which the regressed patient must progress. The pathway to effective treatment involves establishing a terrifying passive dependence. Successful treatment involves the resolution of the struggle against this passive dependence.

The Contributions of Kernberg and Kohut

The contributions of the object-relations theorists have led to an extension of psychoanalytic concepts and practice, including a shift from an emphasis on mental functioning to an interest in experiencing (Lichtenberg, 1979). Basic psychoanalytic concepts of drive and defense have been supplemented by an interest in subjective experiences and concepts of the representational world (Spruiell, 1978). A key question facing contemporary psychoanalysis is "can psychoanalytic theory conceptualize the individual's total experience, his ever shifting yet generally stable sense of self, and his sense of the world of people and things, actual and illusory?" (Lichtenberg, 1979, p. 376). Psychoanalytic concepts now include an interest in the vicissitudes of the instincts, defensive and adaptive functions of the ego, and a concern with the early mother-child interaction and its impact upon the development of object relations and concepts of the self and the object world.

From a historical perspective, Freud (1914), in his pivotal paper *On Narcissism,* raised many questions about the development of narcissistic and object libido, about the development of feelings and concepts about the self and of significant others. Freud's early formulations have been refined and extended to include a consideration of the self as the conscious, preconscious and unconscious representation of the total person, the processes through which self and object representations are internalized as enduring structures, the consideration of self as structure and as experience, the importance of the internal world in psychological functioning, and the importance of a narcissistic object choice as an attempt to correct a deficit in psychological structure (Teicholz, 1978). These elaborations of psychoanalytic theory have contributed to the attempts to broaden the scope of psychoanalytic practice beyond the treatment of the neuroses, in which there are conflicts over sexual and aggressive impulses, to an interest in the treatment of disorders in which the personality is seriously malformed or arrested — the narcissistic borderline and psychotic conditions.

The emphasis on object-relations theory in the past decade has led to a marked increase in interest in borderline and narcissistic disorders. Some investigators consider borderline and narcissistic disorders as a unique diagnostic category, while others regard them as part of a continuum of psychopathology (e.g., Horner, 1980; Kernberg, 1975; Settlage, 1977). The term "borderline" is often used to designate an intermediate area of psychopathology — a diagnosis applied to patients who could be classified as neither neurotic nor psychotic, but who exhibit some features of both. Some (e.g., Green, 1977) argue that, like the hysteric of Freud's time, the borderline patient is the problem of our time. Pruyser (1975) asserts that the concept has become a "star word."

Two primary figures in this expanding scope of psychoanalytic theory and practice are Heinz Kohut (1971, 1977) and Otto Kernberg (1975, 1976). Kernberg's work derives from psychoanalytic ego psychology, and object-relations theory, especially Melanie Klein and the developmental psychology of Jacobson and Mahler. Kernberg has examined the role of aggression and primitive defenses in borderline and narcissistic psychopathology. Kohut, on the other hand, has focused on a psychology of the self and the developmental transformation that takes place as the concepts of the self move from archaic psychological states to more mature levels.

Kohut is particularly interested in the narcissistic patient and has found that the classical theory of drives and defenses, which is useful in understanding neuroses, has relatively little to contribute to the understanding of narcissistic disorders. Neurosis has its origins later in childhood, when self-object differentiations and the structures of the mind (id, ego, and superego) are well established. Libidinal and aggressive drives are experienced as dangerous, anxiety is mobilized, defenses are only partially successful, and neurotic symptoms are a compromise for the tensions between impulse and defense. In psychoanalytic treatment, neurotic patients develop a transference neurosis in which the analyst is experienced as a version of the parents, to whom libidinal and aggressive urges are directed. By contrast, self-pathology begins much earlier in development, at a time when psychological structures are still in the process of formation. Symptoms occur when an insecurely established self is threatened by dangers of psychological disintegration, fragmentation, and devitalization. Because of the absence of a firm cohesive sense of self, the treatment relationship initially is a holding environment that serves as a protective container; it permits consolidation of the self, so that eventually a therapeutic alliance can be established and a more classical analysis of conflicts, defenses, and transference can take place (Topin & Kohut, 1980).

A weakened or defective self, the core of psychopathology in narcissistic patients, is created by an empathic failure in early parent-child relationships. According to Kohut (1971, 1977), an authentic, capable, and vital self can be erected only when the "mirroring" and "idealizing" needs of the child are responded to by parents. Without an adequate sense of self, the child is unable to separate from primitive experiences of the parents as self-objects. The child retains an archaic grandiosity and the wish to continue the fusion with an omnipotent self-object in order to maintain an archaic sense of self as a defense against painful states of anxiety (fragmentation) and depression (devitalization, depletion). Narcissistic disturbances are viewed as primarily structural rather than dynamic disturbances; that is, the patients suffer from a developmental arrest rather than a conflict between drive and defense. Kohut articulates the need of narcissistic patients to reexperience a "self-object transference" ("mirror" or "idealizing") in order to correct their developmental arrest. The primary factor in therapy is the therapist's empathy rather than the interpretation of drives. According to Kohut and Wolff (1978), the patient needs to become aware of, express, and experience the unfulfilled narcissistic needs of childhood in order to develop the basis of an adequate sense of self.

Kohut posits a separate developmental line for narcissism, and traces transformations of narcissism from primitive to mature forms. In normal development, the equilibrium of primary narcissism is disturbed by failures of maternal care, and the child attempts to maintain the narcissistic perfection by establishing grandiose and exhibitionistic images of the self or by attributing the narcissistic perfection onto an omnipotent self-object—the idealized parent image. In normal development, the "grandiose self" and "idealized parent image" are the precursors of mature ambitions, enjoyment, and self-esteem. With inevitable, natural, phase-appropriate failures, misunderstandings, and delays on the part of the mothering agent, the infant gradually withdraws libido from the archaic images of narcissistic perfection and slowly acquires increments of inner psychological structure that gradually take over the mother's function of maintaining narcissistic equilibrium. Gradual and tolerable disappointments in narcissistic equilibrium lead to the development of internal structure and the capacity for self-soothing and tension tolerance.

Serious failures in empathy on the part of the mother, however, may result in narcissistic trauma and a disillusionment with the idealized object. This may lead to a quest for a perfect, idealized external object (and a consequent failure in superego development), or the development of a hypercathected "grandiose self." The "grandiose self" represents "another approach to attempt to recapture the original all embracing narcissism by concentrating perfection and power on the (grandiose) self, and by turning away disdainfully from an outside to which all imperfections have been assigned" (Kohut, 1971, p. 106). The grandiose self and idealized parent image remain unintegrated in the developing personality.

A chronic frustration of legitimate childhood needs interferes with the development of psychological structure and the self perceptions of these patients are fragmented, discontinuous, and unreal. External objects are used as a replacement for psychological structures (Teicholz, 1978). Depending on the quality of interaction with the self-object during development, the adult self may emerge "in states of varying degrees of coherence, from cohesion to fragmentation; in states of varying degrees of vitality, from vigor to enfeeblement; and in states of varying degrees of functional harmony, from order to chaos. Significant failure to achieve cohesion, vigor or harmony, or a significant loss of these qualities after they have been tentatively established, may be said to constitute a stage of 'self-disorders'" (Kohut & Wolff, 1978, p. 414).

Kohut and Wolff (1978) have described specific syndromes of "self pathology" as a consequence of developmental failures. An "understimulated self" develops from a lack of stimulation in childhood. As children, these patients may have exhibited head banging; later, compulsive masturbation and in adolescence, daredevil activities. A "fragmented self" develops as a consequence of an absence of integrating responses from a caring agent. States of fragmentation vary in degree, and more malignant manifestations include profound anxiety and hypochondriacal worry, which can be quasi-delusional. States of fragmentation are frequently induced by empathic failure or rebuff, and often disappear when an empathic response is reestablished. An "overstimulated self" stems from nonempathic, excessive, and phase-inappropriate parental responses to the child's grandiose-exhibitionistic strivings. Unrealistic fantasies of greatness lead to tension, anxiety, and painful inhibitions. Such individuals tend not to perform up to their potential because they are frightened of their intense ambition, perfectionistic tendencies, and archaic grandiose fantasies. An "overburdened self" has been deprived of the opportunity to merge with self-objects representing soothing and calmness. These individuals have failed to internalize a self-soothing modality and insistently dread the trauma of unbridled emotionality, especially anxiety. In order to avoid the dangers of noxious stimuli, these individuals develop chronic attitudes of irritability, suspiciousness, and paranoia.

Kohut and Wolff (1978) also delineate specific self disorders or personality types associated with the narcissistic character or psychopathology within the "narcissistic realm." "Mirror-hungry personalities" seek attention exhibitionistically in order to counterbalance intense feelings of worthlessness and lack of self-esteem. "Ideal-hungry personalities" want others to admire their prestige, power, beauty, and intelligence. They can only experience a sense of positive self-esteem while relating to idealized self-objects; but, because of their structural defect, they continually find defects in the idealized other and are inevitably disappointed. "Alter-ego-hungry personalities" experience a profound inner void that can only be filled by a twinship hollowed by conformity to the self's appearance, values, and ideas, with an awareness that the other is separate and distinct. The alter-ego-hungry personality is prone to feel alienated and estranged. The three narcissistic character types — mirror-hungry, ideal-hungry, and alter-ego-hungry — tend to look relentlessly for self-objects. The mirror-hungry personality manifests a compelling need to control the self-object in an effort to obtain self-structure. The need to merge dominates the clinical picture, the particular type of merger (mirroring, idealizing, or alter-ego) is secondary to structural defects in the self and the need for a self-object in lieu of self-structure. Because of fluidity in the self-other boundary, the merger-hungry personality is intolerant of the self-object's independence, they are acutely sensitive to separations, and they demand the immediate and continuous presence of self-objects. As a reciprocal to the merger-hungry type, "contact-shunting personalities" avoid social contact and isolate themselves as a defense against deep-seated apprehensions that they will be swallowed up and devoured by the symbiotic yearnings for an all-encompassing union.

The work of Otto Kernberg, beginning in 1966, has had a primary influence on psychoanalytic thinking about borderline phenomena. Kernberg's contributions are based on an integration of basic psychoanalytic concepts, psychoanalytic ego psychology, and the object-relations theories of Klein, Fairbairn, and Winnicott. Kernberg discusses specific and nonspecific ego defects and failures of integration that result from disruptions of the internalization of object relations (Kernberg, 1976). Kernberg places his concepts of the borderline personality development within a conceptual model of normal development, and he is specifically concerned about the relation of borderline pathology to issues of pathological narcissism.

Psychological structure is determined by the vicissitudes of internalized object relations, which constitute a crucial determinant of ego integration. Abnormalities in internalization of object relations, regardless of etiology (constitutional or environmental), determine various types of psychopathology (Kernberg, 1975, 1976, 1978). Kernberg (1975) discusses four stages in the internalization of object relations, which range from primary narcissism at the beginning of the developmental continuum to object constancy at the highest level.

In the first three months of infancy there is a primary, undifferentiated self-object matrix based on the pleasurable, gratifying experiences of the infant in interaction with the mother. This undifferentiated self-object representation of gratifying experiences within the infant-mother matrix is juxtaposed with a representation of an undifferentiated, "all-bad" self-object representation based on painful and frustrating experiences. Good and bad or pleasure and pain are the primary differentiations at this stage, and there is no differentiation between self and nonself. Self and object representations become differentiated only with perceptual and cognitive development. Ego boundaries are stablized and self representation gradually becomes separate from object representation. Around one to two years of age, good and bad self images coalesce into an integrated self-concept. Good and bad object images are also integrated in more realistic representation of others. Affects become more differentiated, integrated, and modulated.

In borderline psychopathology, there is a basic and rudimentary differentiation between self and other, but it is based on an extreme juxtaposition and primitive aggression that facilitates the differentiation of "me" and "not me." The active struggle to maintain a differentiation based on contradictory images results in massive anxiety and the ego's use of "splitting" as a major defensive operation. The pathological use of splitting becomes the primary characteristic of the borderline personality.

Borderline pathology is characterized by powerful, untamed affects: a reliance on a constellation of primitive defenses centered in splitting; a lack of impulse control and anxiety tolerance; and premature sexualization of relationships. There is little evidence of internal control and there is an overreliance on external sources for reassurance, praise, and punishment. These characteristics of borderline psychopathology define, according to Kernberg (1975), "a specific, stable, pathological personality organization," well demarcated from both neurosis and psychosis on the one hand, and with a typical constellation of symptoms, defenses operations, instinctual vicissitudes, and quality of self and object representation on the other hand.

The treatment goal with borderline patients includes overcoming developmental arrests, the integration of part-object representations into total-object representations, the development of object constancy, and the achievement of an integrated self-object. The therapist's maintenance of technical neutrality and the interpretation of splitting and other primitive defenses assists the patient to relinquish a contradictory representation of both an overtly idealized and a ruthlessly depreciated therapist. Idealization and depreciation are both attempts to defend against the dread of emptiness and aloneness (Kernberg, 1975, 1976, 1982). Improvement in therapy is a function of the ego strength of the patient and the therapist's skill and empathy in establishing a therapeutic alliance and modulating the patient's primitive aggression. According to Kernberg (1982, p. 26):

> In the severe psychopathologies (including borderline personalities), early, primitive units of internalized object relations are directly manifest in the transference as conflicting drive derivatives reflected in contradictory ego states. In these cases, the predominance of a constellation of early defense mechanisms centering on primitive dissociation or splitting, immediately activates contradictory, primitive but conscious intrapsychic conflicts in the transference. What appear to be inappropriate, chaotic character traits and interpersonal interactions, impulsive behavior, and affect storms are actually reflections of the fantastic early object-relations-derived structures. . . . These highly fantastic, unrealistic precipitates of early object relations, which do not directly reflect the real object relations of infancy and childhood and must be interpreted until the more realistic aspects of the developmental history emerge, determine the characteristics of primitive transference.

While symptoms and pathological character traits reflect intrapsychic conflict, these conflicts are dynamically structured into relatively stable patterns of organization based on the quality of internalized object relations. At severe levels of psychopathology, such as the borderline personality organization, the interpretation of primitive defenses and transference manifestations fosters integration and the transformation of primitive transference into more advanced, neurotic transferences. Relationships based on distorted representations of part properties are replaced by relationships based on more realistic and comprehensive representations of self and others (Kernberg, 1975, 1976, 1982).

This approach to the treatment of borderline patients is part of the "widening scope of psychoanalysis" in that it extends psychoanalytic concepts and methods to the treatment of more severely disturbed patients. It introduces modifications of basic psychoanalytic methods that focus on the primitive transference as the major locus of therapeutic action. The focus of treatment shifts from a traditional emphasis on the content of free associations to a fuller appreciation of the patient-therapist interaction as expressed in the dynamics of the transference. Interpretations of the therapeutic relationship, as expressed through the transference, are made in terms of the patient's predominant level of self and object representations. With seriously disturbed patients, the therapeutic relationship can become a "holding environment" (Winnicott) and the therapist a "container" (Bion, 1959) for the early forms of object relations established by the patient. The therapist's cognitive and affective tolerance provides an integrative function for the patient's chaotic experiences. The interpretation of the primitive borderline defenses of splitting, projective identification, denial, idealization, and devaluation contributes to the gradual development of a capacity to be more observant and reflective. The interpretation of defensive resistance and transference is a major aspect of the treatment process with borderline patients. Kernberg also notes the important role of powerful countertransference reactions in the treatment of borderline patients, and the need to use these emotional reactions in the therapeutic process.

Future Directions

One of the important current debates in contemporary psychoanalysis and dynamic psychology concerns the concept and very nature of narcissism and its role in normal development, in psychopathology, and in the therapeutic process. Kohut (1971) discusses narcissism as an independent developmental line (A. Freud, 1965); impairments in this developmental process create unique forms of pathology. "Narcissism has a development of its own, a pathology of its own, and requires a treatment of its own. . . . Narcissism and object love have side-by-side existences and development that are mutually exclusive" (Goldberg, 1974, p.

245). Kernberg, in contrast, views narcissistic disturbances as part of borderline personality organization. Narcissistic disturbances involve the primitive defenses of splitting and dissociation—the defenses of borderline patients. But, in addition, as "compensation" for the lack of a normal, integrated self-concept, narcissistic patients become grandiose, extremely self-centered, and lack an interest in and an empathy for others, even though they are eager to have the admiration and approval of others (Kernberg, 1975, p. 228). Narcissistic patients have better impulse control and social functioning, including a capacity for work and achievement, than borderline patients because of this compensatory, but pathologically integrated, grandiose self-concept.

There are important theoretical and clinical implications for considering narcissistic disturbances either as specific forms of psychopathology that evolve from a separate developmental line (Kohut, 1971, 1977), or as a subtype of borderline phenomena that evolves out of disruptions in the development of object relations (Kernberg, 1975). The differences in theoretical orientation have significant clinical implications for how one views the role of interpretation, the importance of transference, and the therapeutic alliance in the treatment process. For Kohut, treatment of narcissistic patients involves recognition of the patient's inability to perceive and experience the analyst as a separate person. Therapy involves accepting, for long periods of time, the idealization of the patient as externalizations and projections of the patient's grandiose self. Gradually in treatment, through a series of transmuting internalizations, the narcissistic grandiose self is modified and concepts of the self begin to develop normally and become integrated into the total personality organization. Kernberg, in contrast, views narcissistic structures (grandiose self and idealization) as defenses against primitive oral rage, envy, paranoid fears, and loneliness. Expression of this repressed primitive rage in treatment is a prerequisite for structural change, and this can occur only through the active interpretation of the grandiose and idealizing transferences that are seen as defenses against the underlying rage and negative transference. Kernberg maintains continuity with traditional psychoanalysis in his primary emphasis upon the mutative power of interpreting conflicts and defenses (resistances), as experienced in the transference.

Kohut, in contrast, emphasizes the special

quality of the interpersonal relationship that the patient seeks to establish with the therapist and how important it is to be very attentive to the experiential dimensions of the patient-analyst relationships. Kohut is particularly interested in how the patient constructs concepts of himself and others out of the neutrality and implicit support of the therapeutic relationship. The narcissistic patient has difficulties perceiving the analyst as a separate person, and only gradually, through a process of transmuting internalizations, can this type of patient relinquish primitive forms of narcissism and allow his self-concept to develop in a more realistic form and be coordinated with a developing capacity for object love. Kohut stresses the experiential dimensions of the therapeutic alliance and the mutative role of the unique interpersonal relationship established. He also stresses the manner in which the alliance provides the basis for a series of transmuting internalizations that result in the establishment of more realistic and appropriate concepts of the self and of others.

Blatt and Cooley (1982), in a discussion of therapeutic action from the perspective of processes of separation and individuation, provide a theoretical model of therapeutic action based on integration of the interpretation of conflict and defense as well as transmuting internalizations. They point out that transmuting internalizations can occur only after there has been significant resolution of prior, pathological internalizations. The recognition and relinquishing of pathological introjects that seriously distorted concepts of self and others can come about only through the interpretation of conflict and defense. While this process is essential for therapeutic change, it is not sufficient. Interpretations enable the patient to recognize the power of pathological internalizations and eventually to resolve them. The relinquishing of these well-established but distorted introjects provides the patient with the opportunity to establish new, and it is hoped, more constructive internalizations. These new internalizations occur, initially at least, in the context of the therapeutic alliance. The benign support implicit in the analyst's neutrality enables the patient to explore new concepts of self and of others and new conceptions of actual and potential interpersonal interactions. And the establishment of these new, transmuting internalizations consolidate the patient's relinquishing prior, pathological introjects. The therapeutic process of interpretation and internalization are the mutative forces not

only in the treatment of narcissistic and borderline pathology, but an essential dimension in all dynamically oriented psychotherapy and psychoanalysis (Blatt & Cooley, 1982).

These contemporary considerations about the etiology and treatment of severe psychopathology — the debate between Kernberg and Kohut — indicates an emerging emphasis in psychoanalytic thought on experiential dimensions and the inclusion of a phenomenological point of view. Phenomenological considerations supplement Freud's biological, drive-discharge theory — the economic point of view. There has been substantial criticism of the economic theory of psychoanalysis (Apfelbaum, 1965; Arlow, 1975; Blatt, Wild, & Ritzler, 1975; Dahl, 1968; Holt, 1965, 1967, 1976; Klein, 1976; Peterfreund, 1971; Rubenstein, 1967; Stolorow & Atwood, 1979) as based on outmoded concepts of physiology and physics that are inconsistent with current neurophysiological knowledge. Also, the drive theory postulates impersonal, quasi-physiological forces that ignore personal meaning and motivational dynamics. Likewise, there has been considerable controversy about Freud's "structural theory" — the concepts of id, ego, and superego and how they are often used as reifications and personifications rather than considerations of the individual as an integrated organism with a synthesized orchestration of multiple levels of meanings and motivations. Numerous alternatives have been suggested as replacements for the metapsychological superstructure of psychoanalysis (the economic and structural points of view), including a "protoneurophysiological" theory (Rubenstein, 1967, 1976), a model of information processing and systems theory (Kubie, 1975; Peterfreund, 1971, 1975), and a phenomenological approach which considers issues of intention, meanings, reasons and subjective experiences (Gill, 1976; Home, 1966; Klein, 1976; Schafer, 1976).

It is our belief that the most important of these alternatives is the development of a phenomenological point of view. In the phenomenological approach, concepts of cause, effect, impulse, energy, and drive are supplemented by aspects of subjective experiences such as intentions, decisions, and actions for avowed and disavowed reasons (Anscombe, 1981; Schafer, 1976). Personal meanings and subjective experiences can form the basis of a clinical theory that examines the "whys" of human experiences rather than the "hows" (Sandler & Joffe, 1969). This clinical theory uses what Mayman (1976) calls a "middle-level language" that focuses on subjective meaning, intentions, aims, and motives emerging from "cognitive-emotional schemata" (Klein, 1976) of the representational world (Sandler & Rosenblatt, 1962). These representational configurations have cognitive and affective components and evolve with development and assume "functional significance" (Klein, 1976) in guiding and directing behavior (Blatt, 1974; Blatt et al., 1975). These cognitive-affective representational structures of the self and the object world can be considered not only from a psychoanalytic perspective, but also as they intersect with developmental, cognitive, and social-psychological theory.

This new orientation in psychoanalysis—this addition of a phenomenological point of view—need not replace, but rather it can serve to supplement prior psychoanalytic points of view. The emerging emphasis upon a phenomenological point of view in psychoanalysis can be seen in many aspects of contemporary psychoanalytic research. Much greater attention is being given to the study of infant-mother transaction, such as research on the early, preverbal development of the infant that emerges in significant care taking (e.g., Beebe, 1982). The emphasis upon interpersonal interactions in development can also be seen in investigations of the psychoanalytic situation (e.g., Gill & Hoffman, 1981; Hartley & Strupp, 1982; Luborsky, 1967; Sampson, Weiss et al., 1969; Sampson & Weiss, 1982), on the quality of object and self representations (e.g., Blatt et al., 1976; Blatt & Lerner, 1983a; Blatt, Wein et al., 1979; Mayman, 1973; Urist, 1977), and on the subliminal stimulation of fundamental interpersonal experiences (Silverman, 1982). In fact, a large proportion of articles in a newly developed annual on empirical investigations of psychoanalytic concepts (Masling, 1982a, 1982b) deal with phenomenological issues such as self-deception, self-esteem, and depression (Sackeim, 1982), the definition and assessment of meaning (Dahl, 1982), interests as objects relations (Eagle, 1982), orality and interpersonal behavior (Masling, 1982), needs for fusion and differentiation (Greene, 1982), and on hopelessness and hope (Freedman, 1982).

Conclusion

In this review we have sought to describe recent developments in dynamic theories of personality and especially the increased emphasis on interpersonal relationships and phenomenological experiences as a fundamental data base for the development of a clinical theory of psychoanalysis. The development of a phenomenological point of view in psychoanalytic theory has resulted in a broadening of the scope of psychoanalysis to include interest in more severe forms of psychopathology, including narcissistic disturbances and the borderline and psychotic conditions, an interest in specifying the mutative forces of therapeutic action—the forces that create change in psychoanalysis and psychotherapy, an interest in very early, preverbal development, the normal development of concepts of self and other (the representational world) and their impairment in psychopathology, and the study of a wide range of phenomenological experiences such as hope and hopelessness, wishes, interests, intentions, interpersonal relationships, and the early experiences of dependency, orality, and fusion. This phenomenological orientation has had a profound impact on clinical practice, theory, and research. It has provided a closer link between the basic data base of psychoanalysis—observations made in the clinical context of the psychoanalytic process and theoretical formulations. This closer tie between psychoanalytic data and theory will continue to have significant impact on the nature of clinical practice and it will facilitate empirical investigations of important dimensions of human experience.

References

Abraham, K. A short study of the development of the libido. In *Selected papers on psychoanalysis*. London: Hogarth Press, 1924.

Abraham, K. Notes on the psychoanalytical investigation and treatment of manic-depressive insanity and allied conditions. In *Selected papers on psychoanalysis*. London: Hogarth Press, 1927.

Anscombe, R. Referring to the unconscious: A philosophical critique of Schafer's action language. *International Journal of Psychoanalysis*, 1981, **62**, 225–241.

Apfelbaum, B. Ego psychology, psychic energy, and the hazards of quantitative exploration in psychoanalytic theory. *International Journal of Psychoanalysis*, 1965, **46**, 168–182.

Arlow, J. The structural hypothesis—Theoretical considerations. *Psychoanalytic Quarterly*, 1975, **44**, 509–525.

Balint, M. *Primary love and psychoanalytic technique*. London: Hogarth Press, 1952.

Balint, M. *The basic fault*. London: Tavistock Press, 1968.

Barratt, B. Critical notes on Schafer's "action language." *Annual of Psychoanalysis*, 1978, **6**, 287–303.

Beebe, B. Mother-infant mutual influence and precursors of self and object representations. In J. Masling (Ed.), *Empirical studies of psychoanalytic theories*, Vol. II, Hillsdale, N.J.: Erlbaum, 1982.

Bion, Attack on linking. *International Journal of Psychoanalysis*, 1959, **40**, 308–315.

Blatt, S. J. Levels of object representation in anaclitic and introjective depression. *Psychoanalytic Study of the Child*, 1974, **29**, 107–157.

Blatt, S. J. Paradoxical representations and their implications for the treatment of psychosis and borderline states. Paper read at a meeting of the Institute for Psychoanalytic Research and Training, New York City, May 18, 1978.

Blatt, S. J., & Blatt, E. S. *Cultural continuity and change: A developmental cognitive analysis*. Hillsdale, N.J.: Erlbaum Associates, in press.

Blatt, S. J., Brenneis, B., Schimek, J. G., & Glick, M. Normal development and psychopathological impairment of the concept of the object on the Rorschach. *Journal of Abnormal Psychology*, 1976, **85**, 364–373.

Blatt, S., & Cooley, R. Separation-individuation, internalization and therapeutic action. Unpublished manuscript. Yale University, 1982.

Blatt, S. J., & Lerner, H. Investigations in the psychoanalytic theory of object relations and object representations. In J. Masling (Ed.), *Empirical Studies of Psychoanalytic Theories*. Hillsdale, N.J.: Analytic Press, 1983, 189–249. (a)

Blatt, S. J., & Lerner, H. The psychological assessment of object representations. *Journal of Personality Assessment*, 1983, in press. (b)

Blatt, S. J., & Shichman, S. Two primary configurations of psychotherapy. *Psychoanalysis and Contemporary Thought*, in press.

Blatt, S. J., Wein, S. J., Chevron, E., & Quinlan, D. Parental representations and depression in normal young adults. *Journal of Abnormal Psychology*, 1979, **78**, 388–397.

Blatt, S. J., & Wild, C. M. *Schizophrenia: A developmental analysis*. New York: Academic Press, 1976.

Blatt, S. J., Wild, C. M., & Ritzler, B. A. Disturbances of object representations in schizophrenia. *Psychoanalysis and Contemporary Science*, 1975, **4**, 235–288.

Burnham, D., Gladstone, A., & Gibson, R. *Schizophrenia and the need fear dilemma*. New York: International Universities Press, 1969.

Dahl, H. Panel on "Psychoanalytic theory of the instinctual drives in relation to recent developments." *Journal of the American Psychoanalytic Association*, 1968, **16**, 629–632.

Dahl, H. On the definition and measurement of wishes. In J. Masling (Ed.), *Empirical studies of psychoanalytical theories*, Vol. I. Hillsdale, N.J.: Erlbaum, 1982.

Dare, C. Psychoanalytic theories. In M. Rutter & L. Hersou (Eds.), *Child psychiatry: Modern approaches*. Oxford, England: Blackwell, 1976.

Eagle, M. Interest as object relations. In J. Masling (Ed.), *Empirical studies of psychoanalytical theories*. Hillsdale, N.J.: Erlbaum, 1982.

Fairbairn, W. R. Synopsis of an object-relations theory of the personality. *International Journal of Psychoanalysis*, 1963, **44**, 224–226.

Fairbairn, W. R. D. *An object relations theory of the personality*. New York: Basic Books, 1954.

Federn, P. *Ego psychology and the psychoses*. New York: Basic Books, 1952.

Fenichel, O. *The psychoanalytic theory of neurosis*. New York: Norton, 1945.

Fraiberg, S. Libidinal object constancy and mental representation. *Psychoanalytic Study of the Child*, 1969, **24**, 9–47.

Freedman, N. On depression: From hopelessness to hope. In J. Masling (Ed.), *Empirical studies of psychoanalytical theories*, Vol. II. Hillsdale, N.J.: Erlbaum, 1982.

Freud, A. *Ego and the mechanisms of defense*. New York: International Universities Press, 1936.

Freud, A. The mutual influences in the development of ego and id. *Psychoanalytic Study of the Child*, 1952, **7**, 42–50.

Freud, A. The assessment of borderline cases. Research at the Hampstead Child-Therapy Clinic and other papers. *The writings of Anna Freud*, 1956, **5**, 301–314. New York: International Universities Press, 1969.

Freud, A. *Normality and pathology in childhood: Assessments of development*, Vol. VI. New York: International Universities Press, 1965.

Freud, A. Assessment of pathology in childhood. In A. Freud (Ed.), *Research at the Hampstead Child-Therapy Clinic and Other Papers*, Vol V. New York: International Universities Press, 1969.

Freud, A. Psychopathology seen against the background of normal development. In *Psychoanalytic psychology of normal development*, Vol. VIII. New York: International Universities Press, 1981.

Freud, S. (1900). The interpretation of dreams. *Standard Edition*, Vol. 5. London: Hogarth Press, 1957.

Freud, S. (1905). Three essays on the theory of sexuality. *Standard Edition*. London: Hogarth Press, 1957.

Freud, S. (1914). On narcissism. *Standard Edition*, Vol. 14. London: Hogarth Press, 1961.

Freud, S. (1915). Instincts and their vicissitudes. *Standard Edition*, Vol. 14. London: Hogarth Press, 1957.

Freud, S. (1917). Mourning and melancholia. *Standard Edition*, Vol. 14. London: Hogarth Press, 1957.

Freud, S. (1923). The ego and the id. *Standard Edition*, Vol. 19. London: Hogarth Press, 1961.

Freud, S. (1926). Inhibitions, symptoms and anxiety. *Standard Edition*, Vol. 20. London: Hogarth Press.

Freud, S. (1930). Civilization and its discontents. *Standard Edition*, Vol. 21. London: Hogarth Press, 1961.

Freud, S. (1936). Civilization and its discontents. *Standard Edition*, Vol. 21. London: Hogarth Press, 1961.

Freud, S. (1938). An outline of psychoanalysis. *Standard Edition*, Vol. 23. London: Hogarth Press, 1961.

Gill, M. M. Metapsychology is not psychology. In M. Gill & P. Holzman (Eds.), *Psychology versus metapsychology. Psychological issues*, Monograph, 36. New York: International Universities Press, 1976.

Gill, M., & Hoffman, I. *Analysis of transference: Vol. I & II*. New York: International Universities Press, 1981.

Glover, E. Functional aspects of the mental apparatus. *International Journal of Psychoanalysis*, 1950, **31**, 125–131.

Goldberg, A. On the prognosis and treatment of narcissism. *Journal of the American Psychoanalytic Association*, 1974, **22**, 243–254.

Gouin-Decarie, T. G. *Intelligence and affectivity in early childhood*. New York: International Universities Press, 1965.

Green, A. The borderline concept. In P. Hartocollis (Ed.), *Borderline personality disorders*. New York: International Universities Press, 1977.

Greene, L. Idiosyncratic needs for fusion and differentiation in groups. In J. Masling (Ed.), *Empirical studies of psychoanalytical theories*, Vol. II. Hillsdale, N.J.: Erlbaum, 1982.

Guntrip, H. *Personality structure and human interaction*. New York: International Universities Press, 1961.

Guntrip, H. *Schizoid phenomena, object relations and the self*. New York: International Universities Press, 1969.

Guntrip, H. Psychoanalytic object relations theory: The Fairbairn-Guntrip approach. In S. Arieti (Ed.), *American handbook of psychiatry*, Vol. I. New York: Basic Books, 1974.

Guntrip, H. My experience of analysis with Fairbairn and Winnicott. *International Review of Psychoanalysis*, 1975, **2**, 145–146.

Hartley, D., & Strupp, H. The therapeutic alliance: Its relationship to outcome in brief psychotherapy. In J. Masling (Ed.), *Empirical studies of psychoanalytical theories*, Vol. I. Hillsdale, N.J.: Erlbaum, 1982.

Hartman, H. *Ego psychology and the problem adaptation*. New York: International Universities Press, 1958.

Hartmann, H., Kris, E., & Lowenstein, R. M. Notes on the theory of aggression. *The Psychoanalytic Study of the Child*, 1949, **4**, 9–36. New York: International Universities Press.

Hartmann, H., & Loewenstein, R. M. Notes on the superego. *The Psychoanalytic Study of the Child*, 1962, **17**, 42–81. New York: International Universities Press.

Hoffer, W. The mutual influences in the development of ego and id: Earliest stages. *The Psychoanalytic Study of the Child*, 1952, 7, 31–41. New York: International Universities Press.

Holt, R. A review of some of Freud's biological assumptions and their influence on his theories. In N. Greenfield & W. Lewis (Eds.), *Psychoanalysis and current biological thought*. Madison: University of Wisconsin Press, 1965.

Holt, R. On freedom, autonomy, and the redirection of psychoanalytic theory: A rejoinder. *International Journal of Psychiatry*, 1967, **6**, 524–536.

Holt, R. The past and future of ego psychology. *Psychoanalytic Quarterly*, 1975, **44**, 500–576.

Holt, R. Drive or wish? A reconsideration of the psychoanalytic theory of motivation. In M. Gill & P. Holzman (Eds.), *Psychology versus metapsychology*. *Psychological Issues*, Monograph 36. New York: International Universities Press, 1976.

Home, H. The concept of mind. *International Journal of Psychoanalysis*, 1966, **47**, 43–49.

Horner, A. *Object relations and the developing ego in therapy*. New York: Jason Aronson, 1980.

Jacobson, E. *The self and the object world*. New York: International Universities Press, 1964.

Jones, E. Preface. In W. R. D. Fairbairn (Ed.), *An object-relations theory of the personality*. New York: Basic Books, 1954.

Kernberg, O. Structural derivatives of object relationships. *International Journal of Psychoanalysis*, 1966, **47**, 236–253.

Kernberg, O. Early ego integration and object relations. *Annual of the New York Academy of Science*, 1972, **193**, 233–247.

Kernberg, O. *Borderline conditions and pathological narcissism*. New York: Jason Aronson, 1975.

Kernberg, O. *Object relations theory and clinical psychoanalysis*. New York: Jason Aronson, 1976.

Kernberg, O. Contrasting approaches to the treatment of borderline conditions. In J. Masterson (Ed.), *New perspectives in psychotherapy of the borderline adult*. New York: Brunner/Mazel, 1978.

Kernberg, O. *Internal world and external reality*. New York: Jason Aronson, 1980.

Kernberg, O. The theory of psychoanalytic psychotherapy. In S. Slipp (Ed.), *Curative factors in dynamic psychotherapy*. New York: McGraw-Hill, 1982. (b)

Klein, G. S. *Psychoanalytic theory*. New York: International Universities Press, 1976.

Klein, M. *The Writings of Melaine Klein*, Vol. III, London: Hogarth Press, 1975.

Kohut, H. *The analysis of the self*. New York: International Universities Press, 1971.

Kohut, H. *The restoration of the self*. New York: International Universities Press, 1977.

Kohut, H., & Wolff, E. The disorders of the self and their treatment: An outline. *International Journal of Psychoanalysis*, 1978, **59**, 413–425.

Kubie, L. The fallacious use of quantitative concepts in dynamic psychology. *Psychoanalytic Quarterly*, 1947, **16**, 507–518.

Kubie, L. The language tools of psychoanalysis: A search for better tools drawn from better models. *International Review of Psychoanalysis*, 1975, **2**, 11–24.

Lichtenberg, H. Factors in the development of the sense of the object. *Journal of the American Psychoanalytic Association*, 1979, **27**, 375–386.

Lidz, T., & Lidz, R. Therapeutic considerations arising from the intensive symbiotic needs of schizophrenic patients. In E. Brody & F. C. Redlich (Eds.), *Psychotherapy with schizophrenics*. New York: International Universities Press, 1952.

Loch, W. Some comments on the subject of psychoanalysis and truth. In J. Smith (Ed.), *Psychiatry and the humanities*, Vol. 2. New Haven: Yale University Press, 1977.

Loewald, H. Ego and reality. *International Journal of Psychoanalysis*, 1951, **32**, 10–18.

Loewald, H. On the therapeutic action of psychoanalysis. *International Journal of Psychoanalysis*, 1960, **41**, 16–33.

Loewald, H. Superego and time. *International Journal of Psychoanalysis*, 1962, **43**, 264–268.

Loewald, H. Psychoanalytic theory and the psychoanalytic process. In *The psychoanalytic study of the child*. New York: International Universities Press, 1970.

Loewald, H. On internalization. *International Journal of Psychoanalysis*, 1973, **54**, 9–17.

Loewald, H. Reflections on the psychoanalytic process

and its therapeutic potential. In *The psychoanalytic study of the child.* New Haven: Yale University Press, 1979.

Luborsky, L. Clinicians judgment of mental health: A proposed scale. *Archives of General Psychiatry,* 1962, 7, 407–417.

Mahler, M. *On human symbiosis and the vicissitudes of individuation.* New York: International Universities Press, 1968.

Mahler, M., Pine, F., & Bergman, A. *The psychological birth of the human infant.* New York: Basic Books, 1975.

Masling, J. (Ed.) *Empirical studies of psychoanalytical theories,* Vol. I. Hillsdale, N.J.: Erlbaum, 1982. (a)

Masling, J. Orality, psychopathology, and interpersonal relations. In J. Masling (Ed.), *Empirical studies on psychoanalytical theories,* Vol. II. Hillsdale, N.J.: Erlbaum, 1982. (b)

Mayman, M. Psychoanalytic theory in retrospect and prospect. *Bulletin of the Menninger Clinic,* 1976, 40, 199–210.

Meissner, W. Methodological critique of the action language in psychoanalysis. *Journal of the American Psychoanalytic Association,* 1979, 27, 79–105.

Meltzer, D. The Kleinian expansion of Freud's metapsychology. *International Journal of Psychoanalysis,* 1981, 62, 177–185.

Modell, A. Does metapsychology still exist? *International Journal of Psychoanalysis,* 1981, 62, 391–402.

Parens, H. A contribution of separation-individuation to the development of psychic structures. In J. B. McDevitt & C. F. Settlage (Eds.), *Separation-individuation: Essays in honor of Margaret S. Mahler.* New York: International Universities Press, 1971.

Parsons, T., & Bales, R. *Family socialization and interaction process.* Glencoe, Ill.: Free Press, 1955.

Peterfreund, E. *Information, symptoms, and psychoanalysis: An evolutionary biological approach to psychoanalytic theory.* Psychological Issues, Monograph 25/26. New York: International Universities Press, 1971.

Peterfreund, E. The need for a new general theoretical frame of reference for psychoanalysis. *Psychoanalytic Quarterly,* 1975, 44, 534–549.

Piaget, J. *The Construction of reality.* New York: Basic Books, 1954.

Pruyser, P. What splits in splitting? *Bulletin of the Menninger Clinic,* 1975, 39, 1–46.

Rapaport, D. *Organization and pathology of thought.* New York: Columbia University Press, 1940.

Rubinstein, B. Exploration and more description: A metascientific examination of certain aspects of the psychoanalytic theory of motivation. In R. Holt (Ed.), *Motives and thought: Psychoanalytic essays in honor of David Rapaport.* Psychological issues, Monograph 18/19. New York: International Universities Press, 1967.

Rubinstein, B. On the possibility of a strictly clinical psychoanalytic theory: An essay on the philosophy of psychoanalysis. In M. Gill & P. Holzman (Eds.), *Psychology versus metapsychology. Psychological issues,* Monograph 36. New York: International Universities Press, 1976.

Sackeim, H. Self deception, self esteem, and depression: The adaptive value of lying to oneself. In J. Masling (Ed.), *Empirical studies of psychoanalytic theories,* Vol. I. Hillsdale, N.J.: Erlbaum, 1982.

Sampson, H., & Weiss, J. Testing alternative psychoanalytic explanations of the therapeutic process. In J. Masling (Ed.), *Empirical studies of psychoanalytic theories,* Vol. II. Hillsdale, N.J: Erlbaum, 1982.

Sandler, J., & Joffe, W. Toward a basic psychoanalytic model. *International Journal of Psychoanalysis,* 1969, 50, 74–90.

Sandler, J., & Rosenblatt, B. The concept of the representational world. *Psychoanalytic Study of the Child.* New York: International Universities Press, 1962.

Thomas, R., Chess, S., & Birch, H. *Temperament and behavior disorders in children.* New York: New York University Press, 1968.

Topin, M. & Kohut, H. The disorders of the self: The psychopathology of the first years of life. In S. I. Greenspan & G. H. Pollock (Eds.), *The course of life: Psychoanalytic contributions toward understanding personality development,* Vol. 1: Infancy and early childhood. Washington, D.C.: NIMH, 1980.

Urist, J. The Rorschach test and the assessment of object relations. *Journal of Personality Assessment,* 1977, 41, 3–9.

Vygotsky, L. *Thought and language,* E. Hanfmann & G. Vakar (Trans.). Cambridge, Mass.: MIT Press, 1962.

Werner, H. Comparative psychology of mental development. New York: International Universities Press, 1948.

Winnicott, D. W. Primitive emotional development. *International Journal of Psychoanalysis,* 1945, 26, 137–143.

Winnicott, D. W. Transitional objects and transitional phenomena. *Collected papers: Through pediatrics to psychoanalysis.* New York: Basic Books, 1958.

Winnicott, D. W. The theory of the parent-infant relationship. *International Journal of Psychoanalysis,* 1960, 41, 585–595.

Winnicott, D. W. What do we mean by a normal child? *The child, the family, and the outside world.* London: Penguin Books, 1964.

Winnicott, D. W. The capacity to be alone. In *The maturational processes and the facilitating environment.* New York: International Universities Press, 1965. (b)

Winnicott, D. W. Ego integration in child development. *The maturational processes and the facilitating environment.* London: Hogarth Press, 1965. (c)

Winnicott, D. W. Growth and development in immaturity. *The family and individual development.* London: Tavistock, 1965. (d)

Winnicott, D. W. *The maturational processes and the facilitating environment.* London: Hogarth Press, 1965. (a)

Winnicott, D. W. *Playing and reality.* New York: Basic Books, 1971.

Winnicott, D. W. The use of an object and relating through identifications. *Playing and reality.* London: Penguin Books, 1980.

Wolff, P. H. Cognitive considerations for a psychoanalytic acquisition. In R. Holt (Eds.), *Motives and thought.* New York: International Universities Press, 1967.

7 LEARNING

Howard Rachlin
A. W. Logue

The study of learning has frequently played a role in clinical psychology and in understanding personality. As long ago as the 1920s, Pavlov reported that he could mimic human neuroses in his animal-learning laboratory by exposing his subjects, dogs, to increasingly difficult discriminations (Pavlov, 1927). The dogs became irritable and then began to show many symptoms characteristic of human neurotics. They barked, squealed, whined, and trembled, bit and tore at the apparatus, and lost the ability to make even easy, previously mastered, discriminations. This was one of the first attempts to model clinical phenomena in the learning laboratory. Another early example is Watson's (Watson & Rayner, 1920) experiments on learned fears in infants.

The revelance of laboratory-based learning theory to clinical psychology has rested on three assumptions. The first is that human behavior is at least to some extent learned. There have been no serious quarrels with this assumption. The second assumption is that experiments performed in laboratory settings can have relevance for real life. This assumption has been subject to much criticism, particularly by ethologists who frequently claim that an organism's natural behavior can be studied only in "natural" surroundings (see Johnston, 1981). The argument about this issue continues to rage with much bitter commentary on both sides. It is our belief (Logue, 1981b; Rachlin, 1981) that while an animal's normal activities can be discovered only in a particular ecological niche, the limits of these activities can be tested only in the laboratory. Laboratory experiments, unlike observations of learning in the field, allow the experimenter to control critical variables. For example, in the laboratory it is possible to deprive subjects of food or water to a predetermined level, to isolate them from extraneous noises or lights, and to have a full record of their previous environmental histories. Furthermore, in the laboratory the experimenter is much less likely to succumb to the illusion that he or she "intuitively understands" the subject (animal or person), and is much more likely to rely on the data.

The third assumption is similar to the second in that it also concerns the generality of laboratory experiments. Just as the applicability of the experimental study of learning necessitates the assumption that results obtained from laboratory ex-

*The preparation of this chapter was supported by a grant from the National Science Foundation.

periments are relevant for the real world, so it also often necessitates the assumption that results obtained from nonhuman subjects are relevant for humans. Again, there has been much criticism of this assumption (e.g., Seligman, 1970). Clearly, rats are very different from humans, and so it has been difficult for some psychologists to see any relevance of animal-learning experiments for human behavior. This issue will be discussed in the section of this chapter entitled "General Laws of Learning and Their Biological Limits"; but, for now, suffice it to say that the comparative study of learning has revealed many similarities between species (e.g., Gustavson, 1977).

With these three assumptions in mind, much of what occurs in learning laboratories is of potential relevance for clinical psychology. The remainder of this chapter presents some of the general issues and specific topics of current interest in the field of learning. The general issues are presented without regard for clinical application. In discussing some specific topics, however, we briefly indicate how they may be applied. Finally, some brief observations on the successes, failures, and prospects for clinical application of laboratory work are presented.

Recent Issues within Learning Theory

Molecular and Molar

A problem for any science concerns the level at which information should be examined and principles constructed. In learning theory, a molecular approach usually involves analyzing data and constructing principles at the level of individual responses, such as lever presses or key pecks, often determining the effects of reinforcement on the actual sequence of responses (e.g., Watson, 1970). A molar approach usually involves analyzing data and constructing in principles using units of data that are composed of many individual responses, such as the number of responses in an experimental session, or the number of times that an animal correctly negotiates a maze, or the proportion of an animal's responses on each of two response alternatives during a session (e.g., Herrnstein, 1970; Tolman, 1948).

The reason for concern with the molecular-versus-molar issue is that anyone who claims that organisms learn something at a molar level is promptly faced with a counterargument that some regular-

ity, the real "cause" of the regular behavior seen at the molar level, must exist at a more molecular level. But molar level learning may occur where there is no apparent regularity at a more molecular level (Baum, 1981).

Recent models at all points of the molecular-molar spectrum have contributed much to our understanding of learning. The issue is not which approach, molecular or molar, is the best one, but which best answers a particular question. It will always be possible to describe an organism's behavior in terms of smaller units up to the limits of our physical knowledge. The most truthful level of analysis is, by pragmatic definition, the most useful.

Classical and Instrumental

One of the oldest issues in learning theory is whether there are two kinds of learning or just one. Most of the prominent learning theorists of the 1940s, including Skinner (1938), believed that there are two kinds of learning: classical and instrumental. The first consists of the association of the formerly neutral stimulus (a conditioned stimulus) with a reflex (an unconditioned stimulus and a response); the second consists of the positive and negative laws of effect—the strengthening of a response (or operant) by its favorable consequences (positive reinforcement), and the weakening of a response by its unfavorable consequences (punishment).

While many theorists agree that both kinds of learning are possible, it has been argued that all classical conditioning is really instrumental conditioning (Zener, 1937), and that all instrumental conditioning is really classical conditioning (Moore, 1973). The groundwork of the former argument was actually laid by Pavlov (1927), who asserted that classical conditioning always worked so as to better suit the subject to its environment. Presumably, when classical conditioning is maladaptive, it is less stable.

But the main thrust of the argument that classical conditioning is instrumental is anti-Pavlovian: it comes from the frequent finding of a difference between conditioned and unconditioned responses. For example, in heart-rate conditioning, with electric shock as the unconditioned stimulus, the conditioned response, a decrease in heart rate, is actually the *opposite* of the unconditioned response—an increase (Black, 1979). It is usually the case that where the conditioned response differs from the unconditioned response, the former seems to be a form of preparation for the unconditioned stimulus. Thus, freezing in place (a common conditioned response with shock as the unconditioned response) seems to prepare the animal for shock.

The opposite argument holds that instrumental conditioning is a form of classical conditioning. This argument has gained strength with the finding of autoshaping—that pigeons readily learn key pecking as a conditioned response (Brown & Jenkins, 1968). Simple pairing of a lit key with food generates key pecking. Many other so-called instrumental responses are also susceptible to autoshaping (i.e., can be conditioned responses). Even the various forms of the supposedly arbitrary response of brushing against a pole, learned by cats in the famous experiments of Guthrie and Horton (1946), may well be conditioned responses: the unconditioned response being nuzzling against the leg of the experimenter once out of the puzzle box.

It is hoped that findings and arguments such as the above will eventually lead to a satisfactory unified theory of learning. Meanwhile, however, most researchers still distinguish between classical and instrumental procedures.

Reinforcement and Maximization

Within instrumental conditioning there is currently some controversy about the way that reinforcement acts. One group of theorists holds to the view of Thorndike (1965), Hull (1943), and Skinner (1938) that positive reinforcement automatically acts to strengthen any response that happened to precede it. This automatic action is perhaps epitomized by Skinner's concept of superstition. According to this view, a given environment will frequently provide random reinforcers to a given organism. Such reinforcers, if they are unsignaled, and because they arrive randomly, will strengthen a response and its opposing response in equal degrees, thus having little or no resultant effect (but see the later section on "Learned Helplessness" for research that contradicts this supposition). If, however, the reinforcers are signaled, either externally or internally (by coming at fixed intervals), they may adventitiously strengthen whatever behavior happens to occur just before their delivery—without strengthening its opposite. Each subsequent reinforcer delivery strengthens the behavior more—thus generating idiosyncratic, superstitious responses. Whatever

mechanism is responsible for strengthening the superstitious responses is also responsible for strengthening normal instrumentally conditioned responses, except in the latter case it is usually arranged in the environment (by the contingencies of reinforcement) that only a particular response may precede reinforcement.

Another approach to understanding the effects of instrumental conditioning (Rachlin & Burkhard, 1978) derives from the work of Premack (1965) on the relativity of reinforcers, the work of Herrnstein (1970) on choice, and the work of Staddon (1979) on allocation of time. Instrumental conditioning is seen as an allocation of time to various activities (the instrumental response, consumption of the reinforcer, other behavior) so as to maximize the overall value of the group of behaviors together. The response is seen as no more important than its context (which consists of other responses occurring before and after the target response). Learning is a reallocation of behavior. A change of contingencies is a change of constraints on behavior. For instance, imagine a hungry rat put in a Skinner box for an hour with a dish of food freely available, and a bar that can be pressed or not pressed at will. The rat might spend ten minutes eating, half a minute pressing the bar, and the other 49.5 minutes performing other activities (grooming, scratching, sleeping, etc.). Imagine that a ratio contingency is now imposed which demands ten presses of the lever for each five-second availability of the food dish (say it takes the rat five seconds to make the ten presses), so that now the rat must spend as much time pressing the bar as it does eating. How will the rat reallocate its time? That, according to a form of maximixation theory derived from economics (Rachlin, Kagel, & Battalio, 1980) depends on the degree to which the other activities (grooming, etc.) are substitutable for eating. To the extent that other available responses are substitutable for eating, eating will be reduced. To the extent that other responses are not substitutable for eating, eating will remain rigidly constant. Perhaps surprisingly, experiments with hungry rats show considerable substitutability of these "leisure" activities for food. Similar analyses have been made of the behavior of children playing with toys by adding or removing available toys and making availability of one toy contingent on playing with another. Again, allocation depends on the degree of substitutability of one behavior for another (Rachlin & Burkhard, 1978).

Maximization theory is currently in its early stages of development. It remains to be seen whether it will prove as durable or as fruitful as reinforcement theory.

General Laws of Learning and Their Biological Limits

Pavlov thought of himself as a neurophysiologist rather than as a psychologist, so from the beginning he saw learning in biological terms. It was not surprising to Pavlov that stomach secretions should follow food inserted in the mouth. The nervous system may well connect receptors in the mouth with glands that secrete digestive juices—what could be more natural? But when Pavlov discovered that what seemed to be completely arbitrary stimuli, such as bells and lights, would also generate secretions ("psychic" secretions), it was tempting to suppose (although Pavlov himself did not) that all stimuli could serve equally well as conditioned stimuli with a given unconditioned stimulus.

Skinner also began his career in a neurophysiology laboratory (with Crozier at Harvard), and initially used the Skinner box only as a way of indexing the eating behavior of rats. But, when he discovered the powerful effects of schedules of reinforcement on behavior, it was natural to suppose (although Skinner himself did not) that all reinforcers could serve equally well to strengthen a given response.

Subsequent research has shown that these natural suppositions are only partly true. Certain kinds of conditioned stimuli simply will not work (will not result in conditioning) with certain kinds of reflexes. Certain reinforcers will not work with certain responses. Nowhere is this affinity more clear than with taste-aversion learning, discussed later in detail. Briefly, when a visual or auditory stimulus is paired with sickness animals learn to avoid the stimulus with difficulty, but when a taste stimulus is paired with sickness, animals easily learn to avoid the taste. Thus, there are boundaries, determined by the biological characteristics of the organism, to the degree of arbitrariness with which a given pair of conditioned and unconditioned stimuli may be selected. Nevertheless, within these boundaries, there is still a degree of arbitrariness regarding conditioned and unconditioned stimuli, responses, and reinforcers. It may be that *tastes* must be paired with illness for conditioning to occur easily, but there is a wide range of such tastes.

Given the biological limits on learning, the question arises whether Pavlov, Skinner, and other learning theorists were correct in supposing that there are general laws of learning that transcend biological limits. Are there any such general laws?

Data from several other areas of learning have bolstered the emphasis that taste-aversion learning has placed on the biological origins of behavior. For example, Bolles (1970) has noted the predisposition of animals to make certain responses, and not others, in response to aversive stimuli. He calls these responses species-specific defense reactions. Another example of biological influence is the finding of autoshaping—that pigeons' key pecks are not arbitrary responses that experimenters happened to have chosen to reinforce, but reactions which can naturally be elicited by the presence of food (Gamzu & Schwartz, 1973). In fact, pigeons will even keep pecking when their pecking postpones food (Schwartz & Williams, 1972). Futher, key pecks consistently followed by food are topographically different from key pecks consistently followed by water, although such differences may never have been reinforced (Wolin, 1968). The key pecks followed by food look more like eating pecks, and the key pecks followed by water look more like drinking pecks.

Such results cast suspicion on generalizations from animal-learning experiments. The stimuli and responses studied in these experiments were apparently not arbitrary, and the laws of learning appear to be different for at least some of these predisposed responses. Some authors have gone so far as to say that the learning of each type of task in each species might be described by different laws (Rozin & Kalat, 1971).

Of course, as indicated earlier, learning theorists have not been totally unaware of species and task differences in learning. The following quote from Skinner (1959, pp. 374–375) demonstrates this point:

> Pigeon, rat, monkey, which is which? It doesn't matter. Of course, these three species have behavioral repertoires which are as different as their anatomies. But once you have allowed for the ways in which they act upon the environment, what remains of their behavior shows astonishingly similar properties.

Skinner, like many learning theorists (e.g., Thorndike, 1932), was well aware that the laws of learning are not exactly the same for every organism and every situation. But Skinner chose to investigate some of the myriad aspects of learning that do appear to be general across different species and tasks. Some examples of such general aspects of learning are: better learning the shorter the delay between the CS (or the response) and the reinforcer, stimulus generalization, the eventual disappearance of learning following the removal of reinforcement (extinction), and better learning with a more intense US (Logue, 1979).

There are good evolutionary reasons for general aspects of learning. Since every species has been shaped by evolution, and since certain selection pressures, such as the uniformity of rules of future prediction, are common to all organisms, species-general behaviors could and should result (Lockhard, 1971; Revusky, 1977; Rozin & Kalat, 1971). Further, phyletic closeness (Lockhard, 1971) or economy of the neural wiring of the organism (Rozin & Kalat, 1971) could also result in general laws of learning. Species and task-specific aspects of learning do not have a corner on natural selection. Every law has its limits. But the other side of this coin is that every law has its sphere. So, within biological limits, general laws of learning do exist and can be studied.

Major Topics in Learning

The Rescorla-Wagner Model of Classical Conditioning

There have been several noteworthy recent attempts to construct learning theories that are either distinctly molecular or distinctly molar. A molecular learning theory that has received much attention since its inception is the Rescorla-Wagner model of learning (Rescorla & Wagner, 1972).

The original object of this model was to account for Pavlovian conditioning with more than one conditioned stimulus. One reason for its success is that researchers have come to realize that it is impossible to present only one conditioned stimulus. For example, if a tone is presented as a conditioned stimulus, that tone must be heard by the subject against a background of ambient noise, ambient illumination, ambient smells, tastes, and so on. These stimuli constitute the background (or context) against which the putative conditioned stimulus is presented. As long as the background remains constant between conditioning trials, it can be considered a single stimulus. Thus, the

standard Pavlovian classical conditioning procedure can be viewed as an alternative between:

1. The background alone during the intertrial intervals (without the unconditioned stimulus); and
2. The background plus the conditioned stimulus during the trials (with the unconditioned stimulus).

Thus, the Rescorla-Wagner model is applicable to all classical conditioning procedures.

The theory itself (as originally formulated) contains two critical assumptions. First, the strength gained by the conditioned stimulus on a reinforced trial (a trial with the unconditioned stimulus) is proportional to the difference between the strength of conditioning prior to the trial and the asymptotic strength of conditioning. Unreinforced trials (extinction trials) are treated just like conditioning trials except that the asymptote is zero. This assumption implies the standard negatively accelerated learning and extinction curves. The second critical assumption of the theory is that the strength of conditioning of a compound stimulus (more than one conditioned stimulus) is the sum of the strengths of the individual components. Thus, on a reinforced trial with a compound stimulus, the two conditioned stimuli both contribute to the pretrial level of conditioning. This level determines the amount gained on a specific trial, given a particular unconditioned stimulus. Both conditioned stimuli also share (according to their relative salience) in the added conditioning from the trial itself.

An important consequence of the model is that: if a component conditioned stimuli which has already obtained high conditioning strength through previous reinforced trials with that stimulus alone is paired with a new stimulus that has no conditioning strength and the compound is reinforced, the reinforcement (the unconditioned stimulus) will have little effect; the strength of the compound will be incremented slightly, if at all. This occurs because the strength of the compound must be at least as high, as the strength of the conditioned component. In consequence, the new conditioned stimulus component, the one that had not previously been conditioned, can gain little or no conditioning strength. Thus, the Rescorla-Wagner model explains the phenomenon of "blocking." When the compound consists of background plus a single conditioned stimulus, the model implies that: if the unconditioned stimulus is first presented during the intertrial interval (with no specific conditioned stimulus), the conditioning thus imparted to the background will block furthur conditioning to any conditioned stimulus superimposed upon it. This is indeed the case.

The Rescorla-Wagner model has been challenged and modified considerably during the last ten years, but today it is the reference point for almost all theory and practice in classical conditioning. It accounts for an otherwise vast and confusing mass of experimental findings with a pair of simple, plausible assumptions. It applies to disruption of rats' lever pressing by shock, rabbits blinking their nictitating membranes, and pigeons pecking keys, as well as to dogs salivating. In other words, it is a general law of learning.

A model as general as this is likely to have implications for clinical practice. Let us briefly consider a fairly obvious one, where classical conditioning is deliberately applied as therapy. Suppose a therapist is trying to condition relaxation during previously stressful situations. The conditioned stimuli used in relaxation therapy are often a series of graded verbal statements of increasing threat. The unconditioned and conditioned responses are both relaxation. Consideration of the Rescorla-Wagner model brings our attention immediately to the background of this conditioning situation. What occurs in the therapist's office before and between conditioning sessions? If, as is certainly possible, the therapist's office (the background) itself becomes a conditioned stimulus for deep relaxation, stimuli superimposed upon this background (the graded series of statements) are unlikely to gain conditioning strength. The patient may well relax in the therapist's office during conditioning sessions but in everyday life, outside of the office, the conditioned stimuli will be presented away from the background, which has the greatest share of conditioning strength. It is then that the inherent weakness of these conditioned stimuli as elicitors of relaxation will be made evident. The therapist who wants to condition a given response in a therapeutic setting and intends that conditioning to carry over into everyday life must take care not to condition the response initially to the therapeutic setting itself. Care must be taken, in general, not to make the therapeutic setting the place where any kind of desirable behavior *first* appears. The very conditioning of such behavior would make transfer to everyday life more difficult; conditioning to the therapist's office as background would block conditioning to other stimuli superimposed on that background.

In the light of the Rescorla-Wagner model, the therapist may be better advised to try to transfer elements from those (perhaps few) everyday life situations where behavior is still normal into the therapeutic situation and from there, into those situations where behavior is most dysfunctional.

The Matching Law

The matching law (Herrnstein, 1961) states that animals distribute their responses in proportion to the distribution of reinforcers. For instance, if a pigeon receives twice as much food for pecking one key as another, it will peck that key twice as often. Thus,

$$\frac{B_1}{B_2} = \frac{R_1}{R_2} \tag{1}$$

(Baum & Rachlin, 1969) where B_1 and B_2 correspond to the number of responses made on alternative 1 and 2, respectively, and R_1 and R_2 correspond to the number of reinforcers received for responses on alternatives 1 and 2, respectively, Equation 1 has been confirmed many times with many species (de Villiers, 1977) including humans (Bradshaw, Ruddle, & Szabadi, 1981).

The matching law is a rule of allocation. As such, it has been derived from maximization theory (Rachlin et al., 1980). There is some debate now whether the fundamental principle by which animals allocate time and effort to various activities is maximization of utility, or whether the fundamental principle is matching. It may be that animals have inherited a tendency to match because matching conforms so frequently to maximization and that, in those few instances where matching and maximizing behaviors diverge, animals match. Much research is now being directed toward this question. However the issue is decided, the important fact remains that matching is a widely pervasive empirical finding.

As with the Rescorla-Wagner model, the matching law derives its wide applicability from its consideration of background (or context) of reinforcement. The scope of the matching law was demonstrated by Herrnstein (1970), who extended what was previously a description of choice behavior to a general principle of all instrumental behaviors. If B_1 of Equation 1 is any particular response, then B_2 may be considered the background of that response—all other reinforcement obtained in the experimental situation. That is, the strength of a response is directly proportional to reinforcement dependent on that response and inversely proportional to the overall level of reinforcement.

This principle implies that there are many ways to vary the frequency of (or the time spent at) any behavior: a response may be directly increased in frequency by increasing reinforcement of that response. This is well-known, but a response may also be increased in frequency indirectly, by decreasing reinforcement for (or punishing) *another* response, or by decreasing the background reinforcement. Symmetrically, a response may be directly decreased in frequency by decreasing the reinforcement for (or punishing) that response. But a response may also be indirectly decreased in frequency by increasing the reinforcement for another response or increasing the background reinforcement.

An important caveat to the above comes from maximization theory, which states that the indirect methods work only to the extent that the indirect reinforcer is *substitutable* for the direct reinforcer. If the indirect and direct reinforcers are *not* mutually substitutable (food and water, for example), the *exact opposite* results will occur. Increasing water reinforcement for a response upon which water delivery depends will tend to *increase* the rate of any responses upon which food delivery depends.

The importance of these indirect methods for clinical practice is obvious. Often direct methods of dealing with behavior are impossible either because the behavior is difficult to observe, or infrequent, or is deliberately hidden by the patient. The therapist, nevertheless, may alter the frequency of such behaviors by reinforcing or punishing other behaviors, or by working to increase or decrease the overall level of other reinforcers substitutable for the reinforcers of the response in question.

Self-Control

The matching law, as stated above, describes choice in a situation in which responses produce reinforcers at two separate rates. An expanded form of the matching law is as follows (Rachlin, 1974):

$$\frac{B_1}{B_2} = \frac{R_1 \, A_1 \, D_2}{R_2 \, A_2 \, D_1} \qquad (2)$$

B_1, B_2, R_1, and R_2 are defined as they were above, A_1 and A_2 correspond to the size, or the amount, of reinforcers obtained for responses on alternatives 1 and 2, respectively, and D_1 and D_2 to the

delay between a response and receipt of a reinforcer on alternatives 1 and 2, respectively. Equation 2 states that behavior is directly proportional to the frequency and amount of reinforcement, and inversely proportional to its delay. In situations in which R_1 is equal to R_2, Equation 2 reduces to:

$$\frac{B_1}{B_2} = \frac{A_1 \, D_2}{A_2 \, D_1} \qquad (3)$$

Equation 3 can be used to model self-control. Self-control as defined here is really just one kind of choice, the choice of a larger, more delayed reinforcer over a smaller, less delayed reinforcer. The opposite of self-control, choosing the smaller, less delayed reinforcer, is impulsiveness.

Equation 3 has been quite successful at describing pigeons' choices in self-control experiments; that is, experiments in which a choice must be made between a smaller, less delayed reinforcer, and a larger, more delayed reinforcer (e.g., Green et al., 1981). Suppose, in Equation 3, that A_1 is larger than A_2, but also that D_1 is greater than D_2. Thus, A_1 and D_1 constitute the larger, more delayed reinforcer. If B_1 is greater than B_2, the animal is defined as showing self-control. Otherwise, the animal is showing impulsiveness.

B_1 amd B_2 are entirely determined by the physical values of A_1, A_2, D_1, and D_2. Therefore, according to Equation 3, given two reinforcers of specific sizes and delays, all subjects should make the same choice between these two reinforcers. Nevertheless, we know that individuals within a species and across different species show varying amounts of self-control in similar situations. Equation 3 clearly needs modification in order to express degrees of difference in self-control.

As self-control develops within or across species or within or across individuals, animals come to choose more in accordance with amounts (A_1 and A_2), and less in accordance with delays (D_1 and D_2). Suggested modifications of Equation 3 provide new parameters in the equation, the variation of which would cause delays to be more or less heavily weighted. One suggested modification of Equation 3 (Logue, 1981a; Logue, Rodriquez, Pena, & Mauno, in press) is:

$$\frac{B_1}{B_2} = \left(\frac{A_1}{A_2}\right) \cdot \left(\frac{D_2}{D_1}\right)^{s_D} \qquad (4)$$

Individual differences in self-control may be expressed as individual differences in the exponent of Equation 4. From Equation 4, it can be seen that if the delay exponent, s_D, is very small (i.e., approaching zero), the ratio $(D_2/D_1)^{s_D}$ will approach 1.0, and behavior will mostly be a function of the amounts of the reinforcers. In such cases the subject would be more likely to choose the larger reinforcer irrespective of the reinforcer delays, thus showing more self-control. In the other direction, if s_D were very large reinforcer delays would affect behavior more strongly than reinforcer amounts, thus reducing self-control. Animals' experiences, and perhaps their genes, could affect the size of s_D.

An example of individual differences in self-control as a result of past conditioning history was demonstrated by Logue and Mazur (Logue & Mazur, 1981; Mazur & Logue, 1978). These researchers trained some pigeons to show increased self-control by first giving them a choice between equally delayed large and small reinforcers, and then slowly fading that choice to one between a delayed large reinforcer and an immediate small reinforcer. The experimental pigeons exposed to this procedure continued to choose the large delayed reinforcer significantly more often than control subjects that had not been exposed to this fading procedure (Mazur & Logue, 1978). Research is currently under way to discover whether such learning generalizes to other situations. Logue and Mazur (1981) showed further that colored lights used to illuminate the experimental chamber during reinforcer delays were crucial to the experimental subjects' maintenance of self-control, these lights possibly functioning as conditioned reinforcers. Finally, they showed that the effects of the fading procedure were stable over time.

The implication of this finding for clinical practice is its suggestion that, within biological limits, self-control may be learned in a specific setting. Mischel (1966) has shown that self-control in humans may differ considerably across age, sex, occupation, and wealth. It is still a question whether there exist impulsive personalities. The current research indicates that, to the extent that personality and environment can be separated, we may have more success in looking for "impulsive environments."

The model represented by Equation 4 may, thus, be one way in which individual differences in self-control can be measured and described. At least at the qualitative level, this model does appear to be an improvement over Equation 3, and it is consistent with other research on choice (e.g., Baum, 1974; Green & Snyderman, 1980; Wear-den, 1980). Future research on self-control will be directed at testing the predictions and implications of this model, while concurrently improving methods for training self-control.

Learned Helplessness

Some recent approaches to learning are based on the supposition that organisms can learn correlations between their responses and the occurrences or nonoccurrences of reinforcers; no close contiguity between the responses and reinforcers need occur. One implication is that if the data are reexamined at the level of individual responses and reinforcers, little regularity will be found. The only way that such learning can be observed is by looking at large groups of responses at once: a molar approach.

One recent example of the theories falling within this group is Seligman's (1975) learned helplessness model. The data that initially led Seligman to this model consisted of observations of dogs' behavior following inescapable shock (Overmier & Seligman, 1967; Seligman & Maier, 1967). Dogs strapped in a hammock were given shock regardless of their behavior. Later, it proved extremely difficult to train the dogs to jump to the other side of a shuttle box in order to avoid shock. Seligman and his colleagues concluded that the dogs had learned that they could not avoid shock; they had learned "helplessness." Subsequent experiments were designed (more or less successfully) to show that the results had not been caused by the dogs learning to tense in a certain way to ameliorate shock while in the hammock, or other spurious factors (Seligman, 1975).

Besides describing in a general way how animals can learn that their behavior has no effect on aversive events in their environment, Seligman's learned helplessness theory has been specifically applied to cases of human reactive depression (see Seligman, 1975, for a general discussion on this subject). Seligman and his colleagues have postulated that people who cannot control the aversive events in their lives become depressed. In fact, Seligman believes that the symptoms of depression are themselves the symptoms of learned helplessness. He has even suggested a common biochemical basis for the two phenomena, and attempted to distinguish between chronic and acute depressions (Abramson, Seligman, & Teasdale, 1978; Seligman, 1975).

Several similar approaches to learning, but concerning positive rather than aversive stimuli, have also recently been proposed. One has been termed "learned laziness" (Engberg et al., 1973). Engberg et al. showed that pigeons periodically given food regardless of their behavior learned to be lazy; they learned that their behavior was not connected to food delivery. When pigeons are exposed to the Engberg et al. procedure, it is subsequently more difficult to train them to peck for food.

Mackintosh (1973, 1974) has proposed a general term that encompasses the Seligman and Engberg et al. findings: learned irrelevance. According to Mackintosh, organisms can learn that their responses are uncorrelated with environmental events in general. Mackintosh's primary purpose in identifying this type of learning was to challenge the Rescorla-Wagner model (Rescorla & Wagner, 1972), which, in its original form, could not account for learned irrelevance. Mackintosh's concept, however, has proved to have much broader implications because it provides a formal description of a certain type of learning by organisms at the molar level.

Taste-Aversion Learning

Taste-aversion learning, also known as food-aversion learning, occurs when an organism eats a food, becomes ill (usually with a gastrointestional illness), and subsequently develops an aversion to the food. The terminology of classical conditioning is typically employed to describe taste-aversion learning; whatever causes the illness is called the unconditioned stimulus, and the particular aspect or aspects of the food that become aversive (e.g., the food's taste or smell) is called the conditioned stimulus.

Several aspects of taste-aversion learning appear unusual. First, taste aversions can be learned with very long delays: up to 24 hours between the conditioned and the unconditioned stimulus (Etscorn & Stephens, 1973). This seemed at odds with traditional studies of learning, which have claimed to obtain learning only with delays of up to a few seconds (Kimble, 1961). Attempts to explain taste-aversion learning data by postulating food aftertastes or taste restimulation through vomiting proved futile (Revusky & Garcia, 1970). It has been noted that long-delay aversion learning appeared quite adaptive given that it may take some time before an ingested poison causes illness (e.g., Rozin & Kalat, 1971).

Second, rats, the most commonly used subjects in taste-aversion experiments, appear to form aversions to the taste of food more easily that they form aversions to its visual appearance: hence the name "taste-aversion learning" (Garcia et al., 1968). As previously noted, this characteristic also seemed discordant with traditional views of learning which seemed to assume that any conditioned stimulus should be equally associable with any unconditioned stimulus (Thorndike, 1965).

Third, there appear to be species differences in the predispositions of various types of stimuli to become associated with illness. For example, while rats tended to associate tastes with illness, quail appeared more easily to associate the visual stimuli with illness (Wilcoxon, Dragoin, & Kral, 1971). One explanation of this difference between rats and quail might be that the quail's visual system is far superior to that of rats. But, guinea pigs learn both taste and visual aversions well, although their visual system is no better developed than that of rats (Braveman, 1974, 1975). A more satisfactory explanation is that the manner in which the members of a species hunt for food predicts what stimuli will most easily associate with illness for that species; both quail and guinea pigs search for their food in the daytime using their visual systems, while rats tend to search for food at night using gustation and olfaction (Braveman, 1974, 1975).

Thus, all of the peculiar characteristics of taste-aversion learning seem well suited to help organisms deal with poisons, and particularly poisons in their own ecological niche. Clearly, if feeding were to be understood and properly investigated, each species' own evolutionary history would have to be taken into account (Rozin & Kalat, 1971).

As this issue was examined over a number of years, however, it seemed that those who had advocated taste-aversion learning as something truly unique were too hasty. While there are differences between taste-aversion learning and more traditional laboratory learning tasks, these differences appear to be differences of degree, not of kind (Logue, 1979). For example, it *is* possible to observe learning with more than a few seconds delay between the conditioned and the unconditioned stimulus in traditional learning procedures (Lett, 1977). However no paradigm, has equalled the 24-hour CS-US delays found with taste-aversion learning. As additional examples, very recent research has suggested that taste does play a role in the learning of taste aversions for every species (Gustavson, 1977; Lett, 1980), and that humans learn taste aversions in much the same ways that other animals do (Logue, Ophir, & Strauss, 1981).

Cognition and Learning

Human and animal studies of cognition have been oriented around the notion of representation and representational systems. That is, some aspect of the environment is said to be represented in coded form in the mind (or, in less dualistic conceptions, the nervous system) of the organism. Subsequent behavior is then said to be a function not of the environment directly but of the encoded representation or system of representations.

Many of the early psychology experiments in the United States were attempts to investigate the "mental life" of animals, so as to complement ongoing investigations of the mental life of humans. The first study of rats in mazes (Small, 1901) was such an attempt. Small made observations of the "cognitions" as well as the overt behavior of his subjects. The behaviorist movement (Watson, 1913) grew out of the fact that while overt behavior of rats in mazes was clearly observable and verifiable from one day, one experimenter, and one laboratory to the next, the cognitions of the rats did not seem to be thus observable or verifiable. Behaviorists such as Watson (and later, Hull, 1943) assumed that complex behavior of rats in mazes (and, by extension, behavior of humans in everyday life) could be reduced to a series of observable stimulus-response connections. However, Tolman (1948), with a series of ingenious studies of the behavior of rats in mazes, showed that a rat's behavior could be so complex (while, at the same time, systematic) that immediate observable stimulus-response connections could not reasonably account for that behavior. Tolman suggested that the rat learned a representation of the maze, which he called a mental map or "cognitive map" to which the rat referred while traversing the maze. Tolman felt that he could avoid the problems of nonobservability and nonverifiability by rigidly defining the concept "mental map" in behavioral terms — not as immediate behavior, but as long-term behavior that takes into account the spatial and temporal context of a given experimental trial. The focus on immediate behavior in its context is a molar approach. Tolman (1932) thus referred to himself as a molar behaviorist.

Hull and his followers reacted to Tolman's experiments and arguments by postulating another sort of representation: a representation of the stimulus-response connection itself in the nervous system of the animal (Hull, 1952). They called this representation a "fractional anticipatory goal response" ($r_g - s_g$). The argument between Hullians

and Tolmanians was, thus, not one of cognitive psychology versus behavioral psychology: both camps agreed on the necessity for discussing representation, and, therefore, both were cognitive psychologists. The argument was whether those representations were to be more molecular ($r_g - s_g$'s) or more molar (cognitive maps). It was Skinner ("Are Theories of Learning Necessary," 1950) who rejected the notion of internal representations entirely, on the grounds that representations not defined in behavioral terms suffered from nonobservability and nonverifiability. But once a representation was defined in behavioral terms, the behavior, not the representation, must be the proper object of study.

Recent theory and practice on the relation between cognition and learning has increased and has taken several intertwining paths, all relying on the notion of internal representations of aspects of the external environment. We are unable to explore any of these paths in detail here, or even to label them all. Instead, we will briefly describe some current work with animals under the headings of "response sequences," "matching to sample," and "complex discriminations."

RESPONSE SEQUENCES

In a series of experiments by Olton and his colleagues (e.g., Olton & Samuelson, 1976), rats were placed in a maze containing a central chamber and a number of arms (usually eight) radiating outward from the central chamber. At the outer ends of the arms were goal boxes, some of which contained food. Rats were then trained to choose arms in a specific order, say arms 1, 3, and 7 in three successive trials. After learning had proceeded to criterion, a transfer test was performed; for example, by rotating the arms relative to the central area. Rats in this experiment use cues external to the maze (visually open to the experimental room), and usually enter the rotated arms so as to arrive at the same series of spatial locations as before. Further, they seem able to keep track of which spatial locations they visit (and remove food from), because they tend not to return to a spatial location once it has been emptied of food even though their sequence of responses (and, presumably, stimulus-response connections) has been interrupted. In these experiments, the rats are said to form a cognitive map of the maze and to refer to this map when making choices among arms.

Another series of experiments with pigeons shows that they can learn to peck a series of differently colored keys (say, red-green-blue-yellow) in a specific order regardless of the spatial location of the keys. A pigeon will continue to peck the keys in the specified order even when the sequence is interrupted by removing one of the intermediate colors (Straub et al., 1979). Here, the pigeon's representation cannot be spatial, but is said to be more abstract.

The general nature of these experiments involves transfer tests of various kinds to determine what is learned and, usually, to show that what is learned cannot be "mere" stimulus-response connections. These experiments follow in the tradition of Tolman and his students. For instance, Macfarlane (1930) taught rats to run through a maze for food and then flooded the maze, and found that the rats could now swim correctly through the maze, showing that they must have learned something other than a series of chained movements; they learned something *general* about the maze.

MATCHING-TO-SAMPLE

In a simple matching-to-sample experiment with pigeons, a "stimulus sample" is presented by lighting the response key with a particular color. When the pigeon pecks the key the light is extinguished and two other keys are lit, one with the same color as the sample, the other with a different color. If the pigeon pecks the same colored key, it gets a brief food delivery. If the pigeon pecks the different colored key, no food is delivered. Variations on this procedure involve inserting a delay between the offset of the sample and the onset of the comparison stimuli, or changing the relation of the correct comparison stimulus to the sample (by making the nonmatching color correct, by varying the number of comparison stimuli, or by specifying some specific relationship between the sample and the correct-comparison such as, "If the sample is red, the correct comparison is blue; if the sample is blue, the correct comparison is yellow," etc.). In a still more complex version of matching-to-sample (e.g., Maki & Hegvik, 1980), the presentation of the comparison stimuli is delayed from the offset of the sample but a brief signal is given immediately after the sample. If the signal has one value (a "remember" signal), the comparison stimuli are presented as scheduled. But if the signal has another value (a "forget" signal), the comparison stimuli are not presented. When, contrary to usual procedure, the "forget" signal is followed by the comparison stimuli, the pigeons seem actually to

have forgotten the sample stimulus — their performance is poor.

Here the representation is said to be the rule that regulates reinforcement: "Peck blue if sample was red. Peck yellow if sample was blue. Forget sample if "forget" stimulus is presented," and so on. Whether the postulation of such representations has any meaning beyond the observed behavior is a moot point.

COMPLEX DISCRIMINATIONS

A recent series of experiments by Herrnstein and his colleagues (described in Herrnstein, Loveland, & Cable, 1976) takes the following form. A "library" of slides is formed. Half, called positive slides, contain a picture of an object or a substance (say "a person" or "water") in many different actual forms; the second half, called negative slides, do not contain a picture of the object or substance. The slides are projected in random order and the subject (a pigeon) is rewarded by a food delivery for pecking at the positive slides and is not rewarded for pecking at the negative slides. A *given pigeon never sees the same slide twice*. As far as has been determined, no discrimination can be formed on the basis of lightness, color, texture, or any feature of the slide other than the concept (for example, "person" or "water") itself. Pigeons quickly learn to discriminate between positive and negative slides, pecking the positive slides rapidly and the negative slides slowly. In other words, the pigeons learn the concept. In this case, it is clear that although the concept can be represented by an internal rule such as "Peck slides containing water," the postulation of the rule is not useful in understanding what the pigeons are doing. The question that still remains to be answered is: how do the pigeons learn to discriminate between the two groups of slides?

These three areas of research, again, represent only a sample of the work currently being done in animal cognitive psychology, and that sample is only a fraction of the work in cognitive psychology in general. The resemblance between this work and the clinical practice of cognitive behavior therapy, like the relation among the various areas of cognitive psychology themselves, rests on their common notions of representation and representational systems. In the case of cognitive behavior therapy, the representations postulated are sometimes said to consist of rules for behavior such as, "Everyone must like me for everything I do," and sometimes to consist of sentences or phrases people actually say to themselves. To the extent that these rules are not identifiable with sets of overt behaviors, the problems of observability and verifiability that originally caused the behaviorist revolt still remain. In animal and human experiments, no adequate method has been found to change representations without changing the overt behavior that initially defines those representations. This is not to say that representations of external events do not exist in the nervous system (or the mind), or that people do not talk to themselves; such events may well play a central role in overt behavior. It nevertheless seems to us an illusion that identification and modification of representations will provide a short-cut to identification of reinforcers in the environment and modification of overt dysfunctional behavior.

Future Directions

There are several directions in which we believe learning theory will move in the near future. First, controversial issues that are of recent concern, such as the biological boundaries of learning and the cognitive versus behavioral approaches to learning, will probably becomes less clear-cut. There will be fewer adherents of extreme positions on these issues. Historically, progress in science has been characterized by a group of scientists adopting an extreme position precipitating a theoretical crisis. The crisis is eventually resolved as most scientists adopt a more moderate position, one that is somewhat different from the original, precrisis position (Kuhn, 1962). Psychologists who felt that individual laws of learning would be necessary for every species and every task, and those who felt that cognitive psychology would completely revolutionize animal learning, are examples of scientists whose extreme opinions precipitate theoretical crises and change, but who are probably not representative of future opinions.

A present trend in learning that will probably continue is the development of complex, mathematical models. As experimental techniques become more precise, as psychologists become more sophisticated in mathematics and continue to model psychology or other natural sciences, these models will proliferate. Whether they will ultimately prove a great use to learning theorists is not clear. Hull's (1943) famous elaborate mathematico-deductive learning theory grew so complex that it became unwieldly and untestable, and ultimately died a quiet death. There is always a dan-

ger that this will happen to present and future mathematical models of learning in psychology. Nevertheless, the success of some of the present models bodes well for mathematical models in the future.

Until now, learning theorists have not paid much attention to individual differences. An example of how individual differences could be dealt with was already given with respect to self-control. In the future, there will probably be a greater number of similar attempts in other areas. Finally, the future will undoubtedly see increased application to humans of learning theory obtained from work with animals. Most researchers are concerned about the applications of their work. As the study of learning gains depth, the number of clinical applications of learning studies should increase. For example, since the properties of taste-aversion learning have been worked out in great detail in rats (see Logue, 1979 for a review), and since further studies have shown that humans learn taste aversions much as rats do (e.g., Bernstein, 1978; Garb & Stunkard, 1974; Logue, Ophir, & Strauss, 1981), it should now be possible to take advantage of that knowledge and improve experimental manipulations resulting in strong taste aversions in humans. These developments may then be applied to treatments of alcoholism and other clinical conditions involving excessive cravings or avoidance of specific foods (Logue, Logue, & Strauss, in press).

Conclusions

Studies performed by learning theorists as early as 1920 (e.g., Watson and Rayner's [1920] work on conditioning fears in Little Albert) still have impact for present-day work on human psychological problems (see Harris, 1979). Such impact will undoubtedly continue, allowing clinical psychologists and personality theorists to gain a better understanding of their own areas. However, this will only happen if the more applied researchers and clinicians understand the work being done by learning theorists. In the past, there has been poor communication between the two groups. For example, some therapists (see Wiens et al., 1976) have attempted to treat alcoholism using a taste-aversion paradigm by first making the patients ill, waiting until the patients were actually vomiting, and then giving the patients an alcoholic beverage to drink. As anyone familiar with research on learning could have predicted, this procedure was not very effective. Presenting the unconditioned stimulus prior to the conditioned stimulus, known as backward conditioning, is much less effective than forward conditioning: presenting the conditioned stimulus first (Mackintosh, 1974).

In other cases, perhaps too enthusiastic and too crude application of results obtained in the laboratory has made for poor clinical practice. The use of punishment without proper attention to its side-effects is one example. The use of tokens without proper attention to their context is another (Levine & Fasnacht, 1974). Perhaps most surprising to the learning theorist is the expectation among some clinicians that reinforcement and punishment procedures that have only a temporary effect in the laboratory — a "performance" rather than a "learning" effect — will have a more permanent effect in therapy. Thus, patients are "cured" in the clinic and returned to environments where the contingencies of reinforcement and punishment that originally generated dysfunctional behavior are reimposed. When, as laboratory results predict, the dysfunctional behavior returns, the therapeutic procedures are said to be faulty. But, such procedures are demonstrably effective. They do not need to be replaced by "deeper" methods, cognitive or psychoanalytic. Rather, they need to be modified along lines suggested above in order to take context and background into account — to shift control from the clinic to the everyday environment.

What are such techniques? We have suggested a few possibilities here but we do not believe that it is possible to take a laboratory procedure and apply it straightforwardly to the clinic. No applied science can take the developments of a laboratory science and simply "use" them. Physicists learned much more about physics from steam engines than engineers learned about steam engines from physics. Theory, in this respect, is very limited. It can provide a common language and can relate one applied procedure to another, apparently dissimilar, one. But it cannot prescribe. The theorist has more to learn from the clinician than vice versa. For this reason, we deplore the current tendency toward compartmentalization in psychology.

References

Abramson, L. Y., Seligman, M. E. P., & Teasdale, J. D. Learned helplessness in humans: Critique and reformulation. *Journal of Abnormal Psychology*, 1978, 87, 29–74.

Baum, W. M. On two types of deviation from matching law: Bias and undermatching. *Journal of the Experimental Analysis of Behavior*, 1974, 22, 231–242.

Baum, W. M. Optimization and the matching law as accounts of instrumental behavior. *Journal of the Experimental Analysis of Behavior*, 1981, 36, 387–403.

Baum, W. M., & Rachlin, H. C. Choice as time allocation. *Journal of the Experimental Analysis of Behavior*, 1969, 12, 861–874.

Bernstein, I. L. Learned taste aversions in children receiving chemotherapy. *Science*, 1978, 200, 1,302–1,303.

Black, A. H. Autonomic aversive conditioning in infrahuman subjects. In F. R. Brush (Ed.), *Aversive conditioning and learning*. New York: Academic Press, 1979.

Bolles, R. C. Species-specific defense reactions and avoidance learning. *Psychological Review*, 1970, 77, 32–48.

Bradshaw, C. M., Ruddle, H. V., & Szabadi, E. Studies of concurrent performance in humans. In C. M. Bradshaw, E. Szabadi, & C. F. Lowe (Eds.), *Quantification of steady-state operant behaviour*. Amsterdam: Elsevier/North-Holland Biomedical Press, 1981.

Braveman, N. S. Poison-based avoidance learning with flavored or colored water in guinea pigs. *Learning and Motivation*, 1974, 5, 182–194.

Braveman, N. S. Relative salience of gustatory and visual cues in the formation of poison-based food aversions by guinea pigs (*Cavia porcellus*). *Behavioral Biology*, 1975, 14, 189–199.

Brown, P. L., & Jenkins, H. M. Auto-shaping of the pigeon's key-peck. *Journal of the Experimental Analysis of Behavior*, 1968, 11, 1–8.

de Villiers, P. Choice in concurrent schedules and a quantitative formulation of the law of effect. In W. K. Honig & J. E. R. Staddon (Eds.), *Handbook of operant behavior*. Englewood Cliffs, N.J.: Prentice-Hall, 1977.

Engberg, L. A., Hansen, G., Welker, R. L., & Thomas, D. R. Acquisition of key-pecking via autoshaping as a function of prior experience: "Learned laziness"? *Science*, 1972, 178, 1,002–1,004.

Etscorn, F., & Stephens, R. Establishment of conditioned taste aversions with 24-hour CS-US interval. *Physiological Psychology*, 1973, 1, 251–253.

Gamzu, E., & Schwartz, B. The maintenance of key pecking by stimulus-contingent and response-independent food presentation. *Journal of the Experimental Analysis of Behavior*, 1973, 19, 65–73.

Garb, J. L., & Stunkard, A. J. Taste aversions in man. *American Journal of Psychiatry*, 1974, 131, 1,204–1,207.

Garcia, J., McGowan, B. K., Ervin, F. R., & Koelling, R. A. Cues: Their relative effectiveness as a function of the reinforcer. *Science*, 1968, 160, 794–795.

Green, L., Fisher, E. B., Perlow, S., & Sherman, L. Preference reversal and self control: Choice as a function of reward amount and delay. *Behaviour Analysis Letters*, 1981, 1, 43–51.

Green, L., & Snyderman, M. Choice between rewards differing in amount and delay: Toward a choice model of self control. *Journal of the Experimental Analysis of Behavior*, 1980, 34, 135–147.

Gustavson, C. R. Comparative and field aspects of learned food aversions. In L. M. Barker, M. R. Best,

& M. Domjan (Eds.), *Learning mechanisms in food selection*. Waco Texas: Baylor University Press, 1977.

Guthrie, E. R., & Horton, G. P. *Cats in a puzzle box*. New York: Dahl, Rinehart, & Winston, 1946.

Harris, B. Whatever happened to little Albert? *American Psychologist*, 1979, **34**, 151–160.

Herrnstein, R. J. Relative and absolute strength of response as a function of frequency of reinforcement. *Journal of the Experimental Analysis of Behavior*, 1961, **4**, 267–272.

Herrnstein, R. J. On the law of effect. *Journal of the Experimental Analysis of Behavior*, 1970, **13**, 243–266.

Herrnstein, R. J., Loveland, D. H., & Cable, C. Natural concepts in pigeons. *Journal of Experimental Psychology: Animal Behavior Processes*, 1976, **2**, 285–311.

Hull, C. L. *Principles of behavior*. New York: Appleton-Century, 1943.

Hull, C. L. *A behavior system*. New Haven: Yale University Press, 1952.

Johnston, T. D. Contrasting approaches to a theory of learning. *The Behavioral and Brain Sciences*, 1981, **4**, 125–173.

Kimble, G. A. *Hilgard and Marquis' conditioning and learning*. New York: Appleton-Century-Crofts, 1961.

Kuhn, T. S. *The structure of scientific revolutions*. Chicago: University of Chicago Press, 1962.

Lett, B. T. Long delay learning in the T-maze: Effect of reward given in the home cage. *Bulletin of the Psychonomic Society*, 1977, **10**, 211–214.

Lett, B. T. Taste potentiates color-sickness associations in pigeons and quail. *Animal Learning and Behavior*, 1980, **8**, 193–198.

Levine, F. M., & Fasnacht, G. Token rewards may lead to token learning. *American Psychologist*, 1974, **29**, 817–820.

Lockard, R. B. Reflections on the fall of comparative psychology: Is there a message for us all? *American Psychologist*, 1971, **26**, 168–179.

Logue, A. W. Taste aversion and the generality of the laws of learning. *Psychological Bulletin*, 1979, **86**, 276–296.

Logue, A. W. Effects of experience on self-control. Paper presented at the meeting of the Psychonomic Society, Philadelphia, November 1981. (a)

Logue, A. W. Species differences and principles of learning: Informed generality. *The Behavioral and Brain Sciences*, 1981, **4**, 150–151. (b)

Logue, A. W., Logue, K. R., & Strauss, K. E. The acquisition of taste aversions in humans with eating and drinking disorders. *Behavior Research and Therapy*, in press.

Logue, A. W., & Mazur, J. E. Maintenance of self-control acquired through a fading procedure: Follow-up on Mazur and Logue (1978). *Behaviour Analysis Letters*, 1981, **1**, 131–137.

Logue, A. W., Ophir, I., & Strauss, K. E. The acquisition on taste aversions in humans. *Behaviour Research and Therapy*, 1981, **19**, 319–333.

Logue, A. W., Rodriquez, M. L., Peña-Correal, T. E., & Mauno, B. C. Quantification of individual differences in self-control. In M. L. Commons, J. A. Nevin, & H. Rachlin (Eds.), *Quantitative analyses of behavior* (Vol. 5). Cambridge: Ballinger, in press.

Macfarlene, D. A. The role of kinesthesis in maze learning. *University of California Publications in Psychology*, 1930, **4**, 227–305.

Mackintosh, N. J. Stimulus selection: Learning to ignore stimuli that predict no change in reinforcement. In R. A. Hinde & J. Stevenson-Hinde (Eds.), *Constraints on learning*. New York: Academic Press, 1973.

Mackintosh, N. J. *The psychology of animal learning*. New York: Academic Press, 1974.

Maki, W. J., & Hegvik, D. Directed forgetting in pigeons. *Animal Learning and Behavior*, 1980, **8**, 567–574.

Mazur, J. E., & Logue, A. W. Choice in a "self-control" paradigm: Effects of a fading procedure. *Journal of the Experimental Analysis of Behavior*, 1978, **30**, 11–17.

Mischel, W. Theory and research on the antecedents of self-imposed delay of reward. In B. A. Maher (Ed.), *Progress in experimental research*, Vol. 3. New York: Academic Press, 1966.

Moore, B. R. The role of directed Pavlovian reactions in simple instrumental learning in the pigeon. In R. A. Hinde & J. Stevenson-Hinde (Eds.), *Constraints on learning*. London: Academic Press, 1973.

Olton, D. S., & Samuelson, R. J. Remembrance of places past: Spatial memory in rats. *Journal of Experimental Psychology: Animal Behavior Processes*, 1976, **2**, 97–116.

Overmier, J. B., & Seligman, M. E. P. Effects of inescapable shock upon subsequent escape and avoidance learning. *Journal of Comparative and Physiological Psychology*, 1967, **63**, 23–33.

Pavlov, I. P. *Conditioned reflexes*. (Trans. G.V. Anrep). London: Oxford University Press, 1927.

Premack, D. Reinforcement theory. In D. Levine (Ed.), *Nebraska symposium on motivation: 1965*. Lincoln: University of Nebraska Press, 1965.

Rachlin, H. Self-control. *Behaviorism*, 1974, **2**, 94–107.

Rachlin, H. Learning theory in its niche. *Behavioral and Brain Sciences*, 1981, **4**, 155–156.

Rachlin, H., & Burkhard, B. The temporal triangle: Response substitution in instrumental conditioning. *Psychological Review*, 1978, **85**, 22–48.

Rachlin, H., Kagel, J. H., & Battalio, R. C. Substitutability in time allocation. *Psychological Review*, 1980, **87**, 355–374.

Rescorla, R. A., & Wagner, A. R. A theory of Pavlovian conditioning: Variations in the effectiveness of reinforcement and nonreinforcement. In A. H. Black & W. F. Prokasy (Eds.), *Classical conditioning II*. New York: Appleton-Century-Crofts, 1972.

Revusky, S. H. Learning as a general process with an emphasis on data from feeding experiments. In N. W. Miligram, L. Krames, & T. M. Alloway (Eds.), *Food aversion learning*. New York: Plenum Press, 1977.

Revusky, S. H., & Garcia, J. Learned associations over long delays. In G. H. Bower & J. T. Spence (Eds.), *The psychology of learning and motivation: Advances in theory and research*, Vol. 4. New York: Academic Press, 1970.

Rozin, P., & Kalat, J. W. Specific hungers and poison avoidance as adaptive specializations of learning. *Psychological Review*, 1971, **78**, 459–486.

Schwartz, B., & Williams, P. R. Two different kinds of key-peck in the pigeon: Some properties of responses maintained by negative and positive response-reinforcer contingencies. *Journal of the Experimental Analysis of Behavior,* 1972, **18,** 201–216.

Seligman, M. E. P. On the generality of the laws of learning. *Psychological Review,* 1970, 77, 406–418.

Seligman, M. E. P. *Helplessness.* San Francisco: W. H. Freeman, 1975.

Seligman, M. E. P., & Maier, S. F. Failure to escape traumatic shock. *Journal of Experimental Psychology,* 1967, **74,** 1–9.

Skinner, B. F. *The behavior of organisms.* New York: Appleton-Century, 1938.

Skinner, B. F. Are theories of learning necessary? *Psychological Review,* 1950, **57,** 193–216.

Skinner, B. F. A case history in scientific method. *American Psychologist,* 1959, **11,** 359–379.

Small, W. S. Experimental study of the mental processes of the rat. *American Journal of Psychology,* 1901, **12,** 218–220.

Staddon, J. E. R. Operant behavior as adaption to constraint. *Journal of Experimental Psychology: General,* 1979, **108,** 48–67.

Straub, R. O., Seidenburg, M. S., Bever, T. G., & Terrace, H. S. Serial learning in the pigeon. *Journal of the Experimental Analysis of Behavior,* 1979, 32, 137–148.

Thorndike, E. L. *Animal intelligence.* New York: Hafner, 1965. (Originally published, 1911).

Thorndike, E. L. *The fundamentals of learning.* New York: Bureau of Publications, Teacher's College, 1932.

Tolman, E. C. *Purposive behavior in animals and men.* New York: Appleton-Century, 1932.

Tolman, E. C. Cognitive maps in rats and men. *Psychological Review,* 1948, **55,** 189–208.

Watson, J. B. Psychology as the behaviorist views it. *Psychological Review,* 1913, **20,** 158–177.

Watson, J. B. *Behaviorism.* New York: W. W. Norton, 1970. (Originally published, 1924).

Watson, J. B., & Rayner, R. Conditioned emotional reactions. *Journal of Experimental Psychology,* 1920, **3,** 1–14.

Wearden, J. H. Undermatching on concurrent variable-interval schedules and the power law. *Journal of the Experimental Analysis of Behavior,* 1980, **33,** 149–152.

Wiens, A. N., Montague, J. R. Manaugh, T. S., & English, C. J. Pharmacological aversive counterconditioning to alcohol in a private hospital: One-year follow-up. *Journal of Studies on Alcohol,* 1976, **37,** 1,320–1,324.

Wilcoxon, H. C., Dragoin, W. B., & Kral, P. A. Illness-induced aversions in rat and quail: Relative salience of visual and gustatory cues. *Science,* 1971, **171,** 826–828.

Wolin, B. R. Difference in manner of pecking a key between pigeons reinforced with food and with water. In A. C. Catania (Ed.), *Contemporary research in operant behavoir.* Glenview, Ill.: Scott, Foresman, 1968.

Zener, K. The significance of behavior accompanying conditioned salivary secretion for theories of the conditioned response. *American Journal of Psychology,* 1937, **50,** 384–403.

8 TRAIT APPROACHES

Leon H. Levy

Although it is common practice to speak of "trait theories" and "trait psychologists," this practice is misleading. The psychologists most frequently identified in personality textbooks (e.g., Hall & Lindzey, 1970; Mischel, 1971; Pervin, 1975) as trait theorists—Allport, Cattell, Guilford, and Eysenck—have made extensive use of the concept of traits in their theoretical writings and research, but none can be said to have formulated a fully articulated, comprehensive trait theory of personality—nor would any of them be likely to make such a claim. Cattell (1977), for example, has observed that "the term *trait theory* is as superfluous as a two-legged man theory; for the alternative is a structureless theory of personality structure" (p. 166). Thus, the following recent observation by Jackson and Paunonen (1980) seems most apt: "One encounters the term 'trait theorist,' with all its connotations, in the writings of several authors. Like the witches of 300 years ago, there is confidence about their existence, and even possibly their sinister properties, although one is hard pressed to find one in the flesh or even meet someone who has" (p. 523). Nevertheless, if there is any doubt about the existence of trait theorists, there can be none about the prevalence of traits themselves as important foci of theoretical formula-

tions, methodological developments, and empirical research.

Theoretical development has largely been limited to hypotheses involving individual traits such as extraversion and neuroticism. But even then it has rarely strayed far from the cues provided by the behavioral and test measures by whose factor loadings the traits were defined. Essentially absent have been formulations that allow the derivation of hypotheses about interactions between traits or between traits and other personality and environmental variables. To be sure, exceptions exist, but they are rare. One notable exception, for example, may be found in Eysenck's attempts to link extraversion and introversion with variations in the rate of development of reactive inhibition and with Pavlov's notions about "strong" and "weak" nervous systems (Eysenck, 1953). In the sense of elaborated nomological nets, however, there are no trait theories; at best there are only theories about particular traits, and even these tend not to be very well developed conceptually (Fiske, 1973; Golding, 1978).

This lack of theoretical development is not unique to traits, however; it is widely recognized as characteristic of all of personality psychology (Carlson, 1975; Phares & Lamiell, 1977; Sechrest,

1976). But it is particularly important to bear this in mind in the case of traits since the absence of well-developed theories makes it virtually impossible to assess the significance of much of the research marshalled either in support of, or as a challenge to, trait formulations (Golding, 1978); it also provides fertile ground for the play of ideological biases and for the controversy that appears to be endemic to discussions of traits.

Traits are among the most controversial concepts to be found in the history of psychology. In concluding their exposition on the nature of traits, Carr and Kingsbury (1938) observed that "Much of this literature conveys the distinct impression that psychology at present is grasping somewhat blindly about because of the absence of any definite and accepted principles of orientation in reference to the concept" (p. 524). That statement remains applicable today, over four decades later. Yet, the fact that traits continue to thrive as a focus of research and clinical work, as well as of controversy, suggests that they may be serving certain essential theoretical and practical functions that have not been fully recognized or appreciated by their critics. The alternative interpretation, of course, is that their hardiness simply attests to the obduracy of certain distortions in human cognitive functioning—possibly, a reflection of the operation of "cognitive economics" (Mischel, 1979). Later in this chapter we will consider some of the evidence presented in support of this latter interpretation. For the present, however, it would seem that the wiser course is to assume the validity of the former interpretation, given the vast domain of phenomena with which clinical and personality psychology must deal. We must be careful that our pursuit of the ideal of parsimony in our theories not diminish the range of phenomena with which we are able to deal.

The literature on traits is distinguished from that of other approaches to personality both conceptually and methodologically, and in both of these cases it also differs in being more heavily saturated with empirical content. Conceptually, trait literature is better characterized as metatheoretical than theoretical. Thus, for example, there have been few formal attempts to define the concept of traits (Hogan, DeSoto, & Solano, 1977), nor can one find many formulations concerned with their origins or their role in personality functioning and behavior. Instead, discussions have usually focused on issues associated with the value of traits as explanatory concepts and as bases for prediction and decision making.

Methodologically, trait research is strongly tied to the psychometric tradition in psychology and is more dependent upon a single method of investigation—personality testing, primarily in the form of pencil-and-paper, self-report inventories—and on one method of data analysis—correlational—than any other approach to personality. To be sure, there are trait studies using observational data and objective response measures, but they tend to be in the minority. One consequence of this is that a substantial portion of the trait literature is concerned with technical problems of trait measurement and identification, largely involving methods of test construction and factor analysis. Another possible consequence is that the status of traits as scientific constructs, and of the data concerning them, has suffered because of the predominance of the experimental method in contemporary psychological research (Cronbach, 1957).

This chapter will reflect the current state of the literature on traits by devoting a major portion of its space to conceptual and methodological issues. This will be followed by a section presenting some recent evidence on the two major issues in the trait literature—stability and consistency—and a third section in which I discuss what appear to me to be several interesting recent developments and future trends. I do not consider myself a trait advocate, but I do believe that much of our thinking about traits in psychology has been characterized by a lack of precision and rigor. My intention is therefore to offer readers perspectives and interpretations of research findings that I believe will allow them to arrive at more soundly based judgments concerning the role and value of traits in personality and clinical psychology than has been generally true in the past.

Conceptual and Methodological Issues

The conceptual issues, which seem to have dogged the use of traits in psychology almost from the start, have often been presented as empirical issues or as resolvable by recourse to empirical data. History has revealed that this is not the case, however, and modern, postpositivist thinking in the philosophy of science has shown why this is so. Theory and data are inextricably linked; the kinds of questions raised and the kinds of data collected and their interpretation are dependent upon one's theoretical perspective (Hanson, 1958; Kuhn, 1962; Suppe, 1974). Observations and facts are "theory-laden" (Hanson, 1958). Thus, the major concerns about the concept of traits cannot be answered solely in empirical terms. In this section, we will therefore consider these concerns from a conceptual standpoint. Research relevant to these issues will be reviewed in the following section.

The two issues historically and most commonly raised in connection with traits concern the existence of stability and consistency in personality. Derived from these concerns is the more specific question of behavioral specificity or the extent to which behavior is situationally dependent. A third issue associated with traits, but which extends beyond them, concerns the relative merits of idiographic and nomothetic approaches to personality study. At a different level, and historically more recent, the fourth and most fundamental issue with which we will be concerned is the ultimate question of the utility of traits as conceptual and empirical variables. These are the issues that must be addressed if one is to use trait concepts, whether as a personality theorist or a practicing clinician. Our understanding of these issues will be aided, however, if we first consider a number of issued associated with how traits have been defined, how they are used in psychological discourse, and how they function in theory construction.

Definitional Issues

Among the functions served by definitions, one is stipulative, indicating what the user means by a term or how the term is to be used (Hanson, 1969). Stipulative definitions are essential if confusion is to be avoided in communication in general and science in particular. Such definitions are also essential if we are to know what data are relevant to the use of a given concept or term. Thus, consider the following examples of trait definitions:

a generalized and focalized neuropsychic system (particular to the individual), with the capacity to render many stimuli functionally equivalent, and to initiate and guide consistent (equivalent) forms of adaptive and expressive behavior [Allport, 1937, p. 296].

a covariation or consistency in responses which is a function of past learning in similar situations under similar motivation [McClelland, 1951, p. 229].

a co-variant set of behavioural acts; it appears thus as an organizing principle which is deduced from the observed generality of human behavior [Eysenck, 1953, p. 10].

any distinguishable, relatively enduring way in which one individual differs from others [Guilford, 1959, p. 6].

If we assume that these definitions, taken as a group, contain within them the essential elements of the definition of the concept of traits, several observations seem in order. All definitions agree in identifying observed behavioral covariation or consistency as one criterion for the use of the term. Although this is not explicit in Guilford's definition, elsewhere in his text it is clear that behavioral covariation is implicit. How much consistency or covariation is necessary to justify invoking the trait concept, however, is unspecified by these definitions. This is not an issue for these authors since they use the degree and extent of covariation to distinguish between general and specific traits, although, again, there is no explicit demarcation point between general and specific traits in terms of level of generality. Guilford, for example, states that a trait "may be as inclusive as a general attitude of self-confidence or as narrow as a specific habit, such as a conditioned muscular contraction in response to a sound" (1959, p. 6). Guilford appears to depart here from Allport (1937) and Eysenck, each of whom distinguishes between traits and habits, although in each case the distinction rests upon the degree of generality. Thus, it should be clear that the existence of consistency among some set of behaviors, or intercorrelation between a set of responses, cannot logically serve as a criterion for the use of the trait concept, although it can serve in deciding the level of generality of a particular trait. For this reason, attempts to challenge the validity or meaningfulness of the concept of traits by citing empirical studies that find a lack of consistency among particular behaviors are unlikely to prove successful. Given the distinction between general and specific traits, such evidence can only speak to the degree of specificity of particular traits, not to the scientific status of the concept of traits.

As one illustration of this point, we might compare the views of the same data by two psychologists. As part of a study of dependency motivation, Sears (1963) computed intercorrelations between measures of five categories of behavior that he considered to be forms of dependency in preschool boys and girls. Only 1 of the 20 intercorrelations (computed separately for boys and girls) was statistically significant. Mischel (1968), in what has been commonly taken as a major assault on traits,[1] cited these data, along with other research findings, as grounds for questioning the empirical status of personality traits. Sears, however, concluded only that his findings "suggest that the use of such a term as Allport's *common trait* is not warranted in describing the structure or organization of dependent behavior" (1963, p. 36). Sears did not seem to regard his findings as necessarily hastening the mortality of the concept of traits.

Thus, it appears to be as Allport (1937) concluded: "the consistency of a trait is entirely a matter of degree. There must be some demonstrable relationship between separate acts before a trait can be inferred. Yet occurrence of dissociated, specific, or even contradictory acts is not necessarily fatal to the inference" (p. 332). Although this may not be an intellectually satisfying conclusion in some respects, it appears to be a generally accepted one by trait-oriented psychologists. Nevertheless, because inconsistency has been such a central issue in the trait controversy, we will examine it further from a conceptual standpoint later in this section and review some of the recent research findings bearing on it in the following section.

If we consider the points on which these four definitions differ from each other or on which they are all silent as ones that are not essential to the definition of the concept of traits, it also becomes apparent that they do not: (a) commit users of the term to any single position concerning their nature or origins; (b) identify traits with the absolute absence of change; or (c) limit traits to the role of individual differences variables. Thus, Allport identifies traits as "neuropsychic" systems and Mc-Clelland regards them as products of learning, while Eysenck and Guilford place no constraints on the use of trait terms with regard to either their nature or origins, apparently allowing questions about these to be answered empirically rather than by definition.

Stability is a conceptual issue that we will address shortly. But from a definitional standpoint,

it should be apparent that it is not criterial for the concept of traits. It is explicitly included only in Guilford's definition. This definition makes clear, however, that research showing some degree of temporal or situational variation in a trait measure is not, by definition, fatal to the trait: whatever is being measured is not thereby disqualified from being called a trait. Clearly, personality traits are expected to manifest some degree of stability, but this is relative rather than absolute, and McClelland's definition states two factors—situations and motivation—upon which it may be dependent. Thus, as with consistency, stability serves as a variable characteristic of traits rather than as a test of their existential reality.

Finally, it should be noted that only Guilford's definition identifies traits with individual differences. Allport, as is well known, distinguishes between individual and common traits, regarding only the latter as individual differences variables and then not really "true" traits (1937, pp. 299–300). Thus, while traits may be used in the study of the behavior of individuals, it is a mistake to assume that they necessarily serve as individual differences variables for all psychologists who use them, just as it is a mistake to assume that the study of personality is limited to an individual differences paradigm (Lamiell, 1981).

Where does this brief excursion into definitional exegesis leave us? Better prepared, we hope, to consider the conceptual and empirical issues raised by the concepts of traits. To recapitulate: implicitly, if not explicitly, traits are essentially defined as characteristics of individuals that are expected to contribute in some way to the prediction and/or explanation of particular behaviors by these individuals. Covariation or consistency and stability are behavioral characteristics that are necessary in some degree—but only in some degree—in order for the concept to be invoked. In a word, as they have been commonly defined and used, traits are *dispositional variables*. And so it is to the function of dispositional variables in science and scientific explanation that we turn next.

Dispositional Variables

Although it is common to find traits described as dispositional variables (e.g., Brody, 1972; Mischel, 1971), few writers go on to discuss the nature of dispositional variables as scientific concepts and their implications for our understanding of traits.

---

[1]More recently, Mischel (1979) has said that this was not his intent.

Thus, it will be helpful to consider how dispositional variables have been conceived of in the philosophy of science.

Hempel (1970) discusses the difficulties of defining dispositional concepts in terms of observables and, using "magnetic" as an example, notes that "it designates, not a directly observable characteristic, but rather a disposition, on the part of some physical objects to display certain reactions (such as attracting small iron objects) *under certain specifiable circumstances* (such as the presence of small iron objects in the vicinity)" (p. 676, emphasis added). He goes on to note that the vocabulary of the empirical sciences abounds in dispositional terms. Popper (1965) observes that "words like 'glass' or 'water' are used to characterize the *law-like behavior* of certain things; which may be expressed by calling them 'dispositional words.' . . . we say of a surface that it is red, or white, if it has the disposition to reflect red, or white, light and consequently the disposition to look *in daylight* red, or white" (pp. 424–425, emphasis added). These views, as well as those of psychologists who have been concerned with issues of theory construction in psychology (MacCorquodale & Meehl, 1948) are summed up by Kaplan (1964), who states:

> The characteristics that make up scientific categories are likely to be "dispositional," that is, they identify the characters that *would* be exhibited *if* certain conditions were fulfilled (hostility is the disposition to exhibit anger under a wide range of appropriate circumstances, anxiety the disposition to exhibit fear, and so on). Any proposition containing such a dispositional term is thus a generalization, making a claim about what would happen *whenever* situations of the proper kind might obtain [pp. 52–53].

Two important points become apparent. As theoretical constructs, dispositional variables are essential in the search for lawfulness and the development of scientific theories. They appear to be virtually inescapable if one wishes to formulate empirically based assertions that have any degree of generality. Second, dispositional variables are by nature conditional or interactional; the complete definition and understanding of a dispositional variable necessarily includes assertions about how it will manifest itself under particular conditions. Thus, in the abstract case, statements containing dispositional variables are always of the form: "Let D be the disposition of X to react to a condition C by the characteristic response R" (Carnap, 1956). Dispositional variables are never assumed to operate *in vacuo.*

Traits are obviously not the only dispositional variables in psychology. Habits, needs, drives, states, attitudes, beliefs, and abilities also function as dispositional variables, just as do common clinically descriptive terms such as depressed, enuretic, and phobic. To describe a person as phobic, for example, is to assert that under certain specifiable conditions, the person will engage in one or more forms of avoidance or escape behaviors. Thus, to the extent that psychologists accept any of these other concepts as useful and legitimate, it is unclear why they should question the use of trait concepts. Moreover, it would appear to be vain to expect that traits or other dispositional variables can be avoided in the study of human behavior and personality, for to do so would be to attempt to account for a range of behavioral phenomena without considering any characteristics of the source of those phenomena. This would be analogous to a physicist trying to account for a magnetic phenomenon without considering the characteristics of the material exhibiting it. It might be done, but the explanation is likely to be incomplete at the very least; needless to say, its utility would be correspondingly restricted.

One of the charges most commonly leveled against traits and those who use them is that they fail to take the situation into account. Although it is undoubtedly true that more than a few psychologists have been guilty of this abuse (see Fiske, 1978), it would seem manifestly unjustified to tar traits with the same brush. It should also be apparent that it would be naive. For, as our discussion of dispositional variables has made clear, situations are inextricably bound up in the conceptualization of traits—or at least they should be. Thus, to assert that an individual possesses a particular trait in some degree is to state implicitly the probability that the individual will manifest behavior having certain characteristics *under certain circumstances* (Levy, 1970). For this reason, it would also seem that the recent upsurge of "interactionism" in personality psychology (Endler & Magnusson, 1976a; Magnusson & Endler, 1977) represents less an alternative to traits, as Endler and Magnusson (1976b) have claimed, than a return to some unfinished, but nevertheless important, business. As Costa and McCrae (1980) have observed, "traits are *inherently* interactive" (p. 90). Thus, it should be clear that there is nothing in the concept of traits that is antithetical to the notion of including situations in the explanation, prediction, or modification of behavior, human or otherwise; indeed, the concept requires it. It should also be clear from this discussion that, *in principle*, the issue of the utility of trait concepts should be beyond question.

Stability

Stability may be seen as a special case of consistency, involving a temporal dimension. Whereas consistency refers to covariation of behaviors across situations, generally ignoring their temporal separation, stability refers to covariation of behaviors over time, generally ignoring their differeing situational contexts (Fiske, 1978). Thus, studies of the stability of traits must also perforce count as studies of consistency, and many of the conceptual and methodological issues raised by these studies are the same in both cases. Nevertheless, for ease of exposition, we will maintain the distinction between stability and consistency in studying these issues since the considerations to which they give rise tend to differ in some cases.

If traits are characteristics of individuals, they should be expected to be relatively stable — at least more so than the stream of events that marks the course of their individual lives. Thus, it would appear that the assessment of the stability of traits should be a rather straightforward matter: determine, by some means, the degree of stability of measures of a given trait over some specified interval of time, taking care that these measures are not biased by factors — for example, selective recall or perception in the case of self-report measures or observer judgments — that might spuriously reduce their variability. But reflection on the confusing array of apparently contradictory findings in the literature on the question of trait stability suggests that the problem is far from simple and that the assessment of trait stability entails a number of considerations that have not been adequately addressed thus far.

METHODS OF MEASUREMENT

There are essentially two different ways to conceive of and measure stability, and the distinction between them is usually ignored in the literature. Intuitively, when we talk about a trait being stable we usually mean that it is unchanging within an individual over some extended interval of time. Mischel (1968) seems to mean this when he states:

"If one believes that an individual's position on these continua would be relatively stable across testing situations and over lengthy time periods, then the main assessment emphasis becomes the development of reliable instruments administered under standard conditions to tap accurately the presumably stable, enduring underlying traits and states possessed by the person" (p. 9). The focus appears to be clearly on the person, alone, over time. To assess the stability of a trait so conceived, we might either compute the absolute difference between two measurements of a given trait, if only one time interval were used, or if measurements were taken on the same trait at a number of different points over some period now, we could compute the variance in these measurements. Either approach would provide us with a measure of the intrapersonal stability of the trait in question. And if we wished to enhance the generalizability of our assertion about the trait's stability, we could obtain similar measures for a sample of individuals and compute their mean and standard deviation.

As an alternative, we could define trait stability interpersonally as meaning the maintenance of the same rank-ordering in a sample of individuals on a given trait over some specified period of time. The appropriate measurement of stability in this case, of course, is the correlation coefficient for the measurements of a given trait across a sample of individuals taken at two points in time. What it represents, however, is the stability of *differences between individuals* on a given trait, not the stability of the extent to which the trait is manifested *within individuals* (Lamiell, in press). Moreover, it is unlikely that the two methods of measurement will yield the same values (Golding, 1978; Lamiell, 1981; Norman, 1967). Yet, while writers seem to be referring to intrapersonal stability when they discuss assumptions made about traits, the research they cite most often, if not exclusively, is concerned with interpersonal stability (e.g., Mischel, 1968, pp. 33–36).

Until research is clearly identified as to which kind of stability is being considered, it is obviously impossible to form any sound judgment on this issue. Moreover, we are being deprived of potentially valuable knowledge, pragmatically as well as conceptually. For it seems plausible that traits may vary in the extent to which they manifest one kind of stability or another. Should this be the case, their utility may similarly vary, depending upon our purposes. One might, for example, be more interested in traits with high interpersonal stability if one were designing a personnel selection program, while intrapersonal stability may be of grater concern if one were conducting individual psychotherapy—traits that are highly stable intrapersonally would seem to be poor candidates for criteria in pre-post assessments of psychotherapy outcome.

Recently, the issue of trait stability has become further complicated by the resurgence of interest in idiographic approaches to personality study (Bem & Allen, 1974; Lamiell, 1981). From an idiographic perspective, it is possible that the temporal stability of traits itself may vary over individuals, thus making it impossible to draw any generalized conclusions about their stability. Lamiell (1981; in press) has also demonstrated quite strikingly how interpersonal stability measurement may obscure marked individual differences in trait stability. His work clearly demonstrates the need to take a more differentiated view of the assessment of trait stability than has been the case in the past.

The essentially atheoretical status of trait constructs, their lack of embeddedness within well-articulated theories of personality and behavior, raises two further considerations that must be addressed in any attempt to assess their stability.

THE CHOICE OF MEASURES

If stability is studied over any appreciable length of time, there is a good chance that the measures used on the first occasion will not be appropriate on the second. Crying easily, for example, may be a good behavioral item to include in the measurement of emotionality in children (Buss & Plomin, 1975), but it obviously would be inappropriate in an adult follow-up study of these same individuals. But, then, what would be appropriate? This raises, of course, the more fundamental question concerning the construct validity of trait measures, and will be discussed in more detail in connection with the issue of consistency. Here, it is sufficient to note that, in the absence of a richly elaborated formulation of the concept and its placement within a nomological net of other constructs, the question is usually answered intuitively. As a result, measurements of trait stability are necessarily confounded in unknown (and largely unknowable) proportions with the method variance (Campbell & Fiske, 1959) and differential construct validity of the methods used.

This problem may be less serious when the same standardizd tests are used at the various

times of measurement (Costa & McCrea, 1980) or when expert judges' ratings based upon large age-appropriate data sets are used (Block, 1971). But the problem may exist even in these cases. The tests' construct validity may well vary as a function of age, and the content of the data sets will necessarily differ from one age period to the next, thereby raising the question of differential construct validity and method variance again. These problems are susceptible to empirical study, but as yet they have been given neither the conceptual nor the empirical attention they require. Thus, a best guess is that all measurements of trait stability are probably attenuated in some degree, but how much remains unknown.

AGE AND TIME INTERVAL CONSIDERATIONS

Studies conducted with children generally reveal less stability than those conducted with adults (Moss & Sussman, 1980; Sears, 1977), and stability has been found to correlate negatively with length of time interval (Olweus, 1979). These findings should not be surprising, nor should they be viewed as necessarily damaging to the concept of traits. There may be several reasons for them.

Moss and Sussman (1980) hypothesize that age may be associated with stability because childhood is marked by passage through many more developmental periods than adulthood, and because the variables assessed in children are more likely to be social-interaction variables that are more environmentally dependent than those studied in adults, which are typically motivational and affective traits. Method variance and differential construct validity, as discussed above, may also enter in two ways: (a) because of the more rapid development and change that characterizes the earlier years, it is more likely that different methods of measurement will be required at the two times of measurement for children as compared with adults; and (b) as time intervals increase, regardless of the age of the sample, the probability increases that different methods of measurement will be required on the two occasions.

Again, these considerations point to the need for greater theoretical development, as well as increased concern with psychometric issues, if trait stability is to be adequately assessed. Although even their severest critics do not require that traits be unchanging over time, it is not unreasonable to require that we be able to state how much stability is to be expected in particular traits, and why. In any case, these considerations should make it clear why both the age of individuals studied and the length of time interval involved must be taken into account in evaluating the literature on trait stability.

Consistency

Since covariation or consistency of behaviors is so central to the trait concept, it is understandable that a substantial portion of the attack on the concept should focus on this issue. This criticism usually takes one of two forms. By far the largest effort is directed toward marshalling evidence that suggests that the range of behaviors or situations over which consistency is found is more limited than the trait concept would lead one to expect, or alternatively, that behavior tends to be situation-specific (Mischel, 1968). The second line of attack has drawn upon research that has been interpreted as suggesting that the locus of the consistency that appears to exist in human behavior may reside in the perceptual and cognitive processes of observers rather than in the individuals being observed (D'Andrade, 1965, 1974; Mischel, 1968, 1979; Shweder, 1975). Needless to say, each of these lines of attack has been countered by trait advocates as well as by other investigators who view them more generally as also threatening the very concept of personality (Alker, 1972; Block, 1977; Block, Weiss, & Thorne, 1979; Bowers, 1973; Wachtel, 1973). As with stability, our purpose here is not to enter into the controversy over the issue itself, but to discuss some of the methodological and conceptual considerations that become apparent from a review of its literature and need to be addressed if further progress is to be achieved in its resolution.

RELIABILITY AND VALIDITY ISSUES

The most salient methodological problems associated with attempts to assess the consistency of behavior are largely psychometric, but not exclusively so. The psychometric problems involve both reliability and validity. The nonpsychometric problems concern the choice of research paradigm.

The Hartshorne and May (1928, 1929; Hartshorne, May, & Shuttleworth, 1930) studies continue to serve as the prototype for research on trait and behavioral consistency. The typical study involves measures of behavior in one or more situations, plus measures of the trait presumably manifested by these behaviors obtained from test scores. The intercorrelations between these measures provide the measure of consistency. Although it should be obvious that the magnitude of these intercorrelations is directly dependent upon the reliability of the measures involved, it has been argued by several writers (Block, 1977; Epstein, 1977, 1979, 1980) that most research on consistency has been flawed by a failure to recognize this simple truth. Thus, although no one would expect to be able to construct reliable single-item tests, many consistency studies, as exemplified by Hartshorne and May's work, make use of their logical equivalent in the form of measures based on single instances of behavior. For some reason, many researchers fail to appreciate that the same psychometric principles and standards are applicable whether their information comes from test or nontest behaviors. Yet, once this is appreciated, and one moves away from the use of measures based upon single instances of behavior to more reliable measures based upon aggregates of such instances, Epstein (1979) and others (Rushton, Jackson, & Paunonen, 1981) have shown that it is possible to obtain consistency and stability coefficients far exceeding the .30 to .40 range suggested as typical by Mischel (1968). In fact, Hartshorne and May (1928) showed that combining several tests of honesty into a single score led to a reliability coefficient of .73. Such demonstrations, of course, do not resolve the question of trait consistency; they do, however, cast doubt on the quality of much of the evidence thus far available on the issue.

If insufficient attention has been given to the problem of reliability, the situation is no better in the case of validity. If anything, the problem is more complex since it is conceptual as well as psychometric. As was pointed out earlier, the conceptual formulations of traits and the nomological networks necessary for the systematic assessment of the construct validity of the tests and behavioral measures used in consistency studies do not exist. Intuition and face validity most often guide the choice of measures. This has two consequences. One is that in the absence of theoretical bases for deciding how large correlations should be between particular trait measures, their evidential value for questions of consistency rests largely in the eye of the beholder. The second consequence is that the magnitude and pattern of correlations found between various reputed measures of the same traits are apt to vary widely (Fiske, 1973). Neither consequence is scientifically satisfactory.

Sears' (1963) study of dependency and its treatment in Mischel's (1968) discussion of traits provides a convenient illustration of a number of the problems thus far discussed. As part of a larger study of child-rearing correlates of identification (Sears, Rau, & Alpert, 1965), Sears obtained measures of dependency through a time-sampling procedure in which 5 categories of "dependency behavior" were tallied for each of 40 nursery school children (21 boys and 19 girls), observed in free play for 7 to 10 hours each over a 7-week summer period. Each child received a score in each category which represented the proportion of the total number of half-minute observation periods for that child during which behavior in a given category was observed. The five categories were: (1) *negative attention seeking;* (2) *positive attention seeking;* (3) *touching or holding;* (4) *being near;* and (5) *seeking reassurance.* Assessment of observer reliability for negative attention seeking, of which there were only five occurrences, revealed 40 percent agreement; for the remaining four, it ranged from 67 percent to 82 percent. Observer agreement over all categories was 78 percent.

Intercorrelations between the five categories were computed separately for boys and girls and, as noted earlier, only 1 of the 20 was statistically significant. How damaging is this to the notion of trait consistency? Mischel (1968) apparently found these data so compelling that he reproduced the correlation matrix in his discussion of the questionable empirical status of traits (p. 27). But is the interpretation of this matrix as self-evident as Mischel's presentation of it seems to imply? Several considerations suggest that it is not.

Sears postulated the five categories as representing different aspects of dependent behavior. But no theoretical or empirical support is provided to justify this particular breakdown of dependency. One might question, for example, the justification for regarding "opposing and resisting directions, rules, routines, and demands" (Sears et al., 1965, p. 300) as a form of negative attention seeking and as an aspect of dependency. Other nondependency interpretations seem equally plausible. However, even if it is granted that these categories represent five aspects of dependency, we must then be concerned about the construct validity and reliability of the particular behaviors that are combined to form measures of each aspect, since these behaviors are formally equivalent to test items. But, again, the evidence is lacking. Nor is it apparent in either Sears' (1963; Sears et al., 1965) or Mischel's

(1968) discussions that the need for such evidence was recognized.

Even if the measures possessed acceptable construct validity and reliability, however, it is important to note that they are measures of aspects of dependency, not of the totality of dependency as manifested in particular situations. Thus, the correlation matrix is relevant to the question of the structure or organization of dependency — not its consistency. Sears clearly recognized this (Sears et al., 1965) since he dealt with the question of consistency elsewhere in his monograph. The contrast between Sears' treatment of the issue of consistency in his data and Mischel's portrayal of his findings illustrates the lack of conceptual rigor that characterizes much of the trait literature.

The importance of greater precision becomes evident in this instance when we contrast the data on the structure of dependency with the results of Sears' own analysis of the consistency of dependency. To assess dependency's consistency, Sears made use of all observed instances of dependency across the five categories over the seven-week observation period. Four observers were used in the study. Each observed each child over a prescribed set of periods, distributed over the seven-week period such that each observer contributed an approximately equal share of the total observations on each child. Except when observer reliability was being assessed, no two observers observed the same child at the same time. Thus, Sears obtained four dependency scores for each child, one from each observer. Each score was therefore independent of the other three, but a confound of the idiosyncratic characteristics of each observer, the situations in which the observations were made, and characteristics of the child. Their intercorrelation should therefore provide an indication of the cross-situational consistency of dependency in these children, attenuated in some degreee by observer unreliability.

The mean of the six correlations, based on the z-transformation of the pair-wise correlations between observers, was .42. Correcting this correlation by the Sperman-Brown formula for the fact that it was based upon only one-fourth of the data entering into the total number of observations, yielded a consistency coefficient of .74 for dependency. Analogously, using the total scores of all four observers for each child for each of three time periods (weeks 2–3, 4–6, 7–8), Sears obtained uncorrected and corrected consistency coefficients of .36 and .63, respectively. Thus, a careful reading of Sears reveals that while dependency (in the age group he studied) may not be a broad general trait, it does possess a reasonable level of cross-situational consistency—considerably more, at any rate, than one would have thought from the interrelation matrix reproduced by Mischel.

SAMPLE CHARACTERISTICS:
AGE AND TRAIT SCORE DISTRIBUTIONS

As was noted in our discussion of stability, developmental considerations must also enter into the design and evaluation of studies of trait consistency. While there is some evidence that suggests that a trait such as attention seeking may be fairly consistent among young children, for example, we would not expect comparable consistency in this age group for self-attitudes. For adults, on the other hand, just the opposite would be expected (Sears, 1977). This notion is also proposed by Block (1977) who suggests that one reason that Hartshorne and May failed to find generality for "honest behavior" was that their subjects had not yet reached the stage of moral development where this would be expected. Although such arguments can always be challenged as *ex post facto*, they should alert us to a very real problem. Certain traits may very well vary in their consistency of manifestation as a function of maturity for a variety of reasons. Unless this is taken into account, assessments of the consistency of particular traits are apt to be contradictory and confusing. Once this possibility is granted, however, blanket assertions about trait consistency in general lose much of their credibility. However reasonable these conclusions may appear, we must once again recognize that they also point to the dearth of theory and research—in this case, on the relationship between consistency and maturity for various traits—necessary to address the most fundamental questions about the nature of traits.

If trait measures are conceived of as statements of the probability with which individuals will manifest a particular trait in a given situation (Levy, 1970), then, by definition, it should be expected that the closer individuals are located to the middle of a trait continuum, the less consistency they will manifest with respect to that trait. For individuals located at the midpoint, the probability of manifesting a bipolar trait in any given situation would be .5, and it would increase as they approach either end of the continuum. This also follows from the model upon which trait measurement is most commonly based. For, whether traits are assessed by questionnaires or ratings, their measurement is most often based upon a cumulative measurement model (Wiggens, 1973) that assumes that the number of occasions (or test items) on which a trait is manifested by an individual is an index of the amount of the trait possessed by the individual. For this reason, trait scores may also be conceived as measures of the consistency with which individuals respond to sets of items (stimuli, questions, or situations) appropriate for the elicitation of manifestations of the traits in question (Vaughan, 1977). Recently presented data by Rushton, Jackson, and Paunonen (1981) showing that individuals who are extreme scorers on trait measures rate themselves as more consistent on those traits than do less extreme scorers are consistent with this line of thinking.

Methodologically, these considerations suggest that consistency may be less usefully considered a property of traits than of the individuals possessing them—a view that finds support in the research of Bem and Allen (1974). Consequently, the distribution of trait scores in subject samples may be expected to be critical in determining the outcomes of studies of trait consistency and should be given close attention in the design of such studies and in weighing their evidential value.

Many of the methodological and conceptual problems thus far discussed, as well as several others, are illustrated in a closely reasoned critique of the work of D'Andrade (1965, 1974) and Shweder (1975) by Block, Weiss, and Thorne (1979). The interested reader is referred to Block et al.'s paper for the details of their critique, as well as to Shweder and D'Andrade's (1979) reply. Briefly, as support for their contention that the consistency found in ratings of behavior and in responses to self-report personality inventories represents cognitive distortions that result from the semantic and conceptual similarity of the items either rated or reported upon, D'Andrade and Shweder present a number of studies that all use the same methodology. Drawing upon previously published research, they demonstrate that patterns of intercorrelations between various behavioral or personality dimensions based upon either observe ratings or self-reports correspond better to patterns of similarity ratings between these dimensions made by independent judges than they do to frequency counts of the behaviors identified with each dimension.

In a typical example of this approach, Shweder

(1975) reanalyzed data from a study by Newcomb (1929) of the consistency of extraversion-introversion behavior patterns in boys. Newcomb's data consisted of daily records of the occurrence of particular behaviors and observer ratings of the same 26 items of behavior for two groups of boys observed over a 24-day period in a summer camp. Three examples of these items are: (1) *Speaks with confidence of his own abilities*; (3) *Submits quietly and with good spirit to criticism or discipline from his counselors*; and (6) *Gets up before rising hour.* For each boy, a camp counselor noted the presence of each item of behavior as soon as possible after it occurred, and the measures of "actual behavior" consisted of the percentage of days for each boy on which each item of behavior occurred. The measures of "rated behavior" consisted of ratings made of each boy at the end of the camp period on a five-point scale for each of the same 26 items by six observers, including his counselor. The measures of conceptual similarity between the behavior items were obtained by having ten students in one of Shweder's classes make judgments of similarity for all possible pairs of items, using a seven-point scale. The correlation matrices based upon the actual behavior counts and the rated behavior were then compared with each other and with the matrix of similarity judgments by the use of rank-order correlations between corresponding matrix cells.

For one group of boys, the resulting correlation between the actual behavior matrix and the rated behavior matrix was .51; between the similarity matrix and the rated behavior matrix, it was .83; and between the similarity matrix and actual behavior matrix, it was .47. The corresponding correlations for the other group were .38, .77, and .48. Clearly, in both groups the structure of behavior ratings corresponded more closely to that of the similarity ratings than it did to that of the actual behavior counts. The relatively modest correlations in both groups between the similarity matrix and the actual behavior matrix is taken as evidence that the similarity matrix is not a veridical reflection of the actual structure of behavior. These and other similar findings lead D'Andrade and Shweder to conclude that the behavioral consistency implied by trait concepts, as well as an individual differences conception of personality, are illusory.

While D'Andrade and Shweder prefer to interpret the low correlation between the rated and actual behavior matrix in Newcomb's study and in others they have analyzed as due to the distortion of ratings by raters' preexisting cognitive schemas, this result could equally plausibly be due to the unreliability of either the behavior ratings or the actual behavior counts, or both, as Block et al. (1979) point out. First, the actual behavior counts in all cases were done by single observers, so that there is no possibility of determining their reliability. And second, at least two potential sources of observer unreliability may be identified in their data. One is the varying levels of inference or judgment required in many of the actual behavior counts, as may be seen from the three behavior items cited above from Newcomb's study. Limitations on the information-processing capacity of observers represent the other potential source of unreliability, especially in studies in which Bales' Interaction Process Analysis (IPA) records provided the actual behavior counts. As Block et al. describe it, the single IPA coder had to observe all members of a group and code between 10 and 20 acts per minute into as many as 12 different (not necessarily simple) categories according to the particular actor involved for 50 minutes in one study and 120 minutes in another. It would be surprising if observer reliability under such circumstances was very high. But because it was impossible to assess observer reliability, it was also impossible to know what the correlations between actual and rated behavior matrices would be if they were corrected for attenuation caused by unreliability of measurement.

Questions of validity were involved in two other points raised by Block et al. (1979) as possible sources of attenuation of the correlations between actual and rated behavior matrices. They question whether counts of discrete acts can serve as an adequate operationalization of complex psychological concepts since they fail to reflect these acts' contexts (and, therefore, meaning) or trends in their occurrence — both of which may be taken into account by raters drawing upon long-term memory. They also note that in several studies there is a lack of identity between the behavioral items counted and those rated. This was true for 15 of the 26 items in Newcomb's study and for several in studies using IPA records. For example, for one IPA variable defined as "Shows solidarity, raises other's status, jokes, gives help, reward," the corresponding rated behavior variable was defined as "Shows solidarity and friendliness." The effects that such changes in wording may have on the respective validities of behavior counts and ratings can only be determined empirically, but it would be surprising if they did not contribute to the attenuation of their correlation with each other.

Two conceptual issues are raised in alternative explanations proposed by Block (Block et al., 1979) and Lamiell (1980) for D'Andrade and Shweder's interpretation of the correlations they obtained between rated behavior matrices and similarity matrices — the focal point of their cognitive distortion hypothesis. The mean of these correlations across seven different tests was .75 — impressively higher than the mean correlations of .25 between actual and rated behavior matrices and .26 between actual behavior and similarity matrices (Shweder & D'Andrade, 1979). They take this pattern of correlations as support for their position that "items similar in concept (e.g., 'seeks reassurance' and 'seeks help') are typically judged to be characteristics of the *same person* on verbal report personality assessment procedures, thereby creating the 'illusion' that personality factors are responsible for the consistent display of behaviors expressive of the factor" (Shweder, 1975, p. 477, emphasis added).

Lamiell (1980) pointed out that Shweder had generalized from group data to individual cases, asserting that the covariation found over *n* cases will also be found within individual cases. This is comparable to the failure to distinguish between interpersonal and intrapersonal stability noted earlier. Thus, for example, Shweder implies that an observer who regards "seeks reassurance" and "seeks help" as conceptually similar will be highly likely to apply both in an identical way in describing a particular individual. But Lamiell showed conceptually and empirically that this need not be the case. He was able to show that when analyses were conducted at the level of the individual, correlating responses with conceptual similarity measures, extreme variability was the rule, with correlations ranging between −.18 and .90. Thus, he concluded that "people *are* capable of generating behavior reports which do not correspond highly to their conceptual schemes" (p. 67). It might be noted parenthetically that Lamiell's findings also parallel those of Norman (1967) who found correlations between social desirability and probability of item endorsement ranging between .88 and .91 when they were based on scores averaged over individuals, but only between .22 and .26 when they were computed on values within individuals for the two variables.

The issue raised by Block, Weiss, and Thorne (1979) concerns the need to take into account redundancy characteristics of the sample of variables in investigations such as D'Andrade's and Shweder's. They propose that the strong correspondence found between rated behavior and similarity matrices is the result of the high redundancy and the structure of that redundancy in the particular variable sets D'Andrade and Shweder sampled. Thus, they argue that by varying the amount and structure of redundancy in a set of variables, it is possible to vary the degree of correspondence between rated behavior and similarity matrices. And they demonstrate this empirically in a cleverly designed study in which the average correlation between rated behavior and similarity matrices varied between .21 and .63, depending upon the amount of redundancy built into the set of variables involved.

Both Lamiell's (1980) and Block et al.'s (1970) work provide instructive models of exceptions to Block et al.'s observation that "too often in psychology, crucial experimental points and analytical considerations go unnoticed" (p. 1,059).

Empirical Evidence: Stability and Consistency

Having discussed a number of the central conceptual and methodological issues raised by contemporary research on traits, we shall now review several recent studies that bear upon the critical issues of stability and consistency. The data in most of these studies have only recently reached maturity and so were not available for service in the trait controversy until recently. In presenting these studies, we will distinguish between investigations of the stability of particular traits or attributes (trait stability), and those that might be thought of as assessments of the stability of personality or of the structure of personality traits within the individual (structural stability), a concern to which personality psychologists have paid surprisingly scant attention (Carlson, 1971). As was pointed out earlier, data from longitudinal studies of stability also logically bear upon the question of cross-situational consistency, and so we will not distinguish between consistency and stability in the studies that follow. It should be noted that lawfulness and predictability are also formally equivalent to consistency. Thus, to ask whether behavior is consistent or, more specifically, whether traits and the behaviors associated with them are consistent is to ask whether trait measures and behaviors purported to be manifestations of traits enter into lawful relationships with each other. Hence, in addressing the issue of consistency, we will also review some findings concerned with the predictability of behavior and adjustment from trait measures.

Trait Stability

As part of a study of the changes that occur in personality and interests as a consequence of attending college, Nichols (1965) administered a battery of tests to a group of National Merit finalists, and reported findings on 432 males and 204 females who completed both pretesting, before they entered college, and posttesting, just before graduating four years later. The males attended 104 different colleges, and the females 86. The tests included the 16 Personality Factor Questionnaire (16PF) Form A, the Holland Vocational Preference Inventory, and 10 a priori scales felt to be related to creative and academic achievement. We will consider here only the data from the 16PF.

We will consider changes in magnitude first: there were five scales (Sociability, Adventurousness, Sophistication, Self-Control, and Tension) on which no significant changes were found for either males or females over the four-year period. For males, no significant changes were found on four additional scales (Dominance, Surgency, Suspiciousness, and Anxiety). Females showed no significant changes on three other scales (Femininity, Unconcern, and Radicalism). Stability coefficients for males ranged from .28 (intelligence) to .63 (femininity), with a median of .48; for females, the range was from .21 (sophistication) to .64 (adventurousness), with a median of .52. Nichols (1965) concluded: "Of the changes which occur during the college years the proportion attributable to the gross characteristics of the college is relatively small" (p. 13). If we consider the number of different colleges involved in this major transition period in these students' lives, the amount of stability found in these data is quite impressive.

Olweus (1979) reviewed 16 studies concerned with the stability of aggressive behavior and reaction patterns among subjects (primarily males) ranging in age from 2 to 18 years at time of first measurement. None involved either self-ratings or self-reports, relying instead upon either direct observation, peer nominations, teacher ratings, or clinical ratings. He reported 24 stability coefficients for time intervals ranging from less than one

year to greater than twenty years. The average raw and attenuation-corrected correlations were .55 and .68, respectively, for all 24 coefficients. The corresponding stability coefficients for 12 of the studies with only one coefficient per sample were .63 and .79. Olweus found a correlation between stability coefficients and length of time interval of − .66, but he also found that the estimated attenuation-corrected stability coefficient for a five-year interval of .69 declined only to .60 for a ten-year interval. Several lines of reasoning led Olweus to conclude that it was unlikely that these stability coefficients were due to the stability of the subjects' environment, a not uncommon explanation of such data by trait critics (Mischel, 1969).

On the assumption that error of measurement has been a critical factor in studies failing to demonstrate stability, Epstein (1979) conducted a series of studies in which he varied the size of the sample of occurrences for each variable being assessed. In the typical study, subjects kept daily logs over a specified period, in which they recorded a variety of subjective experiences and objective events by means of ratings or other quantifiable means. To test his assumption, Epstein then computed odd-even reliabilities based on data for two days and for averages of varying numbers of additional days.

Typical of his findings are the following from two of his studies: in one study, in which subjects' ratings of their emotions were analyzed separately for their most pleasant and unpleasant experience each day, as recorded over a one-month period, the average odd-even reliability for emotion ratings for Day 1 versus Day 2 of .36 rose to .88 for all odd versus all even days for pleasant experiences; for unpleasant experiences, the corresponding coefficients were .25 and .79. For reported behaviors engaged in during pleasant experiences the Day 1 versus Day 2 reliability was .06, which increased to .74 for all odd versus all even days. The corresponding reliabilities for unpleasant experiences were .15 and .57. In a second study, mean reliability coefficients for observer-recorded variables increased from .44 for a one-day sample to .84 for a 12-day sample; for self-recorded physiological reactions, the corresponding figures were .27 and .94; and for self-recorded behavior that is externally observable, the corresponding figures were .40 and .96. Epstein also presented data showing that averaged measures of daily behaviors can be fairly well predicted from closely matched inventory items (average rs = .61 and .53 for specific and general forms of the items, respectively), and to a lesser, but still significant, extent by standard personality inventories ($r =$ ca. .40).

Data by Costa and his associates (Costa & McCrae, 1980; Costa, McCrae, & Arenberg, 1980; Costa, McCrae, & Norris, 1981) drawn from the Baltimore Longitudinal Study of Aging provides further evidence on the issue of stability and consistency. For one sample of adult males (aged 25 to 82 initially), divided into three age groups, Costa and McCrae (1980) reported ten-year stability correlations ranging from .58 to .69 for Anxiety or Neuroticism and from .70 to .84 for Extraversion, both variables being represented by scores based upon earlier cluster analyses of the 16PF.

In another study (Costa, McCrae, & Arenberg, 1980), 6-year and 12-year test-retest coefficients were obtained for the ten scales of the Guilford-Zimmerman Temperament Survey (GZTS) for males divided into three different age groups at time of initial testing. The average six-year stability coefficients over the ten scales for the three age groups ranged from .75 to .77; the range for the 12-year stability coefficients was essentially identical, from .72 to .75. Among the individual scales, the lowest stability coefficient obtained was .59 for Objectivity for the 12-year interval for the oldest age group (age 60 to 76 at initial testing); 50 percent of the stability coefficients were .75 or higher.

Finally, neuroticism and extraversion, as represented by the first two factors of the GZTS, were shown to be predictive of personal adjustment to aging, as measured by the Chicago Attitude Inventory (CAI), a test designed for the study of personal adjustment among the aged (Costa, McCrae, & Norris, 1981). A canonical correlation of .46 ($p <$ .001) between neuroticism and extraversion and the ten variables of the CAI was obtained for a two- to ten-year interval between the two measures. The same correlation was obtained for a 10- to 17-year interval, but its significance was reduced to .054 due to the smaller n.

Structural Stability

In an analysis of 226 substantive articles appearing in 1968 in the *Journal of Personality* and the *Journal of Personality and Social Psychology*, Carlson (1971) reported that "not a single published study attempted even minimal inquiry into the organization of personality variables within the individual" (p. 209). Thus, the evidence from which judgments might be made about the structural stability

of personality, within the individual, is exceedingly limited, and only two studies will be reviewed.

Based on a ten-year analysis of data drawn from the extensive archives of the Oakland Growth Study and the Berkeley Guidance Study, Block (1971) has presented findings suggesting a surprising degree of structural stability over time. Using data independently collected on subjects at three points in time—during junior high school, three years later in senior high school, and approximately twenty years later during adulthood—Block had nonoverlapping sets of two to three clinical psychologists describe each subject's personality at each stage by means of Q-sorts. The data upon which the Q-sorts were based consisted of a variety of tests, teachers' comments, conversations, and so forth, for the junior and senior high school years, and extensive interviews, averaging 12 hours, during adulthood. Care was exercised throughout to prevent contamination of data collected at one period by previously collected data, and, because the same psychologists never did more than one Q-sort on a subject, memory contamination of Q-sort descriptions across periods was also ruled out.

The reliability of the Q-sort descriptions was generally satisfactory, ranging between .72 and .78. The average Q correlations for the junior to senior high school interval were .77 and .75 for males and females, respectively; for the senior high school to adult interval the corresponding correlations were .56 and .54, all corrected for attenuation. Although these average correlations are impressive, it should be noted that Block also found considerable dispersion among individual Q correlations: for males the range for the junior to senior high school interval was from −.01 to 1.00, and for the senior high school to adulthood interval it was from −.40 to .97; for females, the corresponding ranges were −.02 to 1.00 and −.30 to .97. In other analyses, he examined the characteristics of high and low changers over time, as well as different patterns of personality development, as revealed through the Q-sort descriptions.

If the personality characteristics making up the items in Block's Q sets are not themselves traits, it can be argued that they are manifestations of traits and that Block's analyses therefore provide evidence for a substantial amount of structural stability in personality, as well as for individual differences in the extent of this stability.

Structural stability was approached in a very different way by Harris (1980) and involved a considerably reduced time frame. Part of his study was concerned with the stability of individual personality profiles as generated by the Personality Research Form (PRF) (Jackson, 1967), by self-ratings, and by peer ratings, the latter two using the same PRF dimensions and the definitions of these dimensions used in the inventory's construction. Subjects consisted of four groups of first year graduate students in clinical psychology, varying in size from six to nine, admitted to the University of Kentucky over a four-year period. Periods of acquaintance among these groups at the time of the first assessment varied from just over five hours to eight months; intervals between first and second assessments varied between three and nine months. Within each group, subjects completed the PRF, rated every other member on each PRF variable, rated themselves on the same variables, and then rated themselves again as they might perceive themselves in the setting of their home cultures. This latter rating was included for comparison purposes with a pilot group of subjects from the East-West Center in Honolulu.

Individual correlations were computed for subjects between their profiles generated by each method on the two occasions and between their composite profiles on the two occasions generated by various combinations of two and three of the methods. The median stability coefficients for PRF profiles ranged between .78 and .83 among the four groups, with an overall median of .81. Individual PRF stability coefficients ranged between .42 and .92. Median stability coefficients for profiles generated by peer ratings ranged between .64 and .85 among the four groups, with an overall median of .74. Stability coefficients for individual profiles generated by this method ranged between − .07 and .92. Self-ratings yielded median stability coefficients within the groups that ranged from .50 to .69, with an overall median of .61. Stability coefficients for individual profiles based on self-ratings ranged between − .02 and .84. Comparable coefficients were found for self-ratings under the home-culture instructions. Stability coefficients for composite profiles were generally slightly enhanced as compared with single-method profiles, with the highest stability coefficients being for profiles based on composites of the PRF, peer ratings, and self-ratings under either of the two instructions. The range in individual stability coefficients for the three methods, including standard self-ratings, was from .49 to .93; for the three methods, including self-ratings under the home

culture instructions, the range was from .54 to .94.

Thus, like Block (1971), Harris found evidence for an impressive level of structural stability, on the average, as well as for variation in its extent at the individual level. Together, these two studies, as well as those on trait stability, clearly provide empirical justification for the assumption of stability and consistency in behavior, upon which the trait concept is based. At the same time, however, they also show that this justification cannot be taken for granted in the individual case—a finding that points to the need for research on the determinants of individual differences in stability and consistency in personality traits.

Recent Developments and Future Trends

Thinking about traits as conceptual entities has been riveted on the issues of stability and consistency. This is reflected in the emphasis of this chapter up to this point. Here we will consider several recent developments that suggest a lifting of this bondage and appear to foreshadow future developments in trait research and theory.

One such development has been the emergence of the life-span perspective in developmental psychology (Baltes, Reese, & Lipsitt, 1980). The work of Block and Costa and their colleagues, discussed in the preceding section, illustrates the value of longitudinal research in dealing with the issues of stability and consistency. Although there are as yet no full-scale life-span developmental studies involving traits, we may anticipate that as existing data bases mature so as to permit such studies, they will shed light on the nature of changes in traits and their structure that occur over time, and on the determinants of these changes. These studies may be expected to move us beyond simple dichotomous thinking about stability and consistency and provide a foundation for substantive theories of traits and human behavior. It is perhaps also worth noting that it would be impossible to study personality development, especially over the life span, without variables such as traits by which to trace the course of its development.

A second development of note is the rise of human behavior genetics (Henderson, 1982). Although there is a long history of research on the genetics of psychopathology, it is only within recent years, with the growth of behavior genetics as a specialty, that research has begun to focus on genetic contributions to personality traits. The evidence thus far suggests that it is likely to become an important area of study in future trait research. In one provocative study, Buss and Plomin (1975) used a rationally constructed survey—the EASI Temperament Survey—to investigate the heritability of emotionality, activity, sociability, and impulsivity. Their subjects were 81 identical twins and 57 fraternal twins, ranging in age from one to nine years, with an average age of 55 months. Their data consisted of mothers' ratings of their children on five simply worded items for each trait. The data, analyzed separately for males and females, revealed a genetic component for the first three traits for both sexes, but mixed evidence for impulsivity. Interclass correlations on all four traits were higher for identical twins than for fraternal twins for both sexes—substantially so for emotionality, activity, and sociability. On impulsivity, there was a large difference between the correlations for identical and fraternal twins for boys (.84 and .04, respectively) but a small one for girls (.71 and .59).

In what has been referred to as a landmark study (Henderson, 1982), Loehlin and Nichols (1976) secured data on a variety of personal characteristics on 850 twins (514 identical and 336 fraternal) who took the National Meit Scholarship Qualifying Test in the spring of 1962. The only standardized personality measure included in their battery was the California Personality Inventory (CPI). On the CPI, the median intraclass correlation on the 18 scales for identical twins was .50; for fraternal twins it was .32. Comparing two randomly divided subsamples of male and female identical and fraternal twins on the 18 scales, they found correlations for identical twins to be higher than for fraternal twins on 69 of the 72 possible comparisons. On the bases of these and other analyses, which effectively ruled out differential treatment of identical and fraternal twins as an explanation for their findings, they concluded that "genes and environment carry roughly equal weight in acounting for individual variation in personality" (p. 90). It is evident, however, that they do not currently receive equal attention by personality researchers.

Finally, Henderson (1982) reported heritability estimates for neuroticism and extraversion (generally measured by either the Eysenck Personality Questionnaire or the CPI) from twin data in nine previously reported studies involving between 287 and over 6,500 twins. The estimates ranged between .41 and .60 for neuroticism and between .50 and .74 for extraversion. Personality and clinical psychologists, reflecting American psychology's strong empiricst bias, have been loath to consider genetic as well as other biological factors in personality; data such as these, however, suggest that the time has come to shed this bias. And as this bias is shed, we may also expect increasing attention to be paid to the biopsychological processes involved in trait acquisition and expression. The value of moving in this direction has been well demonstrated in psychopathology (e.g., Depue, 1979); it can be no less in personality study.

A third development that has portents for the future of personality study is the resurgence of interest in idiographic approaches to personality assessment. Because the idiographic approach to personality study advocated by Allport (1937) seemed incompatible with the development of generalizable principles of personality (Holt, 1962), it has languished as an unattainable ideal for some and as a remnant of romanticism for others. There is reason to believe that this situation may change, however. Bem and Allen (1974), in a widely cited article, made a case for idiographic assessment by showing that cross-situational consistency on particular traits varied among individuals, and suggested that it may not be possible to achieve high cross-situational consistency or predictability using a universal of traits—people may be expected to show consistency and predictability only for those traits that are used similarly by them and the experimenter or clinician.

In support of their position, Bem and Allen reported mean intercorrelations of .57 and .27 between measures of friendliness from several different sources for groups of subjects who rated themselves as consistent and inconsistent on the trait, respectively; for conscientiousness, they reported corresponding correlations of .45 and .09. Using a similar methodology and scales based upon the 16 PF, Kenrick and Stringfield (1980) reported average intercorrelations between self, peer, and parent ratings for self-chosen most and least consistent traits of .61 and .23, respectively, providing further support for individualizing the choice of variables in personality assessment. Although neither study has been without criticism (Rushton, Jackson, & Paunonen, 1981; Tellegen, Kamp, & Watson, 1982), they have served to revive interest in idiographic assessment and to boost the spirits of those who had mistakenly come to believe that consistency coefficients of the order of .30 were the universal fate of personality traits.

Last, recent work by Lamiell (1981, in press)

has the potential for placing idiographic assessment at the very center of personality psychology. Arguing for making a clear distinction between differential psychology and personality psychology, Lamiell maintains that most measures of traits treat them as individual difference variables and thus tell us only about the person relative to others, not about the extent to which traits are possessed by individuals. Similarly, he points out that measures of trait consistency and stability generally represent the extent to which individuals in samples maintain their relative positions on the variable in question; they tell us nothing about how stable or consistent any particular individual is on the variable. High stability coefficients could occur, for example, where the scores of all individuals in a sample change substantially, but approximately equal from T_1 to T_2. This may be no problem for differential psychology. For personality psychology, however, Lamiell proposes that the measure of an individual's possession of an attribute should be defined by the extent to which he or she engages in a range of activities that define that attribute in contrast to those other attribute-related activities in which he or she could but does not engage. Thus, rather than giving meaning to a person's behavior by comparing it to that of others, Lamiell proposes that the comparison should be with other behaviors that the person could have performed but did not. As he sums up the rationale underlying his approach, it is founded on the belief that "the 'kind of person' one *is* is directly reflected in the kind of person one *is not* but *could be* and is only incidentally, if at all, reflected in the kind of person someone else is" (p. 287).

Although this view has been held by others, as Lamiell notes, what makes his work distinctive and most promising is that he has developed a formal measurement model that is consistent with this position, and he has shown how it can be applied in arriving at truly idiographic quantitative personality measurements for individuals. Thus, it is possible, using his measurement model, to utilize idiographic assessment in the development of nomological principles that account for the acquisition, maintenance, and change of personality characteristics in individuals. These are among the basic concerns of personality psychology, and they are of equal importance to clinical psychology in their applied implications; to the extent that Lamiell's notions gain acceptance, they promise a radically different way of empirically addressing these concerns.

Concluding Remarks

Controversy thrives in the absence of sound data and accepted theory by which to interpret data. As we have seen, traits have been chronically afflicted by both of these conditions. It is my hope that this chapter will provide readers with bases for making their own judgments of the data that have been entered as evidence in the case of traits and that it will also make them acutely aware of the need for greater precision in our conceptualization of the issues surrounding traits and of the need for theories that include traits as one of their variables. Although such theories have never existed, in my view, a recent elaboration by Powell and Royce of what they call a multifactor-system theory (Powell & Royce, 1981a, 1981b; Royce & Powell, 1981) suggests one form that they might take. Theories of considerably less complexity than that proposed by Powell and Royce would also represent significant contributions. It is time that we begin lighting candles rather than continue to curse the darkness.

One last point remains to be made. Although it may be clear by now that traits are considerably more substantial as scientific constructs than their critics have portrayed them as being, a question may remain concerning their utility, especially for clinical psychology. Traits may enter into diagnostic formulations, and certainly do in the definition of personality disorders, as illustrated by the DSM-III, but the fact is that no major mode of clinical intervention—neither psychodynamic, cognitive, nor behavioral—systematically utilizes trait information in shaping its strategy and tactics in dealing with individual clients. What should be made of this? Rather than taking this as evidence for the irrelevance of traits for the clinical enterprise, I would argue that it reflects the incompleteness of the theories guiding this enterprise. At present, interventions fail to take into account in any systematic fashion characteristics that might differentially affect the impact of the particular techniques being used by their practitioners. Thus, although clinicians might feel that they are functioning well enough without this knowledge, it should be evident that this confidence lacks any empirical formulation. To the extent that we are committed to counteracting the various "uniformity myths" (Kiesler, 1966) that have plagued psychotherapy research and practice, it would seem clear that traits do have an important role to play in clinical psychology.

Traits also have a significant role to play in primary prevention efforts, an activity of growing importance in clinical psychology. Whether the task is identifying individuals at risk and understanding the nature of their vulnerabilities (Murphy & Frank, 1979; Zubin & Spring, 1977), or the assessment of competence and its enhancement (Bloom, 1979; Sundberg, Snowden, & Reynolds, 1978) as a means of preventing mental disorders, primary prevention is an intrinsically prospective enterprise. Thus, it must have means of identifying and tracking individuals over time in order to test the hypotheses upon which it is based and to evaluate the efficacy of its methods. And for these purposes, as well as for theory building, it is impossible to do without dispositional variables, whether they are called traits or not.

References

Alker, H. A. Is personality situationally specific or intrapsychically consistent? *Journal of Personality*, 1972, **40**, 1–16.

Allport, G. W. *Personality: A psychological interpretation.* New York: Holt, 1937.

Baltes, P. B., Reese, H. W., & Lipsitt, L. P. Life-span developmental psychology. In M. R. Rosenzweig & L. W. Porter (Eds.), *Annual review of psychology,* Vol. 31. Palo Alto, Calif.: Annual Reviews, 1980.

Bem, D. J., & Allen, A. On predicting some of the people some of the time: The search for cross-situational consistencies in behavior. *Psychological Review*, 1974, **81**, 506–520.

Block, J. *Lives through time.* Berkeley: Bancroft Books, 1971.

Block, J. Advancing the psychology of personality: Paradigmatic shift or improving the quality of research? In D. Magnusson & N. S. Endler (Eds.), *Personality at the crossroads: Current issues in international psychology.* Hillsdale, N.J.: Erlbaum, 1977.

Block, J., Weiss, D. S., & Thorne, A. How relevant is a semantic similarity interpretation of personality ratings? *Journal of Personality and Social Psychology*, 1979, **37**, 1,055–1,074.

Bloom, B. L. Prevention of mental health disorders: Recent advances in theory and practice. *Community Mental Health Journal*, 1979, **15**, 179–191.

Bowers, K. S. Situationism in psychology: An analysis and a critique. *Psychological Review*, 1973, **80**, 307–336.

Brody, N. *Personality: Research and theory.* New York: Academic Press, 1972.

Buss, A. A., & Plomin, R. *A temperament theory of personality development.* New York: Wiley, 1975.

Campbell, D., & Fiske, D. Convergent and discriminant validation by the multitrait-multimethod matrix. *Psychological Bulletin*, 1959, **56**, 81–105.

Carlson, R. Where is the person in personality research? *Psychological Bulletin*, 1971, **75**, 203–219.

Carlson, R. Personality. In M. R. Rosenzweig & L. W. Porter (Eds.), *Annual review of psychology,* Vol. 26.

Palo Alto, Calif.: Annual Reviews, 1975.

Carnap, R. *Meaning and necessity: A study in semantics and modal logic.* Chicago: University of Chicago Press, 1956.

Carr, H., & Kingsbury, F. A. The concept of traits. *Psychological Review*, 1938, **45**, 497–524.

Cattell, R. B. A more sophisticated look at structure: Perturbation, sampling, role, and observer trait-view theories. In R. B. Cattell & R. M. Dreger (Eds.), *Handbook of modern personality theory.* Washington, D.C.: Hemisphere, 1977.

Costa, P. T., Jr., & McCrae, R. R. Still stable after all these years: Personality as a key to some issues in adulthood and old age. In P. B. Baltes & O. G. Brim (Eds.), *Life span development and behavior,* Vol. 3. New York: Academic Press, 1980.

Costa, P. T., Jr., McCrae, R. R., & Arenberg, D. Enduring dispositions in adult males. *Journal of Personality and Social Psychology*, 1980, **38**, 793–800.

Costa, P. T., McCrae, R. R., & Norris, A. H. Personal adjustment to aging: Longitudinal prediction from neuroticism and extraversion. *Journal of Gerontology*, 1981, **36**, 78–85.

Cronbach, L. J. The two disciplines of psychology. *American Psychologist*, 1957, **12**, 671–684.

D'Andrade, R. G. Trait psychology and component analysis. *American Anthropologist*, 1965, **67**, 215–228.

D'Andrade, R. G. Memory and the assessment of behavior. In H. Blalock (Ed.), *Measurement in the social sciences.* Chicago: Aldine, 1974.

Depue, R. A. (Ed.). *The psychobiology of the depressive disorders: Implications for the effects of stress.* New York: Academic Press, 1979.

Endler, N. S., & Magnusson, D. (Eds.) *Interactional psychology and personality.* Washington, D.C.: Hemisphere, 1976. (a)

Endler, N. S., & Magnusson, D. Toward an interactional psychology of personality. *Psychological Bulletin*, 1976, **83**, 956–974. (b)

Epstein, S. Traits are alive and well. In D. Magnusson & N. S. Endler (Eds.), *Personality at the crossroads: Current issues in interactional psychology.* Hillsdale, N.J.: Erlbaum, 1977.

Epstein, S. The stability of behavior: I. On predicting most of the people much of the time. *Journal of Personality and Social Psychology*, 1979, **37**, 1,097–1,126.

Epstein, S. The stability of behavior: II. Implications for psychological research. *American Psychologist*, 1980, **35**, 790–806.

Eysenck, H. J. *The structure of human personality.* London: Methuen, 1953.

Fiske, D. W. Can a personality construct be validated empirically? *Psychological Bulletin*, 1973, **80**, 89–92.

Fiske, D. W. Cosmopolitan constructs and provincial observations: Some prescriptions for a chronically ill specialty. In H. London (Ed.), *Personality: A new look at metatheories.* Washington, D.C.: Hemisphere, 1978.

Golding, S. L. Toward a more adequate theory of personality: Psychological organizing principles. In H. London (Ed.), *Personality: A new look at metatheories.* Washington, D.C.: Hemisphere, 1978.

Guilford, J. P. *Personality.* New York: McGraw-Hill, 1959.

Hall, C. S., & Lindzey, G. *Theories of personality.* (2nd ed.) New York: Wiley, 1970.

Hanson, N. R. *Patterns of discovery.* Cambridge, England: Cambridge University Press, 1958.

Hanson, N. R. *Perception and discovery.* San Francisco: Freeman, Cooper, 1969.

Harris, J. G., Jr. Nomovalidation and idiovalidation: A quest for the true personality profile. *American Psychologist,* 1980, **35,** 729–744.

Hartshorne, H., & May, M. A. *Studies in the nature of character: Vol. 1. Studies in deceit.* New York: Macmillan, 1928.

Hartshorne, H., & May, M. A. *Studies in the nature of character: Vol. 2. Studies in service and self-control.* New York: Macmillan, 1929.

Hartshorne, H., May, M. A., & Shuttleworth, F. K. *Studies in the nature of character: Vol. 3. Studies in the organization of character.* New York: Macmillan, 1930.

Hempek, C. G. Fundamentals of concept formation in the empirical sciences. In O. Neurath, R. Carnap, & C. Morris (Eds.), *Foundations of the unity of science: Toward an internation-encyclopedia of unified science,* Vol. II. Chicago: University of Chicago Press, 1970.

Henderson, N. D. Human behavior genetics. In M. R. Rosenzweig & L. W. Porter (Eds.), *Annual review of psychology,* Vol. 33. Palo Alto, Calif.: Annual Reviews, 1982.

Hogan, R., DeSoto, C. B., & Solano, C. Traits, tests, and personality research. *American Psychologist,* 1977, **32,** 255–264.

Holt, R. R. Individuality and generalization in the psychology of personality. *Journal of Personality,* 1962, **30,** 377–404.

Jackson, D. N. *Personality Research Form manual.* Goshen, N.Y.: Research Psychologists Press, 1967.

Jackson, D. N., & Paunonen, S. V. Personality structure and assessment. In M. R. Rosenzweig & L. W. Porter (Eds.), *Annual review of psychology,* Vol. 31. Palo Alto, Calif.: Annual Reviews, 1980.

Kaplan, A. *The conduct of inquiry.* San Francisco: Chandler, 1964.

Kenrick, D. T., & Stringfield, D. O. Personality traits and the eye of the beholder: Crossing some traditional philosophical boundaries in the search for consistency in all of the people. *Psychological Review,* 1980, **87,** 88–104.

Kiesler, D. J. Some myths of psychotherapy research and the search for a paradigm. *Psychological Bulletin,* 1966, **65,** 110–136.

Kuhn, T. S. *The structure of scientific revolutions.* Chicago: University of Chicago Press, 1962.

Lamiell, J. T. On the relationship between conceptual schemes and behavior reports: A closer look. *Journal of Personality,* 1980, **48,** 54–73.

Lamiell, J. T. Toward an idiothetic psychology of personality. *American Psychologist,* 1981, **36,** 276–289.

Lamiell, J. T. The case for an idiothetic psychology of personality: A conceptual and empirical foundation. In B. A. Maher (Ed.), *Progress in experimental personality research,* Vol. XI. New York: Academic Press, in press.

Levy, L. H. *Conceptions of personality: Theories and research.* New York: Random House, 1970.

Loehlin, J. C., & Nichols, R. C. *Heredity, environment, and personality.* Austin: University of Texas Press, 1976.

MacCorquodale, K., & Meehl, P. E. On a distinction between hypothetical constructs and intervening variables. *Psychological Review,* 1948, **55,** 95–107.

McClelland, D. C. *Personality.* New York: Dryden Press, 1951.

Magnusson, D., & Endler, N. S. (Eds.) *Personality at the crossroads: Current issues in interactional psychology.* Hillsdale, N.J.: Erlbaum, 1977.

Mischel, W. *Personality and assessment.* New York: Wiley, 1968.

Mischel, W. Continuity and change in personality. *American Psychologist,* 1969, **24,** 1,012–1,018.

Mischel, W. *Introduction to personality.* New York: Holt, Rinehart & Winston, 1971.

Mischel, W. On the interface of cognition and personality: Beyond the person-situation debate. *American Psychologist,* 1979, **3,** 740–754.

Moss, H. A., & Sussman, E. J. Longitudinal study of personality development. In O. G. Brim & J. Kagan (Eds.), *Constancy and change in human development.* Cambridge, Mass.: Harvard University Press, 1980.

Murphy, L. B., & Frank, C. Prevention: The clinical psychologist. In M. R. Rosenzweig & L. W. Porter (Eds.), *Annual review of psychology,* Vol. 30. Palo Alto, Calif.: 1979.

Newcomb, T. M. The consistency of certain extrovert-introvert behavior patterns in 51 problem boys. Teachers College, Columbia University, *Contributions to Education,* 1929, No. 382.

Nichols, R. C. Personality change and the college. *National Merit Scholarship Corporation Research Reports,* 1965, **1**(2).

Norman, W. T. On estimating psychological relationships: Social desirability and self-report. *Psychological Bulletin,* 1967, **67,** 273–293.

Olweus, D. Stability of aggressive reaction patterns in males: A review. *Psychological Bulletin,* 1979, **86,** 852–875.

Pervin, L. A. *Personality: Theory, assessment, and research.* (2nd ed.) New York: Wiley, 1975.

Phares, E. J., & Lamiell, J. T. Personality. In M. R. Rosenzweig & L. W. Porter (Eds.), *Annual review of psychology.* Vol. 28. Palo Alto, Calif.: Annual Reviews, 1977.

Popper, K. R. *The logic of scientific discovery.* Torchbook edition. New York: Harper & Row, 1965.

Powell, A., & Royce, J. R. An overview of a multifactor-system theory of personality and individual differences: I. The factor and system models and the hierarchical factor structure of individuality. *Journal of Personality and Social Psychology,* 1981, **41,** 818–829. (a)

Powell, A., & Royce, J. R. An overview of a multifactor-system theory of personality and individual differences: III. Life span development and the heredity-environment issue. *Journal of Personality and Social Psychology,* 1981, **41,** 1,161–1,173. (b)

Royce J. R., & Powell, A. An overview of a multifactor-system theory of pesonality and individual differences: II. System dynamics and person-situation interations. *Journal of Personality and Social Psychology,* 1981, **41,** 1,019–1,030.

Rushton, J. P., Jackson, D. N., & Paunonen, S. V. Personality: Nomothetic or idiographic? A response to Kenrick and Stringfield. *Psychological Review*, 1981, **88**, 582–589.

Sears, R. R. Dependency motivation. In M. R. Jones (Ed.), *Nebraska symposium on motivation*. Lincoln: University of Nebraska Press, 1963.

Sears, R. R. Sources of life satisfactions of the Terman gifted men. *American Psychologist*, 1977, **32**, 119–128.

Sears, R. R., Rau, L., & Alpert, R. *Identification and child rearing*. Stanford, Calif.: Stanford University Press, 1965.

Sechrest, L. Personality. In M. R. Rosenzweig & L. W. Porter (Eds.), *Annual review of psychology*, Vol. 27. Palo Alto, Calif.: Annual Reviews, 1976.

Shweder, R. A. How relevant is an individual difference theory of personality? *Journal of Personality*, 1975, **43**, 455–484.

Shweder, R. A., & D'Andrade, R. G. Accurate reflection or systematic distortion? A reply to Block, Weiss, and Thorne. *Journal of Personality and Social Psychology*, 1979, **37**, 1,075–1,084.

Sundberg, N. D., Snowden, L. R., & Reynolds, W. M. Toward assessment of personal competence and incompetence in life situations. In M. R. Rosenzweig & L. W. Porter (Eds.), *Annual review of psychology*, Vol. 29. Palo Alto, Calif.: Annual Reviews, 1978.

Suppe, F. (Ed.) *The structure of scientific theories*. Urbana: University of Illinois Press, 1974.

Tellegen, A., Kamp, J., & Watson, D. Recognizing individual differences in predictive structure. *Psychological Review*, 1982, **89**, 95–105.

Vaughan, G. M. Personality and small group behavior. In R. B. Cattell & R. M. Dreger (Eds.), *Handbook of modern personality theory*. Washington, D.C.: Hemisphere, 1977.

Wachtel, P. L. Psychodynamics, behavior therapy, and the implacable experimenter: An inquiry into the consistency of personality. *Journal of Abnormal Psychology*, 1973, **82**, 324–334.

Wiggins, J. S. *Personality and prediction: Principles of personality assessment*. Reading, Mass.: Addison-Wesley, 1973.

Zubin, J., & Spring, B. Vulnerability—A new view of schizophrenia. *Journal of Abnormal Psychology*, 1977, **86**, 103–126.

9 THE SOCIAL-INTERACTIONAL VIEWPOINT

Robert C. Carson

Social-interactional theories or models in clinical psychology are many and varied and have only recently begun to coalesce into a distinctive set of central thema, usually identified as the "interpersonal" point of view. While they differ considerably in the details of their conceptions, interpersonalists generally accept two main working principles: (a) the most important origins of personality and of psychopathology are to be found in the nature of the personal interactions that characterize the individual's social history; and (b) personality and psychopathology are fundamentally and inextricably matters involving the nature of an individual's current relations with the social environment. An (a) to (b) causal relationship is normally explicitly posited. As is implied in this definition, the intellectual forbear to whom most interpersonalists acknowledge allegiance is Harry Stack Sullivan (1892–1949), the brilliant, if somewhat irascible, *enfant terrible* of early 20th-century American psychiatry.

While Sullivan is the main forebear of this still emerging and evolving viewpoint, he was not the first to perceive the limitations and rigidities of the once dominant medical-taxonomic and psychobiological-psychoanalytic models of psychopathology. Certain of his own mentors, among them

Adolf Meyer and William Alanson White, had already departed from traditional approaches, although in a manner less systematic and complete than Sullivan's. More systematic were the well-known "social" defections from the psychoanalytic ranks, beginning with Adler and subsequently including both Horney and Fromm. Common to the views of all of these theorists was a rejection of major tenets of Freudian theory, among them that: (a) instinctual energies were the ultimate forces in shaping personality; (b) intrapsychic structural and functional properties were the chief determinants of significant behavior; and (c) there are, therefore, certain universals in human behavior that are independent of the "culture" in which a person is reared. Owing to considerations of space and because in most instances there are excellent summaries elsewhere (e.g., Hall & Lindzey, 1978; Smith & Vetter, 1982), no attempt has been made here to outline the specific conceptions of these early socially oriented personality theorists.

The modern era of interpersonal theory in clinical psychology dates from the 1957 publication of Timothy Leary's *Interpersonal Diagnosis of Personality*, which summarized the work of Leary and his colleagues at the Kaiser Foundation on a new system of personality assessment that was avowedly Sullivanian in character. The book is a brilliant *tour de force* that can be profitably read and reread even today. It was undoubtedly the single most important factor leading to Leary's appointment to the Harvard faculty. The remainder of that story is well known and is of little consequence here, except that subsequent career developments for Leary appear to have aborted any extension of the work begun so well in *Interpersonal Diagnosis*.

A central element in what has come to be called "the Leary system" is the now-familiar "interpersonal circle," a circular model systematically arranged around orthogonal axes of "hate-love" and "dominance-submission," whose segments were thought to define in a virtually exhaustive manner the entire realm of discriminable types of interpersonal behavior, normal and otherwise. While Leary and his colleagues appear to have arrived at this conception largely by intuition, it was and continues to be surprisingly concordant with empirical evidence relating to the manner in which our cognitions about interpersonal behavior are organized (Carson, 1969; Wiggins, 1980).

A second important feature of the Leary system that has also had widespread impact is that it attempted to specify the provocative or "pull" aspect of any given type of interpersonal behavior enacted. This idea—that there is an above-baseline probability that the target person's response will be constrained in predictable ways by the particular type of behavior the actor deploys—was not only in itself an original and highly articulated extension of Sullivanian thinking, but it also clarified the "security operation" role of a person's interpersonal behavioral repertoire. In short, one maintains one's security (in the Sullivanian sense of that term) in large part by controlling the feedback one receives from one's interaction partners. Hence, a distinguishing characteristic of the psychologically disturbed person is more or less exclusive reliance on narrow-range security operations (i.e., interpersonal behaviors), that are often deployed with "magnificent finesse."

Notwithstanding the intuitive appeal and potential power of these ideas, they languished in relative obscurity for a number of years following the publication of Leary's book, possibly, as suggested above, because of the notoriety of subsequent unrelated developments in the author's career. An exception to this general neglect was the ongoing work of Lorr and McNair (1963, 1965,

1966, Lorr, Bishop, & McNair, 1965) on the development of an interpersonal circumplex-based assessment instrument; while this was an independent effort, it shared many features with the earlier work of Leary and his colleagues.

The rediscovery of the Leary system by contemporary researchers and theorists appears to have been in large measure an inadvertent by-product of a textbook-writing assignment undertaken by the present author in the mid-1960s. Commissioned to contribute a social-interactional account to a series of what were to be small books in personality, Carson (1969) attempted to update Sullivanian theory by integrating it with the work of Leary, with certain contemporary trends in social psychology, including the social exchange notions of Thibaut and Kelley (1959), and with varied concepts and findings derived from clinical research. Originally intended for students, *Interaction Concepts of Personality* received a surprisingly enthusiastic reception from many established investigators in the field. Clearly, these were ideas whose time was ripe—partly, one suspects in retrospect, because they offered a plausible middle ground to those who felt troubled by the person-situation controversy that was then just beginning to build (Mischel, 1968; Peterson, 1968).

The final noteworthy entry in this brief historical introduction to a now-burgeoning field is Swensen's *Introduction to Interpersonal Relations*, published in 1973. In this book, remarkable for its intellectual scope, Swensen skillfully and comprehensively surveys the entire domain of research and thinking in interpersonal relations. He concludes:

> Sullivanian theory seems to have more potential generality than any other approach to interpersonal relations. However, this potentiality has not yet been realized, nor is it likely to be realized for some time to come. But if I were forced to bet, my bet would be that when a generally accepted paradigm for the study of interpersonal relations comes, it will be a direct lineal descendent of Sullivanian theory. [p. 452]

There is, of course, still no "generally accepted paradigm" for the study of clinical phenomena within an interpersonal perspective. But a great deal is happening; to a necessarily selective summary of which we now turn.

Recent Theory and Research

The last several years have witnessed the development of a number of promising conceptual elaborations and programs of research that have their roots in the interpersonal approach to clinical phenomena. We will focus first on emergent trends insofar as this author can discern them, and then attempt to make some assessment of recent advances and the current state of the field.

Emergent Trends

The prinicipal recent developments in clinically oriented interpersonal research and theory may conveniently be classified under four main rubrics: (1) interbehavioral contingency; (2) rapprochement with other views; (3) cognitive analysis; and (4) behavioral taxonomies. We shall take each of these up in turn, although, as will become apparent, they are not mutually independent categories.

INTERBEHAVIORAL CONTINGENCY

By "interbehavioral contingency" is meant the tendency for a given individual's interpersonal behavior to be constrained or controlled in more or less predictable ways by the behavior received from an interaction partner. As we have seen, this idea was a key element in the Leary system, and it is a prominent feature in the thinking of many more recent theorists. That such contingencies, sometimes called conditional or transitional probabilities, exist is hardly subject to question (Anchin, 1982a). What we have lacked until fairly recently is systematic knowledge concerning the details of these regularities.

By far the most ambitious attempt at systematization in this area is Benjamin's (1974, 1977, 1979a, 1979b, 1982) Structural Analysis of Social Behavior (SASB), an extremely promising approach whose clinical assessment aspects have been computerized under the trade name INTREX (Benjamin, 1980). The SASB model employs three interrelated surfaces projected upon affiliative (hate-love) and interdependence (control-freedom) axes to depict actions of the other, actions of the self, and the "introject" to self related to actions of the other. The interpersonal behavior domain encompassed thus is highly compatible with other attempts to identify the basic properties of interpersonal behavior, including those of Leary (1957) and Wiggins (1979). It also incorporates the affec-tions, inclusion, and control dimensions that were originally proposed in an intuitively sensitive and prescient manner by Schutz (1958). The SASB model has a developmental aspect inasmuch as actions of the "other" are prototypically parentlike in character, for example, "Stroke, soothe, calm," or "Starve, cut out"; correspondingly, actions of the self often seem prototypically childlike, such as, "Sulk, act put upon," "Cling, depend."

The principle of complementarity is utilized within the SASB model to handle the provocational or behavioral induction aspect of contingent interpersonal behavior. Corresponding points on the self and other surfaces are theoretically complementary in this respect. Thus, "Stroke, soothe, calm" behavior on the part of the other is said (normally) to activate a "Relax, flow, enjoy" reaction by the self—and, parenthetically, if turned inwardly, an introject of "Stroke, soothe, self." A particularly interesting and unusual feature of the model is that it also specifies "antitheses," behaviors that would be expected to block or turn aside initiatives of the other. Antitheses are defined as "the opposite of the complement," where "opposite" behavior is both spatially (in terms of the model's pictorial representation) and conceptually at the opposite pole of the behavior in question. Thus, the antithesis of "Stroke, soothe, calm" would be "Sacrifice greatly." The therapeutic implications of the model are largely based on the principle of antithesis.

The product of many years of continuous development, Benjamin's SASB model is thus characterized by high degree of specificity and differentiation in the predictions it makes. Empirical testing of the model has thus far proved encouraging, and the present author can testify from personal experience that an INTREX client assessment can be extremely informative in the planning of therapeutic interventions.

The evocativeness of interpersonal behavior, particularly the in-session behavior of psychotherapy clients, has been subjected to extensive theoretical analysis by Kiesler and his colleagues (1979; Kiesler, Burnstein, & Anchin, 1976). Extending notions advanced by Beier (1966), among others, these authors focus especially on the *impact* upon the observer of the largely implicit interpersonal messages conveyed in the client's verbal and nonverbal behavior. Such messages, when accurately decoded, are a rich source of important diagnostic information. On the other hand, unrecognized impacts may cause the therapist to forfeit a requisite level of therapeutic leadership in the relationship, leading to impass and frustration of therapeutic goals.

The above examples of theory relating to interbehavioral contingency are merely representative of a large number of theoretical and empirical salients of recent years whose net effect is that of rendering obsolete the relatively ancient notion of unidirectional causal influences in interpersonal behavior. Every person in an interpersonal transaction is, behaviorally speaking, both a cause and an effect. There is an unbroken causal loop between the manifest interpersonal behavior of an actor, the reactions that his or her behavior generates in the interpersonal environment, and the feedback received from that environment, which in turn is either assimilated to extant cognitive-affective structures, or more rarely causes an accommodation of those structures to the new information impinging on the person's receptor apparatus. These cognitive-affective structures—altered or not by recent experience—mediate the enactment or initiation of new (or old and stereotyped) behavior (Anchin, 1982b; Carson, 1969, 1979, 1982; Kiesler, 1982).

Unfortunately, our discipline and its scientists and practitioners are ill-equipped at present to deal effectively with this level of complexity in contingent relations among various states of affairs and events that follow from, impinge upon, and possibly alter them. The pertinent methodology and technology appear to be in the realm of so-called stochastic processes, presently in a primitive state of development, although gaining increasing attention from interpersonalists (Benjamin, 1979b; Rausch, 1972).

RAPPROCHEMENT WITH OTHER VIEWS

Goldfried (1980), a scholar long identified with the behaviorist tradition in clinical psychology, has recently called for an end to the quixotic, shortsighted, and conceptually impervious manner in which we as psychologists and change-agents conduct our affairs. Interpersonalists find little to quarrel with in his argument, although it is noteworthy that he hardly acknowledges their point of view in any explicit way. To the present author, that neglect is a welcome indication of the pervasiveness of the influence of interpersonal thinking in contemporary "adjustments" being made to certain more established systems of thought. It now

appears that virtually everyone is, "of course," cognizant of the potency of interpersonal processes in the determination of maladaptive behavior and in its therapeutic amelioration.

A good example of the extent to which unrecognized Sullivanian and interpersonal concepts have invaded the mainstream is to be found in the British "object-relations" emphasis in psychoanalysis (e.g., Guntrip, 1971), now enjoying a surgent interest among American analysts. The cutting edge of contemporary psychoanalytic theory is no longer concerned with the vicissitudes of the libido or even of the ego, but rather with the "objects" a person internalizes and how these internalizations affect subsequent developments, particularly in the interpersonal arena (Fine, 1979). Current interest in the concepts of narcissism and the borderline personality within the psychoanalytic camp is a direct reflection of this distinctly interpersonal thrust. Similarly, Wachtel's (1977, 1982) attempts to reconcile psychoanalysis and behavior therapy are strongly infused with theory and technical recommendations deriving from the interpersonal perspective.

Behavior therapy itself has changed much since Krasner (1962) referred to the psychotherapist as a "social reinforcement machine." On the empirical front, DeVoge and Beck (1978) have comprehensively reviewed and documented the many subtle but powerful interpersonal influences that intrude into what were once thought to be entirely impersonal and "mechanical" behavioral procedures. Similarly, Goldfried and Davison (1976) devote an entire chapter to "The Therapeutic Relationship" in their widely used manual of behavior therapy techniques; they also make clear throughout the book their sensitive concern with interpersonal factors that may impede or facilitate the acceptance of prescribed therapeutic operations, many of which are decidedly interpersonal in character.

Examples of the encroachment of interpersonal thinking into many other superficially divergent conceptual approaches are readily available, but a pursuit of them here would take us too far afield. Let us simply note that the interpersonal viewpoint is increasingly coming to occupy a central position within the domain of the many competing explanations of human behavior and its findings. Sullivan, an ardent believer in the political and even the international ramifications of interpersonal theory, would doubtless have enthusiastically applauded these groping attempts to understand so small an interpersonal unit as the therapeutic dyad.

COGNITIVE ANALYSIS

Virtually all of human psychology has undergone a pronounced "cognitivization" in recent years as psychologists have increasingly recognized that the mechanical stimulus-response psychology of an earlier era is conceptually insufficient to handle the bewildering empirical realities of human performances. Contemporary interpersonal theory has kept apace with these broader developments across a whole array of new conceptual and methodological initiatives. Before sampling some of the latter work, however, it may be pertinent to note how — once again — Sullivan was well ahead of his time.

A convincing argument can be made that the central conception of mind that Sullivan (1953) entertained was that of an information-processing system. As recently pointed out by Carson (1982), his invention of the concepts of *personification* and *parataxic distortion* was undoubtedly inspired by his insight that person-information entering on the input side of a person's receptor apparatus seemed frequently to be transformed dramatically by the time its influence became manifest at the behavioral output side; clearly, some important things were happening inside the "black box," these things being in concept remarkably similar to the stuff of which contemporary cognitive psychology is largely made. Also to be noted here is the ease with which the notion of *selective inattention* can be translated into the modern concepts of cue selection and encoding processes, currently a focus of important work that is being carried out by interpersonalist Stephen Golding and colleagues (Golding, Valone, & Foster, 1980).

In the paper just noted, Carson (1982) attempted to employ a largely cognitive model to account for the commonly observed persistence of interpersonal behavior that is patently maladaptive. In brief, he postulated an unbroken causal loop among expectancies concerning others' behavior, enactment of behavior consistent with those expectancies, and expectancy-confirming reactions thereby generated in the interpersonal environment.

The concept of person-schematas or prototypes — imprecisely organized elements of memory relating to our interpersonal history — was employed prominently in this self-fulfilling ex-

pectancy model, and has in fact become central to much thinking and research in the person perception area (see, for examples, Hastie et al., 1980). Wiggins (1979, 1980, 1982), who has long been concerned with and impressed by the potential richness of circumplex solutions to the description and measurement of interpersonal behavior, has pointed out that our cognitive organizations relating to persons seem — in common with other cognitive organizations — to be composed of categories that have very indistinct boundaries, or "fuzzy sets." Hence, a circumplexly ordered taxonomy of trait-descriptive terms that are not sharply demarcated at the "edges" but rather blend into one another (as do Leary's, Benjamin's, and Wiggins' own) may have the peculiar virtue of corresponding with the manner in which we in fact cognize about persons. Our tendency to think about persons in prototypic rather than in concrete terms has recently received experimental confirmation in the work of Cantor and Mischel (1977, 1979a, 1979b). To put it another way, our thinking about persons seems to a large extent to be *parataxic* in character, which may be one reason why we have so much trouble studying it (see, for example, Golding et al., 1980).

The "problems in living" of which distressed people complain also have strong prototypic elements, as Horowitz and colleagues (Horowitz et al., 1982) have shown. These investigators cogently note that the symptoms presented by psychotherapy clients (e.g., "depression") actually tell us very little until they are decomposed into specific components, which vary from one client to another presenting a particular symptom. The symptom is, therefore, a prototype of a given class of problems, and the underlying problems usually turn out to be interpersonal in nature — frequently having the form, "I can't (do something interpersonal)." Interestingly, the structure of these claimed incompetencies appears to reflect the structure of interpersonal behavior generally. That is, they involve major elements of affection, control, and inclusion (or their opposites).

BEHAVIORAL TAXONOMIES

One of the more important events in the development of an interpersonally based clinical psychology occurred recently with the publication of McLemore and Benjamin's (1979) attack on the traditional psychiatric diagnostic system. In this work, they explicitly urge the abandonment of that system of classification in favor of a concentrated effort to develop systematic descriptions of maladaptive behavior *in interpersonal terms.* Since, they argue, abnormalities of behavior are virtually without exception abnormalities in the manner in which a person relates to others, a classification of abnormality that fails to capture this essence will always be deficient in various essential respects. They tentatively propose the SASB system, described above, as a reasonable beginning for this proposed revolutionary effort. It is an attractive argument, notwithstanding the political realities it perhaps too blithely dismisses.

Psychological "masculinity" and "femininity" (and their blending in certain individuals) have received much attention in the psychological literature in recent years. Spence and Helmreich (1978), accepting evidence—some of it their own—for the dimensional duality and essential orthogonality of these constructs, have, for example, proposed a fourfold classification scheme for individuals who exhibit varying levels of the pertinent behaviors: Masculine, Feminine, Androgynous, and Amorphous. These "types" are representative of the quadrants formed by the orthogogonal axes labeled agentic/instrumental (or their opposites) and expressive/communal (or their opposites). Typing is, of course, conceptually independent of biological gender.

Noting the similarity of this hypothetical space to that proposed by Leary and others (see above), Wiggins (1979, 1980; Wiggins & Holzmuller, 1978) suggests that an integration of gender-role and interpersonal research has the potential of shedding "new light" in both areas. The present author agrees with that assessment. In clinical work, too, there may be some as yet undiscovered relationship between the tendency of our clients' behaviors to concentrate below the horizontal axis (i.e., in the "submissive" ranges) of the Leary Circle, and—looked at in the other way—in the Amorphous and Feminine psychosocial gender classifications. Incidentally, Spence and Helmreich's (1978) data on maladjustment confirm that these are the more trouble-prone categories, for *either* biological sex.

Moving beyond mere attempts to classify individual behavior, Duke and Nowicki (1982) propose a taxonomy of adaptive and maladaptive interpersonal "constellations." A constellation, in their terms, is a particular combination of: (a) the situational appropriateness of behavior dis-played; (b) the congruence/incongruence of the messages transmitted via different (e.g., verbal versus nonverbal) channels; and (c) the level of complementarity obtaining between the behaviors of the interactants. They describe 12 such constellations, half "adaptive" and half "maladaptive." While the details of their analysis cannot be presented here, they make the important point that neither complementarity nor congruence is necessarily essential to an adaptive interaction.

Current State of the Field

Fortunate indeed is the author assigned a task such as the present one to be able to point to a single source—published literally only days before writing deadline—as representing state-of-the-art currency in the field in question. This author enjoys that happy circumstance, and in fact has already employed the source in earlier chapter sections. The work to which reference is made is the *Handbook of Interpersonal Psychotherapy*, edited by Anchin and Kiesler (1982). In this foreword to their volume, Hans Strupp captures the significance of the book for clinical psychology and the interpersonal viewpoint:

> The central theme of this volume is the redefinition of the psychotherapeutic relationship as a two-person system. At first glance, this revision of what used to be seen as a subject-object relationship may not seem radical. As the authors represented in this forward-looking volume demonstrate, however, we stand on the threshold of a revolution in psychotherapy that will predictably have incisive consequences for practice, training, and research in the years to come [p. ix].

Any comprehensive attempt to describe here the current state of the field would be redundant with the Anchin-Kiesler *Handbook*, and especially with Anchin's (1982b) own excellent summary chapter at the end of that work. Instead, the author offers in what follows a general, and to some extent personal, evaluation of the current standing of the interpersonal perspective among "theories of personality" and of its usefulness as a guide to clinical practice.

One of the more extraordinary characteristics of interpersonal theory is the extent to which it is ignored, particularly among writers who purport to survey the field of personality theory. At most, what one finds relating to interpersonal theory in such surveys is a superficial and often simply *wrong* interpretation of Sullivan, usually embedded within a single chapter bearing the rubric of "social theories," or something like that, and including synopses of the ideas of theorists whose contemporary importance approximates that of historical relics. By contrast, the classic global theories that purport to explain all of human behavior with but a few vague and/or utterly untestable propositions are given lavish—one might even say obsessive—attention. As was suggested earlier, the present writer is inclined optimistically to interpret this remarkable phenomenon as evidence of the *success* of interpersonal theory. Now, everyone owns it, and in fact someone else said (or intimated) it first!

Among theories of personality, the most distinguishing features of the interpersonal viewpoint, in this writer's judgment, is that it is burdened neither with closed-system "first principles" nor with constructs that are in principle nonempirical in character. There is no acknowledged leader of the "movement," and hence there is no interpersonal bible to guide the future directions of interpersonal investigation. Rather, there is a marvelous randomness and improvisation among researchers in the interpersonal domain, characteristics that emulate the intellectual style of such innovators as Sullivan and Leary. Because of these qualities, which are almost unique in psychology and particularly in clinical psychology, the future of interpersonal psychology appears bright indeed. May it never succumb to becoming merely another "system."

The practical, clinical implications of interpersonal theory are similarly broad and superordinate in nature, as the Anchin-Kiesler *Handbook* demonstrates. Therapist-client interactions are obviously reciprocally contingent. If psychotherapy is mainly a *learning experience* for at least the client, then it follows that the therapist has, at least, a responsibility to plan and control what it is that the client *will learn* in his or her interactions with the therapist. Much evidence exists that what the successful client "learns" in therapy has less to do with the "content" of his or her problems, whatever they may be, than with the manner in which those "problems" impinge upon and generate aversive reactions in other people—leading to an unnecessarily restricted range of experienced interpersonal satisfactions and securities. In the absence of an understanding of such interpersonal dynamics, the therapist cannot be other than minimally effective.

The "manipulation" of the so-called transference relationship in therapy has been widely condemned, particularly among analysts and other rule-conscious types. Apparently, however, the rule is honored more in the breach than in the practice. The noted psychoanalysts, Alexander and French (1946) recommended many years ago an active style in confronting transferences in the service of shortening treatment duration, and Wachtel (1977, 1982), avowedly writing from the same perspective, presents a not very different rationale of therapeutic strategy. One hardly hears anymore of radically phenomenological, "client-centered" approaches to therapy (notwithstanding their prominence in undergraduate texts), presumably because of the disappointments engendered by the application of that approach to a very seriously disturbed population (Rogers et al., 1967). Behavior therapy, as noted above, has moved much closer to an interpersonal-cognitive orientation than its forebears would have wished or imagined.

In short, the interpersonal viewpoint is alive and well on the current scene. It has demonstrated impressive resilience and ease of accommodation to new research findings, and it continues to have broad overarching appeal as a potential integrating approach to many of the current concerns of clinical psychology—particularly when it is compared with competing systems of thought.

Current Issues

Despite the altogether enviable position of interpersonal theory on the contemporary scene, its full potential has been far from realized and will not be realized until certain rather intimidating, complex problems are overcome. The most important of these problems are briefly surveyed below, and then an attempt is made to predict some of the field's future directions.

Unresolved Problems

The most significant clouds appearing on the horizon of interpersonal theory appear to fall in three main areas.

PROBLEMS OF ASSESSMENT

While great strides in interpersonal assessment have been made since Leary and his colleagues introduced the Interpersonal Check List (ICL) and associated assessment paraphernalia (Leary, 1957), we still lack a comprehensive and psychometrically adequate assessment technology in this area. The ICL, often chosen as a primary assessment instrument by researchers, is plagued with many psychometric problems, including especially a very strong social desirability component. Benjamin's (1980) INTREX system shows much promise for individual clinical assessment, but it is probably too cumbersome and time-consuming to be used extensively in research. Other promising approaches are still in the development stage.

There is, in any event, something of a paradox embedded in any attempt to assess a person's interpersonal behavior, particularly where a traitlike approach is utilized. One of the cardinal principles of interpersonal theory, after all, is that a person's behavior in an interpersonal situation is strongly determined by the behaviors of his or her interaction partners. Indeed, if that is not the case, we tend to render a judgment of mental or personality disorder (Carson, 1969). The assessment issue thus becomes one of determining what *regularities*, if any, exist between behavioral inputs and behavioral outputs. The principle of complementarity, as noted earlier, is one such attempt to specify, at a probabalistic level, a presumed regularity of this type. But, of course, significant interpersonal relationships consist of a long series of input-output exchanges, during the course of which we must assume that each party's behavior undergoes alteration in consequence of the other's behavior. Hence, we are faced with harrowing methodological problems in undertaking any comprehensive assessment program.

The long-term work of Donald Peterson (1982) deserves special mention in this context. With extraordinary diligence and persistence, this investigator has in fact pursued the type of demanding research program that is implied in the above remarks. To date, the main product of this "functional analysis of interpersonal behavior" is a set of thoughtful and well-tried-out procedures for determining what is happening in the enormously complicated transactions that characterize any significant interpersonal relationship. Unfortunately, perhaps, few other investigators would be prepared to invest the time and energy required for a project of this sort; university tenure stringencies alone would bar most young researchers.

TRANSITIONAL PROBABILITY PROBLEMS

A serious difficulty related to relationship change over time is our lack of sufficiently sophisticated mathematical tools for the exposure and analysis of the sequential patterning of interpersonal transactions. As noted earlier, this problem falls within the general domain of stochastic processes. While Markov chain analysis has been effectively employed in an interpersonal context by Benjamin (1979b) and Rausch (1972), their efforts were largely illustrative in nature, and it seems unlikely that the Markov technique is sufficiently powerful to have general utility in disentangling the event networks we need to understand. Presumably, the stochastic analytic techniques that are required will become available some time in the future.

THE PHENOMENOLOGICAL IMPASSE

If — as the present author suspects will happen — interpersonal theory becomes even more "cognitive," it will run headlong into what is perhaps all of psychology's most vexing problem, the problem of objectifying and reliably observing *experience*. It is evidently extremely difficult to observe *one's own* cognitive processes directly (Nisbett & Wilson, 1977). The requirement that we observe and measure the fundamentally private cognitions of *others* may well tax our ingenuity beyond its limits. I am unconvinced that, when we ask a person to describe (typically in linguistic code) his or her experience of another person, we are getting anything very closely correspondent with the actual impact the other has made in terms of primary impressions and interferences made from them. And yet it is difficult to imagine interpersonal theory making much progress in the cognitive direction without being able to ask, and get reliable and valid answers to, *exactly* this form of question.

Notwithstanding the obvious difficulties we face in this area, it would perhaps be a mistake to adopt too pessimistic an attitude. The problem, after all, is an extremely widespread one in psychology (although it is not always recognized), and other kinds of psychologists — e.g., the cognitists themselves — have found ingenious and apparently satisfactory ways around it. Golding et al. (1980) have provided a thoughtful discussion of the issues in the interpersonal realm, and have made a number of constructive suggestions for tapping into this process of "interpersonal construal."

Future Directions

As is already apparent from the foregoing, this author anticipates that major new thrusts in interpersonal theory will originate from judicious incorporations of current and future discoveries in the area of information processing and cognitive psychology in general. Virtually all clinicians, of whatever stripe, accept the proposition (and this is one of Freud's monumental insights) that current interaction patterns with significant others are re-enactments of earlier — often *much* earlier — ones. Conceivable interpretations of this phenomenon are, to this author at least, unconvincing except insofar as they postulate some sort of information-processing mechanism that renders current incoming information functionally equivalent to the earlier inputs that were presumably involved in the establishment of the prototypes or templates by means of which such "new" information is "processed." Put in simpler terms, the past determines the present because the present is interpreted in terms of the past. Much work remains to be done, of course, in establishing the parameters of these functional equivalences.

Interaction Concepts of Personality (Carson, 1969) made a broad plea, both implicitly and explicitly, that the further refinement of Sullivanian theory would depend as much on developments in social psychology as on those of any other of psychology's subdisciplines. That plea is as valid today as it was when those words were written nearly a decade and a half ago. There is no evidence whatever that the plea was heeded by social psychologists, who, like the rest of us, have their own axes to grind. However, the spontaneous and natural development of that field in the intervening years, dominated to a large extent by the seminal ideas of Heider (1958), has in fact contributed richly to our understanding of interpersonal processes — particularly its cognitive aspects, now encompressed under the rubric of "attribution theory." We may hope that social psychologists will one day be freed from their excessive preoccupation with laboratory-based, unidirectional causation, and often analogically contrived, models of research. When and if they are, we will have waiting for them a rich store of questions to which, in many ways, their talents are uniquely suited. In

short, this author still believes in the potential of a rapprochement between clinical and social psychology, and believes that it will in time genuinely be achieved.

Apart from what has already been said in this and earlier sections, other directions that the field may take are not readily discernible. Certainly we will require a much-enhanced research technology to deal with already obvious roadblocks. Whether or not those will emerge from the interpersonal camp remains to be seen, but it is by no means a foregone conclusion that they will. This underscores the enormous strength of the interpersonal viewpoint in its ability to profit from and incorporate advances in areas well beyond its own borders. It is to this strength, in the final analysis, the Sullivan tradition owes its continuous expansion and growth.

On a more pragmatic level, interpersonally based techniques of psychotherapy are expected to continue to proliferate, even though there is already a bewildering array of them (Anchin & Kiesler, 1982). A distinguishing feature of most such therapies is that they prescribe a strikingly active therapist posture in the therapy relationship, in keeping with the interpersonalist view that major changes in personal functioning depend upon dramatic alterations in the interpersonal context in which problem behaviors occur. An unexpected extension of this view is that psychotherapy may occur in the absence of the designated client, provided only that the therapist can effectively control the client's interpersonal milieu (Coyne & Segal, 1982). We may also anticipate the development of specific strategies of interactional psychotherapy for particular types of disorder. Indeed, this has already begun in relation to the problem of depression, and the beginning seems to be an auspicious one (Weissman et al., 1982).

Conclusions

We have — all too briefly — examined in the foregoing pages a point of view on disordered personality and disordered interpersonal functioning (a probably false distinction) that is more open-ended, less "finished," than any other of the broad perspectives purporting to explain personality and its derangements. We therefore run the risk of having depicted a rapidly developing field as it appears within a particular and almost arbitrarily chosen slice of time. We truly do not know where it is headed, although, as we have seen, developments in certain directions are reasonably likely. It may therefore be most appropriate to summarize here where we have been, and what the interpersonal perspective has thus far accomplished with a relatively few active "converts," leaving it to the reader to decide what "conclusions" are warranted at this juncture.

The accomplishments of interpersonal theory would seem to include, to date, at least the following:

1. The approach to personality and psychopathology originally proposed by Sullivan has proven to be a living and dynamic one. It is rich enough to be a constant source of new hypotheses, and flexible enough to accommodate to new findings that emerge from the testing of those hypotheses.

2. We now have the beginnings of an understanding of the structure of interpersonal behavior. In turn, this understanding has shed new light on such venerable problems as the classification of psychopathological conditions and the nature of gender-role behavior.

3. The interpersonal approach has contributed importantly to a revolutionary and highly productive redefinition of psychotherapy and of the psychotherapy relationship, one increasingly incorporated into other systems.

4. We now have the means to analyze — and growing insight into — the relationship between the "presenting complaints" or symptoms of our clients and the interpersonal meaning and function of those symptomatic expressions.

5. The concepts of Sullivan relating to the manner in which we process information, particularly person information, have turned out to be strikingly prophetic in the light of modern cognitive psychology, and important work is underway to understand more fully the processes involved in what Golding calls "interpersonal construal."

6. We have begun to understand some of the rules that govern the influence of one person's interpersonal behavior upon that of another.

7. Interpersonalists have essentially discarded the notion of unidirectional causality in attempting to understand the significant behavior of persons, and in so doing have gained a richer appreciation of how personality traits, adaptive and maladaptive, are maintained.

And, finally:

8. Interpersonal theory is spawning a variety of new and imaginative psychotherapeutic techniques and strategies, often specifically targeted to the rapid resolution of particular types of problems in living — for a sampling of which the reader is referred to the Anchin and Kiesler (1982) *Handbook*.

References

Alexander, F., & French, T. M. *Psychoanalytic therapy.* New York: Ronald, 1946.

Anchin, J. C. Sequence, pattern, and style: Integration and treatment implications of some interpersonal concepts. In J. C. Anchin & D. J. Kiesler (Eds.), *Handbook of interpersonal psychotherapy.* New York: Pergamon, 1982. (a)

Anchin, J. C. Interpersonal approaches to psychotherapy: Summary and conclusions. In J. C. Anchin & D. J. Kiesler (Eds.), *Handbook of interpersonal psychotherapy.* New York: Pergamon, 1982. (b)

Anchin, J. C., & Kiesler, D. J. (Eds.) *Handbook of interpersonal psychotherapy.* New York: Pergamon, 1982.

Beier, E. G. *The silent language of psychotherapy.* Chicago: Aldine, 1966.

Benjamin, L. S. Structural analysis of social behavior. *Psychological Review,* 1974, **81**, 392–425.

Benjamin, L. S. Structural analysis of a family in therapy. *Journal of Consulting and Clinical Psychology,* 1977, **45**, 391–406.

Benjamin, L. S. Structural analysis of differentiation failure. *Psychiatry,* 1979, **42**, 1–23. (a)

Benjamin, L. S. Use of structural analysis of social behavior (SASB) and Markov chains to study dyadic interactactions. *Journal of Abnormal Psychology,* 1979, **88**, 303–313. (b)

Benjamin, L. S. *INTREX users manual.* Madison, Wisc.: INTREX Interpersonal Institute, 1980.

Benjamin, L. S. Use of structural analysis of social behavior (SASB) to guide intervention in psychotherapy. In J. C. Anchin & D. L. Kiesler (Eds.), *Handbook of interpersonal psychotherapy.* New York: Pergamon, 1982.

Cantor, N., & Mischel, W. Traits as prototypes: Effects on recognition memory. *Journal of Personality and Social Psychology,* 1977, **35**, 38–48.

Cantor, N., & Mischel, W. Prototypicality and personality: Effects on free recall and personality impressions. *Journal of Research in Personality,* 1979, **13**, 187–205. (a)

Cantor, N., & Mischel, W. Categorization processes in the perception of people. In L. Berkowitz (Ed.), *Advances in experimental social psychology.* New York: Academic Press, 1979. (b)

Carson, R. C. *Interaction concepts of personality.* Chicago: Aldine, 1969.

Carson, R. C. Personality and exchange in developing relationships. In R. L. Burgess & T. L. Huston (Eds.), *Social exchange in developing relationships.* New York: Academic Press, 1979.

Carson, R. C. Self-fulfilling prophecy, maladaptive behavior, and psychotherapy. In J. C. Anchin & D. J. Kiesler (Eds.), *Handbook of interpersonal psychotherapy.* New York: Pergamon, 1982.

Coyne, J. C., & Segal, L. A brief, strategic interactional approach to psychotherapy. In J. C. Anchin & D. J. Kiesler (Eds.), *Handbook of interpersonal psychotherapy.* New York: Pergamon, 1982.

DeVoge, J. T., & Beck, S. The therapist-client relationship in behavior therapy. In M. Hersen, R. M. Eisler, & P. M. Miller (Eds.), *Progress in behavior modification.* Vol. 6. New York: Academic Press, 1978.

Duke, M. P., & Nowicki, S. A social learning theory analysis of interactional theory concepts and a multidimensional model of human interaction constellations. In J. C. Anchin & D. J. Kiesler (Eds.), *Handbook of interpersonal psychotherapy.* New York: Pergamon, 1982.

Fine, R. *A history of psychoanalysis.* New York: Columbia University Press, 1979.

Goldfried, M. R. Toward the delineation of therapeutic change principles. *American Psychologist,* 1980, **35**, 991–999.

Goldfried, M. R., & Davison, G. C. *Clinical behavior therapy.* New York: Holt, Rinehart & Winston, 1976.

Golding, S. L., Valone, K., & Foster, S. W. Interpersonal construal: An individual differences framework. In N. Hirschberg (Ed.), *Multivariate methods in the social sciences: Applications.* Hillsdale, N.J.: Erlbaum, 1980.

Guntrip. H. *Psychoanalytic theory, therapy, and the self.* New York: Basic Books, 1971.

Hall, C. S., & Lindzey, G. *Theories of personality.* (3rd ed.) New York: Wiley, 1978.

Hastie, R., Ostrom, T. M., Ebbeson, E. G., Wyer, R. S., Hamilton, D. L., & Carlston, D. E. (Eds.). *Person memory: The cognitive basis of social perception.* Hillsdale, N.J.: Erlbaum, 1980.

Heider, F. *The psychology of interpersonal relations.* New York: Wiley, 1958.

Horowitz, L., French, R. de S., Lapid, J. S., & Weckler, D. A. Symptoms and interpersonal problems: The prototype as an integrating concept. In J. C. Anchin & D. J. Kiesler (Eds.), *Handbook of interpersonal psychotherapy.* New York: Pergamon, 1982.

Kiesler, D. J. An interpersonal communication analysis of relationship in psychotherapy. *Psychiatry,* 1979, **42**, 299–311.

Kiesler, D. J. Interpersonal theory for personality and psychotherapy. In J. C. Anchin & D. J. Kiesler (Eds.), *Handbook of interpersonal psychotherapy.* New York: Pergamon, 1982.

Kiesler, D. J., Burnstein, A. B., & Anchin, J. C. *Interpersonal communication, relationship and the behavior therapies.* Richmond: Virginia Commonwealth University, 1976.

Krasner, L. The therapist as a social reinforcement machine. In H. H. Strupp & L. Luborsky (Eds.), *Research in psychotherapy,* Vol. II. Washington: APA, 1962.

Leary, T. *Interpersonal diagnosis of personality.* New York: Ronald, 1957.

Lorr, M., Biship, P. F., & McNair, D. M. Interpersonal types among psychiatric patients. *Journal of Abnormal Psychology,* 1965, **70**, 468–472.

Lorr, M., & McNair, D. M. An interpersonal behavior circle. *Journal of Abnormal and Social Psychology,* 1963, **67**, 68–75.

Lorr, M. & McNair, D. M. Expansion of the interpersonal behavior circle. *Journal of Personality and Social Psychology,* 1965, **2**, 823–830.

Lorr, M. & McNair, D. M. Methods relating to evaluation of therapeutic outcome. In L. Gottschalk & A. H. Auerbach (Eds.), *Methods of research in psychotherapy.* New York: Appleton-Century-Crofts, 1966.

McLemore, C. W. & Benjamin, L. S. Whatever happened to interpersonal diagnosis: A psychosocial alternative to DSMIII. *American Psychologist,* 1979, **34**, 17–34.

Mischel, W. *Personality and assessment.* New York: Wiley, 1968.

Nisbett, R. E., & Wilson, T. D. Telling more than we can know: Verbal reports on mental processes. *Psychological Review,* 1977, **84**, 231–259.

Peterson, D. R. *The clinical study of social behavior.* New York: Appleton-Century-Crofts, 1968.

Peterson, D. R. Functional analysis of interpersonal behavior. In J. C. Anchin & D. J. Kiesler (Eds.), *Handbook of interpersonal psychotherapy.* New York: Pergamon, 1982.

Rausch, H. L. Process and change: A Markov model of interaction. *Family Process,* 1972, **11**, 275–298.

Rogers, C. R.; Gendlin, E. T.; Kiesler, D. J.; & Truax, C. B. *The therapeutic relationship and its impact: A study of psychotherapy with schizophrenics.* Madison, Wisc. University of Wisconsin Press, 1967.

Schutz, W. C. *FIRO: A three-dimensional theory of interpersonal behavior.* New York: Holt, Rinehart & Winston, 1958.

Smith, B. D., & Vetter, H. J. *Theoretical approaches to personality.* Englewood Cliffs, N.J.: Prentice-Hall, 1982.

Spence, J. T., & Helmreich, R. L. *Masculinity and femininity.* Austin: University of Texas Press, 1978.

Strupp, H. H. Foreword. In J. C. Anchin & D. J. Kiesler (Eds.), *Handbook of interpersonal psychotherapy.* New York: Pergamon, 1982.

Sullivan, H. S. *The interpersonal theory of psychiatry.* New York: Norton, 1953.

Swensen, C. H. *Introduction to interpersonal relations.* Glenview, Ill.: Scott, Foresman, 1973.

Thibaut, J., & Kelley, H. H. *The social psychology of groups.* New York: Wiley, 1959.

Wachtel, P. L. *Psychoanalysis and behavior therapy: Toward an integration.* New York: Basic Books, 1977.

Wachtel, P. L. Interpersonal therapy and active intervention. In J. C. Anchin & D. J. Kiesler (Eds.), *Handbook of interpersonal psychotherapy.* New York: Pergamon, 1982.

Weissman, M. M., Klerman, G. L., Rounsaville, B. J., Chevron, E. S., & Neu, C. Short-term interpersonal psychotherapy (IPT) for depression: Description and efficacy. In J. C. Anchin & D. J. Kiesler (Eds.), *Handbook of interpersonal psychotherapy.* New York: Pergamon, 1982.

Wiggins, J. S. A psychological taxonomy of trait-descriptive terms: The interpersonal domain. *Journal of Personality and Social Psychology,* 1979, **37**, 395–412.

Wiggins, J. S. Circumplex models of interpersonal behavior. In L. Wheeler (Ed.), *Review of personality and social psychology,* Vol. 1. Beverly Hills, Calif.: Sage, 1980.

Wiggins, J. S. Circumplex models of interpersonal behavior in clinical psychology. In P. C. Kendall & J. N. Butcher (Eds.), *Handbook of research methods in clinical psychology.* New York: Wiley Interscience, 1982.

Wiggins, J. S., & Holzmuller, A. Psychological androgyny and interpersonal behavior. *Journal of Consulting and Clinical Psychology,* 1978, **46**, 40–52.

10 PHENOMENOLOGICAL-HUMANISTIC APPROACHES

Hugh B. Urban

A generation ago Sir Charles Snow (1959) described and deplored a state of affairs he recognized within British and American universities. In his view, an ominous gap had developed between two strong investigatory traditions — the arts and humanities on the one hand, and the sciences and engineering on the other. Both traditions are concerned with a study of the human condition; both direct their energies to the discovery and pursuit of ways in which the circumstances of people can be enhanced and improved. But, separation had occurred such that two "cultures" had formed, and these two cultures were sufficiently different from each other that useful communication and exchange between them had virtually ceased.

Like divergent enthnic cultures that are geographically separated in different parts of the world, the cultures had grown from different philosophical and ideological foundations, pursued different paradigms and models to guide their efforts, formulated their own languages, developed their own literature, fashioned their own tools, and practiced their own styles of communication and commerce within their own grouping. Snow recognized that the divergencies had been long in developing; by the time he chose to

comment on the situation it was his judgment that the cultural gaps had come to loom large. Philosophical differences as to what was thought to be significant and important to emphasize about the human condition led to sharp and sustained disagreements. Languages had become sufficiently different that efforts to communicate across cultural lines had become burdensome, frustrating, and frequently abandoned. People tended to stay increasingly within their cultural bounds, contenting themselves with their own literature with which they felt compatible, neglecting to remain informed about what was taking place in neighboring areas, and making little if any effort to relate what it was that they were doing to efforts that were being made elsewhere. Finally, cultural barriers had become formed, rendering it unlikely that persons would move freely back and forth between the two cultures; sanctions were sometimes employed to discourage those who were considered "disloyal" to their "cultural traditions"; various hindrances became formed to render collaboration across boundaries more difficult; and the inevitable suspicions and animosities that can develop between segmented human groupings came into being and exerted a dissuasive effect.

Snow regarded the situation as unfortunate for

a great variety of reasons. A major concern, of course, is the jeopardy in which a larger society is placed when deep divisions that become increasingly difficult to reconcile form within it. But developments of this sort are also unsatisfactory if valuable and significant ideas that are necessary to the full development of both fail to be freely exchanged, or if solutions to extant problems that require cross-cultural collaboration cannot be worked out. Each culture is impoverished by the lack of what the other can contribute.

It can be argued that Snow's characterization of the two cultures within the intellective circles of our societies is, like all general analogies, somewhat overdrawn. It is not difficult to find exceptions in particular persons or places. And yet, many agree that his observations hold considerable merit, that his concerns are well founded, and that efforts to remedy the situation are indicated. One of the foremost historians of science (Sarton, 1962) has articulated comparable concerns, pointing out that the humanities without scientific education are essentially incomplete, but that without history, philosophy, art, and letters, and without a living faith, man's life on this planet would cease to be worthwhile.

What can and should be done to correct the difficulty has been much less obvious to those who agree that it exists. Suggested remedies have been numerous. Conferences and committees have been formed and tried; and "two-culture dialogues" are an institutional fixture in some places. Most such efforts have met with only indifferent success, and the two cultures would appear to be maintaining a relatively peaceful, but uneasy, coexistence.

It is tempting to suggest that something akin to all of this has occurred within the arena of psychology as well. We are referring in this instance to the apparently large discrepancies that obtain between the humanistic-phenomenological-existentialist perspectives regarding the proper study of the human and human behavior, in contrast to what appears to be the more prevalent posture known as Scientific Psychology. The parallels with Snow's characterization of two cultures within general academic circles seem, superficially at least, to be rather close. Inspection reveals that the philosophical positions from which these two streams have developed are not only at great variance with one another, but also that the antinomies that exist between them have been with man since earliest times. With variant proposals

as to the nature of being in general and human existence in particular (ontology), as well as divergent views concerning the nature of knowledge and how we know what we think we know (epistemology), the two streams have emerged with sharply different models for characterizing the nature of man, and the methods and means that are required to understand the human person and to render his behavior intelligible.

Separated domains of investigatory activity do seem to have come about. Psychologists with an existential orientation, for example, quite naturally maintain contacts with others of similar persuasion, tend to read the materials of those who are working along comparable lines, and are constrained by limitations of energy and time from remaining conversant with markedly different views and approaches. But, of course, the same can be said of their more laboratory-based colleagues, for whom the task of staying abreast of developments in their particular areas of emphasis is equally seductive as well as demanding. However, even if time and circumstance permitted a greater degree of interplay between persons operating within these different perspectives, productive exchanges would prove problematic. With differences between them at the most basic paradigmatic levels, it should not be surprising that communication problems across these respective streams have proven so difficult, that conceptual units and their definitional terminologies require such lengthy periods of time to share, or that generalizations and conclusions about events generated by one set of models and observational procedures can be regarded as simply nonpersuasive from an alternative perspective.

Separation is recognizable in other respects as well. Persons working within one perspective tend to be concentrated in the world of practice, the other within the world of academia. The respective writings of the representatives of these two perspectives are found in different sources, and in different professional journals. Professional conferences that attract the members of one perspective find few participants who reflect the other. Separate professional associations have become formed. Cross-fertilization of ideas between the two perspectives are difficult to discern; one can look in vain in the literature sources of one seeking references to the findings or discoveries reported in the literature of the other. Often, the two perspectives do not appear in juxtaposition to one another save in comprehensive compendia such as the present volume. As a consequence, success in remaining "bilingual" for any particular psychologist is extremely hard to do.

The suggestion of "two cultures" within the field of psychology is made with considerable diffidence for a number of reasons. Not only is it likely that the analogy, like that of C. P. Snow, is in several respects overstated, there is also a very real question as to whether persons and their points of view can be legitimately "lumped together" in such a fashion. Writers within the humanistic, or the phenomenological, or the existentialist traditions, for example, are exceedingly numerous, and important differences are discernible between and among them. It is more proper to regard these as points of view, rather than as systematic models around which consensus has developed. The citation of commonalities within each of these groupings, insofar as they are discernible, will invariably be found to have done an injustice to the writings of a particular theorist; in few respects do they all sing with the same voice. Furthermore, the legitimacy of clustering the humanist, phenomenological, and existential perspectives together within a common framework is open to challenge, since important differences exist between these perspectives as well.

At the same time, a certain number of commonalities can be identified. Writers within and across these theoretic streams have cited instances where they recognize that their positions are comparable to others; moreover, certain compatibilities between the streams have been noted, as when Sartre (1947) argues forcefully that existentialism is a humanism, or when Perls (1973) asserts that the phenomenalism in his Gestalt approach is existential in character. Finally, the view has become prevalent that a confluence of these perspectives has been taking place, such that with the passage of time they are becoming progressively more similar to one another in the manner in which they are represented (Pervin, 1960).

At the risk, therefore, of misrepresenting the points of view of individual theorists, and with the foreknowledge that the variability they collectively represent cannot be accommodated with a single overarching paradigmatic frame, an attempt will be made to fashion a broad outline of the characteristics of one of these "cultures" so as to explicate and expose the nature and extent of its differences from the other. It is hoped that the deficiencies with which each characterizes the other will become apparent, as will the recognition that

critiques of each by the other can only occur from the standpoint of their own philosophical posture. In order to accomplish this task, it will be necessary first to treat the historical contexts from which the perspectives have emerged.

Historical Antecedents

The seminal origins of all three lines of thought with which we are concerned are older than the titles by which they have come to be known.

The Humanist Tradition

The ingredients that have come to form the humanistic point of view can be traced as far back as the 5th century B.C. Protagoras is cited as having enunciated the fundamental principle underlying this perspective: "Man is the measure of all things; of those that are, that they are; of those that are not, that they are not." In classical literature, Socrates is also linked with this perspective because he eschewed the study of physical nature as a means of dependable insight into the understanding of man and the development of human knowledge, or of developing a satisfactory basis for intellectual and moral value. He looked instead to a study of man himself in search of a rational basis for thought and action.

The preeminence of a theistic view tended to obscure this viewpoint throughout the Middle Ages. It underwent a revival, however, in Italy in the latter part of the 14th century, a revival that rapidly spread throughout the Western world, with Petrarch and Erasmus constituting the major figures in this movement. It was at this time that the term, "Humanism" was explicitly adopted, as a way of asserting a clear break from the sterile, authoritarian, intellectual traditions that had accumulated within scholastic philosophy and theology. It featured a return to, and renewed study of, the classical Greek and Roman writers as a source of inspiration and guidance. Classical Humanism is considered to have been the parent of all modern philosophical, scientific, or social developments.

It is the current thought that Humanism as a perspective contains three major divisions: (1) Classical Humanism, which is exemplified in some college and university circles that have retained a focus upon the study of "The Great Books"; (2) Christian Humanism, which is a God-centered form of Humanism, of which the neo-Thomist

Jacques Maritain is illustrative; and (3) Scientific Humanism, which seeks to wed the contributions of scientific inquiry to the protection and enrichment of man's circumstance on earth by liberating the latent potentialities of human nature. It has in common with the other Humanist positions affirmed a positive attitude toward the development and preservation of human life, the dignity and value of each individual person, and the salience of the human's most distinctive characteristic—rationality. It also supports change and growth in order to enhance the quality of human living, asserts the priority of human needs and values over material things, espouses the necessity for freedom from wants and constraints to enable all people to maximize their personal aspirations and accomplishments within the course of their individual lives, and emphasizes the significance of each person's contribution to the lives and welfare of all human persons who follow (Frank, 1977).

The obvious counterpart to the Humanist position is *Naturalism*, which advocates the study of objects, persons, and events through reliance upon the combined use of empirical observation and rationality, and seeks to explain their origins and functions within the general context of the natural world. There are many varieties of the naturalist position. Those who are persuaded that all energies, forces, and occurrences can be reduced to events comprising the subject matter of physics and chemistry hold a view referred to as *Physicalism*, or *Materialism*.

Humanists as a group take strong exception to most versions of the naturalist position, which they regard as dehumanizing in both its manner of approach and its effects. They would emphasize instead the distinctiveness of humans from the remainder of the natural order. Although they acknowledge that there are continuities between the human and his capabilities and the biological and physical worlds, they would also insist that there are large-scale differences, that these differences are the most significant aspects of the human person upon which attention needs to be focused, and that an explication of these characteristics and what they enable the human person to do can only be discovered by a study of humans themselves. Explanatory extrapolations of human action derived from an analysis of other species would be regarded as biocentric and spuriously metaphorical in character.

Likewise associated with the Humanist position has been the assertion of the legitimacy of the

concept of mind, a concept that is anathema to a thoroughgoing materialist. Attributes of the mind deemed particularly significant include the capabilities for conscious apprehension of the directly experienced world, for the imposition of order and coherence upon the contents of experience, for transcending immediate experience, for intentionality and the pursuit of valued purposes and goals, and for exercising freedom and choice, leading to the necessity for democratic institutions for moral and social behavior.

In keeping with their long tradition, Humanists also maintain a broad-gauged appreciation of the multiplicity of actions in which human persons are everywhere found to engage: art, music, poetry, drama, history, philosophy, and religion. Significant insights and understandings are recognized to arise from the exercise of these pursuits, insights that augment and clarify the characteristics of human nature above and beyond what the more restricted scientific approach might be able to contribute. Reliance upon the exercise of the scientific methodologies alone is characterized as *Scientism*, which humanists view as an extremely narrow and potentially very damaging approach to the human person and his world. The discoveries achieved through scientific method constitute only one small part of the overall knowledge base concerning the human and his capabilities that needs to be built. Appreciation of persons as a whole must capitalize upon knowledge and understandings drawn from the entire spectrum of human activity, and not merely from the scientific investigation carried out by some proportion of humankind.

Finally, a hallmark of the Humanist tradition has been the consistent emphasis placed throughout the ages upon the "classic human virtues," the attainability of these characteristics by each and every individual, the importance of ensuring that the necessary conditions for their acquisition and development are available for all, and the benefits to humans individually and collectively that can be expected to follow. This is the "normative" aspect of Humanism, where "norm" is used in the classical sense of constituting the idealized standard. In contrast to the cynic who supposes that most persons are no more capable of grand passion than they are of grand opera, the humanist remains optimistic, adhering to the notion of the perfectibility of man through the collective exercise of his own resources. Illustrations of the form in which such normative statements tend to occur would be found not only in the classical literature from earliest Greek and Roman times up to the present, but also contemporary humanistic views, such as Maslow's (1950) characterization of self-actualizing people, Rogers' definition of the fully functioning person (1961), and Jahoda's (1958) description of healthy functioning from a mental health point of view.

To attempt to make a listing of persons who have made important contributions to American psychology within the Humanist tradition is a hazardous undertaking. There are the inherent risks in categorizing people and their ideas, the indistinct nature of the categorical boundaries, and the inevitable omissions that can annoy and rankle. However, William James and John Dewey are typically cited as among the more important earlier theorists; Charlotte Buhler (1959, 1964, 1968) and Eric Erikson (1950, 1968, 1975) are ordinarily included as significant figures; Maddi (1963) has shown how both Gordon Allport and Henry Murray stand four-square within this tradition; and of course, Abraham Maslow (1954, 1968) has explicitly labeled his approach as Humanist in character. Also, many theorists who are typically grouped with the related traditions of phenomenology or existentialism, such as Adler (1924, 1927), Rogers (1951, 1961), Perls (1973) or Frankl (1962, 1967) can be identified with many of the elements of the Humanist view. It is to one of these related traditions that we turn next.

The Phenomenological Tradition

The problem of the correspondence between events and objects in the world and our comprehension of them has been with philosophy and science since their beginnings. The ingredients of the phenomenological tradition are every bit as old as that of the Humanist tradition reviewed above.

In ordinary language, the term "phenomenon" refers to a thing, event, or process that is noted and observed by the senses, and from the outset of human thought it has been distinguished from the thing or process itself.

A variety of postures have been adopted over the centuries in an effort to address the problem of the relationship between the phenomenal appearance of such objects and events, and the events themselves. One view has been characterized as the *Realist* position, sometimes referred to as *Presentationism*, which is exemplified in the writings of John Locke (Boring, 1929). In this view, objects are said to have the capabilities of directly affecting other objects (the senses), and hence the phenomenal experience of such objects serves as a faithful representer of the objects themselves. Realism asserts that the intellect conforms to and apprehends objects just as they exist. There is the attraction of simplicity to this theory of knowledge, and it is said that most people — lay and professional — behave in accordance with it. Detractors of this view call it *Naive Realism*.

An alternative view has followed the pattern established by Plato, who noted that if we simply accepted all that we see at face value, and if the comprehension we reached permitted all that we required, there would be no need to search for principles and understandings that lie behind or beyond the surface. But, from a phenomenal standpoint what we encounter is a world of constant change; to rely upon the changing objects of the senses is to notice the inevitable tendency of all things to come into being, to exist, and subsequently to pass away. In addition, the senses too often turn out to be "bad witnesses." With this second line of thought, it has been customary since Plato to conceive of at least two worlds — the world as we experience it, and the world and its objects as they exist independently of our mind's grasp and the structuring of them in our knowledge. From this perspective, we are operating in relation to the objects and events in our world, but our intellect does not have direct and immediate contact with the events as they are in and of themselves. We apprehend them as they are affected by our ways of perceiving and understanding them. We draw upon our collective phenomenal experiences, and through the application of reason we proceed to develop increasingly closer approximations of things as we infer they must be. What we generate are representations, or constructions, that have greater or less merit depending on what it is that they enable us to do. The position is sometimes called *Representationism*.

Still a third resolution of the problem has been to assert the reality and stability of the phenomena themselves; indeed, to assert that it is only such phenomena upon which one can safely rely. An early spokesman of this point of view was Berkeley, an 18th-century English philosopher whose work was elaborated, developed and refined by David Hume in the same period. The posture espoused by these writers is known as *Phenomenalism*, and asserts that what exists is only that which occurs when the senses experience it. Phenomenalists do not presume the existence of a reality independent of human observers to apprehend it. Rather, they affirm that what is known, perhaps directly, is sense experience itself. As a consequence, reality is whatever observers sense or construe it to be. Reality, then, is man-made, constructed by persons out of the sense experiences of themselves and others. For Hume, objects external to the person viewing them have the appearance of substance, with qualities that appear to be inherent in them; however, these appearances, which constitute the real world for the realist, and the real world to be approximated by the representationist, are fictions for Hume. What is real, or at least existent, are the sense impressions that occur, which in turn lead to the formation of ideas concerning them. What the phenomenalist claims is sensation, sense experience, or sense contents. He does not say what they are; they simply occur, and out of them one constructs one's view of physical reality (Eaker, 1972).

Phenomenology began as a philosophical movement devoted to the descriptive analysis and interpretation of existences as they show themselves in the pure form of conscious life. Edmund Husserl was the first to give the name "Phenomenology" to an entire system of philosophy that was intended to develop into an exact, universal, and radical science, capable of serving as a matrix for all theoretical knowledge. The point of view became increasingly influential throughout Europe and the Latin-American world, introduced for example to the Spanish-speaking countries by Ortega y Gasset. Its principal focus was an attempt to give all categories of experience independent and adequate description. Its rather obscure and esoteric method was one of "intuitive abstraction," which sought to identify the essential elements of conscious experience so as to discover the manner in which relations, developed between external events and subjective awareness became generative of meaning.

The translation of this point of view into a study of individual persons occurred comparatively early, taking place initially at the hands of figures such as Adler (1924) and Rank (1945), and later undergoing explicit development with the work of Snygg and Combs (1949) and Rogers (1951, 1961). The Ansbachers' (1956) representation of Adler's essentially phenomenological position, and the significance it played in his break from his mentor, Freud, is a penetrating and important analysis. Most of the emphases that have come to characterize the phenomenological posture in the study of personality (the state or quality of being a person) were reflected in Adler's approach, and were subsequently echoed in work of those who followed. Several of the more important emphases can be cited.

The search for explanations of human behavior must be focused upon individual persons, rather than collectivities of people grouped according to some arbitrary set of categorical arrangements. Information must be sought by means of a detailed analysis of the person's "inner nature," since the principal determinants of what a person comes to do are events that take place "within the skin" rather than events that occur external to the person. The primary events of concern are those with which the person perceives, interprets, and thereby construes his world and himself; what the person elects to do is guided by the particular constructions concerning himself and his surroundings he comes to form. Thus, the behavior of the person, and people in general, is guided and directed by perceptions, images, and thoughts, which are interpretations of actual events but are not isomorphic with them; consequently, they are "fictional" rather than "real." Important among these fictions are the person's constructions about future events or consequences, which the person judges to be attainable. From among a wide variety of such futures deemed to be possible of occurrence, those the person chooses as desirable and worthy of pursuit take on the character of objectives (or goals). It is inherently characteristic of persons that they order their actions not only in terms of the manner in which they construe their present, but also in terms of their current constructions as to the future conditions they seek to bring about. It is toward the latter that a large proportion of their energies come to be directed. The person in whom these events occur has direct and immediate access to them. Access to these "inner" events by others external to the person can be accomplished only by indirection, primarily the verbal report about them by the person in whom they occur. Accordingly, the primary method for studying individual persons (and thus, human behavior) is to view it from the vantage point of the behaving individual, the subject in whom they occur. Reliance is necessarily placed upon the observations of the subject by the subject, and the sharing of these observations by means of verbal report. Attempts to formulate a framework of understanding from the vantage point of an outside observer (e.g., the behavior analyst) will generate spurious accounts. Through the use of a posture of empathic understanding, however, the analyst of behavior can approximate the position of the person to be understood, thereby coming to at least a partial comprehension of the bases for the person's behavior, and some indications of what it is that the person may or may not be likely to do. Initial understandings of the operation of human thought and action must be built upon such intensive studies of the individual case (idiographic analysis). Only after an acceptable number of such studies will it be possible to identify which commonalities appear, thereby permitting one to formulate a limited number of statements that are descriptive of cases in general (nomothetic analysis). However, although such generalizations are useful and informative, they remain limited since they cannot sufficiently account for the behavior of any individual person. Each person in the last analysis constitutes a unique constellation and organization (Ford & Urban, 1963).

It is the phenomenological concern with the analysis of consciousness and the role of conscious events in the regulation and control of human action that has become a hallmark of 20th-century existentialism. Indeed, to many observers, the phenomenological posture has been the intellectual forebear of this tradition.

The Existential Tradition

Despite its frequent characterization as a philosophy, a theory, or a system of thought, existentialism is perhaps more correctly seen as an attitude or a way of perceiving man and the world. As such, one might consider that it has existed since man confronted his frailty and sought to formulate some meaning for his existence (Comerchero, 1970). Job, bemoaning his fate amidst the ashes, but nonetheless asserting the reality of his existence to his rationalizing would-be comforters, was being existential. The writer of Ecclesiastes, sorrowing over the futilities of the everyday world, yet seeking for meaningfulness in life, was speaking from an existential view. Dostoyevsky has shown the confrontation between the existential Christ and the institutions of his day, and all subsequent institutionalized forms of religion. Hamlet's soliloquies bespeak a tormented struggle to discover value and purpose for living. To be consciously aware of happenings, to be anguished by

perplexities, to glory in possibilities, to savor sensations and prize experiences, is to operate within an existential mode. More importantly, though, to recognize that the individual cannot borrow value, truth, and meaning from without, but must create them from within, that they must be a product of his ongoing experiential existing and being, is to be truly existential. Naive and uncritical acceptance of the frameworks of others—no matter how elegantly or persuasively they may be described—is to depart from the necessarily honest and authentic position in which humans are inevitably placed. Life is an unclear gift; there are no useful truths that can serve as guidelines for living; systems of thinking (Christian, Marxist, Psychoanalytic, or Behaviorist) advocated by others are from the standpoint of the individual person a fraud; life is a burden pressed upon each as a result of his inevitable confrontation with the "ultimate concerns" of individual existence—isolation, meaninglessness, responsibility, death; freedom to experience, freedom to choose, indeed freedom to exist, is the "truth" with which each human person must come to terms, and along with it must come an acceptance of responsibility for the form that his existence comes to assume. Not "The Truth shall set you free," but "you are free" is the truth. From an existentialist point of view, when one has said that man exists, and that in his existence he is free—compelled to freedom, ceaselessly free—one has exhausted all useful generalizations about the human person (Comerchero, 1970; Finkelstein, Wenegrat, & Yalom, 1982; Stevenson, 1974).

To say, therefore, that one is an existentialist can be seen to be a contradiction in terms. To do so is to order and abrogate, to fix experience into categories, whereas experience by its very nature is ongoing, fluid, not a thing, but a process. A biography is not to be confused with the person it purports to represent; to formulate generalizations about people is to seek smothering simplicities, tidy proprieties, and packaged answers, which it is possible to make only by pruning away all that is irregular and inconvenient to the illusion of regularity. Pressed to its limits, existentialism is thus a radical perspective—radical in the sense of getting to the root of something, or focusing upon something that is thought to be fundamental. The fundamental questions for each and every individual person are: Who am I? What can my existence represent? What should my existence represent? What shall I do with my freedom?

A large number of writers have come to be called,

or call themselves, existentialists. Given the foregoing discussion, however, one would not expect them to represent some coherent group, necessarily to have a great deal in common among themselves. The contemporaries, Nietzche and Kierkegaard, were perhaps most influential in articulating the characteristics of this posture toward oneself, one's life, and one's world, and prompting a wealth of subsequent writers to explore its multiple ramifications and implications. But there were significant differences between them: Nietzsch's Zarathrustra declared that "God is dead," thereby emphasizing that man is ultimately alone, and Kierkegaard insisted that all sense and meaning must begin with an initial "leap of faith" and excoriating those who supposed it possible to generate meaning through observation and reason, emerging with an opposite conclusion. Likewise, one encounters the contrast between Jean-Paul Sartre who sought to reconcile his existentialist views with Marxism, and Albert Camus who scathingly denounced Marxist efforts to represent human behavior as determined in character.

It should be apparent, however, that the existentialist perspective shares with those of the humanist and phenomenological traditions an intense antipathy to an ontological naturalism or an epistemological realism. The naturalistic view of man with its attempts to use the procedures of science to analyze and explain man as a natural object like any other, eliminates from consideration the very characteristics that render humans distinctive: namely, their awareness of their own existence and their freedom to choose what they will become. Moreover, explanatory generalizations developed by science about human action are inappropriate; they are only possible for objects and events that are determined, not for those that are free. Attempts to use statistical analyses of human behavior cannot unravel causal effects; they can only make things appear to be determined, after the fact. To the thoroughgoing existentialist, such exercises are not scientific, they are merely scholastic. The radical existentialist can also be antiintellectual, viewing systems of thought developed and imposed by others upon persons who abdicate their freedom and their responsibility for architecting their own development, as victimizing the individual with "truth" that is inhuman. The individual is no longer "the measure of all things," and meaning is no longer something with which man invests things and experience. He and his world are something that is interpreted for him; the individual is emptied of his own experiential content and becomes a passive receptacle for the symbolic versions of others. The process, for the existentialist, destroys human responsibility and thereby destroys humans themselves.

One would not have expected that the existentialist viewpoint would enter into the domain of psychology in its most radical form. It would appear to have been introduced by way of a development in European psychiatry, which sought to combine the assumptions of the existential view about the nature of man and his circumstance with the phenomenological viewpoint and its associated methodology. The historical factors that led up to this development are briefly reviewed in Ford and Urban (1963). The intent behind the effort was to develop a more satisfactory understanding of humans, particularly their problems and dilemmas, than was thought to be provided by the standard psychoanalytic, behaviorist, and scientific viewpoints available within Western thought, in order to be of greater assistance in helping troubled people. Influential in this movement have been writers such as Heidegger (1962), Binswanger (1956), and Boss (1958, 1963) writing from a continental vantage point, with May (1961, 1969) representing the foremost American contributor. The movement came to be called Existential Analysis. Subsequent influential contributors to this general movement have been Berne (1972), Frankl (1962, 1967, 1969, 1975), Lowen (1970), and Perls (1973), and the more recent writings of Carl Rogers have come to be more explicitly influenced by the viewpoint as time has gone on.

Although remarkably different in many particular ways, these writers appear to share a set of common principles concerning the nature of man and the appropriate means for comprehending what he is like and what he can and will do. The human person is distinct from other entities within the natural world. One does not simply exist in some state of being; rather, one is in a constant state of becoming something other than what one presently is. The human is an instance of constant activity and change. A second crucial characteristic of the person is one's capability for conscious awareness, comprised of direct and personal experiences that permit one to be immediately aware not only of one's individual surroundings, but also of oneself, of what one is doing, and of what is taking place. One is therefore capable of being self-conscious and of developing a sense of personal identity. The process is burdensome; it entails a constant struggle to come to terms with one's own experience and to render it intelligible. However, the awareness also enables one to be selective in what one responds to and how one chooses to respond. As a consequence, one is able to make decisions about these things and to take responsibility for oneself. In doing so, one creates oneself with one's worlds. What one becomes will be the result of one's inborn potentialities, the opportunities that present themselves, and the choice one makes in the succession of situations that are continuously presented. By the actions chosen, one continually expresses one's innate behavioral possibilities, molding one's environment to oneself and oneself to one's environment, thereby actualizing what has earlier been potential about oneself. Finally, humans have the capacity to transcend the immediacy of the present and to envision alternate states and possibilities; this provides the opportunity for one to invest meaning into one's existence, specifically to formulate intention, sense, purpose, and significance into the pursuit of one's life. To be authentically human is to become increasingly open to experience, to accept the inherent freedom associated with one's fate, to assume fully the responsibility for developing and constantly refashioning one's identity, one's personal commitments, and one's life. To attribute responsibility to factors outside oneself is to deny and distort the essential quality of human existence. Everything of significance with regard to this entire process occurs within the inner or subjective experience of the individual. Comprehension by others of what and where each individual may be operating with respect to their overall life task can only be approximated. The method by which it becomes approximated is necessarily phenomenological in nature.

Some Common Frameworks and Themes

If is has been hazardous to attempt to identify commonalities among writers within these several longstanding traditions of thought, the attribution of commonalities across the traditions will be recognized to be an even more problematic undertaking. Whereas affinities between them are noticeable, and in particular instances similarities are detectable, the process of combining the multiplicity of viewpoints developed by the many persons working within these several traditions can only be accomplished by skipping over the large number of differences among them, and choosing to emphasize the commonalities instead. Emphasis upon the similarities as opposed to the differences reduces to the question of which end of the telescope one chooses to look through. The use of the metaphor of "culture" is thought to be helpful in this regard, since the concept of a culture allows for widespread heterogeneity among the ideas and attitudes of its many members. Few cultures can boast of singular, monolithic systems of thought and action to which even a majority of their members subscribe. A pluralism of ideas is characteristically the norm. And, it has been in keeping with the concept of culture that terms such as system, theory, or model have been deliberately avoided in the representation of the several traditions; it is preferable to speak of perspectives or points of view. Without intending, therefore, to suggest that there is anything specific in the way of an "ethnic character" that can describe a humanistic-phenomenological-existential type of culture and can serve to distinguish it unequivocally from any other, pursuit of the metaphor of "two cultures" leads to the attempt to identify at least some of the "common stock of ideas" within the framework of which the study of human nature and behavior takes place. Accordingly, it is proposed that across these several traditions of thought a common set of emphases have tended to develop, *some* of which can be more readily discerned than others. It is understood that the complexities involved will not permit such a listing of commonalities to be exhaustive.

The Distinctive Character of Humans and Their Behavior

There is, first of all, the prevailing assertion that the human person and human attributes and actions need to be viewed as distinctively different from all other entities in nature and all other forms of life. As Frankl (1962) has expressed it, the human is not seen to be one thing among others, not merely a mechanism or a biological organism, not a member of a herd; rather, the human retains properties and capabilities that are distinctive to the human and to no other creature. To Allport (1955), the human is so unique as a species that efforts to understand human functioning that rely upon information gained from a study of "lower species of animals" are virtually useless. Similarly, Murray (1954) has challenged the "audacious assumption of species equivalence." Ideas about humans drawn from a study of other objects and things are at best only suggestive, and are misleading or damaging at their worst. It follows that any attempt to comprehend the nature of humans and their behavior must derive from an analysis of humans themselves, with particular emphasis placed upon those characteristics that render the human distinctive.

The Significance of the Individual

A second characteristic emphasis has been on the value and significance of each and every individual. All are viewed as equally significant and important, no one showing any inherent merits over any other, each with a legitimate posture and perspective with respect to himself, his life, and the world of others. One reason for this approach has been the view that each person is singular, unique, and hence unrepeatable and irreplaceable. A consequence of this emphasis has been the methodological tendency to generate knowledge about humans and their behavior from the detailed analysis of individual persons taken singly and one at a time. Useful conclusions about persons cannot be gained by looking at the person as a representative of a species, or as a particular kind of machine, or as an element in a social or cultural organization, but rather as an autonomous entity operating in and through the particular arrangements afforded by each individual's peculiar characteristics and environmental opportunities.

It has been existentialists who have argued most strongly for this view; it is conceived by Tillich (1952) to be the essence of the existentialist view—understanding the human situation from the standpoint of, and as experienced by, the individual. Existentialists are concerned with the person under scrutiny rather than with developing generalized theories about him; generalizations about humans are said to leave out what is the most important single feature of each—namely, one's uniqueness. Others, such as Allport (1955), take a similar position to the effect that each person is an idiom unto himself. Allport argued for the development of idiographic methods capable of providing a personal representation of the individual so as to permit the understanding and development of predictions in regard to the individual case. He characterized general principles concerning humans to be merely convenient fictions of only occasional utility when they turn out

to resemble the characteristics and attributes of some persons. Still others, such as Murray (1954) or Maslow (1968), take a broader view, construing humans as comprised of characteristics, aspects of which are species-constant, but others of which are specific and unique for each individual.

Characterizations of persons can be effected in terms of both, as long as the uniqueness of the individual does not become lost in the process. The emphasis upon the individuality and uniqueness of human persons is also reflected in the extent to which variability between and within individuals becomes stressed by this group of writers. To many of them, humans are so exceedingly variable in their modes of thought and action that most any sort of generalizations that others seek to formulate concerning them will have the ring of plausibility, despite the dubious validity associated with them.

The Individual as Complexly Organized

An additional characteristc appears to be a common disposition to seek ways to take into account the enormous complexity that any given human person appears to represent. The observation is repeatedly made that individuals retain an exceedingly large number of different and changing intentions, values, patterns, and styles of behaving, and that these can be manifested in a great variety of ways depending upon the person's circumstance and the nature of the environmental context within which he or she is functioning. An inclination to be critical of efforts to minimize this complexity or to reduce matters to simpler structure occurs, since such efforts tend to be regarded as erroneous and oversimplified. Despite this complexity, each individual is ordinarily regarded as operating in a unified and organized fashion. To Allport (1961), the individual's behavior routinely displays integration, complex and intricate though it may be. He goes on to suggest an inherent "pressing" for a unification of one's self and one's life to be operative within each. The proposal echoes Rogers' notion of an organizing principle underlying human functioning, or Adler's notion of the innate movement within human persons toward self-consistency leading to the formation of the individual's unique life style. Likewise, Murray (1959) chose to argue that each person operates as a temporal whole; one is capable of unified and concerted action at a given point in time, and capable of long-range enterprises that can take weeks, months, or even years of effort to complete (Murray, 1951). Thus, despite the huge number of subsidiary elements that may comprise the human and his behavioral actions, there is said to be the need to recognize that the individual person functions as a unit and operates as an integrated whole. Our knowledge concerning persons at any one time may be incomplete and fragmentary, but the person cannot be understood in terms of such fragments, and ways must be found to encompass the complex whole even if conceptions at very high order of abstraction must be used to accomplish it.

Tha Plasticity of the Individual Person

It has been remarked that two basic postures with respect to the notion of change have been operative throughout the history of Western thought. One of these sees stability as the norm, and change as perturbations of various kinds that serve to deflect things away from a condition of stasis, requiring the exercise of corrective action in order to reinstate the norm. From this standpoint, the world is geared toward equilibrium and the maintenance of similar states (*homeostasis*). The alternative view regards activity and change as the norm (*heterostasis*); conditions of stability occur only as a consequence of some artificial (and often undesirable) interference with an otherwise ongoing and active process.

If such is the case, the viewpoints we have been considering could be said to come down heavily on the side of heterostasis. Once again, using the existentialists as the more obvious group to illustrate a point with, the individual person and everything that he or she represents is an existence, a continuing process, rather than an essence or something fixed and static. This helps account for the proclivity for using a particular set of terms. "Being" traditionally refers to what is actual, or already existent. However, since not all existents are present and available at any one time, the concept is accompanied by a second, "becoming," to reflect the process of things constantly coming into being that were not available earlier. Moreover, we have had to find a way to represent not only what *does,* but also what *will* or *can* exist. This had led traditionally to be concept of "potential." Those entities or states that are not now actual, but will or might become so, are postulated to exist

now, but only in a state of potentiality. The processes by which what exists as potential becomes existent (actual) is called "actualization."

The Western world is indebted to Aristotle for this basic framework, which has been an important ingredient in the thinking of the writers we are currently considering. Rogers (1959) has followed the lead of a number of others in placing heavy reliance upon the process of conversion of the potential into the acutal by postulating an actualizing tendency to be an inherent characteristic of the individual, constituting a kind of master motive around which all activity of the person becomes organized; the self-actualizing tendency is a particularized form of the more general tendency, descriptive of the processes whereby the potentialities of the person undergo progressive development and behavioral expression. Use of the concept of self-actualization has been equally important to many others. Maslow (1954) postulates that each person proceeds in relation to an inner nature: intrinsic, given, to some extent unique, constituting an essential core of the individual, susceptible to being overpowered or suppressed, but never disappearing entirely and persisting underground, forever pressing for actualization.

If one views the individual person as standing in the midst of constant change, where one aspect becomes another, one states changes into another, and the form of the person's being (existence) is an unfolding succession of potentialities that become transformed into actualities, one construes the person as an instance of becoming, as both Rogers (1959) and Allport (1955) have done in the titles of their writings; and one stands in expectation of the essential unpredictability of the person over any extended period of time. Only very proximal predictions could be expected to be made, based upon a thorough knowledge of where the person was at a given instant in anticipation of an immediate instant to follow, or where artificial constraints had been imposed upon, or adopted by, the person to forestall the unfolding process. Cyclical regularities may describe the operation of the planets and the seasons; reversion to steady states may characterize the physical and biological worlds. Not so with the process of human living, it is said, unless the processes are stifled by human action — imposition of blind consistency and regulation upon the process is seen to be the road to ill health.

If one adds to the foregoing the notion that the human is equipped with volition and choice as well, that each has the freedom to change at any instant, the states of the person will be viewed to differ from one to another, from day to day, and from hour to hour, and the individual personality remains essentially unpredictable (Frankl, 1962).

The Significance of Conscious Experience

In the opinions of this group of writers we have been considering, there are a variety of characteristics that are peculiar to the human person, whose operation and functioning must be recognized and understood if an intelligible view of people is to be formed. Space does not permit a review of all of these. However, among the more important would appear to be the emphasis upon conscious experience.

With this phrase, reference is ordinarily made to the capability of humans for extended periods of time in which they are awake and aware, and inwardly sensible of things and happenings. The condition and capability for consciousness was introduced early in American psychology by William James, but has undergone a period of "benign neglect" by academic and experimental psychology for much of the past century. To James, consciousness constituted an inherent capability with certain important characteristics. He regarded it to be invariably *personal* (individual in character), forever *changing* such that no conscious state that has once occurred could ever recur as the exact same state, sensibly *continuous* and thereby producing the impression of continuity of experience despite time gaps as in sleep, and inherently *selective* in that it provided a vehicle for the exercise of choice—the contents of consciousness being governed by the judged relevance of incoming and potential experience to the accomplishment of ends (Boring, 1929).

The centrality of consciousness for understanding human behavior was echoed by the Functionalists, of whom John Dewey and J. R. Angell were the foremost spokesmen, and the theme was maintained by writers in the Humanist tradition, such as Allport and Murray, who provided in their theories for an active and influential consciousness (Maddi, 1963).

The concept of experience has been one for which a variety of other writers have shown a preference. This has been particularly true for those writing within the phenomenological (e.g., Rogers, 1951; Sullivan, 1953) and also the existential tradi-tions (e.g., Binswanger, 1956; May, 1961). The term "awareness" has been preferred by others (Perls, 1973). "Experience" as a term is ordinarily used to refer to the collectivity of the person's impressions or apprehensions (usually conscious) of the world of occurrences, whether these be of an external, bodily, or psychic sort. Experiences are said to accumulate with the passage of time, and an individual's experience at any given time is thought to be the product of happenings personally encountered, undergone, or lived through.

It is difficult to overemphasize the significance these writers have attached to the role of conscious experience for humans and their behavior. In has been customary to start with the observation that the contents of experience are multiple, varied, and change rapidly. In particular, the infant is pictured as entering upon a world that has the phenomenal appearance of being one big booming confusion. The inherent instability and uncertainty that the phenomenal world represents is in principle intolerable, but it is confronted by the inherent hunger within each person for constancy and certainty, and the confluence of these two tendencies initiates a search within the person for some form of order and stability in the midst of change. A process directed toward the institution of order and organization within the person continues in association with the person's development and persists throughout the course of the person's life. In the process, however, each person operates in isolation from his fellows. Each will form some manner of organization that will prove to be more or less serviceable. However, since no two persons are precisely identical, since the extent of experiences undergone will vary from one person to the next, since the manner in which the experiences are ordered in relationship to one another will necessarily be different, the experiential organization with which each person proceeds becomes importantly personal and individual, and in principle unique. It is this inner organization of subjective experience which is said to constitute "reality" from the vantage point of the individual, and is thought to exert the principal influence upon the manner in which the person construes himself and his surroundings, and therefore what the person subsequently comes to be and to do.

Among several writers there has been considerable interest in trying to identify the elements of conscious experience, thought, for example, to include the capabilities for attention and awareness (selective in their functioning), perception and the catagorization of experience, imagery, affect (as distinct from emotion), conception and thought, recollection, anticipation and foresight, symbolization and language, and a set of capabilities thought to permit interpersonal cohesion, variously referred to as projection, empathy, altruism, or social interest (Adler, 1927; Rogers, 1959; Sullivan, 1953; and others). There has also been interest in characterizing what are referred to as modes of experience. This is an approach that endeavors to characterize larger and more inclusive patterns of interactions developed by people to order the complexities of their experiences; illustrations of such proposals would be the prototaxic, parataxic, and syntaxic modes of experiencing of Sullivan (1953), or the modes-of-being-in-the-world suggested by existential writers to constitute different patterns of organization evolved by different persons, including the singular, dual, or plural existential modes, or the modes of *umwelt*, *mitwelt*, and *eigenwelt* (May, Angel, & Ellenberger, 1958). Understanding persons in terms of such larger experiential organizations has been thought to be particularly helpful,

The centrality of conscious experience is recognizable in several additional ways. The proposition is typically advanced that consciousness necessarily has an object; it is always consciousness of something other than itself. This gives rise to another peculiarly human capability: of being aware of the phenomenon of awareness within their experience, and in a sense to "see" that one can see. The ability to sense oneself as a self is asserted to be a power and a possibility of man and man alone (Pervin, 1960). It is this capability that permits the human person to behave as an observer and, when appropriate, a reporter to others, concerning the myriad thoughts, wishes, beliefs, attitudes, memories, sensations, and aspirations that apparently occur continuously during a person's waking experience. It is also suggested that the capability for self-awareness is responsible for the distinctly human process that leads to the idea of a self. It led William James, for example, to propose the concept of "self" as a stream of thought derived from conscious experience, comprised of all those experiences related to oneself as perceptually differentiated from externals (the "me" versus the "not-me"), and out of which was fashioned one's personal identity. Rogers opted for the term "self-concept," thought to be an organized configuration of perceptions (experiences) of one's being

and functioning that are admissible to the person's awareness (1951, 1959). For each person, one's self-concept is who one construes oneself to be, and it constitutes the frame of reference from which all else is observed, interpreted, and comprehended by the individual. The process leads to an awareness of oneself as a unique person of many qualities and values, with an associated feeling of personness. Existentialists have argued that as a consequence of the selectivity of experience, each person continually reformulates and thereby recreates what one is and what one comes to be. In this way, the self is not only a product but is also a producer of experience, serving as the framework within which opportunities are chosen and future experiences are selectively undergone (Combs, Avila, & Purkey, 1971). There has developed an immense literature on the notion of self and various subsidiary selves that observers have suggested are useful: the perceived as opposed to the idealized self (Rogers, 1951); the stable self (Snygg & Combs, 1949); the mutable self (Zurcher, 1972); the acceptable self (Berne, 1972); the subjective, objective, and social self (Arkoff, 1968). And these do not exhaust the alternatives.

Finally, the centrality of experience is reflected in related proposals concerning health and wholeness. A common theme continually recurs. Problems in human behavior are said to arise when incongruities between self and experience are allowed to develop. Jung (1964) observed that modern man's troubles stem from an excessive and debilitating overemphasis upon rationality, with the simultaneous denial of the intuitive, expressive, and esthetic aspects of his nature. Fromm (1955, 1956) characterized modern man as alienated from himself, as well as from his fellow men, and from nature. To Maslow (1962), the denial or suppression of one's inner nature constitutes a crime against one's self—it makes people despise themselves, feel worthless and unloveable because they know that they are guilty of failing to do with their lives all that they know to be possible. "Authenticity" is an important term for existential writers, for to remain authentic is to function in accordance with the actuality of all of one's experience; to be nonauthentic is to practice self-deception. To attempt to escape anguish by pretending one is not free, by trying to convince oneself that one's attitudes and actions are determined by what has been done by others, by situations outside oneself, by the roles to which one has been consigned in life, or anything other than oneself and the choices and decisions one has made, is the epitome of self-deception (Sartre, 1947). Denial of experience to awareness, or distortion of the characteristics of experience by means of faulty symbolization, is the avenue to human misery (Rogers, 1951, 1959).

Correspondingly, by being aware of the myriad transactions between oneself and one's environment on a moment-to-moment basis, one can make the discovery that one is actually making multiple decisions that govern the course of one's life (Perls, 1973). The more people are conscious (aware) of what it is that they are (angry or proud), the more they are not just angry or proud but also more capable of becoming something else be effecting a change or transformation of themselves. Reclamation from misery can occur when persons are led to widen and broaden their fields of awareness so that the entire spectrum of meaning and value becomes accessible to the person's experience. People can be led to become aware of the multiplicity of forces acting upon them, to realize their competencies and capabilities, to comprehend the range of available possibilities and opportunities, to recognize that the exercise of choice governs what their lives become, and to accept the responsibility associated with the process of living (Frankl, 1912, 1919).

The Self-Regulatory Properties of Human Activity

The review of "cross-cultural differences" we have been pursuing could be continued at considerable length. We must content ourselves with a focus upon a final characteristic that should not be overlooked because of the critical role it tends to play in the overall view of the "culture" we have been describing.

The significance of the ingredients of the conscious experience, or "internal proceeding" as Murray (1951) describes them, has been emphasized in the foregoing section; it is these "inner characteristics" that are seen to be the most important aspects of the person and, in turn, lead to one's characteristic patterns of thought and action (Allport, 1961). Among these "internal proceedings" are the human capabilities for initiating action, for directing the course that action will follow, for maintaining direction and sustained activity in the face of barriers and obstacles that inevitably arise, and for exercising overall supervisory control over the behavioral processes in which the person elects to engage. Each person is construed to be an ongoing, self-regulating entity.

Another feature, therefore, that is seen to distinguish the human from all other objects or species in the natural world is the capability for instigating transactions with the environment in relation to thoughts, values, interests, wants, and anticipations of outcomes that are defined as desirable. The depiction of the person as proactive, rather than reactive, was made by Murray (1959) in an effort to designate the manner in which activity is initiated spontaneously from within, rather than by a confronting external situation. It was Murray's view that the activity of people cannot adequately be explained with reference to factors outside the person (1959). He strongly objected to the Freudian view that tends to make the person almost wholly a reactive product of contending forces. His objection to a behaviorist view was equally strong. Murray was impressed with the manner in which humans appear to organize themselves so as to identify goals and objectives judged worthy of pursuit, to initiate and sustain action intended to lead to the attainment of those goals, and to pursue their interests and purposes so as to enhance themselves and their development in ways that they judge to be useful. To Allport (1961), the self-initiating characteristics of humans were equally impressive. He postulated the operation of inner dispositions that have the capability for initiating and guiding consistent forms of adaptive and stylistic behavior.

We have here an emphasis upon the overwhelming importance of the human's orientation toward future states of being. The outlook of the person is seen to be essentially prospective in nature. Attempts to account for man's efforts and activities by focusing upon early fixations, habits, or instincts, are all an effort to trace the behavior of the person in reference to the past; all are misdirected because the person is continuously straining toward the future instead (Allport, 1955).

The directiveness associated with human behavior arises from the capability of humans to be not only *future oriented,* but also *purposive* and *intentional* in operation (Allport, 1961). Each person, it is said, initiates behavioral action for reasons other than simply to achieve and maintain an homeostatic balance, or simply to survive. Rather, people pursue dispositions to construct and create new and useful thoughts, objects, and procedures (Murray, 1959), to acquire greater competence and capability (White, 1959), or to implement a philosophy of living (Allport, 1961). These purposes and goals will vary greatly from one person to the next; they may be proximal or remote, they may be few or many, they may be segmented or ordered into a sequence of subsidiary goals (Murray, 1959). For most, the variety of goals becomes integrated into a coherent cluster of life goals, reflecting the inherent tendency within the person toward an organized integration of the various elements of which he or she is composed (Allport, 1955). The characterization of the teleonomic or purposive nature of the person and its importance in rendering human behavior intelligible is echoed in Adler's depiction of the goal-directedness of human action (1927), and Buhler's emphasis on the study of life goals (1964). The functioning of people is seen to be governed by such conscious characteristics of personality as long-range goals, plans of action, and philosophies of life.

To the existentialist writers, the development of purpose that can provide value and significance to one's existence constitutes the critical task for each to accomplish. To Sartre (1957), there is no ultimate meaning or purpose inherent in human life; in this sense, life is absurd; we are "forlorn," "abandoned" in the world, and must look after ourselves completely. We have not come into being for any purpose, neither created by God, nor predisposed by our biological ancestry, nor anything else. We simply find ourselves existing, and each must decide what to make of him or herself. It is through the exercise of free choice that we decide what will be the purposes and conditions under which we shall live. Frankl (1969), on the other hand, perceives a purpose or meaning inherent in each person's life. Human life is basically purposive, but the meaning or purpose of each individual is unique and specific, and can be discovered and fulfilled by that one person and by none other. Everyone has his or her own specific vocation (calling) or mission in life; each must carry out a concrete assignment that demands fulfillment. In this respect no person can be replaced; nor can another's life be repeated. Each individual's task is as unique as the specific opportunities one has to implement it. The specific purpose or meaning for a person's life cannot be invented or contrived; it can only be encountered and discovered through the process of living. Frankl's position has a number of similarities to those adopted by others, such as Maslow (1950, 1968) and Rogers (1951), who postulate that tendencies toward actualization of personal potentialities are inherent, basic, and primitive, and move the person forward in the search for accomplishment, growth, and human fulfillment (Butler & Rice, 1963).

Critical to the exercise of direction and control is the notion of "volition" and "decisional choice." It is the existential writers who have emphasized the significance of choice to the greatest degree. The term "freedom" is one they have chosen to use in dealing with the decisional capabilities they regard as the premier human feature. Freedom has traditionally meant the absence of outside influence in the action of a thing, such that in the development of its capabilities no block, barrier, or impediment becomes imposed on the exercise of those capabilities. More particularly, freedom is the power to exercise regulatory control without outside interference so as to be or act so that things may be other than they are. In this sense, only a god can be fully free. With humans it has been customary to speak in relative terms; one is more or less free in regard to one or more conditions, since one's knowledge and existence are finite, and one is always subject to, and to some extent governed by, forces, actions, and situations surrounding oneself. To the existentialist, the human is free; it is a freedom not in the sense of indeterminacy, but in the sense of being able to govern the course of one's development and destiny by means of the decisions (choices) made in the "center of one's Being" (Tillich, 1952). To the freedom to envision alternate future possibilities within the contents of consciousness is added the freedom to initiate action to try to actualize them. To be conscious is to be free, although one is not free to cease being free. Humans may not be able to free themselves from any or all conditions; by the same token, however, they are not unwitting victims of such conditions, since it is always possible to take a stand toward them, and thereby choose what one's existence will be, and what it will become in the next moment. Every moment requires new or renewed choice; no motive or past resolution entirely determines what one does in the *now*. There is the invariable necessity of choosing, the inevitable responsibility for one's fate, and the inherent unpredictability of the consequences of one's choices which is the source of so much subjective anguish; namely, the painful awareness of our freedom and the frequent wish by people to avoid it.

The setting of objectives and goals, selecting a pattern of effort to attain those objectives from among alternate courses of action, the initiation and maintenance of activity until such time as the objectives have been achieved, the decision as to whether achievement is sufficient to warrant a shift in direction toward additional goals and objectives—all imply the operation of some kind of command post, or central executive unit within the person whereby such activities can be sensibly coordinated. For this purpose, a variety of suggestions have been made. Murray (1956) found the concept of *ego* useful, characterizing it as the rational, differentiated, and governing establishment of the person, with multiple capacities and functions, including the organization of perceptions into an apperceptive complex, the exercise of intellective operations, the development of serial programs and schedules, the coordination of action, and the exercise of decision. Allport suggested the concept of the *proprium* (1955), a component thought to serve an organizing and integrating role and responsible for producing a sense of body, self-identity, self-image, self-esteem, self-extension, rational coping, and propriate striving. The concept of *self* has enjoyed a long history in this regard; William James relied upon it to refer to an instrumental process of functional utility in regulating and governing the person's entire psychobiophysical functioning. The concept has been a popular vehicle for writers of both phenomenological and existential persuasions. Whether construed as ego, or self, or as some other type of component, there would appear to be no alternative to some such conceptualization, if indeed the person is to be seen as the self-initiating, self-guiding, self-directing, self-maintaining, self-regulating, and self-organizing entity that our group of writers construe each individual to be.

The Two-Cultures Dialogue

One of the defining characteristics of a culture is ordinarily thought to be the existence and operation of a common ideology, or network of belief, around which members of the culture tend to coalesce, the main outlines of which attract their allegiance. Ideologies serve as guidelines for thought and action, providing a common set of conceptions as to the preferred way to look at things, and a set of customary practices related to those ideas that enable the participant members to function collectively to get concrete things done.

The foregoing materials suggest such a development, with the implication that it is around such an ideology that a large number of persons dealing with humans and their behavior on a day-to-day basis have tended to congregate. It must be left to the reader to decide whether a sufficient number of commonalities have been identified to warrant the attribution of an ideology common to the phenomenological, humanistic, and existential groups of writers, and whether at least these ingredients for a culture can be legitimately said to exist. A preoccupation with the task of describing the elements of the ideology of one "culture" precluded a comparable itemization of a suggested cultural counterpart (loosely referred to as scientific psychology), although some of the latter's characteristics are implied in the description of the views of the first.

Critical exchanges between representatives of these two "cultures" have, of course, been taking place since earliest times, and can be recognized to have continued up to the present. Since the philosophical positions from which they are derived are at such variance, each has found much to criticize in the other's position. The differences are basically philosophical in nature for essentially two reasons: (1) they stem from different answers to the most fundamental questions that can be asked, since they speak to one's conceptions of reality (metaphysics) and man's capabilities for apprehending it (epistemology); and (2) the questions are unlikely to be resolved through the exercise of reason alone.

The number of derivatives that follow from the basic positions adopted on these issues are, as one might expect, exceedingly large in number; consequently, their specific criticisms of one another are almost too numerous to catalogue. The essential character of the criticisms has not changed over the decades; moreover, the main outlines of the respective critiques have by now become well known. Thus, a point-by-point account of the critical exchange will not be attempted. However, since indications of the many critical views maintained by the phenomenological-humanist-existentialist group toward the other "culture" have been cited in earlier pages, some of the elements of the counter-critique deserve mention. A number of telling points are frequently made.

While the effect of the phenomenological-humanist view of the person may be positive and optimistic, its effect upon scientific study is considered negative. What, for example, does one do with the processes of consciousness and its successive experiences if one wishes to understand them, other than to fix them "photographically" through their successive states?

Even if it is granted that the operation of both "mental" and "bodily" events is important, and that the "mind" controls much of what the "body" does and hence is more important, assigning it preeminence should not lead to a neglect of the physical and physiological properties of the person, or the blithe neglect of the difficulties occasioned by a dualistic position on the mind-body problem.

Similarly, an emphasis upon the characteristics of the individual person should not lead to an accompanying neglect of environmental factors, both physical and social, and the evident effects of sociocultural influences upon the behavior of individuals and groups.

Adherence to the notion of developmental and behavioral discontinuities from one occasion to the next for any given individual, and from one person to the next across individuals, condemns one to an inherently descriptive posture of analysis; it precludes the possibilities of explanation, prediction, and the prospects for management and control, all of which are made possible by alternate approaches and about which empirical support has been accumulated.

If each event and each integrate of events (the person) is truly unique, then the prospect of developing general laws across an array of humans would appear on the face of it to be impossible; writers who advocate such a view and simultaneously generalize about human action and behavior are contradicting themselves.

The formal properties of the various views (even those that have undergone more detailed development) are characteristically deficient, with conspicuous failure to distinguish between axiomatic presumptions and empirical propositions; as a consequence, they have not as a group proved to be efficient generators of propositions that can be tested satisfactorily; from an empirical standpoint, many are both speculative and sterile.

Reliance upon subjective report as a means of access to the subjective experience said to be so critical precludes the study of all persons in whom the capabilities for such reports is limited (e.g., infants, the mentally retarded), impaired (e.g., senile conditions), or otherwise distorted (e.g., drug-induced psychoses).

The reader will recognize that the majority of the foregoing criticisms, and others like it, speak more to what the "opposition" fails to do and is unable to accomplish, than to what it attempts to do and manages to accomplish. The rejoinders and the counter-criticism by opposite numbers tend to be of the same order, as for example the criticisms of what a reductionist, determinist, materialist position leaves out of consideration in its attempts to render people's lives intelligible. Because of their fundamental underlying divisions, the broad outlines of the dialogue tend to continue and show no sign of abating.

In Search of a Synthesis

An instructive series of articles have appeared of late in the literature of developmental psychology that have relied upon the notion of models. Reese and Overton (1970) characterized models as man-made tools, originating in metaphor, that are constructed in search of the most effective means for representing categories of events in an effort to develop understanding, prediction, and control over occurrences. Following the lead initiated by Kuhn (1962), they noted that models can be said to exist on several levels, ranging from all-inclusive metaphysical models to narrowly circumscribed models of specific theories. First-order models that endeavor to map the world of concrete experience both imply and can be shown to derive from a more general second-order model, which in turn is related to a more encompassing model at a still higher level—on up to the most general order of representation, termed "meta-models" by Reese and Overton, or "paradigms" or world-views in the language of Kuhn.

A consensus had been developing that approaches to the study of human development tend to fall into one of two dominant metamodel frames, one called an organismic model, which is considered to have arisen within the European tradition, and the other called a mechanistic model, considered more distinctively American. In a succession of papers, Reese and Overton (1970) and Overton and Reese (1973) developed the view that these two paradigms served as the major bases for most representations of developmental processes in the human person. By a careful explication of the epistemological and metaphysical propositions of these paradigms, they succeeded in exposing the multiple ways in which the respective metamodels remained incompatible with one another. Moreover, since the differences related to such fundamental issues as the criteria for defining truth itself, it was possible to show that the paradigms and the subordinate models developed in relation to them remained in two separate realms of discourse entirely, and were therefore essentially irreconcilable.

In subsequent writings, Looft (1973) and Lerner (1976) tended to agree. Although both later commentators emphasized that lower-order models derived from these more general paradigms do not necessarily fit perfectly with the metamodels implicit in each, they nonetheless found it possible to catagorize most developmental theories into one or the other, concluding that it was in the metamodel structures — mechanistic and organismic — where it is possible to discern the principal ingredients of their respective representations of the nature of man. They attempted to identify the differences in terms of a listing of issues considered essential or fundamental to any paradigmatic model that attempted to represent human development; they differed only in the number of such issues they thought it was necessary to include. In Lerner's characterization of these differences, the mechanistic paradigm is described as a natural science position, emphasizing quantitative change, continuity, reductionism, a preference for physicochemical representations of events, and concerned with additive effects, whereas the organismic paradigm is described as an epigenetic position, emphasizing qualitative change, discontinuity, emergence, and concerned with multiplicative and interactive effects (Lerner, 1976).

A parallel would appear to exist between what has been taking place in the study of human development on the one hand, and the study of personality on the other. Indeed, one of the ways in which the differences between the two groups under consideration could have been formulated would have been to characterize them as alternate and competing world views, or paradigms. There are several reasons why this avenue was not chosen, the first being the need to take greater pains to establish that the phenomenological, humanist, and existential positions do indeed derive from a common paradigmatic frame. It has been suggested that perhaps in many respects they do; however, the analysis can hardly be said to have been thoroughly accomplished. A second, and more compelling, reason is that to inspect alternate views from the standpoint of models and

metamodels is to adopt the representationalist-epistemological position from the outset, which does immediate violence to one of the views, i.e., the one developed from a phenomenalist posture. Finally, use of the notion of paradigm does not adequately connote the extensive social and professional differences that are present in the behavior of the adherents of these opposing points of view, and the extraordinary difficulties attendant upon their efforts to communicate usefully with one another. It is for reasons such as these that the metaphor of "culture" was used instead.

Inspection of the situation in the domain of developmental psychology left Reese and Overton sanguine over the possibility of reconciling views that were at such variance with each other. They noted that if the metamodels remain cast in their current terms, there is no foreseeable way that their differences could be bridged. To attempt such a reconciliation using the language in which they are currently presented would entail the capitulation by one into the other's terms. This avenue has, of course, been frequently attempted, with advocates of one model attempting to coopt the viewpoint of the other by translating its representations and recasting them into its own terms. However, as Reese and Overton (1973) were able to demonstrate, this cannot be legitimately effected without violating many of the paradigmatic assumptions upon which the second is based.

An alternate route is to seek larger and more encompassing paradigms within which the two may be subsumed. The search for synthetic viewpoints to incorporate those that have gone before is, of course, motivated by profit. Syntheses are designed to capitalize upon the capabilities of the respective elements upon which they become constructed. They aspire to more adequate representations, which will lead to the generation of more adequate information than has been possible with those that have gone before. In developmental theory, Riegel (1975, 1976) pursued this course, proposing that the mechanistic and organismic metamodels could in turn be conceptualized as thesis and antithesis, which would make it possible to architect a dialectic synthesis at more abstract levels of conceptualization within which the two might be subsumed. Looft (1973) likewise argued for the development of a new metamodel, reflecting a different set of developmental models, with more powerful concepts, propositions, methods of inquiry, and generative information.

Urban (1978) suggested that a systems view might in the long run prove to be adequate to the task. Addressing the parallel problem in the domain of behavior theory, Hilgard (1980) applauded the revival of interest throughout the field of psychology in such areas as consciousness, attention, volition, and choice, and expressed the view that developments that use a cognitive paradigm, with its derivative theoretic formulations in information processing, decision theory, serial program analyses, and the like, might eventually turn out to be sufficient.

It is the writer's view that the search for useful synthetic viewpoints needs to continue. Were it not for the extraordinary strength and accomplishments of these respective "cultures," there would be a poor basis for architecting such syntheses; one would be discarded in preference for the other, or both would be discarded to be replaced by a third. However, the capabilities displayed by these respective cultures have earned them a strong measure of respect and admiration. The phenomenological-humanist-existential viewpoint, for example, has proven extremely valuable in the domain of clinical and counseling practice and has been one upon which many procedures for effectively helping troubled people have been based. Its emphases upon the worth of the individual, its positive attitude toward human life, its promotion of freedom and expressiveness, rights and choices, and its advocacy of authentic personalities that reflect candor, honesty, altruism, caring, respect, and empathy toward others, have been requisite elements in effective service. However, the generation of hard information concerning the physical and physiological aspects of persons through the methodologies of experimental science have been equally important, as well as the insights provided from disciplines that have emphasized the sociocultural contexts within which people function and develop.

Formulating such syntheses is no small task. As indicated earlier, the problem is not simply one of reconciliation between antithetical viewpoints. Not only is each incomplete without ingredients drawn from the other, but it also remains very difficult to identify how either paradigm or culture, in combination with the other, can succeed in representing the complexities of human life, the intricacies of human organization and its continuous modification and change in relation to the multiplicity of influences that affect the person, the various ways in which the person in turn affects his environment, the persons' goal-oriented and planful undertakings, or his complex participations in social groups in which he inevitably engages. A position of detachment from both paradigmatic frames discloses that both are inevitably partial in their characterization of the complexities of human behavior and human living; the deficiencies each sees in the conceptualizations of the other can be recognized to have merit.

Thus, the search for syntheses is ultimately motivated by the need to find ways to fill in the gaps left by physicalistic, or biological, or social, or phenomenological, or humanistic, or existential accounts of human process. It is likely that such syntheses will need to eschew the present frameworks, terminologies, and associated methods of inquiry that have developed in relationship to them, and emerge with a framework of analysis of more adequate scope (White, 1952). Such syntheses appear at intervals in the history of thought: for example, the integration between Darwinian evolutionary theory and Mendelian genetics which proved to be so seminal in the advancement of the biological sciences. The appearance of a comparable synthesis in the analysis and study of the person and his or her behavior can be expected to provide an equally significant progression for the human sciences as well.

References

Adler, A. *The practice and theory of individual psychology.* New York: Harcourt Brace, 1924.

Adler, A. *Understanding human nature.* New York: Greenberg Publishers, 1927.

Allport, G. W. *Becoming: Basic considerations for a psychology of personality.* New Haven: Yale University Press, 1955.

Allport, G. W. *Pattern and growth in personality.* New York: Holt, Rinehart, & Winston, 1961.

Ansbacher, H., & Ansbacher, R. *The individual psychology of Alfred Adler.* New York: Basic Books, 1956.

Arkoff, A. *Adjustment and mental health.* New York: McGraw-Hill, 1968.

Berne, E. *What do you say after you say hello?* New York: Grove Press, 1972.

Binswanger, L. Existential analysis and psychotherapy. In F. Fromm-Reichmann & J. L. Moreno (Eds.), *Progress in psychotherapy.* New York: Grune & Stratton, 1956.

Boring, E. G. *A history of experimental psychology.* New York: Appleton-Century, 1929.

Boss, M. *The analysis of dreams.* New York: Philosophical Library, 1958.

Boss, M. *Daseinsanalyse and psychoanalysis.* New York: Basic Books, 1963.

Buhler, C. Theoretical observations about life's basic

tendencies. *American Journal of Psychotherapy*, 1959, **13**. 561–581.

Buhler, C. The human course of life and its goal aspects. *Journal of Humanistic Psychology*, 1964, **4**, 1–18.

Buhler, C., & Massarik, F. *The course of human life.* New York: Springer, 1968.

Butler, J. M., & Rice, L. N. Adience, self-actualization, and drive theory. In J. M. Wepman & R. W. Heine (Eds.), *Concepts of personality.* Chicago: Aldine, 1963.

Comerchero, V. (Ed.), *Values in conflict.* New York: Appleton-Century-Crofts, 1970.

Combs, A. W., Avila, D. L., & Purkey, W. W. *Helping relationships: Basic concepts for the helping professions.* Boston: Allyn & Bacon, 1971.

Eacker, J. N. On some elementary philosophical problems of psychology. *American Psychologist*, 1972, **27**, 553–565.

Erikson, E. H. *Childhood and society.* New York: Norton, 1950.

Erikson, E. H. *Childhood and society.* (2nd ed.) New York: Norton, 1963.

Erikson, E. H. *Identity, youth and crisis.* New York: Norton, 1968.

Erikson, E. H. *Life history and the historical moment.* New York: Norton, 1975.

Finkelstein, P., Wenegrat, B., & Yalom, I. Large group awareness training. In M. R. Rosenzweig & L. W. Porter (Eds.), *Annual review of psychology*, Vol. 33. Palo Alto, Calif.: Annual Reviews, 1982.

Ford, D. H., & Urban, H. B. *Systems of psychotherapy: A comparative approach.* New York: Wiley, 1963.

Frank, J. D. Nature and functions of belief systems: Humanism and transcendental religion. *American Psychologist*, 1977, **32**, 555–559.

Frankl, V. E. *Man's search for meaning: An introduction to logotherapy.* Boston: Beacon Press, 1962.

Frankl, V. E. *Psychotherapy and existentialism.* New York: Washington Square Press, 1967.

Frankl, V. E. *The will to meaning.* New York: World Publishing, 1969.

Frankl, V. E. *The unconscious god.* New York: Simon & Schuster, 1975.

Fromm, E. *The sane society.* New York: Rinehart, 1955.

Fromm, E. *The art of loving.* New York: Harper & Row, 1956.

Heidegger, M. *Being and time.* London: SCM Press, 1962.

Hilgard, E. R. Consciousness in contemporary psychology. *Annual Review of Psychology*, 1980, **31**, 1–26.

Jahoda, M. *Common concepts of mental health.* New York: Basic Books, 1958.

Jung, C. G. (Ed.), *Man and his symbols.* London: Aldus, 1964.

Kuhn, T. S. *The structure of scientific revolutions.* Chicago: University of Chicago Press, 1962.

Lerner, R. *Theories and concepts of human development.* Reading, Mass.: Addison-Wesley, 1976.

Looft, W. R. Socialization and personality throughout the life-span: An examination of contemporary psychological approaches. In P. B. Baltes & K. W. Schaie (Eds.), *Life-span developmental psychology: Personality and socialization.* New York: Academic Press, 1973.

Lowen, A. *Pleasure.* Baltimore: Penguin Books, 1970.

Maddi, S. R. Humanistic psychology: Allport and Murray. In J. M. Wepman & R. W. Heine (Eds.), *Concepts of personality.* Chicago: Aldine, 1963.

Maslow, A. H. Self actualizing people: A study of psychological health. In W. Wolff (Ed.), *Personality symposium*, No. 1. New York: Grune & Stratton, 1950.

Maslow, A. H. *Motivation and personality.* New York: Harper, 1954.

Maslow, A. H. *Toward a psychology of living.* Princeton, N.J.: Van Nostrand, 1962.

Maslow, A. H. *Toward a psychology of being.* (2nd ed.) New York: Van Nostrand, 1968.

May, R. *Love and will.* New York: Norton, 1969.

May, R. (Ed.), *Existential psychology.* New York: Random House, 1961.

May, R., Angel, E., & Ellenberger, H. F. (Eds.), *Existence: A new dimension in psychiatry and psychology.* New York: Basic Books, 1958.

Murray, H. A. Some basic psychological assumptions and conceptions. *Dialectica*, 1951, **5**, 266–292.

Murray, H. A. Toward a classification of interaction. In T. Parsons & E. A. Shils (Eds.), *Toward a general theory of action.* Cambridge, Mass.: Harvard University Press, 1954.

Murray, H. A., & Kluckhohn, C. Outline of a conception of personality. In C. Kluckhohn, H. A. Murray, & D. M. Schnieder (Eds.), *Personality in nature, society and culture.* (2nd ed.) New York: Knopf, 1956.

Murray, H. A. Preparations for the scaffold of a comprehensive system. In S. Koch (Ed.), *Psychology: A study of science.* Vol. 3. New York: McGraw-Hill, 1959.

Overton, W. R., & Reese, H. W. Models of development: Methodological implications. In J. R. Nesselroade & H. W. Reese (Eds.), *Life-span developmental psychology: Methodological issues.* New York: Academic Press, 1973.

Perls, F. *The Gestalt approach and eyewitness to therapy.* Palo Alto, Calif.: Science and Behavior Books, 1973.

Pervin, L. A. Existentialism, psychology, and psychotherapy. *American Psychologist*, 1960, **15**, 305–309.

Rank, O. *Will therapy and truth and reality.* New York: Knopf, 1945.

Reese, H. W., Overton, W. F. Models of development and theories of development. In L. R. Goulet & P. B. Baltes (Eds.), *Life-span developmental psychology: Research and theory.* New York: Academic Press, 1970.

Riegel, K. F. Toward a dialectical theory of development. *Human Development*, 1975, **18**, 50–64.

Riegel, K. F. The dialectics of human development. *American Psychologist*, 1976, **31**, 689–700.

Rogers, C. R. *Client-centered therapy.* Boston: Houghton-Mifflin, 1951.

Rogers, C. R. A theory of therapy, personality and interpersonal relationships, as developed in the Client-Centered framework. In S. Koch (Ed.), *Psychology: A study of science.* Vol. 11. *General systematic formulations, learning and special processes.* New York: McGraw-Hill, 1959.

Rogers, C. R. *On becoming a person.* Boston: Houghton-Mifflin, 1961.

Sarton, G. *The history of science and the new humanism.* Cambridge, Mass.: Harvard University Press, 1962.

Sartre, J. P. *Existentialism.* New York: Philosophical Library, 1947.

Sartre, J. P. *Being and nothingness,* H. Barnes (Trans.). Secaucus, N.J.: Citadel Press, 1957.

Snow, C. P. *The two cultures and the scientific revolution.* New York: Cambridge University Press, 1959.

Snygg, D., & Combs, A. W. *Individual behavior.* New York: Harper, 1949.

Stevenson, L. *Seven theories of human nature.* New York: Oxford University Press, 1974.

Sullivan, H. S. *The interpersonal theory of psychiatry.* New York: Norton, 1953.

Tillich, P. *The courage to be.* New Haven: Yale University Press, 1952.

Urban, H. B. The concept of development from a systems perspective. In P. B. Baltes (Ed.), *Life-span development and behavior.* Vol 1. New York: Academic Press, 1978.

White, R. W. *Lives in progress.* New York: Dryden Press, 1952.

White, R. W. Motivation reconsidered: The concept of competence. *Psychological Review,* 1959, **66,** 297–333.

Zurcher, L. A. The mutable self. *The Futurist,* 1972, **6,** 181–185.

PART III
RESEARCH ISSUES AND PROBLEMS

INTRODUCTION

Advances in clinical psychology have been achieved in part because of developments in research methodology, assessment, and experimental design. Expansion of the range of design options, assessment strategies, and methods of data evaluation have affected the type of research that is done and the substantive yield. With the progress in design has come a clearer focus of the problems and issues that need to be resolved in future research. The chapters in this part detail the advances in clinical research methods and their impact on clinical work, personality, psychopathology, and treatment.

In Chapter 11, Steven Hayes discusses single-case experimental research and its contribution to knowledge in clinical work. Single-case research designs are important because they provide an empirically based research methodology that can be used with individual clients. In this chapter, characteristics of specific designs are detailed with recommendations for their role in treatment evaluation.

In Chapter 12, Thomas R. Kratochwill and F. Charles Mace present methods of experimentation as they pertain to a broad conception of clinical research. Between-group, within-subject, and single-case designs are placed in the larger context of clinical research. Several topics are identified, including the types of experimental validity that need to be met in research, the criteria for evaluating treat-

ment, and the advantages and limitations of alternative design options.

Jean M. Edwards and Norman S. Endler consider advances in personality research in Chapter 13. The impact on methodology on conceptual advances in personality research is evident in the discussion of alternative conceptual models of personality and work that integrates diverse positions. The chapter discusses key issues in personality, including the consistencies and inconsistencies of behavior over time and the impact of trait and situational factors in explaining performance.

In Chapter 14, Richard A. Depue and Scott M. Monroe trace recent advances in psychopathology research. Different views of the nature of psychopathology and different types of disorders are presented. Important issues in conducting research in psychopathology are addressed, including sample section, diagnosis and classification, design, and data analysis.

Finally, in Chapter 15, Alan E. Kazdin examines research issues in relation to the investigation of psychotherapy. Alternative treatment evaluation strategies and the contributions and limitations of analogue and clinical research are discussed. Contemporary issues are examined, including meta-analysis, negative effects of therapy, and integration of alternative treatment techniques.

11 THE ROLE OF THE INDIVIDUAL CASE IN THE PRODUCTION AND CONSUMPTION OF CLINICAL KNOWLEDGE*

Steven C. Hayes

Clinical interventions are largely oriented toward the needs of individual clients. That simple fact has profound implications for the nature of clinical psychology. It implies that understanding the individual is the major *goal* of clinical knowledge. Logically, it also implies that case analyses should be an important *method* in clinical psychology.

It is remarkable that some of the most influential clinical literature is based upon analyses of individual cases. This includes classic case studies, such as Little Hans or Anna O., and schools of thought developed on multiple clinical replications (e.g., Masters & Johnson, 1970; Wolpe, 1958). Unfortunately, these contributions have been criticized by most methodologists. With some exceptions, such as the experimental analysis of behavior (e.g., Johnston & Pennypacker, 1981; Sidman, 1960), most areas of academic psychology are not oriented toward the study of the individual. It is not surprising that their methodological tools do not fit the practicing clinical environment. The cost of this has been very high. It has: (a) helped drive a wedge between clinical practice and research; (b) cut off the practicing clinician

from input into the legitimate knowledge base of the field; and (c) produced research that is not maximally applicable to the clinical situation.

The need for case analysis is usually argued on the basis of the possibility that it can contribute to knowledge, though perhaps not as well as "true experimental" (read "group comparison") research. I will argue that because of the unique goals of clinical psychology, case analyses are not only useful but necessary. Far from being the weak sister in the clinical research enterprise, case analyses are (in practice if not in the models of methodologists) at its core. To make this argument requires that I start at an unusual point—with the consumption not the production, of clinical knowledge.

The Role of the Individual Case in the Consumption of Clinical Knowledge

The generality of findings is a critical issue to the practicing clinician. For practitioners, the ultimate question must always be: which treatment delivered in what way is likely to be most effective for this client with this set of problems and charac-

*Portions of this chapter have been drawn from Hayes (1981) and from Barlow, Hayes, and Nelson (in press).

teristics? This is fundamentally a question of the external validity of our knowledge, whether that knowledge is based on formal research data, direct clinical experience, reports from the clinical experience of others, or even just common sense.

The consumption of research does not depend solely on the kinds of concerns that are critical to the proper design of an experiment. I will argue that in the real world, no amount of care in experimental design will insure that the findings will be relevant because studies do not possess external validity as a matter of logical necessity (Birnbrauer, 1981).

Knowledge that is based on group comparison methods has often been said to be more generalizable than analyses of individual cases. This assertion seems critically flawed, and has had grave consequences for clinical psychology. It has confused issues of numerousness (few versus many) with the level of analysis (the group versus the individual). Clinical science needs many analyses of individuals but has ended up with relatively fewer analyses of groups, all in the name of "external validity." The logic on which this result is based therefore must be examined closely in order to understand the need for concentration on the individual case.

The main basis for claims of greater external validity for analyses of groups is *random selection and assignment.* Suppose we could randomly draw from the population called "schizophrenics," and then randomly assign these subjects to treatment *x*, treatment *y*, or no treatment. We might then be able to say that the particular treatments have particular effects on the population known as schizophrenics. If, furthermore, a new set of patients also constituted a representative sample of the population, then one could know that the results would also apply to those patients, considered as a group. Given all of these requirements, it would be possible to say that an experiment possessed external validity as a matter of logical necessity.

Unfortunately, there are three problems: (1) We are never, or perhaps almost never, able to select randomly from a known population: some clients do not come in for treatment and we do not have access to all that do; (2) even if we solved the first problem, we cannot force all patients to participate in treatment, much less in research; and (3) even if we could resolve the second problem, the results of our research would apply only to representative samples from the population, not to biased samples (e.g., only rich clients, or only clients that like therapist *x*). Our client loads are rarely representative samples.

For these reasons, studies do not logically possess generality—they have it to the degree that they prove to have specified the variable of functional importance to clinical impact. Some authors (e.g., Kazdin, 1981a), have suggested that we accept the lack of random selection and instead try to acquire a large, representative group of patients. We can then correlate patient characteristics with treatment outcome and give these rules of generalization to clinicians. This is a good strategy. It can only be effeciently used, however, if our knowledge is based on an intensive analysis of the individual, repeated many times.

Most clinical research designs are not set up to detect which individuals improved. Rather, they are set up to detect which group improved against the background of individual variability. We cannot then go back and use individual data efficiently. In most group comparison designs, measurement error and other extraneous variables are inseparable from treatment-related variability at the level of the individual. Consider a simple pretest-posttest type study. It is a mistake to say that an individual who improves from pretest to posttest has improved because of treatment. The apparent improvement may actually be due to measurement error, maturation, or a host of similar factors (see Kazdin, 1981b). By random assignment to groups, we equalize these influences for the group as a whole, not for the individual. Since we cannot say which individual improved because of treatment, the correlations with treatment outcome will be necessarily reduced. We are necessarily correlating client characteristics with a mixture of treatment effects and all other sources of variability.

One solution is to conduct intensive analyses of individuals (as described earlier) many, many times. The advantage of this approach is that variability due to sources other than treatment can be identified at the level of the individual, and thus more reliable rules can be generated that relate particular patient characteristics and treatment outcomes. Surprisingly, the total number of clients needed may be as large as in group comparison research. The total amount of work may be greater. But the practicing clinician can contribute to this enterprise, which makes it feasible; and can consume it, which makes it worthwhile.

Assessing External Validity

Generalizability, in the real world, is based on the degree to which the functionally important characteristics in one's own situation are the same as those the analysis presented. Since we usually cannot know this beforehand, we can only make educated guesses about the likelihood of generalization, and then test to see if our guesses were correct. The following is a checklist of important dimensions that practicing clinicians should consider in assessing the generality of findings:

In all cases a "Yes" indicates greater likelihood of generalization to your situation.

1. Are the patients described in detail? Does your patient seem similar to theirs in most or all important respects?
2. Are the procedures they used described in detail sufficient for you to do what they did in all important respects?
3. Did they check the integrity of their treatment, for example, by having others observe and code the application of treatment? Is it adequate?
4. Did they specify the conditions (therapist; therapy environment) under which treatment was applied? Are they similar to your own? Are there therapist effects?
5. Are measures taken repeatedly across time so that an adequate individual sample is obtained?
6. Are several different measures taken if there isn't one universally accepted measure?
7. Are individual characteristics related to treatment outcome? Do your patients share the favorable characteristics?
8. If the results are reported in group form, are the percentage of individuals showing the effect reported? Is it high? Are individual data shown?
9. Have the results been replicated? Several times? By others?
10. Are the effects (and differences between effects) strong and clinically meaningful?
11. Does the study experimentally test differences which might improve generalization? If so, are the favorable conditions present in your situation?
12. Have you tried out the procedures with your clients? Did you achieve similar results?
13. Is the study internally valid? Are competing explanations for the results unlikely? [Barlow, Hayes, & Nelson, in press.]

In the context of this chapter, the reader should take care to note how important issues that are of importance to the intensive analysis of the individual become in the consumption of research, not just in its production. I will discuss each point briefly. To assist assimilation of the information, I ask the reader to picture him or herself having read an experimental article. The following are issues that might be considered.

First, ask yourself if the patients are described in detail. If they are described in detail examine your own patients and see if they seem similar in respects that are probably important (or that are known to be important) to treatment outcome.

One should then ask oneself if the procedures are described in sufficient detail for one to do exactly what was done in all respects that one believes are important to treatment outcome. On this basis, much of the clinical literature must be questioned. It also shows most clearly the difference between internal and external validity. Without specification we may know for sure that an effect occurred, but we can only apply it if we know how it was produced (see Cook & Campbell's [1979] description of construct validity).

The next step is to observe to see if the researchers checked on the integrity of their treatment, for example, by having others observe and code the application of the particular procedure or technique, particularly with complicated clinical techniques. Without this, we will not be sure that the stated treatment was that actually delivered.

One should then examine the conditions under which the treatment was applied. What kinds of therapists were used? What was the therapy environment like? Is there any reason to believe that these factors might have a strong impact on the outcome of treatment (for example, were therapist effects shown)? If there is, are these factors similar to factors that exist in one's own situation?

Were measures taken repeatedly across time so that an adequate individual sample is obtained? An individual clinician would not think of intervening with an individual client until he or she was fairly sure that intervention was needed. A single assessment may not be enough. Paradoxically, one might be quite willing to take seriously the claims that a particular intervention is effective when a single preassessment has been compared to a single postassessment in several clients. We have already analyzed the logical difficulty with this above. If repeated measures are taken, it is usually important that they be presented individually and not just as an aggregate across patients. Among other things, this allows the clinician to assess the goodness of fit between his or her clients' problems and the individuals in the reported research in considerable detail.

One should question whether several different measures are taken if there isn't one universally accepted measure? In many clinical areas the identification of client problems is not a clear cut matter. If several measures have been taken and the results are parallel with these several measures, there is a greater likelihood that the findings will apply to those of one's own clients who are similar on those measures.

Did the study examine whether or not the patient characteristics related to treatment outcome? If it did, what was found? Does the patient currently under consideration share the characteristics of those who were treated most successfully? The need for this kind of analysis has already been evaluated above.

If the results are reported in group form, are percentages of individuals showing the effect reported? Is the percentage high? Are the individual data shown? If one were to look for data on the effect of interventions on individuals, as recommended here, one would usually be disappointed. The methodological posture I have advocated is quite atypical in current clinical science. Recently, however, some researchers have begun to indicate approximately how many individuals in a given group showed the effect. For example, a study in which 90 percent of the patients seemed to improve is probably more likely to generalize to another clinician's individual client than one that might have shown an impact of similar magnitude but only with, say, 60 percent of the clients tested.

Have the results been replicated? How many times? By whom? Every time a finding is replicated, the degree to which it is likely to generalize increases. If the replications are done by several different persons in several different settings and if the findings are relatively consistent, then this is one of the more powerful indications that these findings may be generally applicable.

Are the effects strong? In the usual study, we often examine the level of statistical significance and forget the magnitude of the effect shown. It seems logically likely, however, that strong effects will be more generalizable than weak ones.

Did the study experimentally test client or situational differences that might relate to the impact of treatment? If so, one must assess whether one's own clients or situations show the favorable conditions indicated.

The clinician should consider whether he or she has tried out the procedures with his or her own clients, and if he or she achieved similar results in the past? There is no better way to know that research findings apply to one's situation than by attempting to apply them. The need for application underlines the utility of the advice given in this chapter.

Finally, is the study internally valid? Are competing explanations for the results unlikely? Are the results analyzed correctly? These questions were saved for last simply to underline the importance of other considerations that are so often neglected in discussions of the consumption of research. That being said, it should be obvious that only when findings are valid will they have any hope of generalizing to other situations.

These rules are really nothing more than modified versions of good clinical practice. This is an important point, so let us look briefly at the rules again.

Describing the clients in detail refers to good clinical assessment, careful taking of histories, sensitivity to subtle but critical patient characteristics, and the like. Describing the procedures (and conditions, point number 4) in detail refers simply to a careful and detailed treatment plan. The integrity of treatment simply asks if the clinician is following his or her own treatment plan. Repeated measurement asks if he/she is carefully assessing the client's problems and progress in treatment. The call for multiple measures reminds him/her to do a fairly broad assessment and to keep an eye on the client's overall functioning and well-being. Attention to individual characteristics asks him/her to ensure that the treatment fits the specific needs and strengths of the individual. Attention to individual data asks if he is assessing and working for the progress of each and every client, or is he or she content to say only that the work is generally okay. Replication asks the clinician to use procedures that are likely to work. The call for strong effects asks him/her to make sure treatment goals are met. Situational limitations are a reminder that if therapy is not working, he/she should stop, reassess, and try to determine why not. Testing it himself asks the clinician if this intervention has worked for him? Issues of internal validity ask if he or she is really responsible for change, was the treatment really needed, and are resources being used appropriately?

All this could be summarized by saying that the kind of knowledge that is based on the highest standards of clinical practice is the kind of knowledge that is likely to generalize. Unfortunately, it is all too easy to take short-cuts. Much of our clinical knowledge is not based on the highest standards of practice. The recommendations made in this chapter can be seen as methods to ensure that clinicians produce and consume knowledge that is consistent with both these standards and the goals of clinical psychology.

The Role of the Individual Case in the Production of Clinical Knowledge

If multitudes of intensive analyses of the individual are required for clinical psychology, who will produce them? Who has access to these cases? The answer seems to be active, practicing clinicians. Only they seem to have the resources required. Unfortunately, these professionals have been hobbled in their ability to produce clinical knowledge, largely by cumbersome methodological tools. It has long been recognized that practicing clinicians contribute relatively little to the research base of clinical psychology (Garfield & Kurtz, 1976; Kelly et al., 1978; Levy, 1962). A number of arguments have been advanced about this, from defending it as necessary, to blaming clinicians for some inherent weakness, to chastizing academics for their lack of interest in the clinical environment (e.g., see Leitenberg, 1974; Meehl, 1971; Peterson, 1976; Raush, 1969, 1974; Rogers, 1973; Shakow, 1976). Yet, consider the methodological tools clinicians have been given. Not only are they unwieldy, as I have just argued, but they also tend not to produce the kind of knowledge base that clinical psychology needs, because the level of analysis is incorrect. Group comparison methodologies did not originate with clinical psychology —they were attached to it by methodologists in other areas. These same methodologists have alternately ignored and criticized the clinical research methods developed by early clinicians (e.g., Freud). At best, an intensive case analysis is said to be "heuristic," with the task of developing

real knowledge passed on to the academic who has the resources to grapple with the costly, cumbersome, but "correct" research methodologies.

In the past decade, an explosion of interest has occurred in methodological tools that are built on case analysis (e.g., Barlow, Hayes, & Nelson, in press; Barlow & Hersen, 1973; Browning & Stover, 1971; Chasson, 1967, 1979; Hoyes, 1981; Hersen & Barlow, 1976; Jayaratne & Levy, 1979; Kazdin, 1978, 1980, 1982; Kratochwill, 1978; Leitenberg, 1973; Svenson & Chassan, 1967). These tools are not only scientifically defensible, they are fully applicable to the clinical environment. They, too, have often been presented in ways that have limited their usefulness in the clinical environment. Almost as an overreaction to criticism by traditional methodologists, texts in the areas have tended to emphasize what is ideal over what is essential. Yet, the basic foundation of this methodology seems uniquely suited to clinical evaluation.

The Fundamentals of Single-Case Analysis

The essentials of the treatment-related analysis of the individual case actually parallel the essentials of good clinical practice.

ACCURATE AND SYSTEMATIC ASSESSMENT

All valid clinical knowledge is based upon systematic observation. For example, if what is observed is a function of the needs, biases, or wants of the clinician (i.e., because of "countertransference") and not client behavior, the information gleaned from the case will necessarily be faulty. Anecdotal information has a place in single-case analysis, but the threats to accuracy are so large that little can be learned without going the extra step to assess the client in a systematic way (Kazdin, 1981b). This is good clinical practice. The nature of the observation may include systematic interviews, testing, self-monitoring, direct observation, or other procedures (see Nelson, 1981, for a short review of clinically practical measures). The measures should be practical and taken under consistent and specifiable conditions.

REPEATED MEASUREMENT

Repeated measurement also parallels rules of clinical practice. Practical clinical guides often exhort clinicians to "examine regularly and consistently whether therapy is being helpful" (Zaro et al., 1977, p. 157). In clinical practice, repeated measurement should start early, using several measures if possible. Often, when normal assessment ends, the clinician will have a systematically collected baseline. The use of repeated measurement, more than any other single factor, allows knowledge to be drawn from the individual case, because it eliminates or restricts the plausibility of several alternative explanations for the effects seen (e.g., measurement error).

SPECIFICATION OF CONDITIONS

As will be discussed later, this allows the effects to be "given away." Without a clear understanding of what the clinician actually did, what the client was actually like, and so on, we may know that something worked for someone, but not what worked for whom.

REPLICATION

All valid knowledge should be replicable. This requirement is increased in clinical science because of the many threats to validity.

ESTABLISHMENT OF THE DEGREE OF VARIABILITY

We cannot know if we have had an effect unless we have an idea of where we were headed. Measures should be taken long enough and be stable enough to allow us to know where the problem is going and to see treatment effects, should they occur. These are not absolute qualities — it depends upon what we know about the problem and its treatment. If treatment effects are expected to be large, considerable variability can be tolerated. If the problem is so variable that no effects can be seen, why proceed? In some situations, we know enough about the problem to assume a fair amount of stability, and we may need only a few assessments. An extremely academically deficient child, for example, is unlikely to improve and deteriorate rapidly over short periods of time.

If the measures are too variable, three clinically defensible options are open. First, one could wait to see if a clearer picture emerges. Second, one can search for the events that are causing improvement and deterioration. It may be sloppy measurement, or it could be real and a clue to the actual events influencing the problem. Third, the temporal unit of analysis may be too small. Perhaps the overall pattern is unclear because the specific measures are being examined in terms of

days, when weeks make more clinical sense; hours when days make more sense, and so on.

INVESTIGATIVE PLAY AND THE CREATIVE USE OF SINGLE-CASE LOGIC

The investigation of the individual case should be a dynamic enterprise, produced by the interaction of continuously collected clinical information and ongoing therapeutic actions. When unanticipated effects are seen, the clinician must be ready to abandon previous decisions and to let the client's data be the guide. This is also good clinical practice. Clinicians are told to "be prepared to alter your style of dealing with a client in response to new information" and "be prepared to have many of your hypotheses disproved" (Zaro et al., 1977, p. 28). This is the single greatest difference between the usual methodological tools (e.g., group comparison approaches) and those that fit clinical realities. Even the use of time-series designs may have fallen into this trap, as might be indicated by the literature's emphasis on complete designs rather than on design elements. All single-case analyses are built upon a few core elements. The specific arrangement of elements should be dictated by clinical needs, not by formal categorization of complete designs. One is trying to use these elements to determine if treatment is needed and useful.

In summary, a methodology for the production of clinical knowledge based on the individual case must accord itself with fundamental values of good clinical practice: accurate and repeated assessment; establishment of clinical need; specification of treatment; continuous sensitivity to the needs of clients; and establishment of the role of treatment in client improvement. Whether or not the knowledge developed will be valid will depend upon the degree to which these recommendations are followed. Only the last recommendation is somewhat foreign to trained clinicians, although it is implicit in clinical decision making.

The Design Elements in Single-Subject Analysis

Following the format described in Hayes (1981), the present chapter describes single-case experimental designs in terms of a few core units, organized by the nature of stability estimates and the logic of the data comparisons. These core elements are put together as the needs of the case analysis dictates. The elements can be organized into three types: between, within, and combined series.

The within-series elements draw their estimates of stability, level, and trend within a series of data points across time, taken under similar conditions. Changes are made in the conditions impinging upon the client, and concomitant changes are examined in the stability, level, or trend in a series of data points taken under the new conditions. Thus, changes seen within a series of data points across time are the main source of clinical information.

There are two classes of within-series elements. In the *simple phase change*, the within-series comparison is made one or more times between two conditions (for example, baseline and treatment). In the *complex phase change*, there is an overall coordinating strategy that dictates a particular sequence of three or more conditions. In either case, there is one condition per phase.

Perhaps the most common example is the "A/B" design (by tradition, A always stands for baseline, "B" for the first treatment element, "C" for the second, and so on). The A/B represents a simple case study (but with repeated measurement and careful specification of treatment) in which a period of assessment is followed by a single treatment strategy. If the stability, level, or trend of the data taken in the assessment phase change when treatment is implemented, our confidence increases that treatment is responsible, especially if the change is marked or sudden.

Often, we can think of other reasons for the change, such as the effect of outside events or the effects of assessment itself (see Campbell & Stanley, 1963; Hersen & Barlow, 1976; Kazdin, 1982), so we need to replicate the effect. A simple way is to repeat the phase change in reverse order (an A/B/A) and then perhaps to repeat it again (an A/B/A/B). Each time changes in the data coincide with phase changes, our confidence in the effect increases. This type of design answers the question: Does treatment work for this client?

The alternation of phase changes can continue indefinitely—each sequence constituting a type of completed design. The two conditions could be two treatments (e.g., B/C/B/C), or elements of a treatment package (e.g., B/B + C/B). The logic of these specific types is identical, only the questions being asked and the extent of the compari-

sons differ owing to the specific content of the phases and the number of alternations. In a B/C/B/C design, for example, the question being asked is: Which treatment works best for this client?

When components of a treatment package are being compared, the sequence is called an *interaction element*. It answers the question: What are the combined effects of two treatment components compared to one alone? A number of specific sequences are possible (e.g., B/B + C/B/B + C or B + C/C/B + C).

Several types of complex phase-change elements exist. An example is an A/B/A/C/A sequence. A simple phase change comparing two treatments does not show that either works relative to baseline. If this is not already known, and if the clinician still wants to compare the two treatments, it can be done by combining simple phase-change strategies for determining the effectiveness of each treatment. The sequence A/B/A/C/A combines an A/B/A with an A/C/A. This allows us to ask if treatments B and C are effective, and if they are differentially effective. Because order effects are possible and noncontiguous data are being compared (B and C), it is usually best for other subjects also to receive an A/C/A/B/A/ sequence. If the conclusions are the same, then the believability of the treatment comparison is strengthened.

Another complex phase-change element termed a *changing criterion* is available when a criterion can be set beforehand of the type of behavior that must be seen in the phase to achieve a given outcome (Hartmann & Hall, 1976). If the behavior repeated changes to match a sequence of criterion changes, the therapeutic conditions can be said to be responsible.

This element is often used when changes can only occur in one direction, either for ethical or for practical reasons. The logic of the maneuver, however, allows for criterion reversals when the behavior is reversable. The criteria usually relate to the level of the behavior seen, but it logically also applies to criteria changes based on stability, trend, relationship to initiating conditions, and the like. The weakness of the element is that it is not always clear when observed behavior is tracking criterion shifts. This problem can be alleviated by altering the length, magnitude, or direction of criterion shifts.

Other complex strategies are possible but are seen infrequently in clinical research. For example, the intensity of treatment might be systematically increased and then decreased in a series of phases (see Sidman, 1960). This might be written A/B/B'/B"/B'"/B"/B'/A. A strategy that draws upon similar logic is the *periodic treatments element* (Hayes, 1981). If the frequency of measurement is high (much more often than treatment) and if actual treatment is confined to periodic sessions (e.g., one-hour outpatient visits), then a consistent relationship between the periodicity of behavior change and that of treatment may indicate a treatment effect. This is particularly so if the sessions are irregularly spaced, and if the behavior changes that follow are rapid and stable. That this is a similar type of phase-change design element as the A/B'/B"/B'" (etc.) can be seen if one thinks of phase "B" as "the phase following treatment session one," phase "B" as "the phase following treatment session two," and so on.

BETWEEN-SERIES ELEMENTS

In the between-series elements the estimates of stability level and trend of the data are made in a series of measures taken in a specific condition, not simply across time. Effects are assessed by looking for differences between two or more of these series. There are two basic types. One type is an *alternating treatments design element*, or ATD (Barlow & Hayes, 1979). The ATD is based on the rapid alternation of two or more conditions, in which there is one potential alternation of condition per measurement unit.[1] Since a single data point associated with one condition may be preceded and followed by measurements associated with other conditions, there are no phases. Rather, measurements associated with each condition are put into separate series. If there is a clear separation between the series, differences among conditions are inferred.

Order effects are usually minimized by random or semirandom alternation of conditions. The conditions may or may not include baseline, de-

pending upon the question being asked. The strategy is especially useful for comparing two or three treatments or treatment elements (see Figure 11.1). One could think of the ATD as an extremely rapid simple phase change, but the estimates of variability and source of treatment comparisons are different and it can easily incorporate three or even more conditions into a single comparison sequence (see Barlow & Hayes, 1979).

The ATD is particularly useful for comparing two or more treatments or when measurement is cumbersome or lengthy (e.g., an entire MMPI). Only four data points are absolutely needed (two in each condition), though more are desirable. Alternations may be made after weeks or months, so that a given data point may incorporate many treatment sessions, or on the other extreme, it might occur several times per session (e.g., Hayes et al., in press). "Rapid" alternation refers only to the rate of treatment alternation relative to the rate of measurement.

The only other true between-series element is the *simultaneous treatment design* (Browning, 1967). It requires the simultaneous availability of two or more treatments, while client controls which treatment is actually applied. Thus, a true instance of this design can only measure treatment preference, and it is little used in the applied literature.[2]

COMBINED-SERIES ELEMENTS

Several elements use comparisons both between and within data series to draw conclusions. One is built on several repetitions of a single simple phase change, each with a new series, in which the length of the first phase and the timing of the phase change differ each repetition. This strategy might best be termed a *multiple phase change*, but it is universally known as a *multiple baseline* (whether or not baseline is one of the conditions).

The different series might be based on different behaviors, different individuals, or different

---

[1]At one time the need for a specific stimulus associated with each condition was emphasized (Barlow & Hayes, 1979), but our more recent view of this is that no stimulus is required (Hayes, Levy, & Barlow, n.d.). For example, one could do an alternating treatments design comparing an effective medication with a placebo. A specific stimulus for each condition is usually unavoidable, however, and is needed in certain kinds of situations (see Hayes et al., n.d.).

[2]Unfortunately, there is enormous confusion about the use of terms for design elements. For example, the term "simultaneous treatment design" has also been used (e.g., Kazdin & Hartmann, 1978; Kazdin, 1982) to refer to designs in which an ATD is sandwiched in between phases of baseline, and the most effective treatment as determined by the ATD. The virtues of this specific sequence derive from those of the elements on which it is based so I will not discuss them here (see Kazdin, 1982).

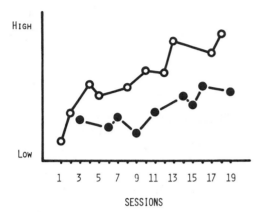

Fig. 11.1. An example, using hypothetical data, of an ATD. The clear difference between the two series shows that more client self-disclosure is produced when the therapist self-discloses. The overall increase across time is not analyzed without the addition of other phases, such as a baseline phase before and after (from Hayes, 1981).

situations, or combinations of these.[3] By replication across different series, the multiple baseline corrects for major deficiencies of a simple phase change, that effects could be due to coincidental extraneous events, assessment, and so on. If the effects are replicated, but with different lengths of baseline for each replication (a strategy that controls for the amount of baseline assessment or mere maturation) and with the actual time of the phase change arbitrarily altered (to reduce the possibility of correlated extraneous events), the conclusions are correspondingly strengthened.

The same first condition must yield to the same second condition, since we are controlling for alternative explanations for a specific phase-change effect. The logic of the comparison does not require baseline. A series of B/C phase changes could easily be arranged into a multiple baseline. The sequence of within- and between-series comparisons are shown in Figure 11.2.

Note that the first comparison is just simple

phase change, but with comparisons with other unchanged series ("B2" and "B3") to see if the change occurred only when the phase changed. The same logic is then repeated.

No set number of phase-shift replications is required between series in a multiple-baseline element, but each additional series strengthens our confidence that much more. The same is true of the differences in initial phase length. If one series has an initial phase that is only slightly longer or shorter than the other, it is less satisfactory than if there are large differences.

If a phase shift is accompanied by changes between as well as within series, either effect is due to extraneous variable (and not treatment) or the effects of treatment are generalized across series. For this reason, the design element is most useful when the series are independent (Kazdin & Kopel, 1975). If several series are being compared, some interdependence can be tolerated (e.g., Hayes & Barlow, 1977; Hersen & Bellack, 1976), without undoing the design (Kazdin, 1980).

Another combined series strategy, termed a *crossover*, is based on two concurrent phase changes on separate series, one the reverse of the other.[4] By changing phases at the same time, this strategy equalizes alternative sources of control that might have produced an apparent phase-change effect (e.g., maturation, phase length). Consistent within-series effects in both series provide some evidence of the superior of one condition over the other. The controls are fairly weak (e.g., for order effects) so additional replications are needed.

A final combined-series element is the *baseline-only control* This is simply an uninterrupted series that can be compared to other manipulated series, allowing a between-series comparison in addition to whatever within-series comparisons are possible. Changes occurring elsewhere and not in the baseline-only control series are more likely to have been produced by treatment (see Campbell & Stanley's [1963] equivalent time samples design)—the logic of this is identical to the between-series comparisons in a multiple baseline.

[3]As with many of these design elements, the literature on the multiple baseline contains many rules that seem unnecessary. For example, it was originally asserted that the additional series must be built on variation along a single dimension (person, place, or behavior; see Baer, Wolf, & Risley, 1968). The logic of the comparison does not require this, although the bredth of the question differs if it is violated. For example, if an effect shown in behavior A in person B and situation C is replicated across behavior A in person X and situation Z, it tests both the person and situational generality of the results.

[4]This is essentially the same as the logic of a true "reversal" design (Leitenberg, 1973).

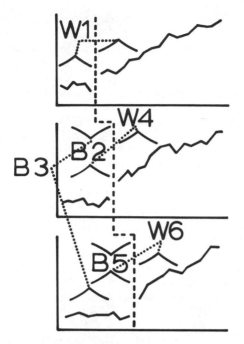

Fig. 11.2. The types of comparisons made in a multiple baseline. W = a within-series comparison, and B = a between-series comparison. The numbers show the usual sequence of comparisons (from Hayes, 1981).

Conducting a Case Analysis

The level of scientific product in a given single-case analysis depends upon the degree to which reasonable alternative explanations can be ruled out. For some clinical issues, especially assessment and etiological questions, careful interviewing or formal assessment may be enough to arrive at valid conclusions. For example, a particular view of depression may claim that a special type of client history or attitude is necessary for depression to occur. Even a single credible instance where this is not true may in itself make a contribution.

In treatment research (as in clinical treatment itself), more is usually required. Accurate and systematic assessment will almost always be needed. Repeated measurement is needed when we do not have certain knowledge of the stability and trend of the behavior of interest. If we are certain that a given disorder is stable and accurately measured, then even a single measurement before-treatment and after-treatment may add to our knowledge base (Jayaratne & Levy, 1979), especially if it is repeated in several cases. Unfortunately, very few

such situations exist. In order to project trends against which effects can be evaluated, we usually need to measure repeatedly. An exception is if it occurs when treatment is very strong. As described earlier, if most individuals improve significantly, a simple pre-post measurement may be sufficient.

Once repeated and accurate measurement is occurring, case studies are really single-case designs. There is no clear division between them. The level of scientific product will vary from one case study to another, but this is not just due to issues of design. It depends heavily on the context in which the information is viewed (what we know about the behavior, etc.).

The most influential case analyses in clinical psychology (e.g., Little Albert) amount to variations of single-case designs, as described earlier. They may at times seem relatively uncontrolled, but they rely on the same logical structure. Unfortunately, single-case designs are often viewed in a fairly rigid way (for example, some claim that treatment must be withheld to be evaluated). This is not logically required. Rather, the obstacles some see to the clinical application of single-case methodology (e.g., Kazdin & Wilson, 1978) are only obstacles presented by specific design elements in specific clinical situations. Other design elements can always be used.

The goodness of fit between single-case methodology and clinical practice is assured because rules of good clinical practice are fundamentally based on the same logical moves (Hayes, 1981). Of course, the amount of knowledge gleaned from a case or series of cases depends upon how precise the analysis can be. Rather than a dichotomy (e.g., research versus practice), the amount of knowledge gained from a case lies on a continuum.

In this section I will describe how single-case methodology fits clinical decision making. Further, I will attempt to show that treatment-related case analyses are actually forms of single-case experimental analysis. The use of within-series and combined strategies provides a good example of this. The following sections describe the sequence of events a clinician might follow in conducting such an analysis.

Within and Combined Series

The clinician typically begins a therapeutic relationship with a period of assessment. If repeated measures are taken, this period amounts to a baseline phase. In order to establish estimates of stability, level, and trend, at least three measurement points seem to be needed (e.g., see Hersen & Barlow, 1976), although more are desirable and may be needed in a given case to discern a trend. Shorter periods of assessment may be justified when there is other information available about the problem being measured. For example, the clinical disorder may have a known history and course (e.g., the social withdrawal of a chronic schizophrenic) or archival baselines may be available (e.g., family reports, records from school, etc.). Note that this issue is a clinical one ("Do I know the nature and course of the problem?"), not an arbitrary addition of single-case methodology.

Even though a baseline would be useful, sometimes treatment must be begun immediately. In this case, scientifically valid information may still be gained by design elements that do not require a baseline (e.g., an ATD), or by replication (e.g., in other cases or later in the same case). When a baseline is taken, it may show the problem to be improving, deteriorating, or staying the same. In general, if substantial improvement is occurring it is not time to change course (i.e., to shift phases and to start treatment). This advice is the same on clinical grounds (why interfere with a good thing?) as it is on methodological grounds (how can you see if you've had an effect?).

At this point, the clinician may be ready to implement treatment. Before doing so, the clinician may want to see if there is a variable that needs to be controlled first. For example, if the client seems susceptible to mild interventions such as family support, therapeutic expectations, social encouragement, and the like (especially if the treatment is dangerous, difficult, or costly), it might be worth trying the less difficult treatment first. If it is not effective, the meaningfulness of subsequent therapeutic effects may be enhanced. When starting treatment, it should ideally be implemented in a powerful way. Excessively gradual implementation will make real effects more difficult to see (Thomas, 1978), though even this would not be lethal.

When the second phase is implemented, only three outcomes are possible: no change, deterioration, or improvement. If there is no change, the clinician can either wait and see if there is a delayed effect, or try another strategy. It is typically assumed that a phase producing no change can be (with caution) considered part of the previous phase (e.g., $A = B/C$). There are limits to this, of course. An $A = B = C = D = E/F/E/F$ design

would not be very convincing and would need to be replicated, but this is true in normal clinical work. If we seem to find the key to a case after extensive floundering, we usually are not sure that we really have it until we try it out with others. Sometimes the new strategies we try are modifications or additions to previous ones (e.g., $A = B = B + C = B + C + D/B + C + D + E$). The methodological considerations here are the same. If treatment produces deterioration, the clinician should withdraw treatment (creating an $A/B/A$). If the behavior improves, an iatrogenic effect is shown, which itself may be a significant (if somewhat disturbing) contribution to the field.

The final possible effect is improvement. Several courses are then opened up: (1) to continue to completion and (perhaps) to try it with similar cases, (2) try the intervention in other areas of the client's life, if appropriate; or (3) withdraw treatment briefly, with an eye toward reimplementation. Since this (an A/B) is the cornerstone of clinical case evaluation, these alternatives will be discussed in some detail.

CONTINUE

An A/B design by itself often produces useful clinical knowledge. This is particularly true if the effects are marked. It makes it unlikely that such things as assessment effects or regression to the mean are responsible (Kazdin, 1981b). It is, of course, always possible that the effects are due to maturation or some extraneous environmental event. This may be more or less likely, depending upon the nature of the problem, its chronicity, past history of treatment, the identification of sudden changes in the client's world, and rapidity and the consistency of improvement in various areas of functioning. In favorable circumstances, a single A/B can produce fairly believable demonstrations of treatment impact because the overall pattern of results significantly undermines competing explanations.

The only way to know for sure is through replication, either within the same client or between different clients. If the A/B can be repeated in other clients, a natural multiple baseline will almost always be formed. This is probably one of the clearest examples of natural design elements that arise in clinical practice. Nothing could be more natural to clinical work than an A/B. Individual cases will naturally have different lengths of baseline (often widely so) and sequential cases usually lead to a multiple baseline across people.

Some of the earliest applied literature on the multiple baseline (e.g., Baer, Wolf, & Risley, 1968) said that multiple baselines across persons should always be one at the same time in the same setting with the same behavior. Saving cases, with perhaps periods of months or even years separating each, violates this rule, but fortunately the logic of the strategy does not really require it. If the time of the phase shift differs in real time from client to client, it is unlikely that important external events could repeatedly coincide with the phase changes. It is true that the external events that were present with case X are not simultaneously present in case Y, but this additional control is unimportant if the effects are clear and replicable.

The multiple baseline controls for the effects of assessment, maturation, and similar effects by varying the lengths of baseline. Multiple A/Bs retain much of this protection, as long as the reasons for changing phases at the precise moment are described, vary from case to case, seem unlikely to be related to sudden improvement, and (ideally) are at times somewhat arbitrary. Thus, while multiple A/Bs have been described as case studies (Kazdin, 1981b), they seem to be legitimate experimental designs.

The clinicians must report all cases attempted, not just those showing the desired effect. If the effect is not seen in some, the clinician should attempt to find out why (e.g., by adding phases to those clients showing an A = B effect). A careful examination of the variables accounting for differences between clients may lead to knowledge about mechanisms of change and boundary conditions.

The multiple baseline across cases also provides a home for those cases in which treatment only is given (B only), and in which treatment is never given (baseline-only control). As anchors in a series of cases, they can provide evidence of the effectiveness of treatment even when no baseline is taken (B only), thus controlling for an unlikely order effect caused by baseline assessment, or of the likelihood of change when no treatment is given (baseline-only control).

A related use of these multiple A/B is as multiple clinical replications (Barlow, 1980). In this use, the focus is on the numbers of cases showing effects of particular types at the A/B shift. While the method of presentation differs, if the baseline lengths differ substantially, this amounts to a method of summarizing multiple-baseline data, more than a new design.

CONDUCT A MULTIPLE BASELINE WITHIN THE CASE.

Multiple baselines often form naturally across behaviors because of the tendency for practicing clinicians to tackle subsets of problems sequentially rather than all at once (e.g., Brownell, Hayes, & Barlow, 1977). Multiple baselines across settings are less common but also naturally occur when clinicians treat problem behavior shown in one specific condition first (e.g., Hayes & Barlow, 1977). If the client has shown a good response to treatment with one problem or in one situation, the clinician should consider trying the same strategy with remaining difficulties. If so, a multiple baseline will be formed.

WITHDRAWAL

Withdrawal of an apparently effective treatment raises ethical issues, client fee issues, potential client morale problems, and possible neutralization of subsequent treatment effects. However, it often seems justified and even clinically useful. It also frequently occurs naturally.

First, a withdrawal can avoid the unnecessary use of ineffective treatment. Physicians recognize this issue in the common practice of "drug holidays" (i.e., withdrawals) to assess the continued need for treatment. Second, withdrawals often present themselves naturally in treatment in the form of vacations, holidays, sickness, temporary treatment drop-outs, or in terms of clinical reassessment, attention to unrelated clinical issues, and the like. When using these kinds of withdrawals, the reasons for the phase change should be described and some interpretive caution should be used, since changes seen could be due to the events causing the natural withdrawal, not to withdrawal per se.

Third, withdrawals can be short and given a good rationale. If this is well done, the client may be helped regardless of the outcome. In some of my own cases, short withdrawals, when connected with deterioration, convinced clients of the need for treatment and produced greater patient involvement. In other cases, withdrawals associated with maintenance lead to greater confidence on the client's part that the problem was now under better control.

If treatment is withdrawn, the behavior will show no change, deterioration, or continued improvement. If it deteriorates, treatment should be reimplemented (an A/B/A/B). If it shows no change (but there is room to improve), treatment could be started again to see if improvement will then occur. If the behavior continues to improve, the case can be saved and the same thing tried again later (forming a multiple baseline).

Between Series

The possibilities to use alternating-treatments design elements in clinical evaluation are great but usually require more planning. One of the advantages of an ATD is its ability to produce information rapidly. When the clinician wants to know if condition B works better than C, there are few finer ways to find out. A situation where this is common is when difficult treatment-related assessment decisions exist. Suppose, for example, that a client is presenting with depression. The clinician may have a difficult time determining if the client is more likely to respond to cognitive-therapy procedures or skills-training procedures. Rather than guess, the clinician might do both, in an alternating-treatments fashion. The better treatment may quickly be revealed and all treatment effort could then go in this direction. We have recently conducted exactly such a clinical series (McKnight, Nelson, & Hayes, n.d.), and were able in just a few sessions reliably to identify "cognitive responders" from "skills responders," based on ATD data.

Combining Elements

Case analyses is an exploration into the world of an individual. This kind of exploration calls for dynamic and creative uses of clinical tools: assessment, intervention, and evaluation. Designs should not be a framework into which clinical procedures are injected; rather, design elements should be used to support clinical decision making. In the ebb and flow of hypotheses that emerge in a clinical case, design tools should be used as needed and discarded as quickly when they're no longer useful. Table 11.1 presents examples of the use of various design elements to answer specific clinical questions. Which design tool is used in any row is determined by which is most feasible in terms of the kind of behavior being analyzed and the situation in treatment.

Summary

In this chapter, I have argued that the nature of clinical psychology puts a fundamental emphasis on the individual, for both the consumption and the production of clinical knowledge. Multiple analyses of the individual case should be a major source of clinical knowledge. The logic applied to this effort should be the logic inherent in rules of good clinical practice. By articulating that logic, the dichotomy between case studies and single-case experimental design is replaced by a gradual continuum of certainty of knowledge; the distinction between research and practice turns out to be essentially artificial, and practicing clinicians are legitimized in their role as producers as well as consumers of clinical knowledge.

References

Baer, D. M., Wolf, M. M., & Risley, T. R. Some current dimensions of applied behavior analysis. *Journal of Applied Behavior Analysis*, 1968, **1**, 91–97.

Barlow, D. H. Behavior therapy: The next decade. *Behavior Therapy*, 1980, **11**, 315–328.

Barlow, D. H., & Hayes, S. C. Alternating treatments design: One strategy for comparing the effects of two treatments in a single subject. *Journal of Applied Behavior Analysis*, 1979, **12**, 199–210.

Barlow, D. H., Hayes, S. C., & Nelson, R. O. *The scientist-professional: Research and evaluation in clinical and educational settings.* New York: Pergamon, in press.

Barlow, D. H., & Hersen, M. Single-case experimental designs: Uses in applied clinical research. *Archives of General Psychiatry*, 1973, **29**, 319–325.

Birnbrauer, J. S. External validity and experimental investigation of individual behavior. *Analysis and Intervention in Developmental Disabilities*, 1981, **1**, 117–132.

Brownell, K. E., Hayes, S. C., & Barlow, D. H. Patterns of appropriate and deviant arousal: The behavioral treatment of multiple sexual deviations. *Journal of Consulting and Clinical Psychology*, 1977, **45**, 1,144–1,155.

Browning, R. M. A same-subject design for simultaneous comparison of three reinforcement contingencies. *Behaviour Research and Therapy*, 1967, **5**, 237–243.

Browning, R. M., & Stover, D. O. *Behavior modification in child treatment: An experimental and clinical approach.* Chicago: Aldine-Atherton, 1971.

Campbell, D. T., & Stanley, J. C. *Experimental and quasi-experimental designs for research.* Chicago: Rand-McNally, 1963.

Chassan, J. B. *Research design in clinical psychology and psychiatry.* New York: Appleton-Century-Crofts, 1967.

Chassan, J. B. *Research design in clinical psychology and psychiatry.* (2nd ed.) New York: Irvington, 1979.

Cook, T. D., & Campbell, D. T. (Eds). *Quasi-experimental: Design and analysis issues for field settings.* Chicago: Rand McNally, 1979.

Garfield, S. L., & Kurtz, R. Clinical Psychologists in the 1970's. *American Psychologist*, 1976, **31**, 1–9.

Hartmann, D. P., & Hall, R. V. The changing criterion

TABLE 11.1 EXAMPLES OF THE USE OF DESIGN ELEMENTS TO ANSWER SPECIFIC TYPES OF CLINICAL QUESTIONS (FROM HAYES, 1981).

Clinical Question	DESIGN TYPE		
	Within Series	Between Series	Combined Series
A. Does a treatment work?	A – B – A – (B – . . .) B – A – B – (A – . . .) A – B (see combined designs) Periodic-treatments design changing-criterion design	Alternating treatments (Comparing A&B)	Multiple baseline (across settings, behaviors or persons) comparing A&B Replicated crossovers (Comparing A&B)
B. Does one treatment work better than another, given that we already know they work?	B – C – B – (C – . . .) C – B – C – (B – . . .)	Alternating treatments (Comparing B&C)	Replicated crossovers (Comparing B&C) Multiple baselines (Comparing B&C, and controlling for order)
C. Does one treatment work, does another work, and which works better?	1. A – B – A – C – A combined with A – C – A – B – A	Alternating treatments (Comparing A&B&C)	Multiple baseline (Comparing A&B&C, and controlling for order)
	2. Or combine *any* element from Row A with *any* element from Row B.		
D. Are there elements within a successful treatment which make it work?	B – B + C – B B + C – B – B + C C – B + C – C B + C – C – B + C	Alternating treatments (Comparing, for example, B & B + C)	Multiple baseline (Comparing B&B + C and C&B + C) Replicated crossovers (Comparing B&B + C and C&B + C)
E. Does the client prefer one treatment over another?		Simultaneous treatments (Comparing B&C)	
F. Does a treatment work, and if it does, what part of it makes it work?	Combine *any* elements from Rows A or C with *any* element from Row D.		
G. What level of a treatment is optimal?	Ascending/descending design B – B' – B – B'	Alternating treatments (Comparing B&B')	Multiple baseline (Comparing B&B'and controlling for order) Replicated crossovers (Comparing B&B')

design. *Journal of Applied Behavior Analysis*, 1976, **9**, 527–532.

Hayes, S. C. Single-case experimental design and empirical clinical practice. *Journal of Consulting and Clinical Psychology*, 1981, **49**, 193–211.

Hayes, S. C., & Barlow, D. H. Flooding relief in a case of public transportation phobia. *Behavior Therapy*, 1977, **8**, 742–746.

Hayes, S. C., Hussian, R., Turner, A. E., Grubb, T., & Anderson, N. The effect of coping statements on progress through a desensitization hierarchy. *Journal of Behavior Therapy and Experimental Psychiatry*, in press.

Hayes, S. C., Levy, R. L., & Barlow, D. H. Single-case designs and the animal laboratory. Unpublished manuscript, n.d.

Hersen, M., & Barlow, D. H. *Single-case experimental designs: Strategies for studying behavior change.* New York: Pergamon, 1976.

Hersen, M., & Bellack, A. S. A multiple baseline analysis of social skills training in chronic schizophrenics. *Journal of Applied Behavior Analysis*, 1976, **9**, 527–532.

Jayaratne, S., & Levy, R. L. *Empirical clinical practice.* New York: Columbia University Press, 1979.

Johnston, J. M., & Pennypacker, H. S. *Strategies and tactics of human behavioral research.* Hillsdale, N.J.: Erlbaum, 1981.

Kazdin, A. E. Methodological and interpretive problems of single-case experimental designs. *Journal of Consulting and Clinical Psychology*, 1978, **46**, 629–642.

Kazdin, A. E. *Research design in clinical psychology.* New York: Harper & Row, 1980.

Kazdin, A. E. External validity and single-case experimentation: Issues and limitations (A response to J. S. Birnbrauer). *Analysis and Intervention in Developmental Disabilities,* 1981, **1,** 133–143. (a)

Kazdin, A. E. Drawing valid inferences from case studies. *Journal of Consulting and Clinical Psychology,* 1981, **49,** 183–192. (b)

Kazdin, A. E. *Single-case research designs: Methods for clinical and applied settings.* New York: Oxford University Press, 1982.

Kazdin, A. E., & Hartmann, D. P. The simultaneous-treatment design. *Behavior Therapy,* 1978, **9,** 912–922.

Kazdin, A. E., & Kopel, S. A. On resolving ambiguities of the multiple-baseline design: Problems and recommendations. *Behavior Therapy,* 1975, **6,** 601–608.

Kazdin, A. E., & Wilson, G. T. *Evaluation of behavior therapy: Issues, evidence, and research strategies.* Cambridge, Mass.: Ballinger, 1978.

Kelly, E. L., Goldberg, L. R., Fiske, D. W., & Kilkowski, J. M. Twenty-five years later. *American Psychologist,* 1978, **33,** 746–755.

Kratochwill, T. F. *Single-subject research: Strategies for evaluating change.* New York: Academic, 1978.

Leitenberg, H. The use of single case methodology in psychotherapy research. *Journal of Abnormal Psychology,* 1973, **82,** 87–101.

Leitenberg, H. Training clinical researchers in psychology. *Professional Psychology,* 1974, **5,** 59–69.

Levy, L. H. The skew in clinical psychology. *American Psychologist,* 1962, **17,** 244–249.

Masters, W. H., & Johnson, V. E. *Human sexual inadequacy.* Boston: Little, Brown, 1970.

McKnight, D., Nelson, R. O., & Hayes, S. C. The assessment of treatment validity in depression. Unpublished manuscript, n.d.

Meehl, P. E. A scientific, scholarly, non-research doctorate for clinical practitioners: Arguments pro and con. In R. R. Holt (Ed.), *New horizons for psychotherapy: Autonomy as a profession.* New York: International Universities Press, 1971.

Nelson, R. O. Realistic dependent measures for clinical use. *Journal of Consulting and Clinical Psychology,* 1981, **49,** 168–182.

Peterson, D. R. Need for the doctor of psychology degree in professional psychology. *American Psychologist,* 1976, **31,** 792–798.

Raush, H. L. Naturalistic method and the clinical approach. In E. P. Willems & H. L. Raush (Eds.), *Naturalistic viewpoints in psychological research.* New York: Holt, Rinehart & Winston, 1969.

Raush, H. L. Research, practice, and accountability. *American Psychologist,* 1974, **29,** 678–681.

Rogers, C. R. Some new challenges. *American Psychologist,* 1973, **28,** 379–387.

Shakow, D. What is clinical psychology? *American Psychologist,* 1976, **31,** 553–560.

Sidman, M. *Tactics of scientific research.* New York: Basic Books, 1960.

Svenson, S. E. & Chassan, J. B. A note on ethics and patient consent in single-case design. *Journal of Nervous and Mental Disease,* 1967, **145,** 206–207.

Thomas, E. J. Research and service in single-case experimentation: Conflicts and choices. *Social Work Research and Abstracts,* 1978, **14,** 20–31.

Wolpe, J. *Psychotherapy by reciprocal inhibition.* Stanford, Calif.: Stanford University Press, 1958.

Zaro, J. S., Barach, R., Nedelmann, D. J., & Dreiblatt, I. S. *A guide for beginning psychotherapists.* Cambridge, Mass.: Cambridge University Press, 1977.

12 EXPERIMENTAL RESEARCH IN CLINICAL PSYCHOLOGY

Thomas R. Kratochwill
F. Charles Mace

As a division of professional psychology, clinical psychology has a strong tradition emphasizing scientific research and empirical evaluation of theory and practice. Although there continues to be heated debate on the role and relevance of certain types of research in training and practice, recent trends suggest that the field of clinical psychology will continue to rely on scientific advances. For example, an emphasis on keeping pace with scientific developments in clinical psychology is integrated into the *Specialty Guidelines for the Delivery of Services by Clinical Psychologists* (APA, 1981). Resolutions of the Virginia Beach Conference (Watson et al., 1981) stressed that training programs should provide training in evaluative research.

Although research is considered an important foundation for the field of clinical psychology, major questions have been raised over the quality of research in the field (Maher, 1978). Indeed, a special issue of the *Journal of Consulting and Clinical Psychology* (1978) was devoted to improving the overall quality of research in the field. In addition to the concern over methodology per se, there has been concern over the relevance of certain types of research for clinical practice (Barlow, 1981).

Again, a special section of the *Journal of Consulting and Clinical Psychology* (1981) was devoted to improving the relevance of research for clinical practice.

Many and varied types of research strategies are used in the clinical psychology field (see Chassan, 1979; Kazdin, 1980; Kendall & Butcher, 1982 for overviews). In this chapter we focus primarily on experimental research methods, discussing variations and considerations associated with their application. We place this form of research strategy in the context of other research methods, and provide an overview of validity and design issues. Thereafter we provide an overview of current issues in experimental methodology in the clinical psychology field.

Perspectives on Experimental Research

Characteristics of Experimental Research

As usually conceptualized, experimental research methods have been regarded as the primary means for establishing cause-effect relations

*The authors wish to express their sincere appreciation to Joel R. Levin for his thoughtful comments on the manuscript.

among variables.[1] In this endeavor, the usual experiment involves comparison of different values of the dependent variable with different values of the independent variable. Both variables can vary on such dimensions as quantity, quality, and type. The independent variable is usually manipulated in order to produce changes in the dependent variable. In this regard, the clinical researcher is interested in determining if the independent variable produces a certain outcome on the dependent variable(s).

There are several different types of experimental methods. The true experiment has usually been defined as a situation in which N subjects (or events) are randomly assigned to some K groups or conditions (see Boruch & Riecker, 1974; Underwood, 1957). Kerlinger (1973) argued that, "If the experimenter does not have the *power* either to assign subjects to experimental groups or to assign experimental treatments to the groups, then his study may be an experiment, but not a true experiment" (p. 315). The true experiment is sometimes referred to as a randomized experiment, to emphasize the random assignment of subjects to conditions for inferring treatment-caused change (Cook & Campbell, 1979). Randomized experiments are usually conceptualized as either within- or between-subject designs (Kazdin, 1980; Mahoney, 1978; these strategies are discussed later in the chapter).

Another class of experimental methods is called quasi-experimental. Such experiments have all the usual features of true experiments described above (e.g., treatments, outcome measures, etc.), but do not use random assignment to infer treatment-caused change (Cook & Campbell, 1979). Quasi-experiments are sometimes used in applied settings because the clinical researcher is unable to assign subjects/clients to conditions randomly. Two general classes of quasi-experiments have been indentified. In the first, nonequivalent group designs, a treatment and comparison condition are measured before and after treatment. For example, a researcher may be interested in comparing two treatments designed to reduce adult depression. In the second type, interrupted time-series designs, the effects of treatment are inferred from repeated observations before and after introduction of the treatment. These designs are sometimes called case studies, intrasubject, and/or single-case designs (see Hayes, chapter 11 in this volume for a review). Many different time-series strategies have been developed and some even employ a randomized sequencing of treatments to infer cause-effect relations.

Considerations in Experimental Research

Experimental methods are sometimes regarded as the method of choice in research. Yet the resolution of such an issue cannot be determined in the abstract and depends on several considerations. To begin with, experimental methods are part of the larger domain of empirical methods used in the scientific community. Yet, scientists have sometimes promulgated the view that associated empirical methods are free from the hazards of less formalized means of knowledge development (such as clinical experience). Science is not free from subjectivity and human bias (Mahoney, 1976). Several specific shortcomings of scientific methods can be described (Craighead, Kazdin, & Mahoney, 1981). First, scientists cannot claim certainty in many cases. Scientific research provides information on the likelihood or probability of certain events, but cannot claim absolute certainty. This is illustrated in the wide-scale use of inferential statistical tests in experimental research. Questions have been raised from time to time over the exclusive reliance on statistical inference. In clinical research, Bergin and Strupp (1972) emphasized that:

> With respect to inquiry in the area of psychotherapy, the kinds of effects that are used to demonstrate at this point in time should be significant enough so that they are readily observable by inspection or descriptive statistics. If this cannot be done, no fixation upon statistical and mathematical niceties will generate fruitful insights, which obviously can come only from the researcher's understanding of the subject matter and the descriptive data under scrutiny [p. 440].

[1]Causal relationships are established along a number of dimensions (Mahoney, 1978, p. 661) including (1) relative temporal contiguity (i.e., occurring together in time); (2) priority (i.e., the cause precedes the effect); (3) noncontradiction (i.e., there are no observed instances of the cause without the effect); (4) factor isolation (i.e., the elimination or control of all influences other than the presumed cause); and (5) replicability (i.e., the capacity to replicate the presumed relationship). Determining cause-effect relations is a difficult task, and as noted by Cook and Campbell (1979) both the epistemology of causation and scientific method are "at present in a productive state of near chaos" (p. 10). We will not digress into this and would refer the reader to Cook and Campbell (1979, chap. 1).

Practical or clinical significance in research has often been raised as one alternative to statistical inference (Barlow, 1981; Hersen & Barlow, 1976).

A second issue is that the knowledge generated through scientific methods generally, and experimental design spcifically, should be viewed as tentative. To begin with, the methods of scientific investigation change over time. New designs and measurement strategies come into existence and revise conclusions in a particular research area. For example, much work in the psychotherapy field has been based on case-study methods. In some areas, uncontrolled case studies provided the basis for theoretical or even treatment approaches (e.g., Little Albert, Little Hans). Watson and Rayner's (1920) work with Little Albert served, in part, as the basis for theoretical notions as to how fear develops and how certain treatment techniques, such as counter-conditioning, operate. Yet major questions can be raised about the study and conclusions that can be drawn from this work (cf. Harris, 1979). Subsequent and better-controlled research has raised new theoretical issues and alternative therapeutic components in conditioning therapies. Future research through a variety of methods will likewise raise new concerns and problems with existing interpretations, making us aware that knowledge is tentative.

Third, scientific methodologies may actually limit what can be known about how certain therapeutic variables will actually operate in practice. Scientific methodologies and especially the experimental type, stress careful operational definition of variables, tight controls on assessment and monitoring of treatment. Yet, these controls may actually limit knowledge regarding how certain techniques will operate when these controls are relaxed as is true in regular clinical practice (Kazdin, 1981).

In summary, it is important to recognize that experimental research contributes greatly to knowledge in the clinical psychology field. Yet, the types of experimental methods available vary in the degree to which they provide knowledge. Perhaps more importantly, it is realistic to perceive experimental methods as forming one domain of understanding complex human behavior and as having certain associated limitations.

Experimental Validity

In experimental research, the focus is on determining whether the independent variable (treatment) is causally related to the dependent variable (client-outcome measures). A formidable obstacle to this pursuit, however, are numerous factors that are extraneous to the treatment-outcome relationship. Consequently, a major concern of the investigator is to exercise adequate control of these factors (called validity threats) in order to ascertain whether variables are related, (i.e., whether cause-effect relations exists), whether the construct under study is the therapeutic variable, and the extent to which findings may be generalized. The degree to which these factors are eliminated represents the extent to which valid cause-effect statements may be made. Because of the complexity of psychological research, however, complete control of all extraneous variables is impossible (Cook & Campbell, 1979; Kiesler, 1981). Thus, the task confronting the investigator is to minimize potential validity threats and thereby strengthen confidence in the inferences drawn.

Most discussions of validity issues in the clinical literature are founded on the original work of Campbell and Stanley (1963); they argued that experiments may be evaluated according to their degree of internal and external validity. Internally valid experiments are those in which alternative explanations for the findings are eliminated, revealing the causal relationship between treatment and client measures. By contrast, external validity is the extent to which findings from one experiment can be generalized to different subjects, settings, and therapist/experimenters. Cook and Campbell (1979) have elaborated on this two-dimensional view of validity. They extend the rubric of internal validity to include statistical conclusion validity *and* internal validity. Similarly, issues pertaining to external validity have been broken down into construct validity *and* external validity. These four types of validity are discussed in the context of their relationships to clinical research.

Statistical Conclusion Validity

In most experimental research, establishing the covariance between treatment and outcome measures is prerequisite to determining cause and effect. Decisions regarding the covariation between the independent and dependent variables are made by evaluating the magnitude of group (or phase) differences and the variability among subjects (or sessions) with respect to a predetermined probability of wrongly concluding that the variables covary. Yet, the use of statistical tests to make decisions regarding the effectiveness of treatment can pose threats to valid inference making. Cook and Campbell (1979) have specified a number of potential threats associated with the use of statistical tests and refer to these collectively as threats to statistical conclusion validity. These include: (1) violated assumptions of statistical tests; (2) fishing and the error rate problem; (3) low statistical power; (4) the reliability of measures; (5) the reliability of treatment implementation; (6) random irrelevances in the experimental setting; and (7) random heterogeneity of respondents. Each of these threats requires consideration, especially in relation to statistical analyses, if accurate statements regarding covariation are to be made.

Major risks associated with statistical analyses have to do with committing a Type I or Type II error. A Type I error occurs when the researcher rejects the null hypothesis, when observed differences are in fact due to "random" or unexplained extraneous factors rather than to the effects of the independent variable. The alpha level (chosen *a priori*) provides the research community with an estimate of the probability of committing a Type I error. In rejecting the null statement, the investigator accepts what is usually a slim chance (e.g., 1 out of 20) that invalid conclusions were drawn regarding the covariance between treatment and outcome. Therefore, inferences are acknowledged to have a 95 percent probability of being valid. Any factors that inflate Type I error beyond the stated alpha level represent a threat to statistical conclusion validity.

Threats (1) and (2) listed above have the potential to inflate Type I errors. Violating assumptions of statistical tests can undermine the validity of research decisions. For example, conducting parametric analyses such as multiple regression, analysis of variance, and *t*-tests on data sets having correlated residuals or errors can result in underestimating the amount of error variance and overestimating error, thereby producing an inflated test statistic. Because of this problem, attempts to apply standard parametric analyses to time-series data (which often have correlated errors) have been generally criticized (see Kratochwill, 1978; McCleary & Hay, 1980). The procedure affectionately known as "fishing" can similarly increase the incidence of Type I errors. Fishing refers to conducting multiple tests or comparisons, often without benefit of theoretical guidance, and without recognizing that a certain proportion of comparisons will be significant by chance alone. This phenomenon led statisticians to recommend reporting the error rate per experiment (i.e., the probability that one or more comparisons in a given experiment will be significant by chance; see Ryan, 1959).

The second risk, that of making a Type II error, results when the experimenter fails to reject the null hypothesis when actual differences exist. This situation arises when the statistical test is not powerful enough to detect "true" treatment effects. Factors contributing to this problem are small sample sizes and effects, low alpha levels, low reliability of measures, and large error variance. In general, sample size and alpha levels are, to a great extent, under experimenter control. The issue of large error variance, however, is considerably more problematic in applied research where numerous factors are allowed to vary. Error variance can increase because of unreliable measures, unreliable treatment implementation, and random heterogeneity of respondents (e.g., clients may respond to different treatments because of their unique characteristics). The resulting inflation in error variance decreases statistical power by reducing the size of the test statistic.

In addition to the consequences of committing a Type II error, there are conceptual problems with failing to reject (or accepting) the null hypothesis (Cook et al., 1979). First, there remains the possibility, albeit remote, that the sample data at hand belong to a distribution whose mean is different from that of the control or comparison distribution. Because in theory all distributions overlap, we cannot be certain to which parent population a group of scores belong. But one can compute power for various effect sizes to obtain some estimate. Second, and more importantly, there is no way to be certain whether the null hypothesis is true or whether the statistical power was insufficient to detect actual differences. Since error is a component of every test statistic, there is always the possibility that treatment effects were obscured by uncontrolled variance. Therefore, in most cases, nonsignificant results pose a threat to statistical conclusion validity and the determination of covariation. Fortunately, steps may be taken to minimize this threat, including conducting power analyses and building logical arguments for accepting the null hypothesis (see Cook & Campbell, 1979).

Internal Validity

Whereas the object of statistical analysis is to determine the covariance among variables, the experimental design is the tool that permits valid statements about causality. The investigator is concerned with making decisions as to whether a specific treatment (A) causes changes in client measures (B). For example, let A be the treatment habit reversal (i.e., repeated performance of a competing behavior) and B represent the frequency of a nervous tic (e.g., leg jerks). At issue is whether implementing the habit reversal procedure contingent upon the occurrence of a tic reduces the frequency of the dependent measure. However, another factor that may bear on this treatment-outcome relationship is the client's increased attention to the occurrence of the tic (C) as a result of performing the habit reversal procedure. If the effects of C are left uncontrolled, there may be some ambiguity as to whether A or C caused changes in B. In this case, internal validity is the degree of certainty that manipulation of the habit reversal procedure changes in the occurrence of leg jerks.

In the example above, failure to control for the therapeutic effects of increased client attention to the tic would constitute a threat to internal validity. Several such internal validity threats have been catalogued and strategies developed for minimizing their effects (Cook & Campbell, 1979). Noted in Table 12.1 are the major threats to internal validity frequently encountered in clinical research. It should be noted that multiple threats may operate concurrently to influence the outcome of a particular study either in an additive fashion to compound invalidity or in opposition to one another to neutralize their biasing effects (Cook & Campbell, 1979). Because of the difficulty in estimating the effects of invalidity, the investigator has few alternatives other than to control as many variables as possible if valid conclusions are to be drawn.

Construct Validity

Along with establishing basic relationships among variables, the investigator must be concerned with evaluating the experiment in terms of its relation to theory. This requires that the operations representing the independent and dependent variables accurately reflect the theoretical constructs under study. That is, there must be a good fit between the specified operations and their referent constructs if valid generalizations are to be made. Thus, construct validity refers to the degree to which operations and constructs overlap.

Assessing construct validity is a twofold process. First, a given measure of construct A will be expected to *converge* or correlate highly with established measures of the same construct. For example, a newly developed self-report inventory purporting to measure behavioral, emotional, and cognitive aspects of fear may establish its *convergent validity* by correlating highly with direct motor, physiological, and cognitive measures associated with the feared situation. Second, the newly developed instrument should *diverge* or correlate lowly with different measures of constructs B, C, D, and so on. For example, the fear inventory should be relatively unrelated to accepted measures of hyperactivity, depression, obsessive/compulsive disorders, etc., in order to demonstrate its *divergent (or discriminant) validity*. Thus, obtaining estimates of convergent and divergent validity represent the vehicles by which construct validity is assessed (Campbell & Fiske, 1959; Cook & Campbell, 1979; Kerlinger, 1973).

Cook and Campbell (1979) identified several threats to construct validity (see pp. 64–68). In general, construct validity becomes threatened when (1) extraneous factors change inadvertently along with the independent variable, or (2) defined operations inadequately represent their referent construct. This first condition is usually referred to as "confounding" and, left uncontrolled, can seriously undermine attempts to infer validity that constructs A and B are causally related. Consider the clinician interested in evaluating the therapeutic effects of Ritalin on the activity level of a child. The biochemical events associated with the medication collectively represent the construct "Ritalin treatment." Yet, a construct that frequently covaries with most medical and psychological treatments is experimenter, client, or caretaker expectancies that improvement will occur. Because such expectancies (commonly known as placebo effects) have a well-documented history of therapeutic benefits (Hersen & Barlow, 1976), there is considerable ambiguity regarding the degree to which each construct, Ritalin treatment or outcome expectancies, produced change in the child's activity level. Double-blind trials are a common method for assessing the relative contribution of each therapeutic construct. With group designs, this involves the use of a group of control subjects who receive an inert substance. Time-series designs, on the other hand, contrast the effects of the active medication and the inert substance over separate phases within each subject.

The second condition that threatens construct validity is defined operations that inadequately represent their referent construct. Obtaining a

TABLE 12.1. THREATS TO INTERNAL VALIDITY.*

History:	The occurrence of events extraneous to the experimental treatment that may affect the dependent measure.
Maturation:	Physical and/or psychological changes occurring within subjects that may affect the dependent measure over time; becomes a threat to internal validity when such changes are not the focus of research.
Testing:	Changes in the dependent variable caused by the process of measuring subject performance; may result from subjects having taken a pretest because of the reactivity of the measurement process.
Instrumentation:	Changes in the dependent measure due to the use of inconsistent measurement procedures over the course of evaluation; instrumentation may occur when data collectors alter their method of recording performance as a result of experience, observer bias or drift, or the malfunction of mechanical recording devices; may also result from tests having unequal intervals leading to so-called ceiling and floor effects.
Statistical Regression:	If subjects are assigned to groups or treatment conditions on the bias of unreliable pretest or baseline measures, high scores will tend to decrease their performance over subsequent measurement occasions while the performance of low scores will increase; regression always occurs toward the population mean of a group; thus, scores in the mid-range will likely be unaffected.
Selection:	When groups are formed by arbitrary rather than random methods, their differential performance may be due to preexisting differences between groups rather than actual treatment effects.
Mortality:	The withdrawal of some subject observed at the pretest or baseline period before the final assessment may result in unequal groups; observed effects may be attributed to differences in subject characteristics or their response to treatment rather than the effects of the independent variable.
Interactions with Selection:	The interaction of history, maturation, and/or instrumentation threats with selection resulting in spurious treatment effects; history-maturation may occur when subjects or groups experience different historical factors that influence performance. Maturation-selection results when subjects or groups mature at different rates to

good fit involves matching the operationalized variables with the constructs they represent such that the particular construct is not under- or overrepresented. Take the case where an investigator successfully employs an implosion therapy procedure to eliminate self-reported feeling of acrophobia (fear of heights). In summarizing the findings, the investigator concluded that "implosion therapy was effective in relieving acrophobia." However, as alluded to earlier, phobic or fear disorder are often multifaceted, affecting motoric and physiological response classes in addition to the cognitive domain. Thus, in this instance, the experimenter seems to have overstated the case for the efficacy of the procedure by referring to a construct (acrophobia) whose scope is broader than the defined variable (self-reported emotions).

Finally, construct validity also becomes relevant when drawing conclusions about the therapeutic effects of a particular treatment. In order to evaluate a therapeutic construct accurately, its operations and administration should reflect the optimal treatment strength and integrity (Yeaton & Sechrest, 1981). Treatment strength refers to the amount and purity of those factors that are responsible for improved client functioning. For example, modeling may be considered a strong treatment when conducted with a high status model, the opportunity for subjects to observe the consequences associated with the model behavior, contingencies for performing the model behavior are clearly stated, and without interference from competing factors. In cases where the administered treatments are of insufficient strength to effect the desired change, conclusions regarding the effectiveness of the therapeutic construct may be understated and invalid. Similar consequences result when the integrity of the treatment is violated. Treatment integrity is the degree to which a

TABLE 12.1 *(continued)*

	increase the disparity between groups over time. Selection-instrumentation occurs when performance is scored differently for different groups owing to observer factors or tests whose intervals are unequal.
Ambiguity about the Direction of Causal Influence:	For many correlational studies in which the temporal ordering of variables is not certain, it is unclear whether A causes B or B causes A. Measures collected at different times provide information about the temporal priority not available in correlational studies that are cross-sectional.
Diffusion of Imitation of Treatments:	When subjects in the experimental and control groups are free to communicate with each other, it is possible that subjects may exchange information about the procedures of conditions of their particular group. The validity of the experiment is therefore threatened because the groups are no longer independent.
Compensatory Equalization of Treatments:	When experimental treatments provide subject desirable services, administrators may find it unacceptable to "deprive" the no-treatment control group of these benefits and insist that comparable or compensatory services be provided. The intended contrast is thus nullified and causal statements about the independent variable are rendered invalid.
Compensatory Rivalry by Respondents Receiving Less Desirable Treatments:	When subjects are aware of their group status (i.e., experimental or control), those not receiving treatment may compete with their experimental counterparts. Observed effects may be the result of this rivalry rather than of the independent variable.
Resentful Demoralization of Respondents Receiving Less Desirable treatments:	Control subjects who are aware that they are receiving less desirable treatment may respond by lowering their standard of performance. Between-group differences following treatment could not be attributed to the effects of intervention.

*Adapted from Cook and Campbell (1979).

particular treatment is implemented according to plans (Sechrest & Redner, 1979).

Administering treatments in any form other than the one operationally defined breeds ambiguity as to the construct responsible for change. Fortunately, these threats to construct validity can be attenuated to some extent by ongoing monitoring of the independent variable.

External Validity

Along with an interest in establishing relations between treatment and client variables, the researcher is usually concerned with identifying lawful relations or principles of behavior that extend beyond a particular study. External validity is the degree to which the findings of a given experiment can be generalized. In clinical research, concern centers on the degree to which results generalize: (1) *to* the population of subjects, disorders, settings, experimenters/therapists, and times targeted within the study, and (2) *across* types of subjects, disorders, settings, experimenters/therapists, and times within and outside the experiment. Valid generalizations *to* targeted populations sampled in the study refers to the ability to replicate results under similar conditions (i.e., were the research goals for a specified population met?). Valid generalizations *across* populations refer to the extent to which different populations (or subpopulations) would be affected by the treatment (i.e., how far can the results be generalized?).

In most clinical studies, we believe the investigator will usually have greater interest in generalizing *across* populations rather than *to* populations. Generalizing *to* a specified population requires that subjects be randomly selected from the entire pool of clients displaying a particular disorder. But true random selection is seldom achieved in psychological research, and there is some question about whether discrete populations of disorders can be specified (Adams, Doster, & Calhoun, 1977). Hence, generalization *to* a population is usually not feasible. Of greater concern, is the extent to which treatment effects are replicable *across* clients sharing the same or different clinical characteristics or when administered by different therapists under different conditions. Confidence in the generality of results is strengthened each time effects are reproduced under varying conditions.

Internal validity and external validity are often inversely related because the rigorous controls needed to establish internal validity pose limits on generalization (Kratochwill, 1978). Similarly, the absence of rigorous controls usually means that variables are free to vary in approximation to the natural clinical situation. Kazdin (1980) identified nine dimensions along which therapy research may differ from the clinical situation. These include the target problem, population, manner of recruitment, therapists, client set, selection of treatment, setting of treatment, variation of treatment, and assessment methods. The more closely these factors resemble the clinical situation, the greater is the external validity of the experiment. According to Ross (1981) and Kazdin (1981), the issues are whether rigorous research that is internally valid identifies treatments that are relevant to clinical practice. They stress the importance of extending knowledge gleaned from internally valid experiments to clinical practice where tight controls are impractical. Nevertheless, whether laboratory results are generalizable to clinical settings is really an empirical question (see Berkowitz & Dounerskin, 1982). One should keep in mind, however, that unambiguous findings are necessary before generalizations become meaningful. In this regard, concern for adequate internal validity should take priority over issues of generalization when attempting to establish fundamental relationships between treatment and outcome.

Experimental Designs

In clinical research, the type of design used is influenced by a multitude of factors. Ideally, the researcher would like to design an experiment sufficiently rigorous to ensure that the treatment variable was responsible for change. In order to make causal statements, the experimenter must adequately control important variables in the study (e.g., accurate measurement, consistent application of the treatments) such that rival hypotheses are deemed implausible. Critical to this pursuit is the ability to assign subjects to conditions randomly and to determine when and to whom the treatment is administered. Unfortunately, the researcher is not always in a position to meet these requirements. Consider, for example, the psychologist interested in evaluating the effects of an ongoing token system on inpatient "schizophrenic" clients on ward A versus a "similar" group receiving milieu therapy on ward B. Because of administrative and practical considerations, the experimenter may be unable to manipulate the treatments or achieve equivalent groups via random assignment. As a result, the experimental methods available to the researcher are determined to a great extent by the degree to which variables are under experimenter control.

The design options available to the clinical researcher can be classified as *quasi-experimental* or *randomized experimental* (Campbell & Stanley, 1963). Quasi-experimental designs provide a systematic method for evaluating clinical research when experimental manipulation and/or random assignment are not possible. Randomized experiments, on the other hand, are those in which threats to internal validity are eliminated through the control of therapeutic variables and the use of equivalent groups. In this section, we will discuss the common quasi- and randomized experimental designs frequently used in clinical research and present some examples of their applications from the research literature.

Quasi-experimental Designs

NONEQUIVALENT GROUP DESIGNS

These quasi-experimental designs are characterized by dividing subjects into nonequivalent groups that are exposed to different treatment conditions. The use of groups, often intact, whose membership is not determined randomly makes it difficult to ascertain whether observed effects are due to the experimental treatment or to the differential characteristics of the group involved. As a result, a number of threats to internal validity are left uncontrolled (e.g., selection-maturation, instrumentation, and statistical regression; Cook & Campbell [1979]).

Cook and Campbell (1979) detailed several nonequivalent group designs covering a broad spectrum of applied social science research. Two of these designs will be discussed here because of their application to clinical investigation. The familiar notation developed by Campbell and Stanley (1963) will be used where O refers to an observations or assessment occasion and X stands for the therapeutic intervention. Subscripts one through n denote the sequential order of recording observations. A broken line separating the experimental and control groups indicates that subjects were not randomly assigned to each condition.

The Untreated Control-Group Design with Pretest and Posttest. The structure of the design is designated as follows:

$$O_1 \; X \; O_2$$

$$O_1 \quad O_2$$

In this experimental paradigm, groups are formed via arbitrary rather than random methods. Following the pretest (O_1), one group receives the experimental treatment (X) while the other group receives either no contact or therapist attention without the active treatment component. Differences between the groups are measured at the posttest (O_2) to determine whether X had the hypothesized effects on client performance.

An example of this nonequivalent group design is found in a study by Taplin and Reid (1977) evaluating the effects of a family intervention on parent-delivered consequences. Twenty-five families participating in the study were referred for treatment by community agencies because of aggressive behavior of at least one male child. Fourteen of the twenty-five families received a social-learning-based intervention designated to train parents to manage deviant child behavior. The remaining 11 families were placed on a waiting list or received an attention-control condition. Prior to and following treatment, parent-child interactions of all families were assessed according to parent use of positive and aversive consequences for prosocial and deviant child responses. A repeated measures analysis of variance was performed on the experimental group and the combined waiting list and attention-control groups. The results suggested that the mothers and fathers receiving parent training engaged in significantly more appropriate interactions than parents exposed to either of the control conditions.

Because random assignment of families to experimental conditions was not specified in the Taplin and Reid (1977) study, interpretation of their findings is difficult. Using nonequivalent groups concedes the possibility that groups responded differentially to treatment because of disparate subject characteristics rather than because of the effects of family intervention (Kazdin, 1980). Also, when random assignment was not used, a group by time (i.e., maturation) problem is definitely of concern, even if groups are initially equivalent. For example, families who received treatment may differ from their control-group counterparts along the following dimensions: (1) motivation to receive treatment and effect change; (2) parental skills and/or responsiveness to training; (3) the severity or intensity of the problem; (4) individual and family histories; and (5) unidentified factors contributing to their selection for treatment. It is unlikely that groups differed systematically along all of these dimensions; however, it is because the possibility exists for any one or a combination of these factors to explain posttreatment differences that the results are rendered ambiguous.

The Untreated Control-Group Design with Posttest Measures at Multiple Time Intervals. This design is a variation of the untreated control-group design with pretest and posttest measures. Its basic form is diagrammed below:

$$O_1 \; O_2 \; X \; O_3$$

$$O_1 \; O_2 \quad O_3$$

The addition of the second posttest (O_2) strengthens the interpretability of the design for a number of reasons. First, any bias caused by a selection-maturation interaction would be expected to surface between O_1 and O_2. If nonequivalent groups are developing at different rates, the disparity should be evident at O_2 prior to treatment, although this would be a function of how close in time O_1 and O_2 are. Measures reflecting comparable growth rates across multiple pretests can be assumed to remain constant between O_2 and O_3. However, this assumption rests on the reliable measurement of performance and therefore may not be valid when measurement error is high. A second advantage of this design is its potential to detect statistical regression. If subjects in the treatment group were selected on the basis of their extreme pretest scores, a second testing would be expected to yield more moderate scores because of the tendency of extreme scores to regress toward the mean (Campbell & Stanley, 1963). Without adequate controls, this change is performance may be mistakenly interpreted as a treatment effect. The present design is sensitive to such spurious treatment effects at the O_1–O_2 comparison.

Although the inclusion of a second pretest improves the ability to conclude that changes in performance were caused by the intervention, this design is not widely used in applied psychology. On the other hand, a variant of this paradigm is commonly employed when experimental subjects are compared to a group of waiting-list controls (Kazdin, 1980). The design can be diagrammed as follows:

$$O_1 \quad X \, O_2$$

$$\text{-----------}$$

$$O_3 \quad O_4 \, X \, O_5$$

The structure is very similar to the untreated control group with pretest and posttest design. An important difference, however, is the delayed administration of treatment to the waiting-list controls following O_4. This arrangement provides two pretest occasions (O_3 and O_4) which permits assessment of trends in performance caused by maturation and statistical regression. Unfortunately, this within-group comparison is limited to clients on the waiting list and provides no information about maturation and regression trends in the experimental group. Consequently, this design is most fruitful when it is used with randomized groups. In this context, the second administration of the intervention permits assessment of the replicability of its effects.

It is important to note that these validity threats do not necessarily render the outcome uninterpretable. The task facing the researcher is to rule out as many factors that are extraneous to the treatment effect as possible in order to improve the ability to draw valid inferences. Two strategies exist for this purpose. The first of these involves a *post hoc* logical analysis in which potential threats are identified and dispelled, if possible, on the

basis of their unlikely occurrence given the data obtained (Cook & Campbell, 1979). The hypothetical data in Figure 12.1 represent the mean performance of two groups of acrophobic clients. Subjects in the treatment group were comprised of clients requiring immediate intervention because of the severity of their condition. In contrast, control subjects were selected from a waiting list and were considered less severe than those accepted for treatment immediately. The results indicate that whereas control subjects outperformed their experimental counterparts at the pretesting, only the treatment group improved at the posttest and to a magnitude exceeding the performance of the control group. Given this pattern of performance, it is most improbable that effects are due to a selection-maturation interaction (few documented cross-over maturation patterns exist; Cook et al., 1975) or to statistical regression of that magnitude (for logical analysis of other data patterns, see Cook & Campbell, 1979).

The second method of enhancing the interpretability of results using quasi-experimental methods pertains to the design of the experiment. Kazdin (1981) argued that valid inferences may be drawn from case studies if several conditions are met. Many of these strategies have similar applications to nonequivalent group designs. The first of these is concerned with the number and characteristics of the clients involved. Heterogeneous subjects tend to inflate error variance and decrease power to detect between-group differences. Yet, obtaining statistical significance using clients with diverse histories, maturation rates, and demographic characteristics builds a strong case for the efficacy of the experimental treatment. Moreover, confidence is further increased

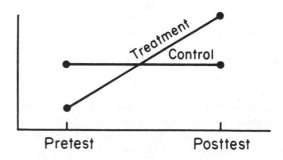

Fig. 12.1 First outcome of the no-treatment control groups design with pretest and posttest. (Adapted from T.D. Cook & D. T. Campbell [Eds.], *Quasi-experimentators: Design and analysis issues for field settings.* Chicago: Rand McNally, 1979, Reproduced by permission.)

when effects are replicated with few subjects in several separate experiments. Second, the inclusion of extensive pre- and postassessment of client perfmance can help substantiate claims for effective therapy. Documentation of subjects' protracted maladaptive behavior by means of archival records or previous evaluation minimizes the likelihood that client change is due to maturational or historical influences. Likewise, demonstrating the durability of improved performance through follow-up assessments is a source of further evidence. A third strategy is to design interventions with considerable therapeutic power to produce immediate and strong treatment effects. Obtaining immediate effects is desirable because the less time that elapses between the pretest and posttest, the more unlikely it is that alternative factors coincided with the treatment to produce client change (Cook & Campbell, 1979). Finally, when the magnitude of change is strong, there is evidence of treatment playing a causal role rather than random extraneous factors operating to produce dramatic results (Kazdin, 1981). Multiple pretests at different points in time permit evaluation of selection-maturation, instrumentation, and statistical regression artifacts. Each of the threats would be expected to surface at the second pretest occasion prior to intervention. Effects that are not evident at this time may be assumed to be inoperative during the period between the second pretest and posttest (see section on the untreated control group design with pretest measures more than one time interval).

Although the procedures outlined above can sometimes improve valid inference making for otherwise inadequate designs, they are no substitute for true experimental methods. Arguments offered can only minimize validity threats rather than totally eliminate them. As noted earlier, however, circumstances in the natural environment often militate against randomization and experimental manipulation. It is in these cases that nonequivalent group designs offer one alternative to randomized experimental designs. Fortunately, there are other design options that are more compatible with clinical practice and are vulnerable to fewer threats to internal validity: Time-series designs.

Time-Series Designs

In contrast to traditional group methods where assessment occasions are limited (e.g., pre- and posttest), time-series designs are characterized by repeated measurement of client performance both prior to and following intervention. Several design options exist for this purpose, each having applications for a range of clinical disorders. (Interested readers will find thorough discussions available in Hersen & Barlow, 1976; Kazdin, 1982; Kratochwill, 1978.)

Time-series design methodology has developed rapidly in recent years, resulting in the emergence of several designs and design variations. Embedded within the diversity and complexity of these procedures are a group of core elements that serve as building blocks from which all time-series designs are devised. Within this framework, three types of time-series designs can be identified (Hayes, 1981): Within, between, and combined series. Each of these can be used to evaluate therapy for a single subject or a group of subjects. In some cases, randomization procedures may be employed to strengthen the validity of the experiment.

WITHIN-SERIES DESIGNS

Procedures in this category are used to evaluate the effectiveness of treatment on the basis of changes in the level or trend of client performance either within or across phases of a study. Correspondence between changes in the therapeutic variable and client measures provide evidence for the value of intervention. Designs of this type include both simple and complex phase changes. Simple phase-change designs include, for example, A/B/A, B/A/B, and A/B/A/B series. Complex phase changes, on the other hand, include interaction designs (e.g., C/BC/C/BC), and the changing criterion design.

Simple phase-change designs assess client performance across experimental phases of the study. Abrupt shifts in the level or trend of the dependent measure that coincide with phase changes serve as the basis for inferring treatment effects. The simplest form of this strategy is the A/B design. Once the pattern of baseline performance is established (A phase), the therapy being evaluated is introduced and client measures are monitored over time (B phase). If client performance shows clear improvement (or a decline) with the onset of therapy, treatment may be responsible. We may begin to make causal statements regarding the relationship between treatment and the dependent response(s) when the withdrawal of therapy is followed by a return or approximation to initial baseline performance (the A/B/A design). Confidence is further strengthened if treatment effects are demonstrated in a second B phase (the A/B/A/B design). This procedure of replicating treatment effects across successive A/B series renders alternative explanations for client change (i.e., validity threats) less plausible. Similar strategies may also be used to compare two different treatments, B and C (e.g., B/C/B and B/C/B/C designs; Hersen & Barlow, 1976).

Complex Phase Changes — Interaction Designs use the same logic in controlling validity threats as do the simple phase-change designs. Rather than examining unitary variables, however, interaction designs evaluate the effects of adding or subtracting treatment components from another treatment component. Consider, for example, a clinical researcher is who is interested in determining the contribution of relaxation training (B) when combined with a contact desensitization procedure (C) in the treatment of a specific phobia. Two phase-change options are possible: C/B + C and B + C/B (B/B + C and B + C/C as well). The degree to which client measures improve in the B + C phase relative to the B or C phase represents the possible therapeutic advantage of including relaxation training (B). As in the case with simple phase-change designs, confidence in the observed effects is enhanced when data patterns are replicated across subsequent phases (e.g., C/B + C/C; B + C/C/B + C/C).

Interaction designs are especially useful for examining treatment interactions and formulating effective and parsimonious treatment packages (Hersen & Barlow, 1976). Often, when treatment variables are combined, their effects will be other than additive. Some variables will enhance the outcome of therapy while others may contribute relatively little or actually detract from the overall effectiveness. Through the joint efforts of reviewing prior research and creatively adding and subtracting variables, researchers strive to determine an optimal combination of treatment components to maximize client improvement.

Clinical researchers interested in employing either of the within-series withdrawal type designs (i.e., single phase-change or interaction designs) should consider the limitations of those procedures. First, the withdrawal of intervention may not result in anticipated changes in client measures. It is quite possible during the course of treatment that effects become generalized to variables other than those involved in therapy. Thus, when a particular aspect of treatment is discontinued, client performance may be maintained by newly developed variables (e.g., conditioned reinforcers

such as increased attention and praise by others for appropriate responses that accompanied tangible reinforcement). When this happens, the logic of the design and experimental control are jeopardized. A related issue of concern is that some measures may not rapidly deteriorate when treatment is withdrawn. When intervention involves the development of relatively immutable skills, gains will typically be maintained once training is completed, thus making the withdrawal-type designs inappropriate. Finally, there is the ethical concern of withholding effective treatment to clients for the purposes of establishing validity. In cases where clients are likely to suffer without a specific therapy, ethical considerations should take priority and designs permitting continuous treatment should be used.

Complex phase changes — changing-criterion design establishes validity by demonstrating that the level of the dependent measure is a function of arbitrarily set criteria for performance (Hall & Fox, 1977; Hartmann & Hall, 1976). Typically, treatment is introduced following a period of baseline measurement and maintained for a varying number of assessment sessions, and then reset at a different level. This procedure is repeated several times, producing a series of stepwise changes in performance criteria throughout intervention. In most cases, criteria are linked with treatment contingencies. For example, a caffeine-dependent client may receive social reinforcement from the therapist on those days in which cups of coffee consumed did not exceed the criterion for that particular day (see Bernard, Dennehy, & Keefauver, 1981). If the dependent measure consistently tracks the stepwise changes in criteria, it becomes improbable that common validity threats were responsible for the observed effects.

The unique nature of the changing-criterion design gives rise to a number of considerations specific to its use. As noted above, this design demonstrates causal relationships through parallel changes in the dependent measure and performance criteria. In order to demonstrate parallel changes, however, it is necessary that each criterion phase be long enough to allow the dependent measure to stabilize before instituting the next stepwise change. Furthermore, the size of the stepwise shift must be large enough to differentiate treatment effects from random variation in performance. To date, most applications of the changing-criterion design have employed criterion phases of consistent length and size that progress either upward or downward depending on the goals of treatment (e.g., Hartmann & Hall, 1976; Bernard et al., 1981). Another strategy suggested by Hayes (1981) involves randomly varying the length, size, and direction of the criterion shifts. This procedure makes more salient the effectiveness of the criteria and the contingencies associated with them on client performance.

BETWEEN-SERIES DESIGNS

Between-series designs are characterized by their comparison of two or more data series over time. Typically, single or multiple clients are administered two or more different treatments during a single experimental phase. Comparisons are made between series on a common dependent variable, taking into account differences in level and trend. The basic between-series elements are the alternating-treatments design (ATD) and the simultaneous-treatment design (STD) (Hayes, 1981). Both provide an alternative to traditional group designs for the comparison of different treatments.

Alternating- and simultaneous-treatment designs are similar in structure. In the ATD, clients are administered different treatments on an equal number of occasions and for equal periods of time (Barlow & Hayes, 1979). Administration of treatments is alternated, usually within a brief time period, according to a counterbalanced or randomly determined schedule. For example, a client might receive treatment B in the morning and treatment C in the afternoon on the first day, the reverse order on day two, and so on over the course of intervention. This arrangement provides control for effects due to time and setting differences and at the same time ensures that time exposed to each treatment is held constant. For the clinical researcher interested in comparing independent treatments expected to have pronounced effects on client performance, the ATD can be a useful strategy. In contrast to group designs, the ATD can compare different therapies for a single client or a small group of clients. Furthermore, the ATD avoids many of the disadvantages of within-series withdrawal designs such as the need for stable baselines and the withdrawal of treatment. Yet there are limitations to consider with this design, including possible multiple-treatment interference and logistical problems involved in administering multiple treatments (for suggestions on

minimizing these problems, see Barlow & Hayes, 1979; Kratochwill & Mace, in press).

The STD also exposes clients to multiple treatments but instead of alternating administrations, treatments are made available to the client simultaneously (Kazdin & Hartmann, 1978). Rather than being under experimenter control, the amount of exposure to the different treatment conditions is determined by the client. Consider, for example, two interventions designed to increase a student's completion of work assignments: teacher praise contingent on completing assignments, and programmed instruction without teacher praise. During work periods, the child has the option of participating in either treatment. Thus, the STD evaluates client preference among treatments rather than comparing the relative effectiveness of different treatments, in that exposure to conditions is not likely (Hayes, 1981; Kratochwill & Levin, 1980).

A study by Barrett, Matson, Shapiro and Ollendick (1982) illustrates the use of the ATD in the treatment of stereotypic finger sucking with a five-year-old retarded girl. Following a period of baseline assessment, two separate treatment conditions (punishment and a DRO procedure plus a no-treatment control condition) were put into effect during phase I. Each condition was administered during separate ten-minute periods that were rapidly alternated in a counterbalanced order for each session. Punishment consisted of screening the client's eyes with the experimenter's hand contingent on each occasion of the stereotyped response. Visual screening was discontinued contingent upon ten consecutive seconds of non-finger-sucking. The DRO procedure involved providing the client a piece of breakfast cereal following ten continuous seconds of nonoccurrence of the target behavior. During phase II of the study, the most effective intervention in phase I (punishment) was implemented in place of the less effective procedure (DRO), and in lieu of no treatment during phase III. The results presented in Figure 12.2 indicate that punishment resulted in dramatic reductions in the problematic behavior while DRO appeared to have only marginal effects. When DRO was discontinued during phase II, performance of the target behavior reached zero rates during periods when punishment was in effect. Finally, when punishment was applied during no treatment periods, the stereotyped behavior was essentially eliminated.[2]

---

[2]The authors appropriately caution against concluding that DRO is ineffective with stereotyped behavior in view of the large literature pointing to the contrary (see Homer & Peterson, 1980).

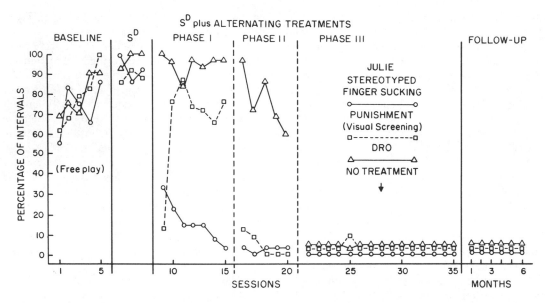

Fig. 12.2 The application of an alternating treatment design to compare a punishment (visual screening) procedure, a DRO procedure, and a no-treatment condition in the treatment of stereotypic finger-sucking with a mentally retarded girl (Julie). (Source: R. P. Banet; J. L. Matson; E. S. Shapiro; & T. H. Ollendick, A comparison of punishment and DRO procedures for treating stereotypic behavior of mentally retarded children. *Applied Research in Mental Retardation*, in press.)

COMBINED SERIES: MULTIPLE-BASELINE DESIGNS

In combined-series designs, comparisons are made both between and within series. Most familiar among the combined-series strategies is the multiple-baseline design (MBD). The basic element of the MBD is a within-series simple phase change (i.e., A/B). To control for common internal validity threats, the A/B element is replicated across two or more clients, settings, or therapists but with different baseline lengths for each series. Staggering the introduction of treatment at different points in time permits within-series baseline-treatment comparisons (i.e., A/B) and comparisons between treated and untreated series. If treatment effects are reproduced at each A/B shift, rival hypotheses explaining behavior change (e.g., history, maturation) become less plausible and confidence in the effectiveness of the treatment is increased.

Several features of MBDs make them especially compatible with clinical research, all of which center on its flexibility. First, the logic and integrity of the design are intact when as few as two data series are available (Hayes, 1981). Since validity is a matter of degree, confidence in the effect of

treatment can be strengthened by simply including additional series. Second, the MBD can accommodate nearly any of the within-series phase-change elements, simple or complex, discussed earlier. Hence, treatments can be compared or interactions examined within subjects and effects replicated across subjects, settings, or behaviors to enhance external validity. Third, some authors have noted that internal validity is jeopardized when generalization of treatment effects occurs across correlated treatment series (e.g., across behaviors or settings within a single subject). When this occurs, however, the investigator has the option to shift to a withdrawal-type design to establish internal validity and assess generalization effects separately (see Kendall, 1981; Rusch & Kazdin, 1981, for suggestions). Finally, the A/B element is compatible with the natural course of treatment. That is, clients typically undergo a period of preintervention assessment followed by the sustained administration of treatment and eventually procedures to ensure maintenance of gains. Thus, the MBD can circumvent the ethical problems involved in withdrawing treatment when clients are likely to suffer. Moreover, the clinician in practice may strengthen the case for a particular intervention strategy by replicating effects with similar subjects as they become available (Hayes, 1981).

Kelly, Urey, and Patterson (1980) used an MBD to evaluate the effects of a conversational skills training procedure on three males diagnosed as schizophrenic. The subjects, each considered deficient in basic conversational skills, were assessed on their frequency of using questions eliciting information, positive self-disclosing statements, and reinforcing or complimentary comments during their interaction with an unfamiliar female. After a period of three baseline sessions, the intervention was initiated targeting "questions eliciting information," while baseline assessment continued for the remaining two target behaviors. Treatment was conducted in a small group (therapist and three clients) and consisted of: (1) identifying the target skill; (2) viewing a modeling tape; (3) discussion/rehearsal of how the subjects might use the target skill in their own interactions; (4) therapist instructions and praise for using the target skill; and (5) rehearsal of specific statements the subjects intended to use in their male-female conversation. Three sessions later, "positive self-disclosing statements" were targeted for increase using the same training procedure; and after eight sessions treatment was applied to "reinforcing or complimentary comments." As shown in Figure 12.3, noticeable increases in the level of each target behavior coincide with the staggered introduction of treatment. Because effects were demonstrated across behavior *and* subjects, clinicians can be more confident that comparable results may be achieved using this procedure with similar clients.

Randomized Experimental Designs

As noted earlier, randomized experiments are distinguished by their use of random assignment and experimental manipulation of the independent variable as a means of inferring causation (Campbell & Stanley, 1963; Kerlinger, 1973). In practice, a pool of N subjects is randomly assigned to each of the treatment(s) and control conditions (see Kazdin, 1980; Kerlinger, 1973 for specific randomization procedures). Thus, each subject has an equal probability of being assigned to each group. As a result, groups are formed free of bias and on this basis are considered equivalent (Cook & Campbell, 1979). The second hallmark of these designs is experimenter control of the treatment variable(s). Holding as many variables as possible

constant across groups, the researcher determines where and to whom the treatments are administered. Any between- or within-group differences following intervention can then be attributed to the effects of treatment.

Randomized experiments fall into two categories: between-group designs and within-group designs. Each of these experimental models is discussed and illustrated with examples of clinical research. An additional notation element, R, is used to denote random assignment of subjects to groups.

Several forms of between-groups designs have been used in clinical psychology. Examples include the posttest-only design (Campbell & Stanley, 1963), the Soloman four-group design (Soloman, 1949), and factorial designs (Myers, 1979). Perhaps the most common between-group design is the pretest-posttest control-group design diagrammed below:

$$R\ O_1\ X\ O_2$$

$$R\ O_1\ \ \ O_2$$

In this paradigm, group membership is determined randomly and both groups receive pretest assessment (O_1). Subjects in the experimental condition are given the treatment while those in the control group receive no treatment or an attention-control condition. Both groups are then posttested (O_2) and the average (mean) performance for each group is analyzed statistically to determine whether significant differences exist.

Haymon and Cope (1980) used a between-group design to assess the effectiveness of assertion training on depression. Twenty-six women meeting Beck's (1976) criteria for depression were randomly assigned to two groups and pretested on two depression inventories and one assertiveness scale. Subjects in the experimental group received eight two-hour sessions of semistructured group assertion training that included modeling, cognitive restructuring, behavioral rehearsal, coaching, goal setting, and individual logs. Treatment for the control subjects were delayed until posttesting on the three measures was completed for both groups. The results indicated that the intervention increased assertiveness in the experimental subjects relative to those in the delayed treatment group. In addition, assertion-training

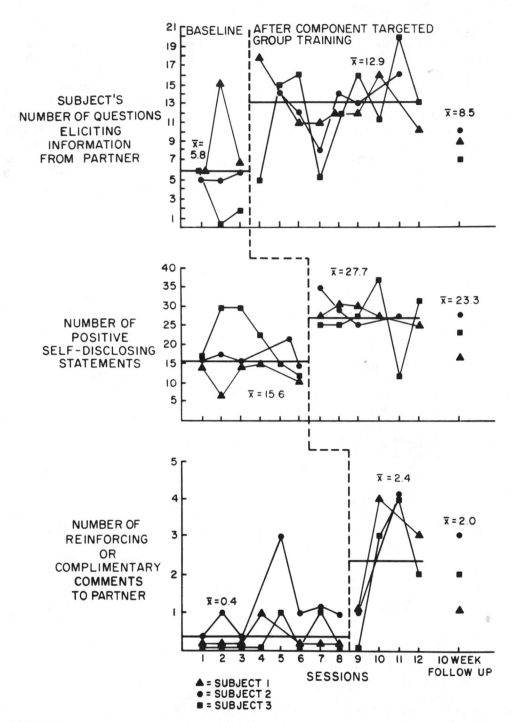

Fig. 12.3 Each subject's frequency of exhibiting component skills during eight-minute unstructured conversations. Data points to the left of the broken vertical line reflect conversational performance before small-group training had targeted the skill; points to the right of the vertical line are ratings of each subject's performance subsequent to group training in that skill. Solid horizontal line across each phase shows the mean for all three subjects' frequency of the skill throughout the phase. (Source: J. A. Kelly; J. R. Urey; & J. T. Patterson, Improving retrosocial conversational skills of male psychiatric patients through a small group training procedure. *Behavior Therapy*, 1980, **11**, 179–188. Copyright 1980 by the Association for Advancement of Behavior Therapy. Reproduced by permission.)

subjects significantly reduced their self-reported depression ratings on one of two inventories, a pattern that was not evident in the control group.

Between-group designs have a number of advantages. First, these designs can analyze a great deal of information relative to treatment efficacy and the variables that enhance it. Second, treatment effects may be demonstrated for several subjects under identical conditions, a feature that single-subject time-series designs achieve only through systematic replication (Hersen & Barlow, 1976). A third advantage of these designs is their ability to compare different treatments while avoiding the possibility of multiple-treatment interference. Finally, assessment requirements are considerably less than those invovled in time-series experiments that may be an important consideration in some applied settings.

A general limitation of between-group designs is their tendency to obscure individual performance. In view of the longstanding tradition in clinical psychology for analysis of the individual, the results gleaned from group studies may have little application to the individual client in therapy (Hersen & Barlow, 1976; Kazdin, 1980; Kratochwill, 1978). Significant differences based on group means and variability are seldom representative of each client within the group. Some clients may evidence remarkable improvement while others receiving the same treatment may be relatively unaffected or actually worsen. Yet the average response to treatment may yield significance and lead to the conclusion that intervention was generally effective. Furthermore, global analysis of this kind may not expose which variables may have produced the differential response to treatment across subjects, an option available through $N = 1$ time-series designs. Another consideration with group designs is their requirement for several subjects to receive experimental conditions at the same points in time. Many clinical problems, however, are of such low incidence that group analysis is either impractical or impossible.

WITHIN-GROUP DESIGNS

Within-group designs are characterized by administering each of the different experimental conditions to each subject over time. Rather than using a separate control group(s), subjects act as their own controls by comparing their performance at separate points in time under different treatment conditions (Kazdin, 1980). Another commonality of these designs is their "counterbalancing" of

treatments between groups to control for order or sequence effects. It is quite possible that treatment effects are influenced by the order in which treatments are presented. By counterbalancing their order of administration, treatment and sequence effects are no longer confounded.

A common within-group design used in clinical research is the *cross-over* design. In its basic form, two randomized groups receive two different treatments in a counterbalanced sequence as shown below:

$$R \; O_1 \; X_1 \; O_2 \; X_2 \; O_3$$

$$R \; O_1 \; X_2 \; O_2 \; X_1 \; O_3$$

Following pretesting (O_1), each group is exposed to a different treatment (X_1 or X_2) and therapeutic effects are assessed at O_2. Groups then receive the alternate treatment and subsequent impact assessment (O_3).

Within-group designs have a number of advantages relative to other experimental procedures. First, these designs focus attention on client performance over time, an emphasis consistent with the purpose of clinical research; this is to assess the magnitude and durability of therapeutic effects over the course of treatment (Nelson, 1981). When time is a critical variable, within-group strategies can accomodate this need by introducing a single treatment that is preceded and followed by repeated measurement of the dependent variable. Structurally, this design is similar to time-series strategies and can be diagrammed as follows (Cook & Campbell, 1979):

$$R \; O_1 \; O_2 \; X_1 \; O_3 \; O_4$$

$$R \; O_1 \; O_2 \; O_3 \; O_4$$

However, important differences do exist including fewer assessment occasions and the use of parametric statistical analyses (e.g., repeated measures ANOVA) for within-group procedures. A second asset of these designs is their efficiency compared to between-group methods. Because subjects can receive multiple treatments and are compared to themselves, fewer clients are required in order to perform adequate data analyses. This becomes an important consideration when clinically relevant disorders are being examined and few subjects are available (Kazdin, 1980).

Within-group designs are not without significant limitations, however. Inherent in all repeated-

measures paradigms is a treatment-by-time confound (Myers, 1979). In other words, the delivery
of treatment coincides with the passage of time,
making it ambiguous whether effects are due
wholly or only partially to therapy. Fortunately,
this problem can be avoided by including a no-
treatment control group that is assessed parallel to
the treatment group(s) (see diagram in the preceding paragraph). Another limitation of these
procedures is the potential for practice effects.
When both treatment and control subjects appear
to improve on the dependent measure, the research may suspect that repeated exposure to the
assessment device has contributed to the observed
change (Kerlinger, 1973). A partial solution to this
problem is the use of unobtrusive measures in
clinical research (e.g., observation from behind
one-way mirrors, behavioral byproducts, physical
traces, and archival records; Kazdin, 1979). A serious limitation of within-group designs in which
groups are administered two or more treatments is
multiple-treatment inference (Cook & Campbell,
1979). Another major limitation is that the assumption of independence of error terms may be
violated, at least if univariate analyses are conducted. In this context, client outcomes may be
influenced by exposure to more than one intervention and may be unrepresentative of performance when singular treatments are involved. The
only alternative to this dilemma is to evaluate
treatments individually using other experimental
methods discussed here.

Current Issues

Three-Mode Response Assessment

An important aspect of assessment in experimental clinical research relates to a framework developed by Lang (1968), and referred to as "triple
response mode" (e.g., Cone, 1978), "multiple response components" (e.g., Nietzel & Bernstein,
1981), or "three response system" (e.g., Kozak &
Miller, 1982). This assessment paradigm is considered an important framework for behavioral assessment (Nelson & Hayes, 1979) and represents a
major characteristic of behavior therapy (Kazdin
& Hersen, 1980).

ADVANCES

In psychotherapy outcome research, the three-
mode assessment framework has provided several
conceptual advances (Kazdin, 1981). To begin

with, the assessment of three response modes has
given recognition to the complexity of various behavior and personality disorders. In the past, experimental outcome research has tended to focus
on a relatively restricted range of measures (e.g.,
self-report or direct measures of overt behavior).
By focusing on self-report, behavioral, and physiological modes, a more comprehensive picture of
the client's problem can be obtained.

Another advance that has occurred with three-
mode response assessment is the recognition that
treatment effects may be specific to a particular
mode. For example, behavioral research on anxiety has suggested that measures of motoric, cognitive, and physiological domains may vary together
(synchrony) or independently (desynchrony), over
the course of therapy (see Agras & Jacob, 1981;
Morris, Kratochwill, 1983, for a review in the adult
and child literature, respectively). For example,
Barlow, Mavissakalian, and Schofield (1980) measured heart rate in three agoraphobic women before, half-way through, and at the end of a 12 session group therapy program consisting of exposure
and cognitive restructuring. The women walked
(or in one case were driven) along a standard 1.2
km course leading away from the treatment setting. Self-report of anxiety was also taken. The authors found that while all clients demonstrated behavioral improvement, patterns of synchrony and
desynchrony were found between heart rate and
self-reports of anxiety. Moreover, increases in
heart rate were noted in one client.

CONSIDERATIONS

While the three mode response system represents
an important advance in experimental therapy research, several issues remain to be resolved. First,
there is still a rather limited research base in this
area. Generally, most of the research has focused
on adult anxiety disorders, and therefore, more effort needs to be directed toward other clinical populations (Barlow & Wolfe, 1981). Also, relatively
little work has been carried out with children
(Morris & Kratochwill, 1983).

In addition to the paucity of studies in this area,
a rather limited number of measures have been used
within the three domains. For example, there are
many different physiological measures that can be
employed, (e.g., GSR, heart rate, respiration). It is
not at all clear which measures would be the most
sensitive to treatment efforts, or even if measures
within a particular mode would correlate highly
with each other.

Another major consideration with the three-mode response system is that it will likely add a great deal of complexity to psychotherapy research. Monitoring three domains presents difficulty for both the therapist and the client. Ultimately, the ease with which this form of asessment can be adopted in practice remains to be demonstrated. Even some members of the NIMH-SUNY, Albany Research Conference (Barlow & Wolfe, 1981) questioned the relative usefulness of physiological data with issues as time, expense, and the unreliability of physiological data raised as problematic.

A final issue that emerges with the three-mode response assessment is the appropriateness of this system for certain personality or behavior disorders. Although employing this paradigm in anxiety assessment might argue for its use with all internalizing problems (e.g., depression), the range of problems for which the assessment framework is appropriate remains to be determined.

Criteria for Evaluation of Outcomes

The experimental research strategies reviewed in the previous sections require certain design and measurement tactics to meet validity concerns. Yet, in recent years criteria have been recommended that take into account a broader range of conceptual and methodological features of clinical research (Kazdin, 1980; Kazdin & Wilson, 1978; Rachman & Wilson, 1980). These include experimental and therapeutic criteria, client-related criteria, efficiency and cost-related criteria, and criteria for generalization and follow-up.

EXPERIMENTAL AND THERAPEUTIC CRITERIA

In therapy research, experimental criteria must be met to establish that the treatment and outcome measures covary. This is usually accomplished through the use of inferential statistical tests, with the possible exception of time-series designs where visual analysis has most often been used. As noted in the previous section on validity issues, choice of an appropriate test represents one of several statistical conclusion validity issues that should be addressed in experimental research. Several considerations must be taken into account in the use of statistical tests to meet experimental criteria. First, the correct test must be selected for the design used and data collected. This is often not as simple as it appears. The variety of statistical tests used in experimental research require many as-

sumptions for their valid application. The researcher must consider the appropriateness of a test and consider alternatives if assumptions are not met. Beyond these usual criteria, researchers should consider the power and sample size needed to determine treatment effects (Cohen, 1970; Levin, 1975).

Brief mention should also be made of the use of visual analysis of data in time-series designs. Traditionally, such designs have not been accompanied by statistical tests. However, statistical tests can be used in many of the time-series designs described in this chapter and the reader is referred to several sources for a review of these issues (e.g., Kazdin, 1976; Kratochwill, 1978).

Therapeutic criteria are also recommended for use in experimental research in psychotherapy. Typically, effect sizes will be large and will surpass the usual experimental or statistical criteria. Some authors have even advocated that effect sizes should be large enough to render the usual statistical criteria redundant (e.g., Bergin & Strupp, 1972; Leven, Marascuilo, & Hubert, 1978).

Therapeutic or clinical criteria can be developed within the context of social validation (Kazdin, 1977; Wolf, 1978). In social validation, the client's behavior can be compared to peers who are not deviant or who do not have a problem. A second procedure involves obtaining subjective evaluations of the client's behavior from individuals in the natural environments (e.g., parents, teachers, ward staff, etc.). Changes in the client's behavior are regarded as clinically significant when the treatment brings the client's performance within the range of acceptable levels of either peer-group comparisons or ratings from those in the natural environment.

An example of the use of social validation procedures is reported by Jones, Kazdin, and Haney (1981) who designed a multifaceted behavioral program to teach emergency fire-escape procedures to five children. Social validation was used to identify situations for the training and responses focused upon and established the importance of outcomes from the study. The appropriate method of responding to fire emergency situations was established by (a) examining published materials describing ways of escaping from a burning house, (b) devising 42 hypothetical fire emergency situations in which children might find themselves and deriving responses from this information, and (c) using responses from (b) to provide sequences of responses that would lead to safety in each of nine different situations in which children would likely find themselves in an actual fire. In addition, social validation of outcome was assessed by obtaining a level of correct responding across all children for the first three sessions of baseline and the last three sessions of training. Levels of overt performance were evaluated. In each of four situations, thirteen local firefighters were asked to rate the child on a five-point scale. The results demonstrated successful performance and positive evaluations from the firefighters.

CLIENT-RELATED CRITERIA

In the usual experiment, differences among groups or comparisons of baseline and treatment conditions are made to determine the impact of therapy. However, several different criteria can be examined to expand knowledge regarding treatment efficacy (Kazdin & Wilson, 1978), including the proportion of patients who improve and the breadth of changes.

1. *Proportion of patients who improve.* A major concern with group psychotherapy research is that the average performance of the group may not reflect the individual differences within groups (Barlow, 1981; Hersen & Barlow, 1976; Kratochwill, 1978). As an option to reporting only mean improvement with a group, Kazdin and Wilson (1978) recommend reporting the proportion of treated clients who improve. By selecting the treatment that provides improvements in the largest number of clients, the therapist/researcher maximizes the probability that a given client will be favorably affected by treatment.

2. *Breadth of changes.* Although the usual criterion for efficacy of treatment is the change of behavior for which the client sought treatment, the breadth of treatment effects should also be used to evaluate efficacy. Side-effects of treatment could be either positive or negative and these should be taken into account. For example, certain types of therapy may teach clients skills that have benefit in solving other problems. Thus, two different treatments might have equal effects, but the one with the most desirable side-effects would be preferred.

EFFICIENCY AND COST-RELATED CRITERIA

Research efforts in clinical psychology can be greatly improved by taking into account several efficiency and cost-related criteria.

1. *Efficiency in duration of therapy.* Several different therapeutic techniques may achieve the same positive results but may vary in the time needed to implement them. Other considerations being equal, the treatment that is most rapidly administered would be preferred. For example, some behavioral treatments for certain types of childhood fears lasted only a few hours or days (Morris & Kratochwill, 1983). Other treatment procedures required several months for implementation. The briefer therapy would generally be preferred.

2. *Efficiency in the manner of administering treatment.* Treatments may vary considerably in the actual time needed for implementation. Some treatments (e.g., token economy, systematic desensitization) may require several weeks or months to administer with an individual client. Yet, if the treatment can be administered in "group" form, it might be regarded as more efficient. Also, a treatment might be efficient because it can be widely disseminated to many clients (e.g., modeling film to treat dental fears, bibliotherapy). For example, standardized treatment packages are frequently efficient because they can be implemented quickly with a large number of clients. Such packages often contain a self-help manual and/or do not involve direct therapist contact or time. Such strategies might be preferred over those that have equal effects but are not as efficient to administer.

3. *Cost of professional expertise.* The cost incurred in training professionals or paraprofessionals in the delivery of the therapy is an important consideration in clinical research. A therapy that is inexpensive to teach might be preferred over one that takes relatively more time and money. As an example, psychological services might be implemented directly with a child. As an alternative, a consultation approach in which the psychologist works through a teacher or parent to effect change in a child is typically more cost efficient. Frequently, the change effected by the parent is more rapid than that of the psychologist.

4. *Client costs.* Several dimensions of client costs should be considered in research. First, there is the cost of actual participation in therapy. For the client, this involves both time and money. The client might also experience certain emotional side-effects from the therapy. For example, although flooding and implosive therapy can be regarded as relatively safe procedures (Shipley & Boudewyns, 1980), these authors did find that .06 percent of 3,493 clients with no history of psychosis were reported to have experienced "acute psychotic reactions" during treatment. Also, "brief panic reactions" were reported to have occurred

in 0.14 percent of the sample. As this report illustrates, it is advisable to assess certain emotional side-effects in some therapies.

COST EFFECTIVENESS

An important consideration in therapy research is the actual cost of providing the services (Kazdin & Wilson, 1978; McMahon & Forehand, 1980; Yates, 1978). A cost-effectiveness analysis can be conceptualized in terms of resources consumed and outcomes produced; that is, an "input" to "output" ratio can be constructed (Yates, Haven, & Thoresen, 1977). Actually, several different variables can be included in a cost analysis, including such dimensions as personnel, facilities, and material. Usually, therapy research requires considerable cost. Efforts should be made by therapy researchers to report this type of information.

Criteria for Generalization and Follow-up

A major criterion for the evaluation of therapy and comparison of different therapies is generalization of the effects and their durability. Debates over the effectiveness of therapy increasingly take into account issues of generalization and durability. Increasing attention to conceptual and methodological features of these research concerns has provided a number of new dimensions to experimental research efforts (Drabman, Hammer, & Rosenbaum, 1979; Stokes & Baer, 1977; Mash & Terdal, 1980; Karoly & Steffen, 1980).

GENERALIZATION

As usually conceived, generalization of therapeutic effects can be measured across time, settings, behaviors, and clients. Generalization across time is usually conceptualized as a maintenance or durability issue and is discussed below under the heading of "follow-up."

One framework for conceptualizing measurement in this area is the Generalization Map presented by Drabman et al. (1979). This conceptual framework presented in Figure 12.4 allows generalized effects of therapeutic program to be categorized within 16 different areas.

Generalization has not always been measured in therapeutic research, but active attempts should be made to assess this dimension. Various single-case or time-series designs can be used to assess generalization (Kazdin & Kopel, 1975; Rusch & Kazdin, 1981; Kendall, 1981). In group designs, the researcher could assess generalization across subjects by including two control groups, one of which has contact with a treatment group and one that does not. Subjects in the contact control may improve with therapy suggesting that some generalization across subjects results from treatment. When generalization is assessed, measures should be taken on the three response modes discussed above. Generalization may occur within modes as well as across modes. Finally, it has become increasingly evident that a passive approach toward generalization may lead to lack of generalized changes. Increasingly, clinical researchers have used the developing technologies for program-

GENERALIZATION MAP

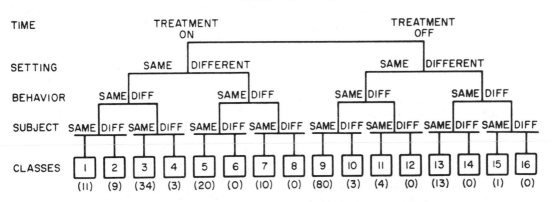

Fig. 12.4 The generalization map depicting the 16 different classes of generalized treatment effects. The numbers in parentheses indicate the number of studies found which illustrated a particular class of generalization. (Source: R. S. Drabman; D. Hammer; & M. S. Rosenbaum, Assessing generalization in behavior modification with children: The generalization map. *Behavior Assessment*, 1979, **1**, 203–219. Copyright 1979 by the Association for Advancement of Behavior Therapy. Reproduced by permission.)

ming generalization in therapeutic work (Stokes & Baer, 1977; Wildman & Wildman, 1975).

An important criterion for evaluation of therapy is the degree to which the effects are maintained or remain durable. Follow-up typically refers to the process of measuring therapy over time. Several different types of follow-up assessments can be distinguished (Mash & Terdal, 1980). First, an *evaluative follow-up* can be conducted to determine whether changes have occurred and whether they continue to occur independent of further intervention. Second, a *diagnostic follow-up* is aimed at making program changes if it is determined that a revised treatment would help the client. Third, a *therapeutic follow-up* is oriented toward further enhancing the positive effects of therapy. Finally, an *investigative follow-up* is designed to answer certain research questions.

Choice of a type or combination of follow-up measures must be determined within the context of the research area under investigation. Also, one type of follow-up might be important at one time while another would be implemented later. For example, the researcher may initially conduct an evaluative follow-up to compare the effects of two treatments, one of which is medication and the other a skill-training program. If it is found that the skill-training program is superior at the first follow-up measurement, a decision to treat the medication group with the skill program might be made. Futher follow-up might consist of both diagnostic and therapeutic approaches.

An important consideration in this conceptual approach to follow-up is that, analogous to the generalization of therapeutic change, the follow-up process need not be considered a passive process. This does raise questions, however, about when therapy stops and follow-up begins. Indeed, various strategies included in the treatment program (self-instruction, self-monitoring) may continue to be implemented by clients (Baer et al., 1981). Clients might even be instructed to reimplement the treatment of a problem reoccurrence.

Summary and Conclusions

We have provided an overview of experimental research methodology in clinical psychology. Some general characteristics and limitations of experimental methods were presented. Yet, despite the limitations of this type of research, we would argue that clinical psychology should adopt a scientific/empirical focus in theory, research, and practice.

Important in clinical experimental research is consideration of four domains of validity, namely: statistical conclusion validity, internal validity, construct validity, and external validity. Each of these validity domains must be addressed in the design of an experiment. Traditionally, there has been great emphasis on addressing various threats to internal validity. Yet it must be emphasized that certain "trade-offs" over which validity issues can be addressed in certain research and settings.

Several classes of experimental designs were reviewed, including quasi-experimental groups and time-series, and randomized between-groups and within-group strategies. Randomized experimental designs use random assignment to draw inferences for observed differences and are usually preferred over quasi-experimental procedures that do not employ randomization. The type of design used, however, depends on a number of issues and cannot be answered in the abstract. Some quasi-experimental designs have unique characteristics (e.g., time-series) and may be the methodology of choice under certain conditions.

A number of current issues were also reviewed as having relevance to experimental clinical research. First, major advances have occurred in assessment of three response domains (motor, cognitive, and physiological). However, use of three response assessment formats in clinical research raises a number of practical and methodolgical issues. Second, criteria for evaluation of experimental outcomes have been expanded in recent years. Increasingly, clinical researchers will need to take into account experimental and therapeutic criteria, client-related criteria, and efficiency and cost-related criteria. Finally, criteria for generalization and follow-up were reviewed. Advances in conceptual and methodological criteria for clinical experimental research have raised major issues in both the quality of past research and what directions future research in the field should take.

References

Adams, H. E., Doster, J. A., & Calhoun, K. S. A psychologically based system of response classification. In A. R. Ciminero, K. S. Calhoun, & H. E. Adams (Eds.), *Handbook of behavioral assessment*. New York: Wiley-Interscience, 1977.

Agras, W. S., & Jacob, R. G. Phobia: Nature and Measurement. In M. Mavissakalian & D. H. Barlow

(Eds.), *Phobia and pharmacological treatment.* New York: Guilford, 1981.

American Psychological Association. Specialty guidelines for the delivery of services by clinical psychologists. *American Psychologist,* 1981, **36**, 640–651.

Baer, D. M., Holman, J., Stokes, T. F., & Fowler, S. A. Uses of self-control techniques in programming generalization. In S. W. Bijou & R. Ruiz (Eds.), *Behavior modification: Contributions to Education.* Hillsdale, N.J.: Erlbaum 1981.

Barlow, D. H. On the relation of clinical research to clinical practice: Current issues, new directions. *Journal of Consulting and Clinical Psychology,* 1981, **49**, 147–155.

Barlow, D. H., & Hayes, S. C. Alternating treatment design: One strategy for comparing the effects of two treatments in a single subject. *Journal of Applied Behavior Analysis,* 1979, **12**, 199–210.

Barlow, D. H., Mavissakalian, M. R., & Schofield, L. D. Patterns of desynchrony in agoraphobia: A preliminary report. *Behaviour Research and Therapy,* 1980, **18**, 441–448.

Barlow, D. H., & Wolfe, B. E. Behavioral approaches to anxiety disorders: A report on the NIMH-SUNY, Albany, Research Conference. *Journal of Consulting and Clinical Psychology,* 1981, **49**, 448–454.

Barrett, R. P., Matson, J. L., Shapiro, E. S., & Ollendick, T. H. A comparison of punishment and BRO procedure for teaching stereotypic behavior of mentally retarded children. *Applied Research in Mental Retardation,* 1982.

Bergin, A. E., & Strupp, H. H. *Changing frontiers in the science of psychotherapy.* Chicago: Aldine-Atherton, 1972.

Berkowitz, L., & Donnerstein, E. External validity is more than skin deep: Some answers to criticisms of laboratory experiments. *American Psychologist,* 1982, **37**, 245–257.

Bernard, M. E., Dennehy, S., & Keefauver, L. W. Behavioral treatment of excessive coffee and tea drinking: A case study and partial replication. *Behaviour Therapy,* 1981, **12**, 543–548.

Boruch, R. F., & Riecken, H. W. *Social experimentation: A method for planning and evaluating social intervention.* New York: Academic Press, 1974.

Campbell, D. T., & Fiske, D. Convergent and discriminant validation by the multitrait-multimethod matrix. *Psychological Bulletin,* 1959, **56**, 81–105.

Campbell, D. T., & Stanley, J. C. *Experimental and quasi-experimental designs for research.* Chicago: Rand McNally, 1963.

Chassan, J. B. *Research design in clinical psychology and psychiatry.* (2nd ed.) New York: Irvington, 1979.

Cohen, J. *Statistical power analysis for the behavioral sciences.* New York: Academic Press, 1970.

Cone, J. D. The behavioral assessment grid (BAG): A conceptual framework and a taxonomy. *Behavior Therapy,* 1978, **9**, 882–888.

Cook, T. D., Appleton, H., Conner, R., Schaffer, A., Tamkin, G., & Weber, S. J. *"Sesame Street" revisited: A case study in evaluation research.* New York: Russell Sage Foundation, 1975.

Cook, T. D., & Campbell, D. T. (Eds.). *Quasi-experimentation: Design and analysis issues for field settings.* Chicago: Rand McNally, 1979.

Cook, T. D., Gruder, C. L., Hennigan, K. M., & Flay, B. R. The history of the sleeper effect: Some logical pitfalls in accepting the null hypothesis. *Psychological Bulletin,* 1979, **86**, 662–679.

Craighead, W. E., Kazdin, A. E., & Mahoney, M. J. (Eds.). *Behavior modification: Principles, issues, and applications.* Boston: Houghton-Mifflin, 1981.

Drabman, R. S., Hammer, D. C., & Rosenbaum, M. S. Assessing generalization in behavior modification with children: The generalization map. *Behavioral Assessment,* 1979, **1**, 203–219.

Hall, R. V., & Fox, R. G. Changing criterion designs: An alternative applied behavior analysis procedure. In C. C. Etzel, G. M. Le Blanc, & D. M. Baer (Eds.), *New developments in behavioral research: Theory, method, and application.* In honor of Sidney W. Bijou. Hilldale, N.J.: Erlbaum, 1977.

Hartmann, D. P., & Hall, R. V. A discussion of the changing criterion design. *Journal of Applied Behavior Analysis,* 1976, **9**, 527–532.

Harris, B. Whatever happened to little Albert? *American Psychologist,* 1979, **34**, 151–160.

Hayes, S. C. Single case experimental design and empirical clinical practice. *Journal of Consulting and Clinical Psychology,* 1981, **49**, 193–211.

Hayman, P. M., & Cope, C. S. Effects of assertion training on depression. *Journal of Clinical Psychology,* 1980, **36**, 534–543.

Hersen, M., & Barlow, D. H. *Single case experimental designs: Strategies for studying behavior change.* New York: Pergamon, 1976.

Homer, A., & Peterson, L. Differential reinforcement of other behavior: A preferred response elimination procedure. *Behavior Therapy,* 1980, **11**, 449–471.

Jones, R. T., Kazdin, A. E., & Haney, J. I. Social validation and training of emergency fire safety skills for potential injury prevention and life saving. *Journal of Applied Behavior Analysis,* 1981, **14**, 249–260.

Journal of Consulting and Clinical Psychology, 1978, **46**, whole issue.

Journal of Consulting and Clinical Psychology, 1981, **49**, (2).

Karoly, P., & Steffen, J. J. (Eds.). *Improving the long-term effects of psychotherapy: Models of durable outcome.* New York: Gardner Press, 1980.

Kazdin, A. E. Statistical analyses for single-case experimental designs. In M. Hersen & D. H. Barlow, *Single-case experimental designs: Strategies for studying behavior change.* New York: Pergamon, 1976.

Kazdin, A. E. Assessing the clinical or applied significance of behavior change through social validation. *Behavior Modification,* 1977, **1**, 427–452.

Kazdin, A. E. Unobtrusive measures in behavior assessment. *Journal of Applied Behavior Analysis,* 1979, **12**, 713–724.

Kazdin, A. E. *Research design in clinical psychology.* New York: Harper & Row, 1980.

Kazdin, A. E. Drawing valid inferences from case studies. *Journal of Consulting and Clinical Psychology,* 1981, **49**, 1,893–1,192. (a)

Kazdin, A. E. Methodology of psychotherapy outcome research: Recent developments and remaining limitations. Paper presented as master lecture at the American Psychological Association, Los Angeles,

August 1981. (b)

Kazdin, A. E. *Single-case research designs: Methods for clinical and applied settings.* New York: Oxford University Press, 1982.

Kazdin, A. E., & Hartmann, D. P. The simultaneous-treatment design. *Behavior Therapy,* 1978, 8, 682–693.

Kazdin, A. E., & Hersen, M. The current status of behavior therapy. *Behavior Modification,* 1980, 4, 283–302.

Kazdin, A. E., & Kopel, S. A. On resolving ambiguities in the multiple-baseline design: Problems and recommendations. *Behavior Therapy,* 1975, 6, 601–608.

Kazdin, A. E., & Wilson, G. T. *Evaluation of behavior therapy: Issues, evidence, and research strategies.* Cambridge, Mass.: Ballinger, 1978.

Kelly, J. A., Urey, J. R., & Patterson, J. T. Improving heterosocial conversational skills of male psychiatric patients through a small group training procedure. *Behavior Therapy,* 1980, 11, 179–188.

Kendall, P. C. Assessing generalization and the single-subject strategies. *Behavior Modification,* 1981, 5, 307–319.

Kendall, P. C., & Butcher, J. N. (Eds.). *Handbook of Research methods in clinical psychology.* New York: Wiley, 1982.

Kerlinger, F. N. *Foundations of behavioral research.* (2nd ed.) New York: Holt, Rinehart, & Winston, 1973.

Kiesler, D. J. Empirical clinical psychology: Myth or reality? *Journal of Consulting and Clinical Psychology,* 1981, 49, 212–215.

Kozak, M. J., & Miller, G. A. Hypothetical constructs vs. intervening variables: A reappraisal of the three-systems model of anxiety assessment. *Behavioral Assessment,* 1982, 4, 347–358.

Kratochwill, T. R. (Ed.). *Single subject research: Strategies for evaluating change.* New York: Academic Press, 1978.

Kratochwill, T. R., & Levin, J. R. What time-series designs may have to offer educational researchers. *Contemporary Educational Psychology,* 1979, 3, 273–329.

Kratochwill, T. R., & Levin, J. R. On the applicability of various data analysis procedures to the simultaneous and alternating treatment designs in behavior therapy research. *Behavioral Assessment,* 1980, 2, 353–360.

Kratochwill, T. R., & Mace, F. C. Time-series research in psychotherapy. In M. Hersen, L. Michelson, & A. S. Bellack (Eds.), *Issues in psychotherapy research.* New York: Plenum, in press.

Lang, P. J. Fear reduction and fear behavior: Problems in treating a construct. In J. M. Schlien (Ed.), *Research in psychotherapy,* Vol. 3. Washington, D.C.: American Psychological Association, 1968.

Levin, J. R. Determining the sample size for planned and post hoc analysis of variance comparisons. *Journal of Educational Measurement,* 1975, 12, 99–108.

Levin, J. R., Marasculo, L. A., & Hubert, L. J. N = Nonparimetric randomization tests. In T. R. Kratochwill (Ed.) *Single subject research: Strategies for evaluating change.* New York: Academic Press, 1978.

Maher, B. A. Preface to the special issue: Methodology in clinical research. *Journal of Consulting and Clinical Psychology,* 1978, 46, 595.

Mahoney, M. J. Experimental methods and outcome evaluation. *Journal of Consulting and Clinical Psychology,* 1978, 46, 660–672.

Mash, E. J., & Terdall, L. G. Follow-up assessments in behavior therapy. In P. Karoly & J. J. Steffen (Eds.), *Improving the long term effects of psychotherapy.* New York: Gardner Press, 1980.

McCleary, R., & Hay, R. A., Jr. *Applied time-series analysis for the social science.* Beverly Hills, Calif.: Sage, 1980.

McMahon, R. J., & Forehand, R. Self-help behavior therapies in parent training. In B. B. Lahey & A. E. Kazdin (Eds.), *Advances in clinical child psychology,* Vol. 3. New York: Plenum, 1980.

Morris, R. J., & Kratochwill, T. R. *Behavioral assessment and treatment of children's fears and phobias.* New York: Pergamon, in press.

Myers, J. L. *Fundamentals of experimental design.* Boston: Allyn & Bacon, 1979.

Nelson, R. O. Realistic dependent measures for clinical use. *Journal of Consulting and Clinical Psychology,* 1981, 49, 168–182.

Nietzel, M. T., & Bernstein, D. A. Assessment of anxiety and fear. In M. Hersen & A. S. Bellack (Eds.), *Behavioral assessment: A practical handbook.* (2nd ed.) New York: Pergamon, 1981.

Rachman, S. J., & Wilson, G. T. *The effects of psychological therapy.* (2nd ed.) Oxford, England: Pergamon, 1980.

Ross, A. O. Of rigor and relevance. *Professional Psychology,* 1981, 12, 318–217.

Rusch, F. R., & Kazdin, A. E. Toward a methodology of withdrawal designs for the assessment of response maintenance. *Journal of Applied Behavior Analysis,* 1981, 14, 131–140.

Ryan, T. A. Multiple comparisons in psychological research. *Psychological Bulletin,* 1959, 56, 26–47.

Sechrest, L., & Redner, R. Strength and integrity of treatments in evaluation studies. In *Evaluation Reports.* Washington, D.C.: National Criminal Justice Reference Service, 1979.

Shipley, R. H., & Boudewyns, P. A. Flooding and implosive therapy: Are they harmful? *Behavior Therapy,* 1980, 11, 503–508.

Soloman, R. L. An extension of control group design. *Psychological Bulletin,* 1949, 46, 137–150.

Stokes, T. F., & Baer, D. M. An implicit technology of generalization. *Journal of Applied Behavior Analysis,* 1977, 10, 349–367.

Taplin, P. S., & Reid, J. B. Changes in parent consequences as a function of a family intervention. *Journal of Consulting and Clinical Psychology,* 1977, 45, 973–981.

Underwood, R. G. *Psychological research.* New York: Appleton-Century-Crofts, 1957.

Watson, J. B., & Rayner, R. Conditioned emotional reactions. *Journal of Experimental Psychology,* 1920, 3, 1–14.

Watson, N., Caddy, G. R., Johnson, J. H., & Rimm, D. C. Standards in the education of professional psychologists: The resolutions of the Conference at Virginia Beach. *American Psychologist,* 1981, 36, 514–519.

Wildman, R. W., II, & Wildman, R. W. The generalization of behavior modification procedures: A review—with special emphasis on classroom applications. *Psychology in the Schools*, 1975, **12**, 432–444.

Wolf, M. M. Social validity. The case for subjective measurement or how applied behavior analysis is finding its heart. *Journal of Applied Behavior Analysis*, 1978, **11**, 203–214.

Yates, B. T. Improving the cost-effectiveness of obesity programs: Three basic strategies for reducing the cost per pound. *International Journal of Obesity*, 1978, **2**, 249–266.

Yates, B. T., Haven, W. G., & Thoresen, C. G. Cost-effectiveness analysis at Learning House: How much change for how much money? In J. S. Stumphauzer (Ed.), *Progress in behavioral therapy with delinquents*, Vol. 2. Springfield, Ill.: C. C. Thomas, 1977.

Yeaton, W. H., & Schrest, L. Critical dimensions in the choice and maintenance of successful treatments: Strength, integrity, and effectiveness. *Journal of Consulting and Clinical Psychology*, 1981, **49**, 156–167.

13 PERSONALITY RESEARCH*

Jean M. Edwards
Norman S. Endler

Personality research is influenced by theories and models, by available methodology, and by sociopolitical factors. We will examine each of these sources of influence, and then turn to an examination of important issues in personality research. We will conclude with an interaction model of anxiety and a program of research that supports that model.

Introduction: Theories of Personality

What is a theory or model? Marx and Hillix (1963) summarize the necessary components of a scientific theory as "abstract formal statements, rules for manipulating these abstract statements, and the definitions that relate the primitive terms of abstract theory to the empirical world" (p. 51). A theory presents a framework for integration of data, a perspective for defining issues, and direction for further exploration. Endler (in press) defines a theory as "a set of postulates from which we can derive testable hypotheses. The psychological theory aids us in explaining, understanding, predicting, controlling and measuring behavior."

Allport (1955) has suggested six criteria for evaluating psychological theories, namely: (1) agreement with facts; (2) generality; (3) parsimony; (4) immediate experimental availability; (5) logical consistency; and (6) explanatory value. Staub (1980) suggests four questions for comparing and evaluating theories: (1) "What are the major concepts of the theory?"; (2) "What are the major assumptions of the theory about human nature?"; (3) "What are the techniques or approaches to the assessment of personality that the theory employs"; and (4) "What are the major research strategies?" (Staub, 1980, p. 25).

"A model is basically an analogical representation of a phenomena. It is less than a theory and is not meant to have as much explanatory value as a theory" (Endler, in press). Models and theories may vary greatly in the scope of the phenomena they seek to encompass, and in the degree of formal elegance of their structure. The theoretical approach or model adopted by a researcher influences his or her definition of the basic concepts and issues in the area of personality. It also affects data collection and data analysis. After reviewing a number of types of definitions of personality, Hall

*The authors wish to thank M. Chown, D. Dubreuil, and L. Litman for their assistance with the literature review.

and Lindzey (1978) concluded that, "[T]he way in which given individuals will define personality will depend completely upon their particular theoretical preference. . . . *personality is defined by the particular empirical concepts that are a part of the theory of personality employed by the observer*" (p. 9). It is important, then, to examine the major theoretical approaches that have influenced research in the area of personality.

Endler and Magnusson (1976b, 1976c) suggest that much of the research and theorizing in the area of personality can be organized in relationship to four major models of personality: the trait model; the psychodynamic model; the situationist model; and the interactionist model. Since Endler and Magnusson have discussed these models extensively, we will only briefly present the major points of each. The various proponents of each model present somewhat different positions and the models have changed over time. Nonetheless,

by comparing and contrasting these models on selected issues, one can illustrate the impact that theory has on one's approach to the study of personality. In addition, an overview of the four models can provide a background for understanding major controversies that recur in this area.

Endler and Magnusson (1976b, 1976c) compared the trait, psychodynamic, situationist, and interactionist models of personality with regard to their positions on the following: (1) the actual determinants of behavior; (2) developmental aspects; (3) research strategies, including methods of data collection, type of data, and treatment of data; (4) populations focused on; (5) the consistency-specificity issue; (6) units of analysis; and (7) types of laws sought (see Table 13.1). They note that, "Perhaps the most important differences between the models are their consequences for research stategies, for methods and models of data collection and for data treatment" (Endler & Magnusson,

TABLE 13.1. FOUR BASIC PERSONALITY MODELS COMPARED ON IMPORTANT RESEARCH ISSUES.

| ISSUE | MODEL | | | |
	Trait	Psychodynamic	Situationism	Interactionism
Basic types of laws	R-R	R-R and S-R	Primarily S-R, but also R-S +	S-R-S-R-S-R . . .
Determinants of behavior	Inner directed	Inner directed	Outer directed	Inner/outer directed
Units of analysis	Traits	Dynamics (underlying motives and instincts)	Situations	Person-situation interactions and other interactions
Consistency versus specificity issue	Consistency of behavior across situations	Consistency of behavior across situations	Inconsistency of behavior across situations (specificity)	Person-situation interactions; behavior varies across situations and subjects (coherence)
Research strategy* Method of data collection	Questionnaires, ratings, tests	Interviews, case histories	Experiments, operant conditioning procedures	Observations, tests, questionnaires, and experiments
Types of data	Questionnaire scores, test scores, rating scores	Verbal descriptions	Experimental data, frequency counts, behavioral checklists	Test scores, questionnaire scores, experimental data
Treatment of data	Correlation, factor analysis	Interpretation of verbal descriptions	Analysis of variance, cumulative records	Analysis of variance, factor analysis, correlations, Markov chains
Populations of prime interest	Adults (normal and abnormal)	Adults and children (abnormal)	Adults, children, and animals (primarily normal, but also abnormal)	Adults and children (normal)

Note: R = Response; S = stimulus.
*Measurement and treatment of data.
Source: adapted from Endler and Magnusson, 1976c, p. 959.

1976b, p. 4). Feshbach and Weiner (1982) similarly contrast and examine the implications of psychoanalytic, social-learning, and cognitive models of personality with regard to their focus on concepts and measurement techniques.

The Trait Model

The trait model of personality has been extremely influential in determining research strategy and, indeed, the definition of personality:

> Throughout the history of the study of personality, considerable effort has been devoted to building taxonomies of traits, developing methods for measuring traits, and finding the ways in which groups of traits cluster together. Indeed, the very concept of personality assumes that there are characteristics or traits that remain stable over time [Feshbach & Weiner, 1982, p. 316].

The trait model assumes that there are various continuous dimensions (traits) along which individuals differ, that traits are the primary determinants of behavior, and that the rank-order of individuals with respect to behavior that is indicative of a certain trait is consistent across situations. The trait model has sought R-R laws, has encouraged the development of formal test theory, and has frequently relied on correlational and factor-analytic techniques of data treatment. The trait approach has encouraged the development of personality tests aimed at assessing specific traits within the individual and on the development of the personality inventory which proposes to assess a number of traits and their patterns or profiles in the individual. While agreeing that traits are the underlying predispositions that determine behavior, trait theorists disagree as to the number, structures, and types of traits. Modern trait theorists continue to emphasize enduring predispositions but also recognize that situational factors are important in accounting for behavior. Influential trait theorists include Allport (1937), Cattell (1957), and Guilford (1959).

Psychodynamic Models

The psychodynamic models also stress internal determinants of behavior, but differ from the trait model in some important respects. The trait model assumes a one-to-one positive, monotonic relationship between underlying hypothetical constructs and responses; the psychodynamic model does not. Psychodynamic models postulate an essential personality core that instigates behavior in various situations. Psychoanalysis emphasizes the structure of the personality (id, ego, and superego), the dynamics of personality, and personality development (Freud, 1959).

The psychodynamic models' discussions of the role of defenses and the unconscious have led to the development of assessment techniques designed to explore the underlying personality dynamics. The projective tests—the Rorschach and the Thematic Apperception test being the best known—have resulted.

The Situationist Model

Situationists emphasize external factors, especially stimulus situations, as the primary determinants of behavior. Social-learning theorists, the leading proponents of a situational approach, do not provide a homogeneous viewpoint. As classical behavior theorists, Dollard and Miller (1950) focused on learning and situational factors but also considered organismic variables such as drives, motives, and conflicts. Modern social-learning theorists (Bandura, 1971; Mischel, 1973; Rotter, 1954), primarily focus on behavior but also incorporate person factors such as cognitive strategies (Mischel, 1973), expectancies (Rotter, 1966, 1975), and personal efficacy (Bandura, 1977). There is also a growing interest among a number of social-learning theorists in the interaction between persons and situations. The situationist model has adopted the research methods of general psychology for its use.

The Interactionist Model of Personality

The interactionist model of personality states that person variables and situation variables interact in an ongoing process to determine behavior (Endler & Magnusson, 1976c; Magnusson & Endler, 1977; Endler, 1982, 1983). Personality is defined broadly by Endler (1983) to include many facets:

> *Personality* is a person's coherent manner of interacting with himself or herself and with his or her environment. It is concerned with how the person affects and is affected by both situational factors and behavioral variables. In processing information, cognitive, motivational, and content variables play an important

role. A comprehensive definition of personality should account for abilities, motives, emotions (feelings), cognitions, traits, content and behavior. It should also account for the strategies (processes) and rules that persons use in processing information and in behaving.

The interactionist model takes the position that it is necessary to consider both persons and situations, and *how* they interact in influencing behavioral outcomes. This interaction is viewed as a continuous, ongoing process. The interactionist view is not a modern one but can in fact be found in the writings of Aristotle (Shute, 1973). In the 1920s and 1930s a number of theorists advocated an interactionist approach (see Kantor, 1924, 1926; Koffka, 1935; Lewin, 1935; Murray, 1938). In the late 1950s and early 1960s, empirical studies of interactionism began (see Endler & Hunt, 1966; Endler, Hunt, & Rosenstein, 1962; Raush, Dittmann, & Taylor, 1959a, 1959b). More recently, theoretical interest in interactionism reemerged (see Bowers, 1973; Endler, 1976; Endler & Hunt, 1969; Endler & Magnusson, 1976b; Hunt, 1965; Magnusson & Endler, 1977; Mischel, 1973; Raush, 1965). The history of theoretical and empirical approaches to interactionism is outlined in detail in Ekehammar (1974) and in Endler (1982).

The term "interactionism" has been used in various ways in the literature (see Ekehammar, 1974; Endler, 1975a; Endler & Edwards, 1978; Magnusson & Endler, 1977; Olweus, 1977; Overton & Reese, 1973). The most pervasive distinction is between mechanistic interaction and organismic (dynamic) interaction (Overton & Reese, 1973). *Mechanistic* interaction refers to the interaction between independent variables, is concerned with unidirectional causality, and employs the analysis of variance as its primary technique of data analysis. Person (P) by situation (S) interactions, person (P) by modes of response (M-R) interactions, S by M-R interactions and P by S by M-R interactions have been studied, although most of the research has focused on P by S interactions. Research within the mechanistic model is concerned with the *structure* of interactions, not with the *process*. It calls for research strategies and measurement techniques that include consideration of both person and situation variables. It is not, however, adequate for studying the dynamic interaction process. *Dynamic* interaction refers to reciprocal causation and process analysis. "*Reciprocal causation* means that not only do events af-

fect the behavior of organisms, but the organism is also an active agent influencing environmental events" (Endler & Magnusson, 1976c, p. 969). The dynamic model of behavior implies that the traditional distinction between independent and dependent variable may not be appropriate (Raush, 1977) and that change over time must be taken into account in understanding the interaction process. Analysis-of-variance designs are not appropriate techniques to study dynamic interaction, and strategies of data analysis that can meet the requirements of process-oriented research are needed (see Kahle, 1979; Peterson, 1977; Raush, 1977).

Endler and Magnusson (1976c) set out the main assumptions of the modern interactionist position: (1) Actual behavior is a function of a continuous process or multidirectional interaction (feedback) between the individual and the situation that he or she encounters. (2) The individual is an intentional active agent in this process. (3) On the person side of the interaction, cognitive factors are the essential determinants of behavior, although emotional factors do play a role. (4) On the situation side, the psychological meaning of the situation for the individual is an important determining factor. Further discussions of the assumption are available in Endler and Magnusson (1976c) and Endler (1983).

One's theoretical approach has a pervasive impact on the type of research one conducts. Trait and psychodynamic theorists emphasize person variables and have devised research techniques to measure and demonstrate the influence of these internal determinants. Situationists have utilized experimental techniques that explore the impact of situational variables on behavior. The interactionist approach insists that persons, situations and their interactions must be considered. Most of the current research has utilized the analysis-of-variance design to investigate mechanistic interactions, but strategies that can investigate dynamic interaction are attracting increasing interest.

The Influence of Sociopolitical Factors on Personality Research

Sociopolitical factors influence the development of any field of research just as do theories and methodology. The influence, however, may be more subtle and more pervasive. Pervin (1978a) has pointed out that "the general public and many scientists have the view of science as a purely objective pursuit and the view of scientists as purely rational individuals. Yet considerable evidence suggests that scientists are very much influenced by their personal histories and by the societal views of the time" (p. 269). As Endler (1982) notes, research in personality may be particularly vulnerable to extra scientific influence since the subject matter is more ambiguous and personally relevant. Stolorow and Atwood (1979) suggested that the life experiences of the scientist influence the theory of personality he or she develops. Pervin (1978a) reviews events in the lives of several theorists that may have been important in their later theory development, although he cautions that retrospective interpretation of these events may be subject to bias. Endler (1982) recounts occurrences in his own life that he feels may have contributed to his development of his model of interactional psychology.

In addition to personal events, specific cultural or societal events and needs influence the development of an area. The development of the intelligence test is an obvious example. In 1905, Binet presented an early intelligence measurement in response to the needs of the Paris school system for a technique for screening children. The advent of World War I and the pressing need in the United States for rapidly classifying the one and one-half million recruits, led directly to the development of group-administered intelligence tests. The Army Alpha and Army Beta tests resulted, and caused a tremendous increase in testing in society in general when they were released for public use after the war (Anastasi, 1976). World War II also spurred research on individual assessment. Henry Murray and his colleagues working for the Office of Strategic Service (OSS) were assigned the task of assessing and selecting men for intelligence work, as undercover agents, spies, and resistance leaders. Their task as presented in the *Assessment of Men* (OSS Assessment Staff, 1948) was to determine which men would do well in a number of different military intelligence situations.

The larger cultural ideologies also play a role in determining which theories will be developed and accepted, which research question pursued, and which strategies of research employed. Pervin (1978a) discusses three psychological issues with regard to the sociopolitical context: (1) Social Darwinism and the controversies concerning gender and I.Q. differences; (2) American ideology and the development of behaviorism; and (3) the relationship between social history and the care and treatment of the mentally ill.

Endler (1979) pointed out that the trait-situation controversy is closely tied to sociocultural events. Ichheiser (1943) has similarly noted the role of sociopolitical factors in personality research. He states that the overestimation of the importance of person factors and the underestimation of the importance of situational factors are rooted in the social system and ideology of 19th-century liberalism, which held that "our fate in social space depended exclusively, or at least predominantly, on our individual qualities—that we, as individuals, and not prevailing social conditions shape our lives" (Ichheisser, 1943, p. 152). Since the 1930s, however, the sociopolitical factors (e.g., World War II, the Cold War, the Depression and recurrent recessions, unemployment, Viet Nam) seem to have shifted emphasis toward social conditions in explaining behavior.

The findings of psychology also have implication for society. Pervin (1978a) has noted, for example, that the results of studies of intelligence were used to influence United States immigration policies in the early part of this century. He concludes that, "Unwittingly, the framing of questions, the design of research procedures, and the interpretation of empirical findings may all be biased by and used in support of prevailing social norms" (Pervin, 1978a, p. 286).

The Influence of Methodology on Personality Research

Research in personality involves three categories of variables: organismic variables, stimulus variables, and response variables (see Edwards & Cronbach, 1953). Response variables refer to behaviors; stimulus variables to situations. Organismic variables imply that some property or attribute of the individual may be inferred from observations of previous responses or knowledge of previous experiences.

Magnusson and Endler (1977) point out that a distinction needs to be made between mediating variables (intervening variables, hypothetical constructs) and behavioral or response variables. They describe three kinds of mediating variables, namely, structural, content, and motivational variables. Abilities, competencies, cognitive styles, and intelligence are examples of *structural* variables. (For specific examples, see Bandura's [1977] concept of self-efficacy and Beck et al.'s [1979] concept of schema.) *Content* variables are situationally determined or stored information (e.g., the content of aggression-arousing situations). *Mo-tivational* variables are actively involved in the arousal, direction, and maintenance of behavior (e.g., attitudes, drives, motives, and needs). Medi-ating variables must be inferred from reaction var-iables. Reaction variables are the organism's re-sponses that are measured or observed. Magnus-son and Endler (1977) classify reaction variables into four categories: overt behavior, physiological reactions, covert reactions (feelings, thought, etc.), and artificial behavior (e.g., behavior on tests, role playing, simulation, etc.). Reaction variables can be measured or assessed by at least four methods: e.g., ratings, self-reports, standardized tests, and objective measures. (For further discussions re-garding distinctions among different kinds of per-sonality data, see Block, 1977; Cattell, 1957, 1973; Magnusson & Endler, 1977.) The distinction be-tween mediating variables and reaction variables is essential, as is the differentiation between reac-tion variables and measurement methods. There is not necessarily a one-to-one relationship between them. For example, anxiety is a mediating vari-able. Reaction variables that assess anxiety may differ for different individuals, in different situa-tions, and at different times. Thus, being silent and withdrawn may indicate anxiety for an indi-vidual in a particular situation, whereas being talk-ative and gregarious may indicate anxiety for an-other individual or in a different situational con-text. In addition, objective measures may not agree with self-ratings of an individual regarding his or her degree of talkativeness.

The various measurement methods are used within laboratory or field settings and with differ-ent research strategies such as experimental and quasi-experimental designs and correlational stud-ies. Each of these research choices is influenced by and to some degree influences the topic of study.

The availability of techniques and measure-ment methods is also an important factor in defin-ing the field of research. Feshbach and Weiner (1982) noted that the development of intelligence testing had a profound effect on personality-as-sessment strategies. The Minnesota Multiphasic Personality Inventory (MMPI), probably the most widely used personality inventory, has generated an enormous amount of research and has been the model for the development of other personality tests (Anastasi, 1976). Similarly, the appearance of the Taylor (1953) Manifest Anxiety Scale and the Rotter (1966) Locus of Control Scale stimulated research in their respective areas (Levitt, 1980; Lefcourt, 1976; Phares, 1976; Rotter, 1975).

Current Issues in Personality Research

A survey of three psychological journals, *Journal of Personality, Journal of Research in Personality,* and *Journal of Personality and Social Psychology,* for 1979, 1980, and 1981 suggests several general conclusions regarding the current direction of re-search. The laboratory setting continues to domi-nate the research methodology, and college stu-dents are the most frequent subjects tested. Very few studies are cross-cultural or draw subjects from cultures other than North America. The analysis of variance is the most common tech-nique of data analysis although a number of stud-ies also employ various correlational analyses.

In the journals we reviewed, no single content area predominated in the studies that focused on personality. Included in the journals reviewed was a substantial proportion of articles focused on is-sues of social interaction and the effects of envi-ronmental or stimulus manipulation. In general, a strong cognitive orientation in the current research is evident. A small percentage of the articles ex-amined person-by-situation interactions from a theoretical perspective. Additional studies includ-ed both person and situation variables within an analysis-of-variance design but without a clear the-oretical rationale. Similarly, a small proportion of the studies focused on the issue of consistency, and very few focused on an analysis of the situa-tion per se. Many of the criticisms that could be leveled with regard the current studies are similar to those raised earlier by Cronbach (1975), Block (1977), Carlson (1971), and Wiesenthal et al. (1978).

Specificity-Consistency— Coherence of Behavior

One of the most controversial issues in the last two decades in the field of personality has been wheth-er behavior is consistent across situations or situa-tion-specific. There appears to be evidence for both sides of the issue. First, there are at least three different meanings of consistency. *Absolute* con-sistency assumes that a person manifests a behav-ioral trait (e.g., aggressiveness) to the same degree in all situations. No theorists support this position. It is recognized that people behave differently in various situations. *Relative* consistency assumes that the rank-order of individuals for a specific be-havior (e.g., aggressiveness) is stable across various situations for a specific group of individuals. It is this interpretation of consistency, derived from the trait model, that has been the focus of much of the controversy. *Coherence* assumes that behavior is predictable and inherent (i.e., lawful) but not necessarily consistent in either the absolute or relative sense. Emphasis is on the person's *pattern* of stable and changing behavior across a wide variety of situations, a pattern that is characteristic for the individual (see Endler, 1977; Magnusson, 1976; Magnusson & Endler, 1977).

The issue of cross-situational specificity versus consistency is closely related to the issue of persons versus situations as the major determinants of behavior. Personologists (Cattell, 1946, 1957; Cattell & Scheier, 1961) and clinicians (Rappaport, Gill, & Schafer, 1945) propose that traits (person factors) are the major determinants of behavior and are manifested in cross-situational (relative) consistency. In contrast, sociologists and social psychologists (Cooley, 1902; Cottrell, 1942a, 1942b; Dewey & Humber, 1951; Lindesmith & Strauss, 1949; Mead, 1934) propose that situations and the perception of situations are the major determinants of behavior, and therefore that behavior is situationally specific.

At least three research strategies have been used to investigate implications of the consistency versus specificity issue: (1) the multidimensional variance components research strategy; (2) the correlational research strategy; and (3) the person-by-situation factorial experimental design (see Endler, 1981a; Endler & Magnusson, 1976c).

THE MULTIDIMENSIONAL VARIANCE COMPONENTS STRATEGY

Raush, Dittmann, and Taylor (1959a, 1959b) and Raush, Farbman, and Llewellyn (1960) studied the behavior of delinquent boys in various settings. Using a multivariate information transmission analysis of ratings of observed behavior, they found that the person-by-situation interaction accounted for more variance than either persons or situations. Endler and Hunt (1966, 1969) employed the S-R Inventory of Anxiousness, a self-report measure that yields a person-by-response-by-situation data matrix (see Endler, Hunt, & Rosenstein, 1962), with subjects varying in age, social class, education, and mental status. Using a variance components technique, they found that persons accounted for about 4 percent of the variance for males and about 8 percent for females, and person-by-situation interactions accounted for about 10 percent. The two-way interactions (persons by situations, persons by response, and situation by response) accounted for more anxiety (about 30

percent) than did the sum of the contributions for situations and persons.

Ekehammar, Magnusson, and Ricklander (1974), Endler (1975b), and Endler and Okada (1975) also report results that support the role of interactions in accounting for variance in anxiety. Similar support for the importance of interactions has been found for honesty (Nelson, Grinder, & Mutterer, 1969), social perception (Argyle & Little, 1972), leisure-time activities (Bishop & Witt, 1970), and conformity (Endler, 1966). Moos (1968, 1969) analyzed observations of subjects' overt behavior and self-ratings in various psychiatric ward settings and found the person-by-situation interaction variance to be important in relationship to the variance due to persons. Reviews of additional studies may be found in Bowers (1973), Endler and Magnusson (1976c), Ekehammar (1974), and Mischel (1973).

CORRELATION RESEARCH STRATEGY

The correlational research strategy provides a direct test of the relative consistency hypothesis. Consistency may be examined either in terms of a temporal (longitudinal) or spatial (cross-sectional) strategy. Magnusson and Endler (1977), however, have suggested that it is more useful to distinguish consistency on the basis of responses to similar and dissimilar situations. Generally, longitudinal studies have examined responses to similar situations over extended periods of time, and cross-sectional studies have focused on responses to dissimilar situations.

The classic study of honesty by Hartshorne and May (1928) found cross-situational correlations of honesty of about +.30. Magnusson, Gerzén, and Nyman (1968), Magnusson and Heffler (1969), and Magnusson, Heffler, and Nyman (1969) systematically varied the situational variables of tasks and group composition and examined consistency in ratings and objective measures of behavior. For similar situations, the correlations were high (about .70) but for dissimilar situations, correlations were low (near zero). Rushton (1976) reviewed studies of children's altruism and found an average cross-situational correlation of about .30. Newcomb (1931) found that correlations for introversion-extroversion behavior patterns across situations averaged about .30. With regard to longitudinal studies, however, Block (1977), Epstein (1979), Olweus (1979), and Backteman and Magnusson (1981) report some support for consistency or temporal stability. The degree of cross-situational consistency found may also depend upon the type of variable investigated, i.e., with respect to intellectual and cognitive variables, there is some evidence for both longitudinal and cross-situational consistency (see Mischel, 1968, 1969; Rushton & Endler, 1977).

PERSONALITY BY TREATMENT
EXPERIMENTAL DESIGNS

Endler (1973) suggests that personality theories and research should address the question: "*How do persons and situations interact* in determining behavior?" The variance component studies demonstrate interactions but do not explain them (Sarason, Smith, & Diener, 1975). The traditional correlational studies either reveal consistency or fail to do so. To increase our understanding of *how* persons and situations interact in eliciting behavior, studies should be designed to incorporate situation and person variables in their designs simultaneously. Edwards and Cronbach (1953), in fact, advocated the use of factorial experimental designs almost three decades ago. Let us briefly summarize some of the person-by-situation (treatment) experimental design studies with regard to various personality variables. Endler's programmatic research on the person-by-situation interaction model of anxiety will be reviewed in a later section.

Cronbach and Snow (1977), after reviewing the school achievement literature, pointed out that there are numerous aptitude-by-treatment (instruction) interactions. Domino (1971) investigated the relationship between person factors and achievement in college. He found an interaction between situation (instructor's teaching style) and person (achievement via independence or achievement via conformance) with respect to course results. Berkowitz (1977) found an interaction of persons and situations with respect to aggression, and Fiedler (1971, 1977) demonstrated that situational variables interact with leadership style (a person variable) in influencing group effectiveness in both field and laboratory studies. Endler and Edwards (1978) reviewed the literature for conformity, internal-external locus of control, and anxiety, and found evidence supporting person-situation interactions.

Evaluation of the Consistency Issue

The research reviewed suggests that person-by-situation interactions are important in accounting for behavioral variance. There has been criticism of the various research areas reviewed, however. Epstein (1977) pointed out that the proportion of variance accounted for by persons, situations, or interactions in any particular study was influenced by the selection of persons, situations, and responses included in that study. With regard to correlational studies, while there is a general finding of *low* cross-situational consistency with respect to personality and social variables, there appears to be some evidence for moderate consistency for measures across similar situations (Magnusson, Gerzén, & Nyman, 1968; Magnusson & Heffler, 1969; Magnusson, Heffler, & Nyman 1968), for longitudinal studies of across similar situations (Block, 1971, 1977), and for some types of variables, i.e., cognitive and intellectual variables (Mischel, 1968, 1969; Rushton & Endler, 1977). The person-by-treatment (situation) experimental designs have demonstrated significant and theoretically meaningful interactions in a number of areas. Some studies, however, have included both person and situation variables in an analysis-of-variance design without a clear theoretical rationale for the selection. The results of such studies often add little to the understanding of the phenomena they sought to address. Cronbach (1975) has raised serious questions for the interactional approach. He points out that two-way interactions may be useful in explaining behavior, but there is no reason for interactions to be limited to the combination of two variables. The number of potential interactions rapidly mounts, however, as additional variables are added to the design. A theoretical basis for selecting and combining variables is crucial for research progress.

The consistency controversy has prompted suggestions for improved methodology and for new research strategies. First, there has been an increasing call for improvement in methodology and measurement techniques (Block, 1977; Epstein, 1977, 1979; Jackson & Paunonen, 1980). Epstein, for example, has called for multiple measures of behavior in order to increase reliability (Epstein, 1979). Bem and others have suggested that not all traits are necessarily applicable to all individuals and that individuals therefore may differ in the degree of variance that they exhibit on any particular dimension (see Bem & Allen, 1974; Kenrick & Stringfield, 1980; Underwood & Moore, 1981). Endler (1981b) has suggested a systematic analysis of the dimensions of persons and situations that interact to affect behavior, with particular attention to be directed to the analysis of situations. Mischel and Peake (in press) have criticized both Bem's and Epstein's approaches and have suggested:

> In our view, an adequate resolution of the many issues raised in the long debate about consistency requires a theoretical reconceptualization of the issues, and of personality and situations constructs themselves (e.g., Cantor & Mischel, 1979; Mischel, 1973) not just more clever methods for applying everyday trait terms to people's behavior in particular contexts [Mischel & Peake, in press].

They propose that persons and situations be conceptualized along similar psychologically meaningful dimensions and have described a method of "prototypical analysis" of persons and situations in order to explore these dimensions.

The Situation as a Variable in Personality Research

An interactional approach to personality is intimately dependent on one's conceptualization of the situation as well as the person. Although the situationists and social-learning theorists have demonstrated the potential impact of situations on behavior and the interactionists insist that it is an integral part of the behavioral equation, we still need, as Frederiksen (1972) asserted, "a *systematic* way of conceptualizing the domain of situations and situation variables before we can make rapid progress in studying the role of situations in determining behavior" (p. 115, emphasis added). A number of strategies for describing and classifying situations have been put forth. Ekehammar (1974) lists five major methods of classifying situations based on "(a) a priori defined variables of *physical* and *social* character, (b) *need* concepts, (c) some single *reaction* elicited by the situations, (d) individuals' *reaction patterns* elicited by the situations; (e) individuals' *perceptions (cognitions)* of the situations" (pp. 1,041–1,042). Moos (1973) proposed six methods whereby "characteristics of environments have been related to indexes of human functionings" (p. 652): (1) etiological dimensions; (2) behavior settings involving both ecological and behavioral properties; (3) parameters of organizational structure; (4) personal and behavioral parameters of the environment inhabitants; (5) organizational climate and psychosocial variables;

and (6) variables related to reinforcement or functional analyses of environments.

Because of space considerations, we will only briefly discuss some of the primary distinctions to be considered in the analysis of situations. (For further discussion of this important area, the reader should consult Magnusson, 1981.)

LEVEL OF ANALYSIS

The breadth of the phenomena to be labeled as the "situation" can vary greatly. Both macro- and microanalysis of the situation is possible. Similarly, one can choose to compare situations-as-wholes or to focus on variations in stimuli within a situation. Pervin (1978b), in discussing the relationship among stimulus, situation, and environment, points out that, "The major distinction appears to have to do with the scale of analysis—ranging from the concern with molecular variables in the case of stimulus to molar variables and behaviors in the case of the environment" (p. 79). He notes, however, that the terms are at times used interchangeably and that the demarcation between them is often blurred.

SYSTEM OF ANALYSIS

The researcher can choose to analyze the situation with regard to either its social or its physical characteristics. Examples of social variables include norms, roles, attitudes, and values. Physical variables can encompass a wide range from temperature, architectural structures, and altitude to seating arrangements (see Barker, 1965; Sells, 1963). One of the most basic and persistent distinctions in the literature is between subjective (psychological) and objective (physical) analysis of the situation (see Ekehammar, 1974; Endler & Magnusson, 1976b, 1976c; Magnusson, 1978, 1980; Pervin, 1978b). Analogous distinctions have also been made by Kantor (1924, 1926) and Murray (1938). It appears that the current emphasis is on the psychological situation (see Endler & Magnusson's [1976c] discussion of the postulates of interactional psychology). Within the psychological analysis of the situation, situations may be described in terms of *perceptions* or *reactions*. Magnusson (1971, 1974; Magnusson & Ekehammar, 1973) has proposed and employed an empirical psychophysical method for investigating the *perception* of situations. Cantor, Mischel, and Schwartz (1982) employed a prototype analysis to explore subjects' conceptualization of situations.

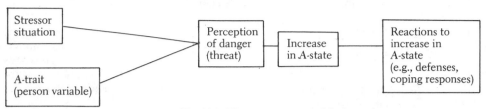

Fig. 13.1. The interaction model of anxiety.

The situation *reaction* studies focus on the individual's responses to situations. Rotter (1954) and Frederiksen (1972) have proposed that situations be classified on the basis of the similarity of behavior they evoke in persons. Bem's template-matching strategy (Bem & Funder, 1978) proposes that situations can be described and categorized with regard to the characteristics of persons who exhibit particular responses in them. Magnusson and Ekehammar (1975, 1978), and Ekehammar, Schalling, and Magnusson (1975) have investigated the relationship between persons' perceptions and situations and their reactions to situations, and found generally high congruence between the two modes.

Finally, it must be noted that in analyzing the situation psychologically — i.e., with regard to the individual's perceptions or responses — the distinction between the situation and the person blurs. This is particularly true when one considers that the individual may have actively chosen the situation to which his or her responses are being measured (see Endler, 1983; Kahle, 1980). Raush (1979) discusses developing appropriate units of analysis for the study of the "person-situation system." The analysis of situations is becoming an active research area (Bem & Funder, 1978; Cantor, Mischel & Schwartz, 1982; Magnusson, 1981). Attempts that provide for the description and categorization of persons and situation along parallel dimensions (see Mischel & Peake, in press) appear promising.

The Person-by-Situation Model of Anxiety

Endler's (1975, 1980) interaction model of anxiety emphasizes the multidimensionality of anxiety in determining reactions to stress. The interaction model of anxiety is schematically presented in Figure 13.1.

A basic conceptual distinction in the interaction model is between state anxiety and trait anxiety. Spielberger (1972) has defined A-state as an emotional reaction "consisting of unpleasant, consciously-perceived feelings of tension and apprehension with associated activation or arousal of the autonomic nervous system" (p. 29). A-trait has been defined as a measure of "anxiety-proneness — differences between individuals in the probability that anxiety states will be manifested under circumstances involving varying degrees of stress" (Spielberger, 1966, p. 15). Spielberger's trait-state theory entails an interaction between person variables (A-trait) and situational variables (stress); however, the measurement instruments developed by Spielberger and his colleagues (Spielberger, Gorsuch, & Lushene, 1970) to assess anxiety focus on ego-threatening anxiety to the exclusion of other dimensions. Endler, Hunt, and Rosenstein (1962) factor-analyzed the situations of the S-R Inventory of Anxiousness, a self-report measure of anxiety. They found three situational factors: interpersonal threat, physical danger, and ambiguous threat. Later work by Endler and his colleagues supports the contention that anxiety, both state and trait, is multidimensional (Endler & Magnusson, 1976a; Endler et al., 1976, Endler & Okada, 1974).

The interaction model simultaneously considers both the person (A-trait) and the situational stress in predicting changes in A-state. The basic prediction of the model, the *differential hypothesis*, is that significant interactions affecting A-state occur when facets of A-trait and situational threats are congruent, and no interactions are anticipated when the person and situation dimensions are not congruent. For example, social evaluation A-trait would be expected to interact with a congruent social evaluation stress situation (e.g., a job interview) to affect A-state changes. This dimension, however, would not be expected to interact with a physical danger stress. The model is predictive of a specific pattern of person-situation interactions. It necessitates research strategies that include both person and situation variables and multidimensional assessment instruments. Endler and his colleagues have developed multidimensional measures of both state anxiety, The Present Affect Reactions Questionnaire (PARQ) (Endler, 1975b, 1980), and trait anxiety, the S-R Inventory of General Trait Anxiousness (S-R GTA) (Endler & Okada, 1974, 1975). The Perception of Situation Rating Forms assesses the type and degree of situational stress as perceived by the subject.

Thirteen studies conducted by the research team at York University have tested the predictions of the interaction model of anxiety. These studies have focused on the various A-trait dimensions, in both field and laboratory settings with a variety of subject groups. Two laboratory studies with college students predicted interactions between the tasks, devised to include the threat of social evaluation, and the interpersonal or evaluation dimensions of A-trait. Endler, Okada, and Flood (1975), however, obtained significant interactions between the laboratory task (a person-perception task) and the ambiguous and physical danger facets of A-trait, with respect to A-state. As predicted, the only significant interaction obtained by Kowalchuk and Endler (1981) was between the interpersonal dimension of A-trait and the task (a sensitivity exercise) in affecting changes in A-state.

A series of field studies in actual classroom settings investigated the effects on A-state of the interaction of an examination stress and the interpersonal or social evaluation dimension of A-trait. Endler and Magnusson (1977) studying a sample of Swedish university students found that the interaction between interpersonal A-trait and the examination situation was significant for the dependent measure of pulse rate and approached significance for the Behavioral Reactions Questionnaire (BRQ), A-state measure. None of the other interactions was significant except for the interaction between physical danger and the examination stress for BRQ scores. Endler, King, Kuczynski, and Edwards (1980), working with Canadian high school students, found that the examination stress by evaluation A-trait interaction was significant. No other interactions occurred. In a study with Canadian university students, similar results were found (Phillips & Endler, 1982).

Two field studies further varied the populations sampled and types of evaluation stress included in this program of research. Diveky and Endler (1977) requested middle-management executives to respond to the PARQ in self-selected "on-the-job" stress situations and "off-the-job" nonstress situations. They found a significant social evaluation A-trait by stress interaction in eliciting A-state changes. Endler, Edwards, and McGuire (1979) studied the responses of actors to rehearsals and important stage performances. They found a trend toward an interaction between social evaluation and stress.

Athletic competitions have also been studied. Flood and Endler (1980) studied the response of male athletes participating in a track meet and also two weeks prior to the events. The interaction between the social evaluation stress of the meet and the evaluation dimension of A-trait was significant. Endler, King, and Herring (1982) studied responses to a karate competition, which was perceived as both a social evaluation and a physical danger situation. They found significant interactions between the stressful events, and both social evaluation and physical danger facets of A-trait, and as anticipated, no other significant interactions.

Medical and dental treatment situations are frequently perceived as stressful along a number of dimensions. King and Endler (1982) assessed women who were required to undergo minor surgery. Although, they found that the medical procedure was perceived primarily as ambiguous, significant interactions with the stress occurred for the ambiguous, physical danger and social evaluation facets of A-trait. Ackerman and Endler (1982) similarly found that adults required to undergo gum surgery perceived the situation as ambiguous and physically dangerous. The only interaction obtained, however, was between the stress and the evaluation dimension of A-trait. Stressful medical procedure appears to be complex and multidimensional.

A laboratory investigation of the interaction of physical danger, threat of shock, and the congruent A-trait dimension found the anticipated pattern of interaction for females but not for males (Endler & Okada, 1974).

Endler, Edwards, and Kowalchuk (1982) examined the interaction model of anxiety with a clinic population requiring crisis-intervention psychotherapy. They found a significant interaction between the social evaluation, interpersonal, and innocuous facets of A-trait for males and females, and the ambiguous dimension for females only. The subjects in this study were experiencing extreme multifaceted stress—a crisis.

The overall support for the interaction model of anxiety offered by this program of studies is encouraging. The studies in the program of research have examined person-by-situation interaction in a mechanistic mode. As noted earlier (see also Endler & Edwards, 1978), this is the current state of most interactional research. The theory in the area of anxiety and stress is increasingly calling for research on the anxiety process—for a transactional or dynamic approach.

Summary and Conclusions

Research in personality is influenced by both theories and models. Historically, personality theories and models of behavior have tended to focus on either person or situation variables. We need to develop models that incorporate both persons and situations, that suggest the important dimensions of each, and that predict how these dimensions interact. Several theorists (e.g., Raush, 1979) suggest that we should examine person-situation systems and Argyle (1977) has proposed that we should examine the generative rules of social interaction rather than concentrating on content. Mischel and his colleagues (Cantor & Mischel, 1979; Mischel, 1973) have suggested exploring people's strategies for categorizing their world. Research in personality is also influenced by sociopolitical factors and by the available technology of measurement and data analysis. We need to be cognizant of the direction and limitations that these factors can impose on research.

Current research in personality journals appears limited in terms of its sampling of both populations and settings. Laboratory research with college students still predominates. The validity of research based on restricted sampling is seriously in doubt. Pervin (1977) has suggested more representative sampling of the situations that subjects encounter. Similarly, current research appears to be deficient with regard to sampling behavior over time. Epstein (1977) and Block (1977) have emphasized the need for longitudinal research. Endler (1980) has suggested that we should examine subjects' diary accounts of their behavior in the situations they encounter in their daily lives.

We discussed the specificity-consistency issue, and found that for social and personality variables across dissimilar situations there is little evidence for consistency. There is some support for consistency in longitudinal studies of similar situations, for cognitive and intellectual variables, and for studies across similar situations. Strategies for studying situations were discussed, and it was noted that the psychological meaning of the situation is crucial in determining its effects on behavior. Fi-

nally, the interaction model of anxiety was presented and relevant research supporting this model reviewed.

References

Ackerman, C., & Endler, N. S. The interaction model of anxiety empirically examined in a dental treatment situation. Unpublished manuscript, York University, Toronto, 1982.

Allport, F. H. *Theories of perception and the concept of structure: A review and critical analysis with an introduction to a dynamic-structural theory of behavior.* New York: Wiley, 1955.

Allport, G. W. *Personality: A psychological interpretation.* New York: Holt, Rinehart, & Winston, 1937.

Anastasi, A. *Psychological Testing.* (4th ed.) New York: Macmillan, 1976.

Argyle, M. Predictive and generative rules models of P × S interaction. In D. Magnusson & N. S. Endler (Eds.), *Personality at the crossroads: Current issues in interactional psychology.* Hillsdale, N.J.: Erlbaum, 1977.

Argyle, M., & Little, B. R. Do personality traits apply to social behavior? *Journal of Theory and Social Behavior,* 1972, **2**, 1–35.

Backteman, G., & Magnusson, D. Longitudinal stability of personality characteristics. *Journal of Personality,* 1981, **49**, 148–160.

Bandura, A. (Ed.) *Psychological modeling: Conflicting theories.* New York: Aldine-Atherton, 1971.

Bandura, A. Self-efficacy: Toward a unifying theory of behavioral change. *Psychological Review,* 1977, **84**, 191–215.

Barker, R. G. Explorations in ecological psychology. *American Psychologist,* 1965, **20**, 1–14.

Beck, A. T., Rush, A. J., Shaw, B. F., & Emery, G. *Cognitive Therapy of Depression.* New York: Guilford, 1979.

Bem, D. J., & Allen, A. On predicting some of the people some of the time: The search for cross-situational consistencies in behavior. *Psychological Review,* 1974, **81**, 506–520.

Bem, D. J., & Funder, D. C. Predicting more of the people more of the time: Assessing the personality of situations. *Psychological Review,* 1978, **85**, 485–502.

Berkowitz, L. Situational and personal conditions governing reaction to aggressive cues. In D. Magnusson & N. S. Endler (Eds.), *Personality at the crossroads: Current issues in interactional psychology.* Hillsdale, N.J.: Erlbaum, 1977.

Bishop, D. W., & Witt, P. A. Sources of behavioral variance during leisure time. *Journal of Personality and Social Psychology,* 1970, **16**, 352–360.

Block, J. *Lives through time.* Berkeley, Calif.: Bancroft, 1971.

Block, J. Advancing the psychology of personality: Paradigmatic shift or improving the quality of research. In D. Magnusson & N. S. Endler (Eds.), *Personality at the crossroads: Current issues in interactional psychology.* Hillsdale, N.J.: Erlbaum, 1977.

Bowers, K. S. Situationism in psychology: An analysis and a critique. *Psychological Review,* 1973, **80**, 307–336.

Cantor, N., & Mischel, W. Prototypes in person perception. In L. Berkowitz (Ed.), *Advances in experimental social psychology*. New York: Academic Press, 1979.

Cantor, N., Mischel, W., & Schwartz, J. C. A prototype analysis of psychological situations. *Cognitive Psychology*, 1982, **14**, 45–77.

Carlson, R. Where is the person in personality research? *Psychological Bulletin*, 1971, **75**, 203–219.

Cattell, R. B. *The description and measurement of personality*. New York: World Book, 1946.

Cattell, R. B. *Personality and motivation structure and measurement*. Yonkers, N.Y.: World Book, 1957.

Cattell, R. B. *Personality and mood by questionnaire*. San Francisco: Jossey-Bass, 1973.

Cattell, R. B., & Scheier, I. H. *The meaning and measurement of neuroticism and anxiety*. New York: Ronald, 1961.

Cooley, C. H. *Human nature and the social order*. New York: Scribner's, 1902.

Cottrell, L. S., Jr. The adjustment of the individual to his age and sex roles. *American Sociological Review*, 1942, **7**, 618–625. (a)

Cottrell, L. S., Jr. The analysis of situational fields. *American Sociological Review*, 1942, **7**, 370–382. (b)

Cronbach, L. J. Beyond the two disciplines of scientific psychology. *American Psychologist*, 1975, **30**, 116–127.

Cronbach, L. J., & Snow, R. E. *Aptitudes and instructional methods*. New York: Irvington, 1975.

Dewey, R., & Humber, W. J. *The development of human behavior*. New York: Macmillan, 1951.

Diveky, S., & Endler, N. S. The interaction model of anxiety: State and trait anxiety for banking executives in normal working environments. Unpublished manuscript, York University, Toronto, 1977.

Dollard, J., & Miller, N. E. *Personality and psychotherapy: An analysis in terms of learning, thinking, and culture*. New York: McGraw-Hill, 1950.

Domino, G. Interactive effects of achievement of orientation and teaching style on academic achievement. *Journal of Educational Psychology*, 1971, **62**, 427–431.

Edwards, A. J., & Cronbach, L. J. Experimental design for research in psychotherapy. *Journal of Clinical Psychology*, 1952, **8**, 51–59.

Ekehammar, B. Interactionism in personality from a historical perspective. *Psychological Bulletin*, 1974, **81**, 1,026–1,048.

Ekehammar, B., Magnusson, D., & Ricklander, L. An interactionist approach to the study of anxiety: An analysis of an S-R inventory applied to an adolescent sample. *Scandinavian Journal of Psychology*, 1974, **15**, 4–14.

Ekehammar, B., Schalling, D., & Magnusson, D. Dimensions of stressful situations: A comparison between a response analytical and a stimulus analytical approach. *Multivariate Behavioral Research*, 1975, **10**, 155–164.

Endler, N. S. Conformity as a function of different reinforcement schedules. *Journal of Personality and Social Psychology*, 1966, **4**, 175–180.

Endler, N. S. The person versus the situation—A pseudo issue? A response to Alker. *Journal of Personality*, 1973, **41**, 287–303.

Endler, N. S. The case for person-situation interactions. *Canadian Psychological Review*, 1975, **16**, 12–21. (a)

Endler, N. S. A person-situation interaction model of anxiety. In C. D. Spielberger & I. G. Sarason (Eds.), *Stress and anxiety*, Vol. 1. Washington, D.C.: Hemisphere, 1975. (b)

Endler, N. S. Grand illusions: Traits or interactions? *Canadian Psychological Review*, 1976, **17**, 174–181.

Endler, N. S. The role of person by situation interactions in personality theory. In I. C. Uzgiris & F. Weizmann (Eds.), *The structuring of experience*. New York: Plenum, 1977.

Endler, N. S. Sociopolitical factors in theory construction. *Ontario Psychologist*, 1979, **11**, 21–22.

Endler, N. S. Person-situation interaction and anxiety. In I. L. Kutash & L. B. Schlesinger (Eds.), *Handbook on stress and anxiety: Contemporary knowledge, theory and treatment*. San Francisco: Jossey-Bass, 1980.

Endler, N. S. Persons, situations and their interactions. In A. I. Rabin (Ed.), *Further explorations in personality*. New York: Wiley, 1981. (a)

Endler, N. S. Situational aspects of interactional psychology. In D. Magnusson (Ed.), *Toward a psychology of situations: An interactional perspective*. Hillsdale, N.J.: Erlbaum, 1981. (b)

Endler, N. S. Interactionism comes of age. In M. P. Zanna, E. T. Higgins, & C. P. Herman (Eds.), *Consistency in social behavior: The Ontario symposium*. Vol. 2. Hillsdale, N.J.: Erlbaum, 1982.

Endler, N. S. Interactionism: A personality model but not yet a theory. In M. M. Page & R. Dienstbier (Eds.), *Nebraska Symposium on Motivation 1982: Personality current theory and research*. Lincoln, Nebraska: University of Nebraska Press, 1983 (in press).

Endler, N. S., & Edwards, J. Person by treatment interactions in personality research. In L. A. Pervin & M. Lewis (Eds.), *Perspectives in interactional psychology*. New York: Plenum, 1978.

Endler, N. S., Edwards, J., & Kowalchuk, B. The interaction model of anxiety assessed in a psychotherapy situation. Unpublished manuscript, York University, Toronto, 1982.

Endler, N. S., Edwards, J., & McGuire, A. The interaction model of anxiety: An empirical test in a theatrical performance situation. Unpublished manuscript, York University, Toronto, 1979.

Endler, N. S., & Hunt, J. M. Sources of behavioral variance as measured by the S-R Inventory of Anxiousness. *Psychological Bulletin*, 1966, **65**, 336–346.

Endler, N. S., & Hunt, J. M. Generalizability of contributions from sources of variance in the S-R Inventory of Anxiousness. *Journal of Personality*, 1969, **37**, 1–24.

Endler, N. S., Hunt, J. M., & Rosenstein, A. J. An S-R Inventory of anxiousness. *Psychological Monographs*, 1962, **76**(17) (Whole no. 536), 133.

Endler, N. S., King, P. R., & Herring, C. The interaction model of anxiety examined in an athletic karate competition situation. Unpublished manuscript, York University, Toronto, 1982.

Endler, N. S., King, P. R., Kuczynski, M., & Edwards, J. Examination induced anxiety: An empirical test of the interaction model. *Department of Psychology Reports*, York University, 1980, no. 97.

Endler, N. S., & Magnusson, D. Multidimensional aspects of state and trait anxiety: A cross-cultural study of Canadian and Swedish college students. In C. D. Spielberger & R. Diaz-Guerrero (Eds.), *Cross-cultural* anxiety. Washington, D.C.: Hemisphere, 1976. (a)

Endler, N. S., & Magnusson, D. Personality and person by situation interactions. In N. S. Endler & D. Magnusson (Eds.), *Interactional psychology and personality*. Washington, D.C.: Hemisphere, 1976. (b)

Endler, N. S., & Magnusson, D. Toward an interactional psychology of personality. *Psychological Bulletin*, 1976, **83**, 956–974. (c)

Endler, N. S., & Magnusson, D. The interaction model of anxiety: An empirical test in an examination situation. *Canadian Journal of Behavioural Science*, 1977, **9**, 101–107.

Endler, N. S., Magnusson, D., Ekehammar, B., & Okada, M. The multidimensionality of state and trait anxiety. *Scandinavian Journal of Psychology*, 1976, **17**, 81–93.

Endler, N. S., & Okada, M. An S-R inventory of general trait anxiousness. *Department of Psychology Reports*, York University, Toronto, 1974, no. 1.

Endler, N. S., & Okada, M. A multidimensional measure of trait anxiety: The S-R inventory of general trait anxiousness. *Journal of Consulting and Clinical Psychology*, 1975, **43**, 319–329.

Endler, N. S., Okada, M., & Flood, M. The interaction model of anxiety: An empirical test in a social situation. *Department of Psychology Reports*, York University, 1975, no. 24.

Epstein, S. Traits are alive and well. In D. Magnusson & N. S. Endler (Eds.), *Personality at the crossroads: Current issues in interactional psychology*. Hillsdale, N.J.: Erlbaum, 1977.

Epstein, S. The stability of behavior: I. On predicting most of the people much of the time. *Journal of Personality and Social Psychology*, 1979, **37**, 1,097–1,126.

Feshbach, S., & Weiner, B. *Personality*. Toronto: D. C. Heath, 1982.

Fiedler, F. E. Validation and extension of the contingency model of leadership effectiveness: A review of empirical findings. *Psychological Bulletin*, 1971, **76**, 128–148.

Fiedler, F. E. What triggers the person situation interaction in leadership? In D. Magnusson & N. S. Endler (Eds.), *Personality at the crossroads: Current issues in interactional psychology*. Hillsdale, N.J.: Erlbaum, 1977.

Flood, M., & Endler, N. S. The interaction model of anxiety: An empirical test in an athletic competition situation. *Journal of Research in Personality*, 1980, **14**, 329–339.

Frederiksen, N. Toward a taxonomy of situations. *American Psychologist*, 1972, **27**, 114–123.

Freud, S. *Collected papers*, Vols I–V. New York: Basic Books, 1959.

Guilford, J. P. *Personality*. New York: McGraw-Hill, 1959.

Hall, C. S., & Lindzey, G. *Theories of personality*. Toronto: Wiley, 1978.

Hartshorne, H., & May, M. A., *Studies in the nature of character: 1. Studies in deceit*. New York: Macmillan, 1928.

Hunt, J. M. Traditional personality theory in the light of recent evidence. *American Scientist*, 1965, **53**, 80–96.

Ichheiser, G. Misinterpretations of personality in everyday life and the psychologist's frame of reference.

Character and Personality, 1943, **12**, 145–160.

Jackson, D. N., & Paunonen, L. V. Personality structure and assessment. In M. R. Rosenzweig & L. W. Porter (Eds.), *Annual Review of Psychology*, 1980, **31**, 503–552.

Kahle, L. R. (Ed.) *New directions for methodology of behavioral science: Methods for studying person-situation interactions*. Vol. 2. Washington, D.C.: Jossey-Bass, 1979.

Kahle, L. R. Stimulus condition self-selection by males in the interaction of locus of control and skill-chance situations. *Journal of Personality and Social Psychology*, 1980, **38**, 50–56.

Kantor, J. R. *Principles of psychology*, Vol. 1. Bloomington, Ill.: Principia Press, 1924.

Kantor, J. R. *Principles of psychology*, Vol. 2. Bloomington, Ill.: Principia Press, 1926.

Kenrick, D. T., & Stringfield, D. O. Personality traits and the eye of the beholder: Crossing some traditional philosophical boundaries in the search for consistency in all of the people. *Psychological Review*, 1980, **87**, 88–104.

King, P. R., & Endler, N. S. Medical intervention and the interaction model of anxiety. *Canadian Journal of Behavioural Science*, 1982, in press.

Koffka, K. *Principles of Gestalt psychology*. New York: Harcourt, 1935.

Kowalchuk, B., & Endler, N. S. The ongoing interaction of interpersonal anxiety with stress: Effect of the assessment situation. Unpublished manuscript, York University, Toronto, 1981.

Lefcourt, H. M. *Locus of control: Current trends in theory and research*. New Jersey: Erlbaum, 1976.

Levitt, E. E. *The psychology of anxiety*. (2nd ed.) Hillsdale, N.J.: Erlbaum, 1980.

Lewin, K. *A dynamic theory of personality. Selected papers*. New York: McGraw-Hill, 1935.

Lindesmith, A. R., & Strauss, A. L. *Social psychology*. New York: Dryden, 1949.

Magnusson, D. An analysis of situational dimensions. *Perceptual and Motor Skills*, 1971, **32**, 851–867.

Magnusson, D. The individual in the situation: Some studies on individuals' perception of situations. *Studia Psychologica*, 1974, **16**, 124–132.

Magnusson, D. The person and the situation in an interactional model of behavior. *Scandinavian Journal of Psychology*, 1976, **17**, 253–271.

Magnusson, D. On the psychological situation. *Reports from the Department of Psychology*, University of Stockholm, 1978, no. 544.

Magnusson, D. Personality in an interactional paradigm of research. *Zeitscrift fur Differentialle und Diagnostiche Psychologie*, 1980, **1**, 17–34.

Magnusson, D. (Ed.) *Toward a psychology of situations. An interactional perspective*. Hillsdale, N.J.: Erlbaum, 1981.

Magnusson, D., & Ekehammar, B. An analysis of situational dimensions: A replication. *Multivariate Behavioral Research*, 1973, **8**, 331–339.

Magnusson, D., & Ekehammar, B. Perceptions of and reactions to stressful situations. *Journal of Personality and Social Psychology*, 1975, **31**, 1,147–1,154.

Magnusson, D., & Ekehammar, B. Similar situations— Similar behaviors? *Journal of Research in Personality*, 1978, **12**, 41–48.

Magnusson, D., & Endler, N. S. Interactional psychology: Present status and future prospects. In D. Magnusson & N. S. Endler (Eds.), *Personality at the crossroads: Current issues in interactional psychology*. Hillsdale, N.J.: Erlbaum, 1977.

Magnusson, D., Gerzen, M., & Nyman, B. The generality of behavioral data: I. Generalization from observation on one occasion. *Multivariate Behavioral Research*, 1968, **3**, 295-320.

Magnusson, D., & Heffler, B. The generality of behavioral data: III. Generalization potential as a function of the number of observation instances. *Multivariate Behavioral Research*, 1969, **4**, 29-42.

Magnusson, D., Heffler, B., & Nyman, B. The generality of behavioral data: II. Replication of an experiment on generalization from observation on one occasion. *Multivariate Behavioral Research*, 1968, **3**, 415-422.

Marx, M. H., & Hillix, W. A. *Systems and theories in psychology*. Toronto: McGraw-Hill, 1963.

Mead, G. H. *Mind, self, and society*. Chicago: University of Chicago Press, 1934.

Mischel, W. *Personality and assessment*. New York: Wiley, 1968.

Mischel, W. Continuity and change in personality. *American Psychologist*, 1969, **24**, 1,012-1,018.

Mischel, W. Toward a cognitive social learning reconceptualization of personality. *Psychological Review*, 1973, **80**, 252-283.

Mischel, W., & Peake, P. K. Beyond Déjà Vu in the Search for Cross-situational consistency. *Psychological Review*, in press.

Moos, R. H. Situational analysis of a therapeutic community milieu. *Journal of Abnormal Psychology*, 1968, **73**, 49-61.

Moos, R. H. Sources of variance in responses to questionnaires and in behavior. *Journal of Abnormal Psychology*, 1969, **74**, 405-412.

Moos, R. H. Conceptualizations of human environments. *American Psychologist*, 1973, **28**, 652-665.

Murray, H. A. *Explorations in personality*. New York: Oxford University Press, 1938.

Nelson, E. A., Grinder, R. E., & Mutterer, M. L. Sources of variance in behavioural measures of honesty in temptation situations: Methodological analyses. *Developmental Psychology*, 1969, **1**, 265-279.

Newcomb, T. M. An experiment designed to test the validity of a rating technique. *Journal of Educational Psychology*, 1931, **22**, 279-289.

Olweus, D. A critical analysis of the modern interactionist position. In D. Magnusson & N. S. Endler (Eds.), *Personality at the crossroads: Current issues in interactional psychology*. Hillsdale, N.J.: Erlbaum, 1977.

Olweus, D. Stability of aggressive reaction patterns in males: A review. *Psychological Bulletin*, 1979, **86**, 852-875.

OSS Assessment Staff. *Assessment of men*. New York: Rinehart, 1948.

Overton, W. F., & Reese, H. W. Models of development: Methodological implications. In J. R. Nesselroade & H. W. Reese (Eds.), *Life span developmental psychology: Methodological issues*. New York: Academic Press, 1973.

Peterson, D. R. A functional approach to the study of person-person interactions. In D. Magnusson & N. S. Endler (Eds.), *Personality at the crossroads: Current issues in interactional psychology*. Hillsdale, N.J.: Erlbaum, 1977.

Pervin, L. A. The representative design of person-situation research. In D. Magnusson & N. S. Endler (Eds.), *Personality at the crossroads: Current issues in interactional psychology*. Hillsdale, N.J.: Erlbaum, 1977.

Pervin, L. A. *Current controversies and issues in personality*. New York: Wiley, 1978. (a)

Pervin, L. A. Definitions, measurements, and classifications of stimuli, situations, and environments. *Human Ecology*, 1978, **6**, 71-105. (b)

Phares, E. J. *Locus of control in personality*. Morristown, N.J.: General Learning Press, 1976.

Phillips, J. B., & Endler, N. S. Academic examinations and anxiety: The interaction model empirically tested. *Journal of Research in Personality*, 1982, in press.

Rapaport, D., Gill, M., & Schafer, R. *Diagnostic psychological testing*. Vols. 1 & 2. Chicago: Year Book, 1945.

Raush, H. L. Interaction sequences. *Journal of Personality and Social Psychology*, 1965, **2**, 487-499.

Raush, H. L. Paradox, levels and junctures in person-situation systems. In D. Magnusson & N. S. Endler (Eds.), *Personality at the crossroads: Current issues in interactional psychology*. Hillsdale, N.J.: Erlbaum, 1977.

Raush, H. L. Epistemology, metaphysics, and person-situation methodology: Conclusions. In L. R. Kahle (Ed.), *New directions for methodology of behavioral science: Methods for studying person-situation interactions*. Vol. 2. Washington, D.C.: Jossey-Bass, 1979.

Raush, H. L., Dittmann, A. T., & Taylor, T. J. The interpersonal behavior of children in residential treatment. *Journal of Abnormal and Social Psychology*, 1959, **58**, 9-26. (a)

Raush, H. L., Dittmann, A. T., & Taylor, T. J. Person, setting and change in social interaction. *Human Relations*, 1959, **12**, 361-378. (b)

Raush, H. L., Farbman, I., & Llewellyn, L. G. Person, setting and change in social interaction: II. A normal control study. *Human Relations*, 1960, **13**, 305-333.

Rotter, J. B. *Social learning and clinical psychology*. Englewood Cliffs, N.J.: Prentice-Hall, 1954.

Rotter, J. B. Generalized expectancies for internal versus external control of reinforcement. *Psychological Monographs*, 1966, **80**(1, whole no. 609).

Rotter, J. B. Some problems and misconceptions related to the construct of internal versus external control of reinforcement. *Journal of Consulting and Clinical Psychology*, 1975, **43**, 56-67.

Rushton, J. P. Socialization and the altruistic behavior of children. *Psychological Bulletin*, 1976, **83**, 898-913.

Rushton, J. P., & Endler, N. S. Person by situation interactions in academic achievement. *Journal of Personality*, 1977, **45**, 297-309.

Sarason, I. G., Smith, R. E., & Diener, E. Personality research: Components of variance attributable to the person and the situation. *Journal of Personality and Social Psychology*, 1975, **32**, 199-204.

Sells, S. B. Dimensions of stimulus situation which account for behavior variances. In S. B. Sells (Ed.), *Stimulus determinants of behavior*. New York: Ronald, 1963.

Shute, C. Aristotle's interactionism and its transformations by some 20th century writers. *Psychological Record*, 1973, **23**, 283–293.

Spielberger, C. D. Theory and research on anxiety. In C. D. Spielberger (Ed.), *Anxiety and behavior.* New York: Academic Press, 1966.

Spielberger, C. D. Anxiety as an emotional state. In C. D. Spielberger (Ed.), *Anxiety: Current trends in theory and research,* Vol. 1. New York: Academic Press, 1972.

Spielberger, C. D., Gorsuch, R. L., & Lushene, R. E. *Manual for the State-Trait Anxiety Inventory.* Palo Alto, Calif.: Consulting Psychologist Press, 1970.

Staub, E. The nature and study of human personality. In E. Staub (Ed.), *Personality: Basic Aspects and Current Research,* Englewood Cliffs, N.J.: Prentice-Hall, 1980.

Stolorow, R. D., & Atwood, G. E. *Faces in a cloud: Subjectivity in personality theory.* New York: Jason Aaronson, 1979.

Taylor, J. A. A personality scale of manifest anxiety. *Journal of Abnormal Psychology*, 1953, **48**, 285–290.

Underwood, B., & Moore, B. S. Sources of behavioral consistency. *Journal of Personality and Social Psychology*, 1981, **40**, 780–785.

Wiesenthal, D. L., Edwards, J., Endler, N. S., Koza, P., Walton, A., & Emmott, S. Trends in conformity research. *Canadian Psychological Review*, 1978, **19**, 41–58.

14 PSYCHOPATHOLOGY RESEARCH*

Richard A. Depue
Scott M. Monroe

Psychologists and psychiatrists have been doing research on psychopathology for approximately four decades. During this period, but especially since 1965, several significant methodological, substantive, and conceptual developments have occurred including: the emergence of psychopharmacotherapies and their prophylactic effects; new diagnostic systems; high-risk paradigms; the role of stress in initiating disorder; the "biological revolution" in general; and new insights into genetic contributions to these disorders. And yet there remain many uncertainties as to the classificatory boundaries of several disorders, the exact mode of genetic transmission is not known for any disorder, and it is still not possible to ascribe a specific pathophysiology to more than a subgroup of any one disorder. Until recently, the typical response to such uncertainties was to plead ignorance of the facts and to suggest that yet more and more studies will enlighten our conceptual darkness. This response is understandable in that it embodies the rationale that has been used successfully by medical scientists to gain public and congressional support in studying other human disorders. Although there is a strong basis to this position, there are other factors as well that contribute to the intractability of psychopathological disorders.

All human disorders are investigated, often implicitly, under the guiding influence of disease models that are in popular use at the time. This is true whether the focus of study is on psychological or biological variables. Which models are used as conceptual frameworks is critical because these models determine, in large part, the type of research strategies applied (Bronowski, 1973). Thus, after four decades of research in psychopathology, it is fruitful to step back and ask whether our current disease models are congruent with what we know of the nature of psychopathological disorders. In fact, comparison of current disease models with the nature of psychopathology suggests that significant incongruencies exist. Previously studied diseases generally fit one of two models: either one based on exogenous or infectious etiology, or one based on metabolic or molecular etiology. In particular, the metabolic disease model has been one of the most influential in

*This work was supported by National Institute of Mental Health Research Grant MH-33195 awarded to Richard A. Depue.

studies of psychopathology. As we will show, however, this type of disorder has very different features from psychopathological disorders. Whether the research strategies currently employed in psychopathology, based largely as they are on concepts of metabolic disease, are maximally effective in revealing the nature of psychopathological disorders is a crucial question.

Historically, the metabolic disease model has greatly influenced major conceptual and research strategies in psychopathology. One of the most significant conceptual frameworks guided by the metabolic model was Kraepelin's (1921) classification system based on patients' phenotypes (observable behaviors). The metabolic model was highly influential during Kraepelin's professional lifetime, and it still is, although there are now other models as well. As discussed later, a taxonomy based on phenotype is congruent with the nature of metabolic disorders because these disorders have a fairly standard set of symptoms that are distinct from the normal phenotype and bear a fairly direct relation to etiology. Psychopathological disorders, on the other hand, do not share these phenotypic features. Indeed, the nature of the phenotype in psychopathology may be incongruent with a taxonomy that is based on a metabolic-disorders framework.

A more recent example of the influence of the metabolic-disease model on conceptions of psychopathology concerns the most influential biological hypothesis in psychopathology to date: the catecholamine hypothesis of depression (Schildkraut, 1965). Biologically, metabolic disorders are homogeneous and their defects tend to be large in magnitude and stable across time. The metabolic model leads one to believe that most disorders will be characterized by a large deficit that is just waiting to be identified. Based in part on this notion, the catecholamine hypothesis was quickly criticized for its simplicity in suggesting that depression is associated with a high-magnitude decrease in the level of essentially one neurotransmitter (e.g., Baldessarini, 1975). It is now clear that the biological nature of psychopathology is more complex than the metabolic model would suggest. Therefore, even in the area of biological research, one must consider other models of human disorders in relation to psychopathology.

In the remainder of this chapter, we systematically evaluate the congruency between metabolic and psychopathological disorders. Although a number of other disease models could be used

rather than the metabolic to highlight the nature of our correct research strategies, the latter best serves this purpose.

The Nature of Psychopathological Disorders

The question of whether current disease models adequately reflect the nature of psychopathological disorders can best be answered by carefully comparing the clinical and biological features of the model disease with those of psychopathology, but first we will provide a brief characterization of the model disease.

Although the notion of a cellular basis of disease had already been well championed by the great 19th-century pathologist, Rudolph Virchow, it was not until the early 20th century that two major forms of disease were recognized as having a significant genetic contribution. These are the inborn errors of metabolism (resulting from incorrect specification of proteins, often enzymes), and the molecular diseases (resulting from deviant DNA codings of polypeptide chains in molecules other than enzymes). Examples of the latter are the hemoglobinopathies and the immunoglobulinopathies (Emery, 1979; Fuller & Thompson, 1978; Vogel & Motulsky, 1982). Both types of disease have served as models for exploring the nature of psychopathology, but the metabolic model has been most influential.

The British physician, Archibald Garrod, developed the notion that metabolic processes proceed in steps, where each step is controlled by a particular enzyme which, in turn, is the product of a particular gene (Garrod, 1923). When some product is being formed through a metabolic process, such as a neurotransmitter molecule, all of these steps taken collectively form a biosynthesis pathway. Garrod proposed that a number of disorders that appeared to aggregate in families were caused by inherited errors in a metabolic process. In line with the one-gene-one-enzyme concept, it was suspected that the genetically determined error in metabolism had its origin in defective enzymes. We now know this to be true in over 120 inborn errors of metabolism. Generally, the activity of the enzyme is abnormally reduced and the synthesis pathway in which the enzyme is located is blocked. In addition, we know that such metabolic errors are generally inherited as autosomal recessives, although a few traits are transmitted as either autosomal dominant (e.g., porphyria) or

X-linked recessive manifested in males in hemizygous form (Emery, 1979; Omenn & Motulsky, 1972; Vogel & Motulsky, 1982). Because of their compliance with Mendelian laws of inheritance, these disorders are often referred to as Mendelian pathologies.

The metabolic disorders may be divided into three broad categories: disorders of amino acid metabolism, disorders of carbohydrate metabolism, and disorders of lipid metabolism. We shall characterize the features of one disorder from the first category because it is best known and serves our purposes well throughout the chapter. Phenylketonuria (PKU), first identified in 1934, is identifiable in infancy and becomes evident early in childhood. Manifest symptoms include:

1. Intellectual retardation: the deficit increases with age to where IQs are generally below 50; institutionalization is often required.
2. Lack of pigmentation: individuals tend to be pale in complexion, blond, blue-eyed, with dry, rough eczematous skin.
3. Musty odor.
4. Irritability.
5. Vomiting.
6. Convulsions in early life.
7. Pithecoid (monkeylike) posture while standing.

Other indicators of PKU require more elaborate measures (Emery, 1979; Fuller & Thompson, 1978; Vogel & Motulsky, 1982):

1. High blood phenylalanine levels.
2. High urinary phenylpyruvic acid levels.
3. Reduction in brain weight with defects in myelination.
4. EEG abnormalities, with spike or wave complexes of the *petit mal* type even in the absence of overt seizures.

The first two indicators directly above can be used to diagnose PKU quite accurately, although not every newborn with high blood phenylalanine concentrations has PKU (Motulsky & Omenn, 1975).

One of the specific etiologies of this disorder has now been determined. In Figure 14.1, the biosynthesis pathway of relevance to PKU is diagrammatically represented. The pathway shows that, in the liver, phenylalanine, an essential amino acid obtained from diet, is synthesized to tyrosine by the catalytic action of the enzyme phenylalanine hydroxylase. Tyrosine may then be synthesized to DOPA, and then DOPA to melanin pigment, both steps requiring the action of different synthetic enzymes. In one form of PKU there exists, for genetic reasons, a basic deficiency in phenylalanine hydroxylase. Because this deficiency blocks the synthesis pathway, it is known as a genetic block. The deficiency results in (a) a large decrease in the synthesis of tyrosine and, hence, a large decrease in melanin pigment, and (b) an increase in blood levels of phenylalanine. The latter activates an alternate metabolic pathway, involving the metabolism of phenylalanine to phenylpyruvic, phenyllactic, and phenylacetic acids (Fuller & Thompson, 1978). These acids are excreted in urine, where the concentration of urinary phenylpyruvic acid is used as a sign of the disorder.

Severe mental retardation results from damage to key functions in the developing brain caused by toxic accumulations of phenylalanine and its ketone metabolites in blood. The convulsions may be of similar origin. The musty odor results from the high concentrations of phenylacetic acid, and the light pigmentation is due to a reduced melanin production resulting from low levels of the melanin precursor, tyrosine.

There are over 100 diseases involving errors of metabolism, and several dozen of these result in

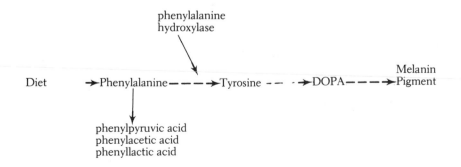

Fig. 14.1. A portion of the biosynthesis pathway where phenylalanine serves as precursor.

mental retardation, as does the error in PKU. Other disorders, such as the Lesch-Nyhan syndrome, manifest much more behavioral disturbance than PKU. Nevertheless, taken together, many (though not all) of the metabolic disorders are characterized by similar features that vary from the nature of psychopathology. There are at least three ways in which these differences become apparent.

Comparison of the Features of Metabolic and Psychopathological Disorders

1. INCIDENCE

Most metabolic disorders such as PKU are very rare (of the order of 1 or fewer in 10,000), whereas most psychopathological disorders are relatively common. For instance, bipolar affective disorder is associated with a 1.2 percent lifetime prevalence for the full syndromal forms (Weissman & Meyers, 1978), and this rate would be significantly higher if subsyndromal bipolar forms (i.e., cyclothymia) were included (Depue et al., 1981).

The rarity of the metabolic disorders is due to their recessive mode of Mendelian inheritance: an afflicted individual must be homozygous for the mutant allele, and thus both parents must be heterozygous carriers. In other words, in order for the enzyme deficiency to cause metabolic disorder, the effect of two mutant alleles coding for the enzyme is required. In contrast, psychopathological disorders do not easily fit Mendelian genetic models, and it is more difficult to provide Mendelian explanations of how these disorders can be so prevalent in the population. Their high incidence has therefore led some geneticists to hypothesize that their genetic basis might lie in the genetic variation inherent in our species (e.g., Gottesman & Shields, 1972). Many traits or variables, such as blood pressure or the activity of enzyme, show continuous, fairly normally distributed variation throughout the population.[1] Under such a model, a psychopathological disorder corresponds to the deviant phenotype observed at one of the extreme tails of a trait's distribution of values (Lerner, 1958). That is, here psychopathological disorders are viewed as the phenotypic expression of extreme values of a biological variable that

has a wide distribution throughout the population.

Thus, a mere comparison of the incidence of some metabolic and psychopathological disorders suggests that a disease process distinct from normal biological functioning is occurring, and their adherence to Mendelian laws of inheritance indicates that this disease process is related to a definite genetic mutation. On the other hand, the genetic model for common disorders suggests that a continuity in biology exists between disease and normal functioning and that the difference in the two states is quantitative, rather than qualitative, in nature. The latter notion suggests that research in psychopathology might profitably focus more on the degree of alteration in normal biological variables as opposed to focusing on distinctly deficient metabolic pathways.

2. PHENOTYPIC FEATURES

There are at least three differences between the phenotypes (here meaning exophenotype, or observable manifestations only) of metabolic and psychopathological disorders.

Heterogeneity. First, psychopathological disorders show much greater symptom heterogeneity within a category than do many of the metabolic disorders. Many metabolic disorders tend to have a standard set of manifestations, most of which reliably occur in most individuals with the disorder, although nongenetic factors can affect the phenotype to some extent (Elston & Namboodiri, 1980). The standard set of symptoms described above for PKU serves as a good example of this: most of these symptoms occur in most PKU individuals. On the other hand, psychopatholgical disorders are characterized by a loosely associated aggregate of symptoms, only a variable subset of which will appear in any one individual. This is in part because psychopathological disorders often have a much larger number of possible manifestations, only a few of which bear a moderately high, reliable association with the disorder.

The difference in symptom pattern between these two forms of disorder could be due to at least two factors. One factor concerns the directness of the association between genetic influence and symptoms. Metabolic disorders are characterized by a much more direct path between genes and

---

[1]The extent to which this variation is due to polygenic effects or to protein polymorphisms is not completely known (Motulsky & Omenn, 1975).

symptoms than is characteristic of psychopathological disorders. In PKU, most symptoms are fairly direct results of pathophysiology, which in turn results directly from genetic influence on the synthetic enzyme, phenylalanine hydroxylase. For instance, many symptoms in PKU are just a few steps removed from genetic influence: (a) the genetic product, phenylalanine hydroxylase, and (b) toxic levels of phenylalanine or its metabolities causing mental retardation, musty odor (phenylacetic acid) and perhaps convulsions. Similarly: (a) the genetic influence, and (b) very low levels of tyrosine and, hence, reduced melanin pigment causing light pigmentation. Thus, in many metabolic disorders, there are few intermediary steps between gene product and symptom to modify the phenotypic expression.

In psychopathological disorders, the variable phenotypic expression may be due in part to the many intermediary steps between gene and symptom. CNS regulation of behavior comprises many separate pathways that operate as a complex adaptive system of excitatory and inhibitory influences (Depue, Monroe, & Shackman, 1979; Roberts, 1972). Dysfunction in one pathway may be counterbalanced by corrective activity in other interactive pathways. This same set of adaptive principles holds even within one pathway. For instance, the biosynthetic pathway for a neurotransmitter has many checks, balances, and feedback circuits that tend to adapt to temporary and chronic disturbances in any one variable (Barchas et al., 1975). Thus, if a psychopathological disorder had a genetically determined enzyme deficiency in certain CNS pathways as its specific etiology, the effect of this enzyme deficiency on behavior could significantly vary owing to the many modulating influences that exist in all the pathways involved in the behaviors' expression. That is, the chain of events between the primary action of the gene to final outward manifestations of the disorder (i.e., behavior) may be extremely complex because of interactions between various tissues, hormonal influences, and so on (Emery, 1979). To the extent that the functioning of each of the modulating pathways is affected by individual differences in biology, one can expect variation in symptoms across members of a particular category. In other words, symptom variation may reflect variation in pathophysiology, which results from individual differences in expressing the specific etiology.

Another factor that could account for the greater phenotypic heterogeneity in psychopathology is the existence of several different biological etiologies within a diagnostic category (Akiskal, 1979; Buchsbaum & Rieder, 1979). Each etiology would produce a set of symptoms and, although a common theme might exist across these sets of symptoms, variation in symptoms would be the rule. Etiologic heterogeneity is further discussed below.

Overlapping. A second phenotypic difference between these two forms of disorder is the much more extensive overlapping of symptoms across categories in psychopathology than in metabolic disorders. Whereas many metabolic disorders tend to have a subset of relatively specific symptoms, the problem of overlapping contributes heavily to diagnostic confusion in psychopathology. This is particularly evident in the confusion over the boundaries between schizophrenia, schizophreniform, schizoaffective, and bipolar affective disorders (e.g., Coryell & Tsuang, 1982; Fowler, Liskow et al., 1980; Fowler, Mezzich et al., 1980; Pope et al., 1980), where thought disorder and affective symptoms are found in each category. In view of this phenomenon of overlapping, it becomes difficult to view psychopathological disorders, as the metabolic disease model would compel us, as a class of relatively specific disorders with homogeneous etiologies.

Range of intensity. The third difference in phenotype concerns the range in phenotypic intensity. In many metabolic disorders, individuals receiving sufficient genetic input for the disease (double dose in recessive transmission, single dose in dominant) almost always manifest the disorder, and show only minimum variation in intensity of the phenotype.[2] Their phenotype is extreme and may be said to be distinctly different from the normal phenotype. Individuals with PKU, for example, have identifiable phenotypes that vary little in intensity and are distinctly different from normal in several ways.

In contrast, psychopathological disorders are characterized by a broad range in intensity of the

[2] This does not take into account heterozygous carriers, who usually show no gross overt manifestations of disease but who may differ from normal on certain biochemical or behavioral measures (Emery, 1979; Fuller & Thompson, 1978; Omenn & Motulsky, 1972).

phenotype. This range may extend from full syn-dromal, hospitalized cases to only minimal indi-cations of disorder. For example, bipolar affective disorder may vary in intensity from full-blown manic and depressive episodes of three months' duration, to the very brief (e.g., three days) mild subsyndromal depressive and hypomanic episodes of cyclothymia (Depue et al., 1981). At very mild intensities, the pathological phenotype will merge almost imperceptibly with the normal phenotype (Meehl, 1973). Note that the occurrence of a broad range of intensity is certainly in keeping with the model of common disorders discussed above: here, a range of phenotypic intensity may, in part, reflect a range in values at the tail of a distribution of a biological variable. This discus-sion implies that an individual could possess the genetic input for a particular psychopathological disorder but, for a host of biological and/or psy-chosocial reasons, show no or only very mild phenotypic manifestations of genetic influence. This condition, of course, implicates the notion of vulnerability or risk to disease, a notion that is less congruent with the more nearly all-or-none rela-tion between genetic input and high phenotypic intensity that is characteristic of metabolic dis-eases (Depue et al., 1979; Weiner, 1977).

Thus, taken together, the psychopathological disorders manifest a much more variable set of symptoms, a much less specific symptomatology, and a much broader range of phenotypic intensi-ties than most metabolic disorders. To clinician and researcher alike, these phenotypic features represent difficult diagnostic problems. Much more problematic is the definition of psychopath-ological disorders on the basis of phenotype, which is suggested by the metabolic disease model. The use of phenotype to define metabolic disor-ders prior to discovery of their etiology is mean-ingful in view of their phenotypic features. But it is much less clear that a taxonomy based on pheno-type is most profitable, or even supportable, in view of the phenotypic heterogeneity so prevalent in psychopathology. Perhaps we need to explore taxonomies based on variables other than, or in addition to, phenotype in order to delimit pheno-typic, and perhaps etiologic, heterogeneity. More-over, our conceptual framework may need to ac-count for the biological continuity between the disordered and normal state suggested by the model of common disorders and the range in phenotypic intensity. The metabolic model enter-tains neither of these alternative ways of looking at psychopathological disorders.

3. THE NATURE OF BIOLOGICAL DISTURBANCES

It is with respect to biological disturbance that the metabolic model of disease has been most gener-ally applied to psychopathology. And yet, there exist a number of very striking differences in the biological disturbances of metabolic and psycho-pathological disorders. For this reason, analysis of these differences may provide the basis for a more compatible framework for conceiving the nature of biological disturbances in psychopathology.

There are at least three major differences be-tween the biological disturbances of metabolic and psychopathological disorders: magnitude, heterogeneity, and variability over time. It is not certain if these differences reflect the operation of qualitatively different etiologic processes, or whether the biological differences simply repre-sent divergent points on a quantitative dimension. Even if the latter were true, the divergence ap-pears to be so great that the two forms of disorder may require different conceptual frameworks.

Magnitude. The first major difference between the two forms of disorder is the magnitude of the biological disturbance. In many inborn errors of metabolism, the magnitude of biological disturb-ance is quite high. That is, the activity of the de-ficient enzyme is usually extremely low, much lower than the lower end of the enzyme's normal range of activity. In fact, in most genetic disorders in which an enzyme deficit has been shown to be causative of the disorder, the enzyme activity it-self is almost undetectable (Wyatt et al., 1980). In cases where only partial deficiency of the enzyme causes clinical disease, such as in porphyria, the enzyme comprises the rate-limiting step in the synthesis pathway (Emery, 1979); this means that the activity of the enzyme determines the upper limit of the rate of synthesis on the entire path-way. Even partial deficiencies in rate-limiting en-zymes, therefore, can have enormous effects on the quantity of synthetic products farther along the pathway.

It should be obvious that if the enzyme disturb-ance is of high magnitude in many metabolic disor-ders, so too is the deficit in products farther along the synthetic pathway. Indeed, these deficits also produce values typically below the normal range. In the example, of PKU, the deficit in pheny-lalanine hydroxylase results in large deficits in the synthetic products of tyrosine and of melanin pig-ment. Recall that the latter deficit is of high enough magnitude to result in a clearly observable lack of pigmentation in eyes, hair, and skin. Furthermore, the pathophysiology of most metabolic disorders is also extreme. The unusually high levels of blood phenylalanine in PKU are one example of this.

Overall, then, the biological changes that occur in many metabolic disorders are of very high magnitude, typically outside the normal range. These high magnitude disturbances result in a biological, and hence a phenotypic, profile that is, practically speaking, distinct from normality. This distinct nature of the biological disturbance in metabolic disorders has no doubt contributed to the development of reliable diagnostic tests for many disorders (Emery, 1979).

The psychopathological disorders, on the other hand, present quite a different picture. To date, there has been no consistent finding of a biological disturbance that is outside normal limits (Depue & Evans, 1981). Certainly, some patients fall outside the limits of control values obtained in a particular sample. But, when several studies are averaged across, biological departures from normal have been of much lower magnitude than in the metabolic disorders.

There are several examples of this in the pathophysiology literature of psychopathology. We will focus briefly on three that represent reliable findings. The enzyme monoamine oxidase (MAO) play an important role in modulating presynaptic levels of the biogenic amine neurotransmitters, such as norepinephrine, dopamine, and serotonin. Therefore, MAO is one very significant factor in the functional processes of these CNS transmitters (Depue & Evans, 1981; Murphy & Kalin, 1980). Because CNS pathways using these transmitters are intimately involved in the expression of a broad range of behaviors, the integrity of MAO metabolism may be highly important in psychopathology.

MAO activity in chronic schizophrenia has been investigated in over 30 studies. All but 6 of these found a decrease in the MAO activity of schizophrenics, and in 22 studies, the decrease was statistically significant (Wyatt et al., 1980). The probability of the latter occurring at the .05 level is less than 1 in 10^{21}. Reductions in MAO activity have also been found, albeit less consistently, in schizoaffective, alcoholic, and bipolar affective disorders (Belmaker, Bracha, & Elstein, 1980; Wyatt et al., 1980). In spite of the rather consistent association of reduced MAO activity and various forms of psychopathology, the reduction of MAO activity is not of high magnitude. When studies on schizophrenia have been averaged across, the mean reduction in MAO activity is approximately 25 percent below the normal mean (Buchsbaum & Rieder, 1979), and no study has reported a mean reduction greater than 68 percent from normal control subjects (Meltzer & Stahl, 1974).

When two other pathophysiology variables are examined, the magnitude of the deficit is similar to the MAO activity deficit. For example, studies measuring the major metabolite of serotonin in cerebrospinal fluid have found reductions of approximately 30 percent in depressed patients (Murphy, Campbell, & Costa, 1978), or at least in a subgroup of these patients (Asberg, Thoren, & Traskman, 1976; Traskman et al., 1981), compared to controls. Similar magnitudes of reduction occur for the major metabolite of norepinephrine in depressed patients (Charney, Menkes, & Heninger, 1981; Depue & Evans, 1981; Schildkraut, 1978). Furthermore, no consistently significant reductions or evaluations have been found in mania for metabolite levels of either of these neurotransmitters (Bunney et al., 1977).

In general, then, psychopathological disorders are characterized by biological disturbances of low magnitude relative to the metabolic disorders. Of course, in psychopathology, the variables measured are not likely to be etiologic factors but rather only pathophysiology (reflections of the etiologic factors). It is possible that etiologic variables of high magnitude will yet be found. If so, unlike the metabolic disorders, their effects on pathophysiology must be greatly reduced in some manner.

Heterogeneity. A second major difference in biological disturbances between metabolic and psychopathological disorders is variability across individuals within a diagnostic category. This refers, of course, to the problem of biologic, and perhaps etiologic, heterogeneity. The issues here are similar to those of phenotype heterogeneity discussed above. And, as was the case with phenotypic heterogeneity, many metabolic disorders present a more uniform biological profile across individuals within a category than do psychopathological disorders. In fact, it is almost axiomatic that any significant biologic disturbance found in a particular psychopathology will not characterize more than a subgroup of individuals with that phenotype (Buchsbaum & Rieder, 1979). Other factors that reflect biological functioning also implicate heterogeneity in most disorders, such as the variabilities of pharmacological response, clinical course, and familial incidence of disorder (Depue & Monroe, 1978a, 1978b).

There are at least two reasons for the difference in biological heterogeneity between metabolic and psychopathological disorders, and both of these were discussed above under the heading of phenotypic heterogeneity. First, as already noted, many metabolic disorders are characterized by a more direct association between the etiologic variable (deficient phenylalanine hydroxylase in PKU) and the resulting pathophysiology (high levels of phenylalanine and its metabolites, reduced melanin pigment, etc.). In psychopathological disorders, the directness of this association is reduced because of the many possible intermediary influences that exist in adaptive CNS systems. Thus, psychopathological disorders would be subject to much more variability in the biological expression of the etiologic factor and, hence, to greater heterogeneity in pathophysiology.

Second, it is equally possible, in addition to the above, that the great biologic heterogeneity of psychopathological disorders is because most are etiologically heterogeneous disorders. This would appear to be a viable alternative conception in that there are many examples of its existence in other disorders. For instance, more than 200 genetic causes of mental retardation have now been identified. Similarly, for each clotting factor, there exists a bleeding disorder (Buchsbaum & Rieder, 1979). Also, there are numerous forms of cancer that probably have very different etiologies. Currently, it is suspected that there may be several schizophrenias: one form associated with low MAO activity (Buchsbaum & Rieder, 1979; Wyatt et al., 1980); another subgroup with a biochemical dysfunction involving CNS dopaminergic pathways (Langer, Brown, & Docherty, 1981; Meltzer & Stahl, 1976; Snyder, 1981); and yet another form that may manifest ventricular enlargement as a reflection of brain atrophy (Andreasen, Olsen et al., 1982; Andreasen, Smith, et al., 1982; Luchins, et al., 1981; Weinberger, et al., 1979). Furthermore, in affective disorders, one finds a similar trend: one form of depression may be characterized by a noradrenergic dysfunction (Maas, 1978; Schildkraut, 1978), another by a serotonergic dysfunction (Asberg et al., 1976; Traskman et al., 1981). Because the pathophysiology of many psychopathologies is associated with disturbances in neurotransmitter metabolism, the magnitude of potential biologic heterogeneity is revealed when it is recognized that there are more than a hundred

known neurotransmitter synthetic and degradative enzymes. Perhaps a large number of these enzymes could become altered in activity owing to genetic reasons and, thereby, comprise a set of etiologies that alter neurotransmitter functioning.

This latter point suggests a more specific hypothesis concerning biological heterogeneity in psychopathology. The biogenic amine neurotransmitters (norepinephrine, dopamine, and serotonin) have been thought to be important in the regulation of many normal behaviors, including sleep, motor, mood, cognition, and reward (Depue & Evans, 1981). They have also been clearly implicated in the pathophysiology of affective disorders (Depue & Evans, 1981; Murphy et al., 1978; Schildkraut, 1978). If the monoamines are associated with the behavioral alterations seen in such different states as depression and mania, then it is possible that they may comprise a significant component of the neurochemistry of *behavioral* disturbance in other disorders. Indeed, to date biogenic amines have been implicated in the pathophysiology of several disorders, including dopamine in schizophrenia (Langer et al., 1981; Meltzer & Stahl, 1976; Snyder, 1981); serotonin (Goldberg et al., 1980), and norepinephrine (Gerner & Gwirtsman, 1981; Gold et al., 1980) in anorexia nervosa; norepinephrine (Hoehn-Saric et al., 1981; Rifkin et al., 1981) and possibly serotonin (Gloger et al., 1981) in anxiety disorders; serotonin (Irwin et al., 1981) and norepinephrine (Reimherr, Wood, & Wender, 1981; Shekim, Dekirmenjian, & Chapel, 1979) in minimal brain dysfunction (or attention deficit disorder); norepinephrine (Knesevich, 1982) and serotonin (Ananth et al., 1979; Thoren et al., 1980) in obsessive compulsive disorder; and norepinephrine (Cohen et al., 1980) and dopamine (Feinberg & Carroll, 1979) in Gilles da la Tourette's Syndrome.

It is intriguing to speculate that psychopathology represents a family of biogenic amine disorders, and that more specific disorders represent one or more subfamilies. Within each subfamily, biological heterogeneity would correspond to the different enzyme variants that result in amine disorder. For example affective disorders may represent a number of norepinephrine and serotonin disorders. Each variant of amine functioning would contribute to heterogeneity, but all would have a common phenotypic theme. Similarly, some forms of schizophrenia may represent a subfamily of dopamine disorders. This conceptualization is compatible with the overlap of symptoms across categories described above. Such phenotypic overlap may reflect a multiple-amine pathophysiology that would be accompanied by a fuller symptomatic picture, such as in schizoaffective disorder where thought disorder and affective symptoms coexist.

How different etiologies could produce a clinical syndrome with a common symptomatic theme is perplexing. One possible explanation for this is that each of the distinct etiologies, as an end result, produces a biologic disturbance in a common CNS system that subserves a set of behaviors. This is the notion of a final common pathway. Akiskal (1979) recently applied this idea to depressive disorders. He suggests that several different types of etiology (in our example, enzymes) may affect the integrity of biogenic amine metabolism in the diecephalon, a brain area that modulates depressive behaviors such as mood, motivation, and psychomotor functions.

It should be clear that biologic heterogeneity is not a basic tenet of the metabolic disease model. One must seriously question, then, whether the standard research procedure used for metabolic disorders of selecting on the basis of phenotype a small group of disordered subjects and of comparing them to an equally small group of normal controls deals adequately with the problem of biologic heterogeneity. Even with the best of sampling luck, the disordered group selected in this way will not be comprised of more than a very small homogeneous subgroup. We will return to this issue again later.

Variability over time. A third difference in the nature of biologic disturbance between some metabolic and psychopathological disorders concerns variability over time. In many metabolic disorders, there exists a distinct block in a biosynthetic pathway that results in a chronic biological disturbance (gout being an exception). Moreover, this is reflected in a constant phenotypic intensity over time. In contrast, most psychopathological disorders are characterized by an episodic course, although there may be a chronic state of mild disturbance between more definite episodes (as in a chronic intermittent course). Thus, the phenotype varies in intensity over time, and so does the intensity of the pathophysiology (Depue & Evans, 1981).

This is a highly important difference between these two forms of disorder. In contrast to many metabolic disorders, it suggests that manifestation of biological disturbance in psychopathology is a probabilistic phenomenon, the likelihood of which varies as a function of several factors. One factor may reside in the fluctuation of vulnerability mechanisms underlying biological disturbance itself. An example of this is the switch process from depression to mania. This switch can occur naturally, but it can also be induced by certain pharmacological agents. The most effective agents are the tricyclic antidepressants (which block the reuptake of biogenic amines) and the MAO-inhibitors (which block the presynaptic degradation of biogenic amines). These effects have been demonstrated in 80 publications reporting on 3,923 patients, so it is a reliable finding (Bunney, 1978). The interesting result relevant to our discussion is that no more than 10 percent (on the average) of patients manifest a drug-induced switch into mania at any one time. This is also true of remitted patients on prophylactic regimens of tricyclic antidepressants (Depue & Monroe, 1978a). These findings suggest that biologic vulnerability to switching from depression to mania, or even from a euthymic state to mania, is not constant within an individual over time. What exactly accounts for fluctuations in biologic vulnerability is not known, but the episodic nature of most psychopathologies indicates that it is an important factor in most of these disorders.

Another factor that contributes to the probabilities nature of biological exacerbation and of phenotypic expression is the individual's physical and interpersonal environment (Depue, 1979; Slater & Depue, 1981). Whereas such factors have not been viewed as important contributors to the etiology or biological expression of gene-influenced enzyme deficiency in metabolic disorders, they have become the focus of intensive scrutiny by psychopathologists within the past decade (Brown, 1979). Because we deal with this literature later, let it suffice here to say that stress-inducement of psychopathology has implications for the nature of biological disturbance similar to drug inducement: that biological vulnerability is increased by strong challenge to the functional system in which the vulnerability resides (Depue et al., 1979).

Elements of a Functional Model of Psychopathology

The most obvious possibility accounting for the differences between metabolic and psychopathological disorders is that most of the inborn errors of metabolism thus far discovered are peripheral to the CNS. In one form of PKU, for example, the deficient synthesis of phenylalanine to tyrosine occurs in the liver. Few psychopathological disorders have been suspected as originating from peripheral sources, although certain pathophysiology may reflect disturbance in peripheral systems resulting from a central source. For instance, the greatly increased secretion of cortisol, a peripherally released hormone, in depressive disorders is thought to be due to the subsensitivity of the norepinephrine receptors involved in the central tonic inhibitory system for cortisol (Charney et al., 1981; Depue & Evans, 1981). Thus, it is generally held that most behaviors that are disturbed in psychopathology are subserved by centrally located neural systems. Indeed, our recent examination of the symptomatic behaviors associated with depressive disorders revealed that most of these behaviors are subserved by various CNS pathways that use biogenic amines as neurotransmitters (Depue & Evans, 1981).

But the peripheral location of the biological disturbance in metabolic disorders is probably not the major factor that accounts for the difference seen between many metabolic and psychopathological disorders. There are metabolic disorders whose enzyme deficiency is located centrally but that are still characterized by a circumscribed, distinct phenotype, and a specific enzyme deficiency that results in a biological disturbance of high magnitude and minimal variability across time and individuals having the disorder. This seems to be true even in metabolic disorders that involve some form of behavioral disturbance. The Lesch-Nyhan syndrome, for instance, consists of involuntary choreoathetoid movements and a bizarre self-destructive behavior with biting of the lips and fingertips, as well as severe gouty arthritis. These behavioral symptoms result from a specific metabolic deficiency of the enzyme hypoxanthine-guanine phosphoribosyl transferase (HGPRT), the highest levels of which are found centrally in the basal ganglia of the brain. Hence, the deficiency is consistent with the involuntary movement disorder (Motulsky & Omenn, 1975). Still, the Lesch-Nyhan syndrome is clearly more similar to the characteristics of metabolic disorders described above than to the nature of psychopathology.

In view of the above comparative discussion on metabolic and psychopathological disorders, is there, then, a principle that can be synthesized

from the many differences between these disorders that characterizes the essential nature of psychopathology? Recall that one needs to account for the fact that the biological disturbance in many psychopathologies is (a) of low-magnitude with respect to normal values, (b) variable with respect to its intensity, suggesting a constantly fluctuating vulnerability, and (c) inducible by particular drugs or environmental stressors.

One conception that encompasses these points is to view many forms of psychopathology as disorders of complex CNS functional systems. An enzymatic deficiency operating directly or indirectly to affect a biogenic amine neurotransmitter system serves as a heuristic example. Neurotransmitter systems have many component parts, and these components are regulated by a complex network of interactive feedback circuits (for more detail on the nature of this form of regulation, see Depue et al., 1979). The major goal of the feedback system is to maintain a dynamic steady-state (a kind of ever-vascillating homeostasis) in the transmitter system.

The functional integrity of such dynamic systems can theoretically be rendered vulnerable by any alteration in one of the component parts, such as an enzyme's activity. This may be true even if the alteration were only of low magnitude, because the alteration is expected to account for only an increased vulnerability in the functional system. That is, the altered component may be viewed as a biological bias in a functional system. The extent of the influence of the bias on the rest of the system under *nonstress* conditions will probably vary as a function of individual differences in (a) direct genetic influence on the biased variable, (b) the functional properties (both genetically and environmentally determined) of the other components of the system, and (c) the corrective activity of other CNS pathways and hormones. The range of individual differences in these three modulating influences is probably great, and this range may contribute directly to the broad range in phenotypic intensity so evident in psychopathology. Moreover, one would expect the phenotypes to extend in their lower values into the normal phenotypic range, thereby suggesting a quantitative definition of disorder.

The fact that many psychopathologies are episodic, and that episodes can be induced by drugs and stress, indicate that phenotypic exacerbations may occur when the biological demands on the vulnerable system exceed its adaptive capacity.

Certainly, the drugs that induce episodes tax the functional properties of CNS neurotransmitter systems (e.g., Charney et al., 1981; Post & Kopanda, 1976). Times of exacerbation may occur because, as discussed above, they coincide with a period of increased biological vulnerability of the system owing to factors endogenous to the bias or to other components of the system, and/or because of intensive, prolonged periods of stress.

Such speculative models are becoming less fanciful as the new field of behavioral neurochemistry expands. There is now evidence that supports at least the thrust of these speculations (Barchas et al., 1975; Stolk & Nisula, 1979). This research investigates the effects of stress on the functioning of genetically variant enzymes used in biogenic amine systems. For instance, Barchas et al. (1975) have shown that inbred rat strains differ with respect to the rate of stress-induced increases in phenylethanolamine N-methyltransferase (PNMT), the adrenal medullary enzyme that converts norepinephrine to epinephrine. After stress is applied, a ten-fold difference in PNMT level across the five inbred strains results. The strain with high baseline PNMT activity shows the greatest stress-induced increase in PNMT. This is a remarkable finding because PNMT normally shows only a two-fold within-animal increase over 20 to 50 days during stress conditions. The significance of such findings is that there may be genetically influenced differences in enzyme properties that result in stress-induced enzyme activity variation across individuals. In the case of PNMT, such differences could result in variation in the amount of norepinephrine and epinephrine secreted from the adrenal medulla under stress. If such genetically determined differences also occur in biogenic amine systems of the CNS, both peripheral and central amine systems could influence long-term response to a variety of stressors. Could it be, then, that low enzyme activity decreases the adaptive capacity of a functional system when it is placed under heavy demand by long-term stressors?

Research Strategies and the Nature of Psychopathology

Thus far, we have explored the nature of psychopathological disorders and found it to be different from that of the metabolic disorders in several significant ways. We now evaluate whether the nature of psychopathology, as we have derived it, is currently being investigated in the most effective manner possible. One way this may be accomplished is first to outline the basic elements of a typical study in psychopathology research, and then to comment on those elements critically. Because each element is plagued with difficulties arising from the nature of psychopathology, we suggest that future research will need to confront several major problems inherent in this nature before more powerful research may be achieved.

Three Elements of Psychopathology Studies

1. SAMPLE SELECTION

Most investigators select research samples on the basis of phenotypic features. Until the development of DSM-III, with the exception of a few research groups, diagnoses were (and often still are) made on the basis of these features without reference to a recognized set of diagnostic rules or criteria. In addition, the selected number of subjects in both the psychopathology and the control groups is usually small, often below 30, too often below 20.

This form of sample selection arises from the framework of many metabolic diseases. It is rational to select in this fashion if the type of disorder studied has a stable set of symptoms that are: (a) distinctly different from the normal phenotype, and (b) directly traceable to pathophysiology. One can expect that the small group of selected individuals will constitute a fairly homogeneous group with respect to phenotype, biological disturbance, and etiology.

In psychopathology, however, selection of a research sample on the basis of phenotype leads to groups with biologic, etiologic, and even phenotypic heterogeneity. Psychopathology research has demonstrated this many times. Consider the problems. Research team A selects a research sample of 30 individuals who probably cluster into several subgroups on practically any psychological or biological measure obtained. Hence, no general finding occurs across the sample: some patients show a deficit, others do not. Moreover, because sampling error is rather large with samples of 30 or less, there is little likelihood that results from a similar-sized sample selected by research team B will correspond to the results of research team A. The sample selected by team B will be comprised of different subgroups than the sample of team A.

How many times in psychopathology have new, exciting findings been reported, only to be irreplicable or only partially replicable by other research teams?

2. RESEARCH DESIGN

The metabolic-disease model provides a framework in which psychopathological defects are expected to be stable and distinct in nature. Accordingly, the large majority of studies of psychological and biological variables in psychopathology have looked for the big deficit. In psychology, this is represented by the search for *the* cognitive deficit in schizophrenia; in psychiatry, by the search for *the* highly deficient metabolite of neurotransmitters. As we have seen, however, deficits in psychopathology are subtle in nature. The search for deficits, moreover, often involves the use of static measures, where the level of a variable is measured at one time. This form of measurement, of course, does not take into account variability over time as we discussed it above. Even in cases where measures do reflect dynamic activity of the variable of interest, only rarely is the study designed to manipulate or challenge the system in which the variable "resides." And yet, the functional nature of psychopathological deficits would strongly suggest the more widespread use of research protocols that challenge the adaptive integrity of functional systems if deficits in these systems are to be detected (Depue & Kleiman, 1979; Gershon, 1978).

3. STATISTICAL ANALYSES

In psychopathology research, statistical analyses are generally comprised of group comparisons, where small groups of psychopathological and control subjects are employed. It is not common, especially but not exclusively in psychology, to explore the data in detail for meaningful subgroups. When group comparisons are made on highly heterogeneous groups, statistical tests, like the t-test, have little power to detect differences: there is generally too much within/group variability, especially in the psychopathology group, in comparison to the between-group difference to reject the null hypothesis. Indeed, the ability to detect a real difference will vary inversely as a function of heterogeneity in the psychopathology sample. Buchsbaum and Rieder (1979) recently demonstrated via computer simulation of sampling from a psychopathology population that as long as heterogeneity exists, the only remedy to the statistical test-

power problem would be to increase sample size so greatly (e.g., $N = 100$ or more for each of the psychopathology *and* control groups) that scientific research in psychopathology would become both unmanageable, in terms of the number of subjects required, and too costly.

We are not likely to solve these problems by running more and more studies with larger and larger samples. The research problems seem conceptual rather than logistical. We must come face to face with two major problems inherent in the nature of psychopathology before our studies yield maximum fruit. These two problems are heterogeneity (both phenotypic and biologic) within categories, and the functional nature of psychobiological disturbance. In recent years, research strategies have begun to emerge to meet these problems.

Problems Inherent in the Nature of Psychopathology and Evolving Research Strategies

1. HETEROGENEITY

Three forms of heterogeneity have led to their own unique research strategies. These three forms are phenotypic heterogeneity with categories, a range in phenotypic intensity, and biological heterogeneity.

Phenotypic heterogeneity. Until recently, the reliability of psychiatric diagnosis was notoriously poor (Spitzer & Fliess, 1974). Indeed, throughout the 1960s and early 1970s, many investigators called for the abolishment of the classification system altogether. Fortunately, cooler heads prevailed, and an effort to ameliorate the system's deficiencies began in the mid-1970s. It is interesting that most of the blame for the unreliability of psychiatric diagnosis was placed on method variables, such as interviewing procedures and the diagnostic process. There is no doubt that these variables play a critical role in determining the reliability of psychiatric diagnoses. We suggest, however, that these variables attain especially high significance in psychiatric diagnosis because of the nature of psychopathological disorders: namely, phenotypic heterogeneity. In psychopathological disorders, there is an absence of a standard, clearly definable, stable set of symptoms across individuals in a category. Moreover, there is an overlap of symptoms across categories. Both of these problems render the diagnostic process in psychopathology especially difficult. Hence, a taxonomy based on phenotype proposed by Kraepelin (1921) using the framework of the metabolic-disease model does not provide a strong concordance with the nature of psychopathology. One way that new efforts to improve diagnostic procedures may be viewed, then, is as an attempt to increase diagnostic reliability within the limits imposed by phenotypic heterogeneity. Within this framework, one can better appreciate the focus on method variables, and more tolerantly evaluate the sometimes modest improvements in reliability.

Much of the method error in diagnostic disagreement has been attributed to: (a) a lack of structure of the clinical interview, allowing the information obtained to vary greatly as a function of both state factors and of the theoretical orientation of the interviewer; and (b) an absence of a set of diagnostic criteria and rules to guide the use of interview material in the diagnostic decision-making process. The first source of error can be remedied without direct concern for phenotypic heterogeneity. The remedy for the second source of error, however, represents a direct attempt to ameliorate the effects of phenotypic heterogeneity on the diagnostic process.

For the remedy for the first source of error, several standardized structured interview schedules have been developed. One such interview, the Schedule for the Affective Disorders and Schizophrenia, or SADS (Spitzer & Endicott, 1977), was initially used with psychiatric inpatients and outpatients; more recently, it has been employed in psychiatric epidemiological research (Weissman & Myers, 1978). The SADS provides the full set of questions necessary to make a clinical diagnosis for a number of psychopathological disorders.

Developed along with the SADS are the Research Diagnostic Criteria, or RDC (Spitzer, Endicott, & Robins, 1978). The RDC represent a set of criteria and diagnostic rules for making a number of psychopathology diagnoses. The RDC may be seen as an attempt to reduce the effects of phenotypic heterogeneity on the diagnostic process. First, whereas a set number of symptoms are required in order to give a particular diagnosis, there is no standard set that each patient must meet. A variable set of symptoms across individuals within a category is tolerated, as long as a sufficient number of symptoms is manifested. Second, the RDC reduce the symptom overlap error resulting from inclusion in a category of individuals who have a disorder that shares common symptoms with the disorder under study. In order to qualify for a particular diagnosis, an individual cannot qualify for a disorder that has similar symptoms. For example, an individual can qualify for a straight diagnosis of schizophrenia if he or she does not qualify for a diagnosis of affective disorder.

When the SADS and RDC have been used together, diagnostic reliabilities for the major psychiatric categories have increased substantially, and this is true whether diagnoses have been derived from patients' current episodes (James & May, 1981; Overall & Hollister, 1979; Spitzer et al., 1978), or from an assessment of an individual's psychiatric features over a number of years (lifetime diagnoses) (Andreasen et al., 1981; Mazure & Gershon, 1979).

This initial success has encouraged others to develop additional structured interview schedules and diagnostic criteria. The Renard Diagnostic Interview (RDI) developed at Washington University is particularly noteworthy because it was constructed so that nonpsychiatric professionals or lay interviewers (i.e., interviewers without previous training in psychology or psychiatry) after one week of training could obtain interviews that provide diagnoses (using the Renard Diagnostic System; Feighner, Robins, & Guze, 1972) both reliably and validly. Early reports have been encouraging (Helzer et al., 1981) and have laid the groundwork for the development of a similar interview for epidemiological purposes (the National Institute of Mental Health Diagnostic Interview Schedule; Robins et al., 1981). In view of the great expense in using professional interviewers in large-scale research projects, the construction of lay-administered interviews must be viewed as a significant development. Equally significant is the fact that these basically research-oriented systems have greatly influenced the form of the clinical manual for the current classification system in psychopathology (DSM-III; American Psychiatric Association, 1980). There are few higher goals in psychopathology than the existence of an interactive exchange between research and clinical activities.

There are other ways in which researchers have attempted to reduce or ameliorate phenotypic heterogeneity. More precisely, they have attempted to delimit phenotypic heterogeneity in order to derive more homogeneous subgroups of patients. The rationale underlying subtyping on the basis of phenotype follows from the metabolic disease model: symptom differences are expected to reflect biological, or even etiological, differences. For example, it has been shown that when affective disorders are subdivided into two groups, one characterized by both manic and depressive episodes (bipolar) and one by depressive episodes only (unipolar), the former manifest psychomotor retardation and hypersomnia in the depressed phase, while the latter show psychomotor agitation and hyposomnia (Depue & Monroe, 1978a, 1979). The discrimiation of bipolar and unipolar cases on the basis of these symptoms is not perfect, but it is very good (85 to 100 percent discrimination). Moreover, there are some data that suggest that the psychomotor and sleep differences observed in these two groups may be related to the functional properties of dopamine and a norepinephrine-serotonin system, respectively (Depue & Evans, 1981). Thus, the unipolar-bipolar distinction may be a useful phenotypic subtyping system that has a grounding in biology.

There are too many examples of subtyping systems based on phenotype in psychopathology to review them here. Some of them are only in experimental stages (Andreasen et al., 1981; Depue, 1976), whereas others are used frequently (Depue & Monroe, 1978a, 1979). In all of these systems, however, one major difficulty generally persists. Even after phenotypically homogeneous subtypes are formed, the subtype system still has less than perfect predictive validity. That is, the individuals in any one subgroup still exhibit heterogeneity with respect to family history, drug response, clinical course, prognosis, and/or just about any psychological or biological variable measured. Our recent reviews of the unipolar-bipolar distinction strongly illustrated this point with respect to treatment response (Depue & Monroe, 1978a, 1979). And this is in spite of the fact that discrimination of the polar subgroups on the basis of certain phenotypic features is quite good. This example strongly indicates that, in psychopathology, *phenotypic homogeneity does not ensure etiology homogeneity* (Buchsbaum & Rieder, 1979; Weiner, 1977).

Is, then, the Kraepelinian classification system workable or has the metabolic model led us astray? One recent attempt to deal with the heterogeneity problem is to use a taxonomy based on other diagnostic characters in combination with phenotype. The basic strategy is to use phenotype to assign patients to a major category (e.g., depression, schizophrenia), and then to use a diagnostic character not based on phenotype to further subdivide

the major category. The attempt here is to use alternative diagnostic characters that may have a more direct relation to etiology.

We proposed one example of this multiple-character diagnostic approach in relation to the unipolar-bipolar distinction in affective disorders (Depue & Monroe, 1978a). The distinction had typically been defined solely on the basis of phenotype (presence or absence of a manic episode) ever since Leonhard (1957) proposed the distinction. Based on phenotype, however, the distinction achieved only moderately high predictive validity (Depue & Monroe, 1978a). Therefore, we proposed a genetic taxonomy of affective disorders. In this system, phenotype is used to assign patients to the affective disorders category. Beyond that point, the system employs a familial definition of polarity, where family history of affective disorder serves as one index of classification. Thus, along with phenotype behavior, the family history of the individual (i.e., presence or absence of manic or hypomanic disorder in first-degree relatives) becomes the determining criterion on which polarity is based. Phenotypic expression *by itself* is therefore not the determining factor and may, in fact, be variable within a polar group. For instance, a patient having depressive episodes only (unipolar phenotype) but a bipolar family history would be assigned to the bipolar group along with patients who actually have a bipolar phenotype. Some evidence indicates that this diagnostic system may have better predictive validity than the system using phenotype alone (Depue & Monroe, 1978a). (Other multiple-character systems exist, but these employ biological variables. They are therefore discussed below under biological heterogeneity.)

Range of phenotypic intensity. At the turn of this century, psychopathologists noted the existence of a range of phenotypic intensities associated with psychopathological disorders (e.g., Kraepelin, 1921). For the most part, however, this phenomenon was neglected until more recent years. Renewed interest in this area stems from the implication of the model for common disorders: that a range in phenotypic intensity is associated with a range in genetic risk for disorder (Shields, Heston, & Gottesman, 1975). Many previous genetic studies had defined disorder only as the full syndromal expression of biological disturbance (Depue & Monroe, 1978a). This definition is perhaps reasonable for genetic studies of many metabolic disorders because of their restricted range of phenotypic intensity. In psychopathology, however, only counting full syndromal cases fails to recognize the many milder, subsyndromal individuals that exist in a proband's first-degree relatives. Because these subsyndromal phenotypes presumably reflect the action of the gene(s) involved in the disorder under study, failure to count these individuals among the afflicted relatives may render genetic model fitting meaningless. Thus, behavior geneticists would like to be able to identify individuals across the entire range of phenotypic intensity so that modes of genetic transmission can be estimated.

Most of the interest in phenotypic range has occurred with respect to schizophrenia and affective disorders. In schizophrenia, a group of behavioral forms of mild intensity have been postulated as being associated with full syndromal process schizophrenia (Heston, 1970; Planansky, 1972; Rosenthal et al., 1968; Shields et al., 1975). There is evidence that some of these mild forms bear some genetic relation to process schizophrenia (Rosenthal, 1975). Moreover, when Heston (1970) included these less intense forms in his analyses of previous familial, twin, and adoption method studies, for the first time data were consistent across methods in suggesting a simple, dominant gene model for schizophrenia. However, there is rather extensive phenotypic heterogeneity in the group with mild phenotypes, and there is little consensus as yet as to which phenotypic forms ought to be included in this schizophrenic spectrum (Shields et al., 1975). Thus, the conclusion reached by Shields et al. (1975) in their review of this problem still holds true today:

> In the absence of good objective criteria for schizoid character and other "borderline" conditions and the consequent lack of adequate epidemiological and family studies of such conditions, it cannot be claimed that we have an improved phenotype for population genetic studies [of schizophrenia]. [p. 191]

There has been more success in relating subsyndromal and full syndromal forms of affective disorders, and this is particularly the case with the relation between cyclothymia and full syndromal bipolar manic-depressive disorder. Kraepelin (1921) suggested these relationships six to seven decades ago, but it was not until very recently that research demonstrated that subsyndromal forms do lie on a continuum with full syndromal forms of disorder.

Recent longitudinal research on cyclothymia by Akiskal, Djenderdejian, Rosenthall, and Khani (1977) and Akiskal, Khani, and Scott-Strauss (1979) has provided support for the continuum model with respect to bipolar spectrum disorder. First, the subsyndromal behavior of well-defined outpatient cyclothymics was qualitatively similar to that of full syndromal bipolar disorder. Indeed, cyclothymia was found to merge imperceptibly with the Bipolar II[3] (and sometimes Bipolar I) form of bipolar disorder. The major reason that cases were not assigned the diagnosis of definite and full bipolar disorder was less a function of the quality of symptoms than a failure to meet the sustained duration criterion. Second, an equivalent rate of bipolar disorder was found in the first- and second-degree relatives of cyclothymic and Bipolar I patients. Third, an equivalent proportion of cyclothymics and Bipolar I patients experienced induction of hypomanic episodes by tricyclic antidepressants. This form of induction has often been thought of as a marker for the bipolar genotype (Akiskal et al., 1977, 1979; Bunney, 1978). And fourth, in a two- to three-year follow-up period, 35 percent of Akiskal et al.'s (1977) cyclothymics evidenced more severe episodes, indicating that cyclothymia is characterized by an increased risk for developing full syndromal bipolar disorder. Indeed, the risk might be higher, but most patients began receiving medication. Whether the risk for developing full syndromal episodes is as high for the entire cyclothymic population as it was for the outpatient cyclothymics studied by Akiskal is unknown. Nevertheless, it is findings such as those above, and data from others showing cyclothymic behavioral disturbance as a precursor to full syndromal bipolar disorder (Kestenbaum, 1979; Waters, 1979a, 1979b), that led to the inclusion of cyclothymia in the affective disorders section of DSM-III.

In view of the support for a continuum between cyclothymia and Bipolar I disorder, we rea-

---

[3]Bipolar I disorder is characterized by both manic and depressive episodes that require treatment and usually hospitalization. Bipolar II disorder is characterized by a family history of mania or hypomania and requires treatment and often hospitalization for depressive episodes; however, where manic or hypomanic symptoms exist, they have not led to hospitalization. Bipolar III disorder is characterized by a family history of mania or hypomania and requires treatment for depressive episodes; however, no manic or hypomanic symptoms exist in the individual's clinical history (Depue & Monroe, 1978a, 1978b, 1979).

soned that perhaps the behavioral and episodic characteristics of Bipolar I disorder could be used to identify very mild cases of cyclothymia (Depue et al., 1981). This would represent a valuable approach because the onset of bipolar disorder generally assumes a mild, cyclothymic form (Akiskal et al., 1979; Depue et al., 1981; Waters, 1979a, 1979b). Only later in life do full syndromal episodes occur in most persons. Thus, this approach has the potential of identifying persons early in life who are manifesting only mild cyclothymia, but who are at increased risk for developing full syndromal bipolar disorder. Because these individuals are identified on the basis of behavior, we have termed our approach the behavioral high-risk paradigm (Depue et al., 1981).

The general framework for the behavioral paradigm as applied to bipolar spectrum disorder is straightforward. The onset of bipolar subsyndromal behavioral disturbance (cyclothymia) usually occurs during early or mid-adolescence (14 years of age on the average) (Akiskal et al., 1977, 1979; Campbell, 1953). For individuals experiencing subsyndromal onset, two outcomes seem possible: (a) the continuation of cyclothymic disorder at similar, reduced, or increased levels of severity, or (b) the onset of some form of full syndromal bipolar disorder (i.e., Bipolar I, II, or III disorder), where initial untreated episodes occur at about 24 years of age on the average (Akiskal et al., 1977, 1979; Depue & Monroe, 1978a, 1978b, 1979). If the ages of sybsyndromal and full syndromal onsets are considered together, this yields an approximately ten-year identification period, during which individuals comprising the subsyndromal risk pool could be potentially identifiable on the basis of full subsyndromal behavioral and episodic features. Of course, the goal in using the paradigm is to identify individuals as early in the identification period as possible.

The paradigm was operationalized in the form of a self-report inventory (the General Behavior Inventory or GBI), which incorporates the behavioral and episodic features of full syndromal disorder described at subsyndromal intensities. The GBI was then subjected to five validation studies using different forms of nontest criteria as the basis of evaluating validity (Depue et al., 1981). The general thrust of these studies was to demonstrate that the group identified by the GBI would "perform" on the nontest criteria in a manner in keeping with that hypothesized for individuals having bipolar affective disorder. The studies were con-

sistent in demonstrating that the disorder of the GBI-identified group is related to bipolar disorder, as reflected in the subjects' own psychiatric diagnoses and clinical characteristics, in their familial disorders, in their roommates' descriptions, and in their behavioral variability over time. Moreover, the psychometric efficiency of the GBI in identifying the cyclothmic group was excellent when a two-cutting-score system was used within a research context.

Thus, the broad range of phenotypic intensity in psychopathology presents difficult questions concerning the value of different definitions of a particular disorder. Researchers are finding it necessary to give up the more comfortable definition of disorder based on full syndromal phenotypic features. Indeed, they are attempting to define disorder more broadly. Just which type of diagnostic character will best identify the full range of intensities is currently unclear. Schizophrenic spectrum disorders have not been identified well when defined by phenotype, whereas mild forms of bipolar disorder do seem to be identifiable on the basis of behavior. Nevertheless, it may be that biological variables will be much better as indices of an individual's risk for psychopathology because they are closer than behavior to the action of genes involved in disorder (Shields et al., 1975). We now turn to this possibility.

Biological heterogeneity. Our above discussion of the elements of the typical group comparison paradigm in psychopathology research raised the critical issue of biological heterogeneity. Biological heterogeneity within categories makes it difficult to find consistent results across research teams. It also makes it difficult for one research team to study a particular biological disturbance across samples: the percentage of patients in any one randomly selected sample who manifest the disturbance will vary greatly, especially if sample sizes are small (Buchsbaum & Rieder, 1979). As we also noted above, thus far, subtyping on the basis of phenotype has not resulted in significant increases in biological homogeneity within subgroups. Therefore, when negative results in a biological variable occur after phenotypic subtyping, one is still uncertain how to interpret this finding. It could be due to the absence of a biological difference between subgroups or subgroups and controls, or it could result from biological heterogeneity.

In response to this enormous problem, which

was not forseen by the metabolic disease model, psychopathologists have been developing several new research strategies. The common theme behind these strategies is to rely more on biological rather than phenotypic taxonomies. By defining subgroups on the basis of a biological variable (or on endophenotype, as opposed to the exophenotype of behavior; Depue et al., 1981), one is subdividing directly at the source of heterogeneity. In addition, because an endophenotype is closer to the action of genes, subtypes based on biological characters may be more likely to correspond to etiological differences (Shields et al., 1975).

An example of this approach is a biochemical-pharmacological taxonomy applied to depressive disorders (e.g., Charney et al., 1981; Schildkraut, 1978). This taxonomy is an elaboration of the catecholamine hypothesis of depression, which states that depression is characterized by a deficiency in norepinephrine in certain CNS pathways (Schildkraut, 1965). Subsequent research on this hypothesis measured the urinary concentration of MHPG, the major metabolite of norepinephrine (Depue & Evans, 1981). The concentration of urinary MHPG determined over time, say 24 hours, reflects the activity or turnover of norepinephrine during that period. Early results showed that depressed patients vary considerably in their 24-hour concentrations of urinary MHPG. Additional work demonstrated that a subgroup of depressed patients, mainly bipolar manic-depressives, were characterized by low MHPG excretion levels (Schildkraut, 1978). There is also some evidence to suggest that schizoaffective depressed patients have low MHPG levels (Schildkraut, 1978), which is of interest because of the possible relation between schizoaffective and bipolar disorders (Pope et al., 1980; Pope & Lipinski, 1978). On the other hand, nonendogenous-unipolar depressives, and a portion of endogenous-unipolar depressives, were characterized by normal or high levels of MHPG. Hence, this represented the first potential biological criterion for the subtyping of depressive disorders.

Stimulated by these findings, several investigators evaluated the predictive validity of the MHPG subtype system. To accomplish this, the ability of pretreatment MHPG level to predict clinical response to specific antidepressant drugs was studied. There appears to be strong support for a low pretreatment MHPG concentration predicting a good treatment response to imipramine. Some evidence suggested that high pretreatment MHPG level predicts a good treatment response to amitriptyline, but results here are inconsistent (Charney et al., 1981). Too few studies have been conducted with other tricyclic antidepressants to draw any firm conclusions about the association between pretreatment MHPG concentration and outcome.

At this point, then, outside of the relation between low pretreatment MHPG concentrations and a good clinical response to imipramine, the MHPG system is limited to a research application. In view of the complexity of pathophysiology in affective disorders, it may be fruitful to use several biological variables together to define subgroups. For instance, Schildkraut found in an initial study that depressed patients who are characterized by low MHPG concentrations also tend to have significantly reduced platelet MAO activity (Schildkraut, 1978). These findings not only add further support to the MHPG subtype system, but they also raise the possibility that multivariate prediction schemes may be more effective than single-variable schemes. Underlying the multivariate model is the concept that one basic defect causes pleiotropic effects on a number of variables, and that by properly weighting and combining these effects, one can uncover the underlying mechanism (Elston & Namboodiri, 1980).

Classification on the basis of biological variables may be applied to other research strategies in addition to studying pathophysiology in full syndromal patients. In genetic studies, one could study the pedigrees of probands selected on the basis of a biological variable, such as MAO. This strategy could be used in two ways (Gershon, 1978). First, if a biological variable is known to be a marker for a certain disorder, the variable can be used in the pedigree to test a genetic hypothesis concerning the mode of transmission of the disorder. Alternatively, if the goal is to determine whether a biological variable serves as a marker for a particular disorder, the variable should show nonindependent assortment with the illness within pedigrees. In a test of this second alternative, Gershon and his colleagues studied the pedigrees of probands selected on the basis of their activity levels on one of several enzymes involved in catecholamine synthesis and metabolism, including MAO (Gershon, 1978; Gershon et al., 1980). Unfortunately, all enzymes assorted independently of affective disorder in relatives, thereby not qualifying as genetic markers of the disorder. It may be that the multivariate approach, mentioned directly above, to identifying "cases" among relatives is needed in this strategy. When Elston applied it to other disorders that also have complex phenotypes and pathophysiologies, correct identification of "cases" in relatives increased dramatically and allowed determination of mode of transmission (Elston & Namboodiri, 1980).

Thus, genetic researchers have dealt with the problems of biologic heterogeneity directly by selecting probands on the basis of a biological character. This approach, perhaps especially within a multivariate framework, represents a very powerful strategy to determining which biological variables should be combined to best identify vulnerable relatives, and which genetic hypotheses seem to best fit the data.

Finally, in recent years the biological classification approach has been developed into a biological high-risk paradigm. In this paradigm, a biological variable that is hypothesized to be related to psychological deviation is used to identify individuals from the general population. Biological variables chosen for this strategy should typically be strongly geneticaly influenced (such as enzymes) and stable over time (Buchsbaum, Coursey, & Murphy, 1980; Gershon et al., 1980). Also, the expectation of an association between the variable and psychological disturbance would typically come from the variable's association with the pathophysiology of a particular disorder, such as MAO and schizophrenia.

This paradigm has several advantages over other strategies used in psychopathology: (a) it directly avoids the problem of biological heterogeneity; (b) it tests hypotheses about a biological variable and its psychological correlates; (c) it avoids unreliable diagnoses in the identification of high-risk subjects; and (d) it allows analysis of the hypothesized expression of the biological variable in the normal as well as the pathological range (Buchsbaum, Coursey, & Murphy, 1980).

The biological high-risk paradigm has successfully employed MAO as the index of risk (e.g., Buchsbaum, Coursey, & Murphy, 1976; Haier et al., 1980). This work is too extensive to be reviewed here, so the interested reader is referred to the special issue on MAO of Schizophrenia Bulletin (1980, Vol. 6, No. 2). Suffice it here to say that low, and to some extent high, levels of MAO activity in general-population subjects and their first-degree relatives is associated with psychological disturbance, particularly of a legal and affective nature (Buchsbaum et al., 1976). Moreover, when MAO activity

and a stimulus intensity modulation measure (average evoked potential) are used together, the group with the highest psychological disturbance (low MAO = stimulus augmentation) is more precisely identified (Haier et al., 1980). Moreover, use of the two variables together also improves prediction of future affective disorder episodes in these subjects, the low MAO-augmenting group having the greatest number of individuals reporting such episodes (Haier, Buchsbaum, & Murphy, 1980). Thus, again, a multivariate approach appears to augment significantly the identification rate of "cases" afforded by univariate analyses alone.

Overall, then, recent strategies for dealing with phenotypic and biologic heterogeneity provide the psychopathologist with new and powerful research tools. Some of these approaches are corrective in nature, such as the development of structured interviews and diagnostic criteria. Others represent totally new paradigms for doing research, such as the use of biological taxonomies and biological and behavioral high-risk paradigms. Even within these new paradigms, however, our thinking may still reflect the notions of the metabolic-disease model. We so often use one variable for typing subgroups or for defining disorder, as if one major variable exists that can provide these distinctions. As we discussed above, there are now several lines of evidence to suggest that a multivariate approach to these issues is warranted.

2. THE FUNCTIONAL NATURE OF PSYCHOPATHOLOGICAL DISORDERS

If psychopathological disorders are characterized by disturbances in CNS functional systems, such as neurotransmitter systems, the manner in which psychopathologists measure variables of interest is critical. Unlike the case of measurement in many metabolic disorders, where deficits are stable and distinct from normal, in psychopathology baseline measures (a measurement taken at one point in time) have not been as differentiating as measures that reflect the dynamic functioning of a system (Depue & Evans, 1981). For instance, urinary measures of cortisol (Carroll & Mendels, 1976; Depue & Kleiman, 1979) and urinary and cerebrospinal fluid measures of biogenic amine metabolites (Depue & Evans, 1981) are more informative when they reflect accumulation over time. Accumulation measures reflect the functional activity of a variable. Thus, in the absence of large deficits in psychopathology, baseline measures are not likely to be as meaningful as measures of the functional properties of a system. Note that this is probably the case even at the level of enzyme measurement. Enzyme activity is a measure of functional activity: the amount of substrate metabolized per unit time. With no major enzyme deficiency as yet identified in psychopathology, we are left to ponder the functional implications for a system of a partially deficient enzyme such as the 25 percent reduction in MAO activity in schizophrenia (Buchsbaum et al., 1980; Buchsbaum & Rieder, 1979; Murphy & Kahn, 1980).

A final point concerning measurement is particularly relevant to the high-risk paradigms discussed above (both behavioral and biological). It is quite possible that high-risk subjects will exhibit no or only mild psychobiological disturbance with baseline *or* dynamic measures. This is because, if a bias in a biological system does exist in a high-risk individual, it is less likely to result in more extensive, functional disturbance in the larger system in which it resides. Thus, how can we detect minor differences between high-risk subjects and controls? There are two potential strategies for this problem. First, the measure used should be highly sensitive to small individual differences. This will allow detection of between-group and subgroup differences if they exist (Depue & Kleiman, 1979). Second, a challenge protocol, where the adaptive capacity of the functional system of interest is challenged pharmacologically or environmentally (laboratory stress), may be employed to evoke a disturbance that would otherwise be undetectable (Gershon, 1978).

We applied both of these strategies recently in studying our subjects who are at risk for bipolar affective disorder (Depue & Kleiman, 1979; in preparation). Using an indwelling catheter system and a constant blood-withdrawal pump, we were able to measure continuously a very sensitive index of cortisol functioning (free cortisol) over a three-hour period. Cortisol is of interest because its release is controlled by a tonic inhibitory pathway in the brain that uses norepinephrine as transmitter. The measure of interest was the slope of recovery of cortisol from venapuncture and from a mild math test. Note that a recovery measure directly reflects the functional integrity of the controlling inhibitory norepinephrine pathway: because full syndromal manic-depressives are characterized by a weak inhibitory influence, they oversecrete cortisol (Depue & Evans, 1981). Thus, if our cyclothymics also have an inhibitory system that operates

in a weak mode, the reinstatement of their inhibitory system after its release during stress should be slower than in controls. Hence, cyclothymic cortisol recovery to baseline following stress should be slower than in controls.

The interesting findings were that the most sensitive measure of cortisol (plasma-free cortisol) best demonstrated a difference in recovery between controls and high-risk subjects. Also, besides the level of accumulated cortisol over the 3 hours, the recovery measure was by far the most discriminating measure, which was not surprising in that the other measures did not reflect the functional activity of cortisol so clearly. In spite of all this planning, however, the results still reflected biological heterogeneity: 50 percent of the high-risk subjects fell beyond the normal range of values, whereas 33 percent were highly deviant (very slow recovery). What was of benefit, though, was that the recovery measure was sensitive enough to separate all subjects, including controls, finely. This allowed the analysis of interesting associations between cortisol values and clinically relevant variables collected in interview.

The functional nature of psychopathological disorders implies that strong adaptive demands may originate from environmental challenge. This is a perspective on psychopathology not provided by the metabolic-disease model. Therefore, there exists a rapidly growing literature that investigates the associations between stress and psychopathology. We, thus, highlight this literature separately below only to outline the major concepts and research strategies evolving in this area.

3. PSYCHOSOCIAL STRESSORS AND PSYCHOPATHOLOGY

Laboratory induction procedures for demonstrating differences in response to stressors ultimately must reflect processes that are generalizable to the individual's psychosocial environment. Consequently, an alternative strategy for delineating predictors of disorder is to study naturally occurring socioenvironmental factors and their implications for psychological functioning and psychiatric disorder. Subsumed under the general concept of stress, this approach to studying psychopathology has become increasingly popular during the past 15 years. A variety of psychosocial phenomena have been studied, ranging from minor daily hassles (Kanner et al., 1981), through less common stressful life events (Dohrenwend &

Dohrenwend, 1974, 1981; Rabkin & Struening, 1976), and ultimately to extremely severe psychosocial circumstances (Gleser, Green, & Winget, 1981; Kinston & Rosser, 1974).

Most of this research has been conceptualized within the volumninous research literature on stressful life events and disease. Although it is a promising area of inquiry, the life-events approach has been increasingly criticized on methodolgical and conceptual grounds (Andrews & Tennant, 1978; Cleary, 1980, 1981; Brown & Harris, 1978; Dohrenwend et al., 1978; Jenkins, Hurst, & Rose, 1979; Lei & Skinner, 1980; Mechanic, 1975, Monroe, 1982, in press; Mueller, Edwards, & Yarvis, 1977; Neugebauer, 1981; Perkins, in press; Rabkin & Struening, 1976; Ross & Mirowsky, 1979; Shrout, 1981; Tennant, Bebbington, & Hurry, 1981; Thoits, 1981; Wershow & Reinhart, 1974; Yager et al., 1981). Furthermore, there has been a lack of attention in this area to particular issues concerning the nature of psychopathology. This is illustrated most clearly by the fact that the majority of life-events studies typically have examined life events in relation to relatively undifferentiated psychiatric distress. Therefore, we limit our discussion to problems concerning disorder as the outcome variable.

The conception of event-induced vulnerability following from earlier life-events work has generally ignored possible differences between various psychopathological disorders. This seems to stem from the postulation of one general mechanism to account for the effects of stress on disorder. "It is postulated that life change events, by evoking adaptive efforts by the human organism that are faulty in kind and duration, lower 'bodily resistance' and enhance the probability of disease occurrence" (Holmes & Masuda, 1974).[4] This hypothesis is based on the notion of the "weakest link" in biology producing dysfunction under stress (Selye, 1976). Within this perspective, groups of disorders have been considered *en masse* as having some common etiologic component stemming from event-induced vulnerability. Although several alternative conceptions of more specific stressor-disorder associations have historically been advanced (Alexander, 1950; Engel, 1968; Hinkle, 1974), the general concept that stress in general increases vulnerability to episodes across disorders has prevailed empirically (Mason, 1975; Selye,

1975). In addition to the issue of the specificity of stressor-disorder associations, studies have not made fine distinctions in outcome variables, such as onset of disorder and clinical course of disorder.

Problems in defining and assessing stressor-disorder associations and outcome variables are factors hindering progress in understanding psychosocial contributions to disorder. Heterogeneity of disorder is an important issue here, and two points are most salient. First, attention to the specific type of disorder under study may help to clarify more specific event-disorder associations and to provide important information concerning the mediating processes involved (Slater & Depue, 1981). For example, in predicting relapse in schizophrenia, Brown and Harris (1978) found that diverse types of events were capable of precipitating florid symptomatology: the characteristic of the event that appeared to be most important for this relationship was that the event caused general emotional arousal (either of a positive or negative nature). In contrast, only particular types of events (negative, long-term threat) were significantly related to the onset of clinical depression. Hence, different events and characteristics of events may be predictive of different classes of disorder.

Second, life events may be differentially important for subgroups of certain diagnostic groupings. For instance, the unipolar-bipolar distinction may be important for clarifying socioenvironmental predictors of depression (Depue & Monroe, 1979). Alternatively, different psychosocial factors may be related to different subtypes of unipolar depression (Akiskal et al., 1979; Benjaminsen, 1981; Cooke, 1980) or to different symptom features of this disorder (e.g., the anxiety component of depressives; Brown & Prudo, 1981; Gersh & Fowles, 1979).

In light of the multifactorial nature of most disorders (Engel, 1977; Hinkle, 1974; Lipowski, 1977; Meehl, 1977), psychosocial factors may be of variable importance for even relatively homogeneous diagnostic groupings. For certain individuals, event-related stress may be *sufficient* but not necessary to *initiate* disorder. For other individuals, biological vulnerability factors may provide a sufficient contribution to evaluate in dysfunction. Again, research in the depressive disorders provides a good illustration. In view of the multiple social, psychological, and biological factors asso-

---

[4]The use of the term nonspecificity can often lead to a certain degree of confusion (see Lazarus, 1976). In the present usage, we are not referring to the nonspecificity of event-induced stress (stressor nonspecificity; see Seyle, 1976), but rather to a general (nonspecific) susceptibility to illness (Najman, 1980).

ciated with depression onset, it is likely that these factors vary in combination for any particular individual under study (Akiskal, 1979; Akiskal & McKinney, 1975). Thus, while life events may be important for particular individuals falling within this nosologic category, they may be irrelevant for others.

Other important issues in the stress literature concern the clinical course of disorder. Much of the research on life events and disorder has failed to distinguish between actual onset of disorder as opposed to fluctuations in symptomatology associated with the stages of a chronic clinical course. This is particularly true of the early work in this area, yet the majority of recent studies are subject to similar criticisms. Many studies confound acute and chronic conditions in the assessment of disorder. This results in attributing to stress the power to initiate onset in persons already experiencing chronic, albeit mild, disorder (i.e., Kobasa, 1979; Wyler, Masuda, & Holmes, 1971). And yet, it is unclear that similar mechanisms are operating in the initiation of acute onset as opposed to exacerbations in an ongoing disorder.

The importance of life events and psychosocial factors for the course of disorder poses another interesting and important, yet relatively neglected, issue (Monroe, 1982). The problem is that many psychopathological disturbances present with either a relatively chronic and/or cycling course of symptoms. Event assessment at one point in time yields very different results depending on the type of course studied. This was well demonstrated by Monroe (1982), who found that the importance of different classes of life events revealed different associations with follow-up symptoms depending upon the initial symptom status of the individual.

In all, then, research on psychosocial stress and psychopathology reflects problems resulting from the heterogeneity of the phenomena under investigation. The problems pertain to the importance of clarifying the psychosocial processes that eventually incur dysfunction, the particular types of dysfunction for which such processes are most relevant, and the type of outcome variable most appropriate to the question under study (onset versus clinical course features). One important extension of stress research would be in using high-risk research strategies. In view of the limited amount of variance commonly attributed to the role of psychosocial stressors in disorder, their role may be clarified through the prospective study of psychosocial influences on high-risk samples. The criteria for selection may vary with respect to the

particular question under study. For example, for studying *onset* of depressive disorder, family history (Winokur, 1979), biochemical (Buchsbaum et al., 1976), behavioral (Depue et al., 1981), or other psychosocial (e.g., divorce; Bloom, Asher, & White, 1978) parameters, may be useful for defining the group at risk. Alternatively, for studying clinical course relationships, psychosocial influences on maintenance and/or remission of disturbed groups — or relapse of recovered persons at risk for subsequent episodes — may provide useful strategies. Such approaches may provide more specific and relevant information concerning basic stressor-disorder associations.

Concluding Remarks

Conceptions of nature, whether of the physical world, societal structures, or man himself, are powerfully influenced by models that depend on time and place (Bronowski, 1973). It is easy to lose sight of the origins and assumptions inherent in our current models. They are readily adopted, almost with the attitude that they are timeless structures that only require further elaboration. We believe that this has occurred in psychopathology to some extent, where the metabolic model has been influential but not always helpful. Our hope therefore, is that this discussion has illuminated some of the inadequacies in applying some forms of the metabolic model to psychopathology, and that future research may converge on modified models of the nature of these disorders.

References

Akiskal, H. S. A biobehavioral approach to depression. In R. A. Depue (Ed.), *The psychobiology of the depressive disorders: Implications for the effects of stress.* New York: Academic Press, 1979.

Akiskal, H. S., Djenderdejian, A. H., Rosenthal, R. H., & Khani, M. K. Cyclothymic disorder: Validating criteria for inclusion in the bipolar affective group. *American Journal of Psychiatry*, 1977, **134**, 1,227–1,233.

Akiskal, H. S., Khani, M., & Scott-Strauss, A. Cyclothymic temperamental disorders. *Psychiatric Clinics of North America*, 1979, **2**, 527–554.

Akiskal, H. S., & McKinney, W. T., Jr. Overview of recent research in depression: Integration of two conceptual models into a comprehensive clinical frame. *Archives of General Psychiatry*, 1975, **32**, 285–305.

Akiskal, H. S., Rosenthal, R. H., Rosenthal, T. H., Kashgarian, M., Khani, M. K., & Pazantian, V. R. Differentiation of primary affective illness from situational, symptomatic, and secondary depressions. *Archives of General Psychiatry*, 1979, **36**, 635–643.

Alexander, F. *Psychosomatic medicine.* New York: Norton, 1950.

American Psychiatric Association. *Diagnostic and statistical manual of mental disorders*. (3rd ed.) Washington, D.C.: American Psychiatric Association, 1980.

Ananth, J., Solyom, L., Bryntwick, S., & Krishnappa, U. Chlorimipramine therapy for depressive-compulsive neurosis. *American Journal of Psychiatry*, 1979, **136**, 700–701.

Andreasen, N., Grove, W. M., Shapiro, R. W., Keller, M. B., Hirschfeld, R. M. A., & McDonald-Scott, P. Reliability of lifetime diagnosis. *Archives of General Psychiatry*, 1981, **38**, 400–407.

Andreasen, N. C., Olsen, S. A., Dennert, J. W., & Smith, M. R. Ventricular enlargement in schizophrenia: Relationship to positive and negative symptoms. *American Journal of Psychiatry*, 1982, **139**, 297–301.

Andreasen, N. C., Smith, M. R., Jacoby, C. G., Dennert, J. W., & Olsen, S. A. Ventricular enlargement in schizophrenia: Definition and prevalence. *American Journal of Psychiatry*, 1982, **139**, 292–296.

Andrews, G. & Tennant, C. Being upset and becoming ill: An appraisal of the relation between life events and physical illness. *Medical Journal of Australia*, 1978, **1**, 324–327.

Asberg, M., Thoren, P., Traskman, L., Bertilsson, L., & Ringberger, V. "Serotonin depression"—A biochemical subgroup within the affective disorders? *Science*, 1976, **191**, 478–480.

Baldessarini, R. J. The basis for amine hypotheses in affective disorders. *Archives of General Psychiatry*, 1975, **32**, 1,087–1,093.

Barchas, J. D., Ciaranello, R. D., Kessler, S., & Hamburg, D. A. Genetic aspects of catecholamine synthesis. In R. R. Fieve, D. Rosenthal, & H. Brill (Eds.), *Genetic research in psychiatry*. Baltimore: Johns Hopkins University Press, 1975.

Belmaker, R. H., Bracha, H. S., & Elstein, R. P. Platelet monoamine oxidase in affective illness and alcoholism. *Schizophrenia Bulletin*, 1980, **6**, 320–323.

Benjaminsen, S. Stressful life events preceding the onset of neurotic depression. *Psychological Medicine*, 1981, **11**, 369–378.

Bloom, B. L., Asher, S. J., & White, S. W. Marital disruption as a stressor: A review and analysis. *Psychological Bulletin*, 1978, **85**, 867–884.

Brenner, M. H. Influence of the social environment on psychopathology: The historic perspective. In J. E. Barrett (Ed.), *Stress and mental disorder*. New York: Raven, 1979.

Bronowski, J. *The ascent of man*. Boston: Little, Brown, 1973.

Brown, G. W. The social etiology of depression—London studies. In R. A. Depue (Ed.), *The psychobiology of the depressive disorders: Implications for the effects of stress*. New York: Academic Press, 1979.

Brown, G. W., & Harris, T. *Social origins of depression*. New York: Fire Press, 1978.

Brown, G. W., & Prado, R. Psychiatric disorder in a rural and an urban population: 1. Actiology of depression. *Psychological Medicine*, 1981, **11**, 581–599.

Buchsbaum, M. S., Coursey, R. D., & Murphy, D. L. The biochemical high-risk paradigm: Behavioral and familial correlates of low platelet monoamine oxidase. *Science*, 1976, **194**, 339–341.

Buchsbaum, M. S., Coursey, R. D., & Murphy, D. L. Schizophrenia and platelet monoamine oxidase: Research strategies. *Schizophrenia Bulletin*, 1980, **6**, 375–384.

Buchsbaum, M. S., & Rieder, R. Biologic heterogeneity and psychiatric research. *Archives of General Psychiatry*, 1979, **36**, 1,163–1,169.

Bunney, W. E., Jr. Psychopharmacology of the switch process in affective illness. In M. A. Lipton, A. DiMascio, K. F. Killam (Eds.), *Psychopharmacology: A generation of progress*. New York: Raven, 1978.

Bunney, W. E., Jr., R. M., Andersen, A. E., & Kopanda R. T. A neuronal receptor sensitivity mechanism in affective illness (A review of evidence). *Communications in Psychopharmacology*, 1977, **1**, 393–405.

Campbell, J. D. Manic-depressive disease: Clinical and psychiatric significance. Philadelphia: Lippincott, 1953.

Carroll, B. J., & Mendels, J. Neuroendocrine regulation in affective disorders. In E. J. Sachar (Ed.), *Hormones, behavior, and psychopathology*. New York: Raven, 1976.

Charney, D. S., Menkes, D. B., & Heninger, G. R. Receptor sensitivity and the mechanism of action of antidepressant treatment. *Archives of General Psychiatry*, 1981, **38**, 1,160–1,181.

Cleary, P. J. A checklist for life event research. *Journal of Psychosomatic Research*, 1980, **24**, 199–207.

Cleary, P. J. Problems of internal consistency and scaling in life event schedules. *Journal of Psychosomatic Research*, 1981, **25**, 309–320.

Cohen, D. J., Detlor, J., Young, J. G., & Shaywitz, B. A. Clonidine ameliorates Gilles de la Tourette's Syndrome. *Archives of General Psychiatry*, 1980, **37**, 1,350–1,360.

Cook, D. J. Conceptual and methodological considerations of the problems inherent in the specification of the simple event-syndrome link. In I. G. Savason & C. D. Spielberger (Eds.), *Stress and anxiety*, Vol. 7. Washington, D.C.: Hemisphere, 1980.

Coryell, W. & Tsuang, M. T. DSM-III schizophreniform disorder. *Archives of General Psychiatry*, 1982, **39**, 66–69.

Depue, R. A. An activity-withdrawal distinction in schizophrenia: Behavioral, clinical, brain damage, and neurophysiological correlates. *Journal of Abnormal Psychology*, 1976, **85**, 174–185.

Depue, R. A. (Ed.) *The psychology of the depressive disorders: Implications for the effects of stress*. New York: Academic Press, 1979.

Depue, R. A., & Evans, R. Psychology of depressive disorders: From pathophysiology to predisposition. In B. A. Maher (Ed.), *Progress in experimental personality research*. Vol. 10. New York: Academic Press, 1981.

Depue, R. A., & Kleiman, R. M. Free cortisol as a peripheral index of central vunerability to major forms of polar depressive disorders: Examing stress-biology interactions in subsyndromal high-risk persons. In R. A. Depue (Ed.), *The psychobiology of the depressive disorders: Implications for the effects of stress*. New York: Academic Press, 1979.

Depue, R. A., & Kleiman, R. M. Free cortisol functioning in persons at risk for bipolar affective disorder. In preparation.

Depue, R. A., & Monroe, S. M. The unipolar-bipolar distinction in the depressive disorders. *Psychological Bulletin*, 1978, 88, 1,001–1,030. (a)

Depue, R. A., & Monroe, S. M. Learned helplessness in the perspective of the depressive disorders: Conceptual and definitional issues. *Journal of Abnormal Psychology*, 1978, 87, 3–21. (b)

Depue, R. A., & Monroe, S. M. The unipolar-bipolar distinction in the depressive disorders: Implications for stress-onset interaction. In R. A. Depue (Ed.), *The psychobiology of the depressive disorders: Implications for the effects of stress.* New York: Academic Press, 1979.

Depue, R. A., Monroe, S. M., & Shackman, S. L. The psychobiology of human disease: Implications for conceptualizing the depressive disorders. In R. A. Depue (Ed.), *The psychobiology of the depressive disorders: Implications for the effects of stress.* New York: Academic Press, 1979.

Depue, R. A.; Slater, J.; Wolfstetter-Kausch, H.; Klein, D.; Goplerud, E.; & Farr, D. A behavioral paradigm for identifying persons at risk for bipolar depressive disorder: A conceptual framework and five validation studies. *Journal of Abnormal Psychology*, 1981, 90, 381–438. (Monograph.)

Dohrenwend, B. S., & Dohrenwend, B. P. (Eds.). *Stressful life events: Their nature and effects.* New York: Wiley, 1974.

Dohrenwend, B. S., & Dohrenwend, B. P. *Stressful life events and their contexts.* New York: Prodist, 1981.

Dohrenwend, B. S., Krasnoff, L., Askenasy, A. R., & Dohrenwend, B. P. Exemplification of a method for scaling life events: The PERI life events scale. *Journal of Health and Social Behavior*, 1978, 19, 203–229.

Elston, R. C., & Namboodiri, K. K. Types of disease and models for their genetic analysis. *Schizophrenia Bulletin*, 1980, 6, 368–374.

Emery, A. E. H. *Elements of medical genetics.* (5th ed.) New York: Churchill Livingstone, 1979.

Engel, G. L. A life setting conducive to illness: The giving-up, given-up complex. *Archives of Internal Medicine*, 1968, 69, 293–305.

Engel, G. L. The need for a new medical model: A challenge for biomedicine. *Science*, 1977, 196, 129–136.

Feighner, J. P., Robins, E., & Guze, S. B. Diagnostic criteria for use in psychiatric research. *Archives of General Psychiatry*, 1972, 26, 57–63.

Feinberg, M., & Carroll, B. J. Effects of dopamine agonists and antagonists in Tourette's disease. *Archives of General Psychiatry*, 1979, 36, 979–987.

Fowler, R. C., Liskow, B. I., Tanna, V. L., Lytle, L., & Mezzich, J. Schizophrenia: Primary affective disorder discrimination. I. Development of a data-based diagnostic index. *Archives of General Psychiatry*, 1980, 37, 811–814.

Fowler, R. C., Mezzich, J., Liskow, B. I., & Van Valkenburg, C. Schizophrenia: Primary affective disorder discrimination. II. Where unclassified psychosis stands. *Archives of General Psychiatry*, 1980, 37, 815–817.

Fuller, J. L., & Thompson, W. R. Foundations of behavior genetics. St. Louis, Mo.: C. V. Mosby, 1978.

Garrod, A. E. *Inborn errors of metabolism.* (2nd ed.) London: Oxford University Press, 1923.

Gerner, R. H., & Gwirtsman, H. E. Abnormalities of dexamethasone suppression test and urinary MHPG in anorexia nervosa. *American Journal of Psychiatry*, 1981, 138, 650–653.

Gersh, F. S., & Fowles, D. C. Neurotic depression: The concept of anxious depression. In R. A. Depue (Ed.), *The psychobiology of the depressive disorders: Implications for the effects of stress.* New York: Academic Press, 1979.

Gershon, E. S. The research for genetic markers in affective disorders. In M. A. Lipton, A. DiMascio, & K. F. Killam (Eds.), *Psychopharmacology: A generation of progress.* New York: Raven, 1978.

Gershon, E. S., Goldin, L. R., Lake, C. R., Murphy, D. L., & Guroff, J. J. Genetics of plasma dopamine-B-hydroxylase (MAO) in pedigrees of patients with affective disorders. In E. Usdin, T. L. Sourkes, & M. B. H. Youdim (Eds.), *Enzymes and neurotransmitters in mental disease.* New York: Wiley-Interscience, 1980.

Gleser, G. L., Green, B. L., & Winget, C. *Prolonged psychosocial effects of disaster: A study of Buffalo Creek.* New York: Academic Press, 1981.

Gloger, S., Grunhaus, L., Birmacher, B., & Troudart, T. Treatment of spontaneous panic attacks with chlomipramine. *American Journal of Psychiatry*, 1981, 138, 1,215–1,217.

Gold, M. S., Pottash, A. L. C., Sweeney, D. R., Martin, D. M., & Davies, R. K. Further evidence of hypothalamic-pituitary dysfunction in anorexia nervosa. *American Journal of Psychiatry*, 1980, 137, 101–102.

Goldberg, S. C., Eckert, E. D., Halmi, K. A., Casper, R. C., Davis, J. M., & Roper, M. Effects of cyproheptadine on symptoms and attitudes in anorexia nervosa. (Letter to the editor). *Archives of General Psychiatry*, 1980, 37, 1,083.

Gottesman, I. I., & Shields, J. *Schizophrenia and genetics: A twin study vantage point.* New York: Academic Press, 1972.

Haier, R. J., Buchsbaum, M. S., & Murphy, D. L. An 18-month follow-up of students biologically at risk for psychiatric problems. *Schizophrenia Bulletin*, 1980, 6, 334–337.

Haier, R. J., Buchsbaum, M. S., Murphy, D. L., Gottesman, I. I., & Coursey, R. D. Psychiatric vulnerability, MAO, and the average evoked potential. *Archives of General Psychiatry*, 1980, 37, 340–348.

Helzer, J. E.; Robins, L. N.; Croughan, J. L.; & Welner, A. Renard diagnostic interview. *Archives of General Psychiatry*, 1981, 38, 393–399.

Heston, L. L. The genetics of schizophrenia and schizoid disease. *Science*, 1970, 167, 249–256.

Hinkle, L. E. The concept of stress in the biological and social sciences. *International Journal of Psychiatry in Medicine*, 1974, 5, 335–357.

Hoehn-Saric, R., Merchant, A. F., & Keyser, M. L. Effects of clonidine on anxiety disorders. *Archives of General Psychiatry*, 1981, 38, 1,278–1,286.

Holmes, T. H., & Masuda, M. Life change and illness susceptibility. In B. S. Dohrenwend & B. P. Dohrenwend (Eds.), *Stressful life events: Their nature and ef-*

fects. New York: Wiley, 1974.

Irwin, M.; Belendiuk, K.; McCloskey, K.; & Freedman, D. X. Tryptophan metabolism in children with attentional deficit disorder. *American Journal of Psychiatry,* 1981, **138,** 1,082–1,085.

James, R. L., & May, P. R. A. Diagnosing schizophrenia: Professor Kraepelin and the research diagnostic criteria. *American Journal of Psychiatry,* 1981, **138,** 501–504.

Jenkins, C. D., Hurst, M. W., & Rose, R. M. Life changes: Do people really remember? *Archives of General Psychiatry,* 1979, **36,** 379–384.

Johnson, J. H., & Sarason, I. G. Moderator variable in life stress research. In I. G. Sarason & C. D. Spielberger, *Stress and anxiety,* Vol. 6. New York: Halstead, 1979.

Kanner, A. D.; Coyne, J. C.; Schaefer, C.; & Lazarus, R. S. Comparison of two modes of stress measurement: Daily hassles and uplifts versus major life events. *Journal of Behavioral Medicine,* 1981, **4,** 1–39.

Kestenbaum, C. Children at risk for manic-depressive illness: Possible predictors. *American Journal of Psychiatry,* 1979, **136,** 1,206–1,208.

Kinston, W., & Rosser, R. Disaster: Effects on mental and physical state. *Journal of Psychosomatic Research,* 1974, **18,** 437–456.

Knesevich, J. W. Successful treatment of obsessive-compulsive disorder with clonidine hydrochloride. *American Journal of Psychiatry,* 1982, **139,** 364–365.

Kobasa, S. C. Stressful life events, personality, and health: An inquiry into hardiness. *Journal of Personality and Social Psychology,* 1979, **37,** 1–11.

Kraepelin, E. *Manic-depressive insanity and paranoia.* Edinburgh: Livingstone, 1921.

Langer, D. H., Brown, G. L., & Doherty, J. P. Dopamine receptor supersensitivity and schizophrenia: A review. *Schizophrenia Bulletin,* 1981, **7,** 208–224.

Lazarus, R. S. Discussion. In G. Serban (Ed.), *Psychopathology of human adaptation.* New York: Plenum, 1976.

Lei, H., & Skinner, H. A. A psychometric study of life events and social readjustment. *Journal of Psychosomatic Research,* 1980, **24,** 57–65.

Leonhard, K. *Aufteilung der endogenen psychosen.* Berlin: Akademieverlag, 1957.

Lerner, I. M. *The genetic basis of selection.* New York: Wiley, 1958.

Lipowski, Z. J. Psychosomatic medicine in the seventies: An overview. *American Journal of Psychiatry,* 1977, **134,** 233–244.

Luchins, D. J.; Morihisa, J. M.; Weinberger, D. R., & Wyatt, R. J. Cerebral asymmetry and cerebellar atrophy in schizophrenia: A controlled post-mortem study. *American Journal of Psychiatry,* 1981, **138,** 1,501–1,502.

Maas, J. W. Clinical implications of pharmacological differences among antidepressants. In M. Lipton, A. DiMascio, & K. Killam (Eds.), *Psychopharmacology: A generation of progress.* New York: Raven, 1978.

Mason, J. A historical review of the stress field. Parts I and II. *Journal of Human Stress,* 1975, **1,** 6–12, 22–36.

Mazure, C., & Gershon, E. S. Blindness and reliability

in lifetime psychiatric diagnosis. *Archives of General Psychiatry,* 1979, **36,** 521–525.

Mechanik, D. Some problems in the measurement of stress and social readjustment. *Journal of Human Stress,* 1975, **1,** 43–48.

Meehl, P. E. *Psychodiagnosis: Selected papers.* Minneapolis: University of Minnesota Press, 1973.

Meehl, P. E. Specific etiology and other forms of strong influence: Some quantitative meanings. *Journal of Medicine and Philosophy,* 1977, **2,** 33–53.

Meltzer, H. Y., & Stahl, S. M. Platelet monoamine oxidase activiy and substrate preferences in schizophrenic patients. *Research Communications in Chemical Pathology and Pharmacology,* 1974, **7,** 419–431.

Meltzer, H. Y., & Stahl, S. M. The dopamine hypothesis of schizophrenia: A review. *Schizophrenia Bulletin,* 1976, **2,** 19–76.

Monroe, S. M. Life events and disorder: Event-symptom associations and the course of disorder. *Journal of Abnormal Psychology,* 1982, **91,** 14–24.

Monroe, S. M. The assessment of life events: Retrospective versus concurrent strategies. *Archives of General Psychiatry,* in press.

Motulsky, A. G., & Omenn, G. S. Special award lecture: Biochemical genetics and psychiatry. In R. R. Frive, D. Rosenthal, & H. Brill (Eds.), *Genetic research in psychiatry.* Baltimore: The Johns Hopkins University Press, 1975.

Murphy, D. L., Campbell, I., & Costa, J. Current status of the indeleamine hypothesis of the affective disorders. In M. Lipton, A. DiMascio, & K. Killam (Eds.), *Psychopharmacology: A generation of progress.* New York: Raven, 1978.

Murphy, D. L., & Kalin, N. H. Biological and behavioral consequences of alterations in monoamine oxidase activity. *Schizophrenia Bulletin,* 1980, **6,** 355–367.

Najman, J. M. Theories of disease causation and the concept of a general susceptability: A review. *Social Sciences and Medicine,* 1980, **14A,** 231–238.

Neugebauer, R. The reliability of life event reports. In B. S. Dohrenwend & B. P. Dohrewend (Eds.), *Stressful life events and their contexts.* New York: Prodist, 1981.

Omenn, G. S., & Motulsky, A. G. Biochemical genetics and the evolution of human behavior. In L. Ehrman, G. S. Omenn, & E. Caspari (Eds.), *Genetics, environment, and behavior.* New York: Academic Press, 1972.

Overall, J. E., & Hollister, L. E. Comparative evaluation of research diagnostic criteria for schizophrenia. *Archives of General Psychiatry,* 1979, **36,** 1,198–1,205.

Perkins, D. V. The assessment of stress using life events scales: A review of current issues. In L. Goldberger & S. Breznitz (Eds.), *Handbook of stress.* New York: Free Press, in press.

Planansky, K. Phenotypic boundaries and genetic specificity in schizophrenia. In A. R. Kaplan (Ed.), *Genetic factors in "schizophrenia."* Springfield, Ill.: Charles C. Thomas, 1972.

Pope, H. G., & Lipinski, J. F. Diagnosis in schizophrenia and manic-depressive illness. *Archives of General Psychiatry,* 1978, **35,** 811–836.

Pope, H. G., Lipinski, J. F., Cohen, B. M., & Axelrod, D. T. "Schizoaffective disorder": An invalid diagnosis? A comparison of schizoaffective disorder, schizophrenia, and affective disorder. *American Journal of Psychiatry*, 1980, **137**, 921–927.

Post, R. M., & Kopanda, R. T. Cocaine, kindling, and psychosis. *American Journal of Psychiatry*, 1976, **133**, 627–634.

Rabkin, J. G., & Struening, E. L. Life events, stress, and illness. *Science*, 1976, **194**, 1,013–1,020.

Reimherr, F. W., Wood, D. R., & Wender, P. H. An open clinical trial of L-Dopa and carbidopa in adults with minimal brain dysfunction. *American Journal of Psychiatry*, 1980, **137**, 73–75.

Rifkin, A.; Klein, D. F.; Dillon, D.; & Levitt, M. Blockade by imipramine or desipramine of panic induced by sodium lactate. *American Journal of Psychiatry*, 1981 **138**, 676–677.

Roberts, E. An hypothesis suggesting that there is a defect in the GABA system in schizophrenia. *Neurosciences Research Program Bulletin*, 1972, **10**, 468–482.

Robins, L. N.; Helzer, J. E.; Croughon, J.; & Ratcliff, K. S. National Institute of Mental Health diagnosis interview schedule. *Archives of General Psychiatry*, 1981, **38**, 381–392.

Rosenthal, D. The concept of subschizophrenic disorders. In R. R. Fieve, D. Rosenthal, & H. Brill (Eds.), *Genetic research in psychiatry*. Baltimore: Johns Hopkins University Press, 1975.

Rosenthal, D.; Wender, P.; Kety, S. S.; Schulsinger, F.; Welner, J.; Ostergaard, L. Schizophrenics' offspring reared in adoptive homes. In D. Rosenthal & S. S. Kety (Eds.), *The transmission of schizophrenia*. London: Pergamon, 1968.

Ross, C. E., & Mirowsky, J., II. A comparison of life event weighting schemes: Change, undesirability, and effect proportional indices. *Journal of Health and Social Behavior*, 1979, **20**, 166–177.

Schildkraut, J. J. The catecholamine hypothesis of affective disorders: A review of supporting evidence. *American Journal of Psychiatry*, 1965, **122**, 509–522.

Schildkraut, J. J. Current status of the catecholamine hypothesis of the affective disorders. In M. Lipton, A. DiMascio, & K. Killam (Eds.), *Psychopharmacology: A generation of progress*. New York: Raven, 1978.

Selye, H. Confusion and controversy in the stress field. *Journal of Human Stress*, 1975, **1**, 37–44.

Seyle, H. *The stress of life*. (Rev. ed.) New York: McGraw-Hill, 1976.

Shekim, W. O., Dekirmenjian, H., & Khapel, J. L. Urinary MHPG excretion in minimal brain dysfunction and its modification by d-amphetamine. *American Journal of Psychiatry*, 1979, **136**, 667–671.

Shields, J., Heston, L. L., & Gottesman, I. I. Schizophrenia and the schizoid: The problem for genetic analysis. In R. R. Fieve, D. Rosenthal, & H. Brill (Eds.), *Genetic research in psychiatry*. Baltimore: Johns Hopkins University Press, 1975.

Shrout, P. E. Sealing of stressful life events. In B. S. Dohrenwend & B. P. Dohrenwend (Eds.), *Stressful life events and their contexts*. New York: Prodist, 1981.

Slater, J., & Depue, R. A. The contribution of environmental events and social support to serious suicide attempts in primary depressive disorder. *Journal of Abnormal Psychology*, 1981, **90**, 275–285.

Snyder, S. H. Dopamine receptors, neuroleptics, and schizophrenia. *American Journal of Psychiatry*, 1981, **138**, 460–464.

Spitzer, R. L., & Endicott, J. *Schedule for the Affective Disorders and Schizophrenia*. New York: Biometrics Research, New York State Psychiatric Institute, 1977.

Spitzer, R. L., Endicott, J., & Robins, E. Research diagnostic criteria: Rationale and reliability. *Archives of General Psychiatry*, 1978, **35**, 773–782.

Spitzer, R. L., & Fliess, J. L. A re-analysis of the reliability of psychiatric diagnosis. *British Journal of Psychiatry*, 1974, **125**, 341–347.

Stolk, J. M., & Nisula, B. C. Genetic influences on catecholamine metabolism. In R. A. Depue (Ed.), *The psychobiology of the depressive disorders: Implications for the effects of stress*. New York: Academic Press, 1979.

Tennant, C., Bebbington, P., & Hurry, J. The role of life events in depressive illness: Is there a substantial causal relation? *Psychological Medicine*, 1981, **11**, 379–389.

Thoits, P. A. Undesirable life events and psychophysiological distress: A problem of operational confounding. *American Sociological Review*, 1981, **46**, 97–109.

Thoren, P., Asberg, M., Bertilson, L., Mellstrom, B., Sjogvist, F., & Traskman, L. Clomipramine treatment of obsessive-compulsive disorder. II. Biochemical aspects. *Archives of General Psychiatry*, 1980, **37**, 1,289–1,294.

Thoren, P., Asberg, M., Cronholm, B., Jornestedt, L., & Traskman, L. Clomipramine treatment of obsessive-compulsive disorder. I. A controlled clinical trial. *Archives of General Psychiatry*, 1980, **37**, 1,281–1,288.

Traskman, L., Asberg, M., Bertilsson, L., & Sjostrand, L. Monoamine metabolites in CSF and suicidal behavior. *Archives of General Psychiatry*, 1981, **38**, 631–641.

Vogel, F., & Motulsky, A. G. *Human genetics*. New York: Springer-Verlag, 1982.

Waters, B. G. H. Early symptoms of bipolar affective psychosis: Research and clinical implications. *Canadian Psychiatric Association Journal*, 1979, **2**, 55–60. (a)

Waters, B. G. H. Risks to bipolar affective psychosis. In B. Shopsin (Ed.), *Manic illness*, New York: Raven, 1979. (b)

Weinberger, D. R., Torrey, E. F., Neophytides, A. N., & Wyatt, R. J. Lateral cerebral ventricular enlargement in chronic schizophrenia. *Archives of General Psychiatry*, 1979, **36**, 735–739.

Weiner, H. *Psychobiology and human disease*. New York: Elsevier, 1977.

Weissman, M., & Myers, J. Affective disorders in a U. S. urban community. *Archives of General Psychiatry*, 1978, **35**, 1,304–1,311.

Wershow, H. J., & Reinhart, G. Life change and hospitalization: A heretical view. *Journal of Psychosomatic Research*, 1974, **18**, 393–401.

Winokur, G. Unipolar depression: Is it divisible into autonomous subtypes? *Archives of General Psychiatry,* 1979, **36**, 47–52.

Wyatt, R. J., Potkin, S. G., Bridge, T. P., Phelps, B H., & Wise, C. D. Monoamine oxidase in schizophrenia: An overview. *Schizophrenia Bulletin,* 1980, **6**, 199–207.

Wyler, A. R., Masuda, M., & Holmes, T. H. Magnitude of life events and seriousness of illness. *Psychosomatic Medicine,* 1971, **33**, 115–122.

Yager, J., Grant, I., Sweetwood, H. L., & Gerst, M. Life event reports by psychiatric patients, nonpatients, and their partners. *Archives of General Psychiatry,* 1981, **38**,343–347.

15 TREATMENT RESEARCH: THE INVESTIGATION AND EVALUATION OF PSYCHOTHERAPY

Alan E. Kazdin

Professional interest in the multiple questions of psychotherapy outcome is high (e.g., Garfield, 1981; VandenBos, 1980). The underlying bases of clinical disorders and the mechanisms of therapeutic change represent major scientific and professional interests. Professional interest also stems from other sources. As a contemporary case in point, proposals to include psychotherapy services as part of national health-care policy in the United States have focused public, professional, and legislative attention on the efficacy of therapy and the cost-benefit issues raised by treatment (Kiesler, 1980; Parloff, 1979).

Psychotherapy research is still at a relatively early stage of development. Basic questions about the efficacy of alternative procedures and the methods by which efficacy should be evaluated occupy a great deal of professional attention (Bergin & Lambert, 1978; Kazdin, 1982a; Rachman & Wilson, 1980; Smith, Glass, & Miller, 1980). Substantive issues continue to foster heated debates, which probably attests to the fact that clear answers to basic questions are still unavailable.

Debates about psychotherapy and its effects can be traced to controversies over conceptual approaches toward human behavior and fundamental methodological issues. How treatment should be evaluated, the conditions under which treatments should be tested, the measures that attest to treatment efficacy, and the point in time after treatment at which effects ultimately are to be evaluated are issues that continue to be debated.

The present chapter discusses current research and evaluation issues of psychotherapy. Psychotherapy as discussed here refers to psychosocial treatments in general rather than to any particular technique or conceptual orientation. The chapter discusses treatment research strategies and the questions they address, the conditions under which treatment can be evaluated, and contemporary issues and controversies surrounding treatment evaluation. The chapter also highlights recent efforts to identify characteristics common to many different psychotherapies and the implications of these efforts for treatment evaluation.

*Completion of this chapter was supported in part by a Research Scientist Development Award (MH00353) provided by the National Institute of Mental Health.

Treatment Evaluation Strategies

The major tasks of psychotherapy research are to identify effective treatment techniques and to understand the underlying bases of therapeutic change. The tasks are not at all straightforward or simple. Indeed, the overall question that has been repeatedly posed to guide outcome research is: What kinds of change are produced by what kinds of treatments, for what kinds of patients, by what kinds of therapists, and under what kinds of conditions? (See Marmor, 1976; Parloff et al., 1978; Paul, 1969.) With a documented list of over 250 psychotherapy techniques (Herink, 1980) and scores of clinical disorders (American Psychiatric Association, 1980), the question as formulated represents a formidible task. Indeed, the question could never be confronted by a single research program or generation of energetic psychotherapy researchers. Gradual progress can be achieved, however, by examining therapy techniques with diverse treatment evaluation strategies. The strategies begin to chisel away at the stone of ignorance to produce a sculpture of knowledge that slowly begins to take shape. Strategies that currently dominate outcome research are reviewed and illustrated below.

Treatment Package Strategy

The treatment package strategy refers to evaluating the effects of a particular treatment as that treatment is ordinarily used. The notion of a "package" emphasizes that the treatment is examined *in toto*. Many techniques are multifaceted and include several components, each of which may exert influences in its own right.

For example, Gruen (1975) evaluated a brief psychotherapy for hospitalized medical patients after they incurred a heart attack. Recovery after an attack may be delayed well beyond the period of physical disability because of psychological concomitants such as excessive anxiety and depression associated with the immediate and unexpected incapacitation. Brief psychotherapy was administered to ameliorate psychological concomitants and to enhance recovery. Patients who had suffered their first heart attack and who were placed in intensive care were randomly assigned to treatment or control procedures while in the hospital. Treated subjects received daily counseling for three weeks, including reassurance, reflection of feelings, discussion and reinforcement of coping responses, encouragement, and general support.

Nontreated subjects did not receive the treatment package. All patients received the usual inpatient medical care. Interestingly, treated patients showed several signs of superior recovery including fewer days in intensive care and in the hospital, fewer arrhythmias and heart failures in the hospital, and superior ratings from nurses and physicians on weakness and mood, and better return to normal routine activities at follow-up. The investigation demonstrated the effectiveness of a multifaceted treatment. Several questions might be asked about the specific ingredients or components that accounted for change. However, these questions extend beyond the treatment package strategy.

The treatment package strategy raises the most basic question about treatment; namely, does it work? In clinical work, the strategy has obvious priority because of its focus on the clinical problem (see Azrin, 1977). Once the technique has been shown to be effective for a particular problem, a variety of other research questions can be raised to understand how the technique works, how it can be improved, and its relative effectiveness when compared to various alternatives.

Dismantling Treatment Strategy

The dismantling strategy consists of analyzing the components of a given treatment package (Lang, 1969). After a particular package has been shown to produce therapeutic change, research that begins to analyze the basis for change assumes importance. To dismantle treatment, individual components are eliminated or isolated from the treatment. In a dismantling investigation, some subjects may receive the entire package, and others may receive the package minus one or more components. Dismantling strategies determine the necessary and sufficient components for therapeutic change.

Dismantling research can serve multiple purposes. First, the strategy points to the specific ingredients or combinations of ingredients that are responsible for change. Hence, clinical practice can be improved by emphasizing those aspects that are more important to outcome than others. Second, the approach often has important theoretical implications. When crucial ingredients are identified, the investigator may be in a position to comment on the reasons *why* treatment produces change. The theoretical uses of dismantling treatment research are important, because they may suggest changes for the technique or new techniques that may prove to be even more effective.

The dismantling strategy has been used extensively in the evaluation of systematic desensitization. When desensitization was first proposed, several specific components were delineated as crucial for therapeutic change (Wolpe, 1958). These included: (1) training the client in a response that could compete with anxiety (e.g., relaxation); (2) developing a hierarchy of items related to the source of anxiety; and (3) pairing the competing response with the individual hierarchy items in a graduated fashion. Such a well-delineated technique lends itself extremely well to dismantling research, and several studies examining the specific components have been completed (e.g., Davison, 1968; Krapfl & Nawas, 1970). The above ingredients, originally thought to be crucial, are not essential for therapeutic change (Wilkins, 1971). The only component that appears to be important is the imagined or overt rehearsal of the response that is to be developed. These findings have important implications regarding the mechanism of behavior change. The original theoretical interpretation of the technique is much less tenable now since the emergence of research that has dismantled the overall package.

The dismantling strategy requires that the treatment package consists of a delimited and reasonably well specified set of treatment components. Dismantling research cannot be done if the ingredients cannot be carefully specified as part of the treatment. Dismantling research is greatly facilitated by having a tentative theoretical basis for explaining the technique. The theory specifies the crucial interpretation of the mechanism of treatment and directs the investigator to a particular set of components that warrant investigation. And the results of the investigation ultimately may reflect on the specific theoretical proposition from which the research was derived.

Constructive Treatment Strategy

The constructive treatment strategy refers to developing a treatment package by adding components that many enhance outcome. In this sense, the constructive approach is the opposite of the dismantling strategy. Constructive treatment research begins with a treatment, which may consist of one or a few ingredients or a larger package,

and adds various ingredients to determine whether the effects can be enhanced. The strategy asks what can be added to treatment to make it more effective? As constructive research continues, in theory a given technique may grow to encompass more and more procedures. Actually, in constructive research some ingredients are likely to enhance treatment and others will not. Those that improve outcome are retained and added, and those that do not are cast aside.

As an example, Kazdin and Mascitelli (1982b) evaluated behavioral rehearsal for outpatient treatment social skills. Clients who were unassertive received treatment in which they rehearsed assertive responses and social interaction with a therapist during their treatment sessions. To determine if the effects of rehearsal could be enhanced, some clients also received self-instruction training and/or homework practice. In self-instruction training, clients were trained to provide self-statements that would prompt use of their newly developed social skills. Clients who received homework practice engaged in prespecified assertive responses in their daily lives between treatment sessions. The results indicated that behavioral rehearsal, relative to no treatment, led to significant changes in self-report and overt behavioral measures of social skills. The addition of self-instruction training and, to a much greater extent, homework practice assignments enhanced treatment at posttreatment and at a six-month follow-up. The study shows that adding procedures to an already effective treatment enhanced outcome.

As with the dismantling strategy, the constructive approach may have implications for the theoretical basis of therapy and perhaps even the nature of the clinical problem. The investigator may select components for treatment on the basis of theory. For example, on the basis of self-efficacy theory (Bandura, 1977), investigators may wish to add an overt behavioral rehearsal component to a treatment that consists of imagining various events (Kazdin & Mascitelli, 1982a). Self-efficacy theory has suggested that greater therapeutic change will be achieved if the client overtly rehearses the desired responses than if rehearsal is omitted.

Constructing treatments need not necessarily rely on theory. Clinical practice or research may provide guidelines for techniques that can be combined to improve outcome, even though underlying theory may not suggest integration of these techniques. For example, medication and various forms of psychotherapy have been combined to treat unipolar depression with the results showing that combined treatment often surpasses individual treatments administered alone (e.g., Roth et al., 1982; Weissman et al., 1979).

Parametric Treatment Strategy

The parametric treatment strategy refers to altering specific aspects of a treatment to determine how to maximize therapeutic change. The dimensions or parameters of the treatment are altered to find the optimal manner of administering the procedure. The approach resembles dismantling and constructive evaluation strategies because variations of a particular treatment are evaluated. However, components of treatment are not withdrawn (dismantling approach) or added (constructive approach). Rather, variables within the existing treatment are altered to find the optimal variation. Essentially, the parametric research focuses on refining a particular technique. In parametric research, variations often are made along quantitative dimensions by presenting more or less of a given portion of treatment. Different groups might receive the same general treatment but differ in quantitative variations of a particular dimension associated with that treatment.

The parametric approach can be illustrated by a study that examined the effects of flooding as a technique to treat agoraphobic patients (Stern & Marks, 1973). Flooding consists of confronting the client with the stimuli that cause distress until the adverse reaction is eliminated. Two parameters of flooding were evaluated, namely, the duration of continuous exposure of the feared stimuli (one long period of exposure versus several short exposures) and the mode of flooding (in imagery or in actual situations). The most effective variation of treatment was the longer exposure period conducted in the actual situations. These results indicate that the two dimensions that can be manipulated within flooding can enhance treatment effects.

Most techniques include several dimensions that are unspecified in practice or research. Moreover, a particular treatment can be conducted in many different ways and still qualify as that technique. For example, modeling generally consists of observing others engage in responses that are to be developed in the client. However, the general procedure leaves unspecified many important variables such as who the model is, how the model

performs, how many models are presented, and so on (Rosenthal & Bandura, 1978). These variables all influence the effectiveness of the procedure as investigated in parametric research.

Parametric treatment research is extremely important because it attempts to develop a particular technique. Relatively little parametric work exists. This is unfortunate because techniques often are proposed as effective and tested against other procedures before basic research has been conducted to explore parametric variations that maximize therapeutic change.

Parametric research can have important implications for the theoretical basis of treatment in addition to developing more effective variations. The parametric variations that influence outcome may suggest the mechanisms responsible for therapeutic change. Also, and as noted with other strategies, understanding the mechanisms of change may lead to eventual improvements in treatment.

Comparative Treatment Strategy

The comparative treatment strategy consists of comparing two or more different treatments. The question addressed by this strategy is which treatment is better (or best) among various alternatives for a particular problem. This strategy is extremely familiar to researchers because of the very wide interest that comparative studies hold. The interest derives from the specific treatments that are compared. Often, the treatments are based on opposing conceptual approaches. Hence, the investigations of alternative techniques are often viewed as critical and even definitive tests of the constituent techniques.

Major comparative treatment studies have been completed in the last several years. For example, Paul and Lentz (1977) compared social-learning and milieu therapies with routine hospital care for chronic psychiatric patients. The social-learning program, based primarily on a token economy to promote adaptive behaviors on the ward, was consistently more effective on measures in the hospital, discharge of patients, and status in the community over the course of follow-up. In another landmark comparative study, Rush, Beck, Kovacs, and Hollon (1977) evaluated the relative effectiveness of pharmacotherapy and cognitive therapy for depressed outpatients. Although both treatments produced significant changes, follow-up over the course of one year showed that cognitive therapy was superior (Kovacs et al., 1981). These studies and others like them (e.g., Sloane et al., 1975) have attracted wide attention in part because they place the many conflicting and hyperbolic claims made for the superiority of one technique over another into the empirical arena.

The comparative treatment strategy has obvious value. In the long run, comparisons are essential to determine which technique should be applied to a given problem. Yet, the importance of comparative research and the wide interest it attracts may lead to premature comparisons. Techniques often are compared long before they are well investigated or well understood. Hence, the versions that are compared may not provide the optimal treatment, and conclusions that are drawn may not be very meaningful or definitive.

Comparative research also introduces a number of special research problems that make it one of the more complex treatment evaluation strategies (Kazdin, 1980). When opposing techniques are compared, special difficulties often arise in keeping the techniques distinct, in holding constant variables associated with treatment administration (e.g., amount of treatment, spacing of treatment), utilizing therapists who can conduct both (or all) of the treatments, and ensuring the integrity of the individual treatments. In many comparative studies, questions can be raised about whether one treatment, usually the one to which the investigator may be less committed, received fair representation.

Client and Therapist Variation Strategy

Previous evaluation strategies emphasize the technique as the major source of treatment outcome. The effectiveness of many treatments, however, is likely to vary as a function of characteristics of the clients and therapists. The client and therapist variation strategy examines whether attributes of the client or therapist contribute to outcome.

The strategy is usually implemented by selecting clients (or therapists) according to a particular subject variable such as age, gender, socioeconomic standing, marital status, education, severity of the disorder, level of anxiety or introversion, and so on. Therapist variables have been studied in a similar fashion by looking at such characteristics as therapist training, years of experience,

age, interests, empathy, warmth, and so on (e.g., Meltzoff & Kornreich, 1970).

An illustration of the impact of therapist characteristics on outcome was reported in a study that evaluated treatment for families of juvenile delinquents (Alexander et al., 1976). Adolescents (ages 13 to 16) and their families were seen in treatment that was designed to alter family communication patterns and interaction. Treatment focused on modeling, prompting, and reinforcement of clear communication, and clearly presenting demands, and generating alternative solutions to problems. Therapist characteristics were rated prior to treatment and included several dimensions such as affective behavior, humor, warmth-directiveness, self-confidence, self-disclosure, blaming, and clarity of communications. Given the intercorrelation patterns, two larger dimensions were generated to describe the therapists and were referred to as relationship (affective behavior, warmth, and humor) and structuring (directiveness and self-confidence) dimensions. The results indicated that treatment outcome, as defined by recidivism among the adolescents, changes in family communication, and continuing in treatment were predicted by relationship and structuring dimensions of the therapist. Indeed, approximately 60 percent of the outcome variance was accounted for by these therapist dimensions.

When clients and therapists are classified according to a particular variable, the main question addressed is whether treatment is more or less effective with certain kinds of participants. The question is directed to the generality of treatment effects by looking at the types of clients to whom treatment can be extended. Examination of the generality of treatment effects in this fashion greatly increases the information about treatment and addresses sophisticated questions about outcome. The question of which treatment or treatment variation produces greater effects is a very global one. It might well be that the techniques are differentially effective as a function of other variables related to the clients and therapists.

General Comments

The above strategies reflect outcome questions that are frequently addressed in current treatment research. The specific question posed by each strategy reflects a range of issues required to understand fully how a technique operates and can be applied for optimal effects. The questions reflect a general progression. The treatment package strategy is an initial approach followed by the various analytic strategies based upon dismantling, constructive, and parametric research. The comparative strategy probably warrants attention after prior work has been conducted that not only indicated the efficacy of the individual techniques but also shows how the techniques should be administered to increase their efficacy. Obviously, comparative research can be conducted before very much is known about the constituent techniques. The yield from such research, however, may be quite limited.

A high degree of operationalization is needed to investigate dismantling, constructive, and parametric questions. In each case, specific components or ingredients of therapy have to be sufficiently well specified to be withdrawn, added, or varied in an overall treatment package. In relatively few therapy techniques are the critical procedures specified to permit careful analytic investigation for dismantling, constructive, or parametric research.

The treatment evaluation strategies outlined above reflect several outcome questions. The process of therapeutic change is another area to which recent therapy research has devoted relatively little attention. Process research traditionally has referred to questions about transactions between the therapist and client, the type of interactions and their interim effects on client and therapist behavior. For example, process research may examine the perceptions of the clients and therapists over the course of treatment (e.g., Orlinsky & Howard, 1975). Although such process factors may eventually be related to outcome, they have been studied independently of treatment efficacy.

Psychotherapy might profit from empirical excursions into the therapy processes. For example, the effects of various techniques and therapist variables that influence change in cognitive processes over the course of treatment might be studied. Cognitive processes may be important because they reflect, lead to, or covary with overt behavioral changes, or because they may ultimately lead to the client's redefinition of the aspects of the environment that were regarded as problematic. Even if interim processes of therapy are not of direct interest, they may be useful as a way of understanding behavior. The correspondence, or rather lack of correspondence, of several modalities of assessment and measures within these modalities may be better understood by looking at the course of changes from the beginning of therapy through outcome as well as follow-up. Also, interim treatment processes may have implications for relapse since they are early signs of the kinds of effects that take place. In general, what happens during treatment, apart from outcome, may provide additional leads for research.

Conditions of Research

The experimental conditions in which treatment questions are investigated can vary widely. The conditions are often delineated by the extent to which they resemble treatment of patients in clinical settings. Analogue research and clinical trials, two points on a continuum of resemblance of research conditions to clinical practice, have been utilized heavily in treatment outcome studies.

Analogue Research

CHARACTERISTICS

Conducting outcome research creates a host of problems that can impede careful experimentation. To begin with, it is often difficult to obtain a sufficient number of clients with the same or similar clinical problems. Similarity among the clients is important so that the same sorts of measures can be used. Even if enough clients with similar problems can be found, there often are restraints in assigning clients to conditions. Random assignment, dictated by sound methodology, often cannot be permitted because of the client's preferences for treatment and administrative restrictions for assigning persons to groups (e.g., inpatient treatment). Difficulties also arise in obtaining therapists who are willing to participate in an outcome study and who can administer alternative treatment or treatment variations.

Even if practical problems could be resolved, certainly ethical issues can impede clinical research. Many of the important questions of therapy require control groups that withhold specific aspects of treatment. Assigning clients to "control" conditions that have a low probability of producing change would be an obvious violation of the professional commitment to treatment. Also, the possible ineffectiveness or relative ineffectiveness of various treatment or control conditions can lead to high levels of attrition that can greatly interfere with research.

The research problems highlighted here suggest

that clinical settings may not be the place to address all or perhaps even most of the questions entailed by therapy. To overcome many of the obstacles, research has been conducted in situations that are *analogous* to the clinical situation. Research that evaluates treatment under conditions that only resemble or approximate the clinical situation has been referred to as *analogue research.*

Different types of analogue research have been employed to evaluate therapeutic processes and behavior change. Analogue research can vary widely in the degree of resemblance to the clinical situation to which the investigator may wish to generalize. Animal (infrahuman) analogues have been used to study behavior change processes that appear to be relevant for therapy (Adams & Hughes, 1976). Alternatively, contrived laboratory arrangements with human subjects provide analogues of specific phenomena or processes that occur in therapy (e.g., Heller, 1971).

In contemporary treatment research, analogue studies refer primarily to investigations of treatment procedures in the context of highly controlled laboratory conditions. Analogue studies, which have proliferated expecially in behavior therapy, have several characteristics (Borkovec & Rachman, 1979; Kazdin, 1978). First, the target problem usually departs from the typical problems seen in inpatient or outpatient treatment. The problems (e.g., fears, social skills deficits) are usually less severe and more circumscribed than those problems patients ordinarily bring to treatment. The problems in analogue research and clinical treatment may differ along quantitative and qualitative dimensions.

Second, the persons who receive treatment in analogue research usually differ from persons seen in clinical settings. Typically, college students and volunteers serve as subjects. Their recruitment differs markedly from the procedures that bring clinical patients to treatment. In analogue research, subjects are actively solicited; course credit or money are often offered as incentives for participation. Apart from the type and severity of target problems that such recruitment procedures are likely to yield, the resulting sample is likely to vary in subject and demographic variables from persons usually seen in clinics.

Third, the motivations and expectancies of persons seen in analogue research are likely to vary from those who ordinarily seek treatment. In clinical settings, persons usually seek treatment for relief from a particular problem that may have reached a crisis point. Patients are likely to expect to benefit from the results and to hope for improvements before and during treatment (Frank, 1973). In contrast, subjects in analogue research may not be interested in treatment or in "cures" for their problems. The expectancies of persons who receive the intervention may be quite different in analogue and clinical research.

Fourth, graduate or undergraduate students usually serve as therapists in analogue research and differ considerably from professional clinicians in subject and demographic variables and clinical experience. The differences may also extend to the credibility of the therapist as a provider of treatment and to the expectations for improvement that therapists generate in the client.

Fifth, the manner of delivering treatment in analogue research varies greatly from treatment in clinical settings. In analogue research, treatments often are highly specified and even explicated in manual form so that a script can be followed. The treatments tend to be standardized so that all persons in a particular treatment condition or group receive the identical treatment with little or no individualization. Many features of treatment, such as duration or number of sessions, and statements that can be made by the therapist, usually allowed to vary in clinical settings, are often meticulously controlled in analogue research. Treatment may be administered in a relatively pure form in analogue research, because it is applied to a circumscribed problem. Because clinical patients usually bring complex problems to treatment, techniques are often combined and included as part of a multifaceted intervention.

ADVANTAGES AND LIMITATIONS

The major advantage of analogue research is its capacity to surmount many of the methodological, practical, and ethical issues associated with conducting research in clinical settings. The limited experimental control allowed in many clinical settings restricts the type of questions that can be asked in clinical outcome studies. The priority of analogue research is the experimental question rather than treatment delivery. Thus, conditions in analogue research can be arranged in ways that usually would not be feasible in clinical settings. Because of obstacles in clinical research, much of what is known about therapeutic processes and behavior change is learned from analogue studies. Analogue research provides opportunities to evaluate mechanisms of therapeutic change and to dismantle treatment by looking at basic elements and their contribution to outcome. The ability to control multiple conditions of the experiment and, consequently, to minimize variability in the data, permits analogue research to address questions that would otherwise be difficult to study.

Analogue research, however, bears potential costs as well as benefits. The obvious concern with analogue research is the extent to which the results can be generalized to the clinical setting. Since analogue studies depart in varying degrees from the clinical situation, perhaps the applicability and generality of the results depart commensurately. Generality of results from analogue studies to clinical situations probably is a complex function of the several variables, including the treatment technique, the clinical problem, and characteristics of the patients and the therapist. Thus, the fact that treatment research is conducted under well-controlled analogue conditions does not automatically delimit the results. Relatively little evidence is available, however, to address the issue.

Clinical Trials

CHARACTERISTICS

Clinical trials refer generally to outcome investigations conducted in clinical settings. In relation to analogue research, the characteristics of clinical trials are usually easily discerned. Instead of students or volunteers, patients who actively seek treatment are included in clinical studies; instead of graduate students, professional therapists and clinicians provide treatment; instead of treatment of relatively mild, subclinical, and circumscribed problems, relatively severe or multifaceted clinical disorders are treated. In short, in a clinical trial, treatment is tested under conditions where it would ordinarily be applied.

In addition to allowing direct evaluation of treatment in the clinical situation, clinical trials meet the methodological requirements of controlled research. Thus, depending on the precise research question, random assignment, double-blind procedures, and placebo controls are used. Because the research is conducted in a clinical setting, methodological compromises and sacrifices often have to be made to meet practical, administrative, and, of course, ethical demands (Kraemer, 1981). For example, withholding treatment is

especially difficult with a clearly identified clinical problem for a patient in distress. Yet the obstacles can be overcome in varying degrees to address the important questions of extending research to clinical settings.

Clinical trials can vary markedly along a variety of dimensions and in their resemblance to the clinical situation where treatment is ordinarily practiced. In clinical trials, as in analogue research, many features of treatment delivery may be altered to permit evaluation of the intervention. The research exigencies may make the situation slightly different from the clinical situation. Thus, in some clinical trials, the most severely disturbed or impaired patients may be excluded. For example, depressed patients whose dysfunctions are severe may be intentionally excluded from the protocol and placed under immediate care because treatments with known efficacy exist. Similarly, screening criteria of patients for clinical trials often select patients who have circumscribed or well-delineated dysfunctions rather than diffuse and multiple disorders. In any case, patients included in clinical trials are not always the same as those seen in routine treatment.

ADVANTAGES AND LIMITATIONS

Clinical trials are conducted under varying conditions that closely resemble clinical settings, but the conditions are not necessarily identical. In the extreme cases, analogue research and clinical trials can be readily distinguished. As analogue research includes dimensions that approach clinical work or as clinical trials include dimensions that move more toward nonclinic characteristics, however, the distinction may become blurred, if meaningful at all.

There is general agreement that clinical trials represent somewhat of a final achievement or end point in outcome research in terms of the evolution of evaluation strategies (Parloff, 1979). Positive leads from case studies, uncontrolled trials, and analogue studies can culminate in a clinical demonstration. Once a controlled clinical trial attests to the efficacy of treatment, the research process has achieved a major accomplishment. The evidence is considered to attest to the effectiveness of treatment when applied clinically.

Even though clinical trials test treatments under clinic conditions, generality of the results to clinical settings may still be a relevant concern. Clinical trials often introduce special features into the situation to meet the demands of research that depart from most clinical applications of treatment (Agras & Berkowitz, 1980; Emmelkamp, 1979; Kazdin, 1982a). The degree of experimental control, the careful application of treatment, and monitoring of treatment administration are some of the features that characterize research rather than clinical applications of treatment. The differences in rigor and care in administering treatment may be quite relevant to the outcome. And, whether the effects of treatment applied in clinical practice achieve the effects demonstrated in research is an open question.

General Comments

Analogue research and clinical trials represent complementary types of research. Analogue research is especially well suited to analyze facets of treatment and to evaluate the underlying mechanism responsible for change, the parameters that influence treatment efficacy, and similar questions requiring careful experimental control. Clinical trials are especially well suited for examining the effectiveness of alternative techniques under conditions that approximate routine clinical care. The complexities and priorities of the treatment settings make evaluation of subtle questions about particular treatments difficult. Hence theory testing, dissection of treatment, and evaluation of subtle treatment parameters that may influence outcome are usually reserved for analogue research.

Contemporary Evaluation Issues

Several issues fundamental to the evaluation and investigation of treatment continue to be actively debated. Many of the debates are part of the continuing saga of therapy research. Yet, advances have been made as well in the methods available for treatment evaluation. Three areas of contemporary concern that relate to treatment evaluation and outcome include meta-analysis as a procedure to evaluate treatment outcomes, negative effects of psychotherapy, and research methods for clinical work with the individual cases.

Meta-analysis

Evaluation of psychotherapy research has continued since Eysenck (1952) criticized the existing literature over three decades ago. Basic questions have been evaluated and reevaluated and include whether psychotherapy produces change and whether some techniques are more effective than others. Literature reviews have repeatedly surveyed the research to address these questions (e.g., Bergin & Lambert, 1978; Kazdin & Wilson, 1978b; Lambert, 1979; Luborsky, Singer, & Luborsky, 1975; Meltzoff & Kornreich, 1970; Rachman, 1971). The conclusions from many literature reviews are familiar. Authors typically state that clear conclusions cannot be drawn or are premature given the methodological problems of existing research; such reviews invariably end with the call for more research. In some reviews, substantive statements about the effects of treatment are provided. Unfortunately, the same studies are often evaluated by different reviewers with very discrepant or diametrically opposed conclusions about their yield (see, for example, Bergin, 1980; Bergin & Lambert, 1978; Franks & Mays, 1980; Mays & Franks, 1980; in press; Rachman & Wilson, 1980).

Recently, a new type of analysis has emerged as a way of evaluating and integrating large sets of investigations using quantitative methods. The procedure, *meta-analysis*, provides a way (or actually several ways) to combine the results from individual investigations and to reach conclusions based on the statistical analyses of these studies *en masse*. A common unit of analysis, referred to as *effect size*, is used across investigations. Effect size consists of the difference between means on a particular measure (e.g., self-report or therapist ratings) for treated and untreated (or alternative treatment) groups divided by the standard deviation of the untreated control group. Essentially, the measure provides information regarding the increment of improvement that treatment provides. Effect sizes can be calculated for separate outcome measures in an individual study. And, of course, the computation can be made separately for changes at different points in time after treatment and over the course of follow-up. Consequently, a single investigation may yield several different effect sizes.

Glass and Smith (e.g., Glass, 1976; Glass, McGaw, & Smith, 1981; Smith, Glass, Miller, 1980; Smith & Glass, 1977) have demonstrated the technique and its application to psychotherapy research. The Smith and Glass (1977) paper provided an initial demonstration of the technique. Meta-analysis was applied to 375 psychotherapy outcome studies. Based on different measures and assessment at different points in time, 833 effect sizes were studied. Studies were included where alternative forms of psychotherapy or psychotherapy and no-treatment were compared. Essentially, effect size represented the dependent measure with alternative treatment conditions across the different studies as the independent variable. Several other independent variables were evaluated by classifying studies according to such factors as duration of treatment, experience of the therapist, patient diagnosis, and so on. Thus, meta-analysis permits evaluation of multiple independent variables that could not be readily examined in individual studies.

Smith and Glass (1977) concluded from this meta-analysis that psychotherapy in its diverse forms is more effective than no treatment. The average effect size was .68, which reflects a difference in means (in standard deviation units) between groups receiving psychotherapy and untreated controls. The .68 standard deviation effect size can be translated into percentages of persons, using the normal distribution as the basis for evaluating the effect. Essentially, bell-shaped distributions drawn for treated and untreated clients will have means separated by .68 standard deviation. In other words, the average patient who does not receive treatment would be at the 50th percentile; the average patient who does receive treatment would be at the 75th percentile of the untreated controls. Although slight superiority was noted for behavioral techniques relative to psychodynamic approaches, the differences were considered negligible. Thus, the analysis was considered to support the conclusion that different techniques tend to differ very little in the effects they produce.

A more extensive meta-analysis of psychotherapy outcome studies was subsequently reported by Smith et al. (1980). The study included a larger set of outcome studies ($N = 475$) and effect-sizes ($N = 1,766$). The results were similar with an effect size slightly larger (.85) than in the previous analysis of the smaller sample of studies. An effect size of .85 translates into the finding that at the end of therapy, the average person who receives treatment would be better off than 80 percent of the persons who did not receive treatment.

The analyses completed by Smith and Glass were novel and provocative. The analyses addressed major questions that have continued to foster debate and research. Perhaps because of the issues involved and the novelty of the method, the controversy stirred by meta-analysis has been

marked. The procedure represents a clear advance insofar as it provides a quantitative way to examine and combine multiple studies with a common unit, effect size. Also, the possibility of examining the impact of independent variables that transcend individual studies on effect size is critical as well. However, controversy has emphasized that application of meta-analysis obscures many problems with the constituent investigations (Eysenck, 1978; Gallo, 1978; Kazdin & Wilson, 1978b; Presby, 1978). Although some objections have been advanced against the analysis itself, concerns more commonly focus on *how* the procedure is used (Strube & Hartmann, 1983).

A major objection to the analysis conducted by Smith and Glass (1977) pertain to the studies that were included. Meta-analysis only refers to a procedure that evaluates a sample of studies. Selection of the sample of studies is obviously critical and determines the ultimate conclusions that will be reached. Objections to the Smith and Glass (1977) analyses have pointed to different features of the sample. First, differences in methodological adequacy of the studies were largely ignored. Thus, the analysis combined studies that varied in factors as random assignment, adequacy of control conditions, and similar design factors that need to be considered when evaluating any particular study or combining that study with others. Second, Smith and Glass (1977) noted that their analyses were comprehensive with respect to the available outcome literature. Other authors have noted, however, that a large number of major studies, especially in behavior therapy, were completely omitted (Rachman & Wilson, 1980).

The objections have been met in varying degrees in the more extended report by Smith et al. (1980) and especially by a recent application by Shapiro and Shapiro (1981), who tried explicitly to address a variety of concerns with the original Smith and Glass (1977) report. In general, the replication attempt also found that treatment was superior to no treatment. Behavioral and cognitive methods were superior to dynamic and humanistic treatments. The treatment conclusions were similar to those of Smith et al. (1980), who also tended to find superiority of behavioral and cognitive methods for selected problems and outcome measures. In each of the demonstrations, however, technique differences were relatively small and their practical significance unclear.

Evaluations of meta-analysis indicate that the procedure is by no means free from interpretive problems (e.g., Cook & Leviton, 1980; Strube & Hartmann, 1983). Despite its quantitative basis, judgment is not eliminated by the procedure. Selection and inclusion of the sample of studies and of course limitations in the available population of studies obviously influence the conclusions that are reached from metaanalysis. Yet, many of the objections applied to meta-analysis also apply to the more traditional literature reviews that have served as a basis to draw general conclusions from masses of data. Meta-analysis not only permits a new way of evaluating outcome evidence, but also extends the range of questions that can be evaluated from existing studies. Multiple variables can be examined by coding studies along different dimensions. Conclusions can be drawn about factors that could not be studied easily in individual investigations or detected in subjective or scholarly reviews from scores of investigations. As with any relatively new method of analysis, caution will need to be exercised in its application and technique refinements will no doubt emerge. However, the method represents a distinct methodological advance in the last few years in treatment evaluation.

Negative Effects of Psychotherapy

A topic that continues to raise substantive and methodological questions in treatment research is the possible negative effects of psychotherapy (see Mays & Franks, in press; Strupp, Hadley, & Gomes-Schwartz, 1977). Negative effects refer generally to the notion that clients may become worse in some way after completing treatment. Bergin (1966) has had primary responsibility for bringing the notion of negative effects into sharp focus by reviewing research and claiming that evidence supports the existence of patient *deterioration* following treatment. Bergin has claimed that psychotherapy produces positive effects (improvements) for some individuals and negative effects (deterioration) for others. The notion has a common-sense appeal since any intervention would not be expected invariably to improve the condition for which it was intended.

The view that psychotherapy produces negative effects and the evidence offered on its behalf are a matter of considerable contemporary debate. The evidence has been reviewed, rereviewed, and critically reexamined on several occasions (see Bergin, 1980; Bergin & Lambert, 1978; Franks &

Mays, 1980; Lambert, Bergin, & Collins, 1977; Mays & Franks, 1980, in press; Rachman & Wilson, 1980). Expert opinion from researchers and clinicians has also suggested the existence of negative treatment effects, but clear evidence on the matter is difficult to obtain (Strupp et al., 1977).

Two obviously related but conceptually separate issues are embedded in the notion of negative effects of psychotherapy. First, negative effects mean that clients have become worse over the course of treatment. Second, the change is considered to result from participation in treatment. These issues raise a large number of different methodological concerns that can only be highlighted here (see Kazdin, in press).

Demonstrating that clients have become worse is not as straightforward as might appear. Simply showing that a client's score on a measure of adjustment has become lower (worse) is insufficient. A lower score must be shown to be of sufficient magnitude that it is unlikely to be from "chance" (expected change given reliability and variability of performance on the measure). Also, the measures used to evaluate change raises problems for demonstrating negative effects. Multiple criteria need to be invoked to evaluate treatment effects (Kazdin & Wilson, 1978a; Strupp & Hadley, 1977). The measures that should serve as the primary basis for inferring deterioration over the course of treatment remain to be resolved.

At present, research suggests that treatments are likely to produce multiple changes. Behavior tends to be organized into clusters or groups of intercorrelated responses, so that change in one area may lead to changes in other areas as well (see Kazdin, 1982c; Voeltz & Evans, 1982; Wahler, Berland, & Coe, 1979). When multiple changes occur, some of them might be viewed as positive and others as negative. It is unlikely that a summary statement can meaningfully proclaim that therapy produced either a positive or a negative effect.

If it is assumed that negative effects were demonstrated by whatever criteria, the next issue would be to determine whether these were induced by treatment. Evidence is needed that clients randomly assigned to treatment and no-treatment groups later differed in the extent or frequency of negative effects. Also, evidence would be needed that group differences could not be explained by other factors. For example, if self-report measures indicated greater negative change for treated than for nontreated subjects, this may not necessarily indicate that deterioration resulted from treatment. Some clients who completed treatment may have responded more negatively to questions assessing their mental health, adjustment, or symptoms than clients who have received no treatment. Treatment may have increased the willingness of treated clients to acknowledge their problems or to evaluate their situations more realistically. Thus, differences in assessment criteria (referred to as instrumentation) across treatment and no-treatment groups rather than actual deterioration might account for group differences.

Another difficulty in showing that negative treatment effects are due to therapy results from the small percentages of persons who show adverse reactions across treatment and no-treatment conditions. Typically, few persons show adverse effects in either treatment or no-treatment conditions. Consequently, the differences in the proportion of persons showing such effects are difficult to detect statistically. Also, the magnitude of change of these few individuals is difficult to evaluate given the small numbers of subjects within each group who become worse on a particular measure.

Whether negative effects of therapy are evident and whether such effects are therapeutically induced require consideration of several assessment and design issues. Analyses of outcome data by and large have been based on *post hoc* evaluation of studies that were not designed to investigate negative treatment effects. Consequently, the assessment and design issues that require consideration naturally were not addressed within the original studies. The debate over negative effects of treatment probably will continue until studies focus directly on the issue.

Evaluation of the Single-Case in Clinical Practice

An important issue for clinical psychology has been the hiatus between research and practice (e.g., Leitenberg, 1974; Shakow, 1976). Although the hiatus represents a larger professional issue with important implications for training, providing credentials, and conceptualizing the field, it raises treatment issues as well. The primary professional activity of clinical psychologists consists of providing direct clinical service (Garfield & Kurtz, 1976). Those who conduct research are rarely engaged in clinical practice and vice versa. Researchers usually work in academic settings and lack access to the kinds of problems seen in routine clinical and hospital care. Consequently, treatment research in these settings often departs greatly from the conditions that characterize clinical settings such as hospitals and outpatient clinics (Kazdin, 1978; Parloff, 1979; Raush, 1974).

Analogue research, discussed earlier, characterizes the type of treatment investigation that is typically conducted in academic settings, where carefully controlled laboratory conditions are invoked and where subjects do not evince the types or severity of problems of persons ordinarily seen in treatment. In research, treatment is usually standardized across persons to ensure that the investigation is properly controlled. Persons who administer treatment are often advanced students who closely follow the prescribed procedures. Two or more treatments are usually compared over a relatively short treatment period by examining client performance on standardized measures such as self-report inventories, behavioral tests, and global ratings. Conclusions about the effectiveness of alternative procedures are reached on the basis of statistical evaluation of the data.

The results of treatment investigations often are considered to have little bearing on the questions and concerns of practitioners who see individual patients (Fishman, 1981). Clinicians often see patients who vary widely in their personal characteristics, education, and background from college students who serve in analogue studies. Also, patients often require multiple treatments to address their manifold problems. The clinician is not concerned with presenting a standardized technique but with providing a treatment that is individualized to meet the patient's needs in an optimal fashion. Rather than presenting a single treatment for a predetermined number of sessions, clinicians are more likely to present multiple treatments and to continue as long as required to ameliorate the problems for which treatment was sought. Also, the clinician is interested in producing a clinically significant change, i.e., one that is clearly evident in the patient's everyday life. The statistically significant changes demonstrated and discussed in research may not be very important or relevant to the clinician. The average amount of change that serves as the basis for drawing conclusions in between-group research does not address the clinician's need to make decisions about treatments for the individual client.

Researchers and clinicians alike have repeatedly acknowledged the lack of relevance of clinical research in guiding clinical practice. Prominent clinical psychologists (e.g., Rogers, Matarazzo) have explicitly noted that their own research has not had much impact on their practice of psychotherapy (Bergin & Strupp, 1972). Part of the problem is that clinical investigations of therapy are invariably conducted with groups of persons in order to meet the demands of traditional experimental design and statistical evaluation. But investigation of groups or conclusions about average patient performance may distort the primary phenomenon of interest, that is, the effects of treatments on individuals. Hence, researchers have suggested that experimentation at the level of individual case studies may provide greater insights in understanding therapeutic change (Barlow, 1980; Bergin & Strupp, 1970, 1972).

The practicing clinician is confronted with the individual case, and it is at the level of the clinical case that empirical evaluations of treatment need to be made. The problem, of course, is that the primary investigative tool for the clinician has been the uncontrolled case study in which anecdotal information is reported and scientifically acceptable inferences cannot be drawn (Bolger, 1965; Lazarus & Davison, 1971). The hiatus between research and practice may exist in part because of the absence of a research methodology that can be feasibly applied in clinical settings. The control over assessment and treatment administration, recruitment of homogeneous patients, standardization, delay or withholding of treatment are not viable options in most clinical settings. Consequently, clinical work at the level of the individual case has remained uncontrolled in part because of the lack of viable alternatives.

Recently, use of the individual case as a basis for research has been advocated. One recommendation has been to reconceptualize the uncontrolled case study as an experiment and to bring to bear multiple sources of information to increase the strength of the inferences that can be drawn (see Kazdin, 1981). The logic of experimentation can be followed in an uncontrolled case study to controvert particular sources of ambiguity. The purpose of experimentation is to make alternative explanations of the results as implausible as possible. At the end of an experimental investigation, the effects of treatment should be the most plausible and parsimonious interpretation of the results.

Case studies can also rule out alternative explanations that might compete with inferences about the impact of treatment.

The major additions required of the case study to make various threats to internal validity implausible include using objective measures (e.g., self-report inventories, ratings, and direct observation), assessing performance at a few points before, during, and after treatment, and obtaining information from research on other cases or from data for the given case about the stability of the problem. Also, the accumulation of a few cases and the evaluation of the pattern of change during treatment can be used to draw valid inferences from uncontrolled case studies. With relatively minor changes in the ways therapists assess individual cases, a quantum leap can be made in the informational yield. The assessment data and the other information the clinician can bring to bear on the case can address specific concerns that ordinarily arise in case studies.

Apart from the valid inference approach highlighted above, several authors have advocated the use of single-case experimental designs to evaluate treatment cases (e.g., Hersen & Barlow, 1976; Kazdin, 1982b; Kratochwill, 1978). The designs consist of different ways of presenting the treatment so that threats to internal validity become implausible explanations of the results. Many designs are available, and their widespread use in clinic research has attested to their methodological strength in demonstrating causal relations (see Hersen & Barlow, 1976; Kazdin, 1982b).[1]

Single-case experimental designs have been advocated for use in clinical practice (Hayes, 1981). The designs, however, make some rather stringent demands on the clinical investigator that may interfere with the usual service delivery priorities of treatment. The requirements for assessing performance continuously, for arranging treatments to evaluate their impact experimentally, and for procuring the resources needed to ensure objectivity of the measures are likely to restrict the use of the designs. Also, the designs have been used heavily in cases where the clinical problems can be readily translated into specific target behaviors that can be observed directly. The multifaceted nature of clinical problems and the unavailability of direct behavioral referents, either in principle or in practice, introduce special prob-

---

[1]Different single-case experimental designs and their place in clinical psychology and treatment evaluation have been elaborated in the chapters by Hayes (Chapter 11) and Kratochwill and Mace (Chapter 12) in this book.

lems for the designs. The important point to convey here, however, is that single-case experimental designs represent a methodology for experimentation with individual clients. Even though the demands the designs place on treatment may restrict their widespread use by practicing clinicians, certainly the methodology is much more feasible than between-group methodology for ordinary clinical practice.

Integration of Alternative Treatments: Implications for Future Evaluation Research

A major issue in the evaluation of psychotherapy is the plethora of techniques that are available. The number of therapy techniques continues to grow. Rarely, if ever, do techniques seem to be discarded for lack of evidence or disuse (Frank, 1982). The obvious difficulty resulting from the glut of available techniques is that their evaluation for any set of clinical problems becomes virtually impossible. Advances can be speeded greatly by integrative work that searches for commonalities among different techniques. Integrative work might look at actual practices that are common to different techniques or identify common underlying mechanisms that account for the many different ways in which interventions are implemented.

The search for commonalities among alternative techniques is reasonable for several reasons. First, it is unlikely that many different interventions claimed to be effective all achieve their effects through different means. Either the techniques are procedurally similar in fundamental ways or are different but work through a common mechanism. The idea that the different procedures are effective and achieve these effects through idiosyncratic mechanisms violates parsimony as well as common sense. Second, despite the different descriptions about alternative techniques in the abstract, techniques appear to be quite similar in clinical practice. Observation of treatment implementation or evaluation of therapist behavior reveals similarities in what actually goes on in allegedly different treatments (Klein et al., 1969; Sloane et al., 1975). Third, the underlying theoretical bases of most techniques are usually unclear. Tests of the theoretical bases of different techniques have often shown that the conditions thought to be necessary for treatment efficacy are not essential (see Kazdin, 1979a). Although proponents of a particular technique are often clear

about the reasons changes are produced by one technique or another, in fact, support for a particular theoretical account is usually unavailable.

Alternative positions have been advanced to help unify alternative treatments. Three positions are outlined briefly below. They are mentioned not only because of the substantive views they reflect but also because they provide important guidelines for future research in psychotherapy.

Demoralization Hypothesis

The view that alternative therapies may include several common ingredients has been consistently advocated by Frank (1961, 1973). The commonalities across different forms of therapy might be reflected in both what the clients bring to different treatments and what they receive once they arrive. Frank (1982) has proposed the demoralization hypothesis to identify the commonalities among the problems that clients bring to treatment. The hypothesis suggests that patients seek therapy not only for their specific symptoms but also because of their demoralization. Demoralization refers to a state of mind characterized by subjective incompetence, poor self-esteem, alienation, hopelessness, and helplessness. The demoralized person, either through lack of skills or confusion of goals, becomes unable to master situations or experiences stress with which he or she cannot cope. Symptoms such as anxiety, depression, and loneliness may result from demoralization. However, despite the different symptoms that patients may bring to treatment, demoralization is a common theme.

Treatments are considered by Frank to be effective because of their characteristics that help ameliorate patient demoralization. Independently of their idiosyncratic features, alternative procedures share the following general ingredients. The treatments provide:

1. An emotionally charged and confiding relationship with a person identified as a helping agent;
2. A setting in which patients' expectancies for help and confidence in the therapist's role as a healer are strengthened;
3. A rationale or conceptual scheme that plausibly explains the symptoms and prescribes a procedure for their resolution; and
4. A set of procedures in which both the patient and the therapist engage that they believe to be the means of restoring the patient.

Frank believes that the rationale to explain the patient's problems (the myth) and the procedures in which therapist and patient engage (the ritual) are critical to combating patient demoralization. The myth and ritual provide new learning experiences, evoke expectancies for help, provide opportunities for rehearsal and practice, and strengthen the therapeutic relationship.

From the standpoint of treatment evaluation, shared ingredients of different therapies provide important research leads. Frank (1982) reviews his own program of research that has produced results consistent with and has helped consolidate his views of the role of patient expectancies for change. Also, existing research for different treatments is consistent with the general model. For example, the role of the therapeutic relationship continues to be recognized as a common and critical ingredient among different techniques (DeVoge & Beck, 1978; Kazdin, 1979a). More direct tests of the model could be provided. For example, common client reactions may be evoked by the myths (rationales) or rituals (procedures) of alternative techniques. Indeed, these characteristics of treatment can be varied to determine their differential impact on client expectations of improvement. Alternatively, client involvement in the treatment might be varied within a given treatment technique to determine if it has impact on client expectancies for change or therapeutic outcome. Some of the research on the common ingredients might need to be evaluated under highly controlled laboratory conditions (analogue research) because of ethical constraints in meeting the needs of patients who seek treatment. Yet, manipulation of aspects of the rationale or procedures might be a matter of degree and hence possible to study in clinical applications of treatment.

Self-Efficacy

Another notion that unites diverse treatment techniques is self-efficacy and has been proposed by Bandura (1977a). Although the notion was originally proposed in the context of analyzing change in the treatment of fear and avoidance, it has been extended to many areas of research including diverse clinical problems and academic performance (DeClemente, 1981; Kazdin, 1979b; Keyser & Barling, 1981).

Self-efficacy refers to a person's expectation that he or she can successfully perform behaviors that will lead to a certain outcome. The expectation of whether one can perform the behavior is distinct from the expectation that a given behavior leads to a certain outcome. A person may believe that particular behaviors will result in a particular outcome (outcome expectancy) but not believe that he or she can successfully perform the behaviors (efficacy expectation). Bandura's notion of self-efficacy is part of a larger social-learning, cognitively-based conceptual framework of behavior change (see Bandura, 1977b). For present purposes, self-efficacy is isolated here from the larger framework, because it has been advanced as the mechanism to explain behavior changes resulting from different treatments. Self-efficacy is the final common pathway through which different treatments are considered to produce change.

Expectations of mastery are proposed to influence a person's initiation and persistence of coping behavior and the situations in which they enter. High-self efficacy persons are more likely to persist or provide greater effort. Those who succeed are likely to have self-efficacy further enhanced. Low self-efficacy persons are more likely to evince little persistence; those who cease to cope or who try unsuccessfully are likely to have their low efficacy expectations further supported.

Bandura and his associates have completed several investigations to evaluate the role of self-efficacy in behavior change (Bandura & Adams, 1977; Bandura, Adams, & Beyer, 1977; Bandura et al., 1980). The research has focused on showing that the extent to which therapeutic change is achieved across different techniques is a function of changes in self-efficacy and that techniques are differentially effective because they vary in their success in altering self-efficacy.

The research has primarily studied volunteer clients who fear harmless snakes but the research has been extended to persons with fears of open spaces, darkness, elevators, and heights (Bandura et al., 1980; Biran & Wilson, 1981). A wide range of behavior therapy techniques have been studied including live, covert, and participant modeling, desensitization, guided exposure, and cognitive restructuring. Self-efficacy has been proposed to explain existing findings that techniques relying on overt performance (e.g., participant modeling, *in vivo* desensitization) are more effective in the outcomes they produce than techniques based on vicarious experiences (e.g., symbolic modeling), persuasion (e.g., interpretative treatments), or emotional arousal (e.g., attribution).

Self-efficacy represents an important advance

in therapy research for different reasons. First, the notion has been couched in terms that permit empirical investigation. The measurement of self-efficacy was described when the notion was first introduced. Thus, self-efficacy is not another abstract construct awaiting operationalization. Second, multiple studies have already been completed attesting to the relationship between self-efficacy and behavior change. Of course, self-efficacy theory or research has not proceeded without criticism. Both the conceptual framework and the methodological problems raised by its assessment have been noted (Kirsch, 1980; Rachman, 1978). Also, the research has been restricted to a relatively narrow set of treatments within behavior therapy and to volunteer clients seen under laboratory conditions. Investigators vary on the extent to which they see this as a relevant issue in evaluation of the underlying mechanisms of therapeutic change (Bandura, 1978, 1979; Woolfolk & Lazarus, 1979). The critical issue for present purposes, however, is the fact that self-efficacy represents a researchable construct designed to describe a common mechanism for changes achieved by alternative treatments. As such, its impact on treatment evaluation in the next several years could be marked.

Integrationism

Commonalities among alternative techniques have been sought without regard to specific notions such as demoralization or self-efficacy. Recently, several investigators have sought a rapprochement among seemingly competing conceptual views on the nature of clinical problems and therapeutic change. The rapprochement has been referred to as *integrationism* and been addressed in different texts (e.g., Goldfried, 1982; Marmor & Woods, 1980; Wachtel, 1977). Over the history of psychotherapy, repeated efforts have been made to integrate competing treatments techniques under a single conceptual scheme (Goldfried, 1982b). The current movement toward integrationism stems from multiple influences, including:

1. The recognition of limitations associated with any singular treatment approach;
2. The infusion of constructs from cognitive psychology in assessment, treatment and conceptualization of clinical disorders, and the broadened perspective it has generated;
3. The recognition that conceptual positions regarded as competing alternatives share many similarities;

4. Acknowledgment that, in practice, treatment techniques tend to be much more similar than their theoretical underpinnings or abstract presentation would suggest; and
5. Increased evidence from individual studies and larger analyses of the literature (e.g., meta-analysis) that the outcomes produced by different techniques are not obviously different (see Goldfried, 1980, 1982a, 1982b).

Although grounds for rapprochement might be sought at an abstract theoretical or concrete procedural level, an intermediate level of similarity has been proposed. Goldfried (1980) has referred to this level as a common set of *clinical strategies* or general principles of change. These strategies include experiences provided in treatment above the level of specific procedures. Different techniques may implement the strategies differently but the overall goal is achieved nonetheless. Similarities in the strategies of different therapies include:

1. Initially inducing client expectancies that treatment will be helpful;
2. Providing a therapeutic relationship in which clients can participate;
3. Encouraging corrective experiences; and
4. Providing clients with the opportunity to reality-test and to obtain an external perspective on their problems.

The movement toward integrationism must be distinguished from simple eclecticism. An eclectic approach recognizes the virtues of different approaches or techniques and tries to sample from them as needed to effect therapeutic change. Thus, an eclectic therapist might adopt and combine desensitization, insight-oriented psychotherapy, and rational-emotive therapy as needed. Eclecticism tends to draw from several different approaches, recognizing their separate integrity. Also, eclecticism can consist of an infinite number of variations depending on which combinations of available techniques clinicians choose (Garfield, 1982; Garfield & Kurtz, 1976). Integrationism is eclectic in that it is open to diverse approaches but it looks at a higher level of abstraction to cull common threads among different treatments. Yet, an integrationist view goes beyond any particular approach and seeks to identify elements embraced by different techniques.

From the standpoint of treatment evaluation, integrationism has the potential for identifying processes and procedures that transcend individual techniques. The processes and procedures can become the focus of research. For example, a common procedure among diverse techniques is the use of extratreatment practice in which the client is encouraged to engage in therapeutically relevant activities to augment therapeutic change. For example, Alexander and French (1946) recommend that psychodynamic therapies require patients to perform in everyday situations those activities that they previously were unable to perform. Other conceptual approaches in varying degrees have advocated similar types of activities (e.g., Ellis, 1962; Fenichel, 1941; Haley, 1963; Herzberg, 1945; Salter, 1949). Interestingly, a recent survey indicated that approximately 60 percent of all outpatient treatment studies of behavior therapy incorporate extratherapy practice for such diverse problems as phobias, obsessive-compulsive disorders, depression, sexual dysfunctions, marital discord, and others (see Shelton & Levy, 1981a, 1981b). Extratreatment practice might be one of the common clinical strategies that spans many different treatments and is worth investigation (see Kazdin & Mascitelli, 1982a, 1982b).

An integrationist approach provides an important initial analysis of commonalities among alternative treatments. The strategies identified in this fashion need to be followed up with theory and research. An integrationism program of outcome research would take a potentially momentous turn away from existing research which tends to focus on individual techniques and their comparison with other techniques that rival for therapeutic superiority.

General Comments

The above discussion highlights three attempts to seek a common ground among alternative treatments. The different views are by no means incompatible or exhaustive. Related attempts to seek commonalities have been identified with other concepts such as nonspecific treatment factors, placebo effects, and others. As already noted, attempts to seek commonalities among different techniques are by no means new. Yet, recent efforts have emerged at a time when research in psychotherapy is particularly active. The area of psychotherapy has never suffered from nonempirical extremes such as armchair theorizing or anecdotal accounts of processes and outcomes of particular treatments. What is new about current proposals is that they are accompanied by recognition of the need to develop new lines of research to make an empirical advance rather than merely to promote conceptual harmony among alternative schools of thought.

Conclusions

Advances in psychotherapy have been slow, a fact that has often been attributed to the inherent complexity and multiplicity of the clinical problems to which treatments are directed. Recent progress has stemmed in part from recognition of the complexity of the topic and the underlying conceptual and methodological issues treatment evaluation raises. A flurry of outcome research alone will not begin to address the many questions — even empirical questions — of psychotherapy. Advances in conceptualization of treatment and evaluation methodology are essential for accelerated progress.

Several areas discussed in the present chapter reflect important methodological advances. For example, the treatment evaluation strategies elaborated earlier codify many of the different ways in which the complex questions of psychotherapy can be divided and conquered in research. The elaborate questions facing psychotherapy cannot be addressed at the level at which they are usually posed. But systematic evaluation of treatments as they progress through the different strategies can yield the desired answers. Also, different conditions of research, as reflected in analogue studies and clinical trials, are both required to address the gamut of questions about a given treatment.

The sources of controversy in the field perhaps now more than ever before are not likely to remain at the armchair level. For example, controversies over meta-analyses have sparked not merely rebuttals but "new and improved" meta-analyses to confront the criticisms directly. Similarly, debates about negative treatment effects, now approaching two decades, will now more than in the past have the methodological criteria for such effects more explicitly spelled out so that the issue can be better studied.

A major advance in the field is the attempt among many to shed rival conceptual positions and the promulgation of narrow orientations or techniques. Many researchers wish to reach a consensus about strategies that apply broadly across techniques and orientations. The explicit movement toward integrationism reflects an ecumenical spirit among researchers and clinicians. Integrationism holds special promise for evaluation of psychotherapy.

References

Adams, H. E., & Hughes, H. H. Animal analogues of behavioral treatment procedures: A critical evaluation. In M. Hersen, R. M. Eisler, & P. M. Miller (Eds.), *Progress in behavior modification*. Vol. 3. New York: Academic Press, 1976.

Agras, W. S., & Berkowitz, R. Clinical research in behavior therapy: Halfway there? *Behavior Therapy*, 1980, 11, 472–487.

Alexander, F., & French, T. M. *Psychoanalytic therapy: Principles and applications*. New York: Ronald, 1946.

Alexander, J. F., Barton, C., Schiavo, R. S., & Parsons, B. V. Systems-behavioral intervention with families of delinquents: Therapist characteristics, family behavior, and outcome. *Journal of Consulting and Clinical Psychology*, 1976, 44, 656–664.

American Psychiatric Association, *Diagnostic and statistical manual of mental disorders*. (3rd ed.) Washington, D.C.: American Psychiatric Association, 1980.

Azrin, N. H. A strategy for applied research: Learning based but outcome oriented. *American Psychologist*, 1977, 32, 140–149.

Bandura, A. Self-efficacy: Toward a unifying theory of behavioral change. *Psychological Review*, 1977, 84, 191–215. (a)

Bandura, A. *Social learning theory*. Englewood Cliffs, N.J.: Prentice-Hall, 1977. (b)

Bandura, A. On paradigms and recycled ideologies. *Cognitive Therapy and Research*, 1978, 2, 79–103.

Bandura, A. On ecumenism in research perspectives. *Cognitive Therapy and Research*, 1979, 3, 245–248.

Bandura, A., & Adams, N. E. Analysis of self-efficacy theory of behavioral change. *Cognitive Therapy and Research*, 1977, 1, 287–310.

Bandura, A., Adams, N. E., & Beyer, J. Cognitive processes mediating behavioral change. *Journal of Personality and Social Psychology*, 1977, 35, 125–139.

Bandura, A., Adams, N. E., Hardy, A. B., & Howells, G. N. Tests of generality of self-efficacy theory. *Cognitive Therapy and Research*, 1980, 4, 39–66.

Barlow, D. H. Behavior therapy: The next decade. *Behavior therapy*, 1980, 11, 315–328.

Bergin, A. E. Some implications of psychotherapy research for therapeutic practice. *Journal of Abnormal Psychology*, 1966, 71, 235–246.

Bergin, A. E. Negative effects revisited: A reply. *Professional Psychology*, 1980, 11, 93–100.

Bergin, A. E., & Lambert, M. J. The evaluation of therapeutic outcomes. In S. L. Garfield & A. E. Bergin (Eds.), *Handbook of psychotherapy and behavior change: An empirical analysis*. (2nd ed.) New York: Wiley, 1978.

Bergin, A. E., & Strupp, H. H. New directions in psychotherapy research. *Journal of Abnormal Psychology*, 1970, 76, 235–246.

Bergin, A. E., & Strupp, H. H. (Eds.), *Changing frontiers in the science of psychotherapy*. Chicago: Aldine-Atherton, 1972.

Biran, M., & Wilson, G. T. Treatment of phobic disorders using cognitive and exposure methods: A self-efficacy analysis. *Journal of Consulting and Clinical Psychology*, 1981, 49, 886–899.

Bolgar, H. The case study method. In B. B. Wolman (Ed.), *Handbook of clinical psychology*. New York: McGraw-Hill, 1965.

Borkovec, T., & Rachman, S. The utility of analogue research. *Behaviour Research and Therapy*, 1979, 17, 253–261.

Cook, T. D., & Leviton, L. C. Reviewing the literature: A comparison of traditional methods with meta-analysis. *Journal of Personality*, 1980, 48, 449–472.

Davison, G. C. Systematic desensitization as a counter-conditioning process. *Journal of Abnormal Psychology*, 1968, 73, 91–99.

DeClemente, C. C. Self-efficacy and smoking cessation maintenance: A preliminary report. *Cognitive Therapy and Research*, 1981, 5, 175–187.

DeVoge, J. T., & Beck, S. The therapist-client relationship in behavior therapy. In M. Hersen, R. M. Eisler, & P. M. Miller (Eds.), *Progress in behavior modification*. Vol. 6. New York: Academic Press, 1978.

Ellis, A. *Reason and emotion in psychotherapy*. New York: Lyle Stuart, 1962.

Emmelkamp, P. M. G. The behavioral study of clinical phobias. In M. Hersen, R. M. Eisler, & P. M. Miller (Eds.), *Progress in behavior modification*, Vol. 8. New York: Academic Press, 1979.

Eysenck, H. J. The effects of psychotherapy: An evaluation. *Journal of Consulting Psychology*, 1952, 16, 319–324.

Eysenck, H. J. An exercise in mega-silliness. *American Psychologist*, 1978, 33, 517.

Fenichel, O. *Problems of psychoanalytic technique*. Albany, N.Y.: Psychoanalytic Quarterly, 1941.

Fishman, S. T. Narrowing the generalization gap in clinical research. *Behavioral Assessment*, 1981, 3, 243–248.

Frank, J. D. *Persuasion and healing*. Baltimore: Johns Hopkins University Press, 1961.

Frank, J. D. *Persuasion and healing: A comparative study of psychotherapy*. (2nd ed.) Baltimore: Johns Hopkins University Press, 1973.

Frank, J. D. Therapeutic components shared by all psychotherapies. In J. H. Harvey & M. M. Parks (Eds.), *Psychotherapy research and behavior change: (Vol. 1): The master lecture series*. Washington, D.C.: American Psychological Association, 1982.

Franks, C. M., & Mays, D. T. Negative effects revisited: A rejoinder. *Professional Psychology*, 1980, 11, 101–105.

Gallo, P. S., Jr. Meta-analysis—A mixed meta-phor? *American Psychologist*, 1978, 33, 515–516.

Garfield, S. L. Psychotherapy: A 40-year appraisal. *American Psychologist*, 1981, 36, 174–183.

Garfield, S. L. Eclecticism and integration in psychotherapy. *Behavior Therapy*, 1982, in press.

Garfield, S. L., & Kurtz, R. Clinical psychologists in the 1970s. *American Psychologist*, 1976, 31, 1–9.

Glass, G. V. Primary, secondary and meta-analysis of research. *Educational Researcher*, 1976, 10, 3–8.

Glass, G. V., McGaw, B., & Smith, M. L. *Meta-analysis in social research*. Beverly Hills, Calif.: Sage, 1981.

Goldfried, M. R. Toward the delineation of therapeutic change principles. *American Psychologist*, 1980, 35, 991–999.

Goldfried, M. R. (Ed.) *Converging themes in psycho-*

therapy: Trends in psychodynamic, humanistic and behavioral practice. New York: Springer, 1982. (a)

Goldfried, M. R. On the history of therapeutic integration. *Behavior Therapy,* 1982, in press. (b)

Gruen, W. Effects of brief psychotherapy during the hospitalization period on the recovery process in heart attacks. *Journal of Consulting and Clinical Psychology,* 1975, **43,** 223-232.

Haley, J. *Strategies of psychotherapy.* New York: Grune & Stratton, 1963.

Hayes, S. C. Single-case experimental design and empirical clinical practice. *Journal of Consulting and Clinical Psychology,* 1981, **49,** 193-211.

Heller, K. Laboratory interview research as an analogue to treatment. In A. E. Bergin & S. L. Garfield (Eds.), *Handbook of psychotherapy and behavior change: An empirical analysis.* New York: Wiley, 1971.

Herink, R. (Ed.) *The psychotherapy handbook.* New York: New American Library, 1980.

Hersen, M., & Barlow, D. H. *Single-case experimental designs: Strategies for studying behavior change.* New York: Pergamon, 1976.

Herzberg, A. *Active psychotherapy.* New York: Grune & Stratton, 1945.

Kazdin, A. E. Evaluating the generality of findings in analogue therapy research. *Journal of Consulting and Clinical Psychology,* 1978, **46,** 673-686.

Kazdin, A. E. Fictions, factions, and functions of behavior therapy. *Behavior Therapy,* 1979, **10,** 629-654. (a)

Kazdin, A. E. Imagery elaboration and self-efficacy in the covert modeling treatment of assertive behavior. *Journal of Consulting and Clinical Psychology,* 1979, **47,** 725-733. (b)

Kazdin, A. E. *Research design in clinical psychology.* New York: Harper & Row, 1980.

Kazdin, A. E. Drawing valid inferences from case studies. *Journal of Consulting and Clinical Psychology,* 1981, **49,** 183-192.

Kazdin, A. E. Methodology of psychotherapy outcome research: Recent developments and remaining limitations. In J. H. Harvey & M. M. Parks (Eds.), *Psychotherapy research and behavior change.* Washington, D.C.: American Psychological Association, 1982. (a)

Kazdin, A. E. *Single-case research designs: Methods for clinical and applied settings.* New York: Oxford University Press, 1982. (b)

Kazdin, A. E. Symptom substitution, generalization, and response covariation: Implications for psychotherapy outcome. *Psychological Bulletin,* 1982, **91,** 349-365. (c)

Kazdin, A. E. Assessment and design prerequisites for identifying negative therapy outcomes. In D. T. Mays & C. M. Franks (Eds.), *Above all do not harm: Negative outcome in psychotherapy and what to do about it.* New York: Springer, in press.

Kazdin, A. E., & Mascitelli, S. Behavioral rehearsal, self-instructions, and homework practice in developing assertiveness. *Behavior Therapy,* 1982, **13,** 346-360. (a)

Kazdin, A. E., & Mascitelli, S. Covert and overt rehearsal and homework practice in developing assertiveness. *Journal of Consulting and Clinical Psychology,* 1982, **50,** 250-258. (b)

Kazdin, A. E., & Wilson, G. T. Criteria for evaluating psychotherapy. *Archives of General Psychiatry,* 1978, **35,** 407-416. (a)

Kazdin, A. E., & Wilson, G. T. *Evaluation of behavior therapy: Issues, evidence, and research strategies.* Cambridge, Mass.: Ballinger, 1978. (b)

Keyser, V., & Barling, J. Determinants of children's self-efficacy beliefs in an academic environment. *Cognitive Therapy and Research,* 1981, **5,** 29-40.

Kiesler, C. A. Mental health policy as a field of inquiry for psychology. *American Psychologist,* 1980, **35,** 1066-1080.

Kirsch, I. "Microanalytic" analyses of efficacy expectations as predictors of performance. *Cognitive Therapy and Research,* 1980, **4,** 259-262.

Klein, M. H., Dittmann, A. T., Parloff, M. B., & Gill, M. M. Behavior therapy: Observations and reflections. *Journal of Consulting and Clinical Psychology,* 1969, **33,** 259-266.

Kovacs, M., Rush, A. J., Beck, A. T., & Hollon, S. D. Depressed outpatients treated with cognitive therapy or pharmacotherapy. *Archives of General Psychiatry,* 1981, **38,** 33-39.

Kraemer, H. C. Coping strategies in psychiatric clinical research. *Journal of Consulting and Clinical Psychology,* 1981, **49,** 309-319.

Krapfl, J. E., & Nawas, M. M. Differential ordering of stimulus presentation in systematic desensitization. *Journal of Abnormal Psychology,* 1970, **75,** 333-337.

Kratochwill, T. R. (Ed.) *Single-subject research: Strategies for evaluating change.* New York: Academic Press, 1978.

Lambert, M. J. *The effects of psychotherapy.* Vol. 1. Montreal: Eden, 1979.

Lambert, M. J., Bergin, A. E., & Collins, J. L. Therapist-induced deterioration in psychotherapy. In A. S. Gruman & A. M. Razin (Eds.), *Effective psychotherapy: A handbook of research.* Oxford, England: Pergamon, 1977.

Lang, P. J. The mechanics of desensitization and the laboratory study of fear. In C. M. Franks (Ed.), *Behavior therapy: Appraisal and status.* New York: McGraw-Hill, 1969.

Lazarus, A. A., & Davison, G. C. Clinical innovation in research and practice. In A. E. Bergin & S. L. Garfield (Eds.), *Handbook of psychotherapy and behavior change: An empirical analysis.* New York: Wiley, 1971.

Leitenberg, H. Training clinical researchers in psychology. *Professional Psychology,* 1974, **5,** 59-69.

Luborsky, L., Singer, B., & Luborsky, L. Comparative studies of psychotherapies: Is it true that "everyone has won and all must have prizes"? *Archives of General Psychiatry,* 1975, **32,** 995-1,008.

Marmor, J. Common operational factors in diverse approaches to behavior change. In A. Burton (Ed.), *What makes behavior change possible?* New York: Brunner/Mazel, 1976.

Marmor, J., & Woods, S. M. (Eds.), *The interface between psychodynamic and behavioral therapies.* New York: Plenum, 1980.

Mays, D. T., & Franks, C. M. Getting worse: Psychotherapy or no treatment—The jury should still be out. *Professional Psychology,* 1980, **11,** 78-92.

Mays, D. T., & Franks, C. M. (Eds.), *Above all do not*

harm: Negative outcome in psychotherapy and what to do about it. New York: Springer, in press.

Meltzoff, J., & Kornreich, M. Research in psychotherapy. New York: Atherton, 1970.

Orlinsky, D. O., & Howard, K. I. Varieties of psychotherapeutic experiences. New York: Teachers College Press, 1975.

Parloff, M. B. Can psychotherapy research guide the policymaker?: A little knowledge may be a dangerous thing. American Psychologist, 1979, 34, 296–306.

Parloff, M. B., Wolfe, B., Hadley, S., & Waskow, I. E. Assessment of psychosocial treatment of mental disorders: Current status and prospects. Report by NIMH Work Group, Advisory Committee on Mental Health, Institute of Medicine, National Academy of Sciences, February 1978.

Paul, G. Behavior modification research: Design and tactics. In C. M. Franks (Ed.), Behavior therapy: Appraisal and status. New York: McGraw-Hill, 1969.

Paul, G. L., & Lentz, R. J. Psychosocial treatment of chronic mental patients: Milieu versus social-learning programs. Cambridge, Mass.: Harvard University Press, 1977.

Presby, S. Overly broad categories obscure important differences between therapies. American Psychologist, 1978, 33, 514–515.

Rachman, S. The effects of psychotherapy. New York: Pergamon, 1971.

Rachman, S. (Ed.) Perceived self-efficacy: Analyses of Bandura's theory of behavioural change. Advances in Behaviour Research and Therapy, 1978, 1, 137–269.

Rachman, S. J., & Wilson, G. T. The effects of psychological therapy. (2nd ed.) Oxford, England: Pergamon, 1980.

Raush, H. L. Research, practice and accountability. American Psychologist, 1974, 29, 678–681.

Rosenthal, T. L., & Bandura, A. Psychological modeling: Theory and practice. In S. L. Garfield & A. E. Bergin (Eds.), Handbook of psychotherapy and behavior change. (2nd ed.) New York: Wiley, 1978.

Roth, D., Bielski, R., Jones, M., Parker, W., & Osborn, G. A comparison of self-control therapy and combined self-control therapy and antidepressant medication in the treatment of depression. Behavior Therapy, 1982, 13, 133–144.

Rush, A. J., Beck, A. T., Kovacs, M., & Hollon, S. Comparative efficacy of cognitive therapy and pharmacotherapy in the treatment of depressed outpatients. Cognitive Therapy and Research, 1977, 1, 17–37.

Salter, A. Conditioned reflex therapy. New York: Straus & Young, 1949.

Shakow, D. What is clinical psychology. American Psychologist, 1976, 31, 553–560.

Shapiro, D. A., & Shapiro, D. Meta-analysis of comparative studies: A replication and refinement. Paper presented at annual meeting of the Society for Psychotherapy Research, Aspen, Colorado, June 1981.

Shelton, J. L., & Levy, R. L. (Eds.). Behavioral assignments and treatment compliance: A handbook of clinical strategies. Champaign, Ill.: Research Press, 1981. (a)

Shelton, J. L., & Levy, R. L. A survey of the reported use of assigned homework activities in contemporary behavior therapy literature. The Behavior Therapist, 1981, 4(4), 13–14. (b)

Sloane, R. B., Staples, F. R., Cristol, A. H., Yorkston, N. J., & Whipple, K. Psychotherapy versus behavior therapy. Cambridge, Mass.: Harvard University Press, 1975.

Smith, M. L., & Glass, G. V. Meta-analysis of psychotherapy outcome studies. American Psychologist, 1977, 32, 752–760.

Smith, M. L., Glass, G. V., & Miller, T. I. The benefits of psychotherapy. Baltimore: Johns Hopkins University Press, 1980.

Stern, R., & Marks, I. M. Brief and prolonged flooding. Archives of General Psychiatry, 1973, 28, 270–276.

Strube, M. J., & Hartmann, D. P. A critical appraisal of meta-analysis. Journal of Consulting and Clinical Psychology, 1983, 51, 14–27.

Strupp, H. H., & Hadley, S. W. A tripartite model of mental health and therapeutic outcomes. American Psychologist, 1977, 32, 187–196.

Strupp, H. H., Hadley, S. W., & Gomes-Schwartz, B. Psychotherapy for better or worse: The problem of negative effects. New York: Jason Aronson, 1977.

VandenBos, G. R. (Ed.) Psychotherapy: Practice, research, policy. Beverly Hills, Calif.: Sage, 1980.

Voeltz, L. M., & Evans, I. M. The assessment of behavioral interrelationships in child behavior therapy. Behavioral Assessment, 1982, 4, 131–165.

Wachtel, P. L. Psychoanalysis and behavior therapy: Toward an integration. New York: Basic Books, 1977.

Wahler, R. G., Berland, R. M., & Coe, T. D. Generalization processes in child behavior change. In B. B. Lahey & A. E. Kazdin (Eds.), Advances in clinical child psychology. Vol. 2. New York: Plenum, 1979.

Weissman, M. M., Prusoff, B. A., Dimascio, A., Neu, C., Goklaney, M., & Klerman, G. L. The efficacy of drugs and psychotherapy in the treatment of acute depressive episodes. American Journal of Psychiatry, 1979, 136, 555–558.

Wilkins, W. Desensitization: Social and cognitive factors underlying the effectiveness of Wolpe's procedure. Psychological Bulletin, 1971, 76, 311–317.

Wolpe, J. Psychotherapy by reciprocal inhibition. Stanford, Calif.: Stanford University Press, 1958.

Woolfolk, R. L., & Lazarus, A. A. Between laboratory and clinic: Paving the two-way street. Cognitive Therapy and Research, 1979, 3, 239–244.

PART IV

ASSESSMENT AND DIAGNOSIS

INTRODUCTION

In the last few decades we have witnessed marked improvements in our ability to assess and diagnose psychopathology. This, of course, is of considerable importance given that diagnosis should be the cornerstone of effective treatment. Indeed, this is especially the case, since more precise treatments have also been developed during this period. Perhaps the most important change in the area of assessment is the greater precision and objectivity with which diagnostic appraisals are being made today. This empirical influence has come from several directions, including DSM-III, standardized interviewing formats, refinements of existing objective tests, more specific neuropsychological batteries with better validity, behavioral assessment, and the evaluation of medical disorders that contribute to a picture of overall psychopathology.

All of the aforementioned are clearly documented in Part IV of this handbook. In Chapter 16, June Sprock and Roger K. Blashfield consider historical developments in classification, as well as DSM-I, DSM-II, and DSM-III. They also look toward future efforts at nosology, arguing for improvements in overall conceptualization. Arthur N. Wiens and Joseph D. Matarazzo, in Chapter 17, relate diagnostic interviewing to current clas-

sification schemes. Such interviewing is viewed as the clinician's more subjective means of accumulating important information about the patient. Skills involved in good diagnostic interviewing are noted. James N. Butcher and Stephen Finn (Chapter 18) document how objective personality assessment is currently at its height of popularity. This apparently is particularly true of the MMPI. A case history is presented to illustrate the use of the MMPI in identifying psychopathology for directed treatment. In Chapter 19, Robert L. Hale presents a historical account of intelligence testing in addition to its current function in the clinician's armamentarium. Controversial aspects of intellectual evaluations are discussed, with attention directed toward a correct interpretation of test scores. Similarly, Barbara Pendleton Jones and Nelson Butters in Chapter 20 outline both the historical and current developments involving neuropsychological assessment batteries. Definitions of several of the batteries are presented, with indications of their advantages and disadvantages provided. In addition, there is a cogent discussion of future trends in the area. In Chapter 21, Stephen N. Haynes documents the dramatic growth of behavioral assessment in the past decade, indicating how this form of evaluation has impacted on clinical psychology in general. Issues particularly germane to traditional assessment, such as reliability and validity, are discussed as they apply to behavioral assessment. Specific strategies of behavioral assessment are considered, with special attention directed to the clear relationship between assessment and treatment in the behavioral arena. Future developments and possibilities in this area also are outlined. Closely related to behavioral assessment is psychophysiological assessment, presented by William J. Ray, Harry J. Cole, and James M. Raczynski in Chapter 22. Here, too, we see an increased use of this mode of evaluation in understanding human functioning. Simplistic notions of mapping physiological events and cognitive functioning on a one-to-one basis are criticized. The complexity of the strategy is underscored as well as a need for a good understanding of physiology as it relates to developmental changes. Much emphasis is accorded to the interrelationship of the physiological systems. Rohan Ganguli (Chapter 23) discusses an important consideration often overlooked by clinical psychologists: the medical evaluation. In each case, the client or patient's medical condition warrants careful evaluation. This is of paramount importance, given that some medical disorders frequently present in masked form as psychological problems. The clinical and ethical considerations here are most obvious, but bear emphasizing.

16 CLASSIFICATION AND NOSOLOGY

June Sprock
Roger K. Blashfield

Classification is the process and/or the product of forming groups of entities. Simpson (1961) divided the study of classification into three areas: (1) *taxonomy* is the theoretical study of classification without regard to content; (2) *classification* is the formation of groups or subsets from a large collection of entities; and (3) *identification* is the process of assigning particular entities or individuals to categories in an existing classification system. In the medical sciences, the preferred term for identification is *diagnosis*. Diagnosis means, literally, to distinguish or differentiate. In Simpson's terminology, the product of the process of classification is the classification system. A *nomenclature* is a specific set of terms used to identify categories. It includes both the names of the categories and technical terms to describe identified entities. A nomenclature is an approved list of terms that is independent of any underlying characteristics of the categories. A classification system of diseases is called a *nosology*.

Kendell (1975) described some ideal characteristics of classification systems. Ideally, the categories are both mutually exclusive and jointly exhaustive. All members possess the defining characteristics of one and only one class. The defining features are never present in partial form (*poly-*

thetic), but are always either absent or present (*monothetic*). All real classification systems, however, depart from this ideal and are polythetic instead of monothetic. For example, within the classification of living things, most classifications are defined by the presence of some or most features, none of which is necessary. The duckbilled platypus is classified as a mammal because it has hair and mammary glands, yet it lays eggs and is not quite warm- or cold-blooded. The problem is more complicated in nosologies because it is possible for an individual to have more than one disease simultaneously, to recover from one disease and subsequently to have yet another.

There are two main components of a classificatory system: the entities being classified called clients or patients, and the categories or classes of patients such as schizophrenia. Categories may be defined in two ways. With an *extensional* definition, all individuals of a category must be listed, which is a monumental and impractical task. Therefore, *intensional* definitions, which list the necessary characteristics for class membership, are used in most classification systems. In psychopathology, symptoms, laboratory results, psychological tests, social history information, demographic characteristics, treatment response, course of the disorder, and prognosis are most frequently used to define categories. In addition, classificatory categories are usually organized into a hierarchy. In the nosology of psychopathology, however, the structural basis for a hierarchical relation among the categories is unclear.

The Purposes of a Classification

A number of investigators have discussed the purposes served by classification. For instance, Weiner (1976) wrote that psychopathological labels are "shorthand" behavioral descriptions and serve no other important function. Recently, Spitzer and Wilson (1975) described classification as a formal process analogous to concept formation, in which individuals attempt to master the environment. Both groups of writers were emphasizing the cognitive conservation function of a classification. Goldenberg (1977) discussed the utility of a classification for communication, research, and understanding etiology.

Blashfield and Draguns (1976b) did a thorough study of the functions of classification. They wrote that classification is the organizing principle that helps clinicians better understand those who seek help. They listed five important functions of classification that are fundamental to any science. First, it provides a nomenclature or consistent set of terms for those working in a field. Consistent usage of the terms independent of specific theoretical orientation reduces confusion and ambiguity and improves reliability. One implication of this purpose is that since nomenclatures are based on linguistic habits that are slow to change, the acceptance of alternative classification systems will not occur quickly.

A second major purpose is the provision for efficient information retrieval by organizing research results and accumulated clinical knowledge according to the classification categories. Knowing a diagnosis allows a clinician to search for information about the typical symptoms, course, and other features the patient is likely to possess. Sarbin and Mancuso (1972), however, argued that the conceptual inadequacy of the terms in the current system makes it useless for the purpose of information storage and recovery. Still, Tryon and Bailey (1970) and others counter by noting that treatment indications, etiology, and epidemiological statistics would be lost if the traditional classification were discarded.

Another major function of a classification is to describe important similarities and differences between psychiatric patients so that learning a diagnosis results in knowledge about the symptoms likely to be seen with the patient. Blashfield and Draguns emphasized how important it is for the categories to be homogeneous in order to derive an accurate summary of significant features, but note that there are a number of possible definitions of homogeneity. McQuitty (1967) offered three alternate definitions, each with different implications for a classificatory system: (1) the members of a homogeneous category are more similar to at least one member of the same group than to any member of another group; (2) the members are more similar to all the members of the same group than to all members of any other group; and (3) the members have a greater average similarity to all members of the same group than to all members of any other group.

Blashfield and Draguns suggested that contrary to the widely held belief that an adequate nosology requires all patients with the same diagnosis to have identical symptoms (i.e., to be monothetic), polythetic classifications are more useful. As mentioned earlier, diagnosis is almost always determined by the presence of several signs, not pathognomic indicators. For example, Yusin, Nihira, and Mortashed (1974) found autism to be highly associated with schizophrenia, but that it is not present in all cases. The current standardized nosology, the DSM-III, is polythetic. For example, the presence of auditory hallucinations or nonpersecutory delusions can both partially fulfill the criteria for schizophrenia, but neither is necessary or sufficient for the diagnosis.

The fourth major purpose—prediction of outcome or prognosis—has been argued to be the most important purpose of classification (Lubin, 1968; Panzetta, 1974). Prediction is related to the third purpose, description, except that prediction deals with data on treatment response, prognosis, and prevention. Many clinicians argue that an adequate psychiatric classification can never be developed by searching for clusters of patients with similar sets of symptoms. Instead, it will be necessary to look at past and future symptoms, and the classification must be validated longitudinally over time. This purpose is also related to communication, since acceptance of the system is partly based on the utility of the predictions that are made.

The final major purpose, according to Blashfield and Draguns, is to provide basic concepts to allow formulations about adequate theories of psychopathology. Hempel (1966) suggested that classificatory terms are extensions of scientific concepts, and must therefore have clear criteria, be empirically determined, and have "systematic import" for a science. While psychiatric classification provides a basis for theories of psychopathology, it also limits the kinds of theories that may evolve from it and guide research.

A number of investigators have noted that the use of classification results in gains and losses for the individual and society. There are three possible detrimental effects to the individual. First, the label cannot contain all relevant information about a patient, so it can function as a stereotype and miss the complexity and individuality of the person. This argument is at the heart of the idiographic approach (Allport, 1961). Nomothetic categories cannot fully describe or explain the behavior of individuals, who are all unique. Also, a label may result in other people modifying their behavior toward the patient and may consequently modify the patient's behavior. This labeling may not be helpful to the patient and may actually cause deviant behavior or result in chronic patient syndromes. Laing (1967) described how a diagnostic label can result in a self-fulfilling prophecy for both the patient and the labeler, influencing both the staff's perception of the patient and, perhaps more seriously, the patient's perception of himself. Finally, the predictions for prognosis and treatment response may be based on the diagnostic label, not on the observed behavior of the patient.

Korchin (1976) also noted that diagnoses emphasize weaknesses rather than strengths. Overemphasis on diagnosis can divert the concern of the clinicians from the ultimate purpose of fostering change. In addition to stigmatizing the patient, the label frequently has serious administrative and legal consequences, including involuntary hospital admissions, monetary compensation, influence on criminal proceedings, and having others make important life decisions for the patient. Use of a diagnostic label creates an illusion of understanding, which distracts the clinician from trying to relieve suffering and from dealing with the serious issues of living that confront a patient (Kendell, 1975).

Szasz (1961) challenged the logical and moral basis of classifying human behavior, and stated that it is a means to control, socially restrain, or demean a person. Laing (1967), another outspoken critic of diagnosis, wrote about the self-fulfilling prophecy. Psychologists have often been skeptical of diagnosis because it implies a medical model, thus ignoring the importance of environmental influences. Kelly (1968) commented that categorization can be a barrier to creative thinking. It is important to distinguish between events themselves and means of classifying them. Albee (1970) also rejected the act of classifying people based on the idea that qualitative differences exist between different types of people, and he criticized the focus on deficits instead of strengths.

The neglect of diagnosis inherent in some of the negative arguments mentioned above has been strongly condemned by Pasamanick (1963). He wrote that it was naive to believe that diagnosticians should view each client as totally unique and then not compare them to previous cases. The elimination of diagnosis would result in the patient being deprived of the benefits of accumulated experience and knowledge.

Diagnosis is vital to epidemiological research to examine differences in incidences of mental disorders across different cultures, races, and socioeconomic classes. Diagnosis by itself is rarely sufficient to make a treatment decision about an individual, but the diagnosis does set limits on what is possible and necessary (Kendell, 1975). The complexity of the individual's situation can only be understood through a comprehensive analysis.

The most damaging criticism of the diagnostic process is the labeling argument, which demonstrates that it is possible that the act of assigning a diagnosis can have negative consequences for the patient. Thus, it is important for clinicians to consider whether the positive gains from making a diagnosis outweigh the negative effects. Diagnostic classification results in more knowledge of psychopathology, benefits patients by guiding the selection of the most effective treatment, and helps to structure the multiplicity of information that is gathered about patients during clinical intervention (Goldenberg, 1977). In addition, the five purposes of classification delineated earlier are of major value to mental-health professionals, patients, and society. Rather than abandoning diagnosis, future efforts should focus on understanding and reducing the negative consequences of a diagnostic label.

The Historical Development of Nosologies of Psychopathology

Ancient Nosologies

Since the beginning of civilization there has been a concern with mental disorders and attempts at classification. Some illnesses, such as mania and melancholia, appear in almost all classifications from Hippocrates on, while others have vanished. The trend has been toward increasing complexity. Spitzer and Wilson (1975) provided a brief summary of ancient nosologies. In the Egyptian literature, the syndromes of melancholia and hysteria were mentioned as early as 2600 B.C. Hippocrates (460–377 B.C.) introduced the concept of psychiatric illness to medicine. He divided the disorders into acute mental disturbances with and without fear, chronic disturbances without fever (melancholia), hysteria and scythian disease (transvestism). Before Sydenham (1624–1663), it was believed that all mental disorders originated from a single pathological process. Sydenham, however, thought that there were multiple disorders, each with a specific course. Pinel (1745–1826), a French physician, simplified the complex diagnostic systems to four fundamental types—mania, melancholia, dementia, and idiotism—that resembled Hippocratic categories. In his 1801 *Traite Medico-Philophique sur la Manie,* Pinel argued for the scientific study and categorizing of mental diseases, for the use of case records and life histories, and for the study of treatment methods. He also proposed that some psychiatric disorders may have psychogenic origins.

19th-Century Classifications of Psychopathology

Before the 20th century, most classifications were of insanity, the only recognized mental illness. Until the end of the 18th century, most nosologies were developed by physicians or philosophers, not specialists in mental disorders. During the middle of the 19th century, however, insane asylums were established that allowed observation of the course of illness. In addition, the growth of insane asylums led to the need for specialized professionals to work with the inmates, and a subspecialty of medicine was formed under the general heading of psychiatry. Also, there was a growing interest in classification. The early systems were crude, the categories were overly broad, and the idiosyncratic terms had questionable validity.

The 19th-century view was that all disorders were manifestations of physical pathology or lesions. Greisinger (1818–1868), for example, said that all mental disorders are brain diseases. Morel (1809–1873) was the first to use the course of a disorder to classify mental disorders. A wide variety of classifications was proposed during this time. Hurd (1881) criticized the variation in classifica-

tion systems between institutions and called for the adoption of a uniform system. In 1885, Morel was appointed as the chairperson of the Congress of Mental Medicine to consider the existing classifications and derive a single system. This congress agreed on eleven categories: mania, melancholia, periodical insanity, progressive systematic insanity, dementia, organic and senile dementia, general paralysis, insane neuroses, toxic insanity, moral and impulsive insanity, and idiocy. Even though this system is different from contemporary classifications, it is interesting to note that most of these terms are still recognizable one hundred years later.

Interest in classification in the 19th century culminated with the work of Emil Kraepelin (1855–1926), who published a series of texts on abnormal psychology. His organization of mental disorders served as a basis of modern nosologies. Kraepelin's intention was not to create a new classification, but to write textbooks of psychopathology. The chapters were organized around generally accepted major categories of psychopathology, and the tables of contents were taken as his classification system. It was Kraepelin's clear description and his case histories, not his diagnostic innovations, that led to his fame. Kraepelin believed that mental disorders reflect an underlying organic etiology, but was less enthralled by the medical model than were many of his contemporaries. He advocated a careful behavioral analysis of the patient and of how to use applied psychological research to improve the understanding of mental disorders. Earlier, Kraepelin had been influenced by his research with Wundt, the father of experimental psychology. He synthesized the clinical-descriptive and somatic approaches with his emphasis on the course of the disorder. He believed that mental disorders could be classified according to symptom patterns, precipitating circumstances, course of conditions, and outcome. However, grouping patients by course of disorders was his major organizing principle. He realized that symptoms could be misleading and thought it was important to differentiate those symptoms that could not be used for diagnosis from those that consistently occurred in the course of the disorder. His sixth edition of the *Textbook of Psychiatry* (1899) became well known and had 16 major categories of psychopathology. In this text, Kraepelin introduced two novel categories. He synthesized seemingly diverse observations to develop the concept of manic-depressive insanity, thereby combining mania and melancholia, concepts that had been recognized for thousands of years. He also introduced the concept of dementia praecox, as distinct from paranoia. He further subdivided dementia praecox into hebephrenic, paranoid, and catatonic forms, and manic-depression into agitated, elated excitement, and retarded melancholy. Kraepelin differentiated psychological disorders from the dementias, and used the concepts of psychogenic neurosis and psychopathic personality.

Later, Bleuler (1857–1937) changed the name dementia praecox to schizophrenia, as the disorder represented a "split" between the intellectual and emotional life of the patient. In contrast to Kraepelin, Bleuler based his classification on inferred psychopathological processes. Bleuler had been influenced by psychoanalytic thinking and was more concerned than Kraepelin with inferences about mental states.

The History of American Classification Systems of Psychopathology

The first system used in the United States had only one category of mental illness and was used as a basis for the 1840 census. In 1880, American psychiatry recognized seven categories of mental illness: mania, melancholia, monomania, paresis, dementia, dipsomania, and epilepsy. In 1917, the American Psychiatric Association developed a system based on Kraepelin's classification that was used until it was revised in 1934. The Standard Classified Nomenclature of Diseases (APA, 1933) had 24 major categories, 19 of which had been described in Kraepelin's textbook. This classsification was considered archaic by psychodynamically oriented psychiatrists and did not gain wide acceptance. Between the two World Wars, psychoanalysis became the dominant theoretical perspective in the United States, and the interest in classification waned. The need to diagnose and treat the casualties of World War II stimulated a renewed interest. The 1934 nosology, which had been designed for use with chronic inpatients, was not suitable for this purpose and did not include categories for acute disturbances, personality disturbances, and psychosomatic disorders. This state of affairs resulted in the Veteran's Administration, the Army, and the Navy each developing their own systems. To reduce confusion, the American Psychiatric Association created a task force to form a standard system for the United States. The DSM-I (*Diagnostic and Statistical Manual for Mental Disorders, first edition*) was the result. The DSM-I empha-

sized the communication purpose of classification as an accepted nomenclature. The DSM-I grew from the VA's classification system as revised by comments from 10 percent of the American Psychiatric Association members.

The DSM-II was published in 1968 and was largely based on the newly released eighth edition of the *International Classification of Diseases* (ICD-8). It attempted to be compatible with the ICD-8 in order to allow exchange of research information between countries. The DSM-II contained ten major categories; mental retardation, organic brain syndromes, functional psychoses, neuroses, personality disorders, psychophysiological disorders, special symptoms, transient situational disturbances, behavioral disorders of childhood, and conditions without manifest psychiatric disorders. There were a number of structural changes from the DSM-I to the DSM-II. The DSM-II contained a larger number of conditions, the number of categories of mental retardation were expanded and the term "reaction," which had been heavily used in the DSM-I to emphasize person-situation interaction, was dropped since the term did little to change thinking about mental disorders.

A critical analysis of the DSM-II system will be presented despite the current use of the DSM-III. Numerous research studies have used the DSM-II, and it is important to have some familiarity with the classification system used from 1968 to 1980. In addition, the currently accepted international classification, the ICD-9, is much more like the DSM-II than the DSM-III.

Numerous criticisms have been made of the DSM-II. A major criticism is that it is based on no single organizing principle (Korchin, 1976). Some disorders are defined by their etiology (Organic Brain Syndrome), and others by age (adjustment reaction of adolescence), behavioral symptoms, or prognosis. Still other categories, such as sexual deviation, are based on apparently arbitrary and subjective decisions (Goldenberg, 1977). Another criticism is that the specific symptoms needed for a given diagnosis were not clearly defined in the DSM-II. Also, the DSM-II did not achieve full coverage and only broadly defined some categories, such as the childhood disorders (Korchin, 1976).

Spitzer and Wilson (1975) presented a detailed description and critique of each of the ten major categories of the DSM-II. The general category of mental retardation was the least criticized. The organic brain syndromes were criticized because most were organized according to etiology. In addition, the dichotomies of acute/chronic and psychotic/nonpsychotic were suggested, but were not applied consistently in clinical practice. The category of functional psychoses was divided into disorders of mood, chronic disorders of thinking (schizophrenia), paranoid states, and disorders of mood due to external stresses. The broad definition of schizophrenia in this section supported the overinclusive use of this term by American psychiatrists. The diagnosis of the neuroses was largely made by exclusion and is based on the psychoanalytic view that anxiety plays a central role in neuroses, despite the likely role of anxiety in the functional psychoses. The personality disorders are described as lifelong, ego-syntonic, but maladjusted behavior patterns. The nonpsychotic mental disorders included sexual disorders and alcoholism. Spitzer and Wilson criticized the sexual disorder subtypes for not being defined, and the subdivisions of alcoholism for being based on a meaningless criteria — number of times drunk per year. The seventh general category, the psychophysiological disorders, are psychologically similar to hysteria, and are categories that were rarely used in clinical practice. In addition, Spitzer and Wilson questioned whether disorders with medical symptoms should be classified as mental disorders. The special symptoms category is a list of symptoms occurring without the presence of other mental disorder (e.g., tics, enuresis). Although anorexia nervosa is included, it is actually a syndrome not a symptom. The transient situational disturbances are divided according to developmental stage and result from overwhelming environmental stress. Regarding the ninth general category, disorders of childhood, psychiatrists and psychologists who worked with children were dissatisfied with the small number of categories and their irrelevance to clinical practice. Finally, Spitzer and Wilson argued that the subtypes of the last general category are not actually mental disorders. This section of the DSM-II is reserved for individuals who are "normal" psychiatrically, but who seek psychiatric help.

During the 20th century, there was a decreased interest in classification. Many felt that the DSM system reflected Kraepelin's 19th-century approach, and "Kraepelinian" became a negative adjective for a psychiatrist who overstressed nosology and diagnosis (Korchin, 1976). In addition, the DSMs were associated with the medical model (which will be discussed later), the diagnoses lacked adequate reliability, and theories about the dehumanization resulting from self-fulfilling prophecies were being proposed.

In the 1970s, a movement by a group of psychiatrists, termed "neo-Kraepelinian" by Klerman (1978), arose as a reaction to the lax state of diagnosis and classification. They emphasized the importance of classification, stressed research, and opposed the psychoanalytic perspective. Initially, they developed two sets of criteria with precise intensional definitions: the Feighner criteria (Feighner et al., 1972) and the *Research Diagnostic Criteria* (RDC). Their work stimulated a rebirth of interest in classification and culminated in the DSM-III, which also included specific diagnostic criteria. After large-scale field trials and the incorporation of recent research findings, the final DSM-III used specific criteria to improve the unreliability that had been reported for earlier editions of the DSM, used a multiaxial system of diagnosis in order to allow for more diverse and complex information retrieval, and reorganized the hierarchical structure of the categories.

Major Theoretical, Empirical, or Methodological Issues

Criteria that Can Be Used to Evaluate a Classification

The most commonly studied criterion to evaluate a classification is reliability. Reliability is essential for the purposes of communication, information retrieval, and generation of theories. Agreement among clinicians is the major type of reliability that has been studied in research over the last three decades. Blashfield and Draguns (1976b) identified four factors that influence interdiagnostician agreement: the specificity of the defining criteria, training of the clinicians, amount and nature of information used in making the diagnosis, and interclinician consistency. The more specific, explicit, and precise the criteria for diagnosis, the less room there is for subjectivity, bias, and disagreement. DSM-II definitions have been criticized for being vague. The authors of the DSM-II tried to excuse their use of vague definitions by remarking that the system was only intended for use by trained professionals. Kendell (1975), however, concluded that more experienced clinicians may not, in fact, give more accurate diagnoses than inexperienced clinicians. Kendell (1973a) found no relationship between length of experience in psychiatry and diagnostic accuracy or confidence, but all clinicians in this study had at least five years' experience.

A number of other factors also affect interclinician agreement. One factor is the amount of information the clinicians are provided. Diagnostic impressions are often formed rather clearly in the first few minutes of an interview (Gauron & Dickinson, 1969; Sandifer, Hordern, & Green, 1970). Additional information in an interview can lead to lowered reliability because the clinicians vary in the information to which they choose to attend, how easily they will change diagnostic decisions, and their strategies for gathering information. Another factor that affects diagnostic agreement is the type of category. The reliability of the organic psychoses is highest, followed by the functional psychoses, the neuroses, and the personality disorders. Also, broad syndromes are more reliably diagnosed than specific subtypes (Kendell, 1973). Katz, Cole, and Lowery (1969) found almost complete consensus on the diagnosis of broad categories of 12 borderline symptom patients, yet found no consensus on the subtypes. Syndromes based on well-defined symptoms that are rarely encountered in other diagnoses (i.e., more distinctive) were also diagnosed more reliably.

A number of statistical measures of interdiagnostician agreement have been employed. Traditionally, percentage of agreement was used. This statistic is biased, however, by the base rate with which clinicians use different categories, and it is necessary to calculate the percentage of agreement expected by chance in order to interpret it (Spitzer & Fleiss, 1974). Cohen (1960) suggested a new statistic, *kappa*, which equals the percentage of observed agreement minus chance agreement divided by one minus the percentage of agreement by chance. Kappa corrects for the base rate with which the clinicians use categories, varies from zero to one, and its meaning is consistent across different samples. Maxwell (1977), however, also criticized kappa because of its assumption that diagnostic disagreement is a random event. Most clinicians assign diagnoses according to a systematic bias, and disagreements among clinicians often occur because of different biases, not because the clinicians made random decisions. Instead of kappa, Maxwell suggested the random-error coefficient (RE), which makes assumptions about diagnostic disagreement that are more plausible than the assumption made by kappa. Janes (1979) found that when the base rates of the disorders and of the clinicians are nearly equal, kappa approximately equals RE. In other conditions, these two statistics can yield fairly different results.

Three influential reviews of the reliability literature have appeared. The earliest of those (Kreitman, 1961), was the most insightful. Kreitman argued that the issue of reliability had been overemphasized and that the research on interclinician agreement was not as negative as many casual commentators on this literature had suggested.

The second influential review was published by Zubin in 1967. Zubin reviewed all studies on diagnostic reliability published before 1965. He grouped the studies into three sets: (1) interclinician agreement, (2) diagnostic consistency over time, and (3) diagnostic frequency across comparable samples. Prior to 1965, research was almost evenly divided among these three types. Since then, the majority of the studies have focused on interclinician agreement. Zubin's review also described how the computational formulae to calculate percentage of agreement varied, and the effect of base rates on the meaning of this statistic.

The third major review was by Spitzer and Fleiss (1974), who analyzed nine major studies of diagnostic reliability. They advocated the use of kappa, since it corrects for chance and has a well-defined formula. Using kappa to reanalyze the results of previous studies, they concluded that only three categories—mental deficiency, organic brain syndrome, and alcoholism—had satisfactory reliability. The reliability of schizophrenia and psychosis was fair, but that of neuroses, affective and personality disorders was inadequate. They concluded that the pre-1975 studies showed the diagnosis of psychopathology to be unreliable for the same reasons cited by Ward et al., (1962): that is, the weakness, ambiguity, and vagueness of the nomenclature. Spitzer and Fleiss emphasized that reliability is a necessary feature of an adequate classification system, a position that has been criticized by Carey and Gottesman (1978).

Two types of validity can also serve as evaluative criteria. The first of these is descriptive validity, which is defined as the degree of homogeneity of the behaviors, symptoms, social history, personality, and other information about members of a category. Although most nosologies were formed on the basis of descriptive validity, two major problems exist in assessing it. First, the characteristics used in defining homogeneity must be specified. Zigler and Phillips (1961) noted that a classification system that is homogeneous for one set of features is not necessarily homogeneous for a different set of characteristics. Descriptive validity may be tested only across features used in the intensional definition, or it may be used across all traits used in diagnosis. Second, homogeneity is a relative concept. There is a continuum from homogeneity to heterogeneity. Also, as previously mentioned, there is no accepted statistical measure of homogeneity. Bartko, Strauss, and Carpenter (1971) arrived at very different classifications using different definitions of homogeneity.

The final criterion to evaluate a classification is predictive validity. Kendell (1975) argued that this criterion is the most important type of validity since it allows predictions of the course, outcome, and therapeutic response. Clinicians are most interested in this criterion since it assesses the practical utility of a classification. A classification is supported if it yields appropriate, accurate predictions about the efficacy of treatment for a particular patient. Predictive validity is usually indirectly studied by the comparison of different diagnostic groups in follow-up on drug trials, and by examining the group- x -drug interaction in an ANOVA. Within psychopathology, no treatment has been found to have a specific action for a single diagnostic category or to be effective for more than two-thirds of the members of any given category. The efficacy of various treatments for particular categories provides some support for their validity, but not as conclusively as would the existence of a treatment effective for all members of a category.

Another recent attempt to demonstrate the validity of categories is to show that they correspond to statistically derived independent clusters of symptoms or behavior patterns. Everitt, Gourlay, and Kendell (1971) used principle components analysis to reduce the number of ratings from interviews of 250 patients in England and 250 patients in the United States, and then cluster-analyzed the data in two ways. In all four analyses, they obtained the same groupings, which included mania, depression, acute paranoid schizophrenia, and chronic schizophrenia. The results from two different cultures and populations provide support that the categories reflect natural groupings.

The Neo-Kraepelinian Movement

As indicated above, the neo-Kraepelinian movement stimulated a rebirth of interest in classification within American psychiatry. This movement consisted of psychiatrists at Washington University in St. Louis, the University of Iowa, the New York State Psychiatric Institute, and Hillside Hospital in New York, the most prominent of which are Guze, Klein, Robins, Spitzer, and Winokur. The movement was developed in reaction to the increasing dissatisfaction with psychiatric classification. Dissatisfaction arose from the studies showing diagnoses to be of low reliability, and because of the negative consequences of labeling. The neo-Kraepelinian movement received its name because it represented a return to Kraepelin's biological orientation and emphasis on the relationship between psychiatry and medicine.

The neo-Kraepelinians emphasized the need for reliable classification largely because of their conclusions that reliability was necessary for validity, that research had shown the traditional categories to be unreliable, and a primary reason was the inherent vagueness of category definitions in the DSM-I and DSM-II. As a result, two sets of diagnostic criteria with precise intensional definitions were developed to overcome this problem and improve reliability, the Feighner criteria and the RDC (Feighner et al., 1972). The Feighner criteria contained clearly defined rules about which characteristics were necessary and how many were sufficient for diagnosing a particular disorder. The explicit criteria were developed for 16 major categories that they felt had been demonstrated to be valid. (The DSM-II contained 180 categories. Perhaps Feighner et al. were implicitly suggesting that most of these 180 had questionable validity.) They also proposed five phases to establish the validity of a particular disorder. These phases included clinical description, laboratory studies, differentiation from other disorders, follow-up studies, and family studies. The Feighner et al. approach rapidly gained popularity (the original article has received over 1,000 citations), partly because it overcame the problems of earlier classification systems and partly because of the increasing prominence of the neo-Kraepelinian movement. The success of these criteria resulted in the development of the Research Diagnostic Criteria (RDC) by Spitzer, Endicott, and Robins (1975), which was modeled after the Feighner criteria and was a precursor to the DSM-III.

The major reliability study involving the Feighner criteria was done by Helzer and associates (Helzer, Robins et al., 1977; Helzer, Clayton et al., 1977). A standard interview was performed on 101 randomly selected admissions to a short-term inpatient unit. Three clinicians rotated interviewing the patients the first and second days after admission. Three measures of agreement were used: overall percentage of agreement, kappa, and percentage of specific agreement. Compared to previous studies using the DSM-I and DSM-II, they found higher reliability values for all diagnostic categories except organic brain syndrome.

Several studies have suggested that although the Feighner criteria have improved reliability, the coverage was less than the DSM-II. In other words, the Feighner criteria could not be used to diagnose as many patients as the DSM-II. This finding is not surprising, since less than 10 percent of the DSM-II categories are included, and Blashfield (1973) has described how overly precise definitions can improve reliability but reduce coverage. Helzer et al. (1977) found that the coverage for the Feighner definition of schizophrenia was poor, with only 3 of the 101 patients receiving this diagnosis—a very low number for an inpatient unit. Morrison, Clancy, Crowe, and Winokur (1972) found that only 31 percent of the patients with a chart diagnosis of schizophrenia met the criteria. The reasons for exclusion included symptom duration of less than six months, an episodic course of the disorder, and the possibility of concurrent affective disorder. Brockington, Kendell, and Leff (1978) found that only 6 percent of two samples of psychotic patients met the Feighner criteria for schizophrenia, while 23 percent of these samples had a hospital diagnosis of schizophrenia and 18 percent exhibited Schneider's first-rank symptoms. They concluded that the Feighner criteria were overly restrictive, especially the requirement of six months' duration of symptoms. Overall and Hollister (1979) also found that only 26.5 percent of patients with a diagnosis of schizophrenia met the Feighner criteria. Most recently, Ries, Bokan, and Schuckit (1980) found that 40 percent of a group of 254 patients were undiagnosable by the Feighner criteria, and 12 percent "just missed" being diagnosed as schizophrenic because of the presence of affective symptoms and/or insufficient duration of symptoms.

The DSM-III

The DSM-III (1980) is the current standard nosology for the United States. It is based on the neo-Kraepelinian ideas about the need for specific intensional definitions to improve reliability, and is modeled after the Feighner criteria and RDC. There are five major changes in the DSM-III compared to the two previous editions. First, the DSM-III is much longer and includes 265 categories compared to 108 in the DSM-I and 182 in the DSM-II. There is a trend toward increasing complexity, and coverage of a wider range of problems dealt with by mental-health professionals (Korchin, 1976). Ancient nosologies usually contained ten or fewer categories of severe, usually psychotic, conditions. As previously mentioned, the DSM-III uses explicit diagnostic criteria, lists separate symptoms for each category, and gives specific rules about which symptoms are necessary for a diagnosis.

Another major innovation in the DSM-III is the use of a multiaxial diagnosis. The idea of using a multiaxial system is relatively new. Essen-Moller (1961) first suggested using two axes, one for clinical syndrome and one for etiology, in order to prevent the confusion that occurs when the two are mixed. Gardner (1968) also suggested a three-axis multidimensional system that included type of reaction or disorder, level and course of disability, and basic pattern of adjustment. Pasamaniak (1968), however, suggested that additional axes would lead to further confusion and unreliability. Mezzich (1978) concluded from his review that three advantages result from a multiaxial system. First, more information is provided so that various facets that may be important for treatment can be represented. A closely related idea is that better and more useful information about mental disorders can be gained. For example, Rutter (Rutter et al., 1969; Rutter, Shaffer, & Shephard, 1975) found that most clinicians only assigned one diagnosis, despite DSM-II's allowance of multiple diagnoses, and he suggested a separate axis for mental retardation in children. Finally, the multiaxial system has educational advantages in that it forces students to examine the patient's personality, medical problems, psychosocial environment, and previous level of functioning, instead of focusing exclusively on symptoms.

In the DSM-III, diagnostic categories have been recognized. The largest changes have occurred in the categories of organic brain syndrome, disorders of childhood and adolescence, affective disorders, sexual deviations/dysfunctions, and the neuroses. In the affective disorders, the distinction between neurotic versus psychotic and endogenous versus reactive depression have been eliminated, with the major division being bipolar versus unipolar disorders. The reason for the change is the widespread disagreement over the classification of depression, and the numerous family and biochemical studies that support a division into bipolar and unipolar categories. Within the category of schizophrenia, the number of subtypes was reduced from 14 to 5 in an attempt to narrow the concept of schizophrenia, thereby making the use of this diagnosis within American psychiatry more consistent with international use. Schizoaffective disorder, which has been a controversial concept since it was first proposed (Kasanin, 1933), was originally considered a subtype of schizophrenia, but feedback from clinicians influenced the committee to move it under the "wastebasket" heading "Psychotic Disorders Not Elsewhere Classified." Finally, the number of subtypes of childhood disorders is greatly expanded from the DSM-II. These disorders are divided into five major categories: intellectual, behavioral, emotional, physical, and developmental disorders. In addition, these disorders are classified by their initial appearance in childhood or adolescence, not by age of the patient, so that a patient of any age can receive these diagnoses.

Despite its advances over previous editions, numerous criticisms have already been leveled at the DSM-III. There are a number of criticisms of the diagnostic criteria themselves. First, despite the emphasis on research, the criteria were developed intuitively by experts based on their knowledge and experience with psychopathology, rather than on empirical determination of which symptoms are most informative. Morey and Blashfield (1981), for instance, performed an empirical analysis of the symptoms of schizophrenia in the DSM-III diagnostic criteria. Their analysis showed two groups of symptoms: one group containing the florid schizophrenic characteristics and a second group of residual/prodromal symptoms. The latter group was found to be of little value in differentiating schizophrenia from other disorders.

Another criticism is that not all criteria for diagnoses are explicit. For example, the criteria for psychogenic amnesia are:

A: Sudden inability to recall important personal information that is too extensive to be explained by ordinary forgetfulness
B: not due to an organic mental disorder.

Part B is simply an exclusionary criterion. Part A does not state how extensive or for what period of time the "inability to recall" information must be. This definition is very reminiscent of the vague prose definitions used in the previous editions of the DSM. As another example of the vagueness of DSM-III criteria, consider Part B of the criteria for passive aggressive personality disorder:

B: Resistance expressed through two of the following:
1) procrastination
2) dawdling
3) stubbornness
4) intentional inefficiency
5) "forgetfulness."

Note that common language terms such as "dawdling" are highly subjective, but also that the last two symptoms imply that motivations and are inferred, rather than directly observed.

A second major criticism involves the use of multiple axes. First, multiple axes require increased time and effort by the clinician, which is a minor point if the gain in information is worthwhile. More importantly, the problems of measurement have not been resolved for the new axes. For instance, Axes IV and V are measured through crude ordinal scales. Although Axes II would have made the most sense if it covered the range of normal personality styles, only categories of personaltiy *disorders* were included, and these categories have been shown to have low reliability. Finally, despite the use of multiple axes to avoid the problems of multiple diagnoses with the DSM-II, multiple diagnoses are still allowed on Axis I. For example, since mental retardation was not made into a separate axis, a retarded child with a psychosis would require multiple diagnoses on Axis I.

A third major area of criticism concerns the role of DSM-III as a book that could be used to help understand psychopathology. Although much factual information is included in the DSM-III, no references are cited: thus, the factual claims cannot be evaluated. In addition, there are no case histories to help illustrate the meaning of a category. Rosche (1975) has suggested that comparing actual patients with prototypic patients (i.e., "textbook cases") is a main process in learning diagnosis. Another problem with the organization of the DSM-III is that there is some inconsistency in providing descriptive information for each diagnosis. The order of presentation of information varies, and under some categories topics are combined. Finally, although a glossary of technical terms is included, many medical terms are not listed, reflecting the DSM-III's psychiatric rather than psychological orientation.

The fourth and last major criticism concerns the reorganization of the categories. First, increasing the number of categories allows for finer differentiation of clinical pictures, courses, and treatments. For example, the DSM-II schizoid personality is divided into schizotypal, schizoid, and avoidant personality disorders in the DSM-III. However, evidence from research has demonstrated that reliability decreases as increasingly fine distinctions are required (Schimdt & Fonda, 1956). Additional categories of "No diagnosis" and "Diagnosis deferred" have the same codes for Axis I and II, even though the difference between the two axes is a major principle of the DSM-III. These categories appear to be administrative additions; little or no criteria or descriptive information is provided, and the terms are not defined in the glossary.

Despite the numerous improvements over the DSM-II in the classifications of childhood disorders, many researchers have been critical of the DSM-III subtypes. When Cantwell, Russel, Mattison, and Will (1979) designed case histories representing different DSM-III childhood disorders, they found only 15 to 55 percent agreement with the diagnoses they were designed to reflect. Rutter and Shaffer (1980) concluded that there is insufficient reliability or validity of many of the specific subtypes, but supported the division into the five major areas of disturbance. Achenbach (1980) argued that there was a general association between the DSM-III categories for disorders and those derived empirically through factor analysis. Factor analysis research has consistently noted two general factors, internalizing and externalizing syndromes, which were respectively similar to the general categories of emotional and behavioral disturbances of the DSM-III. However, not all emotional disturbances are internalizing syndromes. In addition, not all of the specific subtypes in the DSM-III were supported. For example, no category similar to "attention deficit disorder without hyperactivity" as empirically discovered in the factor analysis research. The DSM-III has no categories for depressive disorders of childhood, yet Achenbach noted at least seven factoring studies that discovered a depressive syndrome in children. Kashani et al. (1981) examined recent attempts to operationalize a set of diagnostic criteria for childhood depression. There have been numerous theoretical proposals and organization-

al schemes based on developmental stage, severity, etiology, and various combinations. The DSM-III uses the same diagnostic criteria for childhood depression as for adults, qualified only by a statement that the associated features may differ and vary according to age. Kashani and associates indicated the need for empirical validation of these features. Although they recommended the use of the DSM-III criteria, owing to the absence of reliable and valid criteria for childhood depression, they stated that it is likely that children do not experience depression as adults do, and that research should aim at identifying symptom clusters to allow differential diagnosis and to modify these criteria.

Another area of the DSM-III in which the organization of categories has been criticized involves the personality disorders. Frances (1980) concluded that the lack of clear boundaries among the different personality disorders and between personality disorders and normality results in the personality disorders having the lowest reliability of the DSM-III categories. There is some support from cluster-analysis studies of the validity of the subtypes, but no real reason to believe the 11 types are the most appropriate number or grouping of patients. Finally, it is inconsistent to include dysthymic and cyclothymic personality under affective disorders, as schizotypal personality is in the personality disorders section rather than under schizophrenia.

The logic used to determine the subtypes of schizophrenia is also unclear. Residual schizophrenia was retained even though it is a nonpsychotic disorder. In contrast, latent and simple schizophrenia were deleted, supposedly because patients in these categories were not psychotic. The five subtypes retained (disorganized, paranoid, catatonic, residual, and undifferentiated) have questionable validity and utility (Carpenter & Stephens, 1979). James and May (1981) found a high percentage of agreement between Kraepelin's diagnoses and DSM-III diagnoses of schizophrenia as applied to case histories from Kraepelin's textbooks.

Despite its many weaknesses, the DSM-III remains the most significant restructuring of official psychiatric classification systems during the 20th century. The improvement in reliability (Webb et al., 1981), the reorganization of the categories to improve structural consistency, and the attempt to make classification responsive to contemporary research are all significant advances.

Current Issues

A major difficulty that has persisted in the field of psychopathology is how to define the boundaries of mental disorders and normality. The increasing number of problems being dealt with by mental-health professionals today has further blurred the distinction between normal and abnormal, and has led some to argue that the distinction is need-less (Korchin, 1976). Szasz (1961) argued that there is no qualitative difference between illness and health but rather that there are different degrees of problems in living. Rosenhan (1973) also concluded from his controversial paper "Being sane in insane places" that psychiatrists are unable to differentiate the sane from the insane. Kendell (1975) has suggested that the low reliability of psychiatric diagnosis occurs because the syndromes merge into one another without natural bound-aries. Most patients fit the criteria of several diagnoses while few fit clearly into one category. For this reason, "borderline" categories, such as schizoaffective disorder and borderline personality disorder, became popular.

Kendell (1975) wrote that for a disease entity to be meaningful, it must have a natural boundary or discontinuity between itself and neighboring conditions. The existence of patients with mixed symptoms does not disprove the existence of a category (e.g., the existence of hermaphrodites does not disprove the sexual dualism of humans), but it is necessary to show that a population is bi-modal with more members in either population than in-between. This principle is fundamental to all classification. Divisions must be placed at points of rarity, so that the boundaries correspond to natural divisions.

During the 1960s and 1970s, a multivariate statistical procedure was being developed to define natural groupings of patients that had reasonably clear boundaries between them. This procedure was called *cluster analysis*, because it searches for "clusters" of patients with similar symptom patterns.

A number of different methods can be encompassed by the genetic title of cluster analysis. Examples of these methods are Ward's method, average linkage, k-means iterative partitioning, mode analysis, Lorr's method, inverse factor analysis, and clumping. Readers who are interested in learning about these methods can find interesting introductions by Anderberg (1973), Bailey (1974), Everitt (1980), and Hartigan (1975).

Over the last two decades, there has been a steady increase in the research on psychopathology in which these methods have been applied. At least 200 journal articles and books have been published in which clustering was used to create new classifications of mental disorders. Many of these articles have focused on the topics of alcoholism, depression, childhood disorders, and the psychoses. Probably the clearest results from this research are in the area of depression, where the cluster-analysis studies have consistently found a small cluster described as endogenous/retarded/psychotic depression. In addition, three forms of non-psychotic depression have appeared: hostile, anxious, and agitated. A review of the literature on these clusters has shown that these categories can be descriptively separated and also have important implications for drug treatment.

The other multivariate statistical procedure that has been used to create classification systems is factor analysis. The generic term of factor analysis can be subdivided into two different procedures: principle components analysis and factor analysis. In principle components analysis, a set of variables is transformed into a smaller number of new variables. These components are selected so that the first accounts for the maximum variance, and each succeeding component accounts for successively smaller amounts of variance. Since the first few components usually account for most of the variance, principle components analysis can be viewed as a way to transform a large number of variables to a smaller number without losing too much information. The statistical transformation of the data imposed by principle components analysis is such that patient scores on the components are normally distributed and uncorrelated.

Factor analysis is more than a transformation of the data. Factor analysis attempts to reveal the underlying structure of the data by locating the basic "factors" that account for the interrelationships among the variables. In factor analysis, linear combinations of the variables are selected that account for as much variance as possible. The factors are often rotated after an initial solution is found in order to increase the meaningfulness of the results. Two major decisions in the standard procedures for factor analysis are the determination of the number of factors and the choice of the rotation. Both decisions involve major subjective elements and have been sources of controversy in the statistical literature.

The methodology of factor analysis has been well

known for the past 50 years. Originally, factoring was developed in the studies of human abilities in order to search for the facets of intelligence. The earliest factor studies of psychopathology were performed by Moore (1930, 1933). He used this method in order to organize data from inpatients on 40 symptoms into groups of correlated variables. Thus, Moore was searching for consistent syndromes. The syndromes he did locate were interpreted as being descriptively similar to various syndromes noted in Kraepelin's classification.

Since Moore's early research, nearly 600 articles and books that used factor analysis to study psychopatholgy have been published. Major topics of this research have been the psychoses, depression, and the childhood disorders. For instance, concerning the psychoses, Wittenborn, Lorr, and Overall have all conducted extensive research on the psychoses. From their efforts, several measurement devices to assess the symptoms and behaviors of psychotic patients were developed, such as the *Inpatient Multidimensional Psychiatric Scale* (IMPS) and the *Brief Psychiatric Rating Scale* (BPRS).

There are a number of weaknesses inherent in factor analysis. First, the use of different factoring methods can result in different solutions to the same data set. The various methods include the centroid method, principle axis factoring, and maximum likelihood factor analysis. Furthermore, any changes in the composition of the sample or the dependent measures can result in dramatic changes in a solution. Armstrong and Soelberg (1968) suggested using split samples, Monte Carlo simulations, and confirmation follow-up studies to examine the reliability and validity of the solutions. Further, deciding when to stop the process of selecting the number of factors, rotating the solutions, and interpreting the factors are all highly subjective and at the discretion of the user. Therefore, many distrust the results, and its use is mostly limited to the social sciences.

Factor analysis and cluster analysis are distinctly different procedures. Factor analysis organizes the variables into *syndromes* or groups of correlated data, while cluster analysis organizes the subjects into descriptive *categories* or clusters. In other words, factor analysis assumes a *dimensional* model while cluster analysis is associated with a *typological* model.

In a dimensional system, each patient is assigned a position on one or more dimensions as opposed to a typology, in which a number of rela-

tively homogeneous subpopulations are identified. Dimensional systems require measurement, since there are quantitative linear relationships between different individuals. Factor analysis can be used to create dimensional systems since factors are linear combinations of the variables on which the patients can be given scores. A typology consists of a finite group of categories that are ideally mutually exclusive and jointly exhaustive. The typology has been used much more extensively than the dimensional system. Its ease of use is reflected in the structure of the language and in the classification of natural objects. Only in situations with continuous variables and available measuring devices have dimensional systems been used. In psychopathology, dimensional systems require the use of "tests," which have scales on which patients can be scored.

A controversy has developed in the literature about which model should be preferred: the dimensional or the typological. There is no reason, however, why both models cannot be integrated in the study of mental disorders. Hybrid models can be used in which both dimensional and typological representations of the data are plausible (Skinner, 1981, Strauss et al., 1979). Nonetheless, the controversy has not subsided, partly because it has been associated with a difference between psychological views of mental disorders (i.e., dimensional) versus the medical model perspective (i.e., typological), and partly because a decision has not been made whether a classification of psychopathology should be based on categories (i.e., typological) or on syndromes (i.e., dimensional).

Predictions About the Future of Classification

Computerization of Diagnostic Information Will Become Increasingly Common Over the Next Two Decades

The computer age is having an increasing impact on all segments of our society and the technical changes that are occurring in the computer field are quite impressive. In particular, microcomputers (such as the APPLE II, TRS-80 or IBM Personal Computer) are available at modest prices and have most of the same capabilities as computers that were only available to universities in the 1960s. It is quite likely that by the beginning of the 21st century—which is less than two decades away—computers will be present in the offices of many mental-health professionals to perform billing, record keeping, communication, and other functions.

One of the "other" functions that computers can usefully serve for a clinician is recording, tabulating, and extrapolation from diagnostic information. Ledley and Lusted (1959) demonstrated how clinicians could use a relatively simple tabulation system to record data on the patients they see, to keep follow-up data on these patients, and then to develop personal equations for their patient samples that allow them to relate the initial data to make predictions about future status. These equations could be used, for example, to predict how many therapy sessions will occur, which patients are most likely to require hospitalization, or the probable final diagnosis of the patient.

There has been a growing body of research in which computers have been utilized as part of the diagnostic process. In the early 1970s, two large programs appeared that required data from structured interviews and then used the computer programs to formulate diagnostic hypotheses. These two programs were called DIAGNO (Spitzer & Endicott, 1969), and CATEGO (Wing, Cooper, & Satorius, 1974).

The major advantages of using a computer to estimate a diagnosis is that computers are almost perfectly consistent. When given the same information, computer programs will always formulate the same diagnosis. Human decision makers lack consistency. On the other hand, computers are inflexible. They only can interpret data in the format to which they were programmed. Human decision makers are much more flexible, and can process anomalous data that was not anticipated by the computer program or programmer (Meehl, 1973). Nonetheless, Spitzer and Endicott (1969) showed that DIAGNO was a reasonably reliable program and was as likely to agree with a mental-health professional's diagnosis as was any other clinician.

There Will Continue to be Ambivalent Behavior Within the American Branch of the Mental-health Profession Regarding International Classification

Until some time after World War II, psychiatric classification systems were largely fragmented and showed decided variability from one geographical location to another. Even though the World Health Organization had incorporated a section on mental disorders within its *International Classification of Diseases* (ICD), the sixth edition of the ICD, which was official in the 1950s, was only adopted by four countries. Stengel (1959) reviewed the chaotic state of international classification and recommended the formation of a system that would be adopted by most countries. The result was the ICD-8, published in 1966. The American adaptation of the ICD-8 was the DSM-II, which was virtually identical (Spitzer & Wilson, 1968).

The ICD-9 was published in the mid-1970s. This system was structurally similar to the ICD-8/DSM-II: The major difference was that the number of categories in the ICD-9 was increased, with much of the increase occurring in the area of childhood disorders.

The DSM-III represents a major step by American psychiatry away from a concern with international classification (Kendell, 1980). In structure, the DSM-III is very different from the ICD-9 because of its emphasis on diagnostic criteria and its adoption of a multiaxial system. It is interesting to note that the ICD-10 is scheduled to have a multiaxial system. In addition, the DSM-III organizes certain sections of its categories very differently from the ICD-9, especially the classification of depression, childhood disorders, and the "neuroses."

The pressure for a rapprochement between American classification and the classification generally adopted by the international community will be considerable. In order for epidemiological studies and cross-cultural studies of psychopathology to continue, a consistent nomenclature is necessary. However, a major problem associated with international classification is that the changes within such a system are likely to be very slow. In fact, Kendell (1975) compared international classification to a convoy of ships whose movement is dictated by the speed of its slowest member.

The Conceptual Scope of Classification Will Be Enlarged

The traditional focus of psychiatric classification has been on the patient—on his or her symptoms and deviant behaviors. This focus was maintained in the first two editions of the DSM. However, through its adoption of a multiaxial system, the

DSM-III broadened the focus of classification from symptoms (Axis I), to psychological styles (Axis II), physiological functioning (Axis III), and psychosocial environments (Axis IV).

Although the DSM-III has attempted to broaden the scope of classification, its implementation of multiple axes has been inadequate. More specifically, the de facto focus of the DSM-III is still on the symptoms of the patient. Approximately 95 percent of the DSM-III manual is devoted to Axis I. Axes IV and V are only measured through crude ordinal scales. Axis II, the personality disorders, is defined using diagnostic criteria; evidence to date suggests, however, that these disorders are still so vaguely defined that interclinician reliability is unacceptable (Spitzer, Forman, & Nee, 1979). Thus, the only viable axes from the DSM-III are Axis I (clinical syndrome) and Axis III (medical disorder). The DSM-III does not attempt to define Axis III, but assumes the clinicians will use standard medical classification.

Future efforts could be profitably devoted to developing better measurement systems for the areas of psychological styles and psychosocial environments. Concerning psychological styles, an attempt to provide a more specific approach consistent with the DSM-III is Millon's analysis of personality disorders (Millon, 1981). Millon's classification, based on two dimensions — active/passive and dependent/independent/detached — consists of eight personality types. A very different, but intriguing, approach to psychological styles is inherent in the work of Benjamin (McLemore & Benjamin, 1979), who has suggested a circumplex model and has attempted to show the relevance of this model for the analysis of psychotherapy. Associated with Benjamin's model is a carefully detailed measurement system (Benjamin, 1979).

In the area of psychosocial environments, research has also been undertaken to specify better measurement systems. In Axis IV of the DSM-III, the decision was made just to rate the severity of the psychosocial stressor on an ordinal scale. Better measurements of stressors already exist in the literature (Holmes & Rahe, 1967; Sarason, Johnson, & Siegel, 1979). In addition, scales have been developed to assess family environments (Barker, 1968) and impatient settings (Moos & Houts, 1968). The assessment of psychosocial environments, however, is a monumental task in itself, as the early detailed work by Barker (1968) of small town settings in Kansas has shown. An early version of the DSM-II attempted to list relevant psychosocial environments for Axis IV, but when the list contained nearly 500 categories, the effort was discontinued (Cantwell, 1981).

The DSM-IV Will Contain Fewer Categories and Be Less Innovative than the DSM-III

The DSM-IV is scheduled to appear in 1995. Given the major departure of the DSM-III from its previous two editions, the expectation is that the DSM-IV will not involve similarly large structural changes, but instead, will represent a refinement of the changes that were already made.

Consider, for example, the changes in the diagnostic categories in the DSM-III. Each edition of the DSM has contained about 70 more categories than its predecessor. Linear extrapolation would suggest that the DSM-IV will have about 340 categories. Clinical experience and administrative statistics show, however, that such a large number of categories is not useful. One of the fundamental reasons for a classification system in the first place is to form abstract categories that could help simplify descriptive information. Three-hundred-plus categories is not a simple system.

The other force, in addition to the human issue of simplification, that will pressure for a reduced number of categories is the empirical validation of diagnostic entities. The neo-Kraepelinian perspective has been heavily influenced by research, and as a result, this perspective generated the DSM-III as a system that should be more responsive to research than previous official classifications. Journal articles have already begun to appear that evaluate the validity of various categories, such as the paranoid psychoses (Kendler, 1980), the subtypes of schizophrenia (Carpenter & Stephens, 1979), and the like. As the various categories are further studied, the results should make evident which categories have sufficient support to warrant being retained, and which should be deleted as of either marginal or no validity.

Conclusions

Attempts to classify mental disorders have a long history. As in any science, the need for a standard classification cannot be overemphasized. Although interest in classification waxes and wanes, attention continues to return to the issue of classification because of its fundamental status in the development of a science. The consistent demonstrations of the numerous problems with the current system does not mean it should be eliminated. Instead, it needs to be modified and improved. Cole and Katz (1968) argued that a classification system should be able to tolerate uncertainty. Perhaps it is partly the intolerance of uncertainty that leads many to advocate abandoning classification altogether. A classification also needs to be flexible in responding to empirical findings and evolving theoretical positions. Kendell (1975) emphasized that our current system is simply a convenient model that should be changed or discarded when it outlives its usefulness. However, proving that an alternative to any existing system is an improvement is a very difficult task. Indeed, most studies continue to focus on testing the reliability of the traditional systems rather than evaluating the validity of a new proposal, which is a state of affairs that reflects a reluctance to consider seriously the new alternatives suggested.

The DSM-III in general has been a step in the right direction by providing explicit intensional definitions that result in increased reliability. In addition, the inclusion of background data on each of the disorders may stimulate research on the validity of diagnoses. The use of computers in the diagnostic process will also help improve reliability. The efficiency of the computer should also make more time available for the clinician to perform research and to understand his or her patient; instead of spending time interpreting and organizing the symptoms and then looking through the DSM-III to select a diagnosis, the computer will be able to search for diagnostic criteria and propose diagnostic hypotheses for the clinician to consider.

What will be the nature of future classification systems? Our predictions are that official classifications such as the DSMs will continue to evolve, though, we hope, at a faster rate and with more thought than has been true for psychiatric classification during this century. Classification has been the object of benign neglect since Kraepelin. Most other areas of modern science, including many areas concerning psychopathology, have shown staggering rates of growth during the 20th century. This is not true of the classification of psychopathology, which is still quite similar to Kraepelin's century-old conceptions. The neo-Kraepelinian movement, through its research in developing the DSM-III, has made a major advance by stimulating a rebirth of interest in classification. However, while classification seems to be

a simple activity, it is most complex. Resolving the serious problems associated with classification will not be a trivial undertaking.

References

Achenbach, T. M. DSM-III in light of empirical research on the classification of child psychopathology. *Journal of the American Academy of Child Psychiatry*, 1980, **19**, 395–412.

Albee, G. W. Notes toward a position paper opposing psychodiagnosis. In A. R. Maher (Ed.), *New approaches to personality classification*. New York: Columbia University Press, 1970.

Allport, G. W. *Pattern and growth of personality*. New York: Holt, Rinehart, & Winston, 1961.

American Psychiatric Association. Notes and comments: Revised classified nomenclature of mental disorders. *American Journal of Psychiatry*, 1933, **90**, 1369–1376.

American Psychiatric Association. *Diagnostic and statistical manual of mental disorders*. (1st ed.) Washington, D.C.: American Psychiatric Association, 1952.

American Psychiatric Association. *Diagnostic and statistical manual of mental disorders*. (2nd ed.) Washington, D.C.: American Psychiatric Association, 1968.

American Psychiatric Association. *Diagnostic and statistical manual of mental disorders*. (3rd ed.) Washington, D.C.: American Psychiatric Association, 1980.

Anderberg, M. R. *Cluster analysis for applications*. New York: Academic Press, 1973.

Armstrong, J. S., & Soelberg, P. On the interpretation of factor analysis. *Psychological Bulletin*, 1968, **70**, 361–364.

Bailey, K. D. Cluster analysis. In D. Heise (Ed.), *Sociological methodology*. San Francisco: Jossey-Bass, 1974.

Barker, R. *Ecological psychology*. Stanford, Calif.: Stanford University Press, 1968.

Bartko, J. J., Strauss, J. S., & Carpenter, W. T. An evaluation of taxometric techniques for psychiatric data. *Classification Society Bulletin*, 1971, **2**, 2–28.

Benjamin, L. S. Use of structural analysis of social behavior (SASB) and Markov chains to study dyadic interactions. *Journal of Abnormal Psychology*, 1979, **88**, 303–319.

Blashfield, R. An evaluation of the DSM-II classification of schizophrenia as a nomenclature. *Journal of Abnormal Psychology*, 1973, **82**, 382–389.

Blashfield, R. K., & Draguns, J. G. Towards a taxonomy for psychopathology. *British Journal of Psychiatry*, 1976, **129**, 574–583. (a)

Blashfield, R. K., & Draguns, J. G. Evaluative criteria for psychiatric classification. *Journal of Abnormal Psychology*, 1976, **85**, 140–150. (b)

Brockington, I. F., Kendell, R. E., & Leff, J. P. Definitions of schizophrenia: Concordance and prediction of outcome. *Psychological Medicine*, 1978, **8**, 387–398.

Cantwell, D. P., Personal communication, 1981.

Cantwell, D. P., Russel, A. T., Mattison, R., & Will, L. A comparison of DSM-II and DSM-III in the diagnosis of childhood psychiatric disorders. *Archives of*

General Psychiatry, 1979, **36**, 1,208–1,213.

Carey, G., & Gottesman, I. I. Reliability and validity in binary ratings. *Archives of General Psychiatry*, 1978, **35**, 1,454–1,459.

Carpenter, W. T., & Stephens, J. H. An attempted integration of information relevant to schizophrenic subtypes. *Schizophrenia Bulletin*, 1979, **5**, 490–506.

Cohen, J. A coefficient of agreement for nominal scales. *Educational and Psychological Measurement*, 1960, **20**, 37–46.

Cole, J. O., & Katz, M. M. Introduction and overview of the conference. In M. M. Katz, J. O. Cole, & W. E. Barton (Eds.), *The role and methodology of classification in psychiatry and psychopathology*. Chevy Chase, Md.: U.S. Department of Health, Education & Welfare, 1968.

Essen-Moller, E. On the classification of mental disorders. *Acta Psychiatrica Scandanavia*, 1961, **37**, 119–126.

Everitt, B. S. *Cluster analysis*. (2nd ed.) London: Halstead Press, 1980.

Everitt, B. S., Gourlay, A. J., & Kendell, R. E. An attempt at validation of traditional syndromes by cluster analysis. *British Journal of Psychiatry*, 1971, **119**, 399–412.

Feighner, J. P., Robins, E., Guze, S. B., Woodruff, R. A., Winokur, G., & Minoz, R. Diagnostic criteria for use in psychiatric research. *Archives of General Psychiatry*, 1972, **26**, 57–63.

Frances, A. The DSM-III personality disorders section: A commentary. *American Journal of Psychiatry*, 1980, **137**, 1,050–1,054.

Gardner, E. A. The role of the classification system in outpatient psychiatry. In M. M. Katz, J. O. Cole, & W. E. Barton (Eds.), *The role and methodology of classification in psychiatry and psychopathology*. Chevy Chase, Md.: U.S. Department of Health, Education and Welfare, 1968.

Gauron, E. F., & Dickinson, J. K. The influence of seeing the patient first on diagnostic decision making in psychiatry. *American Journal of Psychiatry*, 1969, **126**, 199–205.

Goldenberg, H. *Abnormal psychology: A social/community approach*. Monterey, Calif.: Brooks/Cole, 1977.

Hartigan, J. *Clustering algorithms*. New York: Wiley, 1975.

Helzer, J. E., Clayton, P. J., Pambakian, R., Reich, T., Woodruff, R. A., & Reveley, M. A. Reliability of psychiatric diagnosis: II. The test/retest reliability of diagnostic classification. *Archives of General Psychiatry*, 1977, **34**, 136–141.

Helzer, J. E., Robins, L. N., Taibleson, M., Woodruff, R. A., Reich, T., & Wish, E. D. Reliability of psychiatric diagnosis: I. Methodological review. *Archives of General Psychiatry*, 1977, **34**, 129–133.

Hempel, C. G. *Aspects of scientific explanation*. New York: Free Press, 1966.

Holmes, T. H., & Rahe, R. H. The Social Readjustment Rating Scale. *Journal of Psychosomatic Research*, 1967, **11**, 213–218.

Hurd, H. M. A plea for systematic therapeutical, clinical and statistical study. *Journal of Insanity*, 1881, **38**, 16–31.

James, R. L., & May, P. R. A. Diagnosing schizophrenia:

Professor Kraepelin and the Research Diagnostic Criteria. *American Journal of Psychiatry*, 1981, **138**, 501–504.

Janes, C. L. Agreement measurement and the judgement process. *Journal of Nervous and Mental Disease*, 1979, **167**, 343–347.

Kasanin, J. Acute schizoaffective psychoses. *American Journal of Psychiatry*, 1933, **97**, 97–120.

Kashani, J. H., Husain, A., Shekim, W. O., Hodges, K. K., Cytryn, L., & McKnew, D. H. Current perspectives on childhood depression: An overview. *American Journal of Psychiatry*, 1981, **138**, 143–153.

Katz, M., Cole, J. O., & Lowery, H. A. Studies of the diagnostic process: The influence of symptom perception, past experience and ethnic background on diagnostic decisions. *American Journal of Psychiatry*, 1969, **125**, 937–947.

Kelly, G. A. The role of classification in personality theory. In M. M. Katz, J. O. Cole, & W. E. Barton (Eds.), *The role and methodology of classification in psychiatry and psychopathology*. Chevy Chase, Md.: U.S. Department of Health, Education and Welfare, 1968.

Kendell, R. E. DSM-III: A British perspective. *American Journal of Psychiatry*, 1980, **137**, 1, 630–631.

Kendell, R. E. Psychiatric diagnoses: A study of how they are made. *British Journal of Psychiatry*, 1973, **122**, 437–445.

Kendell, R. E. *The role of diagnosis in psychiatry*. London: Blackwell Scientific, 1975.

Kendler, K. S. The nosologic validity of paranoia (simple delusional disorder). *Archives of General Psychiatry*, 1980, **37**, 699–706.

Klerman, G. L. The evolution of a scientific nosology. In J. C. Shershow (Ed.), *Schizophrenia: Science and practice*. Cambridge, Mass.: Harvard University Press, 1978.

Korchin, S. J. *Modern clinical psychology*. New York: Basic Books, 1976.

Kraepelin, E. *Psychiatrie. Ein Lehrbuch fur studirende und aerzte*. (6th ed., 2 vols.) Leipzig, 1899.

Kraepelin, E. *Clinical psychiatry: A textbook for students and physicians*. (Trans. A. Ross Diefendorf from the 6th ed. of Kraepelin's *Textbook*.) London: MacMillan, 1902.

Kreitman, N. The reliability of psychiatric diagnosis. *Journal of Mental Science*, 1961, **107**, 878–886.

Laing, R. D. *The politics of experience*. New York: Pantheon, 1967.

Ledley, R. S., & Lusted, L. B. Reasoning foundations of medical diagnosis. *Science*, 1959, **130**, 9–21.

Lubin, A. Discussion: Descriptive and phenomenological approaches. In M. M. Katz, J. O. Cole, & W. E. Barton (Eds.), *The role and methodology of classification in psychiatry and psychopathology*. Chevy Chase, Md.: U.S. Department of Health, Education and Welfare, 1968.

Maxwell, A. E. Coefficients of agreement between observers and their interpretation. *British Journal of Psychiatry*, 1977, **130**, 79–83.

McLemore, C. W., & Benjamin, L. S. What happened to interpersonal diagnosis: A psychosocial alternative to DSM-III. *American Psychologist*, 1979, **34**, 17–34.

McQuitty, L. L. A mutual development of some typological theories and pattern-analytic methods. *Educational and Psychological Measurement*, 1967, **17**, 21–46.

Meehl, P. Schizotaxia, schizotypy and schizophrenia. In T. Millon (Ed.), *Theories of psychopathology and personality*. (2nd ed.) Philadelphia: W. B. Saunders, 1973.

Mezzich, J. E. Evaluating clustering methods for psychiatric diagnosis. *Biological Psychiatry*, 1978, **13**, 265–281.

Millon, T. *Disorders of personality: DSM-III Axis II*. New York: Wiley, 1981.

Moore, T. V. The empirical determination of certain syndromes underlying praecox and manic-depressive psychoses. *American Journal of Psychiatry*, 1930, **86**, 719–738.

Moore, T. V. The essential psychoses and their fundamental syndromes. *Catholic University Studies in Psychology and Psychiatry*, 1933, **3**, 1–28.

Moos, R., & Houts, P. The assessment of the social atmospheres of psychiatric wards. *Journal of Abnormal Psychology*, 1968, **73**, 595–604.

Morey, L. C., & Blashfield, R. K. A symptom analysis of the DSM-III definition of schizophrenia. *Schizophrenia Bulletin*, 1981, 7, 258–268.

Morrison, J., Clancy, J., Crowe, R., & Winokur, G. The Iowa 500: I. Diagnostic validity in mania, depression and schizophrenia. *Archives of General Psychiatry*, 1972, **27**, 457–461.

Overall, J. E., & Hollister, L. E. Comparative evaluation of research diagnostic criteria for schizophrenia. *Archives of General Psychiatry*, 1979, **36**, 1,198–1,205.

Panzetta, A. F. Towards a scientific psychiatric nosology: Conceptual and pragmatic issues. *Archives of General Psychiatry*, 1974, **30**, 154–161.

Pasamanick, B. On the neglect of psychodiagnosis. *American Journal of Orthopsychiatry*, 1963, **33**, 397–398.

Pasamaniak, B. Cited in Wilson, P. T. A plan for refining the nosology of mental illness. In M. M. Katz, J. O. Cole, & W. E. Barton (Eds.), *The role and methodology of classification in psychiatry and psychopathology*. Chevy Chase, Md.: U.S. Department of Health, Education and Welfare, 1968.

Ries, R., Bokan, J., & Schuckit, M. A. Modern diagnosis of schizophrenia in hospitalized psychiatric patients. *American Journal of Psychiatry*, 1980, **137**, 1,419–1,421.

Rosche, E. Human categorization. In N. Warrens (Ed.), *Advances in cross-cultural psychology*, Vol. 1. London: Academic Press, 1975.

Rosenhan, D. L. On being sane in insane places. *Science*, 1973, **179**, 250–258.

Rutter, M., Lebovici, S., Eisenberg, L., Sneznevskij, A. V., Sadoun, R., Brooke, E., & Lin, T. Y. A tri-axial classification of mental disorders in childhood. *Journal of Child Psychology, Psychiatry and Related Disciplines*, 1969, **10**, 41–61.

Rutter, M., & Shaffer, D. DSM-III: A step forward or back in terms of the classification of child psychiatric disorders? *Journal of the American Academy of Child Psychiatry*, 1980, **19**, 371–394.

Rutter, M., Shaffer, D., & Shepherd, M. *A multi-axial classification of child psychiatric disorders*. Geneva: World Health Organization, 1975.

Sandifer, M. G., Hordern, A., & Green, L. M. The psychiatric interview: The impact of the first three minutes. *American Journal of Psychiatry*, 1970, **126**, 968–973.

Sarason, I. G., Johnson, J. H., & Siegel, J. M. Assessing the impact of life changes: Development of the Life Experiences Survey. In I. G. Sarason & C. D. Spielberger (Eds.), *Stress and anxiety*. New York: Wiley, 1979.

Sarbin, T. T., & Mancuso, J. C. Paradigms and moral judgements: Improper conduct is not a disease. *Journal of Consulting and Clinical Psychology*, 1972, **39**, 6–8.

Schmidt, H., & Fonda, C. The reliability of psychiatric diagnosis: A new look. *Journal of Abnormal and Social Psychology*, 1956, **52**, 262–267.

Simpson, G. G. *Principles of animal taxonomy*. New York: Columbia University Press, 1961.

Skinner, H. A. Towards the integration of classification theory and methods. *Journal of Abnormal Psychology*, 1981, **90**, 68–87.

Spitzer, R. L., & Endicott, J. DIAGNO: A computer program for psychiatric diagnosis utilizing the differential diagnostic procedure. *Archives of General Psychiatry*, 1968, **18**, 746–756.

Spitzer, R. L., & Endicott, J. DIAGNO II: Further developments in a computer program for psychiatric diagnosis. *American Journal of Psychiatry*, 1969, **125**, 12–21.

Spitzer, R. L., Endicott, J., & Robins, E. *Research diagnostic criteria (RDC) for a selected group of functional disorders*. New York: New York State Psychiatric Institute, 1975.

Spitzer, R. L., & Fleiss, J. L. A re-analysis of the reliability of psychiatric diagnosis. *British Journal of Psychiatry*, 1974, **125**, 341–347.

Spitzer, R. L., Forman, J. B. W., & Nee, J. DSM-III field trials: I. Initial interrater diagnostic reliability. *American Journal of Psychiatry*, 1979, **36**, 815–817.

Spitzer, R. L., & Wilson, P. T. A guide to the American Psychiatric Association's new diagnostic nomenclature. *American Journal of Psychiatry*, 1968, **124**, 1,619–1,629.

Spitzer, R. L., & Wilson, P. T. Nosology and the official psychiatric nomenclature. In A. Freedman, H. Kaplan, & B. Sadock (Eds.), *Comprehensive textbook of psychiatry*. Baltimore: Williams & Wilkins, 1975.

Stengel, E. Classification of mental disorders. *Bulletin of the World Health Organization*, 1959, **21**, 601–663.

Strauss, J. S., Gabriel, R., Kokes, R. F., Ritzler, B. A., VanOrd, A., & Tarana, E. Do psychiatric patients fit their diagnoses? Patterns of symptomotology as described by the biplot. *Journal of Nervous and Mental Disease*, 1979, **167**, 105–113.

Szasz, T. S. *The myth of mental illness*. New York: Hoeber-Harper, 1961.

Tryon, R. C., & Bailey, D. E. *Cluster analysis*. New York: McGraw-Hill, 1970.

Ward, C. H., Beck, A. T., Mendelson, M., Mock, J. E., & Erbaugh, J. K. The psychiatric nomenclature. *Archives of General Psychiatry*, 1962, **7**, 198–205.

Webb, L. J., Gold, R. S., Johnstone, E. E., & Diclemente, C. C. Accuracy of DSM-III diagnosis following a training program. *American Journal of Psychiatry*, 1981, **138**, 376–378.

Weiner, I. B. *Clinical methods in psychology.* New York: Wiley, 1976.

Wing, J. K., Cooper, J. E., & Sartorius, N. *The description and classification of psychiatric symptoms: An instruction manual for the PSE and Catego System.* London: Cambridge University Press, 1974.

Yusin, A., Nihira, K., & Mortashed, C. Major and minor criteria in schizophrenia. *American Journal of Psychiatry,* 1974, **131,** 688–692.

Zigler, E., & Phillips, L. Psychiatric diagnosis: A critique. *Journal of Abnormal and Social Psychology,* 1961, **63,** 607–618.

Zubin, J. Classification of behavior disorders. *Annual Review of Psychology,* 1967, **18,** 373–406.

17 DIAGNOSTIC INTERVIEWING

Arthur N. Wiens
Joseph D. Matarazzo

Introduction

Classification

A rose is a rose is a rose ... because it remains a rose. The reader will recognize the first phrase as a famous quote from Gertrude Stein. The second phrase was contributed by Donald W. Goodwin in a foreword to a book on psychiatric diagnosis (Woodruff, Goodwin, & Guze, 1974). The two phrases introduce the concept of classification with its two functions of communication and prediction. When you say "rose" to a person who knows something about how a rose is defined and classified, communication results. Goodwin points out that a rose also has a predictable life history: it stays a rose. If it changes into a chrysanthemum, it may not have been a rose in the first place. Of course, just as caterpillars change into butterflies, roses too could routinely change into chrysanthemums. If such a metamorphosis were routine, the classification of rose could still be explicit and predict the natural history of a rose.

The act of classification is basic to all science and to every other aspect of living. Accurate and reliable description that differentiates and predicts is the basis of hypothesis formation and testing in science. Classification makes it possible for us to discriminate days and nights, the seasons, edible and inedible foods, and so on: discriminations that we take for granted but that make survival possible. Matarazzo (1978) has pointed out that diagnosis in clinical practice is essentially no more or and no less than the process of introducing order into one's observations, with an attendant increase in meaningfulness and ultimately control. Placing an object or organism or a set of behaviors into a certain class allows us to infer certain characteristics without needing to demonstrate each characteristic *de novo*. Classification can also help to put individual observations into a different perspective or context, and stimulate new questions for better treatment, prevention, control, and future research.

The specific functions of classification and diagnosis in clinical psychology are many, although four major functions can be delineated: administration, treatment, research, and prevention. Administrative functions of diagnosis include its usefulness in epidemiological reporting and in making it possible for clinicians in different settings to use a common language when communicating about any given classification of patients. As diagnostic criteria have become more detailed, and some therapeutic procedures applied more selectively, specific treatment implications have become attached to such diagnoses as unipolar depression, acute schizophrenic episode, or elevator phobia. Careful diagnostic delineation is critical for researchers who wish to study a homogeneous group of patients or who wish to define a group of patients who are comparable to those being studied by a researcher in another setting. Prevention or control must be based on understanding the development and maintenance of a given diagnostic condition. Reliable diagnosis enhances the search for commonalities across individual observations and allows for the development of abstractions not possible in the single case.

The word diagnosis is derived from the Greek preposition *dia* (apart) and *gnosis* (to perceive or to know). Thus, to know the nature of something requires at the same time distinguishing it from nonmembers of the class to which it belongs. Diagnosis has a long history. As far back as 2600 B.C., what we now label melancholia and hysteria were described in Sumerian and Egyptian literature. The basic descriptions of a set of fairly global classifications appear to have changed very little over several thousand years. These classifications include: psychosis, epilepsy, alcoholism, senility, hysteria, and mental retardation. Yet, the first official system for tabulating mental disorders in this country, used in the decennial census in 1840, contained only one category for all mental disorders and grouped together the idiotic and the insane. Much more diagnostic differentiation has followed. Since 1952, three editions of the *Diagnostic and Statistical Manual of Mental Disorders* (DSM) have been published. DSM-III, which we will discuss at some length in this chapter, includes 18 major classifications and more than 200 specific disorders.

Having just commented on the long history of some diagnostic labels, we would nonetheless caution that diagnoses are conventions to be adopted or discarded depending on whether they contribute usefully to functions of administration, treatment, research, or prevention. Like the term "disease," a given diagnosis may not actually correspond to anything in nature at all and, just as diseases have come and gone, the diagnoses that we presently use may not survive; more useful ones may emerge. Diagnostic nomenclatures represent a way of thinking and communicating with each other. They should not be thought of as defining physical "reality", which will continue to be increasingly differentiated with advances in scientific understanding in the future.

Psychologists as Diagnosticians

Korchin and Schuldberg (1981) point out that treatment interventions are more rational, faster, and more effective if they are based on accurate prior diagnoses, whether we are talking about repairing a car, the human body, a conflict between nations, or the human problems that bring people into psychotherapy. Few would hold that it is better to proceed from ignorance than from knowledge. Yet, interest in clinical psychological testing and diagnosis seems to have been at a low ebb in much of professional psychology for some time. In fact, one cannot help but wonder whether it is third-party payers who have redirected psychologists' attention to diagnosis by making payment contingent on the submission of a diagnosis along with a bill for services. Korchin and Schuldberg (1981) list a number of factors that they believe may have contributed to the relative disinterest shown by psychologists in clinical testing and diagnosis. In recent years, new roles have opened for clinical psychologists, whereas in the early years of professional psychology, psychologists were largely limited to clinical testing. Some new approaches and ideologies in psychology have been theoretically or pragmatically opposed to diagnosis, especially to psychiatric labeling. One example could be the behavioral psychologist, who is more interested in defining the antecedent cues to a particular behavior and modifying this pairing. Psychodiagnosis may also have been oversold; many negative research reports did not support the claims of psychodiagnosticians. In fact, many graduate students seem to have experienced their assessment coursework as an opportunity and a stimulus to disprove the usefulness of psychological tests and psychodiagnosis. Also, for many psychologists, psychodiagnosis has been an effort to comply with another profession's (e.g., psychiatry's) demands, and provided limited one-time interaction with patients who were not the psychologist's clinical responsibility. During the 1970s, many governmental concerns have been addressed to psychologists, and tests have been accused of invading privacy, enforcing conformity, and denying opportunity to disadvantaged people. Patients of a certain race, class, sex, lifestyle, and so on, may be labeled as "sicker" than others, and less apt to gain from treatment, purely on the basis of a stereotype against that class. Assessment and diagnosis at times have been viewed as irrelevant if not detrimental to nonmainstream citizens. Finally, clinical testing and diagnosis are often expensive and if a clinician views diagnosis and treatment as minimally related, diagnosis may be foregone.

There are some settings in which psychologists' interest in psychodiagnostic assessment has not waned in the past decade or two. For psychologists working in the area of health-care psychology, behavioral medicine, or medical psychology, diagnostic consultation has remained important. Just as a medical psychologist might request consultation assessment for medical or neurological diagnosis, the medical psychologist takes it for granted that he or she will be asked to provide consultation and a psychological diagnosis of the patient. A patient's "medical" and "psychological" condition are both deemed important in planning a course of health care.

There are several interfaces between psychological and medical asessment where psychological diagnosis is especially important. One of these is with patients whose psychological dysfunction is quite obviously contributing to their overall status. Examples include the psychosomatic patient and the muscle-tension headache patient. Across a number of other patient types, the persistently stressed patient may reflect this condition in a great variety of somatic symptoms that may be refractory to change until the underlying stress factors are diagnosed and modified. Another important interface is in the diagnostic efforts of the neuropsychologist. The identification of organic brain dysfunction is an important diagnostic task. Detailed assessment of intellectual and emotional functioning is important in treatment and rehabilitation planning for many patients, and can be critical in establishing a baseline against which a patient's further deterioration or recovery may be measured. Although by no means routine or even common as yet, it seems that in the future psychologists and their psychodiagnostic skills should, and will, be employed in the assessment of drug effects when medications are prescribed to alter a patient's behavior or mood.

Medical Model

A rallying cry for many psychologists who wish to limit their diagnostic efforts has been the assertion that available diagnostic schema are based on an inappropriate medical model. What is the medical model? The controversy surrounding the medical model has been confused by the ambiguity and vagueness of the concept of the medical model itself (Macklin, 1973). We would like to call attention to at least two definitions. The first has to do with the medical model as a theoretical basis for the classification and diagnosis of psychological disturbance. The second definition has to do with the use of the medical model as a way of characterizing the medical profession's social and legal control over various aspects of health practices in our society.

One of the most lucid discussions of the medical model is presented by Engel (1977), who challenges psychiatry and medicine more generally to adopt a biopsychosocial model that will incorporate within its framework social, psychological, and behavioral dimensions of illness. He points out that the dominant model of disease today is biomedical, with molecular biology its basic scientific discipline. This model assumes that biological (somatic) variables, when they deviate from the norm, account for disease symptoms. In this model, diseases are dealt with independently of psychosocial behavior. All disease, including mental disease, is conceptualized in terms of derangement of underlying physical mechanisms; mind-body dualism is implicitly assumed. Engel notes that the historical roots of this dualism are in the old arguments between church and science, where the body was given over to science but the mind and soul remained the province of the church. The notion that was fostered is one of the body as a machine, of disease as a consequence of breakdown of the machine, and of the physician's task as repair of the machine. The reductionist psychiatrists who hold to the biomedical model would have to assert that all the behavioral phenomena of disease must be conceptualized in terms of physiochemical principles. The exclusionist psychiatrists would have to say that whatever is not capable of being so explained must be excluded from the category of disease (i.e., they might regard mental illness as a myth). Engel, of course, asserts that the biomedical model is too narrow and that a more comprehensive biopsychosocial model must be adopted. He would have the physician's basic professional knowledge and skills span social, psychological, and biological areas of knowledge.

In this regard, our assertion (Wiens, 1981) is that the physician who sets out to understand the social and psychological aspects of his or her patients' lives soon finds that psychology is as differentiated as medicine, and that there are a variety of specialty and subspecialty areas of study and practice in psychology just as there are in medicine. Both psychologists and physicians may have to accept the idea that a holistic approach to health care, difficult enough to conceptualize, is probably impossible to actualize within a single practitioner. The amount of information necessary to understand "illness" from a biomedical perspective is matched by what has to be learned to understand it from a psychological-behavioral perspective. A given practitioner cannot be a master of all the knowledge and skills necessary for a complete psychobiological approach to health care. Because psychologists and physicians view patient problems and their management from different but complementary perspectives, they can create health-care partnerships that serve the patient's needs more fully. One emerging model for some clinicians who embrace the model proposed by Engel is an active partnership in which physician and psychologist participate jointly in patient evaluation and care, beginning with the patient's first visit to a health-care setting.

We turn now to a second common definition of the medical model (i.e., the one that gives medicine predominant social and legal control over diagnosis and health care). This is a definition presented in Woodruff, Goodwin, and Guze (1977), who state that: "Any condition associated with discomfort, pain, disability, death, or an increased liability to these states, regarded by physicians and the public as properly the responsibility of the medical profession, may be considered a disease" (p.185). They go on to suggest that whether a condition is regarded as a disease can be a function of many factors: social, economic, biological, and so on. At certain times in history a condition or disability may be regarded as a disease, and at other times it may not. From this perspective, the term "disease" is a convention and may be relatively independent of any underlying physiochemical process. Indeed, from this perspective diseases could be expected to come and go, and presumably, if psychologists and the public regarded a given condition as the responsibility of the psychological profession, the condition would not be regarded as a disease, but rather, perhaps, a problem in living. One dysfunction that has alternated between being defined as a disease or a problem in living is alcoholism.

Schacht and Nathan (1977) refer to both definitions of the medical model in their critique of DSM-III. It appears to them that DSM-III makes *a priori* assumptions regarding the locus of problems as within the skin. Their review of the major diagnostic headings in DSM-III, however, suggests that only three headings subsume disorders that are likely to be of organic or physical etiology, and four others categorize disorders for which organic etiology has been implicated. This leaves ten groups of disorders that have not been shown to share such etiologic factors. To lump these three distinct and very different groups of disorders together by calling all of them "medical disorders" seems to make little sense to Schacht and Nathan (1977, p. 1,022). They suggest that lumping together different groups of disorders may actually represent an effort to define the profession of psychiatry. In fact, they report that when the authors of DSM-III were asked why it was so important for mental disorders to be a subset of medical disorders, the answer was in part that there was pressure for the medical profession, and psychiatry in particular, to define its area of prime responsibility. While this definition might enlarge the domain of psychiatry, it would also diminish the domain of other mental-health professionals, including psychologists. Since these disorders include virtually all psychological dysfunctions, if physicians were to be given legislative and third-party-payer primacy in the diagnosis and treatment of the disorders categorized by DSM-III, few patients would be left over for psychologists and other mental-health practitioners to see.

Despite such concerns, clinical psychologists earlier used DSM-II in their practices, and they do now and will continue to use DSM-III in their diagnostic formulations. Miller, Bergstrom, Cross, and Grube (1981) randomly sampled psychologists listed in the *National Register of Health Service Providers in Psychology* (Council for the National Register, 1978) and reported that 90.6 percent used DSM-II to some extent in their practics. The overwhelming reason for using DSM-II was because it was required by third-party payers; 86.1 percent of those who used DSM-II endorsed this reason. Further, 42.9 percent reported that they used DSM-II because it was at that time the only classification system available. While DSM-III was not yet available to the psychologists they studied, at the time the survey took place, nearly all practicing psychologists sampled agreed they soon would use DSM-III because they had no alternative. These authors point out that if the American Psychological Association were to develop an alternative diagnostic schema and manual, its use would be contingent upon reimbursement rather than simply upon improving the ability of scientists and practitioners to assess, treat, and predict human psychopathology. Unfortunately, it seems that, as with the "medical model," an alternative APA system or a "psychological model" would have to promote the professionalization of psychology through a system of economic reimbursement that is free of medical dominance and assured of inclusion in third-party payment programs and in any national health insurance plans (Miller et al., 1981).

Diagnostic Interviewing

Diagnostic Interviewing

The interview is the cornerstone of psychodiagnosis and has surely been used in diagnosis for thousands of years. It has always been the clinician's personal, subjective effort to gain information and understanding, and it remains the most important tool in clinical assessment and diagnosis. Consequently, it is surprising how little is known about its reliability and validity. What data should be recorded in an interview? For example, conclusions that might be drawn from speech content are difficult to separate from inferences concurrently being made from behavioral observations. The latter include the mental notes the diagnostic interviewer makes of shifts in gaze and posture, facial flushes, hesitations, circumlocutions, non sequiturs, delusional content, and other nonverbal or nonlexical communications.

For years it has been assumed that interviewing is an art rather than a science. Hence, it cannot be taught but can only be gradually acquired by means of clinical experience. As we review the current interviewing research literature, we question this assumption. With specification of interview behaviors, it becomes possible to assess the effects of a variety of interviewer and interviewee characteristics and tactics. It also is reasonable to assume that the beginning interviewer can study and should know about some of the psychological forces at work in the interview. Such knowledge can then be a basis for acquiring and insightfully using the specific techniques of interviewing (Wiens, 1976).

In calling attention to the long history of diagnostic interviewing, and its reliability and validity, Matarazzo (1978, p. 49) noted:

> The history of the use of verbal and nonverbal observational cues in early forms of the mental status examination as a basis for classification, nosology, and diagnosis is intimately interwined with the history of medicine, psychiatry, and psychology dating back to the earliest records of the human race. The reader interested in an excellent historical review of the actual nosology system in use for psychiatric classification and diagnosis in each era from the period 2600 B.C., through Hippocrates and Plato of the classic Greek period (fifth and fourth centuries B.C.), through early Christianity, the Dark Ages, the Renaissance, through the great winters of sixteenth-, seventeenth-, and eighteenth-century medicine, and finally into the nineteenth and twentieth centuries will find this history in rich and detailed text in Zilboorg (1941) and in neat but comprehensive outline in the appendix of the book by Menninger, Mayman, and Pruyser (1963). Included in the outline provided by the latter are the specific diagnostic classifications used by each of the well-known and lesser giants, including Hippocrates, Plato, Galen, Avicena, Saint Thomas Aquinas, Paracelsus, Sydenham, Linneaus, Kant, Pinel, Rush, Esquirol, Maynert, Wernicke, Kraepelin, Bleuler, Freud, Meyer, Southard and William Menninger (whose work in World War II led to the American Psychiatric Association's 1952 *Diagnostic and Statistical Manual of Mental Disorders* (DSM-I), and to the revised second edition, DSM-II, published in 1968.

After reviewing research on the reliability (or unreliability) of psychiatric diagnosis, Matarazzo (1978) came to a relatively optimistic conclusion. Given the fact that empirical research on diagnosis is relatively recent, there has been a fair degree of interrater reliability between two interviewers or raters for the more global or major psychiatric classifications. This reliability drops a bit when the judgments within a major category are made more specific. That this state of affairs is even more conducive to optimism today will be seen below when we review the research reported during the last two or three years.

Skillful Diagnostic Interviewing

In later portions of this chapter we discuss the trend in clinical research toward the use of more objective, semistructured, or structured interviews of demonstrable reliability. In this section we call attention again to the assertion that being able to talk with patients is an important skill, and we do not agree with a frequent implicit assumption that it is a skill that cannot be explicitly learned — one either has it or not. Typically, it has been assumed that if interviewing skills were learned, it would probably be through observation and imitation of a more experienced interviewer. We do not disagree that important interviewing skills are learned through observation and modeling. We would call the reader's attention, however, to society's increasing interest in interpersonal communication skills, and to the development of numerous formal courses on interviewing skills for both lay and professional individuals.

Foley and Sharf (1981) suggest that in addition to classroom exposure to an organized body of knowledge concerning doctor-patient relationships and communication, the skilled interviewer will need to engage in continued self-instruction for the purpose of self-assessment, reinforcement, and improvement. The five basic criteria that these writers present as essential to good patient interviewing are: putting the patient at ease, eliciting information, maintaining control, maintaining rapport, and bringing closure.

In putting a patient at ease or estabishing rapport, the clinician must show respect for the patient by attending to his or her needs for privacy and comfort. First of all, the clinician must realize that the patient is anxious. Any waiting beyond the scheduled appointment time will probably add to anxiety and may also stimulate anger. Constant telephone interruptions also are likely to add to the patient's discomfort. Seating arrangements should promote interaction. Also, simple amenities such as ascertaining how a new patient wishes to be addressed and acknowledging memory of material from an established patient's previous visits are important. When there is good clinician-patient rapport, the patient is more likely to trust the clinician's diagnosis and treatment plan.

In eliciting information from the patient, a skillful clinician is likely to use open-ended questions to facilitate patient responses. The necessary corollary to open-ended questions is to give the patient opportunity to explain his or her story in his or her own words, without unnecessary interruption. The experienced clinician, however, intervenes when the patient is unable to supply relevant information, and rephrases or repeats questions if this is needed to enhance understanding and more effective communication. Areas of confusion or inconsistency are clarified, and the clinician inquires into the patient's understanding of the presenting complaints. The skillful clinician uses language that is appropriate to the patient's age and background, and is aware of idiosyncratic verbal habits (uh huh, head nods, etc.) that may be misunderstood by the patient. Clearly, the underlying assumption is that both participants share activity in the process of interviewing, and that both participants are influenced by each other. The outcome of the interview is a result of this interaction. While the clinician may be the expert in diagnosis and treatment, the patient is the expert about him or herself, and it is the latter who has the information that will be needed to make a valid diagnosis and a mutually agreed-upon treatment plan.

Still, the interviewer must maintain control of the interview and be aware of the necessary interview pace needed to cope with time constraints. A brusque, rapid-fire interview will discourage most patients from expressing themselves freely; yet, a very leisurely pace may lead a patient to ramble. The skillful interviewer will make periodic summaries and clear transitions from one step of the interview to another. Unnecessary patient rambling will be interrupted to maintain the interview focus, and pauses will be used as necessary to encourage patient response. Maintaining control of the interview should not be construed as domination. Rather, it should facilitate the clinician-patient interaction in an orderly, comprehensible, and economic fashion.

Maintaining rapport usually means maintaining eye contact and using nonverbal aspects appropriately; the latter can include attention to office arrangement, posture, demeanor, and the like. The skillful interviewer will allow the patient to express feelings about current complaints and allow for sharing of feelings when appropriate. The former accepts the patient's values nonjudgmentally, and is sensitive to aspects of his or her own use of language or behavior that might increase the patient's anxiety. The clinician should explain the need for requesting certain data (e.g., about sexual practices, drug usage) to reduce the patient's anxiety, and deal with the patient's expressed questions and concerns, as well as with the patient's nonverbally communicated concerns. Offhand comments should be avoided; the diagnostic interview is often a situation in which a patient is listening for hidden implications, and the skillful clinician chooses his or her words carefully.

In the end of the interview, the patient is informed about next steps as appropriate, and is given an opportunity to ask additional questions or add to the interview. The patient may actually remember the conclusion of the interview most clearly, and this may be a time for the clinician to maximally influence the latter to participate further in the therapeutic care plan. The close of the interview can be used to engage patients in the choice of alternative treatments or procedures. The patient may need to tell the clinician which alternative is most compatible, given his or her life style, belief system, and past experiences. Stated simply, the conclusion of an interview involves more than ushering a patient out of the office. Foley and Foley and Sharf (1981) have developed an excellent checklist that a skillful clinician can follow in an interview and should use periodically for self-assessment, reinforcement, and improvement.

There are, of course, other characteristics of a skillful interviewer, some of which may seem like plain common sense and others that may be more subtle. Eric G. Anderson (1981) describes an old Scottish doctor who, many years ago, was instructing his new assistant in the ways of his rural practice: "Pay attention tae the way yer patient comes in laddie," he said. "You've got tae give them value for their money. If the man is wearing a clean shirt, it means he expects tae get his chest examined" (p. 16). Patients are increasingly outspoken in their evaluations of health-care professionals and will complain about the clinician who does not maintain confidentiality or who "tunes them out" while they are talking. The clinician who tries to be humorous at the wrong time is likely to be described as a "great guy, great fun, a great doctor to have unless you're ill!" The skillful clinician will not break his promises because of the realization that inconsistency leads to loss of the patient's trust. He or she will not act as if only his or her opinion counts, and will not be dishonest or insincere with a patient. As Anderson (1981) points out, children feel deceit, alcoholics notice disdain, and the dying recognize hypocrisy. Finally, the skillful clinician will not forget that pride goeth before a fall. Anderson tells the delightful story of the family physician who was so omnipotent that all illness disappeared before his magic wand:

> He was called to a home he knew well, to a family he adored, to a problem he handled easily with his skills. His work done, he then sat on the sofa sipping a cup of tea, serenely contemplating his weekend off duty which had now started. He was distracted from his reverie by the children who sat affectionately at his feet sharing his love. Would he look at their faithful hamster who was mysteriously ill? They knew he was not a vet, they knew he could not promise a diagnosis, they knew he could not guarantee a cure, but would he, could he, look at their hamster? Indulgently, he bent over the inert furry shape and gently poked it. Immediately the beast seized his finger in its teeth and bit down hard. The doctor gave an involuntary swing of his arm, the animal let go at the peak of the arc and and flew across the room into the open jaws of the German Shepherd which caught the tasty morsel as cleanly as any baseball center-fielder ever received a sacrifice fly. One gulp and the hamster was gone — the entire episode taking five seconds. There was a dreadful wave of disbelief, a frightening scream of horror, then that wonderful warmth which had surrounded the beloved physician for a decade disappeared in a moment. The doctor picked up his hat, his bag and slunk into the night. Even if a doctor is without sin, he is still not beloved of the gods. [Anderson, 1981, p. 18]

Having described some relevant interviewer characteristics, and a few of the aspects of how a good interview is conducted, we now return to some issues requiring special attention.

Current State of the Art and Science of Differential Diagnosis

Spitzer and Williams (1980) have noted that there are at least three purposes to be achieved in a classification of mental disorders. The first of these is *communication*. A classification schema must allow its users to communicate with each other about the disorders with which they deal. This is not too different from everyday thinking and communication, which is successful to the degree that we have some clear and firm definitions of words and word combinations. This is even more important in science because the material is more complex. The desired outcome of classification in clinical practice is to have terms that communicate a cluster of clinical features about a person without having to list each time all of the features that constitute a given diagnostic entity. In addition to a clear definition of terms, Spitzer and Williams point out that there must also be a high level of agreement among clinicians when the classification categories are actually applied to people. A second purpose in classification is *control* in the service of the client. Ideally, the classification of a psychological dysfunction should include knowledge about how to prevent its occurrence or how to ameliorate it through treatment. As we noted earlier, it has been difficult to derive therapeutic control or treatment implications from past diagnostic categories. Yet, when we look at the changes in diagnosis and treatment over a longer time span (e.g., 50 to 100 years), change and progress are indeed apparent. The third purpose of classification is *comprehension*, which implies understanding the causes of mental disorders and the processes involved in their development and maintenance (Spitzer & Williams, 1980). It is recognized that treatment can often proceed effectively without knowledge of the cause of a particular disorder. However, comprehension is desired because it usually leads to better control of the disorder. The assertion that one does not need to know about diagnosis in order to treat carries the implicit assumption that there is no preferred treatment available. We disagree with such an assumption and assume instead that differential diagnosis does serve to identify patients with similar treatment responses and permits further search for meaningful relationships and differences among them.

There also are three assumptions that are often made when classification of mental disorders is conceptualized and are often thought to be necessary but are not (Spitzer & Williams, 1980). One of these assumptions is that there must be a biological abnormality or dysfunction within the organism to account fully for the condition. One can more reasonably assume that a mental disorder is the result of multiple factors. This assumption, incidentally, also holds true for most instances of physical illnesses. A second frequent, but unnecessary, assumption is that there is a discontinu-

ity between a given mental disorder and other disorders, and between it and normality. There obviously is a continuum of severity for most disorders, and some conditions are defined as a disorder only after they reach a certain point (e.g., interpersonal or job impairment). A third frequent and unnecessary assumption is that there is homogeneity of psychopathology within each diagnostic category. Classification into any category only implies that persons in that category share certain characteristics used as defining features of that category. As Spitzer and Williams (1980) note, Americans, Lithuanians, trees, and cats differ among themselves, yet within each group they share those features that qualify them for membership in those groups. This is equally true for persons falling within any one of our diagnostic categories. A person possesses some defining characteristic that allows classification into a given category but may not possess other characteristics of that category or be exactly like another person similarly classified. In individual assessment and care, we obfuscate our thinking if we refer to a given patient as "the schizophrenic" rather than to "Mr. Jones, who had an acute schizophrenic episode following a job loss."

Diagnostic and Statistical Manual of Mental Disorders

We have employed the term classification in our preceding discussion to describe the process of creating order in our thinking when faced with a multiplicity of observations. Such classification must proceed with a nomenclature (i.e., the names, diagnoses, or other designations we wish to apply to individuals or classes of individuals to convey that they share some important characteristic). Although we can refer to such earlier diagnosticians as Pinel, Kraepelin, and Bleuler, until the 1940s psychiatric diagnosis and classification was often a local hospital or even personal matter, or largely a function of the medical school the physician had attended. Before that time, the diagnostic nomenclatures were oriented primarily to chronic hospital patients.

DSM-I, published by the American Psychiatric Association in 1952, was based heavily on the Veterans Administration classification system developed by William Menninger. It sought to incorporate non-mental-hospital experience for the first time, drawing on the military data of World War II and on data on clinics and private psychiatric practice, which expanded rapidly in the 1940s. Hospital-based classifications of the past did not appear to fit the experiences of psychiatrists and psychologists with WWII casualties, or their patients in private practice. DSM-I expressed the strong environmental orientation of Adolph Meyer, as well as a wide acceptance of psychoanalytic concepts. DSM-I terminology moved away from classical European psychiatry, and concepts of constitutional and assumed organic factors. Instead it stressed the idea that the functional disorders were "reactions" with important social and psychogenic components. This conceptualization included the idea that many diagnostic conditions could be acute versus chronic and that they could be transitory and treatable. DSM-I was widely used, probably more so than any previous system of psychiatric classification and nomenclature. Even so, professional criticisms and discontent accumulated during its use and practical application, and a complete review was called for in the 1960s.

DSM-II was officially accepted throughout the country in 1968. It consisted of ten major diagnostic categories, including for the first time a special category for children and adolescents. The response to DSM-II was decidedly mixed, however, and there were some assertions that it represented a giant leap back into the past by viewing mental disorders as fixed disease entitities. DSM-II essentially eliminated the term "reaction" from diagnostic labels because its authors were apparently concerned that mental disorders and medical diseases were too differentiated; that is, viewing mental disorders as reactions to circumstances differentiated them from medical diseases that were the result of things independent of the patient's nature. One apparent advantage of DSM-II was that it was a system based on the International Classification of Diseases (ICD), and its authors, hoped that this might accrue to international research and communication between psychiatrists and psychologists of different nations.

In 1974, the American Psychiatric Association appointed Robert L. Spitzer to chair a Task Force on Nomenclature and Statistics to develop a new diagnostic manual, the third edition of the Diagnostic and Statistical Manual of Mental Disorders (DSM-III). DSM-III was prepared by this task force with the aid of 14 advisory committees. In 1976, the American Psychological Association was invited to and appointed a liaison committee of three psychologists to provide input into DSM-III.

Unlike DSM-I and II, DSM-III first was field-tested with actual patients and, after numerous drafts, was published in 1980. The final field trial was financially supported by a federal agency (NIMH), required two years, and involved almost 400 clinicians in more than 120 facilities from all parts of the United States. Eighty clinicians in private practice were also included. Spitzer has described, in what clearly must be an understatement, the series of political as well as professional and scientific dilemmas that his task force had to overcome before DSM-III became available to the public (APA, 1980, pp. 1–12).

As noted by Spitzer and Williams (1980), the mandate given to the task force was to develop a classification system that would reflect the current state of knowledge regarding disorders and would be useful in both clinical practice and research. It was also to be compatible with ICD-9. DSM-III was designed to be identical with the mental disorders section of ICD-9; that could not be accomplished, however. Ultimately, the mental disorders section of ICD-9 was modified to be more specific and relabeled ICD-9-CM for use in this country. The task force essentially felt that there was insufficient subtyping for clinical and research use in many specific areas of classification in ICD-9.

DSM-III

BASIC FEATURES

The diagnostic criteria in DSM-III are not the general descriptions found in DSM-II, but rather are specific, denotable features designed to assist clinicians in making a diagnosis. DSM-III attempts comprehensively to describe the specifiable features of each of the mental disorders and only rarely attempts to account for how the disturbances come about, unless the mechanism is included in the definition of the disorder. The general approach can be said to be descriptive in that definitions of the disorders by and large consist of descriptions of the clinical features.

In DSM-I, DSM-II, and ICD-9, the clinician was largely on his or her own in defining diagnostic categories because explicit criteria were not provided. By contrast, DSM-III provides specific diagnostic criteria as guides for making each diagnosis. This was done to enhance interjudge diagnostic reliability. The text in the DSM-III manual begins with a clinical description for each psychiatric or psychological disorder, including its essential features, associated features, age at onset, course, typical level of impairment, complications, predisposing factors, prevalence, sex ratio, and family pattern. The discussion of each disorder ends with a box summary of the operationally denotable diagnostic criteria for that disorder. To emphasize the still evolving nature of this 1980 classificatory system, the following caveat precedes the list of diagnostic classifications included in DSM-III:

> These criteria are offered as useful guides for making the diagnosis, since it has been demonstrated that the use of such criteria enhances diagnostic agreement among clinicians. It should be understood, however, that for most of the categories the criteria are based on clinical judgment, and have not yet been fully validated; with further experience and study, the criteria will, in many cases undoubtedly be revised. [APA, 1980, p. 31]

DSM-I and DSM-II consisted of a single classificatory schema encompassing the whole range of psychiatric diagnostic categories. DSM-III departs from that format and uses instead five separate axes of a considerably more comprehensive schema for classifying the individual patient with a mental disorder. The earlier single-axis schema of DSM-I and DSM-II was separated into two axes in DSM-III emcompassing all the earlier mental disorders of DSM-I and II, plus other categories introduced in the recent past. Axis I of DSM-III includes all the mental disorders, with the exception of the personality disorders and specific developmental disorders that now constitute Axis II. Axis III in DSM-III is to be used for classifying disorders that are predominately physical disorders and conditions rather than mental (e.g., dementia secondary to brain tumor, or childhood conduct disorder secondary to juvenile diabetes).

In recording a diagnosis, the clinician employing DSM-III will use Axes I (mental), II (personality), or III (physical) for classifying the patient being evaluated. A patient may be given a single diagnosis on one of these three axes or may be assigned a diagnosis on two or on all three of the axes concurrently (e.g., on Axis I, major depression; Axis II, dependent personality disorder; Axis III, alcoholic cirrhosis of liver, all may be given as a description of one patient).

Axes IV and V are unique to DSM-III as an offi-

cial classificatory system and were included primarily "for use in special clinical or research settings (to) provide information additional to the official DSM-III diagnoses (Axes I, II and III) that is of value for treatment planning and predicting outcome" (APA, 1980, p. 8). Axis IV is used to specify the judged Severity of Psychosocial Stressors to the diagnostic disorder(s) classified on Axis I, II, or III. Axis IV consists of an eight-point rating scale, from no apparent psychosocial stressor at one end to evidence for the role of a catastrophic stressor on the other end (e.g., a concentration camp experience). Examples of stressors for the intermediate steps on this eight-point scale include change of job, divorce, and death of a parent, and thus are not unlike those stressors assigned a numerical value in the schedule of Recent Events developed by Holmes and Rahe (1967).

Axis V, Highest level of Adaptive Functioning Past Year, assesses in a single composite rating on a five-point scale (from superior to poor) the degree of adaptive success in three major areas of life: social relations, occcuaptional functioning, and use of leisure time. The developers of DSM-III believe that "this information frequently has prognostic significance, because usually an individual returns to his or her previous level of adaptive functioning after an episode of illness" (DSM-III, 1980, p. 28).

An example of the results of a DSM-III multiaxial evaluation of one patient is provided by Spitzer and Williams (1980, p. 1,054):

Axis I: 303.92 Alcohol dependence, episodic
Axis II: 301.60 Dependent personality disorder
Axis III: Alcoholic cirrhosis of liver
Axis IV: Psychosocial stressors: anticipated retirement and change in residence with loss of contact with friends. Severity: 4 moderate
Axis V: Highest level of adaptive functioning past year: 3 good

The idea behind a multiaxial concept is to evaluate and consider all interrelated conditions. One can imagine the patient examined by an internist who might focus on his or her diabetes and ignore the fact that he or she also has an anxiety disorder and a personality disorder. Another clinician might focus on the personality disorder and ignore the anxiety disorder and diabetes. The multiaxial approach records all three different diagnoses on different axes. When attention is directed to each of the three classes of clinical information, all three would be noted by all of the clinicians. It can be seen that the use of a multiaxial system provides for comprehensiveness of diagnosis and evaluation of mental disorders. It also documents multiple classes of information on an individual. Furthermore, it should enhance interclinician diagnostic agreement and assist in the retrieval of statistical and research information.

DSM-III contains explicit definition of 18 classes or groups of conditions and more than 200 distinguishable disorders (APA, 1980, pp. 15–19). Sixteen of these classes of disorder (1–16) are recorded on Axis I; two (17, 18) are recorded on Axis II. The general classifications are as follows:

1. Disorders Usually First Evident in Infancy, Childhood, or Adolescence
2. Organic Mental Disorders
3. Substance Use Disorders
4. Schizophrenic Disorders
5. Paranoid Disorders
6. Psychotic Disorders Not Elsewhere Classified
7. Affective Disorders
8. Anxiety Disorders
9. Somatoform Disorders
10. Dissociative Disorders
11. Psychosexual Disorders
12. Factitious Disorder
13. Disorders of Impulse Control Not Elsewhere Classified
14. Adjustment Disorders
15. Psychosocial Factors Affecting Physical Condition
16. V Codes for Conditions Not Attributable to a Mental Disorder that are a Focus of Attention or Treatment
17. Personality Disorders
18. Specific Developmental Disorders

RELIABILITY OF DIAGNOSIS

Spitzer and Williams (1980) report that over 700 clinicians participated in several phases of the field trials using successive drafts of DSM-III. The last phase involved more than 500 clinicians participating in a formal field trial sponsored by NIMH. A large majority of these clinicians felt that DSM-III was an improvement over DSM-II, that the

multiaxial system was a useful addition, that the diagnostic criteria are a major contribution, and that they agreed with the generally atheoretical approach taken in the description of the diagnostic categories.

In the phase-one reliability study, Spitzer, Forman, and Nee (1979) and Spitzer and Forman (1979) used volunteer clinicians from all parts of the country, including Hawaii. Each clinician was provided a working copy of DSM-III and was asked first to practice using it on 15 patients from his or her own patient population. Following this, the clinician, paired with another local clinician, was to carry out at least four reliability evaluations, with each clinician using each of the five axes in the evaluation. With few exceptions, the reliability interviews were conducted as part of the initial evaluation of a patient whom neither clinician had seen previously. As to format, the two clinicians could either be present at the same evaluation, following which they independently recorded their judgments (joint interview method), or, if that was inconvenient, separate evaluations could be done, preferably within one day of the first interviewer's evaluation (test-retest interview method). Spitzer, Forman, and Nee, (1979, p. 817) report that 40 percent of these test-retest interviews were done within one day of each other, whereas almost half had a test-retest interval of more than three days. In either format, both clinicians were instructed to make use of all the material available on the patient, such as case records, letters of referral, nursing notes, and family information.

In all, 274 clinicians out of 365 recruited participated in the phase-one field trial using the January 15, 1978 draft, and they collectively evaluated 281 adult patients in this first phase. A total of 71 children, under age 18, was evaluated in phase one. The overall kappa coefficient[1] of agreement for Axis I diagnoses of 281 adult patients was .78 for joint interviews and .66 for diagnoses made after separate interviews. For Axis II, coefficients of agreement on the presence of a personality disorder were .61 (joint assessment) and .54 (test-retest). Spitzer, Forman, and Nee (1979) indicate that inasmuch as the kappa reliability coefficients are corrected for chance agreements, a reader may conclude that:

---

[1]See Matarazzo (1978) for a more detailed description of how the Kappa coefficient deals with differences in the base rates of the different diagnostic categories and thus is a more useful statistic for reporting the test-retest reliability of a diagnosis across two clinicians than is Pearson's coefficient of correlation.

High kappa (generally .70 and above) indicates good agreement as to whether or not the patient has a disorder within that diagnostic class, even if there may be a disagreement about the specific disorder within the class. For example, diagnoses of paranoid schizophrenia by two clinicians would be considered agreement on schizophrenia. The overall Kappa for the major classes of Axis I indicates the extent to which there is agreement across all diagnostic classes for all patients given an Axis I diagnosis by at least one of the clinicians and is thus an overall index of diagnostic agreement. [pp. 816–817]

A reader who remembers the relatively low reliability values published only a decade ago on levels of agreement across two clinicians (Matarazzo, 1978), even with their inflation for uncorrected base rate (chance) agreements, cannot help but be impressed with these results. If nothing else, the 12 coefficients that they report that reach the seldom seen value of 1.00 are a remarkable accomplishment. The conclusion that can be drawn from these results is that DSM-III is a remarkably reliable system for classifying the disorders in Axes I and II.

In the companion article on the remaining data of this same phase-one study, Spitzer and Forman (1979) report comparable data for Axis IV (stressors) and Axis V (adaptive functioning). Thus, for the same 281 patients interviewed by the same 274 clinicians, the kappa coefficient of agreement for Axis IV was .62 for joint interviews and .58 for separate test-retest interviews. Reliability for Axis V was even better: .80 for joint interviews and .69 for separate interviews. Importantly, for the acceptability of DSM-III among clinicians, Spitzer and Forman (1979) report that 81 percent of the 274 clinicians participating "judged the multiaxial system to be a useful addition to traditional diagnostic evaluation, although many indicated that they had difficulty quantifying severity of psychosocial stressors" (p. 818).

As stated earlier, this phase-one study was followed by a phase-two study that employed the slightly improved, present version of DSM-III. The interested reader will find the kappa coefficients for the major and specific diagnostic categories that comprise Axes I and II, and the ratings that comprise Axes IV and V, in a sample utilizing adults and a second sample utilizing children and adolescents in three tables in an appendix to the 1980 manual (APA, 1980, pp. 467–472). These

phase-two results are too numerous to discuss in summary fashion here. The following global statement may suffice, however, to indicate their magnitudes: "It is noteworthy that the reliability in general improved in Phase Two, perhaps due to refinements in the criteria used in Phase Two" (APA, 1980, p. 468).

Detailed study of phase-two results contrasted with phase-one results reveals that the kappa values went down for some categories in phase two. Although, as just quoted, the overall trend was for a slight improvement. Whether the reference is the phase-one or the phase-two results, it is clear from these initial kappa values that DSM-III is a remarkably reliable classification scheme for the disorders currently being diagnosed and entered on insurance forms by this country's psychiatrists and clinical psychologists, as well as by mental-health investigators working in local or multicenter, collaborative research projects.

Implications for Diagnostic Interviewing

Later in this chapter we note that information variance can contribute importantly to the unreliability of diagnosis of mental disorders. Information variance is often a consequence of how clinicians conduct diagnostic interviews and can be minimized by the use of structured interview schedules. With an interview schedule, each patient can be asked the same questions in the same order so that differences between patients are likely to be real, rather than a function of differences in the interviewer's questions during the interview.

Traditionally, clinicians have tended to be quite open-ended in their interviews, and diagnosis was often based on their "feel" for the patient, or some other global impression in the mind of the interviewer. With DSM-III, diagnosis is based on specific criteria for each disorder so that when a given diagnosis is used, we can know quite exactly what is meant because we know the precise criteria that have guided the interviewer. Since each diagnostic entity is based on specific information, the interviewer has to proceed in a way that will allow those details to be obtained. Generally, this means that interviewing has to be more focused. Furthermore, the interviewer will usually have to obtain longitudinal as well as cross-sectional data. Duration of symptoms is a diagnostic criterion for a number of mental disorders in DSM-III. Of course, this longitudinal focus also allows the interviewer to search for associations between life events (stressors) and symptoms.

Another interviewing guide included in the DSM-III manual involves decision trees. These decision trees are designed to aid the clinician in understanding the organization and hierarchical structure of the classification. Each decision tree starts with a set of clinical features. When one of these features is a prominent part of the presenting clinical picture, the clinician can follow the series of questions to rule in or out various diagnostic categories (DSM-III, 1980, p. 339). For example, if the presenting symptom is learning difficulty in a child, the clinician might begin by interviewing for and eliciting demonstrable signs of focal central nervous system disease. If such signs are found, he or she could examine further for evidence of a neurological disorder. If there are no focal CNS disease signs, one might go on to assess the possibility of subaverage general intellectual and adaptive functioning. If there are positive findings, one could go on to determine evidence for mental retardation. If there are no indications for subaverage general intellectual functioning, the interviewer looks for evidence of specific delay in development that is not symptomatic of any other disorder. If such evidence is found, one could determine whether a specific developmental disorder is present. If not, the interviewer looks for evidence of developmentally inappropriate short attention span and poor concentration, and so on. Decision trees for seven differential diagnostic problems are presented. They can be invaluable to the novice diagnostic interviewer in planning an interview and equally useful to the more experienced interviewer in pursuing an interview most efficiently.

Another section in the DSM-III manual (Appendix B) that will be of use to many diagnostic interviewers is the glossary of technical terms, which includes a listing and definition of terms that are essential for differential diagnosis. Terms are defined, often with examples, so that it should be possible for students of this manual to use a vocabulary in which there are clear and firm definitions of words and word combinations.

Current Issues

Further Discussion of DSM-III

The members of the task force that developed DSM-III, and their consultants, enunciated the following goals (APA, 1980, pp. 2–3):

- clinical usefulness for making treatment and management decisions in varied clinical settings;
- reliability of the diagnostic categories;
- acceptability to clinicians and researchers of varying theoretical orientations;
- usefulness for educating health professionals;
- maintaining compatibility with ICD-9, except when departures are unavoidable;
- avoiding the introduction of new terminology and concepts that break with tradition, except when clearly needed;
- reaching consensus on the meaning of necessary diagnostic terms that have been used inconsistently, and avoiding the use of terms that have outlived their usefulness;
- consistency with data from research studies bearing on the validity of diagnostic categories;
- suitability for describing subjects in research studies;
- being responsive during the development of DSM-III to critiques by clinicians and researchers.

Clinical psychologists reading and using DSM-III will undoubtedly come to their own conclusions as to how well the task force met its objectives. As stated earlier, its authors recognized that DSM-III is not a final solution in the search for the most useful and reliable diagnostic schema. Rather, it should be viewed as an ongoing, and interim, effort in this search. There will undoubtedly be a DSM-IV in the future. If it will be as much of an improvement as DSM-III is over DSM-II, we can look forward to further great improvements in the meaningfulness and reliability of diagnosis.

For those psychologists who are used to the ICD diagnostic classification system, we note that the original intent was that the mental disorders section of ICD-9 and DSM-III would be identical. In an effort toward compatibility, and to make ICD-9 as acceptable for use in the United States as possible, the ICD-9 codes were changed to ICD-9-CM (for clinical modification) codes whenever greater specificity was required. DSM-III categories are listed in ICD-9-CM, but there are some ICD-9-CM categories that are not listed in DSM-III. It should be remembered that, as with earlier ICD classification systems, as of January 1979, the ICD-9-CM classification became the official system in this country for the statistical recording of all diseases, injuries, impairments, symptoms, and causes of death. There will no doubt be continuing efforts to make the two diagnostic classification systems identical.

Does DSM-III assume that all psychological dysfunctions are mental disorders and that all mental disorders have a physiochemical etiology? DSM-III does not assume that mental disorders have an organic basis or that they are discrete and discontinuous. For most of the DSM-III disorders, etiology is undefined. The approach taken in DSM-III is atheoretical with regard to etiology or pathophysiological process except for those diorders for which this is well established and therefore included in the definition of the disorder (APA, 1980, p. 7). DSM-III takes a phenomenological descriptive approach and chooses the lowest order of inference necessary to describe the characteristic features of the disorder. Furthermore, it classifies disorders, not individuals. It avoids the use of such phrases as "a schizophrenic" and rather uses a phrase like "an individual with schizophrenia": "Although all of the individuals described as having the same mental disorder show at least the defining features of the disorder, they may well differ in other important ways that can affect clinical management and outcome" (APA, 1980, p. 6).

What, then, is a "mental disorder" according to the authors of DSM-III? It is defined as follows:

> In DSM-III each of the mental disorders is conceptualized as a clinically significant behavioral or psychological syndrome or pattern that occurs in an individual and that is typically associated with either a painful symptom (distress) or impairment in one or more important areas of functioning (disability). In addition, there is an inference that there is a behavioral, psychological, or biological dysfunction, and that the disturbance is not only in the relationship between the individual and society. (When the disturbance is *limited* to a conflict between an individual and society, this may represent social deviance, which may or may not be commendable, but is not by itself a mental disorder.) [APA, 1980, p. 6]

Clinical psychologists of different theoretical persuasions need not feel that DSM-III is tied to any particular etiological theory. For example, the field trials with DSM-III have demonstrated that clinicians can agree on the descriptive diagnosis without agreeing on how the disturbance came about. Some may believe that phobic disorders represent a displacement of anxiety resulting from the breakdown of defensive operations for keeping internal conflict out of consciousness. Others may explain phobias on the basis of learned avoidance responses to conditioned anxiety. Others may be of the opinion that certain phobias result from a dysregulation of basic biological systems mediating separation anxiety. Yet all may agree on the diagnosis of an individual with the symptom picture of a phobic disorder.

The authors of DSM-III do not claim that a DSM-III diagnosis is sufficient information to formulate a treatment plan; they do assert that it represents an initial step in a comprehensive evaluation leading to the formulation of a treatment plan. Each therapist will seek additional information (e.g., the behavior therapist will do a functional analysis of the behavior disturbance, the family therapist will want to know how family members relate to each other, and so on for different treatment orientations).

The authors of DSM-III present a noteworthy statement of purpose and a disclaimer, namely:

> The purpose of DSM-III is to provide clear descriptions of diagnostic categories in order to enable clinicians and investigators to diagnose, communicate about, study, and treat various mental disorders. The use of this manual for non-clinical purposes, such as determination of legal responsibility, competency or insanity, or justification for third-party payment, must be critically examined in each instance within the appropriate institutional context. [APA, 1980, p.12]

DSM-III is now in the public domain. Just as with any new knowledge or procedure that is made public, it is not easy to predict what uses it will be put to. We feel it is a valuable contribution to diagnosis and to communication among researchers and clinicians. Of course, we also believe that we should be alert to any political efforts to restrict its use to any one professional group, or to subvert the lofty purposes for which it was developed. It is important to avoid reifying any concepts of classification or diagnosis; they are conventions that have been developed to allow us to communicate better with each other. To assume that DSM-III diagnoses define some physical reality or parameters of professional expertise takes one out of the arena of scientific communication and beyond any available data base.

Several Interview Instruments

As already indicated, we believe that reliability in diagnosis is enhanced with the use of the DSM-III diagnostic schema and manual. We believe that reliability in diagnosis is also enhanced by using more structured interviews than has usually been the case in the past. We want to call attention to two interview instruments that have been well researched and that we believe merit widespread use: the Research Diagnostic Criteria (RDC) and the Schedule for Affective Disorders and Schizophrenia (SADS).

For many clinical psychologists (and psychiatrists), the most used methods of diagnostic study in the past have been relatively open-ended history taking and the mental status examinations. As most clinicians are aware, especially clinical psychologists who emphasize the use of psychological tests, open-ended history taking is likely to omit important questions and leave significant aspects of patient functioning without review. Furthermore, individual clinicians are likely to have their idiosyncratic biases, and they may over- or underemphasize certain aspects of history taking. Related to this is the fact that an initial impression may lead one to miss diagnostic cues that are contrary to the expectations established on the basis of that first impression. Each of us is aware of how likely we are to see and observe what we are looking for in a clinical interview or any other interaction situation.

In thinking about clinical criteria for diagnosis and sources of unreliability in diagnostic formulations, Spitzer, Endicott, and Robins (1975) noted five sources of unreliability and then determined that two of these contributed most heavily to diagnostic unreliability. The first source of unreliability they noted was "subject variance," which occurs when patients actually have different conditions at different times. They gave the example of the patient who may show acute alcohol intoxication on admission to a hospital but develops delirium tremens several days later. A second source of unreliability is "occasion variance," when patients are in different stages of the same condition at different times. An example of this would be a patient with a bipolar disorder who was depressed during one period of illness and manic during another. A third source of unreliability is "information variance," which occurs when clinicians have different sources of information about their patients. Examples here include clinicians who talk with patients' families, and those who do not, or interviewers who question patients about areas of functioning and symptoms that other interviewers might not mention. The fourth area of unreliability they list is "observation variance," which occurs when clinicians notice different things in the presence of the same stimulus complex. Clinicians may disagree on whether a patient was tearful, hard to follow, or hallucinating. Their fifth source of unreliability is "criterion variance," which occurs when clinicians use varying diagnostic criteria (e.g., whether a formal thought disorder is necessary for the diagnosis of schizophrenia or precludes a diagnosis of affective disorder). Spitzer et al. (1975) concluded that the largest source of diagnostic variability by far was criterion variance. Their efforts on behalf of the development of the DSM-III diagnostic criteria obviously reflected their confidence in this conclusion.

Their research efforts to reduce information variance (the second major source of unreliability) and criterion variance led to the development of structured clinical interviews that reduce the portion of the unreliability variance based on differing interviewing styles and coverage. The Research Diagnostic Criteria, or (RDC) (Spitzer, Endicott, & Robins, 1978), provide sets of specific inclusion and exclusion criteria for a large number of functional disorders, with particular emphasis on various ways of subtyping affective disorders. In following RDC, the clinician is required to use these criteria regardless of his or her own personal concept of the disorder. With this approach, the clinician's task is: (1) to determine the presence or absence of specific clinical phenomena, and (2) to apply the comprehensive rules provided for making the diagnosis. A single patient can be categorized in various ways, such as by the presence or absence of endogenous psychopathology, situational stresses, psychotic features, and the like. The kappa values for the RDC were usually above .70 and frequently above .80 (Endicott & Spitzer, 1979), and represent impressive levels of agreement. To temper enthusiasm and to balance this discussion, we should note some limitations of the RDC. Meier (1979) pointed out that one of the limitations of the RDC is that, to date, its use has been with adult inpatients only, so that its usefulness with adult outpatients and with children remains to be demonstrated. Further, the RDC may be more useful to researchers than to clinicians, inasmuch as the researcher can afford to exclude patients to obtain a homogeneous sample, whereas the clinician often does not have the latitude to allow patients to go undiagnosed. The RDC also is time-consuming and complex, and a clinician needs to use it frequently to master it. The proper application of the RDC does depend on experience and knowledge of psychopathology because the criteria involve clinical concepts rather than a mere listing of complaints. Meier (1979) suggests that, despite some limitations, the RDC remains one of the best tools available to a researcher who wishes to study homogeneous patient groups and that the clinician can also use it to good advantage. The RDC is one of about ten structured interview guides distributed through Biometric Research of Columbia University.

Another structured interview guide is the Schedule for Affective Disorders and Schizophrenia, or SADS (Endicott & Spitzer, 1978). The SADS was developed in conjunction with the RDC in an effort to reduce information variance in both the descriptive and the diagnostic evaluation of an individual. Interviewers use the SADS to insure adequate coverage of critical areas of psychopathology and functioning. Part I of the SADS includes items that are used to describe the features of the current episode of illness when they were most severe, as well as the patient's functioning during the week prior to the interview. The SADS is designed both to collect data for the evaluation, diagnosis, prognosis, and phenomenology of the current episode of illness, and to measure change. Part II of the SADS focuses primarily on past history and past illness. The organization of the SADS is similar to that of a clinical interview focused on differential diagnosis. The SADS provides for a progression of questions, items, and criteria that systematically rule in and rule out specific RDC diagnoses. The SADS and the RDC are most suitable for those who have had experience in interviewing and making judgments about manifest psychopathology. Eight summary scale scores can be generated with the SADS. These are: depressive mood and ideation; endogenous features; depressive-associated features; suicidal ideation and behavior; anxiety; manic syndrome; delusions-hallucinations; and formal thought disorder. Both the items and the summary scales of the SADS show high interjudge reliability for test-retest evaluations as well as for joint interviews. Coefficients of reliability for the joint interviews across the eight summary scales range from .82 to .99 and, for the test-retest interviews across the eight summary scales, they ranged from .49 to .93 (Endicott & Spitzer, 1978). The authors point

out that in the test-retest condition it is possible that both subject variance and information variance will be introduced. As examples, a patient may be in a different stage of illness at the time of a second interview, and may also show different behavior or tell one interviewer something he fails to tell the other. Even so, these coefficients of reliability are quite impressive. Interviewers who use the SADS and the RDC can relate their findings to the diagnostic categories in DSM-III. Many of the DSM-III diagnostic categories are virtually identical with those contained in the RDC. The reader interested in a more detailed review of the reliability of psychiatric and psychological diagnosis utilizing DSM-III, SADC, RDC, will find it in Matarazzo (1983).

Behavioral Assessment

Barlow (1981) and Hersen and Bellack (1981) have recently edited major books on behavioral assessment and the interested reader should consult volumes such as these for a detailed exposition of current behavioral assessment. Behavior therapists in the past have made much of the fact that DSM-II diagnostic classifications could not be made reliably, and that these diagnoses did not lead to differential treatment. Behavior therapists have asserted that they could not subscribe to psychodynamic or trait theory, which viewed psychodynamics or traits as consistent, stable, general causes of behavior. Rather, behaviorists espoused a philosophy that did not accept behavioral traits as fixed aspects of a mainly biologically determined temperament. Instead, they believed that environmental contingencies are preeminent, and assumed that behavior could be explained, and should be described in terms of immediate environmental variables. To them, the DSM-II nomenclature seemed to use both trait and psychodynamic concepts in a medical-disease model that made normal and abnormal behaviors discrete entities.

It was recognized, however, that both traditional and behavioral assessment relied heavily on the interview (Haynes & Wilson, 1979; Keefe, Kopel, & Gordon, 1978; Morganstern & Tevlin 1981). Establishment of a positive interpersonal relationship between interviewer and patient was seen to be necessary to facilitate the patient's disclosures about the nature of the presenting problem. The content of the behavioral interview was seen, however, to be on current behaviors (response patterns, antecedents, and consequences) rather than on the generation of hypotheses about the patient based on historical information. The process of assessment may be relatively straightforward once the specific target behaviors are known. Specifying the nature of the presenting problem is surely one of the most useful aspects of a behavioral interview. Often, the patient will initially deny knowing what is wrong or simply complain of being depressed all the time. Even in situations in which the client reports being depressed *all* of the time, or *always* anxious, or a failure at *everything*, careful questions may delimit the problem considerably (Morganstern & Tevlin, 1981). With regard to interviewing and problem specification, these authors make a further point; namely, that the interviewer asks questions only about the specified problem. This caution is presented as both an ethical consideration and one that is ecnomical of time. Ideally, every interviewer question should have the sole purpose of a more thorough functional analysis of the problem behavior.

The assessment schema that most behavioral interviewers refer back to is the one developed by Kanfer and Saslow (1969) that suggests examination of the following areas: analysis of the problem situation (including behavioral excesses, deficits, and assets); clarification of the problem situation that maintains the targeted behaviors; a motivational analysis; a developmental analysis (including biological, sociological, and behavioral spheres); a self-control analysis; an analysis of social relationships; and an analysis of the social-cultural-physical environment. Morganstern and Tevlin (1981) recognize that the beginning interviewer may know what information to seek but still be quite unclear as to the "manner" in which the necessary information is to be obtained. While they recognize the importance of a "complete" functional analysis of a problem behavior, they do assert that an interview should be focused only on content relevant to treatment. This protects the patient's right to minimal intrusion, however interesting other aspects of the patient's life might be to the interviewer and the patient. Discussion of the relationship variables in the interview is much the same as in any other theoretical orientation. That is, the interviewer must be genuinely compassionate and must have the capacity to listen to his or her patients. This would imply that the interviewer does not interrupt with premature questions, does not prematurely reassure or explain away the patient's concerns, and so on. The patient needs to know and to feel that the interviewer is making every effort to understand the problem as the former is experiencing it. Of course, the skillful behavioral interviewer will explicitly define the patient's statements within a behavioral framework. The interviewer-therapist is expected both to model and to shape a behavioral language.

Nelson and Hayes (1981) have pointed out that the earlier orthodoxy of many behaviorists has been modified in that modern behaviorists have adopted an interactionist view that behavior is a function of both environmental and organismic variables. The latter refers to one's physiological state and learning history. Also considered during behavioral assessment are Stimuli-Organism-Response-Consequence (SORC) variables. Behavior samples should be overt motor, cognitive-verbal, and physiological emotional. While behavioral assessment of the single individual is to be the focus, there is nonetheless an interest in classification across individuals. As they point out, an empirical clinical science demands general principles that are universally applicable. They recognize that there are common patterns of response covariation that are much like the syndromes in a diagnostic nomenclature. Nelson and Hayes (1981, p. 13) suggest that these patterns of response covariation are useful in suggesting behaviors, in addition to the presenting problem, that should be examined in an individual client. They acknowledge that the field trials for DSM-III produced respectable reliability figures, and then go on to recognize that DSM-III holds certain advantages for behavioral assessors as a general classification scheme. They write: "For example, DSM-III might help behaviorists to communicate with a professional world that is largely nonbehavioral. Such communication is useful in administrative record keeping, satisfying third-party payers, writing grant proposals, preparing journal articles, referring clients, and as an entry into the psychological and psychiatric literature" (Nelson & Hayes, 1981, pp. 13–14). While still referring back to the need for intervention programs tailored to an individual person, they do admit that some diagnostic categories may suggest appropriate interventions. For example, the depressed individual may respond to an increase in pleasant events, social-skills training, cognitive restructuring, or antidepressant medication.

Nathan (1981) considers even more directly that there may be some diagnostic-assessment situations in which a strictly behavioral assessment may not have much to offer, and vice versa. He presents the diagnosis of a schizophrenic disorder (paranoid), made reliably by use of the DSM-III diagnostic criteria, and concludes that this patient's dysfunctional behavior is not easily explained by any strictly behavioral analysis schema. By contrast, another patient, reliably diagnosed as anxiety disorder using DSM-III criteria, showed behaviors that could be described and modified through a cognitive social learning theory approach. With development of the DSM-III diagnostic criteria, both patients could be described reliably. That is, "With publication of DSM-III, the gap in reliability between behavioral and psychiatric observation has narrowed, though it is probably still true that many of the discrete behavioral units assessed by behavior therapists will yield the highest reliabilities" (Nathan, 1981, p. 6). He also concludes that, in making reliable summary statements about a patient, the DSM-III diagnostician will now probably have an edge over the behavior therapist. Many behavior therapists have pointed out that symptomatic diagnosis does not help in treatment planning. Nathan points out that behavioral analysis also cannot escape the assertion that such an analysis only has utility to the extent that valid treatments exist. The absence of such treatments for the psychoses, for example, makes behavior analysis moot with these disorders, and the DSM-III the diagnostic schema of choice because the diagnosis allows one to plan treatment, (e.g., the use of phenothiazine drugs to treat a schizophrenic disorder). By contrast, behavioral assessment of phobic behavior may be of great help in treatment planning. Nathan concludes that symptomatic diagnosis with DSM-III, and behavioral assessment, now rate about equal in reliability and in utility. Furthermore, in practice, symptomatic diagnosis and behavioral assessment together sometimes work better than either alone.

We would assert that behavioral assessment has had much to offer the practicing clinician and diagnostician. The behavior therapist's emphasis on carefully defining and quantifying symptoms/behavior, treatment/intervention, and outcome variables is surely reflected in all current diagnostic schema and structured interviewing formats. We also believe that DSM-III has considerable advantage as a general classification scheme to allow clinical psychologists to communicate with their general scientific, professional, and public/administrative environment. We view DSM-III as a broad-based, conceptual diagnostic schema to which additional, more specific be-

havioral analyses can be added for specific treatment planning.

Current Diagnostic Needs

Perhaps one area in which clinical psychologists and psychiatrists have most disgraced themselves, because of diagnostic ambiguity and unreliability in the past, is in the courts and in legal testimony. In fact, it might be asserted that the reliability and validity of psychological and psychiatric diagnoses have been so poor in the past that they have been of little value in legal proceedings. In discussing the failure of differential diagnosis in the legal arena, Matarazzo (1978) noted:

Anyone who reads the daily newspapers has known for a long time that experts from the mental health professions disagree with one another on their psychiatric diagnoses when they testify as expert witnesses in court trials. Almost without fail the expert called by the defense offers the opinion that the accused is legally insane. This testimony is followed by that of an expert with similarly impressive credentials who is called by the prosecution and who offers the opinion that the accused is legally sane. The practical effect of such disagreement is to nullify completely, in the minds of the jury and the public, the opinion of either expert. After numerous replays of such public displays of lack of reliability of psychiatric diagnosis, lay persons, jurists, and attorneys have come to expect it and are, in fact, visibly surprised when such experts from opposing sides agree. Disagreement is what is expected, and both sides and the public today routinely place little credence on such testimony in this area of psychiatric diagnosis. [p. 83]

Ambiguous diagnostic criteria probably have been a major factor in such discrepant testimony and have led to unreliability of diagnosis in what is essentially a test-retest situation. With the more clearly defined DSM-III diagnostic criteria, and attendant improvement in diagnostic reliability, both the public and the professional experts should be well served by more credible testimony.

One area of diagnostic interviewing that we are aware of but not addressing in this chapter is linguistic and noverbal analysis of interviewer behavior and its possible diagnostic correlates. We have addressed these issues in the past (Harper,

Wiens, & Matarazzo, 1978; Matarazzo and Wiens, 1972), and will discuss them again in the future because we believe that to understand the interview, we need to be more aware of some of its non-content characteristics. An application of the knowledge of patient speech characteristics is seen, for example, in the assessment of Type A behavior patterns. Patient characteristics of hard driving, competition, and time urgency appear to be reflected most clearly in the rapid and explosive speech patterns that have been associated with the Type A individual. The kinds of linguistic analyses that can be done are almost endless. For example, an interviewer can note that manic patients use more action verbs, adjectives, and acute and concrete nouns compared to depressed patients, who use more state-of-being verbs, modifying adverbs, first-person pronouns, and personal pronouns. In content analysis, manic patients use more words reflecting a concern with power and achievement, while depressive patients show more self-preoccupation (Andreasen & Pfohl, 1976). Related both to personality evaluation and legal-public concerns are efforts to construct personality profiles from various segments of communication and other behavioral indices. Threats from potential terrorists, kidnappers, and assassins are being psycholinguistically analyzed to identify the human needs being expressed by the sender. Indeed, if such needs can be identified, intervention planning may be more successful.

Another diagnostic need that is being increasingly recognized is for efficient screening procedures. We expect clinical psychologists, and especially health-care psychologists, to be increasingly involved in identifying psychological disorders among patients who are presenting themselves for treatment in medical care settings. In such a setting, screening means an effort to apply procedures that can rapidly differentiate persons who do not have a mental disorder from those who may be presumed to have one. The screening procedures are not expected to lead to a definitive diagnosis; further diagnostic procedures must be introduced to follow up the screening procedures. However, the usefulness of a screening procedure will be judged by how well it does separate the person with a mental disorder from one who does not have such a disorder. Further, the screening procedures must be easily administered, often to large numbers of patients, and must be economical in terms of professional time. Self-report inventories often are used for screening purposes. It may well be that brief, structured interviewing procedures

can also be developed to serve screening purposes. Interview procedures would have the advantage of direct patient-clinician interaction and allow the clinician to observe linguistic and nonverbal characteristics in addition to the interview content or other self-report. Observational data in an interview undoubtedly play an important role in a clinician's determination of the patient's well-being. As in other interviewing situations, there must be an effort to put the patient at ease and to assure the patient of the interviewer's complete attention.

Summary

Diagnostic classification is designed to communicate a cluster of clinical features about a person without having each time to list all of the features that clinicians agree constitute a given diagnostic entity. Diagnoses are conventions to be adopted or discarded depending on how useful they are as a way of thinking and communicating, and depending on whether they contribute usefully to functions of administration, treatment, research, or prevention. They should not be thought of as defining physical reality, which will continue to be increasingly differentiated in the future.

Diagnostic interviewing has always been the clinician's personal, subjective effort to gain information and understanding and it remains the most important tool in clinical assessment and diagnosis. Skillful diagnostic interviewing continues to involve classic interview skills such as putting the patient at ease, knowing how to elicit information, maintaining control, maintaining rapport, and bringing about closure. There is a trend in clinical psychology toward the use of more adaptive, semistructured, or structured interviews of demonstrable reliability. The most reliable diagnostic process must provide a nomenclature that defines explicit diagnostic criteria for each diagnosis, and requires the diagnostic interviewer to assess the presence or absence of specific denotable features of any given diagnosis. Current diagnostic nomenclatures are essentially descriptive and atheoretical in regard to the etiology of any given psychological disorder.

References

American Psychiatric Association. *Diagnostic and statistical manual of mental disorders: DSM-III* Washington, D.C.: American Psychiatric Association, 1982.

Anderson, E. G. The seven deadly sins in patient care.

Behavioral Medicine, 1981, **8**, 16–18.

Andreasen, N. J. C., & Pfohl, B. Linguistic analysis of speech in affective disorders. *Archives of General psychiatry*, 1976, **33**, 1,361–1,367.

Barlow, D. H. (Ed.). *Behavioral assessment of adult disorders*. New York: Guilford Press, 1981.

Council for the National Register of Health Service Providers in Psychology. *National Register of Health Service Providers in Psychology*. Baltimore: Part City Press, 1978.

Endicott, J., & Spitzer, R. L. A diagnostic interview: The Schedule for Affective Disorders and Schizophrenia. *Archives of General Psychiatry*, 1978, **35**, 837–844.

Endicott, J., & Spitzer, R. L. Use of the Research Diagnostic Criteria and the Schedule for Affective Disorders and Schizophrenia to study affective disorders. *American Journal of Psychiatry*, 1979, **136**, 52–56.

Engel, G. L. The need for a new medical model: A challenge for biomedicine. *Science*, 1977, **196**, 129–136.

Foley, R., & Sharf, B. F. The five interviewing techniques most frequently overlooked by primary care physicians. *Behavioral Medicine*, 1981, 8, 26–31.

Harper, R. G., Wiens, A. N., & Matarazzo, J. D. *Nonverbal communication: The state of the art*. New York: Wiley, 1978.

Haynes, S. N., & Wilson, C. C. *Behavioral Assessment*. San Francisco: Jossey-Bass, 1979.

Hersen, M., & Bellack, A. S. *Behavioral assessment: A practical handbook*. (2nd ed.) New York: Pergamon, 1981.

Holmes, T. H., & Rahe, R. H. The social readjustment scale. *Journal of Psychosomatic Research*, 1967, **11**, 213–218.

Kanfer, F. H., & Saslow, G. Behavioral diagnosis. In C. M. Franks (Ed.), *Behavior therapy: Appraisal and status*. New York: McGraw-Hill, 1969.

Keefe, F. J., Kopel, S. A., & Gordon, S. B. *A practical guide to behavioral assessment*. New York: Springer, 1978.

Korchin, S. J., & Schuldberg, D. The future of clinical assessment. *American Psychologist*, 1981, **36**, 1,147–1,158.

Macklin, R. The medical model in psychoanalysis and psychotherapy. *Comprehensive Psychiatry*, 1973, **14**, 49–69.

Matarazzo, J. D. The interview: Its reliability and validity in psychiatric diagnoses. In B. B. Wolman (Ed.), *Clinical diagnosis of mental disorders: A handbook*. New York: Plenum, 1978.

Matarazzo, J. D. The reliability of psychiatric and psychological diagnosis. *Clinical Psychology Review*, 1983, in press.

Matarazzo, J. D., & Wiens, A. N. *The interview: Re-search on its anatomy and structure*. Chicago: Aldine-Atherton, 1972.

Meier, A. The Research Diagnostic Criteria: Historical background, development, validity, and reliability. *Canadian Journal of Psychiatry*, 1979, **24**, 167–178.

Menninger, K., Mayman, M., & Pruyser, P. *The vital balance: The life process in mental health and illness*. New York: Viking, 1963.

Miller, L. S., Bergstrom, D. A., Cross, H. J., & Grube, J. W. Opinions and use of the DSM system by practicing psychologists. *Professional Psychology*, 1981, **12**, 285–390.

Morganstern, K. P., & Tevlin, H. E. Behavioral interviewing. In M. Hersen & A. S. Bellack (Eds.), *Behavioral assessment: A practical handbook*. (2nd ed.) New York: Pergamon Press, 1981.

Nathan, P. E. Symptomatic diagnosis and behavioral assessment: A synthesis? In D. H. Barlow (Ed.), *Behavioral assessment of adult disorders*. New York: Guilford Press, 1981.

Nelson, R. O., & Hayes, S. C. Nature of behavioral assessment. In M. Hersen & A. S. Bellack (Eds.), *Behavioral assessment: A practical handbook*. (2nd Ed.) New York: Pergamon, 1981.

Schacht, T., & Nathan, P. E. But is it good for the psychologists? Appraisal and status of DSM III. *American Psychologist*, 1977, **32**, 1,017–1,025.

Spitzer, R. L., Endicott, J., & Robins, E. Clinical criteria for diagnosis and DSM III. *American Journal of Psychiatry*, 1975, **132**, 1,187–1,192.

Spitzer, R. L., Endicott, J., & Robins, E. Research diagnostic criteria rationale and reliability. *Archives of General Psychiatry*, 1978, **35**, 773–782.

Spitzer, R. L., & Forman, J. B. W. DSM-III field trials: II. Initial experience with the multiaxial system. *American Journal of Psychiatry*, 1979, **136**, 818–820.

Spitzer, R. L., Forman, J. B. W., & Nee, J. DSM-III field trials: I. Initial interrater diagnostic reliability. *American Journal of Psychiatry*, 1979, **136**, 815–817.

Spitzer, R. L., & Williams, J. B. W. Classification in psychiatry. In A. Kaplan, A. Friedman, & B. Sadock (Eds.), *Comprehensive textbook of psychiatry: III*. Baltimore: Williams & Wilkins, 1980.

Wiens, A. N. Estimated cost saving for patients treated in a psychological outpatient clinic. In B. Christiansen (Ed.), *Does psychology return its costs?* Oslo: Norweigian Research Council for the Science and Humanities, 1981.

Wiens, A. N. The assessment interview. In I. B. Weiner (Ed.), *Clinical methods in psychology*. New York: Wiley, 1976.

Woodruff, R. A., Jr., Goodwin, D. W., & Guze, S. B. *Psychiatric diagnosis*. New York: Oxford University Press, 1974.

Zilboorg, G. *A history of medical psychology*. New York: Norton, 1941.

18 OBJECTIVE PERSONALITY ASSESSMENT IN CLINICAL SETTINGS

James N. Butcher
Stephen, Finn

The relative importance of personality assessment in clinical practice has been debated for many years. In this chapter we discuss theoretical issues and procedures relating to the use of objective personality testing in clinical settings. Our goal is to present a discussion of traditional clinical personality assessment and to provide a rationale and set of procedures for the clinical use of objective personality instruments. We also review in detail the characteristics of the most widely used clinical objective personality test, the MMPI, and present a case example in which the MMPI had a major impact on the treatment designed for the patient.

The Role of Personality Assessment in Clinical Psychology

Before reviewing the most widely used clinical objective personality instrument, the MMPI, we would like to speak to two of the major criticisms of clinical personality assessment and give our views as to why objective personality assessment continues to have an important place in comprehensive treatment programs. Many of the criticisms of clinical personality assessment fall into two general categories: *validity* and *applicability*

considerations. Critics in these two areas have differed as to whether they identify with the traditional empirical clinical approach and also as to what they propose as a replacement for the personality assessment function in clinical settings.

Validity

The first body of criticism concerning clinical personality assessment raises questions about the imperfect validity of personality assessment devices. By and large, persons offering this type of critique have come from within traditional psychiatry and psychology. The procedure that has been offered as a replacement for personality assessment is that of the clinical interview.

Those who criticize clinical personality assessment on grounds of test validity have pointed out that if the results of a particular test are at odds with the clinical judgment of a practitioner obtained through interview, there is no way for that practitioner to know for an individual case whether the assessment device has yielded a correct or an erroneous (e.g., false positive or false negative) judgment. What, then, these critics have concluded, is the value of using a device with imperfect validity? Why not rely on the clinical interview alone? This dilemma is equally true in research settings, of course, but seems to be less conflict-ridden for researchers in that they are somewhat less likely to interact with the subjects extensively on a case-by-case basis, and are therefore less likely to form strong "clinical" opinions.

The issue of what to do when the clinician and the assessment instrument differ has been discussed at length under the rubric of the "clinical versus actuarial" prediction controversy (Meehl, 1954). Of course, an ardent actuarialist sees an easy solution to the dilemma: If the clinical instrument has greater validity than the clinician's judgment, one should apply it in all cases, even in those instances where the decision of the device differs from that of the clinician. If the opposite is true, one may follow the clinician and discard the instrument.

There are obvious problems with this type of thinking, not the least of which is choosing the clinician or group of clinicians against which the assessment device should be compared. Must the test be more valid than the best clinician, or simply than the average clinician? The question, however, of whether an assessment device should be used need not depend solely on such a comparison. Instead, a rationale for the use of personality tests and a set of procedures governing their use can be given apart from the considerations of agreement with clinical interview information. These procedures are such that even if the overall accuracy of clinical judgment is greater than that of the test alone, there is still benefit to be obtained in using the objective test.

GENERATING HYPOTHESES

In our clinical work, we conceptualize personality assessment as a way of generating hypotheses about patients: their symptomatic pattern, their central conflicts, how their problems compare with other patients in terms of severity or chronicity, what material is likely to emerge in the course of therapy, how the patients are likely to respond to various types of treatment, and so on. These hypotheses may then be corroborated or refuted by further data and by clinical impressions collected in the clinical interview. We believe that this two-step, assessment-interview procedure has the potential of providing clinical judgments of greater validity than those judgments obtained through the use of either procedure alone. This is because the two procedures, in most cases, have different *domains of error* (Cronbach & Gleser, 1965).

The domain of error of an instrument or procedure is that set of stimulus conditions under which the procedure makes invalid or incorrect judgments. At times, this domain of error is found to be systematic and constant. For example, some writers have suggested that the MMPI yields many false-positive judgments of psychopathology when applied to minority populations with the standard ($T \geq 70$) cutoffs. This would be a systematic domain of error of the test, if found to be true. Similarly, a particular clinician would have a systematic domain of error if that clinician always failed to identify from the clinical interview patients with psychopathic characteristics. The domain of error of an instrument or procedure may also be unsystematic (i.e., nonconstant across various stimulus conditions).

Rappaport, Gill, and Shafer (1968) have pointed out that the clinical interview is highly influenced by both subjective and objective variables. This means that, whatever systematic error a particular clinician manifests in interviews (e.g., always failing to identify psychopaths), the clinical interview is also highly subject to random or at least nonconstant sources of error. Personality assessment devices, when administered under standardized conditions, are much less subject to nonconstant error. This is especially true of objective personality tests as compared to projective personality tests. The latter also are highly influenceable by subjective variables. Furthermore, the domain of error of objective personality assessment instruments is further systematized when their interpretation is governed by standard, actuarial procedures, rather than by clinical judgment alone.

By combining the use of personality assessment with the clinical interview, the clinician has the potential of increasing the validity of clinical decisions in two ways. First, the *systematic* domains of error of the clinical interview and the assessment are likely to differ and may be used as checks against each other. For example, the aforementioned clinician who has a blindness for psychopathy may adopt an informal decision rule, such as: "I will be more alert for antisocial tendencies in a patient whenever the MMPI suggest that they exist." Similarly, if the systematic error of a personality assessment instrument involves its use with minority populations, one can circumvent it by weighting the results of the clinical interview more than the test in those cases. A prerequisite for this type of validity *instrument* is that clinicians become aware of their own areas of personal clinical error, and that information be available as to the systematic domains of error of the personality assessment devices they use. Again, we point out that it is much easier to identify these domains of error for objective than for projective personality instruments.

A second reason why combined use of personality test information and clinical interview can improve on the use of interview alone in making therapeutic decisions is that, as stated earlier, personality assessment is less vulnerable than the clinical interview to *nonsystematic* sources of error. This is different from the previous example in that no systematic domain of error is assumed for the clinician: It is not that clinician X has difficulty identifying antisocial personalities, simply that on a particular day clinician X was overtired, or feeling especially trusting, etc., and failed to identify sociopathic tendencies in a certain patient. Use of personality assessment as a check on clinician X's judgment—an objective, outside opinion—could lead to a reexamination of the patient in question and to more valid clinical judgments regarding the patient.

SCREENING FOR PSYCHOPATHOLOGY

In the preceding section, we argued that a two-step clinical procedure, in which each step has a different domain of error, can lead to more valid clinical judgments regarding patients than will a one-step procedure. This reasoning, however, does not necessarily suggest that objective personality assessment should be one part of this two-step procedure. It would, for example, be possible to have each patient interviewed independently by two clinicians. Again, some may argue that if the validity of clinical interview is higher than that of the objective personality assessment device, this is definitely the more desirable procedure. If we assume that two clinicians have different domains of error (which may or may not be true), an increment in the number of valid clinical judgments should occur. Nevertheless, we believe there are several reasons to suggest the use of objective personality assessment as one part of this two-step process.

First, there is the practical issue of the amount of professional time required for objective personality assessment as compared to the time required for a second clinical interview. Our own experience has shown that it is quite possible to train clerical workers or psychometrists to score and graph the results of an objective personality test such as the MMPI. A clinician who is experienced

with the test can then acquire a multitude of information about a patient in very little time. In contrast, a clinical interview may require an hour or more of the clinician's time. It is for this same practical reason that objective personality testing is to be preferred, in our opinion, over projective personality testing as a screening procedure. The time required to record, score, and interpret a Rorschach protocol well exceeds the hour required for a clinical interview.

A second reason for preferring objective personality assessment over an additional clinical interview as part of a two-stage assessment process is that the domains of error of two different procedures (assessment and interview) are more likely to differ than are the domains of error of two administrations of the same procedure (e.g., two clinical interviews). The validity increment of the former two-step procedure is thus likely to exceed that of the latter. This will be especially true if the training, personalities, and biases of two clinicians in a two-step interview procedure are highly similar.

RAPPORT BUILDING

Another justification of clinical personality assessment that is to some extent independent of questions of validity concerns its effects on the relationship between clinician and patient. This justification applies primarily to settings where the clinician who administers and interprets testing to the patient will also be mainly responsible for the patient's ongoing treatment. However, rapport building is also useful for situations other than treatment (e.g., referral). It has been our experience that personality testing often may be used to build rapport with a patient in preparation for or in the preliminary stages of a diagnostic study or course of treatment. This may seem less than obvious to some clinicians, many of whom see personality testing as potentially detrimental to rapport building. For this reason, some elaboration of this point seems in order.

Some patients may have negative preconceptions about psychological testing. Unfortunately, clinicians themselves must take some responsibility for this fact, for psychological testing has been used questionably in some instances for a number of years. We have found that the appropriate use of testing—in a collaborative atmosphere, with full test feedback as to results and post hoc explanation to the patient about the nature of the test, may be the basis for establishing a productive working relationship between clinician and client. We customarily give a minilecture on the MMPI to patients with whom we use this instrument, discussing the development of the test, and other relevant issues. We have found that this usually creates an "attitude of acceptance" on the part of the client, and enables them to incorporate aspects of the test feedback into their understanding of their problems.

For those patients with fears and distrust about both testing and therapy, the appropriate use of testing can serve as a demarcation for the patient that the therapist is worthy of trust and has the best interests of the patient in mind. Even if a patient has no strong negative feelings about psychological services, testing may serve to reassure the patient as to the clinician's expertise. In our experience, many patients have expressed a sense of relief after a test feedback, that finally "someone understood their problems" and was not feeling hopeless or intimidated by their case.

We have found that for certain populations psychological testing is an especially appropriate tool, simply from the aspect of establishing a working relationship between clinician and patient. For example, many adolescents are initially resistive or unable to describe problems directly in their initial contacts with a clinician. They also may be unwilling, unlike younger children, to establish rapport through play. Personality testing gives an opportunity for the clinician and adolescent to interact in a relatively nonthreatening way, in a focused fashion, and in a way that helps to establish personal contact between the two parties. Furthermore, in our experience, a majority of school-aged children are so accustomed to standardized testing that they have few negative feelings about personality assessment.

INTRODUCING MATERIAL INTO THERAPY

The preceding discussion concerned use of personality assessment when it directly precedes a psychological intervention. Some clinicians prefer to do personality testing in the middle of an ongoing treatment process. In this context, another purpose personality assessment may serve is to introduce material for active discussion into therapy. This may be especially useful when the clinician feels that there are issues that are relevant and important, which the patient has not yet brought up for discussion. This is different from the situation described in the preceding section, in that a certain amount of rapport is presumed to exist between the clinician and patient before such a tactic will result in productive therapeutic work.

Why would a clinician prefer to use testing to introduce a therapeutically relevant topic, rather than simply raising the topic with the patient in a session? First, in raising an issue before the patient has introduced it into the course of therapy, the clinician faces the risk that the topic will be rejected or denied by the patient. By referring to testing as an objective source in introducing such material, the clinician may ensure that the patient will not reject an interpretation as readily as if it simply were suggested by the clinician. Alternatively, if the patient truly is unable or unwilling to deal with the issue in question at that time in therapy, the testing provides an easy "out" for both the therapist and the client. The therapist simply may explain that though testing suggests the issue in question is relevant for the patient, the test is not infallible. The therapist may then suggest that both the patient and the therapist be on the look out in the future for material that will definitely either confirm or disprove the test result in question.

This same approach may be used in introducing test-based hypotheses that are not only missing from information presented by the patient in interview, but that appear to be directly contradictory to this information. For example, a patient may claim to have recovered completely from a depression, but still evidence a high score on Scale 2 (Depression) on the MMPI. The patient and clinician may jointly problem solve about such instances of conflicting information, and in the process reach a new level of understanding about the client's problems.

Applicability

Apart from criticisms of its validity, clinical personality assessment also has faced criticism concerning its applicability to the intervention process. Critics state that, even if valid, much of the information with which traditional clinical personality assessment is concerned often is not directly related or is irrelevant to the client's presenting complaint(s) (e.g., Ciminero, 1977; Eisler, 1976; O'Leary & Wilson, 1975). The strongest voices of such a critique have been clinicians who are highly identified with behavioral treatment modes and the procedures that have been offered as a replacement for clinical personality assessment are those that fall under the heading of "behavioral assessment" (Hersen & Bellack, 1976). This is not to suggest, however, that all behavioral clinicians are opposed to traditional personality assessment. Recently, certain behaviorists have urged a reconsideration of the outright rejection of traditional assessment devices (Goldfried & Linehan, 1977; Williams, 1981, in press).

In criticizing traditional assessment, some behaviorally oriented psychologists have pointed out that it is the ethical responsibility of practitioners to respect the confidentiality of patients, and to collect no more information than is necessary to provide an effective intervention (Hersen, 1976). While few clinicians would quarrel with this point, there is obvious disagreement as to what information is or is not necessary for planning an intervention. We would like to offer some reasons why clinical personality assessment is justified, even if the treatment mode to be employed is predominantly behavioral, and even if the information yielded does not appear, at intake, to be directly related to a patient's presenting complaint.

JUDGING THE APPROPRIATENESS OF A CERTAIN TREATMENT

There is increasing evidence in the literature that certain personality variables may be important moderators of the efficacy of given treatment approaches, and that clinicians can save considerable time and energy by being aware of such relationships before initiating an intervention. Pickens, Errickson, Thompson, Heston, and Eckert (1979) found that several of the MMPI basic scales were predictive of point-earning behavior in a token economy psychiatric ward. To choose another example from the behavioral treatment realm, Bellack (1975) and Bellack and Tillman (1974) found that externalizers on Rotter's (1966) Locus of Control Scale are much more likely than internalizers to have difficulty implementing self-evaluation as part of self-control management programs, unless external input is provided. A good behavioral clinician will quickly discover whether or not self-control procedures are tenable with a particular patient, and will tailor a treatment program for those patients who are unable to self-evaluate as part of a prescribed plan. Knowledge of such a probable outcome, however, may prevent an unsuccessful trial of self-control procedures, with the accompanying loss of time, expense, and discouragement on the part of both clinician and patient.

Traditional personality assessment was instrumental in identifying a number of relationships between clinical characteristics and the efficacy of traditional psychotherapy. For example, patients demonstrating elevated scores on Scale 4 (Psychopathic Deviate) of the MMPI show a no-

toriously poor response to traditional psychotherapy. Now that newer therapies are evolving, it seems important to us that objective personality assessment continue to be employed in order to identify such moderator variables. To choose another example from our own clinical work, we have found that although cognitive-behavioral therapy as described by Beck (1972) is extremely effective with certain depressed patients, it is not very successful with patients who show signs of even subtle thought disorder either on the Rorschach, or in an elevation on Scale 8 of the MMPI. Both we and our colleagues who work with cognitive therapies have had the experience of having to change treatment approaches with such patients, after a standard trial of cognitive-behavioral therapy produced no improvement.

IDENTIFYING HOMOGENEOUS CLINICAL GROUPS

Even if known relationships do not exist between patient personality variables and the efficacy of certain treatment modes, there is value in using clinical personality assessment to identify homogeneous clinical groups in the hope that such relationships will emerge. Homogeneous groups exist both within and across patients with similar presenting complaints, and it may be difficult for the clinician to identify such clusters without the aid of personality assessment devices. For example, reliable subgroups of patients in alcoholic treatment programs have been demonstrated using the MMPI (Butcher & Owen, 1975; Penk, 1981). Research remains to be completed as to whether varied treatment approaches are differentially effective with these subgroups. In the meantime, the routine use of the MMPI in alcoholic treatment programs may allow clinicians to make informal observations about such relationships and thus improve their interventions. It seems likely that such subgroups of patients might otherwise go unrecognized. Similarly, use of personality assessment can aid practitioners to recognize similarities between patients with *different* presenting complaints. In this way, clinical experience can be classified and more easily transferred to improve treatment from case to case.

DOCUMENTING (NONBEHAVIORAL) CHANGES DURING THE COURSE OF TREATMENT

Another important function of personality assessment in a clinical setting is to aid in the documentation of changes in the status of patients that are due to, or at least occur during the course of, treatment. Once again, clinicians operating within behavioral paradigms may argue that any changes in status that cannot be observed, objectified, and counted are unimportant. We disagree with this point of view for several reasons. First, there is some evidence that change scores on an objective assessment instrument during therapy are more highly correlated than behavioral ratings with patient satisfaction with therapy (Bergin, 1971). Though not the only, or the most important, therapy outcome variable, patient satisfaction is likely to play a role in such matters as whether the person seeks help in the future from mental-health professionals. Second, we consider change in perceptions and cognitions an appropriate goal for psychotherapy, as is change in behavior. Clinical personality assessment can be used to measure modifications in these variables during the course of a patient's treatment.

Comment

Clinical personality assessment has faced criticism in the past from both within and outside the ranks of traditional psychodynamic psychiatry and psychology. The criticism has taken two major forms: questions regarding the utility of clinical personality assessment because of its imperfect validity, and questions regarding the applicability of personality information to modern treatment processes. We have tried to explicate procedures for, and a way of thinking about, objective personality assessment that show how it is useful in clinical practice. These procedures include a two-step assessment-interview process, in which clerical staff absorb most of the responsibility for administering and scoring the objective testing, and where the clinician uses the results of testing as a way of generating hypotheses regarding clients.

Drawing upon our own clinical experience, we also have presented ways in which the information obtained from personality assessment may aid the clinician in planning, implementing, and evaluating treatment programs. The rationale presented here is applicable both to traditional insight-oriented therapies, and to interventions with a primarily behavioral emphasis. Of course, the utility of clinical personality assessment is, in the end, an empirical question that may be addressed through proper research. Unfortunately, there are few well-designed studies that investigate whether personality assessment is an aid to the treatment process. More research on this question is needed.

In the interim, we hope our comments may be helpful to other clinicians.

Introduction to the MMPI

In the following pages, we present information to acquaint readers with the development, rationale, and workings of one objective personality assessment device: the MMPI. An adequate understanding of the theoretical issues underlying objective clinical personality testing requires that one be highly familiar with the major objective instrument in use today. The MMPI was chosen for this presentation for several reasons. It is the most widely used clinical objective personality test (Dahlstrom, Welsh, & Dahlstrom, 1975), a large amount of validity research has been compiled for the MMPI, and it, unlike some instruments, was specifically designed for use with clinical populations.

Rationale

Objective personality assessment with paper and pencil questionnaires has a long history. One of the first personality scales, and the prototype of present-day inventories, was the *Woodworth Personal Data Sheet* (Woodworth, 1920). The Personal Data Sheet was developed during World War I as an aid to screening out draftees from the Army who were psychologically unsuited for military service. After the war, a large number of personality tests were published that focused upon numerous personality attributes. Most of these scales were developed according to an intuitive or rationale scale construction strategy; that is, the psychologist thought of the quality to be assessed and then generated "from the armchair" the items believed to be related to this attribute. Most of these early scales were never formally validated or proven out against "real-world" behavior.

Unfortunately, when many of these scales were examined in terms of external criteria, they were found to be lacking in validity. Some items were actually shown to work in the *opposite* direction than what the test developer had intended. Criticisms leveled against rationally developed personality scales played an important role subsequently in test development in that empirical validity became a basic means of assuring an item's relevance to the construct being assessed.

In the late 1930s, Starke Hathaway, a psychologist, and J. R. McKinley, a psychiatrist, decided to develop a set of personality scales to aid the clinician in the diagnostic assessment of psychological problems in medical and psychiatric settings. The scales they began to devise, which ultimately became the Minnesota Multiphasic Personality Inventory, were to be unlike existing personality scales in several respects:

1. The scales were to be relevant to clinical problems encountered in medical and psychiatric settings.
2. They were to have substantial norms so that patient scores might be compared to those of people in general.
3. They were to be constructed according to an empirical scale development strategy rather than the intuitive approach. Items were to be included on the scales only if they clearly differentiated the clinical groups from the normal populations; that is, had demonstrated validity.

MMPI Development

ITEMS

Hathaway and McKinley had no preconceived ideas about what an item measured. Rather, they collected items (about 1,000) from various sources—case files, textbooks, other tests, clinical experience, and others. The items covered a wide range of content such as physical symptoms, psychological problems, attitudes toward life, religion, family, and the like. The items were eventually reduced to 504, which comprised the basic pool on which initial normative and clinical group data were collected. In the mid-1940s, two additional item sets, masculinity-femininity and social introversion, were added to the item pool to bring the total on the MMPI to 550. Sixteen items are repeated. The early clinical scales were developed on the basis of the 504 original items. Items were written in such a way as to enable persons with low reading level (Grade 6) to understand them. In order to obtain (or ensure) more self-reference from the examinee, the items were written in the first person. In an effort to prevent "true" responses from always being associated with deviant behaviors, many items were written so that undesirable implication occurred with a "false" response. This served to break up the monotony of responding true or false to numerous items as well as to prevent thoughtless responding or response sets.

The MMPI authors included a number of items to measure the tendency of some people to say overly favorable things about themselves (the Lie Scale). These items (e.g., "I get angry sometimes") were phrased so that an answer of "false" by the respondent suggested "lying," since it was assumed that the statement was actually *true* of nearly all people. Another measure of deviant responding was also included: the F scale or infrequency scale was new with the MMPI. This scale (consisting of 64 items infrequently endorsed) measured the tendency to be overly candid or to place oneself in a bad light. A high score on this scale (the mean score in the general population is about 3) indicated a tendency to admit to symptoms ranging over several problem areas. Because F-scale items are so infrequently endorsed, this scale also provided a measure of "random" scoring such as a poor reader might obtain. Other validity scales (K scale, SD scale) were added later in the MMPI history.

STANDARDIZATION

Prior to the MMPI development, most personality tests were poorly standardized. Hathaway and McKinley launched a substantial empirical study comparing control subjects to clinical groups on the MMPI. The normative group consisted of over 1,500 normal subjects, including 724 visitors to the University of Minnesota Hospital, 265 normal clients from a testing bureau, 254 medical students, and 265 local WPA workers. Over 800 carefully screened and studied psychiatric patients made up the clinical subgroups. The psychiatric criterion groups usually were smaller than 50 patients, but were very homogeneous in terms of clinical problems and symptoms. For example, they obtained patients who had been diagnosed as depressed, hypochondriacal, schizophrenic, psychopathic, etc. Efforts were made to exclude patients with problems that did not fit the "clinical type" being studied.

Items were selected for particular scale *only* if they significantly differentiated between the normal and the criterion or clinical group. Items were not included on a scale if they failed to differentiate the groups or if the frequency of response by both groups was so low or so high as to provide no information. For example, an item that was answered the same way by all subjects was not considered a useful item.

MMPI SCALES

The MMPI scales are groups of items that measure or are associated with the likelihood that an individual is a member of the clinical group on which the scale was developed. Each item answered in the same direction as the clinical group (and opposite that of the normal control subjects) receives one point on that scale. The more items on a given scale the subject answers, the more likely it is that he or she is a "member" of the clinical group. Each MMPI scale has a mean score of 50 and a standard deviation of 10 based on the normative group study. Thus, if a person receives a raw score on the Depression scale that falls at the T-score of 70, or 2 standard deviations higher than the average, his or her score is more like the depressive group than 95 percent of the population. It is considered that extreme scores like this are not likely to be obtained by chance. The greater the scale elevation (i.e., the more deviant a score from the average), the greater the likelihood that the individual is depressed.

The most frequently used MMPI clinical scales, along with a summary of the characteristics they measure, are included in Table 18.1.

Administration and Scoring

The MMPI is easily administered and scored, and little professional time is required since clerks can readily be taught the procedure. Several MMPI forms or administrative formats are available. The most widely used format is the booklet, from which the subject reads items and records answers on a separate sheet that may be scored by either hand or machine. Additional forms have been developed for special purposes, such as an IBM-card form for research purposes and an audio form for use with blind people or individuals with a low reading level. A number of computer-administered formats are being developed at present; for example, subjects respond to the item in interaction with a computer. The MMPI item pool has been widely translated into other languages (over 75 translations presently exist: Butcher & Clark, 1979; Butcher & Pancheri, 1976).

The standard MMPI profile sheet (see Figure 18.1) gives male and female forms on opposite sides of the page. The scoring is very simple — responses to the items on each scale are counted and entered on the bottom of the profile sheet in the space shown. Five of the clinical scales require the addition of a correction factor determined by the individual score on the K or defensiveness scale. The scores may then be plotted on the profile sheet by making a dot at the raw score point on each scale and then connecting the dots by a line.

The standard profile sheet includes four validity scales and ten clinical scales.

A final step in the scoring of an MMPI involves *coding* the profile. The profile code is merely a shorthand way of describing the profile information. Scale number, rather than scale names, are used. A profile elevated to 70 on the Hypochondriasis scale (Scale 1) and Hysteria scale (Scale 3) would be a 1-3 code. This is an example of a two-point code that is widely used. For some purposes it may be desirable to use more than just two-point codes; a person having elevations on Depression (Scale 2), Psychasthenia (Scale 7), and Schizophrenia (Scale 8) would have a 2-7-8 code type.

The code types and single-scale elevations have been the basis of a great deal of empirical validation research on the MMPI. The interpretation of the MMPI is based on well-established empirical literature in which behavioral characteristics have been statistically linked to MMPI scores and indices. The MMPI is a *reliable* instrument in that trained professionals would have a high degree of agreement about what the scale scores and interpretations are. The MMPI is also a *valid* instrument in that the scales measure what they purport to measure.

In spite of its humble beginnings as a diagnostic aid for physicians, psychiatrists, and psychologists in Minnesota in 1940, the MMPI has become the most widely used clinical personality test in the world today. The widespread use of the MMPI actually began during World War II when there was a great need for an objective and inexpensive personality measure for use in military settings. After World War II, with the growth of clinical psychology, the MMPI came to be used extensively in a wide variety of settings across the United States. At present the MMPI is also in use in over 46 other countries around the world (Butcher & Bemis, in press).

MMPI interpretation

There are two basic approaches to MMPI interpretation: *clinical* and *actuarial*. (For further discussion of MMPI interpretation see: Dahlstrom, Welsh, & Dahlstrom, 1972; Graham, 1977; Lachar, 1974). In clinical interpretation, the clinician examines the scale scores for the validity scales and the clinical scales and generates hypotheses and personality descriptions (inferences about the individuals' problems and traits) from their performance in relationship to norms. In clinical inter-

TABLE 18.1 PERSONALITY CHARACTERISTICS ASSOCIATED WITH ELEVATIONS ON THE BASIC MMPI SCALES.

Scale	Characteristics
? Cannot Say	A validity score that, if high, may indicate evasiveness. Attenuated clinical scales are suspected if ? raw score is greater than 30 in the first 400 items.
L Lie Scale	A validity score that measures the tendency to claim excessive virtue or place oneself in an overly favorable light. Elevated scores suggest the need to see or present oneself in a "saintly" manner suggesting an unrealistically positive self-image or life circumstance.
F Fake Bad Scale	A validity scale composed of highly infrequent items. A high score suggests carelessness, confusion, or claiming an inordinate amount of symptoms or "faking illness." Random responding also will result in an elevated F score.
K Subtle Defensiveness	A validity scale that measures defensiveness and a willingness to discuss personal matters. Scores are related to intelligence, education, and social class. Thus, these factors must be considered in scale interpretation. For example, middle-class clients with low K may be viewed as overly frank, complaining, and masochistic while low scores are considered typical in low SES clients. Scores of 55–65 are considered modal for middle and upper SES clients. Scores over $T = 70$ reflect uncooperativeness or unwillingness to discuss problems.
1(Hs) Hypochondriasis	High scorers present numerous physical problems of a vague nature. Their problems tend to be chronic and they do not respond well to psychological treatments. High scorers are generally unhappy, self-centered, whiney, complaining, hostile, demanding, and command attention.
2(D) Depression	Elevations reflect depressed mood, low self-esteem, and feelings of inadequacy. This scale is one of the most frequently elevated in clinical patients. High scorers are described as moody, shy, despondent, pessimistic, distressed, high strung, lethargic, overcontrolled and guilt prone. Elevations may reflect great discomfort and need for change or symptomatic relief.
3(Hy) Hysteria	High scorers tend to rely on neurotic defenses—denial and repression—to deal with stress. They tend to be dependent, naive, outgoing, infantile, and narcissistic. Their interpersonal relations are often disrupted and they show little insight into problems. Higher levels of stress are accompanied by development of physical symptoms in high three people. Scale 3 is the peak score among female medical patients who have negative medical findings. High scorers often respond to client suggestion, however, they resist insight-oriented treatment. They show low psychological-mindedness and interpret psychological problems as physical.
4(Pd) Psychopathic Deviate	Associated with antisocial behavior—rebelliousness, disrupted family relations; impulsiveness; school, work or legal difficulties; alcohol or drug abuse, etc. Personality trait disorder likely among high scorers—they are outgoing, sociable, likable but deceptive, manipulative, hedonistic, immature, hostile, aggressive. They often have difficulty in marital or family relations and trouble with the law. High scores usually reflect longstanding character problems that are highly resistant to treatment. High scorers may enter treatment, but usually terminate quickly.
5(MF) Masculinity-Femininity	High-scoring males are described as sensitive, aesthetic, passive, or feminine. They may show conflicts over sexual identity and low heterosexual drive. Low-scoring males are viewed as masculine, aggressive, crude, adventurous, reckless, practical, and having narrow interests.
	High-scoring females are seen as masculine, rough, aggressive, self-confident, unemotional, insensitive. Low-scoring females are viewed as passive, yielding, complaining, fault finding, idealistic, sensitive.
6(Pa) Paranoia	High elevations on this scale are often associated with being suspicious, aloof, shrewd, guarded, worrisome, and overly sensitive. High scorers may project or externalize blame and harbor grudges against others. High scorers are generally hostile and argumentative and are not very amenable to psychotherapy.
	Low scorers (below $T = 45$) may show guarded, evasive, and paranoid behavior.
7(Pt) Psychasthenia	High scorers are tense, anxious, ruminative, preoccupied, obsessional, phobic, rigid. They frequently are self-condemning, guilt prone, and feel inferior and inadequate.

(continued)

TABLE 18.1　(*continued*)

Scale	Characteristics
	Clients with spike 7 elevations overintellectualize, ruminate, rationalize, and resist psychological interpretation in treatment.
8(Sc) Schizophrenia	High scorers ($T = 70$–80) show unconventional or schizoid life style. They are withdrawn, shy, feel inadequate, tense, confused, and moody. May have unusual or strange thoughts, poor judgment, and erratic mood. Very high scorers ($T = 80$) may show poor reality contact, bizarre sensory experiences, delusions, and hallucinations. High scorers may have difficulty relating in therapy; they tend to lack information and have poor problem-solving skills.
9(Ma) Mania	High scorers ($T = 70$–75) are viewed as sociable, outgoing, impulsive, overly energetic, optimistic, and have liberal moral views, flighty, drink excessively, grandiose, irritable, unqualified optimism, and unrealistic planning. They overvalue self-worth and are manipulative. They show impatience and irritability. Very high scorers (T over 75) may show affective disorder, bizarre behavior, erratic mood, very poor and impulsive behavior, and delusions possible.
0(Si) Social Introversion-Extroversion	High scorers are introverted, shy, withdrawn, socially reserved, submissive, overcontrolled, lethargic, conventional, tense, inflexible, and show guilt.
	Low scorers are extroverted, outgoing, gregarious, expressive, aggressive, talkative, impulsive, uninhibited, spontaneous, manipulative, opportunistic, and insincere in social relations.

Source: MMPI Workshop Series (Butcher, 1980).

pretations, the clinician evaluates such profile features as scale elevation (distance from the norm), profile shape (which scales are elevated together), and whether certain indices such as anxiety states, depressed mood, or phobias, are present. In this approach, the interpreter relies extensively upon his or her personal experience with the test and memory of what scales measure and how different patients typically produce certain profile types.

In the second major interpretive approach, the *actuarial* approach, the clinician relies upon empirically established codebooks (similar to the "experience tables" of insurance actuaries). The primary assumption is that behavioral descriptions, predictions, etc. apply to *all* members of a profile class or code type. Thus, if one were to study the characteristics of a "profile type," then one could apply the same characteristics to describe any person who meets the criteria for that class. A large number of MMPI clinical types have been carefully studied, and extensive information about these "types" has been catalogued. The two main sources of information about MMPI code types were published by Marks, Seeman, and Haller (1974) and Gilberstadt and Duker (1965). These codebooks allow for the classification and description of a large number of patients who appear in both outpatient and inpatient psychiatric facilities.

In the last 15 years a number of computer-

based automated interpretation systems have been developed. These systems are based, in large part, on the actuarial-based codebooks that define the profile types. However, the clinical interpretation procedures are also included to account for the profiles that do not exactly fit the code types.

Most MMPI interpretation involves some combination of the clinical and actuarial approaches. It typically involves the use of *scale* scores and their established empirical correlates, *code types* and their established personality descriptions, and various *MMPI indices* that have been shown to be effective at making important distinctions or predictions. Each of these sources of interpretative decisions will be illustrated to show how they contribute to the MMPI interpretation process.

SCALE INTERPRETATION

As previously described, the MMPI scales are the basic elements of MMPI interpretation. The scale score indicates the likelihood that an individual is responding in a manner similar to the clinical group. In addition to the original scale development research, numerous studies have related each of the MMPI scales to personality attributes or problems in the clinical group. For example, elevations on Scale 4, the Psychopathic Deviate Scale, have been shown to be related to such antisocial characteristics as delinquency, criminal behavior, alcoholism, drug abuse, and the like. Extreme elevations on this scale typically imply impulsivity, poor judgment, uncontrolled behavioral history, acting-out behavior, interpersonal problems, dishonesty, hedonistic behavior, and so on.

Thus, when an individual has elevated scores on a scale (e.g., higher than 95 percent of the population), he or she is believed to possess many of the same characteristics applied to the reference group.

CODE TYPE

Rigorous studies have shown that individuals with common MMPI profile characteristics or code types have similar problems and behaviors. These studies arrived at "experience tables" by defining profile groups and examining actual extratest behavior using outside judgments by clinicians or other people who knew the subjects. It is useful to compare the descriptions of a specific profile type, generated from two distinct clinical samples, to see how the MMPI has cross-sample generality. The following descriptions of the 2-7 profile type were published in the actuarial system of Gilberstadt and Duker (1965), using an all-male Veterans Administration Hospital sample; and in Marks, Seeman, and Haller (1974), using a predominantly female outpatient sample. The symptomatic patterns and behavioral descriptions are highly similar:

Gilberstadt-Duker 2-7 Profile Type

Complaints, Traits, and Symptoms

Anorexia, nausea, vomiting	Nervousness Obsessions
Anxiety	Tension
Cardiac complaint	Weak, tired, fatigued
Depression	Worrying

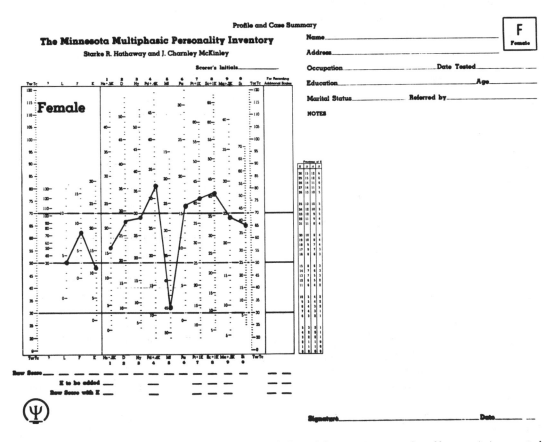

Fig. 18.1 MMPI profile sheet. Copyrighted by The Psychological Corporation, reproduced by permission granted in the test catalog.

Cardinal Features

High standards of performance and achieve well. Capable of emotional ties. Chronically anxious and striving to do well. Vulnerable to accumulated increments of stress from pregnancy of wives, purchases of new houses, illness in families, etc. When unable to tolerate additional anxiety, become depressed, clinging, dependent, self-deprecatory, lose confidence, feel inferior, become overwhelmed. Have somatic manifestations of anxiety (e.g., diarrhea, chest pain, nervous stomach, dizziness, etc.). [Gilberstadt & Duker, 1965]

Marks-Seeman-Haller 2-7 Profile Type

The most salient descriptive feature of persons yielding this profile is depression. The personal tempo is slowed, as is the rate of speech. Although thought processes are retarded, there is no noticeable cognitive slippage; that is, the thoughts, phrases, and ideas are "glued" together in appropriate sequence and in a grammatically and semantically sound fashion. These people are likely to express feelings of pessimism, hopelessness about the future, and even the futility of any treatment. Nevertheless, it is significant that the "projected discharge" profile for this group is within normal limits with no T-score over 70. This constitutes a prognostically hopeful sign which contradicts the gloomy attitude so characteristic of these patients. Furthermore, the discharge MMPI's at termination of therapy conform, in large part, to the "projected discharge" profile—indicating improvement. This is consistent with independent clinical ratings by therapists who judged improvement from "some" to "considerable" and reported an 85% remission rate.

The mean age of onset of disturbance was 49 years; this is significantly older than for any other profile type. In general, the disorder took somewhere from 1 month to 1 year developing and, in 70% of the cases, there were no previous episodes. Eighty-four percent of these patients reported having dated frequently, 78% were married, 87% of those married reported good marital adjustment, and none were divorced. Courtship is typically short for these people and 60% married within 1 month's time.

These patients should be expected to exhibit compulsive, meticulous and perfection-

ist trends. A variety of fears and phobias is possible, as is obsessive thinking. Among multiple neurotic manifestations frequently observed are strong conflicts about self-assertion and a decided tendency toward self-blame and self-punishment. In psychoanalytic terminology, they may be said to be dominated by severe superego constraints. Indeed, they are the most rigid and the most devoutly religious of the profile types.

Tense, high-strung, nervous, anxious, and jumpy are adjectives often applied to these people. Thus, it is not surprising to observe trembling and sweating. Sleep difficulties are characteristic and should be expected. Often these patients are anorexic as well.

There are a variety of ways in which people presenting this profile express their psychological difficulties in a somatic, hypochondriacal fashion. A wide array of body symptoms may be presented; weakness and fatigue, chest pain, constipation, dizziness, and neurasthenia are some of the more common complaints.

These individuals, too, are constant worriers and are very vulnerable to threat—real or imagined. The 2-7 individual is a serious person who is given to anticipating problems and difficulties—the proverbial "crosser-of-bridges-before-the-bridges-have-materialized."

The scholastic history of these patients is average or above. Twenty-eight percent have a college education; 84% for this group is 114 on the Shipley and 119 on the WAIS. They place value on intellectual and cognitive activities, skills, and attitudes.

Behavioral or psychological characteristics very *unlikely* to be encountered in persons with this profile are flippant manner, speech, or resentment of authority figures. Adjectives used *infrequently* to describe them include self-centered and egocentric. Deliberately argumentative behavior or deliberately provocative behavior, verbal or nonverbal, is *not* likely. [Marks, Seeman, & Haller, 1974]

MMPI INDICES

Several useful prediction indices have been developed for the MMPI to aid the clinician or automated interpretation system in making specific decisions about the patient's profile. The index generally is an empirically determined decision rule or set of operations employing MMPI scores in a rather automatic manner: the index is computed and a reference chart or look-up table with recommendations is consulted. One of the most extensively researched and widely used indices is the *Goldberg Index* for discriminating between psychotic and neurotic profiles. In a series of empirical studies, Goldberg examined a number of interpretive strategies, profile characteristics, and scale scores to determine which were more effective at making a valid distinction between profiles of cases that had been clearly diagnosed as neurotic or psychotic.

The Goldberg Index, a simple linear combination of five MMPI scales ($GI = L + Pa = Sc - Hy - Pt$) provides a single score that is compared with scores of the original developmental samples. A patient with a Goldberg Index score greater than 45 is diagnosed as psychotic, while scores below that cutoff are referred to as indeterminate or neurotic. The index is effective at discriminating 70 percent of cases accurately.

Summary

The MMPI is an objective, empirically based personality inventory that has become the most widely used personality test and a standard research and clinical evaluation instrument. The basis of its wide applicability is the empirical foundation of its scales. The scales were developed according to an empirical validation test construction strategy. The empirical correlates for the MMPI scales and indices have been established through a number of rigorous research studies.

A number of scales have been developed to measure behavior and attitudes associated with well defined clinical problems. Individuals who score high on the same scales or combinations of scales, referred to as code types, are found to possess similar personality characteristics and problems.

The MMPI has been found to be an effective clinical assessment instrument in a variety of clinical settings—medical, rehabilitation, correctional, psychiatric, etc. It measures general psychopathology that lies at the source of the presenting complaints or problem behaviors in many situations.

A Case History: Unrecognized Depression in an Adolescent Boy

In the preceding sections of this chapter we have attempted to show how objective personality assessment can be valuable in clinical work. We have also presented detailed information about the most widely used objective personality instru-

ment: the MMPI. We now present an actual case example to demonstrate how the MMPI can contribute to a psychological intervention.

Earlier this year, one of us (SF) was referred a 15-year-old boy for psychological evaluation. The boy had been sent by his school to a pediatric neurologist because of uncontrolled outbursts of destructive behavior, oppositionality, and problems with discipline of approximately two years' duration. The school had attempted a structured behavioral management approach, such as they were accustomed to using with other children with similar problems, with little positive results evident after one and a half years of the program. The pediatric neurologist found no abnormalities on the neurological exam and recommended a psychological evaluation. An interview with the boy and his parents provided more information about behavioral difficulties at home as well as in school. The parents, however, professed to be completely at a loss about the source of their son's difficulties, and the boy himself was extremely resistive about answering questions either alone with the psychologist or with his parents present. There were some reports of rivalry with his nine-year-old brother, and the interviewer noted that parental discipline was inconsistent. After this initial interview, however, there was little understanding of the motivations behind the boy's aggressive behavior. The identified patient agreed to complete an MMPI and to discuss it with the psychologist the following week.

Figure 18.2 presents the boy's MMPI profile, using both adult and adolescent norms (Dahlstrom, Welsh, & Dahlstrom, 1975) to graph the test scores. The following is an excerpt from the blind interpretation of this profile by a psychology graduate student in the clinic where the boy was seen:

The MMPI profile is valid and it appears that the respondent made an attempt to follow instructions and to read the items carefully. There is some indication that he showed a rather unsophisticated defensiveness in answering the test questions. . . . In spite of this defensiveness, however, there are scale elevations that are clinically meaningful.

The response pattern suggests that this boy is significantly depressed at the present time, but without the usual psychomotor retardation or lethargy that is seen in such cases. Insomnia, worry, and tension may be present, and may be expressed in occasional

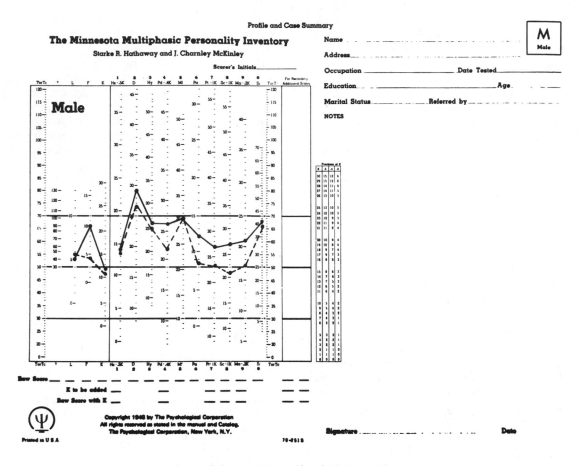

Fig. 18.2 MMPI profile of 15-year-old male.

violent outbursts. Social withdrawal is highly evident. He obviously feels inadequate and insecure in social situations, and a real ineptitude and lack of skill in social interaction probably accompanies his introverted attitudes. The depression appears to be chronic in nature, rather than acute.

Much of this boy's insecurity may revolve around heterosexual situations. His interest patterns are somewhat different from those of the average male. . . . He probably feels . . . insecure of his masculinity in general.

Persons with similar profiles are known to utilize repression and denial in dealing with psychological conflict. . . . They have severe difficulties expressing anger directly and may use passive-aggressive tactics to deal with their anger.

The content of this interpretation was reviewed with the patient and his parents at a follow-up

interview. When alone with the psychologist and faced with the test interpretation, the boy suddenly spoke freely of his distress and voiced feelings of being ostracized in school and unwanted at home. The parents were astonished at the test results and at being informed by the psychologist that their son was experiencing acute depression. They agreed readily to a short-term contract of family therapy.

The family was seen for ten sessions of family therapy. During this period of treatment, the identified patient's role in the family was discussed, and he was able to express, with the support of the therapist, feelings of jealousy about the amount of attention his younger brother received. Activities were scheduled between each of the parents individually and the older boy, and his behavior improved markedly both at home and in schol. At the end of the ten family sessions, the parents decided to discontinue family therapy because of the greatly improved behavior of their older boy. The boy was transferred to an individual therapist to continue to work on issues of identity and low self-esteem.

Comment

This case history illustrates several ways in which objective personality assessment can aid a psychological intervention. For this case, the MMPI was instrumental in identifying an underlying issue (depression) that proved to be responsive to appropriate treatment. Earlier efforts to treat the presenting complaint directly had repeatedly failed with this boy. The MMPI also served another function in this case, which was explicated earlier in the chapter—that of rapport building with a patient. This was a highly important function in that the patient was initially quite resistive to psychological intervention and uncommunicative about his inner experience. The therapist felt that the test feedback session was a turning point in establishing trust and in breaking through the resistance, and that it set the stage for the patient's learning to share feelings with his parents in the family sessions.

Conclusions

Although objective personality assessment has received some criticism from both dynamically oriented and behaviorally oriented psychologists in the past, this approach to understanding personality has survived its critics' major charges and is presently enjoying broader application than it has known at any time in its history. The major objective clinical assessment instrument, the MMPI, has been the subject of over 8,000 books and articles and the literature is growing at the rate of over 200 publications a year. The MMPI is in use in over 46 countries in addition to its application throughout the United States. What accounts for this widespred use of an instrument that was published over 40 years ago? Probably its ease of administration, reliability, established validity, and its demonstrated relevance for clinical decisions. We have attempted to show how the MMPI can be used in conjunction with the clinical interview to gain a diagnostic and treatment perspective that cannot be obtained with either approach alone. We saw, through a case illustration, how the MMPI can be used as an "objective outside opinion" to point out potential problems that might not be recognized in the interview or from the clinical case history. We also described how the MMPI might be useful

as an aid in treatment—as a way of both gaining rapport with the client and perhaps "confronting" the client with problems he or she might not be relating to in the treatment services.

The material presented in this chapter stems from both the clinical validity data on the MMPI as well as the authors' own clinical experience in using the instrument with patients. It is hoped that this approach to the clinical application of objective personality tests will be as valuable to others' clinical practice as it has been to ours.

References

Beck, A. T., *Depression: Causes and treatment*. Philadelphia: University of Pennsylvania Press, 1972.

Bellack, A. S. Self-evaluation, self-reinforcement and locus of control. *Journal of Research in Personality*, 1975, 9, 158–167.

Bellack, A. S., & Tillman, W. The effects of task and experimenter feedback on the self-reinforcement behavior of internals and externals. *Journal of Consulting and Clinical Psychology*, 1974, 42, 330–336.

Bergin, A. E. The evaluation of therapeutic outcomes. In A. E. Bergin & S. L. Garfield (Eds.), *Handbook of psychotherapy and behavior change*. New York: Wiley, 1971.

Butcher, J. N. Personality characteristics associated with elevations on the basic MMPI scores. Monograph. *Clinical Applications of the MMPI Workshop Series*, University of Minnesota, 1980.

Butcher, J. N., & Bemis, K. Abnormal behavior in cultural context. In H. Adams & P. Sutker (Eds.), *Comprehensive Handbook of Psychopathology*, New York: Plenum. In press.

Butcher, J. N., & Clark, L. A. Recent trends in cross-cultural research and application. In J. N. Butcher (Ed.), *New developments in the use of the MMPI*. Minneapolis: University of Minnesota Press, 1979.

Butcher, J. N., & Owen, P. Survey of personality inventories: Recent research developments and contemporary issues. In B. B. Wolman (Ed.), *Handbook of clinical diagnosis*. New York: Plenum, 1978.

Butcher, J. N., & Pancheri, P. *Handbook of cross-national MMPI research*. Minneapolis: University of Minnesota Press, 1976.

Ciminero, A. R. Behavioral assessment: An overview. In A. R. Ciminero, K. S. Calhoun, & H. E. Adams (Eds.), *Handbook of behavioral assessment*. New York: Wiley, 1977.

Cronbach, L. H., & Gleser, G. C. *Psychological tests and personnel decisions*. Urbana: University of Illinois Press, 1965.

Dahlstrom, W. G., Welsh, G. S., & Dahlstrom, L. E. *An MMPI handbook, Volume I: Clinical interpretations*. Minneapolis: University of Minnesota Press, 1972.

Eisler, R. M. The behavioral assessment of social skills. In M. Hersen & A. S. Bellack (Eds.), *Behavioral assessment: A practical handbook*. New York: Pergamon, 1976.

Gilberstadt, H., & Duker, J. *A handbook for clinical*

and actuarial MMPI interpretation. Philadelphia: W. B. Saunders, 1965.

Goldfried, M. R., & Linehan, M. M. Basic issues in behavioral assessment. In A. R. Ciminero, K. S. Calhoun, & H. E. Adams (Eds.), *Handbook of behavioral assessment.* New York: Wiley, 1977.

Graham, J. R. *The MMPI: A practical guide.* New York: Oxford University Press, 1977.

Hersen, M. Historical perspectives in behavioral assessment. In M. Hersen & A. S. Bellack (Eds.), *Behavioral assessment: A practice handbook.* New York: Pergamon, 1976.

Hersen, M., & Bellack, A. S. (Eds.), *Behavioral assessment: A practical handbook.* New York: Pergamon, 1976.

Lachar, D. *The MMPI: Clinical assessment and automated interpretation.* Los Angeles: Western Psychological Services, 1974.

Marks, P. A., Seeman, W., & Haller, D. L. *The actuarial use of the MMPI with adolescents and adults.* Baltimore: Williams & Wilkins, 1974.

Meehl, P. E. *Clinical versus statistical prediction: A the-oretical analysis and a review of the evidence.* Minneapolis: University of Minnesota Press, 1954.

O'Leary, K. D., & Wilson, G. T. *Behavior therapy: Application and outcome.* Englewood Cliffs, N.J.: Prentice-Hall, 1975.

Penk, W. E. Assessing the substance abuser with the MMPI. *Clinical notes on the MMPI.* Nutley, N.J.: Roche Psychiatric Service Institute, 1981.

Pickens, R., Errickson, E., Thompson, T., Heston, L., & Eckert, E. MMPI correlates of performance on a behavior therapy ward. *Behaviour Research and Therapy,* 1979, 17, 17–24.

Rapaport, D., Gill, M. M., & Schafer, R. *Diagnostic psychological testing.* New York: International Universities Press, 1968.

Williams, C. L. Assessment of social behavior: Behavioral role play compared with *Si* scale of the MMPI. *Behavior Therapy,* 1981, 12, 578–584.

Williams, C. L. Can the MMPI be useful to behavior therapists? A case study example. *The Behavior Therapist,* in press.

Woodworth, R. S. *Personal data sheet,* Stoelting, 1920.

19 INTELLECTUAL ASSESSMENT

Robert L. Hale

The Assessment of Intelligence

> The IQ evolved from the interplay between disorder and direction; its natures determined by the problems immigration represented and the solutions education offered; its form and meaning determined by the needs of the society for which it provided solutions, explanations, and ultimately its own future problems [Paula S. Fass, *The IQ: A Cultural and Historical Framework* (1980)].

Two basic approaches have often been taken in discussion of the assessment of intelligence, and authors have often treated these approaches as if they were mutually incompatible. The first approach includes an analysis of the available instruments that purport to measure intelligence. The salient aspects of these tests are analyzed, and some direction concerning which test to use under various assessment circumstances is provided to the reader. Authors who use this approach logically assume that the assessment of intelligence is a legitimate enterprise and that intelligence is a concrete entity that psychologists can measure. They infrequently consider exactly what one is attempting to measure when using an intelligence test. They often fail completely to discuss the constructs underlying intelligence. The second approach discusses intelligence as a hypothetical theoretical construct. Authors who use this approach frequently make little men-

tion of the instruments that are currently used to measure this construct. In fact, it is assumed that the construct of intelligence is so complex that no existing test is capable of measuring it and therefore that the assessment of intelligence is an illegitimate activity. These two positions have recently come into sharp conflict. As Kaufman (1979) notes, "The intelligence testing scene is currently in turmoil, highlighted by litigation, legislation and outbursts by well-intentioned professionals. Advocates of both sides are polarized and many arguments are emotional and uncompromising" (p. xi).

In this chapter, an attempt is made to blend these two approaches. First, the historical development of current intelligence tests is reviewed. Then, the conceptual definitions of intelligence and the more practical uses of the tests are interwoven. Major areas of concern in relation to these current tests are discussed later. These concerns include:

(1) heritability, (2) bias, (3) stability, (4) equivalence, and (5) reporting results. Finally, the future of intellectual assessment is discussed. Recent advances in neuropsychology and microcomputer usage are discussed along with the prospect that the term "IQ" may be dropped altogether.

History

The Development of Intelligence Tests

EUROPEAN INFLUENCES

It is impossible to tease apart the history of intellectual assessment from the greater recent history of man. Sattler (1982) notes that Fitzherbert (1470–1538) proposed a method of measuring a person's mentality by requiring one to count 20 pence, tell one's age, and identify one's father. The real history of intelligence testing, however, is basically confined to 20th-century America. Like a child whose history begins at birth, but is dynamically influenced by events prior to its birth, so too was the development of intellectual assessment influenced by events prior to 1905 when the Binet-Simon Scale was developed. The more important of those early European events included the establishment of Galton's anthropometric laboratory at the International Health Exhibition in 1884, the development of the statistical techniques of correlation by Karl Pearson and Charles Spearman, the concern with precise measurement of various types of perceptual, memory, reading, and conceptual differences in the laboratories in Germany, and the focus on higher mental functions in France. The influences of the researchers from England, Germany, and France on American psychologists, combined with the social-political environment in the United States during the early 20th century, provided the perfect nutritive substrate for the growth and development of intellectual assessment. The influence of the Europeans need not further concern us except that one should keep firmly in mind the fact that the 1905 Binet-Simon was given its impetus for construction by the Minister of Public Instruction in Paris in 1904. The minister appointed a committee, of which Binet was a member, to find a way to separate mentally retarded from normal children in the schools (Sattler, 1982). Originally, mental test results were to be used to determine how well children should do in school.

In the United States the assessment of mental ability provided a way of organizing an American society, which by all accounts was very chaotic at the beginning of the 20th century. It is this social-political turmoil that must be understood if we are to comprehend why the assessment of intelligence became so important in the United States. Fass (1980) and Marks (1976–77) discuss ten factors that were part of the American experience in the early 20th century and that directly contributed to the growth of the mental measurement industry. These ten influences are: (1) massive immigration with ethnic and racial diversity; (2) urbanization; (3) the growing influence of science; (4) the progressive educational movement; (5) World War I; (6) the supposed utility of the Army tests; (7) the putative empirical relation between race and IQ; (8) stricter school attendance laws; (9) the development of child labor legislation; and (10) the belief in a competitive meritocratic society. The men they list as most influential in the development of intellectual assessment in the United States are: (1) Lewis Terman; (2) H. H. Goddard; (3) Walter Lippman; (4) J. M. Cattell; (5) Robert Yerkes; (6) E. L. Thorndike, and (7) John Dewey. Arthur Otis, who is left out of most historical accounts of the development of mental tests, should also be included in this list of influential men.

As Marks (1976–77) clearly points out, the decision to investigate individual differences or similarities is clearly arbitrary. One has to ask, "Why did it become so important to differentiate between people?" (Marks, 1976–77; p. 3). The early development of the mental test by Binet clearly stemmed from an expressed need to differentiate between those French children who could be successful in traditional educational programs and those who could not. Goddard, who first translated Binet's scales into English in 1910, used the test to distinguish among the "feebleminded" children attending the Vineland Training School in New Jersey. Also, Terman incorporated the concept of the intelligence quotient developed by Stern in 1912 and later described in his book (Stern, 1914). This became the Stanford revision in 1916 and was used to identify "feebleminded" children in California. Thus, the test itself had a history that was concerned with the detection of academically related individual differences. As stated previously, the social-political situation in America was quite chaotic. This situation demanded the detection of individual differences so that those differences could be used to order an educational system in a rapidly changing society. This educational system was seen not only as a method by which America could educate its citizens but also as a method of teaching cultural values (good citizenship).

Immigration into America was not evenly distributed in relation to either time or ethnic variables. Immigration patterns into American society took place in distinct waves. As Thomas Sowell (1981a) vividly demonstrates, the reasons for differential immigration are explained by the economics prevalent during the time interval one is considering. Before the widespread use of passenger ships, it was simply less expensive to purchase a ticket to America on a cargo ship. During the era of sailing vessels, America sold large quantities of agricultural and forest products to northern and western Europe and in turn purchased manufactured goods from these countries. Thus, ships returning to the United States carried less bulk than when they left. On returning to America, the ship's extra space could easily be sold to passengers. On the other hand, persons from southern and eastern Europe with whom the United States had limited trade would have to pay the full expense of passage on ships that did not carry cargo to the United States. The high cost of such transportation simply prohibited the development of immigration from these countries. After the development of the steamship, however, the cost of crossing the Atlantic was brought down to a point where formally excluded southern and eastern Europeans could afford to purchase tickets to America. The upshot of this economic situation was that the major immigrations from Ireland and Germany were completed by the 1880s, while immigrants from Italy and Russia were just arriving in the early 1900s:

> The Anglo-Saxons, Germans, and Irish, etc. began their adjustment to American life generations before peoples of Italian, Polish, or eastern European Jewish ancestry. As of the early twentieth-century, the former groups — the "old" immigrants, as they were called — were as a group economically, educationally, and socially well in advance of the "newer" immigrant groups. [Sowell, 1981a, p. 54]

An important point needs to be made. The impact of immigration on the social fabric of America was

enormous. In terms of sheer numbers, "Between 1901 and 1910 alone, nearly nine million people migrated to this country — more than the combined populations of the states of New York, Maryland, and New Hampshire in 1900" (Kownslar & Frizzle, 1967, pp. 600–601).

This was also the end of the age of the robber barons and the beginning of a new social awakening in the United States. No longer was America going to tolerate the building of fortunes for a few on the backs of immigrant labor. In 1901 Theodore Roosevelt succeeded William McKinley as president. Roosevelt and the country took on two broad social aims concerning the immigrant. First, the immigrant was to be set free from the daily grind of work and poverty. Second, the immigrant was to be set free from the liabilities of his native tongue:

> Roosevelt's bravest mission was to try and see through social legislation and the new resources of education, that the immigrants should no longer be looked on as nationally identifiable pools of cheap labor. The country must stop talking about German-Americans and Italian-Americans and Polish-Americans: [As Roosevelt stated] "we have room but for one language here, and that is the English language, for we intend to see that the crucible turns our people out as Americans." There must be no more "hyphenated Americans." [Cooke, 1974, p. 299]

Other evidence of social reform can be noted in the passing of the Keating-Owen child labor act in 1916. Even though it was declared unconstitutional two years later by the Supreme Court, it heralded an age of concern for children. Other evidence of concern for youth and the educational process can be found in the fact that the last state to enact laws requiring child school attendance was Mississippi in 1918. This combination of child labor and compulsory attendance laws assured that most youngsters would be in school. The task of turning these children into competent Americans then fell to the public schools. It was not just a coincidence that Terman, who had served for many years as a public school administrator, completed the Stanford revision of the Binet test in 1916. Necessity, as usual, was the mother of "invention," or in this instance, revision. Intelligence tests were seen as another way to organize the schools so that they could more readily accomplish their task. While these factors might have led to a rapid increase in the utilization of IQs, another event interceded. The demands put on the nation by the First World War were overriding.

Before discussing the effects of the war on the uses of intellectual assessment, another migration should be noted. Blacks from the South, provoked by Jim Crow laws and the rise of the Klu Klux Klan and later reinforced by the availability of jobs during the war effort, migrated in ever-increasing numbers to northern urban centers. They brought with them their unique cultural heritage formed during slavery, which resulted in their having little formal education. It was with this lack of education that both blacks and society at large would later be asked to grapple. The fact that IQ reflected racial (black/white) differences did not hinder its acceptance as a social organizing force. Bias against blacks and the newer immigrants ran high. The fact that the tests indicated racial differences in favor of the older immigrants actually enhanced the acceptance of mental tests as a social organizing force (Gould, 1981). Another important point needs to be underscored. Persons who are currently considered members of the majority culture (Anglo-Saxons, Germans, Irish, etc.) have enjoyed a longer period of adjustment to American life than current minority status members (Italians, Poles, Jews, Blacks, Chicanos, etc.). The meaning and effects of social and racial bias will be taken up more fully later in the chapter.

INFLUENCE OF WORLD WAR I

When the United States declared war on Germany on April 6, 1917, a major task faced America. The country quickly had to form an efficient military unit. Robert Yerkes, the president of the American Psychological Association, offered the services of psychologists to the military:

> In a remarkably short time of about one month, Lewis Terman, Edward Thorndike, Henry Goddard, Robert Yerkes and others designed tests of intelligence for the army. Their purpose was to classify men according to their intellectual ability and to assist in selecting the most competent for leadership positions as well as to eliminate the incompetents. [Marks, 1976–77; p. 5]

Over 1.7 million men were evaluated with the Ar-

my Alpha and Beta tests. It was the publicly assumed success of these intelligence tests in the face of a national emergency that contributed to the increased use of such assessment outside the military.

It was also at this point that misunderstandings and misinterpretations of exactly what these mental tests could and could not do were first pointed out. For example, Goddard accepted the Stanford-Binet 16-year mental age norm as representing the average adult attainment level. He also defined the term "moron" as meaning an adult who could obtain a mental age of up to 12 years. Using the Army test results which indicated that on the Alpha and Beta tests the average mental age was approximately 13, Goddard argued that the Army results established that half the persons in the United States were little better than morons. Walter Lippman correctly argued that Goddard's conclusion stating that the average mental age of adult Americans was only 13 years was neither correct nor incorrect but simply nonsense. "Nonsense because it would be equivalent to the assertion that the average intelligence of adults is below the average intelligence of adults" (Pastore, 1978, p. 323).

Gould (1981) reports that contrary to popular opinion, the Army tests were actually not useful. In fact, he reports that the Army really did not use the scores. Tension between the psychologists and the commanding officers of the army camps became so intense that the Secretary of War asked the officers to give him their opinion of Yerkes' tests:

> He received one hundred replies, nearly all negative. They were, Yerkes admitted, "with few exceptions, unfavorable to psychological work, and have led to the conclusion on the part of various officers of the General Staff that this work has little, if any, value to the army and should be discontinued." [Gould, 1981, p. 202].

Whether or not the Alpha and Beta were useful to the Army is debatable. However, the developments that led to this first group tests of mental ability were certainly significant for testing in general. Arthur Sinton Otis, a graduate student of Terman's prior to the war, developed several of the objective item-scoring formats so necessary for group paper-and-pencil tests. Most notable was his suggestion that instead of asking questions that required recalling answers, one might present a stimulus with several possible response alternatives. This innovation led directly to the multiple-choice item format. Terman introduced Otis's ideas to the committee developing the Army tests. Otis was asked to join the group. His methods of item construction proved to be both effective and economical. It was only a short time before the methods of group assessment found their way into schools, with publication of the *Otis Group Intelligence Scale* and the *National Intelligence Tests* by the World Book Company in 1918.

Before proceeding, a review of what the measures of intellectual functioning had been able to demonstrate is in order. First, on a limited basis, the tests were successful in demonstrating that they could differentiate between children who could be successful in academics and those who could not (they could predict academic achievement). This is not to say that the mental tests could predict standardized achievement test results. The first standardized achievement battery to evaluate the academic areas of reading, spelling, sentence meaning, and vocabulary appeared in the first volume of the *Journal of Educational Research* (Pressey, 1920). However, the Stanford-Binet had been able to differentiate between pupils judged by their teachers to be adequately and inadequately achieving (Sattler, 1974). Second, the public believed that the tests had demonstrated on a very large scale that they could differentiate leadership ability in Army inductees. Third, and perhaps most important, the Army report (Yerkes, 1921) brought to the public's attention the alleged differences in mental ability among blacks and whites as well as inductees from eastern Europe. These racial differences were based on inadequate statistical procedures and analyses. For a detailed discussion of the testing inadequacies during World War I, the interested reader is referred to Gould (1981). Suffice it to say that Gould has more than adequately demonstrated that the Army data were poorly collected and they were misinterpreted. Nevertheless, the racial interpretations given to the data ultimately captured the public's attention. The data fit nicely into the social prejudices then prevalent. This was unfortunate, because as Gould explains, if the data had been properly evaluated:

The army mental tests could have provided an impetus for social reform, since they documented that environmental disadvantages

were robbing from millions of people an opportunity to develop their intellectual skills. Again and again, the data pointed to strong correlations between test scores and environment. Again and again, those who wrote and administered the test invented tortuous, ad hoc explanations to preserve their hereditarian prejudices. [p. 221]

POST–WORLD WAR I INFLUENCES

After the war ended, America was able to turn her attention inward to her own pressing needs. As noted previously, the war interrupted the earlier social reform movement directed toward the European immigrant. The new immigrants were now viewed, however, as an economic enemy. America had just fought a war supposedly to preserve democracy. In 1917, the Bolsheviks had taken over political control of Russia and the immigrants from Europe were considered a threat to democracy in this country. Shortly after the armistice, American soldiers were called upon to break up a socialist rally in New York. The next night, sympathizers of the Russian Revolution were dispersed in a bloody battle.

Blacks also were seen as threatening. They had moved north during the war and had remained there. The economy was slowing down and competition for a declining number of jobs became fierce. In 1919, 23 cities had race riots, and there were many local strikes accompanied by a national steel strike. The social mood in America was a strange mixture of racism combined with isolationism and self-improvement. As examples of the latter two characteristics of this mood, it can be noted that in 1920: (1) prohibition was passed, (2) the Senate rejected the Treaty of Versailles, and (3) the Senate refused to allow the United States to join the League of Nations. With these details about post–World War I America, it is possible to discuss the frequent criticism that intelligence tests based on middle-class values prevented the entry of foreign-born minorities into the United States.

In 1924, Congress established quotas on the number of immigrants who could enter the United States. The English, Irish, and Germans received the largest quotas. Several scholars (i.e., Fass, 1980; Marks, 1976–77) have noted that the low IQs that they believed were "clearly discriminatory" in relation to the new immigrants, caused or contributed to the Immigration Act of 1924. Relatively few intelligence tests were given on Ellis Island. Goddard did, however, send two women to the Island in 1913: "They were instructed to pick out the feeble-minded by sight, a task Goddard preferred to assign to women, to whom he granted superior intuition" (Gould, 1981, p. 165). These women tested a small group of immigrants with Goddard's Binet scale. Goddard eventually concluded that the data indicated that 40 to 50 percent of the immigrants were "feeble-minded." Later, however, it was shown that his version of the Binet scale yielded lower scores than Terman's revision (Gould, 1981). Even though Congressional debates concerning the Immigration Act constantly referred to the Army data to support eastern and southern European exclusion, it does not necessarily follow that the Immigration Act was a direct result of the low mental abilities reported for the foreign immigrants. Many social variables were stacked against the southern and eastern immigrants, most notable being the fact that they were perceived as advocates of socialism:

> Every misfortune that normally follows in the train of a great war—the closing of munitions factories, a cutback in the working week, a slump in the price of crops that for four years had poured into the graneries of the Allies—could be interpreted as tactical triumphs of the Communist strategy to overthrow the American republic. . . . The first law officer of the United States, the Attorney General himself, had his house in Washington blown up. He was Mitchell Palmer. . . .
> Palmer's name should be memorized in schools as the archetype of the paranoid witch hunter with which the Republic is regularly afflicted whenever an unpleasant turn of history . . . seems to be beyond the control of the government of the United States. He ordered or condoned raids on magazine offices, public halls, private houses, union headquarters meetings big and small of anyone—socialists, liberals, atheists, freethinkers, social workers— who could be identified or accused as Bolsheviks. . . . Palmer's hysterical example led, among other horrors, to a drastic revision of the immigration laws. The flow of immigrants from eastern and southern Europe slowed to a dribble, and there was a time when more people were being deported from Ellis Island than were coming in. [Cooke, 1974, p. 310]

This is not to belittle the fact that when a person

was suspected of being mentally deficient, an immigration official would chalk a circle with a cross in the middle on the immigrant's back. This symbol signified that the immigrant was thought to be feeble-minded. It also meant certain deportation. If low IQs were not the direct cause of the Immigration Act, however, they certainly contributed indirectly to its passage. Nevertheless, as Paula Fass (1980) pointed out: "If immigration exclusion was one response to the alien presence, Americanization, remedial socialization, and vocational training, all of which were school centered, were others" (p. 448). Besides exclusion and deportation, the progressive educational movement (founded in 1919 and supported by John Dewey after he joined in 1927) promised educational reform, which would provide some answers to the immigration problem:

> It would be unfair and meanspirited to argue that educators used IQs to cut across the problem and to exclude the newer immigrants from the lines of advancement which the schools now promised. It was never so simple. The schools continued to be theoretically and actually a force that facilitated immigrant access to society's rewards, both as an agency incorporating immigrant children into the mainlines of the culture and as a lever for social and occupational advancement for individuals. [Fass, 1980, pp. 448–449]

SCHOOL ORGANIZATION

Mental ages, or IQs, have never been the primary organizational metric used in schools. Intelligence test results were simply, albeit naively and often inappropriately, used to organize an educational system that had previously adopted chronological age as the primary method for school organization. The complete separation of children into separate "graded" classrooms, each with its own teacher, was reportedly accomplished first by John Philbrick, who reorganized the Quincy, Massachusetts, grammar school in 1847 (Potter, 1967). The Ohio State Commissioner of Education reported that between 1854 and 1855, nearly 150 towns had converted to age-graded schools. Intelligence quotients, which were first available with the 1916 Stanford-Binet, allowed the tracking of pupils within the broader age categories. The claim is often made that these special educational and vocational training programs effectively prevented the upward social mobility of the immigrant groups. The data provided by Thomas Sowell (1981b), however, does not support this conclusion. Jews, who initially scored low as a group on intelligence tests and who have faced centuries of anti-Semitism, presently have the highest family incomes in the United States. Their IQs had risen past the national average by 1920. And, according to Sowell, "Polish IQs which averaged eighty-five in the earlier studies — the same as that of blacks today — had risen to 109 by the 1970s. This twenty-four point rise is greater than the current black-white difference (fifteen points)" (1981b, p. 9). The current Polish family income is well above that of the typical Anglo-Saxon family. Even the traditional black-white income differences have disappeared in college-educated persons with similar family characteristics.

Obviously, the IQ has been misinterpreted; it is not an immutable measure of a person. Few would disagree with the contention that IQs have frequently been misused. Since IQs can change with a person's familiarization with what can broadly be termed the "American Culture," its use in the denial of education, or the provision of relatively poorer educational opportunities to persons not familiar with mainstream cultural standards was, and continues to be, a disservice to those persons. The use of IQs to deny a person's right to fail is always a misuse of the metric. Perhaps a case can be built for using gains in IQs as a measure of a minority's assimilation into the cultural mainstream. Certainly Sowell's data and Gould's reinterpretation of the Army data would support that position.

EARLY ATTITUDES

One of the unfortunate linkages in the history of intellectual assessment is the well-documented prejudicial attitudes of Terman and Goddard. It is really unnecessary to reiterate the racial slurs in their writings. Their Social Darwinistic attitudes did a great disservice to the IQ. Gould (1981) points out that Goddard's views were so myopic on the subject of preventing the "feeble-minded" from having children (he believed intelligence was almost exclusively inherited) that he disfigured photographs of the faces of the Kallikak family who were living in the Pine Barrens of New Jersey to make them "look evil and stupid" (Goddard, 1914). (However, he did not retouch Debora Kallikak's photos. She lived at Goddard's Vineland Institution.) His reasons for altering the other photographs become apparant when one reads the conclusions of his book:

Feeble-mindedness is hereditary and transmitted as surely as any other character. We cannot successfully cope with these conditions until we recognize feeble-mindedness and its hereditary nature, recognize it early, and take care of it. In considering the question of care, segregation through colonization seems in the present state of our knowledge to be the ideal and perfectly satisfactory method. Sterilization may be accepted as a makeshift, as a help to solve this problem because the conditions have become so intolerable. But this must at present be regarded only as makeshift and temporary, for before it can be extensively practiced, a great deal must be learned about the effects of the operation and about the laws of human inheritance. [Goddard, 1914, p. 117]

Through the influence of these men, the original intent of Binet (to identify and assist children who were in need of special educational services) was frequently changed to one of rank-ordering children. Children who scored exceedingly low were often denied any opportunity for an educational experience. This denial of service ended with the *P.A.R.C.* v. *Commonwealth of Pennsylvania* decision in 1972. This legal decision established the right of all children to an appropriate education. Because mentally retarded children could not be denied educational programs, the decision put an end to one of the major misuses of the IQ.

While IQs have been, are, and will continue to be misused, they can also serve well. Intelligence test results can aid practitioners in the decision-making processes concerning certain socially significant criteria. Binet's proposed use of mental tests was noble. When used for like purposes today, the IQ is still a useful device for aiding the decision-making processes of individuals and institutions.

DEVELOPMENT OF TEST ITEMS

One of the startling facts that quickly emerges when one explores the actual test questions over the history of mental measurement is that the items have changed so little. In *The Measurement of Intelligence*, Terman (1916) lists the tests as arranged by Binet in 1911 shortly before his death. Examples include: (1) at age 3 a child is supposed to point to nose, eyes, and mouth; (2) at age 6, distinguish between pictures of pretty and ugly faces; (3) at age 9, answer easy comprehension questions; (4) at age 12, compose one sentence given three words; and (5) at the adult level, give differences between pairs of abstract terms. These items, as well as many others, should be quite familiar to current Stanford-Binet users. Likewise, the interested observer can find many similarities between the 1981 Wechsler Adult Intelligence Scale-Revised (WAIS-R) and the 1939 Wechsler Bellevue.

The reasons given for the stability of the subtests and items making up intelligence tests range from a lack of creativity in the test constructors to the statement that these items have withstood the test of time. The latter interpretation is probably the more correct as various attempts have been made to change the test items. Some attempts have been successful. For example, Wechsler added the new subtests Animal House, Geometric Design, and Sentences to several modified subtests from the Wechsler Intelligence Scale for Children (WISC; Wechsler, 1949) to produce the Wechsler Preschool and Primary Scale of Intelligence (WPPSI; Wechsler, 1967). Other attempts, however, have not been successful. Wechsler continued to experiment with new measures for his intelligence tests:

> Two new tests were tried out experimentally as possible additions to the WAIS-R. The first was a test of Level of Aspiration, which was studied as a possible means of broadening the coverage of the WAIS-R to include a measure of nonintellective ability. It had a number of interesting features, but seemed to require further research before it could be added as a regular member of the battery. The second test was a new measure of spatial ability: although this test also had a number of merits it was too highly correlated with block design to warrant inclusion in the revised scale. [Wechsler, 1981; p. 10].

In summary, however, it can be stated that the actual format of the major intelligence tests has changed little since their initial introductions.

Definition of Intelligence

It is noteworthy that thus far we have talked about the history and development of mental tests and have not yet tendered a definition of the construct those tests are intended to measure. Early in the development of intellectual assessment, the concept of *individual* and *social worth* was tied into the definition of intelligence. Studies like Goddard's *The Kallikak Family* (1912), and *The Criminal Imbecile* (1915), Danielson and Davenport's *The Hill Folk* (1912), and Dugdale's *The Jukes* (1910) firmly implanted in both the professional's and the layperson's minds the concept that mental ability and individual worth were intimately related. This linking of intelligence and worth is reflected in Terman's comment, "In other words, not all criminals are feeble-minded, but all feeble-minded are at least potential criminals" (1916, p. 11). While that linkage has remained close to the surface in lay definitions of intelligence, it is not part of the professional use of the term.

In 1921, the *Journal of Educational Psychology* published the now famous piece that asked 17 of the leading experts to respond to the following questions: (1) What is the definition of intelligence? (2) What are the next important steps needed in intellectual assessment research? A review of the definitions given by the experts who replied shows little evidence of the linkage of these terms. What is apparent, however, is a lack of general agreement on the definition of intelligence. In 1975, Wechsler, reflecting back on the fact that nearly as many definitions of intelligence were offered as contributors who replied, remarked:

> Since 1921, there have been many symposia on intelligence and innumerable articles and books on the subject. A count of the views expressed in them would show no greater percentage of agreement today than it did two generations ago. [p. 135]

An additional seven years and many more scholarly publications have not changed the situation.

Sattler (1982) discusses nine major theorists who have differing views on the definition and measurement of intelligence. Even within the empirical factor-analytic camps (all of which use similar statistical procedures to develop models of intelligence), there remains a great deal of controversy concerning the structure and definition of intelligence. (See, for example, Guilford, 1980; Kelderman, Mellenbergh, & Elshout, 1981.) At present, there does not appear to be a movement toward a consolidated theory of intelligence. Most of the theorists, however, would agree that existing intelligence tests neither are capable of nor attempt to deal with most of the behaviors that might be subsumed under the word intelligence:

When well defined, "intelligence" is too broad to be measured by any test available today. It is a mistake to think we are measuring the full meaning of intelligence with any one test or even several of them. Therefore, it is not only important for test authors to specify the content of their test but also for users to interpret the scores within the limitations of the scores derived and make other observations to fill in around the scores. [French, 1979, p. 756]

Intelligence is not a single entity but is composed of many complex facets. Just because there are numerous definitions, however, does not mean that the term is useless. As Wechsler (1975) stated:

What is not admissible is the assertion that because there are so many views "nobody really knows what one is talking about" when one uses the term intelligence or the equally false assertion that it is all a matter of semantics. . . . An average adult and a normal 12-year-old will understand the word *intelligent* if it is used in a meaningful context. [p. 139]

If, however, one is talking about field-based problems where intelligence is actually being measured with a currently available test, one must emphatically make the distinction between the different definitions of intelligence on the one hand and the tests and scores that are designed to measure intelligence on the other. When Boring (1923) reacted to the seemingly hopeless efforts of others to agree on the definitions of intelligence by stating that it "Must be defined as the capacity to do well on an intelligence test," he focused attention where it belonged — on the tests themselves. Practitioners use the tests to aid in their decision-making processes.

Intelligence tests, and the scores they generate (IQs) have very practical applications. The tests may not measure all (perhaps not even any) of the constructs involved in various formal definitions of intelligence. Intelligence tests, however, allow the persons who use them to make statements about individuals with more confidence in the truthfulness of those statements than they could if the mental test were not used. The practitioner must first determine to what use the mental test is to be put. The answer to this question defines the scores provided by the test. Simultaneously, the usage question determines what kind of validity

the test must demonstrate to justify this usage. It should be remembered that tests are not valid in a general sense. Tests are validated for certain purposes.

Uses of Intelligence Tests

Several uses of IQs that are currently in vogue in education will be taken up and discussed in turn. Education was chosen as the field of IQ application because many of the recent controversies that surround usage of intelligence tests have been generated in this field. The methods of evaluation used in this chapter, however, would remain applicable whether the reader is interested in children and education or adults and psychopathology.

To Measure Intelligence

If one asks psychologists working in public schools why they give intelligence tests to children, a frequent answer (at least in the author's experience) is that they say they administer intelligence tests to measure the child's intelligence. This, of course, begs for a definition of intelligence. The psychologist has responded that he or she uses the test to measure a construct. It therefore follows that the user should be able adequately to define the construct and support the use of the test in that manner by citing construct validity evidence.

Construct validity is not nearly as precisely worked out, from a statistical point of view, as predictive validity. In general, however, the construct validity of a test can be supported through three different approaches. Nunnally (1978) lists the following three aspects of construct validation:

(1) specifying the domain of observables related to the construct; (2) from empirical research and statistical analyses, determining the extent to which the observables measure the same thing, several different things, or many different things; and (3) subsequently performing studies of individual differences and/or controlled experiments to determine the extent to which supposed measures of the construct produce results which are predictable from highly accepted theoretical hypotheses concerning the construct. [p. 98]

While it is well beyond the scope of this chapter to discuss construct validation in any detail, a brief comment concerning each of these aspects with respect to the major individual intelligence tests is in order. First, under the aspect of specifying the domain of observable behaviors related to intelligence, there is still much debate. Wechsler believed that performance items were part of adult intellectual functioning and introduced them into his scales. As noted earlier, he continued to attempt to introduce what he termed "nonintellective" measures into his intelligence tests. He believed that other personality variables were important in the assessment of intelligence, but were not evaluated by present intelligence tests (Wechsler, 1950). Logically, Wechsler would have argued that present tests do not adequately cover the domain of observables that are related to intelligence. Present intelligence tests are narrowly composed of items that are mainly oriented toward scholastic achievements. Berger (1978) argues that intelligence tests measure a certain structure of modern consciousness which is something different from intelligence. Individual items from intelligence tests have also been criticized because certain of them are thought to be unfair to minority groups. This issue will be discussed more fully under the topic of IQ bias.

The second aspect discussed by Nunnally — seeing whether the tests measure one or many things — is often approached through both reliability and factor-analytic studies. High internal consistency reliability estimates indicate that test items are measuring attributes that are similar enough to make adding up the results obtained over all of the items sensible. The reliability estimates for the Wechsler series and the Stanford-Binet are high enough so that the test items can be added together to obtain IQs.

Factor-analytic results of the Wechslers and the Stanford-Binet have been quite consistent across different investigations. The number of factors found on the Stanford-Binet depends upon the age of the subjects being investigated. At the upper age levels, this test is mainly measuring verbal fluency and reasoning, while at the lower age levels the factor composition is more complex (Sattler, 1982). However, Sattler (1982) reports that a single "general" factor appears to carry most of the variance on the Stanford-Binet. The Wechslers are primarily two-factor scales. Exploratory studies (Blaha & Vance, 1979; Carlson & Reynolds, 1981; Kaufman, 1975; Peterson & Hart, 1979; Reschly, 1978; Schooler, Beebe, & Koepke, 1978; Silverstein, 1969; Wallbrown, Blaha, & Wherry,

1974) have indicated that the tests show sometimes either a two- or three-factor structure. However, confirmatory analyses (Ramanaiah & Adams, 1979; Ramanaiah, O'Donnell, & Ribich, 1976) indicate that these tests have a two-factor structure. Research with the Wechsler Intelligence Scale for Children — Revised (WISC-R; Wechsler, 1974) indicates that this test's third factor (Freedom from Distractibility) does not meet the .90 reliability standards needed to make decisions about individuals (Gutkin, 1978). Thus, even when found in some exploratory investigations, the reliability of this factor is not high enough to make it useful for practitioners. In addition, the difficulty in interpreting the Freedom from Distractibility factor as either a measure of the ability to concentrate or a measure of numerical ability has been previously noted by Sattler (1974).

Factor analysis has been the primary tool for studying the structure of intelligence. As a social science research tool, it continues to generate arguments about which techniques should be used. Factor analysis is not a single mathematical technique. The results one obtains concerning a test are dependent upon the factoring technique used. Because factor analysis generally developed within a social science context (Cattell, 1978) and specifically evolved in relation to intelligence tests, a brief description of the problems with respect to Spearman's general intelligence (g) is presented. The reader who is unfamiliar with factor analysis, but who would like an extended discussion of the problems inherent in studying intelligence tests with factor-analytic techniques is referred to an excellent elementary discussion by Gould (1981). Spearman, an English psychologist, initially developed principal components analysis because he noted the positive correlations behind most measures of mental ability. He wondered if there was some simpler structure behind these correlations. Principal components without rotations of the axes assures that a g factor will be found. In the United States, Thurstone developed factor rotations which he termed *simple structure*; these rotations mathematically rotated out g. Thurstone felt that these rotated factors were more representative of the "real" world. Mathematically, both solutions are equivalent. Philosophically, there are large differences. If g exists, and is the most important attribute of an intelligence test, then a single number can be used to summarize the test. However, he continually found simple structures using his technique and therefore proclaimed that the tests measure a small number of "primary mental abilities." Both of the techniques discussed only find mathematically defined factors. Just because a statistical technique grinds out a solution does not assure that the factors(s) found have a necessary correspondence to reality. Several statements made by Gould (1981) about the major factor theorists capture the difficulty in using factor analytic results in interpreting intelligence tests. The first principal component:

> For Spearman it is to be cherished as a measure of innate general intelligence, for Thurstone, it is a meaningless average of an arbitrary battery of tests, devoid of psychological significance, and calculated only as an intermediary step in rotation to simple structure [p. 301].
>
> For Cyril Burt, the group factors, although real and important in vocational guidance, were subsidiary to a dominant and innate g. For Thurstone, the old group factors became primary mental abilities. They were the irreducible mental entities; g was a delusion [p. 303].
>
> The very fact that estimates for the number of primary abilities have ranged from Thurstone's seven or so to Guilford's 120 or more indicates that vectors of the mind may be figments of the mind [p. 309].

Even though factor analysis has not determined the structure of intelligence, and indeed intelligence tests may be developed to conform to almost any *a priori* structure, factor analysis is a useful technique for studying current tests. The evaluation of developed tests through factor analysis will continue as long as the results continue to improve the efficiency of our predictions.

In a study comparing the efficacy of using WISC-R scores to predict academic achievement, Hale (1981) contrasted the utility of using the factor scores with the adequacy of employing the traditional Verbal and Performance IQs. His results indicated that one could account for appreciably more variance in arithmetic using the factor scores. The Performance IQ never aided in the prediction of academic achievement. Hale (1981) also noted that the Freedom from Distractibility factor is highly related to mathematics achievement. These factor-analytic results can be used by test constructors and practitioners to improve their predictions. Another number-related test should be added to the WISC-R to increase the reliability of the predictions using the Freedom from Distractibility factor.

In any event, if the Stanford-Binet is primarily a single-factor test, and the Wechslers chiefly two-factor instruments, it is difficult to see how these particular intelligence tests correspond to the structural theories of Guilford or Thurstone. These tests do not measure as many factors as required by these theorists.

Many investigations have been conducted with reference to Nunnally's third aspect of construct validation: performing studies to verify hypotheses predictable from definitions of intelligence. Most of these investigations, however, are *ex post facto* due to the obvious ethical concerns of varying an independent variable powerful enough to change intelligence. Bereiter (1976–77) has effectively argued that the construct measured by intelligence tests is very important. He shows that a society run by low IQ elites is bound to collapse. This line of evidence, however, does not detract from the position that present intelligence tests measure an ability highly involved in academic achievement. Modern societies require leaders who are efficient learners of academic material.

In summary, if one is using the intelligence test to measure the construct of intelligence, definitions of that construct should be offered. Present intelligence tests appear to measure only one or two factors adequately. These factors appear to be Verbal (Reasoning, Fluency, and/or Comprehension) and Perceptual Organization. It should be remembered that these factors may only be true in a mathematical sense, and may not correspond to any psychological or physiological truth. The factors these tests measure are important, however, because of their relationship with the skills necessary for the successful performance of an individual in a modern technological society.

Subtest Analysis

Subtest analysis of intelligence tests has been mainly confined to the Wechsler series for the obvious reason that the physical structure of the Wechsler series simply lends itself to subtest analysis. The literature on subtest analysis has always been quite controversial. Subtest analysis of the various Wechsler tests has been cyclical. Following the release of new or revised tests, another series of subtest investigations would be published. With both the WISC and the Wechsler Adult Intelligence Scale (WAIS; Wechsler, 1955), the conclusion has eventually been reached that subtest analysis was a relatively useless enterprise (Huelsman, 1970; Rabin, 1965). These results, however, never generalized from one test and its set of researchers to the next test, even though the psychometric properties of the tests are similar. Even though Hirshoren and Kavale (1976) have shown that the relatively low reliabilities of the WISC-R subtests preclude accurate profile analyses, the importance of WISC-R profile analyses is still being debated. Both major texts presently being used by school psychology training programs for teaching WISC-R interpretation (Kaufman, 1979; Sattler, 1982) indicate that subtest analysis procedures may be useful. Many pages of these texts are devoted to analyzing the strengths and weaknesses in a child's cognitive abilities that might be revealed by relatively high and low subtest scores. While the research results in this area are seen as inconsistent by the casual observer, a more intensive investigation will lead the observer to the realization that the literature is quite consistent. From a practical point of view, the literature can be broken down into two types of studies. First are those investigations that start with previously defined groups of children (e.g., reading disabled, conduct disordered, etc.) and ask if significant subtest differences can be found between these groups, or between a group and the standardization sample data. This is termed a *classical validity* study. The second set of investigations start with the subtest results and ask if knowledge of these subtest results can aid in the prediction or differentiation of a socially significant criterion. This criterion might be a child's academic achievement or handicapping condition. These studies are termed *clinical utility* studies. (For an in-depth discussion of the distinctions between classical validity and clinical utility, see Wiggins, 1973.) Miller (1980) contends that the inconsistency that is thought to exist in this body of research exists because, while investigators have found statistically significant WISC-R profiles to be characteristic of certain handicapped groups, there has been a failure to demonstrate that these profiles are distinctive enough to allow practitioners to differentiate between handicapped and normal children. In other words, he argues that significant patterns have been found using the classical validity research strategy, but the clinical research does not support the use of these results. Our review of the literature supports this contention. In those studies starting with intact groups (Ackerman, Peters, & Dykman, 1971; Dean, 1977; Rugel, 1974; Smith,

Coleman, Dokecki, & Davis, 1977; Vance, Wallbrown, & Blaha, 1978), significant subtest differences have been found between children classified as handicapped and those classified as normal. In those investigations that started with subtest results and attempted to classify children into diagnostic categories (Hale, 1979; Hale & Landino, 1981; Hale & Raymond, 1981) or those studies where reclassification could take place (Tabachnick, 1979; Thompson, 1980), high degrees of diagnostic error were encountered. In one investigation (Hale, 1979), a 100 percent error rate was found when classifying reading underachievers using a significant discriminant function identified in the same group of children. In another related investigation, Hale and Landino (1981) found, using significant WISC-R subtest differences to reclassify behaviorally disordered and normal boys, that the results obtained were no better than chance. Other investigations have found that patterns of subtest strengths and weaknesses on the WISC-R derived either through rules provided by Kaufman (1979) or sophisticated profile clustering schemes (Skinner & Lei, 1980) do not aid in the prediction of a child's academic achievement level (Hale & Raymond, 1981; Hale & Saxe, 1982).

In summary, these results suggest that knowledge of a child's subtest profile does not appreciably help the clinician in predicting either academic achievement levels or behavioral difficulties. There is increasing evidence that WISC-R subtest analysis lacks utility for making special education placement decisions (Hale, 1979; Hale, & Landino, 1981; Thompson, 1980; Vance, Singer, & Egin, 1980). In fairness to Sattler (1982) and Kaufman (1979), it should be noted that these authors offer various cautions to profile anaysis: "The hypothese should be treated as tentative, formulated in relation to the child's absolute scaled scores, and not referred to as 'verifiable insights'" (Sattler, 1982, p. 201). If, however, as is presently the case, the procedure is supported as "only" a hypothesis-generating procedure, those hypotheses should be generated and tested. Otherwise, on the basis of these findings, the use of subtest analysis appears unjustifiable.

Predicting Academic Achievement

The primary usage of intelligence tests in the public schools is to help in the determination of special education for children. Thus, the major usage today is the same as that for which Binet developed the test. The major question that school psychologists are still confronted with is, "How well can we expect this child to do in school?" (Hale, 1978). If IQs are employed in this fashion, a presumption is made that they are related to and can be used to predict academic achievement.

More formally, the definition of IQ under this usage might be stated: an IQ allows one to predict a youngster's academic achievement in a typical school environment if the child is left to his or her own devices and all things remain equal. The term "typical school environment" would exclude those academic environs where emphasis was not placed on traditional educational curricular materials. The term "left to his or her own devices" would exclude children from the prediction model if they were given support services (i.e., special education). "All things remain equal" would exclude children where traumatic events, like the death of a parent, might be expected to affect test scores. The prediction definition of intelligence assumes we are predicting in a culturally loaded environment. It also assumes that the IQ is changeable. Intelligence, in any practically meaningful sense of the word, can be increased by education and exposure to the mainstream culture; it is not a fixed, inborn quantity. Sowell's (1981a) earlier reported figures of group IQ changes and Yerkes' (1921) findings that the Army test scores were correlated with years of residence in America certainly corroborate allegations that scores improve with exposure to the American middle-class culture. The final assumption, that these cultural standards and methods of performance are the most appropriate standards on which to measure and train individuals, remains open to debate. Use of intelligence tests in this manner assumes that they can demonstrate adequate predictive validity.

The Primary Predictive Validity Model

The correlation coefficient between a selected test of intelligence and a selected measure of academic achievement is a direct method of evaluating IQs in relation to the academic prediction model. Some tests would fare quite well under this model, and others, of course, would not. Again a discussion that included all of the tests available would deserve a chapter in itself. Therefore, the two major individual tests given to public school children who are deemed serious enough to warrant a psychological evaluation will be discussed in

some detail. These tests are the Stanford-Binet and the Wechsler Intelligence Scale for Children—Revised (WISC-R: Wechsler, 1974).

Correlations between two variables can best be represented by a bivariate plot of their relationship. Figure 19.1 shows a hypothetical situation where there is no relation between intelligence (IQ) and achievement (Ach). The correlation (Rach-iq) in such a circumstance would equal zero. If practitioners found themselves working in that situation and needed to predict a person's score on the criterion variable, knowledge of the person's score on the predictor would not aid the prediction process. The practitioner would be left with predicting the mean criterion score for everyone. The prediction equation would be:

$$\widehat{Ach} = \overline{Ach} \qquad (19.1)$$

Where $\widehat{Ach}$ = predicted criterion score and $\overline{Ach}$ = mean criterion score. To establish confidence intervals around this predicted value, one could add and subtract the standard deviation (SD) of the test:

$$\widehat{Ach} = \overline{Ach} \pm SD_{ach} \qquad (19.2)$$

Equation 19.2 represents the predicted score of a person under the situation represented by Figure 19.1, with 68 percent confidence limits. This is the base rate of prediction. Anyone can predict with this level of accuracy knowing only the descriptive statistics of the criterion variable. This is exactly the situation that is assumed when one expects every child to achieve an average score on an achievement test. Any predictive test of value should allow its user to improve significantly upon the predictions offered by this situation. This situation will be referred to as Case 1.

Figure 19.2 represents a situation where perfect prediction is possible. Every data point falls exactly on a straight line. The more closely the data points can be represented by a straight line, the higher the correlation. Figure 19.2 shows a situation where Rach-iq = 1.0. The question for this straight line (the prediction equation) would be:

$$\widehat{Ach} = b(IQ) + a \qquad (19.3)$$

where b is the slope of the line and a is the intercept (the point where the prediction line crosses the criterion axis when the predictor = 0). In social science research, this situation never occurs. It

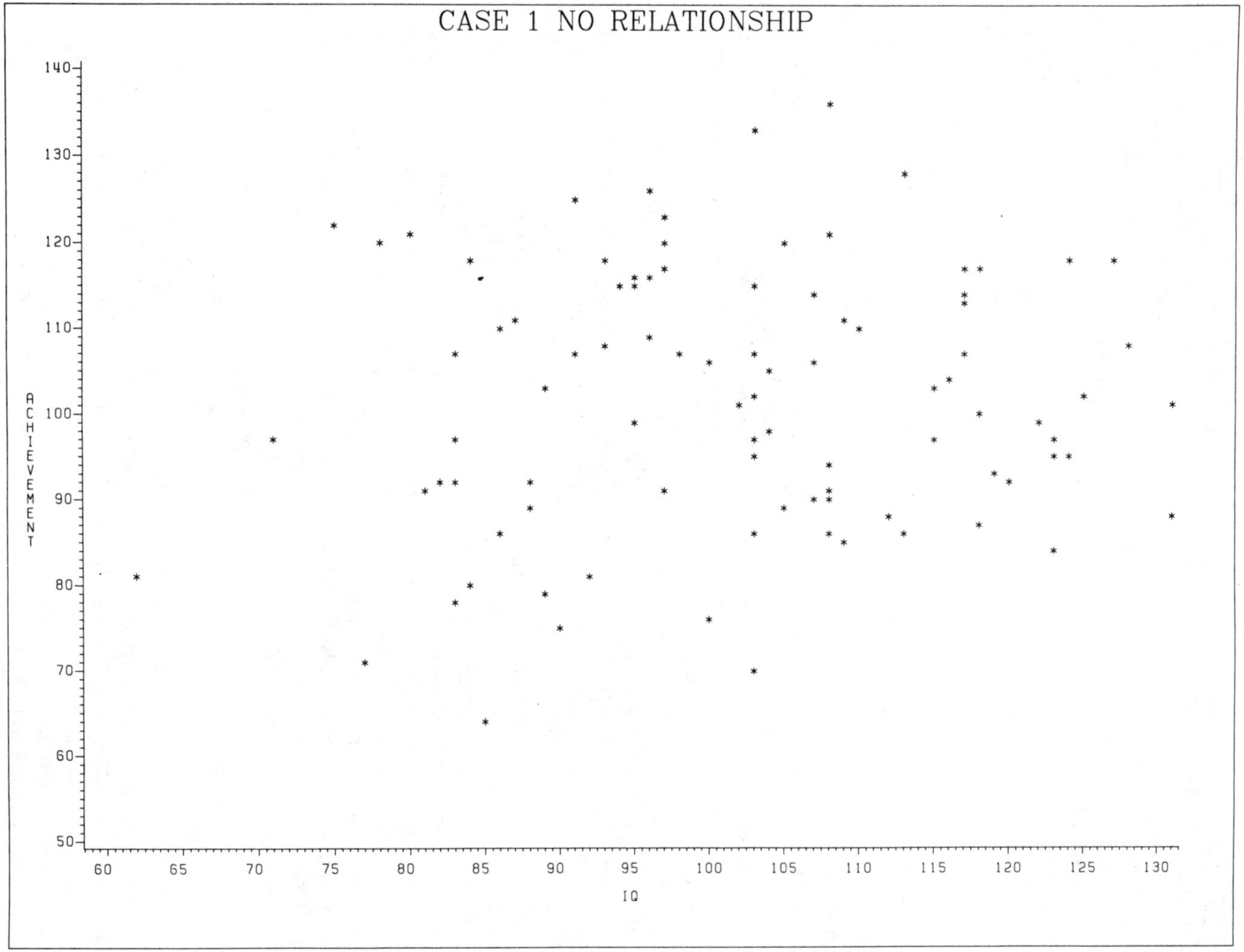

Fig. 19.1. A representation of no relationship between two variables.

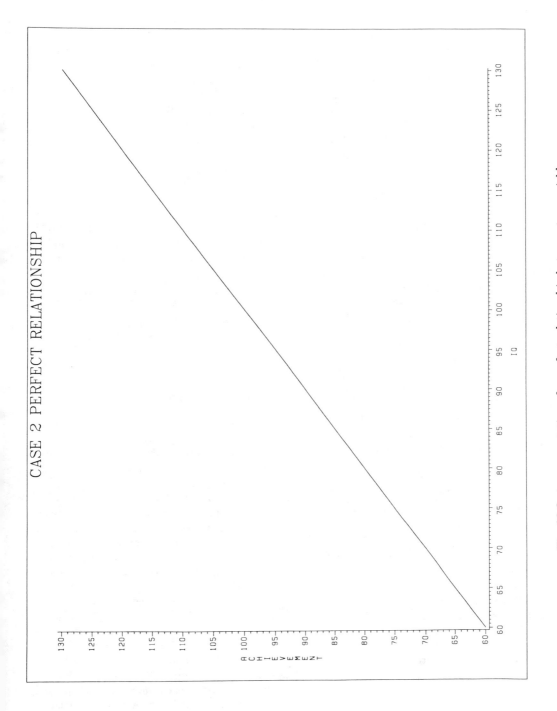

Fig. 19.2. A representation of a perfect relationship between two variables.

might be called the "ideal" situation because there is absolutely no error in the predictions made. If we assume that IQ and achievement scores are distributed in exactly the same manner (i.e., means = 100, SD = 15), then as the child's intelligence scores increased by one point, the achievement scores will also increase by a single point. The slope of the equation would equal one. While for all practical purposes the tests could not measure IQs or achievement indices of zero, if the prediction line were extrapolated to the point where theoretically the IQ equals zero, the achievement score obtained from the prediction equation would also equal zero. Equation 19.4 represents this perfect prediction situation. This situation will be referred to as Case 2.

$$\widehat{Ach} = 1(IQ) + 0 \qquad (19.4)$$

Figure 19.3 represents the more typical situation in the social sciences. It was constructed from the data available from Hale (1978). Hale (1978) was interested in investigating the predictive relationship of the Verbal and Performance IQs from the WISC-R in relation to the Wide Range Achievement Test (WRAT: Jastak & Jastak, 1976). Figure 19.3 however, shows the relationship between the WISC-R Full Scale IQ (FSIQ) and the WRAT Reading standard scores. The solid line through the data points represents the best prediction line. This line is most often called the regression line. If one knows the descriptive statistics for both the predictor and the criterion variables as well as the correlation between them, the equation for the best prediction line is easily found using Equation 19.5.

$$\widehat{Ach} = \left\{ \left[r_{ach\text{-}IQ} \frac{(SD_{ach})}{(SD_{IQ})} (IQ - IQ) \right] + Ach \right\} \qquad (19.5)$$

Sattler (1982) reports the median correlation between WISC-R FISQ and WRAT Reading to be .60. Both WISC-R FISQ and WRAT Reading standard scores are distributed with means equal to 100 and standard deviations (SD) equal to 15. These numbers can be substituted into Equation 19.5, resulting in the following:

$$\widehat{Ach} = \left\{ \left[.6 \frac{(15)}{(15)} (IQ - 100) \right] + 100 \right\} \qquad (19.6)$$

by multiplying and collecting terms, Equation 19.6 can be simplified to:

$$\widehat{Ach} = .6(IQ) + 40 \qquad 19.7$$

Equation 19.7 is equivalent in form to Equation 19.3 where .60 is the slope and 40 is the intercept.

The amount of error in prediction in all three cases is given by the standard error of estimate. Assuming large sample sizes in the investigation, the standard error of estimate (SEe) is given by SD_{ach} $\sqrt{1\text{-}Rach\text{-}iq^2}$. Using the WISC-R FSIQ and the WRAT Reading standard score as the predictor and criterion variables, the SEe for the three cases can be calculated. For Case 1, the SEe = SDach $\sqrt{1\text{-}0}$ = SDach = 15. For Case 2, the SEe = SDach $\sqrt{1\text{-}1}$ = 0. In Case 2 there is no error in prediction. For the achievement data in Case 3, the SEe = 15. $\sqrt{1\text{-}.36}$ = 12. Thus, the entire equation, including confidence intervals, can be written as follows:

$$\widehat{Ach} = \left\{ \left[r_{ach\text{-}IQ} \frac{(SD_{ach})}{(SD_{IQ})} (IQ - IQ) \right] + Ach \right\} \pm SD_{ach} \sqrt{1\text{-}R_{ach\text{-}IQ}^2} \qquad (19.8)$$

using Case 3 data

$$\widehat{Ach} = .6(IQ) = 40 \pm 12 \qquad (19.9)$$

The traditional method of evaluating the utility of the regression equation is to look at the coefficient of determination $Rx\text{-}y^2$. The coefficient of determination tells the investigator the proportion of variance in the criterion which is accounted for by knowledge of the client's score on the predictor variable. Returning to the baseline situation (Case 1), one sees that 15^2 = 225 variance units are unaccounted for. This figure is simply the standard deviation of the test squared. When the prediction situation has changed by knowledge of a predictor score which correlates .60 with the criterion (Case 3) one sees that 12^2 = 144 variance units remain unaccounted for. This figure is simply the standard error of estimate squared. Thus, in moving from Case 1 to Case 3, 225 – 144 = 81 units of variance are accounted for (are removed from the standard error). Therefore 81/225 = .36, is the proportion of variance accounted for under Case 3. Of course, this figure is more simply calculated by squaring the correlation coefficient $.60^2$ = .36. Comparing the standard error of prediction (es-

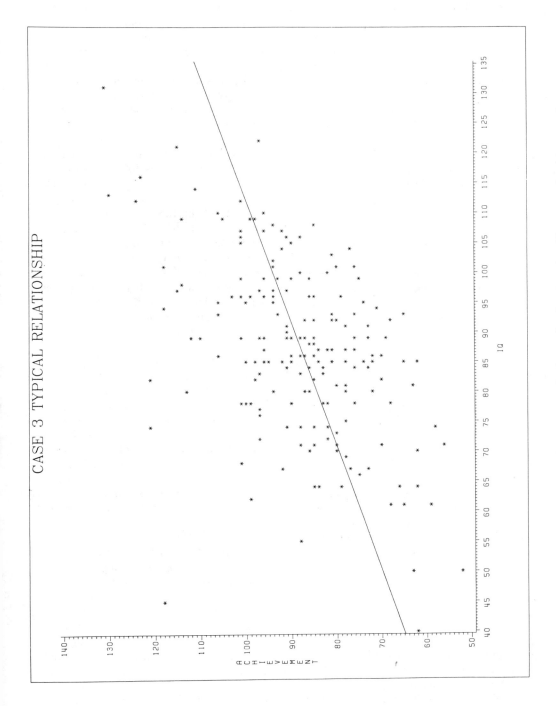

Fig. 19.3. A representation of the typical relationship between intelligence and achievement.

timate) in Case 1 (baseline condition), one sees that at 68 percent confidence intervals the range of prediction has been reduced by six points. Of course, practitioners would probably not make predictions using 68 percent confidence intervals. More appropriate confidence intervals would be 85 or 95 percent. At the 95 percent confidence interval, the practitioner operating under the baseline condition would be adding and subtracting $1.96(15) = 29.4$ points to the predicted score of 100 for each child. The entire 95 percent confidence interval would then encompass a spread of 58.8 points. On the other hand, using an IQ that correlated .60 with the criterion, the point spread at 95 percent confidence is reduced to 47.04 points. The 11.04 point reduction represents a reduction of over three-fourths of a standard deviation on the test. Garrett (1966) gives the formula for calculating the efficiency rate of the regression equation over that available using baseline conditions. Garrett's efficiency statistic is: $E = 1 - \sqrt{1 - Rx - y^2}$ $= .20$. The regression situation encountered in Case 3 is thus 20 percent efficient. This efficiency rate is equivalent to the reduction in points at a given confidence interval divided by the original baseline points at the same confidence level. In our prediction, $(15 - 12)/15 = .20$ or $3/15 = .20$. Both the Stanford-Binet and the WISC-R correlate with achievement tests (using school-age children) at about the same level ($Riq - ach = .60$). Both of these intelligence tests account for approximately 36 percent of the variance in achievement in school-age children and are approximately 20 percent efficient in these prediction situations. Predictions with the Stanford-Binet are less stable for those at the upper end of the scale than for those scoring at the lower end. Also, when the Stanford-Binet is used with preschoolers (ages 2 to 4), the test does not predict future scholastic achievement as well as when the children are tested at older ages.

Current Issues in Intellectual Assessment

Heritability of IQs

A measure of the heritability of a trait is given by the correlation between the genetic constitutions of a group of individuals and the trait in which one is interested. Heritability estimates for intelligence are given by correlating IQs with different degrees of kinship within groups of people, such as mono-

zygotic or dizygotic twins. Sattler (1982) reports that "Studies of European and North American Causasian populations suggest that the heritability of intelligence varies from .40 to .80" (p. 49). The coefficient of determination $(Rx - y^2)$ would therefore indicate that somewhere between 16 and 64 percent of the variance in IQs is accounted for by genetics. This range of numbers in and of itself does not conflict with statements that the environment is important in the expression of intelligence or that supplementary environmental or educational programs can increase intelligence. Academic or social success or failure is more often the real criterion of interest for psychologists using intelligence tests. Remembering that correlations between intelligence and achievement are around .60, even if intelligence scores were 100 percent determined by genetics, it would not necessarily follow that achievement would also be perfectly determined. Much of the confusion begins when the words "inherited" and "inevitable" are thought of as being equivalent. Diabetes Mellitus is inherited, but certainly its debilitating effects are mitigated by the environmental manipulation of insulin. The potential hazards of the disease are certainly not inevitable.

Gould (1981) and MacKenzie (1980) both point out a serious flaw in our statistical thinking about heritability. Both authors note that studies of heritability of IQ are all of the "within-group" type. That is, the investigations permit an estimate of heritability *within* a single, coherent population (white Americans, for example). The extension of this percentage figure derived from the *within-group* study to explain differences *between* groups (differences between blacks and whites) is simply unfounded. Gould (1981) gives the following example.

Human height has a higher heritability than any value ever proposed for IQ. Take two separate groups of males. The first, with an average height of 5 feet 10 inches, live in a prosperous American town. The second, with an average height of 5 feet 6 inches, are starving in a third-world village. Heritability is 95 percent or so in each place—meaning that relatively tall fathers tend to have tall sons and relatively short fathers short sons. This high within-group heritability argues neither for nor against the possibility that better nutrition in the next generation might raise the average height of third-world villagers above that of prosperous Americans. Likewise, IQ could be highly heritable within groups, and the average difference between whites and blacks in America might still only record the environmental disadvantages of blacks. [pp. 156–157]

Again, if we take the practitioner's point of view, the exact heritability index is not of great importance. Even extremely high heritability of IQ should not prevent the provision of environmental and educational support to those persons whose functioning may be enhanced by those social services.

Bias in Intelligence Testing

Recently, a great deal of renewed interest has been focused on the issue of test bias. Two recent events have promoted this renewed concern: (1) the enactment of Public Law 94-142, which requires that handicapped children be found and provided with appropriate educational programming using nonbiased assessment procedures, and (2) the two court cases (*Larry P. v. Wilson Riles* and *PASE* v. *Hannon*), that are diametrically opposed in their findings as to the use of IQs in the determination of Educable Mental Retardation (EMR) as a handicap with minority children. Concern about nonbiased assessment in relation to intelligence testing has been so piqued that major efforts have been expended in the psychology community to educate practitioners. With reference to individually administered intelligence tests, the two recent legal decisions will be briefly discussed. The empirical results concerning bias in relation to Wechler's series of tests and the Stanford-Binet will then be presented.

In the *Larry P.* decision in 1979, Judge Peckham, upholding his earlier judgment, ruled that: (1) California schools could not utilize, permit the use of, or approve the use of any standardized intelligence test for the identification of black EMR children or their placement into EMR classes without securing approval by his court; (2) the disproportionate representation of blacks in EMR classrooms was to be eliminated; and (3) the harm done to blacks misclassified as EMRs was to be remedied and discrimination caused by IQ usage could not be allowed to recur. Also, every black child in EMR placement in California should be reevaluated, but the evaluation was to exclude standardized intelligence tests. Intelligence tests

were found to be biased against blacks and the EMR classes into which they were placed were characterized as "stigmatizing" and "dead-end."

Judge Grady, on the other hand, in *PASE* v. *Hannon*, found that the same tests were not biased with respect to minority status. He faulted Judge Peckham for not looking at and evaluating all of the individual test items himself. Obviously, both Judges cannot be correct. With both cases presently on appeal, it is quite likely that the Supreme Court will make the final determination concerning the use of IQs in minority assessment. In any event, it is the author's opinion that both judges failed adequately to distinguish between the tests' ability to *discriminate* between groups and individuals and whether the tests are *biased* against those same groups and individuals.

Intelligence tests were designed to discriminate between children who were able to be scholastically successful and those who were not. If, as the current research suggests, minority children are not as successful as majority-status children in traditional school environments, then IQs should reflect this. If intelligence tests are doing their job, minority children should have lower IQs as a group than majority children. If IQs are used as a component of remedial educational placement, then proportionally more minority children will be found in specialized educational programs. Proportionally more minority students are experiencing difficulty in scholastic endeavors. If the definition of bias adopted by the reader is that IQs are biased if there are mean differences between ethnic groups or that an intelligence test is biased if its utilization leads to disproportional representation in specialized educational programs of minority groups, then intelligence tests are indeed biased.

In the author's opinion, these definitions of bias incorrectly assume that IQs are a measure of potential and are for all intents and purposes stable characteristics of an individual or group. Those who adopt the mean difference/proportional inbalance definition of IQ bias often believe that intelligence tests have been improperly used to support the proposition that black children have lower intelligence (less potential) than whites (Madden, 1980). A position that is, however, rarely debated is that black children are currently achieving at lower levels in school subjects than are white youngsters. These mean IQ differences can certainly be measuring the relative environmental disadvantages experienced by blacks for generations. The reader is referred back to the same arguments proposed above in the section on heritability. If these differences did not exist, intelligence tests would simply not discriminate between students who are adequately achieving in school and those who are not—the task for which the instrument was devised. The test's ability to *discriminate* is thus a necessary function. *Bias*, on the other hand, refers to the unequal measurement in differing groups, and is detrimental to proper test usage.

Bias in intelligence tests can be evaluated by inspecting the test's differential validity across groups. In other words, if a test does not display the same validity for different groups, it may be said to be biased. Validity is primarily of three types: content, construct, and predictive. An intelligence test may be biased if differential validity can be demonstrated in any one of the three areas for or against one or more groups (Cleary et al., 1975). Excellent reviews of the methods of bias detection under these psychometric definitions may be found in Jensen (1980) and Reynolds (1982). These authors find that, in general, there is very little psychometric evidence for intelligence test bias. The evidence that has indicated that IQs may be biased has generally indicated that the tests are biased in favor of minorities instead of against them. A brief review of some of the research conducted using the Binet and Wechslers is in order. In the following sections, no attempt is made to provide a complete overview of the pertinent research findings. Only a summary of the findings is provided. The interested reader is strongly urged to read the primary sources.

Content Bias

One of the charges in the *Larry P.* decision was that items for intelligence tests are drawn from white middle-class culture. These items are assumed to be more difficult for black and other minority children than they are for white children. If it is assumed for a moment that it is responsible to group persons on some color index, and that blacks should be grouped together and whites should be grouped together, and that differences, if found, would be meaningful, one can ask if the available evidence indicates that some of the test items are more difficult for blacks. As Reschly (1980) points out, there are two distinct methods of "evidence" concerning this hypothesis. The most common method has been subjective "expert" examination of the items. Subjective judgment involves gathering opinion on whether the

items are biased. The item in the WISC-R that is frequently pointed to as being culturally biased is the "Fight" item. The "Fight" item asks what one should do if a same-sex child much younger than yourself starts to fight with you. The opinion of those who believe this item is biased (more difficult) for blacks assumes that urban black children are taught by parents and peers that it is appropriate to strike younger children who are bothering them. As Reschly (1980) notes: "It is doubtful whether such attitudes or behaviors are any more typical or acceptable in that situation than in white, middle class environments" (p. 127).

When these subjective impressions are put to empirical test, the statistical evidence suggests that expert judgments are both unreliable (Sandoval & Millie, 1980) and invalid (Sandoval, 1979). Empirical methods of item analysis simply do not support the subjective judgments.

Schmeiser and Ferguson (1978) evaluated the performance of black and white students and found that test content differing on the amount of material based on black and white cultures did not have a major effect on student performance. Item difficulties for the WISC and WISC-R in several recent studies (Miele, 1979; Oakland & Feigenbaum, 1979; Sandoval, 1979) show that the item difficulty levels are not ordered differently for blacks and whites. Lambert (1981) notes that, "The Race X Items interaction, although it is significant for some items at some age levels, accounts for only 1%–2% of the variance. The only data that supports item bias at present is judgmental" (p. 942).

Construct Bias

One way that construct bias can be empirically evaluated is through factor-analytic techniques. Recent investigations with the WISC-R have consistently shown equivalent factor structures (no construct bias) across race (Dean, 1980; Gutkin & Reynolds, 1980; Reschly, 1978; Reynolds, 1982; Oakland & Feigenbaum, 1979; Vance, Huelsman, & Wherry, 1976; Vance & Wallbrown, 1978). Another concern, in fact a line of defense offered by the defendants in the *Larry P.* case, was that while IQs may not be biased against any of several racial groups, they might be biased against socially and economically disadvantaged groups, irrespective of race. It was proposed by the *Larry P.* defendants that intelligence tests might be biased when used to evaluate minority children because a large proportion of these children are members of lower socioeconomic groups. Hale (in press) presents research evidence concerning the construct validity of the WISC-R in relation to this "poverty principle." The results suggest that under realistic testing conditions, the factor structure of the WISC-R is consistent with respect to socioeconomic status.

Predictive Bias

While we have discussed a variety of models and criteria for defining the presence of test bias, Reynolds (1982) has stated that predictive validity is the most crucial type in relation to test bias. As discussed under "Uses of Intelligence Tests," predictive validity refers to how well a test forecasts a criterion of interest. This definition of bias is especially relevant to evaluating IQs since their ultimate utility depends on their ability to predict academic achievement. The predictive definition of test bias states that bias exists if the regression equations for two separate groups are different. Bias in regression equations can be reflected in the slopes of the lines, the intercepts, or both slopes and intercepts. Figures 19.4, 19.5, and 19.6 demonstrate graphically what bias would look like under these three situations.

Most of the research has been directed toward investigating differences between the regression lines generated for blacks and whites. Recent research has indicated that WISC-R scores are not racially biased according to the predictive definition when only the beta weights or slopes are considered (Reschly & Sabers, 1979; Reynolds & Hartledge, 1979). When the intercepts are included, the evidence is not consistent. When bias in intercepts is found, however, the evidence indicates that most aptitude tests, including the WISC-R, *overestimate* the achievement of blacks (Reschly & Sabers, 1979). This means that for children with identical IQs, the achievement of the black child is more often lower than what one would predict using a regression equation developed using only white children or one developed using both black and white children together. Figure 19.7 was constructed using data provided by Bossard, Reynolds, and Gutkin (1980). They found that the regression lines using Stanford-Binet IQs to predict WRAT achievement scores were not statistically distinct (no bias existed). In Figure 19.7, Stanford-Binet IQs were regressed on WRAT Reading achievement scores. White students are represented by diamonds, black students by crosses. By evaluating Figure 19.7, one can see the extensive overlap between black and white children in the bivariate

space provided by Stanford-Binet and WRAT Reading. The solid line represents the common regression line. The broken lines define 95 percent confidence boundaries for individuals around the common regression line.

Hale, Raymond, and Gajar (in press) have investigated WISC-R bias across socioeconomic status using the predictive bias criterion. Their study provides preliminary evidence that suggests that when bias is defined as significantly different regression lines, the WISC-R Verbal IQ is a nonbiased predictor of WRAT Reading with respect to socioeconomic status.

Stability of IQs

Throughout this chapter, emphasis has been placed on the fact that IQs are not immutable measures of individuals. Just how much they may be expected to change is a complex interaction between many factors such as: (1) the child's familiarization with mainstream cultural standards; (2) the age at which the initial test was administered; (3) the time interval between testing; (4) intervening environmental changes such as special education; (5) whether the child is handicapped, and others. In general, however, the following rules of thumb may be advanced. First, if a youngster is not familiar with the culture, his or her IQ would be expected to change with increasing familiarization. No current intelligence test is "culture-free." Second, infant intelligence tests measure perceptual skills to a greater degree than intelligence tests given to older children. Because more growth may be evidenced by younger children and the material being measured by intelligence tests actually changes over certain ages, IQs are stable if the scores are obtained after five years of age (Sattler, 1982). Third, the longer the time interval between testing, the less stable the measurements tend to be. Fourth, environmental changes, such as special education, may be expected to change IQs (Morris & Clarizio, 1977). Fifth, retarded children tend to have more stable IQs than children with higher IQs. These influences might interact to produce many changes in IQs over a group of children. Hindley and Owen (1978), in a longitudinal study of British children between 6 months and 17 years, found that 50 percent of the children had IQ changes of 10 points or more.

It should certainly be stressed that intelligence tests are measures of *current* levels of functioning. Even though relatively high correlations are found for older children's intelligence test scores over re-

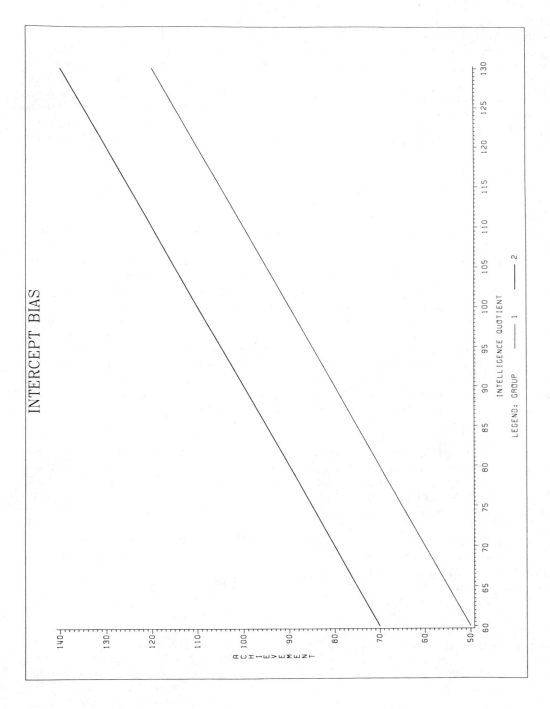

Fig. 19.4. A representation of predictive bias due to differences in regression intercepts.

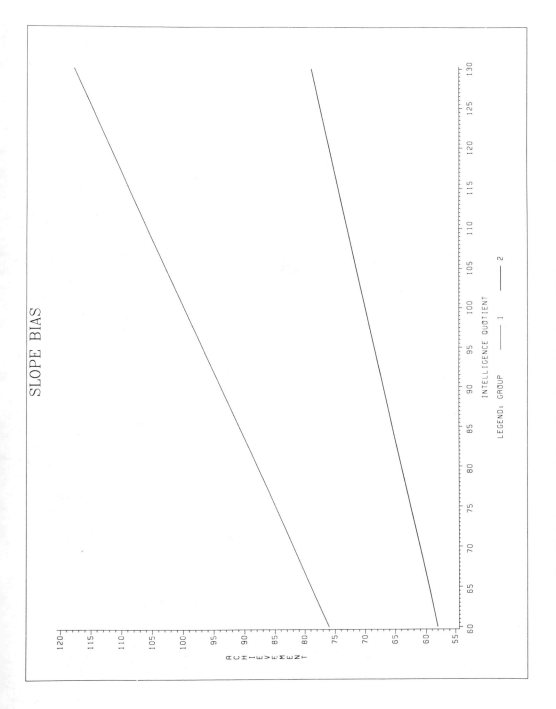

Fig. 19.5. A representation of predictive bias due to differences in regression slopes.

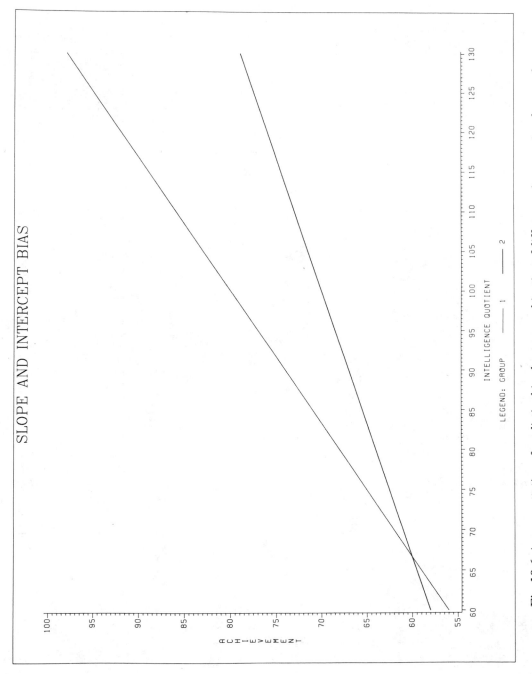

Fig. 19.6. A representation of predictive bias due to a combination of differences in regression slopes and intercepts.

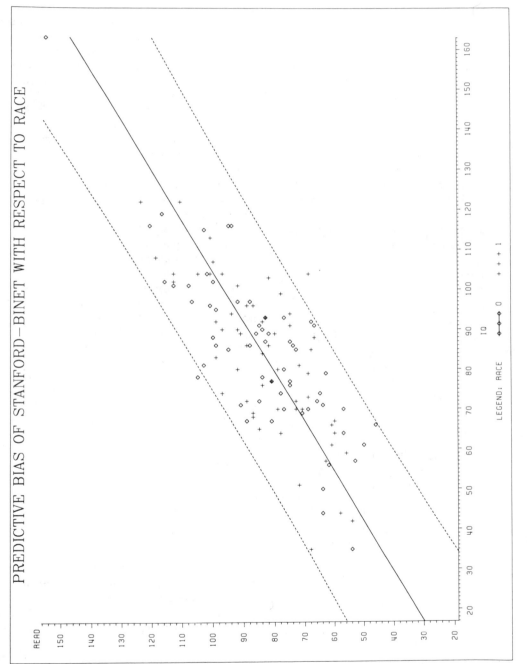

Fig. 19.7. The predictive bias of Stanford-Binet with respect to race. (Diamonds-white children; crosses-black children.)

peated testing, it is necessary to have frequent and periodic evaluations of the individual child's level of functioning. This is especially important if the test scores are to be used to substantiate special educational placement decisions. An interesting point can be made with respect to the intelligence-achievement relationship. Each time one of the major intelligence tests has been renormed or revised, more raw score points have been required for a youngster to receive the same IQ. Intelligence as measured by the Stanford-Binet and Wechsler appears to have increased steadily. Over part of the same time period, academic achievement appears to have decreased. Anastasi (1982) notes that we have experienced a steady 14-year decline in Scholastic Achievement Test results. If the same trend continues, a youngster reevaluated on newer tests may be expected to obtain higher achievement scores and a lower IQ than those found on earlier testing.

Equivalence of Scores across Different Intelligence Tests

A common misconception about intelligence tests is that they all measure the same thing and their scores are equivalent. Definitions of handicapping conditions, like mental retardation, often require measurement of intelligence (frequently the reporting of the IQ is required) but rarely is the instrument used to determine the score specified. State departments of education may formally circulate lists of approved tests (Lambert, 1981) but for the most part, psychologists are free to choose among the tests available. This freedom is necessary for professional flexibility, but the examiner should be aware that not all IQs are equal. As Sattler (1982) reports:

> An evaluation of the IQs provided by the WISC-R and other tests indicates that for group purposes, IQs on the Stanford-Binet and WISC-R are generally similar. The Slosson Intelligence Test, on the average, yields IQs that are about 5 points higher than those of the WISC-R. The McCarthy Scales of Children's Abilities, on the average, yields GCI's (General Cognitive Indexes) that are lower by about 6 points. [p. 149]

Large differences between WISC and WISC-R IQs were noted by Schwarting (1976). Children also obtain higher WAIS than WISC-R IQs. Differences between the WAIS and WISC-R for Verbal,

Performance, and Full Scale IQs were found to be 14, 9, and 13 points, respectively, in favor of the WAIS in a sample of mentally retarded children (Nagle & Lazarus, 1979). When the author was working in the public schools, it was common practice in his Educational Service Unit to tailor the intelligence test to the decision that was believed to be in the child's best interest. For example, while children were in school and believed to be in need of special educational services, WISC-R and Stanford-Binets were given as the intelligence measure of choice. These tests would most often qualify "borderline" children for placement into special education programs. The cost of those programs would then be partially reimbursed by state and federal special educational funding.

Just before these same youngsters graduated from school, they were often reevaluated with the WAIS. Their IQs would frequently increase dramatically and reports would then be written decertifying these youngsters as handicapped. The belief system was that once out of school, the children would no longer need special support services. After graduation, the handicapping label was perceived as detrimental, so an attempt was made to remove it. Another "trick" of the trade involves administering the WISC-R or Stanford-Binet in sequence if the child failed to meet the criteria for admittance to the program for "gifted" individuals on the first administration of one of the intelligence tests. For example, if a child was initially administered a WISC-R and obtained a higher Verbal IQ than Performance IQ and the Performance score was so low that the Full Scale score was pulled below the guidelines for admittance, a retest with the Stanford-Binet (which taps mostly verbal abilities) often provided a second IQ above the cutoff. While professionals may argue that tailoring test usage to desired outcomes may be advantageous to some clients, it should be noted that it is just as easy to tailor the assessment to the institution's best interests. Flexibility in usage with the institutions's best interests in the forefront may not be in the client's best interest.

Reporting Intelligence Testing Results

Often the final product of a psychological evaluation is a written report. In many cases where the presenting problem is an academic learning difficulty, the IQ score is recommended as the anchoring point for the report (Sattler, 1982). Because the IQ is used as a predictor of academic achievement, it provides an expectancy point to which observed achievement can be compared. The actual IQ itself, along with the predictions made from it, are only estimates. Several references on report writing recommend that because IQs are estimates, point scores should not be reported (Kaufman, 1979; Salvia & Ysseldyke, 1978; Sattler, 1982). Instead, these authors recommend that confidence intervals be reported. Some authors recommend reporting confidence intervals around obtained scores, while others recommend reporting confidence intervals around regressed scores (estimated true scores). The reasoning given for reporting confidence intervals is that the child's obtained score would change upon retesting, so the single score generated on a single test administration can be misleading. Confidence intervals represent an interval between which a child's "true" score will lie. The reporting of these confidence intervals is therefore seen as less misleading. Several problems are inherent in this line of reasoning, however. First, as Dudek (1979) points out, even the professionals often use confidence bands that are technically incorrect. Elementary assessment texts have recommended adding and subtracting standard errors of measurement for observed scores to regressed true scores and/or have misinterpreted the meaning of confidence intervals around observed scores. Second, reports are most often written for persons who are not statistically sophisticated. The belief that typical readers can interpret scores written in a confidence interval format with less ambiguity than point scores is, as far as the author knows, unsupported by empirical evidence. There is, however, another alternative: just simply reporting what the raw scores mean and excluding the standard scores altogether. If one is clear about the meaning of the test results, then the actual score is only needed for administrative purposes. An example of a report statement about intelligence test results that excludes standard scores might be: "Jason is currently operating in the mentally deficient ranges of general intellectual functioning. This indicates that without academic support services one would expect that this youngster will not be able to be successful in a regular academic program." Not providing IQs in a psychological report is not the same as refusing to release them. Current legal action with respect to assessment practices makes any recommendations with respect to test scores problematic. The situation changes too rapidly for sound advice to be given.

In the final analysis, however, it is not the IQ that is important. The important point is what the IQ allows one to say with some degree of confidence about the client. Again, in the author's opinion, a psychological report would be less confusing if the conclusions were stated without the use of standard scores. Problems, of course, arise when one has to substantiate that a client meets certain administrative or legal IQ criteria for service provision. With client permission, scores could be reported to agencies that require them without providing them in the psychological report. However, if the report is intended for other professionals, one can be somewhat assured that standard scores will be correctly interpreted. Historically, there is precedence for omitting IQs from reports not intended for other professionals. In the *Casebook on Ethical Standards of Psychologists* (American Psychological Association, 1967), cases 14.B and 14.C point out the difficulties in providing clients with raw scores. In both cases, clients were provided with test scores that were misinterpreted. In both cases, the American Psychological Association's Committee on Scientific and Professional Ethics and Conduct questioned the psychologists' judgments. Again, the reader is cautioned that these judgments are not immutable and were made considering the values of the times in which we live.

Future Directions

Much of *Intelligence* (1979) Volume 3 was devoted to predictions about the form and purposes of intelligence tests in the year 2000. Horn (1979) and Resnick (1979) suggest that realistically, tests very similar to the present ones will be needed. In the near future there is no doubt that the traditional tests will be available. The Riverside Publishing Company is presently planning for a Binet revision and standardization to be completed in late 1983 or early 1984 (Munday, 1982). Both Horn (1979) and Resnick (1979) along with Turnbull (1979) see future intelligence tests as being better able to measure distinct aptitudes and abilities in learners. Brown and French (1979) stress that the test's major function will continue to be prediction. They would like to see an increase in the predictive power of intelligence so that school failure can be accurately predicted prior to its occurrence. As Lambert (1981) notes, IQs presently are not the prime determinants of a child's eligibility for special educational support services—school failure is. A child usually has a substantial history of school failure before he or she is ever given an individual intelligence test. As stressed throughout this chapter, academic prediction is a major function of IQs. To administer the predictor after the criterion of academic failure has been met is a serious underuse of intellectual measurement.

Incorporating Neuropsychology

There is increasing awareness among psychologists that the evaluation of neuropsychological functioning may lead to better understandings of children's educational needs (Gaddes, 1975; Hynd & Obrzut, 1981; Rourke, 1975). Instrumentation available to psychologists to measure these strengths and weaknesses has been very limited. Instruments such as the Bender-Gestalt have been the tests of choice in measuring these strengths and weaknesses (Hynd, Quackenbush, & Obrzut, 1980), even though the limitations of such tests as indicators of neurological strength and weakness are well documented in the literature. Alan Kaufman is currently developing an assessment instrument based on neurological theory that will compete with present IQ measures:

> The Kaufman Assessment Battery for Children (K-ABC), a test of intelligence and achievement of 2 ½–12 ½ year old children, is due to be published in September 1982 by American Guidance Service. The intelligence scales are derived from neuropsychological theories of information processing style, most notably the approaches of Luria and his followers (Das, Kirby, and Jarman) and of cerebral specialization researchers such as Bogen and Gazzaniga and are labeled Sequential Processing and Simultaneous Processing. The achievement scale represents a combination of Wechsler- or Binet-like verbal intelligence tasks along with more traditional achievement tasks (e.g. reading). [Kaufman & Kaufman, 1981, p. 2]

It is interesting to note that Kaufman's intelligence scales are composed of neuropsychological tasks, while the achievement scales are partially composed of items formerly included on verbal intelligence tests. There is some evidence that these neurological tasks may be equal to or better than the traditional intelligence tests in predicting academic achievement. Initial research evidence with another neurological assessment device—

the Luria-Nebraska Neuropsychological Battery (Golden, Hammeke, & Purisch, 1980)—that was initially developed to isolate neurological strengths and weaknesses in adults, suggests that this instrument is able to predict academic achievement in children at a level above that afforded by the WISC-R (Hale & Foltz, 1982). Work is currently being conducted to develop this battery formally for use with children. In theory, these new tests may allow investigators not only the ability to predict learning success and failure in children and adults, but also to link the test results directly to remediational strategies. Remediation studies using the K-ABC are being conducted throughout the standardization process.

Dropping the Term "Intelligence Quotient"

Sattler (1982) lists six misconceptions concerning intelligence tests: (1) IQs measure innate intelligence; (2) IQs are fixed and never change; (3) IQs are perfectly reliable; (4) intelligence tests tell us all we need to know about intelligence; (5) IQs from different tests are interchangeable; and (6) IQs are associated with the essential worth of a person. These misconceptions still exist in the minds of many, even though the evidence does not support these positions. Future assessment tools developed to compete with current intelligence tests may choose not to call themselves intelligence tests and may drop the term "IQ." Turnbull (1979) proposes that future tests will provide users with standard scores like IQs. However, he believes that the term "IQ" may disappear into educational and psychological history. This trend may already by evidenced by noting that the McCarthy Scale of Children's Abilities returns to a General Cognitive Index; the Woodcock-Johnson Psycho-Educational Battery (Woodcock, 1977) provides users with full-scale cluster scores and relative performance indexes. Also, Kaufman's K-ABC will provide sequential and simultaneous processing scores.

Computer Usage

The use of microcomputers in education is a rapidly developing field. Special emphasis is currently being placed on the needs of the handicapped learner. Efficacy studies of remedial programs are appearing in the literature (Jamison, Suppes, & Wells, 1974; Vinsonhaler & Bass, 1972; Watkins & Webb, 1981), as well as assessment systems developed for actual test administration. With the use of microprocessors controlling videodisc equipment, it is only a matter of time before new tests are developed for use in evaluating both children and adults. Initially, these systems will be able to present tests in a manner very much like trained examiners — using both visual and auditory inputs. School psychologists, who currently report that they spend too much time in assessment (Barbanel & Hoffenberg-Rutman, 1974; Cook & Patterson, 1977; Fairchild, 1976; Giebink & Ringness, 1970; Keenan, 1964), will have more time to provide other services to education and children. Like all other applications of microprocessing, developments in measurement and assessment will initially provide the same services that currently are being provided through other methods. Eventually, the new developments in computer science and neuropsychological assessment may combine to provide psychologists with the more accurate predictive tests envisioned by Brown and French (1979). Later, new evaluation procedures we have not even considered will be developed. In the author's opinion, we may be on the leading edge of the first real changes in the measurement of intelligence since Binet was asked to identify those children who would not profit from academics.

Conclusions

Historically, one sees that the measurement of mental abilities received its impetus from concern about children who were unable to learn in school. However, because of the sociopolitical climate in the United States in the early 20th century, intelligence test results were used not only to differentiate between children experiencing academic problems, but also as a measuring stick to organize an entire society. From essentially the very beginning of the intellectual assessment movement, the results of these tests have often been misused. Today, however, intelligence tests still provide practitioners with a method for predicting how well children should be expected to achieve in educational environs when left to their own devices and all other things remain equal.

Several popular conceptions concerning intelligence tests appear to be unfounded. First, even though the heritability of IQs may be high, the acceptance of these high heritability indices does not preclude the possibility that the average difference of 15 IQ points between blacks and whites solely reflects environmental and educational disadvantages experienced by blacks. Second, if psychometric definitions of bias are used, little evidence of racial or socioeconomic bias can be found in the present measures of intelligence. When evidence of bias has been reported in the literature, it has usually been found to favor minority members. Third, IQs may not be highly stable for specific individuals. A set of rules of thumb was proposed to indicate the degree of stability one could expect to find in intellectual testing results. The reader was cautioned that even when the expectation was that the IQ would be stable for an individual, if the score was to be used in educational planning, frequent reevaluations should be conducted. Fourth, IQs from different tests are not the same. To understand fully the meaning of an IQ, understanding the test from which it was derived is also necessary.

An alternative method of reporting results from intellectual assessments was presented. It was proposed that the reporting of standard IQs, even when accompanied by confidence intervals, is not preferential to simply reporting the conclusions that can be confidently arrived at by knowledge of the assessment results. One would expect that more than an intelligence test would be administered in all but the most superficial of psychological evaluations. The information from many sources will then need to be integrated with information from intelligence tests in order to arrive at a complete picture of the client. Breaking that picture back into isolated parts by focusing on individual test scores does not aid in the understanding of the whole client. Finally, future directions were considered. Perhaps, considering the bad press received by IQs, future tests that measure mental or scholastic ability will simply abandon the term. Some evidence of this trend was reported. Most authorities, however, perceive a need for tests like the current ones. With the stress on the prediction of academic failure, some standard score-generating instrument will do doubt exist in the years to come. With the recent advances in neuropsychology and standardized assessment through the use of microcomputers, it is hoped that we will be able to do an even better job of prediction in the future.

References

Ackerman, P. T., Peters, J. E., & Dykman, R. A. Children with specific learning disabilities: WISC profiles. *Journal of Learning Disabilities*, 1971, 4, 33–49.

American Psychological Association. *Casebook on ethical standards of psychologists*. Washington, D.C.:

American Psychological Association, 1967.

Anastasi, A. *Psychological testing.* (5th ed.) New York: Macmillan, 1982.

Barbanel, L., & Hoffenberg-Rutman, J. Attitudes toward job responsibilities and training satisfaction of school psychologists: A comparative study. *Psychology in the Schools,* 1974, **11,** 425–429.

Bereiter, C. IQ and elitism. *Interchange,* 1976–77, **7,** 36–44.

Berger, B. A new interpretation of the IQ controversy. *Public Interest,* 1978, **50,** 29–44.

Blaha, J., & Vance, H. B. The hierarchical factor structure of the WISC-R for learning disabled children. *Learning Disability Quarterly,* 1979, **2,** 71–75.

Boring, E. G. Intelligence as the tests test it. *New Republic,* 1923, **34,** 35–37.

Bossard, M. D., Reynolds, C. R., & Gutkin, T. B. A regression analysis of test bias on the Stanford-Binet intelligence scale. *Journal of Clinical Child Psychology,* 1980, **9,** 52–54.

Brown, A. L., & French, L. A. The zone of potential development: Implications for intelligence testing in the year 2000. *Intelligence,* 1979, **3,** 255–273.

Carlson, L., & Reynolds, C. R. Factor structure and specific variance of the WPPSI subtests at six age levels. *Psychology in the Schools,* 1981, **18,** 48–54.

Cattell, R. B. *The scientific use of factor analysis in behavioral and life sciences.* New York: Plenum, 1978.

Cleary, T. A., Humphreys, L. G., Kendrick, S. A., & Wesman, A. Educational uses of tests with disadvantaged students. *American Psychologists,* 1975, **30,** 15–41.

Cook, V. J., & Patterson, J. G. Psychologists in the schools of Nebraska: Professional functions. *Psychology in the Schools,* 1977, **14,** 371–376.

Cooke, A. *Allister Cooke's America.* New York: Knopf, 1974.

Danielson, F. H., & Davenport, C. B. *The hill folk.* Cold Spring Harbor, Long Island, N.Y.: Eugenics Record Office, 1912.

Dean, R. S. Patterns of emotional disturbance on the WISC-R. *Journal of Clinical Psychology,* 1977, **33,** 486–490.

Dean, R. S. Factor structure of the WISC-R with Anglos and Mexican-Americans. *Journal of School Psychology,* 1980, **18,** 234–239.

Dudek, F. J. The continuing misinterpretation of the standard error of measurement. *Psychological Bulletin,* 1979, **86,** 335–337.

Dugdale, R. L. *The Jukes.* (4th ed.) New York: G. P. Putman's Sons, 1910.

Fairchild, T. N. School psychological services: An empirical comparison of two models. *Psychology in the Schools,* 1976, **13,** 156–162.

Fass, P. S. The IQ: A cultural and historical framework. *American Journal of Education,* 1980, **88,** 431–458.

French, J. L. Intelligence: Its measurement and its relevance for education. *Professional Psychology,* 1979, **10,** 753–759.

Gaddes, W. H. Neurological implications for learning. In W. M. Cruikshank & D. P. Hallahan (Eds.), *Perceptual and learning disabilities in children, Vol. 1: Psychological practices.* Syracuse, N.Y.: Syracuse University Press, 1975.

Garrett, H. E. *Statistics in psychology and education.* (6th ed.) New York: Longmans, 1966.

Giebink, J. W., & Ringness, T. A. On the relevancy of training in school psychology. *Journal of School Psychology,* 1970, **8,** 43–47.

Goddard, H. H. *The Kalikak family, a study of the heredity of feeble-mindedness.* New York: Macmillan, 1914.

Goddard, H. H. *The criminal imbecile.* New York: Macmillan, 1915.

Golden, C. J., Hammeke, T. A., & Purisch, A. D. *The Luria-Nebraska Neuropsychological Battery.* Los Angeles: Western Psychological Services, 1980.

Gould, S. J. *The mismeasure of man.* New York: Norton, 1981.

Guilford, J. P. Fluid and crystallized intelligences: Two fanciful concepts. *Psychological Bulletin,* 1980, **88,** 406–412.

Gutkin, T. B. Some useful statistics for the interpretation of the WISC-R. *Journal of Consulting and Clinical Psychology,* 1978, **46,** 1,561–1,563.

Gutkin, T. B., & Reynolds, C. R. Factorial similarity of the WISC-R for Anglos and Chicanos referred for psychological services. *Journal of School Psychology,* 1980, **18,** 34–39.

Hale, R. L. The WISC-R as a predictor of WRAT performance. *Psychology in the Schools,* 1978, **15,** 172–175.

Hale, R. L. The utility of WISC-R subtest scores in discriminating among adequate and underachieving children. *Multivariate Behavioral Research,* 1979, **14,** 245–253.

Hale, R. L. Concurrent validity of the WISC-R factor scores. *Journal of School Psychology,* 1981, **19,** 274–278.

Hale, R. L. An examination for bias in the WISC-R across socioeconomic status. *Journal of School Psychology,* in press.

Hale, R. L., & Foltz, S. G. Prediction of academic achievement in handicapped children using a modified form of the Luria-Nebraska Pathognomic Scale and WISC-R Full Scale IQ. Unpublished manuscript, 1982.

Hale, R. L., & Landino, S. A. Utility of WISC-R subtest analysis in discriminating among groups of conduct problem, withdrawn, mixed, and nonproblem boys. *Journal of Consulting and Clinical Psychology,* 1981, **49,** 91–95.

Hale, R. L., & Raymond, M. R. Wechsler Intelligence Scale for Children—Revised (WISC-R) patterns of strengths and weaknesses as predictors of the intelligence-achievement relationship. *Diagnostique,* 1981, **7,** 35–42.

Hale, R. L., Raymond, M. R., & Gajar, A. H. Evaluating socioeconomic status bias in the WISC-R. *Journal of School Psychology,* in press.

Hale, R. L., & Saxe, J. Profile analysis of the Wechsler Intelligence Scale for Children-Revised. Unpublished manuscript, 1982.

Hindley, C. B., & Owen, C. F. The extent of individual changes in IQ for ages between 6 months and 17 years, in a British longitudinal sample. *Journal of Child Psychology and Psychiatry and Allied Disciplines,* 1978, **19,** 329–350.

Hirshoren, A., & Kavale, K. Profile analysis of the WISC-R: A continuing malpractice. *The Exceptional Child*, 1976, **23**, 83–87.

Horn, J. L. Trends in the measurement of intelligence. *Intelligence*, 1979, **3**, 229–239.

Huelsman, C. B., Jr. The WISC subtest syndrome for disabled readers. *Perceptual Motor Skills*, 1970, **30**, 535–550.

Hynd, G. W., & Obruzut, J. E. School neuropsychology. *Journal of School Psychology*, 1981, **19**, 45–49.

Hynd, G. W., Quackenbush, R., & Obrzut, J. E. Training school psychologists in neuropsychological assessment: Current practices and trends. *Journal of School Psychology*, 1980, **18**, 148–153.

Jamison, D., Suppes, P., & Wells, S. The effectiveness of alternative instruction media: A survey. *Review of Educational Research*, 1974, **44**, 1–67.

Jastak, J. F., & Jastak, S. R. *Manual, the Wide Range Achievement Test.* (Rev. ed.) Wilmington, Dl.: Guidance Associates of Delaware, 1976.

Jensen, A. R. *Bias in mental testing.* New York: Free Press, 1980.

Kaufman, A. S. Factor structure of the WISC-R at 11 age levels between 6½ and 16½ years. *Journal of Consulting and Clinical Psychology*, 1975, **43**, 133–147.

Kaufman, A. S. *Intelligent testing with the WISC-R.* New York: Wiley, 1979.

Kaufman, A. S., & Kaufman, N. L. The development and current status of the Kaufman Assessment Battery for Children (K-ABC). *Communique*, 1981, **9**, 2.

Keenan, L. A job analysis of school psychologists in the public schools of Massachusetts. *Psychology in the Schools*, 1964, **1**, 185–186.

Kelderman, H., Mellenbergh, G. J., & Elshout, J. J. Guilford's facet theory of intelligence: An empirical comparison of models. *Multivariate Behavioral Research*, 1981, **16**, 37–62.

Kownslar, A. O., & Frizzle, D. B. *Discovering American history.* New York: Holt, Rinehart, & Winston, 1967.

Lambert, N. M. Psychological evidence in Larry P. versus Wilson Riles. *American Psychologist*, 1981, **36**, 937–952.

MacKenzie, B. Hypothesized genetic racial differences in IQ: A criticism of three lines of evidence. *Behavior Genetics*, 1980, **10**, 225–234.

Madden, P. B. Intelligence tests on trial. *The School Psychology Review*, 1980, **9**, 149–153.

Marks, R. Providing for individual differences: A history of the intelligence testing movement in North America. *Interchange*, 1976-77, **1**, 3–16.

McMahon, R. C., & Kunce, J. T. A comparison of the factor structure of the WISC and WISC-R in normal and exceptional groups. *Journal of Clinical Psychology*, 1981, **37**, 408–410.

Miele, F. Cultural bias in the WISC. *Intelligence*, 1979, **3**, 149–164.

Morris, J. J., & Clarizio, S. Improvement in IQ of high risk, disadvantaged preschool children enrolled in a developmental program. *Psychological Reports*, 1977, **41**, 1,111–1,114.

Nagle, R. J., & Lazarus, S. C. The comparability of the WISC-R and WAIS among 16 year old EMR children. *Journal of School Psychology*, 1979, **17**, 362–367.

Nunnally, J. C. *Psychometric theory.* (2nd ed.) New York: McGraw-Hill, 1978.

Oakland, T., & Feigenbaum, D. Multiple sources of test bias on the WISC-R and the Bender Gestalt Test. *Journal of Consulting and Clinical Psychology*, 1979, **47**, 968–974.

Pastore, N. The army intelligence tests and Walter Lippmann. *Journal of the History of the Behavioral Sciences*, 1978, **14**, 316–327.

Peterson, C. R., & Hart, D. H. Factor structure of the WISC-R for a clinic referred population and specific subgroups. *Journal of Consulting and Clinical Psychology*, 1979, **47**, 643–645.

Potter, R. E. *The stream of American education.* New York: Van Nostrand Reinhold, 1967.

Pressey, S. L. Scale of attainment No. 1: An examination of achievement in the second grade. *Journal of Educational Research*, 1920, **1**, 572–581.

Rabin, A. I. Diagnostic use of intelligence tests. In B. B. Wolman (Ed.), *Handbook of clinical psychology.* New York: McGraw-Hill, 1965.

Ramanaiah, N. V., & Adams, M. L. Confirmatory analysis of the WAIS and the WPPSI. *Psychological Reports*, 1979, **45**, 351–355.

Ramanaiah, N. V., O'Donnell, J., & Ribich, F. Multiple-group factor analysis of the Wechsler Intelligence Scale for Children. *Journal of Clinical Psychology*, 1976, **32**, 829–830.

Reschly, D. J. WISC-R factor structures among Anglos, Blacks, Chicanos, and Native-American Papagos. *Journal of Consulting and Clinical Psychology*, 1978, **46**, 417–422.

Reschly, D. J. Psychological evidence in the Larry P. opinion: A case of right problem—wrong solution? *School Psychology Review*, 1980, **9**, 123–135.

Reschly, D. J., & Sabers, D. Analysis of test bias in four groups with the regression definition. *Journal of Educational Measurement*, 1979, **16**, 1–9.

Resnick, L. B. The future of IQ testing in education. *Intelligence*, 1979, **3**, 241–253.

Reynolds, C. R. The problem of bias in psychological assessment. In C. R. Reynolds & T. B. Gutkin (Eds.), *A handbook for school psychology.* New York: Wiley, 1982.

Reynolds, C. R., & Hartledge, L. C. Comparison of WISC and WISC-R regression lines for academic prediction with black and with white children. *Journal of Consulting and Clinical Psychology*, 1979, **47**, 589–591.

Rourke, B. P. Brain-behavior relationships in children with learning disabilities: A research program. *American Psychologist*, 1975, **30**, 911–920.

Salvia, J., & Ysseldyke, J. E. *Assessment in special and remedial education.* Boston: Houghton-Mifflin, 1978.

Sandoval, J. The WISC-R and internal evidence of test bias with minority groups. *Journal of Consulting and Clinical Psychology*, 1979, **47**, 919–927.

Sandoval, J., & Millie, M. Accuracy judgements of WISC-R item difficulties for minority groups. *Journal of Consulting and Clinical Psychology*, 1980, **48**, 249–253.

Sattler, J. M. *Assessment of children's intelligence.* (Rev. reprint.) Philadelphia: W. B. Saunders, 1974.

Sattler, J. M. *Assessment of children's intelligence and special abiities.* Boston: Allyn & Bacon, 1982.

Schmeiser, C. B., & Ferguson, R. L. Performance of black and white students on test materials containing content based on black and white cultures. *Journal of Educational Measurement,* 1978, **15**, 193–200.

Schooler, D. L., Beebe, M. C., & Koepke, T. Factor analysis of WISC-R scores for children identified as learning disabled, educable mentally impaired, and emotionally impaired. *Psychology in the Schools,* 1978, **15**, 478–485.

Schwarting, F. G. A comparison of the WISC and WISC-R. *Psychology in the Schools,* 1976, **13**, 139–141.

Silverstein, A. B. An alternative factor analytic solution for Wechsler's intelligence scales. *Educational and Psychological Measurement,* 1969, **29**, 763–767.

Skinner, H. A., & Lei, H. Modal profile analysis: A computer program for classification research. *Educational and Psychological Measurement,* 1980, **40**, 769–772.

Smith, M. D., Coleman, J. M., Dokecki, P. R., & Davis, E. E. Recategorized WISC-R scores of learning disabled children. *Journal of Learning Disabilities,* 1977, **10**, 437–443.

Sowell, T. *Ethnic America.* New York: Basic Books, 1981. (a)

Sowell, T. *Markets and minorities.* New York: Basic Books, 1981. (b)

Stern, W. *The psychological methods of testing intelligence.* Baltimore: Warwick & York, 1914.

Tabachnick, B. G. Test scatter on the WISC-R. *Journal of Learning Disabilities,* 1979, **12**, 626–628.

Terman, L. M. *The measurement of intelligence.* Boston: Houghton-Mifflin, 1916.

Thompson, R. J., Jr. The diagnostic utility of the WISC-R measures with children referred to a developmental evaluation center. *Journal of Consulting and Clinical Psychology,* 1980, **48**, 440–447.

Turnbull, W. W. Intelligence testing in the year 2000. *Intelligence,* 1979, **3**, 275–282.

Vance, H. B., Huelsman, C. B., & Wherry, R. J. The hierarchical factor structure of the Wechsler Intelligence Scale for Children as it relates to disadvantaged white and black children. *Journal of General Psychology,* 1976, **95**, 287–293.

Vance, H. B., Singer, M. C., & Engin, A. W. WISC-R subtest differences for males and female LD children and youth. *Journal of Clinical Psychology,* 1980, **36**, 953–957.

Vance, H. B., & Wallbrown, F. H. The structure of intelligence for black children: A hierarchical approach. *The Psychological Record,* 1978, **28**, 31–39.

Vance, H. B., Wallbrown, F. H., & Blaha, J. Determining WISC-R profiles for reading disabled children. *Journal of Learning Disabilities,* 1978, **11**, 656–761.

Vinsonhaler, J. F., & Bass, R. K. A summary of ten major studies of CAI drill and practice. *Educational Technology,* 1972, **12**, 29–32.

Wallbrown, F. H., Blaha, J., & Wherry, R. J. The hierarchical factor structure of the Wechsler Adult Intelligence Scale. *British Journal of Educational Psychology,* 1974, **44**, 47–56.

Watkins, M. W., & Webb, C. Computer assisted instruction with learning disabled students. *Educational Computer Magazine,* 1981, September–October, 24–27.

Wechsler, D. *The measurement of adult intelligence.* Baltimore: Williams & Wilkins, 1939.

Wechsler, D. *Manual for the Wechsler Intelligence Scale for Children.* New York: Psychological Corporation, 1949.

Wechsler, D. Cognitive, conative, and non-intellective intelligence. *American Psychologist,* 1950, **5**, 78–83.

Wechsler, D. *Manual for the Wechsler Adult Intelligence Scale.* New York: Psychological Corporation, 1955.

Wechsler, D. *Manual for the Wechsler Preschool and Primary Scale of Intelligence.* New York: Psychological Corporation, 1967.

Wechsler, D. *Manual for the Wechsler Intelligence Scale for Children-Revised.* New York: Psychological Corporation, 1974.

Wechsler, D. Intelligence defined and undefined. *American Psychologist,* 1975, **30**, 135–139.

Wechsler, D. *Manual for the Wechsler Adult Intelligence Scale-Revised.* New York: Psychological Corporation, 1981.

Wiggins, J. S. *Personality and prediction: Principles of personality assessment.* Menlo Park, Calif.: Addison-Wesley, 1973.

Woodcock, R. W. *Woodcock-Johnson Psycho-Educational Battery: Technical report.* Boston: Teaching Resources, 1977.

Yerkes, R. M. Psychological examining in the United States army. In R. M. Yerkes (Ed.), *Memoirs of the National Academy of Sciences,* Washington, D.C.: Government Printing Office, Vol. 15. 1921.

20 NEUROPSYCHOLOGICAL ASSESSMENT*

Barbara Pendleton Jones
Nelson Butters

Neuropsychological assessment is a field with roots in a number of different areas, including clinical psychology, behavioral neurology, experimental neuropsychology (as applied both to animals and man), and aphasiology.[1] As a body of methods, it is used to assess the individual's higher nervous system functioning as reflected in a variety of tasks and to address some or all of the following questions. Does the subject of the assessment show evidence of higher nervous system dysfunction? If so, is the probable locus of dysfunction diffuse or focal, and if focal, affecting which hemisphere(s) and lobe(s)? How severe is the degree of functional impairment in the various areas of cognition, perception, sensorimotor functions, and personality? Is the etiology acute or slowly progressive in onset, and is the course likely to be progressive, static, or admitting of some recovery? What is the nature of the neuropathology (some neuropsychologists are willing to make more specific diagnoses than others)? What are the likely practical consequences of any demonstrated neurological impairment for the individual's professional and interpersonal functioning and daily living activities? And finally, what are the recommendations for remediation? In some instances, neuropsychologists or clinical psychologists with neuropsychological training will become involved in the detailed planning of cognitive retraining and other remediation programs for neurologically impaired patients. And in some cases neuropsychological assessment may be performed at more than one point in time in order to monitor recovery or disease progression or to assess the effects of various treatment interventions.

While the above outline of the scope of neuropsychological assessment has delineated its clinical application, the methods of neuropsychological assessment are also utilized in research on the effects of brain damage. However, because the interests of the readers of the present volume are likely to be oriented toward clinical applications, the focus of this chapter will be on clinical neuropsychological assessment.

*This chapter was funded in part by the Medical Research Service of the Veterans Administration. The authors wish to thank Mrs. Patti Miliotis for help in preparing this manuscript.

[1] Davison (1974) presents a useful discussion of the relation between clinical neuropsychology and allied fields, and of the differences between traditional clinical psychological and clinical neuropsychological approaches to the assessment of brain damage.

Neuropyschological assessment cannot be competently or responsibly undertaken by the professional without some knowledge of neuroanatomy and neuropathology and the basic principles of the neurology of behavior. While even a summary of these foundations is beyond the scope of this chapter, several authorities have attempted to construct reasonably comprehensive theories of brain-behavior relationships (Geschwind, 1974; Hécaen & Albert, 1978; Luria, 1980; Pribram, 1971). As outlined in a recent report by the Task Force on Education, Accreditation, and Credentialing of the International Neuropsychological Society (1981), the clinical neuropsychologist should also be knowledgeable in the following areas: CNS effects of systemic disorders, developmental neuropsychology, the neuropsychology of aging, behavioral psychopharmacology, psychophysiology, sociocultural determinants of performance, personality assessment, and principles of test construction, administration, and interpretation.

This survey of the field of neuropsychological assessment will begin with a brief history, proceed to a presentation and critique of the major contemporary methods, and end with a discussion of future trends and some conclusions on the state of the art.

History of Neuropsychological Assessment

Early Investigations in the East and West

If neuropsychological assessment is defined as the application of psychometric methods to the study of behavioral manifestations of neuropathological conditions, the field can be seen to have its origins in the first quarter of the twentieth century. In the West one might even trace its beginnings to Binet and Simon's testing of brain-damaged and retarded children in Paris in 1905. However, the first studies in the West to use psychological tests in the investigation of the behavioral effects of specified lesions seem to have appeared in the 1930s and 1940s. To cite only some of the better known examples, there were studies of intellectual impairment in aphasia (Weisenburg & McBride, 1935); the effects of frontal lobe lesions on intelligence and other higher functions (Columbia-Greystone

Associates, 1949; Hebb, 1939, 1942; Rylander, 1940); visuospatial impairments in patients with right hemisphere lesions (Paterson & Zangwill, 1944, 1945); the effects of brain lesions on abstraction abilities (Goldstein & Scheerer, 1941); and memory impairments in various amnesic syndromes (Zangwill, 1943). As is evident in the titles of these publications, these studies were for the most part ones in which psychometric methods were used to pursue a topic with a specific focus. In most instances, these early investigators were interested in studying particular functions and chose their tests accordingly; the concept of a neuropsychological battery was not pursued.

In Russia, interest in the behavioral concomitants of neuropathological changes was exemplified in the founding of the Psychoneurological Institute of Bekhterev in 1907. In the early 1930s, A. R. Luria began his neuropsychological studies under Vygotskii; Luria's contribution to clinical neuropsychology will be examined in several following sections.

The Contribution of Ward Halstead

An important line of development in neuropsychology assessment began with the work of Ward C. Halstead. Halstead was a psychologist who was interested in studying the effects of brain damage on a broad range of cognitive, perceptual, and sensorimotor functions. Having established a neuropsychological laboratory at the University of Chicago in 1935, he began his work by carrying out field observational studies of brain-damaged subjects in both work and social settings in order to determine which behavioral characteristics should be measured through formal tests. He then assembled a battery of psychological tests, some modified revisions of existing measures and some newly developed tests, administered them to a number of brain-damaged subjects referred by neurosurgeons and other medical specialists, and subjected the results to factor analytic studies performed by both Holzinger and Thurstone. The results of these analyses led Halstead to the selection of seven tests (10 variables) for inclusion in his neuropsychologic battery (1947); the Category Test, Tactual Performance Test, Speech Sounds Perception Test, Seashore Rhythm Test, Finger Oscillation Test, Critical Flicker Fusion Test, and Time Sense Test.[2] It was also on the basis of these

---

[2]For a description of the tests retained in the current Halstead-Reitan Battery see a subsequent section.

factor analytic studies that Halstead developed his four factor theory of human performance (Halstead, 1947), which included a central integrative field factor C, representing the "organized experience of the individual," whose parameters were "probably reflected" in intelligence test measurements; an abstraction factor A; a power function P (later thought to be an indication of alertness or vigilance); and a directional factor D, specifying the sensory modality or motoric pathway involved.

In his work as a neuropsychologist, Halstead (1950, 1951) developed the concept of "biological intelligence," which subsumed the four factors enumerated above and denoted a basic capacity for controlled adaptability which he felt was not measured by traditional intelligence tests. He was particularly interested in the contributions of the frontal lobes to "biological intelligence," and collected data suggesting that a broad range of performances, which he thought to be reflective of "biological intelligence," was most impaired in patients with frontal lobe excisions (Halstead & Shure, 1954; Shure & Halstead, 1958). The concept of "biological intelligence" never found an enthusiastic audience among other neuropsychologists, probably because of its lack of specificity, and Halstead's overinsistence on it may have detracted from his contributions to the field. His work was of value in that he advocated sampling a wide range of behaviors in order to assess the effects of brain damage; he assembled a battery and performed systematic studies using groups of patients with focal brain lesions in order to observe the effects of lesions in various areas of the cortex; and he undertook to train other neuropsychologists.

Ralph Reitan and the Halstead-Reitan Battery

Halstead's work was continued and expanded by his former student Ralph M. Reitan, who established a neuropsychology laboratory at Indiana University Medical Center in 1951. Reitan (1955, 1966b, 1969) modified Halstead's original battery by deleting two tests (Critical Flicker Fusion and Time Sense Tests) and adding several others (Trail Making Test, Strength of Grip test, Sensory-Perceptual Examination, Tactile Perception, and

Modified Halstead-Wepman Aphasia Screening Test); in addition a Wechsler-Bellevue Scale (Form 1) and MMPI now were routinely performed as part of the Halstead-Reitan Battery (HRB).[3] During and after his modification of Halstead's original battery, Reitan administered his set of tests to a large number of patients with focal and diffuse brain lesions. He also standardized his tests on a group of hospitalized control patients. As he worked with individual patients, he came to use four "methods of inference" to analyze his results. First, as Halstead had done, he looked at the overall level of performance as reflected in the "Impairment Index" (a function of how many scores fall below selected cutting scores). Second, he noted the presence of pathognomonic signs (e.g., inability to draw simple figures) which have a low rate of occurrence but, according to Reitan, are almost invariably associated with brain damage when they do occur. Third, he analyzed the pattern of performance, or the relative strengths and weaknesses in a subject's test scores, which frequently conveyed information about the locus and/or nature of the brain damage; such pattern analysis will be a familiar concept to clinicians accustomed to drawing inferences from WAIS Verbal IQ/Performance IQ discrepancies and WAIS intertest scatter. And fourth, he compared scores on motor, sensory, and sensory-perceptual tasks involving the two sides of the body, as a means of helping to determine both the presence or absence of brain damage (the reasoning was that nonorganic causes of poor performance such as inadequate motivation or emotional disturbance are not likely to affect one side of the body more than the other) and the laterality of the lesions.

Since the late 1950s, Reitan and his collaborators have been using the HRB and related forms in human neuropsychological research (for reviews, see Klove, 1974; Reitan, 1966b). Most of their studies have involved localization (or the ability of the battery to specify the hemisphere and lobe of the lesion), process considerations (or the battery's discrimination of acute, relatively static, and chronic forms of brain damage), and diagnosis of type of brain damage (e.g., intrinsic tumor, extrinsic tumor, cerebrovascular lesion, etc.).

Reitan has had many students, who in turn have trained other psychologists in the Halstead-Reitan method. Indeed, a recent survey of meth-

---

[3]According to Reitan (Davison, 1974), the proper name of the battery is the Halstead Neuropsychological Test Battery for Adults; however, the name Halstead-Reitan has become so widely used (e.g., Boll, 1981) that it will be the term applied here.

ods employed by clinical neuropsychologists in the United States (Hartlage, Chelune, & Tucker, 1980) indicated that this was the most commonly performed battery in the field.

The Post-War Growth of Experimental Neuropsychology and Its Impact on Clinical Assessment

Between the pre-war and post-war decades there was a noteworthy increase in the number of neuropsychological studies being performed, and a more remarkable leap occurred with the advent of the 1960s and the general acceleration of the pace of scientific research both in the United States and abroad. These studies were to prove influential in neuropsychology, not only for the advancement in the understanding of brain-behavior relationships which they provided, but also for their contribution to methodology. While many very significant contributions were made to neuropsychological assessment during this period, those of a few groups stand out.

BRENDA MILNER, DOREEN KIMURA, AND THE MONTREAL NEUROLOGICAL INSTITUTE-MCGILL UNIVERSITY GROUP

From the late 1950s to the present, Brenda Milner and her colleagues at the Montreal neurological Institute and McGill University have been engaged in a series of neuropsychological investigations of behavioral change in neurosurgical patients with focal lesions. Many of these patients came to surgery for the excision of epileptogenic tissue after other means of seizure control had failed. Both the effects of the preoperative focal lesions and those of the surgical excisions themselves have been studied in a remarkably fruitful and influential sequence of experiments. In their series of studies on the effects of temporal lobe lesions, for example, Milner and Kimura found evidence of impaired verbal learning in patients with left temporal lobe lesions and of impaired visual (nonverbal) perception and visual (nonverbal) learning in those with right temporal lobe lesions (Kimura, 1963; Milner, 1958, 1960, 1967, 1968, 1970; Milner & Kimura, 1964). Bilateral mesial temporal (hippocampal) lesions were found to be followed by severe and permanent anterograde amnesia with some degree of retrograde amnesia (Milner, 1958, 1966, 1970; Scoville & Milner, 1957). The role of the temporal lobes in audition was also studied, with the finding of deficits in timbre discrimination and tonal

memory after right temporal lobectomy (Milner, 1962) and impaired overall performance on a dichotic listening task (digits) after left temporal lobectomy (Kimura, 1961). Kimura (1961) also noted a right ear advantage on dichotic digits testing in normal adults and normal children down to the age of 5 and hypothesized that this was due to left hemisphere dominance for speech in the majority of subjects and the greater effectiveness of the contralateral auditory pathway under conditions of dichotic presentation.

Other important findings by this group have included those of impaired abstraction and set shifting on the Wisconsin Card Sorting Task by patients with either left or right frontal lobe excisions, decreased verbal fluency (on Thurstone's Word Fluency Test) in left frontal excision patients, and decreased nonverbal fluency (on a fluency for designs task) and spatial learning in patients with right frontal excisions (Jones-Gotman & Milner, 1977; Milner, 1964). From the perspective of neuroscience, Milner's greatest contribution may be her convincing demonstration that the material-specific memory deficits of her temporal lobe patients are correlated with the amount of hippocampal tissue excised during the operation (Milner, 1970, 1971). The linking of verbal and nonverbal memory deficits with the left and right hippocampi respectively remains the cornerstone of all current research on the neuropsychology of memory.

From these illuminating studies, several techniques either designed by Milner or her colleagues or first utilized by them in neuropsychological research have come into use for neuropsychological assessment purposes. These include Kimura's Recurring Figures Test, the analogous Visual Verbal Memory Test, dichotic listening tests, the Thurstone type of verbal fluency test (Controlled Word Association Test), the Jones-Gotman fluency for designs test, and the Wisconsin Card Sorting Test.

HANS-LUKAS TEUBER AND HIS COLLEAGUES

In the years following World War II, Hans-Lukas Teuber undertook a series of studies to investigate the effects of focal cerebral lesions on a variety of visual and spatial abilities. Working first at New York University College of Medicine and later at the Massachusetts Institute of Technology, he collaborated in these studies with Josephine Semmes, Sidney Weinstein, Lila Ghent, Mortimer Mishkin, William Battersby, Morris Bender, and others. The patient populations in these studies consisted of World War II veterans with penetrating missile wounds. Localization information was obtained from surgeon's records at debridement and from cranial x-rays and was obviously far inferior to that obtainable with current methods. Despite the limitations imposed on the generalizability of their findings by the nature of this population, these studies made significant contributions to human neuropsychology and were influential both in experimental and clinical settings. For example, in a summary discussion of these studies, Teuber (1972) related occipital lobe lesions to abnormalities in the "immediate presentation of visual space" as reflected in extensive studies of visual field defects (Teuber, Battersby, & Bender, 1960). Frontal lobe lesions, he concluded in the same review, were linked to impairment of the "mechanisms for compensation for changes in spatial order, under voluntary changes in posture"; this conclusion was based on studies involving adjustment of a luminous line to the vertical under conditions of body tilt (Teuber & Mishkin, 1954) or adjustment to visual displacements induced by prismatic spectacles under conditions of self-produced movement (Held, 1961). Teuber related parietal lobe lesions to impairments in the representation of spatial relations as reflected in studies of route-finding ability (Semmes, Weinstein, Ghent, & Teuber, 1955). Teuber was particularly interested in the role of the frontal lobes and integrated a number of diverse findings (e.g., impairments in the detection of hidden figures, deficits on a "Personal Orientation Test", and the above-mentioned impairments in compensation for spatial changes) in a theory of corollary discharge (Teuber, 1972).

The work of Teuber in human neuropsychology was particularly valuable in its attempt to integrate findings from human studies with the results of animal experiments and to articulate a *theoretical* basis for current and future research. Teuber was influential in infusing the field of neuropsychological assessment with a spirit of scientific inquiry at a time when it might well have proceeded to a set of repetitive diagnostic procedures lacking adequate conceptual bases. Some of the tests used by Teuber and his colleagues in their studies are still in current use (e.g., Thurstone's Version of Gottschaldt's Hidden Figures Test, optical illusions such as the Double Necker Cube, the Field of Search Test, the Personal Orientation Test, and the Extrapersonal Orientation Test (Lezak, 1976).

THE NEUROPSYCHOLOGY UNIT OF THE BOSTON VETERANS ADMINISTRATION MEDICAL CENTER AND THE BOSTON UNIVERSITY SCHOOL OF MEDICINE

Another active and prominent group of neuropsychologists assembled in the affiliated clinical and research programs of the Boston VA Medical Center and the Boston University School of Medicine. Under the leadership of Harold Goodglass, Edith Kaplan, and Nelson Butters, this group has carried out a large number of influential studies over a period of nearly 30 years and has made important contributions to clinical neuropsychology in the areas of aphasia (e.g., Goodglass & Kaplan, 1963, 1972; Goodglass & Quadfasel, 1954; Goodglass, Quadfasel, & Timberlake, 1964), apraxia (Goodglass & Kaplan, 1963, 1979), amnesia (e.g., Albert, Butters, & Levin, 1979; Butters & Cermak, 1975, 1976, 1980; Cermak & Butters, 1972; Oscar-Berman, 1973; Oscar-Berman & Samuels, 1977), dementia (Albert, Butters, & Brandt, 1981; Butters, Sax, Montgomery, & Tarlow, 1978; Oscar-Berman & Zola-Morgan, 1980a, 1980b), aging (Albert & Kaplan, 1980), and the effects of brain damage on the chemical senses (Jones, Butters, Moskowitz, & Montgomery, 1978; Jones, Moskowitz, & Butters, 1975; Potter & Butters, 1980). Some of the tests developed by this group for research purposes have been widely adopted for general clinical neuropsychological assessment (e.g., the Boston Diagnostic Aphasia Examination [Goodglass & Kaplan, 1972] and the Boston Retrograde Amnesia Battery [Albert, Butters, & Levin, 1979]).

The research efforts of this group have consistently stressed two points with regard to neuropsychological assessment. First, *aphasia, amnesia,* and *dementia* are not unitary disorders each characterized by a single pattern of cognitive deficits. Rather, these neurological disorders are comprised of numerous subtypes, each of which can be characterized by a specific neuropsychological profile. Thus, Goodglass and Kaplan's Boston Diagnostic Aphasia Examination (1972) allows the clinician to differentiate Broca's, Wernicke's, and conduction aphasias on the basis of a standardized battery of tasks of expressive language, comprehension, repetition, reading, and writing. Similarly, much of the clinical research of Butters and Cermak and of Oscar-Berman has successfully demonstrated that the anterograde and retrograde memory disorders of amnesic and demented patients can be differentiated along a number of qualitative and quantitative dimensions (for review, see Butters &

Cermak, 1980; Oscar-Berman, 1980). Second, the Boston group has consistently stressed the importance of searching for the qualititative processes underlying a particularly quantitative score. For example, patients with left or right hemisphere lesions may both earn poor quantitative scores on constructional and drawing tasks, but a close scrutiny of the patients' performances would show that the two patient groups are failing for quite different reasons. Patients with right hemisphere lesions may be unable to grasp the overall contour or "gestalt" of a figure, while the patients with left hemisphere damage may encounter difficulty in the analysis of the inner detail of the figure after successfully reproducing the external configuration. It is the contention of the Boston group that without such qualitative analyses of cognitive disorders much vital diagnostic and prognostic information would be lost (Albert & Kaplan, 1980; Butters, 1980; Butters, Miliotis, Albert, & Sax, 1982; Goodglass & Kaplan, 1972, 1979).

It is important to note that due to the persistence with which the Boston group has applied its process-achievement approach to patient populations, numerous theoretical insights and discoveries concerning cerebral dominance (e.g., Butters & Barton, 1970; Gardner, 1975; Gardner, Ling, Flamm, & Silverman, 1975; Oscar-Berman, Goodglass, & Cherlow, 1973; Shai, Goodglass, & Barton, 1972; Wapner, Hamby, & Gardner, 1981; Winner & Gardner, 1977), the linguistic features of aphasia (e.g., Blumstein, Cooper, Goodglass, Statlander, & Gottlieb, 1980; Blumstein, Cooper, Zurif, & Caramazza, 1977; Caramazza & Zurif, 1976; Milberg & Blumstein, 1981; Zurif, 1980; Zurif & Caramazza, 1976), and the role of encoding in memory (e.g., Cermak & Butters, 1972, 1976; Cermak, Butters, & Moreines, 1974; Cermak & Reale, 1978) have had a major impact upon experimental as well as clinical neuropsychology. Their work best exemplifies the close interdependence of clinical and experimental psychology.

ARTHUR L. BENTON

Beginning with the publication of the now widely-used Benton Visual Retention Test in 1945, A. L. Benton of the University of Iowa has made a valuable series of contributions to human neuropsychology. Among the problems that he has addressed in his experimental and clinical studies are visual memory deficits; the varieties of visuoconstructive disorders; impairments in facial recognition; deficits in right-left discrimination, finger localization, and number operations; the diagnosis and

measurement of aphasic disorders; and differential effects of frontal lobe disease. While his contributions to the field are too numerous to list, some examples are illustrative. In studies of facial discrimination, Benton and Van Allen (1968, 1972) demonstrated that impairment of facial discrimination and prosopagnosia were separate clinicial entities, and that the former occurred more than twice as often in patients with right-hemisphere lesions as in those with left-hemisphere lesions. In the area of constructional apraxia, Benton was able to demonstrate that whereas impairments in two-dimensional block construction (e.g., WAIS Block Design) were equally frequent in left-hemisphere and right-hemisphere lesion patients, defective three dimensional block construction occurred more than twice as frequently in patients with right-hemisphere lesions as in those with left-hemisphere lesions. Interestingly, of those left-hemisphere lesion patients who did demonstrate impaired three-dimensional block construction, a high percentage showed a receptive aphasic impairment (Benton, 1967). In a study of differential behavioral effects of left, right, or bilateral frontal lobe lesions; differential impairments in three-dimensional block construction and design copying in patients with right frontal or bilateral frontal lobe disease, Benton (1968) was able to show differential impairments in verbal association fluency in patients with left, right or bilateral frontal lobe lesions; differential impairments in three-dimensional block construction and design copying in patients with right frontal or bilateral frontal lobe lesions; and differential impairments in paired-associate learning and temporal orientation in bilateral frontal lobe patients.

Among the tests designed by Benton and his colleagues, a number have come into wide use in clinical neuropsychology: the Revised Visual Retention Test (Benton, 1963), the Neurosensory Center Comprehensive Examination for Aphasia (Spreen & Benton, 1969), the Test of Three-Dimensional Constructional Praxis (Benton, 1973), and the Test of Facial Recognition (Benton & Van Allen, 1968). Benton has trained a number of neuropsychologists and has been a distinguished leader in the field of neuropsychological assessment.

A.R. LURIA AND THE LURIA-NEBRASKA NEUROPSYCHOLOGICAL BATTERY

The contributions of Soviet psychologists to the field of neuropsychology were not widely recognized in the West until the publication in 1966 of the English translation of *Higher Cortical Func-*

tions in Man by A. R. Luria. As has been noted, Luria had begun his neuropsychological studies under Vygotskii in the 1930s and subsequently was associated with the Burkenko Neurosurgical Institute in Moscow for many years until his death in 1977. During his long career, Luria worked with a large number of head-injured war veterans as well as with other types of neurological and neurosurgical patients and developed an extensive repertoire of tests for neuropsychological assessment. Whereas the thrust of clinical neuropsychology in the West had been to *measure* the abilities reflective of the integrity of various cortical areas, Luria's emphasis was more on theory-building. He articulated a theory of functional systems in the brain which avoided the worst excesses of both localizationism and holism, and he devised corresponding principles for the evaluation of brain functioning. For example, he advocated breaking complex functions down into the simplest testable components and examining these behavioral components separately in order to see what portions of a functional system were compromised. His methods more resembled those of the neurologist than the psychologist, in that his tests had generally not been standardized or subjected to reliability and validity studies; evaluation procedures were more qualitative than quantitative; and the selection of tests, methods of administration, and scoring criteria were tailored to the individual patient. While these considerations and others limited the application of his methods in the West, his comprehensive theoretical model excited considerable interest.

In 1975, Anna-Lise Christensen, a Danish psychologist, published a detailed description of Luria's method of neuropsychological assessment along with a manual and a set of stimulus cards, without, however, actually attempting to standardize examination procedures (Christensen, 1975). She rather advocated the kind of flexibility that Luria preferred.

The currently much-publicized Luria-Nebraska Battery was developed in an attempt to standardize and validate Luria's procedures (Golden, 1981a, 1981b; Golden, Hammeke, & Purisch, 1978). Charles Golden and his colleagues began with the several hundred items presented by Christensen and administered them first to normal controls and later to neurological patients in addition to normal and psychiatric controls. After discarding items that failed to discriminate between normal and brain-damaged subjects, they were left with a battery of 269 items which could

be administered in two to three hours. Subsequent studies have undertaken to establish the reliability and validity of the battery, as well as to demonstrate the utility of the battery in localizing lesions and in specifying the type of neurological disorder. The Luria-Nebraska Neuropsychological Battery receives further consideration below.

Contemporary Methods in Neuropsychological Assessment

Batteries versus Individualized Approaches: General Considerations

A major dichotomy in the field of neuropsychological assessment is characterized by the use of either a uniform battery for all patients or an individualized approach. Practitioners of an individualized approach usually administer a small, core group of tests to all patients, and they then select further tests for the optimal elucidation of the referral questions and issues that may have been raised in the initial stage of testing.

Batteries undoubtedly have some advantages. These include relative comprehensiveness in the range of functions they sample. They greatly facilitate the combination of research with clinical objectives in that the same data base will automatically be compiled for all patients. They facilitate the use of technicians for the administration of tests, since no expertise is needed for the selection of appropriate assessment measures.

A serious disadvantage of batteries is that they may be providing redundancy of information in some areas of functioning while achieving insufficient exploration of other areas. For example, in the case of a patient who achieves a Verbal IQ of 120, it is hardly necessary to administer a complete aphasia screening battery (although some special language functions, such as word finding, should still be assessed). On the other hand, a patient with a true aphasia by no means will be properly evaluated with the use of an aphasia screening device contained in a battery. A further disadvantage of batteries that is related to the problem of redundancy of information is that of *cost-effectiveness*. Some batteries are sufficiently time consuming that it is becoming increasingly difficult to justify (and recover) the expense incurred in testing, even when technicians are employed for administration and scoring.

A final disadvantage of batteries is that there is usually no opportunity to modify assessment procedures over time to reflect the now rapid advances in the field of human neuropsychology through research. Batteries therefore tend to show an insufficient reflection of recent discoveries and concepts in neuropsychology.

The assets and liabilities of an individualized approach to neuropsychological assessment tend to be the reverse of those noted for batteries. Among advantages of individualized approaches one may list efficiency: in areas where performance in the core group of test demonstrates intact functioning, further tests need not be administered. By the same token, in-depth analysis of areas of impairment may be achieved, as the test selection is tailored to this end. Currency is an important asset to this kind of approach; as research provides more precise instruments for demonstrating and measuring specific types of impairment attendant upon brain lesions, these new instruments can become part of the neuropsychologist's repertoire. Finally, because test selection is not automatic but must be determined in accordance with sophisticated knowledge of brain-behavior relationships, and because there are no rules (much less automated systems) for interpretation of results, use of individualized approaches tends in general to be associated with a higher level of training and experience in neuropsychological assessments.

Disadvantages of the individualized approach include the examiner's inability to rely on the technicians for administration of all tests (some would see this as an advantage) and the length of time required for training in this method. With individualized approaches there is less ease in combining research with clinical objectives, since different patients will have been given different selections of tests.

Now that consideration has been given to some general characteristics of batteries and individualized approaches, the major batteries in current use will be described, followed by a section outlining several well-known individual approaches. Obviously space limitations have necessitated the omission of some batteries and many individualized approaches.

Batteries

HALSTEAD-REITAN NEUROPSYCHOLOGICAL TEST BATTERIES

Composition of the Batteries. As recounted in the historical section, Ralph Reitan's (1969) modification of Ward Halstead's battery of tests (Reitan,

1955, 1966b, 1969) resulted in the now widely used Halstead-Reitan Neuropsychological Test Battery for Adults (HRB). This battery is applicable to individuals aged 15 and older. Also in use are the Halstead Neuropsychological Test Battery for Children (a revision of the adult battery used for children 9 to 14 years old), and the Reitan-Indiana Test Battery for Children (used for 5 to 8 year olds).

The complete version of the HRB now consists of the following tests (for a more complete description see Boll, 1981):

- *Halstead Category Test* — a nonverbal test requiring the formulation of abstract principles for categorizing stimulus displays of visual figures. According to Boll (1981), the test "taps current learning skill, abstract concept formation and mental efficiency."
- *Tactual Performance Test* — a form board test performed in a blindfolded condition with the preferred hand, nonpreferred hand, and both hands. The test is thought to assess "motor speed and the use of tactile and kinesthetic cues to enhance psychomotor coordination, learning, response to the unfamiliar, and . . . (incidental memory)." (Boll, 1981).
- *Rhythm Test* — a rhythm discrimination test that taps "nonverbal auditory perception, attention, and sustained concentration" (Boll, 1981).
- *Speech Sounds Perception Test* — a test of the ability to identify auditorily presented nonsense words. It is thought to measure "auditory verbal perception, auditory-visual coordination of language processing, and sustained attention and concentration . . ." (Boll, 1981).
- *Finger Oscillation Test* — a test of finger-tapping speed, performed with each hand.
- *Trail Making Test* — a test requiring connection of consecutively numbered circles scattered on a page (Trails A) and connection in alternating sequence of numbered and lettered circles scattered on a page (Trails B). The test is thought to assess psychomotor speed, visual scanning, sequencing ability, and the ability to maintain and shift sets.
- *Strength of Grip Test* — a measure of grip strength taken on a hand dynamometer with each hand.
- *Sensory-Perceptual Examination* (Tactile, Auditory, and Visual) — tests of the ability to perceive unilateral stimuli and double (bilateral) simultaneous stimuli to the right and left sides of the body in the tactile, auditory, and visual modalities.

- *Tactile Perception* — tests of tactile finger localization and graphesthesia (deciphering numbers traced on the subject's fingertips while his eyes are closed).
- *Modified Halstead-Wepman Aphasia Screening Test* — a brief screening device of both language and selected non-language abilities.
- *Wechsler Adult Intelligence Scale*
- *Minnesota Multiphasic Personality Inventory*

In the Halstead Neuropsychological Test Battery for Children and the Reitan-Indiana Neuropsychological Test Battery for Children, some of these tests have been modified, some have been retained without alteration, and some have been omitted (for a more complete description, see Boll, 1981); a Wide Range Achievement Test is usually added to the children's batteries.

Methods of Scoring and Interpretation. Perhaps most commonly used is the method of scoring and interpretation developed by Reitan and described in the historical section above. To recapitulate, in using this method the evaluator examines the *level of performance* (reflected in the Impairment Index), the *pattern of performance*, the presence or absence of *pathognomonic signs*, and the *right-left comparison* (relative performances on measures of motor, sensory, and perceptual functioning involving the right and left sides of the body).

It is worth noting that this method of scoring and interpretation, as utilized by Reitan and many of its practitioners, contains a large element of subjective evaluation and is therefore in some measure dependent on the examiner's level of clinical experience and training. For example, the interpreter must make a judgment about what constitutes "pathognomonic signs," and similarly, the evaluation of the pattern of performance and the significance of the right-left comparisons is largely subjective. Reitan (1974) acknowledged that, despite an impressive record of diagnostic accuracy with regard to localization and lesion type when HRB results are qualitatively assessed by a trained evaluator, statistical analyses of test results on groups of brain-damaged patients with focal and diffuse lesions of differing etiologies have generally shown comparatively few significant differences.

In an attempt to objectify clinical inference in the analysis of HRB results, several researchers have developed semi-actuarial systems of interpretation (Adams, 1974; Finkelstein, 1976; Russell, Neuringer, & Goldstein, 1970). Russell et al. developed a neuropsychological key approach. Briefly, in a manner somewhat analogous to that employed by biologists to determine the class into which a species or individual fits (the taxonomic key), they constructed neuropsychological keys based on verbalized rules of inference used by neuropsychologists. Two keys were constructed, one for lateralization of brain damage and one for several major process categories of brain damage (acute, static, and congenital). These keys could be run via computer program when the data from the HRB (with some modifications) were entered. In a recent study comparing the diagnostic accuracy of the Russell et al. system with that of two trained clinicians (Heaton, Grant, Anthony, & Lehman, 1981), it was found that the clinicians were more accurate than the automated system in predicting presence and laterality of lesions but less accurate in predicting chronicity; neither clinicians nor automated procedure exceeded baserate predictions on chronicity. The authors rightly pointed out that as yet the quasi-actuarial method is somewhat primitive; cut-off scores are not adjusted to take account of such critical variables as age and education; test score cut-offs and patterns have not been empirically derived; and base rates of lesion occurrence are not taken into account in the system. In addition to these objective systems of HRB interpretation, alternative methods (e.g., Kiernan & Matthews, 1976; Swiercinsky & Warnock, 1977) have been proposed.

Advantages and Disadvantages. In an assessment of the advantages and disadvantages of the Halstead-Reitan neuropsychological test batteries, it should first be pointed out that Reitan and his followers (e.g., Boll, 1981; Reitan, 1974) emphatically deny that the primary function of these methods is the neurodiagnostic function. Rather, they see these batteries primarily as techniques for research in evaluating brain-behavior relationships. For both purposes the batteries have the advantage of sampling a wide range of functions (intellectual and cognitive, visual-spatial, sensory-perceptual, motor, personality, etc.) by means of tests that have been standardized and normed. Studies have indicated that presence or absence of brain damage can be predicted on the basis of standard HRB summary indices with 70 to 90 percent accuracy (Anthony, Heaton, & Lehman, 1980; Russell et al., 1970; Vega & Parsons, 1967; Wheeler, Burke, & Reitan, 1963).

Furthermore, when dealing with brain-damaged patients, trained HRB clinicians can make inferences as to lesion localization and chronicity with considerable success (for reviews, see Klöve, 1974; Reitan, 1966a). Success in specifying localization and chronicity (process) requires extensive clinical experience and "intuitive" decisions, and recent attempts to use actuarial systems for such specifications have met with disappointing results (e.g., Anthony, Heaton, & Lehman, 1980).

It is important to note that the success of the HRB in determining the presence or absence of organic brain damage declines when the test is applied to psychiatric patients. Heaton and his colleagues have recently reviewed the literature concerning neuropsychological test performances in psychiatric patients (Heaton, Baade, & Johnson, 1978; Heaton, & Crowley, 1981), and Malec (1978) has specifically reviewed neuropsychological assessment of schizophrenia *versus* brain damage. Briefly, while the HRB (and many other neuropsychological tests) performs acceptably in discriminating between the less severe and intractible forms of psychiatric illness and organic brain damage, the HRB and related forms (again, like many other tests) perform at little better than a chance level in discriminating between chronic or process schizoophrenia and organic brain damage (Lacks, Colbert, Harrow, & Levine, 1970; Watson, Thomas, Anderson, & Felling, 1968). While bearing in mind the possibility that schizophrenics, although lacking structural brain lesions, may have some other form of cerebral abnormality (e.g., biochemical), neuropsychologists should ideally be able to distinguish between patterns of neuropsychological impairment commonly seen in psychiatric patients and patterns that would strongly suggest structural brain lesions.

Other disadvantages of the HRB include its length and costliness, its relative lack of portability, and the absence of measures for the assessment of memory. With regard to the time required for administration, Boll (1981) has recently stated that the adult battery "requires about 5 hours . . . but frequently as little as 4 hours for other than the most impaired 20% of the medical center population" (p. 37). Given that it is the most impaired individuals who will usually be referred for neuropsychological testing, one must anticipate frequent overruns of the five-hour limit. Many experienced neuropsychologists will supplement the HRB measures with additional tests in order to gain a more comprehensive data base; this approach, while serving the interests of the individual patient, may not be practicable in many settings because of time and cost limitations.

THE LURIA-NEBRASKA
NEUROPSYCHOLOGICAL BATTERY

Composition of the Battery. As currently published, the Luria-Nebraska Neuropsychological Battery (LNNB) contains 269 items comprising 11 content scales. Three other scales, composed of items from among the content scales, are delineated in the manual (Pathognomonic scale, Left Hemisphere scale, Right Hemisphere scale). As in the case of the MMPI, the number of scales that can be devised using the items is not limited to the original group, and research on experimental scales is proceeding. The 11 content scales are as follows:

- *Motor Functions:* items assessing unilateral and bilateral (hand) motor speed and coordination, various aspects of praxis, motor alternation and inhibition, and verbal control of motor movements.
- *Rhythm and Pitch:* items evaluating pitch and rhythm discrimination and reproduction.
- *Tactile and Kinesthetic Function:* items assessing position sense, tactile discrimination, extinction, graphesthesia, and stereognosis.
- *Visual Functions:* items measuring visual-perceptual skills and visual-spatial abilities.
- *Receptive Language:* items assessing phonemic discrimination and understanding of simple words and phrases and grammatically complex forms.
- *Expressive Language:* items requiring repetition, object naming, automatic speech, spontaneous speech, etc.
- *Reading:* items measuring oral reading ability.
- *Writing:* items assessing writing to dictation, spontaneous writing, and other writing skills.
- *Arithmetic:* items relevant to number recognition, simple calculation, and more complex number operations.
- *Memory:* items assessing verbal and nonverbal short-term memory with and without interference.
- *Intelligence:* items measuring various higher cognitive skills such as abstraction, planning, reasoning, etc.

The Pathognomonic scale consists of items rarely missed by normal subjects and items rarely passed by brain-damaged patients. The Left and

Right Hemisphere scales in the manual comprise the motor and tactile items performed by the right and left limbs respectively.

In addition to the 14 scales specified in the manual, localization and (empirically derived) lateralization scales have been developed in recent studies and are described in published accounts of this research (McKay & Golden, 1979a, 1979b).

Form B, an alternate version of the LNNB, is currently being developed in order to facilitate serial testing of patients. An experimental version of the battery for children aged 8–12 is available presently, and a published version is expected to appear soon.

Scoring and Interpretation. The LNNB employs scaled scores of 0–2 for all items, with 0 representing a normal performance, 1 representing a borderline performance, and 2 representing a clearly defective performance. Depending on the nature of the item, the criterion for assigning a scaled score of 0, 1, or 2 may be accuracy, frequency, time, rate, speed, quality, or appropriateness of the response, or, in some cases, two of the above. The overall score for a scale is determined by adding the scores for all items on the scale; these are then converted into T scores derived from the performance of 50 control subjects.

Currently, the methods of interpretation include a set of recently derived objective clinical rules (Golden, 1981a, 1981b), profile interpretation, localization scales, qualitative evaluation of item patterns, and the presence of specific pathognomonic signs (Golden, Hammeke, & Purisch, 1980). The objective clinical rules begin with a formula for prediction of the average T-score, which includes correction factors for age and education. After calculating the predicted average T-score, one adds 10 to determine the "critical level" and then counts the number of scale scores above this level (considering the basic 11 scales plus the Pathognomonic scale). The cut-off used is three scores above the critical level (Golden, 1981a, 1981b). Golden notes that these rules were derived using a Caucasian, middle-to-lower social class population, and that further studies are necessary to develop rules for other populations.

Other methods of interpretation (profile interpretation, qualitative analysis of item patterns and of specific pathognomonic signs) are dependent on a thorough knowledge of neuropsychological theory (especially Luria's theory) and on clinical neuropsychological training and experience.

The recently proposed localization and lateralization scales (McKay & Golden, 1979a, 1979b) appear to need further validation using large sample sizes.

Advantages and Disadvantages. The LNNB in its present form offers the advantages of brevity and relative comprehensiveness in the screening of a number of areas of higher functioning. Further, in accordance with Luria's approach, complex functions are broken into simpler components so that more information is gleaned about the precise nature of deficits. In the validation studies to date, the developers of the test have reported hit rates in the region of 90 percent in discriminating between brain-injured and control subjects (Golden, Hammeke, & Purisch, 1978; Hammeke, Golden & Purisch, 1978) and between brain-damaged and schizophrenic subjects (Purisch, Golden, & Hammeke, 1978).

On the other hand, there have been a number of criticisms raised against the LNNB. Adams (1980a, 1980b) has criticized the construction of the test and flawed techniques in the standardization, validity, and reliability studies. With regard to test construction, he points out that many items must be scored subjectively, and that ordinal ratings are used throughout the test. In fairness, it must be pointed out that many psychological and neuropsychological tests contain sections that are of necessity scored subjectively on an ordinal scale (e.g., WAIS Comprehension) and that such scores are often subjected to statistical analysis as if they belonged to a ratio scale. Adams (1980a) also criticizes Golden and his colleagues for using multiple T-tests; however, a comparison using a multivariate ANOVA has since been performed (Golden, 1981a, 1981b). Criticisms of the standardization studies have centered around lack of control of subject variables such as age, education, medication, psychopathology, chronicity, number of hospitalizations, and age at onset of disorder, but many of these criticisms have been answered (Golden, 1980). Since Adams' critique, further reliability and validity studies have appeared (Golden & Berg, 1980a, 1980b, 1980c, 1980d, 1981a, 1981b; Golden, Fross, & Graber, 1981; Golden, Hammeke, Osmon, Sweet, Purisch, & Graber, 1981; Golden, Moses, Fishburne, Engum, Lewis, Wisniewski, & Berg, 1981; Golden, Osmon, Sweet, Graber, Purisch, & Hammeke, 1980; Golden, Purisch, Sweet, Graber, Osmon, & Hammeke, 1980; Golden, Sweet, Hammeke, Purisch, Graber,

& Osmon, 1980). As Spiers (1981) points out, however, additional studies are yet needed to establish the (criterion) validity of the content scales of the battery. Spiers presents a detailed critique of the composition of the various content scales of the LNNB, arguing that many items purporting to measure one neuropsychological function in reality reflect another, that items in a number of the scales are too limited in number or too superficial to assess comprehensively the function in question, and that Luria's original method of detailed qualitative analysis of responses is lost in the current LNNB system. Two recent critiques (Crosson & Warren, 1982; Delis & Kaplan, 1982) support such objections.

A fundamental issue raised in virtually all discussions of the LNNB may be expressed in the form of a question: Is the method of neuropsychological assessment developed by A. R. Luria by its very nature one that cannot be operationalized as a fixed battery? Adams (1980b) acknowledges that "the approach may not translate to a battery of tests, and Luria had made this point emphatically" (p. 523) yet he seems to advocate some form of "Luria battery" in order to allow for the validation of Luria's procedures. Spiers (1981) presents a thoughtful discussion of this issue and points out the error in the assumption (implicit in Adams' critiques and also in much of North American psychology) that objectivity can only be achieved through quantitative measurement.

THE MICHIGAN NEUROPSYCHOLOGICAL TEST BATTERY (AARON SMITH)

The Michigan Neuropsychological Test Battery consists of several widely used psychological and neuropsychological tests and several tests that have been developed by Aaron Smith and his colleagues at the University of Michigan. The composition of the battery is as follows:

- *Age-appropriate Wechsler Intelligence Scale*
- *Raven Coloured Progressive Matrices*
- *Revised Benton Visual Retention Test*
- *Purdue Pegboard*
- *Symbol-Digit Modalities Test* (Smith, 1973)
- *Peabody Picture Vocabulary Test*
- *Single and Double Simultaneous (Face-Hand) Stimulation Test* (Centofanti & Smith, 1979)
- *Memory for Unrelated Sentences* (Ostreicher, 1973)

Individualized Approaches

Despite the widespread use of fixed batteries in neuropsychological assessment and the recent promotion of such batteries, a number of influential neuropsychologists active in both training and research continue to prefer an individualized approach. Three such approaches are described in the following subsections.

THE NEUROPSYCHOLOGY UNIT OF THE BOSTON VETERANS ADMINISTRATION MEDICAL CENTER AND THE BOSTON UNIVERSITY SCHOOL OF MEDICINE

The Boston group of neuropsychologists employs a flexible but comprehensive approach that aims at a qualitative analysis of the nature of patients' deficits in addition to the usual specifications as to the presence or absence of brain damage, probable lesion site, severity of deficit, probable etiology, and lesion status (e.g., acute, chronic, progressive, resolving). Attention to the strategies and processes involved in patients' failures and successes in test performance partially determines the selection of tests to be used in addition to those in the core group. Even more importantly, the emphasis on process and strategy contributes to a more than usually detailed analysis of patients' deficits, with the recognition that superficially similar deficits can reflect quite distinctive underlying processes.

The three neuropsychologists most responsible for shaping the Boston approach have been Edith Kaplan, Harold Goodglass, and Nelson Butters. Currently, Edith Kaplan is most involved in training students to conduct neuropsychological assessment. Her core battery for adults now consists of the following tests:

- *Revised Wechsler Adult Intelligence Scale (WAIS-R)*—with several additions, including block pointing span (see Milner, 1971), a sentence arrangement task analogous to Picture Arrangement; a recall task and simple copying task added to Digit Symbol; and use of the automobile item from the WISC-R in addition to the usual Object Assembly items.
- *Wechsler Memory Scale, Form I*—with several additions, including extra items for Current and Personal Information, Orientation, and Mental Control Sections; cued immediate recall and delayed (free and cued) recall of the Logical Memory paragraphs after the usual free recall; recognition, simple matching, copy, and de-

layed recall of the Visual Reproduction designs after usual free recall; reverse testing of paired-associates (second word in pairs given, first word recalled) and delayed recall after the usual administration.

- *Modified Rey Auditory Verbal Learning Test*
- *Rey-Osterrieth Complex Figure* — copy, immediate recall, delayed recall.
- *Screening version of Boston Naming Test*
- *Word list generation tests* — including Controlled Word Association Test.
- *Narrative writing sample*
- *Boston Praxis Test*
- *Tests of response set* — initiation, maintenance, shifting, and inhibition of responses as measured by alternating *m* and *n*'s, reciprocal programs, Trail Making Test B.
- *Drawing to command* (e.g., clocks)
- *Tests of attention* — including simplified visual and auditory versions of Continuous Performance Test; visual scanning and visual search tests.

In cases where the initial referral question or the results of the initial tests suggest the need for further exploration of an area of deficit, additional tests will often be administered. For example, the Wisconsin Card Sorting Test is often used when frontal lobe lesions are suspected (Milner, 1964).

The advantages of the Boston approach include a fair degree of comprehensiveness, especially in the areas of language functions and memory; the emphasis on qualitative analysis; and the emphasis on higher cortical functions. Disadvantages include incomplete standardization and validation of some of the measures used (e.g., clock drawings). Because much of the work upon which the approach is based is at yet unpublished, training in the Boston approach virtually requires an apprenticeship at its source.

MURIAL D. LEZAK

In her volume entitled *Neuropsychological Assessment* (1976), Muriel Lezak presents an insightful discussion of the use of batteries versus individualized approaches in clinical neuropsychology. According to Lezak, in order to be adequate, a test battery must be suitable, practicable, and useful. Her opinion is that no currently available neuropsychological battery fulfills all of these criteria,

and she prefers an individualized approach. Her core battery of tests is composed of two portions: an individually administered part (a WAIS and nine other measures, requiring a total of two and one-half to three hours for administration), and a section of paper and pencil tests that may be given by clinical or nursing staff (six tests tapping a wide variety of areas requiring three to six hours for administration). Additional special tests will usually be selected in order to answer referral questions of a detailed nature (e.g., differential diagnosis, comprehensive description, and analysis of impaired function), or questions raised by the results of the core battery. For a complete discussion of this approach and its rationale, the reader is referred to Lezak (1976).

ARTHUR L. BENTON

Arthur L. Benton and his present and former colleagues[4] at the University of Iowa constitute another prominent school of neuropsychologists who advocate an individualized or patient-oriented approach to clinical neuropsychological assessment. They begin their assessment with a fixed set of tests of minimal length, consisting of a brief test of temporal orientation, two WAIS Verbal subtests (usually Information and Arithmetic), and two WAIS Performance subtests (usually Block Design and Picture Arrangement). The selection of additional tests is governed by the questions raised in the request for examination, by complaints mentioned by the patient during a preliminary interview, and by findings on the initial set of tests. The essential characteristic of their approach is that it is a sequential process leading to a diagnostic decision. They estimate that an experienced neuropsychologist utilizing their approach will complete testing in 60–90 minutes in 80 percent of cases, in less than 60 minutes in 15 percent, and in over 90 minutes in five percent. The armamentarium of tests which they draw from in completing their examinations is listed below.

- *Wechsler Adult Intelligence Scale* (WAIS)
- *Tests of Orientation, Learning and Memory*
  Temporal Orientation
  Presidents Test
  Galveston Orientation and Amnesia Test
  Paired-Associate Learning
  Benton Visual Retention Test

[4]Drs. Harvey Levin, Kerry Hamsher, Nils Varney, Frank Gersh, Max Fogel, and Otfried Spreen.

Serial Digit Learning
Selective Reminding Test
- *Tests of Attention-Concentration and Speed of Information Processing*
  WAIS Digit Span
  WAIS Digit Symbol
  Paced Auditory Serial Addition Task
- *Tests of Abstract Reasoning*
  Abstractions from Shipley Institute of Living Scale
  Raven Progressive Matrices
  Wisconsin Card Sorting Test
- *Tests of Body Schema*
  Right-Left Orientation
  Finger Localization
- *Tests of Visual Performance*
  Test of Facial Recognition
  Judgment of Line Orientation
  Visual Form Discrimination
  Pantomine Recognition
  Dot Localization
- *Tests of Auditory Performance*
  Tactile Form Perception
  Tactile Naming
- *Tests of Constructional Praxis*
  Test of Three Dimensional Construction Praxis
  Copying Designs
- *Tests of Verbal Functions*
  Controlled Word Association Test
  Vocabulary (WAIS and Shipley)
  Token Test
  Reading Section for Wide Range Achievement Test
- *Tests of Psychomotor Performance*
  Purdue Pegboard
  Finger Praxis
  Motor Impersistence
- *Arithmetic Tests*
  Oral Arithmetic Calculation
  Written Arithmetic Calculation
  Arithmetic Reasoning
  Arithmetic section from Wide Range Achivement Test
- *Tests of Lateral Neglect*
  Line Cancellation
  Bisection of Lines
  Geographic Orientation
  Constructional Praxis Tasks
  Double Simultaneous Stimulation
- *Aphasia Batteries*
  Neurosensory Center Comprehensive Examination for Aphasia (NCCEA)

Multilingual Aphasia Examination
- *Tests of Lateralization of Function*
  Dichotic Listening
  Tachistoscopic Visual Field Study
  Somatosensory Threshold Determinations
  NCCEA Handedness Inventory
- *Personality Assessment Tests*
  MMPI
  Rorschach

Single Tests

It is apparent from the discussion of individualized approaches that there are a large number of single tests available for the detailed examination of a variety of higher functions. Lezak's volume (1976) describes a number of the available tests under the following categories: tests of intellectual ability, verbal function, perceptual functions, orientation, attention, self-regulation, and personal and social adjustment. Lezak's book remains the most comprehensive available listing of individual tests in use for neuropsychology assessment, but the reader also is referred to the journals *Clinical Neuropsychology*, *Neuropsychologia*, and *Cortex* for references concerning other commonly used measures.

Reitan (1974) criticizes the use of single tests:

Obviously, we will never develop a meaningful conceptualization of the extent and manner in which brain lesions alter ability structure in individual human beings if each group of subjects is studied with a different set of measurements and the measurements, in turn, are never put in a meaningful overall behavioral context. Thus the use of single tests can scarcely contribute very significantly to an overall understanding of the behavioral correlates of brain lesions nor can a single test, considering the complexity of brain functions, be expected to serve as an adequate diagnostic instrument [p. 22].

One must emphatically agree with the last point. No responsible neuropsychologist would advocate the use of a *single* test as an "adequate diagnostic instrument." The field is no longer at the naive stage of thinking that any single measure can serve as a litmus test for the presence of organic dysfunction. However, a test originally devised and studied in isolation from other tasks can fruitfully be used as a part of a carefully chosen array of tests. The fact that one chooses to use a selection of independently developed tests does not mean that one sacrifices the ability to consider each measurement in a "meaningful overall behavioral context." It is the *selection* of tests that is critical here. Indeed, the same methods of interpretation that Reitan advocates for the HRB are applicable to any well-chosen array of tests. Furthermore, one must always remain cognizant of the possibility that a single test may be shown to detect and/or localize focal lesions more accurately than any single test in a formal battery. For example, in a recent study, the Wisconsin Card Sorting Test was shown to discriminate between frontal and nonfrontal lesions more successfully than any test in the HRB (Robinson, Heaton, Lehman, & Stilson, 1980). In this kind of situation, it is difficult to defend continued reliance on a battery alone, no matter how enshrined in tradition it may be.

Future Trends in Neuropsychological Assessment

The extremely rapid growth of the field of neuropsychological assessment[5] makes prediction difficult; nevertheless, several general trends seem discernible. One of the clearer conclusions to be drawn from the recent public debate over the merits and shortcomings of the LNNB is that no single battery is likely to dominate the field in the foreseeable future. In the case of the LNNB, beyond initial criticisms concerning its construction and the standardization, reliability, and validity studies, such detailed critiques as those of Spiers (1981), Crosson and Warren (1982), and Delis and Kaplan (1982) raise serious doubts about the battery's adequacy as a diagnostic instrument used in isolation from other tests. The HRB approach, on the other hand, is likely to suffer increasingly from the disadvantages imposed by its length, costliness, and the fact that it fails to reflect a number of newer discoveries in the field. The individualized approaches generally require training by one of a small number of their originators and are by definition almost unlikely to be widely adopted. It is probable that the next few years will see more formal comparisons of batteries or diverse systems of interpretation for existing batteries (e.g., Anthony et al., 1980; Golden, Kane,

Sweet, Moses, Cardellino, Templeton, Vicente, Kennelly, & Graber, 1981; Heaton, Grant, Anthony, & Lehman, 1981; Swiercinsky & Warnock, 1977).

A second likelihood is that of development of neuropsychological screening batteries (as distinct from full neuropsychological batteries). As psychologists, psychiatrists, internists, and others involved in patient care become increasingly aware of the incidence of organic cerebral disorders (and the frequency with which they present as behavioral disturbances), the demand for brief, inexpensive screening devices will increase. Considering the inadequacy of the instruments of this type that are already available, it is important that neuropsychologists involve themselves in the task of developing such measures.

A third trend is already in evidence and is likely to increase in strength: the exploration via neuropsychological assessment of the biological substrates of mental illness. At its inception the field was primarily oriented toward the elucidation of the behavioral effects of structural brain lesions. Schizophrenia, depressive psychosis, and manic-depressive illness were lumped together with neuroses and character disorders as "functional" complaints despite repeated findings of abnormalities of cognitive functioning accompanying psychosis (for reviews of these findings, see Heaton, Baade, & Johnson, 1978; Heaton & Crowley, 1981; Miller, 1975; Payne, 1961, 1973). More recently there has been a willingness to consider the possibility that the major psychoses are accompanied by some form of cerebral abnormality, most likely biochemical. For example, neuropsychologists in a number of different settings have found indications of left hemisphere dysfunction in schizophrenia and right hemisphere dysfunction in affective illness (e.g., Flor-Henry, 1976; Flor-Henry, Yeudall, Stefanyk, & Howarth, 1975; Goldstein, Filskov, Weaver, & Ives, 1977; Gur, 1978; Schweitzer, Becker, & Welsh, 1978; Yozawitz & Bruder, 1978).

A trend to be encouraged is the increasing involvement of neuropsychologists in rehabilitation planning for brain-damaged patients. In the emphasis on diagnosis and research that characterized the inception and early development of the field, the need for practical recommendations for

---

[5]The growth of the membership of the International Neuropsychological Society from fewer than 200 members in 1966 to close to 1,500 in 1981 (a growth rate of 10–15% per year) serves as an indication of the increasing size of the field.

treatment strategies all too often was overlooked. This oversight is being remedied in a number of instances, and there are now a dozen or more rehabilitation centers across the United States where neuropsychologists take an active role in designing and implementing programs of cognitive retraining (for an illustration, see Buffery, 1977). A useful resource for psychologists active in neuropsychological assessment would be a directory of such services compiled and maintained by either the International Neuropsychological Society or Division 40 (Clinical Neuropsychology) of the American Psychological Association.

As the field is relatively young, formal requirements for training, accreditation, and credentialing in clinical neuropsychology are still being established. A Joint International Neuropsychological Society/APA Division 40 Task Force on Education, Accreditation, and Credentialing was formed to provide recommendations in these areas and published a report (Task Force on Education, Accreditation & Credentialing, 1981). As a result of this report, the American Board of Clinical Neuropsychology, 'Inc., was formed and is now accepting applications for diplomate status.

Conclusions

From its modest beginnings toward the early part of this century, the field of neuropsychological assessment has become one of the fastest growing subspecialties within psychology and has gained increasing recognition as a valuable and even necessary service in the diagnosis of and treatment planning for a significant subset of psychiatric, neurological, and neurosurgical patients.

There is considerable diversity among neuropsychological assessment procedures in current use. While some neuropsychologists insist on the need for a fixed battery, others are equally convinced of the advantages of a flexible, individualized approach. Among those who favor batteries, opinion is divided as to the relative advantages of the Halstead-Reitan and Luria-Nebraska batteries, and neither seems likely to monopolize the field. The individualized approaches seem by nature destined to limited exposure; training in these methods requires more time and does not easily lend itself to the workshop format.

By all accounts, the "state of the art" in neuropsychological assessment is still somewhat primitive. Although many methodologies yield quite acceptable results in discriminating between brain-damaged subjects and normal controls, distinctions as to lateralization, localization, disease process or course, and differential diagnosis are more difficult and depend in large measure on subjective clinical inference. The clinician's skill in drawing inferences is a function of a sophisticated knowledge of brain-behavior relationships and clinical experience. A problem for most neuropsychological methodologies is the distinction between patients with structural brain lesions and patients with the more severe and intractible forms of psychiatric illness.

It is to be hoped that practitioners in the field, rather than spending too much time debating the relative merits of the current methodologies—all of which have shortcomings—will engage in research to find more effective measures and/or more effective combinations of, and methods of interpretation for, current measures.

References

Adams, K. M. Automated clinical interpretation of the neuropsychological battery. An ability-based approach (Doctoral dissertation, Wayne State University, 1974). *Dissertation Abstracts International,* 1975, **35,** 6085B. (University Microfilms No. 75-13, 289)

Adams, K. M. In search of Luria's battery: A false start. *Journal of Consulting and Clinical Psychology,* 1980, **48,** 511-516. (a)

Adams, K. M. An end of innocence for behavioral neurology? Adams replies. *Journal of Consulting and Clinical Psychology,* 1980, **48,** 522-524. (b)

Albert, M. S., Butters, N., & Brandt, J. Patterns of remote memory in amnesic and demented patients. *Archives of Neurology,* 1981, **38,** 495-500.

Albert, M. S., Butters, N., & Levin, J. Temporal gradients in the retrograde amnesia of patients with alcoholic Korsakoff's disease. *Archives of Neurology,* 1979, **36,** 211-216.

Albert, M. S., & Kaplan, E. Organic implications of neuropsychological deficits in the elderly. In L. N. Poon, J. L. Fozard, L. S. Cermak, D. Ehrenberg, & L. W. Thompson (Eds.), *New directions in memory and aging: Proceedings of the George Talland Memorial Conference.* Hillsdale, New Jersey: Lawrence Erlbaum Associates, 1980.

Anthony, W. Z., Heaton, R. K., & Lehman, R. A. W. An attempt to cross-validate two actuarial systems for neuropsychological test interpretation. *Journal of Consulting and Clinical Psychology,* 1980, **48,** 317-326.

Benton, A. L. A visual retention test for clinical use. *Archives of Neurology and Psychiatry,* 1945, **54,** 212-216.

Benton, A. L. *The Revised Visual Retention Test.* New York: Psychological Corporation, 1963.

Benton, A. L. Constructional apraxia and the minor hemisphere. *Confinia Neurologica,* 1967, **29,** 1-16.

Benton, A. L. Differential behavioral effects in frontal lobe disease. *Neuropsychologia*, 1968, **6**, 53–60.

Benton, A. L. *Test of Three-Dimensional Constructional Praxis Manual*. Neurosensory Center Publication No. 286, University of Iowa, 1973.

Benton, A. L., & Van Allen, M. W. Impairment in facial recognition in patients with cerebral disease. *Cortex*, 1968, **4**, 344–358.

Benton, A. L., & Van Allen, M. W. Prosopagnosia and facial discrimination. *Journal of Neurological Sciences*, 1972, **15**, 167–172.

Blumstein, S. E., Cooper, W. E., Goodglass, H., Statlander, S., & Gottlieb, J. Production deficits in aphasia: A voice-onset time analysis. *Brain and Language*, 1980, **9**, 153–170.

Blumstein, S. E., Cooper, W. E., Zurif, E. B., & Caramazza, A. The perception and production of voice-onset time in aphasia. *Neuropsychologia*, 1977, **15**, 371–383.

Boll, T. J. The Halstead-Reitan Neuropsychology Battery. In S. B. Fisher & T. J. Boll (Eds.), *Handbook of clinical neuropsychology*. New York: Wiley-Interscience, 1981.

Buffery, A. W. H. Clinical neuropsychology: A review and preview. In S. Rachman (Ed.), *Contributions to medical psychology*. Oxford: Pergamon Press, 1977.

Butters, N. Potential contributions of neuropsychology to our understanding of the memory disorders of the elderly. In L. N. Poon, J. L. Fozard, L. S. Cermak, D. Ehrenberg, & L. W. Thompson (Eds.), *New directions in memory and aging: Proceedings of the George Talland Memorial Conference*. Hillsdale, New Jersey: Lawrence Erlbaum Associates, 1980.

Butters, N., & Barton, M. Effect of parietal lobe damage on the performance of reversible operations in space. *Neuropsychologia*, 1970, **8**, 205–214.

Butters, N., & Cermak, L. S. Some analyses of amnesic syndromes in brain-damaged patients. In K. Pribram & R. Isaacson (Eds.), *The hippocampus*. New York: Plenum Press, 1975.

Butters, N., & Cermak, L. S. Neuropsychological studies of alcoholic Korsakoff patients. In G. Goldstein & C. Neuringer (Eds.), *Empirical studies of alcoholism*. Cambridge, Mass.: Ballinger Press, 1976.

Butters, N., & Cermak, L. S. *Alcoholic Korsakoff's syndrome: An information-processing approach to amnesia*. New York: Academic Press, 1980.

Butters, N., Miliotis, P., Albert, M. S., & Sax, D. Memory assessment: Evidence of the heterogeneity of amnesic symptoms. In G. Goldstein (Ed.), *Advances in clinical neuropsychology*. New York: Plenum Press, 1982.

Butters, N., Sax, D., Montgomery, K., & Tarlow, S. Comparison of the neuropsychological deficits associated with early and advanced Huntington's Disease. *Archives of Neurology*, 1978, **35**, 585–589.

Caramazza, A., & Zurif, E. B. Dissociation of algorithmic and heuristic processes in language comprehension: Evidence from aphasia. *Brain and Language*, 1976, **3**, 572–582.

Centofanti, C. C., & Smith, A. *The Single and Double Simultaneous (Face-Hand) Test (SDSS)*. Los Angeles: Western Psychological Corporation, 1979.

Cermak, L. S., & Butters, N. The role of interference and encoding in the short-term memory deficits of

Korsakoff patients. *Neuropsychologia*, 1972, **10**, 89–96.

Cermak, L. S., & Butters, N. The role of language in the memory disorders of brain-damaged patients. *Annals of the New York Academy of Sciences*, 1976, **280**, 857–867.

Cermak, L. S., Butters, N., & Moreines, J. Some analyses of the verbal encoding deficit of alcoholic Korsakoff patients. *Brain and Language*, 1974, **1**, 141–150.

Cermak, L. S., & Reale, L. Depth of processing and retention of words by alcoholic Korsakoff patients. *Journal of Experimental Psychology: Human Learning and Memory*, 1978, **4**, 165–174.

Christensen, A. L. *Luria's neuropsychological investigation*. New York: Spectrum, 1975.

Columbia-Greystone Associates. *Problems of the human brain: I. Selective partial ablation of the frontal cortex*. New York: Hoeber, 1949.

Crosson, B., & Warren, R. L. Use of the Luria-Nebraska Neuropsychological Battery in aphasia: A conceptual critique. *Journal of Consulting and Clinical Psychology*, 1982, **50**, 22–31.

Davison, L. A. Introduction. In R. M. Reitan & L. A. Davison (Eds.), *Clinical neuropsychology: Current status and applications*. Washington: V. H. Winston & Sons, 1974.

Delis, D., & Kaplan, E. The assessment of aphasia with the Luria-Nebraska Neuropsychological Battery: A case critique. *Journal of Consulting and Clinical Psychology*, 1982, **50**, 32–39.

Finkelstein, J. N. BRAIN: A computer program for interpretation of the Halstead-Reitan Neuropsychological Test Battery (Doctoral dissertation, Columbia University, 1976). *Dissertation Abstracts International*, 1977, **37**, 5349B. (University Microfilms No. 77-8, 8864)

Flor-Henry, P. Lateralized temporal-limbic dysfunction and psychopathology. *Annals of the New York Academy of Sciences*, 1976, **280**, 777–797.

Flor-Henry, P., Yeudall, L. T., Stefanyk, W., & Howarth, B. The neuropsychological correlates of the functional psychoses. *IRCS Medical Science: Neurology and Neurosurgery: Psychiatry and Clinical Psychology*, 1975, **3**, 34.

Gardner, H. *The shattered mind*. New York: Knopf, 1975.

Gardner, H., Ling, K., Flamm, L., & Silverman, J. Comprehension and appreciation of humor in brain-damaged patients. *Brain*, 1975, **98**, 399–412.

Geschwind, N. Selected papers on language and the brain. *Boston studies in the philosophy of science (Volume 16)*. Boston: Reidel, 1974.

Golden, C. J. In reply to Adams's "In search of Luria's battery: A false start." *Journal of Consulting and Clinical Psychology*, 1980, **48**, 517–521.

Golden, C. J. A standardized version of Luria's neuropsychological tests: A quantitative and qualitative approach to neuropsychological evaluation. In S. B. Filskov & T. J. Boll (Eds.), *Handbook of Clinical Neuropsychology*. New York: Wiley-Interscience, 1981. (a)

Golden, C. J. The Luria-Nebraska Neuropsychological Battery: Theory and research. In P. McReynolds (Ed.), *Advances in psychological assessment*. Palo

Alto, California: Science and Behavior Books, 1981. (b)

Golden, C. J., & Berg, R. A. Interpretation of the Luria-Nebraska Neuropsychological Battery by item inter-correlations: Items 1–24 of the Motor Scale. *Clinical Neuropsychology*, 1980, **2**, 66–70. (a)

Golden, C. J., & Berg, R. A. Interpretation of the Luria-Nebraska Neuropsychological Battery by item inter-correlation: Items 25–51 of the Motor Scale. *Clinical Neuropsychology*, 1980, **2**, 105–108. (b)

Golden, C. J., & Berg, R. A. Interpretation of the Luria-Nebraska Neuropsychological Battery by item inter-correlation: Items 1–24 of the Motor Scale. *Clinical Neuropsychology*, 1980, **2**, 153–156. (c)

Golden, C. J., & Berg, R. A. Interpretation of the Luria-Nebraska Neuropsychological Battery by item inter-correlation: The Writing Scale. *Clinical Neuropsychology*, 1980, **2**, 8–12. (d)

Golden, C. J., & Berg, R. A. Interpretation of the Luria-Nebraska Neuropsychological Battery by item inter-correlation: The Tactile Scale. *Clinical Neuropsychology*, 1981, **3**, 25–29. (a)

Golden, C. J., & Berg, R. A. Interpretation of the Luria-Nebraska Neuropsychological Battery by item inter-correlation: The Visual Scale. *Clinical Neuropsychology*, 1981, **3**, 22–26. (b)

Golden, C. J., Fross, K. H., & Graber, B. Split-half re-liability and item-scale consistency of the Luria-Ne-braska Neuropsychological Battery. *Journal of Consulting and Clinical Psychology*, 1981, **49**, 304–305.

Golden, C. J., Hammeke, T., Osmon, D., Sweet, J., Purisch, A., & Graber, B. Factor analyses of the Luria-Nebraska Neuropsychological Battery: IV. Intelligence and Pathognomonic Scales. *International Journal of Neuroscience*, 1981, **13**, 87–92.

Golden, C. J., Hammeke, T., & Purisch, A. Diagnostic validity of the Luria Neuropsychological Battery. *Journal of Consulting and Clinical Psychology*, 1978, **46**, 1258–1265.

Golden, C. J., Hammeke, T., & Puisch, A. *The Luria-Nebraska Neuropsychological Battery: Manual (Revised)*. Los Angeles: Western Psychological Services, 1980.

Golden, C. J., Kane, R., Sweet, J., Moses, J. A., Cardellino, J. P., Templeton, R., Vicente, P., Kennelly, D., & Graber, B. The relationship of the Halstead-Reitan Neuropsychological Battery to the Luria-Nebraska Neuropsychological Battery. *Journal of Consulting and Clinical Psychology*, 1981, **49**, 410–417.

Golden, C. J., Moses, J. A., Fishburne, F., Engum, E., Lewis, G. P., Wisniewski, A., & Berg, R. A. Cross validation of the Luria-Nebraska Neuropsychological Battery for the presence, lateralization, and localization of brain damage. *Journal of Consulting and Clinical Psychology*, 1981, **49**, 491–507.

Golden, C. J., Osmon, D., Sweet, J., Graber, B., Purish, A., & Hammeke, T. Factor analysis of the Luria-Nebraska Neuropsychological Battery: III. Writing, Arithmetic, Memory, Left, and Right. *International Journal of Neuroscience*, 1980, **11**, 309–315.

Golden, C. J., Purisch, A., Sweet, J., Graber, B., Osmon, D., & Hammeke, T. Factor analysis of the Luria-Nebraska Neuropsychological Battery: II. Visual, Receptive, Expressive, and Reading Scales. *International Journal of Neuroscience*, 1980, **11**, 227–236.

Golden, C. J., Sweet, J., Hammeke, T., Purisch, A., Graber, B., & Osmon, D. Factor analysis of the Luria-Nebraska Neuropsychological Battery: I. Motor, Rhythm, and Tactile Scales. *International Journal of Neuroscience*, 1980, **11**, 91–99.

Goldstein, S. G., Filskov, S. B., Weaver, L. A., & Ives, J. O. Neuropsychological effects of electroconvulsive therapy. *Journal of Clinical Psychology*, 1977, **33**, 798–806.

Goldstein, K., & Scheerer, M. Abstract and concrete behavior: An experimental study with special tests. *Psychological Monographs*, 1941, **53** (2, Whole No. 239).

Goodglass, H., & Kaplan, E. Disturbance of gesture and pantomime in aphasia. *Brain*, 1963, **86**, 703–720.

Goodglass, H., & Kaplan, E. *The assessment of aphasia and related disorders*. Philadelphia: Lea and Febiger, 1972.

Goodglass, H., & Kaplan, E. Assessment of cognitive deficit in the brain-injured patient. In M. Gazzaniga (Ed.), *Handbook of behavioral neurobiology-neuropsychology*. New York: Plenum Press, 1979.

Goodglass, H., & Quadfasel, F. A. Language laterality in left-handed aphasics. *Brain*, 1954, **77**, 521–548.

Goodglass, H., Quadfasel, F. A., & Timberlake, W. H. Phrase length and the type and severity of aphasia. *Cortex*, 1964, **1**, 133–153.

Gur, R. E. Left hemisphere dysfunction and left hemisphere overactivation in schizophrenia. *Journal of Abnormal Psychology*, 1978, **87**, 226–238.

Halstead, W. C. *Brain and intelligence: A quantitative study of the frontal lobes*. Chicago: University of Chicago Press, 1947.

Halstead, W. C. Frontal lobe functions and intelligence. *Bulletin of the Los Angeles Neurological Society*, 1950, **15**, 205–212.

Halstead, W. C. Biological intelligence. *Journal of Personality*, 1951, **20**, 118–130.

Halstead, W. C., & Shure, G. Further evidence for a frontal lobe component in human biological intelligence. *Transactions of the American Neurological Association*, 1954, **79**, 9–11.

Hammeke, T. A., Golden, C. J., & Purisch, A. D. A standardized, short, and comprehensive neuropsychological test battery based on the Luria neuropsychological evaluation. *International Journal of Neuroscience*, 1978, **8**, 135–141.

Hartlage, L., Chelune, G., & Tucker, D. Survey of professional issues in the practice of clinical neuropsychology. Unpublished report from membership survey, Division 40, American Psychological Association, 1980.

Heaton, R. K., Baade, L. E., & Johnson, K. L. Neuropsychological test results associated with psychiatric disorders in adults. *Psychological Bulletin*, 1978, **85**, 141–162.

Heaton, R. K., & Crowley, T. J. Effects of psychiatric disorders and their somatic treatments on neuropsychological test results. In S. B. Filskov & T. J. Boll (Eds.), *Handbook of clinical neuropsychology*. New York: Wiley-Interscience, 1981.

Heaton, R. K., Grant, I., Anthony, W. Z., & Lehman, R. A. A comparison of clinical and automated interpretation of the Halstead-Reitan Battery. *Clinical Neuropsychology*, 1981, **3**, 121–141.

Hebb, D. O. Intelligence in man after large removals of cerebral tissue: Defects following right temporal lobectomy. *Journal of General Psychology*, 1939, **21**, 437–446.

Hebb, D. O. The effect of early and late brain injury upon test scores, and the nature of adult intelligence. *Proceedings of the American Philosophical Society*, 1942, **85**, 275–292.

Hécaen, H., & Albert, M. L. *Human neuropsychology*. New York: Wiley-Interscience, 1978.

Held, R. Exposure-history as a factor in maintaining stability of perception and coordination. *Journal of Nervous and Mental Disease*. 1961, **132**, 26–32.

Jones, B. P., Butters, N., Moskowitz, H. R., & Montgomery, K. Olfactory and gustatory capacities of alcoholic Korsakoff patients. *Neuropsychologia*, 1978, **16**, 323–337.

Jones, B. P., Moskowitz, H. R., & Butters, N. Olfactory discrimination in alcoholic Korsakoff patients. *Neuropsychologia*, 1975, **13**, 173–179.

Jones-Gotman, M., & Milner, B. Design fluency: The invention of nonsense drawings after focal cortical lesions. *Neuropsychologia*, 1977, **15**, 653–674.

Kiernan, R. J., & Matthews, C. G. Impairment index versus T-score averaging in neuropsychological assessment. *Journal of Consulting and Clinical Psychology*, 1976, **44**, 951–957.

Kimura, D. Some effects of temporal lobe damage on auditory perception. *Canadian Journal of Psychology*, 1961, **15**, 156–165.

Kimura, D. Right temporal lobe damage. *Archives of Neurology*, 1963, **8**, 264–271.

Klove, H. Validation studies in adult clinical neuropsychology. In R. M. Reitan & L. A. Davison (Eds.), *Clinical neuropsychology: Current status and applications*. Washington: V. H. Winston & Sons, 1974.

Lacks, P., Colbert, J., Harrow, M., & Levine, J. Further evidence concerning the diagnostic accuracy of the Halstead Organic Test Battery. *Journal of Clinical Psychology*, 1970, **26**, 480–481.

Lezak, M. D. *Neuropsychological assessment*. New York: Oxford University Press, 1976.

Luria, A. R. *Higher cortical functions in man*. (2nd ed.). New York: Basic Books, 1980.

Malec, J. Neuropsychological assessment of schizophrenia *versus* brain damage: A review. *Journal of Nervous and Mental Disease*, 1978, **166**, 507–516.

McKay, S., & Golden, C. J. Empirical derivation of neuropsychological scales for the lateralization of brain damage using the Luria-Nebraska Neuropsychological Battery. *Clinical Neuropsychology*, 1979, **1**, 1–5. (a)

McKay, S., & Golden, C. J. Empirical derivation of neuropsychological scales for the localization of brain lesions using the Luria-Nebraska Neuropsychological Battery. *Clinical Neuropsychology*, 1979, **1**, 19–23. (b)

Milberg, W., & Blumstein, S. E. Lexical decisions and aphasia: Evidence for semantic processing. *Brain and Language*, 1981, **14**, 371–385.

Miller, W. R. Psychological deficit in depression. *Psychological Bulletin*, 1975, **82**, 238–260.

Milner, B. Impairment of visual recognition and recall after right temporal lobectomy in man. Paper presented at the meeting of the Psychonomic Society, Chicago, September 1960.

Milner, B. Laterality effects in audition. In V. B. Mountcastle (Ed.), *Interhemispheric relations and cerebral dominance*. Baltimore: The Johns Hopkins Press, 1962.

Milner, B. Some effects of frontal lobectomy in man. In J. M. Warren & K. Akert (Eds.), *The frontal granular cortex and behavior*. New York: McGraw-Hill, 1964.

Milner, B. Amnesia following operation on the temporal lobes. In C. W. M. Whitty & O. L. Zangwill (Eds.), *Amnesia*. London: Butterworths, 1966.

Milner, B. Brain mechanisms suggested by studies of temporal lobes. In F. L. Darley (Ed.), *Brain mechanisms underlying speech and language*. New York: Grune & Stratton, 1967.

Milner, B. Visual recognition and recall after right temporal-lobe excision in man. *Neuropsychologia*, 1968, **6**, 191–209.

Milner, B. Memory and the medial temporal regions of the brain. In K. H. Pribram & D. E. Broadbent (Eds.), *Biology of memory*. New York: Academic Press, 1970.

Milner, B., Interhemispheric differences in the localization of psychological processes in man. *British Medical Bulletin*, 1971, **27**, 272–275.

Milner, B., & Kimura, D. Dissociable visual learning defects after unilateral temporal lobectomy in man. Paper presented at the meeting of the Eastern Psychological Association, Philadelphia, 1964.

Oscar-Berman, M. Hypothesis testing and focusing behavior during concept formation by amnesic Korsakoff patients. *Neuropsychologia*, 1973, **11**, 191–198.

Oscar-Berman, M. Neuropsychological Consequences of long-term chronic alcoholism. *American Scientist*, 1980, **68**, 410–419.

Oscar-Berman, M., Goodglass, H., & Cherlow, D. G. Perceptual laterality and iconic recognition of visual materials by Korsakoff patients and normal adults. *Journal of Comparative and Physiological Psychology*, 1973, **83**, 316–321.

Oscar-Berman, M., & Samuels, I. Stimulus-preference and memory factors in Korsakoff's syndrome. *Neuropsychologia*, 1977, **15**, 99–106.

Oscar-Berman, M., & Zola-Morgan, S. M. Comparative neuropsychology and Korsakoff's syndrome. I. Spatial and visual reversal learning. *Neuropsychologia*, 1980, **18**, 499–512, (a)

Oscar-Berman, M., & Zola-Morgan, S. M. Comparative neuropsychology and Korsakoff's syndrome. II. Two-choice visual discrimination learning. *Neuropsychologia*, 1980, **18**, 513–525. (b)

Ostreicher, H. *Memory for Unrelated Sentences Test*. Unpublished test, 1973.

Paterson, A., & Zangwill, O. L. Disorders of visual space perception associated with lesions of the right cerebral hemisphere. *Brain*, 1944, **67**, 331–358.

Paterson, A., & Zangwill, O. L. A case of topographical disorientation associated with a unilateral cerebral lesion. *Brain*, 1945, **68**, 188–212.

Payne, R. W. Cognitive abnormalities. In H. J. Eysenck (Ed.), *Handbook of abnormal psychology*. New York: Basic Books, 1961.

Payne, R. W. Cognitive abnormalities. In H. J. Eysenck (Ed.), *Handbook of abnormal psychology*. 2nd ed.) San Diego: Knapp, 1973.

Potter, H., & Butters, N. Continuities in the olfactory

deficits of chronic alcoholics and alcoholics with the Korsakoff syndrome. In M. Galanter (Ed.), *Currents in alcoholism*. Vol. VII. New York: Grune & Stratton, 1980.

Pribram, K. H. *Languages of the brain: Experimental paradoxes and principles in neuropsychology*. Englewood Cliffs, N.J.: Prentice-Hall, 1971.

Purisch, A., Golden, C. J., & Hammeke, T. Discrimination between schizophrenics and brain-damaged patients using the Luria-Nebraska Neuropsychological Battery. *Journal of Consulting and Clinical Psychology*, 1978, **46**, 1266–1273.

Reitan, R. M. An investigation of the validity of Halstead's measure of biological intelligence. *Archives of Neurology and Psychiatry*, 1955, **73**, 28–35.

Reitan, R. M. Problems and prospects in studying the psychological correlates of brain lesions. *Cortex*, 1966, **2**, 127–154. (a)

Reitan, R. M. A research program on the psychological effects of brain lesions in human beings. In N. R. Ellis (Ed.), *International review of research in mental retardation.*, Vol. 1. New York: Academic Press, 1966. (b)

Reitan, R. M. *Manual for Administration of Neuropsychological Test Batteries for Adults and Children*. Indianapolis: privately published by the author, 1969.

Reitan, R. M. Methodological problems in clinical neuropsychology, In R. M. Reitan & L. A. Davison (Eds.), *Clinical neuropsychology: Current status and applications*. Washington, D. C.: V. W. Winston & Sons, 1974.

Reitan, R. M. Methodological problems in clinical neuropsychology. In R. M. Reitan & L. A. Davison (Eds.), *Clinical neuropsychology: Current status and applications*. Washington, D. C.: V. W. Winston & Sons, 1974.

Robinson, A. L., Heaton, R. K., Lehman, R. A. W., & Stilson, D. W. The utility of the Wisconsin Card Sorting Test in detecting and localizing frontal lobe lesions. *Journal of Consulting and Clinical Psychology*, 1980, **48**, 605–614.

Russell, E. W., Neuringer, C., & Goldstein, G. *Assessment of brain damage: A neuropsychological key approach*. New York: Wiley-Interscience, 1970.

Rylander, G. Personality changes after operations on the frontal lobes. Copenhagen: Munksgaard, 1940.

Selz, M., & Reitan, R. M. Rules for neuropsychological diagnosis: Classification of brain function in older children. *Journal of Consulting and Clinical Psychology*, 1979, **47**, 258–264.

Schweitzer, L., Becker, E., & Welsh, H. Abnormalities of cerebral lateralization in schizophrenia patients. *Archives of General Psychiatry*, 1978, **35**, 982–985.

Scoville, W. B., & Milner, B. Loss of recent memory after bilateral hippocampal lesions. *Journal of Neurology, Neurosurgery and Psychiatry*, 1957, **20**, 11–21.

Semmes, J., Weinstein, S., Ghent, L., & Teuber, H. L. Spatial orientation in man after cerebral injury: I. Analyses by locus of lesion. *Journal of Psychology*, 1955, **39**, 227–244.

Shai, A., Goodglass, H., & Barton, M. I. Recognition of tachistoscopically presented verbal and non-verbal stimuli after unilateral cerebral damage. *Neuropsychologia*, 1972, **10**, 185–191.

Shure, G., & Halstead, W. C. Cerebral localization of

intellectual processes. *Psychological Monographs*, 1958, **72**, No. 12 (Whole No. 465).

Smith, A. *The Symbol Digit Modalities Test*. Los Angeles: Western Psychological Services, 1973.

Spiers, P. A. Have they come to praise Luria or to bury him? The Luria-Nebraska controversy. *Journal of Consulting and Clinical Psychology*, 1981, **49**, 331–341.

Spreen, O., & Benton, A. L. *Neurosensory Center Comprehensive Examination for Aphasia*. Victoria, B. C.: Neuropsychology Laboratory, Department of Psychology, University of Victoria, 1969.

Swiercinsky, D., & Warnock, A. Comparison of the neuropsychological key and discriminant analysis approaches of predicting cerebral damage and localization. *Journal of Consulting and Clinical Psychology*, 1977, **45**, 808–814.

Teuber, H.-L. Unity and diversity of frontal lobe functions. *Acta Neurobiologica Experimentalis*, 1972, **32**, 615–656.

Teuber, H.-L., Battersby, W. S., & Bender, M. B. *Visual field defects after penetrating missile wounds of the brain*. Cambridge, Mass.: Harvard University Press, 1960.

Teuber, H.-L., & Mishkin, M. Judgment of visual and postural vertical after brain injury. *Journal of Psychology*, 1954, **38**, 161–175.

Vega, A., & Parsons, O. A. Cross-validation of the Halstead-Reitan tests for brain damage. *Journal of Consulting Psychology*, 1967, **31**, 619–625.

Wapner, W., Hamby, S., & Gardner, H. The role of the right hemisphere in the apprehension of complex linguistic materials. *Brain and Language*, 1981, **14**, 15–33.

Watson, C.G., Thomas, R. W., Anderson, D., & Felling, J. Differentiation of organics from schizophrenics at two chronicity levels by use of the Reitan-Halstead Organic Test Battery. *Journal of Consulting and Clinical Psychology*, 1968, **32**, 679–684.

Weisenberg, T. M., & McBride, K. E. *Aphasia: A clinical and psychological study*. New York: The Commonwealth Fund, 1935.

Wheeler, L., Burke, C. J., & Reitan, R. M. An application of discriminant functions to the problem of predicting brain-damage using behavioral variables. *Perceptual and Motor Skills*, 1963, **16**, 417–440. (Monograph Supplement 3-VIb)

Winner, E., & Gardner, H. The comprehension of metaphor in brain-damaged patients. *Brain*, 1977, **100**, 719–727.

Yozawitz, A., & Bruder, G. E. Dichotic listening asymmetries and lateralized deficits in affective psychosis. Paper presented to the American Psychological Association, Toronto, August 1978.

Zangwill, O. L. Clinical tests of memory impairment. *Proceedings of the Royal Society of Medicine*, 1943, **36**, 576–580.

Zurif, E. B. Language mechanisms: A neuropsychological approach. *American Scientist*, 1980, **68**, 305–311.

Zurif, E. B., & Caramazza, A. Psycholinguistic structures in aphasia: Studies in syntax and semantics. In H. Whitaker & H. A. Whitaker (Eds.), *Studies in Neurolinguistics*. Vol. 1. New York: Academic Press, 1976.

21 BEHAVIORAL ASSESSMENT

Stephen N. Haynes

Progress in the technology, predictive power, and construct validity of clinical psychology are highly dependent on advances in measurement methods and theory (Korchin, 1976; Weiner, 1976; Wolman, 1965). Measurement systems provide the technology for testing etiological hypotheses and for evaluating intervention effects. One conceptual and methodological basis for the advancement of clinical psychology has been provided by behavioral assessment. It has significantly facilitated the identification and measurement of behavior and its determinants. In addition, it has contributed to the conceptual framework within which behavior is viewed and has facilitated the development of more effective and more efficient intervention programs. In sum, behavioral assessment is contributing to the methodological and conceptual foundations that are necessary for the continued vitality of clinical psychology.

The current vitality of behavioral assessment becomes evident when one examines published research, the history of books and journals published in the area, and its incorporation across disciplines. In a recent survey of the published behavioral intervention literature, Haynes and Wilson (1979) reviewed over 900 studies published in 1977 and 1978 that utilized behavioral-assessment procedures. Although prior to 1976 no general texts on behavioral assessment were available, a number have been published in recent years (Barlow, 1981; Ciminero, Calhoun, & Adams, 1977; Cone & Hawkins, 1977; Haynes, 1978; Haynes & Wilson, 1979; Mash & Terdal, 1981; Nelson & Hayes, 1982). Two journals, *Behavioral Assessment* and *Journal of Behavioral Assessement*, both begun in 1979, focus primarily on methodological and conceptual advances in behavioral assessment.

Advances in research design and in methods of statistical analysis such as time-series analyses and designs have also been associated with behavioral assessment (Hersen & Barlow, 1976; Kratochwill & Brody, 1978; Glass, Wilson, & Gottman, 1975).

Behavioral-assessment methods (e.g., naturalistic observation, analogue observation, self-monitoring, behavioral interviews, behavioral questionnaires, and psychophysiological assess-

*The author would like to express his appreciation to Linda Gannon, A. E. Adams, III, Glenn Swimmer, and Jackie Cuevos for their helpful comments on an earlier version of this manuscript. Preparation of this manuscript was supported, in part, by the Clinical Center, Southern Illinois University at Carbondale.

ment) are used in disciplines as diverse as social psychology (Lindgren & Harvey, 1971); ethology (Hutt & Hutt, 1970); community psychology (Nietzel et al., 1977); mental retardation (Sackett, 1978); behavioral medicine (Davidson & Davison, 1980); and anthropology (Hoebel, 1958). The vitality of behavioral assessment is further indicated by recent applications to diverse personal and social problems such as learning disabilities (Lahey, Vosk, & Habif, 1981); chronic pain (Chapman & Wykoff, 1981); marital dissatisfaction (Jacobson, 1979); depression (Seligman, Klein, & Miller, 1976); headache (Haynes, 1981); sleep disorders (Youkilis & Bootzin, 1981); delinquency (Braukman & Fixen, 1975); and many others (see Turner, Calhoun, & Adams, 1981; Leitenberg, 1976). Behavioral assessment has demonstrated a remarkable record of applicability, utility, and productivity.

The historical roots of specific behavioral-assessment procedures are quite diverse. Behavioral observation was used by early Pavlovian experimentalists (Kazdin, 1978), and can be traced to Hellenic and Egyptian eras (Alexander & Selesnick, 1966; Zilboorg & Henry, 1941). The more systematic methods of behavioral observation currently in use reflect the varied influences of operant psychology (Honig, 1966) and other fields of experimental psychology (Kling & Riggs, 1971; Wolman, 1973); ethology (Hutt & Hutt, 1970); social psychology (Sellitz, Wrightsman, & Cook, 1976); developmental psychology (Wright, 1960); and comparative psychology (see review by Kazdin, 1978). Other behavioral-assessment methods, such as questionnaires, interviews, and self-monitoring, were selectively borrowed or derived from traditionally used clinical and social-psychology assessment instruments (Wolman, 1978; Woody, 1980; McReynolds, 1978). Finally, the technological bases for psychophysiological methods in behavioral assessment were provided by the disciplines of electrophysiology and psychophysiology (Martin & Venables, 1980).

Perhaps the most powerful impetus for the development of behavioral assessment has been the phenomenal growth of the behavioral therapies in the 1960s and 1970s (see Kazdin, 1978). The behavioral therapies differ from the traditional non-behavioral therapies in the type of interventions (Ullmann & Krasner, 1975) and intervention designs (Hersen & Barlow, 1976) that are employed, the underlying assumptions concerning the etiology of behavior (Bandura, 1969), and the be-

haviors targeted for modification (Cone & Hawkins, 1977). During the proliferation of the behavioral therapies in the 1960s, the assessment instruments available were based upon vastly different conceptual systems and were generally unsuited to this new conceptual and technological system (Ullmann & Krasner, 1975).

The high level of activity in the field of behavioral assessment is a recent phenomenon and represents a belated response to the perceived need for assessment techniques and instruments that are more compatible with a behavioral construct system. Although occasional symposia, published articles, and book chapters focused on behavioral assessment throughout the 1950s and the 1960s (Bachrach, 1962; Bandura, 1961; Eysenck, 1960a; Rachman & Costello, 1961; Salter, 1961; Wolpe, 1958), it was not until the early and mid-1970s that behavioral assessment became the subject of more systematic investigation and conceptualization. The 1975 West Virginia Conference on Behavioral Assessment was both a reflection of and impetus to this new field of inquiry. The proceedings were later published as an edited book by Cone and Hawkins (1977). Subsequent to that conference, the number of books, published articles, symposia, and presentations at scientific meetings focusing on behavioral assessment burgeoned and continues to grow.

Conceptual Foundations

Every behavioral, psychodynamic, or biological assessment system is based upon a set of underlying assumptions regarding behavior and its determinants. These assumptions influence the types of assessment instruments utilized, the phenomena upon which they focus, the populations to which they are applied, the types of data acquired, the inferences derived from their applications, and the intervention programs based on these inferences (Haynes, 1978). Behavioral assessment is closely tied to the behavioral construct system, and the conceptual foundations of this model have been previously outlined (Bandura, 1969; Kanfer & Phillips, 1970; Rimm & Masters, 1979). In addition, conceptual and methodological differences between behavioral and traditional clinical assessment systems have been noted frequently (Goldfried & Kent, 1972; Haynes, 1978; Nelson & Hayes, 1979; Mash, 1979; Goldfried, 1977). The purpose of this section is to examine the underlying assumptions of a behavioral construct system that are reflected in and have a major impact on behavior-assessment methods.

Environmental Determinism: An Interactionist Model

Perhaps the assumptions that influence the technology and focus of any assessment system most significantly are those that concern the causality of behavior. For example, assumptions that behavior can best be understood through reference to biological determinants necessitate a focus on physiological events and the use of assessment procedures such as urinalysis, CAT scans, spinal taps, or electroencephalograms. Assumptions that behavior can best be understood through reference to intrapsychic events necessitate a focus on hypothetical intrapsychic factors and the use of assessment procedures such as the Rorschach and TAT.

Within a behavioral construct system, the determinants of behavior are more freqently, but not invariably, attributed to environmental events, particularly phenomena that are consistent with a social-learning model (Bandura, 1969; Goldfried & Kent, 1972; Mischel, 1968). A fundamental assumption of a behavioral construct system is that it is possible to account for a significant proportion of variance in the occurrence or characteristics of behavior through reference to antecedent and consequent environmental events.

The concept of environmental determinism does not presume that individuals are passive recipients of environmental stimuli and that behavior can be treated simply as a dependent variable. Rather, it presumes an *interactionist model* (Bandura, 1981; Mash & Terdal, 1981) in which the behavior of individuals has an impact on the environment, which in turn affects behavior. Interactionist models have been advanced for a number of behavior disorders including depression, insomnia, marital dissatisfaction, psychosomatic disorders, child behavior and family problems, ingestive disorders, learning disorders, and many others (see Hersen, Eisler, & Miller, 1975–1981).

Both the interactionist model and the presumed etiological role of environmental events have had a profound impact upon the targets and methods of behavioral assessment. Assuming that there are causal interactions between behavior and environmental events, behavior analysts carefully evaluate behavior-environment interactions and the role of environmental events occurring before, during, and after target behaviors. For example, an interactionist model stresses the importance of attending to environmental reinforcement decrements that may precede depression and the social-skill deficits that may precipitate reinforcement loss (Lewinsohn, 1975), stressful social interactions that may precede headaches (Haynes, 1981), or peer and parental consequences associated with disruptive child behavior (Wells & Forehand, 1981).

The mechanisms through which behavior-environment interactions operate are complex. It is assumed that the behavior of an individual may affect the reinforcement rate from the environment by differentially consequating those behaviors, can serve as discriminative stimuli for the behavior of others, or can affect the probability of occurrence or degree of exposure to environmental stressors.

The environmental emphasis of behavioral construct systems is relative: there is no presumption that genetic, biochemical, or cognitive events cannot function as significant determinants of behavior or that they cannot interact with behavioral and environmental events (Bandura, 1981). Consequently, these nonpublic phenomena can be relevant targets in behavioral assessment. It is assumed, however, that a systematic examination of environmental events and behavioral-environmental events and behavior-environment interactions will frequently lead to a more useful and comprehensive causal analysis (*functional analysis*) of behavior and facilitate the development of more powerful intervention procedures.

The emphasis on environmental causality influences assessment *methods* as well as *foci*. The hypothesized etiological role of environmental factors underlies the emphasis on *direct observation* of behavior-environment interaction and self-monitoring and participant monitoring of behavior-environment interactions in the natural environment. In addition, behavioral interviews and questionnaires also focus upon behavior-environment interactions. Most importantly, if the assumption of significant environmental causality is valid, it is insufficient to evaluate an individual (or family, classroom, institution, or group) independently of his or her (or their) social-environmental context.

Temporal Continguity of Determinants

Behavioral construct systems also emphasize the importance of determinants in close temporal proximity to the targeted behavior. It is assumed that a greater proportion of the variance in behavior can be accounted for through reference to *current* rather than to *historical* behavior-environment interactions. The deemphasis of historical determinants is based as much on pragmatic as on empirical considerations. It reflects the assumption that events in close temporal proximity to behavior are more amenable to assessment and modification, as well as being more important causal factors. Thus, while the importance of early learning experiences (particularly parent-child interaction patterns) in the development of later behavior disorders such as marital disruption, depression, learning disabilities, and addictive disorders, is acknowledged, the current behavior-environment interactions that may be serving to maintain these behavior problems remain the primary focus of assessment. Support for this assumption is derived from the hundreds of published studies that demonstrate that clinically meaningful behavior change can result when factors that are temporally contiguous with the target behavior are modified.

The deemphasis of historical determinants in behavioral assessment is illustrated by a preference for self-, participant, or external observation and other assessment methods that focus on current behaviors and presumed determinants. Although some authors (Lazarus, 1974; Wolpe, 1973) recommended a fairly exhaustive, historically based assessment, the relative emphasis on more immediate determinants is apparent in most behavioral interviews (Haynes & Jensen, 1979; Linehan, 1977) and questionnaires (Galassi & Galassi, 1980).

Limitations of this relatively narrow focus have been identified. Russo, Bird, and Masek (1980) noted that exclusive attention to temporally contiguous determinants may set upper limits on the validity of the behavioral construct systems. For example, most direct observation procedures are currently used to detect determinants that occur within several minutes of the target behavior. Obviously, powerful causal factors may

occur well beyond that time frame and a number of authors (Gottman, 1979; Margolin, 1981; Russo et al., 1980) have recently recommended extending the interval of temporal analysis. As noted by Haynes (1978), increasing attention to historical and temporally noncontiguous factors might facilitate the development of prevention programs, reduce recidivism, and enhance the predictive validity of the behavioral construct system.

Situationally Determined Behavior Variance

Closely associated with assumptions of environmental determinism is the assumption that a significant proportion of the variance in the occurrence or characteristics of behavior can be accounted for by reference to antecedent or concurrent situational factors (Eisler et al., 1975; Patterson & Bechtal, 1977). In contrast to trait-based "personality" construct systems, which assume a higher degree of cross-situational stability,[1] behavioral construct systems emphasize the importance of situational determinants of behavior. Antecedent environmental stimuli are presumed to operate as *eliciting stimuli* (conditioned or unconditioned stimuli in a *classical conditioning paradigm*), or as *discriminitive stimuli* (stimuli associated with differential probabilities of contingencies for particular behaviors in an *operant conditioning paradigm*) (Kazdin, 1979). For example, sleep disturbances may occur in some sleep environments but not others; headaches may occur at work but not at home; a child's noncompliant behavior may occur in the presence of one parent but not the other. This model suggests that the *conditional probability* of behavior (the probability of behavior occurring following some predetermined event) may vary significantly across situations.

As with previous assumptions, the emphasis on situational determinants is relative. It is illogical to assume that individuals are passive responders to transient environmental stimuli; it is more reasonable to assume that variance in behavior can be accounted for through reference to both situations and persons (Haynes, 1979; Kazdin, 1979). Even within an interactionist model (situation × person interaction), however, the behavior analyst must be cognizant that an individual's behavior in one situation is not necessarily predictive of that indi-

---

[1]Hogan, DeSoto, and Solano (1977) suggest that the contention that trait models presume cross-situational stability is unwarranted. They note that "traits" refer only to stylistic consistencies and that assumptions of cross-situational stability can be ascribed to erroneous inferences by "trait theorists."

vidual's behavior in other situations (Foster & Cone, 1980; Heckerman, Schoen, & Barlow, 1981).

Cross-situational variance in the conditional probabilities of behavior has important implications for identifying etiological factors and for planning and evaluating interventions. For example, differences in the probablility of a child emitting aggressive behavior in the presence of each parent or between home and school environments suggest the operation of different eliciting or contingency operations that are potential targets of intervention. Such differences also suggest caution in presuming generalizability of behavior change from one situation to another (Kazdin, 1979). Behavior analysts therefore, attempt to assess the degree of cross-situational variance in behavior and identify situational factors associated with variance in the targeted behavior (Foster & Cone, 1980; Galassi & Galassi, 1980; McFall, 1982).

Multiple Causality and Individual Differences

Assumptions that a particular behavioral syndrome is homogeneous in topography or that it can be attributed to univariate or nonvariant causes (e.g., neurotransmitter disturbances as *the* cause of depression of schizophrenia; psychosexual conflict as *the* cause of anxiety disorders) are common in clinical psychology and minimize the necessity for preintervention assessment within these models. Behavioral theorists (Bandura, 1969, 1981; Hersen, 1981; Kanfer & Phillips, 1970; Ullmann & Krasner, 1975) have emphasized the concept of multiple causality of behavior: that any behavior can, and usually does, result from multiple and interacting causes. The underlying assumption, that it is difficult to account satisfactorily for behavioral variance within a univariate causal model, suggests that additive and interactive models involving multiple factors are necessary to account for behavioral variance satisfactorily.

A corollary to this assumption is that there are significant individual differences in behavioral topography (Kolko, Dorsett, & Milan, 1981), causality, and response to treatment for any particular disorder. Furthermore, individual differences are assumed to occur both *between* and *within* syndromes. For example, the determinants of depression are presumed to differ from the determinants of other behavior disorders, the topography and determinants among individuals labeled as "depressed," are presumed to vary, and the re-

sponse to a particular intervention by individuals who are depressed are presumed to vary.

The above issues underscore the desirability of *broad-spectrum behavioral assessment:* the use of multiple assessment methods and a focus on multiple targets (Conger & Keane, 1981; Mash & Terdal, 1981; Nelson & Hayes, 1979). A behavior problem such as social-interaction deficits can be the result of various interactive combinations of determinants, including inadequate parental modeling of social behaviors, insufficient exposure to social-learning experiences, reinforcement of inappropriate social-interaction behaviors, interference with social behaviors by elevated "anxiety" responses (*conditioned emotional responses*), cognitive behaviors, or punishment of social interactions. For this reason, intervention programs cannot be based solely on a diagnosis such as "depressed," "alcoholic," "hyperactive," "noncompliant," or "hypertensive," because such diagnoses do not identify relevant parameters. An extensive evaluation of the behavior problem and the etiological role of various possible determinants is necessary to design appropriate interventions and to identify appropriate targets for intervention (Haynes, 1978; Hersen, 1981).

The assumptions of multiple and varying causality within and between behavior disorders do not suggest that a treatment program cannot be applied across individuals manifesting the same disorder. Examples of successful application of such treatments are widespread. It does imply, however, that the *probability* of effective treatment and the *degree* of effectiveness can be significantly improved if treatments are tailored to fit the idiosyncratic determinants identified in pretreatment behavioral assessment.

Minimizing Inferential Qualities

One factor that facilitates the early development of a behavioral construct system was the perceived stagnation of traditional clinical psychology. Many investigators (Eysenck, 1952, 1960b; Ullmann & Krasner, 1975; Wolpe, 1958; see review by Kazdin, 1978) believed that the effectiveness of interventions, the degree of predictive power, and the utility and applicability of traditional clinical paradigms had improved little in the preceding three decades. This lack of development was attributed, in part, to epistemological deficiencies, including an almost exclusive reliance on highly inferential constructs, assessment systems, and intervention targets (Kazdin, 1978). The causes of behavior disorders were presumed to reside in hypothetical mediating and mentalistic variables that were difficult to operationalize, identify, and measure. The resulting construct systems were not amenable to empirical investigation or refutation. This exclusive invocation of inferential, nonpublic, and abstract variables was perceived to be incompatible with the conceptual and technical growth of clinical psychology.

As a partial reaction to the perceived epistemological inadequacy of traditional clinical paradigms, the behavioral construct system has attempted to minimize its inferential qualities. This effect has had far-reaching implications for behavioral assessment (Mash & Terdal, 1981). The emphasis on direct observation of public events is attributable, in part, to the perceived desirability of deriving verifiable and minimally inferential indices of targeted behavior. Behavior analysts are also less likely to ascribe determinants of behavior to internal, nonpublic variables, although the importance of subjective feelings, physiological events, attitudes, expectancies, and other cognitions is recognized (Bandura, 1969).

The avoidance of inferential variables, although an epistemological emphasis that has facilitated the development of behavioral construct systems, has led to some deficiencies and frictions within the discipline. Because of the inferential nature of data derived from interviews and other subjective self-report instruments, such assessment procedures have been applied with greater reticence and have been subjected to less empirical investigation than have other behavioral assessment instruments (Haynes, 1978; Haynes & Jensen, 1979; Linehan, 1977). The recent incorporation of cognitive variables within behavioral construct systems has also precipitated objections that it represents a regression to older models of an excessively inferential, nonparsimonious, nonproductive, and value-laden (Sampson, 1981) discipline. It is too early, however, to determine if such movements within the behavioral construct system serve to enhance its conceptual validity or merely decrease the parsimony of the system without concomitantly enhancing its validity.

Response Fractionation

Response fractionation (sometimes referred to as *response desynchronization*) refers to the assumption that behavior problems such as "aggression,"

"social skills," or "fear" are composed of multiple elements that frequently demonstrate low levels of covariaton (Haynes & Wilson, 1979, pp. 17–21; Nelson & Hayes, 1979; Marinez-Diaz & Edelstein, 1980; Marziller & Winter, 1978; Sartory, Rachman, & Grey, 1977). For example, fear responses may involve components such as specific cognitions, avoidance behaviors, subjective perceptions of discomfort, and elevated levels of autonomic arousal, and these components may not demonstrate a high level of covariation (Borkovec, Weerts, & Bernstein, 1977). Response fractionation may occur between different measures of the same mode (such as low correlations between skin conductance and skin potential responses), as well as between modes (May, 1977; Schwartz, 1977).

As Kaloupek and Levis (1980) and Hartmann, Roper, and Bradford (1979) noted, the degree of response covariation varies across individuals and response systems and is strongly influenced by the methods of measurement. Variables likely to influence the apparent degree of response fractionation include: (1) the unique sources of error associated with each measurement instrument; (2) the degree to which the content of the instruments converge (Kaloupek & Levis, 1980); (3) sources of measurement variance (such as variance in situational stimuli, sampling procedures, duration of samples, and the time frame of comparisons); (4) the degree of similarity in determinants of targeted behaviors (Mischel, 1968); and (5) the variability or intensity of the target variables (McReynolds & Stegman, 1976; Patterson & Bechtel, 1977). Cone (1979) noted that most studies examining response covariation have confounded methods of assessment with the content area, and he recommended using a *multicontent-multimethod-multibehavior* matrix to evaluate the covariation among multiple response systems more validly.

The assumption of response fractionation suggests that no single measure is a valid representation of all components of a complex construct. Therefore, the importance of multimodal measurement identifying specific topographical characteristics of a behavior problem and in evaluating intervention effects becomes more apparent. For example, increases in the probability that a speech phobic will make a speech following intervention may or may not be associated with a concurrent change in perceptions of discomfort or autonomically mediated indices of arousal.

The Importance of an Empirically-Based, Cybernetic Construct System

Most psychological construct systems have been developed through experientially based, rather than methodologically based, processes. They are tied to nonvariant assumptions, and most cease to evolve to a significant degree following their initial development. For example, classic psychoanalysis, client-centered therapy, Gestalt therapy, and rational-emotive therapy, despite numerous derivatives and branches (themselves a product of experientially based dissatisfaction with a particular construct system) retain most of their original concepts and have remained basically unchanged since their original formulation. Unless one adopts the currently indefensible position that a particular construct system can account for most of the variance in human behavior, the nonevolutionary nature of a construct system is a strong indictment against its viability.

The most important characteristic of a behavioral construct system, and one that is supraordinate to all previously discussed assumptions, is its emphasis upon empiricism as the primary method of conceptual and technological development. One of the most important criteria for evaluating the viability of a psychological construct system is its rate of theoretical and technical evolution — the rate of increase in the proportion of variance in behavior that can be accounted for (predictive validity) and the rate of increase in the effectiveness and applicability of intervention strategies based upon the construct system. Thus, the differential emphasis on *methods of inquiry* over fixed concepts is a necessary component of the cybernetic quality of a behavioral construct system — a system that emphasizes self-assessment, self-correction, and self-improvement.

The emphasis on methodological empiricism affects behavioral assessment concepts and procedures in many ways. In addition to minimizing the use of inferential concepts and methods, there is a strong emphasis on quantification. Although qualitative (descriptive) information about clients and behavior is important, behavior analyst also seek data on the rate, duration, intensity, frequency, latency, cyclicity conditional probability, covariates, and degree of change of behavior. Quantitative information is useful in selecting target behaviors, designing intervention programs, and evaluating program effectiveness (Haynes, 1978).

This empirical emphasis is apparent, not only in the efforts to obtain quantitative data through direct observation, self-monitoring, participant monitoring, and psychophysiological assessment, but also in interviews where behavior analysts are likely to seek quantitative indices of behavior problems, associated behaviors, and potentially relevant environmental factors.

The emphasis on empiricism is also reflected in the ongoing assessment of intervention effects and in the application of single-case or time-series clinical research designs (Hersen & Barlow, 1976). The purpose of behavioral assessment is not simply to select target behaviors and facilitate the development of intervention plans, it is also to provide a mechanism for ongoing evaluation of intervention effects and to facilitate the derivation of inferences about what factors are responsible for observed effects. For example, assessment of a family with an aggressive child might include daily parent reports of child behavior throughout the course of intervention, as well as weekly home or clinic observations of parent-child interaction. Intervention would also be designed to maximize *internal validity* by using reversal or replication phases, multiple baseline controls, or combinations of these designs (Kratochwill, 1978).

There are a number of assumptions in a behavioral construct system which affect the concepts, methods, applications, and focus of behavioral assessment. These assumptions emphasize the essential role of assessment in behavioral intervention and in the continued vitality of the behavioral construct system (Goldfried, 1979; Goldfried & Sprafkin, 1976; Haynes, 1978; Karoly, 1981; Patterson & Hops, 1972). The selection of target behaviors, the identification of controlling variables, the interventions designed, and the probability of successful intervention are contingent upon the outcome of valid assessment procedures. In addition, ongoing behavioral assessment provides the bases for evaluating and modifying intervention strategies.

Assumptions of multiple causality and individual differences in the operation of causal factors emphasize the importance of preintervention behavioral assessment in identifying determinants which often become the targets of intervention. However, it should be noted that successful interventions are not *necessarily* contingent upon the manipulation of causal events. There are numerous examples of interventions which are successfully applied across subjects regardless of differences in etiological factors (Leitenberg, 1976).

As noted in the previous section, the assumptions underlying a behavioral construct system also affect the methods used in behavioral assessment. The following section will examine these methods along a number of evaluative dimensions.

Methods of Behavioral Assessment

As noted, behavioral assessment refers to a diverse set of methods. These methods vary considerably in their focus, application, utility, and psychometric characteristics, (Barlow, 1981; Cone & Hawkins, 1977; Ciminero et al., 1977; Haynes, 1978; Haynes & Wilson, 1979; Mash & Terdal, 1981; Nelson & Haynes, 1982). All, however, reflect the behavioral construct system upon which they are based and differ from methods based on other construct systems.

The examination of assessment methods is facilitated by the utilization of several dimensions of evaluation. Assessment methods may be evaluated on dimensions of applicability and utility, cost-efficiency, validity, reliability, sensitivity, social acceptability, and sources of error. These dimensions are outlined below and then used to provide a context for examining specific behavioral-assessment methods.

Dimensions of Evaluation

The evaluation of assessment methods ("methods" typically refers to classes of instruments with similar foci and procedures, such as projectives, analogue observations, or self-monitoring) or of assessment instruments should be based upon several psychometric and qualitative considerations. Clinical psychologists, including behavior analysts, often develop or select assessment instruments and interpret results from assessment instruments without careful considerations of relevant psychometric and qualitative properties. Inferences derived from the application of inadequately developed or evaluated assessment instruments must be viewed with extreme caution because of uncertainty about the validity of the obtained measures. These evaluative dimensions are particularly important in behavioral assessment because of its impact on the development and evaluation of intervention strategies. These dimensions are briefly outlined below; more extensive discussions of qualitative and psychometric aspects of assessment instruments may be found in Anastasi (1968),

Haynes (1978), Kerlinger (1972), Maloney and Ward (1976), Mischel (1968), Nunnally (1967), and Sellitz, Wrightsman, and Cook (1976).

APPLICABILITY AND UTILITY

Applicability and utility refer to the amenability of particular methods or instruments to the assessment of specific populations or behaviors, and within specific environments. The applicability and utility of each instrument varies across populations, behaviors, and settings. Thus, naturalistic observation may be very applicable with high-rate child conduct problems occurring in the classroom but less applicable with low-rate adolescent antisocial behaviors, such as stealing or deviant sexual behavior, that occur in the community.

The applicability and utility of an assessment instrument vary with its purpose. Gottman (1979) has developed a method of analyzing power and reciprocity factors in marital interaction from samples of verbal interaction between the spouses. This time-series analysis of behavior codes derived from dyadic interaction is very useful for research purposes but, because of the extensive time required, is less applicable for clinical assessment purposes.

The applicability and utility of an instrument are also influenced by *cost-benefit ratios* — that is, the amount and utility of information gained per unit of assessment time (or money). Some behavioral-assessment instruments, such as naturalistic observation, provide very useful data but are frequently time-consuming and expensive. Others, such as self-monitoring or behavioral questionnaires, provide less costly but more inferential data.

The clinical psychologist must decide if the type and amount of information gained warrant the use of a particular instrument. This decision is based, in turn, upon the availability of alternative, less costly instruments and the potential significance of the obtained information. A dichotomy between research and clinical applications is apparent because cost factors are frequently weighted more heavily in clinical applications and benefit factors are frequently weighted more heavily in research applications.

A cost-benefit analysis also influences the duration and/or extent of assessment. Although behavioral assessment is a continuous process occurring before, during, and following intervention, there is a point at which additional assessment (more questionnaires, more hours of observation) is not warranted by the information gained. Assessment efforts hould be *parsimonious*, and there is a negatively accelerating relationship between the amount of assessment (hours of observation, weeks of self-monitoring, number of questionnaires) and the amount of information gained: initial assessment efforts have greater impact on our inferences than subsequent efforts.

A number of other factors influence the applicability of an assessment instrument. These include *communicability* (the degree to which assessment procedures can be, or need to be, understood by the individuals being assessed); *social acceptability* (the acceptability of the assessment procedures or goals to the individuals being assessed or the individuals in the social environment of the target individual); *reactivity* (the degree to which the assessment process modifies the behavior of individuals being assessed); and other sources of error (response biases, time-sampling errors, technical difficulties). Most of these will be addressed in subsequent sections of this chapter.

Overall, behavioral-assessment methods demonstrate a remarkable degree of applicability and utility. Methods such as self-monitoring, participant observation, and naturalistic observation, although differing in their focus and application, can be used in diverse environments (mental-health centers, homes, schools, workplaces, psychiatric institutions), across diverse populations (developmentally disabled, teachers, grade-school children, psychiatric outpatients, families) and with diverse behavior problems (attention deficits, sexual dysfunctions, seizures, addictive disorders) (Ciminero et al., 1977; Haynes & Wilson, 1979). No other assessment system has approximated this degree of applicability and utility.

VALIDITY

Perhaps the most important dimension for evaluating an assessment instrument is the degree to which it measures the constructs it is intended to measure. Data derived from an assessment instrument are used to make diagnostic and treatment decisions and to evaluate intervention outcome. If the data are not valid representations of the targeted constructs, erroneous inferences and decisions are more likely and the probability of intervention success is significantly diminished. Examples of the validity dimension include the extent to which data derived from home observation of family in-

teraction are representative of the typical family interaction, the degree to which data derived from self-monitoring of cigarette smoking accurately represents the number of cigarettes smoked, and the degree to which a questionnaire measure of heterosocial anxiety accurately measures social behaviors and/or feelings of distress in heterosocial situations.

Validity is a complex multicomponent construct and is addressed in detail in most books on measurement (e.g., Maloney & Ward, 1976; Mischel, 1977). Aspects of validity include criterion-referenced validity (including internal, external, concurrent, and predictive validity), content validity, and construct validity.

Criterion-referenced validity refers to the degree to which data from an assessment instrument correlate with data from another assessment instrument presumed to measure the same or a similar construct. Examples of criterion-referenced validity evaluation of assessment instruments include correlating two questionnaire measures of marital satisfaction or comparing data derived from self-monitoring and participant monitoring of child noncompliance.

Criterion-referenced validity may be either internal or external. *Internal validity* is closely related to the concept of *accuracy*, while external validity is closely related to the concept of *generalizability* (Cronbach et al., 1972; Tunnell, 1977). For example, the internal validity of data from observing mother-child interactions in a clinic playroom can be assessed by adding a second observer (frequently referred to as *interobserver agreement*). The external validity of the same assessment instrument can be assessed by examining the degree to which the data derived from the clinic observations are representative of data derived from observations of mother-child interactions in the home or the data derived from other instruments such as parent reports.

Validity may also be *concurrent* or *predictive*. The degree to which the data from one assessment instrument are correlated with data from another instrument administered contiguously is a measure of concurrent validity. The degree to which the data are correlated with data from another instrument administered at a later time is a measure of predictive validity.

One method of deriving an estimate of validity is through assessing the *reliability* of data derived from an instrument. Reliability refers to the degree of *consistency* (*external reliability*) or *homo-*

geneity (*internal reliability*) of an instrument: the degree to which data obtained from serial administration of the same instrument correlate (*test-retest reliability*; external), or the degree of covariation of elements of an assessment instrument (such as *split-half reliability* or *internal homogeneity coefficients*; internal).

The implications of low coefficients of reliability vary as a function of the underlying assumptions of the assessment instrument. For constructs that are assumed to be relatively stable across situations and time (such as intelligence, height, defensiveness), they suggest that the instrument does not validly measure the targeted construct. For constructs that are assumed to vary across time or situations (such as social initiation responses, social avoidance behavior, or autonomic arousal), they are consistent with the inference that the instrument is invalid but may also be attributed to real variance in the targeted construct.

Because a behavioral construct system assumes a greater degree of temporal and situational variability, partialling observed variance between measurement error and true sources of variability is a major focus in behavioral assessment (Haynes, 1978). The concept of criterion-referenced validity is based upon traditional psychometric assumptions of cross-situation stability, homogeneous and stable behavioral syndromes, and a high degree of response covariation. This foundation in traditional psychometric assumptions presents challenging conceptual and methodological problems for behavioral assessment. Because of assumptions of situationally controlled behavioral variance and response fractionation, presumed measurement variance would be expected to be greater and validity coefficients lower. As in the case of reliability, low indices of criterion-referenced validity may suggest diminished confidence in the data but may also reflect true behavioral variance, variance in situational factors, or variance in the components of the construct being sampled. Regardless of the source of variance, low validity coefficients suggest cautious interpretation of an instrument's generalizability across situations, components, time, and/or persons.

Because it is difficult to apply traditional psychometric concepts of validity and reliability to an assessment system based upon incompatible theoretical assumptions, a number of authors (Cronbach et al., 1972; Cone & Hawkins, 1977; Coates & Thoresen, 1978) have suggested a *generalizability model* as an alternate conceptual and statistical

framework. Generalizability will be addressed in a subsequent section.

Another form of validity is *content validity*—the degree to which elements of an assessment instrument reflect the relevant dimensions of the targeted construct. A content-valid questionnaire on depression should reflect behavioral conceptualizations of that construct and would include not only items monitoring mood and affect (as in traditional depression inventories), but items focusing on social initiation behaviors, reinforcement decrements, perceptions of control or helplessness, and social consequences for depressive behaviors (Lewinsohn, 1975; Seligman et al., 1976). Although content validity is a qualitatively inferred attribute of an assessment instrument, it is also reflected in coefficients of criterion-referenced validity in that an instrument with a low level of content validity would not correlate highly with more valid measures (Nunnally, 1967).

The degree of content validity of an assessment instrument is influenced by its method of development. Most behavioral, as well as nonbehavioral, instruments are *rationally derived*. However, other methods of selecting elements for an instrument, such as *contrasted groups comparisons* (e.g., selecting observation codes based on behaviors that discriminate between satisfied and dissatisfied marital couples), or drawing from previously validated assessment instruments, can enhance its level of content validity.

Because the behavioral construct system is evolving and conceptualizations of the targeted constructs continue to be refined, the content validity of assessment instruments is never stable. When our conceptualization of behavioral syndromes, such as learning disabilities (Lahey, Vosk, & Habif, 1981), social skills (McFall, 1982), or sleep disorders (Borkovec, 1979) change through the inclusion of additional topographical, mediating, or causal factors, assessment instruments must also change (Messick, 1981).

We are concerned not only with the validity of a particular instrument or method but also with the validity of the construct it is designed to measure—its *construct validity* (Kerlinger, 1972; Maloney & Ward, 1976; Messick, 1981; Nunnally, 1967; Sellitz, Wrightsman, & Cook, 1976). Constructs help summarize observed relationships and provide the basis for their theoretical elaboration (Messick, 1981). They also vary in the degree to which they perform these functions. For example, the individual codes as well as sampling procedures in behavioral observation systems for syndromes such as child aggression (Patterson, Cobb, & Ray, 1973), hyperactivity (Abikoff, Gittelman-Klein, & Klein, 1977), marital dysfunction (Hops et al., 1972), or heterosocial skills (Barlow et al., 1977) are based upon conceptualizations of these syndromes and their determinants. The validity of these coding systems cannot exceed the validity of the constructs upon which they were based.

Construct validity can be evaluated in terms of the proportion of variance in behavior that can be accounted for by the construct (concurrent and predictive validity), and the proportion of variance in behavior accounted for by the construct in comparison to alternative constructs. A particularly important means of construct validation in behavioral assessment is *intervention validity* (or *treatment validity*, Nelson & Hayes, 1979): the effectiveness of intervention based upon assessment procedures derived from the construct.

SENSITIVITY

Another dimension upon which assessment instruments can be evaluated is their *sensitivity* — the degree to which they reflect changes in the various components of a construct. Sensitivity is related to content and criterion-referenced validity and may vary among the components of a construct tapped by an instrument. For example, a questionnaire on social anxiety may be sensitive to changes in subjective discomfort in social situations but not to changes in the frequency with which an individual initiates social contact. Similarly, an observation system for family interaction may be sensitive to changes in parent-delivered contingencies but not to changes in child- or sibling-delivered contingencies.

Instruments may also vary in *temporal sensitivity*. For example, decreases in the rate of classroom aggressive behaviors may be reflected in observation-derived data before it is reflected in data derived from teacher questionnaires.

SOCIAL ACCEPTABILITY

Issues of applicability, utility, validity, and sensitivity are relevant only if administration of the assessment instrument is permitted. Classroom observations may possess excellent psychometric characteristics but the reluctance of school administrators to allow external observers in the classroom renders psychometric considerations irrelevant. The importance of social acceptability underscores the need to discuss carefully with a target individual or important mediators in the individual's environment the rationale, costs, benefits associated with an assessment procedure as well as protection to individual privacy and liberties.

SOURCES OF ERROR

Sources of measurement error vary widely among assessment methods and instruments. They include *observer bias* and *observer drift* (Johnson & Bolstad, 1973), procedures for assessing observer accuracy (Reid, 1970), errors in the content validity or construction of an instrument (Maloney & Ward, 1976), *reactive effects* of the assessment process (Baum, Forehand, & Zegiob, 1979; Haynes & Horn, 1982), errors in time, behavior, or situation sampling (Powell & Rockinson, 1978; Smith, Madsen, & Cipani, 1981), the social influence process of the assessment situation (Haynes et al., 1981), and technical misapplication of assessment instruments (Greenfield & Sternbach, 1972). Sources of measurement error directly affect the validity of inferences derived from an assessment instrument and will be considered in greater detail when specific assessment methods are addressed.

The outcome of behavioral assessment has a significant impact on the design and evaluation of intervention programs and on the growth and refinement of the behavioral construct systems. Because of this impact, behavioral-assessment instruments should be carefully considered on several psychometric dimensions. The previous section has outlined these dimensions. The subsequent section will examine specific assessment methods in their context. Importantly, behavior analysts have recently demonstrated an increasing awareness and application of psychometric principles to behavior assessment (Bellack, 1979; Conger et al., 1980; Galassi & Galassi, 1980; Lahey et al., 1981), which has resulted in a rapid improvement in the quality of the instruments used.

Methods of Behavioral Assessment

NATURALISTIC OBSERVATION

Naturalistic observation is the systematic monitoring and recording of behavior in the natural environment, usually by trained external observers, that is, observers who are not typically part of the natural environment. The frequent use of naturalistic observation in behavioral assessment (Haynes & Wilson, 1979) reflects the emphasis on minimizing the inferential nature of assessment and the importance of acquiring quantitative indices of target behaviors and behavior-environment interactions as they occur in the natural environment. Naturalistic observation has been used with a broad range of target behaviors and settings, including parent-child interaction in the home (Arnold, Sturgis, & Forehand, 1977); and in hospital environments (Bakeman & Brown, 1977); social and institutional behaviors of psychiatric patients in day-treatment settings (Alevizos et al., 1978); children's interactions at a summer day camp (Barret & Yarrow, 1977); janitorial behaviors of mentally retarded adults in institutional bathrooms (Cuvo, Leaf, & Borakove, 1978); work behaviors of mentally retarded adolescents in a halfway house (Johnson & Bailey, 1977); marital interaction in the home (Haynes, Follingstad, & Sullivan, 1979); child behaviors in a ghetto classroom (Jones, Fremouw, & Carples, 1977); and many others (Barlow, 1981; Ciminero et al., 1977; Haynes & Wilson, 1979; Mash & Terdal, 1981).

Methods of naturalistic observation vary widely but most often involve *time sampling*, in which a number of circumscribed observation sessions (e.g., three half-hour sessions per week) are divided into brief intervals (e.g., 15 second segments). Trained observers then record the occurrence of preselected and predefined behaviors within each interval. Behaviors can be recorded in the form of *frequency tallies, response chains* involving a number of social interactions (Patterson et al., 1975), or *contingency matrices* of antecedent-behavior or behavior-consequent chains (Mash, Terdal, & Anderson, 1973). Recording and coding of behavior can sometimes be facilitated with the use of audio or video recordings (Cuvo et al., 1978), electromechanical multiple-event recorders (Gardner et al., 1968), automated data-acquisition systems (Fitzpatrick, 1977), and electronic devices for the direct monitoring of behavior (Schulman, Stevens, & Kupst, 1977).

Naturalisitc observation can provide data on behavior frequencies and/or durations, social interactions, and conditional probabilities, and is a particularly powerful tool for evaluating treatment effects. It is one of the least inferential methods of acquiring information about behavior in the natural environment.

There are several sources of error associated with naturalistic observation (Conger & Keane, 1981; Foster & Cone, 1980; Wasik & Lovin, 1980; Wildman & Erickson, 1977). Some of these sources of error can be attributed to the use of observers: observers may be insufficiently trained, their characteristics or behavior may influence the behavior of target individuals, their accuracy is influenced by observer bias and drift, and the method of assessing interobserver agreement affects coefficients of interobserver agreement (Boykin & Nelson, 1981; Horn & Haynes, 1981; Johnson & Bolstad, 1973; O'Leary, Kent, & Kanowitz, 1975; Sackett, 1978; Wasik & Loven, 1980; Wildman & Erickson 1977). The data derived from naturalistic observation are also influenced by the time-sampling parameters used within sessions, the schedule of sessions over time, the method of collecting data, the complexity of the coding system, observer characteristics, ecological variables, and the environmental context in which observation occurs (Foster & Cone, 1980; Haynes, 1978; Sackett, 1978; Wasik & Loven, 1980; Wildman & Erickson, 1977).

One potential source of error in all assessment methods that is particularly relevant in naturalistic observation is *reactivity*—the process in which behavior is affected by its assessment. While observer errors are associated with threats to the internal validity of observation, reactivity is associated with threats to its external validity. If the process of observing behavior modifies its characteristics or rate, it is impossible to assume that the derived data validly represent behavior when it is not being observed. Two recently published articles (Baum et al., 1979; Haynes & Horn, 1982) have reviewed research on reactive effects in behavioral observation. Both noted strong evidence for reactive effects with some observation procedures and populations, and both identified a number of variables that may affect the occurrence, degree, or direction of reactive effects. The conceptual paradigms offered included *stimulus control, novelty, habituation,* and *obtrusiveness*. Although it is a threat to generalizability, it should be noted that reactivity does not necessarily diminish utility or other forms of validity. For example, functional and dysfunctional families may still behave significantly different when being observed, even though reactive effects to the observation occur. As noted by Haynes and Horn (1982), however, reactive effects may be so great in some cases (e.g., sexual interaction, antisocial behavior) as to preclude the use of naturalistic observation.

Cost-efficiency factors are important when considering the use of naturalistic observation. Despite the utility and importance of observing behavior in the natural environment, it can be time-consuming and expensive. Cost-benefit considerations have led to the development of alternative methods of acquiring data about behavior in the natural environment.

ANALOGUE OBSERVATION

Analogue observation is the direct observation of behavior in environments that are structured to increase observational efficiency. Analogue observation can involve a variety of settings, such as imposed restrictions in the observation of family interaction at home (Patterson et al., 1975), the observation of social interaction in structured clinic rooms (Kent et al., 1977; Reisinger & Ora, 1977), the observation of child behaviors in structured playrooms (Rekers, 1975), the observation of marital interaction in structured clinic situations (Jacobson, 1977; O'Leary & Turkewitz, 1978), the measurement of fear behavior during a *behavioral avoidance test* (Barrera & Rosen, 1977; Gatchel et al., 1978), the assessment of social skills in role-playing situations (Bellack, 1979; Curran, 1977; Curran et al., 1980; Kolko et al., 1981), or the assessment of drinking behaviors in artificially structured bars (Sobell, Schafer, & Mills, 1972). Analogue observation is particularly useful because it facilitates the observation of low-rate behaviors that would be difficult to observe in the natural environment (such as discussion of a problem topic by a marital couple, response in a situation requiring assertion) or that would not normally occur (such as initiating conversation with a member of the opposite sex by an individual with severe heterosexual anxiety).

Analogue observations may involve: (a) *situation analogues*, in which the individual is assessed in an artificial situation such as a simulated bar or playroom that resembles a home environment (Frisch, 1977; Sobel et al., 1972); (b) *stimulus analogues*, in which artificial stimuli are provided, such as in role-played responses to taped assertion situations (Edinberg, Karoly, & Gleser, 1977); and (c) *behavior analogues*, in which observed behaviors are assumed to be part of the same behavioral class as the behaviors of primary interest, such as bar pressing of psychotics (Lindsley, 1964) or marble dropping by children (Patterson, Littmann, & Hinsey, 1964).

The observation methods used in analogue situations are similar to those used in naturalistic situations. Typically, the observation session is divided into short time samples; the occurrence of specific, predefined behaviors within those intervals is recorded by trained observers. Other dependent variables, such as the distance to a feared object, subjective ratings of discomfort, or observer ratings of anxiety or skill (Bellack, 1979; Curran et al., 1980) may also be recorded.

Analogue observation can be more cost-efficient than naturalistic observation. It increases the probability of directly observing behavior-environment interactions (such as interactions between spouses or among family members) without intruding into the natural environment. This efficiency is achieved by structuring the situation so as to increase the probability of observing behaviors of interest (for example, asking parents to deliver commands to a noncompliant child or asking a marital couple to discuss a problem topic). As a result, the number of clinically significant interactions per unit of assessment time is increased.

Some sources of variance and error in analogue observation are similar to those of naturalistic observation, and include factors associated with the use of observers, instructional variables, and temporal parameters. The primary psychometric concern with analogue assessment is the degree of generalizability or external validity of the derived data (Bellack et al., 1979; Forehand & Atkeson, 1977; Hughes & Haynes, 1978). As with naturalistic observation, the most significant potential threat to external validity is reactivity. Because behavior varies as a function of situational factors, the process of observing behavior in a highly structured and novel environment would be expected to affect behavior, perhaps to the extent that it is no longer a valid representation of the targeted constructs.

The external validity of analogue assessment has been examined by a number of researchers. Some (Bellack et al., 1979) have suggested that behavior emitted in analogue situations may not be generalizable to behavior in the natural environment. Others (Reisinger & Ora, 1977; Rollings, Baumeister, & Baumeister, 1977) have noted a satisfactory degree of criterion-referenced validity when compared to measures of behavior in the natural environment. As Foster and Cone (1980) noted, there can be little doubt that threats to generalizability of data can occur. Thus, the most appropriate research strategy is to identify variables that affect the occurrence or degree of generalizability.

Another method of decreasing the expense, and possibly the reactivity, associated with naturalistic observation is to use observers who are normally part of the targeted individual's natural environment. In participant monitoring, a person (such as a parent, spouse, teacher, or peer) in the target individual's natural environment monitors and records selected behaviors emitted by that individual, usually within a time-sampling framework (such as monitoring the number of child "compliance" responses for one hour each night or the number of pleasant events emitted by a spouse each day). Participant monitoring has been a frequently used assessment method and participant observers have included sleeping partners (Bootzin & Engle-Friedman, 1981), parents (Karoly, 1981), spouses (Zeiss, 1977), and teachers (Nunes, Murphy, & Reprecht, 1977). As with analogue observation, participant monitoring is particularly useful in the assessment of low-rate behaviors (such as marital fights, seizures, stealing) or behaviors that might be highly reactive to the presence of external observers (such as sexual interaction, antisocial behaviors, some ingestive behaviors).

While participant monitoring is a cost-efficient method of gathering both qualitative and quantitative data on behavior in the natural environment, it is also subject to numerous sources of error. In addition to the sources of error that are applicable to the use of any observers in the natural environment, participant observation may be more susceptible to *observer bias*. Sources of observer bias in participant monitoring include: (1) the history of interaction between the target individual and the observer, (2) labels placed on the target individual by the observer, and (3) the potential use or impact of acquired data. These sources of error are particularly threatening to the internal validity (accuracy) of the acquired data (Haynes & Wilson, 1978, pp. 68–75).

Another major source of error, and also a threat to external validity, is reactivity. Hay, Nelson, and Hay (1977), for example, noted that participant observation of students by teachers was associated with significant modifications in the behavior of both students and teachers. In contrast, a number of studies (e.g., Broden, Beasley, & Hall, 1978; Nelson & Hayes, 1977; Reid & Hurlbut, 1977) have found a satisfactory degree of criterion-referenced

validity (both internal and external) for participant monitoring. There is little doubt, however, that reactivity and bias can occur and caution should be exercised in assuming external validity of the data acquired through participant observation. Additional study of factors influencing the occurrence and direction of these sources of error is needed. The presumed sensitivity of participant monitoring to oberver bias and reactivity probably accounts for the fact that participant observation is most often used as supplementary, rather than as a primary outcome measure in behavior therapy research (Haynes & Wilson, 1979).

Self-monitoring is another method of efficiently acquiring qualitative and quantitative data on the behavior of target individuals and behavior-environment interactions in the natural environment. In this method, individuals record the occurrence or other characteristics of target behaviors either continuously or within a time-sampling framework (Nelson, 1977). Self-monitoring has been used with a wide range of behaviors such as smoking (Conway, 1977), alcohol consumption (Dericco & Garlington, 1977), food intake (Epstein & Martin, 1977), headaches (Feuerstein & Adams, 1977), sleep patterns (Lick & Heffler, 1977; Youkilis & Bootzin, 1981), fuel consumption (Foxx & Hake, 1977), obsessive ruminations (Emmelkamp & Kwee, 1977), and school-related activities (Hundert & Batstone, 1978). It has also been applied to a wide range of populations including mentally retarded children and adults, outpatient adults, children in classrooms, psychiatric inpatients, families, and institutions (Haynes & Wilson, 1979).

Perhaps the most important threat to the validity of self-monitoring is reactivity. The reactive effects of self-monitoring can be so powerful that self-monitoring is frequently used as an intervention method (Leitenberg et al., 1968; Kilmann, 1968; Wagner, & Sotile, 1977). The reactive effects sometimes associated with self-monitoring are a threat to the external validity of the acquired data in that they may not be valid reflections of the individual's behavior when he or she is not self-monitoring. However, reactive effects appear inconsistently within and between subjects, and it is therefore important to identify those factors that control the occurrence and direction of reactive effects.

A number of factors that may contribute to reactive effects have been identified. These include the number and valence of behaviors monitored, the temporal relationship between the behavior occurrence and its recording, whether the behavior or product of that behavior is being monitored, whether occurrences or nonoccurrences of the behavior are recorded, and social and self-delivered contingencies associated with self-monitoring (Hayes & Cavior, 1980; Haynes, 1978; Kanfer, 1970; Kazdin, 1974; Nelson, 1977).

An additional concern with self-monitoring is that of *accuracy* (Nelson, 1977): the degree to which data derived from self-monitoring reflect the rate or characteristics of targeted behavior during the self-monitoring interval. A number of investigators have addressed this issue (see review by Nelson, 1977). Most studies have found satisfactory levels of agreement between self-monitored data and data derived concurrently from other assessment procedures. However, inaccuracy remains a potential threat to the level of confidence that can be placed in data derived from self-monitoring.

BEHAVIORAL INTERVIEWS

The behavioral interview is the most frequently employed but least researched assessment method (Emmelkamp, 1981; Haynes & Wilson, 1979; Linehan, 1977). It is an indispensible element of any assessment-intervention packages. Data derived from an interview frequently have a strong impact on the selection of additional assessment procedures, the identification of target behaviors, the development of intervention programs, and the evaluation of intervention effects. Until recently, however, the interview has been objected to only minimal empirical investigation (Hay et al., 1979; Haynes, Jensen, et al., 1981; Schiederer, 1977).

Behavioral and nonbehavioral interviews differ in focus, function, and process, reflecting differences in underlying assumptions. The behavioral interview, compared to the nonbehavioral interview, is more likely to focus on current behavior and its determinants, the role of behavior-environmental interactions, and to solicit quantifiable indices of specific behavioral and environmental events. The functions of the behavioral interview include diagnosis, screening of individuals for acceptance into therapy, selection of other assessment procedures, assessment of mediation potential, the identification of cognitive and environmental determinants, identification of problem behaviors, planning interventions, and evaluating the effectiveness of intervention (Bergan, 1977; Brown, Kratochwill, & Bergan, 1982; Kanfer & Grimm, 1977). Other functions of the interview include assessment of mediation potential and of relevant historical factors, reinforcement of the client(s) and the behavior analyst, and informing clients about the assessment and therapy process (Haynes, 1978).

Sources of error in behavioral interviews are multiple and insufficiently studied. Major threats to the validity of data derived from an interview include the subjective and retrospective quality and susceptibility to bias of information derived from an interview and the inherent social influences of the interview situation (Linehan, 1977). Because of a distrust of subjective data, behavior analysts have erroneously presumed that discrepancies in data derived from interviews and more behaviorally-based assessment methods are an indictment against the validity of the interview. However, there is currently a growing awareness that each assessment method has independent sources of measurement error, different determinants and referents, and that they may vary on the continuum of validity.

OTHER ASSESMENT METHODS

A number of other methods are used in behavioral assessment. These include *questionnaires* (Bellack & Hersen, 1977), *checklists*, and *ratings scales* (Walls et al., 1977). These self-report instruments are frequently derivatives of traditional clinical assessment instruments that have been adopted or modified to be more congruent with a behavioral construct system. Compared to nonbehavioral self-report instruments, they tend to be more specifically worded, to include more situational factors, and to focus to a greater extent on overt motor behaviors and behavior-environment interactions (Haynes & Wilson, 1979). The benefits, applicability and utility, and threats to validity associated with self-report instruments have been reviewed extensively (Maloney & Ward, 1976; Mischel, 1968).

Electrophysiology (sometimes referred to as *psychophysiology*) is a frequently used assessment procedure in behavioral assessment. In behavioral-intervention programs, many target behaviors such as erectile dysfunctions, hypertension, migraine headaches, asthma, female orgasmic dysfunction, insomnia, dyspareunia, Raynauds, and vaginismus, are physiologically based. In addition, physiological factors also play important causal roles in these disorders. As a result, electrophysiological measurement procedures such as skin conductance, electroencephalogram, electromyogram, measures of heart rate, blood flow photopletsmography, temperature, blood pressure monitoring, and respiration rate are important methods in behavioral assessment.

Behavior analysts have become increasingly involved with the study and treatment of psychosomatic and medical-psychological disorders. In addition to analyzing the contribution of environmental factors to the development and treatment of these disorders, behavior analysts have borrowed extensively from the methodology of psychophysiology (Davidson & Davison, 1980; Melamed & Siegel, 1980; Haynes & Gannon, 1981).

Psychophysiological methods are very congruent with the assumptions of a behavioral construct system because they provide specific, quantifiable data with minimal inferential qualities. There are, of course, numerous sources of error and threats to the internal and external validity of these measures that have been reviewed extensively in a number of books (Brown, 1967; Greenfield & Sternbach, 1972; Martin & Venables, 1980; Venables & Martin, 1967).

Less frequently used but promising behavioral assessment methods include *product-of-behavior* measures and *critical-event sampling*. Product-of-behavior measures are designed to minimize the reactivity and cost sometimes associated with naturalistic observation by measuring a permanent or transient product of the targeted behavior rather than the behavior itself. Examples include using weight as a measure of caloric intake (Epstein & Martin, 1977), blood or urine analyses as a measure of fluid and food intake for patients undergoing dialysis, (Magrab & Papadopoulou, 1977), and workbook performance as a measure of academic behaviors in the classroom (Hay, Hay, & Nelson, 1977). Product-of-behavior measures have the advantages of being fairly cost-efficient, relatively permanent, available, quantifiable, amendable to psychometric evaluation, and usually unobtrusive. However, there can be significant problems with the internal validity of these measures because it is difficult to attribute the measured product to specific behaviors. For example, weight change may reflect changes in caloric intake, caloric expenditure, fluid intake, or excretion rates.

Critical-event sampling is another promising but inadequately evaluated method of efficiently acquiring data on behavior-environment relationships. In critical-event sampling, an audio or video record is made during time periods or situations in which there is a high probability that targeted behaviors will be emitted. Examples include audio recordings of family interactions during suppertime, parent-child interactions at bedtime, marital interaction during disagreements at home, or heterosocial interactions on dates (Follingstad, Sullivan, & Haynes, 1978; Margolin, 1981). Although this method offers a potentially inexpensive, efficient, and useful method of acquiring data on behavior-environment interactions in the natural environment, issues of external validity or generalizability, sensitivity, reactivity, and other sources of error have yet to be addressed.

One of the most powerful methods of assessment is the *manipulation* of hypothesized controlling variables. For example, the operation of social stimuli as reinforcers for autistic children can be evaluated through response-contingent systematic presentation and withdrawal of these stimuli; the etiological role of stimulus-control factors in insomnia can be evaluated through systematic manipulation of presleep behaviors; the relative discriminative stimulus properties of parents can be evaluated through systematically exposing a child to each parent under similar conditions. As indicated by these examples, systematic manipulation of hypothesized controlling variables can strengthen or weaken our etiological hypotheses. Although such manipulations are normally part of the postassessment intervention process, they are a useful adjunct in behavioral assessment.

Functional Analysis

Perhaps the most complex aspect of the assessment process is integrating the data derived from multiple methods into a comprehensive and valid *functional analysis*: an integrated conceptualization of targeted behaviors, their determinants, and mediational variables. For example, a functional analysis resulting from multimethod assessment of a family with an aggressive child might include qualitative and quantitative information on the specific types of aggressive behaviors emitted, conditional probabilities of aggressive behavior being emitted across various antecedent conditions (school versus home; presence of father versus mother). Also included might be the behavior chains that precede aggressive behaviors and differential contingencies following aggressive behaviors for acquiring social reinforcement. Contingencies placed on alternative social behaviors, avoidance or escape functions of aggressive behavior, other behaviors that covary with aggressive behaviors (forming a *response class*), and events that function as reinforcers for the target child and his or her parents would also be included. A more extensive functional analysis might also include information on causal attributions of the child and his or her parents, other cognitive antecedent or consequent factors, level of intellectual functioning, the presence or absence of learning disabilities or other academic deficits, the possible contribution of the parents' marital relationship, possible models for aggressive behaviors, and the consequent and eliciting effects of peer behaviors.

Because the functional analysis involves the integrated conceptualization of the target individual(s), issues of validity are of paramount importance. Psychometric characteristics of the asessment instruments have a significant impact on the validity and utility of the functional analysis because they affect the validity and utility of the data upon which it is based. Assuming that valid data have been acquired, however, the behavior analyst must still integrate these data set into a valid and useful conceptualization of target and corollary behaviors, interacting causal factors, and most importantly, potential intervention strategies. Valid data do not insure that the resulting analysis will be valid.

Of all the components of the behavioral assessment process, the integration of behavioral data into a valid and comprehensive functional analysis and treatment plan is probably the least understood and researched. The recent volume by Nelson and Hayes (1982) includes chapters on the selection of target behaviors and the selection of treatment procedures, offering the best coverage of this issue to date. However, empirically based discussion of this crucial phase of behavioral assessment is absent.

A number of authors (Emmelkamp, 1981; Goldfried, 1979; Karoly, 1981; Mash & Terdal, 1981) have recently noted deficiencies in traditional approaches to functional analyses. These authors have suggested the need to broaden traditional behavioral functional analyses to include cognitive factors and to recognize the relativity of judgements about target individuals as a function of various comparison groups (social validity). In addition, more research is needed on: (1) the reliability of functional analyses based on a particular data set; (2) the degree to which the quality and quantity of data affect treatment decisions and/or improved treatment results; (3) the relationship of treatment decisions to functional analyses; and (4) the relative efficacy of functional analyses versus conceptualizations based upon traditional clinical assessment.

Recent Developments

A number of recent conceptual and methodological developments in behavioral assessment reflect its vitality and cybernetic quality. These developments involve areas such as research design and statistics, the application of psychometric principles and the identification of sources of measurement error, clinical utility, and the extension of assessment targets. These developments and some of the issues associated with them are briefly discussed below.

Research Design and Statistics

Because behavioral construct systems emphasize empiricism and individual differences, *single-subject designs* have been applied increasingly in the evaluation of behavioral interventions (Chassan, 1967; Hersen & Barlow, 1976; Kratochwill, 1978). Single-subject designs are special classes of *interrupted time-series designs* (Kratochwill & Levin, 1979) involving repeated administration of assessment instruments within carefully controlled parameters and systematic manipulations of independent variables. Such systematic assessment and intervention enhances the validity of inferences about the factors responsible for behavior changes.

Single-subject designs offer exciting possibilities for the clinical researcher. They serve to increase the internal validity of inferences about intervention effects and can facilitate the derivation of causal hypotheses. Although generalizability of effects across subjects cannot be assumed without repeated applications, single-subject designs provide the methodology by which the level of empirical rigor of clinical practice can be increased without excessive disruption of the therapeutic process. Importantly, they also provide for quantitative feedback to the clinician about the effects of his or her intervention strategies and increase the potential impact of clinical findings on the behavioral construct system.

The application of statistics in evaluating intervention effects is an area of growth as well as of conflict in behavioral assessment. As noted by Kratochwill and Brody (1978), Michael (1974) and Sidman (1960), many behavior analysts believe that increased reliance on statistical rather than visual (Pennypacker, Lienig, & Lindsley, 1972; Wampold & Jurlong, 1981) inference will result in less rigorously controlled interventions, an increase in the level of error in research efforts, and a focus on the impact of less significant factors. Proponents of the use of statistical inference note that many important determinants of behavior have relatively "weak" effects, that variability may be a true state of behavior rather than a reflection of uncontrolled sources of error, and that statistical procedures can enhance interpretation of observed effects. Despite conflict over the use of statistics, there is little doubt that they are being used increasingly in evaluating behavioral intervention effects.

Many of the recent developments in statistics have involved the application of time-series analyses (Berstein, 1977; Glass, Willson, & Gottman, 1975; Jones, Vaught, & Weinrott, 1977; Kazdin, 1976) which minimize the impact of serial dependence (Bernstein, 1977; Glass et al., 1975; Hartman et al., 1980; Jones, Vaught & Weinrott, 1977; Kratochwill & Levin, 1979). Other developments in statistical applications are not specifically tied to time-series designs or analyses. These include an increased attention to magnitude-of-effect analyses as adjuncts to typical analyses of variance (Mitchell & Hartmann, 1981), the use of multiple regression to identify proportions of variance in independent variables accounted for by dependent variables (Haynes et al., 1981), *multivariate analysis of variance* to correct for inappropriate confidence levels when using multiple dependent measures (Kaplan & Litrownik, 1977), calculation of *conditional probabilities* to identify possible causal or covariance relationships (Notarious et al., 1981), and calculation of interobserver agreement using a formula that more accurately controls for chance agreement (Harris & Lahey, 1978; Hartmann, 1977; Haynes & Wilson, 1979).

The incorporation of statistical procedures into behavioral paradigms without concurrent reduction in empirical rigor can yield significant benefits, including: (1) increased confidence in the significance of observed effects; (2) identification of relationships between variables that are not readily apparent from visual inspection of data; (3) derivation of indices of magnitude of effects or proportions of variance in variables accounted for by other variables; and (4) identification of sources of experimental and measurement error.

Psychometric Parameters of Assessment Instruments

In the early stages of the behavior therapy movement, behavior analysts developed and applied many assessment instruments that were derived intuitively, rather than empirically (Haynes, 1978). Many were applied without being subjected to prior psychometric evaluation. Questionnaires on fears, assertion, depression, social skills, life history, and marital and family interaction and satisfaction, as well as observation-coding systems were used without regard to psychometric parameters such as reliability or validity. The result was the dissemination and application of assessment instruments of dubious criterion, content, and construct validity.

Behavior analysts have been particularly lax in evaluating the content validity of assessment instruments. Individual behavior codes in observation systems, items on questionnaires, and situations used in analogue observation or role-play assessments have typically been selected intuitively by the instrument's developers. There has been little attempt to apply empirical methods of content derivation or to determine the extent to which and instrument's content reflects the targeted construct. As a result, many assessment instruments are representative of the developer's personal conceptualizations, which may or may not validly reflect the construct being evaluated.

This disregard for psychometric principles was probably based on five factors: (1) the necessity of applying assessment instruments at a time when empirically validated, behaviorally oriented instruments were not available; (2) an assumption that the applicability of psychometric principles was limited to instruments developed within traditional trait construct systems; (3) an excessive reliance on face validity of behavioral-assessment instruments; (4) a lack of training of behavior analysts in psychometric principles and procedures; and (5) a rejection of most assessment instruments associated with traditional clinical paradigms. A number of authors (Goldfried, 1979; Cone & Hawkins, 1977; Haynes, 1978; O'Leary, 1979) have reflected on the problems associated with the use of non-empirically based assessment instruments and have recommended increased attention to psychometric factors. Psychometric evaluation of behavioral-assessment instruments is a necessary component in establishing confidence in the validity of inferences drawn from them.

Recently, behavioral-assessment instruments are being constructed and refined using more empirically grounded approaches such as discriminant function analysis, analytic-synthetic models, contrasted-groups comparisons, and population sampling (Conger et al., 1980; Freedman et al., 1978; Lahey, Vosk, & Habif, 1981; McFall, 1982; Mullini & Galassi, 1981; Twardosz et al., 1979). Increased empirical rigor in the development of assessment instruments is particularly important because the construct validity of the behavioral construct system as well as the validity of treatment decisions are strongly influenced by the content validity of the associated assessment instruments.

Increased attention to other psychometric factors in behavioral assessment has also been evident in the past several years. Examples include studies examining the factor structure of questionnaires (Galassi & Galassi, 1980), the concurrent validity of observation measures (Haynes, Follingstad, & Sullivan, 1979; Robin & Weiss, 1980), the concurrent validity of interview measures (Haynes et al., 1981) and role-play measures (Bellack et al., 1979; Wessberg et al., 1979), and the reliability of measures used in behavioral medicine (Russo, Bird, & Masek, 1980). Further examples include examinations of the sensitivity of psychophysiological measures of female sexual arousal (Henson, Rubin, & Henson, 1979), the accuracy and external validity of self-monitoring (Dericco, Brigham, & Garlington, 1977; Hay, Hay, & Nelson, 1977), and the sources of variance in a variety of assessment instruments (Baum et al., 1979; Hayes & Cavior, 1980; Haynes & Horn, 1982).

Cronbach et al. (1972), Coates and Thoresen (1978), Curren et al. (1980), and Foster and Cone (1980) have proposed a *generalizability* model that parallels traditional psychometric models of reliability and validity. The generalizability model addresses the degree to which data would be representative of those obtained across other dimensions, such as scorer (e.g., interobserver agreement), setting, item, time, and method. Application of this model requires a factorial design involving the dimensions of interest (such as two observers or two settings). The results of the statistical operations provide inferences about the proportion of variance attributed to each of the dimensions. As noted by Coates and Thoresen (1978), there are numerous conceptual, cost-efficiency, and methodological benefits accruing to the application of a generalizability model.

Clinical Utility

Behavioral assessment is a very powerful research tool: it facilitates the acquisition of data across a variety of individuals, behaviors, and settings, and is an important component in etiological and treatment evaluation research. As such, it has been instrumental in the development of powerful intervention strategies.

Behavioral assessment has proved, however, to be less useful for clinical purposes (Barlow, 1980; Emmelkamp, 1981; Keefe, Kopel, & Gordon, 1978; Mash, 1979; Mash & Terdal, 1981; Wickramesekera, 1981). Problems with the clinical utility of behavioral assessment are illustrated by the finding that many behavioral clinicians rely primarily on traditional interviews and questionnaires rather than on the assessment methods more congruent with a behavior construct system (Emmelkamp, 1981; Swan & MacDonald, 1978; Wade, Baker, & Hartmann, 1979).

The insufficient clinical utility of behavioral assessment seems to be a function of cost-effectiveness considerations and contingencies operating in applied settings. For example, behavioral coding systems for marital or family interaction (Gottman, 1979; Patterson et al., 1969; Wahler, House, & Stambaugh, 1976) provide useful and valid data on social interaction among family members and, therefore, are powerful research tools. However, the use of observation-coding systems typically requires many hours for observer training, for application of the system, and for data reduction and analysis. Although these demands do not preclude the use of behavioral observation in clinical settings, in many cases they render it prohibitively costly.

Perhaps a more powerful factor accounting for the infrequent application of behavioral-assessment methods in clinical settings is the contingency systems that frequently operate in those settings. Many mental-health, medical, and other institutional settings operate on a fee-for-service basis in which client-contact hours form the basis of charges and/or allocations from funding institutions. These contingencies strongly encourage the use of assessment procedures that involve traditional psychodiagnostic interviews and testing. For individuals in private practice, the time necessary to develop, apply, and interpret behavioral-assessment instruments is costly, because clients are typically not billed for such activities. In both public and private care-delivery systems, the use of behavioral-assessment methods results in loss of revenue.

Solutions to the financial realities are complex and involve modification of the contingency systems that operate in applied settings and educating the institution administrators and legislators about the benefits associated with more extensive and valid assessment. Additional solutions could involve instituting contingencies for demonstrations of effectiveness (accountability), or modifying the fee-for-service basis of most institutional and private practice operations.

Another solution is to reduce the cost associated with the use of behavioral-assessment instruments. The desirability of developing more cost-efficient instruments has been discussed frequently but infrequently translated into appropriate research efforts. In one recent attempt to address the issue of efficiency in behavioral assessment, Haynes et al. (1979) examined the internal and temporal homogeneity of a marital interaction coding system involving a number of codes applied across three home observation sessions. The results, while tentative, suggested that the amount of information gained may not warrant the use of more than one observation session and that the number of behaviors coded could be reduced without sacrificing satisfactory levels of discriminant validity.

Some behavioral-assessment methods, such as self- and participant monitoring, analogue assessment, or critical event sampling, are fairly inexpensive to apply. Additional research on these methods and greater practitioner familiarity with them will, it is hoped, lead to their increased utilization.

An Expanding Focus

Behavioral assessment has traditionally focused on the relationship between variables in close temporal proximity, interactions between a target individual and immediate environmental events, the behaviors of individuals or families, and observable behavior. Recently, this relatively narrow focus has been expanded to include the examination of: (1) behavioral relationships that are not in close temporal proximity; (2) interactions in extended social systems; (3) community and environmental targets; (4) qualitative and subjective variables; (5) cognitive variables; and (6) behavioral interrelationships.

As noted, most behavioral-assessment methods, particularly those involving observation, are used to identify relationships and determinants that occur within several seconds or minutes of the target behavior. The reciprocity analysis of dyadic verbal interaction is an excellent example of the empirical utility of this approach (Notarius et al., 1981). However, behavior analysts are becoming increasingly aware that many significant relationships and determinants may occur beyond this time frame (Gottman, 1979; Margolin, 1981; Russo et al., 1980). As examples, it may be necessary to examine events that are separated from the target behavior by hours, days, or longer in order to identify factors that influence marital verbal exchanges (Gottman, 1979), the stressors that precipitate migraine headache or ulcers (Haynes & Gannon, 1981), or the stimuli that elicit the aggressive behavior of a child (Bandura, 1973). The primary methods of examining distant relationships involve conditional probabilities and time-lagged correlational analyses. Although it is costly to examine extended relationships and doing so complicates assessment efforts, the potential impact on the validity of the behavioral construct system is enormous.

The focus of behavioral assessment is also being extended to include targets that are consistent with a *systems theory* (Vincent, 1980). A systems model presumes an extended number of interdependent causal paths, all of which may have an influence on the behaviors of individuals in it and all of which may be affected by changes in the behavior of one person within the system (Cromwell & Peterson, 1981). Behavioral assessment has traditionally focused on interactions between primary-target individuals and significant environmental factors (such as parent-child interactions, child-teacher interactions, or spouse-spouse interactions). Behavior analysts are becoming increasingly cognizant of the important causal, maintenance, and mediational role of the larger social network. Thus, it is being recognized that parent-child interactions may be influenced by marital interactions or financial factors, teacher-child interactions in the classroom may be influenced by teacher-principle interactions or the social support system of a teacher. Similarly, marital interactions and satisfaction may be influenced by extramarital relationships.

An excellent example of the impact of an extended systems approach is provided by Wahler (Wahler, Berland, & Coe, 1979) who examined factors affecting recidivism in his child-treatment program. He found a significantly positive relationship between degree of maintenance of parenting skills at follow-up and the level of social support from friends and family of the participating parent. Parents without significant sources of social support in the community demonstrated significantly higher rates of relapse at follow-up periods. This finding suggests the need to assess social support factors prior to treatment and, for some parents, to increase social support systems as part of the intervention program.

The focus of behavioral assessment has also been expanding to include community and ecological targets. Behavioral-assessment procedures have been used in the assessment of such targets as schools attendance and expulsions (Heaton & Safer, 1982), police patrols (Schnelle et al., 1977), energy conservation (Palmer, Lloyd, & Lloyd, 1977), traffic enforcement (Carr, Schnelle, & Kirchner, 1980), sports (Komaki & Barnett, 1977), and program evaluation (Hawkins, Fremouw, & Reitz, 1981; Jones, 1979). These applications underscore the increasing utility of behavioral technology in areas of significant social concern.

Behavioral assessment has also begun to focus on qualitative and subjective variables in addition to observable behavior and environmental variables. This marks a significant departure from sole reliance on quantitative indices of observable behavior in the design and evaluation of treatment. For example, several authors (Deitz et al., 1978; Garfield, 1981; Kazdin, 1977; Kolko et al., 1981; Lebow, 1982; Schreibman et al., 1981; Wolfe, 1978) have emphasized the utility of evaluating the clinical, social, or personal significance and acceptability of assessment and intervention programs: their *social validity*. The concept of social validity implies that behavior analysts should consult with target individuals and mediators regarding their perceptions of desirable target behaviors, attributions of causation, expected methods of intervention, and the outcome of the intervention. These perceptions should be considered not only as major dependent variables but as mediators of inter-

vention outcome. They also involve issues of client rights and informed consent.

The focus on subjective variables does not preclude the application of rigorous measurement techniques. An excellent example of the application of empirical methods to the evaluation of subjective variables is provided by Levis and Plunkett (1979), who applied *magnitude estimation techniques* to quantify subjective reports of anxiety. Empirical methods can also be used in the assessment of perceived causation, credibility of assessment and treatment procedures, and satisfaction with treatment. In addition, *social comparison* procedures (Kazdin, 1977), in which targeted individuals are compared to normative groups to determine the degree of deviance or the clinical significance of treatment effects, can also be used.

The targets of assessment are also being extended to cognitive variables (Bandura, 1981; Kanfer, 1979; Kendall & Hollon, 1981; Korchin & Schulberg, 1981; Merluzzi, Glass, & Genest, 1981; Rimm et al., 1977). The increasing emphasis on the assessment of cognitive variables is a direct effect of their increasing inclusion in conceptualizations of behavior disorders and as integral parts of behavioral intervention programs. Cognitive variables are presumed to function as causal precipitating factors (such as catastrophic thoughts preceding social interactions), as contingencies (such as self-punitive thoughts following failure experiences), as primary target behaviors (such as ruminative or obsessive thoughts or nightmares), and as variables mediating treatment outcomes (such as attributions of causality, expectancies, or perceived credibility). For example, it has been hypothesized that cognitive variables function as causative factors as well as mediating the occurrence and response to treatment of behavior disorders such as obesity (Cooke & Meyers, 1980), depression (Seligman et al., 1976), insomnia (Kamens & Haynes, 1983), headaches (Holroyd & Andrasik, 1978), marital dysfunction (Weiss, 1980), and self-management difficulties (Karoly, 1981).

Behavioral analysts are also becoming increasingly aware of the importance of assessing *behavioral interrelationships*: *covariation* among responses, response hierarchies, and response chains (Kazdin, 1982; Voeltz & Evans, 1982). The presumed importance of behavioral interrelationships is based upon several observations: (1) that responses that are topographically dissimilar can sometimes demonstrate covariation; (2) that modification of one response can sometimes be associated with intended or unintended changes in others; (3) that responses are sometimes organized in hierarchies of probability; (4) that reliable chains of responses sometimes precede a particular target response; and (5) that responses can sometimes function as prerequisites of other responses (Voeltz & Evans, 1982).

These observations represent a significant advancement in the construct validity of a behavioral system and the implications for the theoretical bases and methods of behavioral assessment are far-reaching. Reliable demonstrations of such behavioral interrelationships would suggest that: (1) it is difficult to account satisfactorily for behavioral variance through reference only to situational factors, (2) multimethod/multisituation/multitarget assessment is needed for a comprehensive functional analysis and for a comprehensive evaluation of treatment effects, and (3) examination of response chains and hierarchies may facilitate the derivation of valid and useful functional analyses, and treatment plans. Behavioral interrelationships must, themselves be considered a dependent variable that is under the control of other variables. It is apparent that some responses covary while others do not, that hierarchies may be reliable or unreliable, that behavioral interrelationships may vary across developmental stages, situations, responses, and individuals.

In summary, the behavioral construct system, and therefore the focus of behavioral assessment, have been expanding to include factors in extended temporal relationships, the extended social system of target individuals, a broader range of community and environmental targets, subjective perceptions of clients and significant others, cognitive factors and behavior interrelationships. Although such changes, particularly those that involve subjective reports, are not met with universal enthusiasm (Dietz, 1978; Sampson, 1981), they illustrate the plasticity of behavioral assessment and the behavioral construct systems. Because of its methodological foundation, behavioral assessment is capable of accommodating to conceptual changes within the behavioral construct systems while maintaining an enviable degree of empirical rigor.

Summary

Behavioral assessment has grown dramatically within the past decade. This growth has occurred on several dimensions including applicability, psy-chometric sophistication, research productivity, and clinical utility. Although conceptual and methodological problems remain, behavioral assessment is a viable and important assessment system in clinical psychology.

A number of assumptions affect the goals and methods of behavioral assessment, including a behavior-environment interactionist model of behavioral causality, the importance of determinants in close temporal contiguity to behavior, and the emphasis on situational determinants of behavior. Another important assumption is that behavior is under the control of multiple factors and that there are often significant individual differences in the determinants or topography of behavior. Behavior analysts also strive to minimize the inferential qualities of constructs and assessment methods and assume that there is a significant degree of response fractionation among measures of the same construct. Perhaps the most important characteristic of a behavioral construct system is its emphasis on the development of an empirically based cybernetic system. Because of this empirical emphasis, behavioral assessment is more a methodological than a conceptual system and will therefore continue to demonstrate increasing levels of validity, applicability, and utility.

The methods of behavioral assessment are diverse and include naturalistic observation, analogue observation, participant monitoring, self-monitoring, interviews, psychophysiological measurement, and questionnaires. These methods are derived and adapted from various disciplines but all reflect the concepts and assumptions underlying a behavioral construct system. In addition, each has been the subject of an accelerating amount of empirical investigation, particularly on psychometric issues such as validity, reliability, generalizability, applicability and utility, social acceptability, and sources of error.

The most complex but least researched aspect of behavioral assessment is the functional analysis — the integration of data from various assessment sources into a conceptualization of the determinants, mediational factors, and correlated or covarying elements for an assessment target. The functional analysis is one of the most important aspects of behavioral assessment because it affects treatment decisions, and generalized conceptualization of behavior problems, as well as conceptualizations of specific assessment targets. Additional research is needed on the reliability, validity, and utility of functional analyses.

Behavioral assessment is an evolving conceptual and methodological system and there have been a number of recent developments within it. These include an increased attention to research design and statistics, an increased application of psychometric principles to the evaluation and refinement of behavioral assessment, and an expansion in the focus of behavioral assessment. The focus of behavioral assessment and the attention of behavior analysts is being extended to determinants that are not in close temporal proximity to the targeted behavior, to the social validity of methods, goals, and outcomes, to community and ecological targets, to qualitative aspects of behavior, to cognitive variables, and to the interrelationships among behaviors.

The future viability of behavioral assessment is promising. It is one of the few assessment systems that is experiencing a surge of empirically based activity. As a result, behavioral-assessment methods and concepts in the next decade will be more reliable, valid, comprehensive, applicable, and clinically useful than those of today.

References

Abikoff, H., Gittelman-Klein, R., & Klein, D. F. Validation of a classroom observation code for hyperactive children. *Journal of Consulting and Clinical Psychology*, 1977, *84*, 460–476.

Alevizos, P., DeRisi, W., Liberman, R., Eckman, T., & Callahan, E. The behavior observation instrument: A method of direct observation for program evaluation. *Journal of Applied Behavior Analysis*, 1978, *11*, 243–257.

Alexander, F. G., & Selesnick, S. T. *The history of psychiatry: An evaluation of psychiatric thought and practice from prehistoric times to the present.* New York: Harper & Row, 1966.

Anastasi, A. *Psychological testing.* (3rd ed.) New York: Macmillan, 1968.

Arnold, S., Sturgis, E., & Forehand, R. Training a parent to teach communication skills: A case study. *Behavior Modification*, 1977, *1*, 259–276.

Bachrach, A. J. (Ed.). *Experimental foundations of clinical psychology.* New York: Basic Books, 1962.

Bakeman, R., & Brown, J. V. Behavioral dialogues: An approach to the assessment of mother-infant interactions. *Child Development*, 1977, *48*, 195–203.

Bandura, A. Psychotherapy as a learning process. *Psychological Bulletin*, 1961, *58*, 143–159.

Bandura, A. *Principles of behavior modification.* New York: Holt, Rinehart, & Winston, 1969.

Bandura, A. *Aggression: A social learning analysis.* New York: Prentice-Hall, 1973.

Bandura, A. In search of pure undirectional determinants. *Behavior Therapy*, 1981, *12*, 30–31.

Barlow, D. H. Behavior therapy: The next decade. *Behavior Therapy*, 1980, *11*, 315–328.

Barlow, D. H. (Ed.). *Behavioral assessment of adult disorders.* New York: Guilford Press, 1981.

Barlow, D. H., Abel, G. G., Blanchard, E. B., Bristow, A. R., & Young, L. D. A heterosocial skills behavior checklist for males. *Behavior Therapy*, 1977, *8*, 229–239.

Barlow, D. H., & Hayes, S. C. Alternating treatment design: One strategy for comparing the effects of two treatments on a single subject. *Journal of Applied Behavior Analysis*, 1979, *12*, 199–210.

Barrera, M., Jr., & Rosen, G. M. Detrimental effects of a self-reward contracting program on subjects' involvement in self-administered desensitization. *Journal of Consulting and Clinical Psychology*, 1977, *45*, 1,180–1,181.

Barret, D. E., & Yarrow, M. R. Prosocial behavior, social inferential ability, and assertiveness in children. *Child Development*, 1977, *48*, 475–481.

Baum, C. G., Forehand, R., & Zegoib, L. E. A review of observer reactivity in adult-child interactions. *Journal of Behavioral Assessment*, 1979, *1*, 167–177.

Bellack, A. S. A critical appraisal of strategies for assessing social skill. *Behavioral Assessment*, 1979, *1*, 157–176.

Bellack, A. S., & Hersen, M. Self-report inventories in behavioral assessment. In J. D. Cone & R. P. Hawkins (Eds.), *Behavioral assessment: New directions in clinical psychology.* New York: Brunner/Mazel, 1977.

Bellack, A. S., Hersen, M., & Lamparski, D. Role-play tests for assessing social skills: Are they valid? Are they useful? *Journal of Consulting and Clinical Psychology*, 1979, *47*, 335–342.

Bellack, A. S., Hersen, M., & Turner, S. M. Relationship of role playing and knowledge of appropriate behavior to assertion in the natural environment. *Journal of Consulting and Clinical Psychology*, 1979, *47*, 670–678.

Bergan, J. R. *Behavioral consultation.* Columbus, Ohio: Charles E. Merrill, 1977.

Bergan, J. R., & Tombari, M. L. Consultant skill and efficiency and the implementation and outcomes of consultation. *Journal of School Psychology*, 1976, *14*, 3–14.

Bernstein, G. S. Time-series analysis and research in behavior modification: Some unanswered questions. *Behavior Therapy*, 1969, *7*, 403–408.

Billingsley, R., White, O. R., & Munson, R. Procedural reliability: A rationale and an example. *Behavioral Assessment*, 1980, *2*, 229–241.

Bootzin, R. R., & Engle-Friedman, M. The assessment of insomnia. *Behavioral Assessment*, 1981, *3*, 107–126.

Borkovec, T. D. Pseudo (experiential) insomnia and idiopathic (objective) insomnia: Theoretical and therapeutic issues. *Advances in Behavior Research and Therapy*, 1979, *2*, 27–55.

Borkovec, T. D., Lane, T. W., & Vanoot, P. H. Phenomenology of sleep among insomniacs and good sleepers: Wakefullness experience when cortically asleep. *Journal of Abnormal Psychology*, 1981, *90*, 607–609.

Borkovec, T. D., Weerts, T. C., & Bernstein, D. A. Assessment of anxiety. In A. R. Ciminero, K. S. Calhoun, & H. E. Adams (Eds.), *Handbook of behavioral assessment.* New York: Wiley, 1977.

Boykin, R. A., & Nelson, R. O. The effects of instructions and calculation procedures on observers accuracy, agreement, and calculation correctness. *Journal of Applied Behavior Analysis*, 1981, **14**, 479–489.

Braukmann, C. J., & Fixen, D. L. Behavior modification with delinquents. In M. Hersen, R. M. Eisler, & P. M. Miller (Eds.), *Progress in behavior modification*, Vol. 1. New York: Academic Press, 1975.

Broden, M., Beasley, A., & Hall, R. V. In-class spelling performance: Effects of home tutoring by a parent. *Behavior Modification*, 1978, **2**, 511–530.

Brown, C. C. *Methods in psychophysiology*. Baltimore: Williams & Wilkins, 1967.

Brown, D. K., Kratochwill, T. R., & Bergan, J. R. Teaching interview skills for problem identification: An analogue study. *Behavioral Assessment*, 1982, **4**, 63–73.

Carr, A. F., Schnelle, J. F., & Kirchner, R. E., Jr. Police crackdowns and slowdowns: A naturalistic evaluation of changes in police traffic enforcement. *Behavioral Assessment*, 1980, **2**, 33–41.

Chapman, C. R., & Wyckoff, M. The problem of pain: A psychobiological perspective. In S. N. Haynes & L. R. Gannon (Eds.), *Psychosomatic disorders: A psychophysiological approach to etiology and treatment*. New York: Praeger, 1981.

Chassan, J. B. *Research design in clinical psychology and psychiatry*. New York: Appleton-Century-Crofts, 1967.

Ciminero, A. R., Calhoun, D. S., & Adams, H. E. (Eds.), *Handbook of behavioral assessment*. New York: Wiley, 1977.

Coates, T. J., & Thoresen, C. E. Using generalizability theory in behavioral observation. *Behavior Therapy*, 1978, **9**, 157–162.

Cone, J. D. Confounded comparisons in triple response mode assessment research. *Behavioral Assessment* 1979, **1**, 85–95.

Cone, J. D., & Hawkins, R. P. (Eds.), *Behavioral assessment: New directions in clinical psychology*. New York: Brunner/Mazel, 1977.

Conger, A. J., Wallander, J. L., Mariotto, M. J., & Ward, D. Peer judgements of heterosexual-social anxiety and skill: What do they pay attention to anyhow? *Behavioral Assessment*, 1980, **2**, 243–259.

Conger, J. C., & Keane, S. P. Social skills intervention in the treatment of isolated or withdrawn children. *Psychological Bulletin*, 1981, **90**, 478–495.

Conway, J. B. Behavioral self-control of smoking through aversive conditioning and self-management. *Journal of Consulting and Clinical Psychology*, 1977, **45**, 348–357.

Cooke, C. J., & Meyers, A. The role of predictor variables in the behavioral treatment of obesity. *Behavioral Assessment*, 1980, **2**, 59–69.

Cromwell, R. E., & Peterson, G. W. Multisystem-multimethod assessment: A framework. In E. E. Filsinger & R. A. Lewis (Eds.), *Assessing marriage: New behavioral approaches*. Beverly Hills, Calif.: Sage, 1981.

Cronbach, L. J., Gleser, G. C., Nanda, H., & Rajaratnam, N. *The dependability of behavioral measurements: Theory of generalizability for scores and profiles*. New York: Wiley, 1972.

Curran, J. Social skills: Methodological issues and future directions. In B. Lahey & A. E. Kazdin (Eds.), *Advances in clinical child psychology*, Vol. 1. New York: Plenum, 1977.

Curran, J. P., Monti, P. M., Corriveau, D. P., Hay, L. R., Hagerman, S., Zwick, W. R., & Rarrell, A. D. The generalizability of a procedure for assessing social skills and social anxiety in a psychiatric population. *Behavioral Assessment*, 1980, **2**, 389–401.

Cuvo, A. J. Personal communication, 1982.

Cuvo, A. J., Leaf, R. B., & Borakove, L. A. Teaching janitorial skills to the mentally retarded: Acquisition, generalization, and maintenance. *Journal of Applied Behavior Analysis*, 1978, **11**, 345–355.

Davidson, P. O., & Davison, S. M. *Behavioral medicine: Changing health life-styles*. New York: Brunner/Mazel, 1980.

Deitz, S. M., Slack, D. J., Schwarzmueller, E. B., Wilander, A. P., Weatherly, T. J., & Hilliard, G. Reducing inappropriate behavior in special classrooms by reinforcing average interresponse times: Interval DRL. *Behavior Therapy*, 1978, **9**, 37–46.

Dericco, D. A., Brigham, T. A., & Garlington, W. K. Development and evaluation of treatment paradigms for the suppression of smoking behavior. *Journal of Applied Behavior Analysis*, 1977, **10**, 173–181.

Dericco, D. A., & Garlington, W. K. An operant treatment procedure for alcoholics. *Behaviour Research and Therapy*, 1977, **15**, 497–499.

Edinberg, M. A., Karoly, P., & Gleser, G. C. Assessing assertion in the elderly: An application of the behavioral-analytic model of competence. *Journal of Clinical Psychology*, 1977, **33**, 869–874.

Eisler, R. M., Hersen, M., Miller, P. N., & Blanchard, E. B. Situational determinants of assertive behavior. *Journal of Consulting and Clinical Psychology*, 1975, **43**, 330–340.

Emmelkamp, P. M. G. The current and future status of clinical research. *Behavioral Assessment*, 1981, **3**, 249–253.

Emmelkamp, P. M. G., & Kwee, K. G. Obsessional ruminations: A comparison between thought stopping and prolonged exposure in imagination. *Behaviour Research and Therapy*, 1977, **15**, 441–444.

Epstein, L. H., & Martin, J. E. Compliance and side effects of weight regulation groups. *Behavior Modification*, 1977, **1**, 551–558.

Eysenck, H. J. The effects of psychotherapy: An evaluation. *Journal of Consulting Psychology*, 1952, **16**, 319–324.

Eysenck, H. J. Personality and behavior therapy. *Proceedings of the Royal Society of Medicine*, 1960, **53**, 504–508. (a)

Eysenck, H. J. The effects of psychotherapy. In H. J. Eysenck (Ed.), *Handbook of abnormal psychology: A experimental approach*. London: Pitman Medical Publishing, 1960. (b)

Feuerstein, M., & Adams, H. E. Cephalic vasomotor feedback in the modification of migraine headache. *Biofeedback and Self-Regulation*, 1977, **3**, 241–254.

Fitzpatrick, L. J. Automated data collection for observed events. *Behavior Research Methods and Instrumentation*, 1977, **9**, 447–451.

Follingstad, D. R., Sullivan, J., & Haynes, S. N. Behavioral assessment of a dissatisfied marital couple. In S. N. Haynes (Ed.), *Principles of behavioral assess-*

ment. New York: Gardner Press, 1978.

Forehand, R., & Atkeson, B. M. Generality of treatment effects with parents as therapists: A review of assessment and implication procedures. *Behavior Therapy*, 1977, 8, 575-593.

Foster, S. L., & Cone, J. D. Current issues in direct observation. *Behavioral Assessment*, 1980, 2, 313-338.

Foxx, R. M., & Hake, D. R. Gasoline conservation: A procedure for measuring and reducing the driving of college students. *Journal of Applied Behavior Analysis*, 1977, 10, 61-74.

Freedman, B., Rosenthal, L., Donahoe, C., Schlundt, D., & McFall, R. A. A social behavioral analysis of skills deficits in delinquent and nondelinquent adolescent boys. *Journal of Consulting and Clinical Psychology*, 1978, 46, 1,448-1,462.

Frisch, H. L. Sex stereotypes in adult-infant play. *Child Development*, 1977, 48, 1,671-1,675.

Galassi, M. D., & Galassi, J. P. Similarities and differences between two assertion measures: Factor analysis of the College Self-Expression Scale and the Rathus Assertiveness Inventory. *Behavioral Assessment*, 1980, 2, 43-57.

Gardner, J. E., Pearson, D. T., Berocovici, A. N., & Bricker, D. C. Measurement, evaluation and modification of selected social interactions between a schizophrenic child, his parents and his therapist. *Journal of Consulting and Clinical Psychology*, 1968, 32, 537-542.

Garfield, S. L. Evaluating the psychotherapies. *Behavior Therapy*, 1981, 12, 295-307.

Gatchel, R. J., Korman, M., Weis, C. B., Smith, D., & Clark, L. A multiple-response evaluation of EMG biofeedback performance during training and stress-induction conditions. *Psychophysiology*, 1978, 15, 253-258.

Glass, G. V., Wilson, V., & Gottman, J. M. *Design and analysis of time-series experiments.* Boulder, Colorado: Colorado Associated University Press, 1975.

Goldfried, M. R. Behavioral assessment in perspective. In J. D. Cone & R. P. Hawkins (Eds.), *Behavioral assessment: New directions in clinical psychology.* New York: Brunner/Mazel, 1977.

Goldfried, M. R. Behavioral assessment: Where do we go from here? *Behavioral Assessment*, 1979, 1, 19-22.

Goldfried, M. R., & Kent, R. N. Traditional vs. behavioral personality assessment: A comparison of methodological and theoretical assumptions. *Psychological Bulletin*, 1972, 77, 409-420.

Goldfried, M. R., & Sprafkin, J. N. Behavioral personality assessment. In J. T. Spence, R. C. Carson, & J. W. Thibaut (Eds.), *Behavioral approaches to therapy.* Morristown, Penn.: General Learning Press, 1976.

Gottman, J. M. *Marital interaction: Experimental investigations.* New York: Academic Press, 1979.

Gottman, J. M. Analyzing for sequential connection and assessing interobserver reliability for the sequential analysis of observational data. *Behavioral Assessment*, 1980, 2, 361-368.

Greenfield, N. S., & Sternbach, R. A. *Handbook of psychophysiology.* New York: Holt, Rinehart & Winston, 1972.

Harris, F. C., & Lahey, B. B. A method of combining occurrence and nonoccurrence interobserver agreement scores. *Journal of Applied Behavior Analysis*, 1978, 11, 523-527.

Hartmann, D. P. Notes on methodology: On choosing an interobserver reliability estimate. *Journal of Applied Behavior Analysis*, 1977, 10, 103-116.

Hartmann, D. P., Gottman, J. M., Jones, R. R., Gardner, W., Kazdin, A. E., & Vaught, R. S. Interrupted time-series analysis and its application to behavioral data. *Journal of Applied Behavior Analysis*, 1980, 13, 543-559.

Hartmann, D. P., Roper, B. L., & Bradford, D. C. Some relationships between behavioral and traditional assessment. *Journal of Behavior Assessment*, 1979, 1, 3-21.

Hawkins, R. P., Fremouw, W. J., & Reitz, A. L. A model for use in designing or describing evaluations of mental health or educational intervention programs. *Behavioral Assessment*, 1981, 3, 307-324.

Hay, L. R., Nelson, R. O., & Hay, W. M. The use of teachers as behavioral observers. *Journal of Applied Behavior Analysis*, 1977, 10, 345-348.

Hay, W. M., Hay, L. R., Angle, H. V., & Nelson, R. O. The reliability of problem identification in the behavioral interview. *Behavioral Assessment*, 1979, 1, 107-118.

Hay, W. M., Hay, L. R., & Nelson, R. O. Direct and collateral changes in on-task and academic behavior resulting from on-task versus academic contingencies. *Behavior Therapy*, 1977, 8, 431-441.

Hayes, S. C., & Cavior, N. Multiple tracking and the reactivity of self-monitoring: II. positive behaviors. *Behavioral Assessment*, 1980, 2, 283-296.

Haynes, S. N. *Principles of behavioral assessment.* New York: Gardner Press, 1978.

Haynes, S. N. Behavioral variance, individual differences and trait theory in a behavioral construct system: A reappraisal. *Behavioral Assessment*, 1979, 1, 41-49.

Haynes, S. N. Muscle contraction headache. In S. N. Haynes & L. R. Gannon (Eds.), *Psychosomatic disorders: A psychophysiological approach to etiology and treatment.* New York: Praeger, 1981.

Haynes, S. N., Follingstad, D. R., & Sullivan, J. Assessment of marital satisfaction and interaction. *Journal of Consulting and Clinical Psychology*, 1979, 47, 789-791.

Haynes, S. N., & Gannon, L. R. Psychosomatic disorders: A psychophysiological approach to etiology and treatment. New York: Praeger, 1981.

Haynes, S. N., & Horn, W. F. Reactive effects of behavioral observation. *Behavioral Assessment*, 1982, 4, 443-469.

Haynes, S. N., & Jensen, B. J. The interview as a behavioral assessment instrument. *Behavioral Assessment*, 1979, 1, 97-106.

Haynes, S. N., Jensen, B. J., Wise, E., & Sherman, D. The marital intake interview: A multimethod criterion validity assessment. *Journal of Consulting and Clinical Psychology*, 1981, 49, 379-387.

Haynes, S. N., & Wilson, C. C. *Behavioral assessment: Recent advances in methods and concepts.* San Francisco: Jossey-Bass, 1979.

Heaton, R. C., & Safer, D. J. Secondary school outcome following a junior high school behavioral program. *Behavior Therapy*, 1982, 13, 226-231.

Heckerman, C. L., Schoen, S., & Barlow, D. H. Situational specificity of sex role motor behavior: A preliminary investigation. *Behavioral Assessment*, 1981, **3**, 43–54.

Henson, D. E., Rubin, H. B., & Henson, C. Consistency of the labial temperature change measure of human female eroticism. *Behaviour Research and Therapy*, 1979, **17**, 226–240.

Hersen, M. Complex problems require complex solutions. *Behavior Therapy*, 1981, **12**, 15–29.

Hersen, M., & Barlow, D. H. *Single case experimental designs: Strategies for studying behavior change*. New York: Pergamon, 1976.

Hersen, M., Eisler, R. M., & Miller, P. M. (Eds.), *Progress in Behavior Modification*, Vols I–XI, New York: Academic Press, 1975–1982.

Hoebel, E. A. *Man in the primitive world*. New York: McGraw-Hill, 1958.

Hogan, R., DeSoto, C. B., & Solano, C. Traits, tests, and personality research. *American Psychologist*, 1977, **81**, 255–264.

Holroyd, K. A., & Andrasik, F. Coping and the self-control of chronic tension headache. *Journal of Consulting Clinical Psychology*, 1978, **46**, 1,036–1,045.

Honig, W. K. *Operant behavior: Areas of research and application*. New York: Appleton-Century-Crofts, 1966.

Hops, H., Willis, T. A., Patterson, G. R., & Weiss, R. L. *Marital interaction coding system*. Unpublished Manuscript, University of Oregon, 1972.

Horn, W. F., & Haynes, S. N. An investigation of sex bias in behavioral observations and ratings. *Behavioral Assessment*, 1981, **3**, 173–183.

Hughes, H. M., & Haynes, S. N. Structured laboratory observation in the behavioral assessment of parent-child interactions: A methodological critique. *Behavior Therapy*, 1978, **9**, 428–447.

Hundert, J., & Batstone, D. A practical procedure to maintain pupils' accurate self-rating in a classroom token program. *Behavior Modification*, 1978, **2**, 93–111.

Hutt, S. J., & Hutt, C. *Direct observation and measurement of behavior*. Springfield, Ill.: C. C. Thomas, 1970.

Jacobson, N. S. Problem solving and contingency contracting in the treatment of marital discord. *Journal of Consulting and Clinical Psychology*, 1977, **45**, 92–100.

Jacobson, N. S. Behavioral treatment for marital discord: A critical appraisal. In M. Hersen, R. M., Eisler, & P. M. Miller (Eds.), *Progress in behavior modification*, Vol. 8. New York: Academic Press, 1979.

Johnson, M. S., & Bailey, J. S. The modification of leisure behavior in a halfway house for retarded women. *Journal of Applied Behavior Analysis*, 1977, **10**, 273–282.

Johnson, S. M., & Bolstad, O. D. Methodological issues in naturalistic observation: Some problems and solutions for field research. In L. A. Hamerlynck, L. C. Handy, & E. J. Mash (Eds.), *Behavior change: Methodology, concepts, and practice*. Champaign, Ill.: Research Press, 1973.

Jones, F. H., Fremouw, W., & Carples, S. Pyramid training of elementary school teachers to use a classroom management "skill package." *Journal of Applied Behavior Analysis*, 1977, **10**, 239–253.

Jones, R. R. Program evaluation design issues. *Behavioral Assessment*, 1979, **1**, 51–56.

Jones, R. R., Vaught, R. S., & Weinrott, M. L. Time-series analysis in operant research. *Journal of Applied Behavior Analysis*, 1977, **10**, 151–166.

Kaloupek, D. G., & Levis, D. J. The relationship between stimulus specificity and self-report indices in assessing fear of heterosexual social interaction: A test of unitary response hypothesis. *Behavioral Assessment*, 1980, **2**, 267–281.

Kamens, L., & Haynes, S. N. Presleep cognitions and attributions in insomnia. *Journal of Behavioral Medicine*, 1983 (in press).

Kanfer, F. H. Self-monitoring: Methodological limitations and clinical applications. *Journal of Consulting and Clinical Psychology*, 1970, **61**, 341–347.

Kanfer, F. H. A few comments on the current status of behavioral assessment. *Behavioral Assessment*, 1979, **1**, 37–39.

Kanfer, F. H., & Grimm, L. G. Behavioral analysis: Selecting target behaviors in the interview. *Behavior Modification*, 1977, **1**, 7–28.

Kanfer, F. H., & Phillips, J. *Learning foundations of behavior therapy*. New York: Wiley, 1970.

Kaplan, R. M., & Litrownik, A. J. Some statistical methods for the assessment of multiple-outcome criteria in behavioral research. *Behavior Therapy*, 1977, **8**, 383–392.

Karoly, P. Self-management problems in children. In E. J. Mash & L. G. Terdal (Eds.), *Behavioral assessment of childhood disorders*. New York: Guilford Press, 1981.

Kazdin, A. E. Reactive self-monitoring: The effects of response desirability, goal setting and feedback. *Journal of Consulting and Clinical Psychology*, 1974, **42**, 704–716.

Kazdin, A. E. Assessing the clinical or applied importance of behavior change through social validation. *Behavior Modification*, 1977, **1**, 427–452.

Kazdin, A. E. *History of behavior modification*. Baltimore: University Park Press, 1978.

Kazdin, A. E. Situational specificity: The two-edged sword of behavioral assessment. *Behavioral Assessment*, 1979, **1**, 57–75.

Kazdin, A. E. Symptom substitution, generalization, and response covariation: Implications for psychotherapy outcome. *Psychological Bulletin*, 1982, **91**, 349–365.

Kazdin, A. E., & Hartmann, D. P. The simultaneous-treatment design. *Behavior Therapy*, 1978, **9**, 912–922.

Keefe, F. J., Kopel, S. A., & Gordon, S. B. *A practical guide to behavioral assessment*. New York: Springer, 1978.

Kendall, P. C., & Hollon, S. D. (Eds.), *Assessment strategies for cognitive-behavioral intervention*. New York: Academic Press, 1981.

Kent, R., O'Leary, K. D., Foster, S., & Prinz, R. An approach to teaching parents and adolescents problem-solving communications skills: A preliminary report. *Behavior Therapy*, 1977, **8**, 639–643.

Kerlinger, F. N. *Foundations of behavioral research*. (2nd ed.) New York: Holt, Rinehart, & Winston, 1972.

Kilmann, P. R., Wagner, M. K., & Sotile, W. M. The differential impact of self-monitoring on smoking behavior: An exploratory study. *Journal of Clinical Psychology*, 1977, **33**, 912–914.

Kling, J. W., & Riggs, L. A. *Experimental psychology*. New York: Holt, Rinehart, & Winston, 1971.

Kolko, D. J., Dorsett, P. G., & Milan, M. A. A total assessment approach to the evaluation of social skills training: The effectiveness of an anger control program for adolescent psychiatric patients. *Behavioral Assessment*, 1981, **3**, 383–402.

Korchin, S. J. (Ed.), *Modern clinical psychology*. New York: Basic Books, 1976.

Korchin, S. J., & Schulberg, D. The future of clinical assessment. *American Psychologist*, 1981, **36**, 1,147–1,158.

Kratochwill, T. R. (Ed.), *Single subject research: Strategies for evaluating change*. New York: Academic Press, 1978.

Kratochwill, T. R., & Brody, G. H. Single subject designs: A perspective on the controversy over implying statistical inference and implications for research and training in behavior modification. *Behavior Modification*, 1978, **2**, 291–307.

Kratochwill, T. R., & Levin, J. R. What time-series designs may have to offer educational researchers. *Contemporary Educational Psychology*, 1979, **3**, 273–329.

Lahey, B. B., Vosk, B. N., & Habif, V. L. Behavioral assessment of learning disabled children: A rationale and strategy. *Behavioral Assessment*, 1981, **3**, 3–14.

Lebow, J. Consumer satisfaction with mental health treatment. *Psychological Bulletin*, 1982, **91**, 244–259.

Leitenberg, H. (Ed.), *Handbook of behavior modification and behavior therapy*. New York: Appleton-Century-Crofts, 1976.

Leitenberg, H., Agras, W. S., Thompson, L. E., & Wright, D. E. Feedback in behavior modification: An experimental analysis in two phobic cases. *Journal of Abnormal Psychology*, 1968, **1**, 131–137.

Levis, D. J., & Plunkett, W. J. The use of subjective magnitude estimation technique to validate procedures for pre-selecting "phobic" subjects. *Behavioral Assessment*, 1979, **1**, 191–201.

Lewinsohn, P. M. The behavioral study and treatment of depression. In M. Hersen, R. M. Eisler, & P. M. Miller (Eds.), *Progress in behavior modification*, Vol. 1. New York: Academic Press, 1975.

Lick, J. R., & Heffler, D. Relaxation training and attention placebo in the treatment of severe insomnia. *Journal of Consulting and Clinical Psychology*, 1977, **45**, 153–161.

Lindgren, H. C., Harvey, J. H. *An introduction to social psychology*. St. Louis: Mosby, 1971.

Lindsley, O. R. Characteristics of the behavior of chronic psychotics as revealed by free-operant conditioning methods. *Diseases of the Nervous System*, 1960, **21**, 66–78.

Linehan, M. M. Issue in behavioral interviewing. In J. D. Cone & R. P. Hawkins (Eds.), *Behavioral assessment: New directions in clinical psychology*. New York: Brunner/Mazel, 1977.

Magrab, P. R., & Papadopolou, Z. L. The effect of a token economy on dietary compliance for children

on hemodialysis. *Journal of Applied Behavior Analysis*, 1977, **10**, 573–578.

Maloney, M. P., & Ward, M. P. *Psychological assessment: A conceptual approach*. New York: Oxford University Press, 1976.

Margolin, G. Practical applications of behavioral marital assessment. In E. E. Filsinger & R. A. Lewis (Eds.), *Assessing marriage: New behavioral approaches*. Beverly Hills, Calif.: Sage, 1981.

Martinez-Diaz, J. A., & Edelstein, B. A. Heterosocial competence: Predictive and construct validity. *Behavior Modification*, 1980, **4**, 115–129.

Martin, I., & Venables, P. H. (Eds.), *Techniques in psychophysiology*. New York: Wiley, 1980.

Marziller, J. S., & Winter, K. Success and failure in social skills training: Individual differences. *Behaviour Research and Therapy*, 1978, **16**, 67–84.

Mash, E., Terdal, L., & Anderson, K. The response-class matrix: A procedure for recording parent-child interactions. *Journal of Consulting and Clinical Psychology*, 1973, **40**, 163–164.

Mash, E. J. What is behavioral assessment? *Behavioral Assessment*, 1979, **1**, 23–29.

Mash, E. J., & Terdal, L. G. *Behavioral assessment of childhood disorders*. New York: Guilford Press, 1981.

May, J. R. Psychophysiology of self-regulated phobic thoughts. *Behavior Therapy*, 1977, **8**, 849–861.

McFall, R. M. A review and reformulation of the concept of social skills. *Behavioral Assessment*, 1982, **4**, 1–33.

McReynolds, P. (Ed.). *Advances in psychological assessment*. San Francisco: Jossey-Bass, 1978.

Melamed, B. G., & Siegel, L. J. *Behavioral medicine: Practical applications in health care*. New York: Springer, 1980.

Merluzzi, T. V., Glass, C. R., & Genest, M. *Cognitive assessment*. New York: Guilford Press, 1981.

Messick, S. Constructs and their vicissitudes in educational and psychological measurement. *Psychological Bulletin*, 1981, **89**, 575–588.

Michael, J. Statistical inferences for individual organism research: Some reactions to a suggestion by Gentile, Roden, and Klein. *Journal of Appplied Behavior Analysis*, 1974, **7**, 627–628.

Mischel, W. *Personality and assessment*. New York: Wiley, 1968.

Mischel, W. *Introduction to personality*. New York: Holt, 1981.

Mitchell, C., & Hartmann, D. P. A cautionary note on the use of omega squared to evaluate the effectiveness of behavioral treatments. *Behavioral Assessment*, 1981, **3**, 93–100.

Mullini, S. D., & Galassi, J. P. Deriving the content of social skills training with a verbal response components approach. *Behavioral Assessment*, 1981, **3**, 55–66.

Nelson, R. O. Methodological issues in assessment via self-monitoring. In J. D. Cone & R. P. Hawkins (Eds.), *Behavioral assessment: New directions in clinical psychology*. New York: Brunner/Mazel, 1977.

Nelson, R. O., Hay, L. R., Hay, W. M., & Carstens, C. B. The reactivity and accuracy of teachers' self-monitoring of positive and negative classroom verbalizations. *Behavior Therapy*, 1977, **8**, 972–985.

Nelson, R. O., & Hayes, S. C. Some current dimensions

of behavioral assessment. *Behavioral Assessment,* 1979, **1,** 10-16.

Nelson, R. O., & Haynes, S. C. (Eds.), *Conceptual foundations of behavioral assessment.* New York: Guilford Press, 1982.

Nietzel, M. T., Winett, R. A., MacDonald, M. L., & Davidson, W. S. *Behavioral approaches to community psychology.* New York: Pergamon Press, 1977.

Notarius, C. I., Krokoff, L. J., & Markman, H. Analysis of observation data. In E. E. Filsinger & R. A. Lewis (Eds.), *Assessing marriage: New behavioral approaches.* Beverly Hills, Calif.: Sage, 1981.

Nunes, D. L., Murphy, R. J., & Ruprecht, M. L. Reducing self-injurious behavior of severely retarded individuals through withdrawal of reinforcement procedures. *Behavior Modification,* 1977, **1,** 499-516.

Nunnally, J. *Psychometric theory.* New York: McGraw-Hill, 1967.

O'Donnell, C. R. Behavior modification in community settings. In M. Hersen, R. M. Eisler, & P. M. Miller (Eds.), *Progress in behavior modification,* Vol. 4. New York: Academic Press, 1977.

O'Leary, K. D. Behavioral assessment. *Behavioral Assessment,* 1979, **1,** 31-36.

O'Leary, K. D., Kent, R. N., & Kanowitz, J. Shaping data collection congruent with experimental hypothesis. *Journal of Applied Behavior Analysis,* 1975, **8,** 43-51.

O'Leary, K. D., & Turkewitz, H. Methodological errors in marital and child treatment research. *Journal of Consulting and Clinical Psychology,* 1978, **46,** 747-758.

Palmer, M. H., Lloyd, M. E., & Lloyd, K. E. An experimental analysis of electricity conservation procedures. *Journal of Applied Behavior Analysis,* 1977, **10,** 665-671.

Patterson, G. R., & Bechtel, G. G. Formulating the situational environment in relation to states and traits. In R. B. Cattel & R. M. Greger (Eds.), *Handbook of modern personality theory.* Washington, D.C.: Halstead, 1977.

Patterson, G. R., Cobb, J. A., & Ray, R. S. A social engineering technology for retraining families of aggressive boys. In H. E. Adams & I. P. Unikel (Eds.), *Issues and trends in behavior therapy.* Springfield, Ill.: C. Thomas, 1973.

Patterson, G. R., & Hops, H. Coercion, a game for two: Intervention techniques for marital conflict. In R. E. Ulrich & P. Mountjoy (Eds.), *The experimental analysis of social behavior.* New York: Appleton-Century-Crofts, 1972.

Patterson, G. R., Littman, R. E., & Hinsey, W. C. Parental effectiveness as reinforcers in the laboratory and its relation to child rearing practices and child adjustment in the classroom. *Journal of Personality,* 1964, **32,** 180-199.

Patterson, G. R., Ray, R. S., Shaw, D. A., & Cobb, J. A. *Manual for coding of family interaction.* Unpublished Manuscript, University of Oregon, 1969.

Patterson, G. R., Reid, J. B., Jones, R. R., & Conger, R. E. *A social learning approach to family intervention.* Eugene, Oreg.: Castalia Publishing, 1975.

Pennypacker, H. S., Lienig, C. H., & Lindsley, O. R. *Handbook of the standard behavior chart.* Kansas City, Mo.: Precision Media, 1972.

Powell, J., & Rockinson, R. On the inability of interval time sampling to reflect frequency-of-occurrence data. *Journal of Applied Behavior Analysis,* 1978, **11,** 531-532.

Rachman, S., & Costello, C. G. The aetiology and treatment of children's phobias: A review. *American Journal of Psychiatry,* 1961, **118,** 97-105.

Reid, D. H., & Hurlbut, B. Teaching nonvocal communication skills to multi-handicapped retarded adults. *Journal of Applied Behavior Analysis,* 1977, **10,** 591-603.

Reid, J. B. Reliability assessment of observation data: A possible methodological problem. *Child Development,* 1970, **41,** 1,143-1,150.

Reisinger, J. J., & Ora, J. P. Parent-child clinic and home interaction during toddler management training. *Behavior Therapy,* 1977, **8,** 771-786.

Rekers, G. A. Stimulus control over sex-typed play in cross-gender-identified boys. *Journal of Experimental Child Psychology,* 1975, **20,** 136-148.

Rimm, D. C., Janda, L. H., Lancaster, W., Nahl, M., & Dittmar, K. An exploratory investigation of the origin and maintenance of phobias. *Behaviour Research and Therapy,* 1977, **15,** 231-238.

Rimm, D. C., & Masters, J. C. *Behavior therapy, techniques and empirical findings.* New York: Academic Press, 1979.

Robin, A. C., & Weiss, J. G. Criterion-related validity of behavioral self-report measures of problem solving communication skills in distressed and non-distressed parent-adolescent dyads. *Behavioral Assessment,* 1980, **2,** 339-352.

Rollings, J. P., Baumeister, A. A., & Baumeister, A. A. The use of overcorrection procedures to eliminate the stereotyped behaviors of retarded individuals: An analysis of collateral behaviors and generalization of suppressive effects. *Behavior Modification,* 1977, **1,** 29-46.

Russo, D. C., Bird, B. L., & Masek, B. J. Assessment issues in behavioral medicine. *Behavioral Assessment,* 1980, **2,** 1-18.

Sackett, G. P. *Observing behavior.* Baltimore: University Park Press, 1978.

Salter, A. *Conditioned reflex therapy.* New York: Putnam, 1961.

Sampson, E. E. Cognitive psychology as ideology. *American Psychologist,* 1981, **36,** 730-743.

Sartory, G., Rachman, S., & Grey, S. An investigation of the relation between reported fear and heart rate. *Behaviour Research and Therapy,* 1977, **15,** 435-538.

Schiederer, E. G. Effects of instructions and modeling in producing self-disclosure in the initial clinical interview. *Journal of Consulting and Clinical Psychology,* 1977, **45,** 378-384.

Schnelle, J. F., Kirchner, R. E., Jr., Casey, J. D., Uselton, P. H., Jr., & McNees, M. P. Patrol evaluation research: A multiple-baseline analysis of saturation police patrolling during day and night hours. *Journal of Applied Behavior Analysis,* 1977, **10,** 33-40.

Schreibman, L., Koegel, R. L., Mills, J. I., & Burke, J. C. Social validation of behavior therapy with autistic children. *Behavior Therapy,* 1981, **12,** 610-624.

Schulman, J. L., Stevens, T. M., & Kupst, M. J. The bio-motometer: A new device for the measurement and remediation of hyperactivity. *Child Development,* 1977, **48**, 1,152–1,154.

Schulman, J. L., Stevens, T. M., Suran, B. G., Kupst, M. J., & Naughton, M. J. Modification of activity level through biofeedback and operant conditioning. *Journal of Applied Behavior Analysis,* 1978, **11**, 145–152.

Schwartz, G. E. Biofeedback and patterning of automonic and central processes: CNS-cardiovascular interactions. In G. E. Schwartz & J. Beatty (Eds.), *Biofeedback: Theory and research.* New York: Academic Press, 1977.

Seligman, M. E., Klein, D. C., & Miller, M. R. In H. Leitenberg (Ed.), *Handbook of behavior modification and behavior therapy.* New York: Appleton-Century-Crofts, 1976.

Sellitz, C., & Wrightsman, L. S., & Cook, S. W. *Research methods in social relations.* New York: Holtz, 1976.

Sidman, M. *Tactics of scientific research.* New York: Basic Books, 1960.

Smith, J. B., Madsen, C. H., Jr., & Cipani, E. C. The effects of observational session length, method of recording and frequency of teacher behavior on reliability and accuracy of observational data. *Behavior Therapy,* 1981, **12**, 565–569.

Sobell, M. B., Schafer, H. H., & Mills, K. C. Differences in baseline drinking behavior between alcoholics and normal drinkers. *Behaviour Research and Therapy,* 1972, **10**, 257–267.

Swan, G. E., & MacDonald, M. L. Behavior therapy in practice: A national survey of behavior therapists. *Behavior Therapy,* 1978, **9**, 799–807.

Tunnell, G. B. Three dimensions of naturalness: An expanded definition of field research. *Psychological Bulletin,* 1977, **84**, 425–437.

Turner, S. M., Calhoun, K. S., & Adams, H. E. *Handbook of clinical behavior therapy.* New York: Wiley, 1981.

Twardosz, S., Schwartz, S., Fox, J., & Cunningham, J. L. Development and evaluation of a system to measure affectionate behavior. *Behavioral Assessment,* 1979, **1**, 177–190.

Ullmann, L. P., & Krasner, L. *A psychological approach to abnormal behavior.* Englewood Cliffs, N.J.: Prentice Hall, 1975.

Venables, P. H., & Martin, I. *A manual of psychophysiological methods.* New York: Wiley, 1967.

Vincent, J. P. *Advances in family intervention, assessment and theory.* Greenwich, Conn.: JAI Press, 1980.

Voeltz, L. M., & Evans, I. M. The assessment of behavioral interrelationships in child behavior therapy. *Behavioral Assessment,* 1982, **4**, 131–165.

Wade, T. C., Baker, T. B., & Hartmann, D. P. Behavior therapists' self-reported views and practices. *The Behavior Therapist,* 1979, **2**, 3–6.

Wahler, R. G., Berland, R. M., & Coe, T. D. Generalization processes in child behavior change. In B. B. Lahey & A. E. Kazdin (Eds.), *Advances in clinical child psychology,* Vol. 2. New York: Plenum, 1979.

Wahler, R. G., House, A. E., & Stambaugh, E. E. *Ecological assessment of child problem behavior: A clinical package for home, school and institutional settings.* New York: Pergamon, 1976.

Walls, R. T., Werner, T. J., Bacon, A., & Zane, T. Behavior checklists. In J. D. Cone & R. P. Hawkins (Eds.), *Behavioral assessment: New directions in clinical psychology.* New York: Brunner/Mazel, 1977.

Wampold, B. E., & Jurlong, M. J. The heuristics of visual inference. *Behavioral Assessment,* 1981, **3**, 79–92.

Wasik, B. H., & Loven, M. D. Classroom observational data: Sources of inaccuracy and proposed solutions. *Behavioral Assessment,* 1980, **2**, 211–227.

Weiner, E. B. (Ed.). *Clinical methods of psychology.* New York: Wiley, 1976.

Weiss, R. *Coupling skills: A cognitive behavioral systems approach.* (Cassette). New York: Guilford Publications, 1980.

Wells, K. C., & Forehand, R. Childhood behavior problems in the home. In S. M. Turner, K. S. Calhoun, & H. E. Adams (Eds.), *Handbook of clinical behavior therapy.* New York: Wiley, 1981.

Wessberg, H. W., Mariotto, M. J., Conger, A. J., Farrell, A. D., & Conger, J. C. Ecological validity of role plays for assessing heteroscoial anxiety and skills of male college students. *Journal of Consulting and Clinical Psychology,* 1979, **47**, 525–535.

Wickramesekera, I. E. Clinical research in a behavioral medicine private practice. *Behavioral Assessment,* 1981, **3**, 265–271.

Wildman, B. G., & Erikson, M. T. Methodological problems in behavioral observation. In J. D. Cone & R. P. Hawkins (Eds.), *Behavioral assessment: New directions in clinical psychology.* New York: Brunner/Mazel, 1977.

Wolfe, M. M. Social validity: The case for subjective measurement, or how applied behavior analysis is finding its heart. *Journal of Applied Behavior Analysis,* 1978, **11**, 203–214.

Wolman, B. B. (Ed.), *Handbook of clinical psychology.* New York: McGraw-Hill, 1965.

Wolman, B. B. *Handbook of general psychology.* Englewood Cliffs, N.J.: Prentice-Hall, 1973.

Wolman, B. B. *Clinical diagnosis of mental disorders.* New York: Plenum, 1978.

Wolpe, J. *Psychotherapy by reciprocal inhibition.* Stanford, Calif.: Stanford University Press, 1958.

Woody, R. H. *Encyclopedia of clinical assessment.* San Francisco: Jossey-Bass, 1980.

Wright, H. D. Observation child study. In P. Mussen (Ed.), *Handbook of research methods in child development.* New York: Wiley, 1960.

Youkilis, H. D., & Bootzin, R. R. A psychophysiological perspective of the etiology and treatment of insomnia. In S. N. Haynes & L. R. Gannon (Eds.), *Psychosomatic disorders: A psychophysiological approach to etiology and treatment.* New York: Praeger, 1981.

Zeiss, R. A. Self-directed treatment of premature ejaculation: Primary case reports. *Journal of Behavior Therapy and Experimental Psychiatry,* 1977, **8**, 87–91.

Zilboorg, G., & Henry, G. W. *A history of medical psychology.* New York: Norton, 1941.

22 PSYCHOPHYSIOLOGICAL ASSESSMENT

William J. Ray
Harry W. Cole
James M. Raczynski

The use of psychophysiological measures in understanding human functioning is increasing in popularity. Numerous areas of research, including cognitive psychology, social psychology, marketing research, as well as health psychology and clinical psychology, have utilized psychophysiological measurements. In the areas of clinical and health psychology the use of physiological measures has occurred on both the assessment and intervention levels. Intervention efforts, such as those in biofeedback, have largely focused on the physiological measure alone, whereas assessment strategies have sought to relate physiological processes to broader conceptual formulations such as "anxiety" or "schizophrenia." As we shall see, understanding the relationship between a physiological measure on one level and a conceptual or diagnostic category on another level has given rise to many problems of interpretation that have yet to be adequately resolved.

There are many success stories dating back thousands of years that have kept the promise of psychophysiological assessment alive for both clinicians and researchers. Some of the earliest reports date from the clinical cases of Erasistratos in the third century B.C. and Galen in the second century A.D.(Mesulam & Perry, 1972). Galen, a physician who is considered the father of modern physiology, reported a case in which he was called to treat a woman suffering from insomnia. Observing the woman to be restless and reluctant to answer questions about her condition, Galen looked to the possibility of an emotional problem underlying the insomnia. By chance, on one day when Galen was examining the woman, a person returned from the theater and mentioned the name of a particular male dancer. Galen reports that, "at that instant, her expression and the color of her face were greatly altered. . . . I observed her pulse was irregular . . . which points to a troubled mind." Not wanting to jump to conclusions, Galen had a colleague mention the names of various dancers as Galen was examining the woman over the next few days. There was no physiological reaction to any of the dancers except one. From this reaction, Galen suggested that the woman was in love with one particular dancer, and according to Galen this was confirmed over the next few days.

Although it was not necessary to interpret the work of Galen and others in the following manner, some individuals conceptualized physiological processes as reflecting the "true" feelings of a person toward an event or psychological process. Like the television versions of lie detection, psychophysiology was seen to offer a hard and fast "scientific" answer to diagnostic categories or psychological processing. In early research in the area, attempts were made to identify marker variables (e.g., heart rate changes) that could be used to delineate and define psychological processes (e.g., anxiety). We would like to caution both clinicians and researchers that there is little evidence to support a one-to-one mapping of physiological variables onto psychological constructs, much less the idea that physiological variables somehow give one a truer picture of what is going on. As Lacey (1959) pointed out over 20 years ago, physiology does not measure concepts. Psychophysiological measures may help us to understand concepts such as anxiety or arousal, but anxiety is always something more than an increase in heart rate. It is more consistent with the data to suggest that psychophysiological processes offer one a different level of analysis with a different type of information than may be acquired by other means, such as self-report and behavioral measures. From this develops a very important research question that asks how we can translate one type of language, such as the physiological one into other types such as that of observed behaviors or self-reports. We will raise this issue again in the concluding section of this chapter.

In a chapter that relates psychophysiological measures to clinical process, we are faced with a number of difficulties. One initial difficulty involves the manner in which both areas are structured. Psychophysiology traditionally has been structured around measures such as heart rate, EEG, EMG, and so forth, whereas clinical processes have been structured more around diagnostic classification. Thus, it is often difficult to find a review of interest to the clinician or clinical researcher because of organization. To correct this problem, the present chapter is organized around psychological processes and attempts to include sufficient examples of various psychophysiological measures to be of use. Following a review by area, we turn to some important conceptual questions of psychophysiological processing and assessment. We then conclude with a discussion of future directions and unanswered questions. The present chapter does not emphasize how the psychophysiological measures are to be recorded and the technical questions that arise from these procedures. The interested reader should consult either an introductory book (e.g., Stern, Ray, & Davis, 1980), a more advanced series of readings

(e.g., Brown, 1967; Martin & Venables, 1980) emphasizing recording technique, or publication guidelines such as those available for heart rate (Jennings et al., 1981) and electrodermal activity (Fowles et al., 1981).

Psychopathological Applications

Disorders Usually First Evident in Infancy, Childhood, and Adolescence

Within the behavioral area of attentional deficits, the psychophysiological data on hyperactive children have been reviewed by Satterfield, Cantwell, and Satterfield (1974), and more recently by Hastings and Barkley (1978). Several interesting relationships have emerged, including underarousal of resting cortical activity in hyperactive children, no differences in basal levels of autonomic arousal between normal and hyperactive children, some indication that some children are autonomically underreactive or "underarousable" to environmental stimuli, and a suggestion that stimulant drugs have been found to increase the environmental reactivity or "underarousability" among hyperactive children. Evans and Nelson (1977) have reviewed a very restricted sample of assessment studies (involving children) without drawing any specific conclusions. In the category of physical disorders in infants, Lang and Melamed (1969) have presented an interesting case study in which electromyographic (EMG) activity was used to assess an established criterion in the avoidance conditioning treatment of an infant suffering from chronic ruminative vomiting at the age of nine months.

Stern and Janes (1973) have reviewed autonomic nervous system (ANS) functions among the mentally retarded and cite a review by Karrer (1966) that indicated that the mentally retarded exhibited significantly higher skin conductance levels than nonretarded individuals. Stern and Janes (1973), however, review investigations that contradict that position and also discuss response duration and latency, habituation, and conditioning. In each of these areas, the data are inconclusive and often contradictory. Krupski (1975) has demonstrated significantly lower levels of heart rate, slower reaction time scores, and lower heart rate deceleration prior to reaction signal onset among retarded males than is found in nonretarded males. On a more global level, Venables

(1977) has reviewed autonomic psychophysiological data (primarily electrodermal activity) attempting to identify those children for whom there exists a relatively high risk of psychiatric breakdown. Hall and his colleagues (1976) have suggested that auditory-visual-evoked potentials may be related to both the degree of initial hyperactivity and the degree of decrease in hyperactivity with dextroamphetamine. Friedman, Frosch, and Erlenmeyer-Kimling (1979) present auditory-evoked potential (AEP) data in an attempt to establish some criteria to identify children with high risk for schizophrenia. Their results were not very encouraging, as AEPs were not found to be very accurately predictive. Halliday, Rosenthal, Naylor, and Callaway (1976) have suggested that event-related potentials of hyperactive children may accurately predict significant improvement in attentional deficits as a function of treatment with methylphenidate (Ritalin). Specifically, evoked potential variability increases when responders proceed from tasks requiring active attention to tasks requiring passive observation, whereas evoked potential variability decreases in nonresponders when they go from active attentional tasks to passive observational tasks. Event-related EEG potentials have been investigated as they relate to mental retardation by Galbraith, Squires, Altair, and Gliddon (1979), who report marked hemisphere asymmetry in mentally retarded subjects when compared to nonmentally retarded individuals.

In the category of intellectual disorders, Preston (1979) has discussed literature pertaining to event-related EEG potentials and reading disability. This review concludes that differences exist between normal and reading-disabled individuals, particularly when recording from parietal areas and when using linguistic stimuli. Psychophysiological techniques may also contribute to the assessment of stuttering; Stromer (1979) has noted elevated levels among stutterers of EMG activity that generally occurs in the masseter or laryngeal locations. Each case should be considered as unique, and respective electrode placements for the treatment of this disorder through biofeedback are to be determined on an individual basis.

Organic Mental Disorders

Electrocortical measures have often been employed in the assessment of various neurological disorders. The literature has been reviewed for the assessment of electroencephalographic (EEG) activity during sleep by Feinberg and Evarts (1969), indicating that frequent awakenings and a decrease in total sleep time, as well as rapid eye movement (REM) periods, often accompany neurological disorders. Data concerning contingent negative variation have been reviewed by Tecce (1971) and suggest a decrement in contingent negative variation (CNV) amplitude was evident, especially on the side of the cortex that was lesioned. Visual-evoked potentials (VEPs) have been reviewed by Cracco (1979) and have been found to be useful in identifying patients with visual loss due to optic nerve lesions and in patients with multiple sclerosis when there is no accompanying evidence of visual disturbance. Auditory-evoked potentials (AEPs) provide accurate information in the evaluation of cochlear function and peripheral hearing deficits. Somato-sensory-evoked potentials have been found to add little to information acquired through clinical evaluation or electroencephalographic assessment. Stern and Janes (1973) have reviewed the literature concerning brain damage and autonomic activity (primarily electrodermal data) and report conflicting and inconclusive findings. Pace, Molfese, Schmidt, Mikula, and Ciano (1979) have suggested that auditory-evoked potential data may be successful in the differential assessment of aphasic and nonaphasic disorders.

Substance Use Disorders

Stroebel (1972) has reviewed the utility of psychophysiological assessment of pharmacological effects, while recent investigations have examined the psychophysiological effects of such drugs as marijuana (e.g., Naliboff et al., 1976). The psychophysiological reactivity of drug abusers has been reviewed by Prystav (1975), and he reports that ex-drug addicts matched for sex and age with controls demonstrated significantly lower diastolic but not systolic blood pressure, significantly smaller skin conductance response magnitudes during resting periods, significantly smaller skin conductance response magnitudes and recruitment latencies in response to auditory and visual stimuli, and significantly larger habituation rates of skin conductance response magnitude and recruitment latencies at stimulus offset. These results were interpreted as indicative of decreased autonomic activity in drug-dependent individuals as compared to controls.

Miller (1977) reviewed the articles pertaining to the use of psychophysiological measures to assess changes as a function of treatment. This cursory review of the literature pertained to the addictive behaviors involving drugs and alcohol in an attempt to demonstrate the utility of psychophysiological measures as indices of change following treatment. The review was limited to investigations dealing with reactions to drug and alcohol stimuli as dependent variables to evaluate treatment. Dustman, Snyder, Callner, and Beck (1979) investigated visual-evoked responses among alcoholics as well as young and elderly normals. They reported data that differentiated the elderly from both younger groups and demonstrated significant similarities between the elderly and the young alcoholics. Porjesz and Begleiter (1979) investigated visually evoked responses among normals and chronic alcoholics and reported that the brain functioning impaired by acute doses of alcohol is more permanent among the chronic alcoholics. They have also reported that alcoholics exhibited increased early and decreased late components in addition to delayed latencies, all of which parallel the responsivity among elderly normals. Nirenberg, Ersner-Hershfield, Sobell, and Sobell (1981) reviewed the use of electromyographic and electrodermal assessments in determining anxiety levels of alcoholics. Finally, with respect to the area of tobacco dependence, the electrocortical activity of smokers has been investigated by Knott and Venables (1977). These authors have reported slower dominant alpha frequency in deprived smokers relative to nonsmokers and nondeprived smokers in presmoking assessment and postsmoking assessment, with postsmoking increases in the dominant alpha frequency of deprived smokers to a level comparable to nonsmokers and nondeprived smokers. Pomerleau (1980) calls for an examination of psychophysiological activity to study the manner in which physiological activities are perceived by smokers as well as to determine the influences of physiological responding on smoking behaviors.

Schizophrenic Disorders

Historically, this diagnostic category has received the greatest amount of attention within the literature on psychophysiological assessment. A variety of electrocortical measures have been exhaustively reviewed and include general EEG during sleep as reviewed by Feinberg and Evarts (1969). In their review of the literature pertaining to EEG during sleep among schizophrenics, they reported

decrements in stage four sleep among schizophrenics compared to normals and no differences in the amount of REM sleep. They have interpreted this as an index of increased arousal and argue rather strenuously for greater methodological rigor in the assessment of the physiological correlates of schizophrenia, citing such problems as small sample sizes within the experiments they have reviewed and a failure to control for potentially confounding variables such as anxiety.

Venables (1975) reviews inconsistent skin conductance data on tonic level and the phasic level of activity. Higher levels of spontaneous activity were reported among schizophrenics as compared to normals, yet no differences were reported between normals and schizophrenics on measures of tonic skin potential levels. Few data were available on the phasic skin potential activity among schizophrenics, but greater tonic heart rate among schizophrenics than among normals was reported. However, there were inconclusively sparse data on heart rate responsivity and generally inconclusive electrocortical investigations within this diagnostic category. Itil (1977) concluded that the most important finding in the electrocortical research relating to schizophrenia was that patients seem to have less well organized alpha activity and demonstrate considerably greater amounts of beta activity than normals.

Buchsbaum (1977a) reviews the possibility of converging evidence from experimental approaches in psychophysiology and neuropharmacology in such areas as cerebral circulation and neural activity, skeletal muscle hemodynamics and attention, skin temperature, pupil diameter, electrodermal activity, and finally evidence indicative of left hemisphere dysfunction. An example from the cerebral blood flow literature involved an investigation by Franzen and Ingvar (1975), in which chronic schizophrenics, assessed by means of Xenon-131 carotid injections followed by cerebral blood flow measures to assess the presence of Xenon in the cortex, were found to exhibit low frontal lobe flow and high post central flows. Forearm blood flow data presented by Keely & Waler (1968) suggest that chronic schizophrenics exhibit chronic overarousal on the basis of exceptionally high levels of basal forearm blood flow relative to normals.

Buchsbaum's (1977a) review of the pupil diameter literature concludes that schizophrenics exhibit diminished pupillary constriction to light in comparison to normals. Event-related potentials have been reviewed in response to auditory and visual stimuli (Shagass, 1977a, 1977b, 1979) and in regard to late positive components and slow potentials. Roth (1977) reported that differences do exist between schizophrenics and normals, but the methodology needed to be refined and standardized. Shagass (1979) reported greater than normal somato-sensory-evoked potentials (3/100 msec. post stimulation) in the chronic subtype of schizophrenia, with acute and latent subtypes presenting data similar to normals. Auditory-evoked potential amplitude may be reduced from normal in schizophrenia and studies of visual-evoked potential amplitude vary in their findings, while P300 results are also reduced from normals. Venables (1977) has reviewed the bilateral electrodermal data in an attempt to relate this peripheral measure to lateralized central nervous system activity. It was concluded that the position of left hemisphere involvement in schizophrenia remains unclear. Direct assessment of asymmetric EEG activity has been considered in a review by Alpert and Martz (1977).

Reduced contingent negative variation waves have been reported among schizophrenics as compared to nonpatients by McCallum and Abraham (1973). A variety of autonomic measures have also been reviewed, including electrodermal activity (Depue & Fowles, 1973; Jordan, 1974; Stern & Janes, 1973; Zahn, 1977), electromyographic activity (Goode et al., 1977), skeletal muscle hemodynamics (Buchsbaum, 1977a), eye movement activity (Holzman & Levy, 1977), and skin temperature data (Buchsbaum, 1977a). Spohn and Patterson (1979) have recently provided an excellent review of the application of psychophysiological techniques to this particular disorder and have reviewed data concerning electrodermal activity, cardiovascular activity, smooth pursuit eye movements, electrocortical activity, and evoked potentials. In their review, they conclude that with respect to electrodermal data, schizophrenics are far less responsive than normals regarding skin conductance, and that skin conductance orienting responses may habituate more rapidly in schizophrenics than in normals. Spohn and Patterson (1979) indicate the possibility exists that individual differences in responses and habituation before treatment may reliably predict response to treatment. Their review of cardiovascular activity suggests that studies treating phasic heart rate responding as an orienting response component indicate that schizophrenics differ

from normals in both characteristic and phasic responses to neutral stimuli. These authors also warn that eye-tracking deviance may be a misleading measure in assessing schizophrenia both clinically and etiologically. Finally, Roth and Cannon (1972) compared late positive waves in schizophrenics and controls matched by age and race. They reported that the late waves of schizophrenics were significantly lower in amplitude than late waves in nonpatients.

Dissociative Disorders

Mesulam (1981) has reported on the electrocortical data of 12 cases with a clinical picture reminiscent of multiple personality and supernatural possession, and concluded that dissociative phenomena may be more likely to occur in patients with EEG abnormalities located in the right temporal lobe.

Affective Disorders

Bassett and Ashby (1954) reported that skin resistance was related to recovery in that those patients who eventually recovered failed to habituate the stimuli, whereas habituation occurred in those who eventually were to recover. Zuckerman, Persky, and Curtis (1968) have investigated depressed inpatients and reported nonsignificant correlations between basal skin conductance levels and depression ratings, while significant correlations were found for normals. They also reported that the number of spontaneous fluctuations per minute was positively correlated with depression among psychiatric inpatients but not within a normal population. The two tonic measures employed in this investigation were, therefore, in contradiction with one another. Dureman and Saaren-Seppälä (1963) reported that clinical ratings and self-ratings of depression were not related to conditionability of electrodermal activity. Patients with depressive psychoses were reported to have somato-sensory-evoked potentials (SEPs) greater than normal in amplitude across a variety of stimulus intensities (Shagass & Schwartz, 1963). Shagass, Overton, and Straumanis (1974) have reported higher amplitude SEPs between 50 and 199 msec. and less variable SEPs between 101 and 200 msec. in psychotic depressives as compared to schizophrenics. Shagass, Roemer, Straumanis, and Amadeo (1977) report being able to distinguish neurotic from psychotic depressives on the basis of SEP tracings with patients matched on sex and age. Shagass and Schwartz (1966) have reported reduced amplitude recovery and Shagass (1968) reported enhanced latency recovery among severe depressives as compared to normals. Shagass (1979) reports auditory-evoked potential amplitudes as being lower than normal in patients with psychotic depressions, and Perris (1975) reports lower-amplitude visual-evoked potentials to be associated with depression of increasing severity.

Some investigators claim that this diagnostic category involves an unstable state of hyperexcitability within the organism (Akiskal & McKinney, 1975; Whybrow & Mendels, 1969). Some of the early support for that notion was derived from investigations that revealed greater EMG activity in depressed patients and subsequent decrements in EMG following electroconvulsive treatment (Whatmore & Ellis, 1959, 1962). Lader and Wing (1969) recorded skin conductance, pulse rate, and forearm extensory EMG among agitated depressed, nonagitated depressed, and normal subjects during presentation of auditory stimuli. They reported significant differences between the two major groups of depressed patients. Agitated patients had greater spontaneous skin conductance fluctuations, no SC habituation, and slight pulse rate increases compared to nonagitated depressed patients, while the control group values fell between the two groups of patients. Those findings have been interpreted as contradictory to the excitability model.

More recently, Gruzelier and Venables (1974) have investigated the notion of hemispheric dominance in depressed patients and have recorded skin conductance response characteristics including orienting, habituation, amplitude, latency, recovery time, spontaneous fluctuations, and average skin conductance levels among schizophrenics, depressed patients, and "personality disorder" patients of both inpatient and outpatient status. Their results led them to classify depression as an affective disorder of right-hemisphere dominance, while schizophrenia was classified as a thought disorder of left-hemisphere dominance. Those findings correspond well with the research of Flor-Henry (1976) in which manic-depressive syndromes were found to reflect "disorganization of the nondominant anterior limbic structures" (p. 792).

Finally, investigations dealing with the electrocortical activity of depressives have been reviewed by Feinberg and Evarts (1969) and Mendels and Chernik (1975). Autonomic measures,

in general, have been reviewed by Lader (1975). This review presented the psychophysiological investigations involving depressives and concluded that reduced salivary secretion was reliably more evident in depressed patients than in normals; however, increased salivary flow did not consistently reappear with successful treatment. Lader (1975) also reviewed the EMG data suggesting higher levels among depressed subjects. Skin conductance levels and responses to auditory stimuli were reportedly reduced in the depressed populations compared to normals. As a final note, Lader (1975) indicates that his review of the EEG studies was inconclusive. Other general reviews of autonomic measures have been provided by Lader and Nobel (1955) and Raczynski and Craighead (1980). Specific autonomic measures, such as salivation, have been reviewed by Brown (1970), who has reported inhibition of salivation to be associated with extreme depression, especially retarded depression. In general, the reviews, as well as the specific findings of Lader and Wing (1969) and Raczynski and Craighead (1980), suggest that while ANS measures fluctuate during depressive episodes, the presence of an anxiety component may be a more critical factor in determining the extent and direction of changes in the autonomic nervous system.

Anxiety Disorders

Mathews (1971) has reviewed the psychophysiological measurements utilized in the investigation of systematic desensitization, such as the study by Paul (1966), in which heart rate and skin conductance were assessed before and after treatment for public-speaking phobics and were found to decrease as a function of treatment. Mathews (1971) concluded that psychophysiological measures were useful in the study of process and outcome psychotherapy; the most consistent results were obtained with skin resistance and heart rate, although some success has been noted with respiration and EMG measures. Luiselli, Marholin, Steinman, and Warren (1979) review the literature studying the effects of relaxation training in an attempt to determine what criterion measures are employed. Their review focused on the four dependent measures of self-report, physiological recordings, behavioral ratings, and no report. They found that approximately 70 percent of the articles reviewed provided no indication of how effects of relaxation were assessed. Physiological measures included were heart rate, blood pressure, skin conductance, frontalis EMG, respiration, hand temperature, forehead temperature, and pulse rate. Only 15 percent of the studies reviewed employed any physiological measures, and 58 percent of those used only one measure.

Breggin (1964) reviewed the effects of adrenalin and concluded that initial adrenal medullary secretions may evoke cues that reinforce the anxiety response (sympathetic) while a more prolonged secretion may evoke fatigue or sedative-type effects (parasympathetic). Davidson (1978) has reported being able to distinguish cognitive from somatic anxiety on the basis of psychophysiological specificity. Cognitive anxiety was associated with increased skin conductance responses relative to somatic anxiety whereas somatic anxiety was associated with higher heart rate and EMG activity than was found with cognitive anxiety. Tecce (1971) reports that the contingent negative variation is difficult to establish, developed slowly and inconsistently, or possibly not at all, in anxious as compared to normal subjects.

Katkin and Deitz (1973) have reviewed the electrodermal data as a technique for assessing outcome questions in the systematic desensitization literature. They conclude that larger electrodermal responses are given to real or imagined phobic stimulus objects than to nonphobic stimulus objects by phobic subjects and that phobics also show larger electrodermal responses to phobic objects than matched nonphobic subjects show to the same objects.

Borkovec, Weerts, and Bernstein (1977) review heart rate as the cardiovascular measure of choice in the anxiety literature and conclude that marked increases occur under stress conditions, yet this measure is also receptive to a variety of perceptual, cognitive, and motoric requirements that probably interact with the threat aspect of stimuli and hence require appropriate control measures. The electrodermal responses to fear stimuli habituate at a slower rate, and individual responses recover more slowly than do responses to neutral stimuli. Lader (1975) reviewed the psychophysiological literature relating to anxiety and reports inconsistent findings with respect to differences between anxious and normal subjects and EMG activity. He also reported consistently higher skin conductance levels and number of skin conductance fluctuations in anxious as compared to normals, elevated heart rate with anxiety, decreased alpha and increased beta within the studies of

electrocortical data, and a contingent negative variation decrement among anxious versus normal people. Goldstein (1972) has reported conflicting findings in the anxiety literature with respect to EMG activity. Nietzel and Bernstein (1981) review EMG, heart rate, and electrodermal activity measures and conclude that reliance upon single-site EMG is inappropriate because of fractionation problems, that heart rate should be used with caution as it is sensitive to motor and perceptual artifacts as well as because individual differences are highly prevalent with this measure, and that electrodermal measures were useful as suggested by Borkovec et al. (1977). Mavissakalian and Barlow (1981) review the limited literature available on the obsessive-compulsive disorders and rely primarily on the work of Boulougouris and associates (Boulougouris & Bassiakos, 1973; Boulougouris, Rabavilas, & Stefanis, 1977; Rabavilas & Boulougouris, 1974), which indicated that autonomic nervous system activities, such as heart rate, increased significantly when patients were engaged in obsessional behavior as compared to neutral behavior. Performance of compulsive behaviors seemed to be followed by generally reduced autonomic nervous system activities. However, recent work by Grayson, Nutter, and Mavissakalian (in press) indicates an orienting type of heart rate response is elicited in response to neutral and compulsive scenes, although the latter scenes result in initial heart rate deceleration which is smaller in size and duration when compared to the neutral scene. Phobic scenes elicit defensive-type heart rate responses and phobic compulsive scenes elicit more fully developed defensive responses.

Psychosexual Disorders

The psychophysiological assessment of normal sexual arousal has been reviewed by several authors (Bancroft, 1971; Heiman, 1977; Masters & Johnson, 1966; Stern, Farr, & Ray, 1975; Zuckerman, 1972). This research has been important in drawing attention to the delineation of normal responsitivity as well as the physiological/cognitive interface. Zuckerman (1971) reports on ANS measures that reflect responsivity to stimuli but are not comparable to the same measures taken during coitus, thereby suggesting that responding to much stimuli is not reflective of sexual arousal but rather indicates an orienting response to novelty or emotions other than sexual arousal. In terms of genital responsivity, Barlow (1977) has reviewed the physchophysiological measures that have been employed, including measures of both penile circumference and volume in males and vaginal plethysmographic assessment of localized vasocongestion early in sexual arousal of females.

Karacan (1978) reviews an updated diagnostic procedure for male impotence, nocturnal penile tumescence (NPT), which is recorded in conjunction with EEG and EOG, and is considered useful in differentially diagnosing psychogenic and organogenic impotence. Heiman (1978) reviews the psychophysiological assessment of female genital measurements, concluding that affective and imaginal experiences are closely bound to physiological responsitivity and that the investigation of the relationship among these areas would be most advantageous in acquiring information on functional and dysfunctional sexuality. Freund and Blanchard (1981) have extended the review done by Karacan (1978) regarding NPT as a differential diagnostic assessment procedure. The failure of NPT to co-occur with REM cycles results in the diagnosis of a physiological disorder, suggesting neurological and/or arteriographic assessments. As high as 60 percent of cases of impotence have been diagnosed as having probable organic involvement (Karacan, Salis, & Williams, 1978).

Wincze and Lange (1981) have reviewed the physiological measurements of female arousal, including the vaginal photoplethysmograph and the thermistor method. The latter measure involves the attachment of a temperature-sensitive thermistor probe to the labia majora, and as arousal and vasocongestion occur, the skin temperature increases. They also review the standard circumference and volume measures of change in the penis and discuss a new directional doppler method using ultrasound to determine flow rates in arteries and veins. The authors report successful use of this method on members of both sexes.

Tollison and Adams (1979) review the electrodermal data (e.g., Barlow, Leitenberg, & Agras, 1969) and conclude that electrodermal measures are effected by emotional states not correlated with sex, and therefore do not discriminate between sexual and nonsexual arousal. The validity and utility of this measure is, therefore, seriously undermined. Cardiovascular activity is also reviewed and the conclusion is reached that arousing stimuli do *not* produce consistent heart rate increments (Bernick, Kling, & Borowitz, 1968), facial temperature or finger pulse volume increments,

and although blood pressure shows a reaction to increasingly arousing stimuli, lack of discriminative validity makes this measure unuseful as well. Respiration rates also fail to discriminate sexually relevant from neutral stimuli (e.g., Bancroft & Mathews, 1971). Lack of response specificity also eliminates pupillary responses as valid or reliable assessment measures of sexual arousal (e.g., Chapman, Chapman, & Brelje, 1969). Penile erection responses are conclusively the measure of choice according to these authors. Freund (1981) reviews the psychophysiological assessment of pedophilia and concludes the data are contradictory and inconclusive with respect to EDA and cardiovascular responsivity. The data on respiration are again suggestive of no differentiation among stimuli. However, the pupillary dilation response is considered promising, as is direct assessment of electrocortical activity and phallometric assessment.

Personality Disorders

A number of review articles have been concerned with personality disorders, including Schacter (1971), Schacter and Latane (1964), and Stern and Janes (1973). The latter of these reviews suggests that psychopaths are either not significantly different from normals in terms of resting levels of skin conductance or have significantly lower resting levels on this measure. Significantly fewer nonspecific responses are observed among psychopaths when compared to normals, and the two groups do not differ significantly with respect to orienting responses to simple stimuli. McCallum (1973) and Tecce (1971) have reported reduced CNVs among psychopaths compared to normals; Hare (1975b) suggests that psychopaths are poor EDA conditioners but good cardiovascular conditioners. Hare (1975a) reviews tonic ANS activity and reports that the tonic skin conductance levels of psychopathic inmates are significantly lower than those of other inmates and noncriminal controls (e.g., Shalling et al., 1973). Hare (1975a) also reports that psychopaths exhibit less spontaneous fluctuations in skin conductance than normals and that most investigations have failed to find any significant relationship between psychopathy and tonic heart rate (e.g., Hare & Craigen, 1974). With respect to phasic ANS activity, the EDA of psychopaths suggests this group may be hyporesponsive to intense stimuli that are ordinarily considered stressful. Small cardiac orienting responses suggest that psychopaths are less responsive and/or sensitive to small changes in environmental stimuli than are normals. These findings indicate that the ANS measures reflect dissociation of the ANS. Hare (1975b) has suggested that EDA responses preceding aversive stimuli reflect absence or fear arousal, while anticipatory heart rate activity is a protective response that serves to decrease the emotional impact of the situation. Electrocortical investigations reviewed by Hare (1975b) indicate that approximately 30 to 60 percent of psychopaths exhibit EEG abnormalities, generally widespread slow wave activity (e.g., Aurthers & Cahoon, 1964). Paty, Benezech, Eschapasse, and Noel (1978) recorded visual-evoked responses (VER), auditory-evoked responses (AER), and contingent negative variations (CNV) from two groups of psychopaths and normals. The psychopaths were "hypovigil" double-Y and "hypervigil" Klinefelter psychopaths. The two groups of psychopaths differed significantly on VER and AER, but were alike on CNV measures which differentiated them from normals. Significantly higher amplitudes of the latest associated components of ERs in 47XYY were found, which suggests a potential for differential diagnosis of psychopathic types on the basis of this measure. The CNV distinction is also present in other disorders, such as schizophrenia, autism, and depressive psychoses, and is therefore not a good indicator of psychopathy per se. Fowles (1980) suggests that psychopaths have a deficient behavioral inhibition system and, therefore, show normal approach, active avoidance and heart rate, but demonstrate poor passive avoidance and extinction with reduced EDA in response to threatening stimuli.

Hersen and Bellack (1977) review the social-skills literature and refer to an investigation by McFall and Marston (1970) in which ANS arousal was assessed by pulse rate before and after a role-playing assessment procedure. The results were questionable; no specific information was provided on the relationships between pulse rate, self-report measures, and overt behavioral measures.

Psychological Factors Affecting Physical Condition

The relationship between psychophysiological activity and pain has been reviewed several times (Melzack & Wall, 1975; Schacter, 1971; Sternbach, 1974). Tursky (1974) reviews the literature in which electric shock has been utilized as a painful stimulus in a psychophysiological laboratory, with special reference to ANS activity as assessed by EDA. In summary, Tursky (1974) reported on the comparison of palmar placements to the non-palmar areas of the ventral forearm, inner edge of the forearm, and lower abdomen. The findings indicated that spontaneous responses were almost nonexistent in nonpalmar recordings, most nonpalmar responses were monophasic, and responses could not be classically conditioned. In addition, several recent articles dealing with the psychophysiological treatment of different types of pain reinforce the utility of psychophysiological assessment procedures in this category. For example, Nowen and Solinger (1979) report on the successful EMG biofeedback training for patients experiencing chronic lower back pain. Significant reductions were achieved in both tension and self-reported pain while at a follow-up session EMG activity returned to the previous high level yet pain scores continued to improve. Blanchard (1979) treated a patient with chronic pain due to a reflex sympathetic dystrophy in the hand and arm. The treatment prescribed involved a tradiitional hand warming situation that resulted in marked decrements in pain that remained absent at a one year follow-up. Hartman (1979) reported on two interesting case studies of treatment for angina by hand warming and the subsequent substitution of hand warming for nitroglycerine.

Ray, Raczynski, Rogers, and Kimball (1979) summarize the applications of biofeedback procedures to the treatment of migraine headaches and conclude that hand temperature and extracranial vascular feedback both appear to be effective treatments. These authors also conclude that EMG biofeedback is useful in the treatment of tension headaches and temporomandibular joint pain.

With respect to obesity, Wooley, Wooley, and Dyrenforth, (1979) have stressed the need for metabolic assessment and the assessment of arousal which they suggest may be adequately met only by the inclusion of psychophysiological indices within an assessment package.

V Codes

The DSM III classification scheme has established this category to account for conditions that are not attributable to a mental disorder that are a focus of attention or treatment. Within this category exists an area referred to as noncompliance with treatment. Frederiksen, Martin, and Webster (1979) have suggested that this phenomenon be considered with psychophysiological assessment as a component of the inquiry.

Medical Psychology Applications

As psychology becomes increasingly involved in medical settings, the application of psychophysiological techniques has been extended into the third axis of the DSM III classification scheme involving physical disorders and conditions. Doerr, Follette, Scribner, and Eisdorfer (1980) have suggested that psychophysiological measures may be important in the assessment of renal dialysis patients. Electrodermal responsivity to Valsalva stimulation was assessed in patients suffering chronic renal failure and in a control group of normals. Patients demonstrated significantly reduced phasic skin conductance responses and tonic skin conductance levels when compared to normals. Lubar (1981) has reported on the utilization of EEG assessment prior to biofeedback training for epilepsy as compared to EEG posttreatment, and reports significant changes in both electrocortical activity and decrements in monthly seizure rates as a function of treatment. Goldstein (1981) discusses hypertension and the assessment of blood pressure lability as a function of stressful stimuli.

Psychotherapy

Lacey (1959) reviewed the psychophysiological literature and evaluated psychotherapy process and outcome suggesting the use of a psychophysiological approach. He concluded that autonomic responsivity within the therapeutic context may be somewhat "transactional" in nature and suggested that psychophysiological measures be used not as outcome measures but as process measures. Mathews (1971) has suggested that psychophysiological measures have utility as process and outcome measures based upon his review of these and desensitization procedures. Goldstein (1972) has reviewed literature assessing EMG activity during the process of psychotherapy and concluded that the amount of EMG activity in speech muscles was significantly different in threatening and supportive situations in both therapists and patients (Malmo, Boag, & Smith, 1957). Davis and Malmo (1951) and Shagass and Malmo (1954) investi-

gated EMG activity during psychotherapy and reported on one patient displaying high EMG with depressed mood and low tension in cheerful moods. Paul (1966) assessed EMG activity during desentisitization and reported that progressive relaxation was more effective than hypnotic induction, suggesting relaxation or self-relaxation in reducing tension. Borkovec and Grayson (1980) review the assessment of heart rate data during the systematic desensitization treatment of phobic anxiety and conclude that heart rate increases in the initial presentations of phobic stimuli, decreases initially to increasingly fear-producing scenes, and extinguishes during repeated exposure to phobic scenes.

Applications with the Assessment of Normal Variations in Activity

Psychophysiological assessment has been employed in relation to cognitive processes, personality factors, emotionality, sleep, sexual arousal, deception, aging, and a variety or other organismic and environmental influences. These applications have not been considered in some other discussions of psychophysiological assessment (see Epstein, 1976; Lang, 1971). However, Ray and Raczynski (1981) elected to include these areas in light of the contribution made toward a better understanding of normal human behavior and because environmental and organismic effects revealed in these areas must be accounted for prior to entertaining alternative competing hypotheses.

Cognitive Processes

The effects of such cognitive processes as intelligence, attention, arousal, information processing, performance, motivation, achievement, and learning have been the focus of several literature reviews, the majority of which have stressed electrocortical measures such as evoked potentials and contingent negative variations. Shagass (1972) reviewed the EEG correlates of intelligence and concluded that any relationships that might exist are very weak at best. The EEG correlates with personality were discussed in terms of psychodynamics and test results. In the former category, greater amounts of alpha were associated with passive, dependent individuals, while low levels of alpha activity were associated with consistent and well-directed individuals. In the latter category, the correlations between tests such as the Rorschach and MMPI and EEG measures have been either negative or highly inconsistent from one study to the next. Ritter (1979) reviewed the literature in regard to attention and indicated that an event-related potential (N100) was associated with active attention. Other reviews on cognitive processes and electrocortical activity are available (Donchin, 1979; John, 1967; Naatanen, 1975; Tecce, 1972); Shapiro and Schwartz (1970) review the literature pertaining to ANS activity and achievement, and Ax et al. (1978) review ANS activity and motivation. Finally, Dabbs (1980) has investigated cognitive processes within a cerebral blood flow paradigm, and Pritchard (1981) has reviewed the relationships of P300 with a host of stimulus and subject variables, including such things as information delivery and stimulus salience.

Personality Factors

The relationship between various personality factors and electrodermal activity has been inconclusively reviewed by Edelberg (1972). The personality trait of introversion-extroversion has been assessed by psychophysiological means; the ANS measures of EDA and heart rate suggest greater arousal among introverts than among extroverts (Stern & Janes, 1973). Other reviews have dealt with the development of specific psychosomatic disturbances (Graham, 1962, 1972), introversion and extroversion (Gray, 1970, 1972; Shagass & Canter, 1972), ego strength (Roessler, 1973), and the area of personal development and relationship enhancement (Kiritz & Moos, 1974). Zuckerman, Buchsbaum, and Murphy (1980) present data suggesting that the trait of sensation seeking may be identified by EDA-orienting responses and auditory-evoked potentials. Although some of this literature has been criticized for attempting to predict overt behavior on the basis of assessing hypothetical constructs (Goldfried & Kent, 1972), there is support for the notion that differences exist in psychophysiological responsivity among individuals on whom self-report and behavioral measures vary.

Emotion

Psychophysiological differentiation of emotions has been discussed in a number of reviews (Lang, Rice, & Sternbach, 1972; Pribram, 1967; Schacter, 1971; Schwartz, 1978). Although the litera-

ture regarding the psychophysiological aspects of disorders of affect is rather broad, investigations concerning the psychophysiology of emotionality are less often encountered. Tucker (1981) has reviewed the literature and concluded that high anxiety may engage the left hemisphere whereas high mood might arouse the right hemisphere. Data have been presented in support of a negative emotion (right hemisphere) and positive emotion (left hemisphere) position regarding lateralized emotionality (Davidson et al., 1978; Schwartz, Ahern, & Brown, 1979; Tucker, 1981), as well as the opposite of this, meaning positive/right and negative/left (Harman & Ray, 1977; Erlichman & Weiner, 1980). Finally, Pribram (1981) has attempted to integrate neuropsychological, physiological, and psychophysiological data and summarizes the cortical contribution to emotionality as a complex interaction involving a concept of self, that is organized and enhanced by parietal areas, selectivity inhibited by frontal areas, and affectively regulated by the right hemispere.

Sleep

The associations between psychophysiological measures and sleep have been generally reviewed by Johnson (1970, 1975) and Snyder and Scott (1972), while other reviews have focused upon specific measures, such as electrocortical activity (Feinberg & Evarts, 1969), electrodermal activity (Edelberg, 1972), and electromyographic activity (Goldstein, 1972). The effects of sleep deprivation on psychophysiological measures have also been considered by Naitoh (1975), and the effects of the hypnagogic state by Schacter (1976). Edelberg (1972) reports that stage four sleep is accompanied by greater phasic EDA than is waking state, and Goldstein (1972) reports that the evidence is clear for a marked reduction in head and neck muscle tension during dreaming states.

Sexual Arousal

The psychophysiological effects of normal sexual responsivity to erotic stimuli and during coital activity (and masturbation to orgasm) have been the topic of several reviews, beginning with the pioneering efforts by Masters and Johnson (1966) to Bancroft (1971), Heiman (1977), Stern, Farr, and Ray (1975), and Zuckerman (1972). At one time or another most of the common psychophysiological measures have been employed and, in addition to some rather predictable responses, have been found to be useful in specifying response norms and clarifying the relationship between cognitive and physiological activities.

Detection of Deception

The use of psychophysiological measures to assist in the determination of whether or not an individual is telling the truth has a long history dating back to Munsterberg's (1908) work, suggesting that these techniques can be used to assess guilty knowledge. Recently, the detection of deception literature has been reviewed in the areas of laboratory studies by Podlesney and Raskin (1977) and field investigations by Raskin, Barland, and Podlesney (1977). Other general reviews are available; the consensus of opinions supports the continued use of physiological measures to detect deception (Andreassi, 1980; Barland & Raskin, 1973; Lykken, 1974; Orne, Thackray, & Poskewitz, 1972).

Aging

The psychophysiological effects of aging have been reviewed and summarized recently by Marsh and Thompson (1977), while Woodruff (1978) has reviewed behavioral and electrocortical relationships over the course of the life span. Significant changes have been reported in the area of evoked potentials (Dustman et al., 1979; Perry & Childers, 1969; Shagass, 1972; Tecce, 1971), with SERs and VERs showing a gradual reduction in late wave amplitude with increasing age. Shagass (1972) reviewed EEG data and concluded that increased beta activity accompanies middle age followed by further frequency reductions with increasing age. Electrocortical activity of the aged during sleep has been the subject of a review by Feinberg and Evarts (1969), who report a substantial decrement in stage four sleep with advancing age. Edelberg (1972) has examined the EDA data in regard to the aging process, however, at the opposite end of the continuum, from birth on through adulthood. He reports that resistance levels among children under ten are slightly higher than among adults.

Other Organismic Variations

Many different variables have been reviewed, including literature on sexual differences (Edelberg, 1972; Perry & Childers, 1969; Shagass, 1972), the menstrual cycle (Bell, Christie, & Ven-

ables, 1975), sociocultural differences (Shapiro & Schwartz, 1970), racial and ethnic differences (Christie & Todd, 1975), and circadian rhythm effects (Mefferd, 1975).

Enviormental Influences

In addition to all of the sources of variance reviewed thus far, there remains the interaction between the environment and psychophysiological assessment. Mefferd (1975) has reviewed the existing relationships between physiological assessment and environment variables such as temperature, humidity, barometric pressure, weather fronts, wind speed, amount of sunshine, and geomagnetic activity. In addition, the time of year and day of week have been investigated by Christie (1975), and the time within the academic cycle for students has been implicated as another potential confound by Fisher and Winkel (1979).

Theoretical/Conceptual Issues

General Organization of the Nervous System

The terminology of the nervous system reflects an anatomical organizing principle. The central nervous system (CNS) is composed of all cells within the bony enclosure of the spinal cord and skull, whereas the peripheral nervous system consists of those neurons that are outside of these structures. The CNS is subdivided into the brain and the spinal cord, each of which is further divided along anatomical lines. The peripheral nervous system is also divided into two main parts: the somatic system and the autonomic system. The somatic system is concerned with adjustment between the external world and the organism and the autonomic system deals with the organism's internal regulation. The autonomic nervous system (ANS) is further divided into two parts, depending upon where the neurons originate along the spinal cord: the sympathetic division is within the thoracic and lumbar sections of the spinal cord, while the parasympathetic division originates in the cranial and sacral regions.

The autonomic nervous system and its interaction with the central nervous system has been of particular interest to psychologists because of its important role in the experience of emotion. In general, the sympathetic division activates the body, whereas the parasympathetic division conserves the resources of the body and helps to return physiological functioning to a state of equilibrium. For example, increases in heart rate, sweating, vasoconstriction of the peripheral blood vessels, and stimulation of the sphincters (bladder and intestine) are all controlled in part by the sympathetic nervous system. The parasympathetic system, on the other hand, decreases heart rate, controls erection of the genitalia, stimulates the peristalsis of the gastrointestinal tract, increases tearing and salivation, and has little effect on the peripheral vasculature. In general, the sympathetic system acts more diffusely, whereas the parasympathetic system is capable of independent actions in each of its parts.

As a general formulation, the sympathetic system facilitates activity that aids muscular activity and inhibits activity that would restrict it. The parasympathetic system, on the other hand, tends to conserve and store energy. This generalized view of the nervous system has led some to postulate quickly an opposing role for the sympathetic and parasympathetic system and others to relate these to Cannon's (1939) "fight or flight" notion. In terms of clinical processes, one would find oneself going astray if one were to follow this formulation completely. For example, parasympathetic innervation tends to increase activity in the walls of the stomach and intestive as well as in the glands of the stomach. Thus, one initial reaction in behavioral intervention procedures, such as relaxation training (seen as decreasing sympathetic activity), for certain stomach problems may be counterproductive and may actually exacerbate the situation. Reducing stress to the body is not always equal to decreasing sympathetic activity, although the psychological might mistakenly lead one to this conclusion. Whereas some activities suggest that the two systems work in opposition (e.g., vasodilation and vasoconstriction), there are other cases where this is not so. Thus, we suggest that the parasympathetic and sympathetic nervous system be seen as complementary rather than antagonistic to one another.

Concepts Related to the Interpretation of Psychophysiological Processes

The use of psychophysiological measures as an assessment and intervention procedure draws from a number of disciplines and research strategies. In this section we consider more theoretical work that has been performed in psychophysiology which is necessary for understanding how various measures are to be interpreted. Since psychophysiology is basically a recent science devoted to very old questions, many of the formulations presented are incomplete and are still being developed and refined.

Autonomic Balance

As one examines the effects of sympathetic and parasympathetic innervation, one realizes that some individuals respond with different degrees of sympathetic and parasympathetic innervation, and this in turn may be related to particular psychophysiological disorders. The so-called balance between the sympathetic and parasympathetic aspects of the autonomic nervous system has been a focus of research since the early parts of this century. Eppinger and Hess (1915) performed some of the earliest work in which they classified people as either vagotonic or sympathotonic. Vagotonics (related to the vagus nerve which conducts parasympathetic activity) were individuals who demonstrated large responses to drugs that stimulate the parasympathetic nervous system. Those who showed large responses to drugs that influence the sympathetic nervous system were referred to as sympathotonics. The manner in which a person responds to certain drugs not only reflects the balance within the autonomic nervous system but also serves as an assessment procedure for understanding basic personality differences. Later, work was also performed by Gellhorn and his associates (Gellhorn, Cortell, & Feldman, 1941) and Darrow (1943).

The researcher most associated with the concept of autonomic balance is Wenger (1972). With papers dating back to the 1940s, Wenger researched the idea that a person could be classified by an empirically determined score of autonomic balance ($\bar{A}$). He compared a person's resting score on a number of measures including palmar conductance, heart period, diastolic blood pressure, salivation, and other measures, with the score obtained from different individuals. The scores appear to approximate a normal distribution, with low scores indicating sympathetic dominance and high scores parasympathetic dominance. Autonomic balance has been studied in a variety of populations including children, military personnel, and hospitalized groups. In general, it is reported that low $\overline{A}$ scores are related to both physical and psychological disorders.

The Law of Initial Values

At the heart of the law of initial values is the idea that physiological changes vary within a certain range for a given individual. It follows from this that if a physiological measure such as heart rate is near the upper limit of this range, less upward change would be possible, but in turn the heart rate could decrease more easily. This relationship is referred to as the law of initial values. More formally, the law of initial values states that the psychophysiological response to particular stimulation is related to the prestimulus level of the response being measured. This relationship, not actually a scientific law, was first identified and named by Wilder (1967). Although the relationship was first thought to apply to all autonomic responses, exceptions (such as skin conductance) are reported in the literature that do not follow the suggested relationship. From a practical standpoint, the law of initial values requires that someone interested in assessment take into account the entire experimental context when utilizing psychophysiological measures. To illustrate this point, consider a subject who is late for an experiment and runs over to the building and up the stairs to the laboratory (a condition that usually increases heart rate). When electrodes are attached and this subject is presented with a stimulus that increases heart rate, heart rate activity might not increase and, in some cases, might actually decrease in relation to the prestimulus level. From a practical standpoint, this means that prestimulus levels must be taken into account when calculating heart rate change scores. In conceptual terms, this means that a change from a heart rate of 120 to 125 represents a different amount of effort on the part of the organism than a change from 60 to 65 beats per minute, although both changes are in absolute 5 beats per minute. When correcting for the law of initial values with heart rate, skin resistance, blood pressure or other measures, one of two common techniques is used. The first is to use Lacey's autonomic liability score (Lacey, 1956), a form of residualized gain scores (see Cronbach & Furby, 1970), and the second is analysis of covariance as applied to psychophysiological data (Benjamin, 1967).

Homeostasis

Homeostasis is best understood as part of general systems theory. The homeostatic state is a state of equilibrium that is maintained through a negative feedback loop. For example, when a thermostat is set at 65°, the heating system will be cut off once the temperature rises above this setting. The body has also been conceptualized in this manner as can be illustrated through sweating. As the temperature of the body is increased, negative feedback mechanisms produce perspiration until the temperature is returned to a homeostatic state. Likewise, it has been suggested that there is a normal return to equilibrium after an anxiety-producing event.

The concept of homeostasis was first introduced by Claude Bernard (1877) and made popular by Walter Cannon (1939) in his book, *The Wisdom of the Body*. Cannon suggested that the body is capable of regulating itself without any conscious control. Some recent conceptualizations in biofeedback suggest that physiological disorders are the result of a breakdown in the homeostatic mechanisms and that biofeedback may offer an external means of reestablishing normal homeostatic processes. Likewise, some psychophysiologists suggest that homeostatic mechanisms lie at the basis of the law of initial values.

Habituation

Habituation is the process in which the physiological response diminishes upon continued presentation of the stimulus. It may be generally stated that habituation will be slower the greater the intensity of stimulation, the more unique the stimulus, and the more complex the stimulus (see Graham, 1973). Although many people think of all psychophysiological responses as habituating, Pribram has pointed out that there is little evidence showing habituation of such responses as EEG (Pribram, 1981).

Orienting and Defensive Responses

Pavlov (1927) noticed that previously conditioned dogs did not show conditioning in the presence of a novel stimulus. He described this process as a reflex present in humans and animals that responds immediately to the slightest changes in the environment. This process is now called the orienting response (OR) or the "what is it?" response. Lynn (1966) has summarized the orienting response as follows: (1) an increase in sensitivity of sense organs; (2) body orientation toward sound (turning head, etc.); (3) increase in muscle tone with decrease in irrelevant motor activity; (4) pattern of

EEG activation (faster frequency, lower amplitude); (5) vasoconstriction in the periphery (limbs) and vasodilation in the head; (6) skin conductance increase; (7) after initial delay, respiration shows amplitude increase and frequency decrease; and (8) slowing of heart rate.

Understanding the orienting reponse prevents a researcher from confusing initial OR reactions, as might be displayed to the first few stimuli in a series, from the physiological response to the stimuli themselves. Since it is often difficult to differentiate which psychophysiological responses are to the stimuli themselves and which represent orienting responses, the beginning stimuli are often disregarded in psychophysiological research, especially in those cases where the stimuli are novel to the subject.

Whereas the OR represents attention to a novel stimulus, the defensive response (DR) is thought to represent a turning away from painful and intense stimuli. The DR also habituates much slower than the OR. The psychophysiological reactions of the two are similar except that vasomotor activity in the head shows constriction in a DR, while heart rate shows an increase in the DR (see Sokolov, 1963, 1965). The other psychophysiological responses are similar to those discussed by Lynn (1966) in relation to the OR.

Using Psychophysiological Measures to Understand Psychology Constructs

The emphasis of many who initially use psychophysiological measures is an attempt to understand psychological constructs. Constructs such as anxiety, or emotionality, or attention, or arousal have been the focus of many physiological studies. Given, however, that many constructs such as emotionality have been approached from both a biochemical and an electrophysiological standpoint from a number of broad disciplines, it is not surprising that there is a lack of conceptual clarity concerning many major constructs of interest to behavioral scientists. One of the more researched constructs is that of arousal, which has been equated with activation and even emotionality. Most of this work began at the turn of the century. For example, Cannon (1915) emphasized a general state of arousal that would lead to "fight or flight" behavior. Cannon, and later Papez (1937) and MacLean (1949), pointed research efforts toward the determination of anatomical structures related to emotionality. This led to an understanding of the midbrain and limbic structures in regulating arousal and emotionality. More behaviorally based researchers such as Duffy (1962, 1972), Malmo (1959), and Lindsley (1951, 1952) sought to determine the relationship between physiological changes and behavior. Much of this work viewed arousal as forming a continuum, going from very low arousal (e.g., sleep) to hyperarousal. Arousal was often related to the Yerkes-Dodson law reported in 1908, which suggests that better performance is found with medium arousal than with either low or high arousal. Measures such as heart rate, EEG, and muscle tension were all related to performance in this manner.

Lacey (1967) suggested that this view of arousal was too simple and that it ignored the complexity of the phenomenon. He suggested that in order to understand the construct of arousal, one must determine whether one is discussing cortical, autonomic, or behavioral arousal. In others words, as Borkovec (1976) and Davidson and Schwartz (1976) have recently reported, it is possible to show arousal in one area (e.g., cognitive) and not in another (e.g., somatic). Likewise, the clinician or researcher interested in biofeedback faces a similar assessment issue. For example, it is not uncommon for a patient to report subjective improvement (e.g., fewer headaches) without seeing a reduction in EMG activity or vice versa. Lacey further suggested that even among autonomic variables, it is possible to have a patterning that is inconsistent with a unidirectional arousal continuum. That is to say, it is quite possible to find a situation that produces an increase in skin conductance and muscle tension but a decrease in heart rate and respiration rate.

In an excellent review of the application of psychophysiological measures to the evaluation of psychotheray process and outcome, Lacey (1959) suggests that at least four situations must be considered when performing psychophysiological assessment:

1. Intrastressor stereotypy is descriptive of the case where an individual in response to a certain kind of stimuli gives a reproducible pattern.
2. Interstressor stereotypy occurs when a pattern obtained with one stressor is also found using different stressors.
3. Situation stereotypy, on the other hand, is found when different patterns of responding occur with different task demands. For example, Darrow (1929) suggested that "sensory" stimuli (those that did not require thinking)

would be associated with heart rate decreases, whereas "ideational" stimuli would be associated with an increase in heart rate.

4. Finally, symptom specificity describes the case when a stressor will produce one type of psychophysiological problem (e.g., headaches) in one person and the same stressor will produce another problem (e.g., heart palpitations) in another individual (see Malmo & Shagass, 1949).

Conclusions

We began this chapter with a discussion of the work of Galen in the second century and his ability to infer psychological processing from physiological observation, thus reflecting his knowledge of a mind/body link. However, two thousand years later we have yet to understand this link fully, much less to be able experimentally to replicate consistent physiological responses for specific thoughts, feelings, or movements of any complexity. Part of our problem was the manner in which some individuals conceptualized the search in the first place. Those people sought to find simple indices, such as an increase in heart rate that could be interpreted as *identical* to a psychological construct such as anxiety or arousal. The search has indeed proved fruitless. What we have learned in this search is that the use of psychophysiological measures requires that we give up simplistic notions of a one-to-one mapping between psychological processes and physiological processes. In turn, we are forced to accept the complexity of the nervous system as we view the variety of human interactions both between and within persons and in relation to environmental interactions. If we are to give up the idea that physiological responses somehow lead us to the "truth" about the organism, how then might we conceptualize the measures that we record? The answer is to consider psychophysiological responses as forming a level of analysis and in turn a language of their own. The question, then, becomes one of translation from a psychophysiological languge to a different level of analysis, whether it be motoric, emotional, cognitive, or conceptual. In the same way that one listens to and observes nonverbal responses in therapy as a form of communication that is at times discriminant from the verbal response, one can observe and listen to psychophysiological responses as a separate channel of communication through which we talk to others and ourselves. Asking this type of

question leads one more in the direction of asking about patterns of responding both within and between levels, a question we will return to briefly.

Psychophysiological assessment is not just one field but draws from a variety of sources to gain information and to develop techniques. This diversity has given the approach broad breadth, but the lack of a specific paradigm or even a specific journal in which one would find studies of psychophysiological assessment has also presented the field with problems, especially in terms of communication of information and techniques. Perhaps as the variety of fields from social psychology to clinical psychology, consumer psychology, and cognitive psychology now using psychophysiological measures learn of one another, some of these problems will decrease.

As we have noted, psychophysiological assessment methodologies began with disorders in which there were obvious links between the physiological measure examined and the behavior considered. The utility of psychophysiological procedures was thus quickly realized with disorders such as sexual disorders (Bancroft, 1971), as outcome measures in the assessment of procedures such as systematic desensitization (Mathews, 1971), and in the assessment and modification of psychophysiological disorders (see Ray et al., 1979). Thus, psychophysiology was first considered in assessment simply as a methodology and as a means of assessing and predicting outcome. As psychologists realized the low correlation between physiological activity and cognitive and motoric events (e.g., Lang, 1971), however, the theoretical sophistication of psychophysiology has continued to increase to account for this observed discrepancy in response measures. Following the direction of Lacey (1959), researchers have had to examine the interrelationships of cognitive, motoric, and physiological events. Thus, psychophysiology has had to move to a position in which it is considered as a mechanism (Schwartz, 1978), and psychophysiological measures are utilized to examine the interrelationships between the various response systems.

Thus, while advances are still to be realized in the use of psychophysiological procedures as both a method and a means of assessing outcomes, a major focus of future research will be in terms of examining interrelationships between response systems and even between various physiological measures themselves. The uses of psychophysiological assessment procedures will also increase as researchers gain an increased understanding of the relationships between psychophysiological measures and other processes. Aside from simply using psychophysiological measures as an alternative to cognitive and behavioral measures in the initial assessment of disorders and change treatment, psychophysiological measures may reveal valuable information upon which treatment procedures may be matched, may provide conceptually relevant information for understanding various disorders, and may even provide a criterion base for treatment changes. As technological advances continue to occur, new forms of instrumentation will also become available and may become valuable in psychophysiological assessments, and *in vivo* psychophysiological assessments may become practical. Finally, as behavioral-assessment procedures continue to expand our knowledge of various disorders and even normal ranges of functioning, trends will also be seen in the use of psychophysiological procedures, even in areas where there is no evident link between the behaviors being assessed and the physiological measures being examined.

Psychophysiological Patterning and Interrelationships

In order to further clarify psychophysiological patterning, researchers must turn to the early psychophysiologists such as Darrow (1943), Davis (1957), and Lacey (1959) in considering the psychophysiological patterning of responses with different individuals under different conditions (see Schwartz, 1978; Sternbach, Alexander, & Greenfield, 1969). Psychophysiological principles such as autonomic balance between the sympathetic and parasympathetic branches of the autonomic nervous system (Wenger, 1966), intrastressor stereotypy, interstressor stereotypy, and situational stereotypy emerge as important considerations in understanding the complex relationships between physiological activities in different individuals and in different situations.

This examination of response patterning is already being undertaken with bilateral peripheral autonomic measures. For example, lateralized electrodermal findings have been reported by Gruzelier and Venables (1973, 1974) for schizophrenic and depressed populations, by Myslobodsky and Horesch (1978) for depressed subjects, and

by Hare (1978) for a psychopathic population. Similarly, lateralized findings have been found for hand temperature in test-anxious subjects (McCann & Papsdorf, 1979) and in normal subjects during visual stimulation (van Houten & Chemtolo, 1979); these results suggest lateralization effects in the peripheral vasculature. Lateralization of activity in psychophysiological measures has even been found in the facial musculature (Schwartz, Brown, & Ahern, 1980). Given that some of these investigations of bilateral activity have only found significant effects on one side of the body, these data suggest that researchers should exert caution in generalizing from activity recorded from just one side of the body. Further, while lateralized autonomic events may correlate highly with contralateral events (Bull & Gale, 1975), these results suggest that a patterning of psychophysiological activity should be considered.

On a more general level, since several researchers have attempted to draw implications from lateralized peripheral activity about central nervous system activity (e.g., Flor-Henry, 1976), the need for a more critical examination of the patterning of both autonomic and central nervous system responses to cognitive and behavioral events is indicated. Unfortunately, although several attempts have been undertaken to relate lateralized autonomic activity to central events (Deickhoff et al., 1978; Ketterer & Smith, 1977; Lacroix & Comper, 1979; Myslobodsky & Rattock, 1975, 1977), no consistent relationship has emerged from this literature at the present time. However, clarification of these interrelationships may prove important for both assessment and conceptual reasons (see Galin, 1974).

Apart from further understanding the patterning of autonomic, central, cognitive, and behavioral activities, how these systems are interrelated and influence one another needs to be further examined. This has already been accomplished on the most basic of levels with most contemporary theories of emotion (see Grings & Dawson, 1978; Pribram, 1981; Tucker, 1981); yet, specific mechanisms by which various systems influence one another need to be addressed. Some attempts to clarify these relationships have already been made by the Laceys (Lacey & Lacey, 1970), for example. They have proposed that cardiovascular activity is part of an active feedback mechanism with electrocortical and cognitive activity and with overt behavioral influences.

Uses of Psychophysiological Assessment Procedures

Given the variety of applications of psychophysiological assessment techniques, it is possible to take a broad view and organize these into discrete categories. In particular, we will discuss five uses of psychophysiological assessment.

The first use is as an assessment and diagnostic technique. These types of studies have employed particular psychophysiological measures, such as electrodermal activity, to differentiate established diagnostic categories such as schizophrenia. Other work has followed the line of Jung's original research in using psychophysiological measures to determine areas of conflict in individuals. The main theme of this first area is to learn something about a person from observing psychophysiological changes.

A second use of psychophysiological measures is directed at understanding changes during a particular process. Contained in the Lacey (1959) review, previously cited, are numerous examples of this approach as applied to psychotherapy. In our own laboratory we have observed psychophysiological changes as subjects watch television. The basic theme of this second approach is what can psychophysiological measures tell us about a particular ongoing process.

A third use of psychophysiological measurement focuses on the measure itself and the individual's ability to change it. This is best exemplified by behavioral medicine and biofeedback techniques, in which individuals are taught to control specific physiological responses. The main theme of this approach is control of a physiological response.

The fourth use of psychophysiological measures centers on a search for psychophysiological marker variables; that is, the question becomes one of attempting to find a particular physiological response that will signal occurrence of the particular process under study. For example, in the early eye movement research it was hoped that observing the direction of gaze would tell which hemisphere was processing information. In terms of sleep research REM, activity is often viewed as a marker variable for dreaming. The basic question of this fourth approach involves the search for physiological marker variables.

The fifth use of psychophysiological techniques —and one of the most challenging—seeks to understand patterns of responses both within and across levels of analysis. Within the same level of analysis one can observe patterns of physiolog- ical activity to various tasks. For example, some tasks, such as mental arithmetic, will show an increase in heart rate and decrease in skin resistance, whereas other tasks, such as looking at slides, will also show a decrease in skin resistance but an increase in heart rate. One can also use this type of work to better understand the relationship between the central and autonomic nervous systems or between the sympathetic and parasympathetic parts of the autonomic nervous system. Across levels, one can ask how the language of psychophysiological responding is related to that of cognitive responding, that of emotional responding, or that of motoric responding. Metaphorically, one is faced with problems of translation and difficulty of understanding how each system expresses itself. This question is just beginning to be addressed at the present time.

Trends in Assessment Procedures and Instrumentation

Advances in procedures and instrumentation are likely to be realized in two separate areas. First, technological advances are likely to result in an increase in the types of instrumentation available to the psychophysiologist. Particularly as the behavioral medicine movement results in further collaboration between psychologists and medical personnel, sophisticated medical technology may be more available for psychophysiological assessment. In order to make these advances, however, it will be necessary to include within the domain of psychophysiology all measures of a more macro nature as compared to more micro approaches, such as single-cell recordings. Infrared temperature measurements from the body, doppler measures of cardiovascular functioning, as well as CAT (computerized axial tomography) and PET (position emission tomography) approaches to brain acitivity would be included in this expanded definition of psychophysiology. Some of his work is already available, as exemplified by the preliminary reports on using PET studies with manics (Dagani, 1981).

Second, psychophysiologists are likely to move out of the laboratory and examine *in vivo* measures of physiological activity as telemetry, miniature tape recorders, and integrated circuit devices become more readily available. For example, use of portable automated methods for *in vivo* recording of blood pressure (see Schneider, 1968) may be of value in understanding the range of blood pressure parameters and would be valuable in the assessment of typography in blood pressure levels of hypertensive persons. Even newer methods, such as the use of pulse wave velocity measures (Steptoe, Smulyan, & Gribbin, 1976), might further aid in the endeavor. However, when confronted with million-dollar equipment, psychophysiologists are cautioned not to forget that simple studies of psychophysiological measures are equally useful and should be undertaken. For example, Bell and Schwartz (1975) had individuals self-monitor pulse rate outside of the laboratory with interesting results.

Trends in Disorders that are Assessed Psychophysiologically

Consistent with our discussion of the uses of psychophysiological assessment procedures, future investigations are likely to make use of psychophysiological procedures in an expanded variety of manners with an increased number of disorders. Examinations of disorders that have previously been only minimally investigated with psychophysiological procedures are likely to occur on a more thorough basis. For example, we agree with Wells' (1981) conclusion that although psychophysiological measures with children have only infrequently been utilized, they promise a very useful addition to behavioral-assessment procedures with children. Psychophysiological procedures may also be likely to prove valuable as process variables, such as in evaluating the typography of various behaviors. For example, Pomerleau (1980) has suggested that psychophysiological measures may be important in understanding the manner in which smokers perceive physiological activity and the effect that physiological activity has upon smoking behavior.

Summary

In summary, psychophysiological assessment procedures have proved valuable in providing some objective measures of outcome and as a source of data from which to examine questions concerning the interrelationships of cognitive, motoric, and autonomic events. However, psychophysiological assessment is an area that relies on frequently complex instrumentation with measures that are frequently difficult to interpret. To aid in the interpretation of these measures, it is necessary to give up simplistic notions of a one-to-one mapping between physiological and behavioral activities. Rather, the complexity of the various components of the nervous system and their interactions among themselves and behaviors and cognitions must be appreciated, although this complexity is barely understood even by the best of researchers. Obviously, many questions remain about the utility of psychophysiological assessment procedures, including how physiological responses develop, under what conditions they might be changed, and how flexible or inflexible physiological patternings are. Further, issues, including the nature of psychophysiological changes that occur over the life span, and early developmental studies, offer great potential as developing areas in psychophysiological assessment. With the variety of areas now employing psychophysiological assessment techniques, we expect to witness an expansion of applications with increased methodological sophistication that will have clinical benefit.

References

Akiskal, H. S., & McKinney, W. T. Overview of recent research in depression: Integration of ten conceptual models into a comprehensive clinical frame. *Archives of General Psychiatry*, 1975, **32**, 285–305.

Alexander, A. A. Psychophysiological concepts of psychopathology. In N. S. Greenfield & R. A. Sternbach (Eds.), *Handbook of psychophysiology*. New York: Holt, Rinehart, & Winston, 1972.

Alpert, M., & Martz, M. J. Cognitive views of schizophrenia in light of recent studies of brain asymmetry. In C. Shagass, S. Gershon, & A. J. Friedhoff (Eds.), *Psychopathology and brain dysfunction*. New York: Raven Press, 1977.

Andreassi, J. L. *Psychophysiology: Human behavior and physiological responses*. New York: Oxford University Press, 1980.

Aurthers, R. G., & Cahoon, E. B. A clinical and electroencephalographic survey of psychopathic personality. *American Journal of Psychiatry*, 1964, **120**, 875–882.

Ax, A. F. Psychophysiological methodology for the study of schizophrenia. In R. Roessler & N. S. Greenfield (Eds.), *Physiological correlates of psychological disorder*. Madison: University of Wisconsin Press, 1962.

Ax, A. F., Lloyd, R., Gorham, J. C., Lootens, A. M., & Robinson, R. Autonomic learning: A measure of motivation. *Motivation and Emotion*, 1978, **2**, 213–242.

Bancroft, J. The application of psychophysiological measures to the assessment-modification of sexual behavior. *Behaviour Research and Therapy*, 1971, **8**, 119–130.

Bancroft, J., & Mathews, A. Autonomic correlates of penile erection. *Journal of Psychosomatic Research*, 1971, **15**, 159–167.

Barland, G. H., & Raskin, D. C. Detection of deception. In W. F. Prokasy & D. C. Raskin (Eds.), *Electrodermal activity in psychological research*. New

York: Academic Press, 1973.

Barlow, D. H. Assessment of sexual behavior. In A. R. Ciminero, K. S. Calhoun, & H. E. Adams (Eds.), *Handbook of behavioral assessment*. New York: Wiley, 1977.

Barlow, D., Leitenberg, H., & Agras, W. S. The experimental control of sexual deviation through manipulation of the noxious scene in covert sensitization. *Journal of Abnormal Psychology*, 1969, **74**, 596–601.

Bassett, M., & Ashby, W. R. The effect of electroconvulsive therapy on the psychogalvanic response. *Journal of Mental Science*, 1954, **100**, 632–642.

Begleiter, H. (Ed.), *Evoked brain potentials and behavior*. New York: Plenum, 1979.

Bell, B., Christie, M. J., & Venables, P. H. Psychophysiology of the menstrual cycle. In P. H. Venables & M. J. Christie (Eds.), *Research in psychophysiology*. New York: Wiley, 1975.

Bell, I. R., & Schwartz, G. E. Voluntary control and reactivity of human heart rate. *Psychophysiology*, 1975, **12**, 339–348.

Benjamin, L. S. Facts and artifacts in using analysis of covariance to "undo" the law of initial values. *Psychophysiology*, 1967, **4**, 187–206.

Bernard, C. *Leçons sur le diabete et la glycogenese animal*. Paris: Bailliere, 1877.

Bernick, N., Kling, A., & Borowitz, G. Physiological differentiating, sexual arousal, and anxiety. *Psychosomatic Medicine*, 1968, **65**, 427–433.

Blanchard, E. B. The use of temperature biofeedback in the treatment of chronic pain due to causalgia. *Biofeedback and Self-Regulation*, 1979, **4**, 183–188.

Blanchard, E. B. Behavioral assessment of psychophysiologic disorders. In D. H. Barlow (Ed.), *Behavioral assessment of adult disorders*. New York: Guilford, 1981.

Borkovec, T. D. Physiological and cognitive process in the regulation of anxiety. In G. E. Schwartz & D. Shapiro (Eds.), *Consciousness and self-regulation*, Vol. 1. New York: Plenum, 1976.

Borkovec, T. D. Pseudo (experiential)-insomnia and idiopathic (objective) insomnia: Theoretical and therapeutic issues. *Advances in Behaviour Research and Therapy*, 1979, **2**, 27–55.

Borkovec, T. D., & Grayson, J. B. Consequences of increasing the functional impact of internal emotional stimuli. In K. R. Blankstein, P. Pliner, & J. Polivy (Eds.), *Assessment and modification of emotional behavior*, Vol. 6. New York: Plenum, 1980.

Borkovec, T. D., Weerts, T. C., & Bernstein, D. A. Assessment of anxiety. In A. R. Ciminero, K. S. Calhoun, & H. E. Adams (Eds.), *Handbook of behavioral assessment*. New York: Wiley, 1977.

Boulougouris, J. C., & Bassiakos, L. Prolonged flooding in cases of obsessive-compulsive neurosis. *Behaviour Research and Therapy*, 1973, **11**, 227–231.

Boulougouris, J. C., Rabavilas, A. D., & Stefanis, C. Psychophysiological responses in obsessive-compulsive patients. *Behaviour Research and Therapy*, 1977, **15**, 221–230.

Breggin, P. R. The psychophysiology of anxiety with a review of the literature concerning adrenaline. *Journal of Nervous and Mental Disease*, 1964, **139**, 558–568.

Brown, C. C. *Methods in psychophysiology*. Baltimore: Williams & Wilkins, 1967.

Brown, C. C. The parotid puzzle: A review of the literature on human salivation and its application to psychophysiology. *Psychophysiology*, 1970, **7**, 66–85.

Buchsbaum, M. S. Psychophysiology and schizophrenia. *Schizophrenia Bulletin*, 1977, **3**, 7–14. (a)

Buchsbaum, M. S. The middle evoked response components and schizophrenia. *Schizophrenia Bulletin*, 1977, **3**, 93–104. (b)

Bull, R. H. C., & Gale, M. A. Electrodermal activity recorded concomitantly from the subject's two hands. *Psychophysiology*, 1975, **12**, 94–97.

Caird, W. K., & Wincze, J. P. *Sex therapy: A behavioral approach*. Hagerstown: Harper & Row, 1977.

Callaway, E. *Brain electrical potentials and individual psychological differences*. New York: Grune & Stratton, 1975.

Cannon, W. B. *Bodily changes in pain, hunger, fear and rage*. New York: Appleton, 1915.

Cannon, W. B. *The wisdom of the body* (2nd ed.). New York: Norton, 1939.

Chapman, L. J., Chapman, J. P., & Brelje, T. Influence of the experimental or pupillary dilation to sexually provocative pictures. *Journal of Abnormal Psychology*, 1969, **74**, 396–400.

Christie, M. J. The psychosocial environment and precursors of disease. In P. H. Venables & M. J. Christie (Eds.), *Research in psychophysiology*. New York: Wiley, 1975.

Christie, M. J., & Todd, J. L. Experimenter-subject-situational interactions. In P. H. Venables & M. J. Christie (Eds.), *Research in psychophysiology*. New York: Wiley, 1975.

Cracco, R. Q. Evoked potentials in patients with neurological disorders. In H. Begleiter (Ed.), *Evoked brain potentials and behavior*. New York: Plenum, 1979.

Cronbach, I. J., & Furby, L. How should we measure "change"—Or should we? *Psychological Bulletin*, 1970, **74**, 68–80.

Dabbs, J. M. Left-right differences in cerebral blood flow and cognition. *Psychophysiology*, 1980, **17**, 548–551.

Dagani, R. Radiochemicals key to new diagnostic tool. *Chemical and Engineering News*, November 9, 1981, pp. 30–37.

Darrow, C. W. Differences in the physiological reactions to sensory and ideational stimuli. *Psychological Bulletin*, 1929, **26**, 185–201.

Darrow, C. W. Physiological and clinical tests of autonomic function and autonomic balance. *Physiological Reviews*, 1943, **23**, 1–36.

Davidson, R. J. Specificity and patterning in biobehavioral systems. *American Psychologist*, 1978, **33**, 430–436.

Davidson, R. J., & Schwartz, G. E. The psychobiology of relaxation and related states: A multiprocess theory. In D. I. Mostofsky (Ed.), *Behavior control and modification of physiological activity*. Englewood Cliffs, N.J.: Prentice-Hall, 1976.

Davidson, R. J., Schwartz, G. E., Saron, C., Bennett, J., & Goleman, D. Frontal versus parietal EEG asymmetry during positive and negative affect. Paper presented at the meeting of the American Psychological Association, Toronto, September 1978.

Davis, F. H., & Malmo, R. B. Electromyographic recording during interview. *American Journal of Psychiatry*, 1951, **107**, 908–916.

Davis, R. C. Response patterns. *Transactions of the New York Academy of Sciences*, 1957, **19**, 731–739.

Depue, R. A., & Fowles, D. C. Electrodermal activity as an index of arousal in schizophrenics. *Psychological Bulletin*, 1973, **79**, 233–238.

Deickhoff, G. M., Garland, J., Dansereau, D. F., & Walker, C. A. Muscle tension, skin conductance, and finger pulse volume: Asymmetries as a function of cognitive demands. *Acta Psychologia*, 1978, **42**, 83–93.

Doerr, H. O., Follette, W., Scribner, B. H., & Eisdorfer, C. Electrodermal response dysfunction in patients on maintenance renal dialysis. *Psychophysiology*, 1980, **17**, 83–86.

Donchin, E. Event-related brain potentials: A tool in the study of human information processing. In H. Begleiter (Ed.), *Evoked brain potentials and behavior*. New York: Plenum, 1979.

Dongier, M., Dubrovsky, B., & Engelsmann, F. Event-related slow potentials in psychiatry. In C. Shagass, S. Gershon, & A. J. Friedhoff (Eds.), *Psychopathology and brain dysfunction*. New York: Raven Press, 1977.

Duffy, E. The psychological significance of the concept of "arousal" or "activation." *Psychological Review*, 1957, **64**, 265–275.

Duffy, E. *Activation and behavior*. New York: Wiley, 1962.

Duffy, E. A. Activation. In N. S. Greenfield & R. A. Sternbach (Eds.), *Handbook of psychophysiology*. New York: Holt, Rinehart, & Winston, 1972.

Dureman, I., & Saaren-Seppälä, P. Electrodermal reactivity as related to self-ratings, and clinical ratings of anxiety and depression. 15th Report, December 1963, University of Uppsala, Uppsala, Sweden.

Dustman, R. E., Snyder, W. W., Callner, D. A., & Beck, E. C. The evoked response as a measure of cerebral dysfunction. In H. Begleiter (Ed.), *Evoked brain potentials and behavior*. New York: Plenum, 1979.

Edelberg, R. Electrical properties of the skin. In C. C. Brown (Ed.), *Methods in psychophysiology*. Baltimore: Williams & Wilkins, 1967.

Edelberg, R. Electrical activity of the skin. In N. S. Greenfield & R. A. Sternbach (Eds.), *Handbook of psychophysiology*. New York: Holt, Rinehart, & Winston, 1972.

Epstein, L. H. Psychophysiological measurement in assessment. In M. Hersen & A. S. Bellack (Eds.), *Behavioral assessment: A practical handbook*. New York: Pergamon, 1976.

Eppinger, J., & Hess, L. Die vagotonie. *Mental and Nervous Disease Monograph*, 1915, p. 20.

Erlichman, H., & Weiner, M. A. EEG asymmetry during covert mental activity. *Psychophysiology*, 1980, **17**, 228–235.

Evans, I. M., & Nelson, R. O. Assessment of child behavior problems. In A. R. Ciminero, K. S. Calhoun, & H. E. Adams (Eds.), *Handbook of behavioral assessment*. New York: Wiley, 1977.

Eysenck, H. J. *The biological basis of personality*. Springfield, Ill.: C. C. Thomas, 1968.

Feinberg, I., & Evarts, E. V. Some implications of sleep research for psychiatry. In J. Zubin & C. Shagass

(Eds.), *Neurobiological aspects of psychopathology*. New York: Grune & Stratton, 1969.

Fisher, L. E., & Winkel, M. H. Time of quarter effect: An uncontrolled variable in electrodermal research. *Psychophysiology*, 1979, **16**, 158–163.

Flor-Henry, P. Lateralized temporal-limbic dysfunction and psychopathology. *Annals of the New York Academy of Sciences*, 1976, **280**, 777–795.

Fowles, D. C. (Ed.). *Clinical applications of psychophysiology*. New York: Columbia University Press, 1975.

Fowles, D. C. The three arousal model: Implications of Gray's two-factor learning theory for heart rate, electrodermal activity, and psychopathy. *Psychophysiology*, 1980, **17**, 87–104.

Fowles, D. C., Christie, M. J., Edelberg, R., Grings, W. W., Lykken, D. T., & Venables, P. H. Publication recommendations for electrodermal measurements. *Psychophysiology*, 1981, **18**, 232–239.

Franzen, G., & Ingvar, D. H. Abnormal distribution of cerebral activity in chronic schizophrenia. *Journal of Psychiatric Research*, 1975, **12**, 199–214.

Frederiksen, L. W., Martin, J. E., & Webster, J. S. Assessment of smoking behavior. *Journal of Applied Behavior Analysis*, 1979, **12**, 653–664.

Freund, K. Assessment of pedophilia. In M. Cook & K. Howells, (Eds.), *Adult sexual interest in chidren*. London: Academic Press, 1981.

Freund, K., & Blanchard, R. Assessment of sexual dysfunction and deviation. In M. Hersen & A. S. Bellack (Eds.), *Behavioral assessment: A practical handbook*. (2nd ed.) New York: Pergamon, 1981.

Friedman, D., Frosch, A., & Erlenmeyer-Kimling, L. Auditory evoked potentials in children at high risk for schizophrenia. In H. Begleiter (Ed.), *Evoked brain potentials and behavior*. New York: Plenum, 1979.

Froehlich, W. D. Stress, anxiety, and the control of attention: A psychophysiological approach. In C. D. Spielberger & I. G. Sarason (Eds.), *Stress and anxiety*, Vol. 5. New York: Wiley, 1978.

Galbraith, G. C., Squires, N., Altair, D., & Gliddon, J. B. Electro-physiological assessments in mentally retarded individuals: From brainstem to cortex. In H. Begleiter (Ed.), *Evoked brain potentials and behavior*. New York: Plenum, 1979.

Galin, D. Implication for psychiatry of left and right cerebral specialization. *Archives of General Psychiatry*, 1974, **31**, 572–583.

Geer, J. H. Sexual functioning: Some data and speculations on psychophysiological assessment. In J. D. Cone & R. P. Hawkins (Eds.), *Behavioral assessment: New directions in clinical psychology*. New York: Brunner/Mazel, 1977.

Gellhorn, E., Cortell, L., & Feldman, J. The effect of emotion, sham rage, and hypothalamic stimulation on the vago-insulin system. *American Journal of Physiology*, 1941, **133**, 532–541.

Goldfried, M. R., & Kent, R. N. Traditional versus behavioral assessment: A comparison of methodological and theoretical assumptions. *Psychological Bulletin*, 1972, **77**, 409–420.

Goldstein, I. B. Electromyography. In N. S. Greenfield & R. A. Sternbach (Eds.), *Handbook of psychophysiology*. New York: Holt, Rinehart, & Winston, 1972.

Goldstein, I. B. Assessment of hypertension. In C. K.

Prokop & L. A. Bradley (Eds.), *Medical psychology: Contributions to behavioral medicine.* New York: Academic Press, 1981.

Goldstein, L., & Sugerman, A. A. EEG correlates of psychopathology. In J. Zubin & C. Shagass (Eds.), *Neurobiological aspects of psychopathology.* New York: Grune & Stratton, 1969.

Goode, D. J., Meltzer, H. Y., Crayton, J. W., & Mazura, T. A. Physiologic abnormalities of the neuromuscular system in schizophrenia. *Schizophrenia Bulletin,* 1977, **3,** 121–139.

Graham, D. T. Some research on psychophysiologic specificity and its relation to psychosomatic disease. In R. Roessler & N. S. Greenfield (Eds.), *Physiological correlates of physiological disorder.* Madison: University of Wisconsin Press, 1962.

Graham, D. T. Psychophysiology and medicine. *Psychophysiology,* 1971, **8,** 121–131.

Graham, D. T. Psychosomatic medicine. In N. S. Greenfield & R. A. Sternbach (Eds.), *Handbook of psychophysiology.* New York: Holt, Rinehart, & Winston, 1972.

Graham, F. K. Habituation and distribution of responses innervated by the autonomic nervous system. In H. V. S. Peeke & M. J. Herz (Eds.), *Habituation: Vol. 1, Behavioral studies.* New York: Academic Press, 1973.

Graham, F. K. Constraints on measuring heart rate and period sequentially through real and cardiac time. *Psychophysiology,* 1978, **15,** 492–495.

Gray, J. A. The psychophysiological basis of introversion-extraversion. *Behaviour Research and Therapy,* 1970, **8,** 249–266.

Gray, J. A. The psychophysiological nature of introversion-extraversion: A modification of Eysenck's theory. In V. D. Nebylitsyn & J. A. Gray (Eds.), *Biological bases of individual behavior.* New York: Academic Press, 1972.

Grayson, J., Nutter, D., & Mavissakalian, M. Psychophysiological assessment of obsessive-compulsive neurosis. *Behaviour Research and Therapy.* In press.

Greenfield, N. S., & Sternbach, R. A. (Eds.), *Handbook of psychophysiology.* New York: Holt, Rinehart, & Winston, 1972.

Grings, W. W., & Dawson, M. E. *Emotions and bodily responses: A psychophysiological approach.* New York: Academic Press, 1978.

Gruzelier, J. H., & Venables, P. H. Skin conductance responses to tones with and without attentional significance in schizophrenic and nonschizophrenic psychiatric patients. *Neuropsychologia,* 1973, **11,** 221–230.

Gruzelier, J., & Venables, P. Bimodality and lateral asymmetry of skin conductance orienting activity in schizophrenics: Replication and evidence of lateral asymmetry in patients with depression and disorders of personality. *Biological Psychiatry,* 1974, **8,** 55–73.

Hall, R. A., Griffin, R. B., Moyer, D. L., Hopkins, K. H., & Rappoport, M. Evoked potential, stimulus intensity, and drug treatment in hyperkinesis. *Psychophysiology,* 1976, **13,** 405–415.

Halliday, R., Rosenthal, J. H., Naylor, H., & Callaway, E. Averaged evoked potential predictors of clinical improvement in hyperactive children treated with methylphenidate: An initial study and replication.

Psychophysiology, 1976, **13,** 429–440.

Hare, R. D. *Psychopathy: Theory and research.* New York: Wiley, 1970.

Hare, R. D. Psychopathic behavior: Some recent theory and research. In H. Adams & W. Boardman (Eds.), *Advances in experimental clinical psychology.* New York: Pergamon, 1971.

Hare, R. D. Psychopathy. In P. R. Venables & M. J. Christie (Eds.), *Research in psychophysiology.* New York: Wiley, 1975. (a)

Hare, R. D. Psychophysiological studies of psychopathy. In D. C. Fowles (Ed.), *Clinical applications of psychophysiology.* New York: Columbia University Press, 1975. (b)

Hare, R. D. Psychopathy and electrodermal responses to nonsignal stimulation. *Biological Psychology,* 1978, **6,** 237–246.

Hare, R. D., & Craigen, D. Psychopathy and physiological activity in a mixed-motive game situation. *Psychophysiology,* 1974, **11,** 197–206.

Harman, D. W., & Ray, W. J. Hemispheric activity during affective verbal stimuli: An EEG study. *Neuropsychologia,* 1977, **15,** 457–460.

Hartman, C. H. Response of anginal pain to hand warming. *Biofeedback and Self-Regulation,* 1979, **4,** 355–357.

Hastings, J. E., & Barkley, R. A. A review of psychophysiological research with hyperkinetic children. *Journal of Abnormal Child Psychology,* 1978, **6,** 413–447.

Heath, R. G. Subcortical brain function correlates of psychopathology and epilepsy. In C. Shagass, S. Gerson, & A. J. Friedhoff (Eds.), *Psychopathology and brain dysfunction.* New York: Raven Press, 1977.

Heiman, J. R. A psychophysiological exploration of sexual arousal patterns in females and males. *Psychophysiology,* 1977, **14,** 266–274.

Heiman, J. R. Uses of psychophysiology in the assessment and treatment of sexual dysfunction. In J. LoPiccolo & L. LoPiccolo (Eds.), *Handbook of sex therapy.* New York: Plenum, 1978.

Hersen, M., & Bellack, A. S. Assessment of social skills. In A. R. Ciminero, K. S. Calhoun, & H. E. Adams (Eds.), *Handbook of behavioral assessment.* New York: Wiley, 1977.

Hess, E. H. Pupillometrics: A method of studying mental, emotional, and sensory processes. In N. S. Greenfield & R. A. Sternbach (Eds.), *Handbook of psychophysiology.* New York: Holt, Rinehart, & Winston, 1972.

Holzman, P. S., & Levy, D. L. Smooth pursuit eye movements and functional psychoses: A review. *Schizophrenia Bulletin,* 1977, **3,** 15–27.

Hoon, P. W. The assessment of sexual arousal in women. In M. Hersen, R. M. Eisler, & P. M. Miller (Eds.), *Progress in behavioral modification,* Vol. 7. New York: Academic Press, 1978.

van Houten, W. H., & Chemtolo, C. Lateralized differences in temperature and in the skin's electrical activity in response to visual stimulation. Paper presented at the meeting of the Biofeedback Society of America, San Diego, February 1979.

Itil, T. M. Qualitative and quantitative EEG findings in schizophrenia. *Schizophrenia Bulletin,* 1977, **3,** 61–79.

Jennings, J. R., Berg, W. K., Hutcheson, J. S., Obrist, P.,

Porges, S., & Turpin, G. Publication guidelines for heart rate studies in man. *Psychophysiology*, 1981, **18**, 226–231.

John, E. R. *Mechanisms of memory*. New York: Academic Press, 1967.

Johnson, L. C. A psychophysiology for all states. *Psychophysiology*, 1970, **6**, 501–516.

Johnson, L. C. Sleep. In P. H. Venables & M. J. Christie (Eds.), *Research in psychophysiology*. New York: Wiley, 1975.

Jordan, L. S. Electrodermal activity in schizophrenics: Further considerations. *Psychological Bulletin*, 1974, **81**, 85–91.

Jung, C. G. On psychophysical relations of the associative experiment. *Journal of Abnormal Psychology*, 1907, **7**, 247–255.

Kallman, W. M., & Fuerstein, M. Psychophysiological procedures. In A. R. Ciminero, K. S. Calhoun, & H. E. Adams (Eds.), *Handbook of behavioral assessment*. New York: Wiley, 1977.

Karacan, I. Advances in the psychophysiological evaluation of male erectile impotence. In J. LoPiccolo & L. LoPiccolo (Eds.), *Handbook of sex therapy*. New York: Plenum, 1978.

Karacan, I., Salis, P. J., & Williams, R. L. The role of the sleep laboratory in diagnosis and treatment of impotence. In R. L. Williams & I. Karacan (Eds.), *Sleep disorders: Diagnosis and treatment*. New York: Wiley, 1978.

Karlin, L. Cognition, preparation, and sensory-evoked potentials. *Psychological Bulletin*, 1970, **73**, 122–136.

Karrer, R. Autonomic nervous functions and behavior: A review of experimental studies with mental defectives. In N. R. Ellis (Ed.), *International Review of Research in Mental Retardation*, Vol. 2. New York: Academic Press, 1966.

Katkin, E. S., & Deitz, S. R. Systematic desensitization. In W. F. Prokasy & D. Raskin (Eds.), *Electrodermal activity and psychological research*. New York: Academic Press, 1973.

Kelly, D. H. W., & Walter, C. J. S. The relationship between clinical diagnosis and anxiety, assessed by forearm blood flow and other measurements. *British Journal of Psychiatry*, 1968, **114**, 611–626.

Ketterer, M. W., & Smith, B. D. Bilateral electrodermal activity, lateralized cerebral processing and sex. *Psychophysiology*, 1977, **14**, 513–516.

Kiritz, S., & Moos, R. H. Physiological effects of social environments. *Psychosomatic Medicine*, 1974, **36**, 96–114.

Knott, V. J., & Venables, P. H. EEG alpha correlates of non-smokers, smokers, and smoking deprivation. *Psychophysiology*, 1977, **14**, 150–156.

Krupski, A. Heart rate changes during a fixed reaction time task in normal and retarded adult males. *Psychophysiology*, 1975, **12**, 262–267.

Lacey, J. I. The evaluation of autonomic responses: Towards a general solution. *Annals of the New York Academy of Science*, 1956, **67**, 123–163.

Lacey, J. I. Psychophysiological approaches to the evaluation of psychotherapeutic process and outcome. In E. A. Rubinstein & M. B. Parloff (Eds.), *Research in psychotherapy*. Washington, D.C.: American Psychological Association, 1959.

Lacey, J. I. Somatic response patterning and stress: Some revisions of activation theory. In M. H. Appley & R. Trumbull (Eds.), *Psychological stress*. New York: Appleton-Century-Crofts, 1967.

Lacey, J. I., & Lacey, B. C. Some autonomic-central nervous system interrelationships. In P. Black (Ed.), *Physiological correlates of emotion*. New York: Academic Press, 1970.

Lacroix, J. M., & Comper, P. Lateralization in the electrodermal system as a function of cognitive/hemispheric manipulations. *Psychophysiology*, 1979, **16**, 116–129.

Lader, M. The psychophysiology of anxious and depressed patients. In D. C. Fowles (Ed.), *Clinical applications of psychophysiology*. New York: Columbia University Press, 1975.

Lader, M. H., & Nobel, P. The affective disorders. In P. H. Venables & M. J. Christie (Eds.), *Research in psychophysiology*. New York: Wiley, 1975.

Lader, M. H., & Wing, L. *Physiological measures, sedative drugs, and morbid anxiety*. New York: Oxford University Press, 1966.

Lader, M. H., & Wing, L. Physiological measures in agitated and retarded depressed patients. *Journal of Psychiatric Research*, 1969, **7**, 89–100.

Lang, P. The application of psychophysiological methods to the study of psychotherapy and behavior modification. In A. E. Bergin & S. L. Garfield (Eds.), *Handbook of psychotherapy and behavior change: An experimental analysis*. New York: Wiley, 1971.

Lang, P. J. Physiological assessment of anxiety and fear. In J. D. Cone & R. P. Hawkins (Eds.), *Behavioral assessment: New directions in clinical psychology*. New York: Brunner/Mazel, 1977.

Lang, P. J., & Melamed, B. G. Case report: Avoidance conditioning therapy of an infant with chronic ruminative vomiting. *Journal of Abnormal Psychology*, 1969, **74**, 1–8.

Lang, P. J., Rice, D. G., & Sternbach, R. A. The psychophysiology of emotion. In N. S. Greenfield & R. A. Sternbach (Eds.), *Handbook of psychophysiology*. New York: Holt, Rinehart, & Winston, 1972.

Lindsley, D. B. Emotion. In S. S. Stevens (Ed.), *Handbook of experimental psychology*. New York: Wiley, 1951.

Lindsley, D. B. Psychological phenomena and the electroencephalogram. *EEG and Clinical Neurophysiology*, 1952, **4**, 443–456.

Lolas, R. Event-related slow brain potentials, cognitive processes, and alexithymia. *Psychotherapy and Psychosomatics*, 1978, **30**, 116–129.

Lubar, J. F., Shabsin, H. S., Natelson, S. E. Holder, G. S., Whitsett, S. F., Pamplin, W. E., & Krulikowski, D. I. EEG operant conditioning in intractable epileptics. *Archives of Neurology*, 1981, **38**, 700–704.

Luiselli, J. K., Marholin, D., Steinman, D. L., & Warren, M. Assessing the effects of relaxation training. *Behavior Therapy*, 1979, **10**, 663–668.

Lykken, D. T. Psychology and the lie detection industry. *American Psychologist*, 1974, **29**, 725–739.

Lynn, R. *Attention, arousal and the orientation reaction*. Oxford, England: Pergamon, 1966.

MacLean, P. D. Psychosomatic disease and the "visceral brain": Recent developments bearing on the Papez theory of emotion. *Psychosomatic Medicine*, 1949, **2**, 338–353.

Malmo, R. B. Activation: A neuropsychological dimension. *Psychological Review*, 1959, **66**, 367–386.

Malmo, R. B., Boag, T. J., & Smith, A. A. Physiological study of personal interaction. *Psychosomatic Medicine*, 1957, **19**, 105–119.

Malmo, R. B., & Shagass, C. Physiologic study of symptom neurosis in psychiatric patients under stress. *Psychosomatic Medicine*, 1949, **11**, 25–29.

Marsh, G. R., & Thompson, L. W. Psychophysiology of aging. In J. E. Birren & K. W. Schaie (Eds.), *Handbook of the psychology of aging*. New York: Van Nostrand Reinhold, 1977.

Martin, I. Psychophysiology and conditioning. In P. H. Venables & M. J. Christie (Eds.), *Research in psychophysiology*. New York: Wiley, 1975.

Martin, I., & Venables, P. H. *Techniques in psychophysiology*. New York: Wiley, 1980.

Masters, W. H., & Johnson, V. E. *Human sexual response*. Boston: Little, Brown, 1966.

Mathews, A. M. Psychophysiological approaches to the investigation of desensitization and related procedures. *Psychological Bulletin*, 1971, **76**, 73–91.

Matson, J. L., & Beck, S. Assessment of children in inpatient settings. In M. Hersen & A. S. Bellack (Eds.), *Behavioral assessment: A practical handbook*. (2nd ed.) New York: Pergamon, 1981.

Mavissakalian, M. R., & Barlow, D. H. Assessment of obsessive-compulsive disorders. In D. H. Barlow (Ed.), *Behavioral assessment of adult disorders*. New York: Guilford, 1981.

McCallum, W. C. The CNV and conditionability in psychopaths. *Electroencephalography and Clinical Neurophysiology*, 1973, **33**, 337–343.

McCallum, W. C., & Abraham, P. The contingent negative variation in psychosis. *Electroencephalography and Clinical Neurophysiology*, 1973, **33**, 329–335.

McCallum, W. C., & Walter, W. G. The effect of attention and distraction on the contingent negative variation in normal and neurotic subjects. *Electroencephalography and Clinical Neuropsychology*, 1968, **25**, 319–329.

McCann, B. S., & Papsdorf, J. D. Bilateral hand temperature, test anxiety and anagram solution stress. Paper presented at the meeting of the Biofeedback Society of America, San Diego, February 1979.

McFall, R. M., & Marston, A. R. An experimental investigation of behavior rehearsal in assertive training. *Journal of Abnormal Psychology*, 1970, **76**, 295–303.

McGuinness, D., & Pribram, K. The neuropsychology of attention: Emotional and motivational controls. In M. C. Wittrock (Ed.), *The brain and psychology*. New York: Academic Press, 1980.

Mefferd, R. B. Some experimental implications of change. In P. H. Venables & M. J. Christie (Eds.), *Research in psychophysiology*. New York: Wiley, 1975.

Melzack, R., & Wall, P. D. Psychophysiology of pain. In M. Weisenberg (Ed.), *Pain: Clinical and experimental perspectives*. St. Louis: W. V. Mosby, 1975.

Mendels, J., & Chernik, D. A. Psychophysiological studies of sleep in depressed patients: An overview. In D. C. Fowles (Ed.), *Clinical applications of psychophysiology*. New York: Columbia University Press, 1975.

Mesulam, M., & Perry, J. The diagnosis of love-sickness: Experimental psychophysiology without the polygraph. *Psychophysiology*, 1972, **9**, 546–551.

Mesulam, M. M. Dissociative states with abnormal temporal lobe EEG: Multiple personality and the illusion of possession. *Archives of Neurology*, 1981, **38**, 176–181.

Miller, P. M. Assessment of addictive behaviors. In A. R. Ciminero, K. S. Calhoun, & H. E. Adams (Eds.), *Handbook of behavioral assessment*. New York: Wiley, 1977.

Munsterberg, H. *On the witness stand*. New York: Doubleday, Page, 1908.

Myslobodsky, M. S., & Horesch, N. Bilateral electrodermal activity in depressive patients. *Biological Psychology*, 1978, **6**, 111–120.

Myslobodsky, M. S., & Rattok, J. Asymmetry of electrodermal activity in man. *Bulletin of the Psychonomic Society*, 1975, **6**, 501–502.

Myslobodsky, M. S., & Rattok, J. Bilateral electrodermal activity in waking man. *Acta Psychologica*, 1977, **41**, 273–282.

Naatanen, R. Selective attention and evoked potentials in humans—A critical review. *Biological Psychology*, 1975, **2**, 237–307.

Naitoh, P. Sleep deprivation in humans. In P. H. Venables & M. J. Christie (Eds.), *Research in psychophysiology*. New York: Wiley, 1975.

Naliboff, B. D., Rickles, W. H., Cohen, M. J., & Naimante, R. S. Interactions of marijuana and induced stress: Forearm blood flow, heart rate, and skin conductance. *Psychophysiology*, 1976, **13**, 517–522.

Nelson, R. O., & Hayes, S. C. The nature of behavioral assessment: A commentary. *Journal of Applied Behavior Analysis*, 1979, **12**, 491–500.

Nietzel, M. T., & Bernstein, D. A. Assessment of anxiety and fear. In M. Hersen & A. S. Bellack (Eds.), *Behavioral assessment: A practical handbook*. (2nd ed.) New York: Pergamon, 1981.

Nirenberg, T. D., Ersner-Hershfield, S., Sobell, L. C., & Sobell, M. B. Behavioral treatment of alcohol problems. In C. K. Prokop & L. A. Bradley (Eds.), *Medical psychology: Contributions to behavioral medicine*. New York: Academic Press, 1981.

Nouwen, A., & Solinger, J. W. The effectiveness of EMG biofeedback training in low back pain. *Biofeedback and Self-Regulation*, 1979, **4**, 103–111.

Orne, M. T., Thackray, R. I., & Poskewitz, D. A. On the detection of deception. In N. S. Greenfield & R. A. Sternbach (Eds.), *Handbook of psychophysiology*. New York: Holt, Rinehart, & Winston, 1972.

Pace, S. A., Molfese, D. L., Schmidt, A. L., Mikula, W., & Ciano, C. Relationships between behavioral and electrocortical responses of aphasic and non-aphasic brain-damaged adults to semantic materials. In H. Begleiter (Ed.), *Evoked brain potentials and behavior*. New York: Plenum, 1979.

Papez, J. W. A proposed mechanism of emotion. *Archives of Neurological Psychiatry*, 1937, **38**, 725–743.

Paty, J., Benezech, M., Eschapasse, P., & Noel, B. Neurophysiological study of 47,XYY and 47,XXY psychopaths: Contingent negative variation, evoked potentials and motor nerve conduction. *Neuropsychobiology*, 1978, **4**, 321–327.

Paul, G. L. *Insight vs. desensitization in psychotherapy: An experiment in anxiety reduction*. Stanford, Calif.: Stanford University Press, 1966.

Pavlov, I. P. *Conditional reflexes: An investigation of the cerebral cortex.* London: Oxford University Press, 1927.

Perris, C. EEG techniques in the measurement of the severity of depressive syndromes. *Neuropsychobiology,* 1975, **1,** 16–25.

Perry, N. W., & Childers, D. G. *The human visual evoked response: Methods and theory.* Springfield, Ill.: C. C. Thomas, 1969.

Podlesney, J. A., & Raskin, D. C. Physiological measures and the detection of deception. *Psychological Bulletin,* 1977, **84,** 782–799.

Pomerleau, O. F. Why people smoke: Current psychobiological models. In P. O. Davidson & S. M. Davidson (Eds.), *Behavioral medicine: Changing health lifestyles.* New York: Brunner/Mazel, 1980.

Porjesz, B., & Begleiter, H. Visual evoked potentials and brain dysfunction in chronic alcoholics. In H. Begleiter (Ed.), *Evoked brain potentials and behavior.* New York: Plenum, 1979.

Preston, M. S. The use of evoked response procedures in studies of reading disability. In H. Begleiter (Ed.), *Evoked brain potentials and behavior.* New York: Plenum, 1979.

Pribram, K. H. The new neurology and the biology of emotion: A structural approach. *American Psychologist,* 1967, **22,** 830–838.

Pribram, K. H. Emotions. In S. Filskov & T. Boll (Eds.), *Handbook of clinical neuropsychology.* New York: Wiley, 1981.

Pritchard, W. S. Psychophysiology of P300. *Psychological Bulletin,* 1981, **89,** 506–540.

Prokasy, W. F., & Raskin, D. C. (Eds.), *Electrodermal activity in psychological research.* New York: Academic Press, 1973.

Prystav, G. H. Autonomic responsivity to sensory stimulation in drug addicts. *Psychophysiology,* 1975, **12,** 170–178.

Rabavilas, A. D., & Boulougouris, J. C. Physiological accompaniments of ruminations, flooding and thought-stopping in obsessive patients. *Behavior Research and Therapy,* 1974, **12,** 239–243.

Raczynski, J. M., & Craighead, W. E. A review of the autonomic activity of depressed persons. Unpublished manuscript, 1980.

Raskin, D. C., Barland, G. H., & Podlesney, J. A. Validity and reliability of detection of deception. *Polygraph,* 1977, **6,** 1–39.

Ray, W. J., & Racynski, J. M. Psychophysiological assessment. In M. Hersen & A. S. Bellack (Eds.), *Behavioral assessment: A practical handbook.* (2nd ed.) New York: Pergamon, 1981.

Ray, W. J., Racznski, J. M., Rogers, T., Kimball, W. H. *Evaluation of clinical biofeedback.* New York: Plenum, 1979.

Ritter, W. Cognition and the brain. In H. Begleiter (Ed.), *Evoked brain potentials and behavior.* New York: Plenum, 1979.

Roessler, R. Personality, psychophysiology, and performance. *Psychophysiology,* 1973, **10,** 315–325.

Roth, W. T. Late event-related potentials and psychopathology. *Schizophrenia Bulletin,* 1977, **3,** 105–120.

Roth, W. T., & Cannon, E. H. Some features of the auditory evoked response in schizophrenics. *Archives of General Psychiatry,* 1972, **27,** 466–471.

Rugh, J. D., & Schwitzgebel, R. L. Instrumentation for behavioral assessment. In A. R. Ciminero, K. S. Calhoun, & H. E. Adams (Eds.), *Handbook of behavioral assessment.,* New York: Wiley, 1977.

Rusinov, V. S. (Ed.), *Electrophysiology of the central nervous system.* New York: Plenum, 1970.

Satterfield, J. H., Cantwell, D. P., & Satterfield, B. T. Psychophysiology of the hyperactive child syndrome. *Archives of Child Psychiatry,* 1974, **31,** 839–844.

Schacter, D. L. The hypnagogic state: A critical review of the literature. *Psychological Bulletin,* 1976, **83,** 452–481.

Schacter, S. *Emotion, obesity, and crime.* New York: Academic Press, 1971.

Schacter, S., & Latane, B. Crime, cognition and the autonomic nervous system. In M. R. Jones (Ed.), *Nebraska symposium on motivation.* Lincoln: University of Nebraska Press, 1964.

Schacter, S., & Singer, J. E. Cognitive, social, and physiological determinants of emotional state. *Psychological Review,* 1962, **69,** 379–399.

Schneider, R. A. A fully automatic portable blood pressure recorder. *Journal of Applied Physiology,* 1968, **24,** 115–118.

Schwartz, G. E. Psychobiological foundations of psychotherapy and behavior change. In S. L. Garfield & A. E. Bergin (Eds.), *Handbook of psychotherapy and behavior change: An empirical analysis.* (2nd ed.) New York: Wiley, 1978.

Schwartz, G. E., Ahern, G. L., & Brown, S. L. Lateralized facial muscle response to postive and negative emotional stimuli. *Psychophysiology,* 1979, **16,** 561–571.

Schwartz, G. E., Brown, S. L., & Ahern, G. L. Facial muscle patterning and subjective experience during affective imagery: Sex differences. *Psychophysiology,* 1980, **17,** 75–82.

Shagass, C. Averaged somatosensory evoked responses in various psychiatric disorders. In J. Wortis (Ed.), *Recent advances in biological psychiatry,* Vol. 10. New York: Plenum, 1968.

Shagass, C. Electrical activity of the brain. In N. S. Greenfield & R. A. Sternbach (Eds.), *Handbook of psychophysiology.* New York: Holt, Rinehart, & Winston, 1972.

Shagass, C. Early evoked potentials. *Schizophrenia Bulletin,* 1977, **3,** 89–92. (a)

Shagass, C. Twisted thoughts, twisted brain waves? In C. Shagass, S. Bershon, & A. J. Friedhoff (Eds.), *Psychopathology and brain dysfunction.* New York: Raven Press, 1977. (b)

Shagass, C. Sensory evoked potentials in psychosis. In H. Begleiter (Ed.), *Evoked brain potentials and behavior.* New York: Plenum, 1979.

Shagass, C., & Canter, A. Cerebral evoked responses and personality. In V. D. Nebylitsyn & J. A. Gray (Eds.), *Biological bases of individual behavior.* New York: Academic Press, 1972.

Shagass, C., Gershon, S., & Friedhoff, A. J. (Eds.), *Psychopathology and brain dysfunction.* New York: Raven Press, 1977.

Shagass, C., & Malmo, R. B. Psychodynamic themes and localized tension during psychotherapy. *Psychosomatic Medicine,* 1954, **16,** 295–314.

Shagass, C., Overton, D. A., & Straumanis, J. J. Evoked

potential studies in schizophrenia. In H. Mitsuda & T. Fukuda (Eds.), *Biological mechanisms of schizophrenia and schizophrenia-like psychoses.* Tokyo: Igaku-Shoin Company, 1974.

Shagass, C., Roemer, R. A., Straumanis, J. J., & Amadeo, M. Evoked potential correlates of psychosis. Presented at annual meeting of Society of Biological Psychiatry, Toronto, Canada, 1977.

Shagass, C., & Schwartz, M. Psychiatric disorder and deviant cerebral responsiveness to sensory stimulation. In J. Wortis (Ed.), *Recent advances in biological psychiatry,* Vol. 5. New York: Plenum, 1963.

Shagass, C., & Schwartz, M. Sematosensory cerebral evoked responses in psychotic depression. *British Journal of Psychiatry,* 1966, **112**, 799–807.

Shalling, D., Lindberg, L., Levander, S., Dahlin, Y. Spontaneous activity as related to psychopathy. *Biological Psychology,* 1973, **1**, 83–98.

Shapiro, D., & Schwartz, G. E. Psychophysiological contributions to social psychology. *Annual Review of Psychology,* 1970, **21**, 87–112.

Snyder, F., & Scott, J. The psychophysiology of sleep. In N. S. Greenfield & R. A. Sternbach (Eds.), *Handbook of psychophysiology.* New York: Holt, Rinehart, & Winston, 1972.

Sokolov, E. N. *Perception and the conditioned reflex.* New York: MacMillan, 1963.

Sokolov, E. N. The orienting reflex, its structure and mechanisms. In L. G. Veronin, A. N. Leontrev, A. R. Luria, E. N. Sokolov, & O. S. Vinogradova (Eds.), *Orienting reflex and exploratory behaviour.* Washington, D.C.: American Institute of Biological Sciences, 1965.

Spohn, H. E., & Patterson, T. Recent studies of psychophysiology in schizophrenia. *Schizophrenia Bulletin,* 1979, **5**, 581–611.

Steptoe, A., Smulyan, H., & Gribbin, B. Pulse wave velocity and blood pressure change: Calibration and applications. *Psychophysiology,* 1976, **17**, 488–493.

Stern, J. A., & Janes, C. L. Personality and psychopathology. In W. F. Prokasy & D. C. Raskin (Eds.), *Electrodermal activity in psychological research.* New York: Academic Press, 1973.

Stern, R. M., Farr, J. H., & Ray, W. J. Pleasure. In P. H. Venables & M. J. Christie (Eds.), *Research in psychophysiology.* New York: Wiley, 1975.

Stern, R. M., Ray, W. J., & Davis, C. M. *Psychophysiological recording.* New York: Oxford University Press, 1980.

Sternbach, R. A. *Principles of psychophysiology.* New York: Academic Press, 1966.

Sternbach, R. A. *Pain patients: Traits and treatment.* New York: Academic Press, 1974.

Sternbach, R. A., Alexander, A. A., & Greenfield, N. S. Autonomic and somatic reactivity in relation to psychopathology. In J. Zubin & C. Shagass (Eds.), *Neurobiological aspects of psychopathology.* New York: Grune & Stratton, 1969.

Stroebel, C. F. Psychophysiological pharmacology. In N. S. Greenfield & R. A. Sternbach (Eds.), *Handbook of psychophysiology.* New York: Holt, Rinehart, & Winston, 1972.

Stromer, J. M. Some comments on "Biofeedback in the treatment of psychophysiologic disorders: Stutter-

ing." *Biofeedback and Self-Regulation,* 1979, **4**, 383–385.

Taggart, P., Gibbons, D., & Somerville, W. Some effects of motor-car driving on the normal and abnormal heart. *British Medical Journal,* 1969, **4**, 130–134.

Tecce, J. J. Contingent negative variation and individual differences. *Archives of General Psychiatry,* 1971, **24**, 1–16.

Tecce, J. J. Contingent negative variation (CNV) and psychological processes in man. *Psychological Bulletin,* 1972, **77**, 73–108.

Tollison, C. D., & Adams, H. E. *Sexual disorders: Treatment, theory, research.* New York: Academic Press, 1979.

Tucker, D. M. Lateral brain function, emotion, and conceptualization. *Psychological Bulletin,* 1981, **89**, 19–46.

Tucker, D. M., Stenslie, C. E., Roth, R. S., & Shearer, S. L. Right frontal lobe activation and right hemisphere performance: Decrement during a depressed mood. *Archives of General Psychiatry,* 1981, **38**, 169–174.

Tursky, B. Physical, physiological, and psychological factors that affect pain reaction to electrical shock. *Psychophysiology,* 1974, **11**, 95–112.

Venables, P. H. Psychophysiological studies of schizophrenic pathology. In P. H. Venables & M. J. Christie (Eds.), *Research in psychophysiology.* New York: Wiley, 1975.

Venables, P. H. The electrodermal psychophysiology of schizophrenics and children at risk for schizophrenia: Controversies and developments. *Schizophrenia Bulletin,* 1977, **3**, 28–48.

Venables, P. Psychophysiology and psychometrics. *Psychophysiology,* 1978, **15**, 302–315.

Venables, P. H., & Christie, M. H. Mechanisms, instrumentation, recording techniques and quantification of responses. In W. F. Prokasy & D. C. Raskin (Eds.), *Electrodermal activity in psychological research.* New York: Academic Press, 1973.

Venables, P. H., & Christie, M. J. (Eds.), *Research in psychophysiology.* New York: Wiley, 1975.

Venables, P. H., & Martin, I. A *manual of psychophysiological methods.* Amsterdam: North-Hollands Press, 1967.

Wells, K. C. Assessment of children in outpatient settings. In M. Hersen & A. S. Bellack (Eds.), *Behavioral assessment: A practical handbook.* (2nd ed.). New York: Pergamon, 1981.

Wenger, M. A. Studies of autonomic balance: A summary. *Psychophysiology,* 1966, **2**, 173–186.

Wenger, M. A. Autonomic balance. In N. S. Garfield & R. A. Sternbach (Eds.), *Handbook of psychophysiology.* New York: Holt, Rinehart, & Winston, 1972.

Whatmore, G. B., & Ellis, R. M. Some neurophysiologic aspects of depressed states: An electromyographic study. *Archives of General Psychiatry,* 1959, **1**, 70–80.

Whatmore, G. B., & Ellis, R. M. Further neurophysiologic aspects of depressed states: An electromyographic study. *Archives of General Psychiatry,* 1962, **6**, 243–253.

Whybrow, P. C., & Mendels, J. Toward a biology of depression: Some suggestions from neurophysiology.

American Journal of Psychiatry, 1969, **125,** 1,491–1,500.

Wilder, J. *Stimulus and response: The law of initial value.* Bristol: Wright, 1967.

Wincze, J. P., & Lange, J. D. Assessment of sexual behavior. In D. H. Barlow (Ed.), *Behavioral assessment of adult disorders.* New York: Guilford, 1981.

Woodruff, D. A. Brain electrical activity and behavior relationships over the life span. In P. Baltes (Ed.), *Life span development and behavior,* Vol. 1. New York: Academic Press, 1978.

Wooley, S. C., Wooley, O. W., & Dyrenforth, S. R. Theoretical, practical, and social issues in behavioral treatments of obesity. *Journal of Applied Behavior Analysis,* 1979, **12,** 3–25.

Zahn, T. P. Autonomic nervous system characteristics possibly related to a genetic predisposition to schizophrenia. *Schizophrenia Bulletin,* 1977, **3,** 49–60.

Ziskind, E., Syndulko, K., & Maltzman, I. Aversive conditioning in the sociopath. *Pavlovian Journal of Biological Science,* 1978, **13,** 199–205.

Zubin, J. & Shagass, C. (Eds.), *Neurobiological aspects of psychopathology.* New York: Grune & Stratton, 1969.

Zuckerman, M. Physiological measures of sexual arousal in the human. *Psychological Bulletin,* 1971, **75,** 297–329.

Zuckerman, M. Physiological measures of sexual arousal in the human. In N. S. Greenfield & T. A. Sternbach (Eds.), *Handbook of psychophysiology.* New York: Holt, Rinehart, & Winston, 1972.

Zuckerman, M., Buchsbaum, M. S., & Murphy, D. L. Sensation seeking and its biological correlates. *Psychological Bulletin,* 1980, **88,** 187–214.

Zuckerman, M., Persky, H., & Curtis, G. Relationship among anxiety, depression, hostility, and autonomic variables. *Journal of Nervous and Mental Disease,* 1968, **146,** 481–487.

23 MEDICAL ASSESSMENT

Rohan Ganguli

The need for a medical assessment of persons asking for psychological services or presenting with psychiatric symptoms is not universally accepted (Hollender & Wells, 1980). This may have to do with the sentiment of some mental-health professionals that the "medical model" is not valid and has shortcomings (Siegler & Osmond, 1974). Some have even argued that the therapeutic relationship is altered when the medical aspects of psychological problems are investigated (McIntyre & Romano, 1977). It would appear from this that the widespread recognition that psychological factors can cause or exacerbate physical disorders is not matched by an adequate awareness among mental-health practitioners of the variety of mental symptoms that can be caused by "medical" illnesses.

Because of this situation, serious disorders can go undetected and inappropriate treatment can be administered, sometimes with fatal consequences (Leeman, 1975). The most dramatic examples are provided by the frequent reports of patients with cancer of various organs who initially present with only mental symptoms and who have sometimes received extensive psychiatric and psychological treatment before a correct diagnosis is made (Peterson, Popkin, & Hall, 1981). Less striking, but no less dangerous, are a host of conditions

ranging from such common ones as diabetes mellitus (Sachar et al., 1980) to rare diseases such as myasthenia gravis (Tollefson, 1981) whose primary manifestation may be psychological symptoms. The fact is that those symptoms, such as anxiety, depression, hallucinations, or personality change, that are most common in psychiatric populations are also very common in the physically ill (Koranyi, 1980). Therefore, it should not be surprising that at times the person suffering from a physical illness reports only psychological discomfort. Hence, a medical evaluation is necessary to reduce the chances that appropriate medical treatment will be delayed.

In this chapter, the need for a medical assessment of a proportion of persons who appear to be suffering from psychological distress is explored in the context of the symptoms they may present with and the diseases that may be causing those symptoms. The optimal setting and method of accomplishing the assessment also is discussed.

Historical Background

Since physicians have been involved in the care of the mentally ill for hundreds of years, the relationship between physiological dysfunction and mental symptoms had been noticed long before the formal concepts of psychosomatics (now "behavioral" medicine) were enunciated (Koranyi, 1980). Malzberg (1934) had alluded to the likelihood of serious physical illnesses in the mentally ill when he drew attention to the high mortality rate of psychiatric patients. The earliest systematic studies of the extent of physical disorders in psychiatric patients appear to be those of Comroe (1936) and Phillips (1937). Comroe (1936) followed up 100 outpatients diagnosed as "neurotic" and noted that 24 percent of them were subsequently found to have a significant organic disease. In the study of Phillips (1937), 164 consecutive admissions to a psychiatric hospital were examined for evidence of physical disorders. Forty-five percent of the patients were found to have serious medical illnesses. Phillips also went on to suggest that there was evidence that in 24 percent of the physically ill, the physical disorder had caused or contributed to the psychiatric symptomatology. Numerous subsequent studies yielded similar results. One of these studies was the now famous follow-up of "hysterics" by Slater and Glithero (1965). They traced a sample of 99 patients 8 to 11 years after they had been diagnosed as "hysterical" at the National Hospital in London (one of the best neurological institutes in Great Britain); 12 persons had died, 4 by suicide. Of the nonsuicidal deaths, however, five were caused by diseases that were almost certainly present at the time of the original contact and were probably responsible for the symptoms observed. Of the remainder of the sample, 56 percent had medical illnesses and, in 30 percent, these illnesses were felt to be the "cause" of their psychiatric symptoms. In the same year as Slater and Glithero's study, Davies (1965) published the results of a study of 72 outpatients who were seen by a psychiatrists and then referred to a general practitioner for a medical assessment. According to this study, 51 percent had medical illnesses; in 36 percent, these illnesses were felt to be responsible for the psychiatric symptoms.

Any impression that the results of these earlier studies are not representative of the current situation is dispelled by similar results obtained by Koranyi (1979) and Hall (1980a). Koranyi (1979) had an enormous sample of 2,090 psychiatric clinic patients; he reported that 43 percent of them had physical illnesses, almost a third of which had been missed by *physicians* who saw them. He also felt that in 18 percent of those with physical illnesses, the psychiatric symptoms were caused by the medical disorder. Hall (1980a) reported that of a 100 inpatients studied by him, 80 percent had physical illnesses and in 46 percent of them the medical disorder had caused or contributed to psychiatric symptoms. It should be noted that he reported the discovery of illnesses requiring treatment but unrelated to the psychiatric symptoms in 34 percent of his sample. This is important because the fortuitous discovery of conditions requiring treatment is a tangible benefit of routine medical assessments and one that makes it much more cost-effective.

Apart from these systematic studies, journals such as *Psychosomatics* carry several reports in each issue of persons who present with psychological symptoms that are later found to have been caused by some physical disorder.

It is particularly sobering to note that in a majority of reports the patients have been seen by physicians and the medical diagnoses missed. The mechanisms by which mental symptoms are produced is almost purely a matter of speculation at this point, since we know so little about the physiological processes underlying cognitive and emotional processes — normal or abnormal. However, certain diseases do seem to produce characteristic mental symptoms, and a discussion of the commoner symptoms follows.

Anxiety

Anxiety is one of the commonest psychological discomforts experienced by man and it is therefore not surprising that it is the most frequent way in which a physical disorder may present itself for psychological treatment. Conversely, up to 50 percent of "medical" patients report clinically significant anxiety (Hall, 1980b). In a book on the psychiatric manifestations of medical disease, Hall (1980b) divides conditions by etiology into three classes: (1) those that interfere with stimulus discrimination; (2) those that produce sympathetic nervous system disruption; and (3) those that produce direct end organ change. This formulation is of more theoretical than practical interest. For example, while degenerative brain disease presumably acts via the first mechanism, endocrinal and metabolic disorders could be included in all three. On the other hand, Hall does provide some guidelines for suspecting an organic etiology. Patients often complain of tension, nervousness, and fatigue, rather than of anxiety (Allan, 1944; Bartley, 1957). "Pathological fatigue" (unrelieved by sleep), in particular, might be associated with a range of medical disorders, including neurological problems, chronic infections, metabolic disorders, and heart disease (Allan, 1944). Other symptoms that should arouse suspicion are: sleep disorder, weakness, inattention, memory loss, change in speech, auditory hallucinations, chest pain, intermittently rapid pulse, bed wetting, and confusion (Hall, 1980b).

Table 23.1 lists the more common "medical" causes of anxiety along with procedures that may help in their investigation. Some of the more significant ones will be discussed further. Anxiety often accompanies the onset and occurrence of all physical illnesses. Hence, the following discussion is limited to cases in which symptoms of anxiety might themselves be the recurrent manifestation of the illness.

The association between cardiovascular abnormalities and symptoms of anxiety has been known for a very long time (Da Costa, 1971). Psychiatrists and psychologists have often regarded the cardiovascular responses as secondary to the emotions and "functional." The situation is, however, much more complex than this, and both hyperdynamic states of the cardiovascular system as well as abnormalities of cardiac rhythm might actually be "primary" (Frohlich, Tarazi, & Dunstan, 1969; Lynch, Paskewitz, & Gimbel, 1977). The history is helpful, and one can often detect complaints of "cardiac awareness" (Frohlich et al., 1969), such as palpitations, chest discomfort, and rapid pulse. Holter monitoring, which is relatively simple, can help; it involves having the patient wear a portable, self-contained electrocardiographic monitor for 24 hours. Hemodynamic studies and the response to drugs that block or stimulate the sympathetic system are more elaborate steps taken when the situation remains unclear. It is certainly not being argued here that in every case of anxiety and circulatory abnormality, the latter condition is the cause of the former. In many cases, the question of the direction of causality cannot be rationally determined. It is often true, however, that correction of the hemodynamic abnormality, if marked, can relieve all distressing symptoms (Frohlich et al., 1969).

A recently described condition of the cardiac valves, mitral valve prolapse (O'Rourke & Crawford, 1976), is reported to be found frequently in association with symptoms of chronic and acute anxiety (Dietch, 1981). The physical examination reveals a characteristic abnormal heart sound or "click." Echocardiography, a noninvasive and simple procedure, will confirm the diagnosis. It should be pointed out, however, that this condition exists in large numbers of asymptomatic people as well. Numerous other disorders of cardiac rhythm, conduction, and the like can present for psychological treatment, as pointed out by Ferrer (1968); as he also pointed out, the only way to make an early diagnosis is to have the patient see someone who is likely to be aware of and to suspect these disorders.

Coronary insufficiency and atypical angina (when chest pain is not the prominent symptom) may present in a way that is mistaken for anxiety. Therefore, any history of chest discomfort must be carefully explored and investigated, especially in those at high risk for coronary artery disease, such as older individuals, those who are obese, heavy smokers, people with a family history of heart disease, and perhaps those with a "Type A" personality (Rosenman et al., 1975). Unfortunately, it is not easy to rule out serious coronary artery disease. Negative results from EKGs, enzymes, and stress tests do not rule out serious pathology but are most meaningful if obtained during an acute attack of the symptoms (Hillis & Brunwald, 1977). Angiography and cardiac scanning are more definitive but also are more invasive and risky. The decision of when to stop a negative work-up is a clinical one and ought to be left to the internist or cardiologist.

Cerebrovascular insufficiency or interference with the blood flow to the brain is often a cause of symptoms that might be passed off as anxiety (Hall, 1980b). The history and evaluation of the mental state should give the alert examiner several clues that raise the suspicion of an organic disorder. The occurrence of the symptoms, in persons without abnormal personalities, or an onset before the age of 18 or after 35, are cause for further investigation (Hall, 1980b). Problems with memory, orientation, and attention are also reasons for looking more closely. Screening tests such as the Mini-Mental State and Examination (Folstein, Folstein, & McHugh, 1975) and the "set test" (Isaacs & Kennie, 1973) are simple to administer and reliable enough for clinical use. As is usual for screening tests, they have a high *sensitivity* and an appreciable rate of *false positives*. Hence, negative tests are more definitive than positive ones. Neurological and neuropsychological referral should be the next step in working up a possible case of organic impairment.

TABLE 23.1. DISORDERS THAT MAY BE PRESENT WITH ANXIETY AND
PROCEDURES TO HELP RULE THEM OUT.

DISORDERS	HELPFUL PROCEDURES
Cardiovascular	
Coronary insufficiency	history, EKG, stress testing, angiography, cardiac enzymes scanning
Paroxysmal Tachyarrhythmia	EKG, Holter monitoring
Mitral Valve Prolapse	Physical exam, echocardiography
Hyperkinetic Heart Syndrome	history, exam, hemodynamics, response to isoproterenol and propranolol
Anaemia	exam, blood count and smear
Cerebrovascular insufficiency	history, exam, angiography, flow studies
Endocrine	
Thyroid dysfunction	history, exam, T_3, T_4, TSH, BMR
Pituitary dysfunction	history, exam, T_4, TSH, FSH, TRH stimulation, urinary steroids, insulin tolerance, skull and bone x-rays, etc.
Parathyroid dysfunction	history, exam during episodes, serum and urine calcium and phosphorus, x-rays, alkaline phosphatase, etc.
Pheochromocytoma	VMA and metanephrine excretion, serum and urine catechol amines
Adrenal Cortical dysfunction	exam, blood sugar, potassium, sodium cortisol. Dexamethazone suppression, urinary steroids, etc.
Hypoglycaemia	blood sugar, glucose and insulin tolerance
Carcinoid Syndrome	history, urine 5HIAA
Neurological	
Epilepsy (Complex partial seizures)	history, EEG with sleep, sleep deprivation and other activation
Dementing Conditions	exam, neuropsychological testing
Post-Head Injury	history
Meniere's Disease	history, exam
Post-Encephalitis	history, viral titers of spinal fluid
Miscellaneous Conditions	
Drug Induced Psychosyndromes	history, exam , serum and urine drug screens
Collagen Diseases	exam, antinuclear antibodies, other autoantibodies, serum complement
Chronic Infections	blood counts, ESR, blood, marrow, and other tissue cultures
Malignancies	exam, x-rays, scans, blood tests

Endocrine disorders are another group of illnesses in which anxiety is the predominant symptom. Both hyper- and hypothyroidism can cause anxiety, but the former does this more frequently (MacGrimmon et al., 1979). Typical symptoms of hyperthyroidism are nervousness or restlessness, palpitations, and intolerance of heat. The signs include protrusion of eyeballs, increased pulse rate (especially significant if recorded during sleep), warm dry palms, enlargement of the thyroid gland in the neck, and various abnormalities of eye movements. Hypothyroidism is accompanied by slow pulse, dry coarse skin, changes in voice, intolerance of cold, mental sluggishness, and menstrual irregularity (usually increased frequency of periods). Several tests of thyroid hormone production and stimulation are available as indicated in Table 23.1, but their interpretation requires a full understanding of endocrine physiology.

The recognition of thyroid disorders is important not only from the point of view of correcting the abnormality of hormone production, but it has implications for any planned psychiatric treatment. Patients with these conditions react unusually to many psychotropic medications. For example, hyperthyroid patients may become calmer with phenothiazines, but they increase their heart rate. They also are more susceptible to the toxic effects of antidepressants (Shader, Belfer, & DiMascio, 1970). Hypothyroid patients also may react idiosyncratically to phenothiazines and could go into a hypothermic coma (Jones & Meade, 1964).

Several other endocrine abnormalities can result in symptoms of anxiety, including parathyroid dysfunction (Denko & Kaebling, 1962), adrenal medullary hypersecretion (Pheochromocytoma) (Engelman, 1977), adrenal cortical dysfunction, hypoglycaemia, carcinoid tumors, and others. In recent years, tests have become available for the detection of most of these abnormalities. However, not only are there several endocrine disorders that produce psychiatric symptoms, but more than one may occur at the same time, as in multiple endocrine andenopathies. Alternatively, several endocrine disturbances (thyroid, insulin, estrogens, etc.,) may be a reflection of basic pituitary or hypothalamic disorder. The latter comes about because the pituitary and the hypothalamus are sites from which the regulation and production of many of the body's endocrine systems are conducted. Suffice it to say that the precise definition of the nature of an endocrine disturbance and its etiology is a job for an endocrinologist.

Several neurological disorders, other than cerebrovascular disease, which has already been mentioned, can also cause anxiety as shown in Table 23.1. One deserves special mention: complex partial epilepsy. This is a condition (usually involving the temporal lobe) in which epileptic manifestations occur without loss of consciousness. The experience of fear may be the most common symptom (Williams, 1956). Consequently, the true diagnosis may not be suspected immediately. The EEG, especially with the use of sleep deprivation, all-night recordings, and Metrazol, is the only generally available diagnostic tool. It should be added here that the discovery of abnormalities in the EEG, especially of the nonepileptic variety, should not be regarded as conclusive. This is said because, when epilepsy is suspected in a psychiatric patient, it is often overdiagnosed on the basis of poor evidence.

In the category of miscellaneous conditions listed in Table 23.1, symptoms produced by the ingestion of drugs and other substances (including caffeine, nicotine, alcohol, and over-the-counter diet and "sleeping pills") are particularly frequent causes of anxiety. Consequently, the history of the ingestion of these substances must be very carefully examined with every person who has symptoms of anxiety.

Mood Disorders

This category of disorders includes those conditions that present predominantly with symptoms of euphoria or depression similar to those often seen in the affective disorders. Once again, as in the syndromes associated with anxiety, one has to separate the sadness and despondency with which someone may react to the knowledge that he or she has a serious physical condition from the disability he or she may experience as a result of the alteration of mood caused by a physical disorder. Obviously it is the latter group that we are concerned with in this chapter.

Table 23.2 lists some of the physical disorders that are often manifested by changes in mood. Grouped once again in broad categories and, not surprisingly perhaps, they include many of the same conditions that were listed previously as being associated with symptoms of anxiety. Particular mention will therefore only be made of a few selected conditions.

Among the endocrine disorders, those of the

TABLE 23.2. CONDITIONS OFTEN ASSOCIATED
WITH MOOD DISORDERS

Endocrine

Thyroid dysfunction
Diabetes mellitus
Adrenal cortical disorders
Post-partum and menopause

Neurological

Brain tumors
(? especially of the non-dominant hemisphere)
Post head injury
Degenerative cerebral disorders
(Alzheimer's disease, Huntington's chorea, etc.)
Cerebrovascular accidents
Epilepsy
Infections
(syphilis, mononucleosis, encephalitis, etc.)

Malignancies

Cancer of the pancreas
Some lung cancers
Some leukemias
Some bowel cancers

Nutritional disorders
(vitamin deficiencies, protein-calorie malnutrition, etc.)

Drug induced psychosyndromes

Antihypertensives
(especially reserpine, methlydopa and propranolol)
Sedatives and anxiolytics
(eg. benodiazepines and barbiturates)
Steroids
Phenothiazines and other neuroleptics
(especially depot fluphenazine)
Oral contraceptives
L-Dopa
Appetite suppressants

Miscellaneous conditions

Liver failure
Renal failure
Electrolyte imbalance

adrenal cortex are probably most commonly present with a mood disturbance (Carroll, 1977; Sachar, 1975). Whether there is an excess or a deficiency of the hormones (principally cortisol) does not seem to determine what symptoms are present; depression is the most common mode of psychiatric presentation. Other evidence of the basic disorder may be lacking, making it very difficult to detect cases without a high index of suspicion. In fact, many investigators are coming to believe that an abnormality of the pituitary-adrenal axis may be present in a large proportion of so-called functional depressions, and this is the basis of the Dexamethasone Suppression Test (Carroll, Greden, & Feinberg, 1980). It should also be remembered that steriods (similar in action to those produced by the adrenals) are given to people for a wide range of conditions. They frequently produce changes in mood, usually within a few days of administration (Hall et al., 1978). In this instance, however, the most common symptom is that of euphoria (Prange et al., 1975). Other endocrine disorders, particularly those involving the thyroid gland, also may cause serious mood disturbance.

Among the neurological disorders, tumors of the brain are both fairly comon (Posner & Shapiro, 1978) and liable to cause psychiatric symptoms in 50 to 60 percent of cases (Guvener et al., 1964). They also account for about 365,000 deaths in the United States every year (Posner & Shapiro, 1978). Unfortunately, the clinical presentation of patients with brain tumors can be extremely varied. One simple classification of these modes of presentation is given by Adams, Hochberg, and Webster (1980):

1. those who present with mental symptoms or seizures only;
2. those who have unmistakable evidence of headaches and raised intracranial pressures;
3. specific intracranial tumor syndromes (i.e., being highly characteristic of a particular brain location and even histologic tumor type).

This chapter is concerned primarily with the first type of presentation, though the second kind might also not be recognized for what it is by the nonmedically trained therapist. Besides the symptoms of depression, most cases in which depression is caused by a tumor will show some cognitive impairment, difficulty with memory, and blunting of affect. Of course, these symptoms are occasionally seen in patients who are suffering from de-

pression and clear up along with the mood disorder. Consequently, referral for medical assessment of all cases seems prudent before starting treatment.

Many malignancies not located in the brain can also produce symptoms of depression. The most notorious of these is carcinoma of the pancreas. Over 20,000 deaths per year are attributed to this condition (Greenberger, Toskes, & Isselbacher, 1980), and unfortunately its incidence has been rising—a 300 percent increase since 1930. Clinical experience has shown that depression with feelings of hopelessness and doom might be the first or only symptom of this malignancy; and this has been borne out by many studies (e.g., Fras, Litin, & Bartholamew, 1968). The early detection of this tumor is of the utmost importance because it rapidly progresses to an inoperable stage. And at surgery, only 15 to 20 percent are operable. Even after surgery, only 10 percent of patients survive one year beyond the diagnosis (Greenberger et al., 1980). It has been suggested that any person in his 50s presenting with depression but having no typical prior history and no psychomotor retardation should be investigated for carcinoma of the pancreas (Hall, 1980).

A variety of commonly prescribed drugs, such as many antihypertensives, sedatives and anxiolytics, and oral contraceptives, can all produce depression or elation. Hence, careful inquiry must be made of each person with these symptoms about what he or she *may be ingesting*. Table 23.2 lists some prime suspects, but consultation should be obtained about the effects on mood of any drug the patient may be taking.

Psychotic Disorders

The word "psychotic" is used here not to indicate a specific illness or group of illnesses but rather in the way designated by DSM III (APA, 1980) to indicate that delusions, hallucinations, and incoherence are a part of the clinical picture. This discussion will be kept short as there is more general agreement that persons suffering from psychotic symptoms, who haven't been previously referred to a physician, should be given a medical examination. Table 23.3 lists the commoner causes of psychotic symptoms. Once again, diseases of the nervous system, infections and tumors principally, rank high. Epilepsy should be strongly suspected when there is an episodic and stereotyped pattern of symptoms. Alterations in the level or state of consciousness are fairly pathognomonic. Many

TABLE 23.3. COMMONER CONDITIONS THAT
MAY BE PRESENT AS A PSYCHOTIC STATE.

Infections of the nervous system (e.g., encephalitis, neurosyphilis)
Tumors of the brain
Epilepsy
Endocrine disorders, especially those of the thyroid and the adrenal cortex
Poryphyria
Drugs — prescription and nonprescription

endocrine disturbances could be responsible, led again by disorders of the thyroid and the adrenal cortex. Though not very common, porphyria has been singled out for inclusion in Table 23.3 because it can be an episodic and confusing disease. Attacks are generally characterized by abdominal pain and neurological findings, but may also manifest only with psychotic, delirious, or affective symptoms (Granville-Grossman, 1971; Stein & Tschudy, 1970). Attacks may be precipitated by many drugs, including barbiturates, antiepileptics, oral contraceptives, and alcohol (Meyer & Schmid, 1978). Detection of certain compounds in the urine during attacks is diagnostic. The picture is confused, however, since the findings between episodes may be normal. Only physicians who have had some experience with the disorder are likely to suspect it.

The role of "street drugs" in producing psychotic symptoms is too well known for the point to be belabored here. It does need to be kept in mind, however, that many prescription drugs, especially if taken in larger than prescribed doses, can also produce mental symptoms. Cimetidine (Tagamet), a new and very widely prescribed drug for peptic ulcer, is a case in point (Billings, Tang, & Rakoff, 1981). It had been in use for several years before its ability to produce a confusional state was noticed.

Practical Considerations

Even in clinics attached to psychiatric hospitals, not everyone receives a complete medical assessment. For it to be otherwise would probably waste physician time and the now-dwindling resources available for mental-health care. So, given the variety of psychological presentations of medical illnesses, how should one decide who should be referred for assessment? Hollender and Wells (1980) suggest that for this purpose, patients' complaints be divided into three categories: those involving (1) the body, (2) the mind, and (3) social interactions. Headaches, weakness, and impotence might

be manifestations in the first category, and depression, obsessional symptoms, or hallucinations in the second. Persons with symptoms in these two categories should definitely receive a medical assessment, as their symptoms are the ones that might be the manifestations of physical illness. Persons in the last category, such as those who come for therapy because of persistent difficulty with family spouses or employers, have no compelling need for a medical assessment, since their presenting problems are unlikely to be etiologically related to a physical illness.

How should the evaluation of persons entering psychological treatment be accomplished? Obviously, in settings associated with medical facilities, such as general hospital psychiatric units, this is easily arranged. In other settings, such as when nonmedical therapists are in private practice, special arrangements must be made. Sometimes the therapists arrange group practices with psychiatrists who by virtue of their "M.D.s" fulfill the need for medical consultation. In general, I do not believe this practice is satisfactory. Psychiatrists, especially those who engage principally in outpatient practice, do not usually retain a sufficient degree of skill in physical diagnosis to detect the atypical and subtle forms that illnesses can assume when patients present with psychological symptoms (Hollender & Wells, 1980). The numerous studies mentioned earlier, demonstrating the incidence of undetected physical disease in psychiatric patients, probably is a reflection of this gradual loss (perhaps "atrophy" would be a better word) of skill. There are many reasons for this, including the limited opportunity to see a representative range of pathology and the lack of vigilance that seems to develop from constantly doing "normal physicals." To these reasons must be added the reluctance of many psychiatrists to conduct physical examinations at all (McIntyre & Romano, 1977). The exceptions to these generalizations are those psychiatrists who work on inpatient units in general hospitals and those in consultation-liaison work. In these settings there generally is a much greater contact with serious physical illnesses and hence a tendency to keep up the diagnostic skills learned in medical school.

Therapists ought to have a regular arrangement with a primary medical care clinic or an internist for the examination and evaluation of their clients *before* they start treatment. The advantages of a regular arrangement are that scheduling will be less of a problem, and the clinic or internist often develops a special sensitivity and interest in the type of client referred. The most important benefit of all may be the opportunity it provides for direct discussion with a physician of the results of his examination. Having said earlier that the nonhospital-based practitioners are unlikely to be able to diagnose physical disorders, I should emphasize that they ought to be able to interpret the results of an evaluation to the patient. This is of much practical significance. For example, I have found that it is fairly common for a patient who was told after a routine examination that he has, say, hypertension, to assume automatically that this has some etiologic connection with the symptoms for which he referred himself. If there is no likely connection, it should be possible to explain this to the patient.

What the assessment ought to consist of will now be briefly considered. A careful history and physical examination is still the best way of ruling out medical illnesses. Certainly no amount of "screening laboratory tests" could replace the ability of an alert and experienced clinician to detect subtle clues that distinguish the physical from the psychological origin of common symptoms. For example, the breathlessness that accompanies depression is distinctly different from the respiratory distress of airway disease (Burns, 1971). Laboratory tests can also be misleading when clinical judgment is suspended. The diagnosis of hypoglycaemia, which was once a fashionable explanation of a host of symptoms such as dizziness, exhaustion, and fatigue, is an example of this (Levine, 1974). Most of the time the data from some test have to be coupled with details of the history and from observation. The very difficult problem of distinguishing epilepsy from pseudoseizures is an example of this last point (Delgado-Escueta et al., 1981).

Despite what I have just said, certain laboratory tests are routinely ordered, and these include blood counts, automated serum biochemistry, thyroid function tests, and EEGs. These tests detect a number of diseases that are common in the population at large, and are probably of more use in detecting illnesses that may still be asymptomatic rather than illnesses that cause psychiatric symptoms. To confirm the occurrence of many of the conditions mentioned earlier in this chapter, specific, and often expensive, tests are needed; hence they should only be ordered when there are some clinical grounds for suspicion.

Conclusions

It has been demonstrated that clinical experience and a number of systematic studies show that many physical illnesses may have psychological symptoms — principally anxiety, depression or euphoria, and psychotic symptoms — as their first manifestations. These patients do present themselves for psychological or psychiatric services. In order to avoid dangerous mistakes and delay in applying the appropriate remedies, a medical assessment of all patients with mental symptoms is advisable. Since the illnesses that cause these symptoms are often atypical or rare diseases, the assessment requires an expert and experienced clinician. Once diagnosed, the treatment of the physical disorder generally leads to remission of the presenting symptoms (Hall, 1980a), but this is not always the case. In the later instance, the combination of medical and psychological measures may be necessary to resolve the problem. Unfortunately, the special characteristics of these patients have not been systematically studied, and this is a task for the future. At this point, their special needs will have to be dealt with as common sense dictates.

References

Adams, R. B., Hochberg, F., & Webster, H. F. Neoplastic disease of the brain. In K. J. Isselbacher, R. B. Adams, E. Braunwald, R. G. Petersdorf, & J. D. Wilson (Eds.), *Harrison's principles of internal medicine.* New York: McGraw-Hill, 1980.

Allan, F. N. Differential diagnosis of weakness and fatigue. *New England Journal of Medicine,* 1944, **231,** 414–418.

American Psychiatric Association. *Diagnostic and statistical manual of mental disorders, III.* Washington, D.C.: American Psychiatric Association, 1980.

Bartley, S. H. Fatigue and inadequacy. *Psychological Review,* 1957, **37,** 301–324.

Billings, R. F., Tang, S. W., & Rakoff, V. M. Depression associated with cimetidine. *Canadian Journal of Psychiatry,* 1981, **26,** 260–261.

Burns, B. H. Breathlessness in depression. *British Journal of Psychiatry,* 1971, **119,** 39–45.

Carroll, B. J. Mood disturbances and pituitary adrenal diseases. *Psychosomatic Medicine*, 1977, **39**, 54.

Carroll, B. J., Greden, J. F., & Feinberg, M. Neuroendocrine disturbances and the diagnosis and etiology of endogenous depression. *Lancet*, 1980, **2**, 321–322.

Comroe, B. I. Follow-up study of a 100 patient diagnosed as neurotic. *Journal of Nervous and Mental Disease*, 1936, **83**, 679–684.

Da Costa, J. M. On irritable heart: A clinical study of a form of functional cardiac disorder and its consequences. *American Journal of Medical Science*, 1971, **61**, 2–52.

Davies, W. D. Physical illness in psychiatric outpatients. *British Journal of Psychiatry*, 1965, **3**, 27–37.

Delgado-Escueta, A. V., Mattson, R. H., King, L., Goldensohn, E. S., Spiegel, H., Madsen, J., Crandall, P., Dreifuss, F., & Porter, R. J. The nature of aggression during epileptic seizures. Special report. *New England Journal of Medicine*, 1981, **305**, 711–716.

Denko, J. D., & Kaelbling, R. The psychiatric apsects of hypoparathyroidism. *Acta Psychiatrica Scandinavica*, 1962, **38**, (Supplement 164), 1–34.

Dietch, J. T. Diagnosis of organic anxiety disorders. *Psychosomatics*, 1981, **22**, 661–669.

Engelman, K. Pheochromocytoma. *Clinical Endocrinology and Metabolism*, 1977, **6**, 769–777.

Ferrer, M. Mistaken psychiatric referral of occult serious cardiovascular disease. *Archives of General Psychiatry*, 1968, **18**, 112–113.

Folstein, M. F., Folstein, S. E., & McHugh, P. R. Minimental state—A practical method for grading the cognitive state of patients for the clinician. *Journal of Psychiatric Research*, 1975, **12**, 189–198.

Fras, I., Litin, E. M., & Bartholamew, L. G. Mental symptoms as an aid in the early diagnosis of carcinoma of the pancreas. *Gastroenterology*, 1968, **55**, 191–198.

Frochlich, E. D., & Tarazi, R. C., & Dustan, H. P. Hyperdynamic-adrenergic circulatory state. *Archives of Internal Medicine*, 1969, **123**, 1–7.

Granville-Grossman, K. *Recent advances in clinical psychiatry*. London: J & A Churchill, 1971.

Greenberger, N. J., Toskes, P. P., & Isselbacher, K. J. Diseases of the pancreas. In K. J. Isselbacher, R. B. Adams, E. Braunwald, R. G. Petersdorf, & J. D. Wilson (Eds.), *Harrison's principles of internal medicine*. New York: McGraw-Hill, 1980.

Guvener, A., Bagchi, B. K., Kooi, K. A., & Calhoun, N. D. Mental and seizure manifestations in relation to brain tumors—A statistical study. *Epilepsia*, 1964, **5**, 166–167.

Hall, R. C. Physical illness manifesting as psychiatric disease. *Archives of General Psychiatry*, 1980, **37**, 989–995. (a)

Hall, R. C. W. Depression. In R. C. W. Hall (Ed.), psychiatric presentations of medical illness. *SP Medical and Scientific Book*. New York: 1980. (b)

Hall, R. C., Popkin, M. K., De Van, I. R., Faillace, L. A., & Stickney, S. K. Physical illness presenting as psychiatric disease. *Archives of General Psychiatry*, 1978, **35**, 1,315–1,320.

Hall, R. C., Popkin, M. K., Stickney, S. K., & Gardner, E. Presentation of the "steroid psychoses." *Journal of Nervous and Mental Disease*, 1978, **167**, 229–236.

Hillis, L. D., & Brunwald, E. Myocardial ischemia. *New England Journal of Medicine*, 1977, **296**, 971–972.

Hollender, M. H., & Wells, C. E. Medical assessment in psychiatric practice. In H. I. Kaplan, A. F. Freedman, & B. J. Sadosk (Eds.), *Comprehensive testbook of psychiatry* (3rd ed.) Baltimore: Williams & Wilkins, 1980.

Isaacs, B., & Kennie, A. The set as an aid to the detection of dementia in old people. *British Journal of Psychiatry*, 1973, **123**, 467–470.

Johnson, D. A. W. The evaluation of routine physical examination in psychiatric cases. *Practitioner*, 1968, **200**, 686–691.

Jones, J. H., & Meade, T. W. Hypothermia following chlorpromazine therapy in myxedematous patients. *Geronthology Clinics*, 1964, **6**, 252–256.

Koranyi, E. K. Morbidity and rate of undiagnosed physical illness in a psychiatric clinic population. *Archives of General Psychiatry*, 1979, **36**, 414–419.

Koranyi, E. K. Somatic illness in psychiatric patients. *Psychosomatics*, 1980, **21**, 887–891.

Leeman, C. P. Diagnostic errors in emergency room medicine: Physical illness in patients labelled psychiatric. *International Journal of Psychiatry Medicine*, 1975, **6**, 533–540.

Levine, R. Hypoglycaemia. *Journal of the American Medical Association*, 1974, **230**, 462–463.

Lynch, J. J., Paskewitz, D. A., & Gimbel, K. S. Psychological aspects of cardiac arrhythmia. *American Heart Journal*, 1977, **93**, 645–657.

MacGrimmon, D. J., Wallace, J. E., Goldberg, W. M., & Streiner, D. L. Emotional disturbance and cognitive deficits in hyperthyroidism. *Psychosomatic Medicine*, 1979, **41**, 331–340.

Malzberg, B. *Mortality among patients with mental disease*. Utica, N.Y.: New York State Hospital Press, 1934.

McIntyre, J. S., & Romano, J. Is there a stethoscope in the house (and is it used?). *Archives of General Psychiatry*, 1977, **34**, 1,147–1,151.

Meyer, U. A., & Schmid, R. The porphyrias. In J. B. Stanburg (Ed.), *The metabolic basis of inherited disease*. New York: McGraw-Hill, 1978.

O'Rourke, R. A., & Crawford, M. H. The systolic click-murmur syndrome: Clinical recognition and management. *Current problems in cardiology*. Chicago: Yearbook Publishers, 1976.

Peterson, L. G., Popkin, M. K., & Hall, T. C. W. Psychiatric aspects of cancer. *Psychosomatics*, 1981, **22**, 774–793.

Phillips, R. J. Physical disorder in 164 consecutive admissions to a mental hospital. *British Medical Journal*, 1937, **2**, 363–366.

Posner, J., & Shapiro, W. R. Brain tumor. *Archives of Neurology*, 1978, **32**, 781–786.

Prange, A. J., Breese, G. R., Wilson, J. C., & Lipson, M. A. Pituitary and suprapituitary hormones: Brain behavioral effects. In E. Sacher (Ed.), *Topics in psychoendocrinology*. New York: Grune & Stratton, 1975.

Rosenman, R. H., Brand, R. J., Jenkins, C. D., Friedman, M., Straus, R., & Wurm, M. Coronary heart disease in the western collaborative group study: Final follow-up of 8½ years. *Journal of the American Medical Association*, 1975, **233**, 872–877.

Sachar, E. Psychiatric disturbances associated with endocrine disorders. In S. Arieti & M. Reiser (Eds.), *American handbook of psychiatry*. New York: Basic Books, 1975.

Sachar, E. J., Anis, G., Halbreich, U., Nathan, S., & Halpern, F. Recent studies in the neuroendocrinology of depressive disorders. *Psychiatric Clinics of North America*, 1980, **3**, 313–326.

Siegler, M., & Osmond, H. *Models of madness: Models of medicine*. New York. MacMillan, 1974.

Shader, R. I., Belfer, M. L., & DiMascio, A. Thyroid function. In R. I. Shader & A. DiMascio (Eds.), *Psychotropic drug side effects: Clinical and theoretical perspectives*. Baltimore: Williams & Wilkins, 1970.

Slater, E., & Glithero, E. Follow-up of patients diagnosed as suffering from hysteria. *Journal of Psychosomatic Research*, 1965, **9**, 9–13.

Stein, J. A., & Tschudy, D. P. Acute intermittent porphyria: A clinical and biochemical study of 46 patients. *Medicine*, 1970, **49**, 1–16.

Tollefson, G. D. Distinguishing myasthenia gravis from conversion. *Psychosomatics*, 1981, **22**, 611–621.

Williams, D. The structure of emotions reflected in epileptic experiences. *Brain*, 1956, **79**, 29–67.

PART V
TREATMENT

INTRODUCTION

Of the many areas within clinical psychology, few have attracted such widespread professional and public attention as treatment. Research on the efficacy of psychotherapy and variations of treatment have proliferated tremendously in recent years. The Chapters in this part of the handbook elaborate alternative approaches to treatment, evidence for their efficacy, and major professional, social, and public-policy issues underlying treatment. Diverse approaches are covered, including insight-oriented, behavioral, and cognitive treatments, and individual, group, and family-based procedures. Special topics are also covered, including pharmacotherapy because of its integration with psychosocial treatments in clinical work and health psychology, and behavioral medicine, where the psychology has made important contributions to the treatment and prevention of major health-related disorders. Minority issues are also covered because they raise special considerations that are often neglected in clinical work.

In Chapter 24, Hans H. Strupp discusses verbal psychotherapy from a psychodynamic point of view. Several critical issues are presented that transcend any individual therapeutic approach, including patient variables in treatment, diagnosis, and processes that arise in dyadic interaction. The limits of current research, the hiatus between theory and practice, and changes needed in future research are all addressed.

Constance T. Fischer and William F. Fischer discuss phenomenological-existential psychotherapy in Chapter 25. The authors highlight the underpinnings of this treatment approach and the unique contribution that a phenomenological stance can make to the understanding of psychopathology and treatment. The use of specific treatment techniques, the role of the therapeutic relationship, and the phenomenological approach in clinical research are some of the major topics included.

In Chapter 26, Cyril M. Franks and Christopher R. Barbrack discuss behavior therapy with adults. This chapter presents the development of behavior therapy in clinical psychology and traces its evolution over the last few decades. Advances in cognitive behavior therapy, the integration of behavior therapy and psychoanalysis, and the role of technical eclecticism are addressed. In addition, central topics such as clinical training, licensure and certification, and ethical and legal issues of treatment are raised.

Sandra L. Harris reviews and evaluates behavior therapy with children in Chapter 27. Advances in child behavior therapy are discussed in the context of techniques to treat specific disorders such as phobias, attention deficit disorders, pervasive developmental delays, conduct disorders, and others. Important treatment issues are raised, including the use of medication, cognitive behavior therapy, family treatment, and the need to incorporate research findings from developmental psychology in child treatment.

In Chapter 28, Charles E. Schaefer, Kevin O'Connor, and Anna C. Lee examine psychoanalytic psychotherapy with children. The chapter traces the history of child analysis and the specific processes and therapeutic procedures that are used. Differences in the treatment of children during prelatency, latency, and adolescence are clearly described. Applications of child analysis to psychotic, borderline, handicapped, abused, and deprived children are also elaborated.

In Chapter 29, Philip C. Kendall and Kelly M. Bemis present cognitive-behavioral approaches to psychotherapy. Alternative treatments are discussed, including rational emotive therapy, rational restructuring, cognitive therapy, self-instruction training, stress-inoculation training, and others. The outcome literatures are critically reviewed, and key topics for this area such as the assessment of cognitive processes are elaborated.

Robert H. Klein presents group treatment approaches in Chapter 30. Different types of group therapy are elaborated that represent diverse conceptual models and are directed toward different therapeutic ends. Dimensions for distinguishing among alternative group approaches are proposed, along with critical issues to evaluate progress in establishing the efficacy of group procedures.

In Chapter 31, Neil S. Jacobson and Nicole Bussod discuss current advances in marital and family therapy. Alternative models of marital distress and treatment strategies that they have generated are presented, including psychodynamic, systems, and behavioral approaches. Sexual dysfunction and treatment are also covered, insofar as they often arise in conjunction with marital therapy. The chapter incisively evaluates outcome evidence for alternative marital and family treatment approaches.

Geary S. Alford presents recent work in pharmacotherapy and its integration with psychological treatment in Chapter 32. Basic information is presented on the pharmacological agents that are commonly used in treatment, their classification, and mechanisms of action. Major and minor tranquilizers, neuroleptics, lithium, antidepressants, and stimulants are presented along with evidence for their use, efficacy, and side-effects.

In Chapter 33, Joseph D. Matarazzo and Timothy P. Carmody discuss health psychology, an area where clinical psychology has played an increased role in recent years. Applications of psychology to health-related problem areas are covered, including chronic pain, headache, obesity, coronary heart disease, and other disorders or dysfuctions. The role that health psychology can play in the prevention of dysfunction gives this chapter implications well beyond treatment.

In Chapter 34, Jack O. Jenkins and Knoxice C. Hunter discuss minority issues in relation to clinical psychology and psychological treatment. The impact of assessment, particularly intelligence testing and clinical evaluation, on members of minorities are discussed. The chapter conveys the importance of considering minority issues in clinical evaluation and treatment.

24 PSYCHOANALYTIC PSYCHOTHERAPY

Hans H. Strupp

The birth of modern psychotherapy is commonly traced to Josef Breuer's famous patient Anna O. who, about a hundred years ago, gained relief from her hysterical difficulties by means of the "talking cure." Sigmund Freud, Breuer's young colleague, built on Breuer's early insights, and his subsequent discoveries of psychological dynamics ushered in a revolution that continues to have profound effects on contemporary clinical thinking and practice.

Nonetheless, despite notable advances, modern psychotherapy—much of it based on psychodynamic principles—is in an embattled state. Avidly sought by thousands of troubled people who desire relief from an assortment of problems ranging from the classical neurotic conditions to personality disorder, alienation, loneliness, and existential despair, many diverse forms of psychotherapy are practiced by an expanding cadre of professionals, including among others, psychiatrists, clinical psychologists, social workers, nurses, and pastoral counselors. Psychotherapy continues to be seen as a major weapon against personal and interpersonal difficulties besetting people's lives. On the one hand, it has become a billion-dollar "industry," a set of "treatments," compensable by

the government and private health insurance companies. On the other hand, it is attacked by scores of critics who alternately deny that there is such a "thing" as psychotherapy, question its effectiveness (more recently, in comparison with psychotropic drugs), or advocate interventions claimed to be superior to "traditional" ones. Coupled with these doubts is the public's growing mistrust of science, medicine, and the professions, the professional's preoccupation with economic and political power, their lack of concern for the consumer, and the accumulated frustration of a citizenry that desires simple and cost-effective solutions to the complex problems of our technological society.

Whatever different forms of psychotherapy purport to be, or however they are defined, several things are clear today:

1. Psychotherapy is not a "miracle drug" or a panacea.
2. Although a substantial percentage of people experiencing some form of psychotherapy report marked benefits, it is equally true that others in states of crisis overcome their difficulties through their own adaptive capacities

or with the help of friends, clergymen, and others who may provide counsel.

3. Individuals who have made a better adaptation to adult living and who possess greater personality resources derive greater benefits from psychotherapy than persons who lack these strengths and who suffer from longstanding emotional disorders.

4. No single form of dynamic psychotherapy (or behavior therapy) is uniquely superior to others (except perhaps in a few narrowly circumscribed conditions).

5. A number of psychopathological conditions are not helped significantly by available forms of psychotherapy (or any other known treatment modality).

6. The extent to which intensive or prolonged psychotherapy produces radical reorganization of a patient's personality and therefore lasting change is questionable.

7. The quality of the interpersonal relationship established between a patient and a therapist plays an important part in determining the course and outcome of the therapy.

8. Once the patient has met certain criteria of suitability, the therapist's personal qualities appear to be more potent factors than any specific set of techniques he or she may use.

9. Finally, in the absence of the foregoing considerations, the quest for specific psychotherapeutic techniques for specific disorders (analogous to a drug) may turn out to be futile.

Why, in light of this seemingly gloomy picture, does the practice of psychotherapy continue to flourish? Why do therapists continue to be trained? Why do people continue to enlist the service of psychotherapists? It will become apparent that one cannot speak of psychoanalytic psychotherapy (or any other form) as a unitary treatment procedure apart from the person of the patient and the person of the therapist. Rather, the personal qualities of the participants inevitably become intertwined in any therapeutic encounter. At the same time, it is possible for the therapist to employ his or her clinical acumen in understanding complex cognitive, symbolic, and emotional processes that lead to the formation of "symptoms" or other "difficulties in living" and to help the patient resolve or ameliorate some of these problems. Thus, psychotherapy is both a personal and a technical enterprise, and many of the persistent misunderstandings derive from inadequate appreciation of this fact.

Basic Considerations

In the broadest terms, all forms of psychotherapy are concerned with personality and behavior *change*. The patient who seeks help for a psychological problem desires change: he or she wants to feel or act differently, and the psychotherapist agrees to assist the patient in achieving this goal. The major issues in psychotherapy relate to *what* is to be changed and *how* change can be brought about. The first part of the question entails definition of the *problem* for which the patient is seeking help (e.g., depression, marital difficulties, existential anxiety, etc.); the second pertains to the process and techniques by which change is effected (e.g., support, insight through interpretations, etc.). Ideally, one would like to be able to say that, given problem X, the optimal approach is technique Y. In practice, things are not so simple or straightforward; on the contrary, since many human problems are extraordinarily complex, so are the issues facing the therapist who attempts to deal with those difficulties in therapeutic ways. For the same reason, it is unlikely that there can be a single optimal approach to the solution of a psychological problem. Accordingly, the distinctions between, say, behavior therapy and the therapies based on psychodynamic principles pale in significance. This is not to deny that there may be fundamental distinctions between the philosophies and practices of behavior therapists and dynamically oriented therapists, but in fact no therapist practices a "pure" technique. Indeed, commonalities in all forms of therapy may turn out to be more crucial than differences.

Psychoanalytic psychotherapy generally refers to a broad spectrum of interventions that rest on dynamic principles derived from psychoanalysis. Psychoanalysis as a treatment modality is usually defined in terms of goals (reorganization of personality structure), activity of patient and therapist (free association by the patient, interpretation of transference and resistance by the therapist), the setting (encompassed by the standard definition of the "psychoanalytic situation"), the controlled use of regression leading to a "transference neurosis," frequency and intensity of the treatment, and the use of the couch as an adjunct. No precise definition can be given for the various forms of psychoanalytic psychotherapy. However, many of the techniques may be arranged on a continuum. At one extreme, these therapies approximate "classical" psychoanalysis; at the other, one may distinguish various forms of dynamic psychotherapy that make extensive use of "supportive" techniques, such as encouragement and advice. With regard to the latter class, therapeutic goals are more limited and numerous departures ("parameters") from the classical model regularly occur. (For a detailed discussion of commonalities and differences, see Stewart, 1980.)

Part of the confusion pervading the field of psychotherapy as a whole relates to the definition of psychotherapy as a "treatment modality," analogous to medical treatment in which a physician ministers to a passive patient. This problem is complicated by the fact that modern psychotherapy has its roots in medicine. Thus, terms such as "patient," "therapist," "diagnosis," and "etiology" continue to be used. In truth, psychotherapy bears only a superficial resemblance to this model. However, since it is undeniable that psychotherapy attempts to alleviate human suffering, the medical analogy persists. Furthermore, some conditions (e.g., depressions) appear to yield to psychotherapy as well as to pharmacological interventions, the latter traditionally being the province of physicians. It may therefore be asserted that psychotherapy appears to improve a person's "mental health," a term that has always been fuzzy and whose utility is increasingly being called into question. Nonetheless, psychiatrists (as physicians) have found it advantageous, for political as well as economic reasons, to "remedicalize" psychotherapy. This move runs counter to historical developments, tending to turn back the clock and jettisoning hard-won advances.

Psychotherapy as a Learning Process

It is important to note that psychotherapy bears a much closer relationship to the educational model. As early as 1905, Freud (p. 267) characterized psychoanalytic therapy as a form of "re-education" (or "after-education"), a position he never abandoned. It was clear to him, as it has been to the vast majority of therapists since Freud, that psychotherapy, above all else, is a *collaborative* endeavor in which the patient, from the beginning, is ex-

pected to play an active part. By the same token, the vast majority of neurotic disorders — the prime conditions for which psychotherapy is used — are the product of maladaptive learning in early childhood, resulting in low self-esteem, dependency, and other forms of immaturity. To overcome these impediments, the patient must be helped to become more autonomous, more self-directing, and more responsible. In order to feel better about themselves, their relationships with others, and their behavior in general, patients must learn to make changes within themselves and in their environment. The process of therapy does not impose change on the patient but creates conditions that allow internal changes to occur.

Therefore, psychotherapy is a form of learning and the role of the therapist is analogous to that of a mentor. If troublesome feelings, cognitions, attitudes, and patterns of behavior have been learned, there is the possibility, within limits, for unlearning or relearning. Conversely, where learning is impossible (for example, in conditions, attributable to genetic or biochemical factors), psychotherapy has little to offer. Similarly, if the disturbance is largely produced by factors in the person's social milieu (poverty, oppression, imprisonment) or if patients themselves do not desire change but change is mandated by a court of law, school system, etc., psychotherapy encounters great difficulties. Thus, psychotherapy works best if patients themselves desire change and are motivated to work toward it, if the environment in which they live tolerates the possibility of change, and if the inner obstacles to learning (defenses and rigidities of character) are not insurmountable. Since everyone, despite conscious assertions to the contrary, is deeply committed to maintaining the status quo, psychotherapeutic learning is rarely simple or uncomplicated.

It may prove helpful to compile an "operational inventory" of basic learning experiences occurring in psychoanalytic therapy:

1. The therapist *sets an example* of acceptance, respect, tolerance, nonpunitiveness, reliability, trustworthiness, punctuality, decency, nonretaliation, permissiveness, evenness of temper, predictability, truth, rationality, honesty, steady cooperation in constructive moves by the patient, nonavoidance of anxiety-provoking and "taboo" topics, reasonableness, etc. In this way, he or she provides a certain gratification and stimulates in the patient the expression of wishes and impulses

which become increasingly intense and primitive the less they are interfered with by outside pressure and the more they are guaranteed "safe" expression. The therapist says, in effect: "It is all right for wishes and impulses to be experienced in awareness, but there is no assurance that they will be gratified." In fact, the patient will reject a good many himself once he or she becomes conscious of them. (This paradigm of the permissiveness of the analytic situation has, of course, been abundantly spelled out by Freud and others.)

2. The therapist *sets limits*. He or she strictly limits the time devoted to the patient; the therapist expects payment for services rendered; expects punctuality, respect for his property, rights, privacy, and independence. Most importantly, he or she abstains from participating in the patient's neurotic maneuvers (e.g., sadomasochistic strivings and a wide variety of other techniques of interpersonal control).

3. Through the foregoing and other devices, the therapist teaches the *delay of gratification* — perhaps the most important lesson the patient has to learn. Tolerance of delay is taught by regulated frustration, such as nongratification of dependency wishes, terminating the hour by the clock rather than in accordance with the patient's desires, etc. The principle here is to awaken in awareness strong wishes typically dating back to early childhood and, by failing to gratify them, to educate the patient to tolerate the displeasure, tension, disappointment, discomfort, and unhappiness associated with them. In speaking about this process, Menninger (1958) observed that the patient's gain in psychotherapy is the successful resolution of problems created by early frustrations.

There is little doubt that in normal childhood development, ego strength is acquired in much the same manner: The child learns to accept frustration of his or her wishes (e.g., for dependency, sexual gratification) because he acquiesces in the privations imposed upon him by the parents as trustworthy representatives of reality. The child suffers the pain of frustration and ultimately of separation from his love objects, because his love outweighs his self-centered narcissistic wishes, and he adapts to reality without developing excessive defensive controls resulting in neurotic symptoms. On the other hand, the therapeutic relationship provides a number of real gratifications (e.g., the therapist's commitment, interest, acceptance, caring) that in some measure compensate for the

real privations and injuries the patient sustained in childhood.

The learning occurring in psychoanalytic psychotherapy can thus be reduced to the following basic model:

1. The therapist provides a "good" climate, that the patient can come to recognize as a safe, protective environment. Thus, the therapist fills the role of a reasonable, accepting, and caring parent.

2. The patient — at least consciously — is willing to engage with the therapist in the collaborative venture of psychotherapy.

3. To the extent that the patient can emotionally come to experience the "good" aspects of Condition 1 (although they are controlled, restrained, and dosed), he or she begins to experience hitherto repressed wishes, impulses, and fantasies toward the therapist. Also awakened are the negativistic and obstructionistic tendencies, commonly labeled resistance, by which the patient in accordance with his or her early life experience tries to engage the therapist in a neurotic struggle which, if successful (from the patient's point of view), would spell the failure of therapy. This phase comprises the spectrum of transference reactions.

4. The task of the therapist is to convince the patient of the irrationality, futility, and self-defeating aspects of defensive maneuvers, thus encouraging their abandonment. As a substitute, the therapist implicitly offers his or her own attitudes, beliefs, and values as a new and better model for interpersonal collaboration. This process is both an emotional and cognitive one, and as Freud (1916, p. 445) observed, the balance of forces is determined entirely by the patient's emotional relationship to the therapist. While psychoanalytic therapy in important respects is a process of socialization, this is only a part of it. It is more correct to say that in the ordinary course of the child's socialization, he comes to control (largely repress) his primitive strivings, which remain a central concern of analytic therapy. In the latter, various segments of unconscious processes are worked out in consciousness, interpreted in terms of their infantile roots, and integrated by the patient's adult, rational ego. The essence of analytic therapy is an intensive form of emotional learning in human collaboration and relatedness, carried on within an atmosphere of understanding and respect. The emotional relationship is mediated largely by the use of *language* and linguistic symbols, so that the experiential aspects of the relationship are raised to a

more differentiated cognitive level. Although language serves as a crucial vehicle for therapeutic learning, the products of this learning are reflected in unconscious rearrangements of cognitive structures, which are as yet poorly understood.

Although there is reasonable agreement on the broad outlines of psychoanalytic psychotherapy, no definition has found universal acceptance nor is it likely that any definition ever will. Most therapists, agree, however, that all forms of analytic psychotherapy involve both a human relationship and techniques for bringing about personality and behavior change.

I turn next to a consideration of significant issues relevant to practice and research in psychoanalytic psychotherapy; I believe, however, that the problems are equally germane to other psychotherapeutic modalities.

Issues and Trends

The Problem of Therapy Outcome

The single most important problem overshadowing all others and placing them in perspective is the issue of effectiveness. As precise answers can be given to the question, "What kinds of therapeutic procedures will be helpful to particular patients under particular circumstances?," it will become possible to clarify the nature of the changes produced by *specific* treatment interventions and to delineate the variables that make a particular treatment effective or ineffective. (For a fuller discussion, see Strupp & Bergin, 1969, and Bergin & Strupp, 1972.)

The problem of psychotherapy outcome touches on many facets of human life, and conceptions of mental health and illness cannot be considered apart from problems of philosophy, ethics, religion, and public policy. Inescapably we deal with human existence, the person's place in the world, and ultimately we must confront questions of *value* (Strupp & Hadley, 1977). In the end, someone must make a judgment that a person's compliance with requests from others is a virtue or an indicator of pathological submissiveness; that a decrement of 10 points on the Depression Scale of the MMPI in the 90–100 range is a greater or a lesser "improvement" than a like change between 50–60; that in one case we accept a patient's judgment that he or she feels "better" whereas in another we set it aside, calling it "flight into health,"

"reaction formation," "denial," or the like. These decisions can only be made by reference to a theory of psychological functioning and the values society assigns to feelings, attitudes, and actions. In turn, values are inherent in conceptions of mental health and illness as well as in clinical judgments based upon one of these models.

One of the great stumbling blocks in psychotherapy research and practice has been a failure to realize the importance of values. While researchers have rightfully dealt with technical and methodological issues and made considerable gains in clarifying them, objective assessments and measurements have remained imperfect and imprecise. For example, it is a common finding (Bergin & Lambert, 1978; Garfield, Prager & Bergin, 1971) that outcome assessments by patients, peers, independent clinicians, and therapists correlate only moderately. One may attribute this to the imperfection of the instruments and the fallibility of raters, but one should also be aware that raters bring different perspectives to bear and that the relative lack of correlation results in part from legitimate divergences in their vantage points.

Freud (1916) already saw the outcome issue as a practical one, and this may well be the best way to treat it. When all is said and done, there may be common-sense agreement on what constitutes a mentally healthy, nonneurotic person. Knight (1941), a prominant analyst of his generation, postulated three major rubrics for considering therapeutic change that still seem eminently reasonable: (1) disappearance of presenting symptoms; (2) real improvement in mental functioning; and (3) improved reality adjustment. Most therapists and researchers, while they may disagree on criteria and methods of assessing change, concur that therapeutic success should be demonstrable in the person's (1) feeling state (well-being), (2) social functioning (performance), and (3) personality organization (structure). The first is clearly the individual's subjective perspective; the second is that of society, incorporating prevailing standards of conduct and "normality"; the third is the perspective of mental-health professionals whose technical concepts (e.g., ego strength or impulse control) partake of information and standards derived from the preceding sources but that are ostensibly scientific, objective, and value-free. As Strupp and Hadley (1977) have shown, few therapists or researchers have recognized these facts or taken their implications seriously. Therapists have continued to assess treatment outcomes on the basis of global clinical impressions, whereas researchers have tended to assume that quantitative indices can be interpreted as if they were thermometer readings. Instead, values influence and suffuse all judgments of outcome.

There are other reasons for rejecting the traditional question, "Is psychotherapy effective?," as neither appropriate nor potentially fruitful. Psychotherapy (or behavior therapy) as currently practiced is not a unitary process, nor is it applied to a unitary problem (Kiesler, 1966). Furthermore, therapies cannot be regarded as interchangeable units that deliver a standard treatment in uniform quantity or quality (see Parloff, Waskow, & Wolfe, 1978). Patients, depending on differences in their personality, education, intelligence, the nature of their emotional difficulties, motivation, and other variables, are differentially receptive to different forms of therapeutic influence (Garfield, 1978). Finally, since technique variables are thoroughly intertwined with the person of the therapist, they cannot be dealt with in isolation.

There are, by now, clear indications that these strictures are being taken more seriously by contemporary researchers (e.g., Sloane et al., 1975; Strupp & Hadley, 1979), although as yet by few practicing therapists. There is a longstanding tradition among psychotherapists of viewing their particular approach as the answer to every problem presented by patients, with scant recognition that another technique might be more appropriate in a given case. Freud's consistent refusal to view psychoanalysis as a panacea and his insistence upon carefully circumscribing its range of applicability stands as a notable exception. It is fully apparent that neither therapists nor researchers can evade the necessity of working toward greater *specificity* in describing changes occurring in patients and evaluating the changes by reference to an explicit frame of values.

Research activity in the area of therapy outcomes has been voluminous and sustained (Bergin & Lambert, 1978). In the years since Eysenck (1952) charged that psychotherapy produces no greater changes in emotionally disturbed individuals than naturally occurring life experiences, researchers and clinicians alike have felt compelled to answer the challenge. Analyzing and synthesizing the data from 25 years of research on the efficacy of psychotherapy, Luborsky, Singer, and Luborsky (1975) have concluded that most forms of psychotherapy produce changes in a substantial proportion of patients—changes that are often,

but not always, greater than those achieved by control patients who did not receive therapy. Other reviewers (e.g., Meltzoff & Kornreich, 1970) have reached similar conclusions. In an ingenious analysis, Smith, Glass, and Miller (1980) demonstrated that standardized measures across all types of therapy, patients, therapists, and outcome criteria show the average patient to have improved more than 75 percent of comparable control patients. In short, the preponderance of the evidence, interpreted in the most general terms does not support Eysenck's pessimistic conclusion concerning psychotherapy, nor does it demonstrate behavior therapy as impressively superior to other forms.

The literature also reflects increments in the number of studies that are methodologically sound and clinically meaningful. Major investigations are exemplified by the studies at the University of Chicago Counseling Center with client-centered therapy (Rogers & Dymond, 1954); the Menninger Foundation Project (Kernberg et al., 1972); the Temple study in which treatment results from behavior therapy and psychotherapy were studied under controlled conditions (Sloane et al., 1975); the research by Paul (1966, 1967), DiLoreto (1971), and the Vanderbilt Psychotherapy Project (Strupp & Hadley, 1979). Some of the primary aims of these studies were to contrast variations in treatment and to investigate the impact of patient and therapist variables in determining outcomes. Furthermore, in a host of investigations the impact of patient, therapist, and technique variables upon the *process* of psychotherapy has been explored (Orlinsky & Howard, 1978).

Patient Variables and the Problem of Diagnosis

Therapy outcomes obviously depend to a significant extent on patient characteristics. From the moment he or she meets a patient, the therapist seeks to define the nature of the problem in need of treatment or amelioration. The therapist becomes a diagnostician who attempts to identify a malfunction or a "problem" in order to take appropriate therapeutic steps. This requires clinical understanding and an appreciation of the vast array of individual differences among patients. While seemingly simple, the problem is exceedingly fateful in its implications for therapy and research.

To illustrate, therapists and researchers have come to realize that a phobia, a depression, or an anxiety state in one patient is not identical to a similar problem in another. Accordingly, it is hazardous for a variety of reasons to categorize or type patients on the basis of the presenting difficulty or in terms of standard psychiatric diagnoses. Moreover, the utility of the classical diagnostic categories (hysteria, obsessive-compulsive neurosis), is very limited for either therapeutic practice or research. Other systems of classification (e.g., in terms of defensive styles or ego functions), while sometimes useful, have their own shortcomings. The plain fact, long recognized by clinicians, is that patients differ on a host of dimensions — from intelligence, education, social class, and age, to such variables as psychological-mindedness, motivation for psychotherapy, organization of defenses, and rigidity of character.

Human personality, furthermore, is *organized* and personality organization often forms an integral part of the "therapeutic problem." For example, phobic patients generally tend to be shy, dependent, and anxious in many other situations (Andrews, 1966). In addition, temperament and genetic, social, and environmental factors of various kinds influence the patient's current disturbance. One must also recognize that the patient's life history, particularly interpersonal relationships in early childhood, may be crucially important for understanding and treating the current problem. The foregoing variables are typically intertwined in highly complex ways, resulting in a unique constellation.

Despite the uniqueness of individuals, there are commonalities in patients' "problems." People react in diverse yet limited ways to stresses and crises (such as bereavement, disappointments, or rejection by important persons in their lives). So, while individual variations are real, all members of our culture have had somewhat comparable childhood experiences. For example, most of us have learned early in life that the expression of impulses must be curbed in the interest of social living; in other words, we have learned discipline and to accept authority. To illustrate further, since Americans have grown up in a relatively common culture, share the same language, and have common human desires, conflicts, and goals, others can understand our behavior and motives. For these reasons, as well as others, principles of personality functioning can be abstracted, and psychotherapy has the potential of becoming a scientific discipline. Sullivan's (1953) "one genus postulate" ("We are all much more simply human

than otherwise") underscores the continuity of human experience regardless of ethnic differences or seemingly incomprehensible psychopathology.

In order to be maximally useful to a patient, therapists must sort and integrate the large mass of information that becomes available through clinical interaction and evaluation, formulate the therapeutic problem in terms that are meaningful to both participants as well as to society, and institute appropriate therapeutic procedures. In short, the psychotherapist and the therapy researcher must be sensitive diagnosticians, whose task is different from a one-time effort at pigeonholing individuals into diagnostic classes or categories.

The following implications should be noted:

1. Formulating the therapeutic problem and achieving consensus among interested parties, both from the standpoint of clinical practice and research, is a task of the greatest importance. Thus, progress in studying therapy outcomes, both within and across therapeutic approaches, will remain seriously hampered unless it becomes possible to deal more effectively with this problem.

2. Existing diagnostic schemes have a certain limited utility, as do theoretical formulations of patient problems stated in terms of presenting symptoms, difficulties, or "targets." The latter are often troublesome because they are a statement of the patient's subjective feeling-state or "problem" which, as presented, may not lend itself to therapy. In one case, patient and therapist may agree on the elimination of a phobia as the therapeutic goal. In another instance, however, the patient may state a vague or unrealistic target (like "becoming more popular" or "worrying less"). As therapy proceeds, the therapist often finds it necessary to reformulate the original target.

Moreover, in many instances it is insufficient to focus exclusively on one aspect of the patient's functioning (e.g., overt behavior). Rather, estimates of the *totality* of the patient's personality functioning and performance on a number of dimensions must be obtained even when a specific area is targeted for change. It is gradually being recognized that in all forms of psychotherapy patients will typically experience changes in their self-identity and self-acceptance; that is, regardless of behavioral change, successful psychotherapy produces changes in the patient's *inner experience* (Strupp, Fox, & Lessler, 1969), a realization previously rejected but now often accepted by some behavior therapists (Wachtel, 1977).

3. Diagnosis is a process that calls for the exercise of significant clinical skills. It must be systematic and lead to prognostic judgments that can be translated into therapeutic operations as well as outcome evaluations. In other words, the primary goal of psychodiagnosis should not be to label a patient but to devise a realistic plan for therapeutic action.

4. The personality make-up and behavioral patterns of the individual patient exert the single most important modulating effect on the therapist's total effort and therefore its effectiveness. Disregarding or giving short shrift to this set of variables is tantamount to developing tools without considering the material with which one intends to work.

As society has begun to recognize the importance of making psychotherapeutic services available to a broad spectrum of the population—not merely to its affluent members—the problem of defining and identifying those individuals who can (or cannot) benefit from particular forms of therapy has become increasingly pressing. With it has come the recognition that therapy must be tailored to the needs of individual patients and their problems, rather than the reverse (Goldstein & Stein, 1976). This aim is reflected in research efforts to "socialize" patients prior to psychotherapy (Hoehn-Saric et al., 1964; Orne & Wender, 1968; Strupp & Bloxom, 1973), to increase their understanding of how therapy works, and to prepare them for therapy in other ways.

The study of patient characteristics in relation to therapeutic change, as Strupp and Bergin (1969) noted, has for the most part focused on one basic issue: How do patient variables influence and determine the immediate reaction to as well as the ultimate course of psychotherapy? The following question appears to be more significant: Which constellation of patient characteristics and problems are most amenable to which techniques conducted by which type of therapist in what type of setting? Thus, rather than the more common approach of trying to determine the kind of patient or initial status that will respond best to fairly heterogeneous types of therapy, it may be more important to devise therapies that will benefit particular patients.

The Problem of Technique

Techniques are of course the core and *raison d'être* of modern psychotherapy, and they are anchored in theories of psychopathology or maladaptive learning. Psychoanalysis has stressed the interpretation of resistances and transference phenomena as the principal curative factor, contrasting these operations with the "suggestions" of earlier hypnotists. Behavior therapy, to cite another example, has developed its own armamentarium of techniques, such as systematic desensitization, modeling, aversive and operant conditioning, and training in self-regulation and self-control. In general, the proponents of all systems of psychotherapy credit their successes to more or less specific operations that are usually claimed to be uniquely effective. A corollary of this proposition is that a therapist is a professional who must receive systematic training in the application of the recommended techniques.

So far it has not been possible to show that one technique is clearly superior to another, even under reasonably controlled conditions (e.g., Luborsky et al., 1975; Sloane et al., 1975; Strupp & Hadley, 1979). The commonly accepted finding that approximately two-thirds of neurotic patients who enter outpatient psychotherapy of whatever description show noticeable improvement (Bergin & Lambert, 1978; Garfield, 1978) likewise reinforces a skeptical attitude concerning the unique effectiveness of particular techniques. Finally, it often turns out that initial claims for a new technique cannot be sustained when the accumulating evidence is critically examined. The latter, for example, appears to be true of systematic desensitization in the treatment of phobias (Marks, 1978).

An alternative hypothesis has been advanced (e.g., Frank, 1973; Strupp, 1973) that asserts that psychotherapeutic change is predominantly a function of factors *common* to all therapeutic approaches. These factors are brought to bear in the human *relationship* between the patient and the healer. The proponents of this hypothesis hold that individuals defined by themselves or others as patients suffer from demoralization and a sense of hopelessness. Consequently, any benign human influence is likely to boost the patient's morale, which in turn is registered as "improvement" (Shapiro & Morris, 1978). Primary ingredients of these common *nonspecific* factors include: understanding, respect, interest, encouragement, acceptance, forgiveness—in short, the kinds of human qualities that since time immemorial have been considered effective in buoying the human spirit.

Frank (1974) identifies another important common factor in all psychotherapies: their tendency to operate in terms of a *conceptual scheme* and associated procedures that are thought to be beneficial.

While the *contents* of the schemes and the procedures differ among therapies, they have common morale-building *functions*. Thus, they combat the patient's demoralization by providing an *explanation*, acceptable to both participants, for the patient's hitherto inexplicable feelings and behavior. This process serves to remove the mystery from the patient's suffering and eventually to supplant it with hope.

Frank's formulation implies that training in and enthusiasm for a special theory and method may increase the effectiveness of therapists, in contrast to nonprofessional helpers who may lack belief in a coherent system or rationale. This hypothesis also underscores the continuity between faith healers, shamans, and modern psychotherapists. While the latter may operate on the basis of sophisticated scientific theories (by contemporary standards), the function of these theories may be intrinsically no different from the most primitive rationale undergirding a healer's efforts. In both instances, "techniques" of whatever description are inseparable from the therapist's belief system, which in successful therapy is accepted and integrated by the patient. Some patients may of course be more receptive to, and thus more likely to benefit from, the therapist's manipulations than others.

From a different perspective, Rogers (1957) postulated a set of "facilitative conditions" (i.e., accurate empathy, genuineness, and unconditional positive regard) as necessary and sufficient conditions for beneficial therapeutic change. Thus, both Rogers and Frank deemphasize therapeutic techniques per se; instead, they elevate "relationship" factors to a position of preeminence.

While the hypothesis of nonspecific factors embodies a valuable idea, it may still be possible that some technical operations may be superior to others with particular patients, particular problems, and under particular circumstances. Such claims are made, for example, by therapists who are interested in the treatment of sexual dysfunctions (see Kaplan, 1974) and by behavior therapists who have tackled a wide range of behavior disorders (Marks, 1978). Many of these claims are as yet untested, and a great deal of research remains to be done to document that specific techniques are uniquely effective. Even so, there may be definite limits (largely those set by the patient's personality structure, cited earlier) that no technique per se can transcend. To cite but one example: sex researchers have come to realize that the success of treatment for sexual dysfunctions is often severely circumscribed by more or less deep-seated neurotic problems, of which the sexual difficulty is but one manifestation.

In any event, it is clear that the problem has important ramifications for research and practice. For example, if further evidence can be adduced that techniques per se contribute less to good therapy outcomes than has been claimed, greater effort may have to be expended in selecting and training therapists who are able to provide the "nonspecific factors" mentioned earlier. In light of the existing evidence, there may be definite limitations to what techniques as such can accomplish (Frank, 1974), limits that are set both by patient characteristics and therapist qualities, including level of training.

The Person of the Therapist

As previously suggested, psychotherapy prominently involves the interaction of two or more persons, and the therapeutic influence is by no means restricted to the formal techniques a therapist may use. The patient, like the therapist, reacts to the other as a *total* person, hence both researchers and clinicians must become centrally concerned with the therapist as a human being. What has been said about enormous individual differences among patients applies with equal force to therapists. Indeed, it is difficult to fathom how in early psychoanalysis, as well as in a vast number of later research studies, therapists could have been treated as interchangeable units, presumably equal in skill and influence (Kiesler, 1966). Therapists, like patients, obviously differ on many dimensions: age, gender, cultural background, ethnic factors, level of professional experience, psychological sophistication, empathy, tact, and social values. Any or all of these may have a significant bearing upon a therapist's theoretical orientation, techniques, and the manner in which he or she interact with and influence a given patient. There can be little doubt that the therapist's personality is an important determinant of the therapeutic outcome.

The elusiveness of many therapist qualities has posed serious obstacles to research in this area. It is possible, of course, to specify those human qualities that a good therapist should possess (Holt & Luborsky, 1958), as well as those that may be harmful to patients (Hadley & Strupp, 1976). Because of the recent emphasis on the ancient medical principle, "above all, do not harm" particular interest is currently being shown in those therapist qualities that may be detrimental to patients

(Strupp, Hadley, & Gomes-Schwartz, 1977). At any rate, since therapists represent a combination of personality characteristics and qualities, it has been difficult to dissect strands in the therapist's total influence. Furthermore, patient personality characteristics demonstrably influence the therapist's effectiveness, which provides support for the conclusion that patients must be selected more carefully to match the therapist's capabilities. Finally, therapists appear to be differentially effective with particular patients (Strupp, 1980a, 1980b, 1980c, 1980d).

It has frequently been mentioned that the effective therapist must be able to instill trust, confidence, and hope, and to reinforce the patient's belief in his or her own strength. Yet, real as these variables undoubtedly are, they likewise have eluded quantification. It is becoming increasingly clear that single therapist variables, except perhaps glaring defects in the therapist's personality, are not likely to provide the answers sought by researchers and clinicians; instead, a combination of therapist attributes appears to form an integrated gestalt to which the patient, other things being equal, responds positively, negatively, or neutrally. In order to have a therapeutic impact on the patient, the therapist's personality must have distinctive stimulus value or salience; therapist's can never be impersonal technicians, nor can they apply therapeutic techniques in a vacuum. At times, they must be capable of encouraging the patient to explore a particular feeling, belief, or attitude; at other times, they must wait patiently for the patient to arrive at his or her own solutions. They must be capable of distinguishing between the patient's neurotic and nonneurotic needs and must resist becoming entangled in the patient's neurotic and nonneurotic needs or neurotic maneuvers. Above all, they must make a careful assessment of how much help is needed, what kind of help is needed, and what obstacles prevent the patient from reaching a constructive solution. In short, therapists must have a high level of personal maturity as well as clinical skill and sensitivity. Concerted efforts to specify these qualities may yield important clues to the question of what is ultimately effective in psychotherapy.

The importance of the foregoing considerations has frequently been lost by the artificial distinction between therapist's "personality" and "techniques." For expository purposes, it is of course possible to describe techniques as if they existed apart from the person who is using them.

In practice, however, this is never the case. If demonstrations are needed, all one has to do is listen to a sound recording of any therapeutic interview. It becomes apparent that any therapist, regardless of his or her theoretical orientation, interacts with the patient as a total person. All therapists will ask for clarifications, try to understand the patient's communications, and offer comments of various kinds. To be sure, one therapist may systematically attempt to identify and uproot a patient's neurotic beliefs; another may listen for a long time and offer sparse interpretations of latent meanings in the patient's associations; a third may make "homework assignments," and so forth. None of these techniques, however, is ever "pure"; in all cases they are embedded in the human relationship between the participants. Furthermore, a trained therapist's interventions are guided by his or her understanding of the patient's "problem" at a particular time. This understanding is informed and guided by the therapist's clinical expertise, or his or her knowledge of psychodynamics, the nature of the patient's resistances, and what, in terms of that understanding, might be helpful to say as well as how to say it. The therapist responds in terms of a "cognitive map" that gives direction and guidance. In the absence of such a map, which is essentially a refinement of "commonsense" understanding of another person's interpersonal difficulties, the therapist flounders. In sum, it is basically meaningless to attempt a differentiation of "technique" and "personality." Instead, the two are inextricably intertwined, and reflect the totality of the therapist's personality and professional experience.

The Therapeutic Alliance

In recent years, a number of psychoanalytic theorists (e.g., Greenson, 1967; Langs, 1973; Menninger & Holzman, 1973), have identified the relationship between patient and therapist as a major therapeutic force. As Freud developed the technique of psychoanalytic therapy, he recognized that patients must become active partners who collaborate with the therapist in their cure. Freud distinguished between the patient's "observing" and "experiencing" ego, postulating that the former represents the reasonable and rational part of the patient's personality that forms an alliance and identifies with the therapist's efforts in analyzing the irrational (transferential) aspects of the patient's personality, the principle task of analytic therapy. Thus, the therapeutic relationship is composed of a "real" relationship (that is, the relationship between two adults, one of whom desires therapeutic change) and a "transference" relationship (represented by continual but unwitting tendencies on the patient's part to reenact neurotic conflicts with the therapist).

To the extent that factors within the patient or the therapist interfere with the establishment of a productive therapeutic alliance, therapeutic progress will be retarded or even vitiated. Premature termination or intractable dependency on the therapist are instances of such failure. It is also well known that patients who have relatively strong personality resources have a better chance of succeeding in analytic therapy (Horwitz, 1974; Kernberg, 1976) and perhaps in other forms of therapy as well. Although there are as yet few empirical studies of the therapeutic alliance, preliminary support for its importance comes from several investigations (e.g., Hartley & Strupp, 1982; Horwitz, 1974).

While superficially resembling any good human relationship, the therapeutic alliance provides a unique starting point for the patient's growing identification with the therapist, a point stressed by various theorists (Fairbairn, 1952; Guntrip, 1971; Kernberg, 1976; Kohut, 1972, 1977; Winnicott, 1965) who have spearheaded advances in psychoanalytic theory. According to these authors, the "internalization" of the therapist as a "good object" is crucial for significant psychotherapeutic change. The present writer (Strupp, 1969, 1973), among others, has likewise stressed the importance of the patient's identification with the therapist, which occurs in all forms of psychotherapy. Since the internalization of "bad objects" has made the patient "ill," therapy succeeds to the extent that the therapist becomes internalized as a "good object." However, since the patient tends to remain loyal to the early objects of his childhood, defending their internalizations against modification, therapy inevitably becomes a struggle. Even from this cursory sketch it is apparent that patients' amenability to therapy, that is, their ability to form a therapeutic alliance, is importantly determined by the quality of their early interpersonal relations.

Thus, the quality of the patient-therapist relationship and of the alliance as it manifests itself throughout the interaction appears to be a highly significant prognostic indicator of the forces working in favor of, or in opposition to, progress in therapy. Accordingly, it behooves clinicians and researchers to scrutinize the therapeutic alliance as well as its determinants.

Short-term Psychotherapy: The Wave of the Future?

The question of whether it is possible to shorten the course of psychotherapy, preferably without loss of its effectiveness, has been with us for some time. No sooner had Freud evolved and perfected psychoanalysis—he was straightforward about its length and demands (in those days, nine months to a year!)—than innovators, notably Ferenczi and Rank (1925), began to explore the possibility of shortening it. Freud was ambivalent about these attempts, and the general trend—from psychoanalysis and client-centered therapy to behavior therapy—has always been for treatment to become longer as a therapeutic system developed. Within psychoanalysis, efforts to experiment with the "standard technique" never ceased. Alexander and French's work in the 1940s (1946) was remarkably creative, and while it unleashed a flood of criticism by the establishment, it was far ahead of its time. Today short-term psychotherapy, which includes but is by no means coextensive with crisis intervention, is receiving renewed attention. It may well become the wave of the future. The following are some major reasons for this possibility:

1. Whether openly acknowledged or not, the vast amount of psychotherapy being done today is in fact time-limited (Garfield, 1978). This is particularly true of the clinical work done at outpatient clinics and community mental-health centers; private practitioners, too, are becoming aware that open-ended psychotherapy, following the classical psychoanalytic model, is impractical and unfeasible in the vast majority of instances. In general, the field is overcoming the prejudice that time-limited psychotherapy is superficial therapy, that it is somehow inferior, or an undesirable compromise dictated by circumstances.

2. The search for hard evidence supporting Freud's claim that psychoanalysis, as distinguished from other forms of psychotherapy, produces radical reconstructive personality changes has not borne fruit (Fisher & Greenberg, 1977). By contrast, in our cost-conscious, consumer-oriented society, which is becoming increasingly interested in making psychotherapy available to larger segments of the population, the search for econom-

ical treatments has become markedly intensified. With insurance companies and the government becoming partners in the therapeutic enterprise, there has been a new insistence on efficient modes of treatment whose results can be demonstrated and documented.

3. From the research standpoint it has become obvious that short-term therapy is the only modality that can be effectively researched. While this fact has often been seen as an unwanted limitation, we now recognize that time-limited therapy affords the researcher challenging and unmatched opportunities to learn about the process and outcome of psychotherapy regardless of its form or length. Finally, there have been some promising advances in short-term therapy that strongly suggest that we are only on the threshold of exploring its potentialities.

Despite these promising developments, there remains, as Butcher and Koss (1978) document, a lack of solid knowledge on almost every point one cares to mention: the kinds of patients for whom a particular form of time-limited psychotherapy may be suitable as well as those for whom it may be contraindicated; the kinds of therapeutic changes one may reasonably anticipate and work toward; the most appropriate techniques for reaching these goals; identification of the "active ingredients;" the training and experience a short-term therapist should possess; and the necessary procedures for bringing about an optimal match between a suitable patient and an appropriate therapist. If, as a researcher and as a clinician, one is looking for challenges, no richer ones can be found anywhere.

Furthermore, there is a vast hiatus between what is taught and what is practiced. In the traditional training programs for psychiatrists and clinical psychologists, scant attention is usually paid to the realities of time-limited treatment. Instead, the model that is being taught implies the availability of unlimited time and therapeutic resources. To be more specific: How many young therapists are being taught how to formulate a realistic therapeutic objective for a given patient, how to assess the patient's personality structure in relation to the presenting complaint and in relation to a reasonably specific objective, how to gear therapeutic techniques to the achievement of these objectives, and how to assess whether these goals have been reached? How does one go about identifying a "dynamic focus?" What kinds of activity should one engage in once therapy gets under way? What is the relative promise of particular techniques? What procedures and maneuvers should be avoided, because they are either potentially unproductive or possibly even harmful? These are but a few of the questions that training, practice, and research must address.

There is a great need for a new realism in psychotherapy, a new awareness of what is feasible and practicable. This means that we must deepen and extend our knowledge of the therapeutic process and its outcome. In short, we must infuse the therapeutic enterprise, time-limited or otherwise, with the best knowledge from clinical experience and research. We must become increasingly serious about what psychotherapy can and cannot do. As this process gains momentum, we may have to abandon some cherished notions from the past and we may have to become more modest about our activities. In so doing, we may also evolve a profession that commands increasing respect from the public and one in which we ourselves as practitioners can take greater pride.

The message is by now loud and clear that psychotherapy research must be geared increasingly to clinical realities. In other words, research must provide practicing clinicians useful answers to the key questions: What specific outcomes may be expected when a specific form of treatment is applied to a particular patient with particular problems (Bergin & Strupp, 1972; Kiesler, 1971; Paul, 1969)?

The strategic, technical, and methodological problems that must be confronted along this route have been discussed in considerable detail by a number of researchers and require no reiteration (Bergin & Strupp, 1972; Butcher & Koss, 1978; Fiske et al., 1970; Garfield & Bergin, 1978; Kiesler, 1971; Strupp, 1978).

Conclusion

In conclusion, I wish to restate some implications of the propostion that we need methodologically sophisticated research that is clinically relevant, in the sense that the goal of research is to improve clinical practice.

1. Analogue studies are increasingly becoming of questionable value. Instead we must study genuine patients with real problems. Also, the treatment must serve a real function in the patients' lives; that is, it must be sought and desired by the

candidates, who in turn must have a real commitment to its course and outcome. As research has progressed, there are now compelling reasons for rejecting designs involving volunteers, quasi-treatments, and many laboratory studies. Conversely, the yield of "true" studies of therapy is potentially much greater than any other investment one could name.

2. The isolation of the active ingredients in time-limited as well as other forms of therapy remains one of the most significant research tasks, and its solution, as I have maintained over the years (Strupp, 1973a, 1973b), will mark the most important advance in therapy research. Such advances will place in perspective the relative contribution of nonspecific factors and cast new light on the potential utility of the many new techniques that are presented, often with great fanfare, to the public every year.

3. Furthermore, there is the growing importanc of the therapeutic or working alliance; that is, the quality of the relationship between patient and therapist, which in my view determines the fate of the therapeutic undertaking. Studied here must be those characteristics of patients that enable them to collaborate effectively with a therapist, the characteristics of therapists that make it possible to harness the forces working in favor or against therapy, and the therapeutic management of the dynamics of the patient-therapist interaction upon which treatment outcomes crucially depend.

4. On the basis of my experience in the Vanderbilt Psychotherapy Research Project (Strupp & Hadley, 1979), I am increasingly impressed with the limited utility of traditional research designs involving group comparisons. Such comparisons undeniably represent a first step, but they are only a beginning. Clinicians' skepticism about the value of this research strategy is well taken since it typically obscures precisely those things they most urgently need to know—the dynamic fate of the idiosyncratic patient-therapist dyad. My recommendation here is a stepwise procedure, consisting of traditional group comparisons to be followed by creative analyses of the *process* of individual patient-therapist dyads.[1] Such a combination appears to be one of the best ways for pursuing clinically meaningful research, since it takes advantage of the unique value of $N = 1$ studies, while guarding against faulty inference.

5. Renewed and more incisive attention must be directed at patient variables and their impact upon the selection of a suitable form of therapy, its course, and outcome. A salient example is the patient's amenability, or conversely, resistance, to a particular form of treatment. Categorizations in terms of phenotypical "problems" or "targets" are too crude, and it has long been known that traditional diagnostic categories are not particularly helpful. There is still too much research in which such variables as patients' motivation for therapy, expectancies, and the array of characterological variables that determine a patient's ability and willingness to enter into a therapeutic alliance are ignored. If progress is to be made in selecting the right kind of patient for the right kind of treatment—a task I consider of signal importance—we must provide the clinician with tools for accomplishing these ends. In this respect, the search for *single* variables, within the patient or the therapist, as powerful predictors of outcome has essentially proven futile (Garfield, 1978; Parloff et al., 1978). Instead, we must evolve more complex models of research that take account of idiographic factors inherent in the interaction of a particular patient with a particular therapist. Research focused on factors entering into the therapeutic alliance, in my view, is one such approach.

6. Our knowledge of therapist characteristics is still woefully inadequate (Parloff et al., 1978). My own view, which first received indirect empirical support in a large analogue study (Strupp, 1960), has remained essentially unaltered: I consider the quality of the therapist's commitment and caring as an absolutely necessary but not sufficient condition for therapeutic change. Added to it must be technical expertise which enables therapists, particularly in dealing with deeply engrained neurotic and characterological problems, to maximize their effectiveness. Conversely, I am becoming increasingly skeptical about abstract research on the effectiveness of therapeutic techniques. Thus, I see relatively little promise in

---

[1]The vast majority of process measures have not provided the kind of enrichment in knowledge I have in mind (Orlinsky & Howard, 1978). Many of the earlier approaches have been too simplistic, and they have failed to tap those qualities in the patient-therapist interaction that determine its individual course and outcome. Another stumbling block has been the crudeness of outcome measures and related problems. These shortcomings, coupled with constantly shifting patterns of human adaptation, have conspired to yield the blurred picture that is before us.

efforts to compare different technical approaches per se. This assertion should not be construed as synonymous with the position (Frank, 1974) that common factors in all forms of psychotherapy account for the largest segment of the variance in therapeutic change; instead I propose that the amalgam of technical skills and personal qualities in a particular therapist represents the key to the "active ingredients" in all forms of psychotherapy. In this respect I continue to believe that the psychoanalytic approach, particularly the skillful analysis of transference problems in the here and now of the therapeutic relationship, has a great deal to offer. Since I am thinking here primarily of persistent neurotic patterns that in my experience typically underlie focal conflicts, I am forced to conclude that time-limited psychotherapy that has such analyses (and associated working through) as its goal cannot really be brief (to name an arbitrary figure: say, less than six months or even a year). In keeping with the foregoing, I believe that short-range therapeutic improvements capitalize to a much greater extent upon the curative effects of the common, nonspecific factors. What is needed at this point is research to subject these assertions to empirical test.

7. Concerted efforts must be made to develop a set of standard measures consonant with and responsive to the requirements that have been delineated. Until the ideal battery is developed, we may have to settle for a carefully chosen set of existing instruments (see the recommendations set forth by Waskow & Parloff, 1975). In the long run, however, it will be necessary for clinicians and researchers to join forces in developing a set of measures that embody to a fuller extent than do existing instruments the insights we have gained in recent years. This will be a major undertaking, and it will be demanding in terms of time, money, and energy. In light of society's increasing interest in evaluating the utility, cost-effectiveness, and value of all psychological treatments as well as their safety and potential harmfulness (Strupp, Hadley, & Gomes-Schwartz, 1977), there is no time like the present to mount such a project. The end result, will be a vastly improved set of procedures and measures that will for the first time bring diagnosis in line with treatment and outcome. These will be the tools that, in conjunction with appropriate research, will enable us to make more conclusive and authoritative statements about psychotherapy, its *modus operandi*, range of utility when the

conditions have been specified, and its value for the individual, the mental-health professions, and society.

8. Another problem that has still not been squarely confronted is the meaning and significance of an observed or measured change. Clinical significance is obviously not identical with statistical significance; a decrement of ten points on the Depression Scale of the MMPI may be significantly different from chance, but it is quite another matter whether the individual patient regards it as personally significant. Furthermore, a given change may be valued highly by one patient but not by another. The difficulties alluded to are part of the growing realization among clinicians and researchers that we must seek to individualize assessments of therapeutic change (Bergin & Lambert, 1978; Strupp & Bergin, 1969).

Furthermore, we must take more seriously the subtlety of many therapeutic changes which continues to be missed by our still primitive measuring instruments and assessment procedures. For example, a treated patient may have shifted his or her cognitive framework and achieved a more realistic self-concept. Perhaps the patient has lowered perfectionistic standards for him or herself and has developed greater frustration tolerance, ego strength, and the like. Such changes clearly are subtle; they are intrapsychic and may not be reflected in overt behavior. Thus, they may not be detected by most of our measuring instruments. Nonetheless, for the patient they may be extraordinarily real, and they may reflect true therapeutic change regardless of any numerical values derived from questionnaires, or other test instruments. Of course, one cannot prove that such changes are a function of therapy and that they could not have been brought about in other ways. But I am prepared to argue that perhaps the most important therapeutic changes represent a change in "outlook," an altered view of oneself and one's place in the world. At times such changes may be reflected in responses to structured questionnaire items, but often they are more impressively demonstrated by spontaneous comments a patient may make about his therapy experience in a broader context. To the patient (as well as to the therapist), such comments are extraordinarily real, regardless of whether they can be documented by a test or scale. The lesson to be learned is that we must devise techniques that are appropriately sensitive to clinically and humanly significant changes; concomitantly, we must abandon a blind faith in numbers, scores, and the statistical paraphernalia associated with them.

9. Finally, researchers and clinicians must join hands in the critical task of defining and measuring the competence of psychotherapists. Although serious questions have been raised concerning the quality of training among psychotherapists, there is as yet little agreement, let alone hard evidence, about what constitutes competence. We do know that individuals practicing today typically show a wide diversity of backgrounds; some have extensive didactic training and a wealth of clinical experience while others are grossly deficient in formal preparation. Training programs reflect widely divergent standards. Although professional organizations have formulated criteria, many individuals who call themselves therapists are ill equipped to assume professional responsibilities. Certification and licensing laws now in effect in most states are a salutary development but they are difficult to enforce and guarantee only minimal standards of competence.

Since personal qualities are so thoroughly intertwined with technical skills, we must find ways and means to objectify and evaluate the kinds of therapeutic interactions a given therapist is likely to create. Some patients, as part of their disturbance, have an uncanny ability to evoke anger, hostility, rejection, and other adverse reactions from certain therapists. Consider also the range of problems created by the lack of professional consensus on what constitutes reasonably skillful performance, even within the framework of a particular theoretical orientation. These are but a few of the staggering difficulties confronting a field that society has come to view with growing skepticism.

When all is said and done, public opinion is less likely to be swayed by yet another controlled comparison between therapy A and therapy B than by the seriousness and commitment of scientists and professionals to their discipline, including particularly the expansion of scientific knowledge.

References

Alexander, F., & French, T. M. *Psychoanalytic therapy: Principles and applications.* New York: Ronald Press, 1946.

Andrews, J. Psychotherapy of phobias. *Psychological Bulletin*, 1966, **66**, 455–480.

Bergin, A. E., & Lambert, M. J. The evaluation of therapeutic outcomes. In S. L. Garfield & A. E. Bergin (Eds.), *Handbook of psychotherapy and behavior change.* (2nd ed.) New York: Wiley, 1978.

Bergin, A. E., & Strupp, H. H. *Changing frontiers in the science of psychotherapy.* Chicago: Aldine-Atherton, 1972.

Butcher, J., & Koss, M. Research on brief and crisis-oriented psychotherapies. In S. L. Garfield & A. E. Bergin (Eds.), *Handbook of psychotherapy and behavior change.* (2nd ed.) New York: Wiley, 1978.

DiLoreto, A. O. *Comparative psychotherapy: An experimental analysis.* Chicago: Aldine-Atherton, 1971.

Eysenck, H. J. The effects of psychotherapy: An evaluation. *Journal of Consulting Psychology*, 1952, **16**, 319–324.

Fairbairn, R. *Object relations theory of the personality.* New York: Basic Books, 1952.

Ferenczi, S., & Rank, O. *The development of psychoanalysis.* New York: Nervous and Mental Disease Publishing, 1925.

Fisher, S., & Greenberg, R. P. *The scientific credibility of Freud's theories and therapy.* New York: Basic Books, 1977.

Fiske, D. W., Hunt, H. F., Luborsky, L., Orne, M. T., Parloff, M. B. Reiser, M. F., & Tuma, A. H. Planning of research on effectiveness of psychotherapy. *Archives of General Psychiatry*, 1970, **22**, 22–32.

Frank, J. D. *Persuasion and healing.* (2nd ed.) Baltimore: Johns Hopkins University Press, 1973.

Frank, J. D. Therapeutic components of psychotherapy. *Journal of Nervous and Mental Disease*, 1974, **159**, 325–342.

Freud, S. On psychotherapy. In *The Standard Edition of the Complete Works of Sigmund Freud.* Vol. 7, London: Hogarth, 1963.

Freud, S. Analytic therapy (1916). In *The Standard Edition of the Complete Works of Sigmund Freud*, Vol. 16. London: Hogarth, 1963.

Freud, S. Transference (1916). Introductory lectures on psycho-analysis. In *The Standard Edition of the Complete Psychological Works of Sigmund Freud*, Vol. 16. London: Hogarth, 1963.

Garfield, S. L. Research on client variables in psychotherapy. In S. L. Garfield & A. E. Bergin (Eds.), *Handbook of psychotherapy and behavior change.* (2nd ed.) New York: Wiley, 1978.

Garfield, S. L. & Bergin, A. E. (Eds.), *Handbook of psychotherapy and behavior change.* (2nd ed.) New York: Wiley, 1978.

Garfield, S. L., Prager, R. A., & Bergin, A. E. Evaluating outcome in psychotherapy: A hardy perennial. *Journal of Consulting and Clinical Psychology*, 1971, **37**, 320–322.

Goldstein, A. P., & Stein, N. *Prescriptive psychotherapies.* New York: Pergamon, 1976.

Guntrip, H. *Psychoanalytic theory, and the self.* New York: Basic Books, 1971.

Greenson, R. *The technique and practice of psychoanalysis.* New York: International Universities Press, 1967.

Hadley, S. W., & Strupp, H. H. Contemporary views of negative effects in psychotherapy. *Archives of Gen-*

eral Psychiatry, 1976, **33**, 1,291–1,302.

Hartley, D. E., & Strupp, H. H. The therapeutic alliance: Its relationship to outcome in brief psychotherapy. In J. Masling (Ed.), *Advances in the experimental investigation of psychoanalysis*, in press.

Hoehn-Saric, R., Frank, J. D., Imber, S. D., Nash, E. H., Stone, A. R., & Battle, C. C. Systematic preparation of patients for psychotherapy: I. Effects on therapy behavior and outcome. *Journal of Psychiatric Research*, 1964, **2**, 267–281.

Holt, R. R., & Luborsky, L. *Personality patterns of psychiatrists: A study in selection techniques.* Vol. 1. New York: Basic Books, 1958.

Horwitz, L. *Clinical prediction in psychotherapy.* New York: Jason Aronson, 1974.

Kaplan, H. S. *The new sex therapy: Active treatment of sexual dysfunctions.* New York: Brunner/Mazel, 1974.

Kiesler, D. J. Some myths of psychotherapy research and the search for a paradigm. *Psychological Bulletin*, 1966, **65**, 110–136.

Kiesler, D. J. Experimental designs in psychotherapy research. In A. E. Bergin & S. L. Garfield (Eds.), *Handbook of psychotherapy and behavior change: An empirical analysis.* New York: Wiley, 1971.

Kernberg, O. F. *Object relations theory and clinical psychoanalysis.* New York: Jason Aronson, 1976.

Kernberg, O. F., Burnstein, E. D., Coyne, L., Appelbaum, A., Horowitz, L., & Voth, H. *Psychotherapy and psychoanalysis: Final report of the Menninger Foundation's psychotherapy research project.* Topeka, Kan.: The Menninger Foundation, 1972.

Knight, R. P. Evaluation of the results of psychoanalytic therapy. *American Journal of Psychiatry*, 1941, **98**, 434–446.

Kohut, H. *The analysis of the self.* New York: International Universities Press, 1972.

Kohut, H. *The restoration of the self.* New York: International Universities Press, 1977.

Langs, R. *The technique of psychoanalytic psychotherapy.* New York: Jason Aronson, 1973.

Luborsky, L., Singer, B., & Luborsky, L. Comparative studies of psychotherapies: Is it true that "Everybody has won and all must have prizes?" *Archives of General Psychiatry*, 1975, **32**, 995–1,008.

Marks, I. Behavioral psychotherapy of adult neurosis. In S. L. Garfield & A. E. Bergin (Eds.), *Handbook of psychotherapy and behavior change: An empirical analysis.* (2nd ed.) New York: Wiley, 1978.

Menninger, K. *Theory of psychoanalytic technique.* New York: Basic Books, 1958.

Menninger, K. A., & Holzman, P. S. *Theory of psychoanalytic techniques.* (2nd ed.) New York: Basic Books, 1973.

Orlinsky, D. E., & Howard, K. I. The relation of process to outcome in psychotherapy. In S. L. Garfield & A. E. Bergin (Eds.), *Handbook of psychotherapy and behavior change.* (2nd ed.) New York: Wiley, 1978.

Orne, M. T., & Wender, P. H. Anticipatory socialization for psychotherapy: Method and rationale. *American Journal of Psychiatry*, 1968, **124**, 1,202–1,212.

Parloff, M. B., Waskow, I. E., & Wolfe, B. E. Research on therapy variables in relation to process and outcome. In S. L. Garfield & A. E. Bergin (Eds.), *Handbook of psychotherapy and behavior change.* (2nd ed.) New York: Wiley, 1978.

Paul, G. L. *Insight versus desensitization in psychotherapy: An experiment in anxiety reduction.* Stanford, Calif.: Stanford University Press, 1966.

Paul, G. L. Insight versus desensitization in psychotherapy two years after termination. *Journal of Consulting Psychology*, 1967, **31**, 333–348.

Paul, G. L. Behavior modification research: design and tactics. In C. M. Franks (Ed.), *Behavior therapy: Appraisal and status.* New York: McGraw-Hill, 1969.

Rogers, C. R. The necessary and sufficient conditions of therapeutic personality change. *Journal of Consulting Psychology*, 1957, **21**, 95–103.

Rogers, C. R., & Dymond, R. F. *Psychotherapy and personality change.* Chicago: University of Chicago Press, 1954.

Shapiro, A. K., & Morris, L. A. Placebo effects in medical and psychological therapies. In S. L. Garfield & A. E. Bergin (Eds.), *Handbook of psychotherapy and behavior change: An empirical analysis.* (2nd ed.) New York: Wiley, 1978.

Sloane, R. B., Staples, F. R., Cristol, A. H., Yorkston, N. J., & Whipple, K. *Psychotherapy versus behavior therapy.* Cambridge, Mass.: Harvard University Press, 1975.

Smith, M. L., Glass, G. V., & Miller, T. I. *The benefits of psychotherapy.* Baltimore: Johns Hopkins University Press, 1980.

Stewart, R. L. Psychoanalysis and psychoanalytic psychotherapy. In H. I. Kaplan, A. M. Freedman, & B. J. Sadock (Eds.), *Comprehensive textbook of psychiatry*, Vol. 3. Baltimore: Williams & Wilkins, 1980.

Strupp, H. H. *Psychotherapists in action: Explorations of the therapist's contribution to the treatment process.* New York: Grune & Stratton, 1960.

Strupp, H. H. Psychoanalytic therapy of the individual. In J. Marmor (Ed.), *Modern psychoanalysis.* New York: Basic Books, 1968.

Strupp, H. H. Toward a specification of teaching and learning in psychotherapy. *Archives of General Psychiatry*, 1969, **21**, 203–212.

Strupp, H. H. On the basic ingredients of psychotherapy. *Journal of Consulting and Clinical Psychology*, 1973, **11**, 1–8. (a)

Strupp, H. H. Toward a reformulation of the psychotherapeutic influence. *International Journal of Psychiatry*, 1973, **11**, 347–354. (b)

Strupp, H. H. Psychotherapy research and practice: An overview. In S. L. Garfield & A. E. Bergin (Eds.), *Handbook of psychotherapy and behavior change.* (2nd ed.) New York: Wiley, 1978.

Strupp, H. H. Success and failure in time-limited psychotherapy: A systematic comparison of two cases (Comparison 1). *Archives of General Psychiatry*, 1980, **37**, 595–603. (a)

Strupp, H. H. Success and failure in time-limited psychotherapy: A systematic comparison of two cases (Comparison 2). *Archives of General Psychiatry*, 1980, **37**, 708–716. (b)

Strupp, H. H. Success and failure in time-limited psychotherapy: With special reference to the performance of a lay counselor. *Archives of General Psychiatry*, 1980, **37**, 831–841. (c)

Strupp, H. H. Success and failure in time-limited psychotherapy: Further evidence (Comparison 4). *Archives of General Psychiatry*, 1980, **37**, 947–954. (d)

Strupp, H. H., & Bergin, A. E. Some empirical and conceptual bases for coordinated research in psychotherapy. *International Journal of Psychiatry*, 1969, 7, 18–90.

Strupp, H. H., & Bloxom, A. L. Preparing lower-class patients for group psychotherapy: Development and evaluation of a role-induction film. *Journal of Consulting and Clinical Psychology*, 1973, **41**, 373–384.

Strupp, H. H., Fox, R. E., & Lessler, K. *Patients view their psychotherapy.* Baltimore: Johns Hopkins University Press, 1969.

Strupp, H. H., & Hadley, S. W. A tripartite model of mental health and therapeutic outcomes. *American Psychologist*, 1977, **32**, 187–196.

Strupp, H. H., & Hadley, S. W. Specific versus nonspe-

cific factors in psychotherapy: A controlled study of outcome. *Archives of General Psychiatry*, 1979, **36**, 1,125–1,136.

Strupp, H. H., Hadley, S. W., & Gomes-Schwartz, B. *Psychotherapy for better or worse: The problem of negative effects.* New York: Jason Aronson, 1977.

Sullivan, H. S. *Conceptions of modern psychiatry.* New York: Norton, 1953.

Waskow, I. E., & Parloff, M. B. (Eds.). *Psychotherapy change measures.* Rockville, Md.: National Institute of Mental Health, 1975.

Wachtel, P. L. *Psychoanalysis and behavior therapy.* New York: Basic Books, 1977.

Winnicott, D. W. *The family and individual development.* New York: Basic Books, 1965.

25 PHENOMENOLOGICAL-EXISTENTIAL PSYCHOTHERAPY

Constance T. Fischer
William F. Fischer

This is the first clinical psychology handbook that includes a full chapter on phenomenological psychotherapy. The approach is indeed still young, with its founding clinical publications in North America dating back just 25 years (e.g., Lyons, 1963; May, 1958, 1964; Strasser, 1963; Straus, 1963, 1966; Van Kaam, 1959, 1966a, 1966b). Its theoreticians and its practitioner-spokespersons are still few, although clinicians are increasingly interested in learning more about phenomenological psychology. This chapter is written for those colleagues, rather than as an update for those of us who specialize in this approach. Hence, we have opted for broad coverage of foundational, consensual themes rather than for detailed presentation of representative therapists' understandings of their work. (See Valle & King, 1978, chapter 14, for succinct summaries of Binswanger, Boss, Frankl, May, and Van den Berg; and see Yalom, 1980, for an overview of existential therapy.) Rather than developing a new characterization of this therapy, we also have chosen to orient this chapter toward undoing the prevailing misunderstandings of phenomenological-existential psychotherapy.

The first section presents a series of clarifications of the phenomenological-existential approach. Since philosophy rather than techniques characterizes this psychotherapy, the major section of the chapter describes the philosophy of science and the philosophical anthropology that undergird all phenomenological-existential approaches. A relatively short section then addresses the therapeutic relationship that necessarily flows from that undergirding. Several representative therapeutic interventions are described. The next section addresses the qualitative, empirical research approach that marks phenomenological-existential psychology's development from a philosophically based discipline to a science. The general research approach and the circumstances under which it is useful are reviewed. Examples of basic and clinical research are provided. The chapter concludes by summarizing the status of phenomenological-existential psychotherapy.

Preliminary Clarifications

The following two notions of phenomenology, although legitimate in their own contexts, are *not* what we are concerned with in this chapter. The first is the medical meaning of the term "phenomenology," namely the outward appearance or visible symptoms of a disease or disorder, in contrast to its etiology. For example, one may speak of the phenomenology of schizophrenia, referring to the presence of hallucinations, loose associations, and perceptual distortion, and then go on to say that there may be different courses of developing those apparently similar symptoms, such as dopamine abnormalities, stimulus deprivation during infancy, or double-bind family communications. The second meaning of "phenomenology" also refers to appearances, this time in terms of an individual's own experience and perceptions. Here, "the phenomenology of schizophrenia" would refer to what it is like to be schizophrenic. Both meanings harken back to Kant's distinction between *phenomena* (things as they appear to us) and *noumena* (things as they really are).

Philosophical phenomenology begins with these latter *phenomenal* events, and studies them in their own right to gain understandings of the ways we humans participate in what "appears to" us. This study is in pursuit of the nature of human knowing and of human knowledge, as well as of ontological "Being." Phenomenological *psychology* studies across actual beings to identify patterns of construing and relating to one's world, for example, brain-damaged (Dunn, 1974) and drugged ways of relating (Deegan, 1981). It also studies everyday moments of construing and relating to one's world, such as when one is angry (Stevick, 1971), anxious (W. Fischer, 1974, 1982), learning (Colazzi, 1969), or jealous (Ramm, 1979). As will be seen later, psychologists who identify with this orientation are grounded in a philosophy of science, a method for attending to phenomena, and in a qualitative research tradition. It is this grounding that is referred to by the term "phenomenology," the first half of our hyphenated title. But of course the clinician, while practicing psychotherapy, neither philosophizes nor conducts formal research. Psychotherapy addresses individual lives as such; the person's phenomenal world is attended to in terms of its significance for the individual's life. The therapist's concerns and dealings are necessarily existential; hence the second half of our hyphenated title. The order of the terms, however, is a matter of choice. They easily could be reversed to give priority to existence as the subject matter of phenomenology. Moreover, some theories of existence predate the Husserlian and Heideggerian historical foundations of contemporary phenomenology. Finally, many existential psychologists base their practices on existential philosophy

without concerning themselves with phenomenology.

Although some practitioners have drawn only on partial aspects of existential notions, particularly Sartrean ones, those who have developed a thorough-going theoretical approach do not agree with the typical survey textbook's representation of existential theory: (1) It is true that our lives are not totally determined by natural events; we shape as well as are shaped by circumstances as we act in accordance with our understanding of them. However, "free will" is a misnomer. We are severely constrained by our biological, biographical, and environmental situations. (2) We cannot help but give meaning to circumstances, and hence bear responsibility for subsequent action. However, Sartre's emphasis on this "condemnation" to choice, and to concomitant angst, dread, and the like, is not essential to, or even typical of, existential theory or therapeutic practice. (3) The much-referenced "here and now" is indeed the place where therapeutic intervention occurs. Regardless of how a person arrived at a current crossroad, it is his or her present values, perceptions, habits, and so on, that constrain choice. Nevertheless, phenomenologically grounded therapists, no less than others, find that exploration of the past enrichens and clarifies the present, and indeed can assist the client to see that his or her present is understandable given that past, and to see that alternative courses can now be undertaken.

No particular techniques are essential for phenomenological-existential psychotherapy. Therapists, of course, have contributed diverse techniques such as Frankl's (1962) paradoxical intention and Rogers' (1942) mirroring. However, there are no essential or even prevailing exercises akin to free association in psychoanalysis or to reinforcement in behavior modification. Like these therapies, however, the methodological approach of this one too is characterized by its philosophical anthropology — its prepsychological understanding of the nature of being human. Its therapeutic relationship and its interventional techniques have to do with being open to uniquely human realities. Within that disciplined openness, phenomenological-existential therapists are methodologically eclectic and theoretically pluralistic. The therapist may make use, for example, of desensitization procedures, values clarification exercises, or free association. Likewise, the therapist may draw on the developmental insights of Freud,

Erikson, Sullivan, and others, as well as on contemporary social science research findings.

Like all theorists of therapy, phenomenological-existential authors understand how other therapies actually work in terms of their own theory. Barton (1974) has created a particularly plausible description of the same (fictitious) woman going through three therapies—Freudian, Jungian, and Rogerian, each portrayed sympathetically. Barton shows that each approach works, even as it contributes to the way both therapist and patient give shape to and cope with the presenting problems. Like most phenomenologically grounded therapists, Barton gives credence to the techniques and insights of alternative theories, but is wary of possible inclinations to reduce human affairs to mechanisms, whether biological, environmental, or interactionist. These therapists are equally wary of left-over "sixties" self-help optimism.

Any reader who feels that the above wariness is based on a false image of psychology perhaps should be reminded that phenomenology and existentialism arose as reactions against early and mid-twentieth century physicalism, particularly the fact that the social sciences were modeling themselves after the physical sciences. Today, psychology in general and psychoanalysis and behavior modification in particular have broadened their language and practices to the point that most psychologists, especially clinicians, do not regard themselves as absolute determinists. Nevertheless, mainstream psychology has not developed a philosophy of science that explicitly and systematically takes into account humans' differences from other objects of nature. Likewise, many of humanistic psychology's attitudes have been absorbed into practice without explicit revision and integration at theoretical levels. Phenomenology does provide a viable foundation for such goals.

Phenomenology

Psychoanalysis and then early behavior modification were both grounded in prepsychological conceptions of being human. As mentioned, these conceptions were of people as *homo natura*—things of nature, explicable in terms of, and reducible to, the laws of physical and chemical bodies. *Homo natura* required no principles of understanding beyond those required for any object. Re-

actions against this state of affairs arose independently in Europe and North America. Its advocates, whether individually or in groups, were often unaware of each other's works, at least initially. Further, the specific themes of the revolt—that is, the particular features of the natural scientific philosophies that were rejected—varied from theorist to theorist. For example, in North America, precursors of phenomenology such as Rogers (1942) rejected the analyst's exclusive preoccupation with the patient's past, and questioned the assumption that human life is comprehensible as a constant struggle to control one's animal nature. Twenty or so years later, the humanistic psychology movement in North America, through its multiple spokespersons (e.g., Bugenthal, 1965; Severin, 1965), protested not so much psychoanalysis as American academic empiricism, especially its emphasis in theory and practice on quantification, classification, and explanation solely in terms of antecedent events. In Europe, psychiatrists, such as Binswanger (1963), while accepting Freud's interest in unconscious dynamics and in associative methods of exploring them, explicitly rejected his natural scientific philosophical anthropology (theory of the nature of "man").

The sources of inspiration for these various reactions, which were to become known collectively as Third-Force psychology, differed significantly. Rogers' thought seems to have been an expression of his commitments to "Protestant individualism" and "democratic humanism" (Barton, 1974). The European psychiatrists, Boss (1963), Minkowski (1970), and Straus (1963, 1966) were profoundly influenced by the philosopher Husserl's (1969, 1970) phenomenological method of reflection and findings. The closely related work of Binswanger (1963) was influenced by the existential analyses authored by the phenomenological philosopher, Heidegger (1962). A third group, best exemplified by the German psychiatrist Frankl (1962, 1966), was inspired by existential thinkers such as Kierkegaard (1954), Buber (1965) and Marcel (1965), all of whom were concerned with the spiritual as well as the psychological dimensions of existence. By now the products of these varying early reactions are fairly well homogenized in the thought and work of phenomenological-existential therapists. Of course most psychologists of this orientation do have preferred resource authors, such as the French philosopher Ricoeur (1966) or the French psychologist-philosopher Merleau-Ponty (1962,

1963) for foundational matters, and psychotherapists such as the American Farber (1966) or May (1979) for discussions of existential issues pertinent to theory.

We should offer two further preliminary clarifications before finally addressing the Husserlean philosophy and the existential anthropology that ground existential therapy, either historically as inspiration or in later searches for broader foundations. First, there are practitioners who characterize their orientation as phenomenological and/or existential, but who have only borrowed selected notions or practices. This is akin to practitioners who refer to themselves as behavior modifiers, even though they have not studied how their borrowed practices are based in a philosophical foundation or in empirical research. Second, the majority of practitioners who participated in humanistic psychology's heyday probably were what we might call phenomenalists rather than phenomenologists. That is, they were interested in an individual's immediate experience, usually on the assumption that its expression would lead to growth. Except for a very few researchers (e.g., Severin, 1965), there was little interest in studying phenomenal worlds to build a systematic body of knowledge. Nevertheless, humanistic psychology's protests bear much responsibility for mainstream psychology's broadening its purview to include consciousness and purposiveness. Today's cognitive therapy probably would have been regarded as unscientific 15 years ago.

Husserl and Phenomenology

Edmund Husserl (1859–1938) is the founder of phenomenology and the philosopher upon whose shoulders most existential philosophers, as well as psychologists, stand. Our best way of describing what characterizes phenomenological-existential psychotherapy is to characterize Husserl's contribution, at least as it has been taken up by psychologists. For the reader who wishes to go beyond our highly schematic remarks, and to see what Husserl emphasized, we recommend *Husserl: An Analysis of His Phenomenology* (Ricoeur, 1967). Consciousness is that through which a person is present to his or her world. In other words, consciousness is relational, and it is a key distinguishing feature of human life. To study consciousness is to study how humans differ from other studiable objects. It is also to explore the nature of how humans participate in what they know of their world. Husserl,

himself an expert in mathematics, was particularly concerned that the natural sciences ignored the fact that we do not just go around discovering scientific truths that are independent of our questions. Further, there is no humanly experienceable or knowable world apart from human ways of relating to that world. Hence, Husserl argued that an adequate science required a preliminary study of consciousness. Between 1900 and 1938 Husserl undertook a systematic investigation of consciousness in most, if not all, of its different modalities, such as perception and judgment. In the course of his researches, he demonstrated the fundamentally relational character of human consciousness, and in that process developed and described the guiding principles of the phenomenological method of investigation.

We could say that consciousness is modes (e.g., perceiving, remembering, anticipating, thinking) and types (e.g., anxious, joyful, angry) of being in touch with the world. Of course, what we just referred to as "modes and types" always occur in unity, as in anxiously perceiving. Those pervasive hyphens in existential-phenomenological writing ("person-in-the-world," etc.) are an effort to capture the unity and relational character of consciousness. Much of the awkwardness of phenomenological writing similarly is due to efforts to evoke that relational unity. People are both separate from and yet already incorporative of their worlds. Existential literature sometimes refers to a person's "lived world" as a way of describing this relation that is not merely interactive. "Intentionality" is the philosophical term that points to this nature of consciousness as always consciousness of something, something that, for finite humans, can never be known except through human ways of relating. (The term "intentionality" only indirectly implies purposiveness; we necessarily relate to our worlds in terms of our projects.)

Consciousness is not necessarily self-reflective, that is, conscious of being in relation to something. In fact, consciousness is typically unreflective. For example, as one goes about one's day, one most often is not conscious of oneself *as* present to people, environments, or situations. However, consciousness is not adequately characterized as a trait, such as IQ or dependency. Neither is it a sorting machine or information processor. Above all, consciousness is not a container that could be said to have contents, as a piggy bank has pennies.

Husserl's major effort at clarifying the character of consciousness, however, was addressed to the pervasive inclination of his contemporaries to engage in what came to be known as "psychologism." Husserl's contemporaries were claiming that all presences to objects, others, and the world were mediated by mental representations located somewhere within the mind. They then claimed that without direct access to the world, all knowledge, judgments, and so on of consciousness were "merely psychological"—subjectivistic and dubious. Husserl pointed out that since his contemporaries, by their own argument, could not have direct access to the posited "mediations," their position that the knowledge of consciousness is dubious was itself vulnerable to their own condemnation. An incisive characterization of Husserl's critique of psychologism may be found in Zaner's *The Way of Phenomenology* (1970, pp. 51–62).

In the process of critiquing psychologism, Husserl realized that it was necessary to undertake a systematic study of experience, that is, of consciousness and of how the world appears to it. The method that he developed for this enterprise is known as the phenomenological method. Phenomenology *is* this method and the resulting studies. Of course, his followers have adapted his method to those particular phenomena that have been of interest to them. Still, we can delineate in simplified form the core themes that are present in most, if not all, of the method's variations.

First, a phenomenological method is employed when one seeks to describe and understand the essence of some phenomenon, i.e., the interrelated features without which it would not be what it is. For example, the phenomenon of remembering is re-presenting a past event, as past, from the perspective of the present. If one did not recognize the past event as past, as something one has experienced before and is not experiencing now for the first time, one would not be remembering.

Second, since the method is used when one seeks to understand rather than to demonstrate, explain, or assume, one attempts to suspend judgment about any preconceptions concerning the phenomenon. This suspension is known as "bracketing." For example, a phenomenologically oriented researcher who wants to understand what being anxious is does not presume in advance that it is really a "mental" event, or a physical/physiological event, or a fundamentally quantitatively measureable event. Instead, such a researcher begins with detailed descriptions of his or her own and others' actual experiences of being anxious. Every effort is made to allow the phenomenon, in

this case "being anxious," to become evident in its own right, as it was actually lived and experienced by the subject. In this way, its constituent meanings, whether they be affective, perceptual, bodily, behavioral, or whatever, can be thematized in their interrelationships. The phenomenon as a whole is described; since all described aspects are essential for the phenomenon to be whatever it is, no aspect is regarded as explanatory of the others.

Of course, researchers will not discover in their own or in their subjects' descriptions features that are not either known about or experienced by these persons. Such features might be the neurophysiology of anxiety, or infantile events that are available now only protatoxically. Nor are subjects aware of which aspects of their own reports will turn out to be fundamental to all accounts of the phenomenon. More will be said about research method later; for now it should be noted that the phenomenological method is devised for exploration of what Merleau-Ponty (1963) referred to as the human order. At other times we wish to know about the physical and biological orders, but they are not more real than the human world. Of course, whether or not our research subjects are aware of it, other orders are taken up within and are part of our lived worlds.

Third, the phenomenological method recognizes the fundamentally perspectival character of people's presences to phenomena. This statement is true of traditional experimental research, as well as of phenomenological studies. All research tools provide only partial, interest-laden, technique-bound access to events. The researcher is present to the phenomenon through only certain of its profiles, depending upon which of several modes of access to a phenomenon he or she utilizes. For example, the phenomenological researcher recognizes that being anxious appears somewhat differently to: (1) someone who is concerned with the possibility of becoming anxious, (2) someone who is reflectively living through it, (3) someone who can still vividly recall having been anxious in a situation, and (4) someone who is or has just been present to another person being anxious.

None of these modes of access or the profiles that they reveal is *a priori* the best; no single mode of access guarantees that it will offer "the real meaning" of being anxious. Further, no particular profile of being anxious is mutually exclusive of the others. The researcher asks: "What is revealed about the essential reality of being anxious in each of these profiles, through each of these modes of access?" The researcher describes the phenomenon so that what is revealed in each profile blends into what is revealed in the others. Almost needless to say, standard content analysis is inappropriate for this endeavor. Yes, the written results of the phenomenological method vary with the researcher, much as different authors of psychological assessment reports may write differently even while they agree about their findings. And yes, again not unlike an assessment, repetitions of the method and discussion among researchers do not exhaust what could be said or arrive at *the* best way of saying it. Since our access to phenomena is always perspectival, reality always remains partially ambiguous. This is not due to deficiency in method, but to the nature of human perception and knowledge.

We have stressed notions derived from Husserl because phenomenological-existential philosophy and psychology, at least in their present form, would not have been possible without Husserl's thought. The method provides a framework for a social science explicitly designed for humans, so that we need not rely totally on the framework designed by natural scientists. Phenomenology also provides a foundation for clinicians, one that is consistent with the existential anthropology of phenomenological-existential therapists.

Existential Anthropology

The following characterizations of human nature are found in, or are consistent with, the writings of the previously mentioned philosophers and psychiatrists, as well as with the writings and practices of contemporary North American existential psychotherapists. These perspectives on human nature were developed through bracketing prior conceptions about human functioning, and describing what was then evident.

First, the meanings and significances of one's existence are never given once and for all. Understandings of oneself, others, and the world emerge in the context of particular situations and one's current projects. One continuously re-creates those projects in light of the possibilities as well as the givens of one's existence (a particular body, parents, aging, etc.). To be a person means that one is engaged in a never to be completed task of discovering, positing, and making sense of one's existence. To be a person means that, in actions if not in words, one questions and is questioned by self, others, and the world. Although the questions

vary across developmental stages and from relationship to relationship (Am I a good child, student, spouse, parent, etc.?), the fundamental themes do not vary. They are lived, implicitly if not explicitly, as: What is the world about? Who am I? Who are you? Who have I been? Who can I become?

Second, to be human means that one has no choice but to act and to find meanings in one's actions. But options are restricted by circumstances, and are undertaken without either complete self-awareness or complete knowledge of the consequences. There are no guarantees of success, or even that one will continue to value earlier goals. Yet one recognizes at some level that one is inevitably engaged in a lifelong task for which one is irrevocably responsible.

Third, to be a person is to be in relation to others whether or not they are palpably present. Not only does one shape one's life under the influence of others, especially during formative years, one also comes to know oneself only in relation to others. One never exists first as an absolutely separate individual who subsequently comes to have relations with others. From birth until death we are embedded in and know ourselves in terms of a variety of relationships, whether these have as their singular or multiple themes love, hate, competition, cooperation, and the like. More concretely, I discover the other person's significance, as well as my own, in the ways that he or she calls or allows or demands me to be. For example, it is the child who in being a child calls the mother to be a mother. Relationships are not simple juxtapositions of discrete individuals; a marriage is not a man plus a woman. Rather, one's relation to the other is a mutually and reciprocally implicative phenomenon. Each way of being requires the other's and makes sense only in relation to it. It is for these reasons that the existentialist will ask: "Who does one call the other to be? Who does one demand that the other be? Who does one allow the other to be? How is one co-creating oneself in calling forth or demanding or allowing the other to be in those particular ways?"

Fourth, to be a person is to be an incarnate subject, a *unity* that cannot be adequately comprehended or conceptualized as the parallelistic, interactionistic, or epiphenomenalistic union of two substances, mental and physical. The living human body is itself a subject; it is itself a system of projects through which the meanings of situations are co-created. Could there be near or far if the human body were not self-moving? Could there be tall or short, high or low, if the human body were not itself statured, a being that attains its proper perspective by raising itself from the ground and standing on its feet? Could there be hot or cold, backward or forward, if the human body were not itself temperated and coronally asymmetrical? The questions can be multiplied almost indefinitely; the possible modes of being and dimensions of the human world are co-created by that world and the human body. Hence, a psychologically relevant description of the body can never be given in terms of physiology alone. A psychological account must characterize how the body affords, delimits, and participates in the possibilities of experiencing and acting. By the same token, a person is indeed a body. If not, how could he or she even encounter, let alone comprehend, him or herself, others, and the world in their corporeality? How could one ever experience one's self as visible, as beautiful, as strong, as tired, etc.? It is true that one may objectify one's body and treat it as a thing, just as one may objectify one's styles of approaching problematic situations and treat them as traits over which one has no control. But doing either denies one's subject side.

Psychopathology

All psychopathology involves disordered, restricted existence. The forms of psychopathology that have most interested existential therapists are those that the person has participated in bringing about. The four characteristics of such pathology which are described below are found in the writings of all phenomenological-existential authors, either explicitly in their theory or implicitly in their therapeutic practices. There are, of course, disagreements within the field, mostly about the nature of specific disorders such as schizophrenia, mania, and depression. The disagreements usually have to do with existentialists' inclinations to err on the side of emphasizing choice, just as other schools are inclined to err on the side of determinism. We will not attempt to review the literature on particular psychopathologies because of its complexities and because of space limitations.

The principles of phenomenology and existentialism are useful for understanding and helping people with the everyday difficulties that we all face, as well as for understanding and helping people faced with restricted existences that they were not responsible for bringing about, such as their own brain damage or mental retardation, or the loss of a loved person. The following features of psychopathology, in contrast, are those for which the individual bears etiological responsibility.

First, a psychopathologically disordered person is at an impasse in regard to certain of his or her projects—destinations and ways of being that attempt to answer those inevitable questions about who one is and what the world is about. The person has neither the wherewithal to realize them nor the courage to abandon them (Merleau-Ponty, 1962). On the basis of certain childhood experiences and relationships with significant others, e.g., one's parents, he or she has become committed to those projects in such a way that they are no longer open for discussion, reflection, and modification, even in the face of changing circumstances (Boss, 1963; Gendlin, 1978; Van Kaam, 1966a). For example, efforts to be pure by being clean, to be strong by being all-knowing, and so on, are lived as though they must be true of one's existence for all time in all circumstances. Further, states of affairs that would contradict or undermine these efforts, such as being impure by having "dirty thoughts," are concurrently lived as something that must never be true. In short, to be psychopathological means that one has fled from, or at least placed severe restrictions upon, the general task of openly discovering, positing, and making sense of one's existence. It is through self-deception that one flees from and restricts one's life (W. Fischer, 1981; Sartre, 1956),

Second, the impasse takes on the character of imprisonment as the person continues to live in terms of musts and must-nots, including the necessity of not recognizing that those are one's own terms. The person has turned away from his or her freedom to, and responsibility for, finding and developing alternatives. Occasionally, through anxious or frantic outbursts of activity, the person attempts to will life's meanings rather than to discover them (Farber, 1966). Still, life is generally experienced as superficial, as lacking richness and depth, and the person is unable to find positive meaning in his or her activities and relationships. There is a typically horizontal but occasionally intrusive, oppressive, sense of emptiness and sham (Frankl, 1968). The individual frequently experiences despair and anxiousness over the senselessness of his or her life, but these experiences are fled rather than explored (Frankl, 1968; Keen, 1970).

Third, the self-imprisoned person vigilantly turns away from his or her body's revelations of unwanted meanings. In particular, the anxious body is turned away from; being anxious is always a bodily recognition that one is faced with the possibility of feeling guilty, ashamed, inadequate, or some other "must-not" condition. By heeding instead only what he or she knows with clarity, the person beclouds and evades personal truth (W. Fischer, 1981; Keen, 1970). At the same time, the individual self-deceptively struggles to reaffirm as valid, and as still possible, the impossible, truncated world and projects to which he or she is already committed. Those projects are buttressed and maintained as being unambiguous and unchanging.

Fourth, the psychopathological person's relationships with others, both past and present, are dominated by a past. He or she continues to live in terms of identities and scenarios that are no longer appropriate, that should have been surpassed, and that now preclude ways of being that he or she occasionally longs for but cannot actualize. The unfolding of an I-Other dialectic has been arrested. Instead, this person remains who he or she was with the significant others with whom he or she became "the child," "the rebel," etc. In this effort to continue being what they "must" and to avoid being what they "must not," these persons find themselves increasingly alienated and lonely (Van den Berg, 1971).

To repeat, the above four features of psychopathology are those for which there is broadest agreement among existential therapists. These features emphasize the person's participation in the evolution of his or her restricted existence. The reader readily hears the protests against psychoanalytic and behavioristic positions, neither of which is prevailingly doctrinaire today. Nevertheless, the characterizations are still accurate, and have yet to be formally or thoroughly integrated into mainstream theories. Cognitive therapy, of course, has made room for clients' cognitions, and has characterized them as actively shaping clients' lives. But thus far in both literature and practice, these cognitions have been dealt with in isolation from the clients' broader life course and projects. Moreover, as Mahoney (1977) has pointed out, cognitive therapy is advancing rapidly without conceptual, theoretical clarity about what "cognitive" means. Phenomenological-existential theory in general, and its characterization of pathology in particular, may be helpful in that regard. Moreover, as North American psychiatry continues its biologizing movement, and a new generation of psychiatrists learns pathology primarily in terms of DSM III's behavioral symptoms approach, the above existential themes offer an increasingly pertinent counterpoint.

The reader also readily notes that in their emphasis on client responsibility, existential writers have not attended systematically to the roles of neurophysiology, genetic predisposition, or social environments in psychopathology. Phenomenology, as a philosophical foundation, definitely could ground such an effort. Human-science psychology, to be addressed below under "Research," specifically proposes an approach for psychology that integrates the physical, biological, and human orders. In the meantime, in actual practice, existential therapists have their own individual ways of understanding how the givens of a person's life (constitutional make-up, family history, responsiveness to neuroleptics, etc.) are taken up by that person, and how they may be part of psychopathology. This circumstance is the other side of the prevailing one in North American psychology, where practitioners' schooling had dealt with the givens, but has left them to find their own ways of taking into account the above existential characteristics of restricted existence.

Psychotherapy

As mentioned earlier, most phenomenological-existential therapists are eclectic in their methods. Many existential psychiatrists, for example, were trained in and still practice psychoanalysis. It is the above framework—phenomenology, existential anthropology, and understanding of pathology—that characterizes how existential therapy is different from others.

The Psychotherapeutic Relationship

The invariant theme that appears in all existential understandings of the psychotherapeutic relationship is that of respect. This respect is not just a "nice guy" social presence, nor is it an approval of who the client is or of what he or she may have done (C. Fischer, 1969, 1983). Rather, it is a respect for clients' potential to cope authentically with how they have been part of the trouble they are in, and for their potential to discover viable adaptations of earlier projects and styles. However, this respect is also for the reality that clients, even more than the rest of us, are severely limited in their options. Those limitations are both who the person is trying to be, and his or her present ways of being-in-the-world. The term, "ways," refers not just to habitual actions, but also to the lived world inherent in those actions. In the popular language of our time, to be effective, a therapist must "touch" clients "where they're at," "coming from," and "up to."

Both aspects of this respect foster a context in which personal truths may be discovered, faced, and explored. Even when clients are childlike, compulsive, negativistic, seductive, or whatever, they are understood and addressed in terms of their own worlds, since that is the location of whatever freedom they have. Although therapists from other theoretical orientations may affirm the above statements, it is the existential therapists' radical commitment to them that renders these practitioners least likely to revert to thinking of a client in terms of forces that are out of equilibrium, or of sickness, or of as in need of being made better, made more adaptive, or made free from defenses.

To use an expression that Van Kaam (1966) has stressed, the meeting of the existential psychotherapist with his or her client is understandable as an encounter. This should not be grasped in the sense that others have sometimes given to it, i.e., as an emotionally explosive confrontation where the therapist, if not both parties, deliberately attempts to shake the other radically. Rather, encounter, as Van Kaam characterizes it, is a meeting in which the psychotherapist, while being a disciplined professional in the usual ways, extends to clients "trust," "a defenseless presence," "a commitment to [clients'] autonomous development," and an invitation to be who they would or can be. Clients do differ greatly in the degree to which they can respond to this invitation. Sometimes, for example with institutional patients, the invitation is offered within a case-management context. Nevertheless, the encounter and the invitation characterize the relationship.

Finally, the psychotherapeutic relationship as the existentialist understands it cannot be grasped in terms of transference of feelings and attitudes that really belong to another relationship, such as the relationship of the client to his or her parents. Feelings and attitudes are not entities or forces that a psyche can direct and displace. It is more to the point to say that if the client is still living in the mode of the child, ambivalently struggling with the question of how to be or how to express himself or herself in relation to authority figures, then he or she will be particularly attuned to the parent or authority possibilities of the therapist. Similarly, if the client comes to feel love or hate for the therapist, this cannot be dismissed as merely a transference reaction. The love or hate or whatever is indeed an expression of a person who is struggling at a certain developmental level, and in learned ways, with personal issues. But it is also occurring now in relation to this particular practitioner's ways of being present (and absent) to the person.

Psychotherapeutic Interventions

Existential psychotherapy usually takes the form of typical "talk" sessions, where the therapist assists clients in their efforts to understand how they, along with circumstances, have gotten themselves into their present, truncated lives. The goal is for clients to discover, through reflection and action, that they can continue their lives and identities without remaining committed to earlier, no longer useful, assumptions, goals, and patterns. The further goal, of course, is for clients to begin developing, both within and beyond sessions, more freely chosen ways of being.

There is certainly nothing startling about that paragraph. Many nonexistential psychotherapists share the same goals. The difference is that the therapist whose practices are consistent with an existential anthropology does not also intend to alter hypothetical psychic apparati, maladaptive habit family hierarchies, or even maladaptive cognitions as such. The changes sought are in clients' lived worlds, not in any other level or presumed causal order.

It will be recalled, we hope, that the term "lived world" refers simultaneously to what one apprehends of the world 'out there,' and to the fact that whatever one does apprehend occurs through a believing, feeling, behaving, reflecting, and so on, relation with that world. The term points to a structural unity, respect for which disallows reductive explanations in terms only of parts. Surely standard psychoanalysis, strict behavior modification, rational-emotive therapy and so on all occasion positive results. Existential therapists, however, understand those results as changes in lived worlds. Although we are not aware of existential writings that say so, we believe that medication, life experiences (camping, art classes, for example), and behavior modification exercises could all be suggested within the existential framework. That is, these interventions could all be undertaken in the service of broadening clients' lived worlds, both directly and through occasioning questions about the necessity of prior assumptions.

Just as what is changed via therapy is nonreducible to some substrate reality, so too the change is not understood as occurring just within the client. Nor is it an abstract "world" that changes. Rather, the client is always a very particular existence, changing in the company of a particular therapeutic person. Who that person is varies in each instance, or course, but who he or she is, and what he or she comprehends of that other person are critical aspects of the therapeutic process. The therapist cannot be assumed as a constant.

As mentioned several times, there is no specific intervention that is essential to existential therapy. There are numerous ways to interrupt the client's persistence in evading recognition of past and present (partial) self-determination, and of hence not seeing alternatives as personally viable. The truism, "the timing is all" also applies here. Any intervention, to be effective, must be one that the client is ready to follow to self-discoveries. Therapists differ among themselves as to whether the discoveries must involve reflective insight, or just adaptations of action or mood or the like.

Below we present three interventions that grew specifically out of an existential philosophical anthropology. Frankl (1962) described "paradoxical intention," which he believes is not limited to any particular psychopathology. In a spirit of humor and irony, the therapist invites the client to imagine, think about, or engage in an activity that he or she has typically experienced in an anxious, fearful, guilty, or shamed manner. A woman who complains that she is embarrassed by blushing too readily, for example, is playfully invited to practice blushing until she is really good at it. The suggestion is not primarily aimed at extinguishing the symptom, or even at uncovering its etiology. Rather, client and therapist become attuned to the activity's personal significance—what it reveals to the client about himself or herself as a person. The playfulness of the exercise tells clients that the therapist will not reject them for their activity, that it is speakable, and that it can be safely explored. During this exploration, clients discover that they can themselves take different affective attitudes toward the activity. In that process they also discover that the activity and its past meanings did not "just happen," but that there were pre-

viously unreflected upon reasons for the activity and for its earlier personal meanings.

Boss, who was originally trained as a psychoanalyst, found in the "immediate reality of Freud's psychoanalytic practice an attitude which helps the patient to open himself to his own being" (1963). Boss, however, asserts that rather than ask the patient "Why," the existential psychotherapist should pose the question, "Why not?" In his discussion of this intervention, Boss suggests that, for the most part, patients live in anxiously constricted worlds. Many possibilities—ways of desiring, thinking, imagining, feeling, acting, etc.—are lived as closed off, as taboo. If the possibilities were to be appropriated as their own, it would render patients anxious about their participation in bringing about what they would see as a shameful, guilty, or embarrassing world, one where they could no longer understand themselves as worthwhile, as somebody. In asking "Why not?" the therapist encourages patients "to even greater tests of daring" (Boss, 1963). Not only does this question invite patients to take up possibilities as their own, it also opens the opportunity to explore the inarticulately lived prohibitions that are constricting the patients' worlds. Further, if patients take up such an exploration, they are more likely to discover that the prohibitions do not arise from the world alone, but rather, are actively co-created by themselves. When this happens, they can be helped to experience themselves as co-determining agents in their existence and therefore as people who can make and enact alternative decisions.

Boss also suggests that existential therapists should not be satisfied with patients' explorations, no matter how detailed and candid, of past experiences. The danger is that therapy may readily become nothing more than an endless, sterile, and stereotyped series of accusations and recriminations. Instead, existential psychotherapists must ask: Granted that you now seem to understand who others *were* for you and who you *were* for them, why not abandon these understandings in your present relations and involvements? Why not exercise your freedom to experience or relate to others as well as yourself differently? Aren't there other possibilities?

Gendlin, one of Carl Rogers' original collaborators, has integrated certain themes of Heidegger's existential philosophical anthropology with the general attitude of the client-centered therapist. More specifically, he has accepted Heidegger's claim that persons' moods, i.e., their pervasive yet inarticulately lived and typically ignored modes of being affected, express their unreflectively felt sense of how they are faring in their projects. In other words, a person's moods are understood as revelatory, at least potentially, of both the status and the content of his or her projects. With regard to the general attitude of the client-centered therapist, Gendlin has accepted Rogers' claim that above all the therapist should be oriented toward the client's feelings, should help the latter explicate and own them, and should thereby facilitate the process of self-exploration.

According to Gendlin, neurotic individuals are rigidly committed to their projects. But they are impeded, if not altogether blocked, in their efforts to actualize them. Finally, they are generally disinclined toward exploration and articulation of their projects, and of the ways in which they co-create the moods with which they find themselves assailed.

In his concern with helping these clients to surpass the oppressive and self-defeating impasse that they have participated in bringing about, Gendlin (1978) developed and described "focusing" as an intervention, one that he sees as consistent with the client-centered attitude. More specifically, Gendlin suggests that clients should be invited to dwell with, rather than dismiss or flee from, their various moods. He further suggests that clients should be encouraged to feel these moods in their concrete bodily manifestations, thereby coming to grips with the reality of their being mooded in this or that particular manner. Finally, Gendlin proposes that clients be invited to explore and articulate the various significations of their moods; what do they suggest to clients about the situation in which they find themselves so mooded, and what do they reveal to clients about their projects?

As the clients take up this style of dwelling with, feeling, exploring, and articulating the significations of their moods, they abandon the realm of ideas or rationalizations about themselves and return concretely to themselves in their specific situations. In this way, the processes of self-discovery and self-exploration are radically facilitated, as are the possibilities of letting go of rigid commitments to impossible projects.

Current Status

Today, aside from the actual therapeutic work of existential practitioners, the power of phenomenological-existential literature is primarily its usefulness, in the form of popularized key terms, for practitioners of other persuasions to speak beyond their own theories or pathology and therapeutic method about the person's actual life—his or her lived world. There is indeed a general broadening of theories to acknowledge this realm, and many if not most practitioners refer to themselves as eclectic. Hence, some readers regard existential writings as superfluous. Other readers reject the phenomenological-existential approach because its earlier reactions against absolute determinism frequently were cast in extreme terms, ones that did not give adequate explicit acknowledgment of the contingencies of existence. However, phenomenological-existential theorists and practitioners alike, when not stressing their differences from mainstream psychology, have always acknowledged that freedom is limited to the attitudes with which we take up the conditions in which we find ourselves. Indeed, the potential power of phenomenological-existential psychology lies in its readiness to contribute to an integrated social science. Despite the apparent superfluousness of this approach, in fact at the level of theory (in contrast to therapeutic practice), mainstream psychologies have not made ground-floor room for human characteristics that cannot be explained in terms of "determinants."

So it is up to the minority approach to demonstrate that such an integration is possible. Unfortunately for this effort, phenomenological academicians are usually lone representatives located in a university's philosophy, sociology, or psychology department. Systematic coordination thus is difficult. There are, however, several centers of such activity. At Duquesne University, the philosophy department has one of the strongest phenomenology and existentialism sections in the country. The psychology department's graduate program is totally devoted to development of psychology as a human science (Giorgi, 1970). For nearly 20 years the department has developed phenomenology's implications for a *science* that would integrate "consciousness" (those bodily, affective, behavioral, etc. relations through which the rest of the world is "lived") with the data of physiology, physics, and other realms of natural sciences. The work of the philosopher-psychologist (Merleau-Ponty, 1962, 1963) emphasizing the bodily character of human functioning has been important for this project. Beyond philosophical foundations, the department has developed an empirical qualitative research tradition, stressing both method and the concomitant building of a body of findings. Finally, theory, research, and practice of phenomenologically oriented assessment (C. Fischer, 1979, 1983) and psychotherapy (Burton, 1974) are taught. Diversity within the broad philosophical orientation is a hallmark of Duquesne's efforts. Representative writings from the above areas may be found in the series of *Duquesne Studies in Phenomenological Psychology* (Giorgi et al., 1971, 1975, 1979). The Silverman Phenomenology Collection at Duquesne's library is the most extensive resource in North America. It includes the donated personal libraries of several of the leading early European philosophers and psychiatrists.

Other departments with a strong emphasis on the development of a phenomenologically grounded psychology include those at Seattle University, the University of Dallas, and West Georgia College. Among individuals who are working individually at systematic development, including empirical qualitative research, are Keen at Bucknell University (1970, 1975) and de Rivera (1981) at Clark University. Journals to which psychologists across North America contribute include the *Journal of Phenomenological Psychology*, *Human Studies*, *Review of Existential Psychology and Psychiatry*, and similar specialized philosophy journals. Phenomenologically oriented psychologists, in addition to being involved in such APA divisions as Clinical, Psychotherapy, and Independent Practice, are among the most active members of the Division of Philosophical and Theoretical Psychology, as well as of the Southern Society for Philosophy and Psychology.

So, while these efforts are still underway, what difference does the present state of phenomenological-existential psychology make for the practice of psychotherapy? This orientation encourages grounded, consistent efforts in four major areas: (1) The therapist repeatedly brackets prior theoretical and practical assumptions about clients, therein listening more carefully to clients in terms of their own lives rather than in terms of formulations. (2) The therapist, in being open to, indeed attuned to, the uniquely human characteristic of co-creating one's world through one's relations with it, attends to "process" and "dynamics" in a way that allows so-called "inner" and "external" realities to be addressed in their unity. Even when focused upon separately, these constituents are regarded as mutually implicatory. (3) The therapist does not impose artificial clarity, but instead respects the ambiguity inherent in human reality's always being perspectival—that is, dependent upon historical, personal, technological access. This is not to say that everything is merely relative, however. Although subject to varying expression, and never apprehended once and for all, humanly known reality has its own orderliness. Through joint respect for both ambiguity and orderliness, the therapist encourages clients to respect the complexities of their lives and to be open to what appear as conflicting motives only from the perspective of artificially clear categories. (4) Any active interventions are not directed only to behaviors or to internal dynamics, but to both at once. They are addressed simultaneously in terms of clients' living of the worlds.

The deficit area of phenomenologically grounded psychotherapy is neither theory nor technique, but research on pathological and otherwise restricted aspects of existence, and on what actually happens as clients "get better." Such research helps existential therapists to integrate research findings developed within traditional paradigms, and to refine their approach to individual clients.

Empirical Qualitative Research

There is no body of research literature on phenomenological-existential psychotherapy. Psychologists of that orientation have, however, developed an empirical research approach and a beginning content base that will be described below. The approach is suitable for development of basic research on human experience, on pathological modes of being, and on the therapeutic process.

Existential psychotherapy may, of course, be practiced in accordance with its philosophical anthropology without concern for development of systematized research findings or for a philosophy of science grounding that research. It is our belief, however, that existential psychotherapy will reach its fullest potential if it looks to Husserl's philosophy and method as a foundation for the development of psychology as a human science (Giorgi, 1970). That foundation is, in large part, an explicit acknowledgment that all knowledge, including scientific knowledge, is inescapably co-determined by the knower and the object. Because the knower can never exhaust perspectives on an object, knowledge is necessarily incomplete. When the object (subject matter) is human perception, experience, action, or the like, its radically relational structure leads phenomenologically grounded researchers to respect its essential ambiguity. "Either-

or" and "once and for all" findings are the result of imposed clarity.

With these understandings, faculty and graduate students, especially those from the above-mentioned universities, have been developing methods for studying phenomena in their own right, prior to imposition of measurement schemas. For example, at Duquesne University, Giorgi and his students, following the initial lead of Van Kaam (1959), have systematically developed empirical phenomenological procedures, and have also specialized in the content areas of learning and perception; W. Fischer and his students have focused on affective and emotional states; von Eckartsburg and his students have developed dialogal methods, and have focused on social psychology topics; and Barton and his students are among those who have directly addressed the process of psychotherapy.

Before we characterize the general procedures of empirical research, we offer an example of findings so the reader can see where the procedures lead. C. Fischer studied moments of being in privacy as a means of understanding how assessment and therapy can be intimate and interventional and yet not be experienced as invasions of privacy. The whatness (essence) of being in privacy turned out to be the following:

Privacy is, when: The watching self and world fade away, along with geometric space, clock time, and other contingencies, leaving an intensified relationship with the subject of consciousness lived in a flowing Now. The relationship is toned by a sense of at-homeness or familiarity, and its style is one of relative openness to or wonder at the object's variable nature. [C. Fischer, 1975]

The above example illustrates four points. First, research results are in the form of descriptive structures of the world as lived. The results do not address either a world in itself or internal events, but rather that unity mentioned above. Second, such structures disrupt preconceptions. Here, for example, it turned out that what society usually protects when it attempts to "protect privacy" is secrecy. A structural characterization of moments of disrupted privacy indicated that such disruptions are indeed intrusive, but not so much into a secret life as into reverie, insight, and so on. Indeed, in effective assessment and psychotherapy, the parties often are in *shared* privacy, look-

ing together in openness and wonder at the unfolding and varying nature of the client's life. Third, the results of phenomenological research typically strike one, upon reflection, as familiar, as something we already knew. But we did not know it thematically, and hence we could not make use of it. Both our everyday and our trained ways of thinking about things often cover over unreflective understandings with various cause-effect forms of reasoning. Fourth, phenomenological research is appropriate when we want to know the whatness of a phenomenon, that is, the way people live it. In contrast, our traditional natural-science research methods are appropriate when we want to know about physical and biological events at these levels, and when we want to know "how much" or "how many."

In very brief form, the following are the general steps of empirical, qualitative research as they have been developed at Duquesne University. There are, of course, many variations and alternatives (e.g., de Rivera, 1981). As mentioned in the section on variations on Husserl's method, a first step is to collect verbatim descriptions from subjects of some actual event (e.g., moments of being anxious, being in privacy, feeling understood by a therapist). For workability, transcriptions are demarcated into segments in accordance with shifts in what is being described. The researcher then strives to bracket (shelve, put away for the time being) prior conceptions; implicit conceptions crop up and are also shelved. Segment by segment, the researcher asks: "What is the person saying here that is essential to 'being anxious' [or to whatever the phenomenon is]? In this regard, what is apparent in this segment about the person's lived relations with self, environment, and others?" The researcher writes out the answers to these questions, next to the transcript, sticking as closely as possible to the subject's original language. After finishing the transcript, the researcher writes a synopsis, tying together the segment analyses while also capturing the temporal unfolding of the described event. These steps are repeated for other subjects (anywhere from half a dozen to 50 in research to date). Then the synopses are asked the same question: "What is essential to being anxious (for example) that appears in all these instances?" Again, the language of the subjects is respected, but the resulting structure is necessarily more abstract since it must characterize what is true across all subjects.

Different researchers might word the structure

differently, and researchers do vary in the scope of what becomes apparent to them. The research is empirical, however, in two respects. First, its focus throughout is the reported experience—the original referent for the term "empirical." The focus is not transferred to secondary, derived data such as test scores or behavior tallies. Second, the researcher's procedures and analyses are available for other researchers' inspection and replication. (See C. Fischer & Wertz, 1979, for discussion of how this qualitative research is empirical, of various forms of description the results may take, and for excerpts from different steps of analysis. The exemplar phenomenon in this case was the experience of being criminally victimized.)

Thus far, the bulk of empirical phenomenological research has been carried out in the form of 80 + doctoral dissertations at Duquesne University. The following are representative areas and topics. Among the studies of everyday affective and emotional states are those by Schur (1978) on being disappointed, Ramm (1979) on jealousy, and Mruk (1981) on being pleased with oneself. Among the studies of everyday phenomena that have not lent themselves to traditional research are those by Gratton (1975) on interpersonal trust, Halling (1976) on the recognition of a significant other as a subject, and Wolfe (1980) on the preadolescent "chum" relationship. Representative of studies within established content areas are those by Cloonan (1969) on decision making, Romanysyn (1970) on interracial attitudes, and McConville (1974) on perception of horizontal space. Research on research includes dissertations by Colaizzi (1969) on phenomenological descriptive methods, Perrott (1973) on traditional researchers' constituion of their projects, and Kunz (1975) on perceived behavior as subject matter for phenomenological research.

Studies of restricted existence include Dunn's (1974) on "a brain-damaged existence," Mitchell's (1975) on alcohol addiction, and Murphy's (1978) on low back pain syndromes. Among the dissertations that have addressed the client's experience during specific phases of different forms of therapy are Hofrichter (1976) on trying out a different comportment through psychodrama, Sheridan (1977) on psychoanalysts' perception during initial interviews, and Ward (1977) on clients' experience during the imagining phase of systematic desensitization. Duquesne dissertations addressing therapy process phenomena include Hagan's (1971) on personal transformation in long-term therapy, Tyrrell's (1972) on vivid presence contrasted with technical presence during therapy, and Fessler's (1978) on the client's and therapist's experience of interpretation.

To give the reader a sense of the results of the above research, we present some of the findings from two of them. Fessler (1978) found that the therapist and client experience an intrepretation differently and do not fully understand the other's experience, despite shared speech. Much of what takes place during interpretation is outside both parties' reflective awareness. Nevertheless, success of the interpretation depends upon its closeness to the client's experience. Ward (1977) found that what happens for the client during systematic desensitization is best characterized as "the from-which,. through-which, and to-which of a transformation of self-in-world." This transformation is a "restructurational process in which the subject maintains an engaged presence to the fearsome, thereby allowing familization with, differentiation of, and delimitation of the fearsome to occur. Control of images and of behavior develops as [personally] viable responses are discovered, tried out, practiced, and mastered."

It is no accident that this research does not yet include "outcome" studies. Phenomenological researchers strongly believe that we must first conduct what have traditionally been called "process" studies in order to discover what clients *and* therapists experience during various moments and phases of therapy. Outcome could then be studied in relation to what went on during therapy. This approach would be much more precise than studies that compare ratings and scores of experimental groups without regard for what transpired among their participants. Similarly, studies of what happens in therapy for persons with particular difficulties would add precision to both process and outcome research. Finally, preliminary qualitative (phenomenological) study could identify which dimensions of therapeutic process might most profitably be measured in large-scale quantitative studies.

Summary

This chapter overviewed, in simplified form, existential psychotherapy's grounding in both phenomenology and existential philosophy. It overviewed the understandings, of both psychopathology and the psychotherapeutic relationship, that are most widely agreed upon by practitioners who refer to themselves as existential. The point was made that it is a philosophical stance that most characterizes this approach, rather than specific techniques. There are no subschools or internal controversies, although both language analysis and revisions within psychoanalysis may later prove to be points of departure. At present, despite ever-increasing interest in a phenomenological approach to therapy, and despite a broadening of other theories to accommodate many of its aspects, as Smith (1979) has said, phenomenological psychology offers not so much a school of therapy as a framework for understanding what is unique about human experience, action, and knowledge, as well as a methodology for conducting research into precisely these usually unstudied phenomena.

What is required next, if phenomenological-existential psychotherapy is to grow and to contribute maximally, is an agenda of studies designed systematically to evolve a body of knowledge on usual and restricted ways of being, on growth phenomena, and on what happens during psychotherapy. When more of these "whatness" studies become available, then the agenda will call for systematic comparison and integration with the psychotherapy research that has been conducted within the natural-science tradition.

References

Barton, A. *Three worlds of therapy: Freud, Jung, Rogers*. Palo Alto, Calif.: National Press Books, 1974.

Binswanger, L. *Being-in-the-world: Selected papers of Ludwig Binswanger*. (J. Needleman, Trans.) New York: Basic Books, 1963. (Originally published in 1938-1943.)

Boss, M. *Psychoanalysis and daseinsanalysis*. New York: Basic Books, 1963. (Originally published in 1957.)

Boss, M. Anxiety, guilt and psychotherapeutic liberation. *Review of Existential Psychology and Psychiatry*, 1967, **2**, 173-195.

Buber, M. *Between man and man*. (R.G. Smith, Trans.) New York: Macmillan, 1965. (Originally published in 1926-1939.)

Bugental, J. F. T. *The search for authenticity: An existential-analytic approach to psychotherapy*. New York: Holt, Rinehart, & Winston, 1965.

Cloonan, T. *Experiential and behavioral aspects of decision-making*. Unpublished doctoral dissertation Duquesne University, Pittsburgh, Penn., 1969.

Colaizzi, P. *The descriptive methods and types of subject-matter of a phenomenologically based psychology: Exemplified by the phenomenon of learning*. Unpublished doctoral dissertation, Pittsburgh, Penn., Duquesne University, 1969.

Deegan, P. The use of diazepam to transform being anxious. Dissertation proposal, Duquesne University, Pittsburgh, Penn., 1981.

de Rivera, J. (Ed.). *Conceptual encounter: A method for the exploration of human experience*. Lanham, Md.: University Press of America, 1981.

Dunn, M. *An ideographic reflective analysis of a brain-injured existence*. Unpublished doctoral dissertation, Duquesne University, Pittsburgh, Penn., 1974.

Farber, L. *The ways of the will*. New York: Basic Books, 1966.

Fessler, R. *A phenomenological investigation of psychotherapeutic interpretation*. Unpublished doctoral dissertation, Duquesne University, Pittsburgh, Penn., 1978.

Fischer, C. T. Rapport as mutual respect. *Personnel and Guidance Journal*, 1969, **48**, 201-204.

Fischer, C. T. Privacy as a profile of authentic consciousness. *Humanitas*, 1975, **11**, 27-43.

Fischer, C. T. Individualized assessment and phenomenological psychology. *Journal of Personality Assessment*, 1979, **43**, 115-122.

Fischer, C. T. *Individualizing psychological assessment*. Monterey, Calif.: Brooks/Cole, 1983 (in press).

Fischer, C. T., & Wertz, F. J. Empirical phenomenological analyses of being criminally victimized. In A. Giorgi, R. Knowles, & D. L. Smith (Eds.), *Duquesne studies in phenomenological psychology*, Vol. 3. Pittsburgh: Duquesne University Press, 1979.

Fischer, W. F. Self-deception: An empirical-phenomenological analysis. Paper presented at the convention of the American Psychological Association, Los Angeles, August 1981.

Fischer, W. F. An empirical-phenomenological approach to the psychology of anxiety. In A. de Koning & F. Jenner (Eds.), *Phenomenology and psychiatry*. London: Academic Press, 1982.

Frankl, V. E. *The doctor and the soul: From psychotherapy to logotherapy*. (R. and C. Winston, Trans.) (2nd ed.) New York: Vintage Books, 1966. (Originally published in 1946.)

Frankl, V. E. *Man's search for meaning*. (I. Lasch, Trans.) Boston: Beacon Press, 1962. (Originally published in 1946.)

Gendlin, E. T. *Focusing*. New York: Everest House, 1978.

Giorgi, A. *Psychology as a human science: A phenomenological approach*. New York: Harper & Row, 1970.

Giorgi, A., Fischer, C. T., & Murray, E. (Eds.), *Duquesne studies in phenomenological psychology*, Vol. 2. Pittsburgh: Duquesne University Press, 1975.

Giorgi, A., Fischer, W. F., & Von Eckartsberg, R. (Eds.), *Duquesne studies in phenomenlogical psychology*, Vol. 1. Pittsburgh: Duquesne University Press, 1971.

Giorgi, A., Knowles, R., & Smith, D. L. (Eds.), *Duquesne studies in phenomenological psychology*, Vol. 3. Pittsburgh: Duquesne University Press, 1979.

Gratton, C. *A theoretical empirical study of lived experience of interpersonal trust*. Unpublished doctoral dissertation, Duquesne University, Pittsburgh, Penn., 1975.

Hagan, D. E. *A phenomenological investigation of positive transformation as experienced by persons in long term psychotherapy*. Unpublished doctoral dissertation, Duquesne University, Pittsburgh, Penn., 1971.

Halling, S. *The recognition of a significant other as a*

subject. Unpublished doctoral dissertation, Duquesne University, Pittsburgh, Penn., 1976.

Heidegger, M. *Being and time.* (J. Macquarrie & E. Robinson, Trans.) New York: Harper & Row, 1968. (Originally published in 1927.)

Hofrichter, D. *Trying out a different comportment through psychodrama: The process of the possible becoming viable.* Unpublished doctoral dissertation, Duquesne University, Pittsburgh, Penn., 1976.

Husserl, E. *Ideas: General introduction to pure phenomenology.* (W. R. B. Gibson, Trans.) London: Allen & Unwin, 1969. (Originally published in 1913.)

Husserl, E. *The crisis of European sciences and transcendental phenomenology: An introduction to phenomenological philosophy.* (D. Carr, Trans.) Evanston, Ill.: Northwestern University Press, 1970. (Originally published posthumously in 1954.)

Keen, E. *Three faces of being: Toward an existential clinical psychology.* New York: Appleton-Century-Crofts, 1970.

Keen, E. *A primer in phenomenological psychology.* New York: Holt, Rinehart, & Winston, 1975.

Kierkegaard, S. *Fear and trembling; and the sickness unto death.* (W. Lowrie, Trans.) New York: Doubleday, 1954. (Originally published separately in 1843 & 1849.)

Kunz, G. D. *Perceived behavior as a subject matter for a phenomenologically based psychology.* Unpublished doctoral dissertation, Duquesne University, Pittsburgh, Penn., 1975.

Lyons, J. *Psychology and the measure of man.* New York: Free Press, 1963.

Mahoney, M. J. Reflections on the cognitive-learning trend in psychotherapy. *American Psychologist,* 1977, **32,** 5–13.

Marcel, G. *Being and having: An existential diary.* New York: Harper & Row, 1965. (Originally published in 1949.)

May, R. On the phenomenological bases of psychotherapy. *Review of Existential Psychology and Psychiatry,* 1964, **4,** 22–36.

May, R. *Psychology and the human dilemma.* New York: Norton, 1979.

May, R., Angel, E., & Ellenberger, H. (Eds.), *Existence: A new dimension in psychiatry and psychology.* New York: Basic Books, 1958.

McConville, M. *Perception of the horizontal dimension of space: A phenomenological study.* Unpublished doctoral dissertation, Duquesne University, Pittsburgh, Penn., 1974.

Merleau-Ponty, M. *Phenomenology of perception.* (C. Smith, Trans.) New York: Humanities Press, 1962. (Originally published in 1945.)

Merleau-Ponty, M. *The structure of behavior.* (A. Fischer, Trans.) Boston: Beacon Press, 1963. (Originally published in 1942.)

Minkowski, E. *Lived time: Phenomenological and psychopathological studies.* (N. Metzel, Trans.) Evanston, Ill.: Northwestern University Press, 1970. (Originally published in 1933.)

Mitchell, R. M. *An existential-phenomenological study of the structure of addiction with alcohol as revealed through the significant life-historical drinking situations or alcohol related situations of one self-confirmed alcoholic male.* Unpublished doctoral disser-

tation, Duquesne University, Pittsburgh, Penn., 1975.

Mruk, C. *Being pleased with oneself in a biographically critical way: An existential-phenomenological investigation.* Unpublished doctoral dissertation, Duquesne University, Pittsburgh, Penn., 1981.

Murphy, M. A. *The living of low back pain after injury: A phenomenological investigation.* Unpublished doctoral dissertation, Duquesne University, Pittsburgh, Penn., 1978.

Perrott, L. *Research on research: A human investigation.* Unpublished doctoral dissertation, Duquesne University, Pittsburgh, Penn., 1973.

Ramm, D. *A phenomenological investigation of jealousy.* Unpublished doctoral dissertation, Duquesne University, Pittsburgh, Penn., 1979.

Ricouer, P. *Freedom and nature: The voluntary and the involuntary.* (E. V. Kohak, Trans.) Evanston, Ill.: Northwestern University Press, 1966. (Originally published in 1950.)

Ricouer, P. *Husserl: An analysis of his phenomenology.* (E. G. Ballard & L. E. Embree, Trans.) Evanston, Ill.: Northwestern University Press, 1967. (Originally published from 1949 to 1957.)

Rogers, C. *Counseling and psychotherapy.* Boston: Houghton-Mifflin, 1942.

Romanysyn, R. *A theoretical-empirical investigation of white attitudes toward blacks and black attitudes toward whites.* Unpublished doctoral dissertation, Duquesne University, Pittsburgh, Penn., 1970.

Sartre, J. P. *Being and nothingness.* (H. Barnes, Trans.) New York: Philosophical Library, 1956. (Originally published in 1943.)

Schur, M. *An empirical-phenomenological study of situations of being disappointed.* Unpublished doctoral dissertation. Duquesne University, Pittsburgh, Penn., 1978.

Severin, F. T. *Humanistic viewpoints in psychology.* New York: McGraw-Hill, 1965.

Sheridan, T. *An existential phenomenological study of perception's life in dialogue as exemplified by two psychoanalysts' conduct during interviews.* Unpublished doctoral dissertation, Duquesne University, Pittsburgh, Penn., 1977.

Smith, D. L. Phenomenological psychotherapy: A why and a how. In A. Giorgi, R. Knowles, & D. L. Smith (Eds.), *Duquesne studies in phenomenological psychology,* Vol. 3. Pittsburgh: Duquesne University Press, 1979.

Stevick, E. L. An empirical investigation of the experience of anger. In A. Giorgi, W. F. Fischer, & R. VonEckartsburg (Eds.), *Duquesne studies in phenomenological psychology,* Vol. 1. Pittsburgh: Duquesne University Press, 1971.

Strasser, S. *Phenomenology and the human sciences.* Pittsburgh: Duquesne University Press, 1963.

Straus, E. *The primary world of the senses.* (J. Needleman, Trans.) Glencoe, Ill.: Free Press, 1963. (Originally published in 1935.)

Straus, E. *Phenomenological psychology: Selected papers.* (E. Eng, Trans.) New York: Basic Books, 1966. (Originally published in 1930 to 1962.)

Tyrrell, T. J. *A phenomenological study of the distinction between vivid presence and technical presence in psychotherapeutic encounter.* Unpublished doctoral dissertation, Duquesne University, Pittsburgh, Penn., 1972.

Valle, R. S. & King, M. *Existential-phenomenological alternatives for psychology.* New York: Oxford University Press, 1978.

Van den Berg, J. H. *The phenomenological approach to psychiatry.* Springfield, Ill.: C. C. Thomas, 1955.

Van den Berg, J. H. What is psychotherapy? *Humanitas,* 1971, **7,** 321–370.

Van Kaam, A. L. Phenomenal analyses: Exemplified by a study of the experience of "really feeling understood." *Journal of Individual Psychology,* 1959, **15,** 66–72.

Van Kaam, A. L. *The art of existential counseling: A new perspective in psychotherapy.* Wilkes-Barre, Penn.: Dimension, 1966. (a)

Van Kaam, A. L. *Existential foundations of psychology.* Pittsburgh: Duquesne University Press, 1966. (b)

Ward, W. *Transformation of self-in-world through the imagining phase of systematic desensitization.* Unpublished doctoral dissertation, Duquesne University, Pittsburgh, Penn., 1977.

Wolfe, J. *The experience of chum relationship: An empirical phenomenological study of the best friend relationship of preadolescence.* Unpublished doctoral dissertation, Duquesne University, Pittsburgh, Penn., 1980.

Yalom, I. *Existential psychotherapy.* New York: Basic Books, 1980.

Zaner, R. *The way of phenomenology.* New York: Pegasus, 1970.

26 BEHAVIOR THERAPY WITH ADULTS: AN INTEGRATIVE PERSPECTIVE

Cyril M. Franks
Christopher R. Barbrack

Historical and Conceptual Foundations

It has been said that behavior therapy has "a long past but a short history" (Franks & Wilson, 1973). If many of the techniques of contemporary behavior therapy have been known in one form or another for centuries, it is only recently that behavior therapy emerged as a systematized body of knowledge. How this came about, the present status of behavior therapy, current issues, and future prospects form the substance of this chapter. Formal principles, techniques, how to do behavior therapy and problems of application are not of direct concern here.[1]

Behavior therapy as we know it today began in the late 1950s as an antimentalistic, somewhat blinkered alternative to the prevailing disease-oriented model of psychodynamic psychotherapy.

But conceptually, its roots go back much farther, to the development of exact, quantifiable, and objective ways of thinking about human behavior. It was not until psychology had abandoned the non-experimental speculations of the philosopher and initiated the precise methodology of the experimental laboratory that the ground was ready for behavior therapy to take root.

The names of Pavlov, Thorndike, and Skinner come readily to mind as the precursors of behavior therapy. Each worked with single subjects and each used primarily inductive models of human behavior therapy. Each made signal contributions in the development of behavior therapy. But the implications and translation into practice of their work had to await two developments: The accumulation of sufficient empirical laboratory data and the emergence of the scientist-practitioner model in clinical psychology. It was not until the

---

[1]If theory is to lead to action (and why else study behavior therapy?), such matters are of primary importance. Interested readers might begin with the list of practice-oriented texts appended to the references. These have been selected primarily in terms of timeliness and the ability to translate current thinking about the nature of behavior therapy and its offshoots into clinical practice. For further reading, Wilson and O'Leary (1980) offer a good introduction to the principles of behavior therapy and Kazdin (1978c) deal comprehensively with the history of behavior therapy and behavior modification. Franks and Wilson (1973–1979) and, more recently, Franks, Wilson, Kendall and Brownell (1982) chronicle events in behavior therapy over the years and place them in general perspective. Behavioral assessment and behavior therapy with children are separate chapters in this handbook. The appearance of two discrete chapters reflects an organizational rather than a conceptual distinction.

late 1950s that it was possible to incorporate the early foundations in conditioning and learning established by Pavlov, Thorndike, Watson, Skinner, Hull, and other S-R learning theorists within a methodological framework of behavioral science. Other contributing factors included the burgeoning postwar need for mental-health care, the lack of trained psychiatrists, the limited availability of effective pharmacological therapy, the growing dissatisfaction with the prevailing psychodynamic model—applicable primarily to the more verbal, intact, and better-educated patient—and the increased funds available in the United States for the training of clinical psychologists.

If the times were ripe for the emergence of behavior therapy, it did not emerge without birth pangs and often frank hostility from a variety of sectors: from psychiatrists for reasons both professional and economic, and from traditional clinical psychology and certain segments of the community for reasons to be discussed. For obvious reasons, most behavior therapists were and still are to be found among the ranks of psychologists rather than psychiatrists or social workers, and this served to create further divisiveness. Parenthetically, it might be noted that the first "breakthrough," the first viable alternative to either psychodynamic therapies or drugs that could be applied to the literate, intact patient was developed by Wolpe (1958), a psychiatrist. Prior to the launching of systematic desensitization, a technique allegedly based upon the physiological principles of Sherrington and the classical conditioning of Pavlov, conditioning was something to be applied to either the rat or the hospitalized vegetative idiot but certainly not to a relatively intact literate adult. It might also be noted that, in the first instance, desensitization was applied largely to the treatment of specifically delineated fears and self-contained problem areas. It was only later, as behavior therapy became more sophisticated, that the procedure was adapted to accommodate an increasingly complex range of situations (Kazdin, 1978a).

Early attempts to establish a learning-theory basis for clinical phenomena (e.g., Dollard & Miller, 1950) were essentially exercises in translation. The implicit assumption was that the psychodynamic model was the ideal but that certain elements could be better appreciated and even utilized if translated into an S-R learning-theory terminology. It was not until the advent of systematic desensitization in 1958 and the use of operant techniques to condition socially appropriate behavior in chronic schizophrenics (Ayllon & Michael, 1959; Lindsley, Skinner, & Solomon, 1953), followed a decade later by the design of a viable token economy for institutional application (Ayllon & Azrin, 1968), that behavior therapy as we know it today began to emerge.

Concurrent with these developments were the formation of the Association for Advancement of Behavior Therapy (AABT) in 1966 in the United States and the emergence of several journals devoted exclusively to behavior therapy in the United Kingdom and the United States. Today, there are some 50 behavior therapy journals scattered throughout the world, perhaps as many national and regional behavior therapy associations, and a World Association is in the process of formation.

The term "behavior therapy" was introduced independently by three groups of researchers. In 1953, Lindsley et al. referred to their use of operant conditioning principles with hospitalized psychotic patients as behavior therapy. In 1959, Eysenck used the term in print to refer to a new approach to therapy. Eysenck viewed behavior therapy as the application of "modern learning theory" to the treatment of psychological disorders. Whereas Lindsley conceptualized behavior therapy exclusively in terms of Skinnerian operant conditioning, Eysenck adopted a broader perspective. For Eysenck, behavior therapy encompassed operant conditioning, classical conditioning, and later, modeling, with increasing acknowledgment to Pavlov, Mowrer, and such neobehaviorists as Hull, Spence, and sometimes Bandura. In 1958, Lazarus independently coined the term behavior therapy to refer to the addition of objective laboratory procedures to traditional psychotherapeutic methods. In this respect, Lazarus (then as now) felt that behavior therapy is but one part of a total picture that could include certain elements of traditional psychotherapy and psychiatry, together with validated techniques from any source. The term "behavior modification" was introduced by Watson and popularized by Ullmann and Krasner (see Redd, Porterfield, & Andersen, 1979).

The roots of behavior therapy, then, can be traced back to many schools of thought, to contrasting methodologies, to diverse philosophical systems, to different countries, and to various pioneers. Some stress classical conditioning and its translation into practice by way of such techniques as aversion therapy and systematic desensitization. Others rely upon the Skinnerian legacy of operant conditioning and the experimental analysis of behavior. Others focus on the data of experimental psychology as a whole rather than an exclusive reliance upon conditioning theory per se (Wilson & Franks, 1982). Sometimes behavior therapy takes on peculiarly idiosyncratic aspects, as for example with Yates' (1970) emphasis upon the single case as the conceptual sine qua non of behavior therapy. The general trend is toward increasing complexity. What was once restricted to the application of classical and operant conditioning now encompasses a vast domain that excludes virtually nothing that has even a remote data base in the mental-health field. It is with these developments in mind that we examine behavior therapy as it is today.

The Definition of Contemporary Behavior Therapy

Contemporary behavior therapy is an approach based upon a set of theoretical and methodological assumptions shared in part by most behavior therapists rather than either a compendium of related techniques or a unitary system. Theory and practice complement each other, assessment and intervention are intertwined, scientific rigor and clinical empathy go hand in hand. At least in principle, the hallmarks of behavior therapy are accountability, openness to alternatives, and appeal to data rather than authority.

For Kazdin (1978a), those who call themselves behavior therapists share the following characteristics: (1) a focus on current rather than historical determinants of behavior; (2) an emphasis on overt behavior change as the main criterion by which treatment is to be evaluated; (3) the specification of treatment in objective terms so as to make replication possible; (4) a reliance upon basic research in psychology as a source of hypotheses about treatment and specific therapeutic techniques; and (5) specificity in defining, treating, and measuring target populations.

Within the above context, most definitions of behavior therapy fall into one of two classes: doctrinal or epistemological. Doctrinal definitions attempt to link behavior therapy to doctrines, theories, laws, or principles of learning. Epistemological definitions tend to characterize behavior therapy in terms of the various ways of studying clinical

phenomena. By and large, doctrinal definitions tend to be narrow and fail to accommodate all of behavior therapy, whereas epistemological definitions tend to be excessively accommodating and hence potentially applicable to many nonbehavioral therapies (Erwin, 1978; Franks & Wilson, 1979). The definition of behavior therapy currently endorsed by the AABT attempts to combine the best elements of both:

> Behavior therapy involves primarily the application of principles derived from research in experimental and social psychology for the alleviation of human suffering and the enhancement of human functioning. Behavior therapy emphasizes a systematic evaluation of the effectiveness of these applications. Behavior therapy involves environmental change and social interaction rather than the direct alteration of bodily processes by biological procedures. The aim is primarily educational. The techniques facilitate improved self-control. In the conduct of behavior therapy, a contractual agreement is negotiated, in which mutually agreeable goals and procedures are specified. Responsible practitioners using behavior approaches are guided by generally accepted principles. [Franks & Wilson, 1975, p. 1]

The more flexible and comprehensive the definition, the greater the potential for overlap with nonbehavioral systems, and it may be, as Erwin suggests, that a definition of behavior therapy that is acceptable to the majority of behavior therapists is not possible at this time. Perhaps for this reason, rather than attempt a definition, Davison and Stuart (1975) simply list "several important unifying characteristics." Erwin's (1978) characterization of behavior therapy as "a nonbiological form of therapy that developed largely out of learning theory research and that is normally applied directly, incrementally and experimentally in the treatment of specific maladaptive patterns" (p. 44) is consistent with this position.

Characteristics of Contemporary Behavior Therapy

Contemporary behavior therapy is further characterized by doing as well as talking, by a variety of multidimensional methods, by a growing focus on client responsibility, by an emphasis on current rather than historical determinants, by objectivity and specificity in defining, treating, and measuring the target problems, and by a readiness to go beyond the confining straits of traditional conditioning or S-R learning theory for its data base. Above all, in behavior therapy a theory is a servant that is useful only until better theory and better therapy come along.

Modern behavior therapy is methodology rather than technique oriented. A clinician versed only in the techniques of behavior therapy is not a behavior therapist. Nevertheless, it is techniques that bring about change and behavior therapy has many effective techniques to its credit. Of these, the most well known include systematic desensitiation, assertion training, cognitive restructuring, problem-solving training, token reinforcement systems, and the teaching of coping skills and self-control. Biofeedback, behavioral medicine, environmental psychology, ecology, and systems theory are coming increasingly within the province of behavior therapy. No longer is treatment used primarily with people of limited sophistication or those with specific phobias; behavior therapy is currently applicable to virtually all types of disorder, individual, situation, or setting.

Modern behavior therapy is able to contain considerable diversity within its conceptual borders. There are those who accept trait theories as consistent with a behavioral position and those who avoid them as the plague. There are those for whom physiological and constitutional factors are paramount and those for whom the environment is all-encompassing. There are those for whom self-control is a delusion since they believe there is no such thing as the self, and there are those for whom self-control is a meaningful reality. There are those for whom the guiding framework is that of radical behaviorism and there are those whose only allegiance is to a behavioral methodology and not to any form of philosophical creed at all. For some, the principles of classical and operant conditioning, perhaps with the addition of modeling, are sufficient. For others, conditioning as a primary force in behavior therapy has had its day. For some, data are sufficient and theory is of no consequence. For others—and we fall into this category—theory is essential to the advancement of behavior therapy (Franks, 1969; Franks & Wilson, 1979).

In the formative years, behavior therapists focused upon overt responses and avoided the "stig-

ma" of mentalism by ignoring completely any form of cognitive process. Similarly, in part because the necessary technology did not as yet exist, behavior therapists focused upon the individual rather than the group and upon specific responses rather than complex systems. The more subtle influences of society, community, and system went unrecognized. Over the years, behavior therapy has progressively overcome all of these limitations. The spectrum ranges from cognition, "awareness," and "self" at one extreme to community, system, and interaction at the other. At either end, the word behavior is attached to virtually all facets of scientific endeavor: community behavior therapy, cognitive behavior therapy, holistic behavior therapy, behavioral genetics, and ecological behavior therapy are but a few of the terminological bedfellows that come readily to mind. For all of these, arguments are vigorously, if not always rigorously, advanced by articulate proponents of the various positions. Each is proclaimed a spearhead of the new behavior therapy and each has its own advocate and critic (Franks, 1981).

Bijou and Redd (1975) identify several theoretical models of behavior modification: applied behavioral analysis, predicted on Skinnerian operant conditioning; Pavlovian-based learning or conditioning therapies, as filtered through such neobehaviorists as Hull, Spence, and we would add Eysenck, Rachman, and Wolpe; and social learning, theory, with Bandura (1969) as its foremost spokesman. To these Redd et al. (1979) appropriately add another model: cognitive behavior modification.

These seemingly disparate frameworks share a similar behavioral methodology, a limited rejection of the medical model, and a commitment to empirical validation and accountability. Whether this is enough to establish a unique identity for behavior therapy at large remains to be seen, as does the extent to which the practice of behavior therapy conforms to these principles.

If the first decade of behavior therapy was characterized by ideology and polemics, and the second by consolidation, the third is characterized by sophisticated methodology, innovative conceptual models, and a search for new horizons. In the late 1970s, the "cognitive revolution" swept into behavior therapy as it swept into the rest of psychology. New frontiers with medicine, psychopharmacology, ecology, and systems theory were established. The 1980s is thus the era of biofeedback, behavioral medicine, and the community. If the principles of conditioning and modeling are still of significance, and we believe that they are, contemporary behavior therapy is also free to draw upon other branches of psychology and other disciplines. Private events, the cognitive mediators of behavior, are no longer beyond the psychological pale and a major role is now attributed to vicarious and symbolic learning processes. All of this is a far cry from the simplistic beginnings of little more than two decades ago.

Some Misconceptions about Contemporary Behavior Therapy

There are two kinds of misconceptions in the realm of behavior therapy: those of the world outside and those held by behavior therapists themselves. It is still believed in certain lay and professional circles that behavior therapists reject interpersonal relationships, that behavior therapy cannot encompass the complexities of human behavior, that behavior therapy is a naive treatment of "symptoms" that must inevitably reoccur, that behavior therapy is overly technique oriented, that behavior therapists are not interested in insight and that behavior therapy is limited in its applicability. Another misconception is that behavior therapy is simple to do and does not require any profound training, care, sophistication, or attention to detail (Walker et al., 1981). Most of these faculty perceptions are based upon inadequate knowledge of behavior therapy as it is currently practiced. In its beginnings, behavior therapy was simplistic and some of these misconceptions were valid at that time, but this is no longer so. Further confusion among the general public is engendered by the popular tendency to apply the terms "behavior therapy" and "behavior modification" to all techniques for changing behavior. These can include psychosurgery, drugs, torture, and coercion.

The misconceptions about behavior therapy that many behavior therapists themselves entertain are more subtle and less easily corrected. These include the fiction that behavior therapy consistently rests upon theory derived from experimental psychology, that behavior therapy focuses upon overt behavior, that behavior therapy in practice is invariably empirically based. (For a more extended discussion of these matters, see Franks, 1981, 1982; Franks & Rosenbaum, 1983; Kazdin, 1979; Mahoney & Kazdin, 1979.)

Current Issues in Behavior Therapy

The Role of S-R Learning Theory and Conditioning in Behavior Therapy

To what extent is behavior therapy based on theories and principles of learning? Which learning theories or principles? What is the evidential status of these theories and principles? Is there an alternative scientific foundation for behavior therapy? Do the principles of learning, and in particular those of classical and operant conditioning, apply to covert, inner-directed processes and are they sufficient to account for the data? Should we broaden the foundations of behavior therapy to include principles and knowledge drawn from social psychology, physiology, and sociology? (Kanfer & Grimm, 1980). We can do little more here than draw attention to these issues and refer the reader elsewhere (e.g., Franks, 1982).

Conditioning itself is a word devoid of any precise meaning. It can refer to an experimental procedure, to the effectiveness of this procedure, or to the process believed to account for these effects. Many difficulties arise when one tries to extrapolate data derived from animal experiments to human patients, not least of which stem from the confusion attached to the conditioning model. The precise relationships between classical and operant conditioning remain equivocal and some would doubt whether conditioning as a concept exists at all.

The relationships between conditioning in the laboratory, conditioning in the clinic, and conditioning in daily life are complex and open to many interpretations. We speak liberally of a general factor of conditionability although no such factor has as yet been demonstrated. Neither classical conditioning, operant conditioning, nor applied behavioral analysis accounts adequately for the many complexities of contemporary neuroses. Sophisticated explanations such as Mowrer's (1960) two-factor theory of avoidance behavior of Eysenck's (1982) more recent incubation conditioning explanation of the neuroses fare little better. Attempts to update conditioning theory in terms of cognition (Hillner, 1979), subjective experience (Martin & Levey, 1978), or interaction response patterns (Henton & Iverson, 1978) obscure rather than clarify. The evidence with respect to the utility of concepts of conditioning and their relationships to contemporary behavior therapy is best summed up in terms of the ancient Scottish verdict, "not proven."

The Behaviorism in Behavior Therapy

Closely related to the role of conditioning in contemporary behavior therapy is that of the nature of the behaviorism upon which much of conditioning theory and behavior therapy are predicted. Behaviorism is a far from monolithic concept and has to be understood both within a historic context and in terms of specific individuals (Franks, 1980). At least two major kinds of behaviorism can be identified. First, there is methodological behaviorism, whose proponents insist that behavior can be validly investigated and explained without direct examination of mental state. Methodological behaviorism is mediational, often mentalistic and inferential, and usually employs hypothetico-deductive methodology. It is possible to be a methodological behaviorist and espouse such notions as free will, self-control, and reciprocal determinism. Then there is metaphysical or radical behaviorism in which, by contrast, the existence of mental states is denied: it is nonmediational, antimentalistic, never inferential, and favors induction over hypothesis testing. Individuals such as Watson were metaphysical behaviorists whereas Hull, Spence, Eysenck, and virtually all contemporary behavior therapists can more appropriately be viewed as methodological behaviorists. For such individuals, methodology is of more importance than any philosophical implications in terms of a radical behaviorist underpinning. Be this as it may, the debate about the behaviorism in behavior therapy remains lively and doubtless will continue to do so (see Franks, 1980, 1982; Tryon et al., 1980).

The Relationship between Research and Clinical Practice in Behavior Therapy

In principle, a distinctive feature of behavior therapy is a reliance in the development and use of clinical procedures on knowledge derived from experimental psychology. The investigation of the treatment of agoraphobia by Barlow, Mavissakalian, and Schofield (1980) exemplifies the kind of relationship between research and practice most behavior therapists endorse. Unfortunately, ideals are not always followed in practice and

much of behavior therapy is not based on legitimate scientific evidence at all (Farkas, 1980; Hayes & Nelson, 1981; Kendall, Plous, & Kratochwill, 1981; Swan & MacDonald, 1978). It may be that, even if behavior therapy is more than technology, there is no known set of learning-theory principles that can serve as a viable foundation for what behavior therapists actually do (as contrasted with what they write and talk about). Practitioners are thus only partly culpable with respect to the widening gap between research and practice.

Clinical research has, can, and should lead to the development and improvement of clinical practice. At least publicly, behavior therapists continue to endorse the value of research-practice interaction even though most schools of professional psychology have abandoned the scientist-as-practitioner model in favor of the professional as a consumer of research carried out by others (Peterson, 1976). Which of these models would diminish the gap between research and practice is an empirical question yet to be addressed. Most active researchers report being trained under the scientist-practitioner model (Kendall, Plous, & Kratochwill, 1981). Whether these researchers tend to implement their own findings or those of others has not been investigated.

Cognitive Behavior Therapy

The so-called "cognitive revolution" endorsed with enthusiasm by many behavior therapists departs radically from radical behaviorism and, as such, has provoked many criticisms. For example, Ledwidge (1978) contends that cognitions are no more than hypothetical constructs used to account for relationships between environmental events and behaviors. Thus, cognitions are not behaviors and cognitive behavior therapy is not behavior therapy. These and other views expressed by Ledwidge are critically analyzed and partly rebutted by Rachman and Wilson (1980). Acknowledging the popularity and promise of cognitive behavior therapy, on the one hand, and the continuing controversy over its place in contemporary behavior therapy on the other, Franks (1982) urges that the pertinent issues be moved from the theater of debate to the arena of empirical investigation. Prerequisites would seem to include consensus on the definition of cognitive behavior therapy, precise technical specifications of the methods it employs, and compliance with these methods by behavior therapists (Rachman & Wilson, 1980).

Cognitive behavior therapy has got off to an auspicious start. Because its position is consonant with contemporary behavior therapy, systematic research could accrue to the enhancement of behavior therapy in general. As Mahoney and Kazdin (1979) argue convincingly, all therapies are simultaneously cognitive and behavioral to greater or lesser extents. The quality of clinical research in cognitive behavior therapy in the coming decade may well be decisive in determining the nature of behavior therapy.

Reciprocal Determinism and Social-Learning Theory

Perhaps the most complete, clinically useful, and theoretically sophisticated model within contemporary behavior therapy is that of social-learning theory (Bandura, 1977a, 1977b). Social-learning theory in its most advanced form is interdisciplinary and multimodal. While cognitions are important, it is performance that is paramount. Behaviorists ignore the role of cognition and cognitive therapists tend to minimize the importance of performance. Classical conditioning focuses upon external stimulus events, operant conditioning stresses reinforcement contingencies. Self-efficacy theory, now an essential component of social-learning theory, would seem to provide the necessary means of elucidating the interdependence between cognitive and behavioral changes and integrating the three regulatory systems of antecedent, consequent, and mediational influences into a single comprehensive framework (Bandura, 1977a, 1977b, 1978a, 1978b, 1980). While detailed investigation remains to be carried out, the theory is so formulated that it lends itself readily to experimental scrutiny. For example, according to Bandura (1982), self-efficacy influences thought patterns, actions, and emotional arousal across a variety of levels of human experience ranging from the physiology of the individual to the collective effort. At most levels, it is possible at least in principle, to generate testable predictions, design appropriate investigative studies, and develop crucial experiments to differentiate among alternative models.

Causal processes are conceptualized by Bandura in terms of what he calls "reciprocal determinism." Viewed from this perspective, psychological functioning involves a continuous, reciprocal interaction among behavioral, cognitive, and environmental influence, and it is here that difficulties arise (Franks & Wilson, 1978). Bandura's argument is cleverly conceived in that it creates the appearance of human freedom without either endorsing free will or abandoning the concept of determinism. In a nutshell, Bandura contends that, not unlike human behavior, environments have causes; in other words, the interplay between human behavior and environment is reciprocal. Human actions influence the nature of environmental events which, in turn, influence human actions, and so on.

The notion of reciprocal determinism is particularly enticing to clinicians seeking to reframe behavior therapy in terms that would appeal to those who resent the popular comparison of behavior therapy to coercive manipulation, wholesale promotion of social conformity, and the curtailing of freedom of choice. Regrettably, the use of reciprocal determinism to eliminate or at least diminish the appearance of external control is troublesome. Adverse reactions to determinism stem either from opposing legal, philosophical, and theological conceptions of human nature (e.g., free will prevails) that inevitably lead to the total rejection of deterministic principles as the basis for psychotherapy, or from ethical positions that do not deny the fact of determinism but believe that methods capitalizing on it (e.g., reinforcement schedules) should not be used in psychotherapy. It is unclear how reciprocal determinism resolves these objectives.

Furthermore, it is not clear how the theory of reciprocal determinism changes the nature of determinism as originally conceived. How does reciprocal determinism account for the manner in which human action affects the environment? Specifically, are the principles that govern this process different from those governing the influence of environment on behavior? If the answer is no, then it is not clear how reciprocal determinism adds to human freedom. If the answer is that these influences are different, then it remains to be seen what additional principles govern the behavior-environment interaction. It could be that reciprocal determinism creates more of an illusion of human freedom than freedom itself. But then, perhaps, it is too much to expect anyone to resolve by experiment a dilemma that is fundamentally philosophic.

Integration of Behavior Therapy and Psychoanalysis

Historically, renunciation of psychoanalytic theory and psychodynamic therapies played a central role in the development of behavior therapy and contributed to polarization between the two. Conclusions drawn by Luborsky, Singer, and Luborsky (1975), among others, to the effect that each type of therapeutic intervention has merits convincingly suggested that questions regarding the relative superiority of one approach would probably never be resolved on the basis of empirical evidence alone. Resignation to this state of affairs led to retrenchment and superficial easing of tensions between behavior therapists and psychoanalysts. Factors external to psychology, including questions about psychologists receiving third-party payments and demands that clinicians be held accountable for and demonstrate the efficacy of the therapeutic interventions, created a vexing predicament. On the one hand, it was apparent that questions about comparative effectiveness were complex and not readily amenable to resolution by experiment. On the other hand, external agencies were increasing their demands for scientific evidence that psychotherapy is effective. Neither faction could comfortably endure these pressures, yet there was not apparent way to resolve the dilemma. Integration of behavior therapy and psychoanalysis seemed to offer a solution. Agreement on the utility of shared concepts, the effectiveness of selected interventions and the value of certain outcomes would at least allow therapists from each camp to join forces against an external threat.

Arguing for a perspective that assumed the basic truth of psychodynamic theory, Wachtel (1977) nevertheless endorsed the adjunctive use of behavioral techniques to break neurotic cycles. Arguing from a behavioral perspective Franks (in press) holds that behavior therapy and psychoanalysis are fundamentally incompatible in terms of theory and concept and only appear to be compatible in terms of clinical application. Behavior therapists and psychoanalysists adhere to different paradigms, understand and formulate psychological problems differently, rely on different methods of verification and accept different "facts" as legitimate data. Proponents of either position can be entirely consistent within the assumptions and constraints of their respective paradigms and thereby reach contradictory and apparently irreconcilable conclusions.

For psychodynamicists (Messer & Winokur, 1980, in press), the incompatibility of behavior therapy and psychoanalysis stems from their essentially irreconcilable visions of reality. In the comic vision (in the sense of following the struc-

ture of dramatic comedy), behavior therapy emphasizes the possibility of "non-ambiguous happy endings leading to security and gratification through direct action and removal of situational obstacles" whereas, psychoanalysis emphasizes the tragic "inevitability and ubiquity of human conflict and the limits placed by the individual's early history on the extent of possible change." But in the end, it is a romantic element that seems to prevail for, in spite of their enticing argument, Messer and Winokur refuse to close tight the door to integration. It is suggested that therapists strive to maintain a "dual focus" between subjectivity governed by the ground rules of hermeneutics and objectivity governed by the traditional methods of science." This, in our view, is more akin to sophistry than solution since it requires conditions that cannot coexist. Thus, in discussing how behavior therapy and psychoanalysis might profit from cross-fertilization, Messer and Winokur unwittingly strengthen our position that such integration is not feasible.

Technical Eclecticism in the Practice of Behavior Therapy

Certain individuals recognize the impossibility of philosophic or conceptual integration between psychoanalysis and behavior therapy but insist that some form of interaction is both feasible and desirable at the level of practice. Lazarus (1967, 1981), for example, advises behavior therapists to draw upon a wide variety of clinical techniques without regard to theoretical origin. His only stipulation is that such techniques have empirical support and that empirical methods be used to monitor clinical effectiveness. In so doing, he stresses the necessity to maintain theoretical integrity both in the formulation of conceptual models and in the overall clinical strategy, if not the specifics of such procedures. Unfortunately, Lazarus fails to explain the logical system whereby the practice of technical eclecticism and the holding of an internally consistent philosophical framework can coexist. No technique is utilized in a conceptual vacuum devoid of any explicit or even implicit, underlying theoretical framework.

Empirical evidence bearing on technical eclecticism is sparse. Self-labeled eclectic behavior therapists claim to use a broader range of therapeutic techniques than those who adhere to a particular behavioral orientation (Swan & MacDonald, 1978). The question of whether the use of a broader range of techniques results in more effective, efficient, or durable change has not been addressed seriously. It is conceivable that technical eclecticism could free behavior therapists to develop new ways of treating psychological problems. Conversely, it could foster an overemphasis on techniques to the detriment of theoretical and conceptual understanding. With a myriad of techniques awaiting investigation, what guiding principles would be utilized in selecting priorities (Barlow, 1981; Franks & Wilson, 1979; Wolpe, 1981)?

Technical eclecticism is an appealing and popular trend in behavior therapy. In terms of solid empirical evidence, its theoretical and even clinical utility remains an open and largely unaddressed question (see Swan, 1979). In the long run, greater patient benefits may be more likely to accrue from a disciplined attention to theory and a selection of techniques for empirical study in accord with some guiding framework leading to the posing of meaningful questions than from a capricious endorsement of anything that seems to work.

Methodological Issues in Behavior Therapy

ANALOGUE STUDIES

Analogue studies usually enlist volunteer, nonclinical subjects and expose them to therapeutic intervention of short duration under laboratory conditions. In exchange for the enticing advantages of control over dependent and independent variables, analogue studies suffer from several limitations, the most important of which is probably the extent to which the finding can be generalized to clinical populations (Emmelkamp, 1981; Kazdin, 1978b; Rachman & Wilson, 1980; Rakover, 1980). Until systematic study of the factors influencing the generalizability of analogue research findings is completed, questions regarding the utility of these data will persist.

MAINTENANCE OF THERAPEUTIC CHANGE

Most analogue research does not provide for follow-up evaluation. In fact, surprisingly few follow-up studies of any kind exist in behavior therapy. Evidence bearing on effective maintenance strategies is sparse and equivocal (Rachman & Wilson, 1980). For example, periodic booster sessions for obesity control is logically appealing but the evidence suggests that they do not promote maintenance, whereas there is some evidence that in-

volvement of family members in the therapy is at least one component of an effective maintenance strategy (Wilson, 1980). Developing effective maintenance strategies is on the cutting edge of behavior therapy research, and issues involving the maintenance of initial therapeutic change are likely to receive considerable attention in the coming decade.

SINGLE-SUBJECT EXPERIMENTAL DESIGNS

Traditional designs typically involve the random assignments of relatively large numbers of subjects to various treatment conditions. Independent variables are controlled and manipulated by the experimenter and the significance of their effects is determined by parametric statistical analyses. The excessive time and expense of this approach, together with the limited value of group outcomes that are merely statistically significant, led to the development of strategies geared specifically to the study of the single subject (Hersen & Barlow, 1976; Kazdin, 1978b; Kratochwill, 1978). Single-subject designs range from simple to complex and are technically capable of controlling for most threats to internal and external validity at least as well as their more traditional counterparts. Single-subject approaches are meant to be used in conjunction with rather than to replace traditional large-scale experimental designs.

Problems arise when replication is attempted and the ensuing results are less than clear-cut (see Franks & Wilson, 1978, pp. 176*ff* for a more extended discussion of the salient issues involved). By and large, single-case experimental studies are best viewed as guides for creative application rather than as research strategies for direct use in the clinical setting.

Training in Behavior Therapy

Those responsible for the training of behavior therapists have always espoused a strong commitment to high standards, explicit objectives, accountability, and the monitoring of teaching materials and procedures. These commendable aims notwithstanding, Wolpe, (1981) proclaims that in all of North America there are no more than 200 adequately trained behavior therapists and perhaps a dozen adequate training programs. The specific bases for Wolpe's sweeping judgment, other than perhaps his notions about what constitutes acceptable behavior therapy, are not clear. Nevertheless, Wolpe's indictment is consistent with several more limited criticisms in the recent literature.

Current shortcomings in the training of behavior therapists fall into four general areas. First, behavior therapists are not being trained to do clinical research (Barlow, 1981). Second, behavior therapists are rarely given a thorough understanding of psychopathology (even in behavioral terms) and are not adequately trained in the practice of differential diagnosis (Hersen, 1981). Third, behavior therapists may not be prepared to deal constructively with negative client reactions (Kazdin & Cole, 1981). Fourth, behavior therapists are still not being taught how to enhance client-therapist relationships (Swan, 1979).

With respect to psychopathology and differential diagnosis, behavior therapists seem to be in an uncertain state of transition. Traditionally, these areas involved the medical model, nosological classification, and norm-referenced psychometric assessment, emphases calculatedly rejected by the pioneers of behavior therapy. To the extent that newer conceptions of psychopathology and assessment are connected with the selection of better and more multifaceted interventions, the future training of behavior therapists may well reflect these changes. Training behavior therapists to aniticipate and deal constructively with negative reactions will probably occur incrementally as the factors that contribute to this phenomenon are isolated and clarified (see Kazdin & Cole, 1981).

Not all behavioral training programs practice what they teach. Performance criteria in the determination of goal attainment are available (e.g., Thomas & Murphy, 1981) but are rarely used. Thus, when Heinrich (1980) developed a competency-based curriculum for training first-year psychiatry residents in behavior therapy, a favorable reception from students and faculty did not lead to enthusiasm for contination. Perhaps the effort involved in such endeavors outweighs perceived benefits.

Behavior Therapy in Institution and Community

Behavior therapy is now firmly entrenched in institution, community, and society at large. And in all of these domains, while accomplishments and advances are relatively easy to document, limitations and special problems become increasingly evident. For example, institutional token economies, once relatively straightforward in both concept and application, now present formidable problems. Court rulings tax the ingenuity of the behavior therapist in the development of clinically effective yet legally sanctioned reinforcers. Problems of maintenance and generalization are compounded by the growing recognition that token economies are part of a more total socioeconomic, political and environmental complex (Franks, 1982; Winkler, 1983).

In the 1970s, the appearance of a behavioral community psychology text was an event; in the 1980s it is almost a monthly process (e.g., Cone & Hayes, 1980; Glenwick & Jason, 1980; Hamerlynck, 1980; Martin & Osborne, 1980, are all community behavior therapy texts that appeared in one year). At one end of the spectrum there are concerted attempts to deal with complex issues such as the energy crisis in terms of behavioral principles (e.g., Winnett, 1981). At the other end, there are the ubiquitous studies of such less pressing social problems as litter control (e.g., Bacon-Prue et al., 1980). But as behavior therapy marches boldly into home, school, and community, doubts begin to arise. Too many unresolved issues are beginning to crop up in the transition from laboratory to the outside world. For example, Schneider, Lesko, and Garrett (1980) found that the hypothesized inhibitory effects of hot and cold temperatures on health behavior that emerged very clearly in the laboratory did not appear in real-life situations. Models and strategies that are effective within the research laboratory or even within the natural environment on a small-scale are not necessarily appropriate to larger settings (Franks, 1982).

In contrast to the by now familiar and relatively straightforward functional behavioral analysis of the individual, community behavior therapy is much more complex and a variety of models are beginning to contend with these issues (e.g., Glenwick & Jason, 1980; Hutchinson & Fawcett, 1981). While no single approach dominates, certain common trends are apparent. First, to its credit, community behavior therapy research, program development, and evaluation rest firmly upon behavioral foundations. Second, considerable attention is paid to the ecological intricacies of behavior-environment interactions, with the aim of designing environmental settings to promote adaptive behavior. Third, the practice and process of community behavior therapy stress the active involvement of community members. Fourth, the knowledge base for community behavior therapy is drawn from a variety of sources and disciplines. Fifth, there is a growing appreciation of the tremendous potential of mass media as vehicles for the delivery of behavioral interventions to large segments of society (e.g., Maccoby & Alexander, 1980). Sixth, community behavior therapists espouse a preventive approach. Regrettably, at present, this is more aspiration than fact: a majority of community behavioral psychologists still rely on direct individual treatment or early intervention approaches delivered in small-group settings (Winett, 1979).

Licensing, Certification, and Guidelines for Behavior Therapists

Licensing is mandatory, broad-based, and geared toward minimum standards. Certification is voluntary, focused upon subspecialties and goes beyond minimum standards. Some see the licensing process as a procedure for public protection (Shimberg, 1981). A more negative view suggests that licensing is largely self-serving, designed to allow certain therapists to receive third-party payments and to keep others from doing so (Danish & Smyer, 1981). In either case, few believe that existing licensing procedures establish competency or improve the services offered. Be this as it may, licensing is a fact of life and it is futile to debate its merits. Certification is another matter. Certification of behavior therapists would require specification of competencies in clearly defined areas. Criteria by which such competencies could be judged would have to be empirically establshed, as would methods for evaluation and review. The resources required would be enormous and there is no indication that behavior therapists are currently prepared to undertake this endeavor.

Short of formal certification procedures, behavior therapists have tended to resort to guidelines to govern some aspects of the practice of behavior therapy and to establish some basis for accountability. Franks (1982) reviews the extensive discussion of guidelines in the recent literature and concludes that, at this time, the cons may outweigh the pros.

Ethical and Legal Issues in Behavior Therapy

The ethics of behavior therapy are no different from those of any other mental-health profession. It is the emphasis on total accountability, openness, objectivity, and sensitivity to both societal and inner-directed determinants of behavior that makes behavior therapy unique. Interestingly enough, the mental-health community at large is beginning to follow suit. Witness, for example, the recent interest in accountability and demonstrable validity as one criterion in the reimbursement of clinicians by insurance companies. This, of course, does not imply that behavior therapists are above suspicion. With good reason, and sometimes with not good reason, the value systems of certain behavior therapists have been assailed from within and without. Behavior therapists who are able to modify the behavior of others must be prepared to modify their own behavior if and as need be. House cleaning, like charity, begins at home (Franks, 1982).

Early in the development of behavior therapy, Bandura (1969) distinguished between values and science. Values, argued Bandura, contribute to the selection of the goal, whereas science governs the selection of treatment procedures. In making this distinction, Bandura sidestepped the implicit ethical issues that emerge in both instances, and omission that contributed to Franks and Wilson's (1973) contention that behavior therapy is independent of ethical considerations. Two years later, Franks and Wilson (1975) revised their opinions and concluded that ethical considerations could not be avoided in the application of behavioral technology, a statement now widely endorsed by clinical psychologists in general (Holt, 1978) as well as behavior therapists (Farkas, 1980; Kanfer & Grimm, 1980).

Currently, the topic of ethics is the subject of lively debate in behavior therapy. Kitchener (1981a, 1980b, 1980c) argues that value judgments must be justified and points out serious flaws in the ethical relativism position of Skinner (1971), in which positive reinforcement is equated with that which is morally good or right. From another perspective, Kitchener attacks the so-called "evolutionary ethic" that equates moral goodness with those behaviors that, immediately and ultimately, contribute to the survival of a culture of species. Houts and Krasner (1980) attempt to refute Kitchener's arguments but beg the question by citing clinical examples in which client and therapist agree on treatment goals, thus obscuring the values applied by the therapist in the goal-selection process. One is left to speculate whether the therapist's decision to pursue these goals is morally justified because the client agrees, because therapist and client agree, or because of other considerations (see also Ward, 1980).

If behavior therapists accept that the application of any technology is value-laden and that scientific and strictly logical paradigms cannot be applied to the resolution of issues pertaining to values, then they must step outside the scientific/technological domain to search for an ethical paradigm to detect, understand, and resolve the ethical issues that frequently arise in the course and conduct of behavior therapy. In the interim, it is important for behavior therapists to continue to debate these issues. Individual practitioners might also do well to keep in mind the distinction between science and values (Houts & Krasner, 1980), make their values explicit (Bergin, 1980) and negotiate treatment goals with clients (Kanfer & Grimm, 1980; Turkat & Forehand, 1980) without the obfuscation and pretense of appeal to science and technology alone.

Mental-health legislation, designed to protect the rights of clients, often creates problems because it uses vague terminology, contains conflicting aspirations, and makes assumptions about intrapsychic activity, responsibility, and free will that many behavior therapists find unacceptable (Franks & Wilson, 1979; Martin, 1979; Shah, 1978). The fact that some laws create problems for behavior therapists does not inevitably lead to the conclusion that legal restraints should be abandoned. Many behavioral interventions can be accommodated to current laws and Finesmith (1979) offers specific examples to guide the behavior therapist in this respect.

The Image of Behavior Therapy

The public tend to view behavior therapy as a series of strong, potentially harmful techniques used to promote conformity and to control human behavior without regard for the rights and feelings of others. This view has been promulgated in the press (Turkat & Feuerstein, 1978), in popular books about prisons (Mitford, 1973) and psychotherapy (Ehrenberg & Ehrenberg, 1977), and elsewhere.

These widespread negative reactions alarmed behavior therapists not only because they were distasteful and based on misrepresentation, but also because of their potential impact on the public's willingness to consider behavior therapy as a treatment option and the possible negative effects on treatment outcome. These concerns gave rise to several studies designed to shed light on the factors contributing to this negative public appraisal (e.g., Barling & Wainstein, 1979; Woolfolk & Woolfolk, 1979). The conclusion at that time was that the label "behavior modification" was an important contributor to the prevailing negative image. Consideration was even given to revive an earlier, largely discarded proposal for relabeling behavioral procedures (Repucci & Saunders, 1974). The wisdom of this remedy is now called into question by Kazdin and Cole's (1981) limited-sample demonstration that behavior modification procedures per se are evaluated negatively regardless of how they are labeled. Clearly, further research is indicated.

On the basis of available information, what could be done to improve the public image of behavior therapy? Goldfried and Davison (1976) suggest that a distinction be made between behavior modification and behavior therapy. Investigations might be undertaken to determine under what circumstances behavior therapy has a negative public image and how to make individual (as contrasted with packaged) behavioral treatments more acceptable. We also need to know more about the complex parameters involved in the negative attitudes toward behavior therapy sometimes observed in our nonbehavioral mental-health colleagues. If this involves putting our own house in order as part of the solution, then so be it.

Finally, there is that vexing question of terminology and the medical model. By maintaining the terminology of the medical model, behavior therapy is less likely to be construed as something malevolent. This must be weighed against the advantages of a thoroughgoing departure from the medical model. If a person's psychological problems are construed as signs of illness, it becomes difficult to think in terms of changing specific problem behaviors. If the behavioral alternative is pursued to the hilt, a different vocabulary will need to be devised and, more to the point, used. As the name indicates, behavior therapists are still inclined to use medical terminology and to refer to patients, cures, and treatments. Whether it is possible to modify this state of affairs and whether it is desirable at this stage is unclear.

Future Directions

To paraphrase Evans (1982), when behavior therapists are not questioning their identities, searching for their origins, or reviewing the literature, they are prognosticating about the future. The prevailing mood for the 1980s is best described as one of cautious optimism based upon solid accomplishment. In particular, there is the advent of behavioral medicine; the development of well-established methods of reducing anxiety and fear; progress in the treatment of depression, obsessions, compulsions, the addictions, and sexual disorders; and promising new strategies for coping with complex social problems. What the distant future will bring we cannot say, but the indications are that within the coming decade sustained attention will be given to the considerations that follow.

First, we will have to decide if we are going to become primarily a technology or whether an integrative model of human behavior is to emerge. As the domain of behavior therapy expands, its identity becomes less coherent. Prevailing definitions incorporate all facets of behavioral science and cut across numerous disciplines. Provided that the findings are data-based and in accord with the canons of traditional behavioral science, someone, somewhere calls it behavior therapy. On the one hand, such a grandiose expansiveness could contain within it the seeds of, at the worst, oblivion, or at the very least, loss of that unique identity that is supposed to differentiate behavior therapy from other human sciences. The impact of cognition upon behavior therapy is a case in point. On the other hand, a too narrow definition of behavior therapy could lead to stultification and stagnation. The relationship of learning theory to behavior therapy, it might be noted, is part and parcel of this same problem package. If learning theories and principles constitute too narrow a base to serve as adequate foundations for contemporary and future behavior therapy, then what is the alternative? (See Wilson, 1982.)

Second, we need to accelerate the conceptual shift from the laboratory to a clinical paradigm that utilizes the training of the behavioral scientist but draws its inspirations from real-life situations rather than white rats, college sophomores, or volunteers. More investigations are needed of precisely defined procedures applied *in situ* to clients selected for homogeneity of problem, with follow-up of at least six to twelve months. If the prevailing trend in behavior therapy continues, many of these investigations are likely to fall under the rubric of behavioral medicine. This could bring a fresh look to a new area already tarnished with a jaded medical perspective or we could continue to ape the detrimental features of modern medicine —

simplistic symptomatic treatment for stress, deferential compliance with medical authority, mass screening programs, and more. Time will tell. A fresh perspective is likely to be costly in terms of time, effort, and money but in the long run, highly rewarding for all concerned (Marks, 1981).

Third, behavior therapy has to deemphasize, but not disavow, individual intervention in favor of groups, communities, societies, and systems. Accountability will be one of the pillars of this socially responsive behavior therapy, and meaningful accountability is impossible without some form of sophisticated cost-benefit analysis that goes beyond monetary values. It is essential to include, in addition, less tangible but perhaps equally significant reinforcers, such as prestige and job satisfaction, and take into accunt the many complexities of modern life that make compliance and commitment less than straightforward undertakings (B. T. Yates, 1980). This will almost certainly necessitate a shift from an exclusively individual perspective to some form of systems approach. Traditional systems theory as spelled out by Bertalanffy (1969) is somewhat limited in its behavioral applicability and we will have to develop more appropriate and timely offshoots of this model. In this respect, Miller's (1978) interpretation of general systems theory offers promise in that it is data-based, sympathetic to learning-theory principles, and oriented specifically toward living systems (Franks, 1982).

Fourth, the thoughtful use of behaviorally trained paraprofessionals, an area only beginning to be explored, could be of general economic, social, and psychological benefit to the client, the mental-health profession, the therapeutic assistant, and society at large. Finally, if behavior therapy is to change its public and professional image, it is essential that behavior therapists monitor and, if necessary, modify their own behavior. Professional and public relations campaigns might be required, together with further consideration of the need to develop realistic guidelines and a modified language system that does not reek of either the conditioning laboratory or the medical model. As part of this house-cleaning endeavor, behavior therapists will have to do considerable monitoring. Nowhere is this more evident than in the economically flourishing area of do-it-yourself behavior therapies (Franks & Wilson, 1973, 1979; Franks, 1982; Glasgow & Rosen, 1979). Whether the ubiquitous self-help manual is a viable alternative and under what circumstances is, for the most part, unknown. The fact that prominent behavior therapists publicly endorse such manuals does not, in itself, make them respectable (see Rosen, 1981).

Conclusions

Behavior therapy is no longer a radical alternative, it is part of the establishment. Within less than three decades, an unknown and simplistic application of conditioning principles to the treatment of specific problems has become a highly sophisticated and generally accepted approach to a broad spectrum of individual disorders and societal concerns (Barlow, 1980). If it has not become the solitary wave of the future that was predicted in a surge of initial enthusiasm, neither has it suffered the early demise in the murky depths that the prophets of doom foretold.

The appeal of modern behavior therapy is to those who prefer a coherent conceptual framework rather than a mélange of intuition, anecdotal evidence, and personal preference. Whether this will evolve into a meaningful model of the human species remains to be seen. If behavior therapy is to retain an identity, its advocates will have to effect some working compromise between conceptual and technical overinclusion, on the one hand, and its more narrow historical foundations, on the other.

While in no way attempting to overlook other models of behavior therapy, despite certain limitations cognitively oriented social-learning theory seems to offer particular promise for future advancement and much has already been accomplished within this framework. This, of course, is not to discount certain weaknesses common to social-learning theory and behavior therapy at large such as a narrowness of vision, a still excessive reliance upon the medical model, and a reluctance to develop alternative models of service delivery (Rachman & Wilson, 1980). Behavior therapy is at a vulnerable stage in its short but intensive history. When behavior therapists were busy challenging the traditional dogmas of psychotherapy it was relatively easy to be innovative. Now that behavior therapy is part of the establishment, many behavior therapists tend to be more cautious, more conservative, and to recapitulate the tactical errors of their psychotherapeutic predecessors. For a time it looked as though behavior therapy was an action science, a way of thinking that would provide a methodological link between fundamental re-

search and clinical practice. The danger of losing this interface is now with us.

By way of conclusion, it must be remembered that behavior therapy is still a young psychological discipline, and that learning theory itself is not very old. To expect unifying theories in such a relatively new field when physics and chemistry have failed to do so after 2,000 years seems unreasonable. In many respects behavior therapy, like much of psychology, is still in a preparadigmatic stage. Problems remain, both in theory and in application, and it may be that, at least for the forseeable future, microtheories and circumscribed resolution will be the order of the day, rather than a grand solution. This, of course, need not negate an integrative balance between technology and theory that cuts across behavioral, physiological, and cognitive systems. When all is said, and sometimes even done, it seems appropriate to conclude that, despite theoretical controversies, occasional clinical insufficiencies, confrontations from within and challenges from without, behavior therapy remains alive, well, and in accord with its founding mandate (Franks, 1982; Wilson, 1981).

References

Ayllon, T., & Michael, J. The psychiatric nurse as a behavioral engineer. *Journal of the Experimental Analysis of Behavior*, 1959, **2**, 323–336.

Ayllon, T., & Azrin, N. H. *The token economy: A motivational system for therapy and rehabilitation*. New York: Appleton-Century-Crofts, 1968.

Bacon-Prue, A., Blount, R., Pickering, D., & Drabman, R. An evaluation of three litter control procedures — trash receptacles, paid workers, and the marked item technique. *Journal of Applied Behavioral Analysis*, 1980, **13**, 165–170.

Bandura, A. *Principles of behavior modification*. New York: Holt, Rinehart, & Winston, 1969.

Bandura, A. Self-efficacy: Toward a unifying theory of behavioral change. *Psychological Review*, 1977, **84**, 191–215. (a)

Bandura, A. *Social learning theory*. Englewood Cliffs, N.J.: Prentice-Hall, 1977. (b)

Bandura, A. Reflections on self-efficacy. *Advances in Behaviour Research and Therapy*, 1978, **1**, 237–269. (a)

Bandura, A. The self system in reciprocal determinism. *American Psychologist*, 1978, **33**, 346–358. (b)

Bandura, A. The self and mechanisms of agency. In J. Suls (Ed.), *Social psychological perspectives on the self*. Hillsdale, N.J.: Lawrence Erlbaum, Associates, 1980.

Bandura, A. Self-efficacy mechanism in human agency. *American Psychologist*, 1982, **37**, 122–147.

Barling, J., & Wainstein, T. Attitudes, labeling bias, and behavior modification in work organizations. *Behav-*

ior Therapy, 1979, **10,** 129–136.

Barlow, D. Behavior therapy: The next decade. *Behavior Therapy,* 1980, **11,** 315–328.

Barlow, D. H. On the relationship of clinical research to clinical practice: Current issues, new directions. *Journal of Clinical and Consulting Psychology,* 1981, **49,** 147–155.

Barlow, D. H., Mavissakalian, M., & Schofield, L. Patterns of desynchrony in agoraphobia. *Behaviour Research and Therapy,* 1980, **18,** 441–448.

Bergin, A. E. Behavior therapy and ethical relativism: Time for clarity. *Journal of Consulting and Clinical Psychology,* 1980, **48,** 11–13.

Bertalanffy, L. von. *General systems theory: Foundation, development, applications.* New York: Braziller, 1969.

Bijou, J. W., & Redd, W. H. Behavior therapy for children. *American handbook of psychiatry,* Vol. 5. New York: Basic Books, 1975.

Cone, J. D., & Hayes, S. C. *Environmental problems/behavioral solutions.* Monterey, Calif.: Brooks/Cole, 1980.

Danish, S. J., & Smyer, M. A. Unintended consequences of requiring a license to help people. *American Psychologist,* 1981, **36,** 13–21.

Davison, G. C., & Stuart, R. B. Behavior therapy and civil liberties. *American Psychologist,* 1975, **30,** 755–763.

Dollard, J., & Miller, N. E. *Personality and psychotherapy.* New York: McGraw-Hill, 1950.

Ehrenberg, O., & Ehrenberg, M. *The psychotherapy maze.* New York: Holt, Rinehart, & Winston, 1977.

Emmelkamp, P. M. G. The current and future status of clinical research. *Behavioral Assessment,* 1981, **3,** 249–254.

Erwin, E. *Behavior therapy: Scientific, philosophical, and moral foundations.* Cambrige, England: Cambridge University Press, 1978.

Evans, I. M. Wanted—A good integrative handbook. Review of S. N. Turner, K. S. Calhoun, & H. E. Adams, *Handbook of clinical psychology. Contemporary Psychology,* 1982, **7,** 21–22.

Eysenck, H. J. Learning theory and behavior therapy. *Journal of Mental Science,* 1959, **105,** 61–75.

Eysenck, H. J. The neo-behavioristic (S-R) theory of behavior therapy. In G. T. Wilson & C. M. Franks (Eds.), *Contemporary behavior therapy: Conceptual foundation of clinical practice.* New York: Guilford, 1982.

Farkas, G. M. An ontological analysis of behavior therapy. *American Psychologist,* 1980, **35,** 364–374.

Finesmith, B. K. An historic and systematic overview of behavior management guidelines. *The Behavior Therapist,* 1979, **2,** 2–6.

Franks, C. M. Behavior therapy and its Pavlovian origins: Review and perspectives. In C. M. Franks (Ed.), *Behavior therapy: Appraisal and status.* New York: McGraw-Hill, 1969.

Franks, C. M. On behaviorism and behaviour therapy—Not necessarily synonymous and becoming less so. *Australian Behaviour Therapist,* 1980, **7,** 14–23.

Franks, C. M. 2081: Will we be many or one—Or none? *Behavioural Psychotherapy,* 1981, **9,** 287–290.

Franks, C. M. Behavior therapy: An overview. In C. M.

Franks, G. T. Wilson, P. Kendall, & K. D. Brownell, *Annual review of behavior therapy: Theory and practice,* Vol. 8. New York: Guilford, 1982.

Franks, C. M. Behavior therapy and psychoanalysis: Fundamental incompatibles. In H. Arkowitz & S. B. Messer, (Eds.), *Psychoanalytic and behavior therapy: Is integration possible?* New York: Plenum, in press.

Franks, C. M. & Rosenbaum, M. Behavior therapy: Overview and personal reflections. In M. Rosenbaum, C. M. Franks, & Y. Jaffe (Eds.), *Perspectives on behavior therapy in the eighties.* New York: Springer, 1983.

Franks, C. M. & Wilson, G. T. *Annual review of behavior therapy: Theory and practice.* Vols. 1–7. New York: Brunner/Mazel, 1973–1979.

Glasgow, R. E. & Rosen, S. M. Self-help behavior therapy manuals: Recent developments and clinical usage. *Clinical Behavior Therapy Review,* 1979, **1,** 1–20.

Glenwick, D., & Jason, L. (Eds.). *Behavioral community psychology: Program and prospects.* New York: Praeger, 1980.

Goldfried, M. R. & Davison, G. C. *Clinical behavior therapy.* New York: Holt, Rinehart, & Winston, 1976.

Hamerlynck, L. A. (Ed.). *Behavioral systems for the developmentally disabled. II. Institutional, clinic, and community environments.* New York: Brunner/Mazel, 1980.

Hayes, S. C., & Nelson, R. O. Clinically relevant research: Requirements, problems, and solutions. *Behavioral Assessment,* 1981, **3,** 209–216.

Heinrich, R. Personal communication, 1980.

Henton, W. W. & Iversen, I. H. *Classical conditioning and operant conditioning: A response pattern analysis.* New York: Springer Verlag, 1978.

Hersen, M. Complex problems require complex solutions. *Behavior Therapy,* 1981, **12,** 15–29.

Hersen, M. & Barlow, D. *Single case experimental designs: Strategies for studying behavior change.* New York: Pergamon, 1976.

Hillner, K. P. *Conditioning in contemporary perspective.* New York: Springer, 1979.

Holt, R. R. *Methods in clinical psychology. Volume 2: Prediction and research.* New York: Plenum, 1978.

Houts, A. C. & Krasner, L. Slicing the ethical Gordian Knot: A response to Ketchener. *Journal of Clinical and Consulting Psychology,* 1980, **48,** 8–10.

Hutchinson, W. R. & Fawcett, S. B. Issues in defining the field of behavioral community psychology and certifying (or not certifying) its members. *The Behavior Therapist,* 1981, **4,** 5–8.

Kanfer, F. H. & Grumm, L. G. Managing clinical change. *Behavior Modification,* 1980, **4,** 419–444.

Kazdin, A. E. Behavior therapy: Evolution and expansion. *The Counseling Psychologist,* 1978, **7,** 34–37. (a)

Kazdin, A. E. Evaluating the generality of findings in analogue therapy research. *Journal of Consulting and Clinical Psychology,* 1978, **46,** 673–686. (b)

Kazdin, A. E. *History of behavior modification: Experimental foundations of contemporary research.* Baltimore: University Park Press, 1978. (c)

Kazdin, A. E. Fictions, factions, and functions of behavior therapy. *Behavior Therapy,* 1979, **10,** 629–656.

Kazdin, A. E. & Cole, P. E. Attitudes and labeling biases toward behavior modification: The effects of labels, content and jargon. *Behavior Therapy*, 1981, 12, 56–68.

Kendall, P. C., Plous, S., & Kratochwill, T. R. Science and behavior therapy: A survey of research in the 1970's. *Behaviour Research and Therapy*, 1981, 19, 517–524.

Kiesler, D. J. Empirical clinical psychology: Myth or reality? *Journal of Clinical and Consulting Psychology*, 1981, 49, 212–215.

Kitchener, R. F. Ethical relativism and behavior therapy. *Journal of Clinical and Consulting Psychology*, 1980, 48, 1–7. (a)

Kitchener, R. F. Ethical relativism, ethical naturalism and behavior therapy. *Journal of Clinical and Consulting Psychology*, 1980, 48, 14–16. (b)

Kitchener, R. F. Ethical skepticism and behavior therapy: A reply to Ward. *Journal of Clinical and Consulting Psychology*, 1980, 48, 649–651. (c)

Kratochwill, T. R. (Ed.). *Single-subject research: Strategies for evaluating change*. New York: Academic Press, 1978.

Lazarus, A. A. New methods of psychotherapy: A case study. *South African Medical Journal*, 1958, 32, 660–663.

Lazarus, A. A. In support of technical eclecticism. *Psychological Reports*, 1967, 21, 415–416.

Lazarus, A. A. *The practice of multimodal therapy*. New York: McGraw-Hill, 1981.

Ledgewidge, B. Cognitive behavior modification: A step in the wrong direction. *Psychological Bulletin*, 1978, 85, 353–375.

Lindsley, O. R., Skinner, B. F., & Solomon, H. C. *Studies in behavior therapy*. Status Report 1. Waltham, Mass. Metropolitan State Hospital, 1953.

Luborsky, L., Signer, B. & Luborsky, L. Comparative studies of psychotherapies: Is it true that everyone has won and all must have prizes? *Archives of General Psychiatry*, 1975, 32, 995–1,008.

Maccoby, N. & Alexander, J. Use of media in life style programs. In P. O. Davidson & S. M. Davison (Eds.), *Behavioral medicine: Changing health life styles*. New York: Brunner/Mazel, 1980.

Mahoney, M. J. & Kazdin, A. E. Cognitive behavior modification: Misconceptions and premature evaluation. *Psychological Bulletin*, 1979, 86, 1,044–1,049.

Marks, I. *Cure and care of neuroses: Theory and practice of behavioral psychotherapy*. New York: Wiley, 1981.

Martin, L. & Levey, A. B. Evaluative conditioning. *Advances in Behaviour Research and Therapy*, 1978, 1, 57–102.

Martin, G. L. & Osborne, J. G. (Eds.). *Helping in the community: Behavioral applications*. New York: Plenum, 1980.

Martin, R. Comments on the "Wisconsin Experience." *The Behavior Therapist*, 1979, 2, 7.

Messer, S. B. & Winokur, M. Some limits to the integration of psychoanalytic and behavior therapy. *American Psychologist*, 1980, 35, 818–827.

Messer, S. B. & Winokur, M. Ways of knowing reality in psychoanalytic and behavior therapy. In H. Arkowitz & S. B. Messer (Eds.), *Psychoanalytic and be-

havior therapy: Is integration possible?* New York: Plenum, in press.

Miller, J. G. *Living systems*. New York: McGraw-Hill, 1978.

Mitford, J. *Kind and usual punishment: The prison business*. New York: Knopf, 1973.

Mowrer, O. H. *Learning theory and behavior*. New York: Wiley, 1960.

Peterson, D. R. Is psychology a profession? *American Psychologist*, 1976, 31, 572–581.

Rachman, S. & Wilson, G. T. *The effects of psychological therapy*. New York: Pergamon, 1980.

Rakover, S. S. Generalization from analogue therapy to the clinical situation: The paradox and the dilemma of generality. *Journal of Consulting and Clinical Psychology*, 1980, 48, 770–771.

Redd, W. H., Porterfield, A. L., & Andersen, B. L. *Behavior modification: Behavioral approaches to human problems*. New York: Random House, 1979.

Repucci, N. & Saunders, J. Social psychology of behavior modification: Problems of implementation in natural settings. *American Psychologist*, 1974, 29, 649–660.

Rosen, S. M. Guidelines for the review of do-it-yourself treatment books. *Contemporary Psychology*, 1981, 26, 189–191.

Schneider, T. W., Lesko, W. A., & Garrett, W. A. Helping behavior in hot comfortable and cold temperatures. *Environmental and Behavior*, 1980, 12, 231–240.

Shah, S. A. Dangerousness: A paradigm for exploring some issues in law and psychiatry. *American Psychologist*, 1978, 33, 224–236.

Shimberg, B. Testing for licensure and certification. *American Psychologist*, 1981, 36, 1,138–1,146.

Skinner, B. F. *Beyond freedom and dignity*. New York: Knopf, 1971.

Swan, G. E. On the structure of eclecticism: Cluster analysis of eclectic behavior therapists. *Professional Psychology*, 1979, 10, 732–739.

Swan, G. E., & MacDonald, M. L. Behavior therapy in practice: A national survey of behavior therapists. *Behavior Therapy*, 1978, 9, 799–807.

Thomas, D. R., & Murphy, R. J. Practitioner competencies needed for implementing behavior management guidelines. *The Behavior Therapist*, 1981, 4, 7–10.

Tryon, W. W., Ferster, C. B., Franks, C. M., Kazdin, A. E., Levis, D. J., & Tryon, G. S. On the role of behaviorism in clinical psychology. *Pavlovian Journal of Biological Science*, 1980, 15, 12–20.

Turkat, I. D., & Feuerstein, M. Behavior modification and the public misconception. *American Psychologist*, 1978, 33, 194.

Turkat, I. D., & Forehand, R. The future of behavior therapy. In M. Hersen, R. M. Eisler, & P. M. Miller (Eds.) *Progress in behavior modification*. Vol. 9. New York: Academic Press, 1980.

Wachtel, P. L. *Psychoanalysis and behavior therapy*. New York: Basic Books, 1977.

Walker, C. E., Hedberg, A., Clement, P. W., & Wright, L. *Clinical procedures for behavior therapy*. Englewood Cliffs, N.J.: Prentice-Hall, 1981.

Ward, L. C. Behavior therapy and ethics: A response to

Kitchener. *Journal of Clinical and Consulting Psychology*, 1980, **48**, 646–648.

Wilson, G. T. Current status of treatment approaches to obesity. In W. R. Miller (Ed.), *The addictive behaviors: Treatment of alcoholism, drug abuse, smoking and obesity.* New York: Pergamon, 1980.

Wilson, G. T. Psychotherapy process and procedure: The behavioral mandate. Presidential address to the Association for Advancement of Behavior Therapy, Toronto, November 1981.

Wilson, G. T. The relationship of learning theories to the behavioral therapies: Problems, prospects and preferences. In J. Boulougouris (Ed.), *Learning therapies approaches to psychiatry.* London: Wiley, (1982).

Wilson, G. T., & Franks, C. M. Introduction. In G. T. Wilson & C. M. Franks (Eds.), *Contemporary behavior therapy: Conceptual foundation of clinical practice.* New York: Guilford, 1982.

Wilson, G. T., & O'Leary, K. D. *Principles of behavior therapy.* Englewood Cliffs, N.J.: Prentice-Hall, 1980.

Winett, R. A. Behavioral community psychology: Some thoughts on current status and realistic expectations. *The Behavior Therapist*, 1979, **2**, 14–15.

Winett, R. A. Behavioral community psychology: Integrations and commitments. *The Behavior Therapist*, 1981, **5**, 5–8.

Winkler, R. C. The contribution of behavioral economics to behavior modification. In C. M. Franks, M. Rosenbaum, & Y. Jaffe, (Eds.), *Perspectives on behavior therapy in the eighties.* New York: Springer, 1983.

Wolpe, J. *Psychotherapy by reciprocal inhibition.* Stanford, Calif.: Stanford University Press, 1958.

Wolpe, J. Commentary on the report of the Behavior Therapy Conference. *Journal of Clinical and Counseling Psychology*, 1981, **49**, 604–605.

Woolfolk, A. E., & Woolfolk, R. L. Modifying the effect of the behavior modification label. *Behavior Therapy*, 1979, **10**, 575–578.

Yates, A. J. *Behavior therapy.* New York: Wiley, 1970.

Yates, B. T. *Improving effectiveness and reducing costs in mental health.* Springfield, Il.: C. Thomas, 1980.

A Clinician's Reading List: Recent Texts

Basmajian, J. V. *Biofeedback—Principles and practice for clinicians.* Baltimore: Williams & Wilkins, 1979.

Beck, A. T., Rush, A. J., Shaw, B. F., & Emery, G. *Cognitive therapy of depression.* New York: Guilford, 1979.

Cautela, J. R., & Groden, J. *Relaxation: A comprehensive manual for adults, children and children with special needs.* Champaign, Il.: Research Press, 1978.

Fuller, G. D. *Biofeedback: Methods and procedures in clinical practice.* San Francisco: Biofeedback Press, 1978.

Goldstein, A., & Foa, E. B. *Handbook of behavioral interventions: A clinical guide.* New York: Wiley, 1980.

Goldstein, A. P., Sprafrin, R. P., Gershan, N. J., & Klein, P. *Skill-streaming the adolescent: A structured learning approach to prosocial skills.* Champaign, Il.: Research Press, 1980.

Grieger, R., & Boyd, J. *Rational-emotive therapy: A skills-based approach.* New York: Van Nostrand Reinholt, 1980.

Jacobson, N. S., & Margolin, G. *Marital therapy: Strategies based on social learning and behavior exchange principles.* New York: Brunner/Mazel, 1979.

Jayarotne, S., & Levy, R. L. *Empirical clinical practice.* New York: Columbia University Press, 1979.

Jehu, D. *Sexual dysfunction: A behavioral approach to causation, assessment and treatment.* Chichester, U.K.: Wiley, 1979.

Kelly, J. A. *Social-skills training: A practical guide for interventions.* New York: Springer, 1982.

Melamed, B. G., & Siegel, L. J. *Behavioral medicine: Practical application in health care.* New York: Springer, 1980.

Poser, L. G. *Behavior therapy in clinical practice.* Springfield, Il.: Charles C. Thomas, 1977.

Walker, C. E., Hedburg, A., Clement, P. W., & Wright, L. *Clinical procedures for behavior therapy.* Englewood Cliffs, N.J.: Prentice-Hall, 1981.

27 BEHAVIOR THERAPY WITH CHILDREN*

Sandra L. Harris

hildren are not tiny adults. The research of developmental psychologists, as well as the formal and informal observations of teachers, parents and clinicians all readily verify that children construe the world differently from adults. Although allowed to be dependent and to assume fewer responsibilities than most adults, they are also less in command of their life decisions and for the most part subordinate to the wishes of their adult caretakers. As a result of factors such as these, a specialized clinical psychology of childhood has evolved. Child clinicians are interested in understanding children in their own context and are concerned about meeting the needs of children within the constraints established by society for dealing with children. Behavior therapists, like their dynamically oriented peers, have evolved a distinctive field of child therapy with a variety of techniques, some of which are largely confined to application with children.

This chapter is a selective review of the current status of child behavior therapy. It is not a comprehensive review, but rather an overview of central issues currently visible on the child behavior therapy scene. The targeted population ranges from infancy through the age of 18 years and includes a variety of problems varying from temper tantrums and toilet training to severe self-injury and delinquency.

An author seeking to organize the child behavior therapy literature has several ways to slice the pie. One can, for example, examine various techniques such as time out, overcorrection, and differential reinforcement of other behavior. Alternatively, one can divide the various problems presented by children into those of behavioral excess (e.g., aggression) and those of behavioral deficit (e.g., withdrawal). Ross (1981) used this approach effectively in his textbook. A third approach is to survey the field in relation to various diagnostic categories of the *Diagnostic and Statistical Manual, Edition III* (DSM III, American Psychiatric Association, 1980). Because the present book is intended to be read by people from diverse theoretical orientations, we have followed the latter path. We have selected diagnostic categories that we view as representative of the child behavior therapy literature in general: Anxiety

*The author wishes to thank A. J. van den Blink for his observations about the integration of behavioral interventions and family therapy, and Linda Hoffman for her typing expertise.

Disorder, Functional Enuresis, Attention Deficit Disorder, Mental Retardation, Pervasive Development Disorders, and Conduct Disorder. Special techniques of child behavior therapy such as parent training, family therapy, cognitive-behavioral methods, and modeling will be examined within the context of these various disorders.

The chapter examines how initial attempts to apply behavioral techniques to children have evolved from the somewhat simplistic but sometimes effective early strategies (e.g., Jones, 1924a; 1924b; Watson & Raynor, 1920) into far more complex and sophisticated contemporary techniques. Many of the members of the current generation of researchers in child behavior therapy are acutely aware of clinical as well as theoretical realities and are attempting to shape their interventions to respond to the real demands of children struggling to develop within the stress and complexities of the contemporary social scene. The effective child behavior therapist must be prepared to deal with children's responses to death, divorce, adoption, and step-parents, as well as the more easily definable complaints of bed wetting and temper tantrums.

Phobic Disorders

As Graziano, DeGiovanni, and Garcia (1979) point out, the scientific study of children's fears has been going on for almost 60 years. Children's fears were one of the first childhood problems to attract the attention of learning theorists; Watson and Rayner (1920) and Jones (1924a; 1924b) focused their work on carefully delimited childhood fears. Lazarus (1959) describes an early attempt to apply a variety of behavioral interventions to children's fears. Perhaps this early interest in phobias and fears arose because these behaviors are relatively discrete and frequent. However, the temporary phobias of children have a different and typically less pathological meaning than the phobic responses of adults (Miller et al., 1972a). As we shall see, it is therefore unfortunate that much of the research on children's fears has focused on those of relatively mild intensity and has been conducted in laboratory contexts.

There are two comprehensive and critical reviews of research on children's fears (Graziano et al., 1979; Hatzenbuehler & Schroeder, 1978). The reader can refer to these two sources for a detailed review of individual studies. The present chapter focuses upon major conclusions to be drawn about this body of literature as well as examining research and clinical issues that transcend specific studies.

Systematic Desensitization

One behavioral approach to the treatment of children's fears involves the application of the "standard" systematic desensitization procedures. Hatzenbuehler and Schroeder (1978), in their review of desensitization procedures with children, identified 22 reports that followed the traditional model of pairing a state of deep relaxation with the visualization of the feared stimulus in gradually increasing doses. Eighteen of these reports were case studies and of those, ten cases were sufficiently rigorous to allow one to reach conclusions about probable cause and effect; only five of these ten reported a behavioral improvement in their subjects. Among the four studies that used a treatment control group (Deffenbacher & Kemper, 1974; Mann & Rosenthal, 1969; Miller et al., 1972b; Muller & Madsen, 1970), the data were so inconclusive that it was not possible to draw conclusions about the merits of traditional desensitization as opposed to other modes of intervention (Hatzenbuehler & Schroeder, 1978).

In addition to the standard systematic desensitization package, there have been various efforts to modify these procedures to suit children better. Logically, one could modify the demands made upon the child to: (1) use deep muscle relaxation; (2) use imagery; or (3) do both, while still adhering to the basic concept that the child is passively exposed to the fearful situation. Thus, Lazarus and Abramovitz (1962) modified the visualization process by asking their young clients to incorporate a favorite hero into the fearful situation. The child no longer stands alone as she or he imagines her or himself confronting the neighbor's dog, but is now side by side with Superman in a fantasy woven by the therapist. There have been several case studies of this procedure involving children who were afraid of dogs (Lazarus & Abramovitz, 1962), the dark (Lazarus & Abramovitz, 1962), dentists (Lazarus, 1971) and school (Lazarus & Abramovitz, 1962; Van Der Ploeg, 1975).

One can also alter the systematic desensitization procedure by replacing imagery with external stimuli. For example, Wish, Hasazi, and Jurgela (1973) treated a boy who was afraid of loud noises by teaching him to relax as they played increasingly louder sounds on a tape recorder.

Other case reports using this approach have treated fear of dogs (Lazarus, 1960), school phobia (P. M. Miller, 1972), and fear of bees (Ney, 1968). Nevertheless, Hatzenbuehler and Schroeder (1978) suggest that it may be difficult for children to sustain the necessary level of relaxation while in the presence of the actual anxiety-provoking stimulus.

In addition, one can vary both the relaxation and imaginal components of systematic desensitization at the same time. Instead of relaxation, one uses some other anxiety-antagonistic response such as eating or playing. At the same time, the actual anxiety-provoking stimulus is gradually brought closer and closer to the child. The child is not, however, called upon to emit any behaviors in response to the stimulus object. As with other variations of the standard systematic desensitization package, there have been several case reports applying this paradigm to such fears as water (Bentler, 1962), separation from mother (Montenegro, 1968), and a fire alarm (O'Reilly, 1971).

An important criticism to be raised in connection with these variations of the "standard" desensitization package is that the literature is based almost exclusively upon case reports. The lack of well-controlled studies and our consequent inability to compare the variations in approach, make it impossible to conclude that any of these methods is superior to others or that they are superior to the "standard" procedure or a placebo control. Hence, while the notion of weaving a complex story for the child client, or replacing the possibly difficult relaxation process with sitting on mother's lap while watching a distant dog, is appealing, one cannot yet claim that such choices are data-based.

In the procedures described thus far, the child remains essentially passive while imagining the feared object or while the feared object is brought gradually closer. Another variation on this theme is one in which the child assumes an active role in approaching the stimulus object or observes a model approach to the object. Hatzenbuehler and Schroeder (1978) cite 24 studies that have employed some form of this strategy. Among these two dozen studies are several that used some form of control group (e.g., Leitenberg & Callahan, 1973; Murphy & Bootzin, 1973; Obler & Terwilliger, 1970). Although, in general, the experimental evidence in support of these "active" forms of systematic desensitization is stronger than for the "passive" forms, the data are somewhat limited in scope. Hatzenbuehler and Schroeder (1978) criticize this body of work for faults of design, poor outcome measures, lack of clarity of results, and use of multiple treatment procedures that obscure the identification of active components of treatment.

Modeling

Although Hatzenbuehler and Schroeder (1978) include observation of a model in their discussion of "active" systematic desensitization procedures, we will discuss it here under the general rubric of modeling procedures. Graziano et al. (1979) identified at least 20 studies of modeling to reduce children's fears. They placed these studies in two broad categories: those that dealt with common fears such as dogs or darkness, and those that treated children's fears of medical and dental procedures. This second group of fears includes an essentially realistic set of concerns about experiences the child must undergo.

An example of a symbolic modeling study aimed at reducing a child's fear of an impending medical event was the report of Melamed and Siegel (1975) who showed a film about a fearful child who gradually comes to cope with his fears of an operation to children about to have surgery. The children who saw the film were less anxious and posed fewer postsurgery behavior problems than did the control group. Such studies provide support for the notion that preventive treatment can help a child cope with an impending stress. Graziano et al., (1979) argue that the general efficacy of the procedure has been established, but that we need to press further to identify those ingredients of treatment that are essential for change.

The nonmedical fears that have been studied using modeling procedures include a rather narrow range of mild to moderate fears. The treatment procedure essentially involves having the child first watch a model approach the feared stimulus, and then asking the child to do the same thing. The model may be live or on tape, a child or an adult, male or female, one person or several, initially fearful or fearless (Graziano et al., 1979). Graziano and his colleagues (1979) in their overview of work in this area conclude that the use of modeling as a treatment procedure for childhood fears holds considerable promise although there is a need for extensive research to determine which variables are important to bring about change. They also regard modeling procedures as standing upon a better empirical base than systematic desensitization procedures do.

Cognitive Behavioral Approaches

One of the most recent entries into the marketplace of treatment for children's fears is the use of cognitive behavioral approaches. At least one well-controlled study (Kanfer, Karoly, & Newman, 1975) used this strategy to help children who were afraid of the dark. Their young subjects were asked to say one of the following: "I am a brave girl [boy]. I can take care of myself," or "The dark is a fun place to be," or "Mary had a little lamb." The children who recited the competence sentence ("I can take care of myself") fared best in posttreatment tests of ability to tolerate the dark. One must note, however, that these youngsters suffered a mild fear and were tested and treated in the unnatural context of a laboratory. The study is thus suggestive of clinical application, but requires additional testing before widespread adoption is appropriate. We will discuss cognitive behavioral techniques with children in more detail below under "Attention Deficit Disorder" and "Conduct Disorder."

Research and Clinical Issues

An overview of the research on children's fears suggests that modeling techniques have been the most carefully studied and have the best empirical support while systematic desensitization, with a more limited data base, has not been convincingly shown to be effective, and cognitive behavioral approaches, although interesting, are in a preliminary state of development.

A number of problems become evident as one examines the research on children's phobias. An obvious difficulty is that the literature is based mainly upon case reports with only a few well-designed studies that allow the efficacy of procedures to be compared with one another or with a control group. One must also raise questions about the extent to which relatively minor fears such as those of small animals or darkness are valid models of potentially more complex and debilitating fears such as school phobia. The problem of degree of clinical fear has not been well explored in the study of children's phobias.

We must also be wary of assuming that our knowledge of children's phobia can be built upon the body of research concerning adults. For example, the use of systematic desensitization has not yet shown itself to be very helpful in the treatment of children despite its widespread use with simple phobias in adults. When considering treatments for children, one must take into account the developmental factor—what form of treatment is appropriate to a child at a given level of cognitive, social, and affective development.

One should be careful in the study of children's phobias to control or test for the child's age and sex. It would be an error to compare treatment groups of significantly different ages or different sexes. Such variables can have a substantial impact upon results since treatment has been found to vary with the age of the child (Miller et al., 1972a), and since we believe that girls as a group tend to report more fears than boys (Croake & Knox, 1973).

In clinical practice, it becomes important to do a careful assessment of a young client and to determine exactly where interventions should be aimed. Some phobic behavior may require elimination of the fear per se, while others may demand attention to the child's skill deficits. A child may be afraid to go to school because of poor academic performance, fear of separation from home, or fear of physical violence in school. Each of these situations requires a different intervention.

Functional Enuresis

Functional enuresis provides an excellent example of the developmental factor in diagnosis of a childhood disorder. The diagnosis of enuresis hinges upon the child's age and level of physical development. Babies are in a perpetual state of wet diapers; adolescents are never expected to wet their bed. Although there is debate about the precise age beyond which bed wetting ceases to be simply a source of inconvenience and becomes a clinical problem, there is no doubt that this point is determined largely by the child's age.

The prevalence of enuresis declines steadily throughout childhood and there is very little nocturnal wetting after the age of ten years. Somewhere around school age many parents become concerned if their child is wetting the bed with regularity and may seek help to stop the behavior. Any definition of functional enuresis must, of course, rule out those children who suffer from a neurological or urological disorder that would preclude their developing or maintaining bladder control. Although a number of researchers have made a distinction between primary enuresis (no history of dryness) and secondary enuresis (dryness once established but now lost), Doleys (1977) notes that such a distinction has not been shown to have prognostic significance.

The present discussion briefly examines three major behavioral techniques for treating enuresis: the urine alarm, dry bed training, and retention control training. It is of interest that the behavioral treatment of enuresis constitutes one of the most sophisticated areas of child behavior therapy.

The Urine Alarm

The essentials of the enuresis treatment described by Mowrer and Mowrer in 1938 remain in effect today. When using the urine alarm, the child sleeps in his or her own bed with a special pad placed beneath the sheet. When urine soaks through the sheet and makes contact with the pad, this completes an electric circuit and triggers an alarm that wakes the child. After waking, the child is expected to use the toilet. Parents typically are advised to get up with the child to ensure that the bed is remade and the alarm reset before the child goes back to sleep.

Doleys (1977) summarized 12 studies that met reasonable standards of experimental design in their evaluation of the efficacy of the urine alarm procedure. He identified an overall success rate of 75 percent across this set of studies with the mean length of training running from five to twelve weeks. He also notes that for those studies that provided follow-up data, there was a relapse rate of 41 percent. Among those relapsed subjects who were re-treated, there was a 68 percent success rate. Thus, although the bell-and-pad has a very satisfactory success rate, it is still far from a perfect cure.

The recognition of flaws in the effects of the bell-and-pad led to various efforts to modify the basic package. For example, the use of a delayed alarm triggered three to five minutes after the onset of wetting was examined to determine what benefit there was to an immediate awakening (Collins, 1973; Peterson, Wright, & Hanlon, 1969). Based on these studies, Doleys (1977) concludes that the no-delay contingency is important to the efficiency of the urine alarm.

Another effort to improve the urine alarm procedure examined the schedule of alarm presentations by placing the child on an intermittent schedule with wetting sometimes triggering the alarm and other times not (e.g., Finley & Wansley, 1976; Taylor & Turner, 1975). In general, the continuous versus the intermittent schedules were equally effective in eliminating the wetting, but the intermittent groups showed less relapse over time than did the continuous groups (Doleys, 1977). In addition, the use of an overlearning procedure in which liquid intake is increased once conditioning has occurred seems to lead to a lower rate of relapse than the traditional procedure (Taylor & Turner, 1975; Young & Morgan, 1972).

Along with modifying the treatment procedures, researchers have looked closely at those children who fail to respond to treatment. Doleys (1977) indicates that the single most common reason for treatment failure was lack of parental cooperation. Other difficulties that have arisen include poor sleeping conditions in which to conduct treatment, family problems, the child failing to wake to the alarm, the child being afraid to use the equipment, and incorrect use of the equipment.

Dry Bed Training

Many of the reasons for the clinical failure of the bell-and-pad have been addressed by Azrin, Sneed, and Foxx's (1974) dry bed training. This approach requires the child repeatedly to practice the steps necessary to keep his or her bed dry at night. The youngster practices getting out of bed, walking to the toilet, and so on in the same sequence one might use if waking at night with a full bladder. The parents are fully incorporated into the process with a definite role of reinforcing good behavior and reprimanding wetting. The bell-and-pad is also part of the full package; the alarm is used to wake the child if wetting does occur and the child is required to clean up after himself. Thus, the dry bed training process is a rather intensive one that requires considerable effort of both parents and child and that they have plenty of opportunity to become comfortable and familiar with all the components of the procedure. The package is also complex in learning-theory terms with the conditioning of the bell-and-pad, positive reinforcement for a dry bed, verbal reprimand, and practice for a wet bed. It is difficult to know which elements are critical to the child's learning.

Available studies of dry bed training report good success rates (e.g., Azrin, Sneed, & Foxx, 1974; Doleys et al., 1977). The procedure thus appears to be very promising and in many ways to resemble the steps a therapist might take in practice to ensure that both parents and child are fully committed to change.

Retention Control Training

Retention control training is based upon the notion that the bladder of the enuretic child has a smaller capacity than the nonenuretic child (Zaleski, Gerrard, & Shokier, 1973). Therefore, the child is taught to retain increasingly large amounts of fluid by inhibiting urination and thereby increasing functional bladder capacity (Kimmel & Kimmel, 1970). However, Doleys (1977) in his review of this treatment and Ross (1981) a few years later both agree that the currently available research fails to demonstrate the superiority of this approach to other methods of treatment. They both believe that the technique deserves further study.

Research and Clinical Issues

There clearly are behavioral techniques of demonstrated efficacy for the treatment of enuresis. Contrary to early concerns, there does not appear to be any basis for expecting "symptom substitution" among those children treated with the bell-and-pad (Doleys, 1977). The standard urine alarm as well as the use of the alarm within the context of dry bed training have empirical support. The use of an intermittent schedule and an overlearning process are indicated to strengthen the learning process with the urine alarm.

Unlike many other areas of treatment, the study of enuresis has progressed to the point where it demands sophistication of design. In order to be consistent with the state of the art, one must include appropriate control groups and consider such variables as the age and sex of the child. Follow-up data are essential since relapse is a common problem. One must also attend carefully to the choice of one's outcome measures. This is an area where there is sufficient precedent in quality of design to offer the novice helpful guidelines in the design of a good study. The reader is referred to Doley's (1977) review for a detailed discussion of the subtler aspects of design and evaluation.

Clinically, it is comforting to have available treatment procedures with a reasonable chance of success. One must still take the time, however, to do an appropriate assessment of the conditions in which the child is living. For example, there is an obvious need to rule out a physical problem that would account for the lack of bladder control. Although an extensive and uncomfortable urological examination may not be indicated before one undertakes the relatively benign and short-term intervention described here, one would certainly want to have the assurance of the child's physician that there was no evidence of gross pathology or infection. If the child fails to respond to treatment, a more detailed medical work-up may be indicated.

Attention Deficit Disorder With and Without Hyperactivity

Attention Deficit Disorder, characterized by poor concentration and limited attention span, may or may not occur in conjunction with hyperactive behavior. Therefore, the American Psychiatric Association's (1980) latest diagnostic system (DSM III) provides two categories of Attention Deficit Disorder—with and without hyperactivity. No assumption is made that these disorders are related to one another, nor does DSM III draw any conclusions about the etiology of either condition. In the sections that follow we will compare the use of drugs and behavior modification, the use of cognitive-behavioral techniques, and the application of biofeedback procedures to decrease hyperactivity or increase attention.

Behavior Modification versus Drugs

The widespread popularity of drugs such as Ritalin and Dexedrine to treat hyperactive behavior led to a series of studies comparing this medical approach with behavior therapy procedures. One of the early studies, by Ayllon, Layman, and Kandel (1975), compared a token system with medication for three hyperactive children and found that while medication may make children quiet, it does not improve learning; the use of a token system produced both academic improvement and quiet behavior. Similar findings have been reported in other studies (e.g., Pelham, 1977; Shafto & Sulzbacher, 1977; Stableford et al., 1976). Nevertheless, for some children a combination of medication and behavior therapy may be superior to either treatment alone (Loney et al., 1979; Pelham et al., 1980), and still other studies report medication superior to behavior modification (Gittelman-Klein et al., 1976).

Resolving the inconsistencies among these

studies is a complex problem since they vary along many dimensions, including the subjects' age, IQ, social class, and diagnosis; the setting, including laboratory, home, and classroom; the skill level of the therapists; dosage of medication; measures used to assess outcome; and goals for treatment. Not surprisingly, some studies comparing medication and behavior modification on a variety of measures found the medication superior on some measures, the behavior modification on others (Wolraich et al., 1978; Wulbert & Dries, 1977).

Comprehensive reviews of the use of psychostimulants with children were written by Whalen and Henker (1976) and Barkley (1977). In a highly readable overview of the medication versus behavior modification debate, O'Leary (1980) notes that although it has been documented that the use of medication brings about improved social behavior and attention, there are few if any data indicating that such treatment improves academic performance. By contrast, there is evidence that behavior modification procedures, along with improving social and attending skills, also improve academic performance.

Cognitive-Behavioral Approaches

One of the most recent innovations in the treatment of attention deficit disorders has been the application of cognitive-behavioral techniques. In an important early study, Meichenbaum and Goodman (1971) taught impulsive children to give instructions to themselves as they solved problems on standardized tests. The results showed that the children were able to slow themselves down and decrease their errors with this training. Since that date, a number of other studies have reported that cognitive-behavioral techniques can improve the performance of hyperactive or impulsive youngsters (Bornstein & Quevillon, 1976; Cameron & Robinson, 1980; Cullinan, Epstein, & Silver, 1977; Kendall & Wilcox, 1980).

Hobbs, Moguin, Tyroler, and Lahey (1980) divided cognitive-behavioral techniques for hyperactive and impulsive children into three broad classes: (1) problem-solving techniques in which the child is given a direct description of the necessary behavior (e.g., "Look and think before answering"); (2) self-instruction training in which the child is taught statements to rehearse actively while problem solving (e.g., "If I keep working, I will be a good boy"); and (3) cognitive modeling in

which the child observes a live or symbolic model engaging in the appropriate behavior. These authors note that while a number of studies show that subjects can learn cognitive-behavioral techniques, the generalization of results to clinical settings remains tentative. Important problems including lack of placebo-control subjects, insufficient long-term follow-up data, and the dearth of comparative studies evaluating cognitive-behavioral techniques in relation to other procedures, must be addressed before firm conclusions can be drawn about the efficacy of these interventions.

Biofeedback

The recent, widespread popularity of biofeedback procedures for treating such troublesome complaints as headaches, high blood pressure, and other tension-related disorders led to the exploration of these procedures for treating hyperactive and impulsive behavior in children. In a review of this literature Cobb and Evans (1981) identified 24 studies of biofeedback with hyperactive children. Most of these reports used EMG feedback to facilitate the relaxation process in their young subjects. Although these studies as a group do show that children can learn the necessary muscular control, the absence of placebo-control groups and follow-up data makes it impossible to draw conclusions about the clinical efficacy of the procedures. Cobb and Evans (1981) note that in those studies where the feedback mechanism is directly related to the behavior problem being treated, the results are better than when the feedback mechanism is more indirect. Nevertheless, they conclude that at the present there are insufficient data to indicate that biofeedback procedures are the treatment of choice for hyperactive youngsters or children from any other behaviorally or learning-disordered category.

Research and Clinical Issues

Several conclusions may be drawn about the behavioral treatment of attention deficit disorder. First, although medication has been the treatment of choice among physicians for many years, there are few data suggesting that this approach is superior to behavior therapy. To the contrary, a behavioral aproach has advantages in terms of academic achievement. Second, the area of cognitive-behavioral treatment holds substantial promise for the treatment of hyperactive and impulsive behavior. These techniques are being actively studied and will likely gain increasing popularity among practitioners. Third, biofeedback with the required equipment and special skills has a longer way to go before its clinical efficacy is documented.

A review of the literature on behavior therapy treatment of attention deficit disorders reveals consistent problems, primarily the lack of consistent outcome measures, little regard for placebo-control groups, and limited follow-up data. In addition, aside from the comparisons of medication and behavior modification, there has been little work comparing interventions.

Clinically, our preference for behavior modification techniques rather than medication should be clear. Nonetheless, there are circumstances under which it is difficult to use behavioral procedures. Some children live in families that are so disorganized, chaotic, or indifferent that parents lack the will or ability to help their children. Similarly, some classroom teachers may not be willing to cooperate in the implementation of a classroom program. Under such conditions, medication may be the only option. If one does elect to use a drug, it becomes critically important to monitor the effects in order to demonstrate convincingly that one is bringing about the desired changes.

An important developmental consideration in using cognitive-behavioral procedures is the question of the child's age. Cohen et al. (1981) found no beneficial treatment effects for a cognitive-behavioral program with kindergarten children and suggest that these youngsters were too young to use the strategies independently over time. Copeland (1981) in reviewing the importance of age in cognitive self-instruction programs states that young children typically require explicit and structured self-statements while older children may be able to generate their own strategies.

Pervasive Developmental Disorders and Mental Retardation

Child behavior therapy has had substantial impact upon the treatment of mental retardation and pervasive developmental disorders such as infantile autism. After some early attempts to translate Skinnerian concepts of operant conditioning into direct application with autistic children (Ferster, 1961; Ferster & DeMyer, 1962), there developed a series of successful efforts to use behavioral techniques with these youngsters (Hewett, 1965; Lovaas et al., 1966; Wolf, Risley, & Mees, 1964).

The interested reader will find comprehensive reviews by Harris (1975), Harris and Ersner-Hershfield (1978), and Margolies (1977).

Punishment

In dealing with pervasively developmentally disabled and retarded youngsters one may be confronted by behaviors such as self-injury, temper tantrums, self-stimulation, and aggression, which pose problems for parents, teachers, and others who are responsible for the child's welfare. At the very least, such behaviors reduce the accessibility of the child for learning; at worst they may threaten his or her life. Work with this population therefore often requires an initial phase of suppression of maladaptive behavior. The use of punishment procedures, while controversial, has been shown to have positive effects for many clients (Harris & Ersner-Hershfield, 1978).

In attempting to suppress a behavior, one is ethically obligated to begin with the least aversive alternative. For example, the therapist may simply ignore the unwanted behavior and reward desirable behaviors, a procedure called differential reinforcement of other behavior. Although sometimes beneficial when used alone, differential reward procedures are usually most effective when used in conjunction with some form of punishment that actively suppresses the target behavior (Harris & Ersner-Hershfield, 1978). This is especially true with self-injury or aggression, when it can be impossible to ignore the danger posed by the child.

Time-out and extinction procedures are relatively nonintrusive forms of punishment. These techniques, which involve brief isolation of the child or removal of reinforcement, appear to be most appropriate when the behavior is relatively mild such as tantrums or mild to moderate aggression, rather than with the more dangerous self-injury or severe aggression. These techniques are usually not indicated for self-stimulation since the child may find the isolation a reinforcing opportunity to pursue self-stimulation.

Overcorrection (Foxx & Azrin, 1972) is an innovative attempt to reduce the negative aspects of punishment. It is viewed as an educational procedure that has two components: restitution and positive practice. Briefly, restitution requires the child to restore the surroundings to a better condition than before the offense. For example, if a child stole someone else's dessert, she would have to return it and give the victim her own dessert as well. Positive practice focuses upon the notion that one should engage in behaviors that teach correct responses to replace the unwanted one. For example, a child who puts objects in his mouth might be required to rinse out his mouth with mouthwash. Overcorrection holds considerable promise as a punishment procedure, but requires careful and continued evaluation to identify its essential ingredients and to compare it to other forms of punishment (Harris & Ersner-Hershfield, 1978).

The most dramatic form of punishment used with severely disruptive behaviors is electric shock. This process is painful but not dangerous when properly applied. Electric shock, often delivered to the leg or hand with a unit about the size and shape of a flashlight, enjoyed a brief period of popularity during the late 1960s and early 1970s, but has now diminished in reported use. The decreased popularity of the procedure was probably due to problems of obtaining generalized responding, ensuring maintenance of suppression after treatment was discontinued, and the need to comply with elaborate procedures for the protection of the client's rights. Nonetheless, for some severe cases of self-injury, when other interventions have failed, electric shock remains an appropriate alternative (Harris & Ersner-Hershfield, 1978).

Acquisition of New Skills

Although punishment procedures may be necessary to suppress disruptive behaviors, most of the behavioral techniques used with developmentally disabled and retarded children focus upon the use of positive procedures to teach new skills. Thus, positive reinforcement, physical and verbal prompts, shaping techniques, and chaining of small behaviors into complex sequences are the kinds of behavior therapy techniques one most often uses. For example, Lovaas and his colleagues (1966) used these procedures to establish speech in previously mute children. Since that initial effort, a number of people have demonstrated that behavior therapy techniques can be used to establish at least the rudiments of communicative speech in nonverbal children (Harris, 1975). Behavioral techniques can also teach these children appropriate social skills, play behaviors, self-help skills, and prevocational and vocational activities (Margolies, 1977). Many tasks once thought too complex for the retarded or pervasively developmentally disabled have turned

out to be teachable when broken down into their component parts and taught in a systematic fashion.

Parent Training

The discussion of treatment procedures for the pervasively developmentally disabled and mentally retarded offers us the opportunity to look briefly at the concept of parent training. Behavior therapists have found that parents can become skillful in working with their children to solve a wide variety of problems ranging from stubbornness, noncompliance, and dependency (Wahler et al., 1971) to the profound handicaps of the developmentally disabled child (e.g., Gardner et al., 1968). As a consequence, there has been a widespread incorporation of parents into child behavior therapy programs (Berkowitz & Graziano, 1972; O'Dell, 1974).

In a review of their own research, Rincover, Koegel, and Russo (1978) summarized the skills that were necessary in order to be an effective teacher for an autistic child. The therapist (professional or parent) must be able to present clear instructions, use reinforcement effectively, shape new skills, prompt desired responses, and present discrete trials. Rincover et al. (1978) conclude that parents, classroom teachers, and others can master these skills. In training parents, one must be sensitive to the problems and limitations of the entire family and aware of how the handicapped child fits into the family as a unit (Harris, in press).

Research and Clinical Issues

A large number of single-subject studies have repeatedly demonstrated that operant conditioning procedures can be effective in teaching basic skills to pervasively developmentally disabled and mentally retarded children. These techniques are often tedious to apply, requiring hundreds or even thousands of trials to achieve mastery, but successful outcome typically follows when the clinician is persistent and creative in the application of procedures. Once maladaptive behaviors such as self-injury and self-stimulation are brought under control, these youngsters can be taught a full range of behaviors necessary to function, at least in a limited way, within our society. The procedures do not constitute a cure for these problems, but they do provide the best adaptive techniques available to date.

Almost all of the published studies on the application of operant conditioning techniques with the developmentally disabled and mentally retarded have been based upon case reports and single-subject designs with replications across a small number of subjects. Such studies, while often persuasive, pose problems in terms of our knowledge about the generalized application of the techniques as well as limiting our ability to compare the effects of different techniques. Designs to compare various procedures with the same subject are often difficult to implement since the best planned reversals may not occur when treatment is withdrawn, or the subject may generalize when we least wish him to do so, and thus destroy a nicely designed multiple-baseline design. Of course, researchers turned to single-subject designs at least in part because it is so difficult to obtain a sufficiently homogenous population of these youngsters to do group studies. Nonetheless, with behavior therapy techniques in widespread use for the treatment of the pervasively developmentally disabled and mentally retarded, it seems appropriate that we begin to direct some of our effort toward group studies that would allow us to draw broad conclusions about our procedures. This may be most important for long-term outcome studies that attempt to document that a behavioral approach (as opposed to any single behavioral intervention) is superior to other treatment.

Researchers and clinicians need to be acutely aware of the problem of generalization that may arise with these very handicapped children. It becomes the responsibility of the researcher to demonstrate that a behavior learned in one setting is generalized to other contexts. We know that we cannot take generalization for granted (Harris, 1975).

Conduct Disorder

Children and adolescents are diagnosed as exhibiting a conduct disorder when there is a consistent pattern of violating other people's rights or breaking social rules or norms. Many of these youngsters are the people whom we refer to as delinquent or predelinquent. Child behavior therapists have tried to modify children's antisocial behaviors in many settings including traditional institutions, small-group homes, and the youth's own family. Behavioral techniques have included direct reinforcement and punishment of targeted behaviors, token economies, and cognitive-behavioral tech-

niques. Davidson and Seidman (1974) reviewed much of the early, more traditionally operant interventions that were attempted with delinquent youngsters. We will focus here upon the behavioral treatment of conduct disorders in residential settings, within the family, and using cognitive-behavioral procedures.

Treatment in Institutions

The aggressive, destructive behavior of conduct-disorder children leads to their relatively frequent placement in institutions. Within this setting there is an opportunity for intervention along many dimensions. As Kazdin (1977) points out, while behavior therapists may attempt directly to suppress antisocial behaviors, one must also recognize that skill deficits may underlie many of the delinquent youngster's problems. These young people may lack the ability to obtain satisfactions in ways that do not clash with the demands of the adults around them. Consequently, a number of residential settings employ some form of token economy to reward the child for the acquisition of new, adaptive behaviors.

One important study of the effects of a token economy for boys who had committed serious offenses such as murder and rape was done at the National Training School for Boys in Washington, D.C. The program, entitled Contingencies Applicable for Special Education (CASE) was divided into two parts. CASE I was a demonstration project involving 16 youngsters with a token system to improve academic performance and attitude toward school (Cohen, Filipczak, & Bis, 1968). The success of this project led to an expanded program (CASE II) in which a 24-hour-a-day token economy was used to modify both academic and social behaviors (Cohen & Filipczak, 1971). Both CASE I and CASE II participants made academic progress on standardized measures of achievement. Immediately after release, the CASE I boys showed a reduced rate of recidivism, but within three years they were returning to institutions at rates close to the national norms. Institutional treatment which fails to prepare children fully for their return to the community often encounters such problems of generalization of training.

The National Training School for Boys is a large, restrictive setting. Some behavior therapists have been interested in treating conduct-disorder youngsters in a smaller, more homelike setting that approximates the conditions one might find in a good family. The best known of these home-style settings is Achievement Place, a program for predelinquent youngsters below 16 years of age. These homes are managed with a token economy that includes the use of rewards for such behaviors as cleaning one's room, watching the news on television, doing homework, and being prompt in one's assignments. Tokens are removed for transgressions like fighting, swearing, or being truant from school.

After more than a decade of research, the Achievement Place model has shown itself to be a viable and effective way to treat predelinquent youngsters. Kazdin (1977) points to the model as a successful effort that has been emulated by other projects. He regards this approach to the treatment of young delinquents as superior to the existing traditional approaches and points out that it changes both the attitudes and behavior of the participants.

Family Treatment

Although family-style settings such as Achievement Place are effective in their work with conduct-disorder children, many parents, judges, and clinicians would prefer to keep the child in his or her home, and make changes in that home, rather than removing the child. There have been several attempts to intervene directly with the antisocial youth and his or her parents and siblings. Such work has followed two general paths. One, with younger children, has focused upon parent training, while the other, often with adolescents, has involved both parents and children in a process of family change.

Patterson, Reid, Jones, and Conger's (1975) work with parents of young, aggressive children provided the model for home-based parent training. The fundamental component of their program involves careful observation of parent-child interactions within the home and detailed training for parents in behavioral techniques to diminish aggression and increase appropriate behaviors.

Gurman and Kniskern (1978), in a thoughtful commentary on the use of behavioral parent training, note that some of the children targeted for intervention by Patterson and his colleagues actually differed little if at all in their rates of deviant behavior from nonpatient children. This observation suggests the importance of understanding why this particular child has come to be targeted

as the "identified patient" and argues for a complete assessment of the child within the context of the family before choosing a mode of intervention.

One group of researchers who attempted more broadly family oriented behavioral intervention was Alexander and his colleagues (Alexander & Barton, 1976; Alexander et al., 1976; Alexander & Parsons, 1973). In describing their techniques, Alexander et al. (1976) say, "the focus was not on 'delinquent' target behaviors per se but on the family system functions served by the delinquency, such as maintaining adolescent-parent distance and independence and maintaining parental role relationships" (p. 658). Although traditionalists might regard these interventions as too broad to fit within a behavioral framework, many contemporary behavior therapists view working within the family as a complex and sophisticated application of behavioral procedures within a "real-life" context.

Cognitive-Behavioral Techniques

In addition to the use of token economies within institutions, parent training, and family therapy, there is a growing child behavior therapy literature concerned with cognitive-behavioral techniques for altering conduct-disorder problems. Little and Kendall (1979) provide an extensive review of problem-solving, role-taking, and self-control procedures as they have been applied to delinquents. They point to the importance of assessing the precise deficits of each child since the term "delinquent" can describe a variety of problem behaviors. Three specific areas of potential deficit for the delinquent are: (1) lack of skills in interpersonal transactions (problem solving): (2) difficulty in assuming another person's point of view (role taking): and (3) inability to inhibit one's impulses (self-control). Little and Kendall (1979) contend that cognitive-behavioral techniques to treat these behavioral deficits are not incompatible with the use of token economies or other operant procedures. Cognitive-behavioral procedures might well be integrated into a broad approach of institutional or family treatment. For example, Little and Kendall (1979) suggest that teaching problem-solving skills within a family context (similar to the work of Alexander and his colleagues, above) holds considerable promise, although one could also use the techniques with the delinquent youth alone.

Research and Clinical Issues

Early studies of behavioral interventions for delinquent behavior tended to focus upon specific, narrow behaviors, and frequently reported success in dealing with these circumscribed problems (Davidson & Seidman, 1974). Recent, more broadly based approaches to conduct disorders have led to some substantial success. The Achievement Place model has been shown to be effective with predelinquent youngsters who must be treated outside of their own home. Both parent training and family therapy strategies have had beneficial effects for conduct-disorder children seen while living at home.

Central problems of measurement present themselves to any scientist who wishes to study delinquent behavior. Most delinquent behavior, like criminal behavior in general, escapes detection. For each child caught shoplifting, numerous other youngsters are never identified. A young thief might commit dozens of crimes befor being arrested, then undergo treatment and commit dozens of crimes again, perhaps without being detected. This poses a special problem in single-subject studies where one cannot assume that such errors of measurement will be equally frequent in control and treatment groups. As is the case in studying any form of childhood disorder, one is also confronted by problems of maturation. Without a control group, it becomes difficult to claim much credit for an intervention since many delinquent behaviors decline with age.

As a result of these kinds of measurement problems, it is much easier to measure immediate, short-term changes in narrowly defined target behaviors than it is to assess the broad impact of a program upon such highly desirable long-range objectives as reducing criminal behavior, increasing social conformity, or improving adult adjustment. Consequently, it is not surprising that most researchers confine themselves to measuring such things as number of days missed from school, swear words uttered per hour, or aggressive episodes toward other children in school. Such measures, although valuable, are somewhat limited in utility.

Of all the disorders we have reviewed in the present chapter, none points more pressingly to the need for a comprehensive evaluation of the total environment than does the conduct disorder. The clinician has good reason to anticipate problems in enrolling parental cooperation with many of these families and may well have to work slowly, a step at a time, in order to bring some semblance of organization to a chaotic family situation.

Ethical Issues

The treatment of children imposes upon the therapist unique problems that are not encountered with adults. In large part these special problems arise because it is rare for a child to initiate the request for therapy. Typically, contacts are made by parents and the child comes along as a more or less willing participant. Since the child is, at least initially, a passive member of the therapy process, it is a special obligation of the therapist to act on the child's behalf. When the child refuses to participate in treatment this responsibility becomes even more compelling. It is not always easy to know whether the goals selected for treatment are for the child's welfare or for that of the adults involved.

Who is the Client?

A striking example of a situation where parental objectives and those of the child may clash is found with the child who exhibits gender identity problems (Rekers, 1975; Rekers & Lovaas, 1974; Rekers, Lovaas, & Low, 1974). When a boy shows "an excess of feminine behaviors" or a girl is "too masculine," are we justified in intervening to change the child's behavior? Or should we be working to alter the parental and societal definition of what is acceptable behavior for a girl or boy? Although treatment has been shown to be effective in modifying the selection of toys, styles of motor behavior, and choice of playmates, one must inquire whether adults have the right to determine whether a child will have more or less masculine or feminine activity and behavior preferences. If these youngsters are going to emerge as adult transsexuals or homosexuals, ought we to alter that path of development? Those in favor of treatment argue that growing up with any form of deviant sexual choice is an extremely difficult and painful road to follow in our society. It is much easier to be heterosexual than otherwise. Those opposed to treatment respond that while it is difficult to be deviant, this is nonetheless the choice of the individual and neither parents nor therapists have the right to deny the child that ultimate choice. These issues have been debated at length by Winkler (1977), Nordyke, Baer, Etzel, and Le-Blanc (1977), and Rekers (1977).

The Use of Punishment

The use of punishment procedures with children raises a set of specific ethical problems that must be examined by the behavior therapist. Is it acceptable for us to use procedures that cause physical pain or emotional discomfort for any client, but most especially for a client who is too young to give his or her informed consent to the process? Similarly, may we impose such procedures upon a young client who defiantly refuses to comply with our interventions? Although the use of electric shock for treating self-injurious behavior offers the most dramatic instance of a highly aversive treatment, there are many other, less conspicuous procedures that hold potential for substantial discomfort on the part of the child client.

In reaching a decision about the extent to which punishment procedures are acceptable, one must take care to distinguish between the term "punishment" as used by the layperson and as the same term is used by the behavior therapist. For the layperson, punishment is often used to describe some form of retribution for misbehavior. When one talks about punishment from a behavioral perspective, the goal is not retribution. Rather, punishment is defined as any technique that reduces the probability of the future occurrence of the behavior. There is no issue of moral justification.

The shift from punishment as retribution to punishment as a teaching technique does not eliminate value judgments. One must consistently raise the question of whether the target behavior is sufficiently troublesome or dangerous to warrant a given level of intervention. The case of chronic rumination in infants, a potentially fatal disorder, can justify the use of mild electric shock to punish the vomiting response and thereby teach the infant to retain food. Few clinicians would be willing to draw the same conclusion about using shock to treat tantrums or bed wetting. Painful procedures such as shock or even a slap on the bottom must be reserved for those situations where there is a substantial risk to the individual's welfare and where other procedures of a less drastic nature have proved ineffective. A slap is not appropriate for a ten-year-old of normal intelligence, regardless of the behavior, because this youngster has the cognitive capacity to respond to other forms of management. The punishment must not only be effective, it must be appropriate to the age and cognitive abilities of the client. Children, like adults, must be respected, not demeaned by the procedures we use in treatment.

To what extent do we teach parents how to use punishment procedures as part of their child-management training? Punishment techniques, by their very nature, are open to substantial abuse. It is painfully easy for an effective behavior therapy technique to be subverted into an instrument of abuse by people who are looking for a justification to act against a child. Many of us are familiar with the difficulties that some institutions have in training their staff to use behavioral procedures in ways that are in the best interests of the client. Similar problems can arise within the home.

Accountability

No discussion of child behavior therapy is complete without a mention of the concept of accountability. The notion that we must develop measurement procedures and record-keeping systems that document the efficacy of our procedures is an integral assumption of behavior therapists. The ability to specify goals and to measure change is one of the strong points in favor of a behavioral approach to change. The keeping of appropriate records and the modification of goals and procedures based upon our records increases the likelihood that we will act in our client's best interests. There are guidelines for protecting children who are outpatients (Christian, Clark, & Luke, 1981), students (Pollack & Sulzer-Azaroff, 1981), victims of abuse or neglect (Kuehn & Christopherson, 1981), residents of group homes (Timbers, Jones, & Davis, 1981), or diagnosed as autistic (McClannahan & Krantz, 1981). Many of the recommendations of these authors focus upon specific procedures for enhancing therapist accountability. These same concepts of accountability must be taught to parents when they are initiated into the application of behavioral procedures for child rearing.

Conclusion

Evolution of Treatment

Several themes emerged in our review of the child behavior therapy literature. One of these themes is the pattern of evolution of techniques in the field. In many ways this evolution has paralleled that of behavior therapy in general. Thus, early interventions with children were primarily simple operant or classical conditioning paradigms that worked well for some clearly defined problems such as uncomplicated fears or bed wetting. Nevertheless, the more complex the clinical picture presented by the child, the less satisfactory these early solutions appeared. As one moves into the realm of increasingly complex interpersonal problems, it becomes necessary to develop increasingly sophisticated tools of intervention. The cognitive-behavioral techniques are emerging as one of the important areas of intervention to deal with these clinical realities.

Families

Another important theme in the behavioral treatment of childhood disorders is the increasing involvement of families. Initially, parental participation focused on the notion that parents could be trained to be behavior therapists for their own child. This strategy worked well and continues to be a popular means of treating childhood problems. As Oltmanns, Broderick, and O'Leary (1977) found, pretreatment level of marital discord need not be related to successful treatment of children's behavior problems. All that some families need is a bit of guidance in techniques of child rearing to help them be more effective with their children. However, the traditional parent-training programs have assumed not only the good will, but the unhindered motivation of the parents in their interaction with their child. Clinical experience teaches us otherwise. Parents are sometimes tightly wound up in the behavior problems of their children. The child's pattern of maladaptive behavior has come, in an unfortunate fashion, to be reinforcing for all of the players in the scene. Under these conditions it may not be sufficient simply to teach parents to change their pattern of reward and punishment.

The parents of children seen in clinics typically have less satisfactory marriages than other families in the community (Oltmanns et al., 1977). Recognition of the obvious and subtle ways in which childhood misbehavior may serve purposes within the entire family has led behavior therapists to appreciate the value of intervening with the entire family as well as with its subunits. A family initially coming to a behavior therapist because of a child's behavior disorder may find that the focus of therapy shifts gradually to a concern about the wretched communication between the parents. The widowed mother of a large family with a delinquent son may find that talking as a family about relationships with one another and the deceased father is at least as important as a specific punishment for the boy's shoplifting. One cannot assume that family or marital issues are invariably important to working with a child; neither can one afford to ignore these factors in a behavioral assessment. The behavior therapist who is unable to intervene at this level will be unable to meet the needs of some of his or her child clients.

Development

Yet another theme that emerges as we examine the child behavior therapy literature is that of recognizing the importance of developmental factors in treatment planning. Children are not a uniform bloc of beings. Rather, they have different needs and abilities at different ages. Indeed, developmental psychologists devote their careers to understanding the growth of children's cognitive, affective, and social development. Just as we would not expect a kindergarten child to have the motor ability to do the pole vault, so too would we be ill advised to expect that child to master complex cognitive-behavioral tasks for self-control. The child behavior therapist must choose therapeutic techniques that respect the child's level of development. This need to examine developmental variables, although perhaps implicit in the work and writings of some child behavior therapy researchers, has yet to receive the explicit, empirical respect that is its due.

Research

Finally, as one examines the empirical basis for child behavior therapy, one notes the uneven quality of the data. There are some areas, such as the treatment of enuresis and phobias, where the questions being asked and the designs being used are relatively sophisticated. Other areas, such as the treatment of conduct disorders or pervasive developmental disabilities, while showing considerable progress in the past decade, still demand extensive exploration. We have reached a point where the practitioner can know that there are firm underpinnings upon which to base interventions. Nonetheless, there remain vast areas where treatment choice lies more in the judgment of the therapist than upon a data base.

The coming generation of young researchers and therapists need not despair that all of the important questions have been answered and only trivia remains to be addressed. To the contrary, although we have managed to clarify some of the questions, we have made only modest progress with the answers.

References

Alexander, J. & Barton, C. Behavioral systems therapy with delinquent families. In D. H. L. Olson (Ed.), *Treating relationships.* Lake Mills, Iowa: Graphic, 1976.

Alexander, J., Barton, C., Schiavo, R. S., & Parsons, B. V. Systems-behavioral intervention with families of delinquents: Therapist characteristics, family behavior and outcome. *Journal of Consulting and Clinical Psychology,* 1976, **44**, 656–664.

Alexander, J. & Parsons, B. Short-term behavioral intervention with delinquent families: Impact on family process and recidivism. *Journal of Abnormal Psychology,* 1973, **81**, 219–225.

American Psychiatric Association. *Diagnostic and Statistical Manual of Mental Disorders.* (3rd ed.) Washington, D.C.: American Psychiatric Association, 1980.

Ayllon, T., Layman, D., & Kandell, H. J. A behavioral-educational alternative to drug control of hyperactive children. *Journal of Applied Behavior Analysis,* 1975, **8**, 137–146.

Azrin, N. H., Sneed, T. J., & Foxx, R. M. Dry bed: Rapid elimination of childhood enuresis. *Behaviour Research and Therapy,* 1974, **12**, 147–156.

Barkley, R. A. The effects of methylphenidate on various types of activity level and attention in hyperactive children. *Journal of Abnormal Child Psychology,* 1977, **5**, 351–369.

Bentler, P. M. An infant's phobia treated with reciprocal inhibition therapy. *Journal of Child Psychology and Psychiatry,* 1962, **3**, 185–189.

Berkowitz, B. P. & Graziano, A. M. Training parents as behavior therapists: A review. *Behaviour Research and Therapy,* 1972, **10**, 297–317.

Bornstein, P. H. & Quevillon, R. P. The effects of a self-instruction package on overactive preschool boys. *Journal of Applied Behavior Analysis,* 1976, **9**, 179–188.

Cameron, M. I. & Robinson, V. M. J. Effects of cognitive training on academic and on-task behavior of hyperactive children. *Journal of Abnormal Child Psychology,* 1980, **8**, 405–419.

Christian, W. P., Clark, H. B., & Luke, D. E. Client rights in clinical counseling services for children. In G. T. Hannah, W. P. Christian, & H. B. Clark (Eds.), *Preservation of client rights.* New York: Free Press, 1981.

Cobb, D. E. & Evans, J. R. The use of biofeedback techniques with school-aged children exhibiting behavioral and/or learning problems. *Journal of Abnormal Child Psychology,* 1981, **9**, 251–281.

Cohen, H. L. & Filipczak, J. *A new learning environment.* San Francisco: Jossey-Bass, 1971.

Cohen, H. L., Filipczak, J. A., & Bis, J. S. CASE project. In J. Shlien (Ed.), *Research in Psychotherapy,* Vol. 3. Washington, D.C.: American Psychological Association, 1968.

Cohen, N. J., Sullivan, J., Minde, K., Novak, C., & Helwig, C. Evaluation of the relative effectiveness of methylphenidate and cognitive behavior modification in the treatment of kindergarten-aged hyperactive children. *Journal of Abnormal Child Psychology,* 1981, **9**, 43–54.

Collins, R. W. Importance of the bladder-cue buzzer contingency in the conditioning treatment for enuresis. *Journal of Abnormal Psychology,* 1973, **82**, 299–308.

Copeland, A. P. The relevance of subject variables in cognitive self-instructional programs for impulsive children. *Behavior Therapy,* 1981, **12**, 520–529.

Croake, J. W. & Knox, F. H. The changing nature of children's fears. *Child Study Journal,* 1973, **3**, 91–105.

Cullinan, D., Epstein, M. H., & Silver, L. Modification of impulsive tempo in learning-disabled pupils. *Journal of Abnormal Child Psychology,* 1977, **5**, 437–444.

Davidson, W. S. & Seidman, E. Studies of behavior modification and juvenile delinquency: A review, methodological critique, and social perspective. *Psychological Bulletin,* 1974, **81**, 998–1,011.

Deffenbacher, J. & Kemper, C. Counseling test-anxious sixth graders. *Elementary School Guidance and Counseling,* 1974, **9**, 22–29.

Doleys, D. M. Behavioral treatments for nocturnal enuresis in children: A review of the recent literature. *Psychological Bulletin,* 1977, **84**, 30–54.

Doleys, D. M., Ciminero, A. R., Tollison, J. W., Williams, C. L., & Wells, K. C. Dry-bed training and retention control training: A comparison. *Behavior Therapy,* 1977, **8**, 541–548.

Ferster, C. B. Positive reinforcement and behavioral deficits of autistic children. *Child Development,* 1961, **32**, 437–456.

Ferster, C. B. & DeMeyer, M. K. A method for the experimental analysis of the behavior of autistic children. *American Journal of Orthopsychiatry,* 1962, **32**, 89–98.

Finley, W. W. & Wansley, R. A. Use of intermittent reinforcement in a clinical-research program for the treatment of enuresis nocturna. *Journal of Pediatric Psychology,* 1976, **4**, 24–27.

Fixsen, D. L., Phillips, E. L., Phillips, E. A., & Wolf, M. M. The teaching-family model of group home treatment. In W. E. Craighead, A. E. Kazdin, & M. J. Mahoney (Eds.), *Behavior modification: Principles, issues, and applications.* Boston: Houghton-Mifflin, 1976.

Fox, R. M. & Azrin, N. H. Restitution: A method of eliminating aggressive-disruptive behavior of retarded and brain damaged patients. *Behaviour Research and Therapy,* 1972, **10**, 15–27.

Gardner, J. E., Pearson, D. T., Bercovici, A. N., & Bricker, D. E. Measurement, evaluation, and modification of selected interactions between a schizophrenic child, his parents, and his therapist. *Journal of Consulting and Clinical Psychology,* 1968, **32**, 537–542.

Gittelman-Klein, D. F., Abikoff, H., Katz, S., Cloisten, A. C., & Kates, W. Relative efficacy of methylphenidate and behavior modification in hyperkinetic children: An interim report. *Journal of Abnormal Child Psychology*, 1976, **4**, 361–379.

Graziano, A. M., DeGiovanni, I. S., & Garcia, K. A. Behavioral treatment of children's fears: A review. *Psychological Bulletin*, 1979, **86**, 804–830.

Gurman, A. S. & Kniskern, D. P. Research on marital and family therapy: Progress, perspective, and prospect. In S. L. Garfield & A. E. Bergin (Eds.), *Handbook of psychotherapy and behavior change*. (2nd ed.) New York: Wiley, 1978.

Harris, S. L. A family systems approach to behavioral training with parents of autistic children. *Child Behavior Therapy*, in press.

Harris, S. L. Teaching language to nonverbal children—With emphasis on problems of generalization. *Psychological Bulletin*, 1975, **82**, 565–580.

Harris, S. L. & Ersner-Hershfield, R. Behavioral suppression of seriously disruptive behavior in psychotic and retarded patients: A review of punishment and its alternatives. *Psychological Bulletin*, 1978, **85**, 1,352–1,375.

Hatzenbuehler, L. C. & Schroeder, H. E. Desensitization procedures in the treatment of childhood disorders. *Psychological Bulletin*, 1978, **85**, 831–844.

Hewett, F. M. Teaching speech to an autistic child through operant conditioning. *American Journal of Orthopsychiatry*, 1965, **35**, 927–936.

Hobbs, S. A., Moguin, L. E., Tyroler, M., & Lahey, B. B. Cognitive behavior therapy with children: Has clinical utility been demonstrated? *Psychological Bulletin*, 1980, **87**, 147–165.

Jones, M. C. Elimination of children's fears. *Journal of Experimental Psychology*, 1924, **7**, 382–390. (a)

Jones, M. C. A laboratory study of fear: The case of Peter. *Pedagogical Seminary*, 1924, **31**, 308–315. (b)

Kanfer, F. H., Karoly, P., & Newman, A. Reduction of children's fear of the dark by competence-related and situational threat-related verbal cues. *Journal of Consulting and Clinical Psychology*, 1975, **43**, 251–258.

Kazdin, A. E. *The token economy*. New York: Plenum, 1977.

Kendall, P. C. & Wilcox, L. E. Cognitive-behavioral treatment for impulsivity: Concrete versus conceptual training in non-self-controlled problem children. *Journal of Consulting and Clinical Psychology*, 1980, **48**, 80–91.

Kimmel, H. D. & Kimmel, E. C. An instrumental conditioning method for the treatment of enuresis. *Journal of Behavior Therapy and Experimental Psychiatry*, 1970, **1**, 121–123.

Kuehn, B.S. & Christophersen, E. R. Preserving the rights of clients in child abuse and neglect. In G. T. Hannah, W. P. Christian, & H. B. Clark (Eds.), *Preservation of client rights*. New York: Free Press, 1981.

Lazarus, A. A. *Behavior therapy and beyond*. New York: McGraw-Hill, 1971.

Lazarus, A. A. The elimination of children's phobias by deconditioning. In H. J. Eysenck (Ed.), *Behaviour therapy and the neuroses*. Oxford, England: Pergamon, 1960.

Lazarus, A. A. The elimination of children's phobias by deconditioning. *Medical Proceedings*, 1959, **6**, 261–265.

Lazarus, A. A. & Abramovitz, A. The use of "emotive

imagery" in the treatment of children's phobias. *Journal of Mental Science*, 1962, **108**, 191–195.

Leitenberg, H. & Callahan, E. J. Reinforced practice and reduction of different kinds of fears in adults and children. *Behaviour Research and Therapy*, 1973, **11**, 19–30.

Little, V. L. & Kendall, P. C. Cognitive-behavioral interventions with delinquents: Problem solving, role-taking, and self-control. In P. C. Kendall & S. D. Hollon (Eds.), *Cognitive-behavioral interventions*. New York: Academic Press, 1979.

Loney, J., Weissenburger, F. E., Woolson, R. F., & Lichty, E. C. Comparing psychological and pharmacological treatments for hyperkinetic boys and their classmates. *Journal of Abnormal Child Psychology*, 1979, **7**, 133–143.

Lovaas, O. I., Berberich, J. P., Perloff, B. F., & Schaeffer, B. Acquisition of imitative speech by schizophrenic children. *Science*, 1966, **151**, 705–707.

Mann, J. & Rosenthal, T. Vicarious and direct counterconditioning of test anxiety through individual and group desensitization. *Behaviour Research and Therapy*, 1969, **7**, 359–367.

Margolies, P. J. Behavioral approaches to the treatment of early infantile autism: A review. *Psychological Bulletin*, 1977, **84**, 249–264.

McClannahan, L. E. & Krantz, P. J. Accountability systems for protection of the rights of autistic children and youth. In G. T. Hannah, W. P. Christian, & H. B. Clark (Eds.), *Preservation of client rights*. New York: Free Press, 1981.

Meichenbaum, D. H. & Goodman, J. Training impulsive children to talk to themselves: A means of developing self-control. *Journal of Abnormal Psychology*, 1971, **77**, 115–126.

Melamed, B. G. & Siegel, L. J. Reduction of anxiety in children facing surgery by modeling. *Journal of Consulting and Clinical Psychology*, 1975, **43**, 511–521.

Miller, L. C., Barrett, C. L., Hampe, E., & Noble, H. Factor structure of childhood fears. *Journal of Consulting and Clinical Psychology*, 1972, **39**, 264–268. (a)

Miller, L. C., Barrett, C. L., Hampe, E., & Noble, H. Comparison of reciprocal inhibition, psychotherapy, and waiting list control for phobic children. *Journal of Abnormal Psychology*, 1972, **79**, 269–279. (b)

Miller, P. M. The use of visual imagery and muscle relaxation in the counterconditioning of a phobic child: A case study. *Journal of Nervous and Mental Disease*, 1972, **154**, 457–460.

Montenegro, H. Severe separation anxiety in two preschool children successfully treated by reciprocal inhibition. *Journal of Child Psychology and Psychiatry*, 1968, **9**, 93–103.

Mowrer, O. H., & Mowrer, W. Enuresis: A method for its study and treatment. *American Journal of Orthopsychiatry*, 1938, **8**, 436–447.

Muller, S. D., & Madsen, C. H. Group desensitization for "anxious" children with reading problems. *Psychology in the Schools*, 1970, **7**, 184–189.

Murphy, C. M. & Bootzin, R. R. Active and passive participation in the contact desensitization of snake fear in children. *Behavior Therapy*, 1973, **4**, 203–211.

Ney, P. G. Combined psychotherapy and deconditioning of a child's phobia. *Canadian Psychiatric Associa-*

tion Journal, 1968, **13**, 293–294.

Nordyke, N. S., Baer, D. M., Etzel, B. C., & LeBlanc, J. M. Implications of the stereotyping and modification of sex role. Journal of Applied Behavior Analysis, 1977, **10**, 553–557.

Obler, M., & Terwilliger, R. F. Pilot study on the effectiveness of systematic desensitization with neurologically impaired children with phobic disorders. Journal of Consulting and Clinical Psychology, 1970, **34**, 314–318.

O'Dell, S. Training parents in behavior modification: A review. Psychological Bulletin, 1974, **81**, 418–433.

O'Leary, K. D. Pills or skills for hyperactive children. Journal of Applied Behavior Analysis, 1980, **13**, 191–204.

O'Leary, S. G. & Dubey, D. R. Applications of self-control procedures by children: A review. Journal of Applied Behavior Analysis, 1979, **12**, 449–465.

Oltmanns, T. F., Broderich, J. E., & O'Leary, K. D. Marital adjustment and the efficacy of behavior therapy with children. Journal of Consulting and Clinical Psychology, 1977, **45**, 724–729.

O'Reilly, P. P. Desensitization of fire bell phobia. Journal of School Psychology, 1971, **9**, 55–57.

Patterson, G. R., Reid, J. B., Jones, R. R., & Conger, R. E. A social learning approach to family intervention. Vol. I Families with aggressive children. Eugene, Oreg.: Castalia, 1975.

Pelham, W. E. Withdrawal of a stimulant drug and concurrent behavioral intervention in the treatment of a hyperactive child. Behavior Therapy, 1977, **8**, 473–479.

Pelham, W. E., Schnedler, R. W., Bologna, N. C., & Contreras, J. A. Behavioral and stimulant treatment of hyperactive children: A therapy study with methylphenidate probes in a within-subject design. Journal of Applied Behavior Analysis, 1980, **13**, 221–236.

Peterson, R. A., Wright, R. L. D., & Hanlon, C. C. The effects of extending the CS-UCS interval on the effectiveness of the conditioning treatment for nocturnal enuresis. Behaviour Research and Therapy, 1969, **7**, 351–357.

Pollack, M. J., & Sulzer-Azaroff, B. Protecting the educational rights of handicapped children. In G. T. Hannah, W. P. Christian, & H. B. Clark (Eds.), Preservation of client rights. New York: Free Press, 1981.

Rekers, G. A. Atypical gender development and psychosocial adjustment. Journal of Applied Behavior Analysis, 1977, **10**, 559–571.

Rekers, G. A. Stimulus control over sex-typed play in cross-gender identified boys. Journal of Experimental Child Psychology, 1975, **20**, 136–148.

Rekers, G. A. & Lovaas, O. I. Behavioral treatment of deviant sex-role behaviors in a male child. Journal of Applied Behavior Analysis, 1974, **7**, 173–190.

Rekers, G. A., Lovaas, O. I., & Low, B. The behavioral treatment of a "transsexual" preadolescent boy. Journal of Abnormal Child Psychology, 1974, **2**, 99–116.

Rincover, A., Koegel, R. L., & Russo, D. C. Some recent behavioral research on the education of autistic children. Education and Treatment of Children, 1978, **1**, 31–45.

Rosenbaum, M. S. & Drabman, R. S. Self-control training in the classroom: A review and critique. Journal

of Applied Behavior Analysis, 1979, **12**, 467–485.

Ross, A. O. Child behavior therapy. New York: Wiley, 1981.

Shafto, F. & Sulzbacher, S. Comparing treatment tactics with a hyperactive preschool child: Stimulant medication and programmed teacher intervention. Journal of Applied Behavior Analysis, 1977, **10**, 13–20.

Stableford, W., Butz, R., Hasazi, J., Leitenberg, H., & Peyser, J. Sequential withdrawal of stimulant drugs and use of behavior therapy with two hyperactive boys. American Journal of Orthopsychiatry, 1976, **46**, 302–312.

Taylor, P. D. & Turner, R. K. A clinical trial of continuous, intermittent, and overlearning "bell and pad" treatments for nocturnal enuresis. Behaviour Research and Therapy, 1975, **13**, 281–293.

Timbers, G. D., Jones, R. J., & Davis, J. L. Safeguarding the rights of children and youth in group-home treatment settings. In G. T. Hannah, W. P. Christian, & H. B. Clark (Eds.), Preservation of client rights. New York: Free Press, 1981.

Van Der Ploeg, H. M. Treatment of frequency of urination by stories competing with anxiety. Journal of Behavior Therapy and Experimental Psychiatry, 1975, **6**, 165–166.

Wahler, R. G., Winkel, G. H., Patterson, R. F., & Morrison, D. C. Mothers as behavior therapists for their own children. In A. M. Graziano (Ed.), Behavior therapy with children. Chicago: Aldine-Atherston, 1971.

Watson, J. B. & Rayner, P. Conditioned emotional reactions. Journal of Experimental Psychology, 1920, **3**, 1–14.

Whalen, C. K. & Henker, B. Psychostimulants and children: A review and analysis. Psychological Bulletin, 1976, **83**, 1,113–1,130.

Winkler, R. C. What types of sex-role behavior should behavior modifiers promote? Journal of Applied Behavior Analysis, 1977, **10**, 549–552.

Wish, P. A., Hasazi, J. E., & Jurgela, A. R. Automated direct deconditioning of a childhood phobia. Journal of Behavior Therapy and Experimental Psychiatry, 1973, **4**, 279–283.

Wolf, M. M., Risley, T. R., & Mees, H. Application of operant conditioning procedures to the behavior problems of an autistic child. Behaviour Research and Therapy, 1964, **1**, 305–312.

Wolraich, M., Drummond, T., Salomon, M. K., O'Brien, M. L., & Sivage, C. Effects of methylphenidate alone and in combination with behavior modification procedures on the behavior and academic performance of hyperactive children. Journal of Abnormal Child Psychology, 1978, **6**, 149–161.

Wulbert, M. & Dries, R. The relative efficacy of methylphenidate (Ritalin) and behavior-modification techniques in the treatment of a hyperactive child. Journal of Applied Behavior Analysis, 1977, **10**, 21–31.

Young, G. C. & Morgan, R. T. T. Overlearning in the conditioning treatment of enuresis. Behaviour Research and Therapy, 1972, **10**, 147–151.

Zaleski, A., Gerrard, J. W., & Shokier, M. H. K. Nocturnal enuresis: The importance of a small bladder capacity. In I. Kolvin, R. C. MacKeith, & S. R. Meadow (Eds.), Bladder control and enuresis. Philadelphia: Lippincott, 1973.

28 PSYCHOANALYTIC PSYCHOTHERAPY WITH CHILDREN

Kevin O'Connor
Anna C. Lee
Charles E. Schaefer

Psychoanalysis was first proposed by Freud as a metapsychology and technique by which to understand infantile sexuality in psychic life (Freud, 1900, 1905, 1909). While he based his formulations on child and adolescent cases, his theory was formulated in order to understand the roots of neurosis in adults. Child analysis, considered an extension of adult analysis, officially began in 1908 with Freud's supervision of the case of Little Hans. At that time he presumed that only a parent could adequately act as an analyst for such a young child. He believed that a child could not sufficiently trust a stranger to permit a therapeutic interchange. Hug-Hellmuth (1921) introduced the use of drawings and some free play into the analytic sessions in order to facilitate her direct treatment of children as young as six. Since this time, two schools of child analysis have emerged, led by Anna Freud and by Melanie Klein.

Regarding play as a symbolic representation of the child's inner life, Anna Freud (1936, 1945, 1965, 1974) emphasized it as the child's primary mode of communication. Though she later dismissed it, she introduced the concept of a preparatory period by which a child patient could be engaged in a therapeutic alliance. Her interpretation was held to a minimum while intervention was directed toward the fostering of the working relationship. This preparation was thought to be necessary to maintain the child's participation throughout the subsequent phase, during which the analyst interpreted deep unconscious material. With the advent of ego psychology (A. Freud, 1936) and defense interpretation this preparatory phase was deemed unnecessary. Children experienced defense interpretation as much less threatening than the interpretation of deeper unconscious material, thereby allowing the work of analysis to begin before an intense alliance was established.

Melanie Klein (1955), in contrast, emphasized the direct interpretation of drive material. Though she considered the importance of the therapeutic alliance, she placed greater emphasis on direct interpretation of unconscious and preconscious processes, as revealed by the child's play. An extremely gifted and intuitive clinician, Klein proposed theoretical formulations and technical modifications that have been somewhat integrated into child analytic thinking in Britain. In the United States, however, Anna Freud has proved the theoretician most influential on the development of child analysis.

In the first part of this chapter we shall present

adaptations of the basic child analytic techniques that allow the analyst to treat children at various developmental levels. Regardless of the extent of the adaptation, these approaches retain the following features that characterize them as analysis (Sharfman, 1978, p. 48):

1. The maintenance of the analytic stance which sets as few limitations as possible on the direction of the treatment. As such, the analyst follows the free expression of the patient's thoughts and actions, attending to those derivatives of the psychic structures as they present in their interaction.

2. Interpretation is the basic technique utilized to deal with defenses as they impede the flow of material and with transference manifestations as they appear in the course of treatment.

3. The analyst restricts the use of educative measures or attempts to change the child's environment as much as possible, intervening only where necessary to maintain the continuity of the analytic treatment.

4. The goal of treatment is to allow individuals to fulfill their development as completely as they can by helping to make conscious those unconscious elements which impede effective functioning.

5. The person of the analyst is offered as an object with whom the patient can interact and in whose presence he may experience any thoughts and feelings past, present and future as may arise. The analyst does not limit the patient's varying perceptions of him but continuously analyzes them.

In the second part of this chapter we shall present adaptations of the various child analytic techniques that facilitate the analytic treatment of children with nonneurotic disorders. The adaptations were necessitated by some analysts' desire to treat children who did not necessarily meet the criteria for traditional analysis. Some of the techniques do not retain enough of the features listed above to be considered analysis proper; however, they all share the common framework of psychoanalytic theory.

Before continuing with our discussion of the wide range of techniques broadly referred to as psychoanalytic psychotherapy, it seems necessary to clarify the use of certain terms. First, some authors feel that the different adaptations of the traditional technique are not necessarily equivalent, and that this disparity should be reflected in the terminology. To this end, we have used the terms "modifications" and "parameters." Modifications refer to changes in the technique necessitated by the child's developmental level. Parameters are changes necessitated by the child's particular pathology. Changes made for any other reasons are technical errors. Beyond this a number of terms are used to refer to the treatment and the person performing it. Three terms are used to refer to the treatment: "psychotherapy," "psychoanalytic psychotherapy," and "analysis." Psychotherapy refers to any type of psychological intervention regardless of its theoretical basis. Psychoanalytic psychotherapy refers to techniques that are based on psychoanalytic theory but do not conform to the rigid technical guidelines of child psychoanalysis. Finally, analysis is reserved for the specific technique of using interpretation to resolve a patient's internalized conflicts. As the therapeutic interventions were differentiated, so were the individuals carrying out the treatment. The term "analyst" was used to refer to individuals with specialized training in the performance of child analysis as a specific technique. The term "therapist" was used in reference to any individual performing psychotherapy regardless of theoretical background.

Having briefly reviewed the history of child analysis and the associated terminology, we shall now proceed to a discussion of the child analytic technique.

Modifications of the Analytic Technique for the Treatment of Children at Various Developmental Levels

The Fundamentals of Child Analysis

The conduct of child analysis has traditionally involved several features: frequent contacts, work with the parents, the use of a play setting and materials, interpretation, and the development of the transference. Foremost among these is frequent contact consisting of five-times weekly sessions of 45- or 50-minute duration (Sandler, Kennedy & Tyson, 1980). Such frequency allows for intense observation of the patient's functioning. It also fosters the development of empathy in the analyst in order to understand and interpret properly.

Lastly, it helps the patient develop an optimum intensity of emotional reaction to the analyst (Glenn, 1978a).

In an effort to obtain additional information about the patient's past and present environment, the child analyst generally sees the patient's parents, especially the mother. Initially, the parent-analyst contacts are at weekly intervals; later, their frequency will be determined by the course of the treatment. While the analyst may tell the child what his parents have revealed, he maintains strict confidentiality about the patient's communications. This is essential in the building of the patient's trust in revealing his inner secrets, though such a stance may often cause grief and resentment in parents eager to know the details of their child's feelings and attitudes.

The young patient is seen in either a consultation room or a play room. For those unable or resistive toward verbalization, they are invited to play with materials and toys in the setting. It is preferable to provide materials that enable the child to depict his own wishes and fantasies. These may include crayons, paints, blocks, dolls and doll houses, cars, clay, plasticene, or other materials. Organized games are generally less preferable, as they tend to restrict the child's self-expression.

Typically, children reveal themselves in both verbal and nonverbal ways. Unable to free associate, they express themselves through play, drawing, painting, and bodily movements. Ideally, the child's communication should encompass a balance of primary and secondary process thinking. It should involve sufficient organization for the analyst to understand the communication and evidence enough loosening of control to allow for the emergence of hidden aspects of the personality — i.e., drive derivatives, affects, fantasies, wishes, dreams, defenses, and conflicts. Since some anxiety may attend the child's expression of threatening material, the analyst must gauge his comments or interpretations so as to help the child overcome resistances without inducing panic (Glenn, 1978a).

Interpretations, the primary instrument of therapeutic change in analysis, are generally made in an orderly and systematic way (Harley & Sabot, 1980). Typically, defenses are interpreted before drives, and surface material before deeper, unconscious material. External influences, including the person of the analyst, are taken into account within the interpretation. Interpretations of conflictual material should be timely and offered in an empathic, human way, that respects the patient's affect. The last tenet is especially true in communicating with children, and should preclude heavy, ponderous comments that are seldom effectively received, much less understood. Direct and specific association of the child's play to the interpretation is cautioned since it often leads to constriction of play. The ultimate goal of the analytic work is the revision of psychic structures and functions in order to foster optimum development.

Brody (1974) elucidates the effectiveness with which Berta Bornstein (1949) incorporated all these tenets in the analysis of a five-year-old phobic patient. Bornstein maintained that the key to treatment of children lies in the patient's need to be understood according to his level of ego development. As such, she underscored interpretation of the affect before the drive defense, always with delicacy and tact. Only after interpretation of typical patterns of defense, moreover, could the unconscious content of a child's play be interpreted effectively.

Less stable in child than in adult analysis, the development of the therapeutic and working alliance requires consideration of various aspects and adaptations of the traditional technique. Primary among these is the lack of motivation by the child during the initial stage, and sometimes throughout the treatment. Most often the child is brought into treatment by the parents or on the recommendation of a school. Rarely does the child initiate the treatment process, although some children do acknowledge their suffering and need for assistance. The therapeutic alliance, then, is by necessity affected by the presence of the parents. This presents further complications affecting transferential and countertransferential issues (Blos & Finch, 1975; Kabenell, 1974; Marcus, 1980; Shane, 1980; Wolman, 1978).

Other aspects that merit consideration include the following: (1) the child's poorly developed time sense, thereby precluding projection into the future as to the benefits of treatment and exacerbating the sense of burden imposed by treatment; (2) the child's tendency to externalize the source of difficulties rather than to look inside himself to understand his reactions to the environment; this sometimes creates resentment and disappointment when the analyst refrains from intervening in the external environment; (3) the vicissitudes of psychic equilibrium throughout phases of development often threaten to overwhelm the ego and militate against the ego's active participation in the therapeutic alliance; (4) the child's incapacity for self-observing ego functions, especially before late latency, renders more difficult the task of understanding the nature and meaning of the interaction; and (5) periods of development exist, specifically in latency and adolescence, in which the child experiences a specific turning away from intense affective experiences with parents and other libidinal objects. In consequence, the relationship with the analyst during these phases often poses a threat to defenses against regression to earlier feelings and fantasies that are now viewed as unacceptable (Sharfman, 1978).

Lane (1980) underscores the necessity of developing a significant real-object relationship to the therapist, at least initially, in order to develop a working therapeutic alliance and to lay the groundwork for future transference interpretations. On the other hand, Anna Freud (1974) suggests the use of a preparatory period while Neubauer (1978) recommends special types of "education" regarding the analytic process for some children. Again, these are dictated less by conditions of psychoanalysis than by the reactions and needs of specific patients.

The nature and development of the transference in child and adolescent analysis continue to stimulate controversy. Though she revised her original stance about the inability of children to develop a full transference neurosis, Anna Freud (1965) still doubted that transference neuroses in children equalled the adult variety in every respect. This was based on the difficulty in tracing the development of libidinal transferential components, given the ongoing involvement with primary love objects. The development and understanding of the transference was further complicated by the child's limited ability for free association, the analyst's need to restrict certain types of motor discharge, the multiple object representations invested in the person of the analyst, and the tendency of children and adolescents to seek new objects rather than objects of displacement. On balance, the predominance of transference reactions as the core of experience with the analyst remains less clear, though some children are obviously capable of developing a true transference neurosis within the analytic situation which involves the repetition of specific neurotic conflicts experienced in earlier periods.

The foregoing principles are considered the definitive, basic features of child analysis. Historically, these changes were made in the analytic technique to allow the analyst to treat children. As ex-

perience accrued in the treatment of children, further adaptations were made to allow for differences in the patient's developmental phase. Most of these adaptations were created for children in latency. In the following material, however, we shall also discuss adaptations made for the prelatency child and the adolescent.

The Analysis of Latency-Age Children

Typically used to denote the period between the sixth and the twelfth year, latency was described by Freud (1905) as that period in which there exists a period of sexual quiescence, a period of biologically determined diminution of drive activity. Sarnoff (1976, 1978) and Benson and Harrison (1980) emphasize the relative calm, pliability, and educability of the child at this stage, who has newly emerged from the urgency of the oedipal period. The drives are dealt with through the emergence of repression, sublimation, reaction formation, fragmentation, displacement, symbol formation, synthesis and secondary elaboration, and fantasy formation. The latency-age child will work strenuously to protect these newly acquired defenses, which are threatened by analysis. He is also likely to idealize action and may therefore experience difficulty in containing his activity both in and outside the analysis (Kramer & Byerly, 1978).

Bornstein (1951) divided latency into two stages: early and late. The first period, extending from age 5½ years to 8, is characterized by newly acquired and undependable self-regulating mechanisms defending against the incestuous attachments of the oedipal period. Formed at the end of the latter period, the superego appears inordinately strict at some times and ineffectual at others. Bornstein emphasized temporary regression to pregenital impulses as a characteristic line of defense for this period. Guilt feelings are particularly painful and intolerable and give rise to two defensive measures: identification with the aggressor and projection of guilt.

The second period of latency, lasting from approximately eight to ten years of age, is characterized by more dependable defenses, especially the solidification of reaction formation and sublimation, as well as a less strict superego. Indeed, the developmental task of latency involves warding off drives and their regressive derivatives. Masturbation is quickly forgotten when it occurs. As the child comes to view his parents more realistically, their inner representations in the superego may also become less threatening to the ego, rendering the eight- to ten-year old more content with himself and his world. For these reasons, Bornstein felt that late latency was a less favorable time for analysis than early latency. In contrast, the first period is characterized by defenses that are not yet consolidated. Nor have reaction formations and character formations crystallized. The psychic structure is more modifiable and presents one of the best times for analysis (Becker, 1974).

INDICATIONS

Latency-age children are often capable of feeling bad about their symptoms, and viewing them as ego-dystonic. They may be able to search for their causation and alleviation. Indications for treatment include a well-established neurosis that has resulted in libidinal regression and interfered with the forward progression of development. The analyst should assess the extent to which the child's ego development has been hampered by neurotic symptomatology. These may include excessive reliance on certain defenses—e.g., repression, reaction formation, isolation, denial, and withdrawal into fantasy. Disorders of gender identity and sexual perversion provide other indications for treatment. The application of technique for children with nonneurotic disorders will be further discussed later in this chapter.

GOALS

The essential aim is to modify the child's developmental arrest and reinstate normal development. Concomitant with this are interim goals aimed toward reduction of anxiety and depression and alleviation of the presenting symptoms. These may include school difficulties (school refusal and school phobia), disturbance of object relationships, academic dysfunction unrelated to neurological disturbance, enuresis, encopresis, and others.

TECHNIQUE

Special considerations in the analysis of latency-age children include: how the child communicates his thoughts and feelings to the analyst; how the analyst structures interpretations and statements to the child; and various aspects of the relationship between the child and the analyst.

The child expresses himself with both play and verbalizations. While play may often predominate,

the child's increasing verbal capacity renders him more likely to use words by which he can gain insight into his unconscious affects, fantasies, and drives. Dramatization through play becomes more purposeful, leaving the analyst freer to direct his observations toward what the child does and to choose carefully timed, appropriate interventions. It is imperative in the course of the analysis that the child learns to communicate his internal processes through words rather than rely on action (Kramer & Byerly, 1978).

Kramer and Byerly (1978) further stress three types of verbal communications by the analyst occurring in the analytic interaction: (1) running comments; (2) confrontation; and (3) interpretations. Running comments sum up what the patient has said, thereby familiarizing the patient and the analyst with the patient's productions and laying the groundwork for later confrontations and interpretations. Running comments also demonstrate the analyst's interest in the child's activity, thereby fostering the child's continued output. Closely related to running comments, confrontations draw on both immediate and past material to make the patient aware that a defense is being used. Here the analyst attempts to acquaint the patient with patterns and configurations that are characteristic of the material he brings to sessions. The analyst should prepare the child for interpretation by making comments that show the child that more than one meaning exists for his material and relate the defense to the unconscious material being defended against. By sharing knowledge with the patient, the analyst helps the child to participate in the analytic process and renders the pathological configuration of psychic structures less ego-syntonic.

The relationship between the child and the analyst may often be complicated by issues pertinent to children of this age. While some children do develop transference neuroses, it is more than likely that latency-age children will manifest transference reaction. In addition, they may respond to the analyst as an object of displacement or as a new object. While they are able to develop a therapeutic alliance with the analyst, latency-age children exhibit particularly strong expression of conflicts (Hamm, 1967). In their recovery from the oedipal conflict, the fear of losing the hard-won dominance of secondary process thinking militates against awareness of unacceptable impulses.

Having examined the adaptations of analytic technique for latency-age children, we shall now consider the special modifications necessary for the treatment of prelatency-age children.

The Analysis of Prelatency Age Children

While the term "prelatency" is reserved for all children who have not yet entered the psychosexual stage of latency, the term is typically applied to children under six years of age. The basic issues of the period involve the child's negotiation through the three stages of psychosexual development, as described by Freud (1905), where the libidinal cathexis shifts from the oral to the anal and phallic stages. Mahler (1968) and Mahler, Pine, and Bergman (1975) outline the stages of development of a sense of self separate from, and in relation to, the world. These include: (a) the *autistic stage*, where the child is largely unaware of the external world; (b) the *symbiotic stage*, in which the mother is experienced as a part of the child's self; and (c) the *separation-individuation stage*, which culminates in the achievement of object constancy at three years of age.

Glenn (1978b) emphasizes that children past three who manifest arrests or regressions to earlier stages can be analyzed, depending upon the phase of conflict. Those arrested in the autistic or symbiotic subphase are not amenable to traditional analysis, while the technique has been successful with many prelatency children who have not yet achieved object constancy or who are engaged in intense rapprochement conflicts.

Glenn (1978b) points out two interrelated phenomena characteristic of prelatency children: (1) the gradual diminution of narcissism and the emergence of increased object relations (Freud, 1914) and (2) the gradual change from primary process to secondary process thinking (Freud, 1900). Piaget and Inhelder (1969) describe the evolution of the child's cognitive processes, especially the role played by semiotic (symbolic) function wherein one thing stands for another, enabling the child to speak. The semiotic function allows for increasingly complex forms of play and frequently deals with unconscious conflict: sexual interests, defenses against anxiety, phobias, aggression, or identification with aggressors, withdrawal from fear of risk or competition, etc. (Piaget & Inhelder, 1969). With the development of the semiotic function and the appearance of concrete operations, the child gradually becomes less egocentric and more capable of seeing the world from other points of view. Narcissism decreases and object orientation increases. Thus, the older the prelatency child treated, the more traditional the technique.

Prelatency children are described as imaginative, enthusiastic, and frank. Though egocentric, they evidence a growing cathexis of object representations. The intensity of drives compels the child to express himself in speech and play. Defenses are fluid and less fixed at this period, while superego pressures are relatively weak. Prelatency children are far more willing than latency children to express their wishes, desires, and fantasies. The balance of the child's cognition favors primary over secondary process, although a child over three can sufficiently clarify his thinking through speech and structured play to allow for analysis.

INDICATIONS

Many prelatency children develop symptoms during the phallic oedipal stage, including phobias, conversion symptoms, psychosomatic problems, sleep disturbance, and obsessive-compulsive symptoms. These may represent vicissitudes of developmental conflicts, and may or may not represent an infantile neurosis. Transient symptoms, typical of the pre-oedipal and oedipal stages, simple reactions to external stress, do not warrant analysis. Only when these symptoms appear in a pathological personality would analysis be indicated. A childhood neurosis seems in place where there is indication of a permanently established regression in ego or superego development. Developmental arrests or severe inner conflict unresolved by time and normal development would also suggest analytic treatment (Glenn, 1978b). Lastly, impairment of some areas of ego functioning, depending on the intensity and duration of the child's symptoms, may provide further indication for treatment (Sharfman, 1978). A necessary prerequisite for analysis of children of this age lies in the development of sufficient self and object differentiation and stability of object representation. This allows for the development of a relationship with the analyst as a separate person.

Evaluation of the family is particularly critical when treating a child of this age, especially when societal and/or parental pathology is thought to cause or maintain the child's symptoms or developmental arrest. The parents must also cooperate in providing information to the analyst regarding the child's functioning outside the analysis, bringing him to the sessions, supporting the analysis financially, and tolerating changes in the child as a result of the analysis.

GOALS

As in analysis during latency, the goal with prelatency children is to remove those obstacles impeding development and to facilitate the child's progress in all areas of psychic growth. Interpretation of resistances and transference and unconscious aspects of drive derivatives, ego, and superego all aim at the greater dominance of the ego.

TECHNIQUE

Special considerations in the analysis of prelatency-age children include: how the child communicates his thoughts and feelings; how the analyst structures interpretations and statements to the child; various aspects of the relationship betwen the child and the analyst; and the role of the parent in the child's treatment.

Prelatency children express themselves primarily through direct conversation with the analyst and by using toys, clay, drawings, and paintings in fantasy play. Often, it is necessary for the analyst to participate in the play in order to encourage the child's expression of his or her fantasy life. The analyst may take direct orders from the child about what to say or do within the play. The child is encouraged to describe his or her thoughts and feelings either in simple conversation or while engaged in the play.

Interpretations, according to Glenn (1978b), can be classified thus: (1) defense interpretations; (2) descriptions of conflict; (3) interpretation of drive derivatives and the content of fantasy; (4) reconstructions; (5) transference interpretations; and (6) interpretations of displacements. Especially pertinent in the initial phase of treatment is the interpretation of effects, namely those that are suppressed, displaced, or reversed. The analyst may also ask clarifying questions about an event and how the child experienced it. When interpretations fail and acting out occurs, the analyst may need to resort to physical restriction until such time as the child regains control of secondary process thinking.

A special caveat relevant for this stage lies in the fact that the prelatency-age child is less likely to suffer from his symptoms, which affects the development of the therapeutic alliance. Often, the therapeutic alliance and transference proper are formed simultaneously (Lesser, 1972). Prelatency children tend to externalize rather than recognize some of their problems as of their own making. This may cause them to experience difficulty in forming a mutual, trusting relationship during the initial phase of treatment. The technique of defense analysis has allowed for the work of analysis to begin despite these initial difficulties in developing the relationship between the analyst and the child.

When treating prelatency children, the analyst is put in the position of having to work very closely with the child's parents. With latency-age children the analyst-parent relationship is generally based on an informer-consultant model. The analyst sees the parent in order to keep abreast of changes in the child's life situation, and to ensure the parents' cooperation in their child's analysis. With prelatency-age children, the analyst may actually choose to work with the parent. This working relationship might involve the analyst treating a parent, the analyst and the mother or father jointly treating the child, or the analyst supervising the parent's treatment of the child (Fraiberg, Shapiro, & Spitz-Cherniss, 1980). This last modality is called filial therapy; it is considered the treatment of choice for children under the age of five (Furman, 1979), whose conflict has not yet been internalized (Ack, Beale, & Ware, 1975).

Ack et al. (1975) state that in order for filial therapy to be successful, the child's parent must meet the following criteria: She or he should not be psychotic or have an infantile personality; she or he should not be exclusively engaged in sadomasochistic relationships; she or he should not be so narcissistic that she would be overwhelmed with guilt if the child should improve in treatment, and she or he should be sufficiently motivated to carry out the treatment.

The basic technique of filial therapy involves the analyst interpreting the child's behavior to the parent. The analyst sees the parent one or more times a week and during the session, the parent discusses the child's behavior at length. The analyst then helps the parent "analyze" this material and teaches him or her how to communicate this knowledge to the child (Ack et al., 1975). The purpose of this procedure is to increase the parent's ability to emphathize with the child, thereby creating an environment that will optimize the child's development. A useful adjunct to the procedure is the placement of the child in a therapeutic nursery school. This allows the analyst another arena in which to observe the child's behavior, and creates a situation in which the child can be taught about effects and their management (Furman & Katan, 1969).

Ack et al. (1975) suggest that the major difficulties with this technique involve the management of the parent's affects. First, she or he may try to reenact the parent-child relationship in interactions with the analyst, essentially a transference situation. Second, the parent may have difficulty with her or his own genetic material, which requires direct intervention. Lastly, the parent may need support in order to maintain her or his therapeutic stance as changes in the child's behavior threaten the family's homeostatis.

The Analysis of Adolescents

Analysis of adolescents dates back to Freud's publication of the case of Dora (1905). Much controversy continues about the appropriateness of analysis for this phase. Anna Freud (1958), for instance, cautioned against recommending analysis for adolescents on the premise that the need for adolescents to ward off infantile object ties would jeopardize the development of a workable transference and, hence, the effect of analysis. Adolescents are also likely to experience threatening affects as attached to the analyst's person, and to remove themselves from the analyst as they would from parents. A considerable number of analysts, however, including Blos (1975), Geleerd (1967), and Harley (1974) have undertaken the analysis of adolescents and have contributed significantly to the elaborations and modifications of the conceptual framework of this developmental stage.

As in latency, adaptations of the analytic technique are necessary because of the adolescent's fear of being overwhelmed by drive impulses. Thus, a significant part of the technique focuses on increasing the tolerance of the ego. Analytic effort should also be directed toward superego functions, not only defenses against drives. The latter, however, are undeniably evident in the "Sturm und Drang" of this period, particularly in issues related to the reawakening of sexual impulses and autonomy strivings.

INDICATIONS

Classical neuroses of the hysterical or obessional types are emphasized by those who have worked with adolescents as providing the optimum indication for analysis with adolescents. Anna Freud (1958) suggested analysis for adolescents who manifest narcissistic withdrawal of the libido to the self, where marked grandiose ideas and hypochondriacal preoccupations are evident. Analysis is also indicated for adolescents described as "ascetic" individuals. These are youngsters who typically attempt to ward off their burgeoning sexuality through denial of physical needs and comforts. Other indications include regression in libidinal level, inhibited ego functions and ego restrictions, perverse sexual symptoms and wishes to be of the opposite sex, and impulse disorders that have as their basis a marked defense against depression. Ego constriction is manifested in learning difficulties in school, social withdrawal, and the adolescent's lack of interest in the environment.

Friend (1972) further suggested the following criteria for suitability of analysis in this age group. He emphasizes the capacity to verbalize and delay gratification, the individual's cathexis of a given interest or activity, his ability to achieve fantasy formation, daydreams, and dreams. Further, careful assessment should be made of the individual's capacity for object constancy, for tolerating anxiety without disorganization, and for self-observation. His intellectual capacity for learning and problem solving should also be considered. Lastly, the individual should show some indication of progression along the lines of genital primacy.

GOALS

Analysis with adolescents aims at several aspects of psychic functioning. Friend (1972) further stressed clarifying the genetic aspects of the individual's development with the revival of visual and affective memories. The ego ideal and conscience are expanded with the resolution of ego problems in such areas as learning, memory, sexual inadequacy, or other inhibitions of function. The nature of the anxiety and the responses to it should be better understood. The adolescent should develop an ability to maintain a closer understanding and trusting relationship with another person beyond a level of simple identification. He should attain an increased sense of himself as an individual, along with a better capacity for self-awareness and expression. Lastly, there should be improvement in the psychic relationships as well as in social functioning.

TECHNIQUE

The following presents the adaptations to the technique involving the setting, interpretations, and transference relationship necessary for the treatment of adolescents.

Within the setting, the analyst should expect the period of assessment to take a longer time than with latency or prelatency children, given many adolescents' difficulty in entering into the therapeutic alliance. Prolonged silences should not be allowed, given the adolescent's general intolerance of situations lacking reciprocity and feedback. Further, the adolescent will be testing the analyst during each step for his capacity to empathize and understand his thoughts and feelings. He will often need to experience the analyst as a real object before fully engaging in the therapeutic alliance. Although the adolescent relies on verbal rather than nonverbal communication, the use of the couch is generally experienced as a regressive threat and should, therefore, be avoided.

While the parents continue to play a critical role in their support of the analysis, their participation in the treatment should generally be limited and carefully defined. This is necessitated by the adolescent's developmental pressure to separate from primary love objects during this phase.

With regards to adaptations of the rules of interpretation, Settlage (1974) proposed the following:

1. Recognition should be made of the position of the ego and its need for defenses. Strengthening of the ego is particularly important in the adolescent whose ego is greatly threatened by the intensified emergence of instinctual forces.
2. Analysis of the defense and what it defends against should be undertaken simultaneously. The ultimate goal is to make clear that something is being warded off, how this is done, what is being warded off, and why. Obervation of verbal and nonverbal behavior will lead to inference of the defenses and reasons for them. One should interpret the current behavior before transference and genetic interpretations.
3. Attention should be focused on the most superficial layers of defense with the assumption that the ego will have a greater tolerance for the ex-

posure of warded-off content than at the deeper and more highly defended levels. Interpretations should proceed from the surface.
4. Analysis of the defense neither removes nor entirely destroys the defense. The patient is not forced to yield defenses. Rather, there is a modification and increased appropriateness of defenses.

With regard to the transference neurosis, it must be in mind that its nature is often obscured by the fact that the phase-specific libidinal push and defensive attempts to deal with it involve the analyst in different roles. Since adolescence is characterized by a search for new objects or new levels of relationships, the analyst may not only be seen as a transference object or object of displacement, he may also be seen as a new object. This, too, affects the development of the transference in its purest forms.

As for the intensity and depth of the transference phenomenon, adolescent analysis has shown great variation. The extent to which a patient may develop a full transference experience often depends on the choices made by the analyst in interpreting the transference.

The development of a transference neurosis and its resolution would be the indication for termination, as it would be in adult analysis. Since some adolescents will not develop a transference neurosis, however, an interrupted or periodic analysis seems not an uncommon phenomenon. This variation thereby responds to the adolescent's developmental push to function apart from family and analyst.

Parameters for the Application of Psychoanalysis to the Treatment of Children with Special Problems

Not only have analysts broadened the impact of their treatment by modifying it to include children at virtually every age, they have attempted to define parameters that allow the technique to be applied to children whose disturbances do not fall in the neurotic range. The alternative diagnostic groups to be considered here include: (1) children with gross developmental disturbances; (2) children whose difficulties are, in some way, related to various reality issues; (3) children whose difficulties are the result of exposure to toxic environmental situations; and finally, (4) children whose disorders primarily involve a lack of impulse control.

Children Manifesting Gross Developmental Disturbances

Psychotic Children

INDICATIONS

Relatively early in the history of child analysis various analysts were interested in applying the technique to children with serious disturbances in ego functioning. Two main approaches to the treatment of autism and childhood schizophrenia came out of the 1940s and 1950s. Bender (1956) and Kanner (1942) perceived these psychotic disorders to have a heavy physiological component and advocated the use of specialized educational techniques as the primary mode of treatment. Rank (1949), Szurek and Berlin (1956), and Bettelheim (1967) stressed the psychological origins of the disorders and advocated psychotherapy as the primary mode of treatment. At present the argument over the physiologic versus psychologic origins of these disorders has been temporarily resolved in favor of a multiple-causation model, and pharmacotherapy is widely used as an adjunct to psychotherapy of some type. One of the most comprehensive models of psychoanalytic therapy with psychotic children is outlined by Ekstein, Caruth, Cooper, Friedman, Landres, Liebowitz, and Nelson (1978), who consider any psychotic symptomatology manifested in childhood to be an indication for immediate intervention. No specific criteria are listed to specify children appropriate to the technique discussed, reflecting their bias towards psychoanalytic therapy.

GOALS

The treatment goals for a psychotic child are much the same as those of traditional analysis — namely the reestablishment of the child's normal developmental process. The implications of this goal, however, are very different when one is referring to psychotic as opposed to neurotic children. With neurotic children, one is generally trying to promote movement into the appropriate phase of psychosexual development and to prevent regression to earlier levels of functioning. With a psychotic child, development may never have moved beyond the autistic or symbiotic levels (Mahler, 1968) or the oral or anal levels, or regression to these levels may have already occurred when treatment is initiated. Because the psychotic child is functioning on such a primitive level, an initial goal may be to have the child simply relate to the analyst as an object—already a significant departure from traditional technique.

TECHNIQUE

As was just mentioned, a significant departure from the traditional analytic stance may be necessary in order to help the psychotic child begin to experience the therapist as an object. Kestenbaum (1978), Fe d'Ostiani (1980), and Bender and Gurevitz (1955) all stress the role of the therapist as a person in the therapy of a psychotic child. Although they do not state it as such, these authors recognize the need for the therapist to somehow become a part of the child's fantasy world, to become "real" for the child, before any significant progress is made. The value of this position seems unassailable in that it would be unreasonable to expect the child to respond, either positively or negatively, to an object who is not even a part of his or her own reality.

Within the treatment setting, most psychotic children will communicate with the therapist on the level of primary process. Despite the tendency of many therapists to dismiss these ramblings as reflecting either pure impulse or some terribly distorted view of reality, it is imperative that this not be done. The therapist must attempt to follow the child's thought process and to decipher it (Shafii, 1979). Similarly, the analyst must attempt to understand and sort out the child's behavior and nonverbal communications.

In dealing with a psychotic child, it is imperative that the therapist present a clear and consistent picture of reality (Kestenbaum, 1978). Although this is a requirement of any good intervention throughout the course of the treatment, it may need to be temporarily suspended early on as the therapist tries to engage the child. In the early phase, it may be necessary for the analyst to make interpretations within the child's fantasy or to mirror or imitate some of the child's behavior (Shafii, 1979). As the child becomes more aware of the analyst as an entity to be acknowledged, the therapist must increasingly encourage the child to join in his reality rather than vice versa. The primary way that external reality is emphasized with the child is through the interpretation of affects. The attempt here is to strengthen the child's ego functioning by giving him labels for affects and by relating those affects to concrete experiences. Similarly, the therapist must help the child "translate" his inner fantasy and experience into age-appropriate language.

Certain transferential and countertransferential issues may take on special significance in the treatment of psychotic children. Fe d'Ostiani (1980) suggests that through the transference the psychotic child will repeat the mother's primal failure to cope with his difficulty. That is, the child will manifest the same behaviors and responses that originally created or augmented the mother's inability to relate to him. These manifestations will in turn cause the analyst to respond with behaviors similar to the mother's through the countertransference. Only as this pattern is recognized and then altered by the therapist does the child begin to improve. This formulation counters the traditional view that psychotic children cannot form a transference, but instead the therapist should encourage the child to become identified with him (Bender & Gurevitz, 1955).

A much more fundamental counterference experience that the therapist must manage in treating psychotic children is the anxiety created by the resurgence of his own primary process material. Many a therapist has been overwhelmed by the feelings of loss of control that they experience when just confronted with a psychotic child. Obviously, these feelings can be managed through adequate supervision or by having the therapist treat less severely disturbed children in addition to his caseload of psychotic patients.

SPECIAL ISSUES

A significant issue in the treatment of psychotic children is their very poor prognosis. Bender and Gurevitz (1955), in a follow-up of schizophrenic children, noted that all of the children improved with psychotherapy and that these improvements remained fairly constant throughout latency. They note, however, that most of the children had a recurrence of their symptoms with the onset of puberty. Shafii (1979) acknowledges the poor outcomes of therapy with psychotic children, but

notes that the prognosis is somewhat better if the child has acquired language before the age of five.

Borderline Children

INDICATIONS

The diagnosis and treatment of borderline conditions is a relatively recent phenomenon. In fact, it was not described until the late 1960s and early 1970s by Kernberg (1966, 1975).

> Borderline psychopathology is held to result from a specific developmental arrest or fixation which occurs during the later practicing and rapprochement subphases of separation-individuation (Mahler, Pine, & Bergman, 1975): that is, from ten through twenty-six months postnatally as a consequence of a particular mode of mother-infant interaction during that period. Within that mode of interaction, the mother relates to her infant in such a fashion as to reward . . . his dependency need on her, including all forms of behavior which reflect anaclitic-clinging needs, and to threaten withdrawal of her libidinal supplies in the wake of his normal, oftentimes aggressive efforts toward separation-individuation. [Rinsley, 1980, p. 150]

The general symptoms of the disorder are: a preoccupation with basic survival, a persistent difficulty maintaining reality testing, a view of the environment as excessively demanding, the use of distancing devices to ward off others, and a vulnerability to external stimuli (Engel, 1963). Within this basic pattern, Goldstein and Jones (1975) have identified four subgroups of borderline individuals: those displaying aggressive/antisocial behavior, those engaged in active family conflict, those who display passive negativism, and those who are withdrawn and socially isolated. Each group of patients presents different problems in treatment but all respond, to some extent, to the parameters set forth below.

GOALS

As with all other disorders, the goal is the reestablishment of normal development. Because of the etiology of borderline conditions, the specific goal is the resolution of the separation-individuation process so that further development may occur. To do this, the analyst strives to maintain a predictable environment for the patient while helping the child gain control of his symptomatic behavior. Lastly, there must be concomitant work with the child's family in order to undo the patterns of interaction that maintain the pathology.

TECHNIQUE

The seriously disturbed and sometimes hazardous behavior of the borderline patient often necessitates a more active stance on the part of the analyst than that delimited by the classic technique. Aside from the level of environmental control the analyst may have to exert the individual treatment of children with borderline psychopathologies is generally the same as the treatment of less severe disorders.

On the other hand, there is a push on the part of some therapists to use interventions aimed at the family rather than the individual (Rinsley, 1980). One technique for psychoanalytic family therapy is presented by Herschkowitz and Kahn (1980). They stress that there needs to be a balance between the traditional analytic view that the origins of pathology lie within the individual, and the family-systems view that all pathology has its origins in how family members interact. It is interesting to note that the latter viewpoint is generally seen as operative in borderline conditions despite the analytic origins of the concept and diagnosis of the disorder. Herschkowitz and Kahn (1980) propose looking at the same psychic structures in the family that one would look for in the individual. For example, in a family where none of the members has adequately developed psychic structures, one member may take the role of the ego for the family while another takes the role of the id and another the role of the superego. In contrast, in a healthy family, the assignment of these roles is flexible and each is taken by different members at various times. In addition, the therapist may evaluate how the family as a unit uses various defensive maneuvers and what they are defending against. When evaluating families in this way, it becomes possible to make interpretations on both an individual and a family level.

Finally, the therapist must be aware that in the treatment of a child with borderline psychopathology, the termination phase may involve the bulk of the work of the therapy. This is a consequence of the origins of the disorder in the separation-individuation process. The patient experiences termination as a recapitulation of the developmental phase which was initially stormy, and thus, may find it extremely anxiety provoking. Termination, therefore, may have a number of false trials before it can be accomplished successfully.

Children Contending with Specific Reality Issues

Handicapped Children

INDICATIONS

For children who have any of the handicapping conditions to be discussed here — namely physical, cognitive, sensory, or psychosomatic handicaps — some level of intervention is generally in order to insure that the child's developmental potential is maximized. For the same reason, it is also important that interventions begin early (Poznanski, 1979a). Generally, interventions with these children are either medical or educational in nature, and only recently has psychotherapy of any type been considered appropriate. Decisions regarding the child's need for psychotherapeutic intervention are made on the basis of criteria appropriate for the child's developmental level. In other words, decisions are made as if the handicapping condition did not exist. Once therapy is initiated, however, it becomes imperative that the therapist keep in mind the reality issues confronting the handicapped child and the implications these issues have for the course of the treatment.

In determining whether or not a child with a cognitive handicap is an appropriate candidate for analytically oriented therapy, it is necessary to assess the severity of the handicap. With the mentally retarded child, the therapist must decide whether the child has sufficient cognitive capacities to allow him to identify with objects, shift libidinal and aggressive drive distribution, and work toward a revision of intrapsychic structures. Generally this implies no more than a moderate level of retardation (Schwartz, 1979). When the child has milder cognitive difficulties, such as a learning disability, decisions regarding therapy may become confused with the child's need for academic remediation. Opperman (1978) suggests that learning disabilities, although they usually have some organic basis, frequently interact with more generalized emotional difficulties. When the learning disability represents an established defensive pattern, he suggests the label neurotic learning dysfunction and recommends analytically oriented psychotherapy. He recognizes, however, that not all children with learning difficulties may be either in need of intensive psychotherapy or in a position to sustain such an intervention. And, in these cases he recommends a standard academic tutoring program.

Lastly, the therapist must be aware that a child in an acute phase of a handicapping condition may not have the ego strength needed to sustain traditional analysis and may be better treated with supportive psychotherapy until the medical problem has been brought under control. This is particularly true of children with any type of psychosomatic disorder (Prugh & Eckhardt, 1979).

GOALS

As with any emotionally disturbed child, the primary goal of psychotherapy with a handicapped child is the reinstatement of normal development on all levels. In treating the handicapped child, the analyst has the additional goal of helping the child integrate his handicap into his ego functioning in as realistic a way as possible.

TECHNIQUES

In treating physically handicapped children or those with psychosomatic illnesses, no particular alterations in the traditional child-analytic technique are suggested in the literature. Obviously some allowances for physical limitations may be necessary, but the work of the treatment is still accomplished through interpretations.

The treatment of children with sensory handicaps requires considerable awareness on the part of the therapist and some modification of the technique. The primary problem in treating these children is that a sensory handicap severely alters the child's ego functioning because it alters the ability to form appropriate concepts (Lesser, 1979). For example, blind children often form faulty concepts of real objects. The concepts are usually based on their awareness of their own bodies, such as perceiving an animal to be capable of the same actions of which they are capable. Therefore, when interpreting a blind child's anxiety, the therapist must take pains to determine whether the child's anxiety is real (i.e., based on a danger peculiar to the blind), if the anxiety is based on a faulty conception of reality, or if it is neurotic anxiety. If the anxiety is based on a faulty concept of reality rather than having classical neurotic origin, the therapist may need to move into the role of

a teacher, so as to help correct the child's perception (Burlingham, 1980). Similarly, significant departures from traditional technique are necessary in treating deaf children (Lesser & Easser, 1975). Lesser (1979) suggests that all children with sensory handicaps might be best treated within an ego psychology framework.

The classic techniques of child psychoanalysis might also be considerably altered to be of value in managing mentally retarded youngsters. First, a retarded child's verbalizations may remain on a fairly concrete level requiring that interpretations also be presented through concrete examples whenever possible. Besides this, Schwartz (1979) suggests that the therapist encourage the child to identify with him as an object. The therapist should also prohibit the child's impulsive behavior and generally avoid gratifying the child's basic needs. Having done this, the therapist must then help the child learn to manage and resolve the negative and aggressive feelings that arise from this frustration. This process is thought to promote the child's identification with the therapist and to teach the child to limit impulse gratification.

Therapists who treat children with any type of apparent handicaps may also be faced with serious problems of countertransference. Physical handicaps may generate strong body integrity fears in the therapist, making it difficult for him to help the child cope with certain reality issues involving the disability (Poznanski, 1979a). In addition, when treating children whose handicaps hamper their ability to be independent, the therapist may react negatively to the level of dependency the child exhibits (Schwartz, 1979). Both of these problems are virtually unique to the treatment of handicapped children, and it is imperative that the therapist keep them in mind as the treatment progresses.

Children Responding to Trauma

INDICATIONS

In this segment we will be discussing issues in the treatment of children who have experienced a specific, time-limited trauma. Although the parameters noted can be applied to traumatized children in general, we will give special attention to children reacting to sexual assault, a specific object loss, hospitalization, or divorce.

Usually, children who have been subjected to a specific trauma are not thought to be in need of psychotherapeutic intervention until their symptoms are so severe that they cannot be dismissed by the child's caretakers as transient reactions. When this occurs, a considerable amount of time may have passed and the child may have already internalized his conflicting feelings regarding the incident. The treatment then becomes much more involved. Logically, it seems that very early intervention is in order, particularly if the child shows any signs of withdrawal (Peters, 1976) or play disruption. Play disruption simply means that the child's usual ability and patterns of play behavior change markedly, indicating that he is unable to manage the huge increase in affects and fantasies engendered by his experience (Robles, 1978; Rosenthal, 1979).

Children experiencing any type of trauma may show signs of developmental arrest but this seems to be a particular problem for children who have lost a parent through either death or divorce. The reason for this seems to be that the child no longer has available one of the objects necessary for playing out certain developmental tasks (Chethik & Kalter, 1980). Oedipal crises become difficult to resolve when either parent is absent, but particularly problematic if the same-sex parent is not available as an object with whom the child can identify. Therefore, divorce is often especially problematic for prelatency-age boys as they usually live with their mothers and have minimal contact with their fathers.

Whereas most traumatic events are, by their very definition, unplanned, the hospitalization of a child may often be anticipated. Recent evidence suggests that, no matter how well planned, children experience hospitalization as exceedingly stressful. In light of this, it may be appropriate to initiate a psychological intervention immediately after a child is admitted, if not before. Certainly, interventions need to be initiated when the child's cognitions and affects do not correspond to the severity of his illness (Poznanski, 1979b).

In reviewing the indications for psychotherapy with traumatized children noted above, it should be apparent that analysis may not always be the treatment of choice. Analysis is probably most appropriate for children who have passed the stage of acute response to the trauma and are showing signs of having internalized their conflicting feelings regarding the incident. Psychoanalytically oriented psychotherapy, which is more supportive in nature, may be more appropriate for children whose traumatic experience is very recent. For these children, the conflicting cognitions and affects are not yet internalized and are therefore available for more directed work. Robles (1978) suggests that if it has been less than three months since the traumatic event and the child had good ego strengths with no major regressions prior to the incident, then brief analytically oriented psychotherapy may be very effective. This is particularly true if the mother can be involved in the child's treatment. Lastly, for children who need to be hospitalized, intervention programs that combine a moderate amount of psychotherapy with an educational approach may significantly reduce the child's anxiety and subsequent symptomatology. Each of these four approaches will be briefly reviewed in the following discussion of therapeutic technique.

GOALS

When a traumatized child is thought to be a candidate for analysis, then the goals of the treatment are the same as those for any child at the same developmental level. The primary goal is, of course, the resumption of normal developmental processes.

When the decision is to initiate psychoanalytic psychotherapy, brief psychotherapy, or a therapeutic educational program, the goals are somewhat different. In these interventions the primary goal is the alleviation of the child's anxiety, and consequently a reduction in his symptomatic behavior. The therapist generally takes a much more supportive and directive role than he would in traditional analysis in order to foster a great deal of trust on the part of the child. The goals are circumscribed and usually clear to both the therapist and the patient, thereby creating a therapeutic alliance that is easily sustained over the course of the therapy. The assumption here is that if the child's anxiety can be reduced and his symptoms contained, then he will not internalize the conflict and will not require more intensive intervention.

TECHNIQUE

The analysis of a traumatized child can usually proceed according to the parameters of the classical techniques. The only problem may be if the trauma has resulted in a serious play disruption that drastically reduces the material the child makes available for analysis. Some traumatized children, for example, simply will not play and will only discuss superficial and concrete information. Levy (1938) suggests that the analyst choose play material for the child that might re-create some aspect of the trauma and then initiate play with these materials. More traditional analysts seem to view this procedure as not only intrusive and unncessary, but as a total violation of the analytic technique.

Psychoanalytic psychotherapy can be conceptualized as an intermediate between traditional analysis and the play therapies, such as the technique described by Axline (1947). The external structure of the treatment seems similar to play therapy while the work of the sessions is conducted in an analytic framework. Psychoanalytic psychotherapy is usually only scheduled for one or two sessions per week, and the parents are involved in the treatment to a much greater degree than in traditional child analysis. Within the sessions, the therapist works primarily through interpretations, but these are often aimed at affects and defenses rather than at deep unconscious or drive material. This type of intervention may be particularly effective for the child who is reacting to a divorce. The therapist presents himself as more of an object than he would in analysis so that the child may use him as a prop against which he may work out various developmental issues (Chethik & Kalter, 1980). To this end, it may be helpful if the therapist is the same sex as the missing parent.

Brief psychotherapy lies somewhere between psychoanalytic psychotherapy and crisis intervention on the continuum of duration and intensity. Crisis intervention generally lasts one to several sessions, brief psychotherapy may last between one and six to nine months, and psychodynamic therapy is often six months to two years in length. Because of the time limitations, the goals need to be circumscribed and clearly delimited. Interpretations are kept at a more superficial level, namely that of affect and fantasy, and some educational/supportive work may be necessary (Robles, 1978). For example, in treating sexually abused children it is necessary to protect them against developing the idea that sex of any type is wrong, and to provide them with reassurance that their traumatic experience will not recur (Peters, 1976). Without this support and reassurance, the child's anxiety may be so overpowering that progress in the therapy is virtually impossible. In many instances of trauma the therapist may also have to help reduce the mother's anxiety regarding the incident so that she, in turn, can help to make the child's environment outside the therapy as supportive as possible (Robles, 1978). One final aspect of any of the briefer psychotherapies is the emphasis placed on the child's ability to ventilate feelings and to abreact within the sessions. Peters (1976) points out, for example, that many children are sexually abused by relatives, which makes it difficult for the child to express his or her anger at the abuser within the family setting. In such cases it is crucial that the child have some arena in which he can express his feelings so that they may be integrated on a conscious level.

The value of pretreatment educational programs for the mental health of hospitalized children is still more of a research than a clinical issue (Poznanski, 1979b). Of particular interest are two studies done in 1968. Minde and Mahler (1968) documented the value of providing children with medical information regarding their treatment in reducing the child's immediate anxiety. They used a brief intervention with virtually no psychotherapeutic component. Rie et al. (1968) conducted a study that compared a simple educational approach with a slightly longer intervention involving some psychotherapy along with an educational program. They found that the simple educational intervention was better at reducing the child's immediate anxiety, but that the combined educational and psychotherapeutic program was more effective in maintaining the reduction of the child's anxiety over the course of a prolonged hospitalization. They concluded that the value of early intervention programs is clear. To be optimally effective, however, these programs must take into account the affects and fantasies accompanying medical treatment, as well as presenting and explaining the technical and factual material to the child.

As a final note on the treatment of traumatized children, Greenberg (1975) has noted that the work of treatment with children who have suffered a specific object loss proceeds in relatively predictable stages: announcement, acknowledgment, mourning, and renewal. Announcement is the name given to the period of time during which the child experiences the affective impact of the loss. During the acknowledgment phase the child begins to accept the irreversability of the loss — a stage that may be delayed until the child is cognitively able to conceptualize the permanency of the loss. Mourning is the phase during which the child experiences reactive affects and cognitions such as anger, guilt, and annihilation fantasies. Lastly, during the renewal phase, the child is able to incorporate an image of the deceased individual and to seek out and develop replacement objects. These stages are very similar to those described by Kubler-Ross (1969) as universals in the grief process. No specific alteration of technique is mandated for children who are grieving, but the therapist needs to be aware that these phases are likely and probably necessary to the child's adequate resolution of his loss.

In treating traumatized children, the most frequent countertransference issues for the therapist involve his anger at the individual who is responsible. This is particularly true when the child is the victim of a crime, as is the case with children who are kidnapped or sexually assaulted. If the crime against the child involves a relative, it may be difficult for the therapist to be effective in reintegrating the child into the family setting. The therapist must be able to manage the anguish a victimized child engenders in others if she or he is to be therapeutically effective.

Another problem specific to the treatment of sexual abuse in children stems, in part, from the nature of analytic training. Very early in his work, Freud (1896) postulated that early childhood sexual experiences were the basis for the hysterical neurosis experienced by many of his adult patients. This view appalled the general population of Freud's time and was widely denounced. Then, in 1924, Freud amended the 1896 paper to say that many of the childhood sexual experiences reported by his patients were fantasies and that he had probably overestimated the significance of early sexual experiences as a factor in the development of neurosis. This combination of events led to a rapid decline in emphasis on real childhood sexual experiences and, in fact, most of this material was assumed to be fantasy derived from the very powerful libidinal drives experienced by children. Research, however, indicates that the frequency of sexual assaults on children is so high that a child's reports of such an experience can seldom be dismissed out of hand (Peters, 1976). Obviously, the reality of any report the child makes of potentially harmful behavior needs to be fully explored before the associated fantasies and affects can be analyzed.

Adopted Children

INDICATIONS

As with the other groups of children discussed in this section on children contending with reality issues, the importance of early intervention cannot be overemphasized. The special problems inherent in the adopted child's relationship to his parents makes some degree of pathological development alarmingly likely. The major negative factor seems to be the perceived tenuousness of the relationship, which neither the child nor the parents can rectify. The parents may harbor a great deal of anxiety about the possibility that they may one day lose their child, that the birth mother will return to claim him as her own. They may experience guilt as a result of fantasies that they were in some way responsible for taking this child from a mother who never really wanted to give it up. Or, they may be conflicted regarding the circumstances that put them in the position of having to adopt a child. For the child, there is often a fantasy that the reason he was given up by his birth mother is because he was bad and that, if he is not very careful, he could just as easily drive away his adoptive mother. These very special stresses may make the separation-individuation process difficult for both the patient and the child — a factor that should be explored with the mother through preventative counseling before it becomes problematic. However, once the child has begun to manifest emotional difficulties, decisions regarding treatment are made in the same way they would be for any child at that particular developmental level.

GOALS

There are no goals peculiar to the treatment of an adopted child. There is, however, a special emphasis in therapy on the separation-individuation process and helping the child to develop a distinct identity separate from either his birth or his adoptive parents.

TECHNIQUE

In treating adopted children, special allowances may have to be made in order to help the parents with their anxiety. The therapist may need to be quite supportive with the parents and to help them work through some of their own affective and fantasy material (Wieder, 1978). Further, since the source of the difficulties is often the interaction between the parent(s) and the child, the therapist may want to consider the use of family therapy as it was discussed earlier in the section on the treatment of children with borderline syndromes.

The individual treatment of the child may follow the classical techniques with virtually no alteration. The analyst must be careful, however, not to interpret the child's fantasies too early. This may be more difficult than it appears because the child's play may be so transparent as to virtually beg for interpretation. Despite this, the therapist must wait until there is a sufficient therapeutic alliance or at least trust between him and the patient to begin dealing directly with this material.

Berger, Bandler, Elliott, and Hodges (1980) state that besides the often transparent play material the child presents, he may make extensive use of fantasy figures both outside and within the therapy. They postulate that these fantasy figures often represent the child's attempt to replace his birth parents, the lost objects, or to create a palpable sense of self. Again, interpretation of these figures must often wait until a sufficient working relationship has been established.

One of the areas in which the therapist may have to support the adoptive parent has to do with the transference reactions often manifested during an adopted child's treatment. These children tend to use splitting as a defense. This is seen as a product of the natural split in their lives in which there is a birth mother (usually the "bad" mother), and an adoptive mother (usually the "good" mother). In treatment, the child may develop either a good mother or bad mother transference toward the therapist, and in so doing relegates the remaining role to the adoptive mother (Wieder, 1978). In addition, these transference reactions are usually not stable, and the adoptive mother may find herself alternately in the good or bad parent role depending more on what is happening in the treatment than on her own behavior. If the parents are not prepared for this and do not receive support from the therapist, they may become terribly anxious and, more likely than not, terminate the child's treatment precipitously.

Children from Toxic Environments

Abused or Deprived Children

INDICATIONS

It is rare that a child who has suffered severe abuse or deprivation at the hands of his caretakers does not manifest pathological personality development or symptomatology. This fact does not necessarily make such children candidates for analysis, but it does reflect the desperate need many of them have for some type of psychological intervention. The indications for placing a child from a toxic environment are the same as those for any child at that particular developmental level. The chances are unfortunately high, however, that children from such environments will have serious characterological deficits, which makes it difficult for them to sustain themselves in the work of analysis. These cases may call for either a prolonged preparatory phase before the actual analysis, or for psychoanalytic psychotherapy, as discussed in the section on therapy for traumatized children.

GOALS

One of the earliest goals in the treatment of children from toxic environments is the reestablishment of their ability to trust and interact with an adult, specifically the therapist. Once this has been accomplished, work toward the more traditional therapeutic goals may begin.

TECHNIQUE

Most of the technical adaptations necessary in the treatment of seriously deprived or abused children are the result of their inability to see the world as a predictable place. Most of these children have no expectation of continuity (Boston, 1980), and therefore, the therapist must be absolutely committed to the treatment and consistent in his behavior in order to help build the child's trust and ability to test reality (Blumberg, 1977; Miller, 1980). Further, they may have difficulties with perceptions of time and space (Miller, 1980), a factor that both arises from and perpetuates their experience of the environment as unpredictable and hostile. Also, because they do not expect supplies to be available on a regular basis, they may demand a great deal of concrete gratification (Berse, 1980). The therapist must make decisions regarding his ability and/or desire to gratify the child's needs *a priori*, and then adhere to the decision religiously while explaining his rationale to the child.

Both abused and deprived children tend to have very inconsistent ways of managing their affects, which may in turn cause a problem within the therapy. Two reasons for this inconsistency are postulated. One is that these children lacked a consistent mother figure to absorb the affects they projected as infants (Miller, 1980). With no one to help modulate their feelings, these children never learned to manage their affects, and therefore they either repressed them or projected them violently (Boston, 1980). Further, because the response of the environment was never predictable for either good or bad, these children never learned to make appropriate connections between their affects, cognitions, and events in the environment. To help the child overcome both of these difficulties, the therapist must interpret the child's bodily sensations, relate these to the child's affects and these in turn to the environment, thereby building appropriate cognitions (Berse, 1980). Once this is accomplished, the therapist can go on to interpret affects (Miller, 1980), and only then can the child withstand interpretations of defenses or of the transference.

In a fashion similar to the behavior of some adopted children, children from toxic environments often create make-believe figures in the form of monsters, animals, or people. The tendency to create such figures seems to stem from the perceived instability of both the environment and of interpersonal relationships. Where the adopted child may use fantasy figures to represent lost objects or aspects of himself, the abused or deprived child uses them as vessels for his affects and fantasies (Berse, 1980). It is not uncommon for boys from chaotic homes to develop a great investment in a cartoon superhero. These characters usually represent powerful figures who overcome injustice and punish wrongdoers. During the early 1980s a very popular television character admired by many of the boys in residential treatment was the "incredible Hulk." This is a character whose body responds to his own anger by changing into a giant creature with incredible power who inevitably gets revenge. These fantasy figures provide great insight into the inner world of the child, and interpretations of affect may be readily accepted by the child when they are attributed to the figure.

Finally, if the child is to be maintained in his home environment it is imperative that some type of psychotherapeutic intervention be made at the family level. One option would be the use of family therapy as it was discussed in the section on the treatment of children with borderline syndromes.

If the therapist is consistent and conveys to the child a sense of commitment to the improvement of the child's emotional state, then a strong positive transference is likely to develop. It is as if once the child sees that someone is reliable, he attempts to make up for years of abuse or neglect through one intense, dependent relationship. The therapist must manage this transference very gently in order to maintain the child's desire to work and to

further strengthen the child's reality testing through a positive interpersonal experience.

Countertransference issues may become intense when treating a severely deprived or abused child. These children tend to have such intense needs for narcissistic supplies that the therapist may begin to feel as if he has been drained dry during each session. This is another reason that an *a priori* decision regarding need gratification may be helpful when treating these children. Second, the ability of a child from a toxic environment to project his anger or pain may be so overdeveloped that at times the therapist may feel compelled to act for the child (Miller, 1980). For example, children in residential centers may complain bitterly about their treatment at the hands of the other staff, maintaining that only the therapist really cares about their well-being. It is very easy for the therapist to become angry at the staff for "not understanding" his patient if he is not aware of the degree to which the countertransference may be operating. Last, it may be very easy for the therapist to become angry at the parents for so grossly mistreating the child. Although this attitude may have a certain basis in reality, if it is not managed correctly, it will destroy the therapist's ability to work with the family at stabilizing and correcting the home environment.

Children with Disorders of Impulse Control

Delinquents

INDICATIONS

Generally, the mere appearance of antisocial or delinquent behavior in a child's repertoire is considered sufficient reason for some type of psychotherapeutic intervention. Unfortunately, children displaying this type of behavior rarely respond to any form of individual treatment. They have so externalized their conflicts that they experience little or no anxiety, and therefore have little motivation to change. Only when the acting-out behavior represents some aspect of an internalized conflict is analysis the appropriate intervention. In the rest of the cases one of the most effective treatments appears to be group therapy, which may be carried out within an analytic framework. And, in either case, the chances for success improve if the parents can be involved in the treatment (Marshall, 1979).

GOALS

The primary goal is the reduction or elimination of the child's antisocial behavior. With children whose behavior reflects a serious characterological flaw, this may be the only goal that the therapy has any chance of attaining. With children whose behavior reflects an internalized conflict, the treatment would be analysis, and the goals would be in line with those for any child at the same developmental level.

TECHNIQUE

Rinsley (1980) suggests the use of the following techniques in the individual treatment of a delinquent child. The first step the therapist must take is to encourage the child to develop a narcissistic transference that is to become the child's ego ideal. Since the delinquent child may have little personal motivation for change, the therapist must create the motivation by encouraging the child's symbiosis in treatment. Through this symbiosis the therapist may teach the child the difference between thoughts and actions and their relative impact. He may use the tecnique of joining the child in his feelings to help build the child's ego controls, essentially through modeling. He may also use mirroring and paradoxical intention in helping the child develop some degree of observing ego and in producing some level of discomfort with the behavior on the part of the child. Much later, once alliance between the child and the therapist is firmly established, the therapist may begin to use more traditional analytic techniques and, in fact, to engage in the work of analysis proper.

As previously mentioned, group psychotherapy is often the most effective approach to the treatment of delinquent children. Yalom (1975) lists eleven factors common to therapy groups that contribute to the individual's improvement. These are: (1) the instillation of hope; (2) universality—"I am not the only one with problems"; (3) the imparting of information; (4) the development of altruism; (5) the corrective recapitulation of the primary family group; (6) the development of socialization skills; (7) modeling and imitating new behaviors; (8) interpersonal learning; (9) group cohesiveness; (10) catharsis; and (11) existential factors, such as having to be responsible for one's own behavior. The primary advantage to placing the adolescent in a group is that the presence of peers usually overcomes the adolescent's basic mistrust

of adults and therapy as an attempt, on the part of adults, to undermine his growing independence. In a group, the therapist's impact is diffused and the adolescent may feel comfortable enough to sustain the work of therapy (Kraft, 1979).

Conclusion

Having considered the numerous adaptations to child analysis for the treatment of children at various developmental levels and with specific disorders, consideration of the future of child and adolescent analysis warrants, first of all, some mention of its general contribution to psychoanalytic theory and technique. Though they originated as an extension of the analytic model, the principles derived from child analysis extend to almost all other areas of clinical and scientific investigation of childhood and the psychological development of the child (Lesser, 1972). Moreover, it has formed the base from which all other types of child psychotherapy has been derived. Indeed, the accumulated knowledge from all the forms of psychoanalytic psychotherapy extend beyond the treatment of psychopathology to the awareness of the vicissitudes of normal child development.

Given the proliferation of related forms of child-analytic treatment, one future direction that child analysis as a theory and technique must address is the extent to which child analysis may benefit from recognition and integration of their sizable contributions. While the tendency to dismiss these related forms of treatment as nonanalytic may exist, it seems ill-advised to do so, given the need for treatment of children whose symptomatology does not suit the criteria for analysis and the success they experience.

Indeed, these contributions widen the scope of child analysis, informing and enriching the field to effect a broader impact on child development.

Other future directions for child analysis and therapy may include the need for more rigorous research (Lewis, 1981). There is tremendous need for better controlled research with vigorous methods for testing generalizations. Without such research, there is a danger that the hypothesis and methods of child analysis and therapy may be reified to the point of stagnation. Lewis (1981) further suggests that possible directions for the research may involve more direct, careful observation of children, as well as increased dialogue with other disciplines (i.e., infant development studies, neurology, biochemistry, genetics, language development, epidemiology, etc.).

Anna Freud (1980) specifically suggests necessary research on the following lines of development:

1. The development of secondary process functioning is linked with speech development. The halts and relapses that occur whenever the urge for immediate drive gratification becomes so powerful as to reinstate primary process thinking need to be clarified.
2. The many prestages of adult reality sense need to be considered, beginning with the steps for distinguishing between the inner and outer world.
3. The delineation of the line toward discharging mental excitation via mental, not somatic, pathways should be explored through examination of the holdups, breakdowns, and exemptions associated with repression.
4. The degrees and alternations in successful impulse control should be further considered.
5. The development of a time sense should be addressed, especially the ways in which drive urgency or an environmentally imposed routine weaken this ego function.
6. Clarification of the intermediate steps between the child's egocentrism and adult's objectivity, and those between childish lack of insight and the adult's acknowledgment of internal processes.

As for the future directions of psychoanalytic technique, Lieberman (1976) stresses that the model and essential application have remained the same. What is needed, however, are more refined theories for examining the communication between analyst and analysand. He proposes research into the evolution of the psychoanalytic dialogue both within and outside of sessions. Exploring the variations in new stylistic configurations in the patient's capacity for receiving and sending messages may provide an axiom for mental growth, and inform the analyst in his function to transform these messages to produce change in the psychic structure. In addition, new, more pragmatic ways of dealing with messages are needed so that the ego and superego can gain the upper hand over the id. Thus, the analyst must ascribe new meaning and sense to the messages he hears in order to preclude the risk of distortion of interpretations.

Finally, more careful research into the effectiveness of child analysis and psychotherapy seems especially critical in light of the rapid proliferation of techniques seen in the recent past. Therapy outcome studies are likely to provide greater certainty about the effectiveness of various forms of treatment and strengthen the theory from which they were derived.

References

Ack, M., Beale, E., & Ware, L. Parent guidance: Psychotherapy of the young child via the parent. *Bulletin of the Menninger Clinic*, 1975, **39**, 436–447.

Axline, V. *Play therapy*. Boston: Houghton-Mifflin, 1947.

Becker, T. On latency. *Psychoanalytic Study of the Child*, 1974, **29**, 3–11.

Bender, L. Schizophrenia in childhood: Its recognition, description and treatment. *American Journal of Orthopsychiatry*, 1956, **26**, 499–506.

Bender, L., & Gurevitz, S. Results of psychotherapy with young schizophrenic children. *American Journal of Orthopsychiatry*, 1955, **25**, 163–169.

Benson, R., & Harrison, S. The eye of the hurricane: From seven to ten. In S. Greenspan & H. Pollock (Eds.), *The course of life: Psychoanalytic contributions toward understanding personality development*; Vol. 2, *Latency, adolescence and youth*. Adelphi, Md.: National Institute of Mental Health, 1980.

Berger, M., Bandler, D., Elliott, C., & Hodges, J. Second report on the problems of adopted children. *Bulletin of the Hampstead Clinic*, 1980, **3**, 247–256.

Berse, P. Psychotherapy with severely deprived children: Keith. *Journal of Child Psychotherapy*, 1980, **6**, 49–55.

Bettelheim, B. *The empty fortress: Infantile autism and the birth of the self*. New York: Free Press, 1967.

Blos, P., & Finch, S. Psychotherapy with children and adolescents. In S. Arieti (Ed.), *American handbook of psychiatry*. Vol. 5; *Treatment*. New York: Basic Books, 1975.

Blumberg, M. Treatment of the abused child and the child abuser. *American Journal of Psychotherapy*, 1977, **31**, 204–215.

Bornstein, B. The analysis of a phobic child. Some problems of theory and technique in child analysis. *Psychoanalytic Study of the Child*, 1949, **3/4**, 181–226.

Bornstein, B. On latency. *Psychoanalytic Study of the Child*, 1951, **6**, 279–285.

Boston, M. Psychotherapy with severely deprived children: Introduction: The Tavistock workshop. *Journal of Child Psychotherapy*, 1980, **6**, 45–48.

Brody, S. Contributions to child analysis. *Psychoanalytic Study of the Child*, 1974, **29**, 13–19.

Burlingham, D. Psychoanalytic observations of blind children. *Bulletin of the Hampstead Clinic*, 1980, **3**, 95–126.

Chethik, M., & Kalter, N. Developmental arrest following divorce: The role of the therapist as a developmental facilitator. *Journal of the American Academy of Child Psychiatry*, 1980, **19**, 281–288.

Ekstein, R., Caruth, E., Cooper, B., Friedman, S.,

Landres, P., Liebowitz, J., & Nelson, T. Psycho-analytically oriented psychotherapy of psychotic children. In J. Glenn (Ed.), *Child analysis and therapy*. New York: Aronson, 1978.

Engel, M. Psychological testing of borderline psychotic children. *Archives of General Psychiatry*, 1963, 8, 426–434.

Fe d'Ostiani, E. An individual approach to psychotherapy with psychotic patients. *Journal of Child Psychotherapy*, 1980, 6, 81–92.

Fraiberg, S., Shapiro, V., & Spitz-Cherniss, D. Treatment modalities. In S. Fraiberg (Ed.), *Clinical studies in infant mental health—The first year of life*. New York: Basic Books, 1980.

Freud, A. *The ego and the mechanisms of defense*. New York: International Universities Press, 1936.

Freud, A. Indications for child analysis. *Psychoanalytic Study of the Child*, 1945, 1, 127–149.

Freud, A. Adolescence. *Psychoanalytic Study of the Child*, 1958, 13, 255–278.

Freud, A. *Normality and pathology in childhood*. New York: International Universities Press, 1965.

Freud, A. *The writings of Anna Freud, I, 1922–1935: Introduction to Psychoanalysis. Letters for child analysts and teachers*. New York: International Universities Press, 1974.

Freud, A. Child analysis as the study of mental growth. In S. Greenspan & G. Pollock (Eds.), *The course of life: Psychoanalytic contributions toward understanding personality development*. Adelphi, Md.: National Institute of Mental Health, 1980.

Freud, S. (1896) The aetiology of hysteria. In J. Strachey (Ed.), *The complete works of Sigmund Freud*, Vol. 3. London: Hogarth, 1955.

Freud, S. (1900) The interpretation of dreams. In J. Strachey (Ed.), *The complete works of Sigmund Freud*, Vol. 4, 5. London: Hogarth, 1953.

Freud, S. (1905) Three essays on the theory of sexuality. In J. Strachey (Ed.), *The complete works of Sigmund Freud*, Vol. 7. London: Hogarth, 1953.

Freud, S. (1909) Analysis of a phobia in a five year old boy. In J. Strachey (Ed.), *The complete works of Sigmund Freud*, Vol. 10. London: Hogarth, 1953.

Freud, S. (1914) On narcissism: An introduction. In J. Strachey (Ed.), *The complete works of Sigmund Freud*, Vol. 15. London: Hogarth, 1953.

Friend, M. Psychoanalysis of adolescents. In B. Wolman (Ed.), *Handbook of child psychoanalysis*. New York: Van Nostrand-Reinhold, 1972.

Furman, E. Filial therapy. In J. Noshpitz (Ed.), *Basic handbook of child psychiatry*, Vol. 3. New York: Basic Books, 1979.

Furman, R. & Katan, A. *The therapeutic nursery school*. New York: International Universities Press, 1969.

Geleerd, E. (Ed.) *The child analyst at work*. New York: International Universities Press, 1967.

Glenn, J. The psychoanalysis of prelatency children. In J. Glenn (Ed.), *Child analysis and therapy*. New York: Aronson, 1978. (a)

Glenn, J. General principles of child analysis. In J. Glenn (Ed.), *Child analysis and therapy*. New York: Aronson, 1978. (b)

Goldstein, M., & Jones, J. Adolescent and family precursors of borderline and schizophrenic conditions. In P. Hartocollis (Ed.), *Borderline personality disorders: The concept, the syndrome, the patient*. New York: International Universities Press, 1977.

Greenberg, L. Therapeutic grief work with children. *Social Casework*, 1975, 56, 396–403.

Hamm, M. Some aspects of a difficult therapeutic (working) alliance. In E. Geleerd (Ed.), *The analyst at work*. New York: International Universities Press, 1967.

Harley, M. *The analyst and the adolescent at work*. New York: Quadrangle, 1974.

Harley, M., & Sabot, L. Conceptualizing the nature of the therapeutic action of child analysis. Scientific proceedings: Panel reports. *Journal of the American Psychoanalytic Association*, 1980, 28, 161–179.

Herschkowitz, S., & Kahn, C. Toward a psychoanalytic view of family systems. *The Psychoanalytic Review*, 1980, 67, 45–68.

Hug-Hellmuth, H. On the technique of child analysis. *International Journal of Psycho-Analysis*, 1921, 2, 287–305.

Kabenell, R. On countertransference. *Psychoanalytic Study of the Child*, 1974, 29, 27–33.

Kanner, L. Autistic disturbances of affective contact. *Nervous Child*, 1942, 2, 217–250.

Kernberg, O. Structural derivatives of object relationships. *International Journal of Psycho-Analysis*, 1966, 47(2/3), 236–253.

Kernberg, O. *Borderline conditions and pathological narcissism*. New York: Jason Aronson, 1975.

Kestenbaum, C. Childhood psychosis: Psychotherapy. In B. Wolman, J. Egan, & A. Ross (Eds.), *Handbook of treatment of mental disorders in childhood and adolescence*. Englewood Cliffs, N.J.: Prentice-Hall, 1978.

Klein, M. The psychoanalytic play technique. *American Journal of Orthopsychiatry*, 1955, 25, 223–237.

Kraft, I. Group therapy. In J. Noshpitz (Ed.), *Basic handbook of child psychiatry*. New York: Basic Books, 1979.

Kramer, S., & Byerly, L. Technique of psychoanalysis of the latency child. In J. Glenn (Ed.), *Child analysis and therapy*. New York: Aronson, 1978.

Kubler-Ross, E. *On death and dying*. New York: MacMillan, 1969.

Lane, B. Some vicissitudes in the therapeutic alliance in child psychotherapy. In J. Mishne (Ed.), *Psychotherapy and training in clinical social work*. New York: Halsted, 1980.

Lesser, S. Psychoanalysis with children. In B. Wolman (Ed.), *Manual of child psychopathology*. New York: McGraw-Hill, 1972.

Lesser, S. Sensory handicapped children. In J. Noshpitz (Ed.), *Basic handbook of child psychiatry*. New York: Basic Books, 1979.

Lesser, S., & Easser, B. The psychiatric management of the deaf child. *Canadian Nurse*, 1975, 71, 23–25.

Levy, D. Release therapy in young children. *Psychiatry*, 1938, 1, 387–389.

Lewis, M. Child psychiatry perspectives. *Journal of the American Academy of Child Psychiatry*, 1981, 20, 189–199.

Lieberman, D. Changes in the theory and practice of psychoanalysis. *International Journal of Psychoanalysis*, 1976, 54, 101–107.

Mahler, M. *On human symbiosis and the vicissitudes of*

individuation. New York: International Universities Press, 1968.

Mahler, M., Pine, F., & Bergman, A. *The psychological birth of the human infant: Symbiosis and individuation.* New York: Basic Books, 1975.

Marcus, I. Countertransference and the psychoanalytic process in children and adolescents. *Psychoanalytic Study of the Child,* 1980, **35,** 285–298.

Marshall, R. Antisocial youth. In J. Noshpitz (Ed.), *Basic handbook of child psychiatry.* New York: Basic Books, 1979.

Miller, I. Psychotherapy with severely deprived children: Eileen. *Journal of Child Psychotherapy,* 1980, **6,** 57–67.

Minde, K., & Maler, L. Psychiatric counseling on a pediatric medical ward: A controlled evaluation. *The Journal of Pediatrics,* 1968, **72,** 452–460.

Neubauer, P. The opening phase of child analysis. In J. Glenn (Ed.), *Child analysis and therapy.* New York: Aronson, 1978.

Opperman, J. Tutoring: The remediation of cognitive and academic defects by individual instruction. In J. Glenn (Ed.), *Child analysis and therapy.* New York: Aronson, 1978.

Peters, J. Children who are victims of sexual assault and the psychology of offenders. *American Journal of Psychotherapy,* 1976, **30,** 398–421.

Piaget, J., & Inhelder, B. *The psychology of the child.* New York: Basic Books, 1969.

Poznanski, E. Handicapped children. In J. Noshpitz (Ed.), *Basic handbook of child psychiatry.* New York: Basic Books, 1979.

Poznanski, E. The hospitalized child. In J. Noshpitz (Ed.), *Basic handbook of child psychiatry.* New York: Basic Books, 1979.

Prugh, D., & Eckhardt, C. Psychophysiological disorders. In J. Noshpitz (Ed.), *Basic handbook of child psychiatry.* New York: Basic Books, 1979.

Rank, B. Adaptation of the psychoanalytic technique for the treatment of young children with atypical development. *American Journal of Orthopsychiatry,* 1949, **19,** 130–139.

Rie, H., Boverman, H., Grossman, B., & Ozoa, N. Immediate and long term effects of intervention in prolonged hospitalization. *Pediatrics,* 1968, **41,** 755–764.

Rinsley, D. Diagnosis and treatment of borderline and narcissistic children and adolescents. *Bulletin of the Menninger Clinic,* 1980, **49,** 147–170.

Robles, C. Vulnerability of the traumatized preschool child: Usefulness of brief analytically oriented therapy. In J. Anthony (Ed.), *The Child in His Family,* 1978, **4,** 111–116.

Rosenthal, A. Brief focused psychotherapy. In J. Noshpitz (Ed.), *Basic handbook of child psychiatry.* New York: Basic Books, 1979.

Sandler, J., Kennedy, H., & Tyson, R. *The technique of child psychoanalysis: Discussions with Anna Freud.* Cambridge, Mass.: Harvard University Press, 1980.

Sarnoff, C. *Latency.* New York: Aronson, 1976.

Sarnoff, C. Developmental considerations in the psychotherapy of latency age children. *International Journal of Psychoanalytic Psychotherapy,* 1978–79, **7,** 284–304.

Scharfman, M. Psychoanalytic treatment. In B. Wolman, J. Egan, & A. Ross (Eds.), *Handbook of treatment of mental disorders in childhood and adolescence.* Englewood Cliffs, N.J.: Prentice-Hall, 1978.

Schwartz, C. The application of psychoanalytic theory to the treatment of the mentally retarded child. *The Psychoanalytic Review,* 1979, **66,** 133–141.

Settlage, C. The technique of defense analysis in the psychoanalysis of the early adolescent. In M. Harley (Ed.), *The analyst and the adolescent at work.* New York: Quadrangle, 1974.

Shafii, M. Childhood psychosis. In J. Noshpitz (Ed.), *Basic handbook of child psychiatry.* New York: Basic Books, 1979.

Shane, M. Countertransference and the developmental orientation approach. *Psychoanalysis and Contemporary Thought,* 1980, **3,** 195–212.

Szurek, S., & Berlin, I. Elements of psychotherapeutics with the schizophrenic child and his parents. *Psychiatry,* 1956, **19,** 1–9.

Wieder, H. Special problems in the psychoanalysis of adopted children. In J. Glenn (Ed.), *Child analysis and therapy.* New York: Aronson, 1978.

Wolman, B. The rationale of child therapy. In B. Wolman, J. Egan, & A. Ross (Eds.), *Handbook of treatment of mental disorders in childhood and adolescence.* Englewood Cliffs, N.J.: Prentice-Hall, 1978.

Yalom, I. *The theory and practice of group psychotherapy.* (2nd ed.) New York: Basic Books, 1975.

29 THOUGHT AND ACTION IN PSYCHOTHERAPY: THE COGNITIVE-BEHAVIORAL APPROACHES

Philip C. Kendall
Kelly M. Bemis

Reviews of cognitive-behavioral therapy typically begin with comments about its rapid and surprising emergence from behavior therapy and proceed to discussions of the shared and distinguishing features that can be identified between the two approaches (e.g., Beck, 1970; Kendall & Hollon, 1979; Mahoney & Arnkoff, 1978; Meichenbaum, 1977). While the extent of its present influence on clinical research and practice is indeed remarkable, specification of the exact techniques that define cognitive-behavioral therapy continues to challenge the most creative scholars. The parameters of the approach are not as yet fully established, and the relationship between the various cognitive-behavioral schools remains unclear. This state of affairs is not altogether displeasing, for one aspect of cognitive-behavioral therapy that may be its most distinctive feature is "collaborative empiricism," in which client and therapist work together to evaluate problems and generate solutions. While the cognitive-behavioral therapist's conceptual orientation guides the search for determinants and intervention tactics, the range of potentially useful strategies is not limited to a circumscribed set of techniques that may be said to comprise cognitive-behavioral treatment.

Review papers are also typically accompanied by lists of the premises believed to be held in common by the cognitive-behavioral approaches. While different authors have focused on different themes, there appear to be a number of principles that parsimoniously capture the basic tenets of cognitive-behavioral interventions. The following points are adapted from Kendall and Hollon (1979), Mahoney (1977), and Mahoney and Arnkoff (1978):

1. The human organism responds primarily to cognitive representations of its environments rather than to these environments per se.
2. Most human learning is cognitively mediated.
3. Thoughts, feelings, and behaviors are causally interrelated.
4. Attitudes, expectancies, attributions, and other cognitive activities are central to producing, predicting, and understanding psychopathological behavior and the effects of therapeutic interventions.
5. Cognitive processes can be cast into testable formulations that are easily integrated with behavioral paradigms, and it is possible *and* desirable to combine cognitive treatment strategies with enactive techniques and behavioral contingency management.

6. The task of the cognitive-behavioral therapist is to act as a diagnostician, educator, and technical consultant who assesses maladaptive cognitive processes and works with the client to design learning experiences that may remediate these dysfunctional cognitions and the behavioral and affective patterns with which they correlate.

Within the boundaries of these fundamental principles, there is room for a great deal of variability in the actual implementation of cognitive-behavioral interventions. The commonalities and differences among cognitive-behavioral therapies will be examined through a review of five of the major approaches: rational-emotive therapy; systematic rational restructuring; cognitive therapy for depression; self-instructional training; and stress inoculation.

Rational-emotive Therapy

Theory

Perhaps the first contemporary theoretical and therapeutic system that may be considered an example of the cognitive-behavioral approach was articulated more than 20 years ago by Ellis. Departing from a psychoanalytic background, Ellis (1962) advanced the premise that psychological disturbances result from irrational beliefs. He contends that human beings habitually filter their perceptions through the distorted ideas they hold about themselves and the world, rather than reacting in an objective manner to external events. This basic postulate is expressed in Ellis's "A-B-C" model of the relationship between cognition and emotion, in which private beliefs (B) about particular activating events or situations (A) determine the emotional consequences (C) that are experienced. While individuals are generally acutely aware of their affective responses at point C, they frequently fail to attend to the beliefs that mediate and determine them. When these silent assumptions are inaccurate and are framed in absolute or imperative terms, psychological maladjustment is likely to result. The primary goal of the rational-emotive therapy (RET) Ellis developed is to teach clients to identify and change the illogical notions that underlie their distressing symptoms.

Ellis asserts that "although people have remarkable differences and uniquenesses . . . they also have remarkable sameness in the ways in which they disturb themselves 'emotionally'" (Ellis,

1977a, p. 4). The clinician's task is to ferret out the particular irrational beliefs endorsed by a given client; this is simplified by the consistency of pathogenic beliefs across all clients. In various sources, Ellis has catalogued 10 to 13 of such "basic" beliefs, including "the idea that one must have love or approval from all the people one finds significant" and "the idea that one must prove thoroughly competent, adequate, and achieving" (Ellis & Harper, 1975). Ellis maintains that such beliefs, and the misery they create in the lives of many people, do not derive solely from their lack of empirical validity, but from their "demanding, commanding" nature, which he characterizes as "masturbatory ideology" (Ellis, 1977a). The essence of Ellis's model of psychopathology (as well as the distinctive tone of his writing and therapeutic technique) is captured in the following excerpt:

> Whenever you experience . . . emotional problems, you can assume that your irrational Beliefs take one or more of four basic forms. . . . 1. you think that someone or something *should, ought,* or *must* be different from the way it actually does exist, 2. you find it *awful, terrible,* or *horrible* when it is this way, 3. you think that you can't *bear, stand,* or *tolerate* this person or thing that you concluded *should* not have been as it is, 4. you think that you or some other person (or people) have made or keep making horrible errors and that because you or they must not act the way they clearly do act, you or they deserve nothing good in life, merit *damnation,* and can legitimately receive the label of *louse, rotten person,* or *turd.* [Ellis, 1977a, pp. 9–10]

While Ellis's unidirectional "A-B-C" model has been considered simplistic, if clinically useful (Arnkoff & Glass, 1982; Meichenbaum, 1978), some of the basic tenets of his theory are endorsed by other cognitive-behavioral theorists and have received a degree of empirical support. Some studies have found that merely repeating a list of negative or positive self-statements can induce mood changes in experimental subjects (e.g., Rimm & Litvak, 1969; Velten, 1968). The evidence also indicates a correlation between a variety of psychiatric symptoms and disorders and the tendency to endorse irrational beliefs on paper-and-pencil inventories (e.g., Alden & Safran, 1978; Goldfried & Sobocinski, 1975). However, investigations of the more specific RET hypothesis that acceptance of irrational beliefs is associated with an increased likelihood of emotional arousal in negatively toned situations have yielded equivocal results (e.g., Craighead, Kimball, & Rehak, 1979; Goldfried & Sobocinski, 1975; Sutton-Simon & Goldfried, 1979).

Therapy

In contrast to the explicit rationale underlying RET, few details about specific *procedures* for its optimal implementation have been available to clinicians until quite recently (Goldfried, 1979; Goldfried, Decenteceo, & Weinberg, 1974). Goldfried and his colleagues attempted to remedy this deficiency by delineating specific techniques for the modification of irrational beliefs — in the process developing a related school of therapy that is sufficiently different from RET to warrant a separate discussion (see the following section on Systematic Rational Restructuring). More recently, the publication of *A Practitioner's Guide to Rational-Emotive Therapy* (Walen, DiGiuseppe, & Wessler, 1980) has provided more counsel to therapists wishing to learn about the "orthodox" conduct of RET.

RET is a structured, directive intervention strategy that tends to focus on pervasive patterns of irrational thinking rather than on target symptoms. While increasing emphasis has been placed on the incorporation of emotive and enactive techniques into standard RET treatment, it remains for the most part a semantic, insight-oriented therapy that "largely consists of the use of the logico-empirical method of scientific questioning, challenging, and debating" (Ellis, 1977a, p. 20). Clients are trained to replace maladaptive thoughts such as "I can't *stand* it" or "it *shouldn't* happen" with more rational responses such as "it is unpleasant, but I can tolerate it," or "I wish it hadn't happened" (Lipsky, Kassinove, & Miller, 1980). The goal of this undertaking is to promote a "new philosophy" that will enable the client to view him or herself and others in a more sensible, rational manner. In addition to such discussion and disputation, RET may also include the following techniques: rational role reversal, in which the patient guides the therapist through a problem using the "A-B-C" analysis; rational emotive imagery, in which patients engage in imaginal practice or rational thinking, feeling, and acting; shame-attacking exercises, in which clients are encouraged to perform embarrassing activities deliberately, in order to challenge their

need for conventionality and to demonstrate that the consequences of carrying out socially prohibited acts are rarely catastrophic; and a variety of behavioral assignments such as *in vivo* desensitization and flooding. Bibliotherapy is routinely recommended as a supplement to office sessions, and may draw on an extensive library of self-help manuals written by Ellis and his colleagues (e.g., *A New Guide to Rational Living*, Ellis & Harper [1975]; *Help Yourself to Happiness*, Maultsby [1975]; *Sex without Guilt*, Ellis [1977d]; *A Guide to Successful Marriage*, Ellis & Harper [1973]).

While Ellis views his therapeutic approach as allied to the group of cognitive-behavioral interventions, he has proposed a list of distinctions between what he terms (somewhat pejoratively) "elegant" or "preferential" RET and "nonpreferential" RET or generic cognitive-behavior therapy (Ellis, 1980). The former, more refined version of RET is considered the technique of choice for bright, neurotic, and well-motivated clients because it is believed to be more likely to engender deep or pervasive personality change than its more "superficial" cognitive-behavioral counterparts such as self-instructional training. While Ellis's list of the distinctions between these approaches can be criticized for its assumption of uniformity in non-RET cognitive-behavioral therapies and for some of the specific items erroneously catalogued as "RET-exclusives" (Kendall, 1982), the compilation does at least serve to characterize the "ideal" RET that Ellis advocates. According to this account, "preferential" RET: strives to foster profound philosophical change in clients; espouses a specific existential-humanistic outlook; disparages all forms of self-evaluation; specializes in active disputation; discourages problem solving before basic irrational beliefs have been modified; endorses conditional rather than unconditional self-acceptance; favors forceful emotive interventions such as shame-attacking exercises and encounter or marathon sessions; questions the use of positive reinforcement strategies; and is skeptical about skills-training procedures.

Early Research

The first attempted demonstration of the utility of RET was provided by Ellis's (1957) review of his own effectiveness as a therapist during three periods in his professional career, when he was conducting therapy in orthodox psychoanalytic, directive psychodynamic, and RET modes. A survey of patient records indicated that the improvement rate of clients in his care increased after each shift in orientation, at the same time as the course of therapy became shorter. This review was admittedly deficient in experimental controls, and highly vulnerable to methodological flaws such as differential enthusiasm about the three techniques, incremental development of general therapeutic skills, and the use of subjective and shifting criteria of improvement (Roper, 1976).

Initial experimental support was provided by Meichenbaum, Gilmore, and Fedoravicius (1971) who compared eight sessions of a group "insight" therapy "derived principally from Ellis's RET" to group desensitization, a combined insight-desensitization program, a speech-discussion placebo group, and a waiting-list control. The results indicated that the insight and desensitization treatments were comparably effective for their speech-anxious subjects, with both producing greater reduction of anxiety on behavioral, cognitive, and self-report measures than did the control conditions. The most intriguing finding of the study was that different types of clients received differential benefit from the two effective treatment programs, with insight therapy proving most valuable for clients with high rather than low levels of social distress. While the Meichenbaum et al. (1971) study is frequently cited as supportive of RET, it is evident from reading the published description of the "insight" therapy employed that it departed substantially from the practice of RET prescribed by Ellis. The insight treatment used in this study appears at least as similar to the self-instructional training mode subsequently delineated by Meichenbaum as it was to Ellis's RET, and might be more appropriately cited as providing early support for the former cognitive-behavioral approach.

DiLoreto (1971) compared RET, client-centered therapy, and systematic desensitization to attention-placebo and no-contact groups in a nine-week treatment program for 100 college students with interpersonal anxiety. Posttest measures indicated that all three treatments produced more change than either control condition, with systematic desensitization achieving the greatest amount of symptom reduction. RET proved differentially effective with introverted clients, while client-centered therapy did better with extroverts. A three-month follow-up indicated that students who had participated in the RET group demonstrated more generalization of treatment gains to interpersonal situations than subjects in any other cell. The evaluation of this carefully conducted study must be tempered by several criticisms: the minimal level of symptomatic disturbance of the subjects included (out of a class of 600 undergraduates, no fewer than 100 qualified as socially anxious), and qualitative differences in therapist effectiveness between treatment types (DiGiuseppe & Miller, 1977; Goldfried, 1979; Roper, 1976). Other early studies providing some support for the effectiveness of RET include Karst and Trexler (1970) and Trexler and Karst (1972) with speech anxiety; Thompson (1974) with test anxiety; Maultsby and Graham (1974) with anxiety; and Keller, Crooke, and Brookings (1975) with irrational thinking in a geriatric population. Less positive results were obtained by Tiegerman (1975) with interpersonal anxiety.

Recent Research

It is surprising that it was not until 1980 that a study using a *clinical* population to compare the efficacy of RET to alternative treatments was published. Lipsky et al. (1980) reported on a study carried out with 50 outpatients at a community mental-health center who received diagnoses of "adjustment reaction of adulthood" or "neurosis." Subjects were randomly assigned to one of three RET conditions (RET-cognitive restructuring alone, RET plus rational role reversal, RET plus rational-emotive imagery), an attention-alternate treatment control (a combination of supportive therapy and relaxation training), or no-contact control. Individual treatment sessions were held once a week over a 12-week period. Posttreatment results indicated that RET, either alone or in combination with rational role reversal or rational-emotive imagery, was superior to the control conditions on each of the self-report measures used. Both "extra" RET components seemed to add significantly to the basic RET strategy, with rational role reversal in particular proving a useful adjunct for alleviating symptoms of depression, trait anxiety, and neuroticism. The Lipsky et al. study provides support for the utility of RET as a relatively short-term intervention program for adult outpatient neurotics. However, the conclusions that may be drawn from the study are limited by the exclusively self-report outcome measures used and the absence of a follow-up phase (Kendall, 1982). For other reviews of the outcome literature on RET, the reader is referred to DiGiuseppe and Miller (1977) and Zettle and Hayes (1980).

Issues and Problems

As noted earlier, while the central tenet of RET theory—that thinking influences affect and behavior—has an empirical basis, specific theoretical extrapolations from this premise have been questioned philosophically and experimentally. Ellis's own review of the evidence bearing on RET's conceptual propositions drew very favorable conclusions about their validity (Ellis, 1977b); the strategy he followed in surveying the literature, however, was somewhat unconventional. Ellis began by identifying a series of hypotheses purportedly bearing on RET theory, then listed as supportive of each postulate a broad range of studies, most of which were not designed to test RET constructs. He rarely offered any commentary on the methodological adequacy of these studies or their precise implications for RET hypotheses (Roper, 1976), and frequently neglected to include even a brief synopsis of the findings obtained. Ellis also appears to have employed unorthodox criteria in choosing the studies cited; while other reviewers generally prefer to select studies for inclusion or exclusion on the basis of their experimental rigor, Ellis seems to have done so on the basis of their outcome:

> I found that well over 90% of the published studies supported the RET theory, while less than 10% gave equivocal or negative results. Some of these findings stem from faulty methodology; others pose questions for future research. Because I located so many confirmatory researches and have only limited space in this review, I shall largely omit the nonconfirmatory studies. [Ellis, 1977b, p. 36]

Conceptual criticisms of RET theory include questions about Ellis's identification of a set of "basic" irrational beliefs and his tendency to equate rationality and adaptiveness (Arnkoff & Glass, 1982; Beck, 1976; Kendall & Hollon, 1981b; Mahoney & Arnkoff, 1978; Zettle & Hayes, 1980). While Ellis has suggested that the therapist "can easily put almost all [the] thousands of ideas [expressed by clients] into a few general categories" (Ellis, 1977a, p. 5), Arnkoff and Glass (1982) argue that "there is no 'correct' list of irrational beliefs that can be decided on for all people on an *a priori* basis." They suggest that the conceptual distinction between the lists of 3, 12, or 259 beliefs to which Ellis refers is not clear-cut, and

maintain that there can be no theoretical basis for favoring one hierarchical system of irrational belief classification over another. Arnkoff and Glass (1982) and Beck, Rush et al. (1978) also express a preference for the characterization of problematic beliefs as "maladaptive" or "dysfunctional," rather than "irrational." They contend that a functional view of "rationality" must take the *utility* of each client's beliefs into account, recognizing that "irrational" ideas can sometimes be effective and desirable, while "rational" ones may prove maladaptive in specific situations.

Another area that needs to be addressed more adequately in the RET literature is the lack of attention to diagnostic issues and the failure to provide comprehensive RET analyses of and therapeutic strategies specifically designed for the different forms of psychopathology. While a number of articles discussing the application of RET to particular disorders are available (e.g., Ellis, 1977c, with psychotic and borderline patients; Watkins, 1977, with impulsive individuals), few of these include specific prescriptions for tailoring therapeutic strategies to the target problems.

The most controversial issue in the practice of RET is the general therapeutic style modeled by Ellis. The conduct of orthodox RET has been characterized by proponents as well as opponents as "curt and didactic" (Mahoney & Arnkoff, 1978), "authoritative and aggressive" (Roper, 1976), and argumentative (Goldfried, 1979). While maintaining that critics are incorrect to imply that RET consists exclusively of arguing with clients (Ellis, 1980), Ellis acknowledges the nature of the debate that does occur: "Debating, of course, really consists of rhetorical questions designed to dispute or rip up the *false* belief" (Ellis, 1977a, p. 20). Some clinicians may find this style personally distasteful, while others question its efficacy. Goldfried et al. (1974) comment that the RET method of attacking the client's beliefs and cajoling him into thinking more logically "seems to be a haphazard procedure which can conceivably backfire if the individual feels he is being coerced into changing his beliefs or behavior" (p. 249).

Until quite recently, the most serious indictment of the RET literature has been the high ratio of enthusiastic claims for its clinical efficacy to empirical evidence capable of supporting them. While RET has generated a voluminous amount of written material, most of it has been in the form of self-help manuals, case reports, and noncomparative treatment studies. The few controlled trials that have been carried out have often included analogue subject populations treated by inexperienced therapists using poorly specified and unmeasured intervention techniques, with outcome judged on the basis of inadequate dependent variables and no provision made for follow-up assessment (DiGiuseppe & Miller, 1977; Roper, 1976). It is not clear why such a widely used therapeutic modality should have neglected to establish its credentials in the treatment of genuinely disturbed clients. The situation does appear to be changing in recent years, and perhaps the positive results obtained in the Lipsky et al. (1980) study will encourage other investigators to give RET the serious evaluation it merits.

Systematic Rational Restructuring[1]

Theory

As mentioned in the preceding section, systematic rational restructuring (SRR) developed out of Goldfried's dissatisfaction with the degree of procedural specification of RET, and a desire to fit RET within a self-control-learning framework. The theoretical structure of SRR is not clearly distinguishable from that supporting RET, although the rationale for specific SRR techniques may draw on other cognitive-behavioral concepts. Goldfried's SRR appears to place slightly more emphasis than RET does on the functionality of beliefs rather than their rationality, and on conscious self-statements rather than higher-order irrational beliefs; however, the primary distinction between the two approaches appears to be procedural rather than conceptual.

Therapy

The implementation of SRR is divided into a series of discrete stages (Goldfried et al., 1974):

1. *presentation of rationale* — The therapist explains the cognitive premise that many distressing feelings result from what people tell themselves about situations rather than from the situations themselves. General rather than problem-or client-specific examples are preferred initially.

2. *overview of irrational assumptions* — The therapist presents irrational beliefs, such as those identified by Ellis, in an extreme or exaggerated form, with the goal of getting the client to agree that they are unreasonable. The therapist avoids debates about the logic of these beliefs, encouraging the client to provide his or her own counterarguments instead.

3. *analysis of the client's problems in rational-emotive terms* — The therapist and client then begin to analyze the specific situations with which the latter's problematic affect or behavior has been associated. The therapist attempts to help the client realize that distress is mediated by unrealistic expectations or erroneous beliefs. An examination of the irrationality of the client's self-statements includes a review of both the *likelihood* that the client is interpreting the situation correctly and the *implications* of the way the client views events.

4. *teaching the individual to modify internal sentences* — At this stage the client should be prepared to take what he or she has learned in theory and begin to put it into practice in anxiety-generating situations using the experience of anxiety as a *signal* or *cue* to initiate the process of cognitive reanalysis. The process of training clients to examine their beliefs in anxiety-provoking situations is facilitated by the use of behavioral rehearsal. Through role-play or in imagination, clients practice rational reanalysis of thoughts in a hierarchically-ordered series of relevant situations. The therapist may serve as a model who demonstrates by "thinking aloud" how to cope with unpleasant affect.

Early Research

In their seminal paper outlining the model for SRR, Goldfried et al. (1974) reported on the treatment of four speech-anxious subjects using a modified form of the newly developed therapeutic program. Despite the brief duration of treatment (two to three weeks), the absence of ongoing therapist contact, and a small sample, the results were suggestive of the potential therapeutic benefits. Kanter (1975) conducted a more extensive test of SRR with groups of socially anxious volunteers who responded to newspaper advertisements (see

---

[1]Although the terms "systematic rational restructuring" (SRR) and cognitive restructuring will be used interchangeably in the following discussion, it should be clarified from the outset that the present section will be concerned with the specific intervention strategy (SRR) developed by Goldfried and his colleagues. The term "cognitive restructuring" has a generic meaning covering all therapeutic approaches that employ strategies similar to those endorsed by Ellis, Beck, Meichenbaum, and Goldfried; only the more restricted denotation of the term is intended here.

Kanter & Goldfried, 1979, for a more complete discussion). Subjects were divided into high, medium, and low level of anxiety categories, and were assigned to one of four treatment conditions: SRR, systematic desensitization, SRR plus desensitization, or waiting-list control. After seven weekly group meetings, subjects in all three treatment groups improved significantly more than the control subjects on a variety of measures, with the SRR-alone treatment proving more effective than the combined or desensitization programs. The gains evident at posttest were maintained on self-report measures after a nine-week follow-up period. While the Kanter study represents a significant advance over much of the contemporaneous RET research in that the subject population approximated a clinical sample, it may be criticized for its reliance on a single therapist for its brief follow-up (DiGiuseppe & Miller, 1977).

Recent Research

A study by Hammen, Jacobs, Mayol, and Cochran (1980) compared cognitive restructuring and skills-training programs for nonassertive subjects to a waiting-list control condition. The results indicated that the two forms of therapy were equally effective in the modification of difficulties with assertion. Clients with low levels of dysfunctional attitudes tended to improve most, but no interaction was obtained between level of dysfunctional attitudes and type of treatment.

In a recent report by Biran, Augusto, and Wilson (1981), cognitive restructuring was included as part of a multiple-baseline design for two patients with scriptophobia (fear of writing in public). For five sessions, the subjects participated in a form of cognitive restructuring described as a combination of the techniques recommended by Ellis and Goldfried; they were then given *in vivo* exposure to a hierarchy of relevant situations over five additional sessions. A third subject received exposure treatment alone. An analysis of results indicated that cognitive restructuring did not produce improvement over baseline levels on a behavioral approach test, while therapist-assisted *in vivo* exposure enables subjects to achieve maximal performance within five sessions, and to maintain this improvement at one- and nine-month followups. Although reluctant to conclude that the cognitive restructuring therapy was entirely without benefit, the authors state that it does not appear to be a necessary adjunct to behavioral inerventions for the treatment of phobic disorders.

While the cognitive treatment employed by Biran et al. appears from the published description to be sufficiently similar to SRR to warrant inclusion in the present section, they offer the caveat that "the cognitive restructuring method [used] does not necessarily constitute a faithful replication" of any one cognitive technique (Biran et al., 1981, p. 531). The authors also acknowledge that the cognitive restructuring technique may have been too brief or too focused on the fear of writing rather than broader social anxieties for maximum effectiveness. An additional possibility is not mentioned — that the single therapist who conducted all treatment sessions may have shared the biases of the protocol: "Since it was hypothesized that cognitive restructuring might not be as effective as the exposure treatment, it was applied as the first intervention" (Biran et al., 1981, p. 256).

Among the recent studies that have obtained favorable results with SRR are Linehan, Goldfried, and Goldfried (1979) and Safran, Alden, and Davidson (1980) with assertiveness training; Glogower, Fremouw, and McCroskey (1978) with speech anxiety; Hamberger and Lohr (1980) with anger control; and Jenni and Wollersheim (1979) with Type A behavior. Mixed results were obtained by Woodward and Jones (1980) with an anxious outpatient population. For a more complete review of studies employing SRR in the treatment of anxiety, see Goldfried (1979).

Issues and Problems

As suggested by the Biran et al. study, the limits on the applicability of SRR to a range of clinical problems remains unclear. There is some ambiguity about whether SRR is intended to be applied as a general intervention strategy, a systematized version of RET appropriate to the variety of psychiatric conditions for which Ellis considered his approach indicated, or as a specific treatment package for the remediation of social anxiety. Goldfried (1979) appears to endorse the latter, more restricted view:

there seem to be limits to the effectiveness of this approach to anxiety reduction, and some findings point to the possibility that there may be an interaction between target problem and therapeutic procedure. Although the precise nature of this interaction is far from clear, available evidence suggests that training in realistic thinking may be more appropriate in cases of pervasive anxiety, or in instances in which the anxiety is mediated by concerns regarding the evaluation of others. [Goldfried, 1979, p. 147]

The general topic of interactions between treatment procedures and target behaviors are addressed more fully in Kendall and Bemis (in press); for the specific case of SRR, investigators contemplating an extension of the treatment strategy to other disorders would seem well advised to consider the theoretical rationale for its application carefully, in view of Goldfried's own reservations and the data obtained to date. This caution does not imply that further studies for which such a rationale does exist should be discouraged, for only empirical trials with clinical populations can furnish the data needed to resolve the current questions.

Cognitive Therapy for Depression

Theory

From its inception (Beck, 1963), the cognitive model of psychopathology and psychotherapy has been closely identified with the affective disorders. As a function of this historical emphasis, his approach is often alluded to as "Beck's cognitive therapy for depression." It is apparent, however, when reading Beck's more recent work that he views his cognitive model as a comprehensive framework of psychopathology and psychotherapy, and traces its origins to experience with the whole spectrum of psychiatric disorders. Other researchers and clinicians have begun recently to extend Beck's model to novel populations.

According to Beck (1967, 1970, 1976), psychological problems "are not necessarily the product of mysterious, impenetrable forces but may result from commonplace processes such as faulty learning, making incorrect inferences on the basis of inadequate or incorrect information, and not distinguishing adequately between imagination and reality" (Kovacs & Beck, 1978, pp. 19–20). Beck postulates that early in the developmental period individuals may begin to formulate rules that are overly rigid and absolutistic, and are based on erroneous premises. Schemata, or complex patterns determining how objects or ideas will be perceived and conceptualized, develop out of such beliefs, and begin to channel thought processes even in the absence of environmental data. A

schema also comes to act as a kind of Procrustean mold, shaping the incoming data that are received to fit and reinforce preconceived notions (Beck & Emery, 1979). This distortion of experience is said to be maintained through the operation of characteristic errors in information processing. Beck (1970, 1976; Hollon & Beck, 1979) has postulated that the following kinds of fallacious thinking contribute to the feedback loops that maintain psychological disorders: *arbitrary inference* (or drawing conclusions when evidence is lacking or is contrary); *overgeneralization* (or making unjustified generalizations on the basis of a single event); *magnification* and *minimization* (or exaggerating/ downplaying the meaning or significance of selected incidents); *personalization* (or egocentric interpretation); and *polarized* or *all-or-none thinking* (or the tendency to think in extremes in situations that impinge on sensitive areas). Beck hypothesizes that the form of psychiatric illness is related to the distinctive content of the predominant, aberrant ideation associated with it (Beck, 1970, 1976).

The thought content in depression is said to center on the experience of significant loss, the anticipation of negative outcomes, and the sense of being inadequate. Depressed individuals are characterized as possessing a "negative cognitive triad" (Beck, 1967; Beck et al., 1978; Hollon & Beck, 1979): "they regard *themselves* as deprived, defeated, or diseased, *their worlds* as full of roadblocks to their obtaining even minimal satisfaction, and *their futures* as devoid of any hope of gratification and promising only pain and frustration" (Hollon & Beck, 1979, p. 154). Depressed patients are said to have a limitation in the number, content, and formal qualities of cognitive response categories, and to hold schemata that are global, rigid, and negatively toned (Hollon & Beck, 1979).

A variety of experimental tests have yielded some support for several of the major tenets of cognitive theory. Studies have identified differences in the predicted direction between depressives and nondepressives in expectancy and attribution measures, dream content, endorsement of negatively distorted interpretations of hypothetical situations, and scores on inventories of dysfunctional cognitions such as the Automatic Thoughts Questionnaire (Hollon & Kendall, 1980). Cognitive induction techniques have been shown to depress mood states, and associations have been found between negative thoughts and physiological changes (see Beck, 1976; Hollon & Beck, 1979, for reviews).

Beck's basic cognitive model of psychopathology has been extended to theoretical analyses of anxiety disorders (Beck, 1976; Beck & Emery, 1979; Burns & Beck, 1978; Hollon, 1981a); agoraphobia (Coleman, 1981); paranoid states (Colby, Faught, & Parkison, 1979); substance abuse (Beck & Emery, 1977; Emery & Fox, 1981; Harrison, 1981; Herman, 1981); sexual dysfunction (Fox & Emery, 1981); and anorexia nervosa (Garner & Bemis, 1982). All of these analyses draw on Beck's thesis that distorted underlying assumptions and errors in information processing serve to maintain emotional disturbance. The conceptual models vary widely in their sophistication and comprehensiveness; none has accumulated persuasive empirical evidence for the validity of specific propositions.

Therapy[2]

Beck's cognitive therapy (CT) is an active, structured, and usually time-limited approach to treatment. The intervention involves specific learning experiences designed to teach clients: (1) to monitor negative automatic thoughts; (2) to recognize the connections between cognition, affect, and behavior; (3) to examine the evidence for and against distorted automatic thoughts; (4) to substitute more reality-oriented interpretations for these negative cognitions; and (5) to learn to identify and alter the "higher-order" dysfunctional beliefs that predispose individuals to the distortion of experience (Beck et al., 1978). The basic strategy through which such goals are pursued is that of *collaborative empiricism*, in which the client and therapist work together as active collaborators in the identification of problems, the design and execution of tests of specific hypotheses, and the reanalysis of beliefs. In the ideal practice of CT, the data generated by the client himself or herself in unbiased experiments, rather then therapist credibility, persuasiveness, or authenticity, are seen as the instigators of adaptive change (Hollon & Beck, 1979).

The specific strategies used in CT are an admixture of behavioral and cognitive techniques. Enactive and verbal-symbolic components are always viewed as complementary and interdependent, rather than as discrete elements; behavioral procedures are implemented to collect cognitive data and to enhance the potential for disconfirmation of dysfunction beliefs, rather than simply to get inactive clients moving or desensitize fearful clients to phobic situations (Hollon & Beck, 1979). Predominantly "behavioral" techniques include daily self-monitoring of activities and mood levels, activity scheduling, graded task assignment and "chunking," and role-playing exercises. More "cognitive" procedures include extensive self-monitoring of cognitions and related affect on a structured data form, examination and reality-testing of the kinds of cognitions elicited in therapy sessions or revealed in self-monitoring records, and "reattribution" and "decentering" techniques. "Prospective hypothesis-testing" is considered one of the most important components of CT; the strategy involves helping clients formulate specific predictions relevant to their dysfunctional beliefs, design and carry out extra therapy experiments that bear on these predictions, and reevaluate their original hypotheses with respect to the data that are obtained.

Early Research

As recently as 1970 there was no published evidence that any form of psychotherapy could approximate the positive results obtained with tricyclic antidepressants in the treatment of unipolar depressive disorders (Hollon & Beck, 1979). Since that time, several studies have suggested that CT may equal, or on some parameters even surpass, the benefits of pharmocotherapy in the treatment of depression. An investigation of Rush et al. (1977) compared the efficacy of treatment with individual CT and imipramine, using a clinical sample of 41 unipolar depressed outpatients. After 12 weeks of treatment, both groups improved significantly, with CT patients showing greater relief on both self-report and clinical rating scales. Moreover, a significantly higher proportion of CT pa-

[2]In the following discussion, the acronym "CT" will be used to refer to the specific "cognitive therapy" approach delineated by Beck, as distinct from the much broader category of cognitive based intervention strategies. It should be noted that "cognitive-behavioral therapy" would be a more accurate characterization of the method Beck advocates, as behavioral components figure prominently in the therapeutic program; however, to avoid confusion, Beck's own designation will be followed here.

tients responded favorably to treatment (78.9 versus 22.7 percent), and fewer CT clients dropped out over the course of therapy. Follow-up assessments at six and twelve months indicated maintenance of treatment gains and a continuation of between-group differences (Kovacs et al., 1981).

Group application of CT strategies appeared efficacious in three other studies with depressed clients. Shaw (1977) found CT superior to behavioral therapy, nondirective therapy, and waiting-list control conditions, Comaz-Diaz (1981) found CT superior to a control condition but slightly less effective than behavioral therapy at a follow-up assessment. Taylor and Marshall (1977) reported that cognitive, behavioral, and cognitive-behavioral treatments were superior to waiting-list controls, with the combined cognitive-behavioral treatment demonstrating the greatest gains. Other comparative outcome studies are frequently cited in discussions of the efficacy of CT for depression (e.g., Dunn, 1979; Fuchs & Rehm, 1977; McLean & Hakstian, 1979). However, the specific cognitive or cognitive-behavioral strategies employed in these interventions overlap to varying degrees with the treatment program advocated by Beck, and bear on the merit of "cognitive therapy" in the generic rather than the specific sense of the term.

Recent Research

The somewhat revolutionary finding of the Rush et al. study that a psychological therapy could perform as well as pharmacotherapy in the treatment of clinical depression has stimulated a great deal of interest in replication and expansion of the results. At present, several large-scale studies comparing CT and drug treatment for depression are underway (for example, Waskow et al., 1980; Hollon, Wiemar, & Tuason, 1979). The Hollon et al. project includes two pharmacotherapy alone conditions (12 weeks of medication and 12 weeks plus 1 year of maintenance medication), a CT-alone cell, and a combined-treatment cell.

Blackburn et al., (1981) recently completed a partial replication of the Rush et al. study in England. Patients who met criteria for primary major depressive disorder were drawn from two populations, a hospital outpatient department and general medical practice, and were randomly assigned to "drug of choice" pharmacotherapy, CT, or combined conditions. After a maximum of 20 weeks of active treatment, it was determined that for the hospital outpatient group the combination condition was superior to either treatment alone, with

little difference between the pharmacotherapy and CT-alone cells. For the group of general practice patients, the combined and CT-alone conditions both outperformed the pharmacotherapy-alone condition, and were not significantly different from one another.

Issues and Problems

Unlike some cognitive-behavioral approaches, CT has established solid credentials for conducting research with clinical samples rather than relying on analogue populations of mildly symptomatic college students. This respectability only extends, however, to applications of CT to depressive disorders; the numerous proposals advocating the use of CT in the treatment of other psychiatric disturbances have yet to document its utility for such purposes. Only a handful of systematic case studies of CT with nondepressed clients have been reported, and not one controlled research study has appeared to date. While it seems that CT is being employed by some therapists with the whole range of patients seen in clinical practice, there is a lamentable lack of proof that the strategy is effective in remediating anything other than depression.

Some have suggested that the credibility of CT may be in jeopardy if it is detached from its origins in the affective disorders and applied to the treatment of other conditions. However, a review of the CT model delineated by Beck indicates that it was not conceptualized as a disorder-specific theory or treatment strategy. As a theme rather than a finite set of procedures, the CT model could guide the selection and application of fairly uniform *strategies*, such as collaborative empiricism and prospective hypothesis testing, to arrive at very different *conclusions* about the important issues within each of the emotional disorders. While there is no reason to assume *a priori* that the use of CT should be restricted to depressed patients, it is time for speculation to be supplanted by empirical data supporting or disconfirming its effectiveness with other specific populations.

Paralleling their critique of Ellis's rather arbitrary compilation of "basic" irrational beliefs. Arnkoff and Glass (1982) have pointed out that the major types of information-processing errors identified by Beck (e.g., selective abstraction and polarized thinking) may not be conceptually distinct. A study by Krantz and Hammen (1979) indicated that the boundaries of these categories of distorted reasoning are not sufficiently clear to enable raters to make reliable discriminations among them. Consistent with their comments on RET, Arnkoff and Glass (1982) suggest that the focus of CT should shift to an examination of the adaptiveness of thinking styles rather than their degree of conformity to objective reality.

Self-instructional Training

Theory

The development of self-instructional training (Meichenbaum, 1975a, 1977) can be traced to several independent historical influences. One contributing source was Ellis's RET; as noted in an earlier section, the Meichenbaum et al. (1971) study of speech anxiety incorporated an insight therapy which, although characterized by the authors as a derivative of RET and widely cited as empirical support for the efficacy of that approach, in fact appears to bear a closer resemblance to the self-instructional model articulated by Meichenbaum and his colleagues shortly thereafter. However, the self-instructional approach also derived from such disparate sources as the behavioral tradition and developmental research, and has developed a distinct theoretical and therapeutic identity.

Self-instructional training is an intervention *strategy*; although the application of self-instructional training to the specific population with which it is most often used *does* have a clear conceptual basis, the general model is not associated with a comprehensive theoretical system. Self-instructional training is at present the most widely studied cognitive-behavioral strategy employed with impulsive, hyperactive, and behavior-problem children. As a therapeutic technique, it has also been used to treat other populations (e.g., test-anxious, nonassertive, and schizophrenic individuals), with different and less elaborate theoretical justifications. While several of these applications will be alluded to in the course of this discussion, only the well-developed theoretical rationale for the treatment of impulsive, attention-deficit, and low-self-control disorders in children will be reviewed in detail.

One major impetus to the work on self-instructional training with children has been the developmental theory and research of the Soviet psychologists Luria (1961) and Vygotsky (1962) (Meichenbaum & Asarnow, 1979). These investigators studied the manner in which language

comes to acquire a self-regulatory function over the behavior of young children, suggesting that the internalization of verbal commands from others is a critical step in development. In an extrapolation from this postulate, it has been proposed that impulsive children may have failed to accomplish the transfer from external to internal control. A series of studies of children with self-control deficits has suggested that they do lack appropriate verbal mediation (see Kendall, 1977; Meichenbaum & Asarnow, 1979, for reviews). In contrast to the populations most often treated with cognitive-behavioral interventions such as RET and CT, impulsive children do not appear to have problems with maladaptive or dysfunctional cognitions, but with a *lack* of task-facilitating cognitions in situations where such thinking behavior would be useful (Kendall, 1981a). Therefore, a different sort of cognitive-behavioral intervention would seem indicated — one that tries to prevent automatic behavior and to interpolate thought between stimulus and response.

The self-instructional training program was designed to replicate the developmental sequence through which the overt verbalizations of an adult gradually become internalized in the child's own covert verbal control of his nonverbal behavior (Meichenbaum & Goodman, 1971). The initial formulation of self-instructional training identified the following objectives:

> By using this fading procedure, we hoped to a) train impulsive subjects to provide themselves with internally originated verbal commands or self-instructions and to respond to them appropriately; b) strengthen the mediational properties of the children's inner speech in order to bring their behavior under their own verbal or discriminative control; c) overcome any possible "comprehension, production, or mediational deficiencies;" and finally d) encourage the children to appropriately self-reinforce their behavior. We hoped to have the child's private speech gain a new functional significance, to have the child develop a new cognitive style or "learning set" and thus to engender self-control. [Meichenbaum & Goodman, 1971, p. 116]

Therapy

The conduct of self-instructional training involves a series of sessions in which the therapist and subject work on a variety of training tasks, which may include impersonal-cognitive and/or interpersonal problem-solving exercises. At the beginning of the intervention sequence, the therapist verbalizes a variety of task-relevant self-statements out loud. These verbalizations are intended to *model* a variety of performance skills, including problem definition ("What do I need to do?"); problem approach ("I'm supposed to try to copy this design"); attention focusing ("I should plan ahead and figure out how large I should make this first part"); coping statements and error-correcting options ("I did that part wrong—I can erase that and start again more carefully"); and self-reinforcement ("I finished it—and I did a pretty good job!") (Kendall, 1977; Meichenbaum & Asarnow, 1979). After the child has observed the therapist performing the task while instructing him or herself out loud, then in a whisper, and finally covertly.

The self-instructional treatment package employed in the research program of Kendall and his colleagues places a special emphasis on modeling and behavioral contingencies in addition to self-instruction. In this approach, the therapist models each form of self-instruction in turn (whispering, covert self-instruction) before asking the subject to employ it. The therapist also models instructional problem solving while carrying out his or her own tasks in the training situation, such as searching through a briefcase for test materials. Response-cost contingencies are utilized as an adjunct procedure to help maintain interest in the training procedure and prevent random guessing. In addition, social reward in the form of praise is given for appropriate behavior and correct responses. Several studies have indicated that the combination of cognitive and behavioral techniques may be more effective with impulsive children than either alone (see Kendall, 1982, for a review).

Early Research

In the original paper in which they presented the rationale and procedures for self-instructional training, Meichenbaum and Goodman (1971) reported on two separate studies of its effectiveness in modifying the behavior of impulsive children. In the first investigation, 15 second-graders from a remedial class were assigned to self-instructional, attention-control, or no-treatment control conditions. After four half-hour individual sessions, it was determined that children in the self-instructional group attained higher scores on a variety of nonsocial problem tasks than did subjects in the other groups. However, no generalization of treatment effects to the classroom was obtained on a teacher questionnaire or through a time-sampling observational technique assessing behavior in the classroom. The second study assigned 15 children identified as impulsive on the basis of scores on the Matching Familiar Figures test (MFF, Kagan, 1966) to cognitive modeling alone, cognitive modeling plus self-instructional training, or attention-control groups. The results indicated that while both active treatments were associated with increased response latencies on dependent measures, only the addition of explicit self-instructional training served to decrease error rates.

Recent Research

Kendall and Braswell (1982b) evaluated the contribution of the cognitive component of self-instructional training to the total cognitive-behavioral treatment program by comparing a self-instruction plus contingency management condition to a purely behavioral intervention. Cognitive strategies were not examined in isolation, because of the authors' belief in the fundamental importance of behavioral techniques in the management of impulsive disorders. Twenty-seven children with low self-control were randomly assigned to one of the two treatment cells or to an attention-control condition. All subjects received 12 sessions of individual therapist contact focusing on psychoeducational, play, and interpersonal tasks and situations. The behavioral condition involved the institution of response-cost contingencies and therapist modeling of task-appropriate behavior; the cognitive-behavioral condition added cognitive modeling and training in verbal self-instruction. At the end of the treatment period, both active treatments were associated with improvements on teachers' blind ratings of hyperactivity and on such performance measures as cognitive style and academic achievement; however, only the self-instructional plus contingency management condition yielded improvements in teacher ratings of self-control or on self-report measures of self-concept. Naturalistic observation in the classroom setting evidenced variability, but measures of off-task verbal and off-task physical behavior indicated treatment efficacy. In neither condition did parent ratings of children's behavior at home indicate desired gains. A 10-week follow-up provided additional support for the efficacy of the cognitive-behavioral treatment, whereas 1-year follow-up did not show significant differences across conditions. The authors concluded that while the posttest and short-term follow-up data provided support for the efficacy of cognitive-behavioral treatment and the specific advantage of a combined program over a solely behavioral procedure, the interpretation of these results must be tempered by the lack of long-term maintenance of treatment gains and the absence of generalization to the home setting. Kendall and Braswell speculate that longer treatment periods with a greater focus on home situations and more in-class interventions may be required before truly satisfactory results can be anticipated.

Braswell, Kendall, Braith, Carey and Vye (1983) conducted a process analysis of the audiotapes of the treatment reported in Kendall and Braswell (1982b). Among other findings, multiple regression analyses demonstrated that the frequencies of coded incidents of behavior labeled "involvement" were associated with improvement and maintenance of therapy gains.

The extensive literature on self-instructional training with children includes numerous studies supporting to some degree the utility of the intervention strategy in the modification of impulsivity and hyperactivity, although in almost every instance a variable pattern of results across dependent measures has been obtained (see Barabash, 1978; Cameron & Robinson, 1980; Douglas et al. 1976; Kendall & Finch, 1978; Kendall & Wilcox, 1980; Kendall & Zupan, 1981; Parrish & Erickson, 1981; Varni & Henker, 1979). Positive but uneven results have also been obtained through the use of self-instructional training with aggressive children (Camp et al., 1977), institutionalized adolescents (Snyder & White, 1979), retarded children (Burgio, Whitman, & Johnson, 1980), poor readers (Malamuth, 1979), and adolescents with low mathematics achievement scores (Genshaft & Hirt, 1980). For a more complete review of the literature on self-instructional training with children, the reader is referred to Kendall (1982).

In an extension of self-instructional training to a very different population, Craighead (1979) studied the benefits of using this technique in the treatment of adults with assertion deficits. To investigate the hypothesis that assertion-related therapist communications that are only moderately discrepant from subjects' initial attitudes should produce more change than highly discrepant communications, both moderate and high assertion self-instructional training conditions were

incorporated into the study design. Forty nonassertive subjects were randomly assigned to one of the two self-instructional groups; a placebo control group, or a delayed-treatment condition. Both self-instructional treatments proved significantly superior to the control conditions on behavioral tests and self-report measures of behavior and thoughts. On most indices, the hypothesized discrepancy factor did not produce differential results.

Other studies with adults have found positive results associated with the use of self-instructional training in the treatment of schizophrenics (Meichenbaum & Cameron, 1973a), test-anxious subjects (Cooley & Speigler, 1980; Meichenbaum, 1972), and individuals with dating skills deficits (Glass, Gottman, & Shurmak, 1976). Essentially negative results have been reported in an attempted replication of Meichenbaum and Cameron's (1973a) findings with schizophrenics (Margolis & Shember, 1976), a comparison of *in vivo* exposure with self-instructional training plus exposure for obsessive-compulsives (Emmelkamp et al., 1980), and a study comparing self-instructional training to RET in the treatment of assertion problems (Carmody, 1978).

Issues and Problems

Since the conceptual rationale for self-instructional training involves developing verbally mediated self-control, generalization is an expected as well as a desirable outcome of the treatment approach (Kendall & Finch, 1979). However, a number of self-instructional studies have not found any evidence that such a process has occurred as a consequence of treatment (see Burgio et al., 1980; Douglas et al., 1976; Meichenbaum & Goodman, 1971). In contrast, generalization to at least some tasks and situations has been obtained by Cameron and Robinson (1980), Kendall and Braswell (1982b), Kendall and Finch (1978), Kendall and Wilcox (1980), and Kendall and Zupan (1981). Kendall (1977) has commented that generalization may be affected by the use of incentive contingencies, particular training materials and settings, predetermined versus individualized self-instructions, and concrete versus conceptual verbalizations. It is noteworthy that the series of studies by Kendall and his colleagues that do show evidence of generalization have involved somewhat longer training periods (12 sessions) and modeling, response-cost, and role-playing strategies in addition to basic self-instructional procedures. Further increments in generalization may require even more extensive training with a greater emphasis on involving teachers and families in the treatment process.

Additional areas within self-instructional training that require further research include the identification of active treatment components through dismantling procedures and a more careful examination of the applicability of self-instructional training to other clinical populations. Kendall (1977) has cautioned that while verbal self-instruction procedures are readily modifiable for other behavior problems, consideration of the rationale for such extensions as well as careful assessment and design must precede the decision to implement the approach with novel populations.

Stress Inoculation Training

Theory

Stress inoculation training (Meichenbaum, 1975b; Meichenbaum & Cameron, 1974) is a therapeutic strategy designed to help clients develop and employ a repertoire of skills that will enable them to cope with a variety of stressful situations. The rationale for the training approach is to engender a sense of "learned resourcefulness" in clients undergoing stress (Meichenbaum & Turk, 1976), by providing success experiences in coping with manageable levels of stress, and building a "prospective defense" comprised of skills and positive expectations that will help clients tolerate more aversive situations. In an analogy to medical treatment, this approach is said to build "psychological antibodies" and enhance resistance through exposure to stimuli strong enough to arouse defenses but not powerful enough to overcome them (Meichenbaum & Cameron, 1974; Meichenbaum & Turk, 1976).

As with self-instructional training, it is most meaningful to discuss the conceptual basis for the application of stress inoculation with reference to a specific disorder—although unlike self-instructional training, stress inoculation is not strongly identified with any particular population. Because of its relative sophistication and complexity, Novaco's (1975, 1976, 1978, 1979) application of stress inoculation to the remediation of anger will be highlighted in this discussion.

Novaco conceptualizes anger as an affective stress reaction to aversive events; in strictly cognitive terms, it is said to represent an attempt to extort a validation of one's personal constructs in an effort to control aversive events. While anger is seen as determined by the mutual influences of external events, internal processes, and behavioral reactions, cognitive factors are accorded a central role within Novaco's model: "aversive events have no direct relationship upon anger except as mediated by appraisal, expectations, and private speech" (Novaco, 1978, p. 141). He discusses the role of each of these cognitive processes in anger arousal, concluding that private speech, as the internal dialogue that expresses appraisals and expectations in language form, can itself act as a self-arousal mechanism and can maintain or prolong anger through the repetition of self-statements. However, displaying a rather admirable conservatism in outlining his cognitive model, Novaco notes that:

> it is not necessary [for the implementation of cognitive techniques] to assume that anger is *generated* by self-statements. In fact, this assumption has not been made . . . it has only been hypothesized that the use of therapeutically designed self-instructions can serve as a means to *regulate* anger. [Novaco, 1979, p. 260]

In accordance with this cognitive analysis, the stress inoculation program Novaco recommends for the reduction of excessive anger concentrates on modifying client's perceptions of stressful events, changing negative self-statements and irrational beliefs, and teaching relaxation and coping techniques.

Therapy

The implementation of stress inoculation training is divided into three distinct stages. In a thoughtful review of the literature, Jaremko (1979) identified variations between studies in the manner in which the goals of these phases have been operationalized, and commented on the research data bearing on each.

1. EDUCATION PHASE

The principal aim is to provide clients with a conceptual framework for interpreting the target problem that is compatible with a cognitive-behavioral intervention (Meichenbaum & Turk, 1976). The particular explanatory scheme selected may vary as a function of the client's presenting problems or the preference of the therapist. For example, Meichenbaum recommends the use of Schachter's two-component theory of emotion to teach anxious clients that reactions to stress involve both heightened arousal and negative self-statements, and Melzack and Wall's (1965) gate control model of pain has been employed with subjects who must cope with laboratory-induced pain (Horan et al., 1977; Klepac et al., 1981; Turk, 1975). Meichenbaum also suggests that it is helpful to describe the stress response as a series of phases (preparing for a stressor, confronting a stressor, possibly being overwhelmed by the stressor, and reinforcing oneself for having coped) rather than a single panic reaction, to build the expectation that it is possible to intervene at various points in the sequence (Meichenbaum & Turk, 1976). Jaremko (1979) has observed that no research has as yet been conducted to determine whether or not the education phase of stress inoculation training is really essential, which type of rationale is most useful, or how to increase the plausibility and ease of retention of such conceptual explanations.

2. REHEARSAL OR SKILLS TRAINING PHASE

During the next phase, clients are taught coping skills for the management of stress. A wide variety of techniques have been included within and across different stress inoculation treatment packages. Jaremko (1979) has grouped the array of procedures into three categories: physical means of coping, cognitive restructuring, and generalized coping strategies. Physical coping strategies such as muscle relaxation, mental relaxation, and deep breathing are routinely incorporated into most stress inoculation programs; however, Jaremko (1979) notes that in the absence of empirical investigation, the common assumption that such techniques contribute to the effectiveness of stress inoculation may not be warranted. The cognitive restructuring strategies that have been used in the skills-training phase include RET-like analyses of irrational beliefs, replacements of negative with positive self-statements, and self-instructional training.

3. APPLICATION TRAINING PHASE

In the final stage of stress inoculation training, clients are given the opportunity to practice newly acquired coping skills in stressful situations. This may be accomplished through role-playing exercises, imaginal or *in vivo* presentation of hierarchically ordered situations, or training coping skills to other clients. As with earlier phases, Jaremko (1979) notes that the implementation of this phase differs considerably across studies, with little information available about the optimal type or duration of exposure to practice stressors.

Early Research

Meichenbaum and Cameron (1973b) compared the effectiveness of a modified form of stress inoculation to systematic desensitization and a waiting-list condition in the treatment of multiphobic clients. The stress inoculation program included educational and skill-training phases, but did not provide systematic exposure to stressful stimuli as part of the treatment package. To evaluate the ability of stress inoculation training to promote generalization, half of the subjects were taught directly to deal with fears of snakes, while the other half were treated for fears of rats. The results indicated that stress inoculation was the most effective treatment in reducing avoidance behavior and demonstrating generalization effects.

Turk (1975) employed stress inoculation training to teach subjects how to contend with laboratory-induced pain. In accordance with Melzack and Wall's gate-control theory of pain, subjects were informed that the pain experience consists of sensory-discriminative, motivational-affective, and cognitive-evaluative components. They were then taught coping techniques to counteract pain on each of these levels; for example, motivational-affective components could be dealt with through attention diversion, imaginative inattention, imaginative transformation of pain or context, and somatization techniques. Stress inoculation training was found to be highly effective in increasing subjects' tolerance of the discomfort caused by leaving a tourniquet in place, to a degree superior to that obtained in an attention control group — or though the administration of morphine in a separate study (Smith, Chiang, & Regina, 1974).

Recent Research

An interesting study by Klepac et al. (1981) evaluated the contribution of several different components of stress inoculation training to pain tolerance: (a) the presence or absence of relaxation training; (b) instruction in cognitive coping skill; and (c) exposure to a stressor. Seventy-two subjects with a fear of dentists were assigned to one of eight treatment conditions, each representing a combination of the three components under investigation. "Untreated" subjects received only the education phase of stress inoculation training, in which a modified version of the gate-control theory of pain was offered as an explanation of the pain experience; other subjects also received between two and six therapy sessions, depending on the number of components administered in the cells to which they were assigned. Subjects whose training programs included exposure to stressors were given practice sessions involving shock to the forearm. Dependent measures included tolerance levels for arm and tooth shock and self-reported anxiety. The results on the measure of arm-shock tolerance indicated that each of the treatment components increased the subjects' ability to cope with pain, but none generalized to the tooth shock stressor that had not been available to any subjects during the training phase. Klepac et al. concluded that because treatment effects were found for the training stressor but not the generalization stressor, it would be preferable to use the exact stressor for which increased tolerance is desired in the clinical application of stress inoculation procedures.

The Klepac et al. (1981) study provided useful information yet Kendall (1982) has cautioned that the conclusions that could be drawn from the Klepac et al. study may be restricted by the absence of cognitive assessments to determine which strategies among the many available to them subjects actually *did* employ in coping with the stressors. Admittedly, this task is difficult and few studies have undertaken it, but cognitive assessments are important. In addition, the fact that subjects received different numbers of treatments sessions makes it difficult for this otherwise solid study to rule out rival hypotheses for the differential results obtained.

Other investigators who have obtained positive results using stress inoculation training with a variety of populations include Novaco (1975) with chronic anger problems; Horan et al. (1977) with laboratory-induced pain; Holcomb (1979) with hospitalized patients suffering from severe stress reactions; Hussian and Lawrence (1978) with test anxiety; Fremouw and Zitter (1978) with speech anxiety; Kendall et al. (1979) with the stress associated with undergoing cardiac catheterization; and Denicola and Sandler (1980) with lack of anger control associated with child abuse. For a more complete survey of current applications of stress inoculation procedures, the reader is referred to Meichenbaum and Jaremko (1983).

Issues and Problems

While all of the approaches that have been reviewed incorporate diverse and often overlapping techniques, stress inoculation training appears to be the most inclusive form of cognitive-behavioral therapy surveyed. What sometimes appears to be a haphazard, scattered approach to treatment in fact reflects a deliberate plan with a plausible underlying rationale: that the best way to match particular clients and problems to the techniques that will be most beneficial for them is to present a range of strategies from among which the most appealing and efficacious ones can be selected. In this way the client can serve as a collaborator in helping to generate an individually tailored coping package suited to his or her own needs and experiences (Turk, 1975). While this "cafeteria-style" approach has some intuitive appeal and may well prove clinically advantageous, it also has some disadvantages in both clinical application and research. First, some stress inoculation programs appear to present more alternatives than can be assimilated in the amount of time allotted to the skills training phase. Second, the failure to evaluate the differential contribution of various techniques to treatment outcome may result in the retention of inactive components that unnecessarily clutter the treatment program and may dilute the effects of more potent procedures. Finally, the absence of assessments to determine which technique among the many presented to them clients actually *do* use makes it impossible to understand how successful stress inoculation programs work. Jaremko (1979) has proposed a revised procedural model intended to make the implementation of treatment phases more structured, consistent, and uniform.

Additional comments about the current status of stress inoculation reiterate familiar themes from the review of other cognitive-behavioral approaches: there is an urgent need for more research with clinical populations, and for more studied efforts to promote treatment generalization. As with self-instructional training, one of the theoretical benefits of stress inoculation, inherent in the very name of the therapeutic approach, is that treatment generalization is "built into the therapy package" (Meichenbaum & Turk, 1976).

Jaremko (1979) points out, however, that research has not overwhelmingly supported the ability of such training actually to "inoculate" clients against future stress; clearly, empirical investigations must demonstrate the utility of stress inoculation for such a purpose before claims to the effect can be accepted.

Other Cognitive-Behavioral Approaches

Because of space limitations, it is not possible to provide an exhaustive review of all the cognitive-behavioral aproaches in the present chapter; in the following section, the more visible of the numerous strategies that have been omitted will be summarized briefly.

The *covert conditioning* therapies are more closely aligned with the conceptual model of behaviorism than the other cognitive approaches surveyed. In this perspective, cognitions are viewed as private responses subject to the same laws of operant conditioning as more observable behaviors, and the modification of dysfunctional patterns is attempted through the use of procedures analogous to those employed in traditional behavior therapy. For the most part, covert conditioning methods have been applied to the reduction of undesired behaviors such as overeating and smoking or unwanted cognitions such as excessive rumination (see Mahoney, 1974; Mahoney & Arnkoff, 1978, for reviews).

Coverant control procedures (Homme, 1965) involve teaching clients to alter maladaptive thought chains by substituting and reinforcing more appropriate coverants (covert operants). Subjects are trained to rehearse negative statements such as "I get fat when I eat too much" or "Smoking causes cancer," follow them with positive thoughts such as "I'll look better when I eat less" or "I'll save money by not smoking," and finally to reinforce themselves for the altered cognitive responses by engaging in pleasant activities. Studies with obese subjects have obtained unimpressive results with the use of coverant control strategies (Horan & Johnson, 1971; Tyler & Straughan, 1970).

Covert sensitization techniques (Cautela, 1966, 1967) train subjects to use imagery to associate undesired behaviors with highly aversive consequences, such as the experience of nausea. As with coverant control procedures, attempts to employ this approach in the modification of eating disturbances have yielded minimal and inconsistent results (Diament & Wilson, 1975; Elliott & Denney, 1975; Forety & Hagen, 1973; see Leon, 1979, for a review).

Thought stopping strategies are designed to control obsessive or unpleasant cognitions (Wolpe, 1958, 1969). Clients are instructed to use a loud signal such as a buzzer or the shouted word "Stop!" to terminate episodes of rumination; gradually, the signal is faded to a covert interruption of obsessive thinking. While thought stopping is widely used by behavioral and cognitive-behavioral practitioners, not a single controlled-group study has demonstrated its effectiveness (Mahoney & Arnkoff, 1978). Overall, Mahoney and Arnkoff (1978) conclude that the covert conditioning literature consists of a high ratio of theoretical speculation to empirical evidence, with few adequate trials and still fewer positive findings to support the utility of these procedures.

In contrast, *covert modeling* strategies (Cautela, 1971, 1976) have proven effective in reducing anxiety and increasing assertiveness in a variety of studies with analogue or mildly disturbed subject populations (Cautela, Flannery, & Hanley, 1974; Harris & Johnson, 1980; Kazdin, 1975, 1979, 1980). In this approach, clients are taught to rehearse target performances by imagining models engaging in desired behaviors. A series of studies by Kazdin (1979, 1980) has shown that the spontaneous or directed elaboration of covert modeling scenes by subjects, initially thought to represent a methodological problem, actually enhances the effectiveness of the procedure.

Problem-solving therapy (Shure & Spivack, 1978; Spivack, Platt, & Shure, 1976; Spivack & Shure, 1974) is designed to provide subjects with systematic training in the generation of appropriate options in problematic social situations. The approach is most commonly used with preschoolers and emotionally disturbed children, and has yielded some positive results in facilitating prosocial behavior. Most investigations have failed, however, to rule out nonspecific treatment effects by relying on untreated control-group comparisons (see Urbain & Kendall, 1980, for a review), and some negative findings have been reported (Rickel, Eshelman, & Loigman, 1981).

Multimodal therapy was developed by Lazarus (1980) as a comprehensive framework for assessment and intervention that takes account of seven important areas of human functioning (behavior; affect; sensation; imagery; cognition; interpersonal relationships; drugs). While the emphasis on attending to the variety of modes through which behavioral disorders are influenced and expressed is laudable, interactions between these components and strategies for intervening at each level remain inadequately specified, and as yet the approach has generated little empirical research.

Personal science is a cognitive learning therapy in which the therapist acts as a "technical consultant" to instruct clients in the resolution of their personal problems (Mahoney, 1977b). The approach is similar to Beck's cognitive therapy in underscoring the value of collaborative empiricism, Socratic dialogue, and hypothesis-testing strategies, differing principally in the extent to which it concentrates on structured coping-skills training and emphasizes a pragmatic eclecticism. While some positive results have been obtained with obese clients (Mahoney et al., 1977), few clinical applications of the personal science approach have been reported.

Sorting or Splitting Hairs? Differentiating Cognitive-Behavioral Approaches

Many writers have commented on the essential theoretical and procedural similarity of the cognitive learning therapies that have been reviewed in this chapter. Cognitive-behavioral approaches share the assumption that disturbances in mediational processes give rise to maladaptive emotional states and behavior patterns, and the goal of correcting presumed dysfunctional relationships between external events and cognitions (Sutton-Simon & Goldfried, 1979). This common perspective naturally gives rise to an advocacy of similar techniques and treatment strategies. Proponents often tacitly acknowledge their kinship by citing the empirical findings of other schools as supportive of their own tenets. It is generally recognized, however, that there are differences between these approaches in their theoretical parentage, emphases, specific procedures, and the kinds of target problems for which they are usually deemed most appropriate (Goldfried, 1979; Hollon & Kendall, 1979; Mahoney & Arnkoff, 1978). A number of writers have cautioned against extending the "uniformity myth" identified by Kiesler (1966) to cognitive-behavioral therapy by assuming that all conceptions of cognitive disturbances

are equivalent and that all types of cognitive-behavioral treatment are equally appropriate in a given case (Meichenbaum, 1978; Sutton-Simon & Goldfried, 1979).

At present there are few systems for distinguishing among the variety of cognitive-behavioral therapies conceptually or procedurally. Kendall and Kriss (1983) have offered guidelines for characterizing cognitive learning approaches along five dimensions: the theoretical orientation of the therapy and its associated target of change; the nature of the therapeutic relationship; the presumed principal cognitive change-agent, the source of evidence on which cognitive reappraisals are based; and the degree of emphasis on self-control. According to this system of classification, rational-emotive therapy, systematic rational restructuring, cognitive therapy, and stress inoculation, each has different profiles and evidences degrees of relationship to one another that do not always accord with their historical derivation or stated affiliations. For example, systematic rational restructuring differs from stress inoculation and cognitive therapy on only one dimension; cognitive therapy and rational-emotive therapy emerge as highly discrepant from one another (differing on four of the five dimensions), although they are frequently viewed as closely related.

It is evident that it is possible to distinguish "textbook" or "theoretically specified" implementations of the cognitive-behavioral therapies along a number of dimensions. However, while there are clear differences in what the founders of the respective cognitive schools say *ought* to be done in the conduct of their various brands of treatment, it is not clear that what the practitioners of such therapies actually *do* is as readily discriminable. Even when methods are labeled by different names and acknowledge different sources of inspiration, the practice of therapy in an individual case may be virtually identical across schools (for example, Beck's cognitive therapy, Goldfried's systematic rational restructuring, Meichenbaum's stress inoculation, and Mahoney's personal science). Such confusion in school identification is compounded by the "semantic dilemma" described by Kendall (Kendall, 1982; Kendall & Kriss, 1983). The names given to different intervention programs are often inconsistent, with the label "cognitive" sometimes meaning "cognitive-behavioral," while "cognitive-behavioral" sometimes means solely "cognitive" and sometimes principally "behavioral," and "cognitive-restructuring" may mean anything at all. Moreover, many recent intervention programs profess a deliberate cognitive eclecticism, incorporating elements from a number of relatively independent cognitive-behavioral schools (e.g., Alden, Safran, & Weideman, 1978; Holroyd, Andrasik, & Westbrook, 1977; Taylor & Marshall, 1977). Without observational studies and/or detailed specification of treatment procedures, it is not possible to determine which widely recognized approaches such therapies resemble most closely.

The consequence of this theoretical, terminological, and procedural confusion were clearly apparent in the process of scanning the cognitive-behavioral literature for the purposes of the present review. For example, in a paper outlining a cognitive-behavioral treatment program for the modification of obsessive-compulsive disorders, McFall and Wollersheim (1979) professed an allegiance to RET; in fact, along the contrasting dimensions identified earlier, the principles and procedures they advocate seem to conform at least as closely to those associated with Beck's CT. Most strikingly, a cognitive-behavioral intervention program employed by Holroyd (1976) for the reduction of test anxiety has been variously cited as exemplifying RET (DiGuiseppe & Miller, 1977; Roper, 1976), self-instructional training (Mahoney & Arnkoff, 1978), and stress inoculation (Jaremko, 1979; Kendall & Kriss, 1983); a form of therapy used with obsessive-compulsive patients in a study by Emmelkamp et al. (1980) has been cited as an instance of systematic rational restructuring (Biran et al., 1981) and self-instructional training (Kendall & Kriss, 1983). It is by no means implied that research or treatment programs ought to conform to the specifications of any one cognitive-behavioral approach. However, it is suggested that unless or until the discipline concedes the essential equivalence of most cognitive-behavioral models, more care should be taken by researchers to label treatment programs accurately and identify the precise components included, and by reviewers to evaluate the specific relevance of data obtained in each study to the status of the particular cognitive-behavioral model under review.

At the same time, there is a pressing need for several kinds of research programs to disentangle the confusing array of cognitive-behavioral approaches. First, on the theoretical level, more studies such as those undertaken by Sutton-Simon

and Goldfried (1979) and Gormally et al. (1981) are needed to investigate the involvement of different forms of faulty thinking (such as Ellis's irrational beliefs, Meichenbaum's negative self-statements, and Beck's distorted information processing) in various psychological disorders. Second, process research into the procedures and styles employed by therapists who espouse different cognitive-behavioral models will be required to determine what is actually involved in the implementation of these forms of treatment. The need for this kind of investigation has been underscored in several recent reports (Braswell et al., 1983; DeRubeis et al., 1982; Kendall, 1982; Kiesler, 1980; Mahoney & Arnkoff, 1978). In addition to furnishing information about how closely the cognitive-behavioral therapies resemble one another in practice as well as in theory, such data could be used for therapist training and calibration of the skill with which psychotherapy is executed (Kendall & Hollon, in press). Finally, comparative outcome studies are needed to gauge the relative efficacy of competing cognitive-behavioral approaches with particular disorders (e.g., RET versus SSR versus CT versus stress inoculation for the treatment of interpersonal anxiety). When combined with outcome assessments, the process data could also be applied to an analysis of the "active" components in each treatment modality (Braswell et al., 1983; Hollon, 1981b; Kiesler, 1980).

A related point concerns the need to match particular kinds of cognitive-behavioral strategies to specific types of psychological disorders. In many instances, a logical as well as historical affinity can be identified between specific cognitive-behavioral approaches and particular kinds of disorders, for example, SRR and anxiety, CT and depression, and self-instructional training and impulsivity. However, a trend is evident in the present review for the proponents of various cognitive-behavioral models to claim an "expanded terrain" of appropriate patient populations. For further discussion, see Kendall and Bemis (in press).

Cognitive Assessment

It is beyond the scope of this chapter to offer more than an abbreviated list of the more active issues in cognitive assessment. For a more complete discussion, the reader is referred to Arnkoff and Glass (1982), Hollon and Bemis (1981) Kendall (in press), Kendall and Braswell (1982a), Kendall and Hollon (1981a), and Merluzzi, Glass, and

Genest (1981). The following points may be abstracted from these comprehensive reviews:

1. Clearly, further research is required to refine and evaluate instruments designed for the assessment of the cognitions that are presumed to bear some relationship to psychopathology. For example, the concept of irrational beliefs is a "slippery construct" that has been defined and measured in a variety of ways, and at present the overlap between different conceptualizations and operational definitions remains unclear (Sutton-Simon, 1981). Many of the existing measures of irrational beliefs have serious theoretical and psychometric shortcomings, and often appear to have achieved wide currency on the basis of their availability rather than their merit.

2. Comparative studies of different clinical groups are needed to examine relationships between particular dysfunctional beliefs and modes of information processing and the various forms of psychological disturbances (Sutton-Simon, 1981).

3. The increasing emphasis on the subjective meaning and functionality of cognitions rather than their content and rationality necessitates the replacement of direct assessment methods such as endorsement inventories with strategies such as sequential analysis and the assessment of the "impact" of thoughts (Arnkoff & Glass, 1982; Kendall, in press).

4. New measurement techniques are needed for the study of cognitive schemata, the "organizing principles" hypothesized to underlie conscious self-statements (Kihlstrom & Nasby, 1981; Landau & Goldfried, 1981).

5. In addition to joint process-outcome research designed to identify the "active" ingredients of cognitive-behavioral therapy, attempts should be made to assess ongoing changes in cognition to explore the mechanisms of change within the client through which such components presumably operate (Kendall, 1982; Kendall & Korgeski, 1979). For example, to confirm the proposition that self-efficacy changes with psychotherapy, it is necessary to assess self-efficacy before, during, and after treatment.

6. Additional research is needed to evaluate the utility of the concept of self-efficacy, proposed as a unifying mechanism that can account for the gains achieved through very different modes of treatment (Bandura, 1977; Bandura & Adams, 1977; Bandura, Adams, & Beyer, 1977). While Bandura's formulation has been the subject of

criticism (e.g., Eysenck, 1978; Wolpe, 1978), it has attained considerable prominence in the cognitive-behavioral literature, and is widely invoked as an explanation for the benefits of psychotherapy, particularly when contrasting intervention techniques yield equivalent outcomes that would not be predicted on the basis of cognitive theory. Unfortunately, such interpretations have sometimes been offered without any accompanying data that might implicate changes in efficacy expectations. The difficulties involved in the assessment of self-efficacy have been discussed by several writers (Kazdin, 1978; Poser, 1978). Despite these challenging problems, research designed to investigate the validity of the concept and define its parameters is beginning to accumulate (see Bandura, Adams, Hardy, & Howells, 1980; Gauthier & Ladouceur, 1981; Hammen et al., 1980; Kazdin, 1980; Kirsch, 1982).

Question: "Do You Believe in the Unconscious?" Answer: "Not that I'm Aware of:" Questioning the Place of Dynamic Constructs in Cognitive-Behavioral Therapy

The current popularity of cognitive-behavioral therapy has been attributed in part to its joint emphasis on enactive and verbal intervention strategies, and the ease with which a wide variety of techniques can be integrated into the basic model (Arnkoff, 1981; Glass & Arnkoff, 1982). While the common meaning of the term "eclectic" does not aptly characterize an approach with a clear and relatively consistent framework for interpreting and modifying psychopathology, the cognitive-behavioral model is an "ideological hybrid" (Mahoney, 1977a) that has been influenced by, and continues to express, disparate traditions. The convergent nature of its development is exemplified in the professional backgrounds of some of the most eminent figures in the field, with Ellis and Beck arriving at a cognitive-behavioral approach from the context of training in psychodynamic theory and therapy, and Meichenbaum and Mahoney from experience within the behavioral tradition. At present the cognitive-behavioral orientation continues to draw converts from the ranks of researchers and clinicians on both sides of the gulf between these "veteran enemies" (Mahoney, 1977a).

If cognitive-behavioral therapy may be said to

owe allegiance to both the dynamic and the behavioral models, the influence of the latter is clearly predominant in its current practice. While it is by no means suggested that the commitment to methodological behaviorism or endorsement of enactive techniques should be moderated, it may be that the development of the cognitive-behavioral model would be enhanced by a closer attention to several issues traditionally considered the exclusive province of psychodynamic approaches. Several recent papers have explored the possibility of incorporating more dynamic material into the practice of cognitive-behavioral therapy while retaining the empirical emphasis of its behavioral heritage.

One of the key concepts associated with this trend is that of resistance. The psychodynamic understanding of resistance invokes unconscious processes that actively oppose attempts to explore symptoms that presumably serve a defensive function. The term has been virtually absent from the behavioral and cognitive-behavioral literature, where the prevailing view is that "the notion that some internal process is responsible for most or many treatment failures is simply an unfortunate though convenient evasion of one's clinical responsibilities" (Lazarus & Fay, 1981, pp. 115–116). Recently a number of cognitive-behaviorists, conceding the importance of attending to related issues in the conduct of therapy, have offered alternative definitions of resistance that are consistent with the cognitive model and have proposed a variety of strategies for dealing with its occurrence. Wachtel (1981a) provides a forum for comparing and contrasting the cognitive-behavioral perspective on resistance with the traditional dynamic view.

An analysis of these position papers reveals characteristic differences in how resistance is conceptualized within the two orientations. While psychoanalytic writers are likely to view resistance as a function of the patient's conflicts about change, cognitive-behavioral therapists tend to consider a broad range of variables before making attributions about the cause of resistance or lack of improvement (Glass & Arnkoff, 1982; Goldfried, 1981a, 1981b; Lazarus & Fay, 1981). In cognitive-behavioral approaches, the focus is shifted from active intrapsychic processes hypothesized to underlie noncompliance to the noncompliance itself; patient variables are considered a small subset of the factors that may be responsible for failures to adhere to the treatment program. Cognitive-be-

haviorists are reluctant both to define noncompliance as resistance (nominating such therapist variables as the use of incorrect techniques or the lack of adequate functional analyses as more likely interpretations) and to conclude that the resistance that *is* attributable to client variables represents unconscious conflict (preferring explanations such as pessimism about change and environmental reinforcement of presenting problems) (Goldfried, 1981a; Lazarus & Fay, 1981). Treatment adherence is considered to be most strongly influenced by clients' conscious or preconscious beliefs concerning the therapeutic process. Private monologues about the progress of therapy, the attitudes of the therapist, the feasibility of change, and the meaning of setbacks may all lead to treatment impasses that appear to reflect a vested interest on the client's part in remaining ill (Cameron, 1978; Lazarus & Fay, 1981; Meichenbaum & Gilmore, 1981).

Perhaps as a function of this understanding of resistance, cognitive-behavioral therapists are more likely than their dynamic counterparts to focus on specific procedures for preventing its occurrence and modifying its effects. Recommended strategies for forestalling client resistance include offering a clear rationale for treatment procedures, emphasizing the gradual nature of change, using Socratic dialogue and hypothesis-testing techniques, and conducting thorough task analyses of the patient's problems, skills, and goals that can guide the therapist in the selection of appropriate procedures and homework assignments. When resistance does occur, it is treated as an opportunity for engaging in the same kind of cognitive analysis that is applied to other material; like anomalous data for the scientist, it can provide additional occasions for exploring the nature of the client's thoughts, feelings, and behavior (Meichenbaum & Gilmore, 1981).

As Wachtel (1981b) commented with unusual candor in his preface to the collection of articles he edited, mutual interest in the topic of resistance has not as yet helped to bridge the chasm between dynamic and behavioral approaches; indeed, the marked differences in the ways resistance is conceptualized and dealt with—together with unflattering characterizations of alternative positions—may serve to accentuate it. It is interesting in this context to consider the possibility that the differences in the way resistance is perceived may result not solely from theoretical biases but from the resistive phenomena actually evoked by psychodynamic and cognitive-behavioral therapies. As Goldfried (1981b) observed, the cognitive-behavioral definition of resistance as difficulties in carrying out homework assignments may reflect the fact that the treatment approach is action oriented and places a great deal of emphasis on trying out new behaviors in real-life settings. The dynamic view of resistance as difficulties in facing up to certain thoughts, wishes, and fantasies is equally representative of an approach that attempts to uncover intrapsychic conflicts and defenses. To extend this observation further, it may be hypothesized that both perspectives quite accurately characterize the experience of clients participating in the different forms of therapy, and deal appropriately with resistance on the level that it is manifested; thus, the cognitive-behavioral analysis may be no more "superficial" than the dynamic interpretation is an "evasion of clinical responsibility." Resistance occurs when the client is not doing what the therapist, according to his or her theoretical predilection, says the client should do!

Other traditionally "dynamic" concepts such as insight and the influence of early experience also deserve increased attention from cognitive-behavioral therapists. It has been suggested that insight, defined as a heightened capacity for recognizing and expressing problems through the conceptual system taught in psychotherapy, may contribute significantly to the gains achieved with cognitive-behavioral interventions. Accurate assessment of the processes and mechanisms supporting such cognitive shifts during the course of treatment might prove to be of theoretical and practical benefit (Kendall, 1982). It may also be hypothesized that the "present tense," essentially a historical focus of cognitive-behavioral therapy has led to a neglect of variables such as interaction patterns within the family of origin that could furnish important data bearing on the development of irrational belief systems and distorted styles of information processing.

We are not endorsing a return to a psychodynamic perspective. Rather, we applaud the pivotal gains in the practice of psychotherapy that have resulted from the behavioral influence, and urge a continued alliance with behavior therapy. Nevertheless, members of the field must continue to broaden and deepen their understanding of all the variables involved in the process of intervention. We concur with Goldfried (1981b) that it may be possible to learn much more about the cognitive processes that are confronted in the course of the psychotherapeutic enterprise if we hold fast to the principles of rigorous methodology and systematic research.

References

Alden, L., & Safran, J. Irrational beliefs and nonassertive behavior. *Cognitive Therapy and Research,* 1978, **2**, 357–364.

Alden, L., Safran, J., & Weideman, R. A comparison of cognitive and skills training strategies in the treatment of unassertive clients. *Behavior Therapy,* 1978, **9**, 843–846.

Akiskal, H. S., & McKinney, W. T., Jr. Overview of recent research in depression. *Archives of General Psychiatry,* 1975, **32**, 285–305.

Arnkoff, D. B. Flexibility in practicing cognitive therapy. In G. Emery, S. Hollon, & R. Bedrosian (Eds.), *New directions in cognitive therapy.* New York: Guilford, 1981.

Arnkoff, D. B., & Glass, C. R. Clinical cognitive constructs: Examination, evaluation, elaboration. In P. C. Kendall (Ed.), *Advances in cognitive-behavioral research and therapy.* Vol. 1. New York: Academic Press, 1982.

Bandura, A. Self-efficacy: Toward a unifying theory of behavioral change. *Psychological Review,* 1977, **84**, 191–215.

Bandura, A., & Adams, N. E. Analysis of self-efficacy theory of behavior change. *Cognitive Therapy and Research,* 1977, **1**, 287–310.

Bandura, A., Adams, N.E., & Beyer, J. Cognitive processes mediating behavioral change. *Journal of Personality and Social Psychology,* 1977, **35**, 125–139.

Bandura, A., Adams, N. E., Hardy, A. B., & Howells, G. N. Tests of the generality of self-efficacy theory. *Cognitive Therapy and Research,* 1980, **4**, 39–66.

Barabash, C. A comparison of self-instruction training, token fading procedures, and a combined self-instruction/token fading treatment in modifying children's impulsive behavior. Unpublished doctoral dissertation, New York University, 1978.

Beck, A. T. Thinking and depression. *Archives of General Psychiatry,* 1963, **9**, 324–333.

Beck, A. T. *Depression: Clinical, experimental, and theoretical aspects.* New York: Harper & Row, 1967.

Beck, A. T. Cognitive therapy: Nature and relation to behavior therapy. *Behavior Therapy,* 1970, **1**, 184–200.

Beck, A. T. *Cognitive therapy and the emotional disorders.* New York: International Universities Press, 1976.

Beck, A. T., & Emery, G. *Cognitive therapy of substance abuse.* Philadelphia: Center for Cognitive Therapy, 1977.

Beck, A. T., & Emery, G. *Cognitive therapy of anxiety and phobic disorders.* Philadelphia: Center for Cognitive Therapy, 1979.

Beck, A. T., Rush, A. J., Shaw, B. F., & Emery, G. *Cognitive therapy of depression: A treatment manual.* Philadelphia: Center for Cognitive Therapy, 1978.

Biran, M., Augusto, F., & Wilson, G. T. *In vivo* exposure vs. cognitive restructuring in the treatment of scriptophobia. *Behaviour Research and Therapy*, 1981, **19**, 525–532.

Blackburn, I. M., Bishop, S., Glen, A. I. M., Whalley, L. J., & Christie, J. E. The efficacy of cognitive therapy in depression: A treatment trial using cognitive therapy and pharmacotherapy, each alone and in combination. *British Journal of Psychiatry*, 1981, **139**, 181–189.

Braswell, L., Kendall, P. C., Braith, J., Carey, M. P., & Vye, L. S. *"Involvement" in cognitive-behavioral therapy with children: Process and its relationship to outcome.* Manuscript submitted for publication, University of Minnesota, 1983.

Burgio, L. D., Whitman, T. L., & Johnson, M. R. A self-instructional package for increasing attending behavior in educable mentally retarded children. *Journal of Applied Behavior Analysis*, 1980, **13**, 443–460.

Burns, D. D., & Beck, A. T. Cognitive behavior modification of mood disorders. In J. P. Foreyt & D. P. Rathjen (Eds.), *Cognitive behavior therapy: Research and application.* New York: Plenum, 1978.

Cameron, M. I., & Robinson, V. M. J. Effects of cognitive training on academic and on-task behavior of hyperactive children. *Journal of Abnormal Child Psychology*, 1980, **8**, 405–419.

Cameron, R. The clinical implementation of behavior change techniques: A cognitively oriented conceptualization of therapeutic "compliance" and "resistance." In J. P. Foreyt & D. P. Rathjen (Eds.), *Cognitive behavior therapy: Research and application.* New York: Plenum, 1978.

Camp, B., Blom, G., Herbert, F., & van Doorninck, W. "Think aloud": A program for developing self-control in young aggressive boys. *Journal of Abnormal Child Psychology*, 1977, **5**, 157–169.

Camp, B. W., van Doorninck, W. J., Zimet, S. G., & Dahlen, N. W. Verbal abilities in young aggressive boys. *Journal of Educational Psychology*, 1977, **69**, 129–135.

Carmody, T. P. Rational-emotive, self-instructional, and behavioral assertion training: Facilitating maintenance. *Cognitive Therapy and Research*, 1978, **2**, 241–253.

Cautela, J. R. Treatment of compulsive behavior by covert sensitization. *Psychological Record*, 1966, **16**, 33–41.

Cautela, J. R. Covert modeling. Paper presented at the annual meeting of the Association for Advancement of Behavior Therapy, Washington, D.C.: September, 1971.

Cautela, J. R. The present status of covert modeling. *Journal of Behavioral Therapy and Experimental Psychiatry*, 1976, **7**, 323–326.

Cautela, J., Flannery, R., & Hanley, E. Covert modeling: An experimental test. *Behavior Therapy*, 1974, **5**, 494–502.

Colby, K. M., Faught, W. S., & Parkison, R. C. Cognitive therapy of paranoid conditions: Heuristic suggestions based on a computer simulation model. *Cognitive Therapy and Research*, 1979, **3**, 55–60.

Coleman, R. E. Agoraphobia: Cognitive-behavioral treatment. In G. Emery, S. Hollon, & R. Bedrosian (Eds.), *New directions in cognitive therapy: A clinical casebook.* New York: Guilford, 1981.

Comaz-Diaz, L. Effects of cognitive and behavioral group treatment on the depressive symptomatology of Puerto Rican women. *Journal of Consulting and Clinical Psychology*, 1981, **49**, 627–632.

Cooley, E. J., & Spiegler, M. D. Cognitive versus emotional coping resources as alternatives to test anxiety. *Cognitive Therapy and Research*, 1980, **4**, 159–166.

Craighead, L. W. Self-instructional training for assertion-refusal behavior. *Behavior Therapy*, 1979, **10**, 529–542.

Craighead, W. E., Kimball, W. H., & Rehak, P. J. Mood changes, physiological responses, and self-statements during social rejection imagery. *Journal of Consulting and Clinical Psychology*, 1979, **47**, 385–396.

Denicola, J., & Sandler, J. Training abusive parents in child management and self-control skills. *Behavior Therapy*, 1980, **11**, 263–270.

DeRubeis, R., Hollon, S., Evans, M., & Benis, K. M. Can psychotherapies be discriminated? A systematic investigation of cognitive therapy and interpersonal therapy. *Journal of Consulting and Clinical Psychology*, 1982, **50**, 744–756.

Diament, C., & Wilson, G. T. An experimental investigation of the effects of covert sensitization in an analogue eating situation. *Behavior Therapy*, 1975, **6**, 499–509.

DiGuiseppe, R. A., & Miller, N. J. A review of outcome studies on rational-emotive therapy. In A. Ellis & R. Grieger (Eds.), *Handbook of rational-emotive therapy.* New York: Springer, 1977.

DiLoreto, A. *Comparative psychotherapy.* Chicago: Aldine, 1971.

Douglas, V. I., Parry, P., Marston, P., & Garson, C. Assessment of a cognitive training program for hyperactive children. *Journal of Abnormal Child Psychology*, 1976, **4**, 389–410.

Dunn, R. J. Cognitive modification with depression-prone psychiatric patients. *Cognitive Therapy and Research*, 1979, **3**, 307–317.

Elliott, C. H., & Denney, D. R. Weight-control through covert sensitization and false feedback. *Journal of Consulting and Clinical Psychology*, 1975, **43**, 842–850.

Ellis, A. Outcome of employing three techniques of psychotherapy. *Journal of Clinical Psychology*, 1957, **13**, 344–350.

Ellis, A. *Reason and emotion in psychotherapy.* New York: Stuart, 1962.

Ellis, A. The basic clinical theory of rational emotive therapy. In A. Ellis & G. Grieger (Eds.), *Handbook of rational-emotive therapy.* New York: Springer, 1977. (a)

Ellis, A. Research data supporting the clinical and personality hypotheses of RET and other cognitive-behavioral therapies. In A. Ellis & R. Grieger (Eds.), *Handbook of rational-emotive therapy.* New York: Springer, 1977. (b)

Ellis, A. Characteristics of psychotic and borderline psychotic individuals. In A. Ellis & R. Grieger (Eds.), *Handbook of rational-emotive therapy.* New York: Springer, 1977. (c)

Ellis, A. *Sex without guilt.* Hollywood, Calif.: Wilshire, 1977. (d)

Ellis, A. Rational-emotive therapy and cognitive-behavior therapy: Similarities and differences. *Cognitive*

Therapy and Research, 1980, **4**, 325–340.

Ellis, A., & Harper, R. A. *A guide to successful marriage.* Hollywood, Calif.: Wilshire, 1973.

Ellis, A., & Harper, R. A. *A new guide to rational living.* Hollywood, Calif.: Wilshire, 1975.

Emery, G., & Fox, S. Cognitive therapy of alcohol dependency. In G. Emery, S. Hollon, & R. Bedrosian (Eds.), *New directions in cognitive therapy: A clinical casebook.* New York: Guilford, 1981.

Emmelkamp, P. M. G., van der Helm, M., van Zantan, B. L., & Plochg, I. Treatment of obsessive-compulsive patients: The contributions of self-instructional training to the effectiveness of exposure. *Behaviour Research and Therapy,* 1980, **18**, 61–66.

Eysenck, H. J. Expectations as causal elements in behavioural change. *Advances in Behaviour Research and Therapy,* 1978, **1**, 171–175.

Foreyt, J. P., & Hagen, R. L. Covert sensitization: Conditioning or suggestion? *Journal of Abnormal Psychology,* 1973, **82**, 17–23.

Fox, S., & Emery, G. Cognitive therapy of sexual dysfunctions: A case study. In G. Emery, S. Hollon, & R. Bedrosian (Eds.), *New directions in cognitive therapy: A clinical casebook.* New York: Guilford, 1981.

Fremouw, W. J., & Zitter, R. E. A comparison of skills training and cognitive restructuring-relaxation for the treatment of speech anxiety. *Behavior Therapy,* 1978, **9**, 248–259.

Fuchs, C. Z., & Rehm, L. P. A self-control behavior therapy program for depression. *Journal of Consulting and Clinical Psychology,* 1977, **45**, 206–215.

Garner, D. M., & Bemis, K. M. A cognitive-behavioral approach to anorexia nervosa. *Cognitive Therapy and Research,* 1982, **6**, 123–150.

Gauthier, J., & Ladouceur, R. The influence of self-efficacy reports on performance. *Behavior Therapy,* 1981, **12**, 436–439.

Genshaft, J. L., & Hirt, M. L. The effectiveness of self-instructional training to enhance math achievement in women. *Cognitive Therapy and Research,* 1980, **4**, 91–97.

Glass, C. R., & Arnkoff, D. B. Thinking it through: Selected issues in cognitive assessment and therapy. In P. C. Kendall (Ed.), *Advances in cognitive-behavioral research and therapy.* Vol. 1. New York: Academic Press, 1982.

Glogower, F. D., Fremouw, W. J., & McCroskey, J. C. A component analysis of cognitive restructuring. *Cognitive Therapy and Research,* 1978, **2**, 209–223.

Goldfried, M. R. Anxiety reduction through cognitive-behavioral intervention. In P. C. Kendall & S. D. Hollon (Eds.), *Cognitive-behavioral interventions: Theory, research, and procedures.* New York: Academic, 1979.

Goldfried, M. R. Resistance and clinical behavioral therapy. In P. L. Wachtel (Ed.), *Resistance: Psychodynamic and behavioral approaches.* New York: Plenum, 1981. (a)

Goldfried, M. Thoughts on the resistance chapters. In P. L. Wachtel (Ed.), *Resistance: Psychodynamic and behavioral approaches.* New York: Plenum, 1981. (b)

Goldfried, M. R., Decenteceo, E. T., & Weinberg, L. Systematic rational restructuring as a self-control technique. *Behavior Therapy,* 1974, **5**, 247–254.

Goldfried, M., & Sobocinski, D. Effect of irrational beliefs on emotional arousal. *Journal of Consulting and Clinical Psychology,* 1975, **43**, 504–510.

Gormally, J., Sipps, G., Raphael R., Edwin, D., & Varvil-Weld, D. The relationship between maladaptive cognitions and social anxiety. *Journal of Consulting and Clinical Psychology,* 1981, **49**, 300–301.

Hamberger, K., & Lohr, J. M. Rational restructuring for anger control: A quasi-experimental case study. *Cognitive Therapy and Research,* 1980, **4**, 99–102.

Hammen, C. L., Jacobs, M., Mayol, A., & Cochran, S. D. Dysfunctional cognitions and the effectiveness of skills and cognitive-behavioral assertion training. *Journal of Consulting and Clinical Psychology,* 1980, **48**, 685–695.

Harris, G., & Johnson, S. B. Comparison of individualized covert modeling, self-control desensitization, and study skills training for alleviation of test anxiety. *Journal of Consulting and Counseling Psychology,* 1980, **48**, 186–194.

Harrison, R. Cognitive therapy of substance abuse. Paper presented at the annual meeting of the Association for Advancement of Behavior Therapy, Toronto, November 1981.

Herman, I. Cognitive-behavioral therapy for substance abuse. Paper presented at the annual meeting of the American Psychological Association, Los Angeles, August 1981.

Holcomb, W. Coping with severe stress: A clinical application of stress inoculation therapy. Unpublished doctoral dissertation, University of Missouri, Columbia, 1979.

Hollon, S. D. Cognitive-behavioral treatment of drug-induced pan-situational anxiety states. In G. Emery, S. Hollon, & R. Bedrosian (Eds.), *New directions in cognitive therapy: A clinical casebook.* New York: Guilford, 1981. (a)

Hollon, S. D. Toward a theory of therapy for depression: Concepts and operations. Paper presented at the annual meeting of the American Psychological Association, Los Angeles, August 1981. (b)

Hollon, S. D., & Beck, A. T. Cognitive therapy of depression. In P. Kendall & S. Hollon (Eds.), *Cognitive-behavioral interventions: Theory, research, and procedures.* New York: Academic, 1979.

Hollon, S. D., & Bemis, K. M. Self-report and the assessment of cognitive functions. In M. Hersen & A. S. Bellack (Eds.), *Behavioral assessment: A practical handbook.* (2nd ed.) New York: Pergamon, 1981.

Hollon, S. D., & Kendall, P. C. Cognitive-behavioral interventions: Theory and procedure. In P. Kendall & S. Hollon (Eds.), *Cognitive-behavioral interventions: Theory, research, and procedures.* New York: Academic, 1979.

Hollon, S. D., & Kendall, P. C. Cognitive self-statements in depression: Development of an automatic thoughts questionnaire. *Cognitive Therapy and Research,* 1980, **4**, 383–395.

Hollon, S. D., Wiemer, M. J., & Tuason, V. B. Cognitive therapy in relation to drugs in depression. Unpublished grant proposal, University of Minnesota and St. Paul-Ramsey Medical Center, 1979.

Holroyd, D. A. Cognition and desensitization in the group treatment of text anxiety. *Journal of Consulting and Clinical Psychology,* 1976, **44**, 991–1,001.

Holroyd, K. A., Andrasik, F., & Westbrook, T. Cognitive

control of tension headache. *Cognitive Therapy and Research,* 1977, **1,** 121–134.

Homme, L. E. Control of coverants, the operants of the mind. *Psychological Record,* 1965, **15,** 501–511.

Horan, J., Hackett, G., Buchanan, J., Stone, C., & Demchik-Stone, D. Coping with pain: A component analysis. *Cognitive Therapy and Research,* 1977, **1,** 211–221.

Horan, J. J., & Johnson, R. G. Coverant conditioning through a self-management application of the Premack principle: Its effect on weight reduction. *Journal of Behavior Therapy and Experimental Psychiatry,* 1971, **2,** 243–249.

Hussian, R. A., & Lawrence, P. S. The reduction of test, state, and trait anxiety by test-specific and generalized stress inoculation training. *Cognitive Therapy and Research,* 1978, **2,** 25–37.

Jaremko, M. E. A component analysis of stress inoculation: Review and prospectus. *Cognitive Therapy and Research,* 1979, **3,** 35–48.

Jenni, M. A., & Wollersheim, J. P. Cognitive therapy, stress management training, and the Type A behavior pattern. *Cognitive Therapy and Research,* 1979, **3,** 61–73.

Kagan, J. Reflection-impulsivity: The generality and dynamics of conceptual tempo. *Journal of Abnormal Psychology,* 1966, **71,** 17–24.

Kanter, N. J. A comparison of self-control desensitization and systematic rational restructuring for the reduction of interpersonal anxiety. Unpublished doctoral dissertation, State University of New York at Stony Brook, 1975.

Kanter, N. J., & Goldfried, M. R. Relative effectiveness of rational restructuring and self-control desensitization in the reduction of interpersonal anxiety. *Behavior Therapy,* 1979, **10,** 472–490.

Karst, T. O., & Trexler, L. D. Initial study using fixed-role and rational-emotive therapy in treating public-speaking anxiety. *Journal of Consulting and Counseling Psychology,* 1970, **34,** 360–366.

Kazdin, A. E. Covert modeling, imagery assessment, and assertive behavior. *Journal of Consulting and Clinical Psychology,* 1975, **43,** 716–724.

Kazdin, A. E. Conceptual and assessment issues raised by self-efficacy theory. *Advances in Behaviour Research and Therapy,* 1978, **1,** 177–185.

Kazdin, A. E. Imagery elaboration and self-efficacy in the covert modeling treatment of unassertive behavior. *Journal of Consulting and Counseling Psychology,* 1979, **47,** 725–733.

Kazdin, A. E. Covert and overt rehearsal and elaboration during treatment in the development of assertive behavior. *Behaviour Research and Therapy,* 1980, **18,** 191–201.

Keller, J., Crooke, J., & Brookings, J. Effects of a program in rational thinking on anxiety in older persons. *Journal of Counseling Psychology,* 1975, **22,** 54–57.

Kendall, P. C. On the efficacious use of self-instructional procedures with children. *Cognitive Therapy and Research,* 1977, **1,** 331–341.

Kendall, P. C. Cognitive-behavioral interventions with children. In B. B. Lahey & A. E. Kazdin (Eds.), *Advances in clinical child psychology,* Vol. 4. New York: Plenum, 1981. (a)

Kendall, P. C. One-year follow-up of concrete versus conceptual cognitive-behavioral self-control training. *Journal of Consulting and Clinical Psychology,* 1981, **49,** 748–749. (b)

Kendall, P. C. Cognitive processes and procedures in behavior therapy. In C. M. Franks, G. T. Wilson, P. C. Kendall, & K. Brownell (Eds.), *Annual review of behavior therapy.* Vol. 8. New York: Guilford, 1982.

Kendall, P. C. Methodology and cognitive-behavioral assessment. *Behavioral Psychotherapy,* in press.

Kendall, P. C., & Bemis, K. M. Cognitive-behavioral interventions: Principles and procedures. In N. S. Endler & J. McV. Hunt (Eds.), *Personality and the behavioral disorders.* (2nd ed.). New York: Wiley, in press.

Kendall, P. C., & Braswell, L. On cognitive-behavioral assessment: Model, method, and madness. In D. C. Spielberger & J. N. Butcher (Eds.), *Advances in personality assessment.* Vol. 1. Hillsdale, N.J.: Erlbaum, 1982. (a)

Kendall, P. C., & Braswell, L. Cognitive-behavioral self-control therapy for children: A components analysis. *Journal of Consulting and Clinical Psychology,* 1982, **50,** 672–690. (b)

Kendall, P. C., & Finch, A. J., Jr. A cognitive-behavioral treatment for impulsivity: A group comparison study. *Journal of Consulting and Clinical Psychology,* 1978, **46,** 110–118.

Kendall, P. C., & Finch, A. J. Developing nonimpulsive behavior in children: Cognitive-behavioral strategies for self-control. In P. C. Kendall & S. D. Hollon (Eds.), *Cognitive-behavioral interventions: Theory, research, and procedures.* New York: Academic Press, 1979.

Kendall, P. C., & Hollon, S. D. Cognitive-behavioral interventions: Overview and current status. In P. C. Kendall & S. D. Hollon (Eds.), *Cognitive-behavioral interventions: Theory, research and procedures.* New York: Academic Press, 1979.

Kendall, P. C., & Hollon, S. D. *Assessment strategies for cognitive behavioral interventions.* New York: Academic Press, 1981. (a)

Kendall, P. C., & Hollon, S. D. Assessing self-referent speech: Methods in the measurement of self-statements. In P. C. Kendall & S. D. Hollon (Eds.), *Assessment strategies for cognitive-behavioral interventions.* New York: Academic Press, 1981. (b)

Kendall, P. C., & Hollon, S. D. Calibrating therapy: Collaborative archiving of tape samples from therapy outcome trials. *Cognitive Therapy and Research,* in press.

Kendall, P.C., & Korgeski, G. P. Assessment and cognitive-behavioral interventions. *Cognitive Therapy and Research,* 1979, **3,** 1–21.

Kendall, P. C., & Kriss, M R. Cognitive-behavioral interventions. In C. E. Walker (Ed.), *Handbook of clinical psychology.* Homewood, Ill.: Dow Jones-Irwin, 1983.

Kendall, P. C., & Wilcox, L. F. A cognitive-behavioral treatment for impulsivity: Concrete versus conceptual training non-self-controlled problem children. *Journal of Consulting and Clinical Psychology,* 1980, **48,** 80–91.

Kendall, P. C., Williams, L., Pechacek, T. F., Graham, L., Shisslak, C., & Herzoff, N. Cognitive-behavioral and patient education interventions in cardiac catheterization procedures: The Palo Alto medical psychology project. *Journal of Consulting and Clinical Psychology*, 1979, **47**, 49–58.

Kendall, P. C., & Zupan, B. A. Individual versus group application of cognitive-behavioral self-control procedures with children. *Behavior Therapy*, 1981, **12**, 344–359.

Kiesler, D. J. Some myths of psychotherapy research and the search for a paradigm. *Psychological Bulletin*, 1966, **65**, 110–136.

Kiesler, D. J. Psychotherapy process research: Viability and directions in the 1980's. In W. DeMoor & H. R. Nijngaarden (Eds.), *Psychotherapy: Research and training*. Amsterdam: Elsevier/North Holland Biomedical Press, 1980.

Kihlstron, J. R., & Nasby, W. Cognitive tasks in clinical assessment: An exercise in applied psychology. In P. C. Kendall & S. D. Hollon (Eds.), *Assessment strategies for cognitive-behavioral interventions*. New York: Academic Press, 1981.

Kirsch, I. Efficacy expectations or response predictions: The meaning of efficacy ratings as a function of task characteristics. *Journal of Personality and Social Psychology*, 1982, **42**, 132–136.

Klepac, R. K., Hauge, G., Dowling, J., & McDonald, M. Direct and generalized effects of three components of stress inoculation for increased pain tolerance. *Behavior Therapy*, 1981, **12**, 417–424.

Kovacs, M., & Beck, S. T. Maladaptive cognitive structures in depression. *American Journal of Psychiatry*, 1978, **135**, 525–533.

Kovacs, M., Rush, A. J., Beck, A. T., & Hollon, S. D. Depressed outpatients treated with cognitive therapy or pharmacotherapy: A one-year follow-up. *Archives of General Psychiatry*, 1981, **38**, 33–39.

Krantz, S., & Hammen, C. The assessment of cognitive bias in depression. *Journal of Abnormal Psychology*, 1979, **88**, 611–619.

Landau, R. J., & Goldfried, M. R. The assessment of schemata: A unifying framework for cognitive, behavioral, and traditional assessment. In P. C. Kendall & S. D. Hollon (Eds.), *Assessment strategies for cognitive-behavioral interventions*. New York: Academic Press, 1981.

Lazarus, A. A. *Multimodal therapy*. New York: McGraw-Hill, 1981.

Lazarus, A. A., & Fay, A. Resistance or rationalization? A cognitive-behavioral perspective. In P. L. Wachtel (Ed.), *Resistance: Psychodynamic and behavioral approaches*. New York: Plenum, 1981.

Leon, G. R. Cognitive-behavior therapy for eating disturbances. In P. C. Kendall & S. D. Hollon (Eds.), *Cognitive-behavioral interventions: Theory, research, and procedures*. New York: Academic Press, 1979.

Linehan, M. H., Goldfried, M. R., & Goldfried, A. P. Assertion therapy: Skill training or cognitive restructuring? *Behavior Therapy*, 1979, **10**, 372–388.

Lipsky, M. J., Kassinove, H., & Miller, N. J. Effects of rational-emotive therapy, rational role reversal, and rational-emotive imagery on the emotional adjustment of community mental health center patients. *Journal of Consulting and Clinical Psychology*, 1980, **48**, 366–374.

Luria, A. R. *The role of speech in the regulation of normal and abnormal behavior*. New York: Liveright, 1961.

Mahoney, K., Rogers, T., Straw, M., & Mahoney, M. J. Human obesity: Assessment and treatment. Unpublished manuscript, Pennsylvania State University, 1977.

Mahoney, M. J. *Cognition and behavior modification*. Cambridge, Mass.: Ballinger, 1974.

Mahoney, M. J. Reflections on the cognitive-learning trend in psychotherapy. *American Psychologist*, 1977, **32**, 5–13.

Mahoney, M. J., & Arnkoff, D. B. Cognitive and self-control therapies. In S. L. Garfield & A. E. Bergin (Eds.), *Handbook of psychotherapy and behavior change*. (2nd ed.) New York: Wiley, 1978.

Malamuth, Z. N. Self-management training for children with reading problems: Effects on reading performance and sustained attention. *Cognitive Therapy and Research*, 1979, **3**, 279–289.

Margolis, R. B., & Shemberg, K. M. Cognitive self-instruction in process and reactive schizophrenics: A failure to replicate. *Behavior Therapy*, 1976, **7**, 668–671.

Maultsby, M. C., Jr. *Help yourself to happiness*. New York: Institute for Rational Living, 1975.

Maultsby, M., & Graham, D. Controlled study of the effect of psychotherapy on self-reported maladaptive traits, anxiety scores, and psychosomatic disease attitudes. *Journal of Psychiatric Research*, 1974, **10**, 121–132.

McFall, M. E., & Wollersheim, J. P. Obsessive-compulsive neurosis: A cognitive-behavioral formulation and approach to treatment. *Cognitive Therapy and Research*, 1979, **3**, 333–348.

McLean, P. D., & Hakstian, A. R. Clinical depression: Comparative efficacy of outpatient treatments. *Journal of Consulting and Clinical Psychology*, 1979, **47**, 818–836.

Meichenbaum, D. Cognitive modification of test anxious college students. *Journal of Consulting and Clinical Psychology*, 1972, **39**, 370–380.

Meichenbaum, D. Self-instructional methods. In F. Kanfer & A. Goldstein (Eds.), *Helping people change*. New York: Pergamon, 1975. (a)

Meichenbaum, D. A self-instructional approach to stress management: A proposal for stress inoculation training. In I. Sarason & C. D. Spielberger (Eds.), *Stress and anxiety*. Vol. 2. New York: Wiley, 1975. (b)

Meichenbaum, D. *Cognitive-behavior modification: An integrative approach*. New York: Plenum, 1977.

Meichenbaum, D. Introduction to applied cognitive-behavior therapy. In D. Meichenbaum (Ed.), *Cognitive behavior therapy: A practitioner's guide*. New York: BMA Audio Publications, 1978.

Meichenbaum, D., & Asarnow, J. Cognitive-behavioral modification and metacognitive development: Implications for the classroom. In P. C. Kendall & S. D. Hollon (Eds.), *Cognitive-behavioral interventions: Theory, research and procedures*. New York: Academic, 1979.

Meichenbaum, D., & Cameron, R. Training schizophrenics to talk to themselves: A means of developing attentional controls. *Behavior Therapy*, 1973, **4**, 515–534. (a)

Meichenbaum, D., & Cameron, R. Stress inoculation: A skills training approach to anxiety management. Unpublished manuscript, University of Waterloo, 1973. (b)

Meichenbaum, D. H., & Cameron, R. The clinical potential of modifying what clients say to themselves. *Psychotherapy: Theory, Research, and Practice*, 1974, **11**, 103–117.

Meichenbaum, D., & Gilmore, J. B. Resistance: From a cognitive-behavioral perspective. In P. L. Wachtel (Ed.), *Resistance: Psychodynamic and behavioral approaches*. New York: Plenum, 1981.

Meichenbaum, D. H., Gilmore, J. B., & Fedoravicius, A. Group insight versus group desensitization in treating speech anxiety. *Journal of Consulting and Clinical Psychology*, 1971, **36**, 410–421.

Meichenbaum, D., & Goodman, J. Training impulsive children to talk to themselves: A means of developing self-control. *Journal of Abnormal Psychology*, 1971, **77**, 115–126.

Meichenbaum, D., & Jaremko, M. (Eds.), *Stress management and prevention: A cognitive-behavioral perspective*. New York: Plenum, 1983.

Meichenbaum, D., & Turk, D. The cognitive-behavioral management of anxiety, anger and pain. In P. Davidson (Ed.), *Behavioral management of anxiety, depression and pain*. New York: Brunner/Mazel, 1976.

Melzack, R., & Wall, P. *Pain mechanisms: A new theory*. Science, 1965, **150**, 971.

Merluzzi, T. V., Glass, C. R., & Genest, M. (Eds.). *Cognitive assessment*. New York: Guilford, 1981.

Novaco, R. W. *Anger control: The development and evaluation of an experimental treatment*. Lexington, Mass.: Heath, 1975.

Novaco, R. W. Treatment of chronic anger through cognitive and relaxation controls. *Journal of Consulting and Clinical Psychology*, 1976, **44**, 681.

Novaco, R. W. Anger and coping with stress. In J. P. Foreyt & D. P. Rathjen (Eds.), *Cognitive behavior therapy: Research and application*. New York: Plenum, 1978.

Novaco, R. W. The cognitive regulation of anger and stress. In P. C. Kendall & S. D. Hollon (Eds.), *Cognitive-behavioral interventions: Theory, research, and procedures*. New York: Academic Press, 1979.

Parrish, J. M., & Erickson, M. T. A comparison of cognitive strategies in modifying the cognitive style of impulsive third grade children. *Cognitive Therapy and Research*, 1981, **5**, 71–84.

Poser, E. G. The self-efficacy concept: Some theoretical, procedural, and clinical implications. *Advances in Behaviour Research and Therapy*, 1978, **1**, 193–202.

Rickel, A. U., Eshelman, A. K., & Loigman, G. A. A longitudinal study of social problem solving training: Cognitive and behavioral effects. Manuscript submitted for publication, Wayne State University, 1981.

Rimm, D. C., & Litvak, S. B. Self-verbalization and emotional arousal. *Journal of Abnormal Psychology*, 1969, **74**, 181–187.

Roper, V. C. Rational-emotive therapy: A critical review of the research. Unpublished manuscript, 1976.

Rush, A. J., Beck, A. T., Kovacs, M., & Hollon, S. D. Comparative efficacy of cognitive therapy and pharmacotherapy in the treatment of depressed outpatients. *Cognitive Therapy and Research*, 1977, **1**, 17–37.

Safran, J. D., Alden, L. E., & Davidson, P. O. Client anxiety level as a moderator variable in assertion training. *Cognitive Therapy and Research*, 1980, **4**, 189–200.

Shaw, B. F. Comparison of cognitive therapy and behavior therapy in the treatment of depression. *Journal of Consulting and Clinical Psychology*, 1977, **45**, 543–551.

Shure, M. B., & Spivack, G. *Problem-solving techniques in childrearing*. San Francisco: Jossey-Bass, 1978.

Smith, G., Chiange, H., & Reigna, E. Acupuncture and experimental psychology. Paper presented at Symposium on Pain and Acupuncture, Philadelphia, April 1974.

Snyder, J. J., & White, M. J. The use of cognitve self-instruction in the treatment of behaviorally disturbed adolescents. *Behavior Therapy*, 1979, **10**, 227–235.

Spivack, G., Platt, J. J., & Shure, M. B. *The problem-solving approach to adjustment*. San Francisco: Jossey-Bass, 1976.

Spivack, G., & Shure, M. B. *Social adjustment of young children: A cognitive approach to solving real-life problems*. San Francisco: Jossey-Bass, 1974.

Sutton-Simon, K. Assessing belief systems: Concepts and strategies. In P. C. Kendall & S. D. Hollon (Eds.), *Assessment strategies for cognitive-behavioral interventions*. New York: Academic Press, 1981.

Sutton-Simon, K., & Goldfried, M. R. Faulty thinking patterns in two types of anxiety. *Cognitive Therapy and Research*, 1979, **3**, 193–203.

Taylor, F. G., & Marshall, W. L. Experimental analysis of a cognitive-behavioral therapy for depression. *Cognitive Therapy and Research*, 1977, **1**, 59–72.

Thompson, S. The relative efficacy of desensitization, desensitization with coping imagery, cognitive modification, and rational-emotive therapy with test-anxious college students. Unpublished doctoral dissertation University of Arkansas, 1974.

Tiegerman, S. Effects of assertive training and cognitive components of rational therapy on the promotion of assertive behavior and the reduction of interpersonal anxiety. Unpublished doctoral dissertation, Hofstra University, 1975.

Trexler, L. D., & Karst, T. O. Rational-emotive, placebo, and no treatment effects on public speaking anxiety. *Journal of Abnormal Psychology*, 1972, **79**, 60–67.

Turk, D. Cognitive control of pain: A skills training approach. Unpublished manuscript, University of Waterloo, 1975.

Tyler, V. O., & Straughan, J. H. Coverant control and breath holding as techniques for the treatment of obesity. *Psychological Record*, 1970, **20**, 473–478.

Urbain, E. S., & Kendall, P. C. Review of social-cognitive problem-solving interventions with children. *Psychological Bulletin*, 1980, **88**, 109–143.

Varni, J. W., & Henker, B. A self-regulatory approach to the treatment of three hyperactive boys. *Child Behavior Therapy*, 1979, **1**, 171–192.

Velten, E. A laboratory task for induction of mood states. *Behaviour Research and Therapy*, 1968, **6**, 473–482.

Vygotsky, L. S. *Thought and language*. Cambridge, Mass.: M.I.T. Press, 1962.

Wachtel, P. L. (Ed.). *Resistance: Psychodynamic and behavioral approaches*. New York: Plenum, 1981. (a)

Wachtel, P. L. Resistance and the process of therapeutic change. In P. L. Wachtel (Ed.), *Resistance: Psychodynamic and behavioral approaches*. New York: Plenum, 1981. (b)

Walen, S. R., DiGiuseppe, R., & Wessler, R. L. *A practitioner's guide to rational-emotive therapy*. New York: Oxford University Press, 1980.

Waskow, I. E., Hadley, S. W., Parloff, M. B., & Autrey, J. H. Psychotherapy of depression collaborative research program. Unpublished manuscript, National Institute of Mental Health, Rockville, Md., 1979.

Watkins, J. T. The rational emotive dynamics of impulsive disorders. In A. Ellis & R. Grieger (Eds.), *Handbook of rational emotive therapy*. New York: Springer, 1977.

Wilson, G. T. Cognitive behavior therapy: Paradigm shift or passing phase? In J. P. Foreyt & D. P. Rathjen (Eds.), *Cognitive behavior therapy: Research and application*. New York: Plenum, 1978.

Wolpe, J. *Psychotherapy by reciprocal inhibition*. Stanford, Calif.: Stanford University Press, 1958.

Wolpe, J. *The practice of behavior therapy*. New York: Pergamon, 1969.

Wolpe, J. Self-efficacy theory and psychotherapeutic change: A square peg for a round hole. *Advances in Behaviour Research and Therapy*, 1978, **1**, 231–236.

Woodward, R., & Jones, R. B. Cognitive restructuring treatment: A controlled trial with anxious patients. *Behaviour Research and Therapy*, 1980, **18**, 401–407.

Zettle, R. D., & Hayes, S. C. Conceptual and empirical status of rational-emotive therapy. In M. Hersen, R. M. Eisler, & P. M. Miller (Eds.), *Progress in behavior modification*. Vol. 9. New York: Academic, 1980.

30 GROUP TREATMENT APPROACHES

Robert H. Klein

The prospect of writing a single chapter that adequately encompasses the broad range of group treatment approaches is indeed formidable. For purposes of the present chapter, I have chosen to focus upon group change-induction strategies used primarily with adults. No systematic effort will be made to discuss such work with children or with adolescents.

The diversity of group approaches extends far beyond such conventional classifications as theoretical orientation or leader behavior (e.g., psychodynamic, phenomenologic, behavioral, etc.) Consider, for example, that recent estimates have suggested that over five million Americans have practicipated in some type of encounter group aimed at personal growth or change, several million others have been members of over 250 different varieties of self-help groups, and countless others have been patients in some type of group psychotherapy. Nearly every kind of person with every conceivable psychological or social complaint has participated in some type of group (Lieberman, 1977). The goals of such groups vary from reducing psychotic symptoms to reducing weight. Many participants bring problems that were once taken exclusively to mental health or medical pro-

fessionals, while others seek out groups because they feel oppressed by societal discrimination, or they come with the hope of personal enrichment, growth, and freer access to unused but available personal potential.

Wide variations in group goals, participants, forms of activity, leadership, and settings render classification of current change-induction groups extremely difficult. Unfortunately, the labels (e.g., Gestalt, Transactional Anaysis, Confrontation Therapy, Encounter, Self-Help Groups, etc.) fail to clarify essential ingredients and how they function to promote change, growth, or cure. The methods utilized include talk, action, music, lights, drama, and nonverbal exercises, with or without an appointed or formal leader present. Indeed, the qualifications to become a leader have remained quite ambiguous. In the absence of standards for group leadership, there are some who claim that years of arduous training in prestigious professional institutions are a necessary requirement. Others propose that they are qualified to be leaders by virtue of having participated in a two-week institute or by nature of their personal charisma and commitment. The settings in which these groups take place range from traditional help-giving institutions and private offices of mental-health practitioners, to growth centers, church basements, dormitories, and living rooms.

The situation at first glance is diverse, confusing, lacking in clear boundaries, and in many instances devoid of adequate self-monitoring regulatory functions. In order to begin to assess the current state of the field and the major theoretical, empirical, methodological, and training issues, it may be useful to provide a historical perspective concerning its development.

Theory, Practice, and Research

Historical Perspective

Group therapy was first practiced in Boston in the early 1900s by Joseph Henry Pratt. His treatment regimen for advanced tuberculosis patients included home visits, diary keeping by patients, and weekly class meetings. At each class session, weight gains were publicly recorded, testimonials were given by successful patients, and diary accounts were read by members who were encouraged, admonished, or comforted as the need arose. The forerunner of more modern repressive-inspirational large-group therapy sessions such as Alcoholics Anonymous or Weight Watchers, these class sessions promoted a sense of belonging and emotional support among patients, which relieved their isolation, depression, and pessimism.

Soon thereafter, in both Europe and the United States, psychiatrists began to explore the use of group methods with a wide range of clinical problems, including psychosis, neurosis, psychophysiological disorders, and stammering. Psychoanalytic concepts were applied to inpatient group therapy with nonpsychotic patients. A highly influential contributor during this early period of development was S. Slavson, who adapted a classical psychoanalytic model for work with disturbed children and adolescents.

The utilitization of group psychotherapy was greatly expanded during World War II as a result of a limited supply of psychiatric personnel coupled with an increased need for psychiatric services. A related and important development concerned changing conceptualizations about the nature of mankind and the etiology of psychological ill health. A social rather than an intrapsychic theory of illness became more prevalent. This interpersonal view of man, suggesting that psychological disturbance might be intrinsically related to problems of relationships among people, paved the way for developing multiperson treatment situations.

The 1950s era, characterized by Frank (1979) as "the age of innocence," was a time when group psychotherapy was developed to treat psychiatric patients, and only mental-health professionals were regarded as competent and qualified to conduct it. In general, the clinical practice of group psychotherapy was based upon adaptations of a psychoanalytic individual psychotherapy model in which patients were encouraged to gain awareness of early life experiences that contributed to maladaptive attitudes and behaviors. The primary concern of practicing professionals during this period was to establish psychoanalytically oriented group psychotherapy as a legitimate and valid enterprise. Within this field, there was conflict concerning the acceptability of group dynamics and process-oriented approaches. Limited concern was given to the possibility of negative effects as a result of psychotherapy. This phase of exuberant expansion was marked by the phenomenon of group psychotherapy being offered to persons of all ages with every conceivable type of problem.

Paralleling these developments in the field of group psychotherapy, but in many respects completely separate and independent from them, were a series of developments emanating primarily from the fields of sociology, anthropology, education, and social psychology, which collectively established a growing climate of concern about how groups work. Prior to 1940, relatively little scientific effort was devoted to understanding group processes. However, based upon a desire to understand how methods of leadership influenced the properties of groups and the behavior of their members, social scientists in the early 1940s, led by Kurt Lewin and his associates, began to study group climate, leadership styles, and intergroup conflict. His assumptions about the causes of behavior and his emphasis on forces and constraints in the social field led to a focus on the here and now. It would be difficult to overestimate the impact of his ideas upon both research and training about group life.

During the ensuing decade, research on groups entered an extremely active period of growth. The so-called "small group movement," which emerged against a background of World War II and the fight against totalitarian societies, grew from a concern about human and civil rights plus concerns about personal and group "effectiveness." Behavioral scientists wished to demonstrate that people could employ understanding of their own and others' behavior for positive ends by using the small group as a microcosm for studying interpersonal cooperative and competitive forces. An emotional fervor and intense commitment animated the postwar efforts; research and practice in this area took on an evangelistic aura, one that was often regarded as unscientific by its critics (Lakin, 1979). The ideologic impetus and the financial support for this work appeared to arise from a deep-seated hope that the results of this research would improve democratic methods and shield humanity from the destructive influences of totalitarian leadership. While scientists, physicists, and engineers had guided the country through World War II, the collective wish on the part of society seemed to be that social science would be useful in helping society deal with the problems of group life following the war.

An important development noted by historians in the group field was the initiation in 1947 of the National Training Laboratory (NTL) under the auspices of the National Education Association, in conjunction with the Research Center for Group Dynamics established by Lewin and his associates. The mission of the NTL was to improve the capacities of professional persons to understand groups, to utilize their roles as managers to facilitate changes within organizations, to teach individuals the basic skills of membership, and to train participants in the utilization of democratic methods. Most importantly, NTL maintained a fundamental commitment to conduct research on behavior in groups. Initially, this was an educational and research enterprise; there was no special interest in encouraging personal growth, mental health, sensitivity, and interpersonal relations. However, one aspect of this form of human-relations training, the T-group ("T" for training in human relations), was quickly recognized as a vehicle that could be used to arrive at personal learning and change. The historical forerunner of the encounter group, the T-group emerged from the serendipitous discovery of a powerful technique of human-relations education: experiential learning. It was found that the learning of group members was significantly enhanced by studying the very interactional network they were in the process of establishing.

What began as a rather traditional small discussion group, that considered substantive or "back-home" problems, was followed by a "feedback" session led initially by a member of the research team who reported his or her process observations of the group. Soon the T-group, which had been only one component of the laboratory training procedure, became the core component. The feedback process gradually became an integral part of the T-group and the observer became an assistant trainer. Over the years the T-group came increasingly to focus on interpersonal behavior, with greater emphasis given to feedback, interpersonal honesty, self-disclosure, "unfreezing," and participant observation. Members were encouraged to participate emotionally in group activities while observing themselves and the group objectively. Cognitive aids were provided to assist the participants in organizing their own experiences. Lectures, reading assignments, and theory sessions all demonstrated the basic allegiance of the T-group to the classroom. Soon, two distinct and different emphases resulted in polarization within the NTL: one maintained an allegiance to learning about group dynamics, group development, group pressures, and leadership roles; the other emphasized personal learning and focused on interpersonal style and communication among members.

As summarized by Yalom (1975), the therapy group and the T-group arose from very different traditions. More specifically, the therapy group arose as a form of medical treatment intended to relieve suffering for persons who defined themselves as patients, who were seeking relief from their distress, and who were willing to follow the advice and suggestions of a professional healer. In contrast, the T-group emerged from an educational tradition, with voluntary members who hoped to gain knowledge and skills in circumscribed areas to improve their work effectiveness and their own leadership abilities. Group leaders were designated as teachers, not healers, and presented themselves as co-participants who wanted to decrease unrealistic expectations held of them by group members, rather than to encourage exploration and analysis of such material.

During the 1950s, highly innovative research was being conducted on the social psychology of groups, including investigations of communication in groups, interpersonal power to influence others, sources of coalition, and the nature and consequences of balanced relations within groups (Zander, 1979). By the 1960s, the study of group behavior was an accepted subdiscipline in many academic departments, but research publications were decreasing as essays on the practical applications of groups in education, therapy, and management appeared in increasing numbers. The postwar centers established for conducting research on groups had largely disappeared. This was a decade, too, when group action was primarily utilized not to develop democratic ways of functioning within government and other agencies, but rather to confront, using militancy and the power of demonstrations and disruptions as a means of political action. The ancestral seeds were being sown for what would later become consciousness-raising and self-help groups.

Despite its intellectual heritage and its powerful links with education and research, the intensive small-group experience rapidly became a viable commercial enterprise that attracted numerous adherents. The spread of such groups reached epidemic proportions during the late 1960s and early 1970s. Growth centers proliferated, mushrooming from small organizations offering occasional weekend groups, to year-round operations with massive catalogues of diverse group experiences and with mailing lists numbering in the thousands. As the encounter-group movement grew, it came to exist largely outside of society's traditional help-giving institutions. The strong egalitarian and antiintellectual overtones of this movement seemed in many ways to be a reaction against traditional forms of help giving and traditional dependency on the professional help giver. In the absence of institutional and professional ties, no standards were articulated for leaders. Trainer credentials, roles, and responsibilities remained vaguely defined. Leaders were heterogeneous in terms of levels of competence, training and background, professional discipline, goals, and motives. Although NTL continued to utilize the laboratory training model in a scientific and professional manner, the activities of the individuals, organizations, and growth centers that followed raised an outcry in the professional community about ethical problems and issues.

Concerns about possible adverse consequences or "deterioration effects" of participating in small groups began to appear in the literature with increasing frequency during the latter half of the 1960s and into the 1970s, as the uses and varieties of small-group experiences began to proliferate. Reviewers cautioned about the dangers of "deterioration effects" and the fact that a small but significant proportion of participants could become "casualties" (Hartley, Roback, & Abramowitz, 1976).

Controversies raised within the field of group psychotherapy about theories and techniques that defined the field during the 1950s were dwarfed by the furor that surrounded the emergence of a large variety of new groups during the 1960s and 1970s. These new groups, commonly classified as encounter groups (American Psychiatric Association Task Force Report, 1973), varied in size, shape, composition, leadership, duration, goals, and a host of other parameters. In addition, they were sponsored by both professionals and nonprofessionals working through agencies, institutions, or private practices. During the late 1960s in the northern California Bay Area alone, one might well find on any given weekend a list of groups including psychoanalytic psychotherapy groups, T-groups, Gestalt groups, sensory awareness groups, EST groups, Rolfing groups, behavior therapy groups, Synanon, Recovery, nonverbal therapy groups, verbal sensory awareness groups, psychological karate groups, transactional analysis groups, multimedia groups, truth labs, and more. While many were designated as psychotherapy groups, they tended to straddle the boundary between personal growth and therapy. Despite widely varying formats, most of these groups shared certain common features: (1) they attempted to provide intensive high-contact group experiences; (2) they were generally small and involved considerable face-to-face interaction; (3) they all attempted to maintain a here-and-now focus with an unstructured format; (4) openness, honesty, interpersonal confrontation, and self-disclosure were encouraged; (5) strong emotional expression was stressed; (6) the participants were not called patients; and (7) the experience was not called therapy. The goals of these groups included promoting intimacy, reducing weight, seeking to entertain, "turning on" participants, and searching for joy and truth. In general, overall goals tended to involve some type of personality change with regard to behavior, attitudes, values, or life styles. The goals and the techniques employed often overlapped with those of traditional group psychotherapy.

Despite their involvement as both leaders and participants, many mental-health professionals viewed encounter groups as the equivalent of interpersonal sky diving (i.e., high-risk, high-adrenaline, but only partially controlled endeavors). On the one hand, the tendency was to exaggerate the hazards and to overstress the dangers, while on the other hand, the limited data about the efficacy of such groups made it easy for some to ignore or disregard evidence of adverse consequences. Hartley, Roback, and Abramowitz (1976) note that evaluations of these intensive small-group experiences ranged from "the most significant social invention of this century" (Rogers, 1968), to "a multimillion dollar business . . . callous exploitation and a sham group therapy" (Maliver, 1973). Several comprehensive reviews examined the effects of encounter groups, but depending upon the nature of the leaders, the composition of the membership, the preparation members received, and the criteria for defining a casualty, estimates ranged from less than 1 percent to 50 percent casualties in such small-group experiences.

The development of more traditional group therapy and its increasing professionalization during this era was reflected in the evolution of the American Group Psychotherapy Association (AGPA), the major professional organization in the field. Founded in 1942 by S. R. Slavson, the organization began with a group of about 20 interested individuals who formed an alliance in an effort to encourage further interest in group therapy and to examine issues surrounding theory and practice. By the late 1960s the AGPA had expanded along with the group movement, had over 2,000 members, 16 affiliated national societies, and 6 foreign affiliates. In the early years, this professional organization was largely under the leadership of medical practitioners, but the contributions of other health professionals were widely recognized, and ultimately leadership in the organization came from psychology and social work, as well as psychiatry. During the 1970s, AGPA membership swelled to over 3,000, and various associate and interim membership categories were created to stimulate further interest and support of the field. In my opinion, this organization has consistently provided leadership, stability, legitimacy, and stimulation for interested professionals. The AGPA has had an enormous impact in raising the overall standards of theory, research, training, and practice in the field of group psychotherapy. In addition to providing an important intellectual forum for the exchange of ideas, including an annual conference and institute and a journal sponsored by the organization, the AGPA has provided a source of emotional support for many of its members who have in their own institutional setting often occupied relatively peripheral and/or low-status roles because of their interests in group psychotherapy.

Current State of the Field

During the 1970s, the proliferation of new groups — e.g., encounter groups, T-groups, personal growth groups — plus the rise of the humanistic educational movement, the relative absence of adequate self-regulation and standards within the field, the increasing appeal of the existential approach to treatment with its emphasis on the here and now, and the incorporation of some of the newer technological developments into traditional clinical practices, gave rise to heated debates among group psychotherapists. Pervasive and powerful issues began to dominate the field: concerns about the definition of group therapy, the training and qualification of group leaders, the kinds of settings in which group therapy should be conducted, conflicting therapeutic ideologies, and the efficacy and potential harmfulness of various approaches.

In an effort to lend some clarity to the field, Lieberman (1977) distinguished four major types of groups: (1) psychotherapy groups that are societally sanctioned, professionally led groups with the avowed purpose of improving mental health; these groups have well-defined criteria for acceptance and participants see themselves as patients who are suffering from psychological distress that can be relieved by professional assistance; (2) peer self-help groups where members who share a particular life predicament or symptom believe they can gain relief from their distress through mutual support and without professional aid (e.g., Alcoholics Anonymous, Recovery, Inc., Weight Watchers); (3) human potential groups (including sensitivity training and encounter groups) in which the participants do not consider themselves ill but rather subscribe to an implicit model of personal growth and self-actualization, and where the leader, although viewed as distinct from the members, may at times behave very much like a member; (4) consciousness-raising groups in which the criteria for inclusion for both members and leaders is a shared social characteristic of a large subgroup of people (e.g., being a woman, a black, or a homosexual). Frank (1979) added two additional categories to complete the current scene: (5) marital and family groups, which are naturally occurring rather than artificial and in which therapy in many instances is geared toward achieving individual change by altering the properties of the family or marital system; and (6) counterculture groups in which the members have essentially opted out of society and seek to live by philosophies and codes of conduct that they regard as radically different from and superior to those of the conventional materialistic society around them (e.g., various religious cults, such as the Hare Krishna Society).

While it is often difficult to discriminate between groups on the basis of the clientele who attend them, or those who lead them, groups can be distinguished from one another by examining certain structural and technical differences:

1. *The psychological distance between leader and participants:* this variable can be influenced via the degree of self-disclosure on the part of the therapist, the use of an informal setting, the tendency of leaders to assume the stance of participants, or the diminished importance of the expertise of the leader.
2. *The conception of the group as a mechanism for personal change:* psychotherapy and encounter groups share a view of the group as a social microcosm in which the participants' interpersonal problems are mirrored in their group transactions. Differences exist about which transactions are most important or which emotional states are most conducive to producing change, but change is based on exploration and reworking of relationships in groups. In contrast, self-help groups and consciousness-raising groups view the group as a vehicle for cognitive restructuring and as a supportive environment for developing new behavior that can be used outside of the group. The analysis of transactions between members is not the basic tool of change.
3. *The degree to which groups stress differentiation versus lack of differentiation among members:* consciousness-raising and self-help groups tend to stress member identification with a common core problem, whereas therapy and encounter groups actively promote and encourage individuation.
4. *The nature of the attribution system:* psychotherapy groups, in contrast to consciousness-raising groups, for example, regard the source of human misery and the methods for resolving it as arising from an internal locus, whereas consciousness-raising groups emphasize an external locus of the problem (Lieberman, 1977).

Within the narrower field of traditional group therapy, Bascue (1978) has proposed a set of eight

dimensions (continua) for comparing various theoretical positions:

1. *Temporal dimension.* Here one can examine the extent to which the therapist focuses on the past, present, or future experiences of group members as the primary means for promoting change. The classical psychoanalytic group (Wolf & Schwartz, 1962), for example, focuses on the remote history of group participants, their early childhood events, and subsequent implications. In contrast, reality therapy (Kaltenbach & Gazda, 1975) examines experiences in the more immediate past of the group members, while many encounter groups and interpersonally oriented therapists (Yalom, 1975) prefer to focus on the here-and-now immediate experiences of members within the group itself.
2. *Spatial dimension.* Some therapists encourage members to focus on life experiences external to the group, e.g., rational-emotive therapy (Ellis, 1975), while others encourage a view of the group as a social microcosm geared toward the examination of experiences inside the group itself (Bion, 1961).
3. *Volitional dimension.* This continuum identifies differences between therapists who believe that the modification of thoughts, ideas, and beliefs is crucial to effect change (Glasser, 1965), as opposed to therapists who believe that the experience of intense affect is the most powerful impetus to change (Rogers, 1970).
4. *Actional dimension.* Some theorists (e.g., psychoanalysts and existentialists) rely primarily on verbal communication while other therapists utilize role play, touching, and sensory awareness activities (e.g., Gestaltists). Behaviorally oriented therapists, with a different perspective, may encourage outside activities such as homework for members, modeling, practicing new behaviors, etc.
5. *Systemic dimension.* Some therapists treat the intrapsychic issues of individuals in a group context (Wolf & Schwartz, 1962), others examine the interpersonal relationships between members in the group (Yalom, 1975), and still other therapists emphasize treatment of the group as a whole (Bion, 1961).
6. *Focal dimension.* Some leaders are quite active in groups and are often the center of attention (e.g., classical psychoanalysts, transactional analysts), whereas other therapists who focus on interpersonal interaction or the properties of the group as a system (Durkin, 1981) seem to be less

active and less the focus of group members' overt attention.

7. *Symbolic dimension.* Therapists vary as to whether they focus upon the manifest (obvious) meaning of group members' verbal or behavioral expressions or whether they emphasize the latent (symbolic) meaning of member expressions.

8. *Jurisdictional dimension.* Some therapists focus principally upon problem solving, e.g., those with a behavioral orientation (Harris, 1979); others emphasize elements of both problem solving and personality change (Ellis, 1975), while various psychoanalytic and existential humanistic theorists devote themselves largely to personality change.

One of the most fascinating things about examining the literature on small groups is the nearly complete and utter independence that has been maintained for many years between social psychologists and sociologists (who have been working in the "small-group" naturalistic and laboratory settings studying group dynamics), and clinical psychologists and professional practitioners who have been working in hospitals and consulting settings studying therapy groups. Cross-fertilization between these fields is practically nonexistent. Since both sets of investigators are studying small groups, one might think that there would be areas of mutual concern that could be easily identified and that the sharing of knowledge and information between these two fields would serve to augment the theorizing, research, and practice in each area. Unfortunately, this does not seem to be the case. Only a few well-known group therapists try to make active use of the principles and data that have emerged from small-group research. Similarly, in the small-group research literature, one is hard pressed to find any mention at all of group psychotherapy. Unfortunately, the situation is little better within the more narrowly defined field of group therapy itself, where an extensive schism continues to exist between researchers and practitioners.

During the 1960s there was a decided shift in emphasis among small-group researchers from an interest in groups to an interest in individuals. Individual mental health, personal awareness, growth, and personal security became the focal points of interest. The productivity rate for research in the group area increased significantly, with much effort focused on groups devoted to remediation and education. Reviews of the group

psychotherapy outcome literature dealt largely with the efficacy of group treatment for a variety of clinical populations, while simultaneously the T-group and various new groups were also being evaluated as methods of inducing change with nonpatient participants (Dies, 1979). While earlier assessments reached tentative conclusions about the potency of group treatments, later reviews concluded, in accord with many practitioners, that group therapy was a valuable tool for the helping professions and that group treatments indeed work. Nevertheless, reviewers cautioned that available literature did not support firm conclusions regarding the causal nature of curative factors operating in the group context or the circumstances under which they could be most effectively utilized (Bednar & Kaul, 1978). Similar conclusions were being reached with regard to T-groups. Although T-group training does induce behavioral changes in the back-home setting and is therefore effective, it was not yet possible to clearly identify the important curative components (Smith, 1975). Reviews of empirical investigations of the new groups — encounter, marathon, and personal growth groups — generally indicated that these groups, too, were effective and led to significant attitude or personality change, although more recent reviews have seriously questioned the marathon treatment format as a method for enhancing the efficiency of treatment outcome (Kilman & Sotile, 1976).

Space does not permit a comprehensive review of research on group therapy. It may be useful, however, to summarize briefly some of the recent literature regarding therapeutic efficacy and process. The following general conclusions seem warranted:

1. The vast majority of studies indicate that group treatments are more effective than no treatment, placebo, or nonspecific treatment, but not all groups produce uniformly beneficial results.

2. Changes in self-concept assessment, attitude change, and positive personality development appear to reflect a nonspecific factor of improvement that may or may not be accompanied by behavioral changes.

3. Variations in treatment populations, personality characteristics of therapists, outcome measures, and treatment goals confound most comparative studies. It appears premature to reach conclusions about why therapeutic benefit results from certain procedures; causal state-

ments about curative factors operating in the group context, and the circumstances that promote their utilization also are not clearly supported by available literature.

4. Conceptual, not methodological, problems have fundamentally limited the scope and utility of much contemporary research. Meaningful relevant empirical research on group work still awaits the development of precise comprehensive descriptions of the phenomena we wish to study.

5. With regard to group treatment of specific patient populations: (a) while no clear answer can be provided as to whether group psychotherapy is more effective than some alternative forms of therapy in the treatment of institutionalized schizophrenics, a combination of group therapy and one or more other treatment approaches seems to enhance treatment outcome for schizophrenics; (b) although limited controlled research has been reported in the literature, there is evidence to suggest the efficacy of group therapy in the treatment of neurotic disorders; (c) group psychotherapy appears to offer help for the rehabilitation of juvenile delinquents and adult offenders; and (d) recent studies indicate that group psychotherapy is useful in the treatment of alcoholics; and (e) increasing attention is now being paid by medical practitioners to the utility of group psychotherapy for treating chronically or terminally ill patients.

6. It is difficult to disagree with an overall assessment that documentation regarding the effectiveness of group psychotherapy is disquietingly modest (Parloff & Dies, 1977).

One variable that has yielded some consistent results in the research on group processes is that of expectancy. Individuals who terminate prematurely from group treatment have been found to hold both unrealistic and less favorable expectations about group treatment. This research points to the value of discovering and shaping the expectations of prospective group members before they join the group. Indeed, numerous studies of group therapy have underscored the value of pregroup training. Preparation of prospective patients has taken various forms, including role-induction interviews, information dissemination, vicarious behavioral training, and direct practice of target behaviors. These procedures have varied with respect to the timing of their presentation, the specific content conveyed, and the nature of the behaviors and expectations for which pretraining is being presented. Klein (1982a, 1982b) has summarized significant and constructive effects derived from such procedures. These variables that can be influenced through pretraining have an important impact on the early development of the group, and, when properly shaped, appear to result in more favorable outcomes.

Therapist self-disclosure has been a topic that has received considerable attention in experimental literature. A thorough review of work in this area has recently been provided (Dies, 1979). Methodological difficulties, however, generally dictate a conservative interpretation of the results of these studies (Bednar & Kaul, 1978). The literature regarding members' self-disclosure is equally inconclusive. Unfortunately, these variables cannot be adequately addressed without clear specification of the context of treatment, the nature of the therapeutic contract, patient and therapist expectations, and the relationship between stage of group development, nature of self-disclosure, and therapeutic efficacy.

Research on interpersonal feedback, a crucial therapeutic variable in such groups, also has yielded conclusions of limited relevance for clinical practice. Feedback is a complex concept that has both positive and negative evaluative components, and involves timing, sequence, source, and credibility components, as well as the interaction of these variables with each other (Bednar & Kaul, 1978). The long- and short-term impact of feedback upon the group remains to be explicated empirically, as does its therapeutic effects, vicarious influence, and effects upon group development.

In other areas of research, our information regarding group dropouts, premature terminations, and casualties has tended to remain inpressionistic in nature. Just what constitutes a casualty continues to be a matter of debate. Indeed, the notion of a casualty has no absolute meaning but can only be defined in relation to the purpose of the treatment, specific member and leader characteristics, and the measurement techniques employed. Although considerable research has been conducted with a wide variety of participants observed under varied conditions, with both experienced and inexperienced leaders, we need studies of premature termination and casualty rates that include a clear definition of casualty and how it is measured, relevant base-rate data from no-treatment and placebo-control groups, measurements obtained over a developmental time span relevant to the life of the group, and independent assessment of casualties (Bednar & Kaul, 1978).

Similarly, although the concept of cohesion has occupied a major role in group dynamics and group therapy research over several decades, a lack of clarity surrounds both its definition and its measurement. Differences in definition and measurement procedures have made it difficult to compare results or to build upon previous research. Evans and Jarvis (1980), in their recent review, suggest that while cohesion appears to be uniformly acknowledged in the clinical literature as extremely important in both group process and outcome in all types of groups, research to date has been largely unsystematic and lacking in consistency.

Current Issues

Major Theoretical, Empirical and Methodological Issues

The research literature in group psychotherapy has accumulated at such a phenomenal rate over the past two decades that at least a dozen major reviews have been published during this period (e.g., Bednar & Kaul, 1978; Lieberman, 1976; Parloff & Dies, 1977). This burgeoning literature on change induction in small groups has ushered in an era of increasing methodological sophistication marked by expanded use of control and comparison groups, factorial designs, larger sample sizes, more specific researchable questions, and improved behavioral criteria (Bednar & Kaul, 1978; Gazda, 1978). The pursuit of greater specificity has been noted not only in research efforts but also with the emergence of the specialized review focused upon different types of group formats and particular process variables (Dies, 1979). The more complex interaction effects between group and patient type (Frances, Clarkin, & Marachi, 1980) and the relationship between group processes and specific therapeutic outcomes (Bednar & Kaul, 1978; Lieberman & Bond, 1978) are receiving much needed attention. In addition, an increasingly pragmatic attitude has characterized the group literature, focusing not only upon what to look at in the group but also on how to look at it (Dies, 1979). Suggestions have appeared for conceptualizing group research (Kaul & Bednar, 1978), for solving common methodological and design problems (Weigel & Corrazini, 1978), for assessing therapeutic outcome (Lieberman & Bond, 1978), and for identify-

ing important variables to consider in conducting group research (Parloff & Dies, 1978).

The crucial question in group therapy, however, remains unanswered: What kinds of treatments given what leaders, under what conditions, to what kinds of people lead to what kinds of therapeutic outcomes? Many reviewers of research in group therapy consider hundreds of studies but generally include in their respective reviews only a handful since most fail to meet even minimum standards of adequate research. Certain problems are reliably identified: a poorly defined treatment condition; an inadequately specified and heterogeneous population with whom it is applied; a failure to study patients and to use experienced therapists; a lack of comparable standardized outcome measures; and a failure to replicate results. Many research designs often implicitly assume that potency of group therapy will be manifest independent of the particular composition of the groups tested, the skills and styles of the group leaders, the particular techniques employed, or the amount of time each patient actually attended and participated in group treatment.

Data from studies that do not adequately describe the treatment, the therapists' techniques, the group characteristics, and the like, provide little assistance to the practicing group psychotherapist. In addition, conflicting findings cannot be resolved since it is unclear whether the discrepancies are due to differences among patient populations, therapists' skills, techniques applied, duration of treatment, or to the instrumentation employed (Parloff & Dies, 1977). Furthermore, the outcome variables selected for study often appear to be conceptually unrelated to treatment procedures and/or inadequately assessed. The rationale for what changes are expected as a function of psychotherapy and what instruments can be used to measure these changes accurately, is often not clear. Furthermore, when and from whose perspective these changes should be measured is usually not adequately addressed.

One of the major problems for the investigator of group therapy has to do not with methodological and technological problems, but with the limited level of conceptualization within the field, regarded by some (Bednar & Kaul, 1979) as analogous to that of pre-Galilean astronomy (i.e., primitive, incomplete, and probably based upon questionable assumptions). Research that is technically rigorous often is viewed by practitioners as clinically trivial or irrelevant. In large part, the conceptual malaise in group research is the result of theoretical bases that uncritically incorporate tenets and belief systems generated primarily from individual psychotherapy treatment. Unfortunately, these are often not relevant to the phenomenon of central importance—the group. Each of the major theoretical orientations (i.e., psychodynamic, behavioral, and humanistic) has spawned models for use with groups. Papers continue to appear in the literature, for example, detailing the nature and diversity of psychodynamic approaches (Kauff, 1979), or the range of strategies, techniques, and general guidelines for the conduct of behavioral and social-learning-theory approaches in groups (Harris, 1979). Emphasis continues to be placed upon the importance of interpreting transference and resistance (psychodynamic), the experiencing of unconditional positive regard, accurate empathy, and genuineness (humanistic), or modeling, behavioral rehearsal, and cognitive restructuring (behavioral). Despite innovative technical developments, such approaches have been adapted from dyadic models of intervention. Often, limited attention has been given at a theoretical level to the unique features of the group and the differences between the individual and the group as clinical contexts. Clearly, the one-to-one situation is far less complex; the therapist is treating a single individual without becoming involved in the creation and management of a complex social system with both unique properties for change and unique problems. In the group, however, the therapist is dealing simultaneously with processes occurring at the individual, interpersonal, and group levels. Precisely how to integrate and utilize these processes most effectively to promote change in individual group members remains a source of considerable controversy in the field.

In addition, it has proven difficult to formulate group theory at an adequate level of abstraction and generalizability given the vast range of activities, goals, clientele, and demands on the leader represented by the term group therapy, and the many different cognitive, behavioral, and emotional referents subsumed in its definition. Much published research continues to reflect an individualistic orientation with little attempt to theorize about the therapy group as a system; this research has typically remained centered on variables rather than on theories.

Some contemporary writers, however, have suggested the view of the group as a temporary institution (Singer et al., 1975) or a movable, change-able context of relationships (deMaré, 1977), in which certain norms, values, goals, and institutional factors are negotiated and constructed by the group members. A culture develops that serves as a medium through which the work of therapy is carried out by an exploration of the relationships and changes that occur. Reactivated but distorted or unresolved patterns of relationships (which members replicate within the group) interfere with the movement of the group toward a mature form of institution and become the subject of concern and examination. In essence, each group member eventually reproduces in the group context precisely the kind of difficulty in relationships that led him or her to seek psychotherapy in the first place. The critical difference is that the group has become a work group with a particular culture, set of social processes, values, and structures that permit it to work at certain agreed-upon tasks, namely, understanding members' difficulties. Through the creation of a powerful interpersonal matrix, individual members in the group have an opportunity to change and redefine themselves.

A related underlying issue that directly affects the field of group therapy concerns the nature of our models of illness and treatment and their implications for social policy. Adler, Astrachan, and Levinson (1981) describe various models, including the medical model, which views emotional disturbance as an illness to be controlled, the rehabilitative model, which views it as an adaptive defect or functional limitation to be managed, and the educative-developmental model, which views disturbance as arrests or impediments in normal development which, if removed, can permit further growth. Over the past several decades we have seen an era that places somewhat less emphasis on a medical or illness model, and somewhat more emphasis on a developmental model aimed at promoting personal growth, adaptation, and an examination of the individual's functioning in the context of his or her total group or social situation. But more recently this situation seems to be changing. How mental disturbances are conceptualized and defined will ultimately have considerable bearing on the nature of the treatment provided. Thus, for example, proposed legislation in the health-care field reflects society's views of illness, as well as concerns about the right to treatment and the quality of care. With the emergence of third-party insurance carriers as a major force influencing social policy decisions in the area of psychiatric care, we as a society seem to be moving in a more conservative direction, toward a closer allegiance to a medical model of illness and treatment. Mental-health professionals need to face the fact that third-party payers, whether they be government or private insurers, will increasingly be making decisions about who will be compensated for delivering what kinds of service for what disorders. It will, therefore, be necessary for group therapists to develop their own standards of quality care lest these be imposed upon the field by concerned others. Conflicts between third-party payers and the professionals who deliver the services in part may be mitigated by the development of peer-review standards and relevant continuing education programs. Not only must the field of group therapy be responsive and adaptive to changing social requirements involving health monitoring by external agencies, but it also must be sensitive to areas of social need and costs of services.

However, despite differences in their respective definitions of psychological illness or dysfunction and strategies for promoting change, therapists of different theoretical persuasions generally agree that there may be a set of curative factors that are indigenous to groups. If these can be successfully identified, along with the circumstances and means for utilizing these factors, then a common set of ideas independent of traditional theory that can shape effective clinical practice may be arrived at.

Several efforts have been made to identify such a set of curative factors operative in the group context (Corsini & Rosenberg, 1955; Yalom, 1975). Variables presumed to have curative value in group treatment include: (1) feelings of belonging and acceptance; (2) opportunities for interpersonal learning; (3) the experience of universality; (4) observing and imitating behavior; (5) altruism and role reciprocity; and (6) a corrective emotional experience through a recapitulation of the primary family group. Most group therapists would agree that group members may benefit from group therapy as a result of learning based upon participating in the process of developing, evaluating, and changing an ongoing social microcosm. Social learning may also proceed on the basis of interpersonal feedback and consensual validation, and opportunities to be both helper and helpee in the group setting lead to mutual benefit, particularly in the area of improved self-esteem. It is an oversimplification, however, merely to identify a list of curative factors without an adequate understanding of some of the complex interactions between the goals of the group, the leaders, the patients who are being treated, and the context in which the group is operating.

At the level of the practitioner, the major conceptual issue that continues to plague group therapists is also that of definition. The failure of researchers to define treatment variables adequately appears intimately related to the same dilemma with which clinicians have been struggling. Given the diversity of patient populations, therapists, theoretical models, technical innovations, settings, duration, and a host of other variables that differ across groups, the problem of defining the boundaries of group therapy, as opposed to other kinds of groups, is no small matter. Add to this the social, political, and economic motives of group practitioners and the situation becomes murkier still!

In summary, then, the lack of communication between researchers and clinicians, and the failure of research findings to have much effect on clinical practice has been noted by numerous authors (Frank, 1979; Parloff & Dies, 1977). Several factors have contributed to this lack of integration: (1) the failure to define group therapy clearly and to conceptualize the variables that operate within groups (including member, leader, group, and contextual variables) and the complex interactions between them; (2) inadequate specification in research reports of the nature of the treatment which is being provided; (3) the failure of many research designs to utilize both experienced group psychotherapy leaders and participants who identify themselves as patients seeking therapy; (4) an inability to specify with precision at a theoretical level the linkages between processes, modes of intervention, and expected areas of change; (5) the failure at a methodological level to consider carefully how outcome will be measured, from whose perspective and at what points in time; (6) the lack of standardized populations, criteria, and instrumentation in research studies coupled with the lack of replications; (7) the tendency for rigorous and well-controlled research studies to address clinically trivial issues or to utilize procedures that are not relevant or applicable for clinical practice; (8) inadequate specification by practitioners of their range of therapeutic activities and techniques and the consequences of their application; (9) the tendency of practitioners to maintain strong vested interests in their own theories and techniques and to resist dealing with experimental procedures and findings that call these into question; (10) group psychotherapy may be more of an art than a science (Berger, 1978; Frank, 1979); the scientific methods applicable to objective phenomena that can be quantified may have limited value for measuring the subjective experiences of psychotherapy and indeed may miss the essence of the therapeutic experience.

To make meaningful progress in the area of evaluating psychotherapy procedures, Parloff and Dies (1977) suggest a collaboration between researchers and practitioners aimed at answering:

1. Who and what needs treating or changing?
2. What are the relative dimensions along which group compositions are to be characterized?
3. What are the classes of therapeutic interventions?
4. How are the patterns and styles of patient-patient, and patient-therapist interactions to be characterized?
5. What are the interventions or enabling conditions that are presumed necessary to effect the hypothesized therapeutic process or the ultimate changes desired?

Training Issues

How to train professionals effectively to conduct group psychotherapy has been a subject of widespread concern for many years. In the past decade alone, over 200 articles have been published dealing with the issues of training and supervision of group therapists. A wide variety of training objectives, programs, and methodologies have been proposed. Although the literature is confusing and contradictory at times and the relative effectiveness of different strategies and approaches is difficult to evaluate, most programs have followed the lead of the American Group Psychotherapy Association (AGPA), which developed an initial set of guidelines in 1968 for the training of group psychotherapists. A revised version of these training guidelines was published in 1978, signaling the intent of the AGPA to maintain active leadership in setting standards for professional competence to meet the growing demands of both government and private agencies.

The model proposed by the AGPA identifies prerequisites for specialized training in group psychotherapy, professional discipline-related qualifications for admission to training, and standards for supervisors and agencies conducting training programs. The proposed model includes five elements in the training sequence: (1) seminars in the theory and technique of group psychotherapy; (2) clinical group experience as a responsible therapist or co-therapist; (3) participation in a continuous case seminar on groups; (4) participation as a patient in group psychotherapy; and (5) completion of a minimum number of hours in the direct treatment of patients in individual and group treatment with appropriate supervision.

Although this constitutes a sound and reasonable training model, it also has certain shortcomings. First, the didactic elements of the program appear to be somewhat narrowly focused, and may tend to promote the schism that remains between group psychotherapy and other related areas including group dynamics, the small-group field, large-group and intergroup events, and social systems theories. Second, the guidelines contain no mention of the observation of ongoing groups as a part of the training program, despite the recognized value of such procedures. Third, at a more general level, the guidelines address technical aspects of group psychotherapy training but refrain from addressing the complicated issue of the personal qualifications necessary for adequate group leadership. This remains a sensitive area of concern that is typically avoided by most training programs. Precisely what blend of technical competence and personal qualifications is necessary to produce a good psychotherapist remains regrettably unclear. Fourth, these proposed guidelines do not address the problem of training paraprofessionals to work in group psychotherapy with continuing supervision. With the increasingly widespread demand for services, the extension of group psychotherapy procedures to deal with a variety of clinical problems, the limited supply of professionally trained psychotherapists, and the impact of various other social phenomena including deinstitutionalization, it is likely that in the future it will be necessary to devote more attention to the development of group psychotherapy training programs for paraprofessionals. Minimal training standards, limits of group psychotherapy activity, and the nature of the supervision required will all need to be articulated to establish adequate standards to protect the public and to insure competent practice.

An examination of current practices in the training of group psychotherapists reveals that most training programs are based upon a combination of four components: academic-didactic, observation, experience, and supervision. Although the specific content varies, the academic component usually includes discussion of selected readings, presentation of didactic materials including lectures, films, audio cassettes, etc., and various role-play and simulation procedures. The advantages and disadvantages of various procedural aids including audiovisual aids, role-play techniques, and instrumentation have been discussed in the literature (Dies, 1981). Innovative approaches have been presented for combining didactic and experiential elements within a single course to improve the nature of such academic instruction (Roman & Porter, 1978), and broad-based conceptual models have appeared to facilitate the comparison and integration of various theoretical models (Bascue, 1978; J. Durkin, 1981; Klein, 1979; Singer et al., 1975). A recent survey of 100 professionals from various mental-health fields (Dies, 1980) revealed that the majority of readings endorsed by these senior trainers reflected a highly individualized approach to training. Most readings were technique oriented, with a smaller percentage devoted to theory, of which only a small fraction permitted comparative analysis of different theoretical models of group leadership or group function. Perhaps the most alarming finding was the fact that only a handful of the readings were research oriented. While these trainers clearly favored supervision and experiential groups over academic and observational techniques as more effective training components, research oriented training instruments and questionnaires focused on leadership or group processes were clearly underutilized.

A second training component, observation of ongoing groups, has received relatively little attention in the literature. However, techniques for enhancing observational skills have been suggested, and the value of postgroup feedback and discussion following the observational period have also been noted (Dies, 1980, 1981).

Experiential groups, a third component utilized in training, have included group therapy, T-groups, and various personal growth experiences. A therapeutic group experience has been endorsed by some trainers, while others maintain that experiential groups should be primarily educational rather than therapeutic in nature and therefore they argue in favor of a nontherapy process group as the more appropriate training model. The relative value of these methods has been discussed (Yalom, 1975), but unfortunately much of the literature fails to clarify the goals to which the experiential group is committed. Proponents of various models advocate that such groups should either teach about the dynamics of groups and authority relations, personal learning and insight, or understanding the interpersonal processes involved in group psychotherapy. The kinds of learning anticipated and the kinds of trainee changes being attempted often remain unclear. Furthermore, debate continues about whether such groups should be composed of work peers or unrelated persons.

A fourth training component regarded as essential by most programs is that of supervision. Various supervisory models have been proposed (e.g., dyadic, co-therapeutic, triadic, and group supervision), and the potential contributions of each have been reviewed extensively (Coche, 1977). Special techniques for increasing the educational value of supervision have been presented including instrumentation to refine supervisory feedback (Dies, 1981), methods of obtaining feedback from group members (Roback, 1976), and techniques for incorporating experiential components into group supervision (Mintz, 1978).

While these training components are inextricably interwoven, controversy continues to exist regarding the precise nature, extent, and timing of the various aspects of training, the use of these procedures in conjunction with other (research-oriented) methods, the optimal balance between cognitive and experiential elements in a training program, and the relationship of group therapy to training in individual therapy.

Conclusions

The discussion in previous sections clearly indicates the need for: (1) further conceptual clarification of the definition and boundaries of group therapy; (2) integration of group therapy with theory and research in related disciplines; (3) identification of common underlying active ingredients unique to group treatment approaches; and (4) specification of criteria for determining the best fit between patient, therapist, and group variables to ensure maximum therapeutic benefit for participants. Additional research aimed at linking particular processes with specific outcomes plus the development of self-regulatory agencies to monitor both accreditation and continuing education appear to offer the most promise for establishing acceptable standards for clinical practice.

With regard to the controversies surrounding appropriate training programs, most group therapists agree that prior to obtaining specific training in group therapy, trainees should have a thorough grounding in individual psychotherapy. However, those trainees most experienced in individual therapy often demonstrate the most resistance to using group methods. Individually oriented ideas and techniques appear to be carried over indiscriminately into group therapy without adequate recognition of the differences between these modes of intervention and the unique factors involved in group psychotherapy. In addition, the group method is frequently regarded by individually trained therapists as inferior treatment. Most group training programs are conducted in institutions where the primary emphasis is on individual therapy, so that group therapy may be perceived as "the low-priced spread." Thus, while training in individual therapy is essential for the future group therapist, such training alone is insufficient.

Powerful issues and processes specific to group therapy must be effectively addressed in our training programs. These issues include: the recognition of the group itself as a potential curative force; attention to the features of the group as a system (group culture, hierarchy, pressures, role prescriptions, boundaries, etc.); learning how to operate in a nonauthoritarian indirect role rather than as a sole agent of change; the fact that complex, intense, and often fragmented transference and countertransference reactions emerge more actively in group therapy and threaten trainees' needs for control; the public nature of group work which involves increased vulnerability and exposure of the therapist; and an increased ability to recognize and to make therapeutic use of developmental stages in the group. Programs that prepare trainees for the complexity of the group therapeutic situation need to be designed. Group processes and the unique facets of the group as a therapeutic modality should be emphasized. Readings and instrumentation that focus upon group process phenomena might be included so as to reduce trainees' misunderstandings about the differences between group and individual treatments. An emphasis on experiential groups and supervision using a group-process focus may be useful, rather than relying upon dyadic models that may inadvertently reinforce the tendency of trainees to lapse into one-to-one therapy in the group setting. In addition, experiential groups and supervisory exercises might well examine trainees' interpersonal and leadership styles to promote self-understanding and to decrease trainees' anxieties and uncertainties about their public images and therapeutic roles. Finally, a research orientation needs to be incorporated into training programs, with more attention devoted to acquainting beginning group therapists with relevant research review articles, and research instrumentation in various phases of training.

At this juncture, it is difficult indeed to resist noting the importance of instituting further dialogue and collaboration in the future between practitioners and researchers. Such a process is needed to enrich and to vitalize the work in each area. Researchers need to draw upon the clinical experience and wisdom of practitioners in order to investigate issues that are central to the actual practice of group therapy. Therapists need to incorporate a research perspective into their ongoing clinical work and make use of developing techniques and procedures to insure that their efforts are not guided solely by their personal prejudices. The development of a much needed richer, more comprehensive and generative conceptual structure for group therapy, plus a more sound empirical basis for clinical practice, will require substantial collaborative effort.

In this regard, Basch (1976), discussing the development of psychoanalytic theory, has stated:

> The next few decades should be a time of progress through interdisciplinary interchange. If it is not, it will not be because the necessary conceptualizations and facts are unavailable but because of our inability to acknowledge that theoretical inconsistencies, inadequacies, and myths are challenges to be met and not fortresses to be defended. [p. 386]

Mills (1979) has suggested that in order for the small-group field to make meaningful advances in the future we need to alter our earlier visions of the nature of the group and to reconstruct our current theoretical paradigms. He recommends that we consider eight factors as necessary and strategic for examining groups: (1) *scope*, i.e., we must recognize that the field of forces surrounding groups is more extensive and complicated than imagined by earlier investigators; (2) *collusion*, i.e., both the observed and the observer are in the same field together and exert mutual reciprocal influences upon each other; (3) *depth or thickness*, i.e., group process is multileveled, multifaceted, multifunctional; (4) *reflexivity*, i.e., both the observed and the observer are moving, changing systems that engage in interchanges and transactions with the world around them; (5) *duration*, i.e., time is necessary for group development and the time frame of members within groups may well vary considerably; (6) *autonomy*, i.e., we need to consider how the issue of authority and control between group members and investigators or practitioners is managed; (7) *the notion of a total system*, i.e., the action of elements in the group is to be explained in terms of the functioning of the total system; and (8) *change*, i.e., our paradigms and our findings are bound by context, by culture, and by history.

Several attempts have been made recently to develop a new integrative theoretical structure. Many of these efforts go beyond the mere adaptation of fundamentally dyadic models to the group setting. Emphasis is being placed upon common processes occurring simultaneously at the intrapsychic, interpersonal, and group levels. It appears likely that a holistic model focused upon analysis of pathological boundary structuring will be more widely adopted over the next decade (Liff, 1978). The generic form of this model has been derived from general systems theory (GST). H. Durkin (1981) suggests that GST provides a model of functional behavior that complements the psychodynamic model of dysfunctional behavior. GST may present a conceptual umbrella that can accommodate the major current approaches and incorporate the best of the new techniques.

From a GST perspective, all systems share certain structural features called isomorphies, and also share laws of operations. Whatever one learns about one system can be useful in clarifying another. The group therapist who examines the group, its members, and their individual personality structures as three levels of systems can draw upon new sources of information rather than becoming embroiled in a controversy about whether individual psychodynamics or group factors were the crucial aspects of therapy. By examining these three systems as different levels of complexity in continuous interaction, locating their boundaries and studying how transactions across these boundaries are conducted, the therapist adopts a single uniform approach to all levels. All living systems maintain themselves in dynamic equilibrium by exchanging energy and information with other systems and with the environment through the processes of opening and closing permeable boundaries. The purpose of such exchange is to promote change and growth through restructuring (J. Durkin, 1981). In group therapy, energy/information is exchanged in terms of emotional and cognitive processes. H. Durkin (1981) maintains that GST focuses the therapist's attention on processes and the events that activate change, and it highlights for the therapist the living systems' capacity for growth as well as for self-regulation. GST also influences the therapist's precedures in that the entire repertoire of members' exchange patterns can be identified and amplified in the group and their functional or dysfunctional character can be investigated and, if necessary, transformed.

Thus, GST is devoted to the comparative study of the organizational structure, not the content, of the entire range of living systems. A uniform approach to the three major group therapy systems (intrapsychic, interpersonal, and group) derives from the notion of the isomorphic structure of all systems. The therapist assumes major responsibility for the opening-closing function so as to regulate exchanges between members until they have sufficiently developed their own "steady states" and mechanisms to implement boundary control. The structural bases of dysfunctional systems are examined and the group explores transferential modes of interacting and modes of resistance as a means of facilitating boundary change (i.e., for human systems to restructure themselves).

Nevertheless, despite the contemporary sound of GST tenets and their harmonious blend with recent developments in both the physical and social sciences, it must be recognized that comprehensive and innovative theories about group psychotherapy are few and far between. While some authors express hope about the utility of general systems theory, others decry the fact that it represents little more than a translation from one language system to another. It remains to be determined whether this theoretical framework will lend itself to generative, integrative research and practice, or whether it will merely supply additional clutter and confusion to our already encumbered language systems.

Finally, at a more mundane but practical level, three issues appear destined to elicit further efforts from both researchers and clinicians in the future. First, apart from developing various theoretical and technical approaches to group therapy per se, additional effort will be needed to determine the effects of combining group therapy with other forms of intervention. In the inpatient setting, for example, groups often are combined with other forms of therapy. Various combinations of medication plus individual, group, and/or family therapy constitute an increasingly common clinical treatment approach. While these complex combinations have not been studied in sufficient detail to merit comprehensive discussion of their technical aspects or their efficacy, it will become necessary to identify the unique functions and goals for which group therapy can be most effectively utilized (Klein, 1977, 1979; Klein & Kugel, 1981). While several careful attempts have been made to assess combined individual and group psychotherapy approaches (Porter, 1980), these efforts will need to be greatly expanded in the future.

Second, increased energy will be required to develop more cost-effective short-term modes of intervention. Short-term or time-limited group therapy has only recently been recognized as a valid treatment modality (Klein, 1982a), although the majority of outpatient psychotherapeutic contacts, whether by plan or by premature termination, are brief, lasting less than six sessions. At the inpatient level, the growing use of the hospital as a transient refuge, the impact of the deinstitutionalization movement, the proliferation of day care and other transitional clinical facilities, and changes in the philosophy of inpatient care that diverge from long-term custodial care models have all contributed to the growing demand for short-term intervention strategies. In addition, we are facing the rising costs of psychiatric services on both an in- and outpatient basis and the mounting reluctance of third-party and government agencies to underwrite these costs without adequate assurances as to their benefits. There is a growing body of literature comprised of comparative studies of brief and unlimited therapies administered on either an individual or group level to suggest that short-term therapy is as effective as traditional long-term therapy. Given all of these factors, and the uniquely American penchant for instant food, instant housing, and perhaps instant therapy, it will be increasingly important to explore the uses and limitations of short-term groups systematically, a process that has already begun (Bernard & Klein, 1977, 1979; Imber, Lewis, & Loiselle, 1979; Klein, 1982b).

Another aspect of this issue of cost effectiveness is the preference expressed by many professionals in the area for using a co-therapy model. This practice, endorsed primarily at a clinical,

anecdotal level, is supported by virtually no substantive empirical data as to its therapeutic efficacy. While it may well have considerable value for training and other purposes, it is likely to be subject to severe challenge in the near future.

Third, as we rely more and more upon external social agencies to support our research, training, and clinical efforts, we will be expected to demonstrate increasing accountability, too, in terms of the application of group methods to underserved and overlooked populations. Minorities, children, adolescents, and the aged are all segments of the population for whom group therapists will be asked to develop more finely tuned treatments models. Innovative strategies addressed to the special needs of these populations will be required, not merely grafting old approaches to treat newly identified problems. Just as Pratt, the father of group therapy, began by using a group approach in the treatment of chronic tuberculosis patients, modern group therapists seem determined to rediscover their roots in the treatment of patients with chronic and/or terminal medical illnesses. Attending to the psychological components of chronic illness, whether it be tuberculosis or cancer, is likely to continue to constitute an important and useful form of group intervention in the future.

References

Adler, D. A., Astrachan, B. M., & Levinson, D. J. A framework for the analysis of theoretical and therapeutic approaches to schizophrenia. *Psychiatry*, 1981, **44**, 1–12.

American Psychiatric Association Task Force on Recent Developments in the Use of Small Groups. *Encounter groups and psychiatry*. Washington, D. C.: American Psychiatric Association, 1973.

Basch, M. F. Psychoanalysis and communication science. In The Chicago Institute for Psychoanalysis (Ed.), *The Annual of Psychoanalysis*, Vol. 4. New York: International Universities Press, 1976.

Bascue, L. O. Conceptual model for training group therapists. *International Journal of Group Psychotherapy*, 1978, **28**, 445–452.

Bednar, R. L., & Kaul, T. J. Experiential group research: Current perspectives. In S. L. Garfield & A. E. Bergin (Eds.), *Handbook of psychotherapy and behavior change: An empirical analysis*. (2nd ed.) New York: Wiley, 1978.

Bednar, R. L., & Kaul, T. J. Experiential group research: What never happened. *Journal of Applied Behavioral Science*, 1979, **15**, 311–319.

Berger, I. L. Presidential address: Group psychotherapy today. *International Journal of Group Psychotherapy*, 1978, **28**, 307–318.

Bernard, H. S., & Klein, R. H. Some perspectives on time-limited group psychotherapy. *Comprehensive Psychiatry*, 1977, **18**, 579–584.

Bernard, H. S., & Klein, R. H. Time-limited group psychotherapy: A case report. *Group Psychotherapy, Psychodrama, and Sociometry*, 1979, **32**, 31–37.

Bion, W. *Experiences in groups*. New York: Bask Books, 1961.

Coche, E. Problem-solving training as a special form of group psychotherapy. *Gruppenpsychologie*, 1977, **12**, 49–67.

Corsini, R., & Rosenberg, B. Mechanisms of group psychotherapy: Processes and dynamics. *Journal of Abnormal and Social Psychology*, 1955, **51**, 406–411.

deMaré, P. Group analytic principles in natural and stranger groups. *Group Analysis*, 1977, **10**, 16–21.

Dies, R. R. Group psychotherapy: Reflections on three decades of research. *Journal of Applied Behavioral Science*, 1979, **15**, 361–374.

Dies, R. R. Current practice in the training of group psychotherapists. *International Journal of Group Psychotherapy*, 1980, **30**, 169–185.

Dies, R. R. Group psychotherapy: Training and supervision. In A. K. Hess (Ed.), *Psychotherapy supervision*. New York: Wiley, 1981.

Durkin, H. E. The group therapies and general system theory as an integrative structure. In J. E. Durkin (Ed.), *Living groups: Group psychotherapy and general systems theory*. New York: Brunner/Mazel, 1981.

Durkin, J. E. *Living groups: Group psychotherapy and general systems theory*. New York: Brunner/Mazel, 1981.

Ellis, A. Rational emotive group therapy. In G. Gazda (Ed.), *Basic approaches to group psychotherapy and group counseling*. Springfield, Ill.: C. C. Thomas, 1975.

Evans, N. J., & Jarvis, P. A. Group cohesion: A review and reevaluation. *Small Group Behavior*, 1980, **11**, 359–370.

Frances, A., Clarkin, J. F., & Marachi, J. P. Selection criteria for outpatient group psychotherapy. *Hospital and Community Psychiatry*, 1980, **31**, 245–258.

Frank, J. D. Thirty years of group therapy: A personal perspective. *International Journal of Group Psychotherapy*, 1979, **29**, 439–452.

Gazda, G. M. *Group counseling: A developmental approach*. Boston: Allyn & Bacon, 1978.

Glasser, W. *Reality therapy*. New York: Harper & Row, 1965.

Harris, F. Behavioral approach to group therapy. *International Journal of Group Psychotherapy*, 1979, **29**, 453–470.

Hartley, D., Roback, H., & Abramowitz, S. Deterioration effects in encounter groups. *American Psychologist*, 1976, **31**, 247–255.

Imber, S. D., Lewis, P. M., & Loiselle, R. H. Uses and abuses of the brief intervention group. *International Journal of Group Psychotherapy*, 1979, **29**, 39–49.

Kaltenbach, R., & Gazda, G. Reality therapy in groups. In G. Gazda (Ed.), *Basic approaches to group psychotherapy and group counseling*. Springfield, Ill.: C. C. Thomas, 1975.

Kauff, P. F. Diversity in analytic group psychotherapy: The relationship between theoretical concepts and techniques. *International Journal of Group Psychotherapy*, 1979, **29**, 51–65.

Kaul, T. J., & Bednar, R. L. Conceptualizing group research: A preliminary analysis. *Small Group Behavior*, 1978, **9**, 173–192.

Kilman, P. R., & Sotile, W. The marathon-encounter group: A review of the outcome literature. *Psychological Bulletin*, 1976, **83**, 827–850.

Klein, R. H. Inpatient group psychotherapy: Practical considerations and special problems. *International Journal of Group Psychotherapy*, 1977, **27**, 201–214.

Klein, R. H. A model for distinguishing supportive from insight-oriented psychotherapy groups. In G. Lawrence (Ed.), *Exploring individual and organizational boundaries: A Tavistock open-systems approach*. London: Wiley, 1979.

Klein, R. H. Some problems of patient referral for outpatient group psychotherapy. *International Journal of Group Psychotherapy* (in press). (a)

Klein, R. H. Short-term group therapy on an adult inpatient service. In R. A. Rosenbaum (Ed.), *Varieties of short-term therapy groups: A handout for mental health professionals*. New York: McGraw-Hill (in press). (b)

Klein, R. H., & Kugel, B. Inpatient group psychotherapy: Reflections through a glass darkly. *International Journal of Group Psychotherapy*, 1981, **31**, 311–328.

Lakin, M. What's happened to small group research: Introduction. *Journal of Applied Behavioral Science*, 1979, **15**, 265–271.

Lieberman, M. A. Change induction in small groups. In M. R. Rosenzweig & L. W. Porter (Eds.), *Annual review of psychology*. Palo Alto, Calif.: Annual Reviews, 1976.

Lieberman, M. A. Problems in integrating traditional group therapies with new forms. *International Journal of Group Psychotherapy*, 1977, **27**, 19–32.

Lieberman, M. A., & Bond, G. R. Self-help groups: Problems of measuring outcome. *Small Group Behavior*, 1978, **9**, 221–242.

Liff, Z. A. Group psychotherapy for the 1980's: Psychoanalysis of pathological boundary structuring. *Group*, 1978, **2**, 184–192.

Maliver, B. L. *The encounter game*. New York: Stein & Day, 1973.

Mills, T. M. Changing paradigms for studying human groups. *Journal of Applied Behavioral Science*, 1979, **15**, 407–423.

Mintz, E. E. Group supervision: Experiental approach. *International Journal of Group Psychotherapy*, 1978, **28**, 467–480.

Parloff, M. B., & Dies, R. R. Group psychotherapy outcome research 1966–1975. *International Journal of Group Psychotherapy*, 1977, **27**, 281–319.

Parloff, M. B., & Dies, R. R. Group psychotherapy outcome instrument: Guidelines for conducting research. *Small Group Research*, 1978, **9**, 243–285.

Porter, K. Combined individual and group psychotherapy: Review of the literature 1965–1978. *International Journal of Group Psychotherapy*, 1980, **30**, 107–114.

Roback, H. B. Use of patient feedback to improve the quality of group therapy training. *International Journal of Group Psychotherapy*, 1976, **26**, 243–247.

Rogers, C. R. Interpersonal relationships: Year 2000.

Journal of Applied Behavioral Science, 1968, **4**, 265–280.

Rogers, C. *Carl Rogers on encounter groups*. New York: Harper & Row, 1970.

Roman, M., & Porter, K. Combining experiential and didactic aspects in a new group therapy training approach. *International Journal of Group Psychotherapy*, 1978, **28**, 371–387.

Singer, D., Astrachan, B., Gould, L., & Klein, E. Boundary management in psychological work with groups. *Journal of Applied Behavioral Science*, 1975, **11**, 137–176.

Smith, P. B. Controlled studies on the outcome of sensitivity training. *Psychological Bulletin*, 1975, **82**, 597–622.

Weigel, R. B., & Corrazini, J. B. Small group research: Suggestions for solving common methodological and design problems. *Small Group Behavior*, 1978, **9**, 193–220.

Wolf, A., & Schwartz, E. *Psychoanalysis in groups*. New York: Grune & Stratton, 1962.

Yalom, I. D. *The theory and practice of group psychotherapy*. New York: Basic Books, 1975.

Zander, A. The study of group behavior during four decades. *Journal of Applied Behavioral Science*, 1979, **15**, 272–282.

31 MARITAL AND FAMILY THERAPY

Neil S. Jacobson
Nicole Bussod

T he history of psychotherapy has been dominated by a focus on the treatment of individuals. Ever since the field was inaugurated by Freud and the psychoanalytic movement in the first two decades of this century (Freud, 1915), the predominant treatment approach has been based on a model emphasizing the healing power of a relationship between a single therapist and a single client. Even as the theories of psychopathology underlying these individual treatment approaches attended to the role of familial influences in generating problems of living, clinical practice has depended upon a doctrine that virtually precluded any intrusion of family members on the sanctity of the therapist-client relationship. As alternative theoretical models of psychotherapy emerged to rival, if not supplant, the psychodynamic approach, such as client-centered therapy (Rogers, 1951) and behavior therapy (Wolpe, 1958), the preference for working with individual clients remained virtually unchallenged.

Only in the past two decades have marital and family therapy attained sufficient identity to be considered as distinct and viable alternatives to the hegemony of the individual psychotherapeutic model. This is true, even though the roots of these two modalities were planted much earlier. Broder-

ick and Schrader (1981) have pointed out that the social work movement was involved from its inception in treating the family unit, which means that a rudimentary form of marital and family therapy was standard practice for social caseworkers as far back as the 19th century (Rich, 1956). The absence of a substantive literature, however, and the subsequent submerging of the social work profession by psychiatry beginning in the 1920s prevented the precocity of the social work movement from exerting a major influence on the practice of psychotherapy (see Spiegel & Bell, 1959). Earlier precursors to the development of marital and family therapy can also be found in the writings of neoanalytic theorists such as Sullivan (1953), Horney (1939), and Fromm (1941), who emphasized the interpersonal nature of psychiatric disorders; in the contributions of early sexologists such as Ellis (1936) and Hirschfield (see Broderick & Schrader, 1981), who were actually counseling sexually dissatisfied individuals in the 1920s and 1930s; and in the Family Life Education Movement, whose educational efforts in university settings during the 1930s amounted to the first systematic instances of preventative family counseling.

These early efforts not withstanding, the history of marital and family therapy as major forces influencing the practice of psychotherapy has been much more brief. Although these two modalities are often linked in chapters such as this one, and discussed as if they constituted a monolithic movement, marital and family therapy actually developed and matured in relative isolation from one another. They reached maturity at approximately the same time and have recently begun to merge in both theory and clinical practice (see Gurman & Kniskern, 1981); but for the most part, they are distinct, separate movements, with different origins, different pioneers, and different although parallel courses of development.

Marital therapy, or marriage counseling as it has been called for most of its history, began as a largely pragmatic response on the part of practitioners from numerous disciplines to the necessity of responding to their clients' marital problems. Physicians, lawyers, and social workers, confronted as they were by their clients' marital problems, found themselves doing marriage counseling by necessity rather than because of a firm commitment to the modality itself. The first three institutions primarily devoted to marriage counseling were started by physicians (see Mudd, 1951): the American Institute of Family Relations, founded by Paul Popenoe in Los Angeles in 1930; a clinic in New York City begun at approximately the same time by Abraham and Hannah Stone; and the Marriage Council of Philadelphia, started by Emily Hartshorne Mudd in 1932. These and other pioneers formed the American Association of Marriage Counselors (AAMC) in 1945. Parallel developments were also occurring in England, spearheaded by David Mace.

The growth of marriage counseling into a distinct discipline was slow and rather painstaking. For example, as recently as 1960, the overwhelming majority of marriage counseling consisted of seeing each spouse individually rather than the conjoint format that predominates today (see Gurman & Kniskern, 1978). As of 1965, 75 percent of AAMC members identified primarily with a discipline other than marriage counseling. Prior to 1960, fewer than 100 articles on marriage counseling had been published in professional journals (Gurman, 1973). Most of these articles contained no research, few scientific citations, and in general, were written as if the various authors were unaware of one another (Broderick & Schrader, 1981).

In short, until very recently, marriage counselors were comprised of a loosely organized body of professionals from various disciplines, with no coherent body of theoretical knowledge or research findings. The field was still dominated by psychoanalytic thinking, as evidenced by the preference for treating spouses individually. The development of conjoint marital therapy (Jackson, 1959), in which the two spouses are treated together by the same therapist, did not and could not come about until psychoanalytic thinkers themselves began to relax their position regarding the exclusion of this model. Classical psychoanalysis was based on premises that seemed to preclude even the concurrent therapy of both spouses (see Gurman, 1978). It was not until the 1950s that analytically trained clinicians began to acknowledge the desirability of simultaneous (although separate) therapy with both spouses (Sager, 1966). As psychodynamic theorists began to write about the role of marital relationships in perpetuating neuroses (Dicks, 1967; Eisenstein, 1956), the acceptability of marital therapy grew among psychodynamicists.

The growth of marital therapy over the past 15 years has been quite notable. In addition to the expansion of psychodynamic theories into the analysis and treatment of distressed relationships, new approaches from alternative theoretical perspectives have become widely influential. Two of the most prominent new approaches are the relationship enhancement model of Guerney and his associates (Guerney, 1977), and behavioral or social-learning models (Jacobson & Margolin, 1979; Stuart, 1980; Weiss, Hops, & Patterson, 1973). These contemporary models of marital therapy are discussed below. Moreover, there has been an increasing tendency for the development of marital therapy to become integrated with the growth of family therapy (Broderick & Schrader, 1981).

Family therapy began to emerge in the 1950s as a group of maverick psychiatrists and social scientists reconceptualized many forms of major psychopathology as reflections of dysfunctional family systems. One of the fascinating aspects of this early history is that many thinkers were involved in this reformulation, although each worked independently without awareness of similar work being conducted in other parts of the country. Although most of the pioneers in family therapy were trained in the psychoanalytic tradition, they gradually developed a broad theoretical framework that diverged considerably from this tradition. Instead of emphasizing the unconscious, intrapsychic determinants of the maladaptive behavior of psychiatric patients, these pioneers viewed severe psychiatric disorders in individuals as reflections of a maladaptive family system. It followed from this analysis that the treatment of choice for individual problems was to work with the entire family and attempt to generate positive changes in the functioning of the family as a whole. From this perspective, the identified patient was merely a scapegoat or a messenger, announcing to the world that all was not well in the family.

Ackerman (1959) was one of the seminal figures in the family therapy revolution. Trained as a child psychiatrist in the traditional psychoanalytic mold, during the course of his career he gradually evolved a model that viewed problems in living as a function of factors in the immediate family environment. He was a pioneer not only in the reconceptualization of childrens' problems in family terms, but he was also one of the first advocates of conjoint family therapy as the most thorough and effective treatment modality for working with children.

Like Ackerman, Bowen (1978) was trained as a psychiatrist at that bastion of psychoanalytic thinking, the Menninger Clinic. During the 1950s, while working with schizophrenic patients at the National Institute of Mental Health, he experimented with the hospitalization of the entire family of the schizophrenic patients. This experience convinced him that family therapy was the treatment of choice for schizophrenic patients, and he evolved a family systems theory of schizophrenia. His model of theory and therapy has since been broadened to incorporate other types of dysfunctional behavior, and his work has had an important impact on the field for the past 20 years.

Perhaps the most influential group of pioneers in the field of family therapy worked out of Palo Alto, California, beginning in the late 1950s. This group was organized by the eminent social scientist Gregory Bateson. Along with colleagues Donald Jackson, Jay Haley, and John Weakland, and later Paul Watzlawick and Virginia Satir, this group has had a pervasive influence on the theory and practice of family therapy. First, as a result of their work with schizophrenics and their families, they developed the influential *double-bind* theory of schizophrenia (Bateson et al., 1956). This theory postulated that schizophrenia developed out of persistent exposure to inconsistent or contradictory communication from the parents, especially the mother. Although this theory has not held up under the scrutiny of empirical testing, and no

longer exerts a major impact on the field of schizophrenia itself, the notion that paradoxical or inconsistent parental messages can produce psychopathology in children has endured as a major impetus to the growth of family therapy theory and practice. Second, Haley and his associates (e.g., Haley, 1976) adapted the work of the eminent hypnotherapist, Milton Erickson, to a model of brief psychotherapy that has come to be known as strategic therapy (Bodin, 1981; Haley, 1963; Stanton, 1981). Strategic therapy will be discussed below. More than any other group, this group of creative researchers and clinicians from Palo Alto has nurtured the family therapy revolution, and has popularized the application of systems theory to the analysis of families and of individual psychopathology (Haley, 1963; Jackson, 1959; Satir, 1964; Watzlawick, Beavin, & Jackson, 1967).

The remainder of this chapter surveys the field of marital family therapy. Both the theories underlying the treatment approaches and the treatments themselves will be discussed. When available, evidence from experimental investigations will be offered in support of the efficacy of various approaches. Finally, a number of unresolved but central issues will be delineated.

Theory and Practice

The following section will review the predominant contemporary models of marital and family therapy: psychodynamic, systems theory, behavioral, relationship enhancement, and sex therapy.

Psychodynamic Models of Marital Distress

For most of this century, psychoanalysis has been the dominant theoretical model of practicing clinicians, and the analytic cure the treatment of choice (Broderick & Schrader, 1981; Gurman, 1978). Neither mate selection nor marital dysfunction can be understood from a dynamic perspective without a firm understanding of the form and content of each spouse's unresolved intrapsychic conflicts from early childhood experiences in his or her family of origin. Each spouse evolves into adulthood only after surviving a series of developmental crises in childhood (Bowen, 1978; Meissner, 1978). Each developmental stage, from infancy through adolescence, is viewed as a step toward individuation and separation from the original state of helpless dependency on parental figures.

Adult intimate relationships are adversely affected when these developmental crises are incompletely or insufficiently resolved. For example, if the child's quest toward autonomy and independence is thwarted (e.g., by an overprotective mother), the child may grow up with a need to form interpersonal relationships based on helplessness and dependency. A fragile or incomplete sense of self may lead this individual to draw on the spouse to maintain his or her precarious identity (Erikson, 1959; Meissner, 1978).

When children grow up without an autonomous sense of self, they look for spouses who will help them feel whole or complete. The notion that people unconsciously choose mates who will complement them is a central feature of psychodynamic models of marriage. This complementarity can take many forms. A woman with strong, unresolved dependency needs may choose a man whom she unconsciously views as having resolved such needs. Her unconscious wish is that this man will take care of her and cater to her needs. Another important part of the process is that the emergent adult has unconscious needs in addition to resolving the residues of childhood conflicts. Avoiding these conflicts, preventing them from reaching awareness, is often an important motivating force in mate selection. The anxiety inherent in the conscious experience of these conflicts may prevail over the healthier, more mature strivings toward their resolution. To defend against awareness, adults often develop distorted perceptions of themselves, which then need to be confirmed by the marital partner. Therefore, one of the motivating factors in the choice of a mate is the desire to find a mate who will perceive him or her as he or she perceives him or herself, and thereby allow the distortions in self-image to be maintained. As an example, consider a hypothetical case of a man who defends against low self-esteem and underlying feelings of inferiority by consciously experiencing himself as confident and assertive, which includes the adoption of a life style based on achievement, ambition, and aggressive dominance. This man chooses a mate who idealizes him and validates his view of himself.

The process of choosing mates who confirm each other's sense of self is a dyadic one; that is to say, both partners are actively and simultaneously choosing one another. According to the psychodynamic position, this simultaneous choice is paralleled by an unspoken, unconscious contract between the spouses stipulating that each will protect the other from the anxiety inherent in exposing those self-distortions. This unconscious contract has been termed "collusion" (Dicks, 1967; Gurman, 1978).

Thus, the marital relationship is fundamentally a surrogate of the parent-child relationship. Through the marital relationship, each spouse continues the life struggles begun in early childhood. Marital distress is potentiated by the distortions in each spouse's perception of the other. Spouses choose each other based on *perceptions* suggesting that the other will be a certain kind of person. But to the extent that these perceptions are based on the perceiver's own unresolved conflicts rather than the love object's actual qualities, eventually the discrepancy becomes apparent. Marital conflict occurs in the form of disappointment, hostility, or withdrawal when the spouses find their needs unmet.

TREATMENT STRATEGIES

In traditional psychoanalysis, transference is essential to treatment success: when prior experiences with family members are projected onto the analyst, the analyst becomes the surrogate parent. The patient's past is then reexperienced in the therapist-client relationship, and through this process unresolved conflicts are uncovered, exposed, and then hopefully resolved. The client, freed from repeating past developmental failures, can then resume a more mature adult life with current love objects.

Psychoanalysts used to frown on the inclusion of both spouses in treatment either together (conjoint therapy), or even separately by the same analyst (concurrent therapy), because it was feared that the simultaneous treatment of both spouses would interfere with the therapeutic transference (Gurman, 1978). However, conjoint therapy is now recommended by leading psychodynamic marital therapists (Gurman, 1978; Framo, 1981; Sager, 1976). This modification stems from the belief that when marital conflict is the presenting problem, the therapist can utilize a transference relationship that is already present and more powerful than that between therapist and client, the transference relationship between the spouses (Meissner, 1978; Whitaker, 1981). The therapist can utilize the marital transference to point out concurrent perceptual distortions originating from intrapsychic conflicts within each spouse, clarify lines of communication, and expose both unrealistic expectations and unconscious, collusive contracts between the spouses (Sager, 1976).

The treatment goals include both interpersonal and intrapsychic restructuring. The latter is accomplished by rendering conscious the current perceptual distortions and the transference occurring in the relationship. Unfortunately, the vehicles for accomplishing these ends are not clearly specified by dynamicists. Intrapsychic change in traditional psychoanalysis is thought to require long-term therapy emphasizing the therapist-client transference. Most marital therapy, however, is both conjoint and brief. The psychodynamic marital therapist has to contend with conditions thought by classical analysts to preclude meaningful change. The therapist must be more active and directive. As a result, the technology utilized by psychodynamic marital therapists in treating couples bears little resemblence to classical psychoanalytic therapy. The techniques include the formation of contracts between spouses, direct behavior change instigations, and communication training. These are all strategies used by behavior therapists, and seem to follow much more logically from a behavioral model than they do from a psychodynamic model. To be sure, psychodynamic marital therapists also utilize intervention strategies more clearly derived from their theoretical model: in addition to interpretations, Framo (1981), for example, often conducts sessions where spouses' family of origin are involved, to increase understanding and resolution of those early conflicts. But, to a considerable degree, psychodynamic theories of marriage remain theories in search of a therapy. As a result, most of the prominent psychodynamic theorists are notably eclectic in their approach to marital and family therapy.

Family Therapy: Approaches Derived From Systems Theories

The family therapy movement has been so closely associated with the systems theories that to many the two are virtually synonymous. As we have already stated, there are a number of specific approaches to family therapy that have been derived from a broad-based systems theoretical perspective. Space limitations preclude a detailed specification of all approaches. Happily, there are

some overriding similarities uniting these specific approaches, and it is our view that understanding these similarities is fundamental to grasping the essence of a systems-theory perspective. Therefore, our focus in this section is on these unifying themes as they relate to the theory and practice of family therapy.

MODEL OF INDIVIDUAL PSYCHOPATHOLOGY AND FAMILY DYSFUNCTION

The fundamental tenet of a systems-theory perspective is that traditional problems in living and other psychiatric disorders such as schizophrenia, depression, drug abuse, and anxiety are best understood as manifestations of disturbances in the family (Haley, 1976; Minuchin, 1974; Stanton, 1981; Watzlawick, Weakland, & Fisch, 1974). The family member with "symptoms" is little more than the messenger or family scapegoat; his or her symptoms serve to cover up the generalized family disturbance. In this sense, the symptoms of the "identified patient" are viewed as serving a function for the family as a whole, despite the overt distress that may occur as a consequence of these symptoms. For example, a disruptive or delinquent child may consume an inordinate amount of attention from other family members, and thereby prevent the parents from attending to the emptiness and lack of intimacy in their own marital relationship. As long as the child continues to engage in delinquent acts, the parents are protected from having to focus on their marriage. The functional value of the child's symptoms is usually beyond the awareness of all family members.

The notion that symptoms are functional reflects a view of families as complex interpersonal systems. This family system is relatively stable and organized according to implicit rules governing the behavior of all family members in their interrelationships with one another. The roles and functions of family members' behavior are associated through a series of interconnected feedback loops that defy simple linear causal explanations. These behavior patterns are repetitive and tend to occur in particular sequences. Consider the following example (Stanton, 1981):

Spouse A is driving and Spouse B is in a hurry to get to their destination (and conveys this before the trip). A accelerates through a yellow light, B grasps a dashboard handle and criticizes A, who retorts and steps on the gas. B protests more loudly, A shouts back and the child, C, starts to cry. At this point the argument stops while B attends to C and A slows down. [p. 364]

This sequence exemplifies one form of a repetitive dysfunctional family process, where the child behaves in such a way that attention is withdrawn from the conflict between the spouses and refocused onto the child.

A central concept in family systems theories is *homeostasis,* the notion that patterns of interaction in families are directed toward maintaining the status quo. Family patterns are part of a stable system, and the behavior of the identified patient must be understood as being a part of that system. Despite the expressed concern with the patient's symptoms on the part of all family members, the family is inherently motivated to maintain homeostasis, and will thereby resist any effort on the part of the therapist (or anyone else) to modify the symptomatic behavior of the identified patient. This makes the task of the family therapist exceedingly difficult.

Many of the prominent family theorists have identified *triangles* (e.g., mother-father-son) as the basic unit of family transactions (Bowen, 1978; Haley, 1976; Zuk, 1971). A third person is brought in to diffuse or eliminate tension between the other two. According to Haley (1976), most behavior problems in children are brought about by a cross-generational alliance between the child and an overinvolved parent (usually the mother). The third party in the triangle is the absent parent (usually the father). It is a safe assumption, according to Haley, that symptomatic behavior on the part of the child is maintained by both parents, with the child serving as a buffer between the parents and saving them from a more direct relationship.

FAMILY THERAPY

If symptoms serve to stabilize the family and maintain homeostasis, it follows that the individual cannot be expected to change unless fundamental changes occur in the family system. It also follows that the family will resist the therapist's efforts to make changes either in the identified patient or in the family system. The notion that family members will resist the therapist's change attempts has

lead to the development of *strategic therapy.* Strategic therapy is defined by Haley (1973) as an approach where the therapist directively structures the therapeutic transactions and designs a particular approach for each problem. Although this definition does not follow uniquely from the model of individual psychopathology outlined above, in practice strategic therapy has come to be associated with certain types of intervention strategies that make sense only in light of the systems-theoretical model. The model implies that changes in individuals will effectively come about only when the structure of the family undergoes change. Therefore, whether the therapist is treating one client alone or the entire family, the target of change is the family system. Moreover, since family systems resist change, family members will sabotage any obvious attempts on the part of the therapist to induce structural changes in the family system. In order to counteract the family's resistance to real change, the therapist must maneuver the family into changing by subtle, covert means.

Thus, strategic therapy suggests a framework for conducting therapy more than a set of specific techniques. Nevertheless, certain types of interventions have been associated with the strategic approach. The most controversial but widely publicized are *paradoxical interventions.* Paradoxical interventions involve tasks prescribed by the therapist that appear to run counter to the goals of therapy. Usually these prescriptions consist of variations on the directive, "Don't change!" For example, in a family where the identified patient is an adolescent thief, the therapist might instruct the adolescent to go home and steal money from his mother. At times, the directive may be implicit in the therapist's expression of discouragement or hopelessness regarding the possibility of change (Haley, 1976; Watzlawick et al., 1974). Or, at the other extreme of explicitness, the therapist might instruct the patient to exaggerate their symptoms.

Paradoxical directives are based on the belief that family members will resist the therapist's attempts at direct influence. This resistance, largely beyond the awareness of family members, translates into warding off efforts on the part of any external agent to control the family. However, when the therapist instructs them to continue or increase the intensity of pathological behavior, the only way to resist the influence attempt is by changing for the better. In fact, advocates of paradox argue that once such a directive is delivered, the therapist has improved his or her position regardless of how the family responds. In order to resist the therapist's influence attempts, the family must improve. If they "obey" the directive, they are following the therapist's instructions and the latter has taken control of the pathological behavior. Once they have surrendered control of the symptom, ultimate improvement is thought to be more likely.

Paradoxical directives are potentially risky, if for no other reason than that clients often do what their therapists tell them to do: if paradoxical directives are obeyed, the family has at least temporarily deteriorated on a behavioral level. Haley (1976) and others have tried to specify the context in which such interventions are delivered in order to maximize their benefits and minimize the risks. Unfortunately, the stipulations of context are vague, and leave much room for interpretation and potential misuse by the unskilled or inexperienced therapist. These risks are, of course, more easily justified if the relative efficacy of these interventions is clearly established. As we shall point out in the next section, however, this empirical support has not been forthcoming. Finally, it is appropriate to ask whether or not it is really true that direct strategies to change behavior will not work. This is becoming a controversial topic even within systems theory circles (see Papp, 1979). The empirical support for direct strategies that avoid paradox (see below) suggests that therapists may not need to use paradox in most cases.

Reframing interventions are also common in the repertoire of strategic therapists. This describes the tendency on the part of the strategic therapist to offer a benign or positive interpretation to behaviors labeled by family members as negative. An uninvolved father and husband might be described by the therapist as "feeling too inadequate and caring too much about the family to step in and mess things up." Or a wife who neglects to tell her husband about a major debt might be presented to the husband as "caring about your opinion so much that she was afraid to tell you." The essence of a reframing intervention consists of casting behaviors that are interpreted by family members as malevolent or blameworthy in a context that emphasizes their well-intentioned, but perhaps ineffectual, qualities. The ascription of positive intentions counters the tendency of family members to blame and criticize each other, which consumes their energy and focuses their attention on defending themselves rather than

changing. It is another strategy for countering resistance. The issue of whether or not the therapist actually believes these more benign interpretations is largely irrelevant, although the argument is often made that there is always a positive dimension to even apparently negative family behavior, and the component one chooses to emphasize is largely arbitrary (Barton & Alexander, 1981). In a sense, all symptoms have functions for a family, and are at least adaptive in terms of maintaining homeostasis (Haley, 1976; Minuchin, 1974; Stanton, 1981).

Not all interventions based on systems theories are, strictly speaking, strategic. *Structural family therapy* is a popular alternative approach derived from a systems perspective. The structural approach was developed by Minuchin (1974). Structural family therapy resembles strategic therapy in a number of ways; indeed, Haley was one of the pioneers of strategic therapy and also intimately involved in the structural approach. The structural model, like all systems theories, views psychiatric symptoms in individuals as being generated by pathological family systems. Significant and permanent changes in individuals can come about only when the therapist is successful in altering family structures. For example, if the structure of the family is based on an excessively close (enmeshed) relationship between mother and son with the father detached and uninvolved, a structural intervention might involve directing the father henceforth to make all decisions regarding child discipline, and to take over exclusive responsibility for helping the son with homework. Successful restructuring occurs when the father becomes more involved and the mother more disengaged. Since the presenting problem is viewed as the outcome of faulty family structure, the belief is that the problem will disappear if the therapist can successfully promote more functional family structures.

Although structural family therapists utilize symptom-focused strategic interventions (Aponte & Van Deusen, 1981; Minuchin, 1974), they also utilize a variety of additional intervention strategies. Naturalistic structures are often re-created in the therapy session through task directives such as the manipulation of seating arrangements. Much emphasis is placed upon the therapist "joining" the family through personal interaction and adoption by the therapist of the families' modes of communicating. Once the therapist has "joined" the family, it is believed that restructuring interventions are facilitated.

Behavioral Approaches to Marital and Family Therapy

PARENT TRAINING

Beginning with the seminal work of Gerald Patterson and his associates in the 1960s and early 1970s (Patterson, 1971, 1974; Patterson, Cobb, & Ray, 1972; Patterson & Fleischman, 1979; Patterson et al., 1975), principles of learning theory have been applied to the analysis and treatment of disordered children at a rapidly expanding rate (Allen & Harris, 1966; Berkowitz & Graziano, 1972; Forehand, 1977; Gordon & Davidson, 1981; Graziano, 1977; Johnson & Lobitz, 1974; O'Dell, 1974; Wahler, 1969). Learning-theory principles have produced a method of analyzing family interaction, a theory of child behavior disorders, and a series of treatment innovations based on training parents in behavior modification techniques.

The behavioral approach to parent training is based on the premise that disordered behavior in children is learned, just like any other type of behavior. Parents have inadvertently prompted, shaped, and reinforced their childrens' dysfunctional behavior, and have punished, extinguished, or simply failed to reinforce desired behavior. For example, children who are physically aggressive, verbally abusive, or simply noncompliant have somehow not been effectively punished for such behavior, and more prosocial behaviors, some of which are either incompatible with or would simply supersede these negative behaviors, have not been adequately rewarded. In short, parents, although well-intentioned, have failed to apply learning principles effectively to produce desirable behavior in their children.

To determine how learning principles have been misapplied in a particular family, the behavior analyst first conducts a *functional analysis* to identify the environmental contingencies operating in the family that support deviant behavior and preclude the occurrence of desirable behavior. Then, a treatment plan is set up to restructure the environment in such a way that deviant behaviors are eliminated and desirable behaviors strengthened.

Parents exert considerable control over the contingencies impinging on their children. This fact, combined with the common observation that parents lack skills in the application of learning principles, serves as the rationale for parent training. Parents are instructed in the effective use of rewards and punishments. Training programs have varied from an emphasis on specific instructions to modify a particular behavior to the teaching of general strategies that can be applied to future as well as current problems. An example of the former would be teaching parents to ignore rather than to attend to a child's temper tantrum. The operative principle in this case is *extinction*, and the strategy is often effective because temper tantrums are frequently reinforced by parental attention. Another common strategy is *time out*, where children are removed from a reinforcing environment for a specified period of time, contingent upon the occurrence of an undesirable behavior. But the major emphasis in parent-training programs has been on positive control, using rewards to strengthen positive behaviors such as complying with parental requests, doing homework, or solving conflicts with siblings in a socially desirable manner.

BEHAVIORAL MARITAL THERAPY (BMT)

Like parent training, BMT involves the application of learning principles derived from the laboratories of experimental psychologists to the problems of distressed marital relationships. In addition, BMT has been influenced by social-psychological exchange theories (Thibaut & Kelley, 1959). As is generally true of behavior therapy approaches, BMT focuses on current rather than historical determinants of behavior, emphasizes overt behavior change, specifies treatment procedures in order to potentiate replication, and carefully specifies treatment goals so that the efficacy can be evaluated in a rigorous, objective manner.

According to the learning and exchanges models on which BMT is based, marital satisfaction for each spouse is a function of the ratio of rewards derived from a particular relationship to costs incurred by being in that relationship. The reward/cost ratio is influenced by a variety of factors, ranging all the way from constitutional or genetic to socioeconomic. Behavioral research on marital exchange has elucidated a number of parameters that differentiate between happy and unhappy couples (Birchler, Weiss, & Vincent, 1975; Gottman, 1979; Jacobson & Moore, 1981; Jacobson, Waldron, & Moore, 1980; Margolin, 1981; Margolin & Wampold, 1981; Vincent, Weiss, & Birchler, 1975; Wills, Weiss, & Patterson, 1974); all of these research findings have contributed to the theoretical model of marital distress, as well as to the treatment model that has come to be known as BMT. These studies have shown that distressed couples reward each other less frequently, punish each other more frequently, are more likely to reciprocate punishing behavior, are more emotionally sensitive to immediate relationship events, exhibit greater deficiencies in their ability to deal with conflict, and disagree significantly more often about what events occur in the relationship, than do their nondistressed counterparts. In general, distressed couples seem to be deficient in a number of skills necessary for the effective functioning of a relationship. These deficits are especially striking in the areas of conflict resolution and communication. Thus, helping couples acquire the process skills they lack when they enter treatment is an important part of BMT. But the focus in BMT is also on the content of spouses' presenting complaints. Marital distress occurs not only because of performance or skill deficits, but also because spouses are unable or unwilling to provide those behaviors that the other needs in order to feel "satisfied" with the relationship.

Thus, BMT emphasizes both *content*, the provision of adequate levels of rewarding exchanges, and *process*, the fostering of the communication skills necessary to maintain a satisfying relationship. This dual focus is generally characteristic of BMT, although each couple is treated somewhat differently, depending upon their particular problems. Like parent training, the particular intervention strategy for a given couple is based on a functional analysis of the interaction between the spouses. More than any other theoretical framework, BMT bases its intervention strategy on an individualized assessment of each dysfunctional relationship. Using observations of interaction between spouses in the treatment setting, data collected by the spouses in the home, and a variety of self-report measures, a treatment plan is devised on the basis of the current strengths and weaknesses, the antecedents and consequences of current distressing behaviors, and the reinforcement potential of the couple. A treatment plan is discussed with the couple and a series of goals are mutually decided upon.

Behavior exchange procedures refer to those treatment strategies that attempt to modify the *content* of spouses' presenting complaints. This phase of treatment plays a greater or lesser role in the overall treatment plan depending upon the needs of each couple. The primary goal of behavior exchange procedures is to increase the occur-

rence rate of positive behaviors in the relationship. The emphasis during this phase of therapy is on teaching each spouse how to become more effective at providing the other with what he or she wants in order to feel more satisfied with the relationship. There are many types of specific behavior exchange procedures described by various authors (Jacobson & Margolin, 1979; Stuart, 1980; Weiss, Hopps, & Patterson, 1973). For Jacobson and Margolin (1979), the cardinal rule of this phase of therapy is for each spouse to focus on himself or herself, as opposed to complaining about what he or she is not currently getting from the partner. Each spouse is taught to pinpoint those behaviors that would result in a more satisfying relationship for the partner. Then each spouse is asked to attempt to increase the daily satisfaction of the partner through systematically increasing certain pinpointed behaviors. The positive behaviors that serve as the targets for change are introduced in an incremental, stepwise fashion, and spouses are given maximum latitude to initiate unilateral, noncontingent changes. Once positive changes have begun to occur and spouses report increased daily satisfaction, they engage in exercises such as the request-refusal exercise, in which each asks for specific behaviors from the other that he or she would like to receive more often. During this exercise, spouses would receive practice in asking for and declining behavioral requests in mutually supportive, nonthreatening ways. Collaboration and compromise are further instigated by having spouses state what they would like ideally, and what they are willing to settle for in their requests for change from the partner. The very nature of this exercise implies the presence of unrealistic expectations, and encourages each spouse to moderate his or her requests accordingly, instead of blaming the partner for not fulfilling them.

Over the years, behavior exchange procedures have been modified considerably based on the findings of empirical research. Instead of contingent, *quid pro quo* exchanges, current behavior exchange procedures emphasize unilateral, noncontingent exchanges. This modification has resulted from a number of studies that demonstrate that happy couples deliver positive behaviors without any immediate return, that is, without immediate positive reinforcement (Gottman, 1979; Jacobson et al., 1980). Similarly, Jacobson (in press) recommends that each spouse retain maximum control regarding what behaviors he or she is asked to change. This has positive benefits for both the giver and the receiver. For the giver, the more control he or she has, the less likely it is that directives from the therapist will be resisted. For the receiver, the more control and latitude that the giver has in deciding which behaviors to change, the greater the likelihood that the changes will be well received when they do occur.

In short, behavior exchange procedures are designed to provide each spouse with the maximum benefits potentiated by the relationship that they are currently in. To the extent that reinforcing behaviors currently in the repertoire of each spouse are being withheld, behavior exchange procedures instigate more frequent occurrence of these behaviors. To the extent that one or more spouses are deficient in their potential to gratify the other, procedures that emphasize the development of reinforcement potential are included. By the time the behavior exchange phase of treatment is over, there should be significant increases in the quantity and quality of positive exchanges, these changes should be having an incremental impact on each spouses' subjective satisfaction with the relationship, and each spouse should have developed skills in the process of analyzing his or her impact on the partner and insuring that that impact is as positive as possible.

Communication and problem-solving training is oriented toward teaching couples the communication skills that they need in order to have a maximally positive relationship. One of the best discriminators between distressed and nondistressed couples is the inability of the former to deal with conflict effectively (Gottman, 1979). When distressed couples enter therapy, they exhibit deficiencies in problem-solving and conflict-resolution strategies. Although one cannot infer from this that these deficiencies in communication style precede the development of marital distress (Markman, 1979).

Just like in the case of behavior exchange procedures, a number of strategies have been recommended to teach couples communication skills. Jacobson and Margolin (1979) emphasize problem-solving training, which can be defined as communication training specifically designed toward facilitating conflict resolution. Through practice, instructions, and feedback from the therapist, couples are taught a variety of skills that have been associated with effective conflict resolution and generally positive communication: learning how to express complaints within an overall context of support and appreciation; clear expression of feelings; defining problems specifically and in behav-

ioral terms; accepting responsibility for one's role in the development and maintenance of a problem; and listening skills such as paraphrasing. Couples first receive a manual describing these skills, and practice them on hypothetical or minor problems before using them to tackle major complaints in their relationship. Gradually, as these skills are mastered, the content gradually shifts to more central relationship problems, while the new format provides them with the opportunity to resolve them in a collaborative manner.

If problem-solving training works as it is meant to, couples have not only resolved current problems in their relationship, but have acquired skills that are generalizable to future problems that may occur subsequent to the termination of therapy. Couples learn that all relationship problems are mutual, and that the responsibility toward maintaining a satisfying relationship is shared. The emphasis throughout is on collaboration, compromise, and mutuality. The hope is not simply to teach conflict resolution but actually to promote intimacy. The goal of teaching generalized skills that will be utilized beyond the point where therapy ends is facilitated by gradually fading the influence of the therapist, having the couple practice these skills at home, and by teaching spouses to conduct relationship-enhancement sessions at home independent of therapy.

To summarize, BMT is highly structured, oriented toward relieving present difficulties, and emphasizes the acquisition and maintenance of relationship-enhancement skills. The therapist is both active and directive in instigating behavior change. The underlying assumption that best separates BMT from other approaches to marital therapy is that the two spouses in question are basically well intentioned but ineffectual in their attempts to satisfy one another. The goal of therapy that follows from this assumption is that, if a supportive environment can be created, and if the proper skills can be acquired, the relationship is likely to improve significantly.

Communication and Relationship Enhancement Techniques

In addition to the variety of treatment models for helping distressed and dysfunctional families, a number of approaches have been developed for use with relatively happy or mildly distressed families who either wish to remain so or who wish to attain even greater levels of satisfaction. Often, these approaches emphasize training in communication skills and are offered to relatively young couples either prior to or shortly after marriage. Such programs are often referred to as *marital enrichment*.

Of all the communication-skills training approaches, the most well researched has been the relationship-enhancement model developed by Guerney (1972). The goal of this group-treatment approach is to foster direct and open communication between spouses. The communication process is broken down into distinct modes, and spouses are taught each mode one at a time. The modes include the direct expression of thoughts and feelings, listening skills, and skills in conflict resolution. The content of the skills is derived from the Rogerian, client-centered model of therapy (Rogers, 1951) with its emphasis on the unconditional acceptance of and respect for the feelings of others; the style of training is similar to behavior therapy, with an emphasis on modeling and behavior rehearsal. Guerney's model has, in turn, been influential in the development of behavioral communication training programs (Hahlweg et al., in press; O'Leary & Turkewitz, 1978).

The relationship enhancement program was derived from Guerney's "filial therapy" program, which focused on developing parent-child interaction skills. Both filial therapy and relationship enhancement are highly structured, educationally oriented, and humanistic in underlying philosophy and outlook. Although their application to severely distressed couples may be limited, these and other related approaches may have important implications for the prevention of marital discord.

Sex Therapy

While marital therapy and sex therapy often occur together in clinical practice, we have chosen to treat sex therapy in a separate section for a number of reasons. First, sex therapy has evolved and developed as a field of its own. Second, there is currently little integration between the sex therapy and marital therapy literature. Of course, in clinical practice, marital therapists tend to draw on the techniques of sex therapists and vice versa. But for some reason, empirical research as well as books and articles on therapy have remained separate in the two overlapping disciplines. Third, sex therapy, unlike marital or family therapy, is sometimes applied to single persons without current or available partners.

Unlike marital and family therapy, sex therapy is a form of treatment that remains markedly similar regardless of one's theoretical orientation with respect to the etiology of marital, sexual, or family problems. Whether one's theory of psychopathology is psychoanalytic or behavioral, there is remarkable consistency in the type of sex therapy strategies recommended by experts in the field (e.g., Heiman, LoPiccolo & LoPiccolo, 1981; Kaplan, 1974; Masters & Johnson, 1970). This is mainly due to the influence of the work of Masters and Johnson, who are responsible for both the creation and the proliferation of the field of sex therapy (see Masters & Johnson, 1970).

An overwhelming majority of the work published by sex therapy researchers and theoreticians has been in the area of sexual dysfunctions. Sexual dysfunctions include the following: *erectile dysfunctions* in men, defined as the inability to obtain or sustain an erection long enough for the successful completion of the sexual act; *premature ejaculation* in men, which can be defined as ejaculation which occurs too quickly to satisfy the particular partner; and *orgasmic dysfunctions* in women, which can be defined as the inability to achieve orgasm in the desired sexual situations. Although there are other types of sexual dysfunction, these are the most common and the most frequently studied.

Little is known regarding the etiology of sexual dysfunction. There has been much theoretical speculation regarding the causes and the maintaining factors, but little controlled research. The most common view is that adequate sexual performance is a natural biological concomitant of human functioning, and that for most people it is inhibited only when anxiety interferes. Most sex therapy techniques are based on the view that the elimination of anxiety will lead to normal sexual functioning. In practice, however, many of the common sex therapy techniques also involve training in certain skills.

The goals of sex therapy are numerous and depend on the particular complaints brought in by a given couple. Although sexual dysfunctions are sometimes treated as "just another symptom" (Heiman, LoPiccolo, & LoPiccolo, 1981), the general practice is to pay particular attention to the presenting sexual complaint, and include its elimination as a primary treatment goal. Other therapy objectives include factors thought to be conducive to a satisfying sexual life, such as the reduction of performance anxiety, the provision of sex education and information, communication skills, and the elucidation and acceptance of self and partner preferences.

As in BMT, the therapist functions as a provider of information, an educator, a facilitator, and an expert in relationship and sexual skills. However, the basic model of sex therapy proposed by Masters and Johnson (1970) is based on an anxiety-reduction paradigm, and is similar to the behavior therapy technique known as *in vivo* desensitization (Wolpe, 1958). Anxiety-reduction techniques begin with the directive that the couple cease engaging in sexual behaviors that create anxiety. Then, sexual interaction between the couple is reintroduced in its most rudimentary form, and gradually sexual stimulation is eased back into the relationship, but only when couples are able to tolerate early stages without anxiety. Anxiety-reduction techniques during the early phases of therapy include *sensate focus*, where spouses engage in nonsexual physical stimulation with one another, which gradually becomes more sexual with succeeding assignments. Sensate focus is designed to have the partners experience physical contact in a more relaxed context, and practice giving and receiving information about what pleases them. Sensate focus allows for the pleasurable experience of physical contact, without the anxiety that has come to be associated with sexual interaction.

In addition to the general components common to all sex therapy, such as sensate focus, sex therapy consists of specific techniques tailored to the particular dysfunction of the couple. Premature ejaculation is treated either by the squeeze technique (Masters & Johnson, 1970), or the stop-start technique (Semans, 1956). Heiman et al. (1981) state that there is a recent tendency among sex therapy theorists to prefer the stop-start technique because it is less intrusive than the squeeze technique: the former involves the cessation of thrusting on the part of the male at the point where he feels that ejaculation is imminent. Active thrusting resumes subsequent to the reduction of arousal. Erectile failure is treated with a variety of anxiety-reducing techniques, including desensitization, cognitive reframing techniques, and paradoxical interventions where the male is instructed not to become aroused. Similarly, orgasmic dysfunctions in women are treated in a variety of ways, depending on the nature of the dysfunction. When the woman has never achieved orgasm by any mode of stimulation, the treatment of choice appears to be directed masturbation training, where she is systematically taught to achieve orgasm

through masturbation (LoPiccolo & Lobitz, 1972). Once orgasm is attained through masturbation, the attempt is made to generalize the orgasmic experience to situations involving partner-induced stimulation. When the woman has been able or becomes able to achieve orgasm in some situations, but is in treatment because she wants to attain orgasm in other situations, a variety of techniques have been used. The more delimited and situation-specific the orgasmic dysfunction, the more likely it is that the problem is caused by nonsexual aspects of the marital relationship. Therefore, sex therapy techniques will often be combined with and in many cases preceded by marital therapy focusing on nonsexual issues.

Similarities and Differences among Marital and Family Therapies

As we have shown, and others (Gurman & Kniskern, 1981) have confirmed, there is no such entity as marital and family therapy, but rather a myriad of marital and family therapies. In addition to the major subgroups serving as the basis for organizing this section, each subgrouping has a number of variants. In all, there are dozens of schools of marital and family therapy. The plethora of alternative approaches can be confusing for both students in training and the practitioner trying to stay current with the literature. Fortunately, there is actually less substantive divergence than the number of distinct models would imply. There are several overriding similarities, as well as a few fundamental points of divergence, that, when specified, add clarity and order to this burgeoning field.

First, most of the major models of marital and family therapy focus on current rather than historical determinants of marital and family functioning. In both systems theory and behavioral formulations of marital and family distress, marital and family dysfunctions are viewed within the context of current dysfunctional interaction patterns. Only the psychoanalytic model continues to conceptualize present problems as being caused by distal events in the early history of individual family members.

Second, most forms of marital and family therapy involve an active, highly directive therapist. Here, even psychoanalytic models are characterized by an active therapist who utilizes directive change-inducing intervention strategies presented within a relatively brief period.

Third, most forms of marital therapy view faulty communication as an integral part of marital or family dysfunctions. Treatment approaches differ, however, in the explicitness with which treatment is directed toward modifying communication. Relationship-enhancement, behavioral, and some psychoanalytic approaches emphasize direct communication training, while direct training is deemphasized by systems theorists.

Fourth, the various models differ in the degree of explicitness and overt structure provided during therapy sessions. Behavioral, sex therapy, and relationship-enhancement approaches are highly structured, and specified to a degree that renders them quite teachable and easily replicated. Explicitness and specificity seem to be associated with an educational, skills-training format. Systems and psychodynamic approaches deemphasize skill training, provide little in the way of education, and are comparatively less explicit and specific in their provision of a well-defined technology of a therapy.

Fifth, the approaches differ in their conceptualization of what constitutes meaningful change. All approaches pay attention to the necessity of eliminating the presenting complaints of the particular family with whom they are working. For behaviorists and sex therapists, elimination of the present problem is an end in itself, whereas for systems theorists, there is some variability depending upon the particular systems model employed. Haley's strategic model retains a focus on the presenting problem as a means toward generating changes in the family system, which is the ultimate therapeutic goal. Other systems models, such as Minuchin's structural family therapy or Bowen's family systems theory (Bowen, 1978), tend to focus less on the presenting problem and more on restructuring the family system. Ultimately, the relative merits of these similarities and differences must be evaluated empirically.

Current Issues

Empirical Status of Marital and Family Therapy

GENERAL COMMENTS

Although there has been an incredible proliferation of articles and books on marital and family therapy in the past 15 years (see Gurman & Knis-

kern, 1978, 1981; Jacobson, 1978a, and a number of studies reporting data on the outcome of various therapies), few definitive conclusions can be reached at present regarding either the absolute effectiveness of particular approaches or the relative effectiveness of these approaches. Most of the major theoretical models reviewed in the previous section have been subjected to few if any controlled investigations of treatment efficacy. Much of the outcome research that has been conducted is limited by a variety of methodological flaws including the absence of appropriate control groups, the lack of adequate follow-up data, the use of questionable, poorly validated measures of treatment outcome, and treatment procedures that are so vaguely and poorly specified that they are virtually unreplicable. With these cautions in mind, let us examine what existing evidence there is for the effectiveness of marital and family therapy.

BEHAVIOR MARITAL THERAPY

In contrast to other approaches to marital and family therapy, there is a considerable body of evidence supporting the effectiveness of BMT. Most of the available evidence involves the evaluation of multifaceted treatment packages that include either a communication/problem-solving component, a behavior-exchange/contingency-management component, or both (Jacobson, 1978a). These studies have consistently shown BMT to be significantly more effective than no treatment or minimal treatment (Baucom, 1982; Hahlweg, Shindler, & Revenstorf, in press; Jacobson, 1977, 1978b; Jacobson & Anderson, 1980; Turkewitz & O'Leary, 1981), and more effective than various placebo treatments to which it has been compared (Azrin et al., 1980; Crowe, 1978; Jacobson, 1978, 1979b; Margolin & Weiss, 1978). Most of these studies included at least some follow-up data indicating that treatment-induced gains are maintained subsequent to the termination of active treatment. Attempts to ferret out the effective components of these multifaceted treatments have been strikingly unsuccessful: when single components within the treatment package are compared to one another or to the package as a whole, it has been consistently found that single components are almost as effective as combinations of components (Baucom, in press; Emmelkamp et al., in press; Hahlweg et al., in press; Jacobson, 1979a; Turkewitz & O'Leary, 1981). There is some evidence, however, that behavioral communication training is the most essential component to the success of BMT (see Jacobson, 1978a). There is also some evidence that BMT can be conducted in a couples-group setting without a significant loss in effectiveness (Hahlweg et al., in press). Although there is very little existent data on the types of couples most likely to respond positively to BMT, there is evidence that the age of the couple is inversely related to outcome (Baucom, in press; Turkewitz & O'Leary, 1981).

Thus, BMT has been subjected to a greater number of well-controlled experimental outcome investigations than any other existent model of marital therapy. Although it is unclear at present whether or not BMT is *more* effective than other approaches, it is evident that a substantial majority of couples entering therapy because of dissatisfaction with their marriages derive some benefit from BMT. As to what percentage of couples benefit *significantly* from BMT, there is not much basis for definitive estimates. Many studies report only group means; the studies that do report percentages of improved versus unimproved couples vary from improvement rates of 65 to 80 percent. Still less is known regarding the clinical significance of these improvements; that is to say, how many of these treated couples actually leave therapy with a mutually satisfying relationship, not simply a "better" relationship? In short, a great deal of research is needed to establish how effective the treatment approach is, and for whom that treatment approach is indicated. Although BMT has been subjected to more rigorous experimental scrutiny than any other approach, a great deal of work remains to be done.

COMMUNICATION TRAINING:
LISTENING AND EXPRESSIVE SKILLS

Structured communication-training approaches based on Guerney's (1977) relationship-enhancement model have also been studied extensively in well-controlled clinical research settings (see Jacobson, 1978a). The results of these studies have been generally positive. Communication training that emphasizes listening and expressive skills seems to be a highly effective way to bring about at least short-term positive changes in the quality of a relationship. Studies comparing communication training with BMT have generally found these approaches to be equally effective (Emmelkamp et al., in press; Hahlweg et al., in press; Turkewitz & O'Leary, 1981). It is interesting, however, that Guerney's approach appears to be less effective than BMT when both approaches are compared in a group setting (Hahlweg et al., in press), since the relationship-enhancement model was developed especially for the group setting. In addition to the unknowns already mentioned with respect to BMT, communications-training research suffers form ambiguities regarding external validity; much of the research has been conducted with nondistressed couples seeking an enrichment experience. Although nothing is wrong with studying marital-enrichment programs, it is hazardous to attempt to generalize from such findings to clinical settings with severely distressed couples.

MARITAL THERAPY BASED ON
PSYCHODYNAMIC MODELS OF
MARITAL DISTRESS

Unfortunately, as advocates of these approaches acknowledge, there has been virtually no research conducted on the effectiveness of marital therapy from a psychodynamic perspective (Framo, 1981; Sager, 1981). There is therefore no experimental evidence validating the efficacy of these approaches at this point.

SEX THERAPY

There is a voluminous body of literature supporting the efficacy of sex therapy techniques for the most common types of sexual dysfunctions (see Kaplan, 1974, LoPiccolo & Hogan, 1979; Masters & Johnson, 1970). However, as Heiman et al. (1981) point out, most of this literature is anecdotal rather than experimental, consisting of either case studies, uncontrolled group studies, or controlled studies plagued by methodological problems. Many of the studies that report impressive improvement rates utilize highly selective samples of couples, which makes generalization to clinical practice hazardous. For example, in clinical settings, couples with sexual dysfunctions usually have moderate to severe marital problems in nonsexual domains as well. Yet in many of the influential clinical outcome studies, such difficult-to-treat couples are excluded (Jacobson, 1978a; Masters & Johnson, 1970). Another major problem in interpreting the results of these outcome studies lies in the measures used to evaluate success. Often, global measures of sexual satisfaction are relied upon, rather than specific measures that reflect the presenting problem more accurately. There is a tendency for results to look less promising as the measurements of outcome become more precise.

Keeping these research limitations in mind, one can tentatively conclude that premature ejaculation can be successfully treated 90 to 95 percent of the time using either the squeeze technique or the Semans (1956) method. The prognosis for impotence depends upon prior history of erectile success. When there has been some success at some point in the past (secondary impotence), treatment success rates have varied from 60 to 80 percent. However, with no previous history of adequate sexual functioning (primary impotence), success estimates are lower (40 to 60 percent). Finally, with female orgasmic dysfunctions, the success varies depending on both the generality of the dysfunction and the stringency of the criteria for success. When the woman has never achieved orgasm by any mode of stimulation (primary orgasmic dysfunction), it is usually possible to help her achieve orgasm at least through masturbation (success rates 85 to 95 percent). It is much less likely (30 to 50 percent), however, that sex therapy will lead to orgasms during sexual intercourse. Similar disparities are found with women who have some orgasmic history in at least some situations (secondary orgasmic dysfunction): if the goal is expansion of the experience of orgasm to new situations, success rates are high (70 to 80 percent); but if orgasm during intercourse is the goal, success is less likely (30 to 50 percent).

There has been almost no research conducted on sexual dysfunctions involving loss of interest, low drive, or inhibited desire. These are very common sexual complaints, particularly in distressed married couples, where the field awaits *empirically supported* techniques (Melman & Jacobson, in press).

PARENT TRAINING

Of all existing forms of family therapy where a child's behavior constitutes the presenting problem, parent training has been evaluated most frequently and most rigorously (see Gordon & Davidson, 1981). Literally hundreds of studies report success in modifying deviant behavior in the targeted child. Contrary to predictions derived from systems theories, the available evidence suggests that changes in the deviant child lead to generalized positive changes in the family as a whole (Arnold, Levine, & Patterson, 1975; Karoly & Rosenthal, 1977). The available research has been less conclusive about the permanence of these changes. Gordon and Davidson (1981) point out that desirable changes in fairly discrete child behaviors

appear to be permanent, especially when the changes do not require permanent changes in the behavior of parents. On the other hand, with complex behavior problems requiring substantial and permanent changes in the way parents respond to the child, long-term outcomes are less encouraging. It appears that brief treatment programs that terminate without needed follow-up and booster-session treatment result in relapse (Eyberg & Johnson, 1974; Johnson & Christensen, 1975; Patterson & Fleischman, 1979). Families with severely disturbed children may require long-term treatment with specific steps taken to program in the generalization and maintenance of treatment effects; for families such as these, the concept of termination may be obsolete (Patterson & Fleischman, 1979).

APPROACHES TO FAMILY THERAPY
BASED ON SYSTEMS THEORIES

As our review in the previous section indicates, a number of treatment approaches have been derived from a systems-theory perspective: included among these are Bowen's Family Systems theory (Bowen, 1978), strategic therapy derived from the work of the Palo Alto Group (Haley, 1963; Sluzki, 1978; Watzlowik, Weakland, & Fisch, 1974), and Minuchin's structural family therapy (Minuchin, 1974; Minuchin, Rosman, & Baker, 1978). In addition to these influential models, a number of variants have been reported in the literature, each with their overlapping and distinctive features (Andolfi, 1980; Alexander & Parsons, 1973; Epstein, 1981; Stanton, 1981; Zuk, 1971). Thus, no single approach is subsumed under this theoretical rubric. Given this large number of specific approaches, there have been very few controlled investigations of treatment efficacy. In fact, there have been virtually no controlled outcome studies evaluating the effectiveness of either the Palo Alto approach or Bowen's approach.

Alexander and Parsons (1973) reported one of the most well designed studies in the literature, evaluating the effectiveness of an approach that integrates systems theory and behavioral principles. Compared to alternative treatments based on psychodynamic and Rogerian principles, as well as a control group, this integrative approach reduced recidivism rates in a delinquent population, and also resulted in marked changes for the better on behavioral measures of family functioning. Although these results are impressive, it must be remembered that this study fails to provide a test for the efficacy of a systems-theory-based treatment, since the effective treatment included behavioral techniques.

Minuchin's structural family therapy has led to a number of uncontrolled, clinical outcome studies reporting impressive results for a variety of clinical problems that clinicians acknowledge are exceedingly difficult to treat: delinquency in low-socioeconomic-class families (Minuchin et al., 1967); psychophysiological disorders such as asthma and anorexia nervosa (Liebman et al., 1967; Minuchin et al., 1975; Minuchin, Rosman, & Baker, 1978); psychogenic pain (Berger, Honig, & Liebman, 1977); and elective mutism (Rosenberg & Lindblad, 1978). The only studies, however, that included necessary control groups are two where the identified patient was a drug addict; the results were mixed. One study (Stanton et al., 1979) found that a structural/strategic-therapy approach produced significant reductions in drug use relative to various control groups; generalized improvements in overall social functioning, however, were not apparent. The other study found no significant differences between family therapy and contol subjects (Zeigler-Driscoll, 1977, 1979).

Garrigan and Bambrick (1977, 1979) evaluated the effectiveness of a model of family therapy based on Zuk's work. Although the nature of treatment received by families in the control conditions is not clearly specified, family therapy was effective at eliminating or reducing problematic behaviors in children.

Given the paucity of well-controlled outcome studies, no firm conclusions can be reached at this point regarding the effectiveness of family therapy approaches derived from systems-theory perspectives. However, at least three examples of systems approaches — functional family therapy, structural family therapy, and Zuk's go-between therapy — have generated encouraging findings.

OTHER EMPIRICAL FINDINGS

Gurman and Kniskern (1981) have derived a number of additional conclusions based on their comprehensive review of the family therapy outcome literature. First, the overall success rate of marital therapy is 61 percent, whereas for family therapy the estimated success rate is 73 percent. Second, for some couples and families, marital and family therapy produces deterioration. Third, for nonbehavioral marital therapy, conjoint therapy is the treatment of choice, relative to couples groups and individual psychotherapy. Fourth, family therapy is at least as effective, and probably more effective, than individual therapy for problems where there is significant marital and family conflict. Fifth, brief treatment (up to 20 sessions) may be just as effective as more extended treatment. ment.

Future Directions

Marital and family therapy have become extremely popular treatment modalities in the past decade. In many respects, the recent emphasis on working with more than one family member at a time constitutes a revolution in the practice of psychotherapy. Yet the popularity of marital and family therapy greatly exceeds the empirical evidence supporting the effectiveness of these modalities. As in many areas of psychotherapy, enthusiasm outstrips rigor. We are concerned about this. Marital and family therapy must be made accountable to the consumer. We believe that it is the responsibility of all advocates and enthusiasts of marital and family therapy to document the effectiveness of their techniques. The marked indifference on the part of the major schools of marital and family therapy to experimental demonstrations of efficacy casts a pall on an otherwise creative and vital field. We hope that this changes. Unfortunately, the history of psychotherapy does not lead us to be optimistic about the growing accountability of the marital and family therapy enterprise. Thus, although it is a recommendation for future research, it is, sadly, a hope rather than an expectation.

We would also like to see some definitive work on the role of family systems in generating individual problems in living. Extremists in the field of family therapy view all dysfunctional behavior in individuals as reflecting some sort of family-system problem. It follows from this extreme position that family therapy is the treatment of choice for virtually all traditional psychiatric problems. The question is, exactly what *is* the role of families in generating problems in living for their constituents? How important are faulty or dysfunctional family interaction patterns as causal variables for the major categories of individual psychopathology? Thus far, there is very little evidence in support of the contention that family systems play important etiological roles. In fact, in the earliest and most extensive attempt on the part of family-systems adherents to explain individual psychopathology, the double-bind theory of schizophrenia, subsequent research has repudiated this model as a viable causal explanation for schizophrenic disorders. Although the general etiological contention may seem self-evident to clinicians working with families, science is by definition skeptical about anecdotes. There has been little work done thus far to assuage these doubts.

Third, the method or technology needs to be distinguished from the one who provides the services. The skill level of the therapist must play some role in treatment outcome above and beyond the viability of the therapeutic modality in question. Instead of simply asking, for example, how effective is structural family therapy, it is necessary to add the proviso, "Structural family therapy as conducted by whom?" If clients treated by Milton Erickson respond brilliantly to therapy but their disciples produce a significantly lower percentage of positive outcomes, then the anecdotes provided in seminal works on family therapy tell us little about the method per se. Moreover, the issue of disseminability and teachability is critical to an evaluation of any model of marital and family therapy: How rapidly and thoroughly can students in training learn to treat couples successfully within a particular theoretical framework?

Summary and Conclusions

This chapter has surveyed the rapidly expanding fields of marital and family therapy. We provided an historical introduction, a survey of the major models, and a summary of current empirical research. It is virtually impossible to do justice to the richness and diversity of this area in a brief chapter. It is our belief that some very creative and innovative work has been done in the last 15 years. We hope that such work continues.

References

Ackerman, N. W. *The psychodynamics of family life.* New York: Basic Books, 1958.

Alexander, J. F., & Parsons, B. V. Short-term behavioral intervention with delinquent families: Impact on family process and recidivism. *Journal of Abnormal Psychology*, 1973, **81**, 219–225.

Allen, D., & Harris, F. Elimination of a child's excessive scratching by training the mother in reinforcement procedures. *Behaviour Research and Therapy*, 1966, **4**, 79–84.

Andolfi, M. Prescribing the families own dysfunctional rules as a therapeutic strategy. *Journal of Marital and Family Therapy*, 1980, **6**, 29–36.

Aponte, H. J., & Van Deusen, J. M. Structural family therapy. In A. S. Gurman and D. P. Kniskern (Eds.),

Handbook of family therapy. New York: Brunner/Mazel, 1981.

Arnold, J. E., Levine, A. G., & Patterson, G. R. Changes in sibling behavior following family intervention. *Journal of Consulting and Clinical Psychology*, 1975, **43**, 683–688.

Azrin, N. H., Besalel, V. A., Bechtel, R., Michalicek, A., Mancera, M., Carroll, D., Shuford, D., & Cox, J. Comparison of reciprocity and discussion-type counseling for marital problems. *American Journal of Family Therapy*, 1980, **8**, 21–28.

Barton, C., & Alexander, J. F. Functional family therapy. In A. S. Gurman & D. P. Kniskern (Eds.), *Handbook of family therapy.* New York: Brunner/Mazel, 1981.

Bateson, G., Jackson, D. D., Haley, J., & Weakland, J. H. Toward a theory of schizophrenia. *Behavioral Science*, 1956, **1**, 251–264.

Baucom, D. H. A comparison of behavioral contracting and problem-solving/communications training in behavioral marital therapy. *Behavior Therapy*, 1982, **13**, 162–174.

Berger, H., Honig, P., & Liebman, R. Recurrent abdominal pain: Gaining control of the symptom. *American Journal of Disorders of Childhood*, 1977, **131**, 1,340–1,344.

Berkowitz, B. P., & Graziano, A. M. Training parents as behavior therapists: A review. *Behaviour Research and Therapy*, 1972, **10**, 297–317.

Birchler, G. R., Weiss, R. L., & Vincent, J. P. A multimethod analysis of social reinforcement exchange between distressed and nondistressed spouse and stranger dyads. *Journal of Personality and Social Psychology*, 1975, **31**, 349–360.

Bodin, A. M. The interactional view: Family therapy approaches of the mental research institute. In A. S. Gurman & D. P. Kniskern (Eds.), *Handbook of family therapy.* New York: Brunner/Mazel, 1981.

Bowen, M. *Family therapy in clinical practice.* New York: Jason Aronson, 1978.

Broderick, C. B., & Schrader, S. S. The history of professional marriage and family therapy. In A. S. Gurman & D. P. Kniskern (Eds.), *Handbook of family therapy.* New York: Brunner/Mazel, 1981.

Crowe, M. J. Conjoing marital therapy: A controlled outcome study. *Psychological Medicine*, 1978, **8**, 623–636.

Dicks, H. V. *Marital tensions.* New York: Basic Books, 1967.

Einsenstein, V. W. (Ed.) *Neurotic interaction in marriage.* New York: Basic Books, 1956.

Ellis, H. *Studies in the psychology of sex.* New York: Random House, 1936.

Emmelkamp, P., van der Helm, M., MacGillavry, D., & van Zanten, B. Marital therapy with clinically distressed couples: A comparative evaluation of systems-theoretic, contingency contracting and communication skills approaches. Paper presented at the Symposium, "Marital interaction: Analysis and modification," Munich, July 1981.

Epstein, N. B., & Bishop, D. S. Problem-centered systems therapy of the family. In A. S. Gurman & D. P. Kniskern (Eds.), *Handbook of family therapy.* New York: Brunner/Mazel, 1981.

Erikson, E. H. *Identity and the life cycle.* New York: International Universities Press, 1959.

Eyberg, S. M., & Johnson, S. M. Multiple assessment of behavior modifiction with families: Effects of contingency contracting and order of treated problems. *Journal of Consulting and Clinical Psychology*, 1974, **42**, 594–606.

Forehand, R. Child noncompliance to parental requests: Behavioral analysis and treatment. In M. Hersen, R. M. Eisler, & P. M. Miller (Eds.), *Progress in behavior modification*. New York: Academic Press, 1977.

Framo, J. L. The integration of marital therapy with sessions with family of origin. In A. S. Gurman & D. P. Kniskern (Eds.), *Handbook of family therapy*. New York: Brunner/Mazel, 1981.

Freud, S. *General introduction to psychoanalysis*. New York: Liveright, 1915.

Fromm, E. *Escape from freedom*. New York: Farrar & Rinehart, 1941.

Garrigan, J. J., & Bambrick, A. F. Family therapy for disturbed children: Some experimental results in special education. *Journal of Marriage and Family Counseling*, 1977, **3**, 83–93.

Garrigan, J. J., & Bambrick, A. F. New findings in research on go-between process. *International Journal of Family Therapy*, 1979, **1**, 76–85.

Gordon, S. B., & Davidson, N. Behavioral parent training. In A. S. Gurman & D. P. Kniskern (Eds.), *Handbook of family therapy*. New York: Brunner/Mazel, 1981.

Gottman, J. M. *Marital interaction: Experimental investigations*. New York: Academic Press, 1979.

Graziano, A. M. Parents as behavior therapists. In M. Hersen, R. M. Eisler, & P. M. Miller (Eds.), *Progress in behavior modification*. New York: Academic Press, 1977.

Guerney, B. G., Jr. *Relationship enhancement*. San Francisco: Jossey-Bass, 1977.

Gurman, A. S. Marital therapy: Emerging trends in research and practice. *Family Process*, 1973, **12**, 45–54.

Gurman, A. S. Contemporary marital therapies: A critique and comparative analysis of psychoanalytic, behavioral and systems theory approaches. In T. J. Paolino & B. S. McCrady (Eds.), *Marriage and marital therapy*. New York: Brunner/Mazel, 1978.

Gurman, A. S., & Kniskern, D. P. Research on marital and family therapy: Progress, perspective and prospect. In S. L. Garfield & A. E. Bergin (Eds.), *Handbook of psychotherapy and behavior change: An empirical analysis*, (2nd ed.) New York: Wiley, 1978.

Gurman, A. S., & Kniskern, D. P. Family therapy outcome research: Knowns and unknowns. In A. S. Gurman & D. P. Kniskern (Eds.), *Handbook of family therapy*. New York: Brunner/Mazel, 1981.

Hahlweg, K., Revenstorf, D., & Schindler, L. Treatment of marital distress: Comparing formats and modalities. *Advances in Behaviour Research and Therapy*, in press.

Haley, J. *Strategies of psychotherapy*. New York: Grune & Stratton, 1963.

Haley, J. *Uncommon therapy*. New York: Norton, 1973.

Haley, J. *Problem solving therapy*. San Francisco: Jossey-Bass, 1976.

Heiman, J. R., LoPiccolo, L., & LoPiccolo, J. The treatment of sexual dysfunction. In A. S. Gurman & D.

P. Kniskern (Eds.), *Handbook of family therapy*. New York: Brunner/Mazel, 1981.

Horney, K. *New ways in psychoanalysis*. New York: Norton, 1939.

Jacobson, N. S. Problem solving and contingency contracting in the treatment of marital discord. *Journal of Consulting and Clinical Psychology*, 1977, **45**, 92–100.

Jacobson, N. S. A review of the research on the effectiveness of marital therapy. In T. J. Paolino & B. S. McCrady (Eds.), *Marriage and marital therapy: Psychoanalytic, behavioral, and systems theory perspectives*. New York: Brunner/Mazel, 1978. (a)

Jacobson, N. S. Specific and nonspecific factors in the effectiveness of a behavioral approach to the treatment of marital discord. *Journal of Consulting and Clinical Psychology*, 1978, **46**, 442–452. (b)

Jacobson, N. S. Behavioral treatments for marital discord: A critical appraisal. In M. Hersen, R. M. Eisler, & P. M. Miller (Eds.), *Progress in behavior modification*. New York: Academic Press, 1979. (a)

Jacobson, N. S. Increasing positive behavior in severely distressed adult relationships. *Behavior Therapy*, 1979, **10**, 311–326. (b)

Jacobson, N. S., & Anderson, E. A. The effects of behavior rehearsal and feedback on the acquisition of problem solving skills in distressed and nondistressed couples. *Behaviour Research and Therapy*, 1980, **18**, 25–36.

Jacobson, N. S., & Margolin, G. *Marital therapy: Strategies based on social learning and behavior exchange principles*. New York: Brunner/Mazel, 1979.

Jacobson, N. S., & Moore, D. Spouses as observers of the events in their relationship. *Journal of Consulting and Clinical Psychology*, 1981, **49**, 269–277.

Jacobson, N. S., Waldron, H., & Moore, D. Toward a behavioral profile of marital distress. *Journal of Consulting and Clinical Psychology*, 1980, **48**, 696–703.

Jackson, D. D. Family interaction, family homeostasis, and some implications for conjoint family therapy. In J. Masserman (Ed.), *Individual and family dynamics*. New York: Grune & Stratton, 1959.

Johnson, S. M., & Christensen, A. Multiple criteria follow-up of behavior modification with families. *Journal of Abnormal Child Psychology*, 1975, **3**, 135–154.

Johnson, S. M., & Lobitz, G. K. Parental manipulation of child behavior in home observations. *Journal of Applied Behavior Analysis*, 1974, **7**, 23–31.

Kaplan, H. *The new sex therapy*. New York: Brunner/Mazel, 1974.

Karoly, P., & Rosenthal, M. Training parents in behavior modification: Effects on perceptions of family interaction and deviant behavior. *Behavior Therapy*, 1977, **8**, 406–410.

Liebman, R., Honig, P., & Berger, H. An integrated treatment program for psychogenic pain. *Family Process*, 1976, **15**, 397–405.

LoPiccolo, J., & Hogan, D. Multidimensional behavioral treatment of sexual dysfunction. In O. Pomerleau & J. P. Brady (Eds.), *Behavioral medicine: Theory and practice*. Baltimore: Williams & Wilkins, 1979.

LoPiccolo, J., & Lobitz, W. C. The role of masturbation in the treatment of orgasmic dysfunction. *Archives of Sexual Behavior*, 1972, **2**, 163–172.

Margolin, G. Behavior exchange in happy and unhappy

marriages: A family cycle perspective. *Behavior Therapy*, 1981, **12**, 329–343.

Margolin, G., & Wampold, B. E. Sequential analysis of conflict and accord in distressed and nondistressed marital partners. *Journal of Consulting and Clinical Psychology*, 1981, **49**, 554–567.

Margolin, G., & Weiss, R. L. Comparative evaluation of therapeutic components associated with behavioral marital treatments. *Journal of Consulting and Clinical Psychology*, 1978, **46**, 1,476–1,486.

Markman, H. J. Application of a behavioral model of marriage in predicting relationship satisfaction of couples planning marriage. *Journal of Consulting and Clinical Psychology*, 1979, **47**, 743–749.

Masters, W. H., & Johnson, V. E. *Human sexual inadequacy*. Boston: Little, Brown, 1970.

Meisner, W. J. The conceptualization of marriage and marital disorders from a psychoanalytic perspective. In. T. J. Paolino Jr. & B. S. McCrady (Eds.), *Marriage and marital therapy: Psychoanalytic, behavioral, and systems theory perspectives*. New York: Brunner/Mazel, 1978.

Melman, K. N., & Jacobson, N. S. The integration of behavioral marital therapy and sex therapy. In M. L. Aronson & L. R. Wolberg, (Eds.), *Group and family therapy 1983—An overview*. New York: Brunner/Mazel, in press.

Minuchin, S. *Families and family therapy*. Cambridge, Mass.: Harvard University Press, 1974.

Minuchin, S., Montalvo, B., Guerney, B., Rosman, B., & Schumer, F. *Families of the slums*. New York: Basic Books, 1967.

Minuchin, S., Rosman, B., & Baker, L. *Psychosomatic families*. Cambridge, Mass.: Harvard University Press, 1978.

Mudd, E. H. *The practice of marriage counseling*. New York: Association Press, 1951.

O'Dell, S. Training parents in behavior modification: A review. *Psychological Bulletin*, 1974, **81**, 418–433.

O'Leary, K. D., & Turkewitz, H. The treatment of marital disorders from a behavioral perspective. In T. J. Paolini, Jr., & B. S. McCrady (Eds.), *Marriage and marital therapy: Psychoanalytic, behavioral, and systems theory perspectives*. New York: Brunner/Mazel, 1978.

Papp, P. Paradoxical strategies and countertransference. *American Journal of Family Therapy*, 1979, 7, 11–12.

Patterson, G. R. *Families: Applications of social learning to family life*. Champaign, Ill.: Research Press, 1971.

Patterson, G. R. Interventions for boys with conduct problems: Multiple settings, treatments, and criteria. *Journal of Consulting and Clinical Psychology*, 1974, **42**, 471–481.

Patterson, G. R., Cobb, J. A., & Ray, R. S. A social engineering technology for retraining the families of aggressive boys. In H. E. Adams & I. P. Unikel (Eds.), *Issues and trends in behavior therapy*. Springfield, Ill.: C. C. Thomas, 1972.

Patterson, G. R., & Fleischman, M. J. Maintenance of treatment effects: Some considerations concerning family systems and follow-up data. *Behavior Therapy*, 1979, **10**, 168–185.

Patterson, G. R., Reid, J. B., Jones, R. R., & Conger, R. E. *A social learning approach to family intervention: Families with aggressive children*. Eugene, Oreg.: Castalia, 1975.

Rich, M. E. *A belief in people: A history of family social work*. New York: Family Service Association of America, 1956.

Rogers, C. R. *Client-centered therapy*. Boston: Houghton-Mifflin, 1951.

Rosenberg, J. B., & Lindblad, M. B. Behavior therapy in a family context: Elective mutism. *Family Process*, 1978, **17**, 77–82.

Sager, C. J. The treatment of married couples. In S. Arieti (Ed.), *American handbook of psychiatry*, (Vol. 3). New York: Basic Books, 1966.

Sager, C. J. *Marriage contracts and couple therapy*. New York: Brunner/Mazel, 1976.

Sager, C. J. Couples therapy and marriage contracts. In A. S. Gurman & D. P. Kniskern (Eds.), *Handbook of family therapy*. New York: Brunner/Mazel, 1981.

Satir, V. *Conjoint family therapy*. Palo Alto, Calif.: Science and Behavior Books, 1964.

Semans, J. H. Premature ejaculation: A new approach. *Southern Medical Journal*, 1956, **49**, 353–357.

Sluzki, C. E. Marital therapy from a systems theory perspective. In T. J. Paolino & B. S. McCrady (Eds.), *Marriage and marital therapy: Psychoanalytic, behavioral and systems theory perspectives*. New York: Brunner/Mazel, 1978.

Spiegel, J. P., & Bell, N. W. The family of the psychiatric patient. In S. Arieti (Ed.), *American handbook of psychiatry*, (Vol. 1). New York: Basic Books, 1959.

Stanton, M. D. Strategic approaches to family therapy. In A. S. Gurman & D. P. Kniskern (Eds.), *Handbook of family therapy*. New York: Brunner/Mazel, 1981.

Stanton, M. D., & Todd, T. C. Structural family therapy with drug addicts. In E. Kaufman & P. Kaufman (Eds.), *The family therapy of drug and alcohol abuse*. New York: Gardner, 1979.

Stuart, R. B. *Helping couples change: A social learning approach to marital therapy*. New York: Guilford, 1980.

Sullivan, H. S. *Interpersonal theory of psychiatry*. New York: Norton, 1953.

Thibaut, J. W., & Kelley, H. H. *The social psychology of groups*. New York: Wiley, 1959.

Turkewitz, H., & O'Leary, K. D. A comparative outcome study of behavioral marital therapy and communication therapy. *Journal of Marital and Family therapy*, 1981, 159–169.

Vincent, J. P., Weiss, R. L., & Birchler, G. R. A behavioral analysis of problem-solving in distressed and nondistressed married and stranger dyads. *Behavior Therapy*, 1975, **6**, 475–487.

Wahler, R. G. Oppositional children: A quest for parental reinforcement control. *Journal of Applied Behavior Analysis*, 1969, **2**, 159–170.

Watzlawick, P., Beavin, J. H., & Jackson, D. D. *Pragmatics of human communication*. New York: Norton, 1967.

Watzlawick, P., Weakland, J., & Fisch, R. *Change: Principles of problem formation and problem resolution*. New York: Norton, 1974.

Weiss, R. L., Hops, H., & Patterson, G. R. A framework for conceptualizing marital conflict, technology for altering it, some data for evaluating it. In L. A. Hamerlynck, L. C. Handy, & E. J. Mash (Eds.), *Behavior* change: Methodology, concepts, and practice. Champaign, Ill.: Research Press, 1973.

Whitaker, C. A., & Keith, D. V. Symbolic-experiential family therapy. In A. S. Gurman & D. P. Kniskern (Eds.), Handbook of family therapy. New York: Brunner/Mazel, 1981.

Wills, T. A., Weiss, R. L., & Patterson, G. R. A behavioral analysis of the determinants of marital satisfaction. Journal of Consulting and Clinical Psychology, 1974, 42, 802–811.

Wolpe, J. Psychotherapy by reciprocal inhibition. Stanford: Calif.: Stanford University Press, 1958.

Zeigler-Driscoll, G. Family research study at Eagleville Hospital and Rehabilitation Center. Family Process, 1977, 16, 175–190.

Zeigler-Driscoll, G. The similarities in families of drug dependents and alcoholics. In E. Kaufman & P. Kaufman (Eds.), The family therapy of drug and alcohol abuse. New York: Gardner, 1979.

Zuk, G. H. Family therapy: A triadic-based approach. New York: Behavioral Publications, 1971.

32 PHARMOCOTHERAPY

Geary S. Alford

Although psychoactive drugs have been used for thousands of years for religious, medical, and recreational purposes, the broad-scale use of chemical agents in the treatment of psychological disorders is a relatively recent development. Prior to World War II, comparatively few hospitalized psychiatric patients were regularly maintained on any psychoactive compound, although in instances of acute agitation or violent outbursts, a patient might be given a sedating dose of a barbiturate and subsequently confined in a padded room or placed in a straightjacket. Use of pharmacologic compounds for psychiatric outpatients, aside from occasional sleeping pills, was rare indeed and was even opposed by many leading psychoanalysts. To be sure, there were individuals and institutions that experimented with pharmacological agents in treating various behavioral disorders such as use of heroin or cocaine in treating morphinism or barbiturate-induced prolonged sleep for "irritated" nerves. In general, however, the undesirable pharmacological properties of the available drugs outweighed the limited therapeutic benefits. Barbiturates, for example, might well temporarily sedate a highly aroused psychotic patient. Unfortunately, many patients exhibited a phase of "paradoxical stimulation," the so-called "release phenomenon," shortly after drug administration, and prior to the full sedative effects produced by barbiturates. Thus, patients often exhibited increased arousal, agitation, and sometimes violence prior to sedation. Second, tolerance to barbiturates develops relatively rapidly, requiring increased doses, and thus leading to physical addiction. Finally, sedation on barbiturates left most psychotic patients so intoxicated that they were considered unable, while in such a state, to engage in formal psychotherapy. In short, there was little specificity of action, drug responses were unpredictable, and long-term administration could not be employed without engendering an added major problem of chemical addiction.

Modern psychopharmacology and pharmacotherapy really began at the midpoint of this century, just 30 years ago. In a brief ten-year span between 1950 and 1960, nearly all of the pharmacotherapeutic agents or the prototypes of drugs currently in use were introduced: the first truly antipsychotic compound, chlorpromazine (Thorazine), the first antidepressants, monoamine oxidase inhibitors (e.g., iproniazid) and tricyclic antidepressants (e.g., imipramine), the antimania preparation of the cationic salt Lithium carbonate, and the first compound to be more anxiolytic than simply sedating, meprobamate (e.g., Miltown) and subsequently benzodiazepines (e.g., Librium).

Introduction of these drugs met with a mixed reception (Tourney, 1967). Many traditionally trained psychotherapists tended to ignore what limited clinical pharmacological data were then available. They discounted the utility of pharmacotherapy as treating *symptoms* but not the true, underlying psychiatric disorder (a reaction curiously recapitulated a decade later in response to the emergence of another empirically based mode of behavior change, behavior therapy). On the other hand, the mid-1950s was the period in which science emerged as the preeminent intellectual force of the 20th century. This was the atomic age, the era of Sputnik, the Salk vaccine, DNA, and the fascination and promises of scientific technology exemplified by the electronic computer and the television set. In this atmosphere of excitement in experimentation and optimism in science, biobehavioral researchers saw the psychoactive drugs as a new and additional means of investigating finer, more subtle brain-behavior relationships. Chemical compounds are *real* in the material sense. They can be analyzed, formulated, and quantified. And, as independent variables, they can be experimentally administered and removed or withdrawn. They and their pharmacologic properties can be empirically examined and conceptualized in relation to other physical structures and empirical phenomena: neuroanatomy, neurochemistry, and brain physiology. In addition to their pragmatic clinical potential, it was thought that these new drugs could contribute to the discovery of complex brain processes, and perhaps even to identify the true underlying biological bases of abnormal behavior.

Chemical compounds that alter not only the arousal level of human beings, but indeed alter mood, thought processes, and even content of thinking obviously do so by their chemical action in brain structures and function and not by modifying metaphysical constructs like ego strength or ego integration. This recognition led many behavioral scientists to eschew psychoanalytic formulations of behavior and behavioral disorders and to embrace, perhaps at times equally narrowly, purely biological speculations. Others attempted a rather dissonant integration of biological and psychoanalytic concepts. Picking up on this latter view, pharmaceutical companies throughout the 1960s advertized their drugs with such descriptions as "psychic energizers" (i.e., stimulants and antidepressants), or as "reducing underlying psychic tensions" (anxiolytics), or "ego integrators" (neuroleptics). While adopting somewhat more behavioral terminology in the 1970s, pharmaceutical houses continue this essentially dualistic perspective in part because it reflects the thinking of the majority of practicing clinicians. Nevertheless, the reliance on controlled, experimental investigation, use of measurable dependent behavioral variables, and the conceptualization and interpretation of independent-dependent variable events within the context of empirically derived pharmacological and psychological principles characterizes the core of basic psychopharmacologic research over the last 30 years (see Lipton, DiMascio, & Killam, 1978).

The concurrent clinical use of these compounds, unfortunately, often has not been quite so well guided by either the basic pharmacologic data, controlled clinical research, or a coherent biobehavioral theoretical system. Although new, potentially pharmacotherapeutic compounds must undergo rigorous and extensive tests for safety (i.e., for potentially dangerous and undesirable side-effects to the user or offspring) and for efficacy before being approved by the Food and Drug Admistration (FDA) for general use, actual clinical practices vary greatly among physicians and at times are at variance with basic pharmacological knowledge. Perhaps this is most clearly exemplified in the use of central nervous system (CNS) depressants such as barbiturates and benzodiazepines. Many patients complaining of chronic sleep disturbance have been maintained on regular bedtime doses of barbiturates for months or even years. Yet, controlled laboratory and sleep-EEG studies show that not only do barbiturates interfere with normal sleep cycles, but these compounds begin to lose their effectiveness as sleep-inducing agents within a few weeks of chronic administration (Institute of Medicine, 1979). Similarly, many patients with tension or anxiety-based behavioral problems are maintained over several years on one or more anxiolytics (like the benzodiazepines, Librium and Valium). Pharmacologically, it is known that tolerance develops with these compounds, resulting in decreased pharmacotherapeutic effects, thus requiring either a higher or more frequent dose of a smiliar but more potent agent to achieve the same therapeutic benefit. Moreover, these compounds have physically addicting properties. Further, clinical research literature documents the efficacy of new psychotherapeutic treatments (e.g., systematic desensitization, flooding, cognitive restructuring) for such anxiety-related behavioral problems in which drug therapy is usually unnecessary. Physicians, including psychiatrists, have generally been resistant to learning and applying these new procedures because to do so would require additional training. Particularly for the nonpsychiatric physician, application of these behavioral treatments requires substantially more office time than is usually available for an individual patient. Additional factors in this resistance are that these new therapies were developed primarily by psychologists who are increasingly in competition with medical psychotherapists, that behavioral formulations and concepts are often at variance with traditional psychodynamic theory, and that behavior therapeutic procedures are derived from a body of knowledge in which most physicians have had little education or training (i.e., basic experimental psychology). On the other hand, usually lacking training in pharmacology and unlicensed to prescribe drugs, psychologists generally have downplayed or even ignored pharmacologic contributions to behavior and therapy. In a recent survey of articles published between 1972 and 1980 in three leading psychological journals, Pishkin and Sengel (1982) found that only a small fraction of the studies that involved patients with psychologic-psychiatric diagnoses reported any information about medication the patient-subjects may have been taking. The percentages of articles in which no medication information was reported ranged from 81 percent in one journal to 94 percent in a third (Pishkin & Sengel, 1982). Since many of the patients, particularly the 176,760 inpatients included among these studies, where likely to have been on some type of medication, Pishkin and Sengel justifiably question the validity of conclusions drawn in such articles. In addition, even where medication is mentioned in many psychological studies, such crucial information as dosage, administration schedule, length of time the patient has been on or recently taken off of medication goes unreported. Finally, some articles do provide such information but unfortunately ignore fundamental principles of pharmacokinetics in planning their research design. For example, it is not uncommon to read articles in which drug treatment phases are substantially shorter than the time required for certain classes of pharmacologic compounds to exert clinical therapeutic action.

Even psychological approaches that claim close ties to basic, empirical, laboratory and clinical methods and knowledge bases have only recently begun to recognize and explore specific conjunctive behavioral and pharmacologic intervention programs (Alford & Williams, 1980).

Another area of inconsistency between experimental behavioral pharmacology and clinical conceptualization involved the tendency of many biologically oriented theoreticians to overinterpret the theoretical implications of the data. Perhaps the most common error in this regard is the *post hoc, ergo propter hoc* etiologic-pathogenic conclusion. It usually goes something like this: "Since drugs affect the biological bases of behavior, if a drug effectively results in altering an abnormal behavior pattern toward the direction of normal functioning, this fact supports [often said with force of "proves"] a biologic pathogenesis for that abnormal behavior pattern." Although not often articulated this simply, particularly in written material, such notions are quite commonly offered in lectures, grand rounds, and professional convention presentations, and if carefully structured and eloquently delivered may initially appear persuasive. For example, let us assume that we could document that patients who complain of depression and have such symptoms as sleep disturbance, decreased appetite, and crying spells all have decreased CNS factor-X concentrations. Further, we show that tricyclic antidepressants in fact increase CNS factor-X levels and produce an amelioration of the depression. Here we would have not only the documented clinical effects and probable mechanism of action of these antidepressants, we would also have replicated data that these patients had decreased factor-X concentrations at the time of the depression and that this reversed after drug therapy. Tempting? Yes. Suggestive? Yes. But, of course, not sufficient for any etiologic conclusion. What we would have come close to establishing would be some (possibly *the*) biological *correlates* of depression but not necessarily the *causes* of depression. We might very well find (and, indeed, were this relationship between brain factor-X and depression true, reliable, and invariant, we most certainly would find) that individuals profoundly depressed during the grief reaction to the sudden, accidental death of a spouse also had decreased factor-X. The significant and variance-controlling independent etiologic variable then would be the loss and grief reaction, not the biological mechanism or substrate.

If we return to the initial syllogism and make a few substitutions of terms, perhaps we can identify some ambiguities that lead such theorists astray. First, drugs affect the biological components (or correlates or substrates or mechanisms) of behavior, not necessarily the *bases,* in the sense of *causes,* of behavior. Abnormal behavior does not necessarily imply abnormal physiology. Second, modification of behavior in the direction of desirable overt action by chemicals does not necessarily mean that the underlying biological processes are functioning more "normally." Indeed, "normal" or desirable overt behavior may at times be achieved by chemically inducing "abnormal" physiological processes. For example, low-level alcohol intoxication may temporarily facilitate a socially anxious (phobic) individual's performance of certain social skills, while temporary impairment of normal receptor sensitivity by a topical anesthetic may increase the latency to orgasm in a premature ejaculator. Third, with respect to the initial syllogism, even the identified presence of some abnormal physiological process does not necessarily indicate that this was endogenous and independently produced or caused the abnormal behavior.

A similar fallacy complicating the interpretation and understanding of pharmacotherapeutic-brain-behavior relationships is the tendency to assume that similar abnormal behavior necessarily entails the same biological processes, etiology, and pathogenesis. To return to the hypothetical data and depressed patients, this fallacy is often exemplified as follows: "If *n* number of patients have been found to have a genetically inherited, ribonucleic acid controlled, cyclical abnormal production of brain factor-X whose symptoms include feelings of depression, fatigue, and loss of appetite, and patient A presents complaining of the same symptoms and is also found (at this point in time) to have a lower than normal CNS factor-X concentration, then patient A has the same genetically inherited depressive disorder." If, however, our patient A is the same hypothetical patient in the midst of severe grief described earlier, then we can see the fallacy of assuming similar pathogenesis for similar behaviors even if many of the biological concomitants were found to be the same. Clearly, actual empirical findings analogous to the hypothetical examples described above do raise the possibility of physiological-biochemical pathogenesis. To determine whether such evidence reveals something about pathogenesis as well as

about possible biological substrates, converging sources of data would be necessary. From the biochemical-pharmacological point of view, to establish a purely biological pathogenesis it would be necessary to show that some biochemical, metabolic defect exists prior to the molar behavioral symptoms, that this abnormality was truly endogenous, and that it is both necessary and sufficient for the clinical syndrome to appear. Even this would not exclude the possibility that a similar biobehavioral syndrome might arise from external and cognitive-emotional events and share at least part of a final, common, biological pathway.

Given these caveats, it is also important to recognize that the approach to investigating the causes, physiological processes, and potential cures or treatments for abnormal behavior by biological scientists is not on a track tangential to or inconsistent with empirical behavioral scientists. Converging sources of empirical evidence from psychiatric twin studies and family histories, laboratory genetic studies, research in brain chemistry, pharmacobiochemical as well as clinical pharmacotherapeutic investigations are increasingly persuasive that some behavioral disorders, such as major bipolar affective disorders (manic-depressive disease) and schizophrenias, most probably do have a primarily endogenous biological pathogenesis. The point is that this is not an exclusive track, but one that parallels and interacts with behavioral sciences. Just as early behaviorists tended to ignore, if not dismiss, intraorganismic variables and processes in conceptualizing the development and modification of behavior, many biologically oriented theoreticians tend to ignore the complex, continuous, and inextricable interaction of the internal organism within itself and with its external environment. Such theorists tend to forget that sensory stimuli are not metaphysical constructs, but extraordinarily complex physical events that exert a biological influence, at times a profound and enduring impact upon the physiological activity and indeed chemical structures within the organism. Learning and memory are, after all, ultimately subtle and complex biochemical processes.

Finally, and pragmatically most important, whatever the experimental use of pharmacologic compounds in biobehavioral research may or may not tell us about the pathogenesis, etiology, and underlying biological processes or concomitants of behavior, these drugs do exert a variety of potent effects on sensory, perceptual, cognitive, emotive, motoric, and verbal behaviors. Many of these behavioral pharmacologic properties can provide a valuable and crucial contribution to the therapeutic modification of abnormal behavior.

Basic Pharmacokinetics

Psychopharmacological compounds are classified according to: (1) their chemical structure; (2) their cellular-physiological action, and (3) their effects on molar behavior. For example, trifluoperazine (Stelazine) and perphenazine (Trilafon) may be classed together because they are both piperzine-phenothiazines, (molecular-chemical structure), because they are both dopamine (DA)-blocking agents, that is, they compete with DA or block DA binding sites on the postsynaptic membrane (cellular-physiological action), or because they are both neuroleptic or antipsychotic, that is, they affect a reduction of behaviors that are considered symptomatic of schizophrenic psychoses (molar, clinical behavioral effects). While interrelated, these classifications are not perfectly correlated. Some compounds with similar chemical components and structures may have quite diverse behavioral effects. Similarly, compounds as structurally diverse as ethyl alcohol, phenobarbital, and diazepam (Valium) are all central nervous system (CNS) depressants and can, in varying doses, result in behavioral sedation.

In clinical psychopharmacology, compounds are usually classified primarily by their clinical or molar behavioral action. Secondarily they may be subclassified by their specific cellular-physiological action and by their chemical structure. Thus, the classification "antidepressants" includes the three-ring tricyclic antidepressants whose mode of action is believed to involve blocking reuptake of NE (norepinephrine) by the presynaptic membrane. Also included are the one- or two-ring MAO-inhibitors, whose mode of action is believed to involve inhibition of monoamine-oxidase (MAO), which breaks down (via oxidative deamination) NE and serotonin. Further, drugs are described in terms of their potency, latency of onset of action, and duration and termination of action. Several factors interact to determine a given compound's potency, latency, and duration, as well as its behavioral action.

The elemental components and molecular structure determine the nature and scope of biochemical reactions a given compound will and will not undergo. This provides a degree of specificity of action on the anatomical structures and neurochemical events that a drug can influence or alter, thereby circumscribing the range of its molar behavioral effects. Further, the chemical structure affects the rate at which a drug is absorbed, metabolized, and degraded, its profusion and binding properties, whether it is absorbed and stored in various body tissues (hence its bioavailability and duration of action) and the types of cell tissue, in addition to neuronal tissue, upon which it may exert some or even profound effects.

The rate of absorption and speed required for a compound to reach its target organ is partially determined by route of administration. Route of administration can also influence potency and duration of action. The usual routes of administration for psychoactive pharmaceuticals include: by mouth (per orram, p.o.), intramuscularly (i.m.), and intravenously (i.v.). In behavioral pharmacological studies with animals, additional routes of administration include intraperitoneal (i.p.), and occasionally intraventricular injections are used. Dosage refers to the amount (usually expressed as weight in milligrams) of the active ingredient being administered, not to the composite weight of the active compound and its vehicle. Dosage is usually considered in relation to body weight of the patient or subject, and is commonly expressed as milligrams of drug per kilogram of body weight (mg/kg).

Finally, several idiosyncratic organismic factors interact to influence the nature of drug action. These include: (a) the drug history of the patient or subject; (b) the psychophysiological state of arousal of the subject prior to drug administration; (c) the nature and intensity of external stimuli; (d) the type of environment the subject is in during and following drug administration; and (e) any idiosyncratic hypersensitivity, hyposensitivity, or allergic reactivity a given subject may have for a given compound or class of compounds. When working with infrahuman subjects, species differences account for significant variation in dose-response curves and also for the nature of certain drugs' behavior effects. Occasional articles claim to show that expectancy or environmental setting account for an equal if not greater percentage of the variance as a drug compound itself. Such studies, however, have almost always utilized a nonpatient population and/or administered atypically low doses of the drug under investigation. While expectancy and setting, as noted, can influence behavioral response to a drug, the degree of contribution of such factors is usually inversely proportionate to the potency or dosage of the compound under investigation. In general, as potency or dosage of a psychoactive compound increases, cognitive factors and environmental setting exert proportionately less influence on the central behavioral pharmacologic effect.

Hypnotics, Sedatives, and Anxiolytics

While there are significant differences among the various hypnotic-sedatives and anxiolytics drugs, they share many common properties. All drugs of this type are central nervous system (CNS) depressants. Their administration produces decreased arousal and motor activity, in larger doses, sedation and sleep induction (hence "hypnotic"), and in still larger doses, general anesthesia, coma, and medullary depression resulting in death. They all have some antianxiety (anxiolytic) effects at varying doses. All compounds of this class induce tolerance and physical addiction, though some much more slowly than others. Abrupt cessation of administration once significant tolerance has developed results in a similar abstinence or withdrawal syndrome, including tremors, hallucinations, delirium, and potentially life-threatening convulsions.

The first drug used medicinally as a tranquilizer and as a sleep-inducing agent was, of course, ethyl alcohol. There is evidence that alcohol has been produced and used both socially and medicinally for over eight thousand years. In addition to alcohol, extracts of the poppy and *Cannabis sativa* plants have a long history of use as sedatives and hypnotics. In the 19th century a number of compounds were synthesized that had a more specific pharmacologic action as hypnotics and sedatives. This is in contrast to the use of opium or morphine which we know to be primarily analgesics (pain killers), although in sufficiently high doses they will induce sedation and sleep. These new compounds included the bromide salts (potassium bromide and sodium bromide), the cyclic ether (paraldehyde), and a complex alcohol (chloral hydrate). Although the bromide salts have been abandoned in modern medical practice, paraldehyde and chloral hydrate remain on most hospital formularies and are still administered as sleep-inducing preparations.

In 1864 barbituric acid was first synthesized, and although it has no hypnotic properties itself, it is the core molecule from which numerous effec-

tive hypnotics have been prepared. The first of these was diethylbarbituric acid or barbital (Veronal), introduced in 1903 and found to be an excellent hypnotic, though it has a relatively long duration of action. This ushered in the era of modern hypnotic-sedative pharmaceuticals. Over 2,500 barbiturates have been synthesized, but only a few of these have been found satisfactory for clinical use. Today, there are only a dozen or so barbiturates in wide clinical use; the most common of these are presented in Figure 32.1.

Aside from the fact that barbiturates produce CNS depression, particularly of the ascending reticular activating system (ARAS), little is known of the exact mechanisms of action. More molar behavioral effects, however, are easily observed and have been empirically investigated and documented. While there are individual differences in dose-response reactions, small doses of barbiturates usually result in decreased responsibility to stimulation and subjective feelings of relaxation and tranquilization progressing to sleepiness. Following a somewhat larger dose, a paradoxical state of arousal or excitability is occasionally observed, sometimes having the appearance of drunkenness and, in psychotic patients, agitation or aggressiveness. This "release phenomenon" is

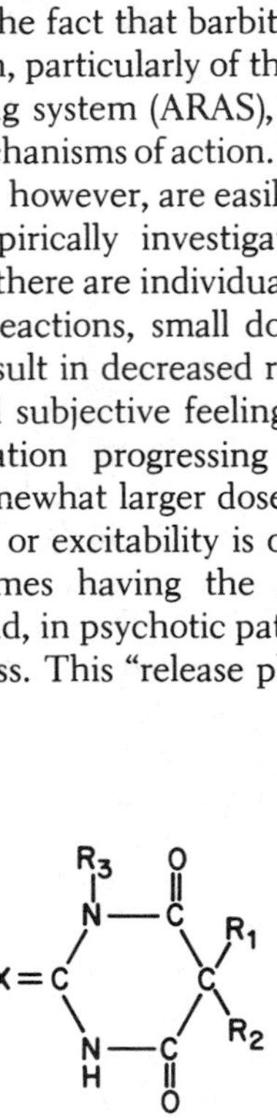

Barbiturate molecule. Substituents attached at X, R_1, R_2, R_3

Ultrashort-acting Barbituates	Intermediate-acting Barbituates
Thiopental (Pentothal)	Amobarbital (Amytal)
Thiamylal (Surital)	
Hexobarbital (Sombucaps)	Long-acting Barbiturates
	Phenobarbital
Short-acting Barbiturates	Mephobarbital
	Metharbital
Pentobarbital (Nembutal)	Primidone (Mysoline)
Secobarbital (Seconal)	

Alchols

Chloral hydrate	Ethchlorvynol (Placidyl)
Ethanol (Whiskey, Beer, Wine)	Phenaglycodol (Ultran)

Fig. 32.1. Hypnotics and sedatives (Trade names given for identification purposes only.)

presumed to result from depression of higher cortical centers thought to exert an inhibitory control on phylogenetically older, lower-brain structures. Unlike the newer benzodiazepine compounds, barbiturates probably do not have an anxianxiety effect apart from their sedative action. Nevertheless, barbiturates have been used not only as hypnotics, but also as anxiolytics.

Since their introduction during the first decade of the 20th century, barbiturates have been used clinically in the treatment of essentially every psychiatric and many neurological disorders. Behavioral disorders for which barbiturates have at one time or another been administered include schizophrenia, manic-depressive disease, alcoholism, insomnia, hyperactivity in children, and all of the neuroses. Aside from their use as anticonvulsants in neurological disorders, barbiturates continue to be used for rapid sedation, in detoxification from hypnotic-sedatives, occasionally for drug-induced hypnotic interviews (e.g., Amytal interview), and for drug-facilitated systematic desensitization and flooding procedures (Alford & Williams, 1980). Because of their significantly increased margin of safety, benzodiazepines have replaced barbiturates as recommended sleep-inducing agents. Similarly, barbiturates are no longer appropriate for use as intermediate or long-action antianxiety agents, although some physicians continue to prescribe them for such purposes. Since 1950, barbiturates have been replaced in the pharmacologic management of schizophrenia by neuroleptics, in control of mania by lithium carbonate, in reduction of anxiety, and even as sedative-hypnotics by benzodiazepine and related compounds. These latter agents are also excellent drugs for detoxification and rapid sedation when administered intravenously. Most have a potent anticonvulsant action. Except for unusual or special circumstances, barbiturates, once a mainstay in the psychiatric pharmacy, are obsolete in the management or treatment of behavioral disorders (see Goodman & Gilman 1975).

Anxiolytics ("Minor Tranquilizers")

Although anxiolytic or antianxiety agents share many common properties with bariturates, there are significant differences that distinguish these subgroups of CNS depressants. While both meprobamates (e.g., Miltown, Equanil) and benzodiazepines (e.g., Valium, Librium, Centrax; see Fig. 32.2) result in CNS depression, their depres-

sant effects are generally less potent and, particularly with benzodiazepines, their margin of safety (i.e., LD_{50}) is substantially greater than that of the barbiturates. Moreover, unlike barbiturates, the antianxiety action of benzodiazepines is largely independent of its hypnotic-sedative action (Goodman & Gilman, 1975). While both barbiturates and benzodiazepines decrease avoidance and escape responding in animals, benzodiazepines can significantly reduce conditioned avoidance responding without impairing appropriate and adaptive escape behaviors (Iverson & Iverson, 1975). Other animal studies have found that operant behaviors established via positive reinforcement (e.g., food-reinforced lever pressing) but subsequently depressed by punishment display substantial reinstatement of high-frequency response rates following benzodiazepine administration. In contrast, administration of amphetamine stimulants (e.g., Benzedrine) or antipsychotic neuroleptics (e.g., Thorazine) to animals so trained either results in no significant change or even further suppresses response rates (Haefely, 1978). Further, some animal studies have found that anxiolytics given in low, nonsedating doses will nonspecifically increase frequency of previously *unpunished* operants as well as those suppressed by punishment training (e.g., Kelleher & Morse, 1964).

Not all the behavioral pharmacologic effects of this class of compounds are desirable. CNS depression from overdose, though significantly less with benzodiazepines than with meprobamates or especially barbiturates, is a serious potential hazard. All of these drugs are essentially cross-tolerant and can potentiate each other. Overdose resulting in death or accidental traumatic injury due to intoxication, particularly when these compounds are mixed with alcohol, are among their most serious liabilities. All of these compounds are potentially physically addicting; abrupt cessation of their use once tolerance and addiction have developed can induce a severe, even life-threatening abstinence syndrome. Intoxication on low to moderate doses resembles intoxication on ethyl alcohol (Smith, Wesson, & Seymour, 1979). And, as with ethyl alcohol, all hypnotic-sedative and minor tranquilizers have state-dependent properties (Alford & Alford, 1976; Overton, 1973). Further, Alford (1981) has described a subclinical abstinence syndrome that may occur during falling drug levels where use of moderate doses of these agents has continued over a long period. Indeed, benzodiaz-

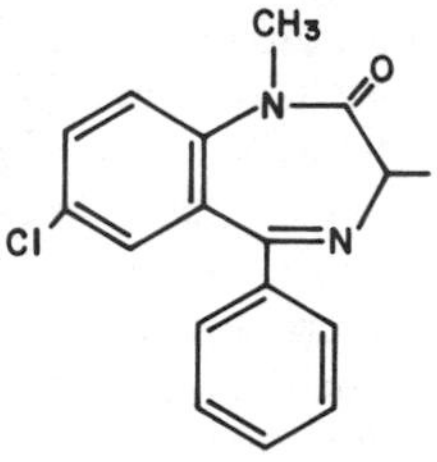

Diazepam
(Valium)

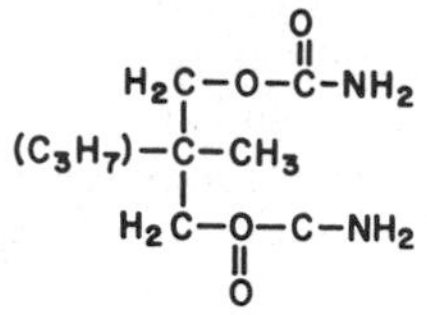

Meprobamate
(Equanil, Miltown)

Short-acting

Methaqualone (Quaalude)
Flurazepam (Dalmane)

Intermediate-acting and Long-acting

Diazepam (Valium)	Chlorazepate (Tranxene)
Meprobamate (Equanil, Miltown)	Chlordiazepoxide (Librium)
Prazepam (Verstran)	Lorazepam (Ativan)
Oxazepam (Serax)	Clorazepate dipotassium (Tranxene)

Fig. 32.2. Sedative-anxiolytics (minor tranquilizers). (Trade names given for identification purposes only.)

epines are among the most used and abused of modern psychopharmacologic agents. Addiction to and dependency on these compounds constitutes one of the most common and serious forms of addictive behavior (see Alford, 1981).

The exact biological mechanisms of action of the different hypnotic-sedative-anxiolytics are still unknown. Some evidence suggests that barbiturates exert their influence on synaptic transmission rather than on neuronal conduction (Nicoll, 1978). Benzodiazepines also may depress synaptic transmission by reducing the turnover rate of the neurotransmitters norepinephrine and serotonin and/or by stimulating the release of gammo-amino butyric acid (GABA), thereby increasing its inhibitory effects (Haefely, 1978; Stein, Wise, & Berger, 1973). While available evidence suggests probable mechanisms for general depressant effects of these compounds, the mechanisms of action for their antianxiety effects, independent of general CNS depression, are unknown. Models that suggest action on the limbic system do so more on the basis of what is known about the role of various limbic nuclei and pathways in "emotional" behavior than on direct evidence of selective action of these drugs on those brain structures.

Clinical Use

Over 90 million prescriptions for nonbarbiturate anxiolytics are filled each year (Cooper, 1978). Although there has been some decline in the number of such prescriptions since a high of 100 million written in 1973, these compounds are among the most prescribed pharmaceuticals in the United States and constitute over 75 percent of all psychoactive medication prescriptions written. Given the potency of these compounds, the available animal and human research literature, their potential hazards and abuse-dependency liabilities, as well as their apparent popularity with physicians, patients, and abusers, one would think that rather clear indications and guidelines for their clinical use would be recommended in standard psychiatric texts. Unfortunately, this is generally not the case. Most texts provide a general discussion of the pharmacology of anxiolytics, note some of their liabilities, and recommend them for control of symptomatic anxiety. Although a few authors strongly recommend only short-term use of anxiolytics (e.g., Freedman, 1981), many influential texts conclude that only the individual physician and patient can determine appropriate indications and protocol of use and, indeed, suggest that anxiolytics may be good for even minor travails of life (e.g., Cole & Davis, 1975a). Although complete data are hard to obtain, studies of prescribing practices (e.g., Cooper, 1978) and anecdotal evidence (such as reviewing patients' charts) indicate that, in practice, anxiolytics are frequently used in the treatment of essentially every form of nonpsychotic, psychiatric disorder in which anxiety or agitation are components. Further, many patients are maintained on anxiolytics over a course of several years. Even patients with primary or secondary diagnoses of chemical dependency are frequently prescribed anxiolytics in attempts to reduce their "psychic tensions," which presumably can trigger episodes of drinking or drug abuse. Many alcoholics, for example, are placed on a benzodiazepine even after detoxification. Others go without specific treatment for their alcoholism and, being advised to reduce their drinking, are placed on an anxiolytic to reduce or control the tension and stress that they and their physician believe causes their excessive drinking in the first place. Since benzodiazepines are almost perfectly cross-tolerant with ethyl alcohol (indeed, they are the current drugs of choice for use in alcohol detoxification) and are themselves potentially intoxicating and addicting, this practice is functionally equivalent to methadone maintenance for opiate-addicted patients. Nevertheless, it is true that most anxiolytics, particularly the benzodiazepines, do have a high margin of safety, are used according to prescribed instructions far more often than they are abused, and can be very effective in reducing anxiety.

Historically, it has been the practice to define "anxiety" as separate and distinct from "fear," primarily on the basis that fears supposedly have identifiable, specific objects, while individuals reporting anxiety cannot (or do not) identify specific stimulus triggers. Similarly, fear is sometimes defined as a reaction to a perceived *physical* threat and anxiety as a reaction to *psychological* threats, such as loss of self-esteem. Psychophysiologically, such distinctions are unwarranted. The physiological components or concomitants (primarily sympathetic hyperarousal and parasympathetic inhibition) of "anxiety attacks," "panic attacks," severe "phobic reactions," and indeed, adaptive *in vivo* fears of actual danger, are biologically identical. The real issue is the extent to which the patient and therapist can identify or uncover the external or internal stimulus events that evoke this aversive autonomic reaction.

Aversive autonomic arousal perceived as anxiety or labeled as tension, stress, nervousness, fear, agitation, or some other name is probably the most common aversive emotional experience. Sometimes these emotional reactions may be associated with relatively discrete and identifiable classes of stimuli. If the stimuli are objectively harmless or entail minimal danger, such reactions are called phobias. If there are a wide variety of stimulus conditions that elicit aversive autonomic arousal or the specific stimuli are vague, obscure, or difficult to identify, the subjective experience may be labeled "free-floating" or even "existential" anxiety. The patient's reported distress may be conceptualized as symptomatic of underlying "psychic conflicts" and as components of other psychological disorders. When one considers how common are the autonomic reactions that can be described or labeled as anxiety, and how often they occur in various physical as well as behavioral disorders, it is easy to see why anxiolytics account for such a large percentage of prescriptions.

In fact, anxiolytics are probably unnecessary in treating the vast majority of anxiety problems. Abundant evidence now exists empirically documenting the efficacy of such procedures as systematic desensitization, flooding, and various cognitive-restructuring strategies for anxiety and anxiety-mediated problems (Leitenberg, 1976). Clinicians evaluating patients who present with such complaints as nervousness, tensions, agitation, anxiety, fearfulness, or apprehension should determine whether the condition appears as a consequence of current, acute life events or whether it constitutes a more long-term or chronic behavioral reaction pattern. If the former is the case, then a short-term course of anxiolytics may be indicated by the degree of disruptive arousal to facilitate the patient's postevent adjustment. If, however, clinical evaluation reveals a more chronic and enduring problem, then appropriate therapeutic intervention aimed at modifying the patient's autonomic and perhaps perceptual-cognitive reaction patterns is indicated. Antianxiety agents may well reduce the patient's anxiety and subjective distress. They do not themselves, however, modify the patient's maladaptive cognitive-emotional repertoire, and undesirable emotional reactions can and indeed theoretically should be expected to return as tolerance to drug effects develops or when anxiolytic pharmacotherapy is discontinued. While the efficacy of many traditional verbal therapies remains questionable, the evidence documenting the effectiveness of behavioral therapies for anxiety disorders is now voluminous (e.g., see Bellack & Hersen, 1977; Leitenberg, 1976). Clinicians who treat chronic anxiety and anxiety-mediated disorders only pharmacotherapeutically (even if ostensibly combined with "psychotherapy"), without a trial of appropriate behavioral psychotherapeutic intervention, are simply not providing their patients with the best interventions currently available.

Anxiolytic pharmacotherapy may, in certain cases, be effectively utilized as a treatment component of various behavioral anxiety-reduction procedures (Alford & Williams, 1980). In cases involving extremely high-level autonomic arousal, for example, some patients may not be able to attain a sufficient state of relaxation through verbal instruction alone to accomplish systematic desensitization successfully. Similarly, some patients may feel unable or unwilling to carry out therapeutic tasks designed to extinguish anxiety reactions, and still others may find certain procedures (e.g., *in vivo* flooding) so aversively anxiety-producing as to withdraw from treatment. In such cases, titrated administration of sedatives or anxiolytics can increase patients' tolerance of previously highly aversive stimulus settings, enhance confrontation and interaction with relevant stimuli, and generally facilitate performance on therapeutic tasks designed to decrease undesirable, disruptive arousal responses. Because of their state-dependent properties, when anxiolytics are used in such therapeutic procedures, it is important to fade drug levels gradually and systematically to zero during active treatment phases (see Alford & Williams, 1980).

No matter how carefully planned and conducted, no set of therapeutics is effective for all patients. Unfortunately, treatment failures often do not make it into journals, especially in those publications primarily identified with the form of therapy that failed. The author, working with medical colleagues, has had a number of patients whose chronic and pervasive anxiety failed to respond to any current behavioral, cognitive, or insight-oriented psychotherapeutic intervention, even when anxiolytics were used as adjuncts. On the other hand, some of these patients whose anxiety seriously impaired their vocational, social, or private behavior were able to function at least adequately when maintained on low to moderate dosage regimens of anxiolytic pharmacotherapy. Some authorities have suggested that many patients with various anxiety disorders are being *undertreated* pharmacologically (Rickels, 1977) and that anxiolytic pharmacotherapy may even be appropriate for individuals who are emotionally overreactive to relatively minor, everyday problems in living (Cole & Davis, 1975a). Although there are no large-scale, hard data on the appropriateness of the 90 million anxiolytic prescriptions written annually, quite a number of patients are prescribed and maintained on anxiolytics agents in lieu of being treated with appropriate, efficacious anxiety-reduction therapies.

In summary, antianxiety agents, particularly the benzodiazepines, have been demonstrated in both animal and human studies to be deserving of the name anxiolytics. Although substantially safer than barbiturates, they do have liabilities, including abuse potential and addictive properties. In view of their behavioral pharmacologic properties together with their liabilities, anxiolytics are indicated where anxiety is at a sufficiently high level to impair an individual's normal behavioral functioning. Mere discomfort is not recommended as a primary indication; rather, evidence of significantly impaired or disrupted function should exist. Second, the clinician should be careful to distinguish between a normal behavioral skill repertoire whose performance is disrupted by anxiety versus behavioral deficits or maladaptive behavior that may be problematic independently of significant anxiety. Indeed, such deficits may produce or contribute to anxiety reactions that are secondary to the individual lacking necessary skills in situations that require or demand the missing repertoire. Further, before embarking on a long-term course of anxiolytic pharmacotherapy, the clinician should provide for a competent, systematic course of behavior therapy, such as systematic desensitization, in cases where anxiety appears *reflexive* to even subtle and obscure stimuli, or cognitive restructuring where anxiety appears to be more the consequence of perceptual and cognitive mediational factors.

Where significantly disruptive anxiety exists, anxiolytics are appropriate: (a) for short-term, transient adjustment reactions, (b) for short-term and gradually reduced or "faded" use, if necessary or significantly facilitory, in systematic anxiety-reduction procedures, or (c) for more long-term use with those few patients who have chronic, disruptively high levels of anxiety *and* for whom a thorough course of an appropriate, empirically documented anxiety reduction procedure has failed. Use of a potentially addicting compound to decrease chronic, minor, autonomic discomfort in response to minor, common, indeed, "normal" life stresses or events should be considered unwarranted, if not contraindicated.

Neuroleptics

The introduction of phenothiazines into the American psychiatry formulary in 1954 ushered in a new age of pharmacotherapy in treating major psychotic disorders. Their clinical use in France for two years before they were approved for use in the United States had already provided some indication of their promise. Neuroleptics, commonly referred to as "antipsychotics" or "major tranquilizers," were found to exert such dramatic and generally desirable effects in most hospitalized schizophrenics that truly revolutionary reforms in mental hospital practices became possible. Not only did physical restraints (straightjackets, padded cells, and traditional sedative compounds) become rarely necessary, but many long-term inpatients were sufficiently improved to be discharged to outpatient status. Even those patients who did not improve sufficiently to be discharged were usually able to be managed in much less restrictive and more constructive ward atmospheres.

Structure and Mechanism of Action

Since the introduction of chlorpromazine (Thorazine), a score of neuroleptic agents have been developed; the more common of these are listed in Table 32.1. The molecular structure and biological mode of actions of neuroleptics are very different from hypnotic sedatives and anxiolytics. Unfortunately, the terms "major tranquilizers" (neuroleptics) and "minor tranquilizers" (anxiolytics)

TABLE 32.1. NEUROLEPTICS (MAJOR TRANQUILIZERS).

DRUG GROUP		CONVERSION FACTOR	SIDE EFFECTS (1=least; 4=most)		DOSE (Range in mg/24 hrs.)
Generic Name	Trade Name		Extrapyramidal	Autonomic	
Phenothiazines					
Aliphatic					
Chlorpromazine	Thorazine	1:1	2	4	300-2500 mg/day
Piperazines					
Trifluoperazine	Stelazine	1:20	4	2	10-40 mg/day
Fluphenazione	Prolixin	1:50	4	2	10-20 mg/day
Perphenazine	Trilafon	1:10	4	2	20-80 mg/day
Piperidines					
Mesoridazine	Serentil	1:2	–	–	150-400 mg/day
Piperacetazine	Quide	1:10	1	–	20-80 mg/day
Thioridazine	Mellaril	1:1	–	4	300-800 mg/day
Butyrophenones					
Haldperidol	Haldol	1:50	4+	1	4-60 mg/day
Thioxanthenes					
Thiothixene	Navane	1:25	4	1	10-60 mg/day
Chloroprothixene	Taractan	1:1	4+	1	
Dihydroindolone					
Molindone	Moban	1:5	–	–	
Dibenzoxazepine					
Loxapine	Loxitane	1:6	3–4+	1	
Dibenzodiazepine					
Clozapine	Leponex	1:2	–	4+	

[1]Estimated dosage ratio in relation to Thorazine. For example, 10 mg. of Stelazine is equivalent to 200 mg. of Thorazine. *Trade names given for identification purposes only

have, at times, led some erroneously to think of neuroleptics as only more potent forms of sedative tranquilizers. Most neuroleptics have a tricyclic nucleus in which two benzine rings are linked by a central ring containing a sulfur atom and a nitrogen atom at which side chains are attached. These tricyclic neuroleptics differ by the constituents of side chains attached to the nitrogen or to the benzine rings. More recently, synthesized neuroleptics, such as haloperidol (Haldol), have altered the tricyclic structure by bonding cyclic components at different points along an alkane chain. All neuroleptics contain one or two amine functions. These variations affect the potency and, to some extent, the side-effects resulting form neuroleptic pharmacotherapy (see Table 32.1).

In spite of a wealth of biochemical research on neuroleptics, the exact mechanisms of action are still unknown. It is known that neuroleptics have multiple biochemical actions in the CNS including effects on alpha-adrenergic, cholinergic, histaminergic, as well as on dopaminergic receptors and on serotonin (5-hydroxytrytamine, 5-HT) metabolism. With respect to antipsychotic effect, the weight of current evidence points to inhibition of dopaminergic function, primarily blockade of postsynaptic dopamine receptor sites as the fundamental mode of action. Although this partial blockade occurs to some extent throughout the brain, a growing body of evidence implicates the mesolimbic dopamine system and its terminals in the paleocortical areas as the critical locus of action (Carlsson, 1978).

In regard to biological theories of schizophrenia, it is interesting to note that amphetamines, known to aggravate schizophrenic psychoses and capable of inducing an acute organic psychosis indistinguishable from paranoid schizophrenia, stimulate release of dopamine (Carlsson, 1978). Further, administration of neuroleptics will usually reverse stimulant-induced psychoses within a few days of initiating pharmacotherapy, and sometimes within a few hours. Still a great deal remains to be discovered about the biological substrates of major psychoses as well as the complex mechanism of action by which antipsychotic compounds exert their influence.

Behavioral Pharmacology and Clinical Use

All neuroleptics have the capacity to produce sedation. While this is not their primary behavioral pharmacologic property, sedation is a useful com-ponent of neuroleptic action particularly when treating extreme arousal, agitation, or aggressive behavior in a psychotic patient. Unlike the hypnotic-sedatives, neuroleptics produce a relatively easily arousable sedation and usually without the ataxia and "intoxication" associated with barbiturate sedation. More importantly, neuroleptics do not have the biphasic action of pseudostimulation or "release phenomenon" preceding sedation that may occur with hypnotic-sedatives. Thus, they can be used to "tranquilize" psychotic excitement without the risk that the medication may initially aggravate the excitement and agitation prior to sedation. Further, neuroleptics are not physically addicting.

It is, however, the antipsychotic action of neuroleptics that constitutes their primary pharmacotherapeutic contribution. Neuroleptics not only reduce arousal symptoms such as agitation, hyperexcitability, and insomnia, but exert a true antipsychotic action on perceptual and cognitive processes. When treated with an adequate dosage of neuroleptics, many, though not all, schizophrenics display a dramatic diminution of cognitive disorganization, looseness of association, thought intrusion or thought derailment, paranoid ideation and general delusional thinking, and remission of bizarre somatic sensation and auditory or visual hallucinations. These effects have been documented in a large number of studies comparing neuroleptics to placebo and other classes of psychoactive compounds. In a survey of 118 clinical studies, Klein and Davis (1969) reported that phenothiazines were significantly superior to placebo in the majority of cases, and that where differences were less striking (particularly in early studies), inadequate dosage had usually been used. In contrast, hypnotic sedatives, such as barbiturates, have consistently failed to produce results superior to placebo in psychotic patients (Baldessarini, 1977). Further, neuroleptic therapy has been shown superior to milieu therapy, group therapy, and individual psychotherapy in schizophrenic populations (Grinspoon, Ewalt, & Shader, 1968; May, 1968). Indeed, the antipsychotic actions of neuroleptics are sufficiently clear and established that it is possible to construct a "time table" of therapeutic response; that is, while there is individual variation, the usual timing, nature, and sequence of behavioral change resulting from neuroleptic therapy for schizophrenia has been identified. Maximum therapeutic response to a neuroleptic requires six to eight weeks on an adequate dose (Baldessarini, 1977; Lehmann, 1966, 1975). Since some clinicians tend to initiate treatment with low or conservative dosages, the time from beginning pharmacotherapy until maximum benefit is obtained may be extended. The first behaviors to be modified are usually the arousal symptoms. Agitation, hyperexcitability, aggressiveness, and insomnia display significant reduction or disappear within the first two weeks. Within four weeks, such affective symptoms as depression, anxiety, and social withdrawal are generally improved. Cognitive and perceptual disturbances, such as hallucinations, delusions, and disorganized cognitive processes (e.g., looseness of association) are usually responsive after six to eight weeks on an adequate dose of a neuroleptic (Lehmann, 1966).

In addition to treating the floridly psychotic schizophrenic, neuroleptics have also been shown to reduce the probability of relapse in schizophrenics who are maintained on them. Davis (1975) reviewed 24 controlled studies on drug maintenance and found a relapse rate of only 30 percent among groups maintained on antipsychotics compared to a relapse rate of 65 percent among placebo groups. Consistent with these findings, Hogarty, Ulrich, Mussare, and Aristigneta (1976) reported that patients who had been thought suitable for drug discontinuation evinced a 67 percent relapse following drug withdrawal.

Like all psychoactive compounds, neuroleptics have a number of undesirable side-effects. Among these are dystonias, muscle spasm and stiffness, stooped posture, shuffling gate, masklike faces, and drooling. The pseudo-Parkinsonian symptoms can usually be reversed or reduced to a minimum by administration of anti-Parkinsonian drugs. Other side-effects accounted are dry mouth, blurred vision, occasionally delayed ejaculation, or even ejaculatory impotence. Again, such side-effects can usually be minimized by modification of drug dosage or switching to an alternative neuroleptic. Two of the most serious potential neuroleptic side-effects are agranulocytosis (a blood dyscrasia) and tardive dyskinesia (a kind of hyperkinesis of muscle groups in the tongue, face, neck, and upper extremities). Patients with tardive dyskinesia exhibit bizarre chewing, smacking, tongue protrusion, facial grimaces, and abrupt flexion and extension of the arms and hands. Fortunately, such severe side-effects are relatively rare. Unfortunately, when they do occur, they often are complicated and, particularly in the case of tardive dyskinesia, are only partially reversible. Careful monitoring

of patient's general health and intermittent blood studies are recommended.

Neuroleptics are all equally effective and thus are essentially interchangeable. However, there are a number of differences in their incidence and severity of various side-effects (see Table 32.1). In addition (although there are few research data that speak to or support this statement), many clinicians report that at least some patients who failed to respond to even aggressive neuroleptic pharmacotherapy with one drug, displayed significant improvement on an equivalent dose of an alternative neuroleptic. Unpublished pilot studies attempting to determine which patients would respond best to which subclass of neuroleptics have produced essentially negative results. Although apparently only occasionally successful, the clinical finding that at least some patients improve following drug substitution has been observed and anecdotally reported by a sufficient number of careful, competent research clinicians to warrant further investigation. Changing from one neuroleptic to another is commonly employed where a given patient has developed side-effects more common to one drug than another or where a patient appears unusually sensitive to a particular neuroleptic.

Clinically, neuroleptics are indicated and used primarily in the treatment of schizophrenic disorders. These agents also are effective in treating acute, drug-induced psychotic behavior, such as that resulting from stimulant abuse and phencyclodine (PCP or "angel dust") intoxication, in treating hallucinations and agitation in some cases of severe organic brain syndrome, and in acute control or manic behavior in a major affective disorder. Although lithium carbonate is the drug of choice for treating mania in major affective disorder, it requires several days to reach a significant serum concentration to exert its behavioral pharmacologic action. During the initial phase, neuroleptics may be used to control the patient's more agitated and psychotic behavior until a therapeutic serum lithium level is achieved.

In treating an actively psychotic schizophrenic, the patient should be hospitalized and the target symptoms identified and systematically monitored. Unless the patient is highly agitated, poses a threat to himself or others, or has a well-documented history of schizophrenia, it is often advisable to delay pharmacotherapy a few days until a firm diagnosis is obtained. Careful history and drug screening should be obtained routinely, particularly for younger patients. Once a diagnosis of schizophrenic disorder is established, pharmacotherapy is usually instituted rather aggressively. Actively psychotic schizophrenics often have a high tolerance for neuroleptics and frequently require doses two or three times what may eventually be found sufficient for maintenance therapy. Though practices vary, many clinicians prescribe a dosage and schedule that initially results in slightly oversedating the patient. As symptomatic behaviors begin to yield to the pharmacotherapy, dosage is adjusted to reduce signs of oversedation. Starting with a lower dosage may have the advantage of avoiding such sedation, but it usually requires a significantly longer hospitalization to achieve an adequate dose to impact on the cognitive and perceptual disturbances.

Once maximum pharmacotherapeutic benefit is obtained, which may take several weeks from the time drug therapy is initiated, dosage is gradually reduced to the lowest level at which maximum symptom remission can be maintained. Often, dosage reduction is begun while the patient is still hospitalized, but may be continued on an outpatient basis. During this time, it is essential that the patient be carefully monitored, through frequent and regular outpatient visits. Once patients are well regulated on an appropriate and effective maintenance dose and adjusted and functioning in their home environments, many can be successfully followed over many years with only intermittent office visits. While long-term neuroleptic maintenance therapy is critical for many schizophrenics, others do quite well over relatively long periods without antipsychotic medication. Unfortunately, no psychological or biological test and no specific symptom or set of symptoms unequivocally predicts which schizophrenic patients can safely discontinue medication. Nevertheless, several factors appear to be correlated with drug-free versus drug-maintenance prognoses. Patients with more gradual and progressive onset of symptoms and poor premorbid level of function frequently do less well on drug-free follow-up than patients who evidenced a more abrupt and rapid onset of psychotic symptoms and who responded relatively rapidly to neuroleptic pharmacotherapy. In addition, patients who have a history of relapse shortly after drug discontinuation would, of course, also be candidates for long-term drug-maintenance therapy.

Although neuroleptic pharmacotherapy has been shown to be the single most effective form of treatment for actively psychotic schizophrenics, it is by no means sufficient. Most schizophrenics have severe and debilitating behavioral excesses and deficits, only some of which are the direct consequence of whatever biochemical abnormality that may exist in their brain. Predictions regarding general long-term outcome have traditionally been considered in reference to a given patient's premorbid personality as well as to the number, frequency, rapidity of onset, and duration of the active psychotic episodes. It is useful to conceptualize "premorbid personality" in terms of performance versus repertoire variables. A careful examination of the patient's prior behavior can yield a great deal of information regarding his intellectual, vocational, emotional, and social functioning and skills (i.e., the premorbid repertoire). The best or optimum benefit neuroleptic pharmacotherapy can provide is to ameliorate the biochemical contribution to the individual's impaired cognitive-emotive-verbal-motoric performance. Pharmacotherapy cannot, of course, instate behavioral patterns the patient never possessed, or modify those maladaptive patterns acquired through environmental experience (learned), including those developed, in part, in reaction to or as a consequence of their psychosis. Instead, specific psychotherapeutic procedures designed to address those problems are necessary additions to the pharmacotherapy.

Such procedures as general ward-token economics aimed at improving patient's self-care, compliance, and general on-ward behavior (see Milby, 1975) and social-skills training (e.g., Hersen & Bellack, 1976) have been found useful. In addition, behavior patterns thought to be the consequence of schizophrenia itself may at times fail to respond to pharmacotherapy, but improve significantly when appropriate psychological procedures are applied. For example, aversion therapy and cognitive restructuring have sometimes significantly reduced or stopped hallucinations in chronic schizophrenics where such behavior persisted in spite of drug treatment, even though most other symptoms had remitted (e.g., Alford & Turner, 1976; Alford, Fleece, & Rothblum, 1982).

In treating schizophrenic disorders, psychological interventions are usually best reserved until adequate response to the medication is obtained. In the first place, some of the behavioral symptoms may be primarily performance deficits which, in many but not all cases, medication alone may help. For example, social withdrawal and diminished social responsivity might initially appear to suggest gross social-skill deficits. Some patients exhibiting such behavior will respond to drug treatment alone, and those behaviors disappear or improve significantly (e.g., Liberman et al., 1973). Second, many schizophrenics may initially fail to respond to psychotherapeutic interventions, but begin responding as maximum pharmacotherapeutic benefit is achieved. Hersen and his associates reported a case in which a patient failed to respond to skills-oriented group therapy or even to a simple, clear token program during the first month of hospitalization. Once medication levels were adjusted and the patient began to remit some of the primary symptomatic behaviors (loose associations, flat affect), he also began to respond rapidly to the token program and to the verbal, occupational, and social-skills training designed to ameliorate those repertoire deficits (Hersen et al., 1975).

Although, as noted, neuroleptics are often useful in the acute management of psychoses other than the schizophrenias, their use in such cases as drug-induced psychosis is almost always time-limited and discontinued as soon as the major psychotic symptoms remit. Use of neuroleptics in the treatment of personality disorders, "latent schizophrenia," or behavioral problems that do not entail clear psychotic symptoms, though endorsed by some clinicians, is not warranted on the basis the current clinical research literature.

Clinical Research and Neuroleptics

Clinical researchers often fail to take into account the pharmacokinetics and behavioral pharmacologic properties of various drugs when conducting psychological studies with patient populations receiving medication. This common, though by no means universal, failure probably occurs most often when the drugs involved are neuroleptics. Several factors previously noted need to be kept in mind. Neuroleptic pharmacotherapy usually requires six to eight weeks for full or maximum benefit to be obtained. Likewise, since neuroleptics are tissue-stored, it may take days or weeks for them to be eliminated from the body. While some patients may relapse within a few days of stopping their medication, others may experience a gradual return of the psychotic behaviors or exhibit a florid psychosis only after several weeks off the medication. Indeed, this is as confusing to many patients as it is to some researchers. In addition, various classes of symptomatic behaviors do not exhibit simultaneous change. Reduction or elimination of

delusional and hallucinatory behavior may occur several weeks after a schizophrenic patient has displayed dramatic changes in some of his or her arousal symptoms. Finally, it should go without saying that not all schizophrenics respond well to medication. While many display a dramatic remission of symptoms, some are only slightly improved, and others not at all. Failure to take such pharmacologic properties and effects into account when conducting clinical research can result in very confounded data from which fallacious conclusions may be derived.

Lithium

The introduction of lithium carbonate into the American pharmacopoeia has a curious history. In 1949, an Australian psychiatrist named John Cade reported successful treatment of ten manic patients with lithium carbonate. Shortly after this anecdotal report appeared, controlled studies of lithium treatment for manic psychoses were conducted and confirmed its efficacy (Shou, Amdisen, & Baastrup, 1970). Lithium therapy was rapidly incorporated into Australian, British, and European psychiatric pharmacotherapy. In the United States, however, the Food and Drug Administration did not approve the use of lithium carbonate until 1970. Lithium chloride had long been used as a substitute for common table salt (sodium chloride) by patients on low sodium diets. Unfortunately, at about the time of Cade's original report, several deaths and cases of severe intoxication were reported among individuals using lithium chloride as a sodium-salt substitute (Corcoran, Taylor, & Page, 1949). This occurrence combined with the lack of enthusiasm among pharmaceutical companies (lithium carbonate is a simple, cheap, unpatentable compound) resulted in a 20-year delay in the approval and use of lithium carbonate in America.

Pharmacology

Lithium carbonate is rapidly and almost completely absorbed through the gastrointestinal tract, making oral administration as efficient as any other route. Not bound by plasma proteins or metabolized, lithium is excreted unchanged by the kidneys. In solution, such as in CNS extracellular fluid, lithium carbonate yields the cationic lithium ion. While it is known that lithium ion is more evenly distributed between intra- and extracellular spaces than is sodium or potassium and is believed to behave like those ions at the cell membrane, it remains unknown how this relates to lithium's effect on molar behavior. Perhaps the lithium ion somehow interferes with the sodium pump (substituting for sodium ions), which would increase the time for cellular repolarization, hence increasing the refractory period between neuronal "firing." But this is still speculation. In addition to its possible direct effect on cellular function, lithium has a number of other CNS effects. It reduces or prevents release of norepinephrine and dopamine at aminergic synapses, it interferes with the production of adenycyclase, and it stimulates the synthesis of serotonin while inhibiting its turnover. Just how these properties interact to result in lithium's behavioral pharmacological properties is still unknown. More is known about lithium's more molar and clinical behavioral pharmacologic properties than about its mechanisms of action.

Clinical Efficacy and Use

In a variety of controlled studies, lithium has been shown effective in significantly reducing manic behavior and in preventing recurrence of manic episodes in patients with carefully documented or diagnosed bipolar depressive illness (major affective disorder, manic or bipolar). In a review of the international literature up to 1973, Gershon and Shopsin (1973) found improvement rates between 60 and 100 percent in studies of lithium treatment for acute mania. The majority of controlled studies comparing lithium to placebo in treating acute mania show lithium distinctly superior (Walker & Brodie, 1978). A large-scale, collaborative study comparing lithium to chlorpromazine found that chlorpromazine was more effective in rapidly quieting highly agitated patients. In less highly agitated manic patients, however, lithium proved superior in diminishing manic behavior, with fewer side-effects than chlorpromazine (Prien, Caffe, & Klett, 1971). Although lithium is rapidly absorbed, it usually requires a week to ten days or so before a serum concentration sufficient to control manic behavior is achieved (.5 to 1.2 mEq/liter). Thus, administration of a neuroleptic is often used initially to control the agitated manic patient during the first week after lithium therapy has been initiated.

In addition to its efficacy in controlling acute manic behavior, controlled studies have also documented lithium's prophylactic value in preventing or reducing the frequency, intensity, and duration of manic episodes (Baastrup & Schou,

1967; Quitkin, 1976; Schou, Baastrup, & Grof, 1970). In reviewing controlled studies from four countries, Davis (1976) calculated the relapse rate (i.e., recurrence of manic episodes) as averaging only 36 percent among the lithium maintenance groups compared to a 79 percent relapse rate among placebo groups. In spite of clinical reports to the contrary, there is little in the research literature showing that lithium is of significant value in treating depression or psychotic depressive episodes associated with bipolar major affective disorder. The use of lithium carbonate in treating other conditions for which it has sometimes been suggested, such as alcoholism or tardive dyskinesia, does not have adequate controlled empirical documentation and must be assumed for now to be no more than placebo.

Since there is a delay ranging from four to ten days between initiating lithium therapy and its clinical behavioral effects on manic behavior, most severely disturbed or highly active manic patients are often given neuroleptics for the management of hyperactive, disruptive behavior. As the manic behavior remits and therapeutic lithium level is achieved (assessed by taking periodic blood samples from which serum lithium concentration is calculated), neuroleptics are discontinued and lithium dosage reduced (Cohen, 1975). In patients with a history of manic episodes, lithium maintenance therapy usually is indicated. Maintenance doses vary between 600 mg and 1800 mg a day and are adjusted to each individual patient to maintain a serum lithium concentration between 0.5 and 1.2 mEq/liter. Immediately following discharge from the hospital, blood samples are drawn frequently, usually at least once or twice a week. Once the patient, having returned to routine daily activities and home diet, demonstrates a stable dose-serum concentration, dosage is maintained and blood samples may be taken only once a month or so. Still later, if a consistent level has been maintained with no complications, the physician may elect to test even less frequently for serum lithium concentrations. Patients and at times concerned others such as spouses are warned of toxic effects of overdose and instructed on the effects of exercise or physical exertion and dietary changes on lithium concentration toxicity.

As in the case of schizophrenic disorders, acute manic episodes in major affective disorders usually require medication as the cornerstone of treatment. Systematic psychological evaluation and behavioral assessment may provide means for more careful and objective monitoring of changes in the patient's behavior as pharmacotherapy exerts its effects. However, specific individually tailored psychological interventions are best reserved until maximum medication effects are obtained. Also, like schizophrenic patients, those suffering from cyclic mania or bipolar major affective disorders may appear to have behavioral repertoire excesses or deficits that are, in fact, performance problems resulting from the biological aspects of the psychosis. Careful examination of the patient's history and behavior (e.g., from self-report, siblings, spouses, etc.), as well as from evaluation after the primary psychotic symptoms have remitted, can guide the clinician's planning of specific psychotherapeutic interventions once the patient is pharmacologically controlled. Patients with psychotic disorders commonly exhibit a variety of acquired, maladaptive behavior patterns that are unresponsive to medication and require specific psychotherapeutic procedures. Such problems, unfortunately, are sometimes overlooked by some clinicians who focus on the management of the primary symptoms of the major thought or affective disorder per se.

Antidepressants

Feelings of depression, sadness, or dysphoria are, like anxiety, universally experienced aversive and disquieting affective states. Most human beings intermittently experience mild degrees of acute and transient depression throughout their lives in response to adverse life events. Similarly, nearly everyone will experience moderate to severe depressive feelings occasionally in the course of life in reaction to personal tragedies, loss of loved ones, or catastrophic events. For most people, such experiences are short-lived and only temporarily disrupt normal functioning. When depressive feelings are chronic, too frequent, too intense, of abnormally long duration, or out of proportion to or even without external precipitants such as major losses, they are usually considered clinically significant and require professional attention. Two types of pharmacologic compounds effective in treating depression were developed during the 1950s. These are the monoamine oxidase (MAO) inhibitors and the tricyclic antidepressants. As in many scientific discoveries, a bit of luck and serendipity intersecting a current theoretical notion played a role in the discovery and development of both classes of compounds.

In 1951, anecdotal reports indicated that some patients who were being treated for pulmonary tuberculosis with isoniazid displayed marked elevation in mood. Initial trials of isoniazid for depression yielded some promising results, but the drug proved to be too hepatotoxic for clinical use. However, molecularly similar compounds were formulated, such as iproniazid, that were less hepatotoxic and were found to have antidepressant properties. Subsequently, the MAOIs that are currently approved for use were developed. These include isocaboxazid (Marplan), phenelzine (Nardil), and tranylcypromine (Parnate). Monoamine oxidase plays a major role in regulating the metabolic degradation of epinephrine, norepinephrine (NE), and dopamine (DA), in addition to oxidatively deaminating serotonin, 5-hydroxytryptamine (5-HT). Put simply, MAO inhibition is known to increase concentrations of norepinephrine in the central nervous system, and this is believed to be related to reduction in depressive feelings.

Clinical trials produced inconsistent results, but generally supported the antidepressant effects of MAO inhibitors. Unfortunately, MAOIs also interfere with the metabolism of amines involved in blood pressure regulation. Relatively high concentrations of pressor amines are found in a variety of common foods such as cheese, beer, yeast extract, chocolate, red wines, sour cream, broad beans, and raisins, to name a few. This presented a risk of possibly fatal hypertensive crisis, mandating rather strict dietary constraints for patients on MAOIs. Apart from the inconsistent evidence documenting their efficacy, MAOIs fell into disfavor because of these restrictions and side-effects and because alternative antidepressants were available: the tricyclic antidepressants. Although there has been a recent revival of interest in MAOIs, there current use is so limited that they will not be discussed at length here.

Tricyclic Antidepressants

Like MAOIs, the tricyclics were discovered during a search for something else. The success of the early neuroleptics in the treatment of schizophrenia led pharmacologists to synthesize related compounds in the hope of producing new, more effective, or at least equally effective and patentable antipsychotics. One of these new compounds was imipramine. In 1957, Kuhn reported that imipramine was not effective with schizophrenia, but had relieved symptoms in patients suffering from depression (Kuhn, 1957). The era of tricyclic antidepressants was begun (Fig. 32.3).

Structure and Mechanism of Action

Tricyclics, so named because of their three-ring molecular core, are rapidly absorbed after oral administration. They block reuptake of amines at presynaptic nerve endings, which is important since presynaptic reuptake is necessary for inactivation of endogenous sympathominetic amines (Axelrod, 1971). This is thought to be their primary mechanism of action in relieving depression. Although exactly how blockade of amine reuptake relates to relief of depressive behavior remains unknown, current biological theories of depression hypothesize that it is associated with decreased bioavailability of neurotransmitters norepinephrine (NE), dopamine (DA), and serotonin (5-HT). By blocking presynaptic uptake, these amines remain and accumulate in the synaptic cleft, thereby increasing their concentration and/or duration of action at postsynaptic receptor sites, facilitating aminergic transmission (Hollister, 1978).

More recently, tetracyclic (four-ring molecular core) antidepressants have been developed. Al-though initially thought to be faster acting than the tricyclics, recent studies question this claim. Research on tetracyclics such as maprotiline is ongoing. Thus far, most of the evidence indicates that they are about as effective as the tricyclics, with no significant advantages yet clearly documented. Because current data indicate that tetracyclics have essentially the same clinical action and side-effects as the tricyclics, they are not discussed separately.

Side-effects

If rare and atypical adverse reactions are included, the list of tricyclic side-effects is quite long. Fortunately, the more common side-effects are usually medically innocuous, though perhaps at times uncomfortable. These may include dry mouth, drowsiness, dizziness, blurring of vision, difficulty urinating, constipation, mild tremor, and increased perspiration. Even where one or more of these reactions occur, they usually fade within a few days after treatment. In some cases, the side-effects may be useful in the primary treatment. For example, amitriptyline (e.g., Elavil) is known to produce a greater degree of drowsiness, even sedation, than many other tricyclics. Although this side effect is also temporary and di-

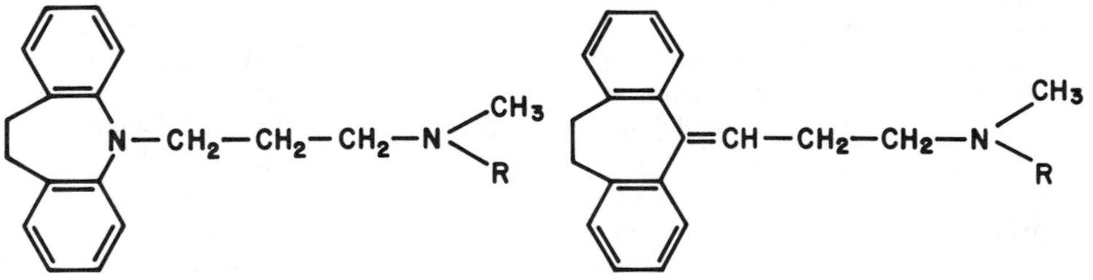

Basic molecules for Tricyclic Antidepressants

Impramine (Tofranil)   Amitriptyline (Elavil)

Desipramine (Norpramine, Pertofrane)   Nortriptyline (Aventyl, Pamelor)

                                                   Protriptyline (Vivactil)

TETRACYCLIC ANTIDEPRESSANT*

Maprotiline (Ludiomil)

Fig. 32.3. Tricyclic antidepressants (Trade names given for identification purposes only.)

minishes rapidly, it can be useful in facilitating sleep induction in depressed patients who have significant sleep disturbance. Tricyclics occasionally result in cardiac arrhythmias and other cardiovascular abnormalities. Thus, physicians need to assess patients' general physical health and cardiac status carefully, particularly those patients with a cardiac history, before prescribing tricyclics. In addition, overdose on tricyclics can be fatal. Since suicidal feelings and ideation are frequent components in severely depressed patients for whom tricyclic antidepressant therapy is being considered, it is usually recommended that such individuals be prescribed the lowest number of doses (or lowest total dosage) practical between office visits.

Clinical Use

Controlled clinical research investigating the efficacy of tricyclics in treating depression (e.g., Bielski & Friedel, 1976), while not uniformly positive, has provided generally strong support for their efficacy, particularly with severe depression (i.e., where vegetative symptoms such as middle and terminal sleep disturbances, poor appetite and weight loss, and psychomotor disturbance are present). In their review of controlled double-blind studies evaluating antidepressants, Cole and Davis (1975b) found that 49 of 65 published reports indicated that tricyclics were significantly superior to placebo in treating depression. Better performance is seen in trials where less severe depressions are eliminated and adequate dosages are used (Baldessarini, 1977). Most evidence indicates that depressive symptoms associated with neurotic, hysterical, or hypochondriacal traits consistently respond poorly to tricyclics. This observation is consistent with current models that distinguish endogenous from exogenous depression. Unfortunately, most of the symptoms supposedly associated with "endogenous" depression also occur in severe reactive depressions. The concept of *endogenous* depression is probably useful or even valid with respect to severe and/or cyclical major depressions that are unrelated to identifiable environmental or cognitive precipitating events to which the depression could be reasonably attributed. Depressions, however, cannot be dichotomized into endogenous versus exogenous or reactive solely on the basis of whether particular symptoms are present or absent. Rather, severity, duration, and patterns of particular symptoms considered within the context of and in relation to life events pro-

vides a more rational basis for such clinical judgments. Symptoms usually considered indicative of severity of depression such as decreased appetite with weight loss, midphase and terminal sleep disturbance, psychomotor changes, and the like also occur in some reactive depressions and may persist over several weeks. Current evidence indicates that tricyclic antidepressants are often effective in alleviating these types of depressive symptoms whether or not they occur as part of a biological pathogenesis or a neurotic-reactive clinical picture (Hughes, 1981). Thus, rational clinical use of tricyclics at this time is best guided by the symptomatology rather than inferred pathogenesis. For example, a 38-year-old female in the midst of an unwanted and conflictual divorce may suffer from feelings of despair and worthlessness, experience crying spells, sleep disturbance, decreased appetite, anhedonia, and decreased energy. Such symptoms may well endure over several weeks and confound therapeutic procedures designed to reduce the depression. If such symptoms have persisted for two or three weeks, have not shown evidence of improvement, and appear likely to continue, perhaps impairing the patient's capacity to respond to psychotherapeutic interventions, then a trial on tricyclics would be indicated. This is so even though the patient's history and current life events suggest that her depression occurred in reaction to the divorce.

Prior to initiating pharmacotherapy, it is essential that pretreatment measures be taken along with a careful and detailed history. Assessment instruments useful in determining the nature and severity of depression include the Beck Depressive Inventory (Beck et al., 1961), the Hamilton Rating Scale (Hamilton, 1960), the Behavioral Rating Scale (Williams, Barlow, & Agras, 1972), and the Minnesota Multiphasic Personality Inventory (Marks, Seeman, & Haller, 1974). In addition to providing some indices of depression (particularly the relationship among scales D, Pt, Ma, and Si), other profile features on the MMPI (such as scales Hs, Hy, and Pd) can provide some clues regarding hypochondriacal, histrionic, and other personality features. These may be associated with types of depressive behavior that are generally less responsive to antidepressant pharmacotherapy.

Clinical features usually associated with good drug response are: (1) depression where significant vegetative symptoms are present including two or more of the following: midphase or terminal sleep disturbance, loss of appetite with weight loss, psychomotor retardation, marked diurnal mood variation, anhedonia, and lack of responsivity to environmental and previously reinforcing activities; (2) clear and rapid onset of depressive symptoms; and (3) relatively good premorbid adjustment and functioning. Other factors predictive of good response to antidepressants include prior history of therapeutic response to tricyclics, a family history of affective disorders, and family history of good antidepressant response.

Clinical features frequently associated with poor response to antidepressants are: (1) depressive symptoms of longstanding duration; (2) depressive symptoms occurring as part of or an exacerbation of longstanding, chronic negativistic, "depressive" personality; (3) depressive symptoms associated with alcoholism or chemical dependency; and (4) prominent features of hysteria, hypochondriasis, and/or preoccupation with multiple somatic complaints, complaining, blaming others, and strong or rigid externalization of locus of emotional control or "causation." Also, poor previous response to antidepressants, hypersensitivity to side-effects, and presence of schizoid or schizoaffective features are typically associated with poor response to tricyclic pharmacotherapy.

There is, of course, no single pathognomonic sign or symptom of depression that invariably predicts drug response. Likewise, these two sets of clinical features are not mutually exclusive. Patients whose clinical picture is consistent with many of the features enumerated in the second set also may exhibit one or more of the symptoms listed in the first set associated with good antidepressant response. Careful examination of the patient, the patient's history, personality or cognitive-behavioral repertoire, response patterns or style, life situation and environmental events, and the interrelationships among such factors can help the clinician determine the relative prominence of good versus poor drug-response features.

Antidepressant pharmacotherapy usually is not recommended as a single modality therapy in treating depression. Rather, where indicated, tricyclics are used in conjunction with psychotherapeutic interventions. Because of the lag between initiating antidepressant therapy and the onset of their antidepressant effects, patients who are severely depressed may require hospitalization or other close supportive measures. Decisions regarding hospitalization should be made on the basis of the patient's current clinical condition rather than on anticipated effects of pharmaco-

therapy, even if the patient has a history of good or even rapid drug response. Although some patients may respond rather rapidly on an adequate dose, others may not evidence much change for two or more weeks. Therefore, if a trial on antidepressants is indicated and elected, the patient should be kept on an adequate dose for a minimum of three weeks. Patients need to be informed not only of side-effects, but that improvement in their mood and feelings may be gradual and may not occur for several days. Further, it is important that patients understand they should continue taking the medication exactly as prescribed, even if they initially do not feel it is helping them very much. If no significant improvement occurs after three weeks on an adequate dose, then the probability of therapeutic response can be considered low and drug therapy discontinued.

When patients do display therapeutic response to antidepressants, the decision of how long to maintain drug therapy is determined by their evolving clinical picture and by etiologic considerations. Where depressive symptomatology is associated with a major affective disorder of probable biologic pathogenesis (e.g., recurrent or cyclical depressions), then antidepressant therapy is usually maintained for six to twelve months after remission. Clinical follow-up studies indicate that patients on maintainence therapy in such cases do significantly better and experience fewer relapses than similar patients whose medication was discontinued shortly after symptom remission (Klein & Davis, 1969). Alternately, where severe depression occurs in response to an interaction between enviromental events and cognitive-emotive or "personality" factors, then reduction of tricyclic therapy is guided by the evolving clinical picture, including both evidence of symptom remission and changes in relevant cognitive-emotional processes. Protracted drug therapy in such cases usually is unnecessary.

In addition to use in treating depression, imipramine has been found of value in the treatment of obsessive-compulsive behavior and agoraphobia. For example, Foa and associates (Foa, Stekett, & Groves, 1979) combined behavioral and pharmacologic treatment for a severe obsessive-compulsive patient. Following behavior therapeutic intervention involving stimulus exposure and response prevention, the patient exhibited a marked reduction in ritualizing, but evidenced little change in fear of contaminants, obsessive thinking, or depression. Administration of imipramine resulted in significant improvement in these targeted behaviors. Similarly, Zitrin, Klein, and Woerner (1978) reviewed the use of imipramine in treating agoraphobia, particularly the drug's effect in reducing panic attacks commonly involved in the agoraphobic syndrome. Aside from ameliorating the depressive component frequently involved in these disorders, it remains unclear by what mechanism imipramine's "antiobsessive" and "antipanic" effect is achieved.

Stimulants

Stimulants are compounds that exert an excitatory effect on neuronal tissue, resulting in an increased biochemical, physiological, and molar behavioral activity. Although common stimulants such as nicotine and caffeine have been in use both recreationally as well as medicinally for several hundred years, those of interest here are the more powerful pharmacologic stimulant compounds including amphetamines (Benzedrine, Dexedrine), methylphenidate (Ritalin), and magnesium pemoline (Cylert). The prototypic stimulants are the amphetamines. In the central nervous system, these compounds induce the local release of norepinephrine and also potentiate dopamine at central synapses. This is thought to be their primary mechanism of action. Behaviorally, amphetamines' stimulatory effects can be observed, for example, in that intravenous administration of an amphetamine can largely reverse light anesthesia previously induced by i.v. administration of amobarbital. An oral dose of 10 to 20 mg of amphetamine given to adult subjects usually results in wakefulness, alertness, decreased sense of fatigue, and often increased verbal and motor activity. For these reasons, such stimulant compounds have been popular on college campuses since World War II for the purpose of staying up to cram for exams. High frequency or chronic use of stimulants in higher doses can produce a schizophreniform psychosis that is clinically indistinguishable from schizophrenia, although the drug-induced psychosis will usually reverse within one to two weeks upon discontinuation of stimulant abuse, particularly if neuroleptics are used acutely in treatment. Tolerance does develop to stimulants, although marked abstinence symptoms are usually seen only in persons taking relatively higher doses. Side-effects of stimulants include headache, nausea, insomnia, and anorexia. In longterm and/or high-dosage use, depression and psychosis may develop.

Clinical use

First used in inhalants for asthmatics, stimulants were subsequently employed in treating morphine addiction, depression, and, because of the anorectic side-effect, obesity. Because of their lack of efficacy and the development of more effective alternate therapies, stimulants are no longer appropriate for those disorders. Currently, stimulant pharmacotherapy is approved for narcolepsy (a neurologic disorder involving sudden, uncontrollable sleep onset) and attentional deficit disorder in children (formerly minimal brain dysfunction or hyperkinetic impulse disorder).

The use of stimulants in the treatment of socalled "hyperactive children" has been and continues to be surrounded by controversy. Fueling this controversy are a variety of factors and complex and emotionally loaded issues. Stimulants have high abuse potential and were among the most misused drugs during the 1960s an early 1970s. Further, the long-term effects of such drugs when taken for protracted periods during childhood are not fully known. For these reasons, parents and professionals express legitimate concerns over forcing young children to take these relatively potent compounds. In addition, the syndrome of behavioral symptoms currently called attentional deficit disorder is poorly understood and is often misdiagnosed. This results in some children being placed on stimulant therapy who could have responded to alternative, drug-free interventions. Finally, some professionals who are untrained in pharmacology and not licensed to prescribe medications often ignore if not dismiss the potential therapeutic contribution of pharmacotherapy. Indeed, there are some who even deny the existence of the disorder. On the other hand, professionals generally untrained in empirically based, efficacious behavioral management procedures often rely solely on drug therapy with such children.

The third edition of the *Diagnostic and Statistical Manual* (DSM III) of the American Psychiatric Association (1980) lists a variety of symptoms under Attentional Deficit Disorder (ADD), including easy distractibility, difficulty concentrating on schoolwork, difficulty organizing work, excessive motor activity, etc. These behavioral symptoms were derived from clinical investigators who, over the years, have been struggling to identify the necessary and sufficient symptoms for the diagnostic entity formerly called minimal brain dysfunction (e.g., Wender, 1978). Complicating this process is the fact that all of the behavioral symptoms associated with ADD occur to some extent in normal children. Moreover, most of these behaviors, even in excessive form, can result from maladaptive learning and environmental influences or are associated with other childhood problems (such as childhood grief and situational adjustment reactions). It can be seen, then, how some clinicians may mistakenly overdiagnosis ADD, while others question its very existence. As Wender (1978) points out, and DSM III stipulates, the crucial factor in determining a diagnosis of ADD is not whether one specific symptomatic response class is present or absent. Rather, it is based on the constellation of the various problematic behavioral classes, their history, intensity, and duration, and the absence of alternative etiologic evidence that could account for the clinical picture (Cantwell, 1977; Wender, 1978). In clinical studies where child patients who met the diagnostic criteria for ADD served as subjects, results have shown that many of the symptomatic behavioral excesses and deficits do improve with stimulant therapy. Therapeutic improvements resulting from pharmacotherapy have included increased vigilance, time-on-task, accuracy of performance (Sprague & Sleator, 1977), improved reading and arithmetic (Sulzbacher, 1972), significantly increased scores on standard IQ tests (Wiens, Anderson, & Matarazzo, 1971), decreased motor activity such as fewer "out of seats," "jump ups," and "talk outs" (Sulzbacher, 1972; Zike, 1972), and improved "social behavior" and responsiveness to reinforcement (Sprague & Sleator, 1977; Wender, 1978). By contrast, similar behaviors associated with other childhood disorders such as mental retardation (Lipman et al., 1978) or infantile autism-childhood schizophrenia have not been found to improve with stimulant therapy (Campbell, 1978).

Although nondrug treatments such as various behavioral shaping and contingency-management procedures have been found effective in reducing hyperactive behavior, improving scholastic performance, and establishing more adaptive and appropriate social skills (e.g., Ayllon, Layman, & Kandel, 1975), few studies have systematically compared stimulant pharmacotherapy to psychotherapeutic interventions with children who met the criteria for ADD. In one of the better designed and controlled investigations comparing stimulant therapy to behavioral therapy, Gittelman-Klein and her associates compared meth-

ylphenidate, placebo, behavior therapy, and combined pharmaco-behavior therapy (Gittelman-Klein et al., 1976). Results revealed that while medication alone, behavior therapy alone, and combined pharmaco-behavior therapy were all effective and superior to placebo, methylphenidate was found significantly superior to behavior therapy alone in modifying the targeted problematic behaviors. Teachers who made global, subjective ratings favored the combined therapy.

Medication, however, cannot add new components to an individual's behavioral repertoire; it can only influence its performance or help create conditions under which new skills can be acquired. While clinical studies demonstrate the efficacy of stimulant therapy with respect to hyperexcitability, abnormally short attention span, impaired learning capacity, scholastic performance, and socially disruptive motor-verbal activity, those academic, emotional, and social skills that entail a relatively longer acquisition phase do not show parallel levels of improvement via pharmacotherapy alone. Further, the long-term outcome in the absence of conjunctive psychological therapy is rather poor (Barkley, 1977). Thus, it is crucial that clinicians working with ADD children employ additional therapeutic procedures with documented efficacy in conjunction with pharmacotherapy.

When the diagnosis of attentional deficit disorder is being considered, extremely careful data gathering is important. Unlike the psychotic, the ADD child may not display the full range of symptoms necessary for the diagnosis in the office or even in the observational playroom. Further, parents and even teachers may not be accurate reporters. Experienced teachers, however, have a better subjective model than parents against which to judge the normalcy or appropriateness (in terms of intensity, frequency, and topography) of a child's behavior. In addition, some parents may be reluctant to reveal certain information that might suggest an alternative diagnosis and etiology, such as a grossly disturbed family or home life. Although there are no definitive tests specific for ADD, there are a variety of assessment devices and procedures that can provide more objective data for making diagnostic and treatment determinations (see Barkley, 1981).

If stimulant pharmacotherapy is indicated, medication should be used conservatively. After a careful diagnostic and behavioral analysis with baseline evaluation have been made, it is usually advisable to determine the extent to which targeted problem behaviors might be responsive to nonpharmacologic interventions. Second, it is important to determine which classes of problem behaviors are most serious or crucial and which might be more or less responsive to alternative therapies such as behavior modification. Dose-response studies (e.g., Sprague & Sleator, 1977) have found that positive drug effects on one class of behavior (e.g., scholastic learning) may display optimal response with one dosage, while optimal improvement of another class of behaviors (e.g., "hyperactivity") might occur at a higher or lower dosage. For example, "jump ups," "talk outs," and other hyperactive behaviors may show greatest improvement at 1 mg/kg of methylphenidate. But this dosage may significantly exceed the dosage at which optimal attentional behavior and scholastic learning are achieved. By exceeding the peak dosage (e.g., .3 mg/kg) at which maximum improvement in academic learning results in order to obtain a desirable effect on motor behavior, the clinician sacrifices the more crucial behavioral target by trying to cover all bases with a single modality treatment. Instead, if stimulant pharmacotherapy is indicated, clinicians should systematically determine which problematic response class responds best to medication, while carefully considering those problem behaviors that may be amenable to alternative treatment strategies. In the previous hypothetical example, "jump ups," "talk outs," and other motoric-verbal excesses may respond to contingency management and other environmental-social influence tactics, such that the stimulant dose could be selected to target the attentional deficits.

Where stimulant therapy proves effective with a specific case, it is not always necessary to maintain drug treatment indefinitely. Pharmacotherapy can sometimes be used to decelerate the rate or intensity of disruptive behaviors to a point where they may be brought under the control of environmental and intraorganismic variables. Similarly, such drug-induced reduction of problem behaviors can allow opportunities for more appropriate behavior to be shaped and instated, thus replacing deviant acts. Since the metabolic turnover rate of stimulants is relatively rapid, medication-reduction trials can be attempted once optimum functioning has been achieved and appears to be stabilized. That is, the pharmacokinetics of stimulants, unlike neuroleptics, allow for relatively shorter and more clearly delineated drug and no-drug treatment-assessment phases. Therefore, clinical case protocols can be planned along programmatic research lines, allowing the clinician to monitor progress systematically over time. By including drug-reduction or reversal phases, it is possible to determine the quantitative and qualitative pharmacotherapeutic contribution. In many cases, protracted stimulant therapy will prove warranted; in many others it will not. This can only be determined on a case-by-case basis by skilled and careful clinical management within the context of a comprehensive intervention program.

Conclusions

Psychopharmacologic research and clinical advances over the past 30 years have been extensive and, at times, astounding. Not only do current pharmacotherapeutic agents have greater specificity of action, they also are substantially safer and have fewer side-effects than most of their chemical predecessors. Psychopharmacologic compounds cannot, as yet, "cure" psychological disorders. Rather, their action is in controlling symptoms. In some cases, as with many schizophrenics, pharmacotherapy is crucial; without it, environmental or social influence therapies would have little or no impact. In other cases, pharmacologic compounds serve to create or enhance conditions under which psychological interventions can be efficiently applied to attain maximum therapeutic results more rapidly. Rarely are psychopharmacologic agents appropriate as a single modality treatment for behavioral and biobehavioral disorders. Instead, concomitant therapeutic programs aimed at behavioral deficits or acquired, maladaptive cognitive-emotive and overt behavior patterns are usually necessary. Psychological and pharmacological sciences, and their respective therapeutic contributions, are not inconsistent, much less incompatible. Indeed, their boundaries increasingly overlap. For example, this is so as we begin to discover how certain experiences and thoughts or thought patterns affect the chemical and physiological processes of the nervous system. Or, for example, how do chemical compounds effect the biological mechanisms of sensation, perception, and memory by which those external and internal stimulus events are detected, organized, stored, and utilized? Not only coordination, but active collaboration between pharmacological and psychological researchers and clinicians is fundamental to establishing an empirical knowledge base from which the best possible therapeutic procedures can be derived for now and in the future.

References

Alford, G. S. Sedatives, hypnotics, and minor tranquilizers. In S. J. Mule (Ed.), *Behavior in excess: An examination of the volitional disorders*. New York: Free Press, 1981.

Alford, G. S., & Alford, H. Benzodiazepine induced state-dependent learning. A correlative of abuse potential? *Addictive Behaviors*, 1976, 1, 261–267.

Alford, G. S., Fleece, L., & Rothblum, E. Hallucinatory-delusional verbal behavior: Modification by self-control and cognitive restructuring. *Behavior Modification*, 1982, 6, 421–435.

Alford, G. S., & Turner, S. M. Stimulus interference and conditioned inhibition of auditory hallucinations. *Journal of Behavior Therapy and Experimental Psychiatry*, 1976, 7, 155–160.

Alford, G. S., & Williams, J. G. The role and uses of psychopharmacological agents in behavior therapy. In M. Hersen, R. M. Eisler, & P. M. Miller (Eds.), *Progress in behavior modification*, Vol. 10. New York: Academic Press, 1980.

American Psychiatric Association. *Diagnostic and statistical manual of mental disorders — III.* (DSM-III.) Washington, D.C.: American Psychiatric Association, 1980.

Axelrod, J. Noradrenaline: Fate and control of its biosynthesis. *Science*, 1971, 173, 598–606.

Ayllon, T., Layman, D., & Kandel, H. J. A behavioral-educational alternative to drug control of hyperactive children. *Journal of Applied Behavior Analysis*, 1975, 8, 137–146.

Baastrup, P., & Schou, M. Lithium as a prophylactic agent: Its effect against recurrent depressions and manic depressive psychosis. *Archives of General Psychiatry*, 1967, 16, 162–172.

Baldessarini, R. *Chemotherapy in psychiatry*. Cambridge, Mass.: Harvard University Press, 1977.

Barkley, R. A. A review of stimulant drug research with hyperactive children. *Journal of Child Psychology and Psychiatry*, 1977, 18, 137–165.

Barkley, R. A. Hyperactivity. In E. J. Mash & L. G. Terdal (Eds.), *Behavioral assessment of childhood disorders*. New York: Guilford, 1981.

Beck, A. T., Ward, C. H., Mendelson, M., Mock, J., & Erbaugh, J. An inventory for measuring depression. *Archives of General Psychiatry*, 1961, 4, 561–571.

Bellack, A. S., & Hersen, M. *Behavior modification: An introductory text book*. Baltimore: Williams & Wilkins, 1977.

Bielski, R. J., & Friedel, R. O. Prediction of tricyclic antidepressant response. *Archives of General Psychiatry*, 1976, 33, 1,479–1,489.

Campbell, M. Use of drug treatment in infantile autism and childhood schizophrenia: A review. In M. A. Lipton, A. DiMascio, & K. F. Killam (Eds.), *Psychopharmacology: A generation of progress*. New York: Raven, 1978.

Cantwell, D. P. Drug treatment of the hyperactive syndrome in children. In M. E. Jarvik (Ed.), *Psychopharmacology in the practice of medicine*. New York: Appelton-Century-Crofts, 1977.

Carlsson, A. Mechanisms of action of neuroleptic drugs. In M. A. Lipton, A. DiMascio, & K. F. Killam (Eds.), *Psychopharmacology: A generation of progress*. New York: Raven, 1978.

Cohen, J. M. Current status of lithium threrapy: Report of the APA task force. *American Journal of Psychiatry*, 1975, 132, 997–1,001.

Cole, J. O., & Davis, J. M. Minor tranquilizers, sedatives, and hypnotics. In A. M. Freedman, H. I. Kaplan, & B. J. Sadock (Eds.), *Comprehensive textbook of psychiatry*, Vol. 2. Baltimore: Williams & Wilkins, 1975. (a)

Cole, J. O., & Davis, J. M. Antidepressant drugs. In A. M. Freedman, H. I. Kaplan, & B. J. Sadock (Eds.), *Comprehensive textbook of psychiatry*, Vol. 2. Baltimore: Williams & Wilkins, 1975. (b)

Cooper, J. R. *Sedative-hypnotic drugs: Risks and benefits*. Washington, D.C.: U.S. Government Printing Office, 1978.

Corcoran, A. C., Taylor, R. D., & Page, I. H. Lithium poisoning from the use of salt substitutes. *Journal of the American Medical Association*, 1949, 139, 685–688.

Davis, J. M. Overview: Maintenance therapy in psychiatry: I. Schizophrenia. *American Journal of Psychiatry*, 1975, 132, 1,237–1,245.

Davis, J. M. Overview: Maintenance therapy in psychiatry: II. Affective disorders. *American Journal of Psychiatry*, 1976, 133, 1–12.

Foa, E. B., Stekett, G., & Groves, G. Use of behavior therapy and imipramine: A case of obsessive-compulsive neurosis with severe depression. *Behavior Modification*, 1979, 3, 419–430.

Freedman, R. Neurochemical and psychopharmacological factors in mental illness. In R. C. Simons & H. Pardes (Eds.), *Understanding human behavior in health and illness*. Baltimore: Williams & Wilkins, 1981.

Gershan, S. & Shopsin, B. (Eds.), *Lithium ion, its role in psychiatric treatment and research*. New York: Plenum, 1973.

Gittel-Klein, R., Klein, D. F., Abikoff, H., Katz, S., Gloisten, A. C., & Kates, W. Relative efficacy of methylphenidate and behavior modification in hyperkinetic children. An interim report. *Journal of Abnormal Child Psychology*, 1976, 4, 361–379.

Goodman, L. S., & Gilman, A. *The pharmacological basis of therapeutics*. New York: Macmillan, 1975.

Goodwin, D. V., Powell, B., Bremer, D., Hoine, H., & Stern, J. Alcohol and recall: State-dependent effects in man. *Science*, 1969, 163, 1,350–1,360.

Grinspoon, L., Ewalt, J. R., & Shader, R. Psychotherapy and pharmacotherapy in chronic schizophrenia. *American Journal of Psychiatry*, 1968, 124, 1,945–1,952.

Haefely, W. E. Behavioral and neuropharmacological aspects of drugs used in anxiety and related states. In M. A. Lipton, A. DiMascio, & K. F. Killam (Eds.), *Psychopharmacology: A generation of progress*. New York: Raven, 1978.

Hamilton, M. A rating scale for depression. *Journal of*

Neurology, Neurosurgery and Psychiatry, 1960, 23, 56–62.

Hersen, M., & Bellack, A. S. Social skills training for chronic psychiatric patients: Rationale, research findings, and future directions. Comprehensive Psychiatry, 1976, 17, 559–580.

Hersen, M., Turner, S. M., Edelstein, B. A., & Pinkston, S. G. Effects of phenothiazines and social skills training in a withdrawn schizophrenia. Journal of Clinical Psychology, 1975, 31, 588–594.

Hogarty, G. E., Ulrich, R. F., Mussare, F., & Aristigrieta, N. Drug discontinuation among long term, successfully maintained schizophrenic outpatients. Diseases of the Nervous System, 1976, 37, 494–500.

Hollister, L. J. Tricyclic antidepressants. New England Journal of Medicine, 1978, 299, 1,106–1,109.

Hughes, J. R. Interaction between drugs and psychotherapy for depression. Paper presented at the annual convention of the Association for Advancement of Behavior Therapy, Toronto, December 1981.

Institute of Medicine. Sleeping pills, insomnia, and medical practice: Report of a study by a committee of the Institute of Medicine. Rockville, Md.: NIDA, 1979.

Iverson, S. D., & Iverson, L. L. Behavioral pharmacology. New York: Oxford University Press, 1975.

Kelleher, R. T., & Morse, W. H. Escape behavior and punished behavior. Federal Proceedings, 1964, 23, 808–817.

Klein, D. F., & Davis, J. M. Diagnosis and drug treatment of psychiatric disorders. Baltimore: Williams & Wilkins, 1969.

Kuhn, R. Über die behandlung depressives zustande mit einem iminodibenzylderivat (G-22355). Schweizer Medicinischer Wissenschaftschrift, 1957, 87, 1,135.

Lehmann, H. E. Pharmacotherapy of schizophrenia. In P. Hoch & J. Zubin (Eds.), Psychopathology of schizophrenia. New York: Grune & Stratton, 1966.

Lehmann, H. E. Psychopharmacological treatment of schizophrenia. Schizophrenia Bulletin, 1975, 13, 27–45.

Leitenberg, H. Behavioral approaches to treatment of neuroses. In H. Leitenberg (Ed.), Handbook of behavior modification and behavior therapy. Englewood Cliffs, N.J.; Prentice-Hall, 1976.

Liberman, R. P., Davis, J., Moon, W., & Moore, J. Research designs for analyzing drug-environment behavior interactions. Journal of Nervous and Mental Disease, 1973, 156, 432–439.

Lipman, R. S., DiMascio, A., Reatig, N., & Kirson, T. Psychotropic drugs and mentally retarded children. In M. A. Lipton, A. DiMascio, & K. F. Killam (Eds.), Psychopharmacology: A generation of progress, New York: Raven, 1978.

Lipton, M. A., DiMascio, A., & Killam, K. F. (Eds.) Psychopharmacology: A generation of progress. New York: Raven, 1978.

Marks, P. A., Seeman, W., & Haller, D. L. The actuarial use of the MMPI with adolescents and adults. Baltimore: Williams & Wilkins, 1974.

May, P. R. A. Treatment of schizophrenia: A comparative study of five treatment methods. New York: Science House, 1968.

Milby, J. B. A review of token economy treatment programs for psychiatric inpatients. Hospital and Community Psychiatry, 1975, 26, 651–658.

Nicoll, R. Selective actions of barbituates on synaptic transmission. In M. A. Lipton, A. DiMascio, & K. F. Killam (Eds.), Psychopharmacology: A generation of progress. New York: Raven, 1978.

Overton, D. A. State-dependent learning produced by addicting drugs. In S. Fischer & A. M. Freedman (Eds.), Opiate addiction: Origins and treatment. Washington, D.C.: Winston, 1973.

Pishkin, V., & Sengel, R. A. Research in psychopathology, 1972–1980: Unreporting of medication and other relevant demographic data. The Clinical Psychologist, 1982, 35, 13–14.

Prien, R., Caffey, E., & Klett, C. A. A comparison of lithium carbonate and chlorpromazine in the treatment of mania. Cooperative studies in psychiatry. Prepublication Report 86. Perry Point, Md.: Central Neuropsychiatric Research Laboratory, 1971.

Prien, R., Caffey, E., & Klett, C. Prophylactic efficacy of lithium carbonate in manic depressive illness. Report of the VA and NIMH collaborative study group. Perry Point, Md.: Central Neuropsychiatric Research Laboratory, 1972.

Quitkin, R., Rifkin, A., & Klein, D. F. Prophylaxis of affective disorders. Archives of General Psychiatry, 1976, 33, 337–341.

Rickels, K. Drug treatment of anxiety. In M. E. Jarvik (Ed.), Psychopharmacology in the practice of medicine. New York: Appelton-Century-Crofts, 1977.

Schou, M., Admisen, A., & Baastrup, P. C. The practical management of lithium treatment. British Journal of Hospital Medicine, 1970, 6, 615–619.

Schou, M., Baastrup, P. C., & Grof, P. Pharmacological and clinical problems of lithium prophylaxis. British Journal of Psychiatry, 1970, 116, 615–619.

Smith, D. E., Wesson, D. R., & Seymour, R. B. The abuse of barbiturates and other sedative-hypnotics. In R. I. Dupont, A. Goldstein, & J. O'Donnell (Eds.), Handbook on drug abuse. Washington, D.C.: U.S. Government Printing Office, 1979.

Sprague, R. L., & Sleator, E. K. Methylphenidate in hyperkinetic children: Differences in dose effects on learning and social behavior. Science, 1977, 198, 1,274–1,276.

Stein, L., Wise, C. D., & Berger, B. D. The benzodizepines. New York: Raven, 1973.

Sulzbacher, S. Behavior analysis of drug effects in the classroom. In G. Semb (Ed.), Behavior analysis and education. Lawrence, K.: University of Kansas Press, 1972.

Tourney, G. A history of therapeutic fashions in psychiatry, 1800–1966. American Journal of Psychiatry, 1967, 124, 784–796.

Walker, J. I., & Brodie, H. K. H. Current concepts of lithium treatment and prophylaxis. Journal of Continuing Medical Education, 1978, 19–30.

Wender, P. H. Minimal brain dysfunction: An overview. In M. A. Lipton, A. DiMascio, & K. F. Killam (Eds.), Psychopharmacology: A generation of progress. New York: Raven, 1978.

Wiens, A. N., Anderson, K. A., & Matarazzo, R. G. use of medication as an adjunct in the modification of behavior in the pediatric psychology setting. Professional Psychology, 1972, 157–163.

Williams, J. G., Barlow, D. H., & Agras, W. S. Behavioral measurement of severe depression. *Archives of General Psychiatry*, 1972, **27**, 330–334.

Zike, K. Drugs in maladaptive school behavior. Unpublished manuscript, 1972, obtainable from author at Harbor General Hospital, Los Angeles, California.

Zitrin, C. M., Klein, D. F., & Woerner, M. G. Behavior therapy, supportive psychotherapy, imipramine and phobias. *Archives of General Psychiatry*, 1978, **35**, 307–316.

33 HEALTH PSYCHOLOGY*

Joseph D. Matarazzo
Timothy P. Carmody

In the past decade, we have witnessed the solidifying of a professional and scientific partnership between psychology and medicine. An accumulating empirical literature establishing the role of psychological factors in the etiology, treatment, and prevention of physical illness has led to this expansion of the psychologist's role as a *health*, in contrast to only a *mental-health*, professional. This rapidly accelerating partnership between psychology and medicine is, in part, the result of the annually increasing numbers of studies that now offer support to the *biopsychosocial* model, which again has gained prominence in medicine and that holds that physical illness is best understood as a disruption of a biological, psychological, and social system (Engel, 1977; Guze, Matarazzo, & Saslow, 1953; Leigh & Reiser, 1977; Lipowski, 1977; Weiner, 1977). The plethora of recent studies reporting empirical findings that life style, behavioral predisposition, and related mental processes can affect bodily functioning, a hypothesis that appeared in the earliest writings of Western civilization, has provided the impetus for the

modern restatement of this biopsychosocial perspective.

Psychologists working in hospitals, medical schools, and other health settings, constituting the largest single group of nonphysician social-behavioral scientists working in such settings (Buck, 1961), have had a significant influence in the development of the biopsychosocial perspective of illness. Increasing numbers of medical sociologists and other social-behavioral scientists also are becoming involved in the field of health. This growing collaboration among the social, behavioral, and biomedical sciences has led to the evolution of a new field, *behavioral medicine,* an interdisciplinary field of scientific inquiry, education, and practice concerning itself with health and illness (Matarazzo, 1980; Schwartz & Weiss, 1978a, 1978b). A variety of professional disciplines are presently contributing to the field of behavioral medicine. These include psychologists, cardiologists, physicians from other specialties, epidemiologists, nutritionists, biochemists, dentists, and nurses. *Health psychology* refers to the collective

*Preparation of this chapter was supported in part, by National Heart, Lung, and Blood Institute Grants, 5T32-HL07332, HL24233 and HL20910.

activities of psychologists who work as scientists, health professionals, and teachers in the interdisciplinary field of behavioral medicine (Matarazzo, 1980, 1982). Within the area of health psychology, clinical, social, personality, and other psychologists have expanded their scientific research and practice beyond the domain of their earlier predominant concern with mental health in an effort to contribute to the better understanding and more effective management of a much wider variety of health problems (Matarazzo, 1980; Stone, Cohen & Adler, 1979).

Increasing numbers of collaborative efforts between psychologists and other health professionals have been prompted by an increase in the number of well-designed studies that confirm the age-old hypothesis of a high prevalence of psychological problems among individuals seeking medical care (e.g., Olbrisch, 1977). Bakal (1979), a modern spokesperson of this position, concludes that 60 to 90 percent of health problems have a significant psychological component, and epidemiological studies show that at least 50 percent of our population in the United States suffer from psychophysiologically related symptoms such as headaches, hypertension, or gastrointestinal disease (Schwab, Fennell, & Warheit, 1974). The yearly expenditures for health care of all types in our country now exceed 200 billion dollars, or more than 10 percent of our nation's annual gross national product, much of which is spent on disorders associated with life style and individual behavior. This unfortunate fiscal trend has prompted health experts and government officials to support and encourage psychological research and practice in the areas of primary prevention (e.g., to deter children from becoming smokers, to encourage Americans to use less salt, and so on), an interdisciplinary field recently given the name "behavioral health" (Matarazzo, 1980; 1982).

In the present chapter, the historical emergence of health psychology will first be reviewed. Second, examples of the application of social-psychological and behavioral principles in the health field will be presented, including the operant treatment of chronic pain, behavioral-biofeedback intervention with headaches, and coronary rehabilitation. Third, the role of psychology in the primary prevention of physical illness will be reviewed, focusing on the prevention and modification of smoking, obesity, alcohol abuse, high-fat diet, and Type A (coronary-prone) behavior pattern. Fourth, contemporary issues in health psy-

chology will be addressed, such as what the training of health psychologists might involve and how the collaboration among psychologists, physicians, health educators, and others can be made most productive. Finally, an attempt will be made to examine possible future directions in health psychology on the basis of recent trends in teaching, research, and practice in hospitals, medical schools, and other health settings.

Historical Emergence of Health Psychology

The partnership between psychology and medicine is not a new development, rather, it may be traced to the era of the early Greeks, when both disciplines were for all intents and purposes practiced by philosophers. In the area of modern medical education, psychologists first joined the faculty of a school of medicine at the turn of the 20th century (Franz, 1913). At the 1911 annual meeting of the American Psychological Association, courses in psychology were recommended for medical students by Franz and Watson and by their physician-colleagues, Meyer and Prince (Matarazzo, Carmody, & Gentry, 1981). Thus, what we have observed in the last decade is a reemergence rather than an initial emergence of the relationship between psychology and medicine (Gentry & Matarazzo, 1981).

Tracing Earlier Developments

References to the influence of the mind on the body in understanding disease date back to the earliest writings of civilization in ancient Greece, in the 5th century B.C. (Ehrenwald, 1976; Lipowski, 1977). In later centuries, mind-body dualism was promoted by the church, in its view of physical disease as a breakdown in the biological processes of the body in contrast to the corruption of the soul (Engel, 1977). In the 19th and early 20th centuries, the work of Freud, Pavlov, and Cannon set the stage for the heuristically more effective empirical study of mind-body interaction. The field of psychosomatic medicine during this latter era still reflected the mind-body dualism that had been doctrine for centuries. Still, it represented an initial bridging of the gap between medicine and psychology based on empirical, in contrast to philosophic, reasoning. Nevertheless, building upon the work of these pioneers, decades later in the 20th century the field of psychosomatic medicine took on two different directions. This bifurcation included the work of psychoanalytic clinical investigators such as Franz Alexander, on the one hand, and the laboratory experiments of psychophysiologists such as Harold Wolff at Cornell, on the other. Applying psychoanalytic theory, Alexander studied the relationship between personality and disease. Wolff, on the other hand, and coworkers such as Thomas Holmes and Stewart Wolf, examined the relationship between laboratory-induced stresses and physiological responses.

Until the last several decades, even in the traditional perspective of psychosomatic medicine diseases were classified as either *psychosomatic* (i.e., physical dysfunctions arising from psychological processes) or *organic* (i.e., physical disorders arising from pathophysiological factors). In contrast, the more recent biopsychosocial perspective toward illness suggests that psychosocial factors are involved in all diseases because illness occurs in individuals, who have not only a biological make-up but a psychological and social make-up as well.

This modern biopsychosocial view of illness has been proposed by interdisciplinary teams consisting of internists, psychiatrists, and behavioral scientists. As examples, Guze, Matarazzo, and Saslow (1953) proposed a single view of illness in which physical and psychological factors played a role, in varying degrees of prominence, in *all* physical and in *all* mental disease states. Leigh and Reiser (1977) also proposed that all health problems can be considered "psychosomatic" in the sense that psychological factors are involved in all cases where individuals seek professional help for physical symptoms. Engel (1977) added his criticism of the organically focused, traditional biomedical model of disease, pointing out that it excludes social, psychological, and behavioral dimensions of illness. In like manner, Lipowski (1977) defined the "new" psychosomatic medicine as the study of the biological, psychological, and social determinants of health and illness. Schwartz (1978) also has added his voice to the thesis that behavioral, physiological, and neurological assessment and treatment procedures each focus on the same unitary organism at different levels. Thus, reasons Schwartz, environmental and behavioral interventions such as psychotherapy focus on the modification of biopsychosocial processes which are being expressed as verbal, behavioral, and physiological responses. Finally, Mishler and his colleagues (Mishler et al., 1981) have recently presented a comprehensive critique of the biomedical model, examining the social, historical, political, and economic factors associated with its evolution, and defining illness as a disturbance in social relationships.

Escalating Health-Care Costs: An Impetus to Health Psychology

The cost of health care in the United States continues to escalate at an alarming rate. As shown in Table 33.1, taken from Vischi et al., (1980), the national total expenditure for health in 1950 was only 4.5 percent of that year's gross national product (GNP). By 1978, the comparable expenditure for health care had risen to 9.1 percent of that year's GNP. Furthermore, the average per capita health expenditure increased tenfold, from $82 in 1965 to $968 per capita in 1979. Health analysts attribute a justifiable proportion of this escalating cost of health care to the willingness of citizens to pay for hospital intensive care units, computerized axial tomography (CAT) scanners, and other very costly technological advances. These elements of the rising costs are associated with rapid progress in medical technology. But, less justifiable are the rising health costs associated with preventable diseases such as lung cancer, drug and alcohol abuse, motor vehicle accidents, and cardiovascular disease, which represent a needless waste of human and fiscal resources (Matarazzo, 1982).

Developments in the basic and applied health sciences in areas such as infectious disease, immunology, and epidemiology during the past 80 years have dramatically changed the illness patterns of Americans by reducing or eliminating the incidence of previously highly prevalent conditions such as tuberculosis, influenza, measles, and poliomyelitis. The human and dollar toll of these four diseases has been reduced significantly in our lifetime. Unfortunately, as shown in Figure 33.1, during this same time period, there has been an increase in other conditions, including lung cancer and cardiovascular disease.

The federal government, using the power of its funding arms, has mandated that scientific, educational, and health-care resources be directed toward the task of curtailing the human and dollar costs associated with the preventable aspects involved in the health of our citizens. Within this social, economic, and political climate, medical practitioners and biomedical scientists increasing-

TABLE 33.1. TOTAL AND PER CAPITA NATIONAL HEALTH
EXPENDITURES BY PERCENTAGE OF GROSS NATIONAL
PRODUCT (GNP).

Calendar Year	GNP (in billions)	TOTAL		
		Amount (in billions)	Per Capita	% of GNP
1950	$ 284.8	$ 12.7	$ 82	4.5
1955	398.0	17.7	105	4.4
1960	503.7	26.9	146	5.3
1965	688.1	43.0	217	6.2
1970	982.4	74.7	359	7.6
1975	1,528.8	131.5	605	8.6
1976	1,700.1	148.9	679	8.8
1977	1,887.2	170.0	769	9.0
1978[a]	2,107.6	192.4	863	9.1
1979[b]		212.9	968	

[a]Preliminary estimates. Adapted from Vischi et al., 1980, p. 131.
[b]The *total* health expenditure costs of 1979 data are from the *American Medical News*, December 26, 1980–January 2, 1981, p. 9.

ly are seeking collaborative relationships with psychologists and other social-behavioral scientists who have expertise in the area of human behavior that can be targeted toward the alleviation of health problems among the sick and the continued maintenance of health among the currently healthy.

Institutional and Governmental Support for Health Psychology

Until the present decade, the majority of clinical psychologists concentrated their efforts in three general areas: psychotherapy, schizophrenia, and mental retardation (Schofield, 1969). This concentration of effort was largely the result of a strong alliance formed during the post–World War II years between clinical psychology and psychiatry. As stated above, more recently, psychology has extended its contributions beyond a preeminent focus on mental illness to the study of *illness behavior in all of its physical and psychological manifestations*, using general hospital wards, the school and employment settings, and even whole communities as laboratories for investigating the role of life style in illness and in health.

This expanding role of psychology in the health field was made possible, in part, because of the advances in knowledge produced by many disciplines, and in part by the collective contribution of an increasing number of psychologists employed in medical schools and universities as well as community hospitals throughout the country. For example, the number of psychologists employed in

medical schools rose from 255 in 1953 (Mensh, 1953) to 2,336 in 1976, a figure that is almost 5 percent of the nearly 50,000 members of the American Psychological Association (APA) (Lubin, Nathan, & Matarazzo, 1978; Matarazzo, Lubin, & Nathan, 1978). The most recent figures (for 1975–1978) reveal that this percentage is holding at 4.3 percent for the proportion of newly graduated Ph.D.s in psychology who join a full-time medical

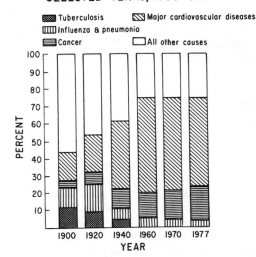

Fig. 33.1. United States deaths from selected causes expressed as a percent of all deaths (adapted from Califano, 1979a, p. 4).

school faculty (Stapp et al., 1981, p. 1,231). Moreover, there has been a linear growth in the size of the average medical psychology faculty within the university medical centers from a mean of 4.4 faculty members in 1953 to 20.7 per school in 1976 (Nathan et al., 1979). In addition, professional psychologists were employed in virtually each of our country's then 115 medical schools (98 percent) in 1976, as compared with 73 percent of such institutions in 1953 (Matarazzo et al., 1981). This growing representation by psychologists employed in medical schools and hospitals, and their concomitant desire for formal recognition for their activities in the field of medicine, provided impetus for the establishment in 1978 of the Division of Health Psychology (38) within the American Psychological Association.

The growth of health psychology has paralleled the recent revitalization of activity in the larger interdisciplinary fields of behavioral medicine and behavioral health (Matarazzo, 1980, 1982). Several developments have provided impetus to the recent formal recognition of behavioral medicine and behavioral health as vital fields in their own right. Prominent among these developments were the establishments of the *Journal of Behavioral Medicine*, the Behavioral Medicine Branch of the National Heart, Lung and Blood Institute (NHLBI), the Behavioral Medicine Study Section within the Division of Research Grants of the National Institutes of Health (NIH) and, in 1982, the new journal of the APA's Division 38 called *Health Psychology*. In addition, both federal and nonfederal sources of monetary support of predoctoral and postdoctoral research training in behavioral medicine as well as basic and applied research in etiology, treatment, and prevention have increased owing to the initiatives of a number of the institutes that comprise the NIH. The NHLBI has been particularly active in funding predoctoral and postdoctoral research training programs in both health psychology and other areas that collectively constitute behavioral medicine and its sister discipline, behavioral health.

Behavioral Medicine, Behavioral Health and Health Psychology

At the 1977 Yale Conference on Behavioral Medicine and again at a 1978 conference hosted by the National Academy of Science, health experts representing several scientific and professional disciplines met to discuss current issues and future directions in the newly emerging interdisciplinary field of behavioral medicine. Based on these discussions, the following definition of behavioral medicine was formulated and has gained wide acceptance:

> *Behavior Medicine* is the interdisciplinary field concerned with the development and integration of behavioral and biomedical science, knowledge, and techniques relevant to health and illness and the application of this knowledge and these techniques to prevention, diagnosis, treatment and rehabilitation. [Schwartz & Weiss, 1978a, p. 250; 1978b, p. 7]

Behavioral medicine does not limit itself to the contributions of any single discipline or theoretical mode. Psychology is but one of many disciplines contributing to the interdisciplinary field of behavioral medicine. The other disciplines include medicine, sociology, epidemiology, nutrition, anthropology, biochemistry, and dentistry, as well as others.

Wishing to give added emphasis to the element of *prevention* in the definition of behavioral medicine, Matarazzo (1980) coined the term "behavioral health" and defined it as follows:

> Behavioral Health is an interdisciplinary field dedicated to promoting a philosophy of health that stresses *individual responsibility* in the application of behavioral science, knowledge, and techniques to the *maintenance* of health and the *prevention* of illness and dysfunction by a variety of self-initiated individual or shared activities. [Matarazzo, 1980, p. 813]

Although sister disciplines such as sociology and epidemiology have much to offer the field of behavioral health (i.e., primary prevention), psychology has the longest history of formal research on individual human behavior, a well-established scientific knowledge base, the practical applied experience, and the educational-institutional supports to make substantial early contributions in the parallel fields of behavioral health and behavioral medicine. Recognizing this potential, and wishing to capitalize on a number of the developments cited above, Matarazzo offered the following as an interim definition of the emerging field that encompasses these collective efforts of psychologists:

Health Psychology is the aggregate of the specific educational, scientific, and professional contributions of the discipline of psychology to the promotion and maintenance of health, the prevention and treatment of illness, and the identification of etiologic and diagnostic correlates of health, illness and related dysfunction. [Matarazzo, 1980, p. 815]

A poll of the members of Division 38 recently suggested that the following underlined additional clause be added at the *end* of the just cited definition: "related dysfunction, *and to the analysis and improvement of the health care system and health policy formation.*"

Thus, the activities encompassed within health psychology are discipline-specific, and refer only to psychology's contributions as a science and profession to the broad interdisciplinary fields of behavioral medicine and behavioral health. According to this definition, health psychology encompasses not only clinical practice but also teaching, research, and administration. Furthermore, it is meant to encompass *all* the subspecialties of psychology; e.g., clinical, social, industrial, developmental, experimental, physiological, as well as others. Included under this general umbrella range the contributions, among many others, of psychotherapists working in medical settings (Olbrisch, 1977; Rosen & Wiens, 1979), utilizers of the behavior therapies with physically ill persons (Williams & Gentry, 1977), the contributions to biofeedback theory and application by experimental psychologists (Miller, 1969), and the contributions to medicine and behavioral health made by social psychologists such as Evans (1976) and Janis and Rodin (1979).

A wide range of opportunities for collaboration with other disciplines in the health field are becoming available to psychologists interested in health. One example of this partnership currently in the process of development among the disciplines of psychology, epidemiology, nutrition, biochemistry, and cardiology is the subspecialty of behavioral medicine which focuses on cardiology and behavior and has recently been named "behavioral cardiology." Deliberately crafted as an offshoot of the above definition of behavioral medicine, the following is one possible definition of this newly emerging field:

Behavioral cardiology is an interdisciplinary field concerned with the development and integration of behavioral and biomedical sci-

ence, knowledge, and techniques relevant to *cardiovascular* health and illness *and related conditions* and the application of this knowledge and these techniques to prevention, diagnosis, treatment, and rehabilitation. [Matarazzo et al., 1982]

Behavioral cardiology, only one of a potential multitude of outgrowths or subspecialties within the scope of behavioral medicine and behavioral health, focuses on the study of processes by which people develop certain behavior patterns, attitudes, and life styles that prevent or are associated with coronary heart disease and other cardiovascular dysfunctions. Psychologists involved in behavioral cardiology are working, among others, in the weight loss, smoking cessation, nutritional, attitude change, and stress reduction areas, where they collaborate with cardiologists, nutritionists, biochemists, epidemiologists, and others to collectively form the discipline of behavioral cardiology (sometimes called "preventive cardiology" by interdisciplinary teams that specialize exclusively in the preventive aspect). In identifying with behavioral cardiology, such psychologists are able to apply their expertise in concert to the coronary heart disease epidemic in a more concentrated, systematic, and coordinated manner. A more detailed discussion of the interrelationships among such currently extant subspecialties as "health psychology" and "medical psychology," on the one hand, and their relationships to such interdisciplinary fields as "behavioral medicine," "behavioral health," and "behavioral cardiology" may be found in Matarazzo et al. (1981, pp. 307–312).

Current Applications in Health Psychology

Numerous books, chapters, and review articles describing recent advances in health psychology (e.g., Ferguson & Taylor, 1981; Prokop & Bradley, 1981; Rachman, 1981; Stone et al., 1979) attest to the many contributions being made by psychologists who are collaborating with other behavioral and biological scientists in the treatment of physical illness (behavioral medicine) and in the area of primary prevention (behavioral health). In the following section, contributions of health psychologists in both of these areas will be described, focusing first on the behavioral treatment of chronic pain and rehabilitation, and next on the role of psychology in the emerging field of behavioral health as it relates to the primary prevention of coronary artery and other diseases. Given the marked growth in the number of potential areas for research and intervention in the field of health psychology, the following examples are not intended as an exhaustive list of all the currently active areas, but rather as examples of a few of the many tributaries that are contributing to this still emerging field.

Chronic Pain

The effective, two-way collaboration between psychology and medicine has led to significant advances in the treatment of chronic pain, as well as in the more general area of the long-term rehabilitation of pain patients as well as other chronic patients. The development of psychological intervention programs in the management and rehabilitation of chronic pain patients has been described in detail in several recent texts on behavioral medicine and health psychology (e.g., Goldensen, Dunham, & Dunham, 1978; Melamed & Siegel, 1980; Pomerleau & Brady, 1979; Weisenberg, 1981).

The operant treatment of chronic pain represents a major contribution of health psychology (Melamed & Siegel, 1980; Roberts, 1981; Weisenberg, 1981). Based on the assumption that environmental factors play a major role in the development (learning) of chronic pain behaviors, Fordyce (1974; 1976a, 1976b) and other behavioral scientists (e.g., Wooley, Blackwell, & Winget, 1978) have developed a behavioral (operant) treatment program in which attention and rest for the hospitalized chronic pain patient are made contingent upon the occurrence of specific desirable behaviors, such as increased physical activity and social interaction. Also, to counteract the addiction to or dependence on analgesics shown by the majority of such patients, medication is given by the floor nurse on a fixed time schedule in the form of a "cocktail" in which the amount of analgesic is gradually reduced (faded). Operant pain programs have been established at several medical centers throughout the country, achieving high levels of success (e.g., Wooley et al., 1978). Despite the published reports from these university-based centers that describe the efficacy of the pain programs, Roberts (1981) has recently pointed out the need for more controlled outcome studies that compare operant treatment programs with alternative psychotherapeutic approaches. Also currently underway are efforts to develop reliable ways of identifying potential chronic pain patients

before long-term patterns of pain behavior, invasive surgery, or life-long dependence on analgesics begin. It is hoped that prevention programs can be utilized with such high-risk patients when first treated and before chronic pain patterns begin.

Headaches

Other forms of pain also are being treated behaviorally. For example, migraine and tension headaches, if they reoccur for months or years, can develop into a new life style built primarily around these chronic pain symptoms. It is estimated (Turner & Stone, 1979) that as many as 90 percent of the population in this country experience muscle contraction (tension) or vascular (migraine) headaches. Some of these individuals suffer such pain regularly. Various forms of biofeedback, stress-management, and psychotherapy techniques have been used in the treatment of chronic tension and migraine headaches with what appear initially to be high levels of success. This literature has been reviewed extensively elsewhere (Cinciripini, Williamson, & Epstein, 1981; Epstein & Cinciripini, 1981; Melamed & Siegel, 1980). Electromyographic (EMG) biofeedback and progressive muscle-relaxation training have been shown to have comparably high levels of success in assisting patients to achieve deep levels of muscle relaxation, a physiological response assumed to have therapeutic effects in treating headaches (Cox, Freundlick, & Meyer, 1975). One advantage of biofeedback is that it provides an initial, symptom-oriented, nonthreatening foot-in-the-door for somaticizing headache patients who, as treatment continues, will derive the greatest benefit and relief from their symptoms by resolving psychological issues or learning to cope better with stress in psychotherapy. In addition to biofeedback, Holroyd and his colleagues (Holroyd, Andrasik, & Westbrook, 1977) have developed what are reported to be successful cognitively oriented stress-management approaches to the treatment of headaches that are based on the assumption that headaches are a result of cognitive responses to stressful situations.

Thermal biofeedback procedures have been employed successfully in the treatment of migraine headaches, based on the assumption that such procedures increase blood flow away from the forehead and thereby decrease arterial dilation (Budzynski, 1973). Research shows that both thermal and EMG biofeedback procedures are effective with migraine patients (Bakal, 1979; Cinciripini et al., 1981; Epstein & Cinciripini, 1981). However, Phillips (1978) has suggested that while biofeedback may be useful when physiological and self-report measures of headache pain correspond, cognitive and other stress-management procedures (such as psychotherapy) may be more effective when self-report and physiological variables do not correspond. Studies in this area are still too few to adequately reconcile the issues being debated.

Rehabilitation

The behavioral treatment of chronic pain, chronic disability, and specific symptoms such as tension headaches often constitute a central component in a comprehensive program of rehabilitation. Therefore, in an increasing number of university hospital or large medical-center rehabilitation programs, psychologists, physiatrists, orthopedic surgeons, occupational therapists, physical therapists, nursing staff, speech therapists, social workers, and vocational counselors are integrating their professional services into the behavioral perspectives described below. These interdisciplinary rehabilitation teams work in a variety of health settings, including hospital pain wards, medical rehabilitation centers, developmental disability diagnostic and treatment units (Lindemann, 1982), outpatient medical clinics, psychiatric hospitals, and schools and institutions for the mentally retarded and physically handicapped. Pain patients as well as other young and elderly patients needing such comprehensive rehabilitation services present many cognitive, sensory, and motor symptoms of pain associated with a variety of chronic illness and metabolic disorders (chronic headaches, diabetes, nephrotic syndrome, coronary artery disease), psychiatric disorders, and accidents and injuries. Within institutional settings, behavioral strategies (e.g., token economies) have been used to increase participation in rehabilitation activities (Michael, 1970). Fears regarding increasing physical activity or performing new tasks (e.g., transferring from a bed to a wheelchair for paraplegics) have been alleviated using cognitive behavioral therapy and systematic desensitization (DiScipio & Feldman, 1971). The opportunities for psychologists working in these areas have yet to be fully identified, let alone exploited (Greif & R. G. Matarazzo, 1982).

The rehabilitation of cardiac patients following myocardial infarction has presented a unique and difficult challenge to health professionals working in this area. It is well documented that the return to a productive and satisfying life style following myocardial infarction is often hampered by depression, family problems, and fears regarding physical exertion (Gentry & Williams, 1979). For example, Wishnie, Hackett, and Cassem (1971) reported that 88 percent of the cardiac patients surveyed in their study were depressed from six months to one year after their myocardial infarction. Nagle, Gangola, and Picton-Robinson (1971) found anxiety or depression in 55 percent of such patients surveyed who had not returned to work.

Patterns of invalidism or perceived helplessness have been found to be reinforced by anxious and overprotective spouses, who themselves report severe emotional problems (Gulledge, 1979; Skelton & Dominian, 1973). Individual, family, and group therapy (Hoebel, 1976; Wynn, 1967) have been employed with cardiac patients, encouraging family support to facilitate rehabilitation. Baile and Engel (1978) have reported the successful application of behavioral strategies in facilitating compliance in seven cardiac patients who had previously ignored or defied the guidelines of other rehabilitation programs.

Physical exercise training is considered an important part of rehabilitation for the coronary patient (Gentry & Williams, 1979). However, studies of physical exercise rehabilitation programs for cardiac patients extending over 12 months have demonstrated high dropout rates and poor attendance (Carmody et al., 1980; Kavanaugh et al., 1973; Kentala, 1972). Oldridge et al. (1978) found that early dropouts in these exercise rehabilitation programs were more likely to be patients who show the Type A behavior pattern, who smoke and who have had more than one previous myocardial infarction. These programs represent only a few of those in which psychologists are working in collaboration with physicians and other health professionals in an attempt both to better understand the process of rehabilitation and then to help design more effective intervention programs with cardiac patients.

Also in the area of behavioral approaches to chronic pain, rehabilitation, and related dysfunctions, other beginning successes have been reported in the behavioral treatment of Raynaud's disorder (Surwit, Pelon, & Fenton, 1978), sexual dysfunction (Masters & Johnson, 1970), essential hypertension (Agras & Jacobs, 1979), and pre-surgical anxiety and postsurgical recovery (Olbrisch, 1977). In addition, the behavioral medicine literature cited earlier contains many other examples of specialized behavioral, family, and group intervention programs that are being used in the hope of more effectively treating chronic pain or to better facilitate rehabilitation.

Addressing a wider range of areas of potential collaboration, Rosen and Wiens (1979) have advocated a more active partnership between physicians and psychologists, participating in joint decision making in patient evaluation and care from the patient's very first contact with the health-care setting. Examples of such already established physician-psychologist partnerships working with pain patients include those in the Department of Rehabilitation Medicine at the University of Washington School of Medicine (Fordyce, 1976a), the Rush Multiple Sclerosis Center established through the Department of Neurology at Rush-Presbyterian-St. Luke's Medical Center (Pavlou, et al., 1979), the Psychosomatic Unit at the University of Cincinnati (Wooley et al., 1978), and the Oregon Health Sciences University headache screening clinic which is co-directed by a neurologist and a psychologist (Rosen & Wiens, 1979).

Examples of Primary Prevention (Behavioral Health) Approaches

Health experts agree that the costly toll from heart disease, cancer, alcohol abuse, and accidents could be dramatically reduced if healthy people would not begin to smoke or use alcohol, would consume less cholesterol and salt, exercise regu-larly, and apply a few basic safety standards such as wearing seat belts (Matarazzo, 1980; 1982). Published reports during the last few years indicate that psychologists with experience and expertise in the areas of smoking, alcohol abuse, obesity, and stress are collaborating with health professionals from several other disciplines to develop ways of keeping healthy people healthy. Examples of a few of these collaborative efforts follow.

CIGARETTE SMOKING

Despite a massive national education program following the first Surgeon General's Report on Smoking in 1964, and despite a decrease in the number of adult males who presently smoke, there was an increase in adult female smokers from 25 percent in 1955 to 29 percent in 1979 (Califano, 1979). More alarming, as shown in Table 33.2, the percentage of smokers among 15–16-year-old girls doubled from 10 percent to 20 percent from 1968 to 1974, and even exceeded in 1974 the smoking rates of similarly aged boys, whose increase was only from 17 to 18 during that same six year period (Califano, 1979; Harris, 1980). It was concluded from these and related data that 12- and 13-year-old girls and boys are most susceptible to becoming regular smokers.

Given these findings for the epidemiology of smoking, psychologists and other behavioral scientists and their colleagues from medicine mounted a number of programs to prevent onset of smoking among preteenage youth. Green (1977), in a study aimed at discerning why children initiate smoking behavior, surveyed 5,200 school children regarding cigarette smoking, factor-analyzed their responses, and found that peer pressure and ambivalence toward authority figures were related to the

TABLE 33.2. PERCENTAGES OF CURRENT, REGULAR TEENAGE CIGARETTE SMOKERS IN THE UNITED STATES BY AGE GROUP (ADAPTED FROM CALIFANO, 1979c, p. 14, APPENDIX).

Year	AGES 12–14		AGES 15–16		AGES 17–18		AGES 12–18	
	Male	Female	Male	Female	Male	Female	Male	Female
1968	2.9	0.6	17.0	9.6	30.2	18.6	14.7	8.4
1970	5.7	3.0	19.5	14.4	37.3	22.8	18.5	11.9
1972	4.6	2.8	17.8	16.3	30.2	25.3	15.7	12.3
1974	4.2	4.9	18.1	20.2	31.0	25.9	15.8	15.3
1979[a]	3.2	4.4	13.5	11.8	19.3	26.3	10.7	12.7

[a]1979 data (12–18) are from the American Cancer Society's five-year study entitled "Target Five" (*Sunday Oregonian*, January 25, 1981, p. 5) and 12–14- and 15–16-year-old data from Harris (1980, p. 36).

onset of cigarette smoking among this large sample of teenage boys and girls. Following similar baseline research in other cities, several smoking prevention programs have been conducted with seventh, eight, ninth, and tenth grade children in Texas, California, Minnesota, and New York. These smoking prevention programs incorporate variants of techniques developed by Evans (1976) in the Houston, Texas, elementary schools. Such techniques include videotaped presentations, peer modeling, group discussion, role playing ways of resisting social pressures to smoke, and repeated monitoring of smoking and measures of knowledge and attitudes toward smoking. Evans et al., (1978) successfully applied principles derived from the social-learning-theory (modeling) literature to develop the first such smoking prevention program with 750 seventh-graders in Houston. The efficacy of similar programs was studied in Stanford, California (McAlister, Perry, & Maccoby, 1979; Perry et al., 1980), in Minnesota (Hurd et al., 1980), and in New York (Botvin, Eng, & Williams, 1980). A brief description and the results of these studies are summarized in Table 33.3. The intervention programs investigated were conducted within each city's schools with seventh, eighth, and tenth graders. Since the goal of each program was prevention, the outcome criterion was the lowering of the percentages of youngsters who were smokers, measured either by the absolute number of smokers in the group or by the number of *new* smokers. As may be seen in Table 33.3, in each of the five studies reviewed, there was a lower percentage of smokers in the group of youngsters exposed to an intervention than in those in the control groups. Also, in some cases the number of smokers was found to decrease, suggesting that some youths actually quit smoking in response to the program. Although the "gains" in these studies are generally small as expressed in percent (albeit not in numbers of individual children), they point out the value of such school programs aimed at one of the most important areas of controlling smoking behavior: that is, preventing the onset of smoking in the first place.

ALCOHOL ABUSE

Problem drinking appears to be quite prevalent among teenage youths. Alarmingly, recent reports by Galanter (1980) and by Parker et al. (1980) reveal that even *social* drinking in young adults may produce a marked loss of cognitive and neuropsychological functioning. The costs, associated with chronic alcoholism across all age groups in the United States are estimated to approach 42 billion dollars annually for the total

TABLE 33.3. SMOKING PREVENTION STUDIES WITH ADOLESCENTS.

Study	Subjects	N	Conditions	% Smoking	Length of Intervention
Evans et al., 1978	7th-graders	750	Full Treatment	10.0[a]	10 weeks
			Feedback only	8.6	
			Control (pre-posttest)	9.6	
			Control (pretest)	18.3	
McAlister et al., 1979	7th-graders	550	Intervention	5.6[b]	21 months
			Control (pre-posttest)	9.9	
Perry et al., 1980	10th-graders	498	Intervention	9.7[c]	6 months
			Control	13.1	
Hurd et al., 1980	7th-graders	1530	I Monitoring	9.6[d]	12 months
			II Monitoring (Saliva)	21.1	
			III Peer pressure plus modeling film plus role play	20.3	
			IV Peer III plus public commitment	5.9	
Botwin et al., 1980	8–10th-graders	281	Intervention	4.0[a]	12 weeks
			Control		

[a]Smoking onset rate.
[b]% Smoking in past weeks.
[c]% Smoking in past day; 16.3 and 21.9, respectively for past week; and 23.6 and 30.4, respectively for past month.
[d]"Regular" smokers (i.e., smoking at least twice per month).

economic costs, and an incredible 864 million dollars for the costs related to the treatment of alcoholism (Vischi et al., 1980). In addition, recent literature reviews by Streissguth et al. (1980) and by Abel (1981) reveal that the effect on the fetus of alcohol ingested by pregnant women who are merely *social* drinkers (i.e., two to three drinks per day) may be even more devastating than is the effect of tabacco on the fetus. Sulik, Johnston, and Webb (1981), using a mouse model, duplicated the teratogenic effect of alcohol produced in the human offspring and caution that these results provide clear evidence that social drinking early in pregnancy may be as deleterious to the human embryo as is constant heavy drinking. Abel (1981) concluded that there is considerable evidence indicating that alcohol per se, rather than other factors associated with alcohol consumption, is responsible for these Fetal Alcohol Syndrome effects in humans.

There has been an increasing emphasis on the prevention of alcohol and drug abuse among teenage youths. Health-education courses in high schools throughout the country are focusing on this important area. Programs similar to those developed for the prevention of the onset of smoking have been formulated in a like manner to prevent the onset of alcohol and drug abuse in teenage boys and girls (Schaps et al., 1980). According to Alden (1980), three strategies have been used in primary prevention of alcoholism: alcohol education classes, public information campaigns, and attempts to modify government policy. Alcohol education programs have been shown to be effective in increasing knowledge about alcohol but not in producing attitude or behavior change (e.g., Swisher, Warner, & Hern, 1972; Tennant, Weaver, & Lewis, 1973). The application of behavioral techniques such as self-management, controlled drinking, and coping-skills training have been recommended by several experts in the area (Berg, 1976; Haggerty, 1977) to enhance the effects of alcohol and drug abuse prevention programs. In a review of drug abuse prevention programs including alcohol use, Schaps et al. (1980) reported that over 70 percent of the programs using behavioral techniques (e.g., social-competency training) showed positive effects, whereas only 46 percent of information programs were shown to be effective. Botvin and his colleagues at the American Health Foundation in New York have developed the *Know Your Body* program for risk reduction (e.g., Botvin et al., 1980). Drug abuse is one of the target areas in their primary prevention program. The early prevention of alcohol abuse appears to be an area ripe for collaboration between psychologists and health educators, especially those teaching our children in this country's vast network of local educational systems (Dwore & Matarazzo, 1981).

OBESITY

Overconsumption, sedentary living, and other lifestyle habits associated with obesity often can be traced to problem childhood and adolescent food and exercise patterns. Estimates of the prevalence rates of obesity in children in our country range from 10 to 25 percent, and 80 percent of these overweight youngsters become obese adults (Coates & Thoresen, 1981; Stunkard, 1979). The end result is that an estimated 40 to 80 million adults in the United States are currently overweight (Hagen, 1981).

Achieving ideal body weight is one of the primary dietary concerns in the treatment of numerous diseases, including coronary heart disease, hypertension, and diabetes (Stunkard & Mahoney, 1976). Obese individuals have a higher risk of developing complications during surgery, have a mortality rate 50 percent greater than for normal-weight people, and have a higher incidence of medical problems including respiratory infections, skeletal-joint dysfunction, hernias, and gall bladder disease (Hagen, 1981; Mann, 1974). They also suffer a high incidence of emotional problems, including low self-esteem, depression, and interpersonal difficulties (Stuart, 1980).

Unfortunately, traditional medical and dietary approaches to the treatment of obesity have generally not been effective (Stuart, 1980). Obese persons are able to lose weight but quickly regain it (Mahoney & Mahoney, 1976). In addition, the dropout rate from traditional weight-control programs has been reported as high as 80 percent (Hagen, 1981). In contrast, behavioral approaches have been more effective in producing greater weight loss and have lower dropout rates (Abramson, 1977; Leon, 1976; Stuart, 1980). The behavioral weight-control literature has been comprehensively reviewed elsewhere (Hagen, 1981; Leon, 1976; Ley, 1981, Stuart, 1980; Stunkard, 1979). Behavioral strategies of stimulus control and contingency management (i.e., arranging reinforcement for appropriate eating and exercise behaviors) have been modified to include spouse-training procedures to enhance family support and facilitate maintenance of desired habit changes (Brownell et al., 1978). In addition, motivation to lose weight is essential for successful lifestyle change. One strategy used to enhance motivation has been to require the person to make a public committment to lose weight by informing family, friends, or group members of the intention to make specific habit changes (Hagen, 1981).

Jeffrey and Lemnitzer (1981) have recently suggested that increased physical exercise to control weight might be encouraged by: establishing national goals of physical fitness (as has been done in the People's Republic of China); improving physical education programs; expanding employer-sponsored sports programs; examining tax policies and other incentives; and redirecting school athletic programs away from the emphasis on the most talented athletes. In each of these areas, opportunities are present for psychologists to collaborate with health educators, public health nurses, epidemiologists, physicians, and program administrators to implement research studies, policy changes, and intervention programs to facilitate a more prudent diet and physical exercise (Dwore & Matarazzo, 1981).

Health experts in the area of obesity are also turning their attention to the early prevention of lifelong patterns of overeating and sedentary living by conducting intervention programs for overweight children and adolescents. Given the unnecessarily high incidence of obesity, hypertension, and hyperlipidemia among children in our country, the importance of such programs cannot be overstated. One representative program is the Stanford Adolescent Obesity Project (Coates & Thoresen, 1981). In this program, behavioral strategies, including self-observation, cue elimination, and social and family (parental) support, are used to facilitate weight control in obese adolescents. In one of the studies, behavioral intervention was found to be more effective when parents were involved (Coates & Thoresen, 1981). The Stanford group is also investigating the effect of peer leaders in obesity discussion groups similar to those employed by Evans et al. (1978) in smoking prevention programs with seventh-graders in Houston.

TYPE A BEHAVIOR PATTERN AND CORONARY HEART DISEASE

Major epidemiological studies have shown a positive relationship between Type A behavior and coronary heart disease (Haynes, Feinleib, & Kannel, 1980; Rosenman et al., 1964). The Type A behavior pattern involves a chronic sense of time urgency, competitive striving, involvement in multiple activities with self-imposed deadlines, a rapid pace in mental and physical actions, and an aggressive interpersonal style (Glass, 1977). Friedman and Rosenman's structured interview and standardized questionnaires such as the Jenkins Activity Survey (Jenkins, Zyzanski, & Rosenman, 1979) have been developed to measure Type A behavior objectively and reliably. There has developed an extensive body of research literature describing the relationship between Type A behavior and coronary heart disease, the theoretical development of the Type A construct, situation-specific behaviors associated with the Type A pattern, and possible biobehavioral mechanisms mediating the relationship between Type A behavior and coronary risk (e.g., Dembroski et al., 1978; Glass, 1977; Jenkins, 1978; Krantz et al., 1982). Although some studies (Friedman & Rosenman, 1959; Rosenman & Friedman, 1974) have shown that extreme Type A persons have higher cholesterol levels, faster clotting times, and higher epinephrine than Type B individuals, the bulk of the evidence suggests that Type As and Bs are not different in average levels on these *physiological* measures, per se. Rather the evidence suggests that Type As *react* more than Type B individuals to various stressors and challenging tasks; for example, showing greater increases in catecholamine response or blood pressure when presented with a stressor (Glass, 1977). As yet, however, the exact link between Type A behavior and specific pathophysiologic manifestations of coronary heart disease has not been determined.

Several attempts to modify Type A behavior have been reported in the literature. Suinn (1974), for example, developed a Cardiac Stress Management Program to modify Type A behavior. This behavioral treatment program consisted of relaxation and coping-skills training to help persons to recognize the early signs of stress and to reduce such stress by visualizing effective coping behaviors. In a study with cardiac patients (Suinn, 1974), this cardiac stress-management program was shown to reduce daily tension and self-reported speed and impatience. However, in a later study with healthy volunteers (Suinn & Bloom, 1978), significant reductions in Type A pattern, plasma lipid values, and blood pressure measures were not achieved. Roskies et al. (1978) reported reductions in perceived time pressures and amount of actual overtime work following a behavioral intervention group. Improvements were also noted in job satisfaction, stress, and cholesterol and blood pressure values. Still, changes in Type A behavior were not directly measured. To date, a variety of methods have been used in attempts to modify Type A behavior, including anxiety-management training, cognitive-behavior therapy, and self-monitoring (Suinn, 1981). But, the results of this Type A treatment outcome research have been inconsistent; evidence for treatment effectiveness is not conclusive because of the small sample sizes and failure to measure directly pretest versus posttest changes in Type A behavior in many of the studies.

According to Suinn (1981), Type A modification programs should attempt: (1) to modify stress-induced cognitions; (2) to eliminate the effects of specific stressors via emotional deconditioning; (3) to alter environmental factors such as the size of one's workload or number of appointments scheduled in a day; or (4) to modify stress-inducing behaviors such as rapid speech, walking, eating, or quick movements, each of which disturbs a sense of calm or relaxed control. Differential motivational issues must also be addressed, as suggested by Friedman (1979), who concluded that such interventions are most likely to be successful with Type A cardiac patients. Unless the Type A individual is convinced that reducing stressful behaviors will facilitate the achievement of personal goals, the modification of stress-generating behaviors will be difficult, if not impossible.

MODIFYING THE HIGH CHOLESTEROL, HIGH FAT AMERICAN DIET

There is a growing consensus among health experts that the typical American diet, which is high in fat, cholesterol, and salt, contributes to our country's increased morbidity and mortality due to cardiovascular disease. Several large-scale national, as well as local, research teams made up of psychologists, physicians, and other health scientists have provided examples of approaches developed to reduce the human and dollar costs associated with these dietary-based coronary risk factors.

The National Diet Heart Study (1968), a nationwide primary prevention trial, tested the effects of dietary intervention in preventing coronary heart disease in "normal" free-living male volunteers. Initial diet changes and reduced risk in biologic endpoints were achieved, but backsliding subsequently occurred. The Lipid Research Center study (Haback, Schrott, & Connor, 1974), another nationwide dietary intervention trial, also was aimed at reducing coronary risk in high-risk males. This study was designed to determine whether males with elevated plasma cholesterol could reduce their risk by lowering cholesterol levels via diet and, in some cases, pharmacologic treatment. The results showed initial lipid reduction which, unfortunately, again was followed by backsliding.

Foreyt et al. (1979) reported a diet intervention aimed at reducing plasma lipids in volunteer subjects. An educational intervention package was used that included either a diet booklet, education in nutrition, behavioral intervention utilizing group discussion, or a combination of these procedures. Foreyt et al. (1979) showed that plasma cholesterol levels in their target population initially could be reduced significantly. However, as shown in Figure 33.2, these initial cholesterol reductions were not maintained beyond six months.

Finally, at the Oregon Health Sciences University, a five-year dietary intervention program is currently being conducted to investigate the acceptance of a low-fat, low-cholesterol, low-sodium "alternative diet" among free-living Portland families and to examine the effects of dietary change on plasma lipids, blood pressure, and body weight (Matarazzo et al., 1982). The behavioral intervention approach is modeled after the technique used by Lewin with Iowa housewives in the 1940s, and requires spouse-participants to attend monthly group sessions conducted by psychologist-dietician co-leaders. The two critical features of this diet-change study are its focus on the family instead of the individual, and the gradual, phased approach

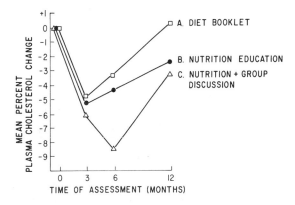

Fig. 33.2. Mean percentage change in plasma cholesterol in three groups receiving different interventions (adapted from Foreyt et al., 1979, p. 449).

to nutritional life-style change over a five-year period. The project is still in the intervention stage but early indications are that only a relatively small percentage of the families beginning the program are dropping out.

MULTIPLE RISK FACTOR REDUCTION

In three California communities near Stanford, Meyer et al. (1980) used a mass-media campaign (including television, radio, newspaper, billboards, bus posters, and direct mail leaflets as well as face-to-face instruction) and produced what the investigators believed were significant decreases concurrently in several targeted risk factors associated with cardiovascular disease. There were methodological problems with this research program, which have been addressed by Leventhal, Safer, Cleary, and Gutmann (1980) and rebutted in turn by Meyer, Maccoby, and Farquhar (1980). It is clear, however, that the Stanford group and the Houston research team are conducting important research on the potential of applying psychological knowledge in the prevention of a number of behavioral or life-style risks associated with cardiovascular disease. The Multiple Risk Factor Intervention Trial (Kuller et al., 1980), another national intervention study, was designed to evaluate the effects of reducing plasma cholesterol, hypertension, and cigarette smoking on subsequent mortality and morbidity due to coronary heart disease. The final results of this large-scale study, when available, should have a major impact on the coronary prevention field. Unfortunately, the design will not permit the determination of the individual contributions of (1) reducing plasma lipids via diet, (2) lowering blood pressure via diet and medication, and (3) quitting smoking on mortality and morbidity because, as a cost-saving measure, the intervention was aimed at all three of these risks collectively in each participating city, rather than using a design that focused on one intervention at a time.

It is clear even from these brief overviews of various programs that psychologists are making important contributions in the development of large-scale community and national programs for coronary risk-factor reduction. The accumulating literature also makes clear that psychologists working on the prevention of smoking, alcohol abuse, and obesity, and attenuating Type A behavior, have begun to collaborate with other health professionals in a joint effort to reduce multiple risk factors and to study how healthy people can be helped to remain healthy. Opportunities in behav-

ioral health, focusing on primary prevention, will continue to grow as the impact of psychological interventions is recognized and documented in well-designed and controlled research studies. There is by now ample evidence from long-term, prospective, longitudinal studies with clinically healthy individuals that everyday life-style risk behaviors markedly increase morbidity and mortality. The interested reader will find this evidence in reports from the 24-year prospective study conducted in Framingham, Massachusetts (Dawber, 1980), and from the 8½-year Western Collaborative Group Study carried out in 10 California companies (Rosenman et al., 1976).

Training and Research Issues in Health Psychology

As will be clear from earlier sections, numerous research, teaching, and professional practice opportunities are arising from psychologists working in a variety of health settings. As the field of health psychology grows, several important issues have emerged. These include the need for well-articulated standards for training in health psychology, the need for developing theoretical models to enhance the quality of research, further study of the diverse professional roles and responsibilities of psychologists in hospitals, clinics, schools, health-maintenance organizations (HMOs), private industry, and other current or potential health and health-care settings, and examination of various models with which to integrate clinical psychology most effectively with other specialty areas of psychology in health research and practice. Obviously, how these issues are resolved will influence the future direction of health psychology.

Training Clinical Psychologists in Health Psychology

Clinical psychologists, particularly those trained within the guidelines of the 1947 scientist-practitioner (Boulder) model, have been and continue to be particularly well suited to make a significant contribution in both the basic research and applied areas of health psychology. Their professional knowledge and experience in the areas of psychopathology, personality, human lifespan development, behavior change, human motivation, and psychological assessment and intervention prepare them well for helping to accumulate new knowledge and for applied work in the growing numbers of present and potential areas of health psychology discussed in the previous sections of this chapter. As a matter of fact, a significant portion of the research published by clinical psychologists since 1950 falls directly in the area today being labeled health psychology. Thus, until the past few years no other specialty area of psychology provided its new doctoral graduates with the range of academic, scientific, professional, and hospital-based experiences needed for immediate entry in the field of health psychology. As early as a quarter of a century ago, Matarazzo (1955a, 1955b) charted some of the opportunities offered psychologists working in medical settings. Writing for the present generation, and in discussing recent trends and future applications of clinical psychology, Hartman (1981) repeated these earlier observations and emphasized that most clinical psychologists already have the requisite skills and expertise concerning abnormal behavior, diagnosis, and intervention that can be applied to the understanding, treatment, and prevention of medical problems. Schofield (1979) reinforced this theme and described at length the potential contributions of clinical psychologists in such areas as patient compliance, preparation for surgery, and the patient-doctor relationship. For those preparing for a career of research, it is readily discerned that clinical psychologists have expertise in research design, methodology, and quantitative analysis which easily may be applied to questions related to prevention, mechanisms in the etiology of dysfunction, the effects of intervention procedures, and a host of other empirical questions related to health psychology. In addressing the issue of potential further advances, Hartman (1981) emphasized that psychological intervention techniques applied to the treatment and prevention of medical disorders and other health-related behaviors must be based on rigorous scientific methodology, and will benefit from the clinical-experimental perspective and expertise of the clinical psychologist. Whereas these arguments highlighting the contributions of clinical psychology are cogent, it is also important to point out that much of what is today the best of health psychology also has built upon the contributions of experimental psychologists such as Miller and Skinner, physiological psychologists such as Lindsley and Lacey, social psychologists such as Shachter, Rodin, Singer, Leventhal, and Evans, and representatives of a number of other subspecialties of psychology.

Unfortunately, because of the years of lead time universities require to introduce new curricular offerings, at the present time training in health psychology is being offered in ad hoc, isolated curricular segments, and mostly in traditional graduate programs in the several core areas of psychology which then are augmented by specialized research and practicum experiences in health-care, educational, and research settings. A recent survey by Belar, Wilson, and Hughes (1982) indicated that most APA-approved doctoral and internship training programs offer only a smattering of some form of training (i.e., coursework, practica, research) in health psychology. A Ph.D. degree in Health Psychology per se is presently granted in only three programs: University of California at San Francisco, Albert Einstein College of Medicine, and the Uniformed Services University of the Health Sciences in Bethesda, Maryland. The most frequently reported training opportunities in health psychology cited in the Belar et al. survey were within clinical psychology programs. Also directly related to training in health psychology are a number of predoctoral and postdoctoral training programs in behavioral medicine and behavioral health that are being funded by the National Heart, Lung, and Blood Institute (see Table 33.4). There is a likelihood that other NIH institutes may also fund training programs related to health psychology (Matarazzo, 1982) in the future.

It has been recommended by Olbrisch and Sechrest (1979) that individuals interested in pursuing a career in health psychology should first take extensive course work in the core areas of psychology, including social psychology, personality theory, development, physiological psychology, learning, motivation, and cognition before extending this with more formal training in health psychology. Both in applied areas and in basic research in health psychology, training in the core areas of psychology, including statistics and research methodology as well as the theoretical foundations of psychology, seems necessary to provide the health psychologist with the professional skills needed to interact effectively with other professionals, as well as to design and conduct research in a multidisciplinary health setting while maintaining a clear identity as a psychologist. In this regard, it seems clear that the training derived by clinical psychologists as scientist-practitioners continues to provide one of the optimal pathways for careers in both research and applied work in health psychology. The coursework, research opportunities, and practicum experiences provided in most APA-approved doctoral programs in clinical psychology enable those state-

TABLE 33.4. DOCTORAL AND POSTDOCTORAL RESEARCH TRAINING PROGRAMS
RELATED TO HEALTH PSYCHOLOGY AND SUPPORTED BY THE NATIONAL
HEART, LUNG, AND BLOOD INSTITUTE.*

Institution	Type	Training Director
Cornell Medical College	Two-year postdoctoral training in central nervous system control of circulation	Donald J. Reis Professor of Neurology
Johns Hopkins University	Pre- and postdoctoral multidisciplinary training in disciplines related to health	Lawrence W. Green Associate Professor of Health Education
Stanford University	Multidisciplinary postdoctoral training in cardiovascular disease prevention	John W. Farquhar Professor of Medicine
University of California, Berkeley	Pre- and postdoctoral training in cardiovascular disease etiology and prevention	S. Leonard Syme Professor of Public Health and Preventive Medicine
University of Houston	Pre- and postdoctoral training in social psychology and cardiovascular disease	Richard I. Evans Professor of Psychology
University of Minnesota	Predoctoral training in human behavior and cardiovascular disease	Russell V. Luepker Assistant Professor of Pharmacology
University of Oregon Health Sciences Center	Pre- and postdoctoral training in behavioral cardiology	Robert D. Fitzgerald Professor of Medical Psychology
University of Miami (Coral Gables)	Behavioral medicine research in cardiovascular disease	Neil Schneiderman Professor of Psychology
Washington University in St. Louis	Nutrition–behavioral cardiovascular disease prevention	Ruth E. Brennan Assistant Professor of Nutrition
University of Minnesota	A one- to three-year postdoctoral training program in cardiovascular disease prevention.	Henry W. Blackburn Professor and Director, Laboratory of Physiological Hygiene

*Updated from Matarazzo, 1980, p. 810.

licensed psychologists working in the applied areas of health psychology to contribute their doctoral-based research skills both in intervention-focused activities with patients and in the empirical investigations of such intervention techniques, thereby avoiding the possibility of being relegated to the position of behavior-change technicians.

For subsets of psychologists preparing for a research career who wish to acquire more specialized training in health psychology, Stone (1979) described examples of clinical research placements that have been arranged for graduate students in the health psychology program at the University of California at San Francisco. However, although university hospitals have long provided segments of training in health psychology for students in clinical psychology, there are currently few internship and other practicum facilities available to provide supervised training in psychological intervention exclusively with medical patients suffering from physical disorders associated with their life styles, or with healthy

individuals in schools and in the workplace (i.e., behavioral health). Accordingly, Olbrisch, Kurz, and Matarazzo (1981) have encouraged the development of formal internship programs in health psychology per se. Increasingly over the past decade, supervised training in health psychology has been added as a supplement to internship programs in clinical psychology: e.g., selected experiences in pain management, headache clinics, relaxation training, stress management, and consultation with surgical patients. The internship program at the Palo Alto VA Medical Center (Swan, Piccione, & Anderson, 1980) was the first to offer an integrated set of experiences in health psychology. The question has been raised as to whether such training should supplement or supplant more traditional training with psychiatric patients. At this early stage it is impossible to predict whether, in the long run, full-time internships in health psychology or supplemental packages of health psychology added to the current clinical psychology internship would be the better model for furthering the training of practitioners of health psychology. Accordingly, a diversity of such training approaches, offered in high-quality settings, would appear to maximize the chances that a model for health psychology, as effective as was the 1947 Boulder model for clinical psychology, will be developed.

Training Experimental Psychologists in Health Psychology

Optimally, psychologists working closely with physicians in health settings need and should receive some training in the biomedical and clinical sciences to facilitate communication with medical colleagues from other disciplines, as well as to understand better the physiological correlates of their behavioral variables. For example, in the predoctoral and postdoctoral graduate training program in experimental psychology focused on behavioral cardiology in the Department of Medical Psychology at the Oregon Health Sciences University, young psychologists receive almost two years of formal training in the physiology and anatomy of the cardiovascular system, lipid metabolism, nutrition, pathophysiology of coronary disease, and biochemistry in order to facilitate their ability to carry out effective basic and applied research with cardiologists and the other health professionals working in behavioral (and preventive) cardiology. Representative examples of the variety of these research undertakings have been reported by Brown, Eaton, and Cunningham (1979); Cunningham (1981); Fitzgerald and Stainbrook (1978); and O'Brien and Quinn (1979). Comparably suitable training packages have been developed in the Ph.D. programs related to health psychology for graduate students in social psychology trained by Evans (Houston), Leventhal (Wisconsin), Singer (Uniformed Services University of the Health Sciences), and Schwartz (Yale), and by Stone in health psychology policy and administration (University of California, San Francisco), to mention only a few such programs.

Changing Theory and Perspectives in Health Psychology

Among others, Leventhal and his colleagues frequently have argued in favor of strengthening the theoretical basis for research in health psychology (Leventhal, Meyer, & Nerenz, 1980). For example, in the study of patient compliance, numerous investigations have been designed to identify factors predicting compliance despite the absence of any comprehensive theory capable of generating specific hypotheses or integrating the numerous and often inconsistent findings in this area of research. Accordingly, Leventhal et al. (1980) described a theoretical model of health and illness based on the assumption that patients' attributions about their symptoms significantly influence the course of their illness and medical treatment. This model appears to represent a heuristically important advance over previously constructed theories, such as the Health Belief Model (Becker, 1974), in that it describes specific psychological processes involved in determining how patients perceive and deal with their illnesses. With such a theory base, such processes may now be better studied empirically in prospective research.

In addition, psychology's several learning theories (i.e., operant, respondent, and social-learning theory) have markedly influenced the development of health psychology (Hunt & Matarazzo, 1970, 1973, 1982). In their most recent theoretical conceptualization of the psychology of smoking, Hunt, Matarazzo, Weiss, and Gentry (1979) defined the smoking habit as a stable pattern of behavior marked by automaticity and unawareness, and influenced by associative learning as well as reinforcement. Hunt et al. also concluded that habits such as smoking are maintained primarily through practice and repetition and, thus, they recommend that interventions aimed at developing new healthful habits must provide cues for these desired habits that are compatible with the individual's daily routine. As described earlier, approaching risk factors and health psychology from a similar perspective, behavior therapists working in such areas as pain management have applied the principles of operant, associative, and social learning to the study of other habit patterns related to health and illness (e.g., smoking, diet, exercise, and pain behavior).

A third perspective emerging as an important contribution in health psychology is human development or lifespan psychology. Numerous articles in a recent (1979) issue of *Professional Psychology* devoted to health psychology supported this notion. Budman and Wertlieb (1979) suggested that preventive health interventions might be most effective when based on a model of human development, urging that graduate training programs in health psychology include coursework in lifespan psychology. Sank and Shapiro (1979) recommend that preventive therapeutic programs be provided to help people cope with difficult transition periods or life events (e.g., birth of one's first child, graduation, and entrance into the job market). Bibace and Walsh (1979) note that clinical-developmental psychologists and family-practice physicians share an interest in normal human (lifespan) development. This perspective is also consistent with the formulation of intervation programs designed for particular target groups such as the elderly (e.g., Lebray, 1979). The evolution of such theoretical perspectives will help promote and define productive avenues of research and practice in health psychology, but, clearly, additional training opportunities must be developed by our universities to help launch such initiatives and exploit the resulting opportunities.

The construct of self-efficacy (Bandura, 1977, 1982) has numerous applications in health psychology. According to the thesis of self-efficacy, an individual's expectations of personal efficacy, along with external cues and motivation, influence and direct behavior. For example, Marlatt and Gordon (1980) have suggested that perceived self-efficacy is a contributing factor in the common relapse process postulated in alcoholism, smoking, and heroin addiction. Studies of addictive behaviors such as cigarette smoking confirm that perceived inefficacy in specifiable situations increases vulnerability to relapse (Condiotte & Lichtenstein, 1981; DiClemente, 1981). Research on postcoronary rehabilitation offers one of many opportunities in health psychology to study the impact of perceived self-efficacy on health-promoting behaviors. For example, Bandura (1982) argues that in recovery from a heart attack, the restoration of perceived physical self-efficacy is an essential ingredient in the rehabilitation process.

Finally, as in each generation during the last century there is a growing trend in medicine once again to return to a focus on the patient (as opposed to the symptom) and on his or her family, to avoid the pitfalls of compartmentalized practice and to provide more humane and comprehensive medical services. Health psychologists are focusing more attention on family-based interventions to enhance their understanding of both illness and health behavior, and to promote life-style changes associated with the treatment and prevention of physical disorders. Examples of family-oriented interventions may be found in communitywide primary prevention programs such as the Family Heart-Alternative Diet Study at the Oregon Health Sciences University (Matarazzo et al., 1982), behavioral programs aimed at weight control (e.g.,

Brownell et al., 1981), and cardiac rehabilitation (Hoebel, 1976).

Possible Future Directions in Health Psychology

The field of behavioral health (i.e., helping healthy people to stay healthy) should continue to provide numerous opportunities not only for clinical psychologists working in applied aspects of health psychology but also for each of the other subdisciplines of psychology (e.g., experimental, social, physiological, developmental). It will be clear from our earlier discussion that a consensus has emerged that the behavior or life style of the individual is today's frontier in the study and understanding of health and illness; for example, the use of tobacco and alcohol, consumption of cholesterol and salt, poor dental hygiene, and failure to use automobile seat belts. As detailed elsewhere (Matarazzo, 1982), every specialty of academic, scientific, and professional psychology has within its ranks psychologists with the potential to contribute to this relatively unexplored frontier of the health behavior of currently healthy individuals who wish to decrease their risk of losing this healthy state. Some examples of challenges and new opportunities will now be highlighted.

Collaboration with Health Educators

Psychologists in university, school, and industrial settings who are interested in charting new directions in behavioral health or preventive medicine have available numerous opportunities to teach, do research, and carry on a practice with one group of professional colleagues (health educators) who already possess a wealth of readily applicable skills. Although overlooked by psychologists until recently (Dwore & Matarazzo, 1981), health-education specialists are experts in the applied aspects of helping healthy people to stay healthy. They already have classes full of elementary, secondary, and college-based students eager to learn, and the space and facilities within which to practice and perfect their ideas and teaching-intervention techniques. Psychologists and health educators can pool their skills to develop health life-style-change programs in physical exercise, diet, prevention of smoking and alcohol abuse, weight control, and stress management. Furthermore, these primary prevention approaches also could be applied to as yet unexploited but potentially equally challenging areas such as preventive intervention with primary-grade children who are facing or have faced parental death, divorce or remarriage, and comparable crises of early life (see Felner et al., 1981, for one example). To such programs psychologists can bring to bear their expertise in research design and behavior-change modalities while, concurrently, health educators can contribute a set of practical professional skills based on a didactic educational base and decades of application in the classroom setting.

Both the behavioral-science and health-education field are oriented toward studying human behavior and improving the quality of life through teaching, research, and service. Both fields have a need to collect data to document progress toward established goals. Dwore and Matarazzo (1981) have suggested that behavioral scientists (including psychologists, anthropologists, sociologists, and others) and health educators can all benefit from "interchanges of perspective through visiting faculty exchanges, team taught classes and seminars on the same campus, and interdisciplinary research and service projects" (p. 7). The collaboration of behavioral scientists (especially psychologists) and health educators will enhance the teaching, research, and service programs that currently are aimed at the investigation and actual modification of health-related habits, thereby reducing the costs associated with health care in this country. In addition, considerable new knowledge will be added to the current scientific base that supports these respective disciplines.

In what settings will the collaboration between psychologists, physicians, health educators, and other health professionals take place? We believe health psychologists soon will find themselves working in a variety of school, community, and workplace settings other than hospitals and medical clinics. Particularly in the area of primary prevention (behavioral health), psychologists are already working in a variety of settings, including schools, industry, the military settings, YMCAs, senior citizens' centers, and other community agencies conducting risk-factor reduction, stress-management workshops, and "wellness" clinics.

Departments of Medical or Health Psychology

Recent developments suggest that medical school psychologists quite likely will continue for a period of time to be one of the dominant forces in the field of health psychology, inasmuch as they far outdistance sociologists and anthropologists in total numbers and, as licensed health professionals in their states and as voting members of the medical staff at some university hospitals (Matarazzo et al., 1978), they have the unique capacity both to provide treatment to patients and to do research on health and illness behavior.

Within medical schools in particular, there will most likely be a continued increase in the number of psychologists employed on medical school faculties. The increase in the numbers of medical school psychologists during the last 30 years has been a linear one, and there is no reason to suspect that the growth period is over. In addition, unlike the 1950–1970 era which saw them administratively housed in Departments of Psychiatry, recent academic employment patterns suggest that increasingly more medical school psychologists will find themselves housed administratively in Departments of Pediatrics, Medicine, and Neurology, as well as in Departments of Medical (or Health) Psychology themselves (Matarazzo et al., 1981, pp. 312–315). Given the acceleration in the requests for consultations to university hospital and community hospital-based psychologists from physicians, one also may expect an increase in this present number of autonomous departments of psychology in community and university hospitals and in schools of medicine. This same change to full department status in medical schools occurred for Psychiatry, which in the pre-1950 era was a division within the Department of Medicine; for Anesthesiology, Obstetrics and Gynecology, Opthalmology, and Otolaryngology, which until recently were divisions within the Department of Surgery; and for Neurology and Dermatology which were also formerly divisions within Departments of Medicine. This anticipated important administrative recognition of psychology as an autonomous medical school and hospital department will probably be promoted by members of the emerging discipline of psychology, as well as by specialists from other medical school and hospital departments who are in positions of influence. This will likely occur for several reasons, including the establishment of national and local professional and scientific societies in health psychology; offers of federal and private funding for research, training, and service in this newly emerging specialty; the emergence of relevant scientific professional specialty journals (e.g., Division 38's new journal, *Health Psychology*); and the creation of discipline-specific housestaff and postgraduate fellowship programs (in health psychology). These myriad forces operated to give full specialty status (and next, full departmental status) to neurology, dermatology, psychiatry, anesthesiology, obstetrics and gynecology, etc., and one may realistically expect a comparable elevation of health (or medical) psychology to the status of a full department in many more universities and community hospitals (Matarazzo, Carmody, & Gentry, 1981).

Future Trends in Psychotherapy

What form will psychotherapy as a modality for psychological intervention take in the newly developing field of health psychology? The 1960s and 1970s witnessed the growth of behavioral and cognitive-behavioral approaches to therapy, along with a proliferation of group and family therapy modalities, as traditional psychoanalytic and psychodynamic therapies lost their standing as the preferred form of psychological intervention. Now, with the emergence of health psychology, the question has been raised whether or not individual psychotherapy will continue, as in the 1952–1975 era, to represent the mainstream of one-to-one intervention for psychologists working in health settings. Several early studies have suggested that individual psychotherapy may offer considerable utility as a cost-containment strategy even with medical patients. These studies attempted to document changes in health-care utilization following referral for psychological services. Olbrisch (1977), in her review of the literature on the effects of psychotherapy on "overutilizers" of medical care, found that a large number of persons who seek medically based health-care services are under some form of emotional distress and that, likewise, individuals with emotional problems tend to use medical services excessively, looking for answers to their life problems. In a similar vein, Rosen and Wiens (1979) found significant declines in the number of outpatient visits, drug prescriptions, emergency-room visits, and medical diagnostic services following referral to the medical psychology clinic. These findings appeared to corroborate the results reported earlier by Follette and Cummings (1967), and Goldberg, Krantz, and Locke (1970). However, in a critique of these three studies Olbrisch (1980, 1981) cautioned against an overly enthusiastic interpretation of

these early findings because of potential methodological weaknesses, such as patient self-selection into treatment and the interaction of selection with regression. Rosen and Wiens (1980), in response to Olbrisch, indicated that a reduction in medical-care utilization persisted even when a substantial portion of high-frequency users were dropped from the analysis. More recently, Olbrisch (1981) described a brief one-hour educational intervention with college students who were high utilizers of medical-health services, and again concluded that neither the effectiveness of psychotherapy nor that of educational approaches has been demonstrated in reducing inappropriate utilization of medical services. This important issue is far from settled, and represents an area in which research as well as applied health psychologists could make a very important contribution to science as well as to society in general.

Recent trends suggest that more traditional individual and group psychotherapy will continue to be practiced but that, additionally, well-organized psychoeducational and behavioral-group intervention programs aimed at specific target areas such as weight control, the prevention of smoking and alcohol abuse, reduction of absenteeism, and the human and dollar costs associated with chronic illness and pain, treatment of somatic symptoms such as headaches, and stress management in the workplace (and in our primary and secondary schools), will be increasingly utilized. As implied in Olbrisch's criticisms of prior research, the growth of such programmatic intervention, prevention, and treatment approaches will be fostered by well-designed and controlled outcome research documenting effective components of intervention with specific populations with particular deficits or lifestyle problems.

Preventive (Behavioral) Cardiology

As discussed briefly in earlier sections, a considerable amount of scientific knowledge has accumulated in the past two decades on the effects of life style on cardiovascular health. For example, there is now extensive evidence relating high-fat diet, smoking, Type A behavior, and other risk factors to the development of atherosclerotic coronary disease. As detailed by Matarazzo (in press), recent publications by the National Heart, Lung, and Blood Institute (NHLBI) Working Group on Arteriosclerosis (1981), the National Academy of Sciences (1978), and the three major reports from the Surgeon General's office all clearly demonstrate the importance this nation's leading health experts place on using knowledge from the behavioral sciences in promoting the physical health of our citizens. Thus, in the Surgeon General's report on "Promoting Health—Preventing Disease: Objectives for the Nation, 1980," 15 specific goals were outlined for promoting the health of our citizens during the next decade. Among these goals are: control of high blood pressure; smoking cessation; better nutrition; better physical fitness and exercise; and control of stress. Consistent with these goals, the NHLBI predicts that the following appear to be promising areas for future research: (1) Role of behavior in such life-style factors as smoking, Type A pattern, hypertension, obesity, poor diet, lack of exercise, and stress; (2) Compliance; (3) Animal models of the role of social stressors and conditioning on sudden death; and (4) Promotion of cardiovascular health in currently healthy people. To accomplish these and many related research objectives too numerous to be repeated here, highly skilled behavioral scientists will be needed with the requisite background of interdisciplinary training at the interfaces of cardiology and behavior. The developments in the past decade in research on risk factors combined with these recently published national goals for 1990 make it clear that the number of young behavioral scientists with appropriate predoctoral interdisciplinary training in cardiology (and young cardiologists with training in the behavioral sciences) must be increased considerably if these goals are to be met (Hollis, Connor, & Matarazzo, 1982; Matarazzo et al., 1982).

Summary and Conclusions

The educational, scientific, and professional contributions of health psychology within the broader context of behavioral medicine and behavioral health that were reviewed above reinforce the growing observation that the psychologist has emerged as a full-fledged, respected health professional. In the applied areas of health psychology, examples of the psychologist's expanding role in the treatment and prevention of physical illness can be found in numerous health, school, community, and workplace settings. Considering the current economic climate in our country, reflected in the federal mandate for reduced government spending, health psychologists will be looking more to the private sector (business and industry) for financial support for these efforts. As described by Matarazzo (1980), the corporate world is becoming increasingly concerned about maintaining the health of its employees and executives to improve the quality of life and increase productivity and profit. More and more businesses are welcoming psychologists and other health specialists who, as examples, conduct health-screening clinics and carry out intervention programs designed to promote healthy behaviors (e.g., physical exercise) and to prevent, alleviate, or reduce life-style-risk behaviors.

As primary prevention in targeted areas continues to present opportunities for psychologists to develop ways of keeping healthy people healthy, other professional and scientific partnerships will develop along with the psychologist-physician collaboration that has become prevalent during the past decade. Health educators at numerous colleges and universities throughout the country appear ready to collaborate with behavioral specialists to improve the quality of health education in such areas as preventing the onset of smoking, alcohol and drug abuse, and obesity in primary-grade and teenage youth. At the same time, there will be continued demand for psychological intervention with already self-identified medical patients suffering from physical dysfunctions associated with their life styles (e.g., headaches, back pain, dysmenorrhea), recent life-threatening myocardial infarction, mutilative surgery, and the prospect of a lifelong chronic disease (diabetes, asthma, renal failure, etc.). The intervention strategies described in this chapter aimed at promoting life-style change, stress reduction, psychological rehabilitation of the chronic patient, and early prevention are applicable to both sick and disabled patients (behavioral medicine), and currently healthy people trying to stay healthy (behavioral health). According to our projections, both areas will continue to offer professionally and scientifically rewarding challenges as long as psychologists continue to be creative in applying their clinical and scientific skills and expertise in human behavior, in collaboration with other health professionals in a variety of hospital, school, individual, and other health-promotion and health-remediation settings. The Second World War required that our government rehabilitate a large number of disabled veterans and help millions more reassimilate themselves into our nation's colleges and workforce. These urgent societal needs helped rapidly increase the development of modern clinical psychology during the past four decades. Recent advances in biomedical science and practice have wiped out many infectious diseases and other major earlier killers of the 20th century, but other diseases, disorders, and dysfunctions remain in which life-style behavior plays a very prominent role. This fact is recognized by policy makers in medicine, in psychology, and in funding agencies both in the public and the private sectors. In our opinion, these interrelated recent developments present health psychology with opportunities for rapid growth comparable with those faced by clinical psychology in the first years after the Second World War. What is required immediately is that psychologist-leaders in our institutions of higher learning, our scientific and professional societies, and our state licensing boards in psychology recognize these opportunities and exploit them in the service of society.

References

Abel, E. L. Behavioral teratology of alcohol. *Psychological Bulletin*, 1981, **90**, 564–581.

Abramson, E. E. Behavioral approaches to weight control: An updated review. *Behaviour Research and Therapy*, 1977, **15**, 355–363.

Agras, S., & Jacobs, R. Hypertension. In O. Pomerleau & J. P. Brady (Eds.), *Behavioral medicine: Theory and practice*. Baltimore: Williams & Wilkins, 1979.

Alden, L. Preventive strategies in the treatment of alcohol abuse: A review and a proposal. In P. O. Davidson & S. M. Davidson (Eds.), *Behavioral medicine: Changing health lifestyles*. New York: Brunner/Mazel, 1980.

Bakal, D. A. *Psychology and medicine*. New York: Springer, 1979.

Bandura, A. Self-efficacy: Toward a unifying theory of behavioral change. *Psychological Review*, 1977, **84**, 191–215.

Bandura, A. Self-efficacy mechanism in human agency. *American Psychologist*, 1982, **37**, in press.

Baile, W. F., & Engel, B. T. A behavioral strategy for promoting treatment compliance following myocardial infarction. *Psychosomatic Medicine*, 1978, **40**, 413–419.

Becker, M. H. (Ed.) The health belief model and personal health behavior. *Education Monographs*, 1974, **2**, 326–508.

Belar, C. D., Wilson, E., & Hughes, H. Doctoral training in health psychology. *Health Psychology*, 1982, **1**, 289–299.

Berg, R. L. The high cost of self-deception. *Preventive Medicine*, 1976, **5**, 483–495.

Bibace, R., & Walsh, M. D. Clinical developmental psychologists in family practice settings. *Professional Psychology*, 1979, **10**, 441–451.

Botvin, G. J., Eng, A., & Williams, C. L. Preventing the onset of cigarette smoking through life skills training. *Preventive Medicine*, 1980, **9**, 135–143.

Brown, J. S., Eaton, N. K., & Cunningham, C. L. Motivation. In M. E. Meyer (Ed.), *Foundations of psychology*. New York: Oxford University Press, 1979.

Brownell, K. D., Heckerman, C. L., Westlake, R. S., Hayes, S. C., & Monti, P. M. The effects of couples training and partner cooperativeness in the behavioral treatment of obesity. *Behaviour Research and Therapy*, 1978, **16**, 323–333.

Buck, R. L. Behavioral scientists in schools of medicine. *Journal of Health and Human Behavior*, 1961, **2**, 59–64.

Budman, S. H., & Wertlieb, D. Psychologists in health care settings: An introduction to the special issue. *Professional Psychology*, 1979, **10**, 397–401.

Budzynski, T. H. Biofeedback procedures in the clinic. *Seminars in Psychiatry*, 1973, **4**, 537–547.

Califano, J. A., Jr. *Smoking and health: A report of the Surgeon General*. Washington, D.C.: Superintendent of Documents, U.S. Government Printing Office, Stock Number 017-000-0218-0, 1979.

Carmody, T. P., Senner, J. W., Malinow, M. R., & Matarazzo, J. D. Physical exercise rehabilitation: Long-term dropout rate in cardiac patients. *Journal of Behavioral Medicine*, 1980, **3**, 163–168.

Cinciripini, P. M., Williamson, D. A., & Epstein, L. H. Behavioral treatment of migraine headaches. In J. M. Ferguson & C. B. Taylor (Eds.), *The comprehensive handbook of behavioral medicine*, Vol. 2. New York: Spectrum, 1981.

Coates, T. J., & Thoresen, C. E. Treating obesity in children and adolescents: Is there any hope? In J. M. Ferguson & C. B. Taylor (Eds.), *The comprehensive handbook of behavioral medicine*, Vol. 2. New York: Spectrum, 1981.

Condiotte, M. M., & Lichtenstein, E. Self-efficacy and relapse in smoking cessation programs. *Journal of Consulting and Clinical Psychology*, 1981, **49**, 648–658.

Cox, D. J., Freundlick, A., & Meyer, R. G. Differential effectiveness of electromyograph feedback, verbal relaxation instructions and medication placebo with tension headaches. *Journal of Consulting and Clinical Psychology*, 1975, **43**, 892–899.

Cunningham, C. L. Association between the elements of a bivalent compound stimulus. *Journal of Experimental Psychology: Animal Behavior Processes*, 1981, **7**, 425–436.

Dawber, T. R., *The Framingham study: The epidemiology of atherosclerotic disease*. Cambridge, Mass.: Harvard University Press, 1980.

Dembroski, R. J., Weiss, S. M., Shields, J. L., Haynes, S., & Feinleib, M. (Eds.) *Coronary-prone behavior*. New York: Springer-Verlag, 1978.

DiClemente, C. C. Self-efficacy and smoking cessation maintenance: A preliminary report. *Cognitive Therapy and Research*, 1981, **5**, 175–187.

DiScipio, W. J., & Feldman, M. C. Combined behavior therapy and physical therapy in the treatment of a fear of walking. *Journal of Behavior Therapy and Experimental Psychiatry*, 1971, **2**, 151–152.

Dwore, R. B., & Matarazzo, J. D. The behavioral sciences and health education: Disciplines with a compatible interest? *Health Education*, 1981, **12**, 4–7.

Ehrenwald, J. *The history of psychotherapy: From healing*

magic to encounter. New York: Jason Aronson, 1976.

Engel, G. L. The need for a new medical model: A challenge for biomedicine. *Science,* 1977, **196,** 130–136.

Epstein, L. H., & Cinciripini, P. M. Behavioral control of tension headaches. In J. M. Ferguson & C. B. Taylor (Eds.), *The comprehensive handbook of behavioral medicine.* Vol. 2. New York: Spectrum, 1981.

Evans, R. I. Smoking in children: Developing a social psychological strategy of deterrence. *Preventive Medicine,* 1976, **5,** 122–127.

Evans, R. I., Rozelle, R. M., Mittlemark, M. B., Hansen, W. B., Bane, A. L., & Havis, J. Deterring the onset of smoking in children: Knowledge of immediate physiological effects and coping with peer pressure, media pressure, and parent modeling. *Journal of Applied Social Psychology,* 1978, **8,** 126–135.

Felner, R. D., Norton, P. L., Cowen, E. L., & Farber, S. S. A prevention program for children experiencing life crisis. *Professional Psychology,* 1981, **12,** 446–452.

Ferguson, J. M., & Taylor, C. B. (Eds.) *The comprehensive handbook of behavioral medicine.* New York: Spectrum, 1981.

Fitzgerald, R. D., & Stainbrook, G. L. The influence of ethanol on learned and reflexive heart rate responses of rats during aversive classical conditioning. *Journal of Studies on Alcohol,* 1978, **39,** 1,916–1,930.

Follette, W., & Cummings, N. A. Psychiatric services and medical utilization in a prepaid health plan setting. *Medical Care,* 1967, **5,** 25–35.

Fordyce, W. E. Treating pain by contingency management. In J. J. Bonica (Ed.), *Advances in neurology (Vol. 4) International symposium on pain.* New York: Raven, 1974.

Fordyce, W. E. Behavioral concepts in chronic pain and illness. In P. O. Davidson (Ed.), *The behavioral management of anxiety, depression, and pain.* New York: Brunner/Mazel, 1976. (a)

Fordyce, W. E. *Behavioral methods for chronic pain and illness.* St. Louis: Mosby, 1976. (b)

Foreyt, J. P., Scott, L. W., Mitchell, R. D., & Gotto, A. M. Plasma lipid changes in the normal population following behavioral treatment. *Journal of Consulting and Clinical Psychology,* 1979, **47,** 440–452.

Franz, S. I. On psychology and medical education. *Science,* 1913, **38,** 555–556.

Friedman, M. The modification of Type A behavior in post-infarction patients. *American Heart Journal,* 1979, **97,** 551–560.

Friedman, M., & Rosenman, R. H. Association of specific overt behavior pattern with increase in blood cholesterol, blood clotting time, incidence of arcus senilis and clinical artery disease. *Journal of the American Medical Association,* 1959, **169,** 1,286–1,296.

Galanter, M. Young adult social drinkers: Another group at risk? *Alcoholism: Clinical and Experimental Research,* 1980, **4,** 241–242.

Gentry, W. D., & Matarazzo, J. D. Medical psychology: Three decades of growth and development. In C. K. Prokop & L. A. Bradley (Eds.), *Medical psychology: Contributions to behavioral medicine.* New York: Academic Press, 1981.

Gentry, W. D., & Williams, R. B. *Psychological aspects of myocardial infarction and coronary care.* St. Louis: Mosby, 1979.

Glass, D. C. *Behavior patterns, stress, and coronary disease.* New York: Wiley, 1977.

Goldberg, I. F., Krantz, G., & Locke, B. Z. Effect of short-term outpatient psychiatric therapy on the utilization of medical services in a prepaid group practice medical program. *Medical Care,* 1970, **8,** 419–428.

Goldenson, R. M., Dunham, J. R., & Dunham, C. S. (Eds.). *Disability and rehabilitation handbook.* New York: McGraw-Hill, 1978.

Green, D. E. Psychological factors in smoking. In M. E. Jarvik, J. W. Cullen, E. R. Gritz, T. M. Vogt, & L. J. West (Eds.), *Research on smoking behavior* (NIDA Research Monograph No. 17). DHEW Publication 78-581. Rockville, Md.: DHEW, 1977.

Greif, E., & Matarazzo, R. G. *Behavioral approaches to rehabilitation: Coping with change.* New York: Springer, 1982.

Gulledge, A. D. Psychological aftermaths of myocardial infarction. In W. D. Gentry & R. B. Williams (Eds.), *Psychological aspects of myocardial infarction and coronary care.* St. Louis: Mosby, 1979.

Guze, S. B., Matarazzo, J. D., & Saslow, G. A formulation of principles of comprehensive medicine with special reference to learning theory. *Clinical Psychology,* 1953, **9,** 127–136.

Haback, Y. A. Schrott, H. G., & Connor, W. D. The coronary primary prevention trial. *Journal of the Iowa Medical Society,* 1974, **64,** 19–28.

Hagen, R. L. Behavioral treatment of obesity: Progress but not panacea. In J. M. Ferguson & C. B. Taylor (Eds.), *The comprehensive handbook of behavioral medicine.* Vol. 2. New York: Spectrum, 1981.

Haggerty, R. J. Changing lifestyles to improve health. *Preventive Medicine,* 1977, **6,** 276–289.

Harris, P. R. *The health consequences of smoking (the changing cigarette): A report of the Surgeon General.* Washington, D.C.: Superintendent of Documents, U.S. Government Printing Office, Stock Number 1980-335-339:7063, 1980.

Hartman, L. M. Clinical psychology: Emergent trends and future applications. *Journal of Clinical Psychology,* 1981, **37,** 439–445.

Haynes, S. G., Feinleib, M., & Kannel, W. B. Relationship of psychosocial factors to coronary heart disease in the Framingham study. *American Journal of Epidemiology,* 1980, **111,** 37–58.

Hoebel, F. C. Brief family-interactional therapy in the management of cardiac-related high-risk behaviors. *Journal of Family Practice,* 1976, **3,** 613–618.

Hollis, J. F., Connor, W. E., & Matarazzo, J. D. Lifestyle, behavioral health and heart disease. In R. J. Gatchel, A. Baum, & J. E. Singer (Eds.), *Behavioral medicine and clinical psychology: Overlapping disciplines.* Hillsdale, N.J.: Erlbaum, 1982.

Holroyd, K. R., Andrasik, F., & Westbrook, T. Cognitive control of tension headache. *Cognitive Therapy and Research,* 1977, **1,** 121–133.

Hunt, W. A., & Matarazzo, J. D. Habit mechanisms in smoking. In W. A. Hunt (Ed.), *Learning mechanisms and smoking.* Chicago: Aldine-Atherton, 1970.

Hunt, W. A., & Matarazzo, J. D. Three years later: Recent developments in the modification of smoking behavior. *Journal of Abnormal Psychology*, 1973, **81**, 107–114.

Hunt, W. A., & Matarazzo, J. D. Changing smoking behavior: A critique. In R. J. Gatchel, A. Baum, & J. E. Singer (Eds.), *Behavioral medicine and clinical psychology: Overlapping disciplines.* Hillsdale, N.J.: Erlbaum, 1982.

Hunt, W. A., Matarazzo, J. D., Weiss, S. M., & Gentry, W. D. Associative learning, habit and health behavior. *Journal of Behavioral Medicine*, 1979, **2**, 111–124.

Hurd, P. D., Johnson, C. A., Pechacek, T., Bast, L. P., Jacobs, D. R., & Luepker, R. V. Prevention of cigarette smoking in seventh grade students. *Journal of Behavioral Medicine*, 1980, **3**, 15–28.

Janis, I. L., & Rodin, J. Attribution, control, and decision-making: Social psychology and health care. In G. C. Stone, F. Cohen, & N. E. Adler (Eds.), *Health psychology: A handbook.* San Francisco: Jossey-Bass, 1979.

Jeffrey, D. B., & Lemnitzer, N. Diet, exercise, obesity, and related health problems: A macroenvironmental analysis. In J. M. Ferguson & C. B. Taylor (Eds.), *The comprehensive handbook of behavioral medicine,* Vol. 2. New York: Spectrum, 1981.

Jenkins, C. D. Behavioral risk factors in coronary artery disease. *Annual Review of Medicine*, 1978, **29**, 543–562.

Jenkins, C. D., Zyzanski, S. J., & Rosenman, R. H. *Jenkins Activity Survey Manual.* New York: Psychological Corporation, 1979.

Kavanaugh, T., Shephard, R. J., Doney, H., & Randit, V. Intensive exercise in coronary rehabilitation. *Medical Science and Sports*, 1973, **5**, 34–39.

Kentala, E. Physical fitness and feasibility of physical rehabilitation after myocardial infarction in men of working age. *Annals of Clinical Research*, 1972, **4**, 1–84.

Krantz, D. S., Glass, D. C., Schaeffer, M. A., & Davia, J. E. Behavior patterns and coronary disease: A critical evaluation. In J. T. Cacippo & R. E. Petty (Eds.), *Focus on cardiovascular psychophysiology.* New York: Guilford Press, 1982.

Kuller, L., Neaton, J., Caggiula, A., & Falvo-Gerard, L. Primary prevention of heart attacks: The multiple risk factor intervention trial. *American Journal of Epidemiology*, 1980, **112**, 185–199.

Lebray, P. R. Geropsychology in long-term care settings. *Professional Psychology*, 1979, **10**, 475–485.

Leigh, H., & Reiser, M. F. Major trends in psychosomatic medicine: The psychiatrists evolving role in medicine. *Annals of Internal Medicine*, 1977, **87**, 233–239.

Leon, G. R. Current directions in the treatment of obesity. *Psychological Bulletin*, 1976, **83**, 557–578.

Leventhal, H., Meyer, D., & Nerenz, D. The common sense representation of illness danger. In S. Rachman (Ed.), *Medical psychology,* Vol. 2. London: Pergamon, 1980.

Leventhal, H., Safer, M. A., Cleary, P. D., & Gutmann, M. Cardiovascular risk modification by community based programs for life-style change: Comments on the Stanford study. *Journal of Consulting and Clinical Psychology*, 1980, **48**, 150–158.

Ley, P. The psychology of obesity: Its causes, consequences, and control. In S. Rachman (Ed.), *Contributions to medical psychology.* New York: Pergamon, 1981.

Lindemann, J. (Ed.) *Psychological and behavioral aspects of physical disability: A manual for health practitioners.* New York: Plenum, 1981.

Lipowski, S. J. Psychosomatic medicine in the seventies: An overview. *American Journal of Psychiatry*, 1977, **134**, 233–244.

Lubin, B., Nathan, R. G., & Matarazzo, J. D. Psychologists in medical education: 1976. *American Psychologist*, 1978, **33**, 339–343.

Mahoney, M. J., & Mahoney, K. Treatment of obesity: A clinical exploration. In B. J. Williams, S. Martin, & J. Foreyt (Eds.), *Obesity: Behavioral approaches to dietary management.* New York: Brunner/Mazel, 1976.

Mann, G. V. The influence of obesity on health, Parts 1 and 2. *New England Journal of Medicine*, 1974, **289**, 178–186, 226–232.

Marlatt, G. A., & Gordon, J. R. Determinants of relapse: Implications for the maintenance of behavior change. In P. O. Davidson & S. M. Davidson (Eds.), *Behavioral medicine: Changing health lifestyles.* New York: Brunner/Mazel, 1980.

Masters, W. H., & Johnson, V. E. *Human sexual inadequacy.* Boston: Little, Brown, 1970.

Matarazzo, J. D. Comprehensive medicine: A new era in medical education. *Human organization*, 1955, **14**, 4–9. (a)

Matarazzo, J. D. The role of the psychologist in medical education and practice: A challenge posed by comprehensive medicine. *Human organization*, 1955, **14**, 9–14. (b)

Matarazzo, J. D. Behavioral health and behavioral medicine: Frontiers for a new health psychology. *American Psychologist*, 1980, **35**, 807–817.

Matarazzo, J. D. Behavioral health's challenge to academic, scientific, and professional psychology. *American Psychologist*, 1982, **37**, 1–14.

Matarazzo, J. D. Behavioral health: An overview. In J. D. Matarazzo, N. E. Miller, S. M. Weiss, J. A. Herd, & S. M. Weiss (Eds.), *Behavioral health: A handbook of health enhancement and disease prevention.* New York: Wiley, in press.

Matarazzo, J. D., Carmody, T. P., & Gentry, W. D. Psychologists on the faculties of United States schools of medicine: Past, present and possible future. *Clinical Psychology Review*, 1981, **1**, 293–317.

Matarazzo, J. D., Connor, W. E., Fey, S. G., Carmody, T. P., Pierce, D. K., Brischetto, C. S., Baker, L. H., Connor, S. J., & Sexton, G. Behavioral cardiology with an emphasis on the Family Heart study: Fertile ground for psychological and biomedical research. In T. Millon, C. J. Green, & R. B. Meagher (Eds.), *Handbook of health care psychology.* New York: Plenum, 1982.

Matarazzo, J. D., Lubin, B., & Nathan, R. G. Psychologists' membership on the medical staffs of university teaching hospitals. *American Psychologist*, 1978, **33**, 23–29.

McAlister, A. L., Perry, C., & Maccoby, N. Adolescent smoking: Onset and prevention. *Pediatrics*, 1979, **63**, 650–658.

Melamed, B. G., & Siegel, L. J. *Behavioral medicine: Practical applications in health care.* New York: Springer, 1980.

Mensh, I. N. Psychology in medical education. *American Psychologist*, 1953, **8**, 83–85.

Meyer, A. J., Maccoby, N., & Farquhar, J. W. Reply to Kasl and Leventhal et al. *Journal of Consulting and Clinical Psychology*, 1980, **48**, 159–163.

Meyer, A. J., Nash, J. D., McAlister, A. L., Maccoby, N., & Farquhar, J. W. Skills training in a cardiovascular health education campaign. *Journal of Consulting and Clinical Psychology*, 1980, **4**, 330–334.

Michael, J. L. Rehabilitation. In C. Neuringer & J. L. Michael (Eds.), *Behavior modification in clinical psychology*. New York: Appelton-Century-Crofts, 1970.

Miller, N. E. Learning of visceral and glandular responses. *Science*, 1969, **163**, 434–445.

Mishler, E. G., AmaraSingham, L. R., Hauser, S. T., Liem, R., Osherson, D. S., & Waxler, N. E. *Social contexts of health, illness, and patient care*. Cambridge: Cambridge University Press, 1981.

Nagle, R., Gangola, R., & Picton-Robinson, I. Factors influencing return to work after myocardial infarction. *Lancet*, 1971, **2**, 454–456.

Nathan, R. G., Lubin, B., Matarazzo, J. D., & Persely, G. W. Psychologists in schools of medicine, 1955, 1964, and 1977. *American Psychologist*, 1979, **34**, 622–627.

National Diet-Heart Study Research Group. The National Diet-Heart Study Final Report. *Circulation*, 1968, **37**, 761–777.

O'Brien, J. H., & Quinn, K. J. Changes in cortical sensory responses with a cryogenic blockade of nucleus ventralis posterolateralis. *Brain Research Bulletin*, 1979, **4**, 539–548.

Olbrisch, M. E. Psychotherapeutic interventions in physical health and economic efficiency. *American Psychologist*, 1977, **32**, 761–777.

Olbrisch, M. E. psychological intervention and reduced medical care utilization: A modest interpretation. *American Psychologist*, 1980, **35**, 760–761.

Olbrisch, M. E. Evaluation of a stress management program for high utilizers of a prepaid university health service. *Medical Care*, 1981, **19**, 153–159.

Olbrisch, M. E., Kurz, R. B., & Matarazzo, J. D. Internships in health psychology: Or bolder than Boulder. *Health Psychologist*, 1981 **3** (1).

Olbrisch, M. E., & Sechrest, L. Educating health psychologists in traditional graduate training programs. *Professional Psychology*, 1979, **10**, 589–596.

Oldridge, H. B., Wicks, J. R., Hanley, C., Sutton, J. R., & Jones, N. L. Noncompliance in an exercise rehabilitation program for men who have suffered a myocardial infarction. *Canadian Medical Association Journal*, 1978, **118**, 361–364.

Parker, E. S., Birnbaum, I. M., Boyd, R. A., & Noble, E. P. Neuropsychologic decrements as a function of alcohol intake in male students. *Alcoholism: Clinical and Experimental Research*, 1980, **48**, 129–142.

Pavlou, M., Johnson, P., Davis, F. A., & Lefebvre, K.A. program of psychologic service delivery in a multiple sclerosis center. *Professional Psychology*, 1979, **10**, 503–510.

Perry, C., Killen, B. A., Telch, M., Slinkard, M. A., & Danaher, B. K. Modifying smoking behavior of teenagers: A school-based intervention. *American Journal of Public Health*, 1980, **70**, 722–725.

Phillips, C. Tension headache: Theoretical problems. *Behaviour Research and Therapy*, 1978, **16**, 249–261.

Pomerleau, O., & Brady, J. P. (Eds.). *Behavioral medicine: Theory and practice*. Baltimore: Williams & Wilkins, 1979.

Prokop, C. K., & Bradley, L. A. (Eds.). *Medical psychology: Contributions to behavioral medicine*. New York: Academic Press, 1981.

Rachman, S. *Contributions to medical psychology*. Oxford, England: Pergamon, 1981.

Roberts, A. H. The behavioral treatment of pain. In J. M. Ferguson & C. B. Taylor (Eds.), *The comprehensive handbook of behavioral medicine*. New York: Spectrum, 1981.

Rosen, J. C., & Wiens, A. N. Changes in medical problems and use of medical services following psychological intervention. *American Psychologist*, 1979, **34**, 420–431.

Rosenman, R. H., Brand, R. J., Sholtz, R. L., & Friedman, M. Multivariate prediction of coronary heart disease during 8.5 year follow-up in the Western Collaborative Group Study. *American Journal of Cardiology*, 1976, **37**, 903–910.

Rosenman, R. H., & Friedman, M. Neurogenic factors in pathogenesis of coronary heart disease. *Medical Clinics of North America*, 1974, **58**, 269–279.

Rosenman, R. H., Friedman, M., Straus, R., Wurm, M., Kositchek, R., Hahn, W., & Werthessen, N. T. A predictive study of coronary heart disease. The Western Collaborative Group Study. *Journal of the American Medical Association*, 1964, **189**, 15–22.

Roskies, F., Spevak, M., Surkis, A., Cohen, C., & Gilman, S. Changing the coronary prone (Type A) behavior pattern in a non-clinical population. *Journal of Behavioral Medicine*, 1968, **1**, 201–216.

Sank, L. I., & Shapiro, J. R. Case examples of the broadened role of psychology in health maintenance organizations. *Professional Psychology*, 1979, **10**, 402–409.

Schaps, E., Churgin, S., Palley, C. S., Takata, B., & Cohen, A. Y. Primary prevention research: A preliminary review of program outcome studies. *The International Journal of the Addictions*, 1980, **15**, 657–676.

Schofield, W. The role of psychology in the delivery of health service. *American Psychologist*, 1969, **24**, 565–584.

Schofield, W. Clinical psychologists as health professionals. In G. C. Stone, F. Cohen, & N. E. Adler (Eds.), *Health psychology—A handbook*. San Francisco: Jossey Bass, 1979.

Schwab, J. J., Fennell, E. B., & Warheit, G. J. The epidemiology of psychosomatic disorders. *Psychosomatics*, 1974, **15**, 88–93.

Schwartz, G. E. Psychobiological foundations of psychotherapy and behavior change. In S. L. Garfield & A. E. Bergin (Eds.), *Handbook of psychotherapy and behavior change: An empirical analysis*. New York: Wiley, 1978.

Schwartz, G. E., & Weiss, S. M. Behavioral medicine revisited: An amended definition. *Journal of Behavioral Medicine*, 1978, **1**, 249–251. (a)

Schwartz, G. E., & Weiss, S. M. Yale Conference on Behavioral Medicine: A proposed definition and statement of goals. *Journal of Behavioral Medicine*, 1978, **1**, 3–12. (b)

Skelton, M., & Dominian, J. Psychological stress in wives of patients with myocardial infarction. *British Medical Journal*, 1973, **2**, 101–103.

Stapp, J., Fulcher, R., Nelson, S. D., Pallak, M. S., & Wicherski, M. The employment of recent doctorate recipients in psychology: 1975 through 1978. *American psychologist*, 1981, **36**, 1,211–1,254.

Stone, G. C. A specialized doctoral program in health psychology: Considerations in its evolution. *Professional Psychology*, 1979, **10**, 596–604.

Stone, G. C., Cohen, F., & Adler, N. E. *Health psychology: A handbook*. San Francisco: Jossey-Bass, 1979.

Streissguth, A. P., Landesman-Dwyer, S., Martin, J. C., & Smith, D. W. Teratogenic effects of alcohol in humans and laboratory animals. *Science*, 1980, **109**, 353–361.

Stuart, R. B. Weight loss and beyond: Are they taking it off? In P. O. Davidson & S. M. Davidson (Eds.), *Behavioral medicine: Changing health lifestyles*. New York: Brunner/Mazel, 1980.

Stunkard, A. J. Behavioral medicine and beyond: The example of obesity. In O. Pomerleau & J. Brady (Eds.), *Behavioral medicine: Theory and practice*. Baltimore: Williams & Wilkins, 1979.

Stunkard, A. J., & Mahoney, M. J. Behavioral treatment for eating disorders. In H. Leitenberg (Ed.), *Handbook of behavioral modification and behavior therapy*. Englewood Cliffs, N.J.: Prentice-Hall, 1976.

Suinn, R. M. Behavior therapy for cardiac patients. *Behavior Therapy*, 1974, **5**, 569–571.

Suinn, R. M., Pattern A behaviors and heart disease: Intervention approaches. In J. M. Ferguson & C. B. Taylor (Eds.), *The comprehensive handbook of behavioral medicine*, Vol. 1. New York: Spectrum, 1981.

Suinn, R. M., & Bloom, L. J. Anxiety management training for pattern A behavior. *Journal of Behavioral Medicine*, 1978, **1**, 25–37.

Sulik, K. K., Johnston, M. C., & Webb, M. A. Fetal Alcohol Syndrome: Embryogenesis in a mouse model. *Science*, 1981, **214**, 936–938.

Surwit, R. S., Pelon, R. N., & Fenton, C. H. Behavioral treatment of Raynaud's disease. *Journal of Behavioral Medicine*, 1978, **1**, 323–335.

Swan, G. E., Piccione, A., & Anderson, D. C. Internship training in behavioral medicine: Program description, issues and guidelines. *Professional Psychology*, 1980, **11**, 339–346.

Swisher, J. D., Warner, R. W., & Hern, J. Experimental comparison of four approaches to drug abuse prevention among 9th and 11th graders. *Journal of Counseling Psychology*, 1972, **19**, 328–332.

Tennant, F. S., Weaver, S. C., & Lewis, C. E. Outcomes of drug education: Four case studies. *Pediatrics*, 1973, **52**, 246–251.

Turner, D. B., & Stone, A. J. Headache and its treatment: A random sample survey. *Headache*, 1979, **19**, 74–77.

Vischi, T. R., Jones, K. R., Shank, E. D., & Lima, L. H. *The alcohol, drug abuse, and mental health national data book*. Washington, D.C.: Superintendent of Documents, U.S. Government Printing Office, Stock No. 017-024-00983-1, 1980.

Weiner, H. *Psychobiology and human disease*. New York: Elsevier-North Holland, 1977.

Weisenberg, M. Understanding pain phenomena. In S. Rachman (Ed.), *Contributions to medical psychology*. New York: Pergamon, 1981.

Williams, R. B., & Gentry, W. D. (Eds.), *Behavioral approaches to medical treatment*. Cambridge, Mass.: Ballinger, 1977.

Wishnie, H. A., Hackett, T. P., & Cassem, N. H. Psychological hazards of convalescence following myocardial infarction. *Journal of the American Medical Association*, 1971, **215**, 1,292–1,296.

Wooley, S. C., Blackwell, B., & Winget, C. A learning theory model of chronic illness behavior: Theory, treatment, and research. *Psychosomatic Medicine*, 1978, **40**, 379–401.

Wynn, A. Unwarranted emotional distress in men with ischemic heart disease. *Medical Journal of Australia*, 1967, November, 847–851.

34 MINORITIES

Jack O. Jenkins
Knoxice C. Hunter

While many individuals in America have been able to realize the "American dream," too many minority group members have found the American dream to be just that—a dream. Although presently many Americans are unemployed and adversely affected in other ways by the economy, Blacks, Hispanics, and Native Americans bear much more than their share of these hard times. Even when times have been good, minority group members have had much reason for despair. Poverty, high unemployability, substandard housing, unequal treatment by the criminal justice system, and substandard nutrition and health care can be cited for disproportionate numbers of Blacks, Chicanos, and Native Americans. Figures available from the 1979 Census indicated that 30 percent of Black Americans and 24 percent of Hispanics were living in poverty as compared to 9 percent of White Americans; for Asian Americans, 14 percent were listed as having incomes below the poverty level in 1979 (U.S. Bureau of Census, 1982).

The number of Blacks with four years of high school in 1979 was 3,802,235, or 29 percent of their population as compared to 36 percent (40,628,258) of the White population. The percentage of the Black population with four or more years of college was 8 percent as compared to 17 percent of the White population. For individuals of Spanish origin, 24 percent of their population had four years of high school and 8 percent had four or more years of college work; 24 percent of Asian Americans had four years of high school and 33 percent had four or more years of college (U.S. Bureau of the Census, 1982).

While each major minority group in America has a different history in this country, racism and its effects have played a major role in creating the deplorable state of affairs in which many minority group members find themselves today. Black Americans were either slaves or existed in situations where, while free, they were less than equal to Whites. The debilitating effects of slavery, including the disintegration of Black families, cruel treatment, and sexual abuse are well documented (e.g., Saunders, 1974, 1976) although not read widely enough by all Americans. Liberation from slavery did not liberate Blacks from oppression and prejudice. The unemployment rate for Blacks in 1979 was 14 percent (U.S. Bureau of Census, 1982).

Mexican Americans (Chicanos) are a disadvantaged group who have experienced little social progress, even though they have lived in the

United States longer than most other ethnic groups (Acosta, 1977). In 1979, 24 percent of all Mexican Americans lived under the poverty level; in addition, the unemployment rate was 9 percent for Mexican Americans aged 16 or older (U.S. Bureau of Census, 1982). Mainstream-culture social scientists have explained the lack of social mobility and economic advancement by Chicanos as a result of their approach to life and their distinct cultural values (Madsen, 1964; Saunders, 1954). Their ascribed values, such as greater concern for the present than the future, being more dependent than individualistic, and being more non-goal-oriented than goal-oriented, are usually viewed as the opposites of Anglo-American values and impediments to success in the United States (Vaca, 1970).

The plight of Native Americans on reservations is more severe than any minority group in the Unites States (Levitan, Johnston, & Taggart, 1975). High unemployment, poor educational resources, and alcoholism represent only a few of the problems of these people. The unemployment rate for all Native Americans in 1969 was 11.29 (Sowell, 1981). These figures had worsened with the 1974–75 recession. Native Americans are more likely than any other racial or ethnic group to be unemployed and have a family income below the poverty level (Office of Special Concerns, 1974). Native Americans living on reservations have attempted farming, raising stock, and timber production, but basically have been unsuccessful. It should be noted that many Native Americans were not farmers traditionally and had to make tremendous cultural changes when forced to become farmers. At some reservations the people are able to secure jobs nearby or are bused or drive themselves to and from work—often 60 to 100 miles away. The economic opportunities available to Indians on reservations are so limited that over a fourth of them are estimated to have left for relocation into urban ghettos, with some overall improvement in their socioeconomic condition (Levitan, Johnston, & Taggart, 1975).

There also exists a problem in terms of education for Native Americans. On the average, only 33 percent of Native Americans aged 25 and over are high-school graduates (Bahr, Chadwick, & Strauss, 1979).

In summary, many minority group members in America lead lives that are vastly different from mainstream America in terms of culture, education, and economic resources. Nevertheless, such differences in experience have not always been recognized by mainstream social scientists when therapy issues are examined.

Psychology and Minorities: A Historical Perspective

Psychologists are human beings, and therefore influenced by the society around them. A Black psychologist, Robert Guthrie (1980) states:

> The academic profession of psychology has been faced with many obstacles in grasping objective truth in the psychological study of Black Americans. Among these barriers have been submission to faulty and in many cases unworthy authority, influence of custom, and racial prejudices. [P. 15]

According to Guthrie, the discipline of psychology emerged during the time when the "Western environmental atmosphere was infected by overt racism and social Darwinism. Black people were scarcely out of the bonds of legalized slavery" (Guthrie, 1980, p. 15).

Psychology was strongly influenced by four events that not only affected philosophical biases and research stances concerning Black America, but in addition provided a gestalt, impacting upon attempts to study the psychology of Black Americans objectively. The major thesis of these events was an affirmation of nativistic themes, asserting that human difference resulted from innate causes within people rather than environmental forces in society (Guthrie, 1980). These four events were Darwinian theory, Galton's eugenics, McDougall's theory of instincts, and Mendelian genetics.

Black Americans received the most early attention by American psychologists. It would be quite naive, however, to assume that Native Americans, Hispanics, and Asian Americans escaped negatively based theorizing by mainstream psychologists. In addressing the issue of "When is a Scientist Political?" Rappaport (1977) cites a paper by Kamin (1974) on "Heredity, intelligence, politics, and psychology," describing the involvement of some of the most esteemed American psychologists in an effort to limit European immigration to the United States. According to Kamin, the renowned psychologist Henry Goddard used "mental tests" to examine large numbers of immigrants; he concluded that 83 percent of Jews, 80 percent of Hungarians, 79 percent of Italians, and 87 percent of Russians were "feebleminded" (cited in Rappaport, 1977, p. 32).

Other famous early 1900s psychologists such as Robert M. Yerkes and Carl Brigham also provided data to support the notion that America should have immigration quotas to keep out the undesirables. According to Rappaport (1977):

> If men like Yerkes, Goddard, and Brigham had decided that the intelligence test data used to justify limited immigration were actually so culturally biased as to be unfair and unscientific, and had used their considerable influence to argue for more opportunities for immigrants, one wonders what their fate would have been. [P. 32]

We will not belabor the historical abuses of Blacks and other minorities by psychologists. It is noteworthy that the American Psychological Association (APA) has supported the integration of Blacks and other minorities into its organization.

Assessment Variables

Assessment is the set of processes used by a person or persons for developing impressions and images, making decisions, and checking hypotheses about another person's pattern of characteristics, which determine his or her behavior in interaction with the environment (Sundberg, 1977). For minority groups, however, assessment is often biased and provides an inadequate view of the problem. Biases often observed in assessment will be discussed in the following section.

Intelligence Testing

The first attempts at mental testing in the United States were in the 1890s. One of the first uses of mental tests was to determine if there were any mental differences that could be attributed to race. The psychologist R. M. Bache tried to measure the quickness of sensory perception and compared twelve Whites, eleven Indians, and eleven Blacks. The Indians had the fastest reactions, the Blacks were second, and the Whites were the slowest. These results did not stop Bache, however, from proclaiming that the test had proved that Whites were the superior group. He maintained that they "were slower because they belonged to a

more deliberate and reflective race than did the members of the other two groups" (Berry & Tischler, 1978).

In 1905, Alfred Binet and Theodore Simon, working in France, developed a series of tests designed to measure intelligence. These tests were to be used to distinguish among various levels of "feeble-mindedness." Even in these early days of intelligence testing, Binet and Simon admitted that environmental and educational opportunity would invariably affect the scores; they concluded that the tests would only be appropriate for comparing children from closely similar environments (Berry & Tischler, 1978). Unfortunately, many psychologists ignored this warning and viewed the tests as measures of inherited intelligence that were virtually uninfluenced by the environment. When Binet died, the intelligence-testing research laboratories were moved to the United States and came under the control of Lewis Terman.

In 1916, Lewis Terman revised the Binet scales; however, the revisions were overshadowed by his declarations to future psychologists: "Mental retardation represents the level of intelligence which is very, very common among Spanish Indians and Mexican families of the Southwest and also among negroes. Their dullness seems to be racial" (p. 92). He also predicted that there would be significant racial differences when future IQ testing of these groups was done, and that "these racial differences cannot be wiped out by any scheme of mental culture" (p. 92). Finally, speaking of minorities again, Terman (1916) stated: "There is no possibility at present of convincing society that they should not be allowed to reproduce, although from a eugenic point of view they constitute a grave problem because of their unusually prolific breeding" (p. 93).

The Stanford-Binet is still being employed. Of the major intelligence tests currently in use today, only the Wechsler scales for adults and children have provided more normative data for minorities.

The purpose of this chapter is not to pursue any exhaustive argument on this issue. However, since it is clinicians who do a great deal of intelligence testing, it is important that the problems regarding the accurate intellectual assessment of minorities be addressed at least briefly.

Questions have arisen in recent years over the controversy of intelligence tests. The debate revolves around whether intelligence tests accurately assess the intelligence of Blacks, Hispanics, and other culturally diverse individuals. There are a number of reasons why the intellectual assessment of many minority group members may lead to erroneous conclusions. One explanation, as indicated earlier, is that normative samples of most intelligence tests do not systematically include minorities (Bernstein & Nietzel, 1981; Berry & Tischler, 1978; Jones, 1980). Second, the items on the tests are not culture-free. Hilliard (1982) defines "culture" as the shared creativities of a group of people, including language, values, experiences, symbols, tools, rules, etc. While there are cultural commonalities among American citizens, there are nonetheless a variety of subcultures whose members, for a number of reasons, have some experiences that are different from other individuals in American society. These experiences may be negative in nature and include discrimination, poor schools, poverty, unemployment, malnutrition, and the like. On the other hand, these cultures may also manifest variations in the usage of standard English, different values in dressing, and even different cognitive styles in learning and problem solving (Cooke, 1980). Intelligence, according to Hilliard (1982), is reflected in both common and unique cultural behavior.

The dominant intelligence tests in use represent White American middle-class values and culture. Many Blacks, Hispanics, and Native American children have been raised in somewhat different settings than White middle-class children (Berry & Tischler, 1978; Hilliard, 1982; Jones, 1980; Mercer, 1972). Mercer (1972) and her colleagues found that when they controlled for social background such as occupation, income, and educational level, there were no significant differences in intelligence between Whites and Blacks or Chicanos. In fact, Chicano individuals who had all of the sociometric characteristics of their White counterparts actually averaged IQs that were a little higher. No one has yet been able to devise a culture-free test, and there is some doubt as to whether a culture-free intelligence test is even possible. Third, there is the problem in the language of the intelligence tests and the individual taking the test. Many non-English-speaking individuals (e.g., some Hispanics) have been administered intelligence tests in English; those test scores were used to label them as mentally retarded (Acosta, 1977; Jones, 1980). This abysmal situation has recurred more often than one would think. Another issue in the recent intelligence controversy has been the race of the examiner in the testing situation.

Some studies over the years have been used to support the notion that Blacks on the average obtain lower scores when the test is adminstered by White examiners as opposed to a Black examiner.

A recent review by Sattler and Gwynne (1982) suggests that the hypothesis that the race of the examiner produces different IQ scores for Blacks than for Whites is a "myth." These authors note that of 27 reports, only four studies indicate positive results supporting the hypothesis of examiner bias. The authors pointed out that the results of these studies were obviated by methodological problems. Sattler and Gwynne (1982) concluded that there is no substantial evidence that the race of the examiner really has any effect on IQ scores. While their conclusions may be entirely accurate, it is noteworthy that they did not closely scrutinize the other 23 studies in which the race-of-examiner effect was not supported. Another group of authors (Graziano, Varca, & Levy, 1982) have also reviewed the current literature on race-of-examiner effects in intelligence testing. These authors concluded that the evidence for race-of-examiner effects at this time is equivocal. Therefore, while it may be true that there is no definitive evidence of the race-of-examiner effect at this time, it is also not true that the race-of-examiner effect should be considered merely a myth, as Sattler and Gwynne suggest. Graziano et al. (1982) argue that the reasons for differences observed in Black and White intelligence scores is a complex issue and that much research remains to be done.

Given the present evidence for the race-of-examiner hypothesis, it would probably be too hasty to dismiss the effect as a myth. It is simply naive to believe that persons high in prejudice who administer intelligence tests obtain the same IQ scores from low SES minority individuals, than individuals who are less prejudiced. To believe Sattler and Gwynne (1982) is to believe we should ignore the possibility for the long-term damage that can be done by giving the wrong IQ score. Psychologists of all races and ethnic backgrounds ought to examine their own biases and prejudices when they evaluate culturally diverse populations. Furthermore, Sattler and Gwynne (1982) only address obtained IQ scores and not the test reports that are based on such testing.

Hilliard (1982) cogently notes that until the definitive experiment of exposing all individuals to the same environmental variables before testing and then assessing intelligence has been done, there is no evidence to suggest that these tests accurately assess anything except differences in environment.

Recently, the National Assessment of Educational Progress (1982) conducted surveys that yielded data from the assessment of reading and writing skills for Black children at ages 9, 13, and 17 for the years 1969, 1974, and 1979. The most recent survey revealed that by 1979 Black students excelled significantly in the areas of reading and writing. In fact, Black nine-year-olds improved in reading skills by 9.9 percentage points, while White nine-year-olds improved by 2.8 percentage points. According to this organization, the increase in the Black nine-year-old's reading skills was one of the largest gains ever reported. In addition, Black 13- and 17-year-olds improved on almost all of their writing tasks, thus decreasing the gap between themselves and the nation. One may hypothesize that this is because of the integration and exposure of Black children to the same materials that the average White American child has typically received in public schools.

While some other factors might be mentioned, suffice it to say that the clinician must be aware of these issues and also quite careful in the conclusions he or she reaches from reading an IQ report on a minority-group member.

Clinical Assessment

Clinical assessment may occur in three spheres: (1) self-report, which is comprised of the clinical interview, various pencil-and-paper self-report measures, and self-monitoring; (2) behavioral measures; and (3) physiological measures.

Of self-report measures, the clinical interview represents the most often used method of assessment (Adams, 1981; Bernstein & Nietzel, 1980; Calhoun, 1982). According to Walsh (1967) and Yarrow, Campbell, and Burton (1968), in many instances interview data may not always be reliable and valid. These authors found that interview data may be distorted in various ways as a function of: (1) characteristics of the interviewer and the questions he or she poses, (2) client characteristics such as memory and willingness to disclose accurate information, and (3) the circumstances under which the interview takes place.

Interviewer error and bias often are problems for the clinician. Schwitzgebel and Kobb (1974) stated that sometimes "errors" are deliberate.

They quoted an interviewer hired to conduct structured inquiries as saying: "One of the questions asked for five reasons why parents had put their child in an institution. I found most people can't think of five reasons. I didn't want [the boss] to think I was goofing off, so I always filled in all five." Bernstein and Nietzel (1980) also stated that personal biases, preferences, and various kinds of prejudice may strongly affect the conclusions reached by clinical interviewers. This view was supported by previous studies (Mehlman, 1952; Raines & Rohrer, 1955, 1960; Temerlin, 1968), in which it was found that interviewers tend to have favorite diagnoses that are applied more often than any others. Temerlin (1968) found that clinicians' diagnoses of a client may be determined by prejudicial information given to them before they ever hear the client speak. Carkhuff and Pierce (1967) assessed the effects of therapist race and social class upon the patient's depth of self-exploration in a clinical interview. These authors found that patients explored themselves more in the clinical interview when they were more similar to the race and social class of the counselor involved. Patients who were less similar tended to explore themselves less. Hollingshead and Redlich (1958) found that therapists reported greater ease of communication and more positive assessments of clients who were White and middle class. Differences in language, values, and racial prejudice may all lead to less than accurate information being obtained from minority clients by individuals unfamiliar with or perhaps hostile to their subculture. These findings definitely have implications for the psychological treatment of culturally diverse groups.

For example, imagine a therapist who has ultraconservative negative opinions of welfare and believes that those on welfare are "shiftless and lazy" interviewing a poor Black patient. He ignores the old Black lady's report of how depressed she is about her state of affairs and concludes it is all her fault. He withholds any kind of psychotherapy and prescribes drugs because "that's all you can do with these people." Any therapist who regularly interviews minority clients should not assume that he or she knows all about these people and should seek out information from appropriate individuals (i.e., minority therapists) about variables important in conducting meaningful interviews with them.

Language of the client also is an issue with minority clients. The language barrier makes it impossible for many Spanish-speaking persons to communicate effectively with monolingual therapists (Acosta, 1977; Hilliard, 1982; Olmendo, 1981). (Some Asian Americans may also have difficulty as well as Black Americans, who are heavily into nonmainstream English.)

A few non-Hispanic therapists have probably learned enough Spanish at least to communicate with Spanish-speaking patients, but their numbers are likely to be small, and the depth of communication is probably not the same (Acosta, 1977; Olmendo, 1981). Native Americans, especially those residing on reservations, also may have difficulty because of the almost impossible task of translating some Native American languages into English while keeping intact the exact meaning of the terms. Other problems in communication occur with Black and Asian Americans. The therapist should be aware of the problems in communication he may have with particular members of minority groups.

Other issues therapists should take into consideration include basics, such as establishing trust and rapport with the minority client. In many instances, minority clients may not automatically provide the therapist with the detailed information necessary for adequately assessing the problem. This may be attributed to a lack of knowledge in the area of psychological assessment and treatment on the part of the minority client. However, these problems may be alleviated by the sensitivity, interest, and open-mindedness that the therapist shows toward the minority client.

Paper-and-Pencil Self-Report Measures

Paper-and-pencil self-report measures for evaluation of psychopathology primarily have been developed on Whites and administered without reservation to minorities. These self-report measures include projective devices, such as the Rorschach and Thematic Apperception Test, trait measures such as the Edwards Personal Preference Scale (Edwards, 1959), empirically derived measures such as the Minnesota Multiphasic Personality Inventory (Dahlstram & Welsh, 1960; Hathaway & McKinley, 1951), and behavioral inventories.

The projective tests (e.g., Rorschach) probably are the most easily abused, because they involve a great deal of subjective interpretation (Adams, 1981; Bernstein & Nietzel, 1980; Jones, 1980). Such a heavy emphasis on subjective inter-

pretation based upon Freudian theory may be easily affected by prejudice (Jones, 1980).

Research with the MMPI comparing the results for Blacks and Whites has found that Blacks typically obtain significantly higher scores than Whites on scales measuring nonconformity, alienation, and impulsivity (Gynther, 1972). Gynther (1981) stated that clinicians often interpret these differences as indicating that Blacks are more maladjusted than Whites, but there is no empirical evidence to support this conclusion. Gynther (1981) went on to suggest that misinterpretations could be reduced by developing behavioral correlates for MMPI profiles for blacks.

Behavioral self-report measures, such as the Rathus Assertiveness Schedule (Rathus, 1973), Fear Survey Schedule II (Wolpe & Lang, 1964), Fear Survey Schedule III (Geer, 1965), Social Avoidance and Distress Scale, and Fear of Negative Evaluation Scale (Watson & Friend, 1969) are designed to obtain descriptions of an individual's behavior in situations without drawing gross personality interpretations from such data. While the goal of a quick method of behavioral description is very worthwhile, these inventories may or may not be useful for all minority-group members. The normative samples for these measures and the White middle-class perspective from which they were developed may be problematic when administered to minorities.

It is interesting that history does repeat itself. Despite all of the furor over the normative samples of intelligence tests, behavioral self-report measures that have been standardized and validated almost exclusively on White middle-class college subjects continue to be administered to poor and/or minority individuals. Many of the measures do not even provide cautions as to the populations with whom these inventories should be used. While there may be fewer problems in the use of behavioral tests with various minority clients, we do not know this. It has not yet been documented at this point. For example, the tests may be appropriate for Black, Chicano, and Native American college students but not for poor individuals from the same minority groups.

Self-Monitoring

Self-monitoring consists of the detection and tabulation of discrete internal or external behavioral events by an individual. Self-monitoring has proven itself useful as an assessment strategy and occasionally as an intervention strategy (Adams, 1981;

Jenkins & Peterson, 1977; Lahey, 1981). It is particularly useful in the assessment of difficult-to-verify covert events (e.g., obsessive thoughts) or behavior, where it is important to detect their occurrence in the natural environment. The problem with self-monitoring may not be self-monitoring per se, but how its usefulness is viewed by poor and minority clients. It may be that the way this middle-class therapist describes the utility of the self-monitoring to his poor and minority clients in no way motivates the individual to believe in the utility of such a strategy. Or, it may be that the way self-monitoring is arranged to occur for this poor, old Native American is impossible given her environmental constraints. The therapist should utilize a good deal of common sense in applying this useful strategy.

Behavioral Measures

Behavioral measures may be obtained in two ways. The first is through naturalistic observation, whereby the therapist observes the behavior as it occurs in the natural environment. The second involves the observation of behavior in the laboratory, in a behavioral analogue. Both types of behavioral observation may have implications for the accurate assessment of minority-client behavior.

During naturalistic observation, the therapist should already be aware of the possible reactivity of his presence, regardless of the race or ethnic group of his subjects. When the client involved is a minority individual, the observer ought to be aware that not only is his presence reactive, but that because he is of one race and his clients are of another, his presence may be *doubly reactive*. First, there are some actions that minority individuals will avoid because of their fear that such behavior (while in fact normal) will confirm the prejudices of the observer. Second, there is the natural tendency of any individual to react to being observed.

With analogue situations, the therapist may feel more at ease with his client, but there still may be problems. First, the therapist may arrange an analogue situation that does not accurately assess this minority person's behavior. For example, the Chicano client may have excellent assertive skills but not in the presence of Whites in authority. These data may be overlooked by the therapist. Another observer may place his or her minority client in a role-play situation to determine conversational skills, but because this Black male is trying to speak standard English rather than nonstandard English, he gives the impression of being less effective. It is imperative that the therapist take culture into account when arranging behavioral analogues.

Physiological Assessment

Kallman and Feuerstein (1977) stated that the purpose of physiological assessment is to qualify physiological events as they are related to psychological variables. The use of physiological measures, such as the electrodermal response, in cross-cultural studies has not been extensive. Lazarus (1976) and his associates, however, have been exploring this area of research. The research has been based on experimentation with American subjects in which motion picture films are used to produce stress reactions. Lazarus et al. (1966) presented benign and stressful films to Japanese students and adults and compared their physiological and subjective responses with data from American experiments. The stressful film dealt with subincision rites involving the mutilation of male adolescent genitals. The benign film dealt with rice farming in Japan, which was intended as a Japanese version of a corn farming film used in American studies. The results indicated that in many respects, the Japanese reaction to stress was similar to that of Americans. Unlike Americans, however, the Japanese's skin conductance was almost as high during the benign films as during the stressful film. Lazarus et al. (1966) even suggested that Japanese subjects resembled "high anxious" individuals in American studies. He reported that skin conductance data on Japanese subjects indicated a general state of apprehension, maintained throughout both films, while their self-reports reflected small variations in perceived distress. Lazarus hypothesized that lack of experience of Japanese subjects in the laboratory and general apprehension about the total experimental situation produced the variations observed with the physiological measures.

With regard to other ethnic groups, research has shown significant differences between Blacks and Whites in terms of electrodermal-level reactivity. It appears that Blacks have lower skin conductance than Whites when contrasted to the Japanese in Lazarus' study, who manifested higher skin conductance values. Differences have even been found in electrodermal response reactivity between Jewish subjects born in America, Europe, or Israel.

The degree to which genetic factors are operative in addition to cultural processes has not as yet been clarified. It is quite clear that differences in autonomic reactivity may be a function of many social and psychological variables. But until this area is thoroughly researched across ethnic groups, assessment by means of physiological measures may always be interpreted in terms of the race of the subjects being assessed.

The foregoing discussion of assessment should be tempered with the knowledge that this discussion is in no way designed to stereotype any minority group or minority clients. Too much of that has been done in the past, and in fact, many liberal White psychologists have avoided considering racial topics for this reason.

The purpose of the foregoing discussion is to delineate some variables, which may be important in assessment and ought to be taken into account when evaluating a minority client. We are not stating that anything will have to be done differently with a minority client. It is quite likely, however, that therapists will have to attend to even more than the usual variables important in assessment. Because of racism, poverty, unemployment, level of stress, language, and other variables, the minority client is almost always different in some manner. These differences may be relevant or they may not be relevant, but they should be given their due consideration.

Therapy Issues

According to Kardiner and Ovesey (1962) (two psychoanalysts), American Blacks do not have a single personality trait that is not derived from their difficult living condition (i.e., their life of oppression). In addition, these psychoanalysts believe that psychotherapy or counseling for Blacks is useless (Maultsby, 1982). Kardiner and Ovesey (1962) believe that the only way to increase the self-esteem of Blacks is to eliminate all racial prejudice and discrimination in America. While this is a noble ideal, the assertion that Blacks cannot benefit from therapy is an extremely pessimistic view. It should be noted that Kardiner and Ovesey (1962) drew their conclusions from a very limited sample of nonsuccessful Blacks (Maultsby, 1982).

While Freud himself did not advance conceptualizations of psychopathology that were biased in nature, many American psychoanalytic writers did. In the first issue of their journal, *The Psycho-*

analytic Review, White and Jeliffe (1913) devoted three articles to mental illness among Blacks. A note by the two editors declared that "the existence side by side of the white and colored races in the United States offer an unique opportunity not only to study the psychology of a race at a relatively low cultural level, but to study their material effects upon one another" (cited in Thomas & Sillen, 1972, p. 8). Writing in the *American Journal of Psychiatry,* Bevis (1921) stated that, "All Negroes have a fear of darkness . . . careless, credulous, childlike, easily amused, sadness, and depression have little part in his psychic make-up" (cited in Thomas & Sillen, 1972, p. 11).

The famous European psychiatrist, Carl Jung, on a visit to America, examined Black patients in a mental hospital. He declared that, "The different states of the mind correspond to the history of the races" and that the Negro "has probably a whole historical layer less" than the White man (cited in Thomas & Sillen, 1972, p. 14). Erikson (1950), a developmental psychologist, observed that, "Negro babies often received sensual satisfactions which provide them with enough oral sensory surplus for a lifetime, as clearly betrayed in the way they move, laugh, talk, sing" (p. 214). This "sensory treasure helped to build a slave's identity: mild, submissive, dependent, somewhat querulous, but always ready to serve with occasional empathy and childlike wisdom" (Erikson, p. 214). Erikson goes on to state that the "so-called opportunities offered the migrating Negro often turn out to be a more subtly restricted prison which endangers his only successful historical identity (that of the slave)" (p. 214). Eventually Blacks would retreat into "hypochondria invalidism" a condition analogous to the safety of being a slave (Erikson, 1950).

Several years ago, Hollingshead and Redlich's (1958) investigation revealed that the most severe diagnoses and least amount of psychotherapy were offered to those who were poor and Black. Results of a study conducted recently by Jenkins (1981) found similar results in a community mental-health center. Jenkins found that White males and females received less severe diagnoses and more psychotherapy than Black males and females. Other minorities are similarly affected. According to Padilla, Ruiz, and Alvarez (1975), although highly disadvantaged and subject to multiple stresses, the Mexican American has been substantially underrepresented among those who receive mental-health services. Native Americans experience similar problems.

Several factors probably have contributed to this depressing state of affairs. The major culprit has been the failure of doctoral clinical programs to recruit, train, and graduate enough minority psychologists. While many schools have made great strides in recent years in the recruitment and training of minority psychologists, the problem remains acute. Problems caused by the paucity of minority psychologists has meant that it has been relatively easy for mainstream psychology to ignore factors related to the treatment of minorities. The modal number of minority faculty for most psychology departments is zero. Hence, most mainstream psychology members rarely even get to converse with a minority psychologist on a regular basis. Second, the absence of minority faculty has resulted in fewer courses on ethnic concerns (e.g., Black psychology or Chicano psychology). Third, minority faculty members could direct mainstream faculty to journals in which many minority psychologists publish (which often are not mainstream psychology journals, e.g., the *Journal of Black Psychology*). Fourth, minority psychologists often are more vigorous and have the connections to recruit minority students and assist in their retention. Fifth, the culturally aware minority psychologist can generally sensitize other faculty and nonminority students to minority issues.

However, most therapists will continue to be White and most of them have little or no formal training in working with non-White clients. Much more attention needs to be paid to educating present and future nonminority psychologists to minority issues. It should be noted, however, that until substantial curriculum changes are made, even minority graduate students will receive only mainstream-oriented education. Those minority psychologists who have addressed minority or cultural issues have studied nonmainstream psychology independently and have benefited from organizations such as the Association of Black Psychologists.

A well-researched problem in clinical psychology relates to why clients drop out of therapy prematurely. According to Garfield (1971), premature termination of therapy is a widespread finding across a large number of therapies.

Social class has been established as a very important factor in why clients prematurely terminate therapy. Sue, McKinney, and Allen (1976) reviewed the cases of 13,450 clients in 17 mental-health centers and found that individuals with low levels of education and who were members of minority and ethnic groups were more likely to leave therapy early.

It should be noted that several investigators (e.g., Roessler & Boone, 1979) have failed to find any real differences between premature terminations and remainers (Sultan, 1982). It may well be that clinics and individual therapists through their differential expectation for the success of some clients and their varying levels of ability to provide "relevant" services may, in fact, discourage some clients from continuing in treatment (Sultan, 1982).

A major point to be drawn from the literature on dropouts is that there is evidence that socioeconomic status and other variables *are* related to client dropout rate. There also is other evidence that therapists tend to accept those individuals most like themselves (e.g., Hollingshead & Redlich, 1958; Jenkins, 1982). With Blacks, Native Americans, Hispanics, and Asian Americans constituting a disproportionate number of the lower-socioeconomic-status individuals in our society, it is important that therapists address the special needs of such clients in therapy. There are reasons why lower socioeconomic clients drop out. Socioeconomic status may account for much of the high dropout rates for minority group members. However, racial prejudice and failure to understand and to appreciate completely the cultural differences of these minorities most assuredly accounts for some of the dropout rate as well.

The traditional therapies do not hold much promise for many minority group members because of their long duration, relative ineffectiveness, and extremely select client population. Most traditional therapies are best suited for the YAVIS (Young-Attractive-Verbal-Intelligent-Successful) type of client (Schofield, 1964) and not the HOUNDs (Homely-Old-Unsuccessful-Nonverbal-Dull). Behavior therapy, while lagging in its attention to cultural variables, seems to hold the most promise for minority group members, because of its proven efficacy in the treatment of diverse problems, its heavy emphasis on experimentation, and its propensity to be more flexible in dealing with problems in living. The remainder of this chapter, then, focuses most heavily on the possible utilization of cultural variables to improve and strengthen empirically-based treatment strategies.

Client Variables of Minority Individuals that May Affect Treatment

The first notion that must be advanced here is that the variables we will address are those that therapists need to take into account when treating minority patients. The goal of this section is not to stereotype the Black, Hispanic, or Native American client. The assumption underlying this discussion is that individuals in America who have been forced into different experiences by the dominant culture have both deliberately and inadvertently developed many different cultural values and perspectives from those of mainstream America. The minority client will always be different in some way from his White middle-class therapist. It may be that some or all of these differences must be taken into account before maximum success in therapy can be achieved.

Black Clients

Since most clinical programs do not have required courses addressing issues of culture as they relate to therapy, the non-Black therapist who sees a Black client should first assume that he or she does not view a Black client objectively. The therapist should also be aware that all of his training (even if he has seen some Black clients) has been White, middle class, and geared to the dominant culture. No matter how liberal the non-Black therapist, his perceptions of the world must be based on his past experiences (Maultsby, 1982). These past experiences do not include growing up as a Black American. Cheek (1976) has suggested 34 questions Black and non-Black therapists should ask themselves before assuming readiness to work with Black clients. The questions are rated on a "very much," "somewhat," "not at all" format. Nine of the most crucial questions of the 34 that Cheeks suggests are: (1) Are you comfortable with Black language? (2) Do you desire Black supervision of your work with Black clients? (3) As a parent, would you approve of your son or daughter dating an average (whatever you consider average) Black youth? (4) Would you seek out competent Black consultation or supervision in working with different Black patients? (5) Have you had exposure to professional training conducted by Blacks (classes, workshops, seminars)? (6) Have you been exposed to professional views of Black women as well as Black men? (7) Are you familiar with the current literature, journals, and periodicals in which Blacks express

their professional views? (8) Have you ever exposed your approach to counseling Blacks to other Blacks in the profession (as individuals or in a group) for a response (or advice)? (9) Have you had specific formal training in dealing with ethnic minorities? Cheek (1976) feels that a "not at all" response to any of these questions means that the therapist is not yet "ready" to counsel Blacks effectively.

This test should be taken by Blacks and Whites alike. However, since we can safely assume that most non-Black therapists who work in environments that require they see Black clients will persist in their attempt to "counsel" or otherwise disposition Black clients, a number of variables should be taken into account by such therapists.

First, while discrimination in America has led to similar experiences for many Black Americans, not all Black Americans are alike. Each Black client is an individual, as is each poor client, each rich client, each Hispanic client, and each Asian American client.

Second, the fact that this client talks and dresses differently from the therapist has nothing to do with his or her intellect or worth as a human being. Third, if the person is on welfare, has only a sixth-grade education, and does not speak excellent English, this does not mean that he cannot benefit from therapy.

Fourth, cultural variables should be taken into account in assessment and treatment. These cultural variables include: (1) Where does this client live and what are the norms of the area? (2) What is the meaning of certain expressions in this area? Am I going to be more or less accepted if I use such expressions with this client? (3) How can I enhance the generalization of the effects of therapy to this client's environment? (4) Are the assessment instruments I am using relevant for Black clients? (6) What is the extent of my knowledge of Black culture both historically and at present as obtained from Black writers, not just my mainstream literature? (7) Last, do I have a repulsion to working with or feel ill at ease with Black clients? If the answer to the last question is yes, then the therapist should seek some assistance in resolving these feelings.

Other Minorities

We will not make the mistake of writing from any supposedly expert sense about other minority clients. What is important is that all of the questions raised in regard to Black clients may apply to other minority clients. Where we have used the word Black, the reader may substitute Native American, Hispanic, Asian American, or others. Nevertheless, there are other variables that might be taken into account almost entirely within the context of certain groups.

For Hispanics, there is the "problem" of bilingualism. Many Hispanics do not speak fluent English and consequently do not receive maximum therapy benefits from their Non-Spanish-speaking therapists. Most of those who need psychotherapy do not seek services offered by mental-health agencies (Acosta, 1977). In addition, there are numerous stereotypes perpetrated by social scientists and mainstream America in general that therapists should know and scrutinize in him or herself before beginning therapy.

Historically, Native Americans are certainly among the most discriminated groups in the United States (Joint Commission on Mental Health, 1978). Among all the minorities in American society, Native Americans hold a unique status, in that they were acquired in 1871 as official wards of the federal government. The attitudes of White people toward Native Americans in the United States have varied widely, from disdain to pity. Nonetheless the Native American in addition to and because of his problems of poverty, poor education, and discrimination has great need of psychological services.

Dauphinais, LaFramboise, and Rowe (1980) surveyed 150 American Indian and 50 non-Indian 11th- and 12th-grade students to assess self-reported problem areas and persons perceived as potential sources of help. While the Indian students had much in common with the White students in terms of problems most likely to be taken to a counselor, there were differences. Indian students indicated a large likelihood of talking to no one about getting along with friends, being depressed, and not caring (Dauphinais, LaFramboise, & Rowe, 1980).

Two other groups of Indian students (those from boarding schools and metropolitan schools but not those from rural areas) expressed a reluctance to talk to anyone about problems with parents and family members, whether to stay in school, and making a decision. The majority of non-Indian students indicated that they would talk with some other person about these concerns.

LaFramboise, Dauphinois, and Lujan (1981) investigated verbal indicators of insincerity as perceived by American Indians. These authors found that attempting to show affinity, the use of ethnic stereotypes, denial of ethnic differences, displaying a misunderstanding of Indian-related problems, use of accusatory or derogatory phrases, attempts to gain confidence, displaying a "run-around" or "put off" maneuver, attempting to show an understanding of Indian experiences, and attempting to antagonize or satisfy curiosity were most often named as indicators of insincerity.

It should be noted that the word "American Indian" must be carefully used and the exact individuals being discussed specified (this is also true for Hispanics). The variability of individuals within the category called American Indian is great. Our goal of the presentations of the two studies above was to give some information that may prove useful in counseling some American Indians, but we would caution that each individual— White, Black, Hispanic, or Native American— must be viewed as just that, *an individual*.

Suggestions for the Use of Cultural Variables in Behavior Therapy

Many studies have been conducted demonstrating the efficacy of behavioral strategies (see Rimm & Masters, 1979), but there are very few in the behavioral literature that address the systematic assessment and utilization of cultural variables in treatment. The reasons for this oversight vary from an attempt by liberal White psychologists to avoid race in their research as a reaction to previous abuses, to simply viewing race and culture as unimportant variables. It is noteworthy that Kanfer and Saslow (1967), in their article "Behavioral Diagnosis," present a schema for assessment that includes an analysis of the individual's environment. Below, we explore the possible use of cultural variables in behavior therapy with regard to well-known strategies.

Systematic desensitization (Wolpe, 1958) now is a standard therapeutic technique principally used to treat maladaptive anxiety occurring in the presence of specific environmental cues. There is no evidence, however, that the technique has been used widely with poor persons and minority-group members. The strategy probably does not need any substantial modification with a client who accepts the rationale and is induced to begin.

However, there are some ways in which cultural variables may play an important role. The first concerns getting the client to believe the treatment rationale. The second involves the actual administration of the treatment procedure. The former requires taking into account many of the cultural variables addressed thus far. The latter involves the use of cultural variables in scene preparation (i.e., anxiety and relaxation elicitation stimuli) and scene description (i.e., perhaps the scene is made more vivid by terms more familiar to the client). In some scenes, perhaps an appropriate Spanish accent or Black voice may facilitate treatment.

Social-skills or assertiveness training (Wolpe, 1958) has been the primary treatment modality for maladaptive anxiety as it occurs in the realm of interpersonal relations. However, the effects of social-skills or assertive-training procedures have not always generalized to the natural environment (e.g., McFall & Twentyman, 1973), or endured. It is our contention that one major factor in the failure of social-skills training to generalize to the natural environment is that cultural variables have been ignored. Many Black patients have taken part in social-skills training experiments in inpatient settings, but never does the reader see that the client's environmental context was assessed. Moreover, it is not clear that the patient was taught skills most likely to be reinforced in his or her environment. The White middle-class therapist may teach White middle-class social-skills to a Mexican American person who does not use them because they make him appear odd in his environment. Important variables in social-skills assessment and training may include description of the interpersonal partners and his or her race and sex. Cheek (1976) has argued rather convincingly that the race of a respondent may alter the exact nature of an assertive response. Hazzard (1979) found that Whites and Blacks altered their responses on a self-report measure when the race of the respondent changed.

The reader should not assume from this discussion that there are no instances when training in White middle-class social-skills is necessary. It may well be the case that this Chicano, Black, or Native American person needs to know more about how to operate effectively in a White middle-class environment. As Cheek (1976) asserts, however, Blacks and other minorities are raised to be White and not vice versa. Minorities understand the values and skills of the dominant culture much more than the dominant culture understands the values and behavior of its minorities.

Punishment and aversive counterconditioning procedures should be avoided whenever possible,

no matter what the race of the subject. Since there are behaviors that respond best to certain procedures, however, the cultural variables should be taken into account whenever such procedures are administered. Cultural variables in terms of language and values may increase the aversiveness of covert sensitization scene content or the removal of one type of reinforcer instead of another in response-cost procedures. In addition, the effects of therapy will be enhanced when the minority client is capable of developing a good relationship with his or her therapist who has considered culturally relevant materials.

With regard to operant strategies, the greater the knowledge the clinician has about his client's culture, the greater the likelihood that he will accurately assess potential reinforcers, maintaining stimuli and ways to effect generalization of results. The rationale given to the client should take into account who this client is and how such a rationale will be accepted. Using polysyllabic words with clients who do not understand them only shows your ignorance, not theirs.

Conclusions

The future status of the treatment of minorities will depend on several factors: (1) Larger numbers of minority clinical psychologists should be trained. The number of minority psychologists in the country (i.e., Black, Chicano, Asian American, and Native American) remains well below what one would expect given their representation in the population of the United States. (2) Larger numbers of minority clinical psychologists should be hired for faculty of academic institutions and community mental-health agencies. (3) Larger numbers of nonclinical minority psychologists should be trained. (4) Larger numbers of nonclinical minority psychologists should be hired in appropriate job placements. (5) All psychologists who write about or do research on minority groups but who are not members of such minority groups should consult with appropriate psychologists who are of that minority. If this is not accomplished, then the research should not be undertaken. (6) The APA· committee on accreditation should require that all doctoral-level clinical students receive formal instruction in ethnic concerns. (7) Departments of psychology should institute core courses on ethnic concerns taught by minority psychologists and require all of their doctoral (clinical, social, industrial, etc.) students to take them.

(8) All students and faculty should be made aware of materials written by minority psychologists on minority concerns that frequently are not found on the shelves of mainstream faculty and in college libraries. (9) Research regarding the role of culture in behavior therapy assessment and treatment should be conducted.

If these actions are taken, conditions regarding treatment of minority group members surely will improve.

References

Acosta, F. X. Ethnic variables in psychotherapy: The Mexican American. In J. L. Martinez (Ed.), *Chicano psychology*. New York: Academic Press, 1977.

Adams, H. E. *Abnormal psychology*. Wm. C. Brown, Dubuque, 1981.

Bernstein, D. A. & Nietzel, M.T. *Introduction to clinical psychology*. New York: McGraw-Hill, 1980.

Berry, B., & Tischler, H. L. *Race and ethnic relations*. Boston: Houghton-Mifflin, 1978.

Bevis, W. M. Psychological traits of the southern negro with observations as to some of his psychoses. *American Journal of Psychiatry*, 1921, **1**, 69–78.

Carkhuff, R. R., & Pierce, R. Differential effects of therapist race and social class upon patient depth of self-exploration in the initial clinical interview. *Journal of Consulting Psychology*, 1967, **31**, 632–634.

Cheek, D. K. *Assertive Black . . . Puzzled White*. San Luis Obispo, Calif.: Impact Publishers, 1976.

Cooke, B. G. Nonverbal communication among Afro-Americans: An initial classification. In R. L. Jones (Ed.), *Black psychology*. (2nd ed.) New York: Harper & Row, 1980.

Dahlstrom, U. G., & Welsh, G. S. *An MMPI Handbook: A quide to use in clinical practice and research*. Minneapolis: University of Minnesota Press, 1960.

Dauphinais, P., LaFromboise, T., & Towe, W. Perceived problems and sources of help for American Indian students. *Counselor Education and Supervision*, 1980, 37–44.

Edwards, A. L. *Edwards Personal Preference Schedule*. New York: Psychological Corp., 1959.

Erikson, E. H. *Childhood and society*. New York: Norton, 1950.

Garfield, S. L. Research on client variables in psychotheapy. In A. E. Bergin & S. L. Garfield (Eds.), *Handbook of psychotherapy and behavior change*. New York: Wiley, 1971.

Geer, J. H. The development of a scale to measure fear. *Behaviour Research and Therapy*, 1965, **3**, 45–53.

Graziano, W. G., Varca, P. E., & Levy, J. C. Race of examiner effects and the validity of intelligence tests. Unpublished manuscript, University of Georgia, 1982.

Guthrie, R. V. *Even the rat was white: A historical view of psychology*. New York: Harper & Row, 1976.

Guthrie, R. V. The psychology of Black Americans: An historical perspective. In R. L. Jones (Ed.), *Black psychology*. (2nd ed.) New York: Harper & Row, 1980.

Gynther, M. D. White norms and black MMPI's: A prescription for discrimination? *Psychological Bulletin*, 1972, **78**, 386–402.

Gynther, M. D. Is the MMPI an appropriate assessment device for blacks? *Journal of Black Psychology*, 1981, **7**, 67–75.

Hathaway, S. R., & McKinley, J. C. *The Minnesota Multiphasic Personality Inventory Manual*. (Rev. ed.) New York: Psychological Corp., 1951.

Hazzard, M. An assessment of assertive behavior: Black and white differences. Unpublished doctoral dissertation. University of Georgia, 1979.

Hilliard, A. IQ thinking as the emperor's new clothes: A critique of Jenson's *Bias in Mental Testing*. Unpublished manuscript, Georgia State University, 1982.

Hollingshead, A. B., & Redlich, F. C. *Social class and mental illness: A community study*. New York: Wiley, 1958.

Jenkins, J. O., & Peterson, G. L. Self-monitoring plus aversion in a case of bruxism. *Journal of Behavior Therapy and Experimental Psychiatry*, 1976, **9**, 387–388.

Jenkins, J. O. An analysis of the delivery of services to black and white individuals in a community mental health clinic. Unpublished manuscript, 1981.

Jones, R. L. *Black psychology*. (2nd ed.) New York: Harper & Row, 1980.

Jung, C. G. Your negroid and Indian behavior. *Forum*, 1930, **83**, 193–199.

Kallman, W. M., & Feuerstein, M. Psychophysiological procedures. In A. R. Ciminero, K. S. Calhoun, & H. E. Adams (Eds.), *Handbook of behavioral assessment*. New York: Wiley, 1977.

Kamin, L. J. Heredity, intelligence, politics and psychology. Paper presented at the meeting of the Eastern Psychological Association, Philadelphia, April 1974.

Kanfer, F. H., & Saslow, G. Behavioral diagnosis. In C. M. Franks (Ed.), *Behavior therapy: Appraisal and status*. New York: McGraw-Hill, 1969.

Kardiner, A., & Ovesey, L. *The mark of oppression*. New York: World Publishing, 1962.

LaFromboise, T., Dauphinias, P., & Lujan, P. Verbal indicators of insincerity as perceived by American Indians. *Journal of Non-White Concerns*, 1981, 87–93.

Lahey, B. B., & Ciminero, A. R. *Maladaptive behavior: An introduction to abnormal psychology*. Scott, Foresman, 1980.

Lazarus, R. S. Psychological stress and the coping process. In W. F. Prokasy & D. C. Raskin (Ed.), *Electrodermal activity in psychological research*. New York: Academic Press, 1973.

Lazarus, R. S., Tomita, M., Opton, E. M., & Kodama, M. A cross-cultural study of stress-reaction patterns in Japan. In W. F. Prokasy & D. C. Raskin (Ed.), *Electrodermal activity in psychological research*. New York: Academic Press, 1973.

Levitan, S. A., Johnston, W. B., & Taggart, R. *Minorities in the United States: Problems, progress, and prospects*. Washington, D.C.: Public Affairs Press, 1975.

Madsen, W. *The Mexican-Americans of south Texas*. New York: Holt, Rinehart, & Winston, 1964.

Maultsby, M. C., Jr., A historical view of blacks' distrust of psychiatry. In S. M. Turner & R. T. Jones (Eds.), *Behavior modification in black populations: Psycho-social issues and empirical findings.* New York: Plenum, 1982.

McFall, R. M., & Twentyman, C. T. Four experiments on the relative contributions of rehearsal, modeling, and coaching in assertion training. *Journal of Abnormal Psychology,* 1973, **81,** 199–218.

McNair, D. M., Lorr, M., & Callahan, D. Patient and therapist influences on quitting psychotherapy. *Journal of Consulting Psychology,* 1963, **27,** 10–17.

Mehlman, B. The reliability of psychiatric diagnosis. *Journal of Abnormal and Social Psychology,* 1952, **47,** 577–578.

Mercer, J. R. IQ: The lethal label. *Psychology Today,* September 1972.

National Assessment of Educational Progress, Winter 1981–82, **15**(4).

Office of Special Concerns, Office of the Secretary, Department of Health, Education and Welfare. A study of selected socio-economic characteristics of ethnic minorities based on the 1970 Census: Volume III: American Indians. Washington, D.C.: U.S. Government Printing Office, 1974.

Olmendo, E. L. Testing linguistic minorities. *American psychologist,* 1981, **36,** 1,078–1,085.

Padilla, A. M., Ruiz, R. A., & Alvarez, R. A. Community mental health services for the Spanish-speaking surnamed population. *American Psychologist,* 1975, **30,** 892–905.

Raines, G. N., & Rohrer, J. H. The operational matrix of psychiatric practice, II. Variability in psychiatric impressions and the projection hypotheses. *American Journal of Psychiatry,* 1960, **117,** 33–139.

Rappaport, J. *Community psychology: Values, research, and action.* New York: Holt, Rinehart, & Winston, 1977.

Rathus, S. A. A 30-item schedule for assessing assertive behavior. *Behavior Therapy,* 1973, **4,** 398–406.

Report of the United States Joint Commission on Mental Health. Washington, D.C.: U.S. Government Printing Office, 1978.

Rimm, D. C., & Masters, J. C. *Behavior therapy: Techniques and empirical findings.* (2nd ed.) New York: Academic Press, 1979.

Roessler, R. T., & Boone, S. E. Comparison of rehabilitation center dropouts and completers on demographic, center environmental perceptions, and center problems. *Psychosocial Rehabilitation Journal,* 1979, **3,** 25–33.

Sattler, J. M., & Gwynne, J. White examiners generally do not impede the intelligence test of black children: To debunk a myth. *Journal of Consulting and Clinical Psychology,* 1982, **50,** 196–208.

Saunders, D. E. *The ebony handbook.* Chicago: Johnson, 1974.

Saunders, L. *Cultural differences and medical care: The case of the Spanish-speaking people of the southwest.*

New York: Russell Sage, 1954.

Schofield, W. *Psychotherapy: The purchase of friendship.* Englewood Cliffs, N.J.: Prentice-Hall, 1964.

Schwitzgebel, R. K., & Kolb, D. A. *Changing human behavior.* New York: McGraw-Hill, 1974.

Smythe, M. M. *The black American reference book.* Englewood Cliffs, N.J.: Prentice-Hall, 1976.

Sowell, T. *Ethnic America.* New York: Basic Books, 1981.

Stern, S. L., Moore, S. F., & Gross, S. J. Confounding of personality and social class characteristics in research on premature termination. *Journal of Consulting and Clinical Psychology,* 1975, **43,** 341–344.

Sue, S., McKinney, H. L., & Allen, D. B. Predictors of the duration of therapy for clients in the community mental health system. *Community Mental Health Journal,* 1976, **12,** 365–375.

Sultan, F. E. Factors contributing to dropout in a psychosocial rehabilitation program for the chronically emotionally disabled. Unpublished doctoral dissertation. University of Georgia, 1982.

Sundberg, N. D. *Assessment of persons.* Englewood Cliffs, N.J.: Prentice-Hall, 1977.

Temerlin, M. K. Suggestion effects in psychiatric diagnosis. *Journal of Nervous and Mental Disease,* 1968, **147,** 349–353.

Terman, L. M. *The measurement of intelligence.* Boston: Houghton-Mifflin, 1916.

Terman, L. M., & Merrill, M. A. *Measuring intelligence.* Boston: Houghton-Mifflin, 1937.

Thomas, A., & Sillen, S. *Racism and psychiatry.* New York: Brunner/Mazel, 1972.

U.S. Bureau of the Census. *Census of populations: Detailed characteristics.* Washington, D.C.: U.S. Government Printing Office, 1970.

U.S. Bureau of Census. *Statistical abstract of the United States: 1974.* (95th ed.) Washington, D.C.: U.S. Government Printing Office, 1974.

U.S. Bureau of the Census. *Supplementary report: Provisional estimates of social, economic, and housing characteristics.* Washington, D.C.: U.S. Government Printing Office, 1982.

Vaca, N. A. The Mexican-American in the social sciences. Part II: 1936–1970. *El Grito,* 1970, **4,** 17–51.

Walsh, W. B. Validity of self-report. *Journal of Counseling Psychology,* 1967, **14,** 18–23.

Watson, D., & Friend, R. Measurement of social evaluative anxiety. *Journal of Consulting and Clinical Psychology,* 1969, **33,** 448–457.

Wolpe, J. *Psychotherapy by reciprocal inhibition.* Stanford, Calif.: Stanford University Press, 1958.

Wolpe, J., & Lang, P. J. A fear survey schedule for use in behavior therapy. *Behaviour Research and Therapy,* 1964, **2,** 27–30.

Yarrow, M. R., Campbell, J. D., & Burton, R. V. *Child-rearing: An inquiry into research and methods.* San Francisco: Jossey-Bass, 1968.

PART VI

COMMUNITY APPROACHES

INTRODUCTION

Community psychology has had a remarkably checkered course in its short history. Spurred by the idealistic visions and ample dollars of the Kennedy-Johnson years, community psychology and community mental health began a meteoric rise. There were expectations that the entire mental-health-care delivery system would be transformed from an office-bound resource of the middle class to a truly community-based system. Prevention and social change were seen as the most appropriate province of the new mental-health workers, which included nonprofessional community residents and paraprofessionals, as well as the traditional professional groups. Unfortunately, by the end of the Vietnam era, the proverbial bubble had burst. The flow of dollars to the community mental-health system was dramatically restricted, resulting in a marked curtailment of existing programs, to say nothing about the dashed hopes for expansion. Moreover, much of the early idealism was shattered by the harsh realities of the "real world." Prevention was easier said than done and political leaders and community residents had far different ideas about their needs and how they could be met from the ideas of academically trained professionals.

While some critics have written the epitaph of the community movement, the chapters in this section indicate that it is still alive and well. First, Donald G. Forgays (Chapter 35) describes current perspectives on prevention. He lucidly discusses definitional issues, examines the role of community mental health in prevention, and then considers the important ethical issues involved in early identification and social action. Next, Gonzales, Hays, and Kelly (Chapter 36) provide an overview of the current status of the field of community mental health. They highlight some of the innovative programs that have been developed in work with ethnic minorities, the elderly, rural groups, and women. Richard K. McGee discusses crisis intervention and brief therapy in Chapter 37. He details the conceptual and tactical distinctions between the two approaches, and presents guidelines for their use. In the final chapter (Chapter 38) Shulberg and Jerrell examine consultation. They distinguish between mental health, behavioral, and organizational development models. They then describe the stages of consulting relationships, and consider the thorny issue of evaluation of consulting services.

35 PRIMARY PREVENTION OF PSYCHOPATHOLOGY

Donald G. Forgays

When one examines the literature on the primary prevention of psychopathology, one is reminded of many examples of constantly recurrent themes. In the film retrospective *That's Entertainment* there is a marvelous series of clips drawn from several of Mickey Rooney's early MGM movies. In each, at the point of maximum buildup of anxiety over the need to demonstrate adult responsible behavior or the desire to earn needed money, someone, usually Mickey, says: "Let's put on a show!" The phrase always seems new and most appropriate to the needs in question at the time. The redundancy appears glaring only when the film retrospective juxtaposes the relevant scenes. Such is the case with the review of primary prevention literature. In each of the last several years, definitional issues arise, the mislabeling of programs as primary prevention occurs, the great need for more primary preventional effort is espoused, the argument between treatment and prevention foci is drawn, and the very existence of primary prevention is questioned. Efforts to bed these concerns are repeatedly made (Bloom, 1968, 1979; Cowen, 1973, 1977a, 1977b, 1980; Kessler & Albee, 1975), but to little effect, as evidenced by the repetition of the same concerns across time.

What are the reasons for this continuing state of affairs? There appear to be several. First is the issue of what is being prevented (Cowen, 1977a, 1980; Kessler & Albee, 1975). Is it behaviors reflecting social malaise or is it mental "illness"? If one accepts the answer of mental "illness," the point is made that since we know little about the etiology of most mental "illness," how would it be possible to prevent such conditions? This, of course, is the stance of those who accept the medical-model approach to mental disorder, and this definitional self-entrapment is commonly associated with an entreaty to expand treatment and other direct-service programs (e.g., Beigel, Sharfstein, & Wolfe, 1979; Borus, 1978; Langsley, 1980; Reinstein, 1978; Ribner, 1980). If one feels that social malaise behaviors are what primary prevention is all about, then such prevention is certainly possible. But, of the myriad of possibilities, what specific techniques are to be used to prevent which target behaviors? This level of ambiguity is disturbing indeed (DeWild, 1981). A second reason concerns the personnel to be involved in or responsible for primary preventive efforts. Those professionals who are deeply occupied with problems of psychopathology (mainly psychiatrists and clinical psychologists) follow treatment and direct-service priorities and are not trained, or apparently interested, in manipulating social systems or working with communities (Bloom, 1968; 1969; Cowen, 1973, 1977a, 1980). A related issue is the fear that mucking about in social variables and systems runs an antilibertarian risk (Bloom, 1968; DeWild, 1981). That is, manipulating value-laden social dimensions may impose inappropriate restrictions on individual behaviors, suggesting social control in the guise of furthering mental health. These and other reasons relating to the slow development of a recognized field of primary prevention will be dealt with more completely below.

Goldston (e.g., Goldston, 1978; Klein & Goldston, 1977) has said on several occasions that primary prevention is an idea whose time has come. It is to be hoped that this point of view will not turn out to be chimerical, although the evidence for it is less than reassuring. For example, a recent analysis of articles in the *Community Mental Health Journal* reports a 50 percent decrease in prevention reports over the period 1969–1976, and the absolute number of such papers was very small to begin with (Lounsbury et al., 1979).

Where did the idea of primary prevention come from? For nearly two decades after World War II the focus of mental health was clearly the provision of direct service and treatment to those with disordered minds. These unhealthy minds had to be restored to soundness, and the restorational model was, for the most part, a medical one. By the 1960s, two ideas were growing that were to have an important influence on the thrust of the mental-health movement. The first was the realization that some aspects of psychopathology were likely associated with, and probably partly caused by, social forces (i.e., life stresses), and perhaps these disablements were preventable. The second concerned the impossibility of training a sufficient number of high-level mental-health professionals to deal with the ever-burgeoning number of disordered minds (Albee, 1969, 1970). President John F. Kennedy, reflecting his own personal interest and the advice of various study panels, issued a plea to seek out the causes of mental retardation and mental illness and to eradicate these disabilities altogether (Kennedy, 1963). This message signalled the third revolution in the history of mental health. The armory of the revolution consisted of the Community Mental Health Clinics, which were instituted in all of the states. The army was comprised, of course, of the mental-health professionals manning the clinics. These front-line troops waged attacks, unbloody for the most part, on mental-health problems whose relationship to the community and social causation seemed to become clearer. The important distinctions between a treatment model and a prevention model were quick to arrive.

The community-based, prevention approach to problems of mental health was depicted in public health terminology by Gerald Caplan (1964). Public health has undergone its own revolutions from the miasmatic model in medieval days, to the germ theory of the late 19th and early 20th centuries, to the present model which emphasizes the interactions among germs, the environment, and the individual. One could have undertaken preventive activities within each of these theoretical bases, albeit in quite different ways. The miasmist, who associated disease with the corruption of lands and waters, might prevent ill health as Lord Snow did in London during the cholera epidemic in the 19th century. After a bit of epidemiological detective work in which he discovered that the greatest incidence of the disease occurred in that group of Londoners who drew their water supply from the Broad Street pump, Snow simply had the handle of the pump removed. Instant prevention! He did not know what was causing the illness, but whatever it was, it was associated with the Broad Street water supply. Apparently, one does not have to know all aspects of the etiology of a disorder to develop preventive strategies, a point to be remembered in discussions below. Prevention efforts based on the germ theory or the interaction model would likely take other forms and be more specific in operation, such as quarantine and innoculation.

Caplan (1964) adapts the public health model of the prevention of disease and applies it to emotional disorder or mental illness. He bases this application on the public health tenet that treating the victims of a disease will never lead to preventing the disease. In his definition of community psychiatry, Caplan described what he means by prevention and the various levels of prevention. Thus, community psychiatry is "the body of professional knowledge, both theoretical and practical, which may be utilized to plan and carry out programs for reducing (1) the incidence of mental disorders of all types in a community (primary prevention), (2) the duration of a significant number of those disorders which do occur (secondary prevention), and (3) the impairment which may result from those disorders (tertiary prevention)" (Caplan, 1964, pp. 16–17). Further, he states that:

> Primary prevention is a community concept. It involves lowering the rate of new cases of mental disorder in a population over a certain period by counteracting harmful circumstances before they have had a chance to produce illness. It does not seek to prevent a specific person from becoming sick. Instead, it seeks to reduce the risk for a whole population, so that, although some may become ill, their number will be reduced. When a program of primary prevention deals with the individual, he is seen as a representative of a group, and his treatment is determined not only by his own needs but in relation to the extent of the community problem he represents and the resources available to deal with it. [Caplan, 1964, p. 26]

While this definition of primary prevention appears clear enough, its translation into actual program application has not reflected its pellucidity. For example, Cowen (1977a, 1977b, 1978, 1980) has repeatedly criticized the definitional slippage of the term "primary prevention." Authors state what primary prevention is, and then present programs that do not follow their own definitions (Cowen, 1977a). Some professionals either do not understand what primary prevention is, or else suggest that they have been "doing it" for years. In other cases, old programs are described in primary prevention terms (Cowen, 1980). For example, Klingman and Ben Eli (1981) describe an interventional program that began in an Israeli border town after a terrorist attack. The local school board provided various services to teachers and others to prevent further buildup in anxiety. They refer to these initial services as primary prevention because they are provided generally to the community, and they refer to services subsequently provided to the children of the community as secondary. But, the initial program is provided to persons already identified as victims, so it is difficult to call these efforts prevention. If the program had been available to communities that had not already been attacked, it could properly be labeled primary. Cowen (1977b) states that his own longstanding interventional program in Rochester, New York, called the Primary Mental Health Program, is frequently cited as a "shining beacon of primary prevention," but in reality

it is not. Rather, it is "one in ontogenetically early secondary—not primary—prevention" (p. 485). To emphasize the point further, he states that, "if Cowen indeed is the most important psychologist contributor to primary prevention in mental health, we do not have a primary prevention" (pp. 485–486).

There are those who say it does not matter if the primary and secondary levels of prevention are confused. For example, Murphy and Frank (1979), after discussing certain examples of interventional programs, ask the question: Are they primary or secondary programs? They say that some are primary because they nip problems in the bud and prevent the development of further problems. But they are secondary as well, because they treat an existing emotional problem. So, to them the distinction is not an important one. We will suggest below that it *does* matter and that we should be clear about the distinctions because they have much importance in determining the nature of one's interventional programs. Primary prevention is clearly oriented toward the population while secondary prevention is aimed at the individual.

Those who hold to the medical model of psychopathology emphasize secondary and tertiary prevention almost to the exclusion of a concern for primary prevention. For example, Adler, Levinson, and Astrachan (1978) state that prevention has different meanings and functions in the four major task areas of psychiatry (medical, rehabilitative, social control, and humanistic tasks), and that the concepts of primary and secondary prevention are most useful in the medical task area. However, the primary prevention of mental illness can be of only limited effectiveness because we know so little of the etiology of these disturbances. Therefore, secondary prevention (early diagnosis and treatment) is central to medical caring tasks, while tertiary prevention is assigned to the rehabilitative task area. Because they focus on the disease model, social-change factors are not considered pertinent. This is essentially because the etiological relevance of social factors, including stress, for mental *disease* has not been demonstrated. They sound the warning bell of liberty infringement when they state that the "application of models of prevention in the social control and humanistic task areas has led to serious confusion" (p. 786), and that preventing deviance is a political act!

Caplan (1964) has confused some issues in

characterizing prevention of psychopathology in public health terms. His interpretation still follows the medical model and is disease oriented. To avoid this unnecessary snare, we should perhaps return to language antedating Caplan's classificatory schema, as proposed by Wagenfeld (1972) and later by Kessler and Albee (1975). They propose the attractively seductive position that *prevention* refers to the prevention of mental disorders, *treatment* to the interventional processes applied to existing disorders, and *rehabilitation* to the reparation of systems affected by the disorder. Therefore, primary prevention "can be anything which prevents the occurrence of disorder" (Kessler & Albee, 1975, p. 559). This approach certainly allows for and even encourages the investigation of social factors as related to mental disorder, in contrast to the medical model described above. It clearly points to a distinction between prevention and treatment and also intimates, however unclearly, that prevention is to be considered a group or population concept, as Caplan has proposed (1964).

But we are not home free, yet, in our definitional perquisition. While we agree with Kelly (1977) that "the topic of primary prevention is a most exciting and overdue challenge for psychology," it is still not clear what constitutes this form of intervention. Cowen (1977a) says that "Primary prevention is a glittering, diffuse, thoroughly abstract term" (p. 1). The core dilemma of this very complex area is that virtually any event or structure can affect one's psychological well-being and, therefore, we must separate the near-infinity of manipulations that could potentially affect well-being into those we know something about and those we know little or nothing about. He nominates for special consideration social-system analysis and competence training (Cowen, 1977a, 1978). Kessler and Albee (1975) compare the field of primary prevention to the Okefenokee Swamp: "Attractive from a distance and especially from the air, it lures the unwary into quagmires, into uncharted and impenetrable byways. There are islands of solid ground, sections of rare beauty, unexpected dangers, and violent inhabitants" (p. 338). Colorful language that dramatically articulates an important point! They further list nearly a score of areas and programs that have been referred to as primary prevention in the articles they reviewed, including group homes, titanium paint, Sesame Street, antipollution laws, special diets, free VD clinics, and more.

Below, I will attempt to provide an expanded definition of primary prevention to reflect the prepossessing aspects of definitions referred to above, and also the kinds of prevention programs that have appeared in the literature in the past seven years or so. I will also attempt to differentiate clearly between primary and secondary prevention and describe illustrative programs for the latter area, as well. It is hoped that these attempts will not be subverted by any violent inhabitants. The Kessler and Albee (1975) review article has 381 references and is an excellent summary of the prevention literature through 1973. That report is highly recommended reading. Literature citations for the present analysis will mainly reflect the period from January 1974 through the end of January 1982.

Primary Prevention Defined

It appears clear that prevention is neither treatment nor the development of new treatment programs (Heller & Monahan, 1977). Kessler and Albee (1975) state that primary prevention is the prevention of the occurrence of mental disorders and it is generally something that is applied to groups or made available to everyone. Munoz, Snowdon, and Kelly (1979) state that primary prevention refers to reductions in the incidence of new cases of dysfunction and that currently accepted definitions imply that the targeted population must be defined demographically; that is, by characteristics other than individual behavior: "Thus a group defined by sex, age, ethnic background, and socioeconomic class would be a proper focus of primary prevention" (p. 6). This latter statement seems to reflect Caplan's (1964) suggestion that populations might be selected for primary prevention programs on the basis of "host factors" such as age, sex, socioeconomic class, and ethnic group since these factors may relate to degree of vulnerability for psychopathology. On the other hand, if primary prevention involves the modification of social systems and the development of competence, as Cowen proposes (1977a, 1978), programs based on such goals would influence everyone and should be made available to all. Demographically defined populations would only aid in determining the beginning steps in what would necessarily become massive programs.

DeWild (1981) has suggested a scheme for clarifying the concept of primary prevention. Stating that two commonly suggested barriers are the ambiguity of the concept and the fear that it may have antilibertarian implications, he proposes dividing intervention targets and sociopolitical values as a new classificatory tactic. Thus, the targets are either populations of individuals or social institutions, while the sociopolitical values are either those that emphasize individual freedom or those that emphasize collective harmony. This plan results in four intervention models: population welfare (assisting people in need); population adjustment (changing individuals to comply with social standards); social action (changing social structures to fulfill the needs of the population); and social ecology (modifying the social system to produce better people). He feels that this form of classification helps to remove much of the ambiguity associated with primary prevention. Further, he suggests that the antilibertarian fear can be overcome by avoiding the population adjustment and social ecology prevention activities and concentrating on the other two areas. His system, therefore, helps to distinguish between threatening and nonthreatening preventive programming.

Cowen (1980) provides a quite different classificatory scheme. He has done so because he feels that little has yet been done in primary prevention. One reason for this state of affairs is the lack of adequate conceptual analyses of the defining properties of potential primary prevention approaches and their promise for reaching certain goals. He claims that the goal of primary prevention is "to engineer structures, processes, situations, events, and programs that maximally benefit, both in scope and tempered stability, the psychological adjustment, effectiveness, happiness, and coping skills of large numbers of individuals" (p. 264). In preventing dysfunction and/or promoting health, this approach frequently uses educational rather than restorative models, and the professional skills called for may differ substantially from those used by the mental-health fields in the past. With Cowen, we clearly see a general positive building focus for primary prevention, in contrast to the medical model concerned with the diagnosis and treatment of individuals.

Cowen's classification system proposes a three-way breakdown of prevention approaches (Cowen, 1980). The system asks initially if the approach is directed at promoting health or preventing maladjustment. Then it inquires whether the approach is programmatic or relational. Lastly, it asks if the approach has mental-health dependent variables or nonmental-health dependent variables. This scheme comprises eight cells, of which Cowen states only two are direct primary prevention. They are the cells that are programmatic and employ mental-health dependent variables in studies that manipulate independent variables to promote health or prevent maladjustment. The remaining six cells form the potential generative component of primary prevention. While his classification system is recent, Cowen has proposed in the past several years that the analysis and modification of impactful social systems and competence training should be the foci of early programs, or "baby steps," in primary prevention (Cowen, 1977a, 1978). Cowen's emphasis on competence building is shared by Bloom (1979). He suggests that the physical health paradigm for primary prevention may not operate for emotional disorders. Stressful life events might result in depression, alcoholism, psychosis, or coronary disorders, and, therefore, our focus should not be on specific ailments but on the reduction of the incidence of particular stressful life events. Recent precipitating factors would be accented rather than longstanding predisposing factors in psychopathology. While primary prevention is concerned with disorder prevention, it also emphasizes the promotion of growth through competence assessment and competence building. The latter can be accomplished by enhancing social or interpersonal problem-solving skills in the young and in helping children, especially the disadvantaged, to avoid learned-helplessness behaviors.

In the analysis below, I have accepted that psychopathology and mental disorder are synonymous, and that many of these difficulties are referred to as problems in living, and likely related to life stressors. Further, I accept that some of these disorders are related to organic damage while many follow the psychogenic hypothesis, so ably defended by Kessler and Albee (1975). Thus, as these authors state: "efforts at primary prevention, in addition to being concerned with prevention of organic and physical damage, must also be directed at the social and emotional experience of children" (p. 566). I would add that, since primary prevention can be undertaken with targets of any age, we also direct our attention to the social and emotional experiences (life stressors) that occur later in life as well. We must keep in mind that the definition of emotional disturbance is subject to sociopolitical bias and pressure. The moral-treatment movement in this country and in

England over 100 years ago characterized the "lunatic" as a human being lacking a self-restraint and order. These qualities are restored to the person through tenderness and reinforcement, so that he will return to being a sober, rational person (Scull, 1979). In a very recent article, Bower (1982) suggests less-than-objective motives in the definition of "emotional disturbance" accepted by the federal government, as specified under Public Law 94-142. This definition is, essentially, that offered by Bower in 1957, but with important modifications. Bower argues that the modifications make the definition contradictory in intent and content with the research from which it came. He states that, "It combines a clinical, intrapsychic concept of emotional deviance with a school-related behavioral one. It makes a zero-sum game of services to the seriously, non-socially maladjusted children and youth. It negates the school as a prime, potentially effective, preventive institution in reducing the problem and helping children in need at critical times. . . . It recommends that acting-out aggressive children be differentiated from neurotic, personality problem children in service needs, despite the fact that the differentiation is psychologically and educationally untenable (p. 60)." Bower laments this breach of communication between policy makers and social and behavioral scientists, and states that these two groups should respect each other's assumptions and concepts if the public is to be served best.

Society and politics notwithstanding, I will accept the suggestions of Bloom (1979), Cowen (1977a, 1978, 1980), and Kessler and Albee (1975) that we are attempting to prevent mental disorder and to promote positive mental health, and offer the following triadic breakdown of primary prevention. It is an attempt to resolve the ambiguity associated with the identification of the targets of primary prevention intervention. The crux of the definitional difficulties of primary prevention depends on whether the interventional targets are singled out because they represent some level of risk for the development of emotional disturbance or whether they are provided a program that enhances behaviors thought to be desirable for all. Viewed from this stance, primary prevention can be of at least three types:

PRIMARY PREVENTION I

This category refers to the provision of programs for nontargeted groups that represent the general population. Such programs may take the form of competence training through the enhancement of social and interpersonal skills for citizens of any age; for example, all third-graders or all third-graders in Hoboken, New Jersey. Other programs in this grouping may be more organically based, including genetic counseling and accident-reduction campaigns. Still other programs may be social-action oriented, directed, for example, at the reduction of poverty, or the improvement of educational institutions. The focus here is clearly on the community, and it is quite in keeping with the description of primary prevention offered by Caplan (1964).

Some of these programs will, indeed, be offered to the entire community, probably making use of the mass media and other general communication agencies. Others, however, will be offered only to segments of the community. In this latter case, I am proposing that the targets be identified only by the nature of the program. For example, a program for initial social-skills training would likely be made available to preschoolers or to children in the elementary-school grades, while genetics counseling would likely be provided to an older population, and so on. Targets are not identified in terms of *risk*, but rather in terms of the *relevance* of the program for that segment of the population.

Few will argue with the importance of most programs falling within this category; those programs that will threaten most will be those that take the form of social action or arouse antilibertarian rhetoric, for any reason.

PRIMARY PREVENTION II

This category refers to the provision of programs for segments of the population identified as subject to *mild risk* for the development of emotional disturbance. "Mild risk" is determined on the basis of demographic variables that suggest some maladjustment or a reduction in potential happiness on the parts of entire segments of the population or substantial portions of those segments. The recipients of these programs will be targeted, but only in demographic terms. Thus, the children of low socioeconmic families in the community may not be provided with even a modicum of sex education or social and interpersonal skills in their homes and neighborhoods. Prevention efforts here might take the form of parental training programs directed to the schools that these children attend. Or, in much the same way, special nutritional information may be provided to the children of disadvantage either through their parents or through their schools.

Programs in this second category may be offered at any age level, and may well be tied to certain stress points. Bloom (1968), for example, has proposed "milestone" interventional programs in which the targets are exposed to relevant programs at specified times in their lives; for example, at initial school attendance, or the beginning of adolescence, or at retirement. The targets comprise a large group of persons who may face stressful conditions and risk emotional disturbance and who may be aided by intervention. The targets are identified generically, and there is no necessary implication that any individual in the target group would become disturbed without the intervention.

PRIMARY PREVENTION III

This category refers to the provision of interventional programs for segments of the population identified as *high risk* for the development of serious mental disorder. The concern here is with groups referred to in vulnerability terms. Thus, the children of two schizophrenic parents are frequently labeled as vulnerable to the development of this disorder. The children of the ghetto are seen as vulnerable to the development of subnormal or borderline-normal IQs. Other vulnerable groups might include the children of alcoholic parents, children who have experienced great trauma (e.g., death of parents) when they were quite young, or children who have been physically or sexually abused by parents, relatives, and/or others. These segments of the community may represent only a small proportion of the population but their potential disturbances are seen as so overwhelming or catastrophic as to license deep community concern.

Targets for these programs are identified in terms of whole groupings; for example, all those children of the ghetto, or all of those who have one or both parents classified as schizophrenic or alcoholic, and so on. Again, there is no necessary implication that any individual in the target group would become deeply disturbed without the intervention, but the disorder is so disquieting to the community at large that even a small chance of becoming so disordered is viewed as sizable enough to warrant attention. Keep in mind that the focus is on community values, and that low IQs in large ghetto populations may not disturb us to the same degree as smaller numbers of schizophrenic citizens. This is another reminder of the import of sociopolitical considerations.

In the classificatory system proposed here, Primary Preventions II and III differ only in the severity of the behaviors at risk and not in the probability of their occurrences. The probability of disturbance may be high or low in either category and for different behavior patterns. For example, a large proportion of children who may become targets for category II programs may develop antisocial behaviors without intervention, while only a small number of children of schizophrenic parents (category III) may develop schizophrenia without intervention. Or, conversely, only a small proportion of category II children may become hardened criminals, while a larger percentage of ghetto children (category III) may display quite low IQ scores and are labeled as maladjusted in school. Probability of occurrence of disorder should be considered a variable that is orthogonal to the present schema, and one to be incorporated as sufficient empirical data justify its inclusion.

It should also be kept in mind that it is the category II and category III intervention programs that are the most threatening to society. Category I programs should bother only the most extreme liberations among us. Szasz (1970), for example, might suggest that there is little basis for the broad community-oriented programs, and that citizens should be permitted to die from lung cancer if they so choose, and so on. Szasz, along with most of the rest of us, would likely prefer that each of us has a choice, and meaningful choice is dependent on general informational and educational programs. The other two categories, however, threaten many for two reasons. The first is the libertarian complaint that society has no reason for singling out these high-risk groups and applying programs of change to them. Here the spectre of social control of deviant populations is raised. This caution is one that we cannot ignore. We should, rather, respond to it by increasing the precision of our programs and the specific relevance of such programs for the targeted populations. The second type of threat is illustrated in the criticism of overprediction made about some intervention programs (Bloom, 1968; Heller & Monahan, 1977; Monahan, 1975). Many of the disorders may be low base-rate behaviors, such as the development of delinquency of schizophrenia. In such cases it is quite likely that more persons will be labeled inaccurately than accurately. This is a serious ethical problem that should not be slighted. It becomes less serious if one can plan the intervention program so that there is less chance of negative effects, including the labeling of participants or the development of self-fulfilling prophesies. It is also less important a criticism to the extent that the behaviors involved are high base-rate behaviors, such as the incidence of low IQs among children of the ghetto. A third criticism of prevention programs of all three types is their cost. For the category I programs, perhaps the intervention is not required at all or perhaps not for all of those intervened. For the category II and III programs, especially in light of the possibility of overprediction, most of those exposed to the program will not need it. The agreeable goal of cost efficiency will demand increased precision in our efforts and a great deal more empirical information than is presently available. The metaphor of Kessler and Albee (1975) comes to mind: "Perhaps in our present efforts at social overhaul, sweeping clean with a wide broom will be efficacious only because we may inadvertently hit the appropriate dirt" (p. 567). Society will demand that we sweep with smaller and smaller brooms, and more predictably hit the right dirt.

Secondary Prevention

We have suggested above that primary prevention refers to programs that are provided to groups and populations either not identified at all, or identified in terms of demographic variables, depending on the nature of the intervention program or expectancy of development of mild- or high-risk behaviors because of subgroup membership. What, then, is secondary prevention?

Caplan (1964) states that secondary prevention refers to "programs which reduce the disability rate due to a disorder by lowering the prevalence of the disorder in the community. 'Prevalence' is the rate of established cases of the disorder in the 'population at risk' at a certain point or period in time. . . . A reduction in prevalence can occur in two ways: either the rate of new cases can be lowered by altering the factors which led to the disorder, . . . or the rate of old cases can be lowered by shortening the duration of existing cases through early diagnosis and effective treatment. It is customary to restrict the discussion of secondary prevention to the latter, with the realization that secondary prevention also includes primary prevention" (p. 89). There is a bit of confusion in this definition, at least as the term is employed by most writers in the field. Caplan allows the label to be used when the rate of new cases is lowered through the modification of etiological factors. This sounds preciously like our definition of primary prevention, assuming that the preventive techniques are group-applied. The confusion disappears if Caplan means only that the treatment of problem 1 at time 1 for a target-identified individually can help that person avoid problem 2 at time 2. In that case, most secondary prevention will include primary prevention; or, the example may simply reflect the difficulty of applying physical health models to mental disorders, where the fit is not as good (Bloom, 1979). In any event, the problem may not be too important because Caplan makes it clear that one usually applies secondary prevention to those interventions that shorten the duration of existing cases through early diagnosis and effective treatment. This is certainly the manner in which the term is employed in the current literature review. We should, however, keep in mind Caplan's statement that secondary prevention also includes primary prevention, and, perhaps, look for indications that this principle of physical health may hold in the area of emotional disturbance.

Secondary prevention refers to those interventional programs that are applied to individuals who are already identified as targets. The labeling process may be applied quite early in life, such as Cowen's ontogenetically early secondary prevention program (Cowen, 1977b), or quite a bit later in life, such as programs for the aged, or at any time between, such as after separation or divorce. The defining characteristic of secondary prevention is that the *individual* is already labeled as disordered. He or she may be a likely candidate for greater disorder and a long rehabilitative program, especially without intervention. But, at the time of selection for intervention, the person is assigned to a disordered classification. Providing an effective program for this person may help to prevent further difficulties from occurring, or it may exacerbate such difficulties. This is a matter for empirical study.

Examples of Primary Prevention Programs

Primary Prevention I

As indicated above, this category refers to the provision of intervention programs for nontargeted groups that represent the general population. I could identify only a few such programs in the recent literature that were carried out systematically. These programs are usually rather limited in scope. There are other programs that have been applied to whole communities. These are larger in number, but because they frequently provide no control comparisons, only a few will be discussed for illustrative purposes.

A study reported by Weissberg et al. (1981) appears to be one of the first truly primary prevention attempts of Cowen's Primary Mental Health Project in Rochester, New York. It began in October 1978, at which time *all* second-, third-, and fourth-grade teachers from five suburban and three urban schools were invited to participate in the intervention. Of the 97 teachers contacted, 18 volunteered to teach problem-solving skills to their pupils and 12 agreed to be in the control condition. The subjects were 332 children in the training group, and 231 controls. The intervention itself was a 42-lesson training program based on a 143-page manual that offered a systematic approach to solving interpersonal problems. The program included small-group role playing, videotape modeling, cartoon workbooks, and class discussion. This special curriculum was taught 3 times a week for 14 weeks, and the program ended in March 1979. The "trainer" teachers and assigned undergraduate aides were themselves taught in weekly two-hour workshops by clinical psychology graduate students and by a "master teacher."

Results indicate clearly that the program improved the problem-solving skills and the adjustment of both the suburban and the urban children, as indicated by teacher ratings. The trained children improved more than the control children in such tasks as offering solutions to hypothetical problem situations, independently attempting to resolve a simulated behavioral peer conflict, and in expressing confidence about handling interpersonal difficulties. However, no relationship was found between SPS skill attainment and adjustment gain.

So, while these results suggest that the SPS competence-training approach is a potentially useful primary intervention strategy, we still need to know what specific training components enhanced social adaptation. There is the possibility that this enhancement reflects only a halo bias from the teachers but the authors suggest that this is probably not the case.

In a related study, Weissberg, Gesten et al. (1981b) assessed the effects of a 52-lesson, class-taught, social-problem-solving (SPS) training program for third-grade children. They wished to ascertain if the program improved interpersonal problem-solving abilities, whether it enhanced behavioral adjustment, and whether the problem-solving skills and adjustment gains were related. The experimental and control subjects were 243 third-graders representing 12 classes in three schools, two in White suburban middle-class neighborhoods and one in a low-income Black urban neighborhood.

The children exposed to the SPS program improved more than controls on several cognitive skills, including problem identification, alternative-solution thinking, and consequential thinking, as well as on behavioral problem-solving performances. The intervention positively affected the adjustment of the suburban children but not that of the urban children. There were no signs of radiation from the SPS skills to adjustment in these urban children. There was also no linkage (i.e., significant relationships) found between SPS skills and adjustment change in either group. This linkage, of course, is quite important to those who argue the primary prevention potential of competence building. The authors conclude that we have to consider and better understand program curriculum, age and sociodemographic attributes of children in exploring the potential of SPS training in the promotion of behavioral adjustment.

In the two studies described above, it should be remembered that there was no early identification of maladjustment of the children involved, nor was there any assessment of mild or high risk of these subjects, except in the most generic way in the case of the urban children. In addition, the second program described was carried out in twelve classes in three different schools representing at least two socioeconomic levels. The program carried out in the first study was made available to nearly 100 teachers in eight different schools, and nearly one-third of them participated in the program. This latter program comes very close to true primary prevention as we have classified it above.

While the results of the two programs are limited, and while the finding of no relationship between SPS skill attainment and rated adjustment is bothersome, especially since both measures increased overall (for all children in the first study and for the suburban children in the second), these "baby steps" in true primary prevention are to be admired and further such studies encouraged.

One hopes that the use of control-group comparisons will become contagious in further studies, and that attempts will be made to obtain more direct measures of skill attainment and adjustment, in addition to teacher ratings.

Other programs that fit into this primary prevention category include those reported by Basker (1981), Hartman (1979), Saunders (1979), and Gaughan et al. (1975). The Hartman report describes controlled intervention with high school students who are trained in coping and social skills. The other three describe communitywide interventions in this country and in Israel. These may represent primary prevention at its best but without control observations (not even within-group comparisons across time), it is difficult to evaluate their efficacy.

Primary Prevention II

This category of prevention refers to the provision of intervention programs for segments of the population identified as subject to mild risk for the development of emotional disturbance. The recipients of these programs are targeted, but only in demographic terms. A program outlined by Shure and Spivack (1979) is identified as first-order primary prevention by Munoz, Snowden, and Kelly (1979) and it is described in some detail in their book. I classify the project as Primary Prevention II because, while the targets are not identified individually, they do represent a group whose members might be expected to display some amount of emotional disturbance, including lowered IQ, school adjustment difficulties, and the like.

The intervention in this program is the provision of interpersonal cognitive problem solving (ICPS). The subjects were 40 Black mother-child pairs, recruited from the Philadelphia area. Twenty of these pairs received the training, while the remaining 20 pairs, equated with the trained group for initial ICPS ability, were controls. The children of the two groups were comparable in age (mean = 4.3 years), school behavioral adjustment level, and sex distribution (10 males and 10 females in each group). All children regularly attended federally funded day-care programs. Each experimental mother was given ICPS training so that she could adminster the games and dialogues to her child 20 minutes a day over a 3-month period.

Before and after the training program, several measures of the thinking and problem-solving abilities of the mothers and children were made, and the behavioral adjustment of the children was also measured. Various scales, tests, and games were used to measure the thinking and problem-solving variables and teachers rated the adjustment of the children.

The most general finding of this study is that ICPS training clearly improved impulsive and inhibited behaviors of these inner-city four-year-old children. The strongest direct ICPS-mediator of these improved abilities is the child's ability to think of alternative solutions to interpersonal problems, and the child's ability to foresee possible effects of his or her own actions on others. It was also found that ICPS and behavior changes in children trained by their mothers are very similar to those in children trained by their teachers, as seen in other studies in this research program. The children taught in the home generalized their problem-solving solutions to the school, where they were observed by teachers who were unaware of the training procedures or goals. The training program helped those children who were impulsive to show less anger and impatience, and those children who were inhibited to retreat less from confrontation with others. The mothers also improved their own problem-solving skills in this relatively short time.

These kinds of training interventions have been applied to older children and other kinds of children (e.g., retarded-educable children) successfully in other parts of their program, although longer training periods were required in some. The authors state that such training has been demonstrated to have preventive effects. For example, teacher-trained four-year-olds showed no noticeable behavior problems during the nursery year and they were also significantly less likely than controls to begin showing varying degrees of behavior difficulties a year later in kindergarten. Also, trained children whose impulsive or inhibited behaviors had decreased subsequent to the intervention were likely to maintain adjusted behavior for at least two years without further training. They suggest that this finding might also obtain for mother-trained children; the effect might even be larger there.

Sarason and Sarason (1981) report an attempt to strengthen the cognitive and social skills in a high school whose students have quite high dropout and delinquency rates. Subjects are 127 students, 63 females and 64 males with an average age of 14.8 years, assigned either to the experimental or to the control group. The intervention was provided through live or videotaped modeling to encourage these adolescents to think of more adaptive ways of approaching problematic situations and to perform more effectively in a self-presentation situation (a job interview).

The experimental subjects demonstrated the acquisition of these social and cognitive skills at the end of the training program, as compared with the control subjects. In addition, in a one-year follow-up, they tended to show lower rates of tardiness and fewer absences and behavior referrals. The authors feel that, "This research suggests a potentially useful and cost-effective approach to the prevention of behavioral problems" (p. 908). We have included the study under Primary Prevention II because the subjects, although not targeted individually, represent a mild-risk grouping because they are drawn from a school whose students demonstrate extensive problem behavior.

Felner, Norton, Cowen, and Farber (1981) describe an intervention to provide help to elementary-school children who were experiencing "crisis" at the time. Subjects were 57 children. Most (39) were children of parents who had been separated, divorced, or remarried; others (11) were from families who were experiencing illness, major elective surgery, or had given birth to a sibling. The remaining children (7) were from families in which a parent had died. Each child was seen by a trained, nonprofessional child aide in the school setting. The aides employed abreactive and problem-solving techniques in twice-weekly meetings over a six-week period. The program lasted from the beginning of 1976 to the middle of 1977.

The children showed significant improvement on measures of school adjustment problems and competencies, as well as on a measure of trait anxiety. The post measures were taken two weeks after the intervention was ended. Analyses of the data indicated that the intervention was most effective for children for whom the life event seemed most crisis precipitating. It is unfortunate, however understandable, that no control comparisons were made in this study. It would also have been desirable to have measures of later adjustment.

The reader may wonder why this particular study is listed under Primary Prevention II. Admittedly, it is a judgment call. These children fit into the mild-risk description of category II, but they are identified by the life event and the intervention is individually administered. Since each child was not identified as emotionally disturbed

or maladjusted as a condition of entry into the program, the project was included here. In a very real sense, this study falls between Primary Prevention II and Secondary Prevention.

Primary Prevention III

This category of prevention refers to the provision of intervention programs for segments of the population identified as being at high risk for the development of severe mental disorder; such groups are frequently referred to as highly vulnerable for intellectual or emotional disturbance or both. I will not describe programs dealing with the reduction of physical ailments in high-risk persons, such as the programs described by Maccoby and Alexander (1979) of the Stanford Heart Disease Prevention Program. While there may well be emotional and other mental correlates of such physical diseases, I will deal here only with disorders that can be more directly subsumed under the psychopathology rubric.

The two most extensive and important studies in this category reported to date are those by Heber (1978) and Ramey, MacPhee and Yeates (in press). Heber's study, called the Milwaukee Project, was designed to add to knowledge of the etiology of cultural-familial mental retardation and its susceptibility to preventive measures. In an epidemiological survey, Heber found that the "slum" area of Milwaukee yielded by far the highest prevalence of identified mental retardation among school children in the entire city. Further study indicated that the best single predictor of the level of intellectual development in the child was the IQ of the mother. In an earlier study, Heber, Dever, and Conry (1968) showed that the mean measured IQ of children of mothers with IQs above 80 is relatively constant over the first 14 years of life, while that of children of mothers with IQs below 80 show the progressive decline in mean IQ as age increases, a frequently reported finding. The survey data also indicated that the lower the maternal IQ, the greater the probability was that the children would demonstrate a low IQ.

Heber used maternal IQ as the basis for selecting the newborn subjects of his intervention program, confident that a large proportion of these children would be identified as mentally retarded as they grew older. Screening procedures yielded 40 newborn infants with mothers whose measured IQ was less than 75. Twenty of these mothers and infants were assigned to an experimental group, with the remaining 20 pairs assigned to the control group. Only Black family members were used in the study, to take advantage of their lowered mobility as a protection against sample loss in a longitudinal study.

The 20 families in the experimental group were entered into an intense rehabilitation program that emphasized education, vocational rehabilitation, and home- and child-care training for the mother, and an intense, personalized program for the infant that began in the first three months of life. The infant intervention mainly took place in a day-care center that the child attended seven hours per day, five days per week, on a year-round basis. The curriculum of the infant program emphasized perceptual-motor development, cognitive-language development, and social-emotional development. The program ended when the child was six years of age and entered the public school system.

A variety of developmental and intellectual measures were made on the 40 children over the 70-month period of the intervention. At 12 months of age there are no reliable differences between the two groups, and both score within the normal to above-normal ranges. The control group begins to drop in these scores at about 18 months of age, while the experimental children maintain their performance levels. At the end of the intervention (72 months of age), the mean IQ for the experimental children is about 120, while that for the control children is in the high 80s. This difference is greater than two standard deviations on the IQ scale, certainly a substantial one. Three years into follow-up, data show that the experimental children continue to perform within the normal range while control children, as a group, perform at the borderline level.

While the intervention program for the mothers of the experimental children did not result in an increase in their IQs or in important changes in their social patterns or patterns of interaction with their children. It was reasonably successful in preparing these mothers for employment, which was one of its goals. In addition, there was a small but reliable difference in the IQs of the siblings of the children in the study, in favor of the siblings of the experimental children. Also, among older siblings of the subjects, about twice as many from control families as from experimental families have been placed in special classes for the mentally retarded. So, it is possible that there has been a radiation ef-

fect from the intervened children to their older siblings.

Here, then, is dramatic evidence for "the hope that it may indeed prove possible to prevent the high frequency of mental retardation among children reared by parents of limited intellectual competence under circumstances of severe economic deprivation" (Heber, 1978, p. 62).

Ramey, MacPhee, and Yeates (in press) report a program similar to Heber's except that it involves several waves of children rather than a single sample. It is called the Carolina Abecedarian Project. It began in 1972 and is coordinated through the Frank Porter Graham Child Development Center of the University of North Carolina. Ultimately, the program is geared to intervene at the level of the child, caregiver, family, neighborhood, and society. The underlying model follows a general systems approach.

The project staff developed a High Risk Index based on maternal IQ, family income, parent education, intactness of family and several other factors, and used it to select 112 children or families with normal biology over the years 1972 to 1977. Fifty-seven are in the experimental group and 55 in the control group. Over 90 percent of this sample was intact after six years; the oldest children were in public school in 1980 and the youngest were less than four years old. Over half of the selected families are headed by females; their average earned income is less than $1,500 and the mothers have about a 10th-grade education and a mean IQ of about 85. Ninety-five of the children are Black. Another study done in North Carolina indicated that school failure was reliably related to maternal education and race. On this basis, the targeted children are viewed as being high-risk candidates for school failure.

The children begin the program in the specially devised day-care center as early as six weeks of age, and may begin no later than by three months of age. The program takes place from 7:45 A.M. to 5:30 P.M. each weekday, 50 weeks per year. The children are grouped by age, and there are 12 experienced teachers and assistants and 3 administrative staff members. The teacher ratio is between 1:3 and 1:6, depending on the age of the children. The overall program is designed to foster language development and concept attainment and to promote appropriate and adaptive social behavior, including independence and self-help. The teachers encourage middle-class verbal interactions. The infant curriculum contains 300 items in the areas of language, motor, social, and cognitive behavior. After three years of age, the children are exposed to more and more structured educational curricula.

The experimental and control children (who do not receive the intensive day-care program) are compared on several occasions over the period of intervention. Findings indicate that the program influenced the stimulus properties of the experimental children; they adapt more readily to unfamiliar situations and people, respond more vigorously and appropriately to the demands of a task, and are more advanced in language development than the control children. A variety of IQ measures were used over the years. Both groups score at about the mean IQ level of 105 at 12 months. At the two, three, four, and five-year-old testings, however, the experimental group has a mean IQ of about 95 and the control group mean score is between 80 and 90; the control children display the expected IQ drop but the experimental children do not. The control children are nearly four times more likely to have IQs under 85 than the experimental children. If the IQ analysis is done in terms of infant temperamental ratings of Easy or Difficult based on scores on the Bayley Infant Behavior Record, the Easy experimental children score around 115 to 120 on the IQ scale, and the Difficult score in the high 80s to high 90s. The Easy control children score around the mean IQ level of 100 to 110, and the Difficult in the high 70s to about 100. Other tests administered at 42 months and 54 months of age indicate that the experimental children were significantly better than the control children on verbal, perceptual-performance, and quantitative measures, but not on the motor scale used.

This program also studies the influence of the intervention on the dyadic relationship between the child and the mother and on the mother alone. With respect to the former, experimental children were four times more likely than control children to try to modify the behavior of the mother. For example, they were more likely to ask the mother to watch, to read a book, or to play with them. Interplay activities between mother and child lasted twice as long in the experimental dyads as compared with the control dyads. The researchers correlated the child's IQ with that of the mother for both groups. The general finding has been that a child's IQ will correlate with that of the parent at

about the 0.5 level. Ramey and colleagues find that the child-mother coefficients for the control group are about at the expected level of 0.5 correlation. However, the relationship for the experimental dyads is not different from zero. This finding would indicate that the parent/child intellectual resemblance pattern has been significantly altered by the intrvention program. Furthermore, the mothers of the experimental children of this program obtained more education and were more likely to be employed than the control mothers.

The Heber and the Ramey studies both indicate that cognitively stimulating programs provided to children from infancy through the preschool years can *prevent* the reduced intellectual functioning predicted for such children. Heber has also presented evidence that positive effects of the intervention may continue for at least a number of years. It is very important that such children be followed throughout the school years, and beyond, to study the maintenance of these desirable effects and to learn how such maintenance may be aided through the deployment of social supports later in the lives of the targeted children, These interventions are expensive ones. Thus, it is also important to pinpoint those elements of the programs that most especially contribute to the positive effects so that future interventions may be more easily and less expensively provided. The reader will recall that the experimental children in the Heber study have a mean IQ of about 120 while those in the Ramey study have a mean IQ of about 95 at program end. If it does not reflect random variation, this difference is an important one. One difference in the two programs that may deserve direct study is that the Heber program provided a consistent one-to-one teacher-child relationship throughout the child's first year in the program. This teacher actually established rapport with the family in the home before the child entered the day-care program. There is no indication that this closeness was part of the Ramey program. Other research indicates that specific reciprocal relationships during the latter part of the first year of life may be important for more optimal cognitive development. If so, then the Heber program may be more desirable.

A well-publicized study of the children of Mauritius was first described in brief detail by Bell et al. (1975) and later by Mednick and Witkin-Lanoil (1977) and by Schulsinger (1980). The project was begun as a follow-up to studies reported by Mednick and Schulsinger (1968) and Mednick (1973), which indicated that the speed with which skin conductance returns to baseline value after response to stimulation may be a reliable predictor of later psychopathology, specifically schizophrenia. The present prospective study was started in 1972 on Mauritius, an island off the coast of Africa, under the auspices of the World Health Organization.

Out of 1,800 tested children, 200 were selected to represent three electrodermal levels, two of them considered to be high risk for later psychopathology. The high-risk children were assigned at random to both experimental and control groups. The intervention is an intensive nursery-school educational and day-care program. The study plan is to test the two groups until the children have reached the age of maximum risk for schizophrenia, implying that complete results will not be available until around the year 2000.

Initial results indicate that high-risk children cry more in initial testing and display more fear and anxiety. They also later show more disturbing and aggressive behavior in the nursery schools. The latest report of this project describes the high-risk children spending more time in interaction with others and less time just watching them than their nonschool controls. The normal school children also spend less time watching, but they spend less time interacting and more time with constructive play than the normal nonschool controls.

Other projects fitting into this category include those reported by Klein, Alexander, and Parsons (1977) and by Rolf and Harig (1974). Klein et al., studied the impact of family-systems intervention on delinquency recidivism and also in its effect on sibling delinquency. They report that their behaviorally oriented family-systems approach produced significant improvements in process measures and a significant reduction in recidivism. Rolf and Harig outline the high-risk group method and the early childhood observation of vulnerable children.

The important methodological difficulties of high-risk research, especially studies having the dependent variable of schizophrenia, are described very clearly by Garmezy (1977).

Early Secondary Prevention

It will be remembered that this category refers to the provision of interventional programs to targets who have been identified as emotionally disturbed

or maladjusted, or socially different. We focus here only on studies in which the targets are children and the intervention is applied to groups, not individuals.

The Primary Mental Health Project of Emory Cowen and his colleagues at the University of Rochester has a history of over 20 years of research and has undergone many model changes. Cowen, Pesten, and Wilson (1979) described the latest evaluation of this program, which is designed to detect early and to prevent school adjustment problems. The children are typically referred to the PMHP program by their teachers and the training intervention is generally administered by trained but nonprofessional child aides.

This study had as subjects 215 primary-grade children who had been referred during the 1975–1976 school year. Children from four schools participated and four grades were primarily involved (kindergarten, first, second, and third; about 10 percent of the children were fourth- or higher-graders).

Pre- and postprogram assessments of the children were available, including teacher ratings of problem behaviors and competencies and child-aide ratings of problems. In addition, school mental-health professionals judged the educational and behavioral changes in the project children during the year.

Significant across-the-board improvements were found on all criterion measures, and the authors state that the improvements appear to be due to the intervention rather than to halo effects. The PMHP children also improved significantly more than did a matched, retrospectively selected group of control children.

The authors feel that these results support all of their prior findings that the PMHP approach effectively serves young children with school adjustment problems and adds to the evidence that justifies the provision of programs conderned with early identification and prevention of school adjustment problems.

In another study, Gesten, Cowen, and Wilson (1979) compared primary-grade children who have been referred to PMHP with a nonreferred but matched group on several sociopsychological and competence measures.

They found that teachers rated the referred children as having more serious school adjustment problems. Teachers knew the referred children less well, judged them to have fewer competencies, and liked them less than the control children, probably because they caused more problems in the class.

The authors concluded that these results suggest that the goal of strengthening the competencies of the referred children may be as important as reducing their symptoms. We should keep in mind, of course, that all of the measures were obtained from the same teachers and they may not be without bias.

Other recent early secondary prevention studies include those of Blechman, Taylor, and Schrader (1981), Durlak (1977), Fresham and Nagle (1980), Jason (1977), Jason, DeAmicus, and Carter (1978), Kirschenbaum (1979), LaGreca and Santogrossi (1980), and Sandler, Duricko, and Grande (1975). In virtually all of these studies, social-skills training is provided to young children who vary in age from about three years to twelve years. While control observations are made in most, these studies provide little follow-up data and certainly no long-term follow-up. However, most do report desirable short-term effects of the training.

The reader may wish to refer to more general reviews of secondary prevention programs. An excellent summary has been made by Jason (1975) of intervention programs for three young disadvantaged groups: infants, toddlers, and preschoolers. Jason concludes that the findings of the reviewed studies suggest that early intervention helps materially to reduce the intellectual and linguistic problems of the young disadvantaged. Murphy and Frank (1979) also review a number of local (that is, not national) programs designed to prevent future maladjustment of disadvantaged and high-risk persons. They also review two national secondary prevention programs dealing with the problems of alcoholism and crime and delinquency.

Scores of studies of crisis intervention could have been included within the secondary prevention rubric but space does not permit this coverage here.

Variables Relating to Early Identification

A few studies have been made of warning cues that may be useful in predicting later maladjustment. These analyses of "host factors" (Caplan, 1964) are included here because they point to studies that can be undertaken within the Primary Prevention II and III and the Secondary Prevention categories described above.

Friedrich and Boriskin (1978) review the litera-ture on child abuse and present evidence that certain children are overrepresented in the abused population. For example, children who are born prematurely (those of low birth weight), handicapped children (mentally retarded, blind, or crippled), sickly children, and unusual children (irritable children or those who cry a lot) are at high risk for abuse. The authors suggest that these relationships may obtain because of a lack of maternal-child bonding due to early separation due to the physiological difficulties of the child, or to a lack of care knowledge on the part of the mother, or to the increased stress of having a "special" child. They also propose several specific techniques that may be useful in preventing the development of abuse patterns.

Spivack and Swift (1977) report longitudinal data in which correlational and multiple-regression analyses were made to relate overt classroom behaviors exhibited in kindergarten and the first grade to academic achievement and classroom behaviors exhibited at the end of the third grade.

Results indicate that the earliest high-risk signs include behaviors suggesting a lack of self-confidence in decision making, difficulty in taking action without specific adult support and guidance, inability to attend to and use support and guidance when offered, and a lack of personal involvement and reflectiveness while in the classroom. These children are easily swayed; they look to see what others are doing; directions have to be precise for them; they get fidgety and their minds seem to be elsewhere. They also do not interact with others verbally or get involved in the learning and social process.

Somewhat less salient for predicting high risk are early defiant behaviors and behaviors reflecting poor self-control. These enter into the picture as risk signs only after the child has been in the school system for a year or so. It is interesting to note that of the two types of possible warning cues, cognitive and interpersonal, the cognitive cues turn out to be better predictors of later maladjustment.

Other warning cue studies include Comstock and Helsing (1976), Moos and VanDort (1979), Rolf (1976), and Taylor and Watt (1977), who have examined the probability of having depression symptoms, the prediction of college students having physical symptoms, the poor adult outcome of vulnerable children, and subsequent delinquency behaviors of school children, respectively.

Life Stresses, Social Supports, Environmental Factors, and Mental Health

While some researchers continue to propose physiological models and organic etiology for antisocial behavior and emotional disturbance (for example, Mednick, 1981; Volavka et al., 1977), most emphasize the importance of social and environmental factors in mental disorder and the use of social systems in the prevention of disorder or its treatment. For example, Ho (1974) describes the prevention and treatment of mental illness in the People's Republic of China. He describes the social aspects of such programs as the therapeutic community, community mental health, and milieu therapy. In the Republic of China, whole groups are organized to produce better adjustment; many are involved and not simply mental-health personnel. This country does not plan to train a lot of mental-health personnel or to build many special mental-health facilities. Mental-health problems are seen in a social light.

Such a view reminds one of the moral-treatment program in the 19th century which was dedicated to the social rehabilitation of the emotionally disturbed who were assumed to be socially disordered (Scull, 1979). Such interpretations are not shared by all. Adler, Levinson, and Astrachan (1978), for example, feel that social manipulations are political acts and that preventionists should avoid such domains. On the other hand, those following the medical model have been criticized for using chemotherapy as a social control. For example, Koumjian (1981) states how Valium "treatment of anxiety is a process which redefines social problems as medical problems and, by providing symptomatic relief from stress, discourages approaches which attempt to make more structural changes in society" (p. 245).

While these two points of view continue to be expressed without any appreciable reduction in misguided hyperbole, the resolution of the inherent conflict is not in sight, probably because of all of the sociopolitical consequences of a settlement. Nonetheless, there continues to appear in the literature a large number of articles that catalog the effects of life stressors and environmental factors on mental disorder and the importance of social systems and networks to the prevention or treatment of these disorders.

The significance of life stresses for emotional disturbance has been the subject of speculation and investigation for many years. An early systematic approach to their listing and interrelationships and possible contribution to mental disorder was provided by Caplan (1964). This prospectus, importantly influenced by the work of Lindemann (1944), appears to have laid the groundwork for much of the later work of the Dohrenwends and others who have written many articles on life stresses over the years. In a recent statement, Dohrenwend and Dohrenwend (1981) suggest that mental disorders are largely socioenvironmental in origin. Social causation is more prominent than social selection in producing inverse relations between social class and schizophrenia, antisocial personality, and problem drinking. In this article, they present a variety of theoretical models for linking low social class to relatively high rates of various types of psychopathology.

In this section I will describe recent research concerned with the relationship of life stresses to health, go on to discuss social support systems as potential buffers for the negative influence of stress, outline briefly the impact of environmental settings and stimulation as they contribute to stress or its dissipation, and end with a few lines about one special stress variable, that of old age.

Recent Research on Life Stresses

Godkin and Rice (1981) studied the relationship between psychosocial stress and physical illness on the basis of computerized data on 21,000 patients who were clients of four family health centers in Massachusetts. They found a significantly higher age-sex rate of somatic complaints in patients demonstrating one of four indicators of psychosocial stress (anxiety, depression, couple conflict, and child abuse/neglect) as compared with a patient population not diagnosed as stressed. Such evidence does not support causality statements but these findings do support the accumulating evidence that psychosocial stress is a contributory factor to a wide variety of physical complaints.

Fifty-eight married couples were studied in 1979–1980 by Bird, Schuham, and Gans (1981). Twenty-nine had voluntarily sought psychotherapy because of communication and marital-role problems, and 29 presently reported satisfactory marital and family life. Scalar measures were made of stressful life events in the two groups. The experimental (in-therapy) group reported more sources and a greater incidence of stress than the control group but there were no group differences in the magnitude of stress reported. The experimental group reported over twice the frequency of stressful events over the three-year period before referral and a significant increase in stress for the year immediately before referral. Stresses involved for both groups were similar and included changes in family structure or family interaction patterns. The authors conclude that there is a significant relationship between stressful life events and marital dysfunction and that the clinical assessment of life events can play a meaningful role in evaluation and treatment planning.

Paykel (1978) addresses the contribution of life events to psychiatric disorder and suggests that such events may increase the risk for developing schizophrenia in the six-month period after the stressor by a factor of 2 to 3, of depression by a factor of 2 to 5 times, and suicide by a factor of 6. For all disorders, risks decrease with length of time after the event. Events may not result in psychiatric disorder but rather in medical illness or emotional distress, and the event interacts with many other factors to determine the outcome. This suggests that the appropriate model for event/disturbance research is one of multifactorial causation, and prospective studies are called for in this area.

Brown and Prudo (1981), in a study of a random sample of women in a South London area, later extended to the Outer Hebrides, report that new occurrences of depressive disorders were brought about by certain kinds of life events and ongoing difficulties (provoking agent) and that the risk was increased by the presence of certain other social conditions (vulnerability factors). For example, working-class females were much more likely to develop depression because they experienced more of these factors than middle-class females. They confirmed their city findings in the rural Outer Hebrides sample, although provoking agents occurred far less frequently there. Integration into a traditional way of life, rather than middle-class status, was related there to a lowered chance of developing depression.

In a still ongoing longitudinal study of the influence of the psychosocial environment on health status, McFarlane et al. (1980) report that positive (desirable) life events do not relate to their strain index of health but that negative ones do. Anticipation and control of the event are important variables. The absence of either control or anticipation appears to strengthen the disruptive influence of even desirable events, and the person's perception of not being in control increases the impact of undesirable events. Fortification against the negative effects of life events may be provided through marriage. Morgan (1980) reports that mortality rates are higher for males than for females but lower for married males than for unmarried females. In addition, though women have a higher rate of hospital use than men, the rate for married females is smaller than for nonmarried males. Thus, the differences between the sexes in terms of mortality rate and use of hospital inpatient care facilities appears to be influenced by marital status. Fortification may also be provided by having clear goals and values and feeling in control of matters. For example, Kobasa (1979) studied over a period of three years 75 executives who got ill and 86 who did not after stressful life events. The high-stress/low-illness executives showed more control, commitment, and interest in change as a challenge. They tended to have clear values and goals, active involvement in the environment, and an internal locus of control as compared with the ill group. All of these data were obtained from self-report methods.

Other recent studies have added to the evidence for the relationship between life events and health. Paykel and Tanner (1976), for example, compared relapsed depressed females with those who had recovered and did not relapse and found more life events in the former group in the three months before relapse. Eaton and Lasry (1978) studied immigrant Jews in Montreal and found that job stresses involved in upward mobility can lead to mild psychiatric symptoms. This finding supplements older evidence that severe mental disorder tends to follow downward mobility.

These studies and many earlier ones seem to indicate the importance of life events (stresses) as a major contributor to physical and mental health. The evidence appears so pervasive as to suggest major programs of further study and attempts to build prevention programs around these relationships. We should keep in mind that virtually all of these studies are post hoc, correlational, and make use of self-report data. As such, no cause-and-effect relationships have been established. One would hope that well-known students of these relationships would invest some of their time in the pursuit of clean, prospective studies, rather than in the continued repetition of the same themes, often accompanied by elaborate theoretical models based on weak data.

There have been critics of this approach to

identify prevention variables. Susser (1981), for example, says that "much current life stress research can add little to our ability to control health disorders. The demonstration that the cumulation of a wide array of undifferentiated stressful events can generate stressful states does not point to the means of prevention or treatment" (p. 6). He feels that specific major events ought to be studied to point the way to prevention possibilities and suggests such events as widowhood or cirrhosis. Essentially, he is espousing the high-risk approach in which target groups are identified and various interventions can be tested.

Other authors have found a universal effect of life events on health. Krupinski (1980), for example, found no general relationships between ill health and a large number of social factors, including such objective indicators as work, income, housing, time spent on specific activities, and subjective perception of life. On the other hand, marked relationships were found between level of fulfillment in specific areas and the prevalence of psychiatric disorders. He suggests that we should not aim in health-education programs at imposing our values on the population at large but rather to try to help individuals to determine and to fulfill their desires in actual life. Similarly, Michalos (1979) found no substantial linear relationships between life experiences, measured in the usual way with the Holmes and Rahe scale, illness as measured by several indices, and personal life satisfaction, as measured by a 12-item scale. Haney (1980) has written a review article on the relationship between life events and coronary heart disease. After examining much of the literature in the area, he raises many issues about artifactual findings, the role of retrospective bias, the possibility that individuals who report stress may change their behavior because of the report, and a variety of other methodological difficulties in the reported research. He assesses the most commonly reported generalizations and presents a model to link these disparate generalizations. Andrews (1978) states that the early promise in the area of life-event stress and psychiatric illness has turned more recently into questions of methodology and that a lot of current studies lack power to add materially to what is already known. He suggests that we suspend judgment on the issues until more and better evidence is available.

Perhaps one way of improving research in this area has been suggested by Redfield and Stone (1979). They studied 85 students enrolled in the introductory psychology course at the State University of New York at Stony Brook. They were between the ages of 17 and 39, 61 percent were females, and 82 percent non-Hispanic White. Using bipolar scales based on Holmes and Rahe and Dohrenwend and others, they obtained ratings of 44 life events, both desirable and undesirable, and factor-analyzed the results. They found large individual differences in the perception of life events. These individual differences are so potent a source of variance in life-events ratings that averages taken over large samples do not adequately represent individual perceptions of life events. The analysis revealed three important independent dimensions of variation among events: Change, Desirability, and Meaningfulness. They conclude that life events cannot be equated with subjective stress.

This latter study would indicate that the relationship between life events and health is not a very direct one or an uncomplex one, and that much of the research in this area has been naive in its simplicity. More complicated and meaningful models will have to be developed, more precise and sophisticated measures of life events and stresses devised, and more direct and independent measurement of dependent variables will have to be made. Throughout all of these future efforts, we should keep in mind the advice of Heller and Monahan (1977) that since certain society stressors are more easily preventable than others, we should concentrate on those that appear to be modifiable. They further provide the dictum that the goal of preventive efforts need not be a completely stress-free environment.

Importance of Social Support Systems

Some insight into the difficulty in finding consistent relationships between life events and health is provided by a consideration of the availability of social support factors. There is evidence that suggests that a life event will have quite different effects on the health of the person to the extent that appropriate social props are at hand.

Williams, Ware, and Donald (1981) report a longitudinal study undertaken by the Rand Corporation (Rand's Health Insurance Experiment) of 2,234 persons sampled from the general population in Seattle, Washington. Sociodemographic variables, measures of physical limitations, and measures of mental health, social supports, and stressful life events were measured twice, one year apart. They developed a best-fitting model on half of the sample of subjects and validated it on the other half. They found that social support availability predicts improvement and that life events and physical limitations predict a deterioration in mental health over time. Further, the negative effects of life events and physical limitations do not vary according to the amount of social supports available. This latter finding confirms that of other studies that report that *type* is more important than *amount* of social supports in dissipating the effect of a life event.

Liu et al. (1979) found no direct relationship between stressful life events and psychiatric measures, confirming other studies mentioned in the section above. They report, however, that social support contributes significantly and negatively to illness symptoms. The social support scale explained more than twice as much of the illness variance as the combined variance of the stressful life events and the demographic variables used. Their findings suggest that social support may be just as important if not more important than stressful life events in influencing illness symptoms.

Social support may contribute to psychological well-being, as well as being a protection against the life-event crunch. Turner (1981) looked at the findings of four studies, the results of which suggested a modest, but reliable, association between the availability of social supports and feelings of psychological well-being. Evidence indicated that some part of the causation involved goes from social support to psychological well-being and some part vice versa. Thus, these two variables may have different major determinants. On the basis of studies of the effect of stress upon the support/well-being relationship, Turner concludes that support is most important in stressful circumstances and that these relationships vary across social-class groupings.

The availability of social support may also lower the predisposition to using counseling services. Linn and McGranahan (1980) found that greater contact with close friends diminishes the effect of personal disruptions on individual well-being, but this greater contact also diminishes the predisposition of these persons with disruptions to use professional counseling services. They also found, unexpectedly, that greater interaction with close friends in cases where individuals have no physical, social, or emotional crises does *not* produce increments in life satisfaction.

Larger social support systems are frequently referred to as networks. Evidence linking network variables to psychiatric disorder has been reviewed by Mueller (1980) in three areas: network structure, supportiveness of network relationships, and recent changes or disruption of the network. Findings indicate that social networks may be especially important in the onset and course of depression, although the studies referred to are only suggestive and not definitive. Mueller states that there is a need for systematic study of the relationship of social network characteristics to specific psychiatric disorders, and especially that of depression. Boman (1979) also emphasizes the great value of a supportive and cohesive social network in enabling the individual to cope with events of a stressful nature. He suggests that in intervention work we pay attention to the availability of a social network. He feels that this support system is so important that, if one is not available to the client, one should be provided.

There are a number of factors that may influence the availability of social supports, such as size of community. Oxley, Barrera, and Sadalla (1981) did a telephone survey of four communities of varying size in which the respondents provided information regarding the social support provided by their network members, relations with neighbors, and extent of their social participation. Path-analysis results suggested that larger communities are associated with lower average social support and a pattern of social interaction that limits social participation and, in turn, network size. Larger size of community not only limits the richness of the family network system but also that of voluntary and important nonfamily relationships. The area studied was one of the faster growing in the United States (Arizona), with many newcomers, so the results may not be generalizable to other areas.

Several authors refer to social support or the network system as a buffer between the individual and maladjustment. For example, Sandler (1980) presents evidence showing the effectiveness of older siblings and two-parent families as natural support resources that moderate the effects of stress on young, economically poor children. He suggests that community psychology should augment and advocate these natural support systems and avoid interventions that usurp the role of these systems. He agrees with Boman (1979) that the professional might assist community residents in providing them if the systems do not exist for the client. La-Rocco, House, and French (1980) support the buffering hypothesis but only for certain dependent variables. Their evidence suggests that social support will buffer effectively for physical- and mental-health variables, including anxiety, irritation, and somatic symptoms, but, as in other studies, not for job-related strains, including job satisfaction, boredom, and dissatisfaction with work load. Wilcox (1981) provides clear support for the notion that social support mediates as a buffer between life events and psychological stress. He finds that at high levels of life change, social support protects the person from deleterious effects of stressful life events but that social support is unrelated to level of psychological stress at low levels of life change.

Mitchell and Trickett (1980) have provided a general summary of research on social networks as mediators of social support. They feel that the study of social networks has significant implications both for an understanding of community life and for the design of intervention programs. Further, they feel that mental-health personnel using the network orientation will increase emphasis on understanding the social systems in which individuals are embedded, perhaps decrease their historical emphasis on intrapsychic interpretations, and also plan intervention protocols that increase contact with and collaboration of nonprofessional community resources.

Social support systems have, of course, been provided to clients as intervention to avoid potential disturbance. Recent examples include the work of Kagey, Vivace, and Lutz (1981), who instituted a mutual support group for parents of newborns. The program was founded in 1975 in Lynn, Massachusetts, by a Community Mental Health Center Primary Prevention Team in collaboration with a Regional Maternity Center. The project developed to 28 ongoing groups led by 9 volunteer facilitators. A survey of the parents in 1977 revealed that 94 percent of respondents felt the support group to be helpful and 97 percent would recommend such support groups to others. The groups was found to be helpful for social contact, helpful to feel more positive about being a parent, helping to feel less alone in the role of parenting, and increasing the understanding of the parents of child development and their skills in caring for their child. On the other hand, the group did not help to improve the relationship of the respondent with his or her spouse. Belsky (1982) suggests that such a parent-support group should be instituted in the hospital right after the birth and

then followed up later in the home. Heller (1975) describes an interesting program operated out of the Staten Island Children's Community Mental Health Center. A series of discussions was begun for parents who recently moved to the area and had been subjected to considerable stress. Parents were helped with concerns about their children, who were displaying some minor maladjustment. The program goal was to prevent the need for costly, long-term help that might become necessary if these problems were not dealt with immediately. Parents were recruited through take-home notices to the school children. Nine groups were run over eight months. Each group consisted of about ten parents and it met for ninety minutes once a week for ten weeks. The groups were led by a psychiatric social worker. Parents rated the program highly and the schools involved requested that it be continued. The program was made a continuing part of the consultation and education division of the center.

Occasionally, social support services are tailored to the characteristics of a particular cultural subgrouping of the population. For example, Yee and Lee (1977) describe a high-school program to provide Asian-American youngsters with a positive view of their cultural identity by providing a comfortable arena within the school curriculum for the students to discuss the strengths of their subculture and how the values and behavior of their subculture differed from those of the mainstream. Similarly, Johnson et al. (1974) describe a parent-education program designed especially for Mexican-American families. The training here included home training of the mother and weekend sessions for the entire family. Significant achievements on the part of the children and mothers in the program are reported, as compared with control families. Both of these studies can, in some respects, be viewed as primary prevention programs dealing with mild-risk populations (i.e., Primary Prevention II). They are included here because they appear to provide specific social support to the targets identified in subcultural terms.

The Importance of Environmental Settings and Environmental Stimuli

Aspects of the physical environment have frequently been linked to the development of stress and therefore to emotional disturbance. In this brief section I will present some information on how the environment may be conceptualized to be involved in this process and then present recent data on one very objective environmental influence, that of noise.

The Council on Prevention of the National Council of Community Mental Health Centers identified environmental assessment as a major priority and set up a task force to study the area. Swift (1980) describes the background of this project and introduces several reports stemming from the task force. In one of these latter reports, Monahan and Vaux (1980) comment on three models of the environment and of person-environmental relations. Two of these follow a stress-theory approach, in which environmental stimuli may increase the cognitive and emotional arousal of the individual, with physiological and behavioral implications. Social disruption may occur when the finite human capacity to process information is exceeded. The third is based on behavior-setting theory in which too many or too few participants may have important consequences for those involved in a setting. They outline noise and density as important factors in the physical environment, and socioeconomic status, unemployment, and societal economic change as important factors in the economic environment. They feel that mental-health personnel must pay greater attention to the physical and economic aspects of their community. Further, they emphasize that these professionals should prevent physical stressors, such as noise, when possible, and try to mitigate the influence of unavoidable stressors, such as economic change. The latter can be accomplished by predicting the demand for services and also the demographic characteristics of the population groups most at risk and, then, setting up appropriate service programs.

Wittman and Arch (1980) describe behavior settings and the general relationships between built environments and human activity and the need for a close fit between the two. They suggest that the community should be involved in the planning of mental-health settings and incorporate the physical environment into such planning. Population groups and their settings should be emphasized rather than individual problems or particular situations. They propose a closer alliance between mental-health professionals and environmental psychologists in these planning efforts.

Insel (1980) states that prevention of mental illness requires understanding and assessment of the social environment. Environmental research has shown, for example, a U-shaped relationship between inside density and mental-illness rates; both isolation and overcrowding increase stress at the extremes and become associated with more mental illness. He outlines urban stress factors, including physical threat, stimulus-information overload, frustration of goal-directed behavior, and so on, and suggests how the mental-health consequences of various environments may be predicted. Once environments that are harmful to mental health are identified, social-climate information can be used as a basis for making changes and designing optimal environments. Such planning should always involve the users and should be continually monitored.

Another recent emphasis on environmental planning was suggested by Levine and Perkins (1980). They state that the Task Panel on Prevention to the President's Commission on Mental Health recommended the teaching of coping skills, a person-centered approach, and the modification of social systems as the most important primary prevention programs to be instituted. These authors suggest an alternative approach that would emphasize the development of social-setting prevention programs through the identification of environmental settings that influence relevant behaviors. Taxonomies of settings would be developed to help individuals to define, select, or create environments optimal for their own well-being. They feel that primary prevention efforts should focus on all developmental milestones, not just on early childhood.

Studies on the relationships between the physical environment and psychosocial health have been undertaken. For example, Tyler and Dreyer (1975) analyzed the impact of the location of a new business on Indian reservation life, and suggest that coordinating carefully these types of environmental changes would minimize the pathogenic influences of business development. Brogan and James (1980) studied 100 city blocks of Atlanta, Georgia, by relating 21 indices of deviant psychosocial behavior to 104 indices of the physical environment and 106 sociocultural indices, and factor-analyzing the results. Results indicated that characteristics of the physical environment are about as important as characteristics of the sociocultural environment in explaining variations in psychosocial health. One implication of such findings is that urban and other planners must incorporate advice of community psychologists into their programs.

With respect to contribution of more specific aspects of the physical environment on mental health, the reader is referred again to the Kessler and Albee (1975) review article, to the Monahan and Vaux (1980) task force report, and to many excellent general treatments of the issues within environmental psychology, for example, Bell, Fisher, and Loomis (1978). I will add here only a few quite recent citations relevant to this area.

Chaiklin (1979) again raises the issue of lead poisoning. He states that this form of poisoning is still prevalent, that it can lead to important learning difficulties, and that it may be misdiagnosed as Minimal Brain Damage. He laments that the removal of lead from the environment is not a very popular environmental cause.

Studies of the influence of aircraft noise on human behavior continue to be conducted. In one by Watkins, Tarnopolsky, and Jenkins (1981) of the London Heathrow environs, the authors found that no main effects were significant but degree of disturbance depended on how annoyed the people were. Greater annoyance was associated with the greater use of psychotropic drugs, and greater use of general physicians and outpatient services. This was true for both high- and low-noise areas, leading to the conclusion that vulnerability of the person seems to be importantly involved in determining the influence of some potentially noxious environmental stimuli. Studies such as these suffer because they are essentially correlative and they cannot be expected to entertain all possible important factors. Experimental study of the influence of such stimuli would be far preferable, but is difficult to carry out.

One such study has recently been reported on the physiological, motivational, and cognitive effects of aircraft noise on children (Cohen et al., 1980). Experimental studies of the influence of noise have typically taken place in the laboratory, as in the important work of Glass and Singer (1972). In the present investigation, the impact of aircraft noise on attentional strategies, feelings of personal control, and physiological processes related to health is studied in a controlled situation in the natural setting. They compared third- and fourth-grade children attending several noisy schools in the air corridor of the Los Angeles airport with matched children attending several schools outside of the corridor. All of the children were tested in a noise-insulated trailer parked outside of the school. They found that children from noisy schools had higher blood pressure and were more

likely to give up on a task, and that years of exposure to noise leads to children being more distractable, not less. Performance on puzzle and distractability tasks supports the hypothesis that prolonged noise affects cognitive processes. While some habituation of physiological stress responses seemed to occur, there was no similar adaptation of the cognitive and motivational effects of noise. The authors feel that these kinds of naturalistic field studies accomplished with laboratory precision should be the model for further studies of environmental influences in order to increase the influence of psychological research in the formation of public policy.

The Special Problem of Aging

Aging as a stressor has been studied for several decades and much excellent gerontological research has appeared, especially in the past 15 years. This brief section is not included as a review of that research but only as a repository for a few recent citations that appear to be relevant to our prevention theme.

Schaie (1981) states that the older person's behavioral competence is related to his state of health and the opportunities to be involved in a stimulating environment. To assure the successful transition from midlife to old age, a major educational effort should be provided by the mass media and the public service sector to counter the stereotypes about aging that often become self-fulfilling prophecies. The media should focus on the 95 percent of the aged who are not hospitalized, show successful older persons, and generally train the public to understand that only moderate changes are occurring with age and that older persons should be valued. In addition, health education should be provided to the aging. Mental-health information presently provided is far worse than physical-health information. Since mental-health problems are as important in later life as in the younger ages, stress management and personal energy conservation should be taught. Finally, help in transition from the world of work to that of leisure should be made available to the aging. A lot of uncertainty has been introduced with the advent of more recent flexible retirement plans, and Schaie feels that mental-health professionals should become increasingly involved in preretirement counseling programs to aid in retirement decisions.

Quite a few specific programs have been provided to the elderly as attempts to prevent institutionalization. For example, Rouch and Solomon (1978) describe an outreach gerontological program by a prevention unit of a mental-health center serving the elderly in Miami. The aim of the unit was to provide services to prevent institutionalization. Counseling and group-therapy programs were available and individual evaluations were made. Consultation and education were provided to other facilities. The unit appears to be an important new source of assistance to the community. Group participants have increased their social interactions for the portion of their time not involved in the program, and the number of inappropriate referrals to the center decreased. Similarly, Deutsch and Kramer (1977) report on a program that provides group psychotherapy for elderly outpatients of a municipal hospital in Baltimore. Most of their clients were depressed about physical, mental, or social losses. Therapy was arranged for 5 groups of 12 members each for 1½ hours once a week for 12 weeks, in the hospital. Additional group therapy could be obtained on request. They found that many of the participants became involved in volunteer or part-time work, they renewed contact with family and friends, and they were better able to deal with life stresses.

The Role of Community Health in Primary Prevention

It has been stressed above that, ultimately, primary prevention refers to intervention programs provided to the community at large and not to individuals, as such. Bloom (1980) states that there are basically three types of social and community interventions. The first is the planned short-term therapy, as exemplified by mental-health consultation and crisis intervention. He accents this model and even single-session therapy and suggests that reimbursement ought to be made in reduced amounts as sessions accumulate. The second type of intervention involves mental-health education, whose role is to promote positive mental health by influencing knowledge, attitudes, and behavior patterns. This process demands the exchange of information and not simply the presentation of information. The third type of intervention is illustrated by the patient rights and patient advocacy movement. Bloom feels that community interventions have become less global in intent over the years and more tied to empirical and experiential knowledge, that more recent community change efforts have been increasingly effective,

and that the objectives of such intervention include the strengthening of social supports, the building of social competency, and the management of stressful life events.

Community-oriented interventions can take the form of broad-stroke influence on all or nearly all of the persons in a community. We have already described two such programs in Israel (Basker et al., 1981; Klingman & Ben Eli, 1981). Or, on the other hand, Cowen and Lorion (1975) provide one of many descriptions of their Rochester Primary Mental Health Project which was in only one school for the first 11 years and had expanded to 16 schools by 1975. They obtained evaluation information on the project from 35 mental-health professionals associated with the program in some way. Sixteen of these were mental-health professionals who were founders of the Primary Mental Health Project, while the remaining 19 were psychiatrists, psychologists, and social workers who were consultants, trainers, project directors, and research coordinators. They found that the different groups valued project activities differently. For example, program founders tended to value the project more highly than did those who carried out its "line" functions. Some differences were identified between what was valued about the project theoretically and how participants actually allocated their time. The authors view these differences as sources of potential friction, and that such difficulties tend to increase as initially simple program models are extended to diverse settings with different needs, problems, resources, and personnel. The latter is a most important point. I have already suggested above that primary prevention programs are typically not developed for very large populations. Rather, demonstration and small experimental studies are undertaken and if the model appears to be efficacious, the effort is expanded. Such institutionalization of a model is not without its important problems, as Cowen and Lorion have pointed out.

Some insight into what community mental-health professionals have been concerned with in recent years is provided by Novaco and Monahan (1980). They made an analysis of the work published in the first six years (1973 to 1978) of the *American Journal of Community Psychology*. Referring to their screening, they state that the research articles over this period "have little theoretical foundation, lack methodological sophistication, and give considerable attention to the assessment of person variables." They report that concern with theory has decreased over time, while, at the same time, there was a large increase in the number of articles dealing with the assessment of persons independent of their environment. Further, they report that articles reflecting the study of environments and environment-person interactions are virtually absent, and that this is especially true for studies of community mental-health centers and police studies. They conclude that "the majority of research published in the field's leading journal has little to do with the stated objectives of the discipline."

What is responsible for this disturbing state of affairs? Are there problems inherent in community mental health that mitigate against the development of theory, the conduct of acceptable research, and the inclusion of community, environmental, and prevention foci in its programs? Are the underlying problems related to the difficulties in the definitional properties of the concepts used in community mental health, or to the interests and training of the mental-health professionals involved? Each of these possibilities will be dealt with below.

The community mental-health movement of the 1960s shared many commonalities with the health-center movement of the early decades of this century, as Boyajian (1975) has pointed out. Each emphasized district location, preventive care, the participation of community members, and a bureaucratic organization. Both movements were expressions of the reform spirit of the times and later were undermined by the shift to conservative domestic politics. Boyajian laments that the Community Mental Health Center (CMHC) program of the "great society" has already been truncated, but he feels strongly that "there are those who are still committed to the fundamentally progressive ideas of citizen participation and comprehensive care for all, and who have the firm belief that prevention is better than cure."

Definitional problems and program prioritization have certainly limited the amount of primary preventional activities of Community Mental Health Centers. Saunders (1979) states that while President Kennedy emphasized the prevention aspects of the CMHC program in 1963, several factors have confounded this effort. Included are the lack of agreement about the nature of primary prevention of emotional and mental disorders, the inability of professionals to pinpoint the etiological underpinnings of these disorders, the lack of

theoretical and practical guidelines for the implementation of systematic preventive services in a designated area, only limited data about the effectiveness of trial approaches, and the general disinclination of mental-health professionals to become involved in preventive efforts. Broskowski and Baker (1974) state that while mental-health agencies acknowledge the importance of primary prevention, they continue to devote major resources to diagnosis, treatment, and rehabilitation. They suggest four barriers to the design and implementation of primary prevention programs, including definitional problems (difficulty of defining various forms of prevention, especially as these definitions are influenced by the medical illness model), systemic complexity (the things we wish to prevent are so complexly mediated and interventions are so difficult to develop that trial efforts are often trivial), difficulties of demonstration (intervention effectiveness is difficult to demonstrate because the research methodology used is inadequate and professionals are resistant to new methodologies; this leads to erosion of public acceptance and funding), and lack of constituent demands (there are fewer constituents demanding prevention as compared with those demanding treatment and rehabilitation). The authors conclude that such "barriers have led to a situation in which many talk about primary prevention but few are adequately supported to do anything about it." They fear that interest in prevention will disappear before it has been given an adequate chance to demonstrate its worth.

Perlmutter, Vayda, and Woodburn (1976) made an attempt to clarify some of the definitional issues surrounding prevention concepts and programs. They obtained information from all CMHCs in Region 3 (Pennsylvania, Delaware, Maryland, Virginia, West Virginia, and Washington, D.C.). Based on Caplan's definitions of primary, secondary, and tertiary prevention, they developed a list of 30 items, 10 items each representing the 3 levels. For construct validity, they got independent ratings from a variety of experts as to which item referred to which level of prevention. They then presented the items in a random order to the CMHC staff members and got their ratings of each as to prevention level. They found that there was great and significant agreement for the secondary and tertiary prevention items but much greater dispersion (less agreement) for the primary prevention items. Apparently, CMHC personnel are not familiar with primary prevention areas, likely because they are not much involved in these areas.

The position that mental-health centers are not very actively involved in prevention efforts is supported solidly by Matus and Nuehring (1979), who state that CMHCs in 1973 spent only about 7.7 percent of staff time in prevention work and about two-thirds of their time in direct treatment. They feel that this reflects confusion regarding what primary prevention is. They surveyed 84 mental-health professionals from three centers on the basis of a clear specification of prevention activities and confirmed that about 7.8 percent of staff activities were of prevention orientation.

Of the various roles mandated for CMHCs, the one that subsumes primary prevention activities is the category of "consultation and education." Vayda and Perlmutter (1977) made a survey of such activities in all 43 CHMCs in Region III. They site-visited each center and interviewed directors and others involved in consultation and education. Defining prevention activities as institutional (caretaker training and program consultation) or individual (developmental and situational crises), they found that the mean number of consultation and education activities per center is 10, with a range of from 0 to 28. Prevention activities total about one-half of consultation and education activities; the mean number is 5 and the range is 0 to 23. Most of these activities are institutional and the situational crises are very infrequent. The authors feel that prevention activities must increase and that this can be accomplished by developing programmatic packages and exposing the practitioners to them. They feel further that there is a need to stipulate the prevention needs to CMHCs, particularly the consultation and education personnel, and that such personnel should become lobbyists to get existing community structures to take on appropriate prevention responsibilities.

In addition to definition problems and staff confusions about primary prevention, there is also the issue of CMHC staff interest in the primary prevention area. Bloom (1978) surveyed 211 psychologists in 51 CMHCs in the western United States. He found that two-thirds of their work was involved in the provision of traditional clinical services, 19 percent in community mental-health activities, and the remaining 15 percent in program development, administration, research, and pro-

gram evaluation. Thus, these psychologists spend little time in research, even though one associates psychologists with research. These personnel also express the need for additional training in clinical areas rather than in community mental-health functions. Bloom concludes that CMHC psychologists spend their time in much the same way that mental-health professionals did before the CMHC program began; that is, in traditional, direct diagnostic and treatment services.

Matus and Neuhring (1979) report that their survey of three CMHCs indicates that social workers do most of the primary prevention activities, even though psychologists obtain a higher score on a scale that indicates acceptance of primary prevention. Social workers appear to be more experienced in these activities than their professional colleagues in other disciplines. Interestingly enough, the social workers don't conceptualize these activities as prevention, nor do they espouse an especially preventive philosophy. This, of course, may reflect their historical focus on action and not on theory. These findings may account, at least in part, for the low primary prevention involvement estimate of 7.7 percent of total time. If social workers are doing most of these activities and they do not view them as primary prevention, perhaps much more primary prevention is being accomplished than we are aware of.

Where does the psychiatrist fit into this convoluted and disappointing picture of primary prevention activities in the CMHC program? The relationship appears to be an unhappy one, and one that is decreasing in variety of contribution to and in frequency of membership in these programs. Albee (1980) points out that while it was mandated that a psychiatrist be the chief administrator of each CMHC when they were initially introduced, this policy was discontinued and now about half of the centers are headed by persons trained in other disciplines. The activities of psychiatrists in these centers have decreased over time and their roles appear to have been truncated. These changes are perceived to represent serious problems, mainly, of course, by psychiatrists. In an article provocatively entitled, "Issues Critical to the Survival of Community Mental Health," Borus (1978) demonstrates that community mental health is moving away from medicine, while psychiatry is getting more biological. Such programs have gone into societal areas and somewhat away when their highest priorities should be to serve patients with debilitating illnesses. Inexperienced persons have been providing client evaluations that should be done by the most experienced personnel, usually psychiatrists. Borus feels that there is a false egalitarianism in community mental health. Since the psychiatrist has medical, psychological, and management expertise and skills, he should really be responsible for the diagnostic and treatment programs of a center's activities. However, the number of psychiatrists has dropped from 6.4 percent to 4.7 percent of all CMHC staff from 1972 to 1976, and psychiatrists frequently use the center as a stepping stone to private practice, partly because of financial incentives. Finally, he claims that effectiveness evaluations are rare in community mental health and that the funding for such programs is unstable. The latter problem, he feels, can be dealt with by providing national health insurance which will allow a free choice of program and therapist for the client. Let the marketplace determine the success or failure of the program and the professional!

Reinstein (1978) supports many of the points raised by Borus. He states that in 1976 he felt very disenchanted being a community psychiatrist and felt that his patients could be better served in a private practice setting. To see if others felt as he did, he surveyed 33 psychiatrists in mental-health centers all over the country. Most of these centers were not hospital based and most had nonmedical directors. Many of these respondents complained that they were not allowed to do psychotherapy, they were not responsible for the full management of the patients, they were unable to provide medical care, they were responsible to a nonmedical director, and that there was an obligation to treat all patients, even those who were poorly motivated. More than 80 percent of those responding, said that they were inadequately reimbursed, only six said that they were happy, and only seven said that they were going to stay in community mental health. Reinstein recommends several solutions to these problems. One is to support only those centers in which the psychiatrist has an appropriate role. He also proposes, as did Borus, that all clients be provided equal access to private psychiatric care as well as to community programs. This could only be done, of course, through some sort of national insurance voucher program.

Beigel, Sharfstein, and Wolfe (1979) state that the presence of psychiatrists in CMHCs has diminished in recent years, especially in non-hospital-based centers, rural centers, and in urban centers in disadvantaged areas. The decrease of psychiatric leadership in these centers is especially noticeable. The reasons for these decreases include low salary levels, the decrease in the number of patients with severe mental disorders coming to centers, and impact of a decrease in specialized training programs in community psychiatry. As a solution for these problems, these authors suggest that the hiring of an appropriate ratio of psychiatrists to other clinical staff be made a condition of funding for the center. They also propose that there be an increased medical involvement in the centers and that psychiatrists be given more time for research, evaluaton, and teaching.

These sympathies are echoed by Ribner (1980) who also lists the difficulties of the medical model and the hostility of nonpsychiatric mental-health staff as additional reasons for psychiatrists leaving centers for private practice. Langsley (1980) even more specifically highlights the differences between the medical models and the social services approaches to community mental health. He claims that the original intent of the CMHC program was to treat those who were mentally ill, and that the more than 750 centers now operating are drifting away from that form of health service toward a socially oriented model offering crisis intervention and counseling for predictable problems of living. One result of this shift in focus is the marked decrease in the number of medically trained personnel and a neglect of the mentally ill, especially chronic and deinstitutionalized patients. He advocates a return to the original mandate, in which centers deal with professionally diagnosed psychiatric illness, become involved with hospitals, and hire an adequate number of psychiatrists.

On the other side of the coin, Adler (1981) states that it is acceptable to maintain a medical model in psychiatry but that the field should use other models as well. He feels that psychiatry should clarify its appropriate use of the medical model. Even more extremely, Burstein (1981) suggests that psychiatry drop the medical model as a rallying cry. He feels that much of psychiatry is not medical and that the field ought to recognize this fact.

Finally, Magaro, Gripp, and McDowell (1978) state that the core of psychiatric research is increasingly biochemical and genetic despite the growing evidence for social and economic issues as those most salient for the genesis and maintenance of chronic mental health disability. The mental-health system is seen in this country as a legitimate mechanism of social control for chronic patients. The alternative community programs are obtaining less support and are being forced into a fee-for-service mode. They argue for the right of the disadvantaged to be able to choose their own rehabilitation. Such persons should be provided the funds and be able to choose their "therapist." This is certainly preferable, they feel, to attempting to restructure a bankrupt social system.

So what are community mental-health programs doing? Apparently a good deal of direct treatment and service and very little primary prevention. The staffs of the centers appear to be treatment oriented and this appears to reflect the training and orientation of these professionals and also the increasing financial pressures for fee-for-service funding. Psychiatrists are disassociating themselves from centers for private gain, and also because their medical model approach appears to conflict with the social service model of most of the remaining center personnel. There is one small hopeful note with respect to primary prevention: since center personnel do not appear to know what this form of intervention is, perhaps they are doing more of it than has been catalogued to date.

Primary Prevention: The Future and Conclusions

The past and the present of primary prevention have been difficult enough to describe, and so it may appear unsagacious to outline possible futures for this field. I will do so here in the hope that these words may encourage further interest in prevention efforts.

First of all, I think that we will soon bury the now trite conventionalism that knowledge of the etiology of psychological disorder is necessary before we can establish prevention programs. This is usually the position of those who accept an organic or medical model of mental disorder. However, in public health itself quite a few preventive measures have been instituted without a complete knowledge of etiology and even, in some cases, with an incorrect knowledge of etiology of some disorders (Heller & Monahan, 1977; Kessler & Albee, 1975). The programs I have described above as primary prevention and early secondary prevention should encourage even those most umbrageous about the etiology issue to take heart. Thus, we should develop additional programs based on our best guesses about relevant independent variables and important dependent variables. We will be wrong occasionally, even frequently, but the work is too important to avoid on the basis of possible imperfection. There have been three encouraging signs in recent years that attest to the growing importance of the area of primary prevention. The first has been the creation in 1980 of a Center on Prevention within the National Institute for Mental Health. The second has been the initiation of the *Journal of Primary Prevention* (called the *Journal of Prevention* for the first year), also in 1980. The third has been the development and success of the Vermont Conference on the Primary Prevention of Psychopathology. These annual conferences began in 1975 and are held in the summer at the University of Vermont. Each is concerned with imporant aspects of prevention theory and programs, and the conference proceedings are published each year (Albee, Gordon, & Leitenberg, in preparation; Albee & Joffe, 1977; Bond & Joffee, in press; Bond & Rosen, 1980; Forgays, 1978; Joffe & Albee, 1981; Kent & Rolf, 1979). No conference was scheduled for 1982 but it is expected that they will resume in 1983.

Assuming that there will be greater involvement in primary prevention efforts in the future, what will be their nature? Future research in the field will become more empirical and especially more experimental, and attempts will be made to develop theories or at least miniature models of relationships among variables important to the development of mental disorder. I agree with Heller and Monahan (1977) that we should take a multiple risk factor orientation to the etiology issue and attempt to develop predictive equations comprising genetic, constitutional, developmental, and environmental dimensions. Loading would be ascertained for each of these areas for a variety of mental disorders, and these, in turn, related to different interventional strategies to determine which produces the best result at the least cost to society, its financial resources, and its mental health. It would likely be wise in early efforts to focus prevention programs on important specific behaviors rather than on specific etiological elements. Heller and Monahan (1977) also remind us that prevention research will have to face the methodological difficulties involved in making accurate counts of disorders, due to problems in the definition of disorder, how the count is made, and who is involved in the supply of such information.

Much more research has to be done within the

area of primary prevention and this research will have to be an improvement over that published in the past ten years or so. Lounsberg et al. (1979) analyzed the topic trends represented in the *Community Mental Health Journal*, certainly one of the leading outlets for prevention research, over the years 1965 through 1977. For this entire period, prevention articles represented 2.3 percent of total articles — not an impressive proportion. With respect to trend, for the period 1965–1968 the prevention proportion was 1.4 percent, for 1969–1972 2.4 percent and for 1973–1976 1.6 percent of the total. For an area that "appears" to be burgeoning in interest, this trend is alarming. Lounsbury, Leader, and Meares (1980) made a content analysis of all of the empirical articles appearing in the *American Journal of Community Psychology* from 1973 through 1978. While the themes of these articles included many other than prevention, they found that the studies suffered from many methodological difficulties, including unrepresentative sampling of subjects, nonequivalent comparison groups, small samples, few variables examined, use of only limited methods, and simple statistical analyses. They conclude that few practical decisions can be made on the basis of these kinds of studies. Clearly, then, prevention research will have to become more sophisticated and much more of it will have to be done.

If the CMHC program is going to be continued in roughly its present form in the future, changes will have to be made in its approach if prevention is to become viable. A much higher priority will have to be assigned to prevention efforts within centers. This may necessitate training in the definition of prevention and in the kinds of interventions that may be undertaken at the local level. It will be especially important to involve members of professional disciplines other than social workers, who presently constitute the prevention workforce of the centers. Funding for prevention activities will have to be provided. This can be done in part by reducing pressure on center personnel to increase income through the fee-for-service route, and also in part by training these personnel in the ways of "billing" for preventional efforts. Center personnel must also be provided training in evaluation and research techniques, and then provided time to apply this new learning to improve their general programs as well as those in prevention. Many of these objectives would occur more readily and, apparently, improve the morale of most center personnel if the CMHC structure

could be bifurcated into two quite distinct components. One set of centers would be treatment and direct-service oriented. The focus here would be on the individual client, it would reflect the major portion of current activities of centers, and it would be a more attractive arena for psychiatry to consider rejoining. The second set of centers would be prevention oriented. The focus here would be on the group and on the community, it would reflect a greatly expanded consultation and education set of activities, and it would be the appropriate forum for mental-health personnel to engage with other disciplines and community agencies and resources on prevention problems. To suggest an increase in the mental-health bureaucracy at a time when national commitment to social service appears to be in retrenchment may appear foolish, but the bicameral approach suggested here solves a good many of the logistical, practical, and morale problems of the existing structure, it may not increase costs importantly over present levels if other programs are assigned to the new centers, and, most of all, it will provide the needed impetus to prevention progress.

What specific prevention projects or programs offer the most appeal for early study? Cowen (1980), after providing a conceptual framework for primary prevention, suggests three types of primary prevention programs that have been or should be developed: the effects of natural, unpredictable events or crises (e.g., floods), predictable crises or events (e.g., divorce), and health-building programs (e.g., education, bonding, enrichment). Heller and Monahan (1977) offer as early candidates: anticipating the stress of surgery, dealing with the stresses of college life, and the study of factors associated with resistance to stress. In addition to these areas, we should expand research on the contribution of social supports and networks to prevention, as Davis (1977), Leighton (1979), Turner (1981), and Williams, Ware, and Donald (1981) suggest. We should develop further the good beginnings of the analysis of child abuse (e.g., Gil, 1975) and studies of the newborn period (e.g., Belsky). Competency-training programs should be generalized from the Cowen Rochester PMHP to many geographical areas, be provided as both secondary and primary prevention attempts (as Cowen and others already have done), and also extended to other kinds of trained behaviors. In the area of the prediction of violence, the environmental task of predicting dangerous situations, as proposed by Monahan (1975), and the multidimensional view espoused by Halleck (1975) should be developed further. The very promising area of behavioral settings research in prevention should be a high priority, as suggested by Leighton (1979). More communitywide prevention attempts, such as those described by Basker, Meir, and Kleinhauz (1981) and Klingman and Ben Eli (1981), should be undertaken. Perhaps we should evaluate the contribution that periodic developmental assessments might make to prevention designs, as proposed by Miller (1977). Since a great deal of personpower will have to be available to accomplish larger-scale prevention programs, we should study how the church, clergy, physicians, teachers, parents, college students, and others can contribute as prevention volunteers, or in the provision of social support, as Carver (1977), Haugk (1976), and Signell (1976) have recommended, and even the provision of a mental-health ombudsman, as Wolkon and Moriwaki (1977) have suggested.

Whichever of the above courses we decide to pursue, we must realize that primary prevention endeavors are saturated with ethical and moral issues that must be faced squarely. The chief such issue is the potential of violating civil liberties and invading privacy. Since primary prevention, in its truest form, involves the provision of interventions before a clear need for the intervention has been determined, there are important concerns here. The violation of liberty and the infringement of privacy must be minimized in any program, and protections provided by frequent reviews, overseeing boards of professionals and community members, and so on. In this latter regard, users of prevention services must be actively involved in the development of programs and in the monitoring function, and not merely participate in some sort of token committee capacity. Care should be taken lest we propose programs only for statistically extreme targets. Prevention should be directed to the deviants in society only if they represent meaningful categories of mental disorder. Those who make these decisions must do so carefully, publicly, and with accountability.

Another important ethical problem is the likely overprediction of targets in prevention interventions. This may not be too serious an issue if the intervention involves social-skills training for those felt to be at some risk for minor school maladjustment. It becomes more important in interventions involving the prevention of more stigmatizing conditions, such as criminality or schizophrenia. This will become less of a problem when we begin

to sort out the multiple factors involved in the etiology of such behaviors, and will disappear altogether when we begin to apply prevention programs to the community at large.

Other ethical questions concern the appearance of treating an entire community as mentally disordered and the power struggle that may seem to be at the heart of prevention tactics. In the first case, communitywide interventions must take on a positive demeanor and be concerned with the development of competency, mental health, and happiness. In the second case, the apparent power orientation of the preventionists can be less alarming to others if they become part of the planning and monitoring rubric.

Is primary prevention an idea whose time has come? Indeed, yes, although the revolution is slow in the making. On the other hand, when the definition of primary prevention is more clearly presented and becomes more generally known, we may find that the revolution is well underway and many of us have simply not recognized it.

References

Adler, D. A. The medical model and psychiatry's tasks. *Hospital and Community Psychiatry*, 1981, **32**, 387–392.

Adler, D. A., Levinson, D. J., & Astrachan, B. M. The concept of prevention in psychiatry: A reexamination. *Archives of General Psychiatry*, 1978, **35**, 786–789.

Albee, G. W. Who shall be served? *Professional Psychology*, 1969, **1**, 4–7.

Albee, G. W. The uncertain future of clinical psychology. *American Psychologist*, 1970, **25**, 1,071–1,080.

Albee, G. W. The fourth mental health revolution. *Journal of Prevention*, 1980, **1**, 67–70.

Albee, G. W., Gordon, S., & Leitenberg, H. (Eds.). *Primary prevention of psychopathology. Vol. VII: Promoting sexual responsibility and preventing sexual problems.* Hanover, N.H.: University Press of New England, in preparation.

Albee, G. W., & Joffe, J. M. (Eds.). *Primary prevention of psychopathology. Vol. I: The issues.* Hanover, N.H.: University Press of New England, 1977.

Andrews, J. G. Life event stress and psychiatric illness. *Psychological Medicine*, 1978, **8**, 545–549.

Basker, E., Meir, A. Z., & Kleinhauz, M. Community intervention and mental health: A case study of a neighborhood in Jaffa. *Community Mental Health Journal*, 1981, **17**, 123–131.

Beigel, A., Sharfstein, S., & Wolfe, J. C. Toward increased psychiatric presence in community mental health centers. *Hospital and Community Psychiatry*, 1979, **30**, 763–767.

Bell, B., Mednick, S. A., Raman, A. C., Schulsinger, F., Sutton-Smith, B., & Venables, P. H. A longitudinal psychophysiological study of three-year-old Mauritian children: Preliminary report. *Developmental Medicine and Child Neurology*, 1975, **17** 320–324.

Bell, P. A., Fisher, J. D., & Loomis, R. J. *Environmental psychology*. Philadelphia: W. B. Saunders, 1978.

Belsky, J. A principled approach to intervention with families in the newborn period. *Journal of Community Psychology*, 1982, **10**, 66–73.

Bird, H. W., Schuham, A. I., Benson, L., & Gans, L. L. Stressful life events and marital dysfunction. *Hospital and Community Psychiatry*, 1981, **32**, 486–490.

Blechman, E. A., Taylor, C. J., & Schrader, S. M. Family problem solving versus home notes as early intervention with high-risk children. *Journal of Consulting and Clinical Psychology*, 1981, **49**, 919–926.

Bloom, B. L. The evaluation of primary prevention programs. In L. M. Roberts, N. S. Greenfield, & M. H. Miller (Eds.), *Comprehensive mental health: The challenge of evaluation*. Madison: University of Wisconsin Press, 1968.

Bloom, B. L. Prevention of mental disorders: Recent advances in theory and practice. *Community Mental Health Journal*, 1979, **15**, 179–191.

Bloom, B. L. Social and community interventions. *Annual Review of Psychology*, 1980, **31**, 111–142.

Bloom, B. L., & Parad, H. J. The psychologist in the community mental health center: An analysis of activities and training needs. *American Journal of Community Psychology*, 1978, **6**, 371–379.

Boman, B. Behavioral observations on the Granville train disaster and the significance of stress for psychiatry. *Social Science & Medicine*, 1979, **13A**, 463–471.

Bond, L. A., & Joffe, J. M. (Eds.), *Primary prevention of psychopathology. Vol. VI: Facilitating infant and early childhood development*. Hanover, N.H.: University Press of New England, in press.

Bond, L. A., & Rosen, J. C. (Eds.), *Primary prevention of psychopathology. Vol. IV: Competence and coping during childhood*. Hanover, N.H.: University Press of New England, 1980,

Borus, J. F. Issues critical to the survival of community mental health. *The American Journal of Psychiatry*, 1978, **135**, 1,029–1,035.

Bower, E. M. Defining emotional disturbance: Public policy and research. *Psychology in the Schools*, 1982, **19**, 55–60.

Boyajian, L. Z. History strikes again: Two twentieth-century reform ventures. *Hospital and Community Psychiatry*, 1975, **26**, 17–21.

Brogan, D. R., & James L. D. Physical environment correlates of psychosocial health among urban residents. *American Journal of Community Psychology*, 1980, **8**, 507–522.

Broskowski, A., & Baker, F. Professional, organizational, and social barriers to primary prevention. *American Journal of Orthopsychiatry*, 1974, **44**, 707–719.

Brown, G. W., & Prudo, R. Psychiatric disorder in a rural and an urban population: 1. Aetiology of depression. *Psychological Medicine*, 1981, **11**, 581–599.

Burstein, B. Rallying 'round the medical model. *Hospital and Community Psychiatry*, 1981, **32**, 371.

Caplan, G. *Principle of preventive psychiatry*. New York: Basic Books, 1964.

Carver, J. Prevention. Begin at the beginning. *Mental*

Hygiene, 1977, Winter, 7–10.

Chaiklin, H. The treadmill of lead. *American Journal of Orthopsychiatry*, 1979, **49**, 571–573.

Cohen, S., Evans, G. W., Krantz, D. S., & Stokels, D. Physiological, motivational, and cognitive effects of aircraft noise on children. *American Psychologist*, 1980, **35**, 231–243.

Comstock, G. W., & Helsing, K. J. Symptoms of depression in two communities. *Psychological Medicine*, 1976, **6**, 551–563.

Cowen, E. L. Social and community interventions. *Annual Review of Psychology*, 1973, **24**, 423–472.

Cowen, E. L. Demystifying primary prevention. In D. G. Forgays (Ed.), *Primary prevention of psychopathology. Vol. II: Environmental influences*. Hanover, N.H.: University Press of New England, 1978.

Cowen, E. L. Baby-steps toward primary prevention. *American Journal of Community Psychology*, 1977, **5**, 1–22. (a)

Cowen, E. L. Psychologists and primary prevention: Blowing the cover story. *American Journal of Community Psychology*, 1977, **5**, 481–489. (b)

Cowen, E. L. The wooing of primary prevention. *American Journal of Community Psychology*, 1980, **8**, 258–284.

Cowen, E. L., Gesten, E. L., & Wilson, A. B. The primary mental health project (PMHP): Evaluation of current program effectiveness. *American Journal of Community Psychology*, 1979, **7**, 293–303.

Cowen, E. L., Izzo, L. D., Miles, H., Telschow, E. F., Trost, M. A., & Zax, M. A preventive mental health program in the social setting: Description and evaluation. *Journal of Psychology*, 1963, **56**, 307–356.

Cowen, E. L. & Lorion, R. P. Multiple views of a school mental health project: A needed focus in community programs. *Community Mental Health Journal*, 1975, **11**, 203–207.

Cowen, E. L., Zax, M., Izzo, L. D., & Trost, M. A. prevention of emotional disorders in the school setting: A further investigation. *Journal of Consulting Psychology*, 1966, **30**, 381–387.

Davis, M. S. Women's liberation groups as a primary preventive mental health strategy. *Community Mental Health Journal*, 1977, **13**, 219–228.

Deutsch, C. B., & Kramer, N. Outpatient group psychotherapy for the elderly: An alternative to institutionalization. *Hospital and Community Psychiatry*, 1977, **28**, 440–442.

DeWild, D. W. Toward a clarification of primary prevention. *Community Mental Health Journal*, 1981, **16**, 306–316.

Dohrenwend, B. P., & Dohrenwend, B. S. Socioenvironmental factors, stress, and psychopathology. *American Journal of Community Psychology*, 1981, **9**, 128–159.

Durlak, J. A. Description and evaluation of a behaviorally oriented school-based preventive mental health program. *Journal of Consulting and Clinical Psychology*, 1977, **45**, 27–33.

Eaton, W. W., & Lasry, J. C. Mental health and occupational mobility in a group of immigrants. *Social Science and Medicine*, 1978, **12**, 53–58.

Felner, R. D., Norton, P. L., Cowen, E. L., & Farber, S. S. A prevention program for children experiencing life crisis. *Professional Psychology*, 1981, **12**, 446–452.

Forgays, D. G. (Ed.), *Primary prevention of psychopathology. Vol. II: Environmental influences.* Hanover, N.H.: University Press of New England, 1978.

Friedrich, W. N., & Boriskin, J. A. Primary prevention of child abuse: Focus on the special child. *Hospital and Community Psychiatry,* 1978, 29, 248–250.

Garmezy, N. On some risks in risk research. *Psychological Medicine,* 1977, 7, 1–6.

Gesten, E. L., Cowen, E. L., & Wilson, A. B. Competence and its correlates in young normal and referred school children. *American Journal of Community Psychology,* 1979, 7, 305–313.

Gil, D. Unraveling child abuse. *American Journal of Orthopsychiatry,* 1975, 45, 346–356.

Glass, D., & Singer, J. *Urban stress.* New York: Academic Press, 1972.

Godkin, M. A., & Rice, C. A. Psychosocial stress and its relationship to illness behavior and illnesses encountered commonly by family practitioners. *Social Science and Medicine,* 1981, 15E, 155–159.

Goldstein, S. E. A national perspective. In D. G. Forgays (Ed.), *Primary prevention of psychopathology. Vol. II: Environmental influences.* Hanover, N.H.: University Press of New England, 1978.

Gresham, F. M., & Nagle, R. J. Social skills training with children: Responsiveness to modeling and coaching as a function of peer orientation. *Journal of Consulting and Clinical Psychology,* 1980, 48, 718–729.

Halleck, S. L. A multi-dimensional approach to violence. In D. Chappell & J. Monahan (Eds.), *Violence and criminal justice.* Lexington, Mass.: Lexington Books, 1975.

Haney, C. A. Life events as precursors of coronary heart disease. *Social Science and Medicine,* 1980, 14a, 119–126.

Hartman, L. M. The preventive reduction of psychological risk in asymptomatic adolescents. *American Journal of Orthopsychiatry,* 1979, 49, 121–135.

Haugk, K. C. Unique contributions of churches and clergy to community mental health. *Community Mental Health Journal,* 1976, 12, 20–28.

Heber, F. R. Sociocultural mental retardation: A longitudinal study. In D. G. Forgays (Ed.), *Primary prevention of psychopathology. Vol. II: Environmental influences.* Hanover, N.H.: University Press of New England, 1978.

Heber, F. R., Dever, R. B., & Conry, J. The influence of environmental and genetic variables on intellectual development. In H. J. Prehm, L. A. Hamerlynck, & J. E. Crosson (Eds.), *Behavioral research in mental retardation.* Eugene, Ore.: University of Oregon Press, 1968.

Heller, K., & Monahan, J. *Psychology and community change.* Homewood, Ill.: Dorsey Press, 1977.

Heller, M. Preventive mental health services for families new to the community. *Hospital and Community Psychiatry,* 1975, 26, 493–494.

Ho, D. Y. F. Prevention and treatment of mental illness in the People's Republic of China. *American Journal of Orthopsychiatry,* 1974, 44, 620–636.

Insel, P. M. Task force report: The social climate of mental health. *Community Mental Health Journal,* 1980, 16, 62–78.

Jason, L. Early secondary prevention with disadvantaged preschool children. *American Journal of Community Psychology,* 1975, 3, 33–46.

Jason, L. A. A behavioral approach in enhancing disadvantaged children's academic abilities. *American Journal of Community Psychology,* 1977, 5, 413–421.

Jason, L. A., DeAmicus, L., & Carter, B. Preventive intervention programs for disadvantaged children. *Community Mental Health Journal,* 1978, 14, 272–278.

Johnson, D. L., Leler, H., Rios, L., Brandt, L., Kahn, A. J., Mazeika, E., Frede, M., & Bisett, B. The Houston parent-child development center: A parent education program for Mexican-American families. *American Journal of Orthopsychiatry,* 1974, 44, 121–128.

Joffe, J. M., & Albee, G. W. (Eds.), *Primary prevention of psychopathology: Vol. V: Prevention through political action and social change.* Hanover, N.H.: University Press of New England, 1981.

Kagey, J. R., Vivace, J., & Lutz, W. Mental health primary prevention: The role of parent mutual support groups. *American Journal of Public Health,* 1981, 71, 166–167.

Kelly, J. G. The search for ideas and deeds that work. In G. W. Albee & J. M. Joffee (Eds.), *Primary prevention of psychopathology. Vol. I: The issues.* Hanover, N.H.: University Press of New England, 1977.

Kennedy, J. F. Message from the President of the United States relative to mental illness and mental retardation. Feb. 5, 1963, 88th Congress, First Session, House of Representatives, Document No. 58.

Kent, M. W., & Rolf, J. E. (Eds.), *Primary prevention of psychopathology. Vol. III: Social competence in children.* Hanover, N.H.: University Press of New England, 1979.

Kessler, M., & Albee, G. W. Primary prevention. *Annual Review of Psychology,* 1975, 26, 557–590.

Kirschenbaum, D. S. Social competence intervention and evaluation in the inner city: Cincinnati's social skills development program. *Journal of Consulting and Clinical Psychology,* 1979, 47, 778–780.

Klein, D. C., & Goldstein, S. E. *Primary prevention: An idea whose time has come.* DHHS Publication No. (ADM) 80-447, 1977.

Klein, N. C., Alexander, J. F., & Parsons, B. V. Impact of family systems intervention on recidivism and sibling delinquency: A model of primary prevention and program evaluation. *Journal of Consulting and Clinical Psychology,* 1977, 45, 469–474.

Klingman, A., & Ben Eli, Z. A school community in disaster: Primary and secondary prevention in situational crisis. *Professional Psychology,* 1981, 12, 523–533.

Kobasa, S. C. Personality and resistance to illness. *American Journal of Community Psychology,* 1979, 7, 413–423.

Koumjian, K. The use of Valium as a form of social control. *Social Science and Medicine,* 1981, 15E, 245–249.

Krupinski, J. Health and quality of life. *Social Science and Medicine,* 1980, 14A, 203–211.

La Greca, A. M., & Santogrossi, D. A. Social skills training with elementary school students: A behavioral group approach. *Journal of Consulting and Clinical Psychology*, 1980, **48**, 220–227.

Langsley, D. G. The community mental health center: Does it treat patients? *Hospital and Community Psychiatry*, 1980, **31**, 815–819.

La Rocco, J. M., House, J. S., & French, J. R. P. Social support, occupational stress, and health. *Journal of Health and Social Behavior*, 1980, **21**, 202–218.

Leighton, A. H. Research directions in psychiatric epidemiology. *Psychological Medicine*, 1979, **9**, 235–247.

Levine, M., & Perkins, D. V. Social setting interventions and primary prevention: Comments on the report of the Task Panel on Prevention to the President's Commission on Mental Health. *American Journal of Community Psychology*, 1980, **8**, 147–157.

Lindemann, E. Symptomatology and management of acute grief. *American Journal of Psychiatry*, 1944, **101**, 141–148.

Linn, J. G., & McGranahan, D. A. Personal disruptions, social integration, subjective well-being, and predisposition toward the use of counseling services. *American Journal of Community Psychology*, 1980, **8**, 87–100.

Liu, N., Simeone, R., Ensel, W. M., & Kuo, W. Social support, stressful life events, and illness: A model and an empirical test. *Journal of Health and Social Behavior*, 1979, **20**, 108–119.

Lounsbury, J. W., Leader, D. S., & Meares, E. P. An analytic review of research in community psychology. *American Journal of Community Psychology*, 1980, **8**, 415–441.

Lounsbury, J. W., Roisum, K. G., Pokorny, L., Sills, A., & Meissen, G. J. An analysis of topic areas and topic trends in the *Community Mental Health Journal* from 1965 through 1977. *Community Mental Health Journal*, 1979, **15**, 267–276.

Maccoby, N., & Alexander, J. Reducing heart disease risk using the mass media. In R. F. Munoz, L. R. Snowden, & J. G. Kelly (Eds.), *Social and psychological research in community settings*. San Francisco: Jossey-Bass, 1979.

Magaro, P. A., Gripp, R., & McDowell, D. J. *The mental health industry: A cultural phenomenon*. New York: Wiley-Interscience, 1978.

Matus, R., & Nuehring, E. M. Social workers in primary prevention: Action and ideology in mental health. *Community Mental Health Journal*, 1979, **15**, 33–40.

McFarlane, A. H., Norman, G. R., Streiner, D. L., Roy, R., & Scott, D. J. A longitudinal study of the influence of the psychosocial environment on health status: A preliminary report. *Journal of Health and Social Behavior*, 1980, **21**, 124–133.

Mednick, S. A. Studies of children at high risk for schizophrenia. In S. R. Dean (Ed.), *Schizophrenia: The first ten Dean award lectures*. New York: MSS Information, 1973.

Mednick, S. A. ANS functioning and antisocial behavior. *Psychophysiology*, 1981, **18**, 202–203 (abstract).

Mednick, S. A., & Witkin-Lanoil, G. H. Intervention in children at high risk for schizophrenia. In G. W. Albee & J. M. Joffe (Eds.), *Primary prevention of psychopathology. Vol. I: The issues*. Hanover, N.H.: University Press of New England, 1977.

Mednick, S. A., & Schulsinger, F. Some premorbid characteristics related to breakdown in children with schizophrenic mothers. *Journal of Psychiatric Research*, 1968, **6**, 267–291.

Michalos, A. C. Life changes, illness and personal life satisfaction in a rural population. *Social Science and Medicine*, 1979, **13A**, 175–181.

Miller, E. Out to protect a vital resource. *Mental Hygiene*, 1977, Spring, 15–17.

Mitchell, R. E., & Trickett, E. J. Task force report: Social networks as mediators of social support. *Community Mental Health Journal*, 1980, **16**, 27–44.

Monahan, J. The prediction of violence. In D. Chappell & J. Monahan (Eds.), *Violence and criminal justice*. Lexington, Mass.: Lexington Books, 1975.

Monahan, J., & Vaux, A. Task force report: The macroenvironment and community mental health. *Community Mental Health Journal*, 1980, **16**, 14–26.

Moos, R. H., & Van Dort, B. Student physical symptoms and the social climate of college living groups. *American Journal of Community Psychology*, 1979, **7**, 31–43.

Morgan, M. Marital status, health, illness and service use. *Social Science and Medicine*, 1980, **14A**, 633–643.

Mueller, D. P. Social networks: A promising direction for research on the relationship of the social environment to psychiatric disorder. *Social Science and Medicine*, 1980, **14A**, 147–161.

Munoz, R. F., Snowden, L. R., & Kelly, J. G. *Social and psychological research in community settings*. San Francisco: Jossey-Bass, 1979.

Murphy, L. B., & Frank, C. Prevention: The clinical psychologist. *Annual Review of Psychology*, 1979, **30**, 173–207.

Novaco, R. W., & Monahan, J. Research in community psychology: An analysis of works published in the first six years of the *American Journal of Community Psychology*. *American Journal of Community Psychology*, 1980, **8**, 131–145.

Oxley, D., Barrera, M., & Sadalla, E. K. Relationships among community size, mediators, and social support variables: A path analytic approach. *American Journal of Community Psychology*, 1981, **9**, 637–665.

Paykel, E. S. Contribution of life events to causation of psychiatric illness. *Psychological Medicine*, 1978, **8**, 245–253.

Paykel, E. S., & Tanner, J. Life events, depressive relapse and maintenance treatment. *Psychological Medicine*, 1976, **6**, 481–485.

Perlmutter, F. D., Vayda, A. M., & Woodburn, P. K. An instrument for differentiating programs in prevention—primary, secondary and tertiary. *American Journal of Orthopsychiatry*, 1976, **46**, 533–541.

Ramey, C. T., MacPhee, D., & Yeates, K. O. Preventing developmental retardation: A general systems model. In L. A. Bond & J. M. Joffee (Eds.), *Primary prevention of psychopathology. Vol. VI: Facilitating infant and early childhood development*. Hanover, N.H.: University Press of New England, in press.

Redfield, J., & Stone, A. Individual viewpoints of stressful events. *Journal of Consulting and Clinical Psychology*, 1979, **47**, 147–154.

Reinstein, M. J. Community mental health centers and the dissatisfied psychiatrist: Results of an informal survey. *Hospital and Community Psychiatry*, 1978, **29**, 261-262.

Ribner, D. S. Psychiatrists and community mental health: Current issues and trends. *Hospital and Community Psychiatry*, 1980, **31**, 338-341.

Rolf, J. E. Peer status and the directionality of symptomatic behavior: Prime social competence predictors of outcome for vulnerable children. *American Journal of Orthopsychiatry*, 1976, **46**, 74-88.

Rolf, J. E., & Harig, P. T. Etiological research in schizophrenia and the rationale for primary prevention. *American Journal of Orthopsychiatry*, 1974, **44**, 538-554.

Rouch, J. L., & Solomon, J. R. An outreach and prevention unit in a mental health center serving the elderly. *Hospital and Community Psychiatry*, 1978, **29**, 710-711.

Sandler, I. N. Social support resources, stress, and maladjustment of poor children. *American Journal of Community Psychology*, 1980, **8**, 41-52.

Sandler, I. N., Duricko, A., & Grande, L. Effectiveness of an early secondary prevention program in an inner-city elementary school. *American Journal of Community Psychology*, 1975, **3**, 23-32.

Sarason, I. G., & Sarason, B. R. Teaching cognitive and social skills to high school students. *Journal of Consulting and Clinical Psychology*, 1981, **49**, 908-918.

Saunders, S. Primary prevention from a neighborhood base: A working model. *American Journal of Orthopsychiatry*, 1979, **49**, 69-80.

Schaie, K. W. Psychological changes from midlife to early old age: Implications for the maintenance of mental health. *American Journal of Orthopsychiatry*, 1981, **51**, 199-218.

Schulsinger, F. Biological psychopathology. *Annual Review of Psychology*, 1980, **31**, 583-606.

Scull, A. T. Moral treatment reconsidered: Some sociological comments on an episode in the history of British psychiatry. *Psychological Medicine*, 1979, **9**, 421-428.

Shure, M. B., & Spivack, G. Interpersonal problem solving thinking and adjustment in the mother-child dyad. In M. W. Kent & J. E. Rolf (Eds.), *Primary prevention of psychopathology. Vol. III. Social competence in children*. Hanover, N.H.: University Press of New England, 1979.

Signell, K. A. On a shoestring: A consumer-based source of personpower for mental health education. *Community Mental Health Journal*, 1976, **12**, 342-354.

Spivack, G., & Swift, M. "High risk" classroom behaviors in kindergarten and first grade. *American Journal of Community Psychology*, 1977, **5**, 385-397.

Susser, M. The epidemiology of life stress. *Psychological Medicine*, 1981, **11**, 1-8.

Swift, C. Task force report: National Council of Community Mental Health Centers Task Force on Environmental Assessment. *Community Mental Health Journal*, 1980, **16**, 7-13.

Szasz, T. *The manufacture of madness*. New York: Harper & Row, 1970.

Taylor, T., & Watt, D. C. The relation of deviant symptoms and behaviour in a normal population to subsequent delinquency and maladjustment. *Psychological Medicine*, 1977, **7**, 163-169.

Turner, R. J. Social support as a contingency in psychological well-being. *Journal of Health and Social Behavior*, 1981, **22**, 357-367.

Tyler, J. D., & Dreyer, S. F. Planning primary prevention strategy: A survey of the effects of business location on Indian reservation life. *American Journal of Community Psychology*, 1975, **3**, 69-76.

Vaughan, W. T., Huntington, D. S., Samuels, T. E., Bilmes, M., & Shapiro, M. I. Family mental health maintenance: A new approach to primary prevention. *Hospital and Community Psychiatry*, 1975, **26**, 503-508.

Vayda, A. M., & Perlmutter, F. D. Primary prevention in community mental health centers: A survey of current activity. *Community Mental Health Journal*, 1977, **13**, 343-351.

Volavka, J., Mednick, S. A., Rasmussen, L., & Sergeant, J. EEG spectra in XYY and XXY men. *Electroencephalography and Clinical Neurophysiology*, 1977, **43**, 798-801.

Wagenfeld, M. O. The primary prevention of mental illness. *Journal of Health and Social Behavior*, 1972, **13**, 195-203.

Watkins, G., Tanopolsky, A., & Jenkins, L. M. Aircraft noise and mental health: II. Use of medicines and health care services. *Psychological Medicine*, 1981, **11**, 155-168.

Weissburg, R. P., Gesten, E. L., Carnrike, C. L., Toro, P. A., Rapkin, B. D., Davidson, E., & Cowen, E. L. Social problem-solving skills training: A competence-building intervention with second- to fourth-grade children. *American Journal of Community Psychology*, 1981, **9**, 411-423.

Weissburg, R. P., Gesten, E. L., Rapkin, B. D., Cowen, E. L., Davidson, E., Flores de Apodaca, R., & McKim, B. J. Evaluation of a social-problem-solving training program for suburban and inner-city third-grade children. *Journal of Consulting and Clinical Psychology*, 1981, **49**, 251-261.

Wilcox, B. L. Social support, life stress, and psychological adjustment: A test of the buffering hypothesis. *American Journal of Community Psychology*, 1981, **9**, 371-386.

Williams, A. W., Ware, J. E., & Donald, C. A. A model of mental health, life events, and social supports applicable to general populations. *Journal of Health and Social Behavior*, 1981, **22**, 324-336.

Wittman, F. D., & Arch, M. Task force report: Sociophysical settings and mental health. *Community Mental Health Journal*, 1980, **16**, 45-61.

Wilkon, G. H., & Moriwaki, S. The ombudsman: A serendipitous mental health intervention. *Community Mental Health Journal*, 1977, **13**, 229-238.

Yee, T. T., & Lee, R. H. Based on cultural strengths, a school primary prevention program for Asian-American youth. *Community Mental Health Journal*, 1977, **13**, 239-248.

36 COMMUNITY MENTAL HEALTH

Linda R. Gonzales
Robert B. Hays
Meg A. Bond
James G. Kelly

The field of community mental health can be appraised from a variety of viewpoints; one can emphasize the adaptation of clinical services for new clients, evaluate community mental-health services, elaborate the role of the federal Community Mental Health Center program, or highlight the administrative and logistical issues when designing services for geographical areas with widely varying characteristics and needs. We have elected another option: we present examples of novel services that illustrate methods and processes when citizens and professionals work together.

We have selected community mental-health services for four special populations: (1) ethnic minorities; (2) the elderly; (3) rural groups; and (4) women. We have chosen as examples those services that strengthen a community's capacity to develop personal and social competences.

Following a brief presentation of the exemplary services, we review three topics that contribute directly to the operation of these novel services: social support networks, self-help groups, and citizen participation. These three topics are reviewed in terms of knowledge that directly enhances service delivery. The four populations and the three topics are intertwined. When designing preventive services, knowledge about social support networks, self-help, and citizen participation is considered essential.

[1]Those who designed the programs we cited in the chapter shared additional insights about their work. We have benefited very much from their commitment to their own work and their interest in this chapter. Our appreciation is expressed to Donna Yee (On Lok), Bob Knight (Senior Outreach Services), John Shybut (Nebraska Linkage), and Nelba Chavez (La Frontera).

We also benefited from critical appraisals by colleagues who gave us detailed comments on an initial draft of the manuscript. We thank the following persons for their interest and help to us: Bernard L. Bloom, Cary Cherniss, Ben Gottlieb, Ellen Greenhouse, Tom Gullotta, Ira Iscoe, Chris Keys, Charles Kieffer, Donald C. Klein, Alice Lemme, Ed Lichtenstein, David J. McKirnan, Peggy Peterson, Stephanie Riger, Myrna B. Shure, Lonnie R. Snowden, Thomas J. Thompson, Charles Windle, and Marc A. Zimmerman. We also acknowledge the help of Jacqueline Kurzeja of the University of Illinois, Chicago, who at the typewriter and one Wylbur generated multiple revisions and the final draft.

This chapter is dedicated to the unique contributions and memory of Erich Lindermann who gave initial meaning to the field of community mental health (Lindemann, 1952, 1953, and 1977).

The history of community mental-health services in the United States is a history of at least two social processes. One process has been the search for public support to maintain the federally initiated Community Mental Health Center program. A second process, the evolution of community mental-health services per se, can be understood as the struggle to create services that can meet community needs. It is this second process that is the theme of this chapter.

Developing mental-health services with active participation by citizens has produced some substantial success even though there has not been extensive publication about this activity in traditional journals. It is this commitment of citizens and professionals working together to create community-based services that we acknowledge here. In noting this collaborative enterprise we hope that the reader will be encouraged, join in, and then contribute to the continued development of community mental health.

Special Populations

Considerable gains have been made in recent years in identifying the mental-health needs of ethnic minority groups, the elderly, rural populations, and women and in designing programs to serve them. Although on the surface these groups are quite dissimilar, an analysis of the issues for each reveals that there are common elements for effective service delivery. We will consider the issues pertaining to these four special populations and cite several exemplary programs, including some that serve people who are members of two of these populations (e.g., ethnic minority women, and elderly ethnic minority persons). Special considerations for designing and evaluating community mental-health programs for these groups will be highlighted.

Ethnic Minorities

Although ethnic minority groups in the United States differ greatly from one another in social history, level of acculturation, and demographic attributes, they nonetheless share a number of characteristics that bear on our discussion. Ethnic minority groups whose language, cultural, and physical features make them readily visible continue to suffer from high levels of environmental, economic, and social stresses, and they must deal with both personal and social problems created by discrimination against them (President's Commis-

sion, 1978). In response to their status as minorities, these groups have developed coping strategies and subcultures that paradoxically have given ethnic minority individuals both strengths and vulnerabilities (Kobata, Lockery, & Moriwaki, 1980). Subcultures give their members pride in their ethnic identity, and collective values and norms for guiding behavior; on the other hand, differences in education, languages, values, life style, and other variables have often served as reasons to exclude minorities from positions of influence and access to resources in mainstream society (Vontross, 1976). These strengths and vulnerabilities must be considered when designing mental-health services for ethnic minorities. For example, the medical model of mental illness has been identified as particularly inappropriate for a comprehensive, intervention-oriented analysis of minority group members' psychopathology since it is based on the assumption that illness is internally caused and treatment focuses on the individual, with scant attention to environmental contributors (Bloom, 1983; Davis, Owens, & Critton, 1980).

The strict adherence to a medical model may also be inappropriate for ethnic minority individuals in another way. Assumptions about what constitutes and causes mental illness or health vary widely from culture to culture, as do opinions about what constitutes therapy (Sue & Sue, 1977). Differences between the client's and the professional's belief systems and expectations for the therapeutic process may constitute a psychological barrier influencing the ethnic minority person's willingness to seek and/or complete treatment (Higginbotham, 1977).

Besides psychological barriers created by differing assumptions about causes of illness and appropriate treatment, many additional barriers to service exist (Acosta, 1979). Geographical barriers have been identified as an important factor lessening accessibility to mental-health services (Burreal & Chavez, 1974; Torrey, 1972). Services may be inaccessible owing to physical distance from the ethnic minority neighborhood, lack of public transportation, or neighborhood boundaries. Language barriers are a second major problem, in both obvious and subtle ways. Sue and Sue (1977) note that difficulty in using English as a second language may mitigate against clients' benefiting from talk-oriented therapy. Further, lack of staff conversant in the ethnic-minority language, and lack of signs and advertising in the language are barriers to minorities' awareness and utilization of mental-health services (Torrey, 1972).

A third barrier is that of cultural relevance of treatment. Mental-health centers have attempted to address this problem by hiring bilingual, bicultural staff. This practice is supported by Wu and Windle's (1980) study in which they concluded Blacks, Hispanics, Asian-Americans and American Indians do increase their utilization rates at community mental-health centers as a function of the proportion of staff from their respective ethnic group.

There is also evidence, however, that providing bilingual, bicultural therapists is not in itself sufficient. Miranda and Castro (1977) indicated that among female Mexican American outpatients, client acculturation level was directly related to length of stay in therapy, despite the fact that bilingual, bicultural therapists were being used. Client social class was not related to length of stay, which led the authors to conclude that differences in cultural expectations about the therapeutic process may have been operating in this situation. Miranda and Castro speculate that receiving training and working within the context of traditional mental-health models may cancel out the advantages of cultural similarity between staff and clients.

Another caveat should be added with regard to the goal of increasing the proportion of ethnic minority staff. Often, because of the scarcity of ethnic minority mental-health professionals, an over-reliance on paraprofessionals has occurred. One study noted a number of abuses, including failure to match client and paraprofessional cultural background, use of paraprofessionals to conduct insight-oriented therapy without special training, and an informal policy of assigning the least desirable clients to paraprofessionals (Satow & Lorber, 1978). The quality of supervision given these staff also varied greatly. Neither the interests of ethnic minority mental-health consumers nor those of staff are advanced by such practices (Delgado & Scott, 1979).

Another set of barriers stems from social-class differences between mental-health professionals and ethnic minority individuals, since many ethnic clients are from the lower socioeconomic class (Padilla, Ruiz, & Alvarez, 1975). Since substantial literature exists detailing these problems (see Garfield, 1978; Lorien, 1973, 1974, 1978), we limit our comments to noting that both practical programming (setting fee policies and hours of service) and less tangible aspects of community mental health, such as implicit treatment goals within services, are mediated by values and day-to-day realities that differ across social class.

Finally, ethnic minorities criticize the fact that their communities have lacked control over the development and administration of services and interventions aimed at them (Davis et al., 1980; Smith et al., 1978; Zwerling, 1976). The definition of social problems and related personal mental-health difficulties by White professionals who have not themselves experienced the cause of these hardships can often result in misdefinitions of problems and in sensitivity to societal contributions and, thus, to "victim-blaming" types of solutions (Rappaport, 1977; Ryan, 1971).

The goal of ethnic community control over the definition of problems and solutions speaks to the tension that continues to exist in community mental health between systemic change and service orientations. Ethnic minority group members maintain that a major problem in our society is unequal access to power, and resources. Changing this at the administrative and policy levels within community mental-health agencies should be equally or more important than redesigning services for ethnic minorities (Zwerling, 1976). A true commitment to ethnic minority community control is demonstrated by recruiting ethnic minority professionals, training indigenous community members as both professionals and paraprofessionals, and including ethnic minority service providers and citizens in policy making.

The list of barriers presented above is formidable, and spans the domains of geographical, lingual, cultural, and social-class accessibility, as well as community control over defining problems and solutions in these areas. But these barriers are not insurmountable or inevitable. We next consider an example of culturally responsive programming that speaks to all these problems with some success.

La Frontera, a private, nonprofit, comprehensive community mental-health center in Tucson, Arizona, represents an effort to adapt services to the needs of Mexican Americans, who in 1971, comprised 41 percent of its catchment's population (Chavez, 1979). At La Frontera, bilingual, bicultural individuals are a vital part of both the staff and board of directors. The range of services offered includes an outpatient clinic, services for older adults, substance abuse programs, aftercare, two separate halfway-house programs, day treatment, and a unique preschool therapeutic and educational day-treatment program for children. Various services are offered in a dozen locations to provide geographical accessibility, including rural programming for several outlying areas.

Examples of culturally responsive approaches that the center has adopted at every level include an open-door self-referral policy; the careful effective use of paraprofessional community supportive service workers to do home assessments and help clients with "bread and butter" problems of locating and obtaining needed resources, the development of psychotherapies incorporating Mexican American cultural practices, attitudes, gender-roles, familial patterns, etc.; and ongoing research on such topics as utilization patterns and client expectations for therapy.

In addition, La Frontera's consultation and education division has developed several outreach programs. Education about mental health is the main objective of biweekly radio programs by La Frontera's staff on the Spanish radio. The show, called "Tabus y Realidades" (Taboos and Realities) considers a different mental-health topic during each program, and call-in questions from listeners are discussed. The radio program has been very popular since its beginning over a year ago.

Another very successful prevention-oriented effort has been "La Linea Tibia" (The Warm Line), a bilingual, over-the-phone question-answering, referral, and counseling service for "parents bringing up children and children bringing up parents" (Chavez, personal communication, 1982). La Linea Tibia also offers a puppet presentation (in Spanish and in English) for school-age children, dealing with issues of identity, self-esteem, and values. This educational outreach service is well utilized by public and private schools in the area.

La Frontera's Domestic Violence Program illustrates how the center has adapted treatment strategies to the specific cultural aspects of clients' presenting problems. In response to needs-assessment findings in 1979, a program has been developed including individual counseling for adult victims of violence, a weekly evening open-group meeting for women, and a children's group that runs concurrently. The program averages about one referral per day, and 65 percent of the clients are Mexican American (Lackey, personal communication, 1982). In the adult group (offered in English and in Spanish) one component of exploring the options available to women is the identifi-

cation of the cultural norms that have served to maintain the domestic violence. The traditional Latino ideas that wives must accept a domestic situation defined by the husband and that women must always put their needs second to those of the family are discussed, and alternative notions are considered.

In the children's group, for ages 6 to 11, besides dealing with the practical questions of how to cope in a violent domestic situation, children are able to express their feelings and are helped to explore alternative ways to cope with conflict, other than through violent behavior. Thus, the children's group provides a preventive, educational service, designed to help children realize that violence is not an inevitable aspect of the Mexican American culture.

The rate of client utilization at La Frontera showed a noticeable increase in 1972, when the commitment to culturally relevant programming began (Chavez, 1979). The rate of utilization continues to grow, over 30 percent from 1979 to 1980 (Chavez, personal communication, 1981), attesting to the success of its methods.

In summary, community mental-health approaches for ethnic minorities must address issues on a variety of levels from interpersonal cross-cultural communication, to culturally relevant programming, to the empowerment of communities so that they control the agencies that serve them. To accomplish this, a variety of methods must be brought to bear, ranging from traditional therapy outcome research to initiating change in social policy. A committed, comprehensive approach to serving ethnic populations, and a willingness to be accountable to these groups are paramount.

The Elderly

Persons over 65 comprise one-tenth of the U.S. population, and number 25 million. By the year 2010, an elderly population of 32.2 million is expected (Cohen, 1980). The elderly represent an extremely diverse population, having nothing necessarily in common besides their age; however, certain trends can be observed. Most elderly (78 percent) live independently at home (President's Commission, 1978) and only 5 percent over the age of 65 are living in institutions (Cohen, 1980). However, 86 percent of the elderly have chronic health problems, that can be assumed to be a source of considerable psychological stress (Cohen, 1980). A 1975 national survey indicates that the immediate family (spouse and/or children) is the major source of care and social support for the noninstitutionalized elderly person in time of illness (Shanas, 1979). Seventeen percent of men, and 54 percent of women over the age of 65 are widowed. In the mid-1970s, one in six elderly was living below the poverty level. Women over the age of 65 had a median income about half that of men over 65 (Cohen, 1980).

Cohen (1980) has noted that the prevalence of psychosis is more than twice as common among those over 75 than in 25- to 35-year-olds; senile dementia is the fourth leading cause of death; and 25 percent of recorded suicides are committed by the elderly.

Clearly, the need for mental-health services is great, but what is more disturbing are the service-delivery problems experienced by this group. Only 4 percent of clients seen at outpatient mental-health clinics are age 65 and older (President's Commission, 1978). The elderly comprise 30 percent of inpatients of public mental hospitals, and the current system of Medicare coverage for mental-health treatment strongly favors inpatient treatment (President's Commission, 1978).

Major barriers between appropriate mental-health services and the elderly include: a discrepancy between the quantity of available services and the size of the rapidly growing senior population; lack of geographical and psychological accessibility of services (if the services are available, the elderly may not be aware of or understand them); biased attitudes of mental-health professionals against treating the elderly; lack of specialized approaches or programs developed for the needs of senior citizens; and deficiencies in reimbursement mechanisms and policies for services to the elderly (Cohen, 1980; Hagebak & Hagebak, 1980; President's Commission, 1978). Interwoven through all of these barriers is the theme of the combination of social-psychological-physical health problems that many elderly have. A multidisciplinary approach is necessary for effective assessment, treatment programs, and community interventions.

Two community mental-health methods particularly effective in reducing the barriers between the elderly and adequate mental-health care are those of consultation/education, and outreach. The two may be effectively combined, as has been the case with *Senior Outreach Services*, a geriatric outpatient service within the consultation and education division of Ventura County

Mental Health Services in Southern California (Knight, 1981; Slaughter & Peterson, 1981). This unorthodox arrangement makes possible a wide range of traditional and nontraditional treatment services closely coordinated with consultation and education services. The program's two major goals are the prevention of unnecessary institutionalization for the frail and mentally impaired elderly, and making mental-health services more accessible to them.

To meet the first goal, four strategies are employed: early comprehensive assessment and intervention; case management and advocacy to secure various community support services; strengthening family support, including the provision of both tangible aid and emotional support (via the creation of mutual support groups); and strengthening the capability of the Ventura community aging network through in-service training and consultation with agencies. The outreach team is multidisciplinary, including a clinical geropsychologist, a clinical social worker, two mental-health nurses (including one who is bilingual and bicultural), a part-time psychiatrist, and a part-time psychologist. In order to increase accessibility, offices are maintained in towns and neighborhoods with high concentrations of seniors, and a large proportion of services (51 percent) is given in the homes of those who cannot come to a treatment center. Overcoming psychological barriers to service is approached through consultation and education. Education is offered at senior meal sites and senior recreation centers on topics such as "using medication wisely" to acquaint elderly with the idea of improving mental health, with services available, and with staff members (Knight et al., 1981).

The basic premise of Senior Outreach Services is that the care of the elderly's many needs can be accomplished through careful assessment, brief psychotherapy, and establishing close working relationships with the network of service providers who are also concerned with caring for the community's elderly. Ventura County Mental Health is committed to careful program evaluation, and the center's records show that there has been a significantly greater utilization rate of outpatient services by persons over 65 since the implementation of Senior Outreach Services (Knight, personal communication, 1982). The "no-show" rate for appointments in the program was only 7.4 percent, comparing very favorably with rates of 25 percent to 50 percent for other services within Ventura

County Mental Health. A preliminary evaluation of inpatient service utilization levels of seniors for periods before and after the program was implemented showed no significant differences, although there was a trend toward lower rates after implementation (Knight, personal communication, 1982).

In contrast to the outreach-preventive orientation of Senior Outreach Services, *On Lok Senior Health Service* of San Francisco begins with the assumption that a comprehensive program for the elderly must offer all services through its own auspices. Besides demonstrating an original, multifaceted approach for the elderly, On Lok is an exemplary community program in that it was designed in large part by and for the members of a specific multiethnic minority community. The program was founded in 1973 out of community concern for Chinese, Filipino, and Italian American seniors who were being prematurely institutionalized away from their cultural, familial, and neighborhod social support systems and comforts because of a lack of services for the elderly in the Chinatown Northbeach area (Lurie et al., 1976).

On Lok's program offers comprehensive day health services and social services to the dependent, frail elderly, using a threefold strategy to maintain independent living. Participants are offered rehabilitative therapy and training, and physical modifications of their home environments. Second, the familial and social helping network of the elderly person is educated and supported to meet the person's needs. Third, service needs that cannot otherwise be met are provided by On Lok (*On Lok Annual Report*, 1981).

Services are given at participants' homes, nursing homes, and hospitals as well as at the On Lok Day Health Centers, and include primary physician services; nursing care; counseling and advocacy; physical, occupational, speech, and recreational therapies; socialization; nutritional counseling; onsite and at-home hot meals (including special diets, Chinese and Western menus); transportation; home health care; homemaker services; respite care; and inpatient medical care (*On Lok Annual Report*, 1981). Participants are assigned to a specific combination of services, based on their individual needs and the helping resources they already have.

The average age of On Lok participants is 78. Most are poor, non-English-speaking, and live alone. They have multiple medical problems, cognitive impairments, and mobility and perceptual disabilities (Zawedski & Ansack, 1981). In order to serve this population effectively, quite unusual measures are taken in program design and clinical practice. Grooming and bathing is scheduled for those who need assistance; toilet retraining is offered for the incontinent; laundry is done for participants who are unable to use community laundry facilities (Lurie et al., 1976). About 75 percent of the staff are bilingual or multilingual, and reality-orientation therapy is offered daily in both English and Cantonese (Yee, personal communication, 1981). Many cultural aspects of the ethnic groups served have become an integral aspect of programming, ranging from observance of cultural holidays to the staff's understanding of the Asian philosophy of mind-body integration and wholeness.

It is noteworthy that community members were instrumental in conceptualizing and supporting the inception of On Lok. Originally a local nursing home had been sought to meet the needs of the area's elderly, but after some investigation and careful thought, the community constituency turned instead toward the senior-day-care concept as practiced by the English (*On Lok Annual Report*, 1981). Careful adaptation of this basic model has occurred since 1973, taking into account the aspects of participants' culture and life style. The program does not purport to be oriented toward any single ethnic group; rather, the multilingual and multicultural characteristics of the community are linked to a high valuation of cultural aspects in programming.

On Lok's centralized, community-based management system is inseparable from the financing method employed. Participants must be residents of the Chinatown Northbeach district and must be certified as appropriate for institutional placement by the state in order to be enrolled as lifetime members. On Lok receives a single, noncategorical capitation from Medicaid, based on enrollment levels and a prospective budget. This means the program is not required to itemize how much money will be spent on each participant for each type of service given. The goal of a single service system such as On Lok is to eliminate gaps and overlaps in services to the elderly, as well as to provide accountability to the community served. A preliminary study has found that the program's cost has been under $1,000 per "participant-month" in a community where the average cost of the long-term institutional care is near $2,000 a month (*On Lok Annual Report*, 1981). A comparison-group study that follows the progress of On Lok participants and matched subjects not in the program is currently underway (Zadwaski & Ansak, 1981). Over a period of many months, the variables of medical and cognitive status, of both consumers and controls, their health service utilization, as well as their expressed satisfaction, are all being assessed. This study will provide a thorough cost-benefit analysis of the system.

Although On Lok does not formally consider itself a mental-health program, it demonstrates that for some groups, mental-health needs are perhaps best dealt with in the context of the total life situation of the individual in the community. This general theme will continue to be explored in the next section on rural community mental health.

Rural Community Mental Health

The importance of developing viable rural community mental-health models is underscored by the fact that for the first time in over 160 years, the United States population growth rate was higher in rural and small-town communities than in metropolitan areas, according to a preliminary count from the 1980 census (U.S. Department of Agriculture, 1981). The modest shift of urban dwellers moving back to the land, and the boom-town growth occurring in many areas have been known to create cultural clashes and social upheaval in conservative rural communities (Bachrach, 1977, 1981; Berry & Davis, 1978). However, the mental-health needs created by population influx and environmental change represent only one aspect of the many challenges facing rural CMHCs. In this section we outline the diverse constraints of rural settings that have influenced some practitioners to view rural CMHCs as "ideological misfits" (Berry & Davis, 1978, p. 674). On the other hand, the opportunities for creating innovative rural community psychology approaches will be discussed and an example will be presented. On the surface, it may seem a great paradox that many of the more successful rural mental-health approaches have not followed the traditional community mental-health service model of maintaining a wide variety of carefully articulated separate programs tailored to various clienteles. This is more easily understood in light of the fact that the Community Mental Health Act and its amendments represented an urban-oriented concept. Despite this, there is room for optimism about rural community men-

tal health. Whereas several years ago authors tended to focus on identifying the many problems resulting from inappropriately applying an urban community mental-health approach, a plethora of unorthodox rural approaches has recently appeared in the literature (Agnew & Dodgion, 1982; Libertoff, 1979; Smyer, Davis, & Cohn, in press). Rigorous evaluative research is still scarce, and only a few graduate training programs for the mental-health professions exist in rural community mental health (Solomon, 1980). Nonetheless, the topic of rural community mental health seems to be experiencing the beginning of a promising new surge of interest and inquiry.

To understand the many influences that shape rural mental-health needs and approaches, some background information is in order. The usual way of defining rurality is according to population density, by county. According to the U.S. Census Bureau, a "nonmetropolitan" county is basically one with fewer than 50,000 population, and approximately 30 percent of the U.S. population live in counties so classified (U.S. Department of Agriculture, 1981). However, only 11 percent of operating federal community mental-health centers are rural (Solomon, 1980). This low proportion of rural centers is directly tied to the fact that although rural areas have greater mental-health needs, they have fewer resources for addressing them. In contrast to the popular myth of bucolic, wholesome living available in the country, rural areas in actuality have a greater proportion of people living in poverty, a lower level of formal education, and a higher proportion of "high-risk" groups such as the elderly, ethnic minorities, migrant workers, and persons in poor physical health (Bachrach, 1981; Flax et al., 1979). Another influential factor in rural areas is the shortage of health and mental-health care providers—for example, less than 3 percent of the nation's psychiatrists practice in rural areas (Jones, Wagonfeld, & Robin, 1976). Recruitment and retention of professionals is a major problem because of such factors as poorer working conditions, lower remuneration, and lack of opportunity for professional education and specialty development, to name but a few (Bachrach, 1981; Miller, 1981).

Another important factor salient for mental-health service design and delivery in rural areas is a cultural values system that emphasizes self-determined, active resolution of personal and community difficulties (Cedar & Salisan, 1979), a high valuation of personal and kinship ties, and a resistance to change and distrust of outsiders (Flax et al., 1979). The notion of "mental health" is often misunderstood; instead, a holistic view of personal and community well-being is endorsed, assessed by the individual's ability to fit into the community and the community's ability to serve the individual (President's Commission, 1978). A characteristic social organization predominates in rural communities—a proclivity toward homogeneity and lack of specialization. In the aggregate, these sociocultural characteristics can help us understand the differing expectations about mental-health needs, service design, and delivery, and the difficulties encountered by urban-trained outsiders attempting to set up traditional types of programs. Too often, mental-health practitioners have labeled rural populations as victims of a "culture of poverty" because of low service utilization levels (Flax et al., 1979). Similarly, "community poverty" has been used to explain the lack of specialized services available or desired by rural communities (Ford, 1969). An alternative explanation is that designers of urban-oriented, middle-class programs have failed to adapt to rural values, belief systems, and resources.

Although rural communities generally lack the substantial tax base and local support for specialized services, they often express ample interest in community activities and greater sense of civic pride and self-sufficiency than is common in urban areas (Parrott & Sebastian, 1977; Solomon, 1980). Other advantages of rural communities for mental-health practitioners include the opportunity to circumvent bureaucracy and employ more flexibility in program design and service delivery (Jeffrey & Reeve, 1978; Parrott & Sebastian, 1977), and the ease of problem identification, as well as the immediate feedback about efficacy of interventions, due to small community size and high visibility of individuals and programs (Bachrach, 1981; Parrott & Sebastian, 1977).

If mental-health planning is approached in partnership with the community, so that mental-health programs are "owned" by citizens, much can be accomplished. For example, satellite office services intended to be more accessible geographically and psychologically to small-town dwellers at a distance from the main community mental-health program, are effectively designed and developed according to this principle (Shane & Seibert, 1977). Because only one or two professional staff are assigned to the satellite, much collabora-

tion with local volunteers, from board members to volunteer receptionists, is necessitated. The day-to-day maintenance and operation of the program is used for mutual awareness and education around local mental-health issues, and community support is mobilized around concrete issues as a matter of course.

A different kind of collaboration between professional service providers and the community focuses on identifying rural community "natural helpers" and integrating their efforts with the formal service system. There are some decided advantages to the use of informal helpers: they are readily available, easily accepted by the community, of minimal cost to the taxpayer, and less stigmatizing for clients (Bertsche, 1979). At the same time, in setting up a system involving natural helpers, it is essential to remember that helping networks are fragile social arrangements and that intervening in the network should be approached with great care. For example, service-delivery structures, such as categorical requirements for funding, should not be imposed on these natural systems from the outside (Bachrach, 1981).

An application of the natural helpers strategy is found in the *Emergency Mental Health/Paraprofessional Training Program* (EMH/PTP) linkage project in Nebraska (Agnew & Dodgion, 1982; Shybut, in press). The Nebraska EMH/PTP linkage project was created to dovetail natural helping systems and professional services, in order to facilitate the appropriate use of both natural and professional services throughout a 22-county catchment area in northern Nebraska (Agnew & Dodgion, 1982; Shybut, in press). The training project's design and implementation were based on a recognition of several salient factors: the need among a variety of natural helpers for paraprofessional mental-health training; the necessity to build and maintain linkages between the professional mental-health staff and community caretakers; and the goal of respecting and protecting individual communities' self-determination about whether they want involvement in the project. To address these concerns, the following strategies were pursued: a Community Advisory Council was created that advised the program designers of local needs, helped identify natural caretakers, and advocated for the project in local communities. A careful entry process was begun in each community, including a series of organizational meetings to contact participants not yet connected to formal systems of care. The meetings were held to encourage natural caretakers to discuss how the proposed training might affect their own roles in the community and to decide whether they did wish to host the program. At the same time, collaboration with emergency response system leaders (e.g., police chiefs, nursing directors) was initiated to gain entry and develop training curricula for emergency response systems workers.

Ultimately, five different groups were identified and training programs were developed for each: Law Enforcement Personnel, Hospital Personnel, Emergency Medical Technicians, Crisis Line Volunteers, and Community Caretakers. Local ownership of the project was enhanced by having volunteers in each community involved in arranging logistics for the training. The local junior college agreed to grant either continuing education or regular academic credit for the various courses, enabling participants to receive concrete benefits. The project had a number of desired effects in addition to raising the skill level of the natural helpers, including the side-effects of generating more referrals from natural networks to the mental-health center (Shybut, in press), increasing the number of community-based mental-health projects developed collaboratively by local citizens and mental-health professionals (Agnew & Dodgion, 1982), and creating channels for mental-health professionals to make referrals back to local community resources (Shybut, personal communication, 1982). In addition, the creation of a Crisis Line Volunteers Program served as a structural link between communities and the formal mental-health system.

The success of the federally funded EMH/PTP program has led to a new, similar, state-supported project, the development of community-based paraprofessional support systems for the chronically mentally ill with emphasis on residential alternatives, advocacy, and psychosocial habilitation. Although it is too early to evaluate the results, the idea of applying this approach to meet the needs of rural chronically mentally ill is definitely intriguing. Paradoxically, the specific constraints and opportunities of rural communities may serve as a catalyst to create new methods of citizen involvement in the design and delivery of services, as essential component of community mental-health practice in any setting. The significance of citizen involvement in the delivery of services is an essential element in the design of preventive services, as will be noted in the next section on community mental-health services for women.

Community Mental Health Services For Women

Women make up the majority of the patient population in most mental-health facilities and yet can also be considered an underserved population since present mental-health services do not appear to be responding to women's mental-health needs (Russo & Sobel, 1981). A diversity of mental-health services are needed for women that: (1) recognize the depth and variety of women's mental-health needs; (2) promote understanding of and change in the *social context* of women's problems; and (3) emphasize primary *prevention* through change in societal attitudes and beliefs about women and through encouraging the competencies women need to assume to gain control of their lives. These topics will be addressed with illustrative examples.

UNDERSTANDING WOMEN'S NEEDS

Understanding the range and depth of women's mental-health needs requires recognition of the multiple stresses unique to women's lives: employed women are clustered in the lowest paying occupations and at the bottom of the occupational ladder, with one in four living on an annual income of less than $4,000 (President's Commission, 1978). The physical and psychological processes of child birth unique to women are universally noted but still not understood as stressors for women. Women's role within the family also carries with it conflicts when a woman is simultaneously performing roles of mother, spouse, and employed person (Rapoport & Rapoport, 1978). An increasing number of women are reporting that they have been beaten, abused, or raped, and the fear of rape pervades their lives regardless of whether or not they have actually been victimized (Riger & Gordon, 1981).

Stressors such as economic burdens, lack of career opportunities, role strain, and feelings of powerlessness have been associated with mental and physical disorders (Rabkin & Struening, 1976; Dohrenwend & Dohrenwend, 1974). It is not surprising, then, that more women than men seek services from mental-health centers, private mental-health hospitals, general hospital inpatient units and outpatient facilities (Russo & Sobel, 1981), particularly since there is more societal encouragement for women to express weakness and discomfort than for men. Even though many women seek help, mental-health service providers seem reluctant to recognize the diverse needs resulting from these pervasive social and economic stresses on women. Russo and Sobel (1981) attribute this phenomena in part to mental-health professionals' reluctance to provide services for women when the disorder is not consistent with societal stereotypes about what problems women should have (e.g., alcoholism). For example, women are commonly treated for depression, schizophrenia, social maladjustment, and neurotic disorders (Russo & Sobel, 1981), whereas women with drinking problems are unserved (Lindbeck, 1972) or misdiagnosed more often then men with such problems (Lindbeck, 1972; Gomberg, 1981). As a result, women alcoholics are a sorely underserved population. Russo and Sobel (1981) attribute the relative lack of recognition of such problems as rape, spouse abuse, and incest to a reluctance on the part of professionals to recognize problems congruent with society's devaluation of women.

Single mothers, lesbians, minority women, rural women, and elderly women are among the many subgroups of women who have unique mental-health needs. The specific circumstances of such groups define special mental-health considerations. Single mothers typically experience an increased number of stressors yet are without the time or flexibility to seek the financial and emotional support they need to deal with such stress. Lesbian women often live in a tension between discrimination or hiding their sexual preference — either way experiencing alienation and invalidation of who they are as individuals. Minority women have to confront both sexism and racism in their lives with their cultural values often directly conflicting with a value on sexual equality or androgeny. The stress on rural women is intensified by their isolation, lack of access to resources and community constraints on expressing a variety of roles. Elderly women face constraints of sex, age, and poverty. As a group they are among the very poorest in our country. The challenge is to increase women's choices without destroying their historical, economic, sexual, or social bases of support and identity.

Fortunately, there are examples of how communities recognize the need for a diversity of services for women. Consciousness-raising groups have, for example, been proposed as alternative mental-health resources for women to help them recognize the sources of stress in their lives, and thereby move beyond self/victim blaming and begin to define their own needs more clearly

(Brodsky, 1973, 1977; Kirsh, 1974; Kravetz, 1980; Warren, 1976). Women's self-help groups, which typically incorporate consciousness raising, have emerged around such themes as sexuality, physical and sexual abuse, and life transitions. Many alternative feminist agencies have evolved out of this movement, e.g., rape crisis centers, battered women's shelters, and women's health collectives. Self-help groups and feminist service organizations represent important grass-root efforts to meet the needs of women that have not been addressed by established mental-health facilities. In recognizing the value of women as resources for one another, women have been increasingly active in defining both problems and solutions for themselves.

Complementing the emergence of consciousness-raising, self-help, and feminist agencies is the expanded development of support services and service delivery patterns that insure women's access to mental-health resources. Mental-health services need to face the fact that they are unavailable to some women by virtue of the increased role demands and financial strain placed on women who do seek help. Single mothers or mothers who have primary responsibility for their own children, are faced with both the cost and the effort of finding child care while they are in treatment. This situation can unwittingly increase rather than decrease the stress on such women. The provision of child care in conjunction with low-cost community-based child-care centers is critical in increasing the accessibility of mental-health services to women.

This call for greater accessibility and diversity of services also argues for specific networking services for women. Women's resources and referral centers, often university- or YWCA-based, and some feminist bookstores, play this role in many communities. Some community groups have developed printed directories of resources for women (e.g., *Portland Women's Yellow Pages*, 1981). National clearing houses, such as the National Center for Prevention and Control of Rape which publishes a nationwide inventory of rape-related prevention and treatment services (*National Directory: Rape Prevention and Treatment Resources*, 1981), provides guides to available services across the country. As these networking services expand, it seems particularly critical that mental-health professionals and the networking staff work collaboratively to provide accessible, varied, and high-quality services for women.

Critiques of traditional approaches to mental-health service delivery have emphasized the importance of expanding upon individual intrapsychic therapy approaches by emphasizing the social context in understanding and promoting the mental health of women (Brodsky & Hare-Mustin, 1980; Frieze et al., 1978; Sturdivant, 1980). Research findings are available to suggest that the status of women's mental health is linked to their social and employment circumstances. For example, some studies show that married women are at a greater risk for depression than single, separated, or divorced women (Gove & Tudor, 1973; Weissman & Klerman, 1977). Women who are full-time child-care providers often experience both a lack of respect for their work and isolation, and thereby become a risk for psychological distress (Brown & Harris, 1978). Employed women show fewer signs of psychosomatic illness (Bane, 1976) and higher self-esteem than full-time home makers (Nye, 1974). This type of research illustrates the importance of viewing women in the context of their work and home relationships.

Social context can be addressed by focusing upon interpersonal relationships and by changing the structure and policies of social institutions. Several writers have emphasized the need for educational programs that change the basic power relations between men and women to improve the mental health of women (e.g., Russo & Sobel, 1981). For example, since the exaggeration of the traditional role of the authoritative male within the family has been associated with such problems as incest (Herman, 1981) and spouse abuse (Walker, 1981; Bayes, 1981), community programs have been designed for abusing men. One such program, offered in conjunction with a shelter for battered women, involves group treatment for men who batter (Purdy & Nickle, 1979). Group discussion revolves around why the men use physical and verbal violence to try to control others, how they can learn alternative interpersonal skills for dealing with their anger, and how they can unlearn destructive myths about the roles for men and women that serve to justify anger and aggression. This work shows promise as an illustration of integrating of clinical and educational services and as a strategy for promoting women's mental health through changing couple relationships.

The workplace is a second important context for facilitating women's social competencies and enhancing their mental health. As mentioned earlier, there is some evidence that women who work outside the home are generally healthier than those who do not (e.g., Bane, 1976; Nye, 1974). Yet there are numerous barriers that serve to keep women out of the workforce or that hinder their advancement, thereby preventing women's equal participation (Kanter, 1977; Nieva & Gutek, 1981; Zellman, 1976). Legal remedies aimed at equal employment opportunities, sex discrimination, and sexual harrassment are important community strategies for improving the conditions of women's work. An increasing number of national, state, and local business and professional women's networks (e.g., National Federation of Business and Professional Women, Catalyst, Alliance for Career Advancement) are emerging to help women cope with barriers of the workforce. Support networks are primary settings not only to lobby for improvement in the working conditions of women but also to encourage the integration of work and family roles.

Primary prevention strategies are resources to strengthen the role of women in the family, in the workplace, and in society at large. School-based sex equality programs have been designed to educate both boys and girls about sex-role socialization and to increase their awareness of sex roles that are open to both sexes. The Southern California Rape Prevention Study Center (1981) has proposed that such educational programs within the high school curriculum be a first priority for the prevention of rape. They suggest teaching adolescent women to act assertively and to feel confident about their intellectual and social abilities while adolescent males learn how to deal constructively with their anger.

Strengthening the role of women working in the school system and combating sexism in the learning environment constitute a complementary school-based preventive strategy. The Women's Equity Action League (WEAL) has described a program to deal with sexism in schools that proposes a multilevel focus ranging from changing individual awareness to emphasizing policy changes. WEAL suggests that interested citizens invest in their local schools and talk with community members, teachers, and principals about such topics as the sex segregation of jobs in the school, or how the career plans of boys versus girls are shaped, or the use of nonsexist curriculum materials. At the broader policy level, WEAL emphasizes the importance of electing women to decision-making boards, lobbying for changes in laws (e.g., toward mandatory inclusion of curriculum materials about women), and resorting to legal action when other efforts get nowhere. This program is one illustration of integrating school-based preventive services with community-based policy development.

There is also a need for preventive services that enhance women's competencies. Enabling women to deal creatively with stresses in their lives is an altogether different goal than aiding women to adjust or deal with the problems created by the stress. Preventive programs that focus on the acquisition of competencies such as assertiveness (Jakubowski, 1978), problem-solving skills (Wycoff, 1977), leadership, and physical self-defense have enabled women to deal with such topics as depression, role overload, discrimination, and victimization, and given women more choices for control over their lives. Rowledge, Bond, and Schradle (1980), for example, developed a four-part portable curriculum to increase women's skills for dealing with the negative effects of sexist attitudes and changing sex roles. The curriculum contained small-group exercises, minilectures and discussion topics focusing on problem-solving strategies, power and resource management, and the development of support networks as they connect to the particular stresses women experience related to sexist attitudes and sex-role constraints.

This section on women has emphasized the need for services that address a broad range of women's needs. The call is for programs that go beyond the reduction of pathological behavior to include the development of positive competencies, that are offered in a context that decreases rather than increases role demands on women and that involve aspects of women's social and work settings as the foci of change.

The illustrations presented above affirm the value of a diversity of community-based women's programs and underline the need for programs with multiple components. A compelling feature of future mental-health services for women will be models, like La Frontera's battered women's shelter, that integrate clinical services with education and preventive services, and involve collaboration between mental-health professionals and citizens and citizen groups. The future challenge is to increase women's access to economic opportunities, and to varied supports and resources, while helping women acquire the social and political competencies needed to perform their preferred and chosen roles.

Promising Topics

Designing services to meet the mental-health needs of these four special population groups has illuminated three topics that have not as yet received major attention. Because these topics are essential for the continued delivery of community mental-health services, we have reviewed them here. The topics are social support networks, self-help, and citizen participation. In presenting these three topics, it is hoped that the principles noted in the delivery of services to the special populations are highlighted and clarified.

Social Support Networks

An individual's social support network can be defined as those enduring social ties that link the individual to beneficial resources for effective personal adaptation. Components of one's support network may include family, friends, work associates, neighbors, social, religious, or organizational ties, or contacts for mutual help. Among the resources provided may be emotional support, task-oriented assistance, communication about expectations and feedback, access to new and diverse information and social opportunities, and a sense of belongingness (Gottlieb, 1981; Mitchell & Trickett, 1980; President's Commission, 1978; Weiss, 1974). A growing body of opinion and some empirical research shows that the quality of the social network is a significant contributor to physical and psychological well-being (Caplan, 1974; Gottlieb, 1981; Mitchell & Trickett, 1981; President's Commission, 1978). Social support has been found to be especially valuable in buffering the potentially harmful effects of personal crises and life transitions (Gottlieb, 1981; President's Commission, 1978). Social support is also indicated as a preventive resource for increasing job satisfaction, particularly for these citizens and professionals who are doing community mental-health work (Cherniss, 1980; Cherniss & Egnatios, 1978; Maslach, 1976). Although mental-health professionals have long recognized the importance of social ties and social support, it has only been within the past decade that social network concepts have begun to be significantly incorporated into the design and delivery of mental-health services (President's Commission, 1978; Turkat, 1980).

An understanding and utilization of natural support networks can be valuable to the community mental-health practitioner in several ways. Network analysis (e.g., Froland et al., 1979; Wellman, 1981) can help in both assessment (e.g., identifying individuals whose lack of supportive ties places them "at risk") and evaluation (e.g., assessing the degree to which former mental patients have been integrated into a community). The identification of a community's networks may be a first step in finding key informants for mental-health needs assessment (e.g., Gonzales, 1978). In this way, a more representative sampling of opinions may be obtained, a decided advantage over surveying only human-services providers. For example, in order to assess public opinion about mental-health service needs in a rural mining county, Gonzales (1978) identified and sampled four networks: the political network, social service network, mining company network, and a bartender network. It was felt that the individuals surveyed were not only knowledgeable, but influential, which maximized the potential for community support of later mental-health services based on the needs-assessment results.

Programs that help promote a community's natural support systems hold promise as means by which community mental-health workers can contribute to the prevention of community members' psychological problems and strengthen citizens' personal competence and sense of community. Tapping natural support systems as sources of informal care giving can be cost-effective in expanding the range of services available within the community. Such programs also help insure accessible and responsive care appropriate to the unique characteristics of the community and avoid categorization or stigmatization of the helpee into a formal "client" role (Collins & Pancoast, 1972; Gottlieb, 1981; Mitchell & Trickett, 1980; President's Commission, 1978).

The strategies by which community mental-health professionals have attempted to mobilize natural social support systems fall into two main categories: (1) strengthening a community's existing systems of social support, and (2) stimulating the formation of new social linkages for individuals who lack adequate support networks. One approach toward strengthening the quality of support provided through a community's existing networks has been offering consultation or training to natu-ral help-givers. Collins and Pancoast (1972), for example, described how their "Day Care Neighbor Service Project" sought to prevent child abuse and neglect in a low-income community through collaboration with central network figures. Social welfare workers identified residents of a trailer court who played central roles as informal help-givers among their neighbors and extended consultation to them aimed at increasing their skills. The project was valuable not only in helping the residents deal effectively with problems encountered, but also in enhancing the social workers' understanding of the strengths and needs of the trailer court community. The "Day Care Neighbor Project" is noteworthy in that the consultants did not try to supplant or "professionalize" the help-giving methods used by the residents, but rather provided them with support, feedback, and relevant information to supplement their natural helping strategies.

Mental-health workers have often included a more formal training component in their consultations with natural help-givers. In the rural Nebraska linkage project (Agnew & Dodgion, 1982) discussed earlier, community caretakers were identified and offered training in a variety of topics including crisis intervention, communication skills, and methods of referral and client advocacy, Similarly, as part of a community health-education program, Salber, Beery, and Jackson (1976) identified community members to whom other citizens turned for advice on health-related problems and offered "health-facilitator" training designed to increase their competency in advising and referring community residents to appropriate community resources.

Considerable enthusiasm has recently been generated for providing consultation on mental-health issues to individuals whose occupational role brings them into repeated contact with large numbers of citizens who confide in them about personal problems (e.g., bartenders, hairdressers, store clerks, etc.). Bissonette (1977), for example, notes that a bartender's role is well suited for such "gatekeeping" functions as case finding, referral, and limited crisis intervention. Weisenfeld and Weis (1979) offered training in informal helping skills to interested hairdressers in Rochester. Using pre- and postmeasures of the hairdressers' responses in hypothetical help-giving situations, they found that the relatively brief consultation program did affect the participants' helping strategies (i.e., the hairdressers significantly increased their frequency of reflecting clients' feelings). However, actual effects on the hairdressers' clients were not determined. Similar programs have been initiated with bartenders and hairdressers (cited in Bisonnette, 1977) and Cub Scout den mothers (Conter, Hatch, & D'Aguelli, 1980). Critics of such approaches, however, question whether formal training may actually have an adverse effect on the relationship between the worker and the consumer by hindering the spontaneity of the relationship, altering the worker's view of the consumer, or reducing those behaviors that the professional trainer, perhaps shortsightedly, considers "unhelpful" (Collins & Pancoast, 1972; Gottlieb, 1981). Gottlieb (1981) further emphasizes that the psychological distance and norms about interaction between network contacts must be taken into account when selecting responses for training. For contacts such as hairdressers, bartenders, or shop clerks who typically are not psychologically close, consultation in providing referrals may be more beneficial than training in informal counseling skills (e.g., Leutz, 1976). More systematic and controlled evaluations of the impact of such programs are certainly needed.

Community mental-health workers also can be helpful in stimulating the formation of new support networks for community members who lack them. This basically involves bringing together individuals who share a common life experience and providing them with the opportunity to share resources (i.e., problem-solving information, emotional support, feedback, tangible assistance, etc.). Silverman's (1974) "widow-to-widow" program is exemplary. In this program, designed to promote psychological adaptation of the newly bereaved, Silverman enlisted volunteers who themselves had survived the death of a spouse, to visit and assist recent widows. The aides provided emotional support and understanding and helped the widows to build networks of new social contacts and support.

Budman (1975) describes an effective model for the formation of mutual support groups for individuals who share a common life crisis such as new parents, disabled Vietnam vets and hypertensive patients. Budman's approach involves bringing together interested individuals and providing initial structuring and information sharing about the common life experience, but then group members are allowed to take the major role in the group's functioning. Budman reports that group members often develop a strong sense of cohesiveness and continue to meet informally after the group has officially terminated. Similar uses of support groups have been reported for new parents (McGuire & Gottlieb, 1979), parents of premature infants (Minde et al., 1980), and males adapting to changing sex roles (Wong, 1978).

Gottlieb (1981) notes two important caveats regarding the use of mutual support groups. First, linking individuals with similar others could backfire if members of the devised network are not equipped to offer support, or recommend unproductive coping strategies. Second, individual variables such as need for affiliation and level of social skills will influence the effects of membership in a support group. Before attempting such a community service program, community mental-health workers should carefully assess the skills, resources, and potential compatibility of those to be involved.

Community mental-health workers also can have a significant effect on the quality of citizens' social support systems without directly intervening at a network level. Services that influence community members' interpersonal competencies or orientations toward drawing upon network resources may increase the use of their social networks. For example, Todd (Gottlieb & Todd, 1979) conducted "support development" workshops for college students that included self-evaluations and group discussion of the participants' own social networks, and found that the increased awareness stimulated participants toward taking productive action to improve their networks. Along this same vein, Gottlieb and Schroter (1979) suggest that community workshops and public forums on such topics as "How to Find a Helping Network" and "Ways of Building Mutual Help Communities" may be beneficial.

At an environmental level, the mental-health staff can be instrumental in creating social settings within the community through which isolated individuals can develop their social networks. Neighborhood-strengthening programs, such as barter networks or skills-banks (Exchange Networks newsletter, 1980), can serve a dual benefit of providing opportunities in which individuals can meet potential friends and expand their social networks (1972). Ellis (1972), for example, initiated a program for "latchkey" children in which elderly community members were recruited to plan and run after-school recreational activities for the children. The program not only succeeded in providing mutually satisfying involvements for both elderly volunteers and the children but also promoted the development of peer-helping networks for both groups.

Gottlieb and Schroter (1979) propose that mental-health professionals can be useful by offering consultation during community planning operations on ways to design social settings that increase the likelihood of social support networks forming and preserving existing ones. Unfortunately, little research exists comparing the effectiveness of the various network approaches described here. Mitchell (1981), in discussing the design of social network programs, stresses the importance of attending to a neighborhood's social-structural characteristics. In cohesive, integrated neighborhoods, consultation with central figures (e.g., Collins & Pancoast, 1972) may be quite effective, while in more socially diffuse neighborhoods, creating new linkages or offering training to neighborhood gate-keepers (e.g., bartenders, shop clerks, hairdressers) in providing referrals may be a more beneficial approach. Above all, professional mental-health workers must be cautious that their actions do not disrupt the delicate balance of a community's natural support systems. A careful assessment of potential positive and negative side-effects of proposed network approaches should be performed before attempting a social network program.

Self-Help

Self-help groups are associations of people sharing a common concern, interest, or life experience who join together for the purpose of mutual aid. The President's Commission (1978) estimated that there were a half-million self-help groups operating in the United States. Self-help groups vary greatly in form, structure, and type of services offered (see Killilea, 1976, for a comprehensive review), but can be distinguished by the following characteristics: (1) the group membership consists of individuals who share a common life experience or interest, (2) the group relies on its own group members' efforts, skills, and knowledge as their primary source of help, and (3) the group's structure and mode of operation are under the members' control (Gartner & Reissman, 1977; Killilea, 1976; Levy, 1976). A self-help organization exists for nearly every major illness or stressful life situation, with help for both the afflicted and for their relatives and friends (President's Commission, 1978). For example, *Make Today Count* is an organization for persons with cancer and their families to share support and practical informa-

tion about daily living. *Parents Anonymous* is a crisis-intervention and support group to help parents who have abused their children. The *Delancey Street Foundation* in San Francisco offers a self-help residential program for drug addicts and criminal offenders (Hampden-Turner, 1976).

The tremendous rise of the "self-help movement" in the last decade can be traced to the convergence of several contemporary social forces: mounting frustration of nonmainstream groups who felt their needs were not adequately met through professional mental-health services; the increased recognition of the importance of advocacy and consumer-control; and the rise of group "pride" and consciousness-raising movements among disenfranchised groups (Dumont, 1976; Gartner & Reissman, 1977; Katz & Bender, 1976). As expressed by Dumont (1976), "the increasingly powerful technologies of mental health professionalism . . . in prevention and control of deviant behavior tended to blur the distinctions between health care and social control" (p. 125). Self-help groups represent citizens' attempts to wrest control over their own destinies.

Self-help groups can be categorized into two types, according to their primary function (Levy, 1976): (1) behavior control groups in which members seek a change in a particular nonproductive behavior (e.g., Alcoholics Anonymous, Gamblers Anonymous, Take Off Pounds Sensibly), and (2) mutual support groups that emphasize facilitating the members' adaptation to a stressful situation or role transition which the group does not attempt to change (e.g., Parents Without Partners, Stroke Clubs, Mastectomy Recovery Plus). In addition, many self-help organizations are politically active, seeking to change public attitudes and policy regarding their condition (e.g., Gray Panthers, National Gay Task Force, National Organization for Women).

The *Center for Independent Living* in Berkeley, California, which addresses the needs of disabled individuals, illustrates the multiple functions a self-help organization can serve. Started in 1972 by six disabled individuals, the center has grown to a multipurpose enterprise serving approximately 2,000 people each month with a staff of 100 (most of whom are disabled). The center offers a wide array of personal services, including counseling, education, health care, housing and job placement, wheelchair repair, transportation, financial advocacy, sex counseling, and legal assistance. In its role as a political and social advocate for the dis-

abled, the center's accomplishments include securing civil rights for disabled persons in obtaining
driver's licenses and bank accounts, pressuring for
the removal of barriers and the enforcement of
rights of access, and lobbying at state and national
levels (Kirshbam, Harveston, & Katz, 1976).

Unfortunately, very little research exists on the
effectiveness of self-help groups, partly because of
the relative newness of self-help groups as foci of
professional interest, but also because of inherent
methodological difficulties in conducting valid
evaluation studies (Levy, 1976). For example, self-
help group members are self-selected; groups often
keep few written records and members may shun
scrutiny by outsiders, especially by professionals.
Several studies, however, document the effectiveness of self-help groups. An evaluation study of
Parents Anonymous (1977) found that members
showed a significant decrease in physical abuse of
their children immediately after joining the group,
as well as a reduction in social isolation patterns
and an increase in knowledge of child development. Reduced recidivism was reported in Delancey Street programs in which ex-offenders worked
with other ex-offenders (Hampden-Turner, 1976).
Members of TOPS weight-reducing group showed
significant degrees of weight loss and maintenance of that loss (Stunkard, 1972).

Investigations of the processes by which self-
help groups operate suggest that their effectiveness
lies in the sharing of useful information about the
problems and effective coping strategies, social
support and reinforcement for effecting change,
and an improvement in the self-esteem of members through identification with a supportive reference group (Gartner & Reissman, 1977; Killilea,
1976; Levy, 1976; President's Commission, 1978).
A major advantage of self-help group involvement
is that members can progress from helpee to helper (i.e., older members or veterans assist newer
members), thus instilling a new self-image to the
individual in a way that traditional therapy by a
professional can seldom achieve. Further, as Spiegel (1976) notes, whereas traditional psychotherapy tends to isolate clients in individual treatment,
mutual-help groups provide an opportunity to draw
strength from a collectivity of similar others. Thus,
self-help groups serve not only to reduce the individual's symptomology, but foster a new sense of
identity, pride, and support base from which
members can begin to shape more personally fulfilling lives.

Self-help groups are clearly a valuable resource
in promoting community mental health and are
increasingly being recognized as such by mental-
health professionals. In a nationwide survey of
community mental-health professionals, Levy
(1978) found that professional opinion of the effectiveness of self-help groups was 85 percent favorable. Forty-eight percent of the respondents reported making frequent or occasional referrals to
self-help organizations.

There is a danger, however, in romanticizing
self-help to the point of not recognizing its limitations for certain individuals. Some self-help groups
function in an authoritarian manner, and in some
cases may actually foster long-term dependence
on the group (Gartner & Reissman, 1977). Omark
(1979), for example, questions the effectiveness of
self-help groups, such as Recovery, Inc., that do
not provide channels by which members' successful improvement is clearly evaluated. Further,
Gartner and Reissman (1977) point out that the
client-oriented approaches of many self-help
groups may lead to victim blaming rather than action toward changing societal factors contributing
to the problem. Moreover, the assumption that
needy populations can be served through self-help
must not be mistaken for justification for curtailing professional programs or reducing systemic responsibility for the plight of disadvantaged groups
(see Gartner & Reissman, 1977, for a fuller discussion of these issues). The goal, then, is not an elimination of professional input, but rather a recognition of the value of nonprofessional resources and
an integration of professional services with self-
help activities. Community mental-health professionals can usefully coordinate their services with
self-help organizations in a number of ways, including: encouraging referrals to self-help groups;
co-developing directories of self-help organizations operating within the community; providing
education and favorable publicity about self-help
groups and how to start them; training agency
personnel to understand and work with self-help
groups; and communicating a willingness to provide professional or technical assistance to them as
desired. In addition, both self-help groups and
professionals could benefit from more research
that not only verifies the effectiveness of self-help,
but also helps identify the types of problems and
populations for which self-help groups are most
effective. Community mental-health workers are
urged to contact the National Self-Help Clearing-

house (33 West 42nd Street, New York, New York 10036) for information on self-help organizations in their geographical area. In addition, Gartner and Reissman (1980) provide a practical guide on organizing and locating self-help groups useful to both professionals and nonprofessionals. The beauty of self-help organizations is their autonomy and self-directedness. The challenge for the community mental-health professional is to facilitate self-help organizations within the community without compromising or coopting the essence of self-help.

Citizen Participation

The community approach to mental-health services offers both an opportunity and a mandate for citizens to participate in the operation of services that affect them. Only through the active involvement of community participants in the planning, development, operation, and evaluation of community mental-health programs as noted in the discussion of services to the special populations, can it be insured that those programs will be responsive to the needs of the community, have optimal visibility and utilization, and enjoy broad-based public support (Cravens, 1981; Gershon & Biller, 1977; Morrison, Holdridge-Crane, & Smith, 1978; Ragland & Zinn, 1979; Silverman, 1981). The principle of citizen participation in community mental-health services became a legal requirement for Community Mental Health Centers with the passage of Public Law 94-63, the Community Mental Health Centers Amendments Act of 1975. This law mandated that centers be governed by a representative board of community residents charged with establishing general policies for the center, approving its annual budget, and approving the selection of its director (Cravens, 1981). Unfortunately, significant progress toward true citizen participation in community mental health has been slow, owing partly to ideological and personal resistance by mental-health professionals about sharing power with nonprofessionals (Chiarmonte, 1981; Gershon & Biller, 1977; Morrison, Holdridge-Crane, & Smith, 1978), and partly to genuine uncertainty about how to bring about meaningful participation (Holton, New, & Hessler, 1973; Ragland & Zinn, 1979).

A consumer-control model is often advocated as the ideal form of governance for community mental-health programs (Holton, New, & Hessler, 1973; Ragland & Zinn, 1979). A governing board consisting of a cross-section of community residents holds final authority in establishing an agency's basic policies and priorities, monitoring its functioning, and assessing the quality of its service delivery. As stated by Ragland and Zinn (1979), "According to this governance model of citizen control, the citizens' voice should be the ultimate in community decision-making, while the professionals who run the social service programs would provide technical background and advice on policy issues—citizens in the decision-making role, technicians in the advisory role" (p. 57).

The case of the Lincoln Hospital in the Bronx dramatically illustrates the critical role of consumer control over community mental-health services (Ruiz, 1973). Established in 1963 to serve an extreme poverty area in 90 percent Puerto Rican and Black southeast Bronx, the Lincoln Community Mental Health Center after only a few years developed a broad range of clinical and outreach services and was highly acclaimed. In 1969, the center received the American Psychiatric Association's Silver Medal for its "imaginative and innovative services for a deprived urban population." Ironically, one year later, protests by community groups resulted in a cessation of the center's services and forced the resignations of the center's top professional leaders. The absence of meaningful community participation was cited as the major cause of the crisis (Ruiz, 1973). The center's administrators—none of whom lived in the local community—had failed to develop a true partnership with the community; there were no Black or Spanish-speaking professionals in top positions in the center's staffing and no channels for significant influence in decision making by community residents. In rebuilding the center, the approval of local community groups was sought before appointing a new director. The new director (who was Hispanic) then began to institute significant community participation in the center's operation. He organized a central community board with representatives from local community organizations to advise the center's administration on virtually all aspects of the center's programs, and gave control over the center's outreach services to local groups. In addition, high-level staff positions were made representative of the community's ethnic composition. According to the director, Dr. Ruiz, in the four years following these changes, "the center has moved from a phase marked by almost constant conflict over issues of community control to one of tranquility in which we are employing what we consider a very advanced model of genuine community control" (Ruiz, 1973, p. 38).

Theoretically, citizen advisory boards are useful in insuring that community mental-health services are responsive and accountable to the communities they serve. However, the degree to which citizen boards have had real control or influence over center activities has varied greatly (Holton, New, & Hessler, 1973; Morrison et al., 1978; Ragland & Zinn, 1979). Many boards have been merely tokens, composed of prominent citizens whose functions mainly include fund raising and public relations, with substantive matters of program planning and policy setting initiated by the professional staff. In instances where meaningful participation was sought, problems such as ambiguity of responsibilities and procedures, lack of access to necessary information, lack of comprehensive orientation to service operation, absence of training in group process and problem-solving skills, and perceived lack of support from professional staff have frequently hampered the board's ability to achieve that objective (Chairmonte, 1981; Morrison et al., 1978). The reader is urged to consult Ragland and Zinn (1979) for an excellent, comprehensive discussion of methods and guidelines for developing an effective advisory or governing board.

An exemplary project that involved citizens in the planning of community mental-health programs at a community mental-health center in Rochester, New York, is reported by Saunders (1979). The center's staff recruited and organized citizens into 12 action groups representing each of the districts within the center's 180,000-person predominantly middle- and working-class catchment area. Each action group was given responsibility and resources to identify mental-health needs within their district and develop appropriate local programs to address those needs. In the initial stages of the groups' development, the staff provided an orientation to community mental health and to the services offered by the center, and assigned a staff person to each group who served as a consultant to the group. Each group selected its own leadership, developed its own operating structure, budget, and work focus, and elected a representative to the CMHC's advisory board. The groups' early activities included disseminating information about mental-health resources in the community and developing intracommunity networks with the media, town officials, and general public. Their later and major focus was in developing primary prevention programs within the community. The group members themselves assumed leadership in identifying the community's needs and developing, implementing and marketing programs to address those needs. The community groups conducted interviews, public hearings, and surveys as part of their needs assessment. From the data gathered, they developed the specific goals and objectives for projects, decided the projects' content, format, and setting, divided the tasks into citizen and professional tasks, and then contracted with the community mental-health and human-service agencies for desired staffing and services. Professionals thus provided technical assistance as requested (e.g., preparing workshops, presenting lectures and audiovisual displays, designing surveys, providing skills training, etc.). Chairpersons of the action groups met quarterly with the agency administration to discuss organizationwide issues, strategies, and problems. Training was also provided for group leaders in communication, group process, and conflict-resolution skills. According to Saunders, in their first 5 years, the groups sponsored over 50 health-promotion and primary prevention projects within the community, with approximately 1,500 community residents participating in one or more of the services.

The types of projects implemented are quite impressive in their creativity and diversity, including, for example: discussion and support groups for single parents, physically disabled individuals, older adults, individuals interested in stress management, and divorced individuals; educational seminars on child development, depression, alcoholism, family communication and parenting; workshops on birth and bonding, being single, self-concept development, mortality, and interpersonal attraction and intimacy; projects co-sponsored with the police department on burglar-proofing homes and developing "neighborhood watch teams"; training programs for teachers in human relations; and a citizen-industrial partnership to develop services in response to mental-health needs of factory employees. Though it is too early to determine the long-range impact of the projects, Saunders reports that the program has been valuable in educating the community mental-health service staff about the needs, values, and processes of the community, facilitating their entry into the community and establishing productive relationships with community leaders and agencies. Further, the citizen volunteers report increased sense of self-esteem, competence development, and feeling of integration within their community.

The process by which the Rochester CMHC organized the groups is noteworthy. The staff provided enough structure and statement of objectives to the citizens to facilitate the development of the groups, but gave them enough freedom in decision making and access to resources that they could function autonomously. Equally impressive is the scope of the project, demonstrating that meaningful citizen participation can be accomplished on a large scale.

Community members have also demonstrated their effectiveness in the delivery of mental-health services. As volunteers and paid paraprofessionals, citizens have been actively involved in a wide variety of areas, including: casework and supportive counseling, crisis intervention, outreach work, community action and development, behavior modification, and mental-health education (see Gershon & Biller, 1977; Nash, Lifton & Smith, 1978; Silverman, 1981, for comprehensive reviews). In Lincoln Hospital, for example, over one-third of the staff consists of indigenous paraprofessionals who perform such diverse functions as providing supportive counseling, organizing community projects, and helping clients fill out applications, obtain financial aid, find employment and housing, seek legal advice (Gershon & Biller, 1977).

Participation by community members is valuable in increasing both the quantity and quality of available mental-health services. Further, citizen participation is cost-effective and promotes a reciprocally beneficial relationship between the program and the community (O'Donnell & George, 1977). Utilizing indigenous nonprofessionals helps bridge the gap between the middle-class-oriented professional and the typically lower socioeconomic and minority client. As Gershon and Biller (1977) say, "Through their ability to do things professionals have difficulty doing, such as identifying with the client's life situation, language, values and attitudes, indigenous paraprofessionals may serve important advocacy and liaison functions" (p. 125).

Research on the effectiveness of nonprofessionals has generally shown them to be quite successful (Gershon & Biller, 1977; Nash et al., 1978). In fact, several studies found them to be more effective than the professionals (Nash et al., 1978). More research is needed, however, to identify the conditions in which utilizing paraprofessionals is optimal (i.e., type of client, techniques, methods, settings, etc.). In their review, Nash et al. (1978) state that factors found to reduce the effectiveness of paraprofessionals include: role ambiguity, divergent role expectations, little supervision, inadequate training programs, and sharply drawn boundaries between professional and nonprofessional responsibilities. Further, as discussed earlier with regard to services for ethnic groups, citizen volunteers and paraprofessionals have occasionally been exploited or misused by professionals (e.g., Satow & Lorber, 1978). For this reason, a necessary prerequisite for meaningful and appropriate citizen involvement in service delivery is citizen input in the design and management of the services offered.

Conclusion

In this chapter, we have presented community mental-health approaches for serving four special populations: ethnic minorities, the elderly, rural communities, and women. We have also discussed three topics of major promise for advancing the field of community mental health: social support networks, self-help, and citizen participation. Some of the key themes that have emerged from this review are now discussed. These principles are significant for nonmainstream groups, and salient for community mental-health work with all types of populations.

First, each topic directs community mental-health workers to focus on the natural strengths and health-promoting resources inherent within communities, and affirms the value of optimally utilizing—with care not to exploit or exhaust—these resources. Informal social networks, paraprofessionals, citizen advisory and planning boards, and self-help organizations all represent strong forces for the promotion of community mental-health goals. By drawing upon and developing a community's natural resources, mental-health professionals can improve both the quantity and the quality of services available within the community and, importantly, help reduce the likelihood of overextending or "burning out" the professional resources available. An excellent example of this approach was seen in the rural Nebraska program which linked traditional professional services with informal systems of care, provided training to the informal caregivers, and offered consultation programs with natural gatekeepers. As funds for professional services become increasingly scarce, the maximal use and development of non-professional resources becomes even more critical to insure adequate community mental-health service.

Second, it is considered particularly important that communities and individuals are able to define problems and solutions for themselves, rather than have definitions imposed on them by professionals and persons not from the community. This principle rests on the implicit assumption that a component of social change (e.g., the empowerment of community members) is as important as service delivery for the practice of community mental health. Effective community work necessitates a recognition and respect by professionals of the many potential topics of expertise of community residents, and an egalitarian commitment to involve citizens who will be affected by services in the planning and decision-making process. This was excellently demonstrated in the Rochester prevention project and the case history of the Lincoln Hospital. Consumer control of mental-health services, and the promotion of natural support systems and self-help approaches are processes by which community members can meaningfully participate in the delivery of services that affect them.

The advantages of citizens playing a control role in the formation of services are twofold. The basis for problem solving by community members may be quite different from that of professionals, and it is the former that should be the focus of attention in a community-based program. The On Lok senior day health program and the Center for Independent Living for disabled individuals illustrate how community constituencies can seek out solutions and adapt them in innovative ways in order to meet the needs as they are perceived by the community members themselves. Another advantage of community ownership is that the degree to which a program is supported and utilized is enhanced by having citizens in a sanctioned planning role.

A third principle stresses the importance of professionals carefully attending to the process of community mental-health practice. This principle is closely linked with citizen participation, since highly valuing citizen involvement is necessary but not sufficient to bring it about. Profes-sionals must design settings and methods that encourage community participation in decision making, and facilitate citizens' ability to contribute ideas and energy. The rural Nebraska linkage project, in particular, demonstrates a careful attention to the process of community entry. The Rochester program illustrates how professionals can serve as technical resources for citizen-defined preventive interventions. Both show the type of attention to process necessary for citizen involvement to have impact.

Another aspect of process relates to evaluation of potential side-effects — both positive and negative — that community programs generate. Community mental-health program designers must take care that their work does not destroy or disrupt natural systems within the community.

In order to be effective, mental-health programs and preventive interventions must be tailored to meet the needs and preferences of community members, beginning with assumptions about mental health and illness and continuing through every aspect of every service. For example, as discussed with regard to each of the four special populations, the accessibility of services is a critical determinant of their effectiveness. Outreach and consultation services as demonstrated by La Frontera and Senior Outreach Services are especially important for bringing mental-health services to those who would not otherwise receive them. Outreach efforts serve community members by noting and building on familiar social settings and valued cultural and psychological traditions, indirectly serving individuals rather than simply pushing them into a client role. Many other ways in which services can be made accessible have been mentioned, from offering bilingual services, to having child care available, and to setting up satellite offices in isolated rural communities.

Finally, each topic offers the challenge for community mental-health workers to be creative and flexible in developing dynamic, nontraditional approaches to mental-health service delivery that are truly *community* in spirit. Saunders' citizen action groups for designing prevention programs, Collins and Pancoast's consultation with natural help-givers, the rural Nebraska linkage project, and La Frontera's listener-involvement radio shows on mental-health issues are all examples of innovative methods of responding to citizens' needs. A systemic perspective is essential in designing programs that are adapted to and compatible with the unique needs, resources, and patterns of informal social networks, self-help capabilities, and nonprofessional resources within the individual communities. There is a particular need to integrate professional efforts with those of natural community caretakers so as to achieve a productive relationship between the community's professional resources and the informal systems of care.

This chapter has presented examples of services and topics that can contribute both meaning and vitality to community mental-health work. Most importantly, it is hoped that this chapter has described the challenges and opportunities provided when professionals and citizens work together to create new services. This active collaboration increases the potential that the resulting services can not only meet mental-health needs but increase opportunities for citizens' self-development and self-direction. In so doing, the spirit of community mental health is preserved along with its validity.

References

Acosta, F. A. Barriers between mental health services and Mexican-Americans: An examination of a paradox. *American Journal of Community Psychology*, 1979, **7**, 503–520.

Agnew, K., & Dodgion, D. A. A paraprofessional linkage network in rural areas. In J. D. Murray & P. A. Keller (Eds.), *Innovations in rural mental health*. New York: Human Sciences, 1982.

Bachrach, L. L. Deinstitutionalization of mental health services in rural areas. *Hospital and Community Psychiatry*, 1977, **28**, 669–672.

Bachrach, L. L. Human services in rural areas: An analytical review. *Human Services Monograph Series*, 1981, **22**. Washington, D.C.: Project Share, Department of Health and Human Services, 1981.

Bane, M. J. *Here to stay: American families in the twentieth century*. New York: Basic Books, 1976.

Bayes, M. Wife battering and the maintenance of gender roles: A sociopsychological perspective. In E. Howell & M. Bayes (Eds.), *Women and mental health*. New York: Basic Books, 1981.

Berry, B., & Davis, A. E. Community mental health ideology: A problematic model for rural areas. *American Journal of Ortho-Psychiatry*, 1978, **48**, 673–679.

Bertsche, J. Research and demonstration project: Improving the utilization of informal helping systems by child welfare workers. *Rural Community Health Newsletter*, 1979, **8**, 5.

Bissonette, R. The bartender as mental health service gatekeeper: A role analysis. *Community Mental Health Journal*, 1977, **13**, 92–99.

Bloom, B. L. *Community mental health: A general in-*

troduction. (2nd ed.) Monterey, Calif.: Brooks/Cole, 1983.

Brodsky, A. The consciousness-raising group as a model for therapy with women. *Psychotherapy: Theory, Research and Practice*, 1973, **10**, 24–29.

Brodsky, A. Therapeutic aspect of consciousness-raising groups. In E. I. Rawlings & O. K. Carter (Eds.), *Psychotherapy for women: Treatment toward equality*. Springfield, Ill.: C. C. Thomas, 1977.

Brodsky, A., & Hare-Mustin, R. T. (Eds.), *Women and psychotherapy: An assessment of research and practice*. New York: Guilford, 1980.

Brown, G. W., & Harris, T. *Social origins of depression: A study of psychiatric disorder in women*. London: Tavistock, 1978.

Budman, S. H. A strategy for preventive mental health intervention. *Professional Psychology*, 1975, **6**, 394–398.

Burreal, G., & Chavez, N. Mental health outpatient centers: Relevant or irrelevant to Mexican Americans? In A. B. Tulipan, C. L. Attneave, & E. Kingstone (Eds.), *Beyond clinic walls*. Tulane: University of Alabama Press, Poco Perspectives, 1974.

Caplan, G. *Principles of preventive psychiatry*. New York: Basic Books, 1964.

Caplan, G. *Support systems and community mental health*. New York: Behavioral Publications, 1974.

Cedar, T., & Salisan, J. *Research directions for rural mental health*. McLean, Va.: MITRE Corporation, 1979.

Chavez, N. Personal communication. September 1, 1981.

Chavez, N. Personal communication. April 9, 1982.

Chavez, N. Foreword. *La Frontera perspective: Providing mental services to Mexican-Americans*. Monograph No. 1. Tucson: La Frontera, 1979.

Cherniss, C. *Staff burnout: Job stress in human services*. Beverly Hills, Calif.: Sage, 1980.

Cherniss, C., & Egnatios, E. Is there job satisfaction in community mental health? *Community Mental Health Journal*, 1978, **14**, 309–318.

Chiarmonte, F. The constant battle: The politics of advisory boards. In W. H. Silverman (Ed.), *Community mental health*. New York: Praeger, 1981.

Cohen, G. D. Prospects for mental health and aging. In J. E. Birren & R. B. Sloan (Eds.), *Handbook of mental health and aging*. Englewood Cliffs, N.J.: Prentice-Hall, 1980.

Collins, A. H., & Pancoast, D. L. *Natural helping networks*. Washington, D.C.: National Association of Social Workers, 1976.

Conter, K., Hatch, D., & D'Aguelli, A. Enhancing the skills of Cub Scout den leaders. *American Journal of Community Psychology*, 1980, **8**, 77–85.

Cravens, R. B. Grass roots participation in community mental health. In W. Silverman (Ed.), *Community mental health*. New York: Praeger, 1981.

Davis, R. J., Owens, C., & Critton, B. The delivery of mental health services to blacks. *Clearinghouse for Civil Rights Research*, 1980, Spring, 10–17.

Delgado, M., & Scott, J. F. Strategic intervention: A mental health program for the Hispanic community. *Journal of Community Psychology*, 1979, **7**, 187–197.

Dohrenwend, B. S., & Dohrenwend, B. P. *Stressful life*

events: Their nature and effects. New York: Wiley, 1974.

Dowell, D. A., & Ciarlo, J. A. Overview of the Community Mental Health Centers Program from an evaluation perspective. Unpublished manuscript. October 1981.

Dumont, M. P. Self-help treatment programs. In G. Caplan & M. Killilea (Eds.), *Support systems and mutual help.* New York: Grune & Stratton, 1976.

Ellis, J. B. Love to share: A community project tailored by oldsters for "latch-key" children. Paper presented at the 49th Annual Meeting of the American Orthopsychiatric Association, Detroit, Michigan, April 1972.

Exchange Networks Newsletter. Washington, D.C.: National Center for Citizen Involvement, July–August 1980.

Flax, J. W., Wagonfeld, M. O., Ivens, R. E., & Weiss, R. J. *Mental health and rural America: An overview and annotated bibliography.* (DHEW Publication No. 78-753). Washington, D.C.: U.S. Government Printing Office, 1979.

Ford, T. R. Rural poverty in the U.S. In *Rural poverty and regional progress in an urban society.* Washington, D.C.: U.S. Chamber of Commerce, 1969.

Fozouni, B., & Schulberg, H. C. Research paradigms and mental health policy. Paper presented at University of Pittsburgh Conference of Knowledge Use, Pittsburgh, March 1981.

Frieze, I. H., Parsons, J. E., Johnson, P. B., Ruble, D. N., & Zellman, G. L. *Women and sex roles: A social psychological perspective.* New York: Norton, 1978.

Froland, C., Brodsky, G., Olson, M., & Stewart, L. Social support and social adjustment: Implications for mental health professionals. *Community Mental Health Journal,* 1979, **15,** 82–93.

Garfield, S. L. Research on client variables in psychotherapy. In S. L. Garfield & A. E. Bergin (Eds.), *Handbook of psychotherapy and behavior change: An empirical analysis.* (2nd ed.) New York: Wiley, 1978.

Gartner, A., & Reissman, F. *Self-help in human services.* San Francisco: Jossey-Bass, 1977.

Gartner, A., & Reissman, F. *Help: A working guide to self-help groups.* New York: Viewpoints, Franklin Watts, 1980.

Gershon, M., & Biller, H. B. *The other helpers.* Lexington, Mass.: D. C. Health, 1977.

Gomberg, E. S. Women, sex roles, and alcohol problems. *Professional Psychology,* 1981, **12,** 146–155.

Gonzales, L. R. *Mental health needs assessment of Shoshore County.* (Technical Report) Wallace, Id.: Idaho Department of Health and Welfare, 1979.

Gottlieb, B. H., & Schroter, C. Collaboration and resource exchange between professional and natural support systems. *Professional Psychology,* 1978, **9,** 614–622.

Gottlieb, B. H., & Todd, D. Characterizing and promoting social support in natural settings. In R. Munoz, L. Snowden, & J. Kelly (Eds.), *Social and psychological research in community settings.* San Francisco: Jossey-Bass, 1979.

Gottlieb, B. H. (Ed.) *Social networks and social support.* Beverly Hills, Calif.: Sage, 1981.

Gove, W., & Tudor, J. Adult sex roles and mental illness. *American Journal of Sociology,* 1973, **78,** 812–835.

Grady, M. A., Gibson, M. J., & Trickett, E. J. *Mental health consultation, theory, practice, and research, 1973–1978.* Washington, D.C.: U.S. Government Printing Office, 1981.

Hagebak, J. E., & Hagebak, B. R. Serving the mental health needs of the elderly. *Mental Health Journal,* 1980, **4,** 263–275.

Hampden-Turner, C. *Sane asylum: Inside the Delancey Street Foundation.* San Francisco: San Francisco Book, 1976.

Herman, J. Father-daughter incest. *Professional Psychology,* 1981, **12,** 76–80.

Higginbotham, H. N. Culture and the role of client expectancy in psychotherapy. In R. W. Brislin & M. P. Hammett (Eds.), *Topics in culture learning.* Vol. 5. Honolulu: Cultural Learning Institute, East-West Center, 1977.

Hodges, W. F., & Cooper, S. (Eds.) *The field of mental health consultation.* New York: Human Sciences Press, 1982.

Holton, W. E., New, P. K., & Hessler, R. M. Citizen participation and conflict. *Administration in Mental Health,* 1973, Fall, 96–103.

Iscoe, I. Social and community interventions. In *Annual Review of Psychology.* Vol. 34. Palo Alto, Calif.: Annual Reviews, 1983.

Jakubowski, P. Facilitating the growth of women through assertive training. In L. W. Harman et al. (Eds.), *Counseling women.* Monterey, Calif.: Brooks/Cole, 1978.

Jeffrey, M. J., & Reeve, R. E. Community mental health services in rural areas: Some practical issues. *Community Mental Health Journal,* 1978, **14,** 54–63.

Jones, J. D., Wagonfeld, M. D., & Robin, S. S. A profile of the rural community mental health center. *Community Mental Health Journal,* 1976, **12,** 176–181.

Kanter, R. M. *Men and women of the corporation.* New York: Basic Books, 1977.

Killilea, M. Mutual help organizations: Interpretations in the literature. In G. Caplan & M. Killilea (Eds.), *Support systems and mutual help.* New York: Grune & Stratton, 1976.

Kirsh, B. Consciousness-raising groups as therapy for women. In V. Franks & V. Burtle (Eds.), *Women in therapy.* New York: Brunner/Mazel, 1975.

Kirshbaum, H. R., Harveston, D. C., & Katz, A. H. Independent living for the disabled. *Social Policy,* 1976, **7,** 59–62.

Knight, B. A geriatric outreach program in community mental health. *Newsletter of the Division of Community Psychology, American Psychological Association,* Summer 1981, 2.

Knight, B. Personal communication, March 30, 1982.

Knight, B., Slaughter, M., & Peterson, B. *Senior outreach team annual report, 1980–81.* Ventura County Mental Health Service, 1981.

Kobata, F. S., Lockery, S. A., & Moriwaki, S. Y. Minority issues in mental health and aging. In J. E. Birren & R. B. Sloan (Eds.), *Handbook of mental health and aging.* Englewood Cliffs, N.J.: Prentice-Hall, 1980.

Kravetz, D. Consciousness-raising and self-help. In A.

Brodsky & R. T. Hare-Mustin (Eds.), *Women and psychotherapy: An assessment of research practice.* New York: Guilford, 1980.

Lackey, C. Personal communication, March 18, 1982.

Leutz, W. N. The informal community caregiver: A link between the health care system and local residents. *American Journal of Orthopsychiatry,* 1976, **46,** 678–688.

Levy, L. H. Self-help groups: Types and psychological processes. *Journal of Applied Behavioral Science,* 1976, **12,** 310–313.

Levy, L. H. Self-help groups viewed by mental health professionals: A survey and comments. *American Journal of Community Psychology,* 1978, **6,** 305–313.

Libertoff, K. National helping networks in rural youth and family services. Paper presented at the meeting of The American Psychological Association, New York, September 1979.

Lindemann, E. Use of psychoanalytic constructs in preventive psychiatry. *Psychoanalytic Study of the Child,* 1952, **7,** 429–437.

Lindemann, E. *Interrelations between the social environment and psychiatric disorders.* New York: Milbank Memorial Fund, 1953.

Lindemann, E. *Beyond grief: Studies in crisis intervention.* New York: Jason Aronson, 1979.

Lorion, R. P. Socioeconomic status and traditional treatment approaches reconsidered. *Psychological Bulletin,* 1973, **79,** 263–270.

Lorion, R. P. Patient and therapist variables in treatment of low income patients. *Psychological Bulletin,* 1974, **81,** 344–354.

Lorion, R. P. Research on psychotherapy and behavior change with the disadvantaged. In S. L. Garfield & A. E. Bergin (Eds.), *Handbook of psychotherapy and behavior change: Empirical analysis.* (2nd ed.) New York: Wiley, 1978.

Lurie, E., Kalish, R. A., Wexler, R., Ansak, M. On Lok Senior Day Health Center: A case study. *The Gerontologist,* 1976, **16,** 39–46.

Mannino, F. V., MacLennan, B. W., & Shore, M. F. (Eds.). *The practice of mental health consultation.* New York: Gardner, 1975.

Maslach, C. Burned out. *Human Behavior,* 1976, **5,** 16–22.

McGuire, J. C., & Gottlieb, B. H. Social support groups among new parents: An experimental study in primary prevention. *Journal of Clinical Child Psychology,* 1979, **8,** 111–116.

Miller, R. S. Successful rural to urban professional role transition. *Community Mental Health Journal,* 1981, **17,** 143–152.

Minde, K., Shosenberg, N., Marton, P., Thompson, J., Ripley, J., & Burns, S. Self-help groups in a premature nursery: A controlled evaluation. *Journal of Pediatrics,* 1980, **96,** 933–940.

Miranda, M. R., & Castro, F. G. Culture distance and success in psychotherapy with Spanish-speaking clients. In J. L. Martinez (Ed.), *Chicano psychology.* New York: Academic Press, 1977.

Mitchell, R. E., & Hurley, D. J. Collaboration with natural helping networks: Lessons from studying paraprofessionals. In B. H. Gottlieb (Ed.), *Social networks and social support.* Beverly Hills, Calif.: Sage, 1981.

Mitchell, R. E., & Trickett, E. J. Task force report: Social networks as mediators of social support. *Community Mental Health Journal,* 1980, **16,** 27–44.

Morrison, J. K., Holdridge-Crane, S., & Smith, J. E. Citizen participation in community mental health. *Community Mental Health Review,* 1978, **3,** 1–9.

Nash, K. B., Lifton, N., & Smith, S. E. Paraprofessionals and community mental health. *Community Mental Health Review,* 1978, **3,** 1–8.

National Center for the Prevention and Control of Rape, U.S. Department of Health and Human Services. *National directory: Rape prevention and treatment resources.* DHHS Publication No. (ADM) 81-1008, 1981.

Nieva, V. F., & Gutek, B. *Women and work: A psychological perspective.* New York: Praeger, 1981.

Nye, F. I. Husband-wife relationship. In L. W. Hoffman & F. I. Nye (Eds.), *Working mothers.* San Francisco: Jossey-Bass, 1974.

O'Donnell, J. M., & George, K. The use of volunteers in a community mental health center emergency and reception service. *Community Mental Health Review,* 1977, **13,** 3–12.

Omark, R. C. The dilemma of membership in Recovery, Inc.: A self-help ex-mental patients' organization. *Psychological Reports,* 1979, **44,** 1,119–1,125.

On Lok annual report, 1980–1981. San Francisco: On Lok Development Corporation, 1981.

Padilla, A. M., Ruiz, R. A., & Alvarez, R. Community mental health services for the Spanish-speaking/surnamed population. *American Psychologist,* 1975, **30,** 892–905.

Parents anonymous self-help for child abusing parents: Project evaluation report. Tucson, Ariz.: Behavior Associates, 1977.

Parrot, C., & Sebastian, J. Rural mental health: A partnership with the community. Paper presented at the 1977 Summer Study Program on Rural Mental Health Services, University of Wisconsin Extension, June 1977.

Portland women's yellow pages. (3rd ed.) Portland, Oreg.: Portland Women's Yellow Pages, 1981. (Available from 14550 S. E. Fairoaks Lane, Milwaukie, Oregon 97222.)

Presidents' Commission on Mental Health, Vols. 1–4. Washington, D.C.: Superintendent of Documents, 1978.

Purdy, F., & Nickle, N. Practice principles for helping men who batter. Unpublished manuscript, 1979. (Available from Washington State Shelter Network/ 1063 S Capital Way #217/Olympia, Washington 98501.)

Rabkin, J., & Streuening, E. Life events, stress, and illness. *Science,* 1976, **194,** 1,013–1,020.

Ragland, S. L., & Zinn, H. K. *Citizen participation in community mental health centers.* Washington, D.C.: Department of Health, Education and Welfare Publication, No. 79-737, 1979.

Rapoport, R., & Rapoport, R. (Eds.) *Working couples.* New York: Harper & Row, 1978.

Rappaport, J. *Community psychology: Values, research and action.* New York: Holt, Rinehart, & Winston, 1977.

Ribner, D. S. Psychiatrists and community mental health: Current issues and trends. *Hospital and*

Community Psychiatry, 1980, **31,** 338–341.

Riger, S., & Gordon, M. T. The fear of rape: A study of social control. *Journal of Social Issues,* 1981, **37,** 71–92.

Rowledge, L., Bond, M. A., & Schradle, S. A few more baby steps: Reflections on social support, sexism, power, problem solving and prevention. Paper presented at the meeting of the Oregon Psychological Association, Portland, November 1980.

Ruiz, P. Consumer participation in mental health programs. *Hospital and Community Psychiatry,* 1973, **24,** 38–40.

Russo, N. P., & Sobel, S. D. Sex preferences in the utilization of mental health facilities. *Professional Psychology,* 1981, **12,** 7–19.

Ryan, W. *Blaming the victim.* (Rev. ed.) New York: Random House, 1976.

Salber, E. J., Beery, W. L., & Jackson, E. J. The role of the health facilitator in community health education. *Journal of Community Health,* 1976, **2,** 5–19.

Sataw, R. A., & Lorber, J. Cultural congruity and the use of paraprofessionals in community mental health work. *Sociological Symposium,* 1978, **23,** 17–26.

Saunders, S. Primary prevention from a neighborhood base: A working model. *American Journal of Orthopsychiatry,* 1979, **49,** 69–80.

Schulberg, H. C. The evaluation of community mental health program models. In H. Schulberg & M. Killilea (Eds.), *Principles and practices of community mental health.* San Francisco: Jossey-Bass, in press.

Shanas, E. The family as a social support system in old age. *The Gerontologist,* 1979, **19,** 169–174.

Shane, D. W., & Seibert, M. The sattelite office: Development and planning, current practice, and new directions. Paper presented at the 1977 Summer Study Program on Rural Mental Health Services, University of Wisconsin Extension, June 1977.

Shybut, J. Use of paraprofessionals in enhancing mental health service delivery in rural settings. *Journal of Rural Community Psychology,* in press.

Shybut, J., Personal communication, January 4, 1982.

Silverman, M. M. Volunteers in mental health settings. In W. Silverman (Ed.), *Community mental health.* New York: Praeger, 1981.

Silverman, P. R. The widow as a caregiver in a program of preventive intervention with other widows. In G. Caplan & M. Killilea (Eds.), *Support systems and mutual help.* New York: Grune & Stratton, 1976.

Smith, D. W., Burlew, A. K., Mosley, M. H., & Whitney, W. M. *Minority issues in mental health.* Reading, Mass.: Addison-Wesley, 1978.

Smyer, M. A., Davis, B. W., & Cohn, M. A prevention approach to critical life events of the elderly. *Journal of Prevention,* in press.

Solomon, G. *Problems and issues in rural community mental health: A review.* Lubbock: Texas Tech. University, 1980. (ERIC Document Reproduction Service, No. Ed 182101.)

Southern California Rape Prevention Study Center, Division of Didi Hirsh Community Mental Health Center. Consensus and controversy in sexual assault, prevention and intervention: A delphi study. Unpublished manuscript, 1981.

Spiegel, D. Going public and self-help. In G. Caplan &

M. Killilea (Eds.), *Support systems and mutual help.* New York: Grune & Stratton, 1976.

Stunkard, A. J. The success of TOPS, a self-help group. *Post-Graduate Medicine,* 1971, **18,** 143–147.

Sturdivant, S. *Therapy with women: A feminist philosophy of treatment.* New York: Springer, 1980.

Subpanel on the Mental Health of Women, President's Commission on Mental Health. *Task panel report,* Vol. 3, Appendix 1,022–1,116. Washington, D.C.: U.S. Government Printing Office, 1978.

Sue, D. W., & Sue, D. Barriers to effective cross-cultural counseling. *Journal of Counseling Psychology,* 1977, **24,** 420–429.

Torrey, E. F. *The mind game: Witchdoctors and psychiatrists.* New York: Emerson Hall, 1972.

Turkat, D. Social networks: Theory and practice. *Journal of Community Psychology,* 1980, **8,** 99–109.

U.S. Department of Agriculture. *Rural and small town population change, 1970–1980.* Washington, D.C.: Economic and Statistics Service, February 1981.

Vontross, C. E. Rural and ethnic barriers in counseling. In P. Pederson, W. J. Lonner, & J. Draguns (Eds.), *Counseling across cultures.* Honolulu: University of Hawaii Press, 1976.

Walker, L. Battered women: Sex roles and clinical issues. *Professional Psychology,* 1981, **12,** 81–91.

Warren, L. W. The therapeutic status of consciousness-raising groups. *Professional Psychology,* 1976, **7,** 132–140.

Weisenfeld, A. R., & Weiss, H. M. Hairdressers and helping: Influencing the behavior of informal caregivers. *Professional Psychology,* 1979, December, 786–792.

Weiss, R. S. The provisions of social relationships. In Z. Rubin (Ed.), *Doing unto others.* Englewood Cliffs, N.J.: Prentice-Hall, 1974.

Weissman, M., & Klerman, G. Sex differences and the epidemiology of depression. *Archives of General Psychiatry,* 1977, **34,** 98–111.

Wellman, B. Applying network analysis to the study of support. In B. H. Gottlieb (Ed.), *Social networks and social support.* Beverly Hills, Calif.: Sage, 1981.

Women's Equity Action League. What you can do about sexism in the schools. In K. Paulsen & R. Kuhn (Eds.), *Woman's almanac.* New York: J. B. Lippincott, 1976.

Wong, M. R. Males in transition and the self-help group. *Counseling Psychologist,* 1978, **7,** 46–50.

Wu, I., & Windle, C. Ethnic specificity in relative use and staffing of community mental health centers. *Community Mental Health Journal,* 1980, **16,** 156–168.

Wycoff, H. *Solving women's problems through awareness, action and contact.* New York: Grove, 1977.

Yee, D. Personal communication, December 31, 1981.

Zawedski, R. T., & Ansak, M. *On Lok's CCODA: The first two years.* (Tech. Rep. No. 300). San Francisco: On Lok Senior Health Services, 1981.

Zellman, G. L. The role of structural factors in limiting women's institutional participation. *Journal of Social Issues,* 1976, **32,** 33–46.

Zwerling, I. (Ed.). *Racism, elitism, professionalism: Barriers to community mental health.* New York: Jason Aronson, 1976.

37 CRISIS INTERVENTION AND BRIEF PSYCHOTHERAPY

Richard K. McGee

The decision to combine discussions of crisis intervention and brief psychotherapy into a single chapter may imply that the author conceives of them as two similar psychological intervention strategies, and that the reader might likewise consider them to be interchangeable methods for understanding and treating emotional and behavioral dysfunction. There is a grave danger in drawing this conclusion, although, to be sure, the terms are used so casually and interchangeably in the literature of the past ten years as to blur the important distinctions between them. Several authors (Aguilera & Messick, 1982; Ewing, 1978; Marmor, 1979; Smith, 1977; Stuart & Mackey, 1977) have addressed the similarities and differences between crisis intervention and brief psychotherapy. It is important for an understanding of the material that follows to identify a group of concepts that will help to develop a definitional set, or frame of reference, from which to view crisis intervention as a method of treatment separate and distinct from brief psychotherapy.

Community mental-health centers and other public clinic facilities provide both crisis intervention and brief psychotherapy for a wide range of presenting problems without necessarily having a clear understanding of their differences. They fo-

cus only on the similarities, and the result is that all patients tend to be treated in much the same way. Moreover, most community mental-health programs equate the terms "crisis" and "emergency," and the important distinction between crisis intervention and emergency psychiatric care is likewise obliterated. Stuart and Mackey (1977) distinguish between these concepts by means of a model that involves three elements: person, stress, and reaction. The model says simply that: "Person plus Stress yields a Reaction." The person is defined as everything that the patient brings to the clinic, including certain demographic characteristics, a family background, a developmental history, a set of values and beliefs, and a history of previous attempts at coping with life. Stress is the immediate situation the person is experiencing in the here and now, that resulted in the current request (or referral) for help. The final element in the model—the reaction—is the total configuration of responses and symptoms that the person is displaying at the time of intake. In applying this model, a clinician performing an initial intake assessment must determine which of the three elements seems most highly charged and in greatest need of attention. When it is the symptomatic behavior (i.e., the reaction) that must be controlled, then we have a case of psychiatric emergency and intervention in the form of hospital admission and/or psychotropic medication is indicated. Should the clinician's assessment reveal that the reaction could be managed by the patient if only the level of stress from the presenting situation were reduced, the treatment method becomes crisis intervention. However, when the presenting data suggest that the problem goes beyond the current stress to the person, then brief psychotherapy is the treatment of choice.

Aguilera and Messick (1982) have developed a presentation of the differences between psychoanalysis, brief psychotherapy, and crisis intervention which is found in Table 37.1. Their scheme calls attention to the focus on treatment and usual activity of the therapist in the two forms of treatment.

Another distinction that may be made focuses attention on a sequential factor in the actual practice of the two forms in community clinic operations. Marmor (1979) places crisis intervention, emergency care, and short-term dynamic psychotherapy as significant points on a continuum of psychiatric intervention. Crisis intervention is rarely a "stand-alone" procedure, especially in the more severe and active crises involving threatened suicide or actual self-injury. Even in non-life-threatening cases in which the patient is experiencing a major disruption in life circumstances,

such as traumatic bereavement, divorce, or vocational failure, crisis intervention has as one of its goals the transferring of the patient to other appropriate services in the network of helping agencies that can assist in the total restoration of the individual to the former, precrisis level of functioning. Brief psychotherapy, administered by a private therapist or a clinic, is one of the many options available for the crisis intervener to use in transferring the patient, after initial intervention, as a part of the crisis intervention process. In some cases, brief psychotherapy is the only appropriate option. In this system, brief psychotherapy would take over where crisis intervention leaves off. The two treatments would ordinarily be administered by two different therapists, and often by persons of different levels of professional skill and training.

This latter distinction is often lost in community mental-health centers that claim to provide crisis intervention services through their emergency mental-health service, but refer all crisis cases to the clinic staff for psychotherapy. Crisis intervention becomes merely the intake contact that occurs by telephone or in the hospital emergency room after hours and on weekends, and all crisis cases are treated as if, *a priori*, they have some degree of psychiatric disturbance. Some crisis agencies defuse the immediate situation, and when the patient is once more able to cope with the stress,

TABLE 37.1. MAJOR DIFFERENCES BETWEEN PSYCHOANALYSIS, BRIEF PSYCHOTHERAPY, AND CRISIS INTERVENTION METHODOLOGY.*

	Psychoanalysis	Brief Psychotherapy	Crisis Intervention
Goals of therapy	Restructuring the personality	Removal of specific symptoms	Resolution of immediate crisis
Focus of treatment	1. Genetic past	1. Genetic past as it relates to present situation	1. Genetic present
	2. Freeing the unconscious	2. Repression of unconscious and restraining of drives	2. Restoration to level of functioning prior to crisis
Usual activity of therapist	1. Exploratory	1. Suppressive	1. Suppressive
	2. Passive observer	2. Participant observer	2. Active participant
	3. Nondirective	3. Indirect	3. Direct
Indications	Neurotic personality patterns	Acutely disruptive emotional pain and severely disruptive circumstances	Sudden loss of ability to cope with a life situation
Average length of treatment	Indefinite	From one to twenty sessions	From one to six sessions

*From Donna C. Aguilera and Janice M. Messick, *Crisis Intervention*, 4th ed. (St. Louis: C. V. Mosby, 1982). Reprinted with permission.

transfer the case to whatever kind of help is appropriate.

It is this important distinction between crisis intervention and professional mental-health service that the full-service crisis intervention centers have been providing in the community for the past two decades. These centers have learned to work collaboratively with mental-health agencies, but have been most effective when they were neither a substitute for nor a component of them (McGee, 1974).

The reader who seeks an opposing view to the one discussed above should consult Small (1979). Small believes that there are no basic differences in the approach taken to a crisis, a neurosis, or an emergency. He discusses crises that have a neurosis at their base and will not resolve unless the neurosis is cured. While this is clearly a minority opinion in the literature concerning crisis, it articulates the blending and blurring of concepts that lies behind much of the current practice of crisis intervention in community agencies.

There are two widely recognized aspects to the delivery of crisis intervention services that do not receive attention in the literature on brief psychotherapy. The first of these is the requirement for immediate response, and the second relates to the level of professional training required. These issues will be discussed in greater detail later in this chapter, but in drawing out our conceptual guidelines for a distinction between the two forms of service, it is important at this point at least to cite them. Crisis intervention service cannot be rendered in the therapist's office by prescheduled appointment. Crisis intervention is practiced when and where the situation demands; it is always, and only, an "on-call" type of service. Crisis intervention services are often provided best and most economically in the community by trained and supervised volunteers, whose credentials do not include advanced academic degrees or profesional affiliations.

In this chapter, we shall always refer to *crisis intervention* as that form of service that:

1. focuses only on the precipitating event or situation,
2. seeks to enhance the patient's problem-solving and coping behavior,
3. is immediately available on demand, at all hours every day, and
4. may be provided effectively by trained crisis counselors without traditional professional backgrounds.

In contrast, by *brief psychotherapy* we mean that service form that:

1. focuses on the person primarily, and the situation secondarily,
2. seeks to educate the patient concerning the role of past experience and relationships in determining present problems and behaviors,
3. is scheduled to occur by appointment like any form of psychotherapy, but over a shorter interval of time, and
4. should only be practiced by professionally trained psychotherapists.

In addition, we use the term "brief psychotherapy" to include all of the similar labels found in the literature, including: short-term psychotherapy, planned short-term therapy, and time-limited psychotherapy. Similarly, we make no distinction between crisis intervention and terms such as crisis therapy, crisis counseling, and crisis management, which seem to be used almost interchangeably in the current literature.

Evolution of the Methods

Brief Psychotherapy

Bloom (1980) has drawn an association between the emergence of brief psychotherapy in the professional literature and the formal beginning of the community mental-health movement. He identified several major volumes that began appearing in 1963 when the first of a long series of important theoretical and empirical works was published by Malan and his colleagues at Tavistock (Malan, 1963). Soon to follow were discussions by Bellak and Small (1965), Wolberg (1965a, 1965b), Phillips and Wiener (1966), Parad and Parad (1968a, 1968b), and Sifneos (1967, 1972). Marmor (1979) has prepared a general synthesis of the views found in the foregoing references, and he describes quite succinctly the present state of the art in short-term dynamic psychotherapy.

There is a clear consensus that brief psychotherapy grew out of the classical psychoanalytic tradition. In retrospect it can be seen as the means by which dynamically oriented therapists responded to the twin challenges posed by the advent of psychopharmocological agents introduced in the 1950s, and the professional manpower studies of the Joint Commission on Mental Illness and Health (1961). The response was reluctant at first, and many pages of the early works were devoted to overcoming the resistance practitioners offered to reducing the length of psychotherapy. But it was clearly a practical necessity. Bellak and Small (1965) report that their first introduction to brief therapy was forced upon them as early as 1946, when the Veterans Administration began limiting the amount of psychiatric service it would authorize for GIs returning from World War II. Units of three or four interviews were allowed, but there was absolutely no certainty of more than one such unit per veteran. By the end of the 1950s, large social agencies in metropolitan cities were attempting to deliver psychiatric services to new populations of mental-health patients. Caseloads were large and waiting lists were impossibly long. A trouble-shooting clinic appeared in the Psychiatry Department at the City Hospital at Elmhurst, Queens, in 1958, and became a focal setting for the practice and study of brief psychotherapy (Bellak & Small, 1965). Mann (1973) describes the establishment of a similar program at Boston University School of Medicine. The primary purpose was to manage the long waiting lists with limited therapeutic resources. The mental-health needs of America in those early days of the community mental-health movement were being demonstrated on a daily basis. The demand was to treat more and more patients, and produce significant results in a shorter period of time. Bellak and Small (1965) refer to the conclusion of the Joint Commission report, which completely accepted the findings of Albee's (1959) mental-health manpower study. Albee had insisted that every professional person should do those things that most help the largest number of persons needing help. The development and utilization of brief psychotherapy became recognized as a means by which an enormous mental-health problem in the United States might be alleviated (Straker, 1977). Indeed, Fenichel (1954) had been prophetic when, ten years earlier, he described brief psychotherapy as "the child of bitter practical necessity."

An obvious corollary of this development was the fact that many patients began to seek psychotherapy who did not have the personal financial resources to pay for the long-term psychoanalytic treatment that had been the previous model. There was a new need to gear treatment plans to the patient's financial situation. Fortunately, some insurance companies were beginning to show an interest in adding coverage for psychiatric services to the list of subscriber benefits. It would take a demonstration of the efficacy of a therapy program shorter than conventional analysis to attract these third-party payment programs. Avnet (1965a, 1965b) recognized that short-term therapy was the only practical solution to the dilemma facing the mental-health planners. Consequently, she conducted and reported a study sponsored by Group Health Insurance, Inc., the American Psychiatric Association, and the National Association for Mental Health, in which the benefits of short-term therapy were recorded by patients of 1,139 participating psychiatrists. The results were promising and a new era in the economics of mental-health treatment was born.

Crisis Intervention

Meanwhile, another response to the mental-health *Zietgeist* was taking shape in the form of crisis intervention. If brief psychotherapy was the method by which the psychoanalytic establishment attempted to hold on to its traditional roles and prerogatives in the face of the new community mental-health movement, crisis intervention was the avenue by which a few pioneers of the time began to disregard tradition and redistribute prerogatives.

The earliest roots of this treatment form are universally attributed to the work of Erich Lindemann with survivors of the Cocoanut Grove fire in Boston in the early 1940s. Lindemann (1944) recognized that people with a history of good emotional health and adjustment often face critical events in the normal process of life, and unless appropriate help is immediately available, become vulnerable to psychological casualty. His concern became the maintenance of good mental health, and the prevention of emotional disorganization on a communitywide level. Aguilera and Messick (1982) have traced the early origins of the crisis intervention method, attributing them, as in brief psychotherapy, to the traditional psychoanalytic school.

It may appear something of a mystery that these two quite divergent approaches to patient care could spring from the same theoretical and cultural beginning. The explanation is to be found in the work of the Wellesley Project, established by Lindemann and Gerald Caplan in Cambridge in 1946 (Lindemann, 1979). It was through this program that Caplan (1964) began to formulate his definitions of crisis periods, and his theoretical conceptualizations of the psychological response to "obstacles to important life goals." But more importantly, it was in this context that Caplan and his associates began looking for examples of people and families in crisis, and developing organized helping responses that the community could make. He taught public health nurses to intervene with mothers of premature infants. He consulted with social workers who helped manage crises in family relationships. It is of subtle but very important significance that the first clear, concise, and articulate set of instructions on how to intervene in a crisis was published as an appendix to Caplan's classic textbook, *Principles of Preventive Psychiatry,* in 1964. This appendix was authored by Cadden, and appeared as a reprint from a January 1962 issue of *Redbook* magazine (Cadden, 1964).

Brief psychotherapy came into the mental-health armamentarium as a modern form of practice of psychoanalytic therapists, but crisis intervention emerged primarily as the contribution from social work and public health nursing (Parad, 1965). The chief difference between the two approaches was in the concept of the problem. One was a pathology concept, emanating from the traditional medical model. The other was a concept of normal responses of psychologically healthy people to hazardous life events. Ewing (1978) has prepared a comprehensive analysis of the difference between crisis intervention and the medical model of treatment. Erikson's (1963) characterization of an orderly sequence of normal development through defined stages over the entire lifespan contributed heavily to the development of crisis theory. Developmental crises came to be seen as the potential building blocks of heavily psychosocial development, just as traumatic or disastrous events could lead to enhanced problem-solving capacity if effective intervention were provided.

Crisis intervention methodology and practice were aided by an additional dynamic social force during the 1960s in the form of the paraprofessional, or volunteer counselor, that formed the core of the suicide prevention movement (Butcher & Maudal, 1976; McGee, 1974). The work of Rioch et al. (1963) on the training of nontraditional counselors was adopted by the Los Angeles Suicide Prevention Center, and spread throughout the country in less than five years. The principles of the new community mental-health movement, as introduced by the Joint Commission (1961), were the key factors in the success of the better-established suicide prevention centers.

McGee (1965, 1968) has described the suicide prevention center as a model for demonstrating the larger community mental-health concepts. At the heart of this relationship was the crisis intervention service paradigm.

Current Development

There is no doubt that both brief psychotherapy and crisis intervention are now thoroughly established forms of treatment in a wide range of settings. Clarkin et al. (1980) surveyed approved psychiatric residency programs in 1978 and found that 88 percent of them offer direct training in brief psychotherapy via supervised clinical practica, seminars, and supervised reading. Similar data are not available for the extent of crisis intervention education in medical and psychological training programs. It is, however, a standard clinical course in schools of nursing and social work throughout the country.

An exhaustive review of the current literature in either topic would be an impossible task, so extensive are the reports of research and clinical cases. A quick inspection of Volumes 65 and 66 of *Psychological Abstracts* published during 1981 revealed 22 and 27 references, respectively, to brief psychotherapy under the subject index. Cursory observation of the number of references to articles indexed under the crisis intervention heading suggests three to four times those frequencies. An annotated bibliography on brief psychotherapy (Mandel, 1981) contains 1,552 entries on 647 pages. One would have to conclude that the time was right, the need was great, and the services rendered were effective. In this context, the development of crisis intervention and brief psychotherapy has been reinforced to the point where they are both integral and permanent aspects of the mental-health scene in the 1980s.

Method and Theory of Brief Psychotherapy

Although early, now classical, writings on brief psychotherapy were prepared by therapists of the traditional analytic school (Davanloo, 1978; Wolberg, 1965b), more recent articles and chapters have discussed applications of brief psychotherapy in the practice of transactional analysis or Gestalt therapy (Grayson, 1979; Jensen et al., 1980). Hence, we must conclude at the outset that there is no one form or method of brief therapy, any more than there is a single form of psychotherapy that isn't brief. There is, however, a common set of issues that must be considered in any form of brief psychotherapy. We will consider these issues under the headings of: (1) selection of patients, (2) the therapist's role, (3) the issue of duration, and (4) evidence of effectiveness.

Criteria for Selecting Patients

Wolberg (1965b) was among the first to define the goals of brief psychotherapy, and the patients for whom shortened treatment was appropriate. He is emphatic that if the goal is to eliminate a neurosis completely and bring about a radical change in the personality of the patient, a brief form of therapy is simply out of the question. Rather, brief therapy is appropriate when one is seeking a rapid restoration of balance in an acute neurosis, or the resolution of an acute upset in a chronic character disorder. The goal of personality reconstruction, according to Wolberg, is only appropriate in cases where patients are unable to avail themselves of long-term therapy. In a more recent analysis, Wolberg (1980) defines five classes of patients seeking therapy. In Class 1 patients there is a history of good adjustment until the onset of current difficulties. Class 5 patients seek and require extensive reconstructive personality changes. Between these two extremes are those whose chief problem is maladaptive behavior or disturbing symptoms (Class 2), those whose symptoms and behavior are associated with deep-rooted intrapsychic problems or personality disturbances (Class 3), and those whose problems are so severe that therapy can only keep them reasonably functioning in reality (Class 4). Brief psychotherapy could conceivably be applied to all but Class 5 patients, but would be expected to be most successful with Classes 1 through 3. There are many who would reserve Class 1 patients for crisis intervention treatment, leaving Classes 2 and 3 as the ideal candidates for brief psychotherapy.

Wolberg suggests a set of criteria for brief psychotherapy patients (1977). He suggests that patients should: (1) already have worked out most of their difficulties on a nonverbal level; (2) need a helping hand in clarifying these difficulties; (3) have strong motivation to work on their problem; (4) have good ego strength; (5) have environmental situations that are remedial; and (6) have a keen intelligence and an ability to work on their own solutions between therapy sessions.

Hoch (1965) concludes that, generally speaking, shorter-term therapy is useful for: (1) the resolution of acute conflicts, (2) the relief of situations where the patient's neurotic response is a reaction to the environment, or (3) anxiety states or hysterical reactions. The cases Hoch finds clearly unsuited for brief psychotherapy are those with: (1) chronic psychotic disorders, (2) chronic psychosomatic or character disorders, or (3) obsessive-compulsive states. In addition, Hoch doubts the possibility of a good therapeutic result with brief psychotherapy for marked sexual aberrations, except cases of acute homosexual panic.

A somewhat similar position is advocated by Castelnuovo-Tedesco (1975), when he suggests that suitable patients must be motivated, have a mature personality, and present a focalized, acute problem situation. In general, candidates for brief therapy should possess good ego strength and not be grossly incapacitated. Brief psychotherapy is not considered appropriate for patients with phobias, hypochrondriacal reactions, psychoses, character disorders, disabling psychosomatic illness, or deep depressions. Those with poor impulse control, especially suicidal patients, are not appropriate for brief treatment.

All of these criteria have raised the criticism that brief psychotherapy is only useful to those patients who don't really need it, while those who do require therapy really need the conventional long-term form. Bellak and Small (1965), on the other hand, take the position that brief therapy may be of some use in nearly every kind of emotional disturbance. It is, admittedly, most clearly beneficial where there is an acute presenting situation, or a relatively mild disorder involving real-life events. The major contraindication, according to Bellak and Small, is that brief therapy has already been tried and found to be insufficient. Other contraindications are when restructuring of the personality or character is desirable and feasible, and where circumstances permit the prolonged, classical analysis.

Sifneos (1967, 1972) discusses two types of brief psychotherapy he has developed and described frequently in the literature. The first of these is brief anxiety-suppressive psychotherapy, which he believes is useful for patients even though they present with lifelong emotional problems. The criteria for selecting patients for this therapy are that they: (1) have the ability to maintain a job; (2) make a strong appeal for help to overcome their difficulties; (3) are willing to recognize that the symptoms they manifest are psychological in origin; and (4) are willing to cooperate with the therapist.

The major contribution Sifneos has made to the field of brief psychotherapy is his development of short-term anxiety-provoking psychotherapy, or STAPP (1967, 1972, 1978, 1979; Sifneos et al., 1980). He describes this form of treatment as the best available help for patients who have been unable to deal with their emotional crises, and who may, as a result, develop a variety of fairly well circumscribed psychoneurotic illnesses. As Sifneos' work has proceeded, he has continually refined the list of criteria for patient psychodynamics. They must show evidence of: (1) above-average intelligence and psychological sophistication; (2) having had at least one meaningful relationship with another person in which they have been capable of altruistic and reciprocal relations; (3) an ability to verbalize feeling and show emotions; (4) an ability to verbalize a specific chief complaint; and (5) motivation for change, not just symptom relief, and willingness to work hard to get it.

Strupp (1978; Keithly, Samples, & Strupp, 1980) has cited only two criteria for brief therapy patients, but they are the most encompassing. He says patients must be willing and able to explore feelings, and be able to work within a therapeutic relationship with interpretation. In brief psychotherapy, the quality of the relationship is far more important than the diagnosis or other patient variables.

Malan and his colleagues have written extensively on their studies of brief psychotherapy (1963, 1975, 1976a, 1976b, 1978). He cites the confusion in the brief therapy literature concerning what types of patients are suitable for the method (1975). Malan identifies two opposite views, which he calls "conservative" and "radical." The conservative view, which tends to be dominant in the literature, holds that only the mildest and most recent illnesses may be helped by brief therapy. The problems and the treatment are both superficial, and the results are usually no more than palliative. The radical view, by contrast, proposes that severe and longstanding illness can sometimes be helped; and, where this is the case, the effects are far-reaching and permanent. Malan confesses to having begun his work in 1963 in sympathy with the conservative view, and finds himself embracing the radical view by 1975.

There is also the distinct possibility, referred to directly by a number of authors (Bellak & Small, 1965; Malan, 1975; Strupp, 1978; Wolberg, 1977), that the key variable in selecting patients for brief therapy lies not in the patients, but in the therapist. Wolberg (1977) insists that the shortening of therapy depends to a considerable degree upon the therapist and his understanding of psychodynamics and ability to use self in the treatment relationship. To Wolberg, the therapist must be capable of: (1) rapid rapport, (2) sensitivity, (3) perceptive analysis, and (4) constant focus on the conflict area.

Malan (1976b) observed that one of the most favorable prognostic factors for outcome in brief therapy was what he termed "focality," which was defined as the *therapist's* ability to concentrate on the focus of the therapy as it was originally defined. Moreover, Malan cites 12 factors that tend to lengthen therapy, four of which are clearly therapist variables (1975b). These are a tendency toward passivity and willingness to follow where the patient leads, a sense of timelessness which is conveyed to the patient, therapeutic perfectionism which requires total cure or personality change, and an increasing preoccupation with ever deeper and earlier experiences.

Strupp (1978) emphasizes the therapist's ability to arrive at an understanding of the patient in dynamic terms and the ability to formulate and follow a circumscribed therapeutic plan. Similarly, Bellak and Small (1965) put primary emphasis on the therapist's capacity to conceptualize the patient's disturbance clearly in terms of psychodynamics, and the potential response (of the disturbance) to psychotherapy.

A brief concluding statement may be helpful in summarizing the several points of view concerning when and for which patients brief psychotherapy is an appropriate form of treatment. The earliest, more conservative views stressed diagnostic categories that connoted the less severe forms of functional psychological disorder. The emphasis has gradually shifted away from diagnosis to the quality of the relationship that can be developed in the therapy program. With this shift has come a realization that a wider range of patients can be helped with brief therapy than was originally felt to be the case. Responsibility for the quality of the therapy relationship is currently being placed as much on the therapist as upon the patient. The common threads of opinion and experience in brief psychotherapy indicate that the patient must be motivated to work hard, and the therapist must be able to do in a shorter time those things that would ordinarily be done over a long period of treatment. Together they must be capable of a dynamic, interpretative, and intense human relationship in order for brief psychotherapy to be effective. What is actually done in that relationship is the subject of our next section.

The Therapist's Role in Brief Psychotherapy

Just how different is brief psychotherapy from its longer-term, traditional parent forms? The answer one receives to this question varies considerably from one writer to another. Brief therapy is obviously different in duration, but the major differences in methods used to achieve patient change are those that are the direct results of the shorter time frame. Bellak and Small (1965) argue that brief psychotherapy is really just the shorter application of traditional psychotherapy. With the time reduced, however, the therapist cannot wait for insight to develop, nor can he leisurely develop a diagnosis as therapy proceeds. He must arrive at an early understanding of the problem, and the diagnosis becomes the starting point. Similarly, he must foster insight actively, and encourage or stimulate the "working-through" behaviors of the patient. Otherwise, the principles of psychic determinism, overdeterminism, continuity of personality and unconsciousness, and homeostasis that permeate traditional analysis apply equally to brief therapy. Bellak and Small (1965) also address the use of specific treatment methods in brief therapy. They are of the opinion that free association is not a basic tool, primarily because it requires the therapist to remain passive while the patient moves at his own pace. They also suggest that it is not typical for the patient to lie on a couch with the therapist properly located just out of sight. However, the therapist's interpretation is still the chief device by which the patient gains insight and effects behavior change. In brief therapy it is often necessary to couple the interpretations with other forms of interventions, such as medication and environmental manipulation. In every case of brief therapy, however, the transference relationship remains as important to a successful outcome as in classical analysis. The only difference is that with a shorter time in which to work, the therapist must actively seek and maintain a *positive* transference, rather than permit it to develop in the usual, more passive style of analysis.

The process of brief psychotherapy, as described by Bellak and Small (1965), assumes the principles common to all dynamic forms of therapy: communication, insight, and working through. They identify five essential aspects to this process. First, the patient communicates to the therapist. The communication involves the patient's problems, his developmental and behavioral history, and his contemporary life situation. Second, the therapist forms an insight by evolving the common denominator from the patient's contemporary behaviors and experiences, the genetic precursors of the current condition, and the patient's behavior toward the therapist. Third, the therapist communicates the insight back to the patient in a way that gives meaning to the behavior patterns and feelings the patient is experiencing. Fourth, the patient gains insight by perceiving the pattern or configuration of meaning in the feelings being experienced. This insight may be both an intellectual as well as an emotional perception and may occur as a sudden "aha experience," or like the gradual dawning of the light of day. Finally, in the fifth stage, the patient works through the problem by applying the insight he has gained to specific situations in his current life circumstances.

Probably no issue is more consistently considered in the literature of brief psychotherapy than the role of transference. Malan (1976b) reports that one clear statistical finding of his initial study (Malan, 1963) was that thorough interpretation of the transference played an important part in favorable outcomes of brief psychotherapy. The most critical part of this was the therapist's consistent interpretation of the transference link back to the patient and his parents. In reviewing the findings of several studies, Malan (1976a) concludes that brief therapy produces effective and permanent changes in patients in proportion to the amount of working through of nuclear conflicts within the transference relationship. He asserts unequivocally that the more radical the technique in terms of transference, depth of interpretation, and link to childhood, the more radical are the therapeutic effects.

Alexander (1965) identifies the key to shorter forms of therapy as the ability of the therapist to experience and control the transference. Strupp (1978) and Brogen (1978) use the term "transference" sparingly, but there is no mistaking that they are referring to the process by which the therapist uses the therapeutic relationship to achieve treatment goals. To Strupp, the goal of any form of psychotherapy is to correct the maladaptive adjustment patterns that have been learned in significant early relationships. These corrections must be made within the context of an interpersonal experience that resembles the earlier ones, but is different in important respects. It is the therapist's job to facilitate and encourage the development of a relationship between himself and the patient, wherein the patient can experience the conflicts existing between himself and other significant people in his life. Consequently, Strupp believes that therapy is successful to the extent that the therapist can bring the patient's maladaptive patterns into focus within the therapy relationship and allow the patient to experience them with sufficient vividness that he can use the experience to feel, think, and act differently. He has issued a series of reports that compare a success and a failure in brief psychotherapy, largely in terms of the ability or inability of the patient and the therapist to develop a productive working relationship early in therapy (Strupp, 1980a, 1980b, 1980c, 1980d; Strupp & Hadley, 1979). Differences in process and outcome are shown by these studies to be due to the quality of the therapeutic interaction. Brogen's (1978) report, also involving college students as patients, leads to a remarkably similar conclusion.

Hoch (1965) identifies only one difference in the therapist's role in brief therapy as compared to classical analysis. This is his level of activity, which must be far greater in brief treatment. The therapist must be keenly aware of what he is doing, since there is not time to experiment with various strategies as he aggressively pursues the patient's conflicts. Otherwise, Hoch concludes, every technique known to standard long-term therapy can be used effectively in brief therapy.

The universal factor that sets the method of brief therapy apart from its conventional counterpart is the need to identify and focus on specific complaints and/or goals of the patient. Wolberg (1965a, 1965b) originally discussed goals as being, like the therapy itself, abbreviated in nature. Suitable goals are relief of symptoms, restoration of functioning to the pre-illness level, an understanding of what initiated the upset, the identification of pervasive personality patterns and their relationship to the present illness, and determining remedies for the environment. Sifneos (1972, 1979) makes the ability to verbalize a chief specific complaint the first critical selection factor when assessing a new patient for brief therapy. There just isn't time to permit the goal or direction of therapy to evolve and change throughout its course if a time limit is to be placed on the process.

Bender and Smokler (1980) suggest that the therapist should collect a number of early memories from the patient during the evaluation process. They show how these early memories are a reflection of central and enduring life themes, and can be used as an aid to focusing on the specific issue of therapy when duration is limited.

What else does the therapist do in brief psychotherapy? Wolberg (1965b, 1977, 1980) has listed the topics that should be included under an outline of brief treatment. Interestingly, the list grew from 14 items in the first writing to 15 in 1977, and 20 in the 1980 version. The 20 recommended therapist operations Wolberg cites are:

1. rapidly establish a positive working relationship
2. deal immediately with initial resistances
3. gather historical data
4. select a specific focus
5. define the precipitating event
6. evolve a working hypothesis
7. make a tentative diagnosis
8. convey the need for the patient's active participation in the therapeutic relationship
9. make a verbal contract with the patient (which may include the number of sessions and the termination date)
10. utilize all therapeutic techniques in an active and flexible manner
11. study the reactions and defenses of the patient to the techniques used
12. relate present-day behavior to long-established patterns
13. watch for and deal with transference
14. examine possible countertransference
15. be alert to other forms of resistance in the patient
16. assign homework
17. accent the termination date
18. terminate therapy as planned
19. assign continuing self help activities
20. arrange for further treatment if necessary

Undoubtedly, there will be some who find little in this list that is unique to brief therapy as opposed to conventional forms. If so, one must remember that whereas these therapist behaviors seem quite common in 1980, some of them were quite revolutionary when Wolberg first listed them in 1965. The central feature of brief therapy, both then and now, is not so much what the therapist does, but how actively and aggressively he directs the process and drives it along its truncated trajectory toward termination.

Despite his list of specific behaviors for the therapist to follow, Wolberg (1977) also believes that there are basically three things that really matter in brief psychotherapy. First is the therapist's acceptance of eclecticism which leads him to adopt whatever specific techniques from psychiatry, psychology, sociology, or philosophy may be of help in the total treatment effort. Second, the therapist must exercise flexibility in adjusting his strategems to the immediate needs of the patient, and the treatment hour. Finally, therapy is dependent on the deliberate employment of activity in the relationship.

This degree of activity and direction has caused Sifneos to formulate a quite different model for brief psychotherapy, one that emphasizes the role of teacher, or instructor, rather than therapist in the traditional sense. The model Sifneos has developed (1967, 1972, 1978, 1979) can be described by its eight essential elements, as follows:

1. The patient is asked to assign top priority to the one of a variety of presenting complaints that he wishes to overcome.
2. The therapist acts as an evaluator and teacher.
3. The therapist interviews and takes a history in order to set up a tentative psychodynamic hypothesis to use in formulating the patient's underlying emotional conflict.
4. The therapist directs the process and concentrates on these conflicts throughout the therapy.
5. The therapist must create an atmosphere, establish an alliance with the patient, agree on a definition of the problem to be solved, and utilize positive transference as the main therapeutic tool.
6. The therapist substantiates or modifies his working hypothesis by using anxiety-provoking questions.
7. The therapist also uses confrontations and clarifications to stimulate the patient to examine areas of difficulty he otherwise tends to avoid.
8. If the therapist is successful, the patient uses the novel learning experience and new problem-solving techniques to deal with new situations encountered in the future.

Thus, for Sifneos, brief therapy is an intensive learning process that offers vast learning opportunities to both therapist and patient, who are, he believes, better labeled as teacher and student.

In his earlier work, Sifneos (1967, 1972) described both short-term anxiety-suppressive therapy, and the anxiety-provoking brief therapy (STAPP) that he developed extensively. The descriptions of the former method suggest a very close similarity to what is now generally thought of as crisis intervention, rather than a form of psychotherapy. This is because Sifneos has also developed a theory of crisis, and the psychological deterioration that may result when life crises go unresolved. His position is clearly consistent with that of the crisis intervention school, and thus, his work may be thought of as a theoretical and methodological bridge between crisis intervention and brief psychotherapy.

The phases of brief therapy encountered in STAPP will serve as an effective summary of the role of the therapist in brief psychotherapy. Sifneos describes them as follows:

1. *Patient-Therapist Encounter:* This period of treatment is characterized primarily by efforts to establish rapport, the development of positive feelings between the patient and therapist, the formulation of a dynamic working hypothesis, clarification of expectations, history taking and evaluation, and an initial focus on conflicts, presenting complaints, and the chief priority for the work to follow.
2. *The Early Treatment:* In this phase, the patient's positive feelings for the therapist are at their highest level. The therapist must, therefore, confront the patient with these transference feelings and use them as the main tool of the therapy. The therapist confronts, invites, and stimulates the positive transference as quickly as possible.
3. *The Height of Treatment:* During this phase, the therapist begins to move in on the patient's intrapsychic space with anxiety-provoking questions to concentrate on unresolved conflicts. The patient must be confronted with his anger, fear, anxiety, and sadness that result from a confrontation with these suppressed or repressed emotions.
4. *Evidence of Change:* Following anxiety-provoking confrontations, the patient begins to give evidence of improved interpersonal relationships occurring in experiences outside the therapy hour. There is a notable reduction of tension, and the patient is able to give examples of how the new learnings are put to work and experienced in the outside world.
5. *Termination:* This is a most important phase of treatment. The therapist must demonstrate his

willingness to abandon the traditional tendency to continue until every last issue is resolved, and personality reconstruction is achieved. He must be alert to the desire to continue for his own pleasure, or other professional rewards. It is important at this phase to encourage the patient to take over the role of the therapist in his own life, and to learn from the therapist how to anticipate situations and handle them effectively on his own.

Once more, this description of brief psychotherapy will sound like a description of any well-planned and well-executed dynamic treatment program. What makes it uniquely brief psychotherapy is that the therapist structures his activity so that these five phases are accomplished by predetermined design in an average of three to five months, although it may take as few as two, and occasionally as many as twelve months to complete (Sifneos, 1972).

If the duration of the treatment is really the major variable separating brief from conventional psychotherapy, how long should the therapy be to the be most effective? We now turn to an analysis of this critical issue.

The Duration of Brief Psychotherapy

Wolberg (1977) has reviewed the evidence in the literature, and suggests there is much controversy as to how long brief psychotherapy is. Whether or not the discrepancies represent active disagreement, or merely individualized cognitive styles applied to time spans, is not at all clear. A brief review of the time frames used by the major writers in the field may shed some general light on the confusion, or at least inconsistency, that is to be found.

Bellak and Small (1965), probably as a result of their early experience with the four-session limit placed by the Veterans Administration, consider brief psychotherapy to be bounded by from one to six interviews.

Malan (1963) included in his first study of brief therapy those cases in which the patient was seen from 10 to 40 times. In a later discussion, however, Malan (1975) identified clear therapeutic effects arising from the single diagnostic interview. Hence, he talks about the existence of one-session psychotherapy. Mendelsohn (1978) summarizes the critical aspects of short-term therapy and includes in his discussion all therapy lasting up to one year,

with sessions as frequent as one or two per week. Harrower (1965) considers brief therapy to last less than nine months. However, she specifically excluded from her study a group of 193 patients who were seen for treatment less than four times. Avnet (1965a, 1965b) reported on the benefits of therapy that was limited by the insurance coverage to a maximum of 15 sessions. To be included, all patients received a minimum of five treatment visits. Hoch (1965) is not very specific in defining the length of therapy, but implies that he considers it to last between 15 and 20 sessions. Mann (1973) developed a brief therapy program at Boston University Medical Center that limited therapy provided by the residents to a maximum of 12 treatment hours, but left the distribution and duration of individual visits to be determined by the patient needs. Hoyt (1979) proposed a series of 12 50-minute therapy sessions for working through bereavement problems, but distributed them twice per week for 6 weeks. Marmor (1979) concludes from his own practice that between 20 and 30 visits is appropriate for nearly all patients, but he suggests allowing for a return visit three to six months after termination if this helps the patient. Straker (1977) advocates only 15 to 20 sessions, but allows for up to 30 sessions under "rather unusual circumstances," which he does not describe or define. Finally, Sifneos (1972) has already been cited for his conceptualization that anything up to two months is merely crisis support, and that brief psychotherapy lasts from two to twelve months.

To be sure, the number of therapy sessions or duration of treatment in terms of months is the least important consideration. The differences cited above should not be interpreted as prescriptions for conducting brief therapy. Rather, we should conclude that they are merely descriptive data by which authors defined the work they had done, and the actual numbers quoted represent limits that were chosen because they seemed at the time, for whatever reason, to be the best ones to use in selecting cases for study, or for establishing new programs.

Appelbaum (1972, 1975) addresses the issue of therapy duration in terms of the well-known Parkinson's law. His thesis is that the task of psychotherapy, like any other work to be done, will expand or contract to fill the time that is allotted for it. Hence, it is not the patient's problem or the therapist's technique that determines duration, but the tendency of the therapist to keep it going, as opposed to his willingness to cut it short, that distinguishes brief therapy from longer forms.

A similar view is expressed by Weiner (1975), when he observes that the extent to which the needs and capacities of the patient affect the necessary duration of psychotherapy serves as a challenge to the current practice of distinguishing between long-term and short-term treatment on the basis of some arbitrary number of sessions or months until termination. Weiner's concern is that the nature of the treatment and the skill and orientation of the therapist must be appropriate to the patient's needs. If this is the case, then there is no such thing as brief or prolonged treatment, only treatment that lasts for a particular length of time.

It must be concluded that as the mental-health professions have grown accustomed to the reality that therapy need not last for extended periods of time to be effective, the central issue of "How long?" with which we were once preoccupied has evolved into one of "How effective is shortened therapy?" There are some data on this question.

Evidence for the Effectiveness of Brief Psychotherapy

The several reports published by Malan and his associates have been mentioned repeatedly in the foregoing discussion. His primary data, however, are to be found in the original study (1963) and his replication, which was published in 1976 (Malan, 1976b). Malan's chief concern seemed to be related to whether or not cases seen in therapy for periods shorter than that required for traditional psychoanalysis could be shown to result in beneficial change in the patient. His conclusions were based on both clinical observations and statistical findings. The variables selected for study included such factors as patient motivation, depth and extent of transference interpretation, severity of pathology, and duration of pretherapy symptoms. All of these were related to judgments of outcome following therapy. Malan's replication of the 1963 data and a further replication by Marziali and Sullivan (1980) have both yielded positive results confirming the value of brief therapy. The chief findings are consistently that severity of pathology does not predict outcome, but high patient motivation and therapist interpretation of the parent-to-therapist transference do significantly correlate with effective treatment.

Sifneos et al. (1980) discuss the preliminary findings of an ongoing outcome study of STAPP. He compared the results of treating 22 experimental patients with the outcomes of 8 delayed-treatment controls. Of the experimental group, 14 were rated by two evaluators as "recovered," 4 were "much better," 3 were "little better," and 1 was found to be "unchanged." By contrast, 5 of the 8 controls were "unchanged," 3 were a "little better." When they were actually treated, 4 of the controls were "recovered," 2 were "much better," and 2 withdrew from treatment. Sifneos cites these data as confirming the effectiveness of anxiety-provoking confrontations during therapy lasting five months or less.

In an early research program, Harrower (1965) measured the effects of psychotherapy by asking the therapist to rate the degree of recovery or progress achieved by the patient, and also by administering a battery of projective tests before and after treatment. She found that therapists have much less satisfaction with results from brief therapy than with the outcome of the classical forms of treatment that require a longer time. Cases rated as "failures" occurred much more frequently among those that received brief therapy than those who received classical analysis. The mean duration of therapy for the "improved" group was four times greater than the mean for the "unimproved" patients. Some very interesting data emerged, however, when Harrower extended her study over a period of 15 years, and included long-term follow-up testing. She compared her projective test data collected from responses given prior to therapy with those observed at the termination of therapy. She generally found little change in the projective records. But ten years after the therapy was terminated, a large number of the patients were again retested and showed marked improvement in performance. Harrower concludes that there is a factor that is operative over the therapeutically empty time interval that somehow allows even the patients treated briefly to show significant gains that were not evident at the end of treatment.

Wolberg (1977) has reviewed the results of a variety of studies and he also concludes that the evidence is persuasive that the time prior to demonstration of recovery need not be spent in all cases in continuous psychotherapy. Johnson and Gelso (1980) have presented data from an extensive and critical review of the literature on outcome studies in psychotherapy, especially time-limited or brief therapy, in which they analyze both the results reported and the methodology used to gather the data. Their primary conclusion concerning methodology is that there are so few controls exercised consistently that comparisons across studies are next to impossible. Different sources of outcome measures, and different times for taking the measures clearly confound the results in most of the current literature. Nevertheless, given this limitation, they review 36 studies, reporting 51 different measures of treatment as a function of time in therapy. They conclude that the general results of these studies favor the hypothesis that the more treatment, the greater the improvement. This is primarily true when the outcome measures are taken at termination. However, when long-term follow-up studies are performed, the differences disappear, and the positive effects of short- and long-term therapy are equal. The conclusion of the Johnson and Gelso review is a clear restatement of the discovery made by Harrower 15 years earlier. It is simply that with at least weekly treatment contact to begin the improvement process, time alone — either with or without active therapy —seems to be the critical variable in producing optimal improvement in clients. In short, it is not that "the more therapy, the better improvement," but "the more time after the beginning of therapy" that makes the difference.

If we were to draw a dominant conclusion from the foregoing discussion, it would have to be that brief psychotherapy is properly seen as an introduction to effective, healthy adjustment. When the therapist uses the time to develop a learning environment wherein his clinical insights and his behavior as an interpersonal stimulus are actively employed, the therapy sessions become a laboratory in which learning to live constructively outside therapy becomes a challenge to the patient motivated for change. At the end of therapy, whenever it occurs, the patient will have learned how to learn, and will have successfully begun a process that may be completed just as easily and effectively without the therapist as with him.

A Concluding Statement about Brief Psychotherapy

It has not been the goal of this chapter to undertake an exhaustive review or to evaluate critically the theoretical, methodological, or research literature on brief psychotherapy. Our intent has been to identify for the serious reader who wishes to delve deeper into specific areas the leading references that will constitute a profitable place to begin that search. The rate at which new articles and books are appearing would suggest that the scholar interested in brief psychotherapy for either academic or clinical practice pursuits will not be frustrated in his quest for new ideas or data in the foreseeable future.

Theory and Methodology in Crisis Intervention

A thorough discussion of the topic of crisis intervention must not only provide a meaningful contrast to the method of brief psychotherapy reviewed in the last section, but should indicate the unique features of crisis intervention itself. To accomplish this, we address three major topics in the crisis literature: (1) crisis theory and the nature of a crisis, (2) techniques for effective intervention, and (3) the issue of professional and paraprofessional interveners.

It should be noted that in crisis intervention we must adopt a new set of terms. Since a crisis is a normally occurring event, rather than a sickness, treatment for it is typically referred to as intervention, rather than therapy. Consequently, the person who provides the intervention is most often referred to as a "worker," or "counselor," but rarely as a "therapist." The language used in the remainder of this chapter is selected to emphasize, rather than blur, the distinction between crisis intervention and psychotherapy.

Crisis Theory and the Nature of a Crisis

Caplan (1964) and Sifneos (1972) have described crisis theory in very similar terms, and it must be assumed that one was influenced, at least in part, by the other. In fact, the recent discussions of crisis theory by Aguilera and Messick (1982), France (1982), Hoff (1978), and Puryear (1979), as well as some of the earliest articles by Rapoport (1965) and Parad and Caplan (1965), all base their notions on the conceptual formulations by Lindemann and Caplan.

According to the basic theory, a crisis develops in stages, beginning with the encountering of an emotionally hazardous event or situation in the individual's life space. The event is initially perceived as a threat to current psychological adjustment, and in response to this threat, the individual mobilizes well-learned and practiced methods of problem solving and coping. If these procedures are effective in removing the threat, the event or situation is controlled, and what might have become a crisis is really just a demonstration of good psychological adjustment processes. However, it is when these usual coping methods fail to reduce the tension effectively in the face of this particular hazardous event that the roots of a personal crisis begin to grow. France (1982) reviews the mechanism whereby this may lead to the development of learned helplessness in the individual if he should come to believe that all his efforts will have no effect in preventing bad outcomes, or in producing desired ones (Abramson, Seligman, & Teasdale, 1978). Caplan (1964) identifies the general feature of the threatening event that initiates a crisis as some barrier to an important life goal. This means it can occur in any one of a wide variety of forms, depending upon the individual's particular life style and psychosocial environment.

After the initial impact with the precipitating event, and the person's realization that usual problem solving is not effective, the next phase is one of increased efforts and coping. During this phase, the individual strives with a marked increase in effort to overcome the barrier, or to resolve the situation. There is a notable increase in urgency, or motivation for a solution. Anxiety or agitated depression are the major symptoms, but they may also appear with signs of confusion, disorganization, or panic. Moreover, the individual will show evidence of reduced cognitive flexibility, and be unable to entertain alternatives or to comprehend options available. Efforts at coping take on a stereotyped or repetitive character. They may also be defensive reactions to the frustration and other unpleasant feelings being experienced. This leads to repression and denial, magical thinking or distortions of the facts, projection of blame to the wrong people or circumstances, or conversion of the psychological stress to physiological symptoms. Avoidance through sleep, drinking, tranquilizing medication, or other diversions may temporarily serve to dull the psychological pain, but will not lead to resolution of the precipitating event. France (1982) and Hoff (1978) have provided exceptionally vivid descriptions of the development of this second phase of a crisis situation.

A very significant aspect of the second phase of crisis was identified long ago by Caplan and his co-workers (Caplan, 1964; Parad, 1965). This is the fact that, because of the increased anxiety and tension of the coping phase, an individual will be especially vulnerable—or amenable—to intervention. Almost any help that is offered will be accepted. Effective interventions made at this time

will result in beneficial resolution, and poorly planned or implemented interventions will also be embraced uncritically by the person in need of assistance.

If intervention occurs and leads to problem resolution, the incident will end successfully, usually with the person having learned new coping strategies that may serve to make him less vulnerable to problems in the future. On the other hand, if there is no intervention, the crisis will progress to the third stage, which is characterized primarily by withdrawal. The individual will cease his attempts at resolution, and give up. Obviously, this signals an even more ineffective response, and sets the stage for the beginning of psychological deterioration and potential psychiatric casualty. It is important to recognize that up to this point, the individual in crisis has displayed anxiety, agitation, confused thinking, disorganized problem solving, and even projection and magical thinking. At this point apathy, withdrawal, and indifference may look like a genuine depression. However much these signs of crisis may look like or mimic the symptoms of psychiatric disorder, they are not the same, and should not be confused with them. They are the normal responses of an individual facing a temporary crisis in the process of living. They serve as indicators that intervention is necessary, but not as symptoms of psychopathology.

After a crisis situation has progressed to phase three, the standard crisis theory in the literature holds that it will not last much longer without some kind of resolution taking place. A crisis is, by its nature, a short-lived psychological condition, lasting probably six to eight weeks. Either an intervention will result in new coping mechanisms to alleviate the precipitating event or modify the perception of it, or withdrawal, repression, and denial will dissipate its lingering impact on the individual. The concern is not whether or not the crisis will be resolved, but the condition in which it leaves the individual. During the third stage of crisis, the individual may be so convinced of his helplessness to change circumstances and so in need of something to help him stop living in this situation, that he may elect to stop living, *period*! Suicide becomes a high risk in some crisis cases during this stage, and it is important that suicidal behavior be properly interpreted as a "cry for help" (Farberow & Shneidman, 1961) in response to the crisis, rather than as a form of psychiatric illness. France (1982) has pointed out that suicidal behavior will have a higher degree of lethality during phase three than under phase two, when self-injury behavior may be a coping technique, the intent of which is to promote rescue rather than to die (Farberow & Litman, 1970; Freeman et al., 1974). Even when suicide is not chosen as one alternative for resolving the crisis, it is still possible that the individual will be left with more learned helplessness, or with fewer psychological strengths and resources for solving future problems. This, according to Caplan (1964), is the real concern in a crisis. He portrays the situation as a waystation out of which the individual may emerge in the direction of greater psychological health and stability, or in the direction of increased psychological deterioration and vulnerability. Crises can induce growth, or they can be debilitating. The difference lies in what happens to assist the individual's efforts to cope during the six or eight weeks after the precipitating event.

The majority of writers in crisis theory have explained this process in terms of the concept of homeostasis borrowed directly from the field of physiology (Caplan, 1964; Parad & Parad, 1968a; 1968b; Puryear, 1979; Sifneos, 1972). According to this notion, the individual resolves a crisis by returning to a normal, precrisis level of functioning. It is the tension produced by an excess or deficiency of some important factor—in this case, an increase in tension or threat to the achievement of life goals—that motivates the individual to take adjustive reaction. When the actions are appropriate and sufficient, they result in a restoration of the homeostatic balance and a precrisis state of normal functioning is resumed. Taplin (1971) has taken issue with the use of homeostasis as a descriptive model because it is apsychological and fails to account for the opportunities for growth, development, change, learning, or actualization. He believes that these processes characterize the essential aspects of human behavior in crisis situations, and that homeostasis is not useful in explaining how they can occur. Instead, Taplin substitutes a cognitive theory that he shows can explain the observations and implications of the crisis literature. Whether or not Taplin's cognitive model has been adopted is unclear, for recent books fail to include it. At the same time, it is also true that there is less use of the principle of homeostatic balance to describe what happens in a crisis. Major books on crisis intervention no longer refer to it in their sections on theory (France, 1982; Hoff, 1979).

From the foregoing discussion of theory, it is evident that a crisis is the result of a hazardous emotional event with which the individual is unable to cope using previously learned and effective problem-solving techniques. Distinctions between the stressful events and the crisis itself have been developed by Bloom (1963), Klein and Lindemann (1961), and Sifneos (1972), and may be of some academic interest. Beyond that, it is important to recognize other aspects of a crisis.

Hansell (1976) offers a framework for conceptualizing a crisis as a state in which a person experiences a loss of one or more of the basic attachments that are developed as sources of support in life. Hansell lists these attachments that we all have to: (1) food, oxygen, and other physical supplies; (2) a strong sense of self-identity; (3) at least one person in a close, mutually supportive relationship; (4) at least one group that accepts us; (5) one or more roles that we perform with self-respect and dignity; (6) financial security; and (7) a set of meanings and values that we use to set goals and understand ourselves and the world. Hansell uses these attachments, or the loss of them, as his definition of the nature of a crisis.

In fact, it is possible to formulate a comprehensive explanation of the perceptions and behaviors of an individual in crisis in terms of just one of these attachments: the strong sense of self-identity. Throughout crisis literature, the definition of a crisis is given in terms of it being a time of transition, of change, or as a turning point in a person's life. A crisis signals the end of something, and the beginning of something else. This is very easy to see when we consider the developmental crises, such as when an individual is faced with the transition from adolescence to adulthood, and the former ways of coping are no longer effective in resolving new problems. Extending this same concept of a transitional state to any crisis that might occur not only between, but within phases of life, we can ask, "What is it that is changing?" Whereas Hansell would say it is any one of seven basic attachments, it also can be claimed that in every crisis situation it is the individual's self concept that is undergoing a painful transition. A crisis is essentially an attack upon the very core of our psychological being—how we perceive and define ourselves.

It is helpful, both in understanding the nature of crisis generally, and specifically in assessing an individual at the beginning of crisis counseling, to determine what has *changed* in the way an individual describes himself. One can effectively approach this by exploring the list of adjectives that a person would use in this description, and how it is changed as a result of some precipitating event. Today such adjectives as healthy, employed, married, and friendly may describe a person in terms of major social and psychological support systems. If one of these adjectives must be eliminated from the list tomorrow as a result of some event that occurs in the meantime, we have an individual in a potentially severe crisis. The search for changes in the entire set of adjectives a person uses to describe himself will uncover the scope of the crisis in his life, as well as define the type of crisis to be resolved. This technique aids in the task of focusing attention on the specifics of the precipitating event, and its unique impact on the individual. It helps define the personal nature of the crisis and explains why the event leads to specific responses in the person being helped.

Whether or not one finds this notion of a self-identity in transition as helpful to understanding a crisis, it must be recognized that any crisis situation must be understood in terms of two necessary elements. First, there must always be some identifiable and specific precipitating event. Second, there must always be evidence of an acute elevation of psychological tension in the form of anxiety or depression. Otherwise, if both are not present, the situation is not a crisis. It is inappropriate to think of a crisis as an acute exacerbation or a recurrent episode in a chronic state of psychopathology or social maladjustment. Family disputes that occur regularly on Friday and Saturday nights are *not* crisis events, despite the fact that police agencies have developed "crisis intervention" teams of officers to handle family disturbance calls. Alcoholics and drug addicts who are arrested and sent to holding tanks or detoxification units are *not* in crisis, despite the fact that mental-health centers and other state-supported agencies have created "crisis intervention" procedures to allow clients to "crash" in a safe and supportive environment. Schizophrenics are *not* in a crisis when they run out of medication on the weekend, or experience an acute return of symptoms under stress, despite the fact that emergency mental-health services have professed to be doing "crisis intervention" when they establish procedures for admitting patients to the in-patient service after normal clinic hours. These situations do not represent a crisis either because there is no new specific precipitating event, or there is no acute elevation of anxiety or depression, or both. Crisis intervention will not be an effective technique to use in treating such cases. The adoption of the crisis intervention language to describe the services only indicates a lack of clarity and understanding of the agency's real role in relation to the client, or the community.

In summary, a crisis should always be defined, as France (1982) has described it, in terms of: (1) its having been precipitated by a specific identifiable event; (2) its being a normal event that will be experienced by everyone at one time or another; (3) its very personal nature for the individual involved; (4) its certainty of being resolved in some way in a brief period of time; and (5) the possibility it holds for either growth, development, and increased psychological health, or increased maladaptive functioning and psychological deterioration.

Techniques for Effective Crisis Intervention

In recent years a number of books have appeared that present comprehensive guidelines for understanding crisis situations and offer step-by-step directions for undertaking actual crisis intervention services with individuals in need. Three excellent discussions designed for a wide audience of both professional and paraprofessional crisis workers are those by France (1982), Hoff (1978), and Puryear (1979). McGee (1974) has described the principles of crisis work in terms of community agency organization and concepts directing service procedures. Mitchell and Resnik (1981) have discussed a wide range of issues relevant to specific crisis intervention delivery procedures and practices. Their book is relevant to crisis work in many types of applied settings.

Wolberg (1980) lists some practical points that a worker should pursue in the course of crisis intervention. He includes the following:

1. See the patient within 24 hours of calling for help.
2. Be alert to patients with a high risk of suicide.
3. Handle evidence of depression immediately.
4. Evaluate the nature of the current stress, present resources, and previous methods for coping.
5. Identify and evaluate exisitng support systems available to the patient.
6. Estimate the patient's own ego resources.
7. Help the patient to an awareness of the factors involved in his reaction to the crisis.

8. Provide empathic listening and supportive reassurance.
9. Utilize tranquilizers only when anxiety is so great the patient cannot make decisions.
10. Deal with the immediate present and avoid probing the past.
11. Avoid exploring dynamic factors.
12. Aim for increasing self-reliance and finding alternative soultions.
13. Always involve family and significant others.
14. Use group treatment as an adjunct to individual sessions.
15. Terminate within six sessions.
16. If patient is in need, and is motivated, institute or refer for dynamically oriented brief psychotherapy.

Wolberg's guidelines for crisis intervention cover the entire range of significant issues in the current literature. Among the most important is the issue of immediate availability of the service. Crisis intervention programs that merely take calls and refer for scheduled appointments during regular business hours are of questionable service to the client. Hansell (1971) has proposed a unique criterion for effective crisis management when he says that treatment in the patient's home environment (rather than in the hospital) is preferred. Hansell claims that the quality of intervention can be measured by the number of feet of distance between the place where treatment is given and the patient's ordinary space of life. This statement has been adopted as "Hansell's Law" within the crisis intervention field, and it has a corollary, devised from paraphrasing Hansell, which holds, similarly, that the quality of crisis intervention service can be measured in minutes that pass from the time the individual asks for help until it is provided. One cannot be an effective crisis worker in the security of one's own familiar surroundings, and at the convenience of one's own orderly schedule of appointments.

Consequently, many crisis intervention programs have developed action-oriented crisis teams that provide an outreach service in the community. They follow up initial telephone contact with on-the-scene interventions where family and other resources can be assessed and brought into active involvement, and where the client is most comfortable dealing with acutely painful fears and anxieties (McGee, 1974; Richard & McGee, 1973).

Among the few areas where there is controversy in the crisis intervention literature is the question of whether or not psychotropic medication should be used. Initially, Caplan (1964) discouraged the excessive use of tranquilizers because they dull the sense of awareness, and prevent the individual from confronting the stressful situation. Hoff (1978) has addressed the issue in her book and taken an emphatic stand against ever using tranquilizers as a substitute for crisis counseling and problem solving. As an adjunct to a managed crisis intervention, she admits that tranquilizers may be helpful when the client is experiencing extreme anxiety and fears losing control, or when sleep is prevented for long periods of time. Sleeping pills such as barbiturate preparations should always be avoided in crisis situations because of the ever-present possibility of lethal overdose. Similarly, Wolberg (1980) suggests a conservative attitude toward tranquilizers as a regular part of crisis intervention. A distinctly opposing and minority opinion is that of Lieb, Lipsitch, and Slaby (1973), who advocate that psychotropic agents may be freely employed for symptomatic relief. They also indicate that when liberally used, medication will alleviate ego-alien symptoms and facilitate rapid return to premorbid levels of functioning. These authors are admittedly writing for mental-health professionals only, and are describing a crisis team approach that is being carried out in a more conventional medical and psychiatric setting. One should use extreme caution, however, in concluding that tranquilizers are beneficial or even necessary in the majority of personal crisis situations. Unless genuine psychiatric illness is involved in the case, which usually does not occur, tranquilizing medication may only retard the return of normal coping behavior, and delay the emergence of healthy psychological adjustment.

Many authors discuss crisis intervention techniques not so much in terms of what is done, but of how it is done. France (1982) devotes several pages to the importance of communication style and the development of an effective relationship as part of the basic techniques of crisis intervention. Knickerbocker and McGee (1973) and McGee et al. (1972) have reported on a major research activity in crisis intervention where the critical variables of worker performance were assessments of the levels of empathy, genuineness, and warmth provided by the person making the intervention. Although no selection criteria could be identified that would predict which trainee applicants would prove to be most effective counselors, the levels of empathy, genuiness, and warmth evidenced in the interventions were shown to relate to level of client satisfaction with the service, and effectiveness of the intervention.

Without question, the key features of a crisis intervention are: (1) the assessment, (2) the action plan, and (3) the follow-up. A full discussion of these important elements of the process has been provided by McGee (1974) in a chapter on the "Four-Phase Process of Crisis Intervention." The assessment activity is critical because it enables the worker to gain an understanding of the nature of the problem facing the client in terms of the details of the precipitating event and previous methods for coping. Even more important, however, is the need to assess completely the full range of the client's resources that can be made available in solving the current situation. Assessment of lethality, or the probability of an overt suicidal behavior must be done in every crisis case, and this takes specific training and skill on the part of the worker. Hoff (1978) has provided an excellent discussion of crisis case assessment.

The action plan is the *sine qua non* of crisis intervention. It is based upon the assessment, and builds a prescription of behaviors that the client and the worker jointly undertake to reach a resolution. Hoff (1978) has listed and discussed the criteria for a good action plan. She includes the following features:

1. Action plans should be problem oriented.
2. Action plans must be appropriate to the individual's functional level and dependency needs.
3. They must be consistent with the person's culture and life style.
4. An action plan must include the significant others and the social network of the community.
5. The plan must be realistic, time limited, and concrete.
6. An action plan is dynamic and renegotiable.
7. The action plan must include provision for follow-up.

The value of the action plan is that it adds structure to the client's problem-solving efforts. It directs his efforts along lines that the worker helps to identify. The action plan is jointly developed with the client playing a role, but with the worker leading the way. It is through participation in the planning as well as the implementation that the client gradually looses his cognitive rigidity and is able to see more and more options.

The action plan is the means by which the worker utilizes and builds bridges toward all of the helping resources in the community network. When marital separation and threatened divorce is the precipitating event, the client may need, more than anything else, the kind of information that can only be provided by an attorney. The action plan should provide for meeting this need.

Follow-up in crisis cases is often confused with the process of determining whether or not a transfer or referral to another agency had been effective, or whether or not the client can keep an appointment for intake. This is a short-sighted notion of follow-up, and is really a standard part of active case management. The follow-up activity that is often neglected is that which occurs several weeks or months after a case is closed. There are two values to this longer-range view of follow-up. First, it forces both the worker and the client to have a deliberate, conscious agreement that the case is in fact being closed. This closing discussion reviews the client's progress in terms of identifying the specific steps taken during the intervention to use new coping methods when the original ones failed. It specifically prepares the client for self-initiated use of similar techniques for future crises. This session also rewards the client's efforts by calling attention to the fact that while he once felt helpless, he is now once more functioning independently. Finally, it prepares the client for the follow-up contact at an agreed-upon time some weeks in the future.

The follow-up has two primary purposes, that are equal in importance and legitimacy. The first of these is obviously to insure that the client is still functioning well and determine if subsequent difficulties have been successfully encountered. The second is to elicit an evaluation from the client. It is appropriate for the crisis worker, and the sponsoring agency, to learn whether or not their procedures were really useful and well regarded by the client. Often, constructive suggestions for changing the form of service delivery have been gathered from these follow-up interviews. If the client never returns, the crisis intervener may never know whether it is because the client has had no future problems, or because he may feel the crisis service is not a good place to get help. This kind of self-evaluation is essential for crisis services, and can only be obtained from long-term follow-up.

Finally, no discussion of the method of delivering crisis intervention would be complete without at least mentioning the discussion by Cadden (1964), of those behaviors on the part of the worker that provide the service a client needs most during periods of crisis. Cadden's article was developed out of many experiences wherein workers engaged the mothers of premature infants. The mothers and the rest of the families were grouped into categories based upon the quality of their psychological adjustment several months after the child was born. It was found that those mothers and families who failed to adjust satisfactorily had certain common response tendencies that distinguished them from those whose adjustment was as good as, or even superior to, the prepartum adjustment level. To help people deal with crisis and avoid the psychological deterioration Cadden observed, she identified the following ways a crisis worker should help:

1. Help the client confront the crisis. Avoidance via denial, repression, or tranquilizing medication is to be prevented.
2. Help the client confront in manageable doses. The worker must have an empathic sense of how much the client can take at one time, and be prepared to discontinue and resume later if confrontation becomes too painful.
3. Help the client get information. The client needs as much factual data as he can get, and it must be from knowledgeable sources. Reliance on rumor is to be avoided. Wishful thinking must be replaced with reality.
4. Help should be provided with everyday tasks if necessary. Crisis workers often provide transportation, or engage in actual physical labor alongside the client when it is appropriate to do so. Here is where accurate assessment of resources is vital, for it never benefits a client if we do something for him which, in fact, he can provide for himself.
5. Help the client avoid placing blame. Being able to determine who is to blame for the situation is not constructive in solving the problem, and may encourage the client to overlook his own role in the problem.
6. Avoid giving false assurances. The client in crisis needs all the help he can get in facing and accepting the new reality which has been imposed by the precipitating event. Naive and inexperienced helpers who give false reassurances are treating the client like a child, and may be assisting the client to deny rather than confront the situation.
7. Help the client to accept help. People in crisis are very reluctant to perceive themselves as needing assistance especially from the mental

health sector. Cultural and religious mores often advocate "being strong," avoiding displays of emotion, and denying any personal deficiency. The crisis worker must expect, and be prepared to deal with resistance which, if allowed to persist, will foster denial and repression, and decrease the probability that the crisis will yield a positive outcome.

These seven elements of crisis intervention were among the first prescriptions for how to intervene in a personal crisis. They have never been improved upon. When they are included in the process of assessment, action planning, and follow-up, they constitute all that a crisis intervener needs to know and do in order to insure that the crisis work will give the client maximum opportunity to emerge from his temporary waystation in the direction of greater psychological health and stability.

The Issue of the Professional or Paraprofessional in Crisis Intervention

Probably no issue was more thoroughly debated in the early years of the community mental-health movement than whether or not persons with less than professional qualifications as psychotherapists should attempt crisis intervention work. McColskey (1973a, 1973b) has taken a firm position favoring the professional crisis worker. Beginning with the premise that professional training in one of the mental-health disciplines is requisite for managing psychological problems, she then argues that acute adjustment crises demand the utmost, rather than the least, in expertise.

On the other hand, if one looks carefully at Wolberg's (1980) list of activities for the crisis worker, it is apparent that he is asking the professional therapist to ignore the skills and theories in which he is so thoroughly and carefully trained. Crisis workers do not probe past experiences. They do not develop psychodynamic formulations of the problem. They do not interpret transferences or symbolic manifestations of conflicts. They do not engage for extended periods of time in treatment. What is there about professional training that prepares a person for crisis intervention work? Empirical evidence actually indicates that professional training may make an individual even less effective in crisis work, especially if he is unwilling to respond immediately and in the client's environment rather than his own. Knickerbocker and McGee (1973) and McGee and Jennings (1973) have presented data that indicate rather clearly that persons who are not professionally trained tend to be more friendly, more empathic, and provide more warmth than professional therapists.

Aguilera and Messick (1982) suggest that there are two approaches to crisis intervention: generic and individual. They agree that nonpsychiatrically trained persons can perform well in generic crisis therapy, but they reserve any individual crisis work for those who are capable of understanding the psychodynamic aspects of the client's problem.

One example of generic crisis intervention may be seen in the application of crisis principles to victims of natural and man-made disasters. France (1982) discusses crisis work with residents in the area surrounding the Three Mile Island nuclear plant incident in 1979. McGee and Heffron (1976) and Richard (1974) have discussed a philosophy for intervention that emerged from the delivery of crisis services to the victims of the Susquehanna River flood at Wilkes-Barre, Pennsylvania, in 1972. Parad, Resnik, and Parad (1976) include chapters in their comprehensive text on disaster management that report on a variety of crisis applications in disaster situations. A thorough analysis of methods for planning and implementing crisis intervention services following natural disasters in smaller communities may be found in an excellent NIMH project report by Tierney and Baisden (1979). They review the experiences of mental-health teams serving flood and tornado victims at Buffalo Creek, West Virginia, and Xenia, Ohio, and draw conclusions for directing future programs in disaster recovery. A common finding in these events is that disaster victims do not define themselves as psychiatric patients. They welcome assistance in their strenuous efforts to cope with the overwhelming efforts at recovery, until the assistance is identified with the mental-health establishment. If trained paraprofessional persons were not available to render these services, they would not be performed in large-scale disaster situations.

Butcher and Maudal (1976) have discussed the characteristics of the worker that are essential to effective crisis intervention. They include among their list the following essential minimum requirements.

1. Ability to be empathic.
2. Ability to listen attentively and selectively, and to elicit appropriate and relevant material from the client.
3. Ability to listen objectively without imposing one's own views.

4. Must be able to assess problems, conflicts, assets, and resources, including suicide potential and motivation to receive help.
5. Must have an up-to-date knowledge of the community resources and procedures for calling them into action.
6. It may also help to be a member of the particular subculture that might utilize the agency.

The last characteristic is especially helpful when the services are being rendered primarily to members of the youth culture, or where drug abuse treatment is part of the agency's role.

It is obvious that nothing in the Butcher and Maudal list of minimum requirements excludes persons with professional training. All that is necessary for a professional therapist to become a crisis intervention worker is that he acknowledge that he is performing a different task, unlike the one for which he was carefully trained, and that he is willing to discard one role and assume another one consciously, deliberately, and without a sense of diminished importance. If this can be done, there is no distinction between a paraprofessional and a professional in crisis intervention. There are just two empathic human beings who may have attended the university for different lengths of time.

Finally, it should be noted that in the recent literature, only Ewing (1978) makes reference to the early controversy about paraprofessional crisis workers. For all practical purposes that issue has been laid to rest, and it is only raised again in this chapter because it is a significant part of the history of crisis intervention, and the references to it may be of academic interest to those who wish to review the arguments on both sides.

Summary

This chapter has traced the development of two forms of personal treatment that have emerged from the community mental-health movement in the early 1960s and have found their way into the mainstream of the current psychological literature. Both are tied conceptually to the community agencies that respond to large numbers of persons for whom traditional psychoanalytic treatment has never been available or feasible.

Brief psychotherapy is clearly and unequivocally a form of professional service that requires the clinical expertise of well-trained therapists. Almost any kind of psychological problem or patient condition may be helped by brief therapy providing the therapist is able to focus on a specific and limited goal of the interaction within the context of a close and intensive personal relationship. It really doesn't matter whether the therapy lasts a few weeks or nearly a year. There is evidence that the formal treatment sessions merely initiate a process that will continue after therapy is over, to enable the patient to regain his premorbid level functioning, or even grow into a more healthy individual.

Crisis intervention is a procedure that is often successfully employed by persons with training specific to the work, but without a professional mental-health education. Crises are the result of encountering hazardous emotional events in the course of daily living when the usual problem-solving techniques are not sufficient to reduce the tensions. They can lead to psychological growth or to even greater impairment. Interventions are designed to focus on the precipitating event and reduce the acute elevation of anxiety or depression by means of careful assessment of the situation, implementation of a relevant action plan, and follow-up.

There are many current applications for both brief psychotherapy and crisis intervention. They are permanently entrenched in the mental-health disciplines, and there is an abundance of new theoretical and empirical work being published in both areas. The clinician who allows himself to become proficient in brief psychotherapy or crisis intervention or both will have ample opportunity to utilize these skills in his practice, whether in a public agency or a private clinic.

References

Abramson, L. Y., Seligman, M. E. P., & Teasdale, J. D. Learned helplessness in humans: Critique and reformulation. *Journal of Abnormal Psychology*, 1978, 87, 49–74.

Aguilera, D. C., & Messick, J. M. *Crisis intervention: Theory and methodology.* (4th ed.) St. Louis: Mosby, 1982.

Albee, G. W. *Mental health manpower trends.* Joint Commission on Mental Illness and Health Monograph Series, No. 3. New York: Basic Books, 1959.

Alexander, F. Psychoanalytic contributions to short-term psychotherapy. In L. R. Wolberg (Ed.), *Short-term psychotherapy.* New York: Grune & Stratton, 1965.

Appelbaum, S. A. How long is long-term therapy? *Bulletin of the Menninger Clinic*, 1972, 36, 651–655.

Appelbaum, S. A. Parkinson's law in psychotherapy. *International Journal of Psychoanalytic Psychotherapy*, 1975, 4, 426–436.

Avnet, H. H. Short-term treatment under auspices of a medical insurance plan. *American Journal of Psychiatry*, 1965, 122, 147–151. (a)

Avnet, H. H. How effective is short-term therapy? In L. R. Wolberg (Ed.), *Short-term psychotherapy.* New York: Grune & Stratton, 1965. (b)

Bellak, L., & Small, L. *Emergency psychotherapy and brief psychotherapy.* New York: Grune & Stratton, 1965.

Bender, J. L., & Smokler, I. Early memories: A technical aid to focusing in time-limited dynamic psychotherapy. *Psychotherapy: Theory, Research, and Practice*, 1980, 17, 52–62.

Bloom, B. L. Definitional aspects of the crisis concept. *Journal of Consulting Psychology*, 1963, 27, 498–502.

Bloom, B. L. Social and community interventions. *Annual Review of Psychology*, 1980, 31, 111–142.

Brogen, K. Time-limited psychotherapy with university students. *Australian and New Zealand Journal of Psychiatry*, 1978, 12, 151–155.

Butcher, J. N., & Maudal, G. R. Crisis intervention. In I. B. Weiner (Ed.), *Clinical methods in psychology.* New York: Wiley, 1976.

Cadden, V. Crisis in the family. Appendix B. In G. Caplan (Ed.), *Principles of preventive psychiatry.* New York: Basic Books, 1964.

Caplan, G. *Principles of preventive psychiatry.* New York: Basic Books, 1964.

Castelnuovo-Tedesco, P. Brief psychotherapy. In S. Arieti (Ed.), *American handbook of psychiatry*, Vol. 5. (2nd ed.) New York: Basic Books, 1975.

Clarkin, J. F., Frances, A., Taintor, Z., & Warburg, M. Training in brief therapy: A survey of psychiatric residency programs. *American Journal of Psychiatry*, 1980, 137, 978–979.

Davanloo, H. (Ed.) *Basic principles and techniques in short-term dynamic psychotherapy.* New York: Spectrum, 1978.

Erikson, E. H. *Childhood and society.* (2nd ed.) New York: Norton, 1963.

Ewing, C. P. *Crisis intervention as psychotherapy.* New York: Oxford University Press, 1978.

Farberow, N. L., & Litman, R. E. A comprehensive suicide prevention program. Suicide Prevention Center of Los Angeles, 1958–1969. Unpublished final report DHEW NIMH Grant Nos. MH 14946 & MH 00128. Los Angeles: Suicide Prevention Center, 1970.

Farberow, N. L., & Shneidman, E. S. (Eds.) *The cry for help.* New York: McGraw-Hill, 1961.

Fenichel, O. Brief psychotherapy. In H. Fenichel & D. Rapaport (Eds.), *The collected papers of D. H. O. Fenichel.* New York: Norton, 1954.

France, K. *Crisis intervention: A handbook of immediate person-to-person help.* Springfield, Ill.: C. C. Thomas, 1982.

Freeman, D. J., Wilson, K., Thigpen, J., & McGee, R. K. Assessing intention to die in self-injury behavior. In C. Neuringer (Ed.), *Psychological assessment of suicidal risk.* Springfield, Ill.: C. C. Thomas, 1974.

Grayson, H. (Ed.) *Short-term approaches to psychotherapy.* New York: Human Sciences Press, 1979.

Hansell, N. Casualty management method: An aspect of mental health technology in transition. In H. H. Barten (Ed.), *Brief therapies.* New York: Behavioral Publications, 1971.

Hansell, N. *The person in distress.* New York: Human Sciences Press, 1976.

Harrower, M. A clinical psychologist looks at short-term therapy. In L. R. Wolberg (Ed.), *Short-term psychotherapy*. New York: Grune & Stratton, 1965.

Hoch, P. H. Short-term versus long-term therapy. In L. R. Wolberg (Ed.), *Short-term psychotherapy*. New York: Grune & Stratton, 1965.

Hoff, L. A. *People in crisis: Understanding and helping*. Menlo Park, Calif.: Addison-Wesley, 1978.

Hoyt, M. F. Aspects of termination in a time-limited brief psychotherapy. *Psychiatry*, 1979, **42**, 208–219.

Jensen, S. M., Baker, M. S., & Koepp, A. H. TA in brief psychotherapy with college students. *Adolescence*, 1980, **15**, 683–689.

Johnson, D. H., & Gelso, C. J. The effectiveness of time limits in counseling and psychotherapy: A critical review. *Counseling Psychologist*, 1980, **9**, 70–83.

Joint Commission on Mental Illness and Health. *Action for mental health*. New York: Basic Books, 1961.

Keithly, L. J., Samples, S. J., & Strupp, H. H. Patient motivation as a predictor of process and outcome in psychotherapy. *Psychotherapy and Psychosomatics*, 1980, **33**, 78–97.

Klein, D., & Lindemann, E. Preventive intervention in individual and family crisis situations. In G. Caplan (Ed.), *Prevention of mental disorders in children*. New York: Basic Books, 1961.

Knickerbocker, D. A., & McGee, R. K. Clinical effectiveness of nonprofessional and professional telephone workers in a crisis intervention center. In D. Lester & G. W. Brockopp (Eds.), *Crisis intervention and counseling by telephone*. Springfield, Ill.: C. C. Thomas, 1973.

Lieb, J., Lipsitch, I. I., & Slaby, A. E. *The crisis team: A handbook for the mental health professional*. Hagerstown, Md.: Harper & Row, 1973.

Lindemann, E. Symptomatology and management of acute grief. *American Journal of Psychiatry*, 1944, **101**, 141–148.

Lindemann, E. *Beyond grief: Studies in crisis intervention*. New York: Jason Aronson, 1979.

Malan, D. H. *A study of brief psychotherapy*. New York: Plenum, 1963.

Malan, D. H. Psychoanalytic brief psychotherapy and scientific method. In D. Bannister (Ed.), *Issues and approaches in the psychological therapies*. New York: Wiley, 1975.

Malan, D. H. *The frontier of brief psychotherapy*. New York: Plenum, 1976. (a)

Malan, D. H. *Toward the validation of dynamic psychotherapy: A replication*. New York: Plenum, 1976. (b)

Malan, D. H. Exploring the limits of brief psychotherapy. In H. Davanloo (Ed.), *Basic principles and techniques in short-term dynamic psychotherapy*. New York: Spectrum, 1978.

Mandel, H. P. (Ed.) *Short-term psychotherapy and brief therapy techniques: An annotated bibliography 1920–1980*. New York: Plenum, 1981.

Mann, J. *Time-limited psychotherapy*. Cambridge, Mass.: Harvard University Press, 1973.

Marmor, J. Short-term dynamic psychotherapy. *American Journal of Psychiatry*, 1979, **136**, 149–155.

Marziali, E. A., & Sullivan, J. M. Methodological issues in the content analysis of brief psychotherapy. *British Journal of Medical Psychology*, 1980, **53**, 19–27.

Mendelsohn, R. Critical factors in short-term psycho-therapy: A summary. *Bulletin of the Menninger Clinic*, 1978, **42**, 133–149.

McColskey, A. S. Professional crisis counseling. In G. A. Specter & W. L. Claiborn (Eds.), *Crisis intervention*. New York: Behavioral Publications, 1973. (a)

McColskey, A. S. The use of the professional in telephone counseling. In D. Lester & G. W. Brockopp (Eds.), *Crisis intervention and counseling by telephone*. Springfield, Ill.: C. C. Thomas, 1973. (b)

McGee, R. K. The suicide prevention center as a model for community mental health programs. *Community Mental Health Journal*, 1965, **1**, 162–170.

McGee, R. K. Community mental health concepts as demonstrated by suicide prevention programs in Florida. *Community Mental Health Journal*, 1968, **4**, 144–152.

McGee, R. K. *Crisis intervention in the community*. Baltimore: University Park Press, 1974.

McGee, R. K., & Heffron, E. F. The role of crisis intervention services in disaster recovery. In H. J. Parad, H. L. P. Resnik, & L. G. Parad (Eds.), *Emergency and disaster management: A mental health sourcebook*: Bowie, Md.: Charles Press, 1976.

McGee, R. K., & Jennings, B. Ascending to "lower" levels: The case for nonprofessional crisis workers. In D. Lester & G. W. Brockopp (Eds.), *Crisis intervention and counseling by telephone*. Springfield, Ill.: C. C. Thomas, 1973.

McGee, R. K., & Knickerbocker, D. A., Fowler, D. E., Jennings, B., Ansel, E. L., Zelenka, M. H., & Marcus, S. Evaluation of crisis intervention programs and personnel. *Life-Threatening Behavior*, 1972, **2**, 168–182.

Mitchell, J. T., & Resnik, H. L. P. *Emergency response to crisis*. Bowie, Md.: Robert J. Brady, 1981.

Parad, H. J. (Ed.) *Crisis intervention: Selected readings*. New York: Family Service Association of America, 1965.

Parad, H. J., & Caplan, G. A framework for studying families in crisis. In H. J. Parad (Ed.), *Crisis intervention: Selected readings*. New York: Family Service Association of America, 1965.

Parad, H. J., & Parad, L. G. A study of crisis-oriented planned short-term treatment: Part I. *Social Casework*, 1968, **49**, 346–355. (a)

Parad, H. J., Resnik, H. L. P., & Parad, L. G. (Eds.) *Emergency and disaster management: A mental health sourcebook*. Bowie, Md.: Charles Press, 1976.

Parad, L. G., & Parad, H. J. A study of crisis-oriented planned short-term treatment: Part II: *Social Casework*, 1968, **49**, 418–426. (b)

Phillips, E. L., & Wiener, D. N. *Short-term psychotherapy and structured behavior change*. New York: McGraw-Hill, 1966.

Puryear, D. A. *Helping people in crisis: A practical family-oriented approach to effective crisis intervention*. San Francisco: Jossey-Bass, 1979.

Rapoport, L. The state of crisis: Some theoretical considerations. In H. J. Parad (Ed.), *Crisis intervention: Selected readings*. New York: Family Service Association of America, 1965.

Richard, W. C. Crisis intervention services following natural disaster: The Pennsylvania recovery project. *Journal of Community Psychology*, 1974, **2**, 211–219.

Richard, W. C., & McGee, R. K. Care team: An answer

to need for suicide prevention center outreach program. In D. Lester & G. W. Brockopp (Eds.), *Crisis intervention and counseling by telephone.* Springfield, Ill.: C. C. Thomas, 1973.

Rioch, M. J., Elkes, C., Flint, A.A., Usdansky, B., Newman, R. G., & Silber, E. National Institute of Mental Health pilot study in training mental health counselors. *American Journal of Orthopsychiatry,* 1963, **33,** 678–689.

Sifneos, P. E. Two different kinds of psychotherapy of short duration. *American Journal of Psychiatry,* 1967, **123,** 1,069–1,074.

Sifneos, P. E. *Short-term psychotherapy and emotional crisis.* Cambridge, Mass.: Harvard University Press, 1972.

Sifneos, P. E. Short-term anxiety-provoking psychotherapy. In H. Davanloo (Ed.), *Basic principles and techniques in short-term dynamic psychotherapy.* New York: Spectrum, 1978.

Sifneos, P. E. *Short-term dynamic psychotherapy: Evaluation and technique.* New York: Plenum, 1979.

Sifneos, P. E., Apfel, R. J., Bassuk, E., Fishman, G., & Gill, A. Ongoing outcome research on short-term dynamic psychotherapy. *Psychotherapy and Psychosomatics,* 1980, **33,** 233–241.

Small, L. *The briefer psychotherapies.* New York: Brunner/Mazel, 1979.

Smith, L. L. Crisis intervention and planned short-term treatment. *Bulletin of the Menninger Clinic,* 1977, **41,** 273–279.

Straker, M. A review of short-term psychotherapy. *Diseases of the Nervous System,* 1977, **38,** 813–816.

Strupp, H. H. The challenge of short-term dynamic psychotherapy. In H. Davanloo (Ed.), *Basic principles and techniques in short-term dynamic psychotherapy.* New York: Spectrum, 1978.

Strupp, H. H. Success and failure in time-limited psychotherapy: A systematic comparison of two cases: Comparison 1. *Archives of General Psychiatry,* 1980, **37,** 595–603. (a)

Strupp, H. H. Success and failure in time-limited psychotherapy: A systematic comparison of two cases: Comparison 2. *Archives of General Psychiatry,* 1980, **37,** 708–716. (b)

Strupp, H. H. Success and failure in time-limited psychotherapy: With special reference to the performance of a lay counselor. *Archives of General Psychiatry,* 1980, **37,** 831–841. (c)

Strupp, H. H. Success and failure in time-limited psychotherapy: Further evidence (Comparison 4). *Archives of General Psychiatry,* 1980,. **37,** 947–954. (d)

Strupp, H. H., & Hadley, S. W. Specific vs. nonspecific factors in psychotherapy: A controlled study of outcome. *Archives of General Psychiatry,* 1979, **36,** 1,125–1,136.

Stuart, M. R., & Mackey, K. J. Defining the differences between crisis intervention and short-term therapy. *Hospital and Community Psychiatry,* 1977, **28,** 527–529.

Taplin, J. R. Crisis theory: Critique and reformulation. *Community Mental Health Journal,* 1971, 7, 13–23.

Tierney, K. J., & Baisden, B. *Crisis intervention programs for disaster victims: A sourcebook and manual for smaller communities* (DHEW Publication No. (ADM) 79-675). Washington, D.C.: U.S. Government Printing Office, 1979.

Weiner, I. B. *Principles of psychotherapy.* New York: Wiley, 1975.

Wolberg, L. R. Methodology in short-term therapy. *American Journal of Psychiatry,* 1965, **122,** 135–140. (a)

Wolberg, L. R. (Ed.) *Short-term psychotherapy.* New York: Grune & Stratton, 1965. (b)

Wolberg, L. R. *The technique of psychotherapy.* (3rd ed.) New York: Grune & Stratton, 1977.

Wolberg, L. R. *Handbook of short-term psychotherapy.* New York: Grune & Stratton, 1980.

38 CONSULTATION

Herbert C. Schulberg
Jeanette M. Jerrell

A major proportion of the psychologist's efforts as a clinician generally are spent interacting directly with patients. The many skills required to function as a diagnostician and therapist are the subject of the preceding chapters in this volume. While direct contact with patients will always be a central function of clinical psychologists, many of these professionals are aware that they can participate in the assessment and treatment process without having direct, personal contact with patients. In fact, psychologists who adopt the public health concern for populations at risk rather than just for identified cases can readily expand the number of persons upon whom they impact through consultation to other caregivers. Clinical psychologists are also recognizing that their consultative skills can be practiced not only in human-service centers but in various other organizational settings as well.

Korchin (1976) notes that consultation is as old as clinical practice itself, being an inevitable by-product of specialization in any function. The interest of psychologists in consulting with others is a relatively recent phenomenon, however. Spurred by the federal requirement in the mid-1960s that consultation be included as an essential community mental-health center service, numerous clinicians have since trained themselves or been trained in it. Indeed, clinical psychologists are among the prime practitioners of consultation. Unlike other mental-health specialists, many psychologists have been willing to venture from the security of their offices into the unfamiliar domain of other human-service providers. Psychologists displaying an ideological affinity for primary prevention have particularly viewed consultation as a relevant technique for furthering primary prevention and have become proficient at it.

Mental-health consultation is considered one of community mental health's unique technologies and an extensive literature about its process and goals has emerged in the last two decades. Caplan's (1964, 1970) seminal writings laid the foundation for much of this specialty and Grady, Gibson, and Trickett's (1981) annotated bibliography reveals that mental-health consultation continues to evolve in increasingly sophisticated directions. Although the roles and functions of mental-health consultants generally are specific to the service setting within which consultation occurs (e.g., schools and nursing homes) Grady et al. also note the recent trend of interdisciplinary conceptualization and interaction that can potentially lead to more universal and less setting-specific consultative practices.

Despite state and federal requirements that consultation be provided as an essential community mental-health service and the conceptual attractiveness of multiplying professional effectiveness through this activity, the potential envisioned for consultation as an essential mental-health center service has not been realized. Within several years of the establishment of consultation as a required service, caution was being expressed about the validity of its theoretic framework and the effectiveness of its process. Practical dilemmas grew into insurmountable barriers, such as how to assign limited staff time for indirect services in the face of incessant demands for direct patient care. These and other factors led to the repeated survey finding during the 1970s that only 4 to 6 percent of available CMHC staff time was being expended for consultation and education (Ketterer, 1981). Now, in the 1980s, the prospects for consultation within CMHCs are even more unclear. Paradoxically, as the technology of consultation is becoming increasingly sophisticated, its viability as even a limited CMHC service is threatened. Unlike direct patient care, which generates income for service rendered, consultation produces but meager, if any, revenue. In these times of fiscal austerity, it is not surprising that mental-health consultation and education are among the first services to be reduced as administrators grapple with the deficits produced by shrinking federal staffing funds.

The present developments are real and their significance cannot be minimized. Nevertheless, even though the future of consultation as a community mental-health center service is ambiguous, consultation continues to be practiced by psychologists under numerous other auspices. Using not only mental-health consultation techniques but behavioral consultation and organizational development as well, psychologists are playing a key role in rectifying problems experienced by individuals, groups, and organizations. The purpose of this chapter, therefore, is to review the role of consultation in the clinical psychologist's armamentarium, particularly as it has evolved from a technology focused primarily upon patient care to that of a specialty practiced in diverse environments for multiple purposes. We will analyze the several models within which consultation is practiced, the significant stages in the consultation process, opportunities for and constraints upon consultation in differing facilities, and strategies for evaluating consultation's efficacy. On the basis of this analysis, implications for the training of clinical psychologists will be considered. In essence, this chapter aims to succinctly assess the present state of the art regarding the practice of consultation.

Consultation Models

Just as there are differing models of psychotherapy within which the process of direct patient care can be formulated and practiced, so there are now varying models of consultation to guide the activities of those seeking to influence individual and group behavior through this alternative intervention. Heller and Monahan (1977) consider the mental-health, behavioral, and organizational development models the major models influencing psychological consultants. Each of these theoretical perspectives evolved from a different historical mission and developed goals and methods specific to that mission. Given the diversity of these consultation models, we will analyze their fundamental principles and the skills pertinent to their practice.

Mental-Health Consultation

Community mental-health practitioners who are concerned about populations at risk and not just with identified cases have long understood that all human-service providers dealing with these populations must be involved in the battle to reduce psychiatric morbidity. Subscribing to an ideology that posits the need to include providers who are untrained as well as trained in psychodynamic and psychoanalytic principles (Baker & Schulberg, 1967), community mental-health leaders started 25 years ago to experiment with procedures to sensitize non-mental-health personnel to the emotional problems of their clients. Much of this seminal work was conducted at the Harvard School of Public Health under the direction of Gerald Caplan, whose formulations of the consultation process remain pertinent to the present time. Caplan (1970) restricted the term "consultation":

> to denote a process of interaction between two professional persons—the consultant, who is a specialist, and the consultee, who invokes the consultant's help in regard to a current work problem with which he is having

some difficulty and which he has decided is within the other's area of specialized competence. The work problem involves the management or treatment of one or more clients of the consultee, or the planning or implementation of a program to cater to such clients. [p. 19]

From the logistical point of how to maximize the effectiveness of limited resources, mental-health consultation has been deemed by Caplan and others to have particular merit since it permits a relatively small number of experts (consultants) to influence a large group of nonexperts (consultees), each of whom interacts with many clients.

Much of the early consultation performed at Harvard and elsewhere was client- or consultee-centered. During the mid-1960s, however, practical requirements and theoretical developments made it evident that program-centered consultation is an equally legitimate and vital activity for skilled mental-health consultants. The traditional focus of client- and consultee-centered consultation on the dynamic-laden conflicts of individuals was expanded to consider the similar struggles faced by organizations. Their executives could benefit from the insights of a consultant capable of objectively appraising complex situations and recommending solutions; the exponential growth of human-service programs during the 1960s created fertile opportunities for program consultation. Ironically, the fiscal cutbacks and staff reductions experienced by the human-services sector during the initial years of the Reagan administration have again reinforced the need for skilled program-centered consultants. The several forms of mental-health consultation continue to be utilized by psychologists functioning in this role, and developments with regard to each will be noted briefly.

CLIENT-CENTERED CONSULTATION

The most commonly practiced form of mental-health consultation occurs in situations where human-services providers have difficulty assessing and/or treating a client. Help is sought from a specialist who may or may not meet with the client to formulate an expert opinion. The consultant's recommendation is shared with the consultee and it is the latter's responsibility to determine which aspects can be translated into a feasible plan and implemented. While this form of mental-health con-

sultation is primarily intended to meet the needs of a specific client, helping the consultee deal better with the general category of problems can also be a goal of this consultation. When the latter is the aim, the consultant probably will spend less time meeting directly with clients and instead will concentrate upon improving the consultee's ability to present valid, pertinent data for joint analysis.

Client-centered consultation is practiced in a variety of settings. The psychologist's involvement has been spurred in those instances that by statute or by regulation require that expert opinion be involved in the formulation of treatment plans. For example, school programs for students with special needs and rehabilitation programs for the mentally retarded in institutional facilities often require client-centered consultation reports. Psychologists may also contribute their expertise on a routine or ad hoc basis in general hospitals, vocational rehabilitation centers, penal facilities, substance abuse centers, and police stations. As psychologists are increasingly perceived as specialists with regard to the needs of such client populations and as their recommendations are deemed cogent and feasible, requests for client-centered consultations can be expected to grow in volume and diversity.

CONSULTEE-CENTERED CONSULTATION

In contrast to interventions focused upon a specific client or category of client problems, consultee-centered consultation focuses primarily upon those aspects of the consultee's functioning that impede his or her ability to manage the client. The goal, thus, is to improve the consultee's capacity to function effectively in relation to a broad category of cases, rather than to benefit a particular individual. Clients are not seen directly in this form of mental-health consultation; the consultant's analysis and recommendation emerge from the consultee's material, which is subject to possible distortion. Caplan (1970) considers the four most common reasons for consultee-centered consultation to be lack of knowledge, skills, self-confidence, or professional objectivity.

Given the more complex aims of consultee-centered consultation, its use is more circumscribed and a greater skill level is required to practice it. Caplan (1964, 1970) has described theme interference reduction, in particular, as a major technique of this consultative mode, and its practice requires a sophistication in psychodynamic concepts. Although proponents of mental-health consultation initially devoted much effort to consultee-centered interventions and emphasized its centrality to the upgrading of a caregiver's functioning, this approach has receded in significance with the passage of time. It remains highly useful, but in a selective rather than a universal way. We have come to realize that many of the consultee's problems cannot be readily interpreted within this conceptual framework. Furthermore, consultee-centered consultation is constrained by the fact that the consultant often must first pass through the time-consuming process of demonstrating his or her value through client-centered assistance before developing the trusting relationship essential to this consultation strategy.

PROGRAM-CENTERED CONSULTATION

As mental-health specialists became familiar with the human-services organizations in which they consulted, they realized that, in certain instances, program-centered intervention was needed if client care was to be improved. When fundamental organizational obstacles or gaps affect the quality of service, consultation must be organizationwide and not limited to specific clients or consultees. At this level of functioning, the consultant must devise a strategy for entering the organization, assembling needed information, assessing the situation, and presenting recommendations. While the process of client-centered consultation in many ways resembles that of the program-centered type, in the latter the consultant is expected to formulate a plan of action, not simply to help improve the consultee's level of understanding.

Given the action-oriented purpose of this consultative mode, it is critical that the consultant be highly skilled in acquiring pertinent data. Procedures for doing so may range from the essentially clinical-intuitive questioning of only key respondents to the gathering of information through highly structured survey instruments from all organizational members. While Caplan's (1970) approach to obtaining needed information is largely clinical, Levinson (1972, 1982) has for many years used a systematic mode of organizational diagnosis based upon a highly detailed case-study outline. The outline has a genetic orientation and it produces a comprehensive, cross-sectional description of how an organization is functioning at the present time.

The practice of program-centered consultation requires that the psychologist not only be a sophis-

ticated clinician but also proficient in organizational theory and practice, fiscal and personnel management, planning and administration, and the like. Relatively few clinical psychologists possess this array of skills and knowledge. For those who do, program-centered consultation is a particularly challenging function in the 1980s when human-services organizations are experiencing significant programmatic reductions. Hirschowitz (1982) emphasizes that these critical workplace changes provide the program-centered consultant with unusual opportunities to promote healthy organizational adaptation. Psychologists afforded such opportunities should appraise: their knowledge and skills to determine whether they can be effective; the consultee's motivation for and commitment to this type of intervention; and whether adequate resources will exist to conduct the extensive assessments and interventions associated with program-centered consultation (Birney, 1981). The significance of this latter issue is emphasized by Berlin (1979a) in his description of the various ways in which resistance to change can be manifested and some of the educative counterefforts that may be effective.

Behavioral Consultation

In contrast to mental-health consultation whose development and refinement occurred in settings with a psychodynamic if not medical orientation, behavioral consultation has emerged from more traditional psychological roots. Its theoretical constructs are derived not only from the operant and classical conditioning approaches to behavioral change but also from social-learning theory and studies of such processes as persuasion, conformity, and modeling (Bandura, 1977). Key assumptions underlying behavioral consultation are that: behavior involves complex person-environment interactions, with situational events influencing performance, cognition, and affect; behaviors are directly observable in the natural environment; and behavioral assessment (i.e., problem identification and analysis) is closely related to consultation-intervention.

Consultation was previously defined as a process in which a specialist assists another professional to resolve a difficulty the latter is experiencing in dealing with clients. In behavioral consultation, a professional skilled in behavioral-change techniques collaborates with a consultee to solve learning or adjustment problems demonstrated by the latter's clients. As with mental-health consultation, responsibility for implementing change in the client's behavior rests with the consultee; the consultant does not engage in direct behavioral interventions with the client, and the interactive process between consultant and consultee may focus upon the client or the consultee. Behavioral consultation has been utilized for program-centered purposes (e.g., establishing token economies) but these experiences are not well documented.

Behavioral consultation, like mental-health consultation, encompasses three key phases of assessment, intervention, and evaluation, but in the former they are well specified, clearly structured, and utilize highly defined techniques. Assessment is vital for identifying those variables that influence and maintain the client's focal behavior; it may be accomplished through intensive interviews, checklist or rating scales, or direct observation. The consultant's function in the assessment phase is to convey its purpose and process through a systematic framework so that the consultee may readily implement appropriate procedures. Studies by Bergan and Tombari (1975, 1976) and Tombari and Bergan (1978) indicate that the nature of the consultant-consultee interaction during the assessment stage critically influences outcome. Indices of consultant effectiveness in an assessment interview include message and content relevance, message control, and interview focus.

The intervention stage of behavioral consultation pertains to the consultee's implementation of a jointly determined remedial strategy. During this phase, the consultant's role is primarily collaborative. He or she seeks to insure through teaching, modeling, review, and feedback that the consultee possesses adequate knowledge and skill. While the variables affecting this collaborative process have only been investigated to a limited extent, some data are available regarding consultant, consultee, and system characteristics relating to the intervention phase of behavioral consultation.

The consultant must not only be knowledgeable about a wide range of behavioral strategies, he or she should also be capable of applying them flexibly. Woolfolk and Woolfolk (1979) suggest that use of technical terms detracts from consultee effectiveness. Frequency of consultant-consultee contacts and sensitivity to the consultee's affective concerns and listening skills are also related to intervention outcomes (Greiger, Mordock, & Breyer, 1970; Abidin, 1977).

Consultee characteristics affecting behavioral consultation include knowledge level, behavior, and attitudes. With regard to knowledge about principles and techniques, being provided with instruction alone is insufficient for successful implementation (O'Leary & O'Leary, 1976). An equally critical determinant for interventions based upon operant principles is the extent to which clients find the consultee's attention rewarding. The consultee's degree of personal organization and attitudes toward the client are additionally significant correlates of successful consultation.

Although little empirical research has been conducted on the relationship of organizational variables to behavioral consultation, several themes have been emphasized. Inadequate training programs, lack of administrative support, and resistance to procedural changes can impede the implementation of a behavioral consultation program. Assuming that negative employee attitudes can be diagnosed and altered so as to improve successful outcomes, Dubno et al. (1978) have developed a scale for assessing attitudes toward behavioral-modification techniques.

In summary, the sizable literature on behavioral assessment and therapy offers a rich understanding of these techniques and of how they might be used for behavioral consultation purposes. On the other hand, the very process of behavioral consultation is presently less well understood than is mental-health consultation. This is somewhat surprising considering the key role that empirically oriented psychologists have played in the former's development, and it offers a rich opportunity for productive investigations.

Organizational Development

The third model guiding the consultation activities of psychologists to public and private entities is that of organizational development. This model is rooted in diverse substantive areas, each of which represents a particular view of how organizations function, develop maladaptive procedures, and can regain stability with the aid of external consultants. The research foundation for "organizational theory" has been pursued by sociologists, and social and industrial psychologists, whereas the intervention strategies of "organizational development" have emanated from the work of social, clinical, and organizational psychologists.

In contrast to mental-health and behavioral consultation, which focus on the functioning of specific clients and consultees, organizational development is concerned with the critical components of interactive systems, i.e., people, structure, tasks, and technology. Organizational functioning can be improved by manipulating any one of these components; such manipulations, however, are likely to affect the other components as well. Furthermore, human-service facilities are subject to environmental influences so that consultants must understand that these organizations are open rather than closed systems. A major contribution of psychologists, in fact, has been their refinement of the theoretic and practical implications of organizational development in open systems (Baker, 1973; Leavitt, 1972).

The objective of organization development is generally considered to be to optimize personal and social processes and task accomplishment so as to enhance organizational performance (Friedlander & Brown, 1974). This objective is pursued through the strategies of survey feedback, small-group and intergroup development, and techno-structural interventions. In survey feedback, data are systematically collected from organizational members, analyzed, and reviewed with selected managers and/or employees. This method evolved from attitude-survey research conducted at the University of Michigan and a sizable literature points to the circumstances under which it can be used effectively for organizational development. For example, the participation of an external consultant in this process has long been recognized as facilitating problem solving and group participation (Alderfer & Ferris, 1972; Chase, 1968).

Small-group and intergroup development is rooted in the seminal research on group dynamics during the 1950s. In the ensuing decades, principles of group dynamics have evolved into such team-building techniques as sensitivity-training groups. They have been shown to improve group climate and decision making (Jerrell & Kouzes, 1982) as well as other factors related to organizational effectiveness. The use of small-group techniques in human-service facilities requires that goal setting be emphasized and concern for interpersonal issues per se reduced (French & Holliman, 1975; Plovnick, Fry, & Rubin, 1975). This diminished focus on human relations stems from the growing sophistication of sociotechnical interventions now applied in human services organizations. The complexity of contemporary medical technology and the expanded range of services provided by any single health facility, for example, require that consultants appreciate the structure of work tasks and production units. Thus, psychologists consulting within the organizational

development model have been challenged to make recommendations about the degree of specialization versus the degree of generalization to be used in the design of clinical units, the composition of management-information systems for planning and evaluation purposes, and other relevant areas.

Consultation Processes

Consultation, like most purposeful interactions between clinicians and clients, proceeds through a series of complex but definable phases. Unless the psychologist recognizes the characteristics of each phase and understands their intrinsic requirements, the risk of a nonsuccessful consultation is high. These working phases, which are common to all three of the previously described consultation models, have been defined as assessment, entry, goal development, relationship building and implementation, and termination. Since assessment, entry, and relationship building have received the greatest attention in recent years and are perhaps the most crucial phases for effective consultation, they are emphasized in the following section.

Assessment

An organization's request to undertake a consultation presents the psychologist with the challenge of analyzing the facility's covert as well as overt features. Argyris (1970) has viewed the assessment as being intended to develop valid and pertinent information, assist the consultee to appreciate the possible options for resolving identified problems, and facilitate internal commitment to change. In order to stimulate change, the consultant should be knowledgeable about the organization's present functioning, and various frameworks can be utilized for this diagnostic purpose. For example, the consultant's assessment work can be conceived as proceeding within a systems-analysis paradigm, focusing upon the organizations's formal and informal structures while building relationships with consultees. Potential problems in clarifying the informal structures include communication breakdowns, discrepant views among consultees about organizational objectives and production functions, and resistance to change. Nine steps for determining the real goals of a school system have been suggested by White (1978). A variety of quantitative as well as qualitative data-gathering procedures suited to this general purpose are described by Goodstein (1978). He emphasizes that the resulting information must be viewed as jointly owned by the consultant and consultee to facilitate cooperation.

A diagnostic model based upon six interrelated organizational factors has been developed by Weisbrod (1978). These factors are the organization's purposes and goals; the structure within which tasks are performed; the interactive patterns between people, people and tasks, and people and technology; the nature and clarity of the organization's reward system; the leadership structure and its effectiveness; and the mechanisms available to foster staff cohesiveness and commitment to organizational goals. Each of these dimensions must be considered in terms of the goodness of fit between structure and goals, and the environmental milieu within which the organization exists. It is evident then that the assessment process must incorporate organizational as well as environmental considerations for effective consultation, regardless of whether it occurs within the mental-health, behavioral, or organization development models.

Entry

Entry is the complex process whereby a consultant encounters and establishes a working relationship with the consultee and his or her organization. This process involves crossing the organizational boundary and gaining access to those members possessing knowledge of the problem and/or experiencing it so as to facilitate problem resolution. In a seminal analysis of these issues, Glidewell (1961) conceptualized the entry phase as being one of achieving a "goodness of fit" between the consultant and consultee. Factors affecting this fit include perceptions of: the problem and need for expert help; role expectations; the allocation of resources and rewards; and dependency and control. Cherniss (1976) contends that when perceptual differences vary too widely in the preentry or entry phase, they must be resolved before the consultation can proceed. Resolution of these differences is viewed by others, however, as part of the ongoing consultation process with the consultant striving to achieve sanction for potential interventions.

The organizational level at which entry occurs is critical to the success of this phase of the consultation process and to the interventions subsequently to be attempted. A "top-down" approach that provides sanctions and legitimates the consultation usually is advocated so that problems and

priorities may then be defined within the subordinate levels of the organization. However, as Berg (1979) notes, many organizations lack a sufficiently clear-cut structure to guide the consultant as to the proper entry level; in such situations, judicious judgments are required lest this process be prematurely undermined. An empirical framework to guide the consultant's judgment about entry was described by Mann (1972), who focused upon the power an organizational unit possessed relative to technical expertise, rewards, and legitimation. Significantly, Mann found that the desire for consultation is inversely related to organizational power. Hirschman (1974) also attempted to explore the consultee's position of power within an organization as it affects the use of consultation. When the consultee's self-ratings of importance and influence were correlated with the time elapsing before expert help was sought, Hirschman found a positive relationship. Personnel with high ratings waited longer to initiate consultation requests than co-workers who attributed low status to their organizational roles.

A similar but also differing conception of the entry process was offered by Baizerman and Hall (1977) who describe consultation as a bargaining process marked by various sociopolitical characteristics. Expertise, organizational position, and personal and organizational reputation are the currency of the bargaining; the consultant and consultee each attempt to maximize his or her currency at minimal personal cost. Within this perspective, many of the entry processes usually considered dysfunctional are actually the substance and focus of the consultant/consultee interaction.

A further perspective on the entry process is provided by Engelberg (1980), who suggests that it be understood in terms of open systems concepts. Drawing upon his experience as a consultant to schools in the United States and Australia, Engelberg emphasizes that various transactional processes are operating when a consultant from a mental-health system enters the educational system, and that a *modus vivendi* must be developed if intersystemic contacts are to be viable. Conceptualizing the entry process in open systems terms can produce a closer congruence between the consultant's understanding of the setting being entered and its actual reality.

In his review of the entry issues, Pipes (1981) points to the differing dynamics created when the consultant is internal or external to the organization; when the consultation is voluntarily solicited or mandated; and when the contract is fixed or subject to renegotiation in the light of evolving information. Considerably more empirical analysis is needed so that systematic decision frameworks will be available to guide those involved in this complex and often subtle process.

Relationship Building

Since the manner in which the consultant establishes a working relationship with the consultee can influence the change process and its outcome, this phase has received much attention. Caplan (1970) has detailed the tasks specific to the consultation relationship in contrast to those tasks associated with supervisory and therapeutic interactions. Sandoval, Lambert, and Davis (1977) extended Caplan's framework by pointing to the unique tasks challenging the consultee, i.e., learning the parameters of a new professional relationship, using it effectively, and discerning the manner in which he or she contributes to the problem situation. These tasks must be accomplished expeditiously given the limited resources commonly expended for consultation. Techniques available to the consultant for furthering the consultative relationship have been described by Eisdorfer and Batton (1977), and Hollister and Miller (1977). The former focus upon the consultant's attitudes toward a problem and their implications for the role to be played by him or her, e.g., buddy, provocateur, superior expert, and the like. The latter authors emphasize a problem-solving perspective that pays careful attention to the relationship's modeling component and explicitly considers additional resources that may be needed to rectify the consultee's problem.

The "goodness of fit" between consultant and consultee characteristics as it affects relationship building has been examined by several investigators. Fine, Grantham, and Wright (1979) suggest that success is enhanced when the consultant and consultee's personal and professional orientations to help giving are congruent; by their flexibility to possible solutions and comfort with ambiguity; and a willingness to spell out mutual expectations and the terms of a consultation contract. While most analysts of the relationship-building process view discrepancies between the consultant and consultee's training, style, and personal characteristics as likely impediments, Conoley (1981) views the discrepancies as potential sources of creativity and innovation.

In terms of specific consultant characteristics affecting relationship building, the literature contains much speculation but few empirical studies. Among the latter are Bergan and Tombari's (1976) finding that efficient responses to referrals, flexible application of psychological principles, and skill in eliciting information contributed to the consultant's acceptance and ability to identify the focal problem. Interestingly enough, virtually all problems that were properly identified were resolved through the consultation. Consultants perceived as collaborative were found to be more highly rated in a study by Schowengerdt, Fine, and Poggio (1976).

Finally, relationship building between consultant and consultee may occur in a dyadic or group setting. The latter is very much like a seminar experience and has many of the characteristics of a small group. Particularly pertinent to the choice of a dyadic or group setting is the difficulty some consultees have in sharing feelings with colleagues, and the issues of trust and confidentiality that arise in group consultation. When these aspects of relationship building are surmounted, consultees deem group consultation to be equally or more effective than individual consultation.

Having reviewed three of the several phases intrinsic to the consultation process, it is useful now to consider an empirical study by Martin and Curtis (1981) in which they analyzed consultant perceptions of causality for success and failure. Drawing upon attribution theory, the investigators found that school psychologists attributed both success and failure in the consultation relationship to consultee factors more than to such other factors as consultant and organizational characteristics. However, consultee factors were assigned a significantly greater role in negative than in positive relationships. Martin and Curtis note that the attributional factors of motivation, expertise, and rapport are general and relatively unsophisticated, so that further research is needed.

Consultation Settings

Consultation's early practitioners were primarily trained in schools of public health and these professionals focused upon the potential for reducing the prevalence of mental illness. Many persons at high risk for mental illness are served in public schools and public health nursing agencies and these organizations were natural targets for an indirect intervention. Consultation soon flourished in these settings, but in the last decade the practice has grown far beyond its initial environs and psychologist consultants can now be found in virtually all human-service arenas. Rogawski (1979) and Grady et al. (1981) review the practice of consultation in such additional settings as correctional agencies and police departments, the military, industry, hospitals, churches, and community residences. While the full scope of current consultation practice cannot be conveyed here, a sampling of these efforts is presented to illustrate the richness of opportunity awaiting psychologists willing to utilize their expertise in improving the skills of other human-service professionals.

The range of educational and other human services provided preschool and school-age children has grown exponentially as the result of Great Society legislation in the late 1960s. Although some efforts at aiding socially, physically, and psychologically handicapped youngsters have decreased as the result of funding cutbacks in the 1980s, consultation still continues as a vital practice at countless schools and other agencies serving youngsters and adolescents. In this regard, Berlin (1979b) reviews the changing nature of schools and emphasizes that educational institutions now play a different societal role because of increased urbanization, busing decisions, heightened community organization activities, and the like. The schools have assumed responsibility for the early identification and education of children with developmental disabilities, and even early intervention with infants of high-risk mothers. While the psychologist's role in consulting with grade-school teachers is reasonably clear-cut, consultative opportunities in these more recent undertakings still need to be refined. The work of Frank and Gordetsky (1976), and Birney (1981) in preschool settings suggest directions in which these efforts may be pursued.

With regard to troubled adolescents, the school's educational and guidance roles in many ways have been supplanted by alternative, nontraditional agencies such as runaway houses and crisis intervention centers. Effective consultation in these settings requires a keen awareness of their historical context, the community dynamics affecting their viability, and the service flexibility that they need to remain responsive. Gordon (1979) suggests, furthermore, that the consultant to alternative agencies cannot maintain the usual posture of external observer but must become an integral part of these organizations if his or her expertise is to be accepted and utilized.

Despite the high prevalence of emotional illness in the clients of public welfare agencies, mental-health professionals have devoted scant effort to this sector of the human services. Psychologists in particular have displayed little appreciation for the complex needs of public welfare workers and their clients, generally concluding that consultation cannot be effectively utilized in this context. The frequent personnel changes that plague public welfare agencies, the political reorganizations to which they are susceptible, and their unpredictable funding status undoubtedly contribute to the above conclusion. Nevertheless, the prevalence of pathology in public welfare clients and the proneness of their caseworkers to rapid burnout makes this less than hospitable environment deserving of continued consultation effort on the part of the psychologists.

Another client group with high need that could benefit from consultation are persons living in community residences. The consultant's role in helping with the development and operation of such facilities for the psychiatrically ill are described by Budson (1979) and Peterson (1979). Budson suggests that in contrast to the usual developmental sequence in which program consultation succeeds client and consultee-centered consultation, the unique needs of community residences require that the process be reversed. Only when the staff of such facilities are comfortable with their own roles and have established a viable therapeutic environment can they meaningfully consider the issues typically raised in client-centered consultation.

While psychologists have a long history of consulting within various human-service programs, their ability to perform this role within general hospitals is a more recent development. The psychologist's expertise has long been utilized on such services as those serving tubercular patients but it is only in the past several years that other medical units have recognized the psychologist's potential contribution (Gabinet & Friedson, 1980). Among the most promising consultation opportunities at present are those in pediatric hospitals, where the intense emotional needs of seriously ill children often overwhelm the staff responsible for their care. Emerging roles for psychologists in these pediatric facilities include client-centered and consultee-centered consultation on surgical and neurological wards (Geist, 1977; Hartlage & Hartlage, 1978). Building upon several years of experience in client-centered consultation with the staff of a pediatric oncology service, Koocher, Sourkes, and Keane (1979) evolved their roles from a crisis orientation to one in which the overall care-giving system became the focus of attention.

Another sector of the human services in which psychological consultation is having a growing impact is that serving elderly clients. In nursing homes, psychologists may consult on individual residents, educate staff, advocate for program change, and perform community liaison tasks (Hyerstay, 1979). Since the psychologist's role in nursing homes and hospices still is a relatively unfamiliar one, he or she must be careful not to impose professional opinions upon the staff and volunteers of these facilities. The psychologist should instead help clarify client-centered or organizational problems, and facilitate staff and volunteer ability to manage routine problems (Noll & Sampsell, 1978).

Finally, consultation opportunities exist for psychologists to enhance the skills of nonprofessionals whose contributions are vital for a community's mental health. Consultation with the clergy has been well accepted for many years but it has proceeded slowly at best. Kaseman and Anderson (1977) emphasize the great potential that the clergy have with regard to primary prevention and the consequent value of enhancing their pastoral skills. The psychologist's work with self-help organizations has grown in recent years but the dynamics of consulting to these groups still requires much investigation.

Evaluating Consultation Services

The early years of consultation's development were marked primarily by a concern for theoretical principles and techniques. Little attention was devoted through the 1960s to systematic research and evaluation, although nascent awareness of this need was already evident in the nearly 20 such reports reviewed by Mannino and Shore (1975). The number of studies evaluating consultation programs has escalated over the past decade, and while obstacles to the evaluation process still continue (Ahmed & Tims, 1977; Meyers et al., 1978; Windle & Flaherty, 1979), the quality of evaluations has improved markedly. Medway (1982) states that, "today we recognize that it is misleading to ask if consultation is effective or if one technique is better than another without taking into account the particular consultation model that is being evaluated, since the adoption of one or an-

other model will at least theoretically determine whether treatments will be directed at consultees, clients, and/or systems and whether evaluation will be exclusively behavioral or will include affective and attitudinal components" (p. 423). In addition to this conceptual refinement, methodological advances can be discerned as well in the study of consultation's effectiveness. The use of experimental and control groups has become routinized, standardized instruments are now employed to gather data about process and outcome, and the limitations of a study's generalizability are readily acknowledged. In particular, it is recognized that many of the previous evaluations were conducted at exceptional demonstration projects and so are not directly useful to administrators of more typical consultation services.

Given these advances and the need for an evaluation framework applicable to typical as well as exceptional consultation programs, the following section presents an assessment model useful for those requiring routinized planning and evaluation tools. The four components of the evaluation model pertain to systems resource management, process evaluation, outcome evaluation, and impact evaluation. The relevant assessment functions and domains of executive responsibility are considered for each component, thus emphasizing Attkisson and Broskowski's (1978) conviction that effective evaluations depend upon proper administrator-evaluation roles and an adequate informational capacity within the agency.

Systems Resource Management

Systems resource management is concerned with the internal operations of an organization. With regard to consultation activities, evaluation's function includes assisting in the formulation of program goals that are based on statutory mandates or documented need; framing information needed to set program priorities; identifying and allocating resources; and translating program priorities into measurable intervention strategies.

Needs assessment is a common starting point in the design of new services and frequently is accomplished through the analysis of social-indicator and public-survey data. While this approach is useful for planning clinical interventions, it rarely provides the information relevant to consultation. More specific data are needed to determine which client populations or provider groups would benefit from this indirect service. No comprehensive format yet exists for evaluators to assess the need for consultation but an example of pertinent data-gathering procedures is found in Taylor and Vineberg's (1978) survey of school problems potentially amenable to this form of external intervention. They assembled data on: the demographic characteristics of the school and its surrounding community; environmental factors affecting school programs and procedures; school characteristics such as curriculum and resources; staff characteristics; and the principal's appraisal of school strengths and weaknesses. Taylor and Vineberg's approach has many features of the organizational assessment strategy discussed earlier and could be utilized with each of the three consultation models.

A monitoring system is a means of continuously collecting data relevant to policy and service-delivery decisions. Much of the data presently collected by mental-health centers is used to satisfy administrative reporting requirements, with little understanding of its relevance to agency decision makers. Mannino and MacLennan (1978), therefore, explicate the uses that can be made by mental-health centers of data derived from their consultants' activity logs or checklists about the community's need for this service and the degree to which it is being met.

Process Evaluation

The delivery of consultation services can be monitored through data that reliably describe consultee characteristics and the volume of services provided them. Although these data typically are assembled primarily for external reporting purposes, when combined with outcome measures they can also suggest strategies for improving consultation's efficiency, effectiveness, and relevance. The consultation activities monitored in process evaluation differ among agencies but they are generally selected within the framework of: *Who did what to whom, when, where, and how often?* When such indices are constructed, the monitoring process can document not only consultation's very occurrence but also the relative use of specific consultation techniques, shifts in orientation and goals, and other factors potentially germane to the consultation's outcome.

A decade ago, Mannino and Shore (1972) considered process evaluation as still being a nascent state. The prior studies had indeed focused upon variables pertinent to the consultation process but they were hampered by methodological and con-

ceptual limitations. Norman and Forti (1972), for example, investigated how the developing consultant-consultee relationship affects the latter's objectivity, problem-solving ability, and work competency. However, the lack of adequate instruments for measuring the unfolding relationship obscured the meaning of their findings. Bergman and Tombari (1976) similarly investigated the effect of process variables on consultation outcome but their data collection was more valid and more credence can be ascribed to their finding that consultant efficiency, interviewing skill, and flexibility in applying psychological principles enhance problem identification. While process evaluations have limited utility in the absence of outcome studies, when the latter are available they significantly advance our comprehension of which facets of the consultant-consultee interaction contribute to success and which to failure.

Not all data collected for process-monitoring purposes are readily quantified. For example, the recently developed Joint Commission on the Accreditation of Hospitals quality-of-care indices for consultation services pertain to abstract organizational policies and procedures rather than measurable consultative services. Administrators, evaluators, and consultants should, therefore, consider the quality and utility of the information needed relative to the decisions to be made when undertaking process evaluation.

The manner in which utilization review and quality assurance data can be used to assess the consultation process is described by Hoven et al. (1979). Questionnaires completed by consultees at the start of the relationship and every six months thereafter provide a systematic record of the service's daily operations, its client populations, goals, and resources utilized. In this approach to quality assurance, the performance attributes associated with effective consultation can serve as observable criteria, i.e., whether specific goals were established with the consultee, anticipated services were rendered, and goals achieved within the expected time frame.

Outcome Evaluation

The effects of a consultation program can be investigated through a comparison of the obtained results with expected goals and/or other criteria that judge the program's value. Data required for this type of evaluation may be obtained through either routine monitoring procedures or from special studies; the type of clinical or administrative decision to be made will determine whether the former or the latter strategy is more appropriate. When maximal validity is needed, such as for determining whether to maintain a controversial service, special studies are preferable but they usually require highly skilled evaluators and expensive data collection.

Early studies of consultation's effectiveness focused essentially upon goal achievement. In their initial review of consultation outcome studies, Mannino and Shore (1972) distinguished between immediate outcome (affecting change in the consultee's knowledge and skills), intermediate outcome (affecting change throughout the consultee's organization), and long-range outcome (affecting change in the clients served). Of the studies focused upon immediate outcome, Mannino and Shore determined that about half demonstrated significant positive results. Studies concerned with intermediate and long-term outcome essentially yielded insignificant findings. Mannino and Shore, therefore, concluded that consultation's far-reaching consequences were difficult to demonstrate.

In their more recent review of outcome studies, Mannino and Shore (1979) found that a growing number of evaluations are attempting to determine whether consultation produces change beyond the consultee. Over two-thirds of such studies have utilized control or comparison groups, a development that represents significant movement toward greater research rigor. As in the past, Mannino and Shore found that consultation's effectiveness with consultees is reasonably well demonstrated. However, they also determined in this more recent analysis that even the more complex goal of producing change beyond the consultee was partially or totally achieved in 81 percent of the studies reviewed.

Schools are the dominant setting within which outcome evaluations have been conducted; only 5 of the 54 studies reviewed by Mannino and Shore (1979) were performed in another setting. These assessments of school consultation have been concerned with pre-post teacher perceptions of and attitudes toward student behavior; they have utilized direct observations of student performance, direct observations of teacher-student interaction, and student performance on achievements tests as criterion measures. Other pertinent outcome criteria include the teacher's knowledge of child development, teacher's self-concept, and school-community relationships. Outcome assessments in nonschool settings have employed a wide variety of indices and data-gathering procedures suited to their particular purpose.

Curiously, much of the recent outcome literature is comprised of doctoral dissertations. While this is a positive trend among academic advisors, indicating their acknowledgment of consultation as an area for scholarly pursuit, Mannino and Shore (1979) also note that student research cannot substitute for that conducted by professionals whose experience, competence, and sensitivity to consultation surpass those of graduate investigators. In particular, Mannino and Shore urge that sophisticated assessments be performed of program-centered consultation since this intervention has been deemed to have great potential payoff. The methodologies and results of such an investigation of program-oriented consultation provided to 80 mental-health organizations were reviewed by Larsen (1982). Using an experimental design, she found that a four-month follow-up, organizations receiving the consultation reported no greater problem-solving ability than the control facilities that received no such consultation. However, upon eight-month follow-up, the former facilities were significantly more successful than the latter ones at solving problems. Larsen's data suggest that program-centered consultation takes time to manifest its effects and evaluators must be aware of this gestation phase in selecting follow-up time frames.

Impact Evaluation

Impact evaluation is the least technically developed evaluation strategy but it is also the most pertinent for ascertaining consultation's preventive effects. This level of analysis seeks to determine whether consultation activities such as advising about the structure of comprehensive service-delivery networks or stimulating citizen input to program planning ultimately affect the nature and quality of services provided to clients. Such assessments require that evaluators shift their focus away from typical criteria of intraorganizational effectiveness and examine instead the consultant's functioning across organizational boundaries.

The National Institutes of Mental Health and other groups have formulated criteria for ascertaining the broad impact of clinical services upon a community, but no similar guidelines have been established with respect to consultation. Several elements of such a framework for consultation were described by Hagedorn et al. (1976), but their material does not sufficiently distinguish criteria evaluating consultee outcomes from those assessing impact upon other agencies or professionals. The present reality, then, is that each attempt to evaluate consultation's impact must specify the particular goals and criteria uniquely suited to that study. An example of this approach to impact evaluation is seen in Rinn, Turner, and Markle's (1979) analysis of the percentage of clients discussed in consultation who later became direct-service recipients at a mental-health center. This rate was monitored over several years; the resulting data suggested that consultation was effective in reducing the number of clients later needing clinical care.

Training Implications

The preceding review of consultation frameworks and their continuing application in a wide variety of human-service settings suggests that the issue for clinical psychologists is not whether they should be trained in consultation techniques but rather how those skills should be acquired. Indeed, the greatest complaint expressed by students who evaluated their graduate clinical training was their poor preparation to play the consultant role thrust upon them after leaving the university (Swensen, 1978). This problem undoubtedly persists for the graduates of many university training centers and solutions are long overdue. While informal educational strategies of the type described by Manos (1981) have merit, they leave too much to the vagaries of particular circumstances, and the acquisition of needed conceptual frameworks is rendered unduly difficult. Given the need for systematic approaches to the training of psychologists for the role of consultant, several such efforts were analyzed in a 1973 APA symposium. Its contents remain pertinent almost a decade later; features of some of these presentations will be described briefly here.

Psychologists often are called upon to consult with educators, parents, and childcare workers about a variety of issues pertaining to childhood development. Stollack (1978) describes courses, material, and techniques to help graduate students acquire experience with and knowledge of child development from conception through eight years of age. The students are taught how to impart this knowledge to prospective and exsiting

parents, teachers, and others involved in early child care, education, and rearing. Stollack presents a scheme for evaluating the effects of this consultation; he suggests that change be assessed in the student consultants, the parent consultees, and the children whom these adults encounter.

The behavioral consultation model described earlier is commonly utilized in school settings, and Dorr (1978) offers guidelines for the training of graduate students in its use. He emphasizes distinctions between the behavioral approach and psychodynamically oriented consultation, noting that the former makes heavy use of *in vivo* modeling as the major procedure for communicating with teachers. The consultant lectures very little and starts direct interaction with youngsters as soon as possible to ensure that the consultee fully understands what is being advocated. A description of how behavioral consultation can be taught to school psychologists is provided by Kratochwill and Bergan (1978), whose major focus is upon the design of psychological service systems that would link the family, school, and other institutions responsible for guiding childhood development. Their training model is developed in the context of applied behavioral psychology which articulates training competencies and service goals in school settings.

The emergence of these and similar training programs for refining the psychologist's consultation skills has created the need to evaluate the efficacy of such educational efforts. Broskowski (1978) suggests that the assessment of training is quite formidable because it involves the distinct yet interrelated domains of consultation, education, and program evaluation. Strategies of varying methodological stringency can be utilized for this purpose but Broskowski espouses a fairly rigorous one incorporating the features of quasi-experimental design. Its application in assessing the postgraduate functioning of consultants trained at Harvard Medical School illustrates that such educational evaluations are indeed feasible. However, Broskowski's evaluative model focuses primarily upon the consultant and does not examine the consequences of his or her training upon clients served and/or the organizations within which consultations are conducted.

The proclivity of clinical psychologists for functioning as consultants will vary in keeping with their orientation to the process of change, their capacity for appreciating that indirect services provided through others can be as effective as those provided personally, and the demands of the organizational setting within which they are functioning. Regardless of their position on these and similar issues, psychologists inevitably will be called upon to function as consultants. Therefore, it behooves them to be prepared when this challenge arises and to be familiar with the role characteristics and tasks associated with consultation in contrast to therapy, supervision, and education.

Summary

Psychologists are practicing consultation in increasingly diverse settings and it is now one of the key skills that members of this discipline can offer to groups requiring the expertise of a mental-health professional. Community mental-health centers spawned much of the interest in consultation during the 1960s and 1970s. While the involvement of these centers is presently tenuous because of funding restrictions, psychologists working in numerous other facilities have developed and maintained their proficiency as consultants. The dominant conceptual models within which consultation is practiced are mental-health, behavioral, and organizational development. Psychologists have a particular affinity for the behavioral approach, given its foundation in learning theory; they have refined its practice in schools and elsewhere. The evaluation of consultation's efficacy continues to be a major need. Methodological advances in such studies are evident and the recent involvement of universities in outcome research is particularly welcomed. Procedures for the training of graduate students in the practice of consultation have advanced as well. Here again, a major commitment by universities to this task would be of great help in advancing the state of the art.

References

Abidin, R. Operant behavioral consultations as conducted by master's and doctoral level psychologists in Virginia. *School Psychology*, 1977, **15**, 225–229.

Ahmed, P., & Tims, F. Some considerations in evaluating school consultation programs. In S. Plog & P. Ahmed (Eds.), *Principles and techniques of mental health consultation*. New York: Plenum, 1977.

Alderfer, C., & Ferriss, A. Understanding the impact of survey feedback. In W. Burke & H. Hornstein (Eds.), *The social technology of organizational development*. Fairfax, Va.: NTL Learning Resources, 1972.

Argyris, C. *Intervention theory and method*. Reading, Mass.: Addison-Wesley, 1970.

Attkisson, C., & Broskowski, A. Evaluation and the emerging human service concept. In C. Attkisson, W. Hargreaves, M. Horowitz, & J. Sorensen (Eds.), *Evaluation of human service programs*. New York: Academic Press, 1978.

Baizerman, J., & Hall, W. Consultation as a political process. *Community Mental Health Journal*, 1977, **13**, 142–149.

Baker, F., & Schulberg, H. The development of a Community Mental Health Ideology Scale. *Community Mental Health Journal*, 1967, **3**, 216–225.

Baker, F. *Organizational systems: General systems approaches to complex organizations*. Homewood, Ill.: Richard D. Irwin, 1973.

Bandura, A. *Social learning theory*. Englewood Cliffs, N.J.: Prentice-Hall, 1977.

Berg, D. Failure at entry. In P. Mirvis & D. Berg (Eds.), *Failures in organization development and change*. New York: Wiley, 1977.

Bergan, J., & Tombari, M. The analysis of verbal interactions occurring during consultation. *School Psychology*, 1975, **13**, 209–226.

Bergan, J., & Tombari, M. Consultant skill and efficiency and the implementation and outcomes of consultation. *School Psychology*, 1976, **14**, 3–14.

Berlin, I. Resistance to mental health consultation directed at change in public institutions. *Community Mental Health Journal*, 1979, **15**, 119–128. (a)

Berlin, I. New approaches in school mental health consultation. In A. Rogawski (Ed.), *Mental health consultation in community settings*. San Francisco: Jossey-Bass, 1979. (b)

Birney, D. Consulting with administrators: The consultee-centered approach. In J. C. Conoley (Ed.), *Consultation in schools*. New York: Academic Press, 1981.

Broskowski, A. Evaluation of consultation training programs. *Professional Psychology*, 1978, **2**, 210–219.

Budson, R. Consultation to halfway houses. In A. Rogawski (Ed.), *Mental health consultation in community settings*. San Francisco: Jossey-Bass, 1979.

Caplan, C. *Principles of preventive psychiatry*. New York: Basic Books, 1964.

Caplan, G. *Theory and practice of mental health consultation*. New York: Basic Books, 1970.

Chase, P. A survey feedback approach to organization development. In *Proceedings of the Executive Study Conference*. Princeton: Educational Testing Service, 1968.

Cherniss, C. Creating new consultation programs in community mental health centers. *Community Mental Health Journal*, 1977, **13**, 133–141.

Conoley, J. The process of change: The agent of change. In J. Conoley (Ed.), *Consultation in schools*. New York: Academic Press, 1981.

Dorr, D. Training for rapid behavioral consultation. *Professional Psychology*, 1978, **9**, 198–202.

Dubno, P., Hillburn, D., Robinson, G., Sandler, D., Trani, J., & Weingarten, E. An attitude toward behavior modification scale. *Behavior Therapy*, 1978, **9**, 99–108.

Eisdorfer, C., & Batton, L. The mental health consultant as seen by his consultees. *Community Mental Health Journal*, 1972, **8**, 171–177.

Engelberg, S. Open systems consultation: Some lessons learned from case experience. *Professional Psychology, 1980, **11**, 972–979.

Fine, M., Grantham, V., & Wright, J. Personal variables that facilitate or impede consultation. *Psychology in the Schools*, 1979, **16**, 533–539.

Frank, T., & Gordetsky, S. Child-focused mental health consultation in settings for young children. *Young Children*, 1976, **32**, 339–344.

French, W., & Holliman, R. Management by objectives: The team approach. *California Management Review*, 1975, **17**, 13–22.

Friedlander, F., & Brown, L. Organization development. *Annual Review of Psychology*, **25**, 313–341.

Gabinet, L., & Friedson, W. The psychologist as front-line mental health consultant in a general hospital. *Professional Psychology*, 1980, **11**, 939–945.

Geist, R. Consultation on a pediatric surgical ward: Creating an empathic climate. *American Journal of Orthopsychiatry*, 1977, **47**, 432–444.

Goodstein, L. D. *Consulting with human service systems.* Reading, Mass.: Addison-Wesley, 1978.

Gordon, J. Consultation with youth programs. In A. Rogawski (Ed.), *Mental health consultation in community settings.* San Francisco: Jossey-Bass, 1979.

Grady, M., Gibson, M., & Trickett, E. *Mental health consultation theory, practice, and research, 1973–1978.* DHHS Publication No. (ADM) 81-948. Washington, D.C.: U.S. Government Printing Office, 1981.

Greiger, R., Mordock, J., & Breyer, N. General guidelines for conducting behavior modification programs in public school settings. *School Psychologist*, 1970, **8**, 259–266.

Hagedorn, H., Beck, K., Neubert, S., & Werlin, S. A *working manual of simple program evaluation techniques for community mental health centers.* Washington, D.C.: U.S. DHEW, 1976.

Hartlage, L. C., & Hartlage, P. L. Clinical consultation to pediatric neurology and developmental pediatrics. *Clinical Child Psychology*, 1978, **7**, 19–20.

Heller, K., & Monohan, J. *Psychology and community change.* Homewood, Ill.: Dorsey, 1977.

Hirschman, R. Utilization of mental health consultation and self-perceptions of intra-organizational importance and influence. *Journal of Consulting and Clinical Psychology*, 1974, **42**, 916.

Hirschowitz, R. Consultation to changing organizations. In H. Schulberg & M. Killilea (Eds.), *The modern practice of community health.* San Francisco: Jossey-Bass, 1982.

Hollister, W. G., & Miller, F. T. Problem-solving strategies in consultation. *American Journal of Orthopsychiatry*, 1977, **47**, 445–450.

Hoven, C., Schwartz, A., Seiffer, S., & Mandell, D. Quality assurance and utilization review in evaluating consultation and education services. In G. Landesberg, W. Neigher, R. Hammer, C. Windle, & J. Woy (Eds.), *Evaluation in practice: A sourcebook of program evaluation studies from mental health care systems in the United States.* Washington, D.C.: U.S. DHEW, 1979.

Hyerstay, B. The role of the psychologist in a nursing home. *Professional Psychology*, 1979, **10**, 36–41.

Jerrell, J., & Kouzes, J. Organization development in mental health agencies. *Administration in Mental Health* (in press).

Kaseman, C. M., & Anderson, R. G. Clergy consultation as a community mental health program. *Community Mental Health Journal*, 1977, **13**, 84–91.

Ketterer, R. *Consultation and education in mental health.* Beverly Hills, Calif.: Sage, 1981.

Koocher, G., Sourkes, B., & Keane, W. Pediatric oncology consultations: A generalizable model for medical settings. *Professional Psychology*, 1979, **18**, 467–474.

Korchin, S. *Modern clinical psychology.* New York: Basic Books, 1976.

Kratochwill, T., & Bergan, J. Training school psychologists: Some perspectives on a competency-based behavioral consultation model. *Professional Psychology*, 1978, **9**, 71–82.

Larsen, J. Does consultation work? Reviewing the research evidence. *Consultation*, 1982, **1**, 25–33.

Leavitt, H. J. *Managerial psychology.* (3rd ed.) Chicago: University of Chicago Press, 1972.

Levinson, H. *Organizational diagnosis.* Cambridge, Mass.: Harvard University Press, 1972.

Levinson, H. Organizational diagnosis: Manner and method. In H. Schulberg & M. Killilea (Eds.), *The modern practice of community mental health.* San Francisco: Jossey-Bass, 1982.

Mann, P. A. Accessibility and organizational power in the entry phase of mental health consultation. *Journal of Consulting and Clinical Psychology*, 1972, **38**, 215–218.

Mannino, F., & MacLennan, B. *Monitoring and evaluating mental health consultation and education services.* Washington, D.C.: U.S. DHEW, 1978.

Mannino, F., & Shore, M. Research in mental health consultation. In S. Golan & C. Eisdorfer (Eds.), *Handbook of community mental health.* New York: Appleton-Century-Crofts, 1972.

Mannino, F., & Shore, M. The effects of consultation: A review of the literature. *American Journal of Community*, 1975, **3**, 1–21.

Mannino, F., & Shore, M. Effects of consultation: Problems and prospects. In A. Rogawski (Ed.), *Mental health consultation in community settings.* San Francisco: Jossey-Bass, 1979.

Manos, N. Resistances encountered in the consultation-training of the community mental health worker. *International Journal of Social Psychiatry*, 1981, **1**, 33–36.

Martin, R., & Curtis, M. Consultants' perceptions of causality for success and failure of consultation. *Professional Psychology*, 1981, **12**, 670–676.

Medway, F. School consultation research: Past trends and future directions. *Professional Psychology*, 1982, **13**, 422–430.

Meyers, J., Pitt, N., Gaughan, E., & Friedman, M. A research model for consultation with teachers. *Journal of School Psychology*, 1978, **16**, 137–145.

Noll, G., & Sampsell, M. The community and the dying. *Journal of Community Psychology*, 1978, **6**, 275–279.

Norman, E., & Forti, T. A study of the process and outcome of mental health consultation. *Community Mental Health Journal*, 1972, **8**, 261–267.

O'Leary, K., & O'Leary, S. (Eds.), *Classroom management: The successful use of behavior modification.* (2nd ed.) New York: Pergamon, 1976.

Peterson, C. Consultation to residential facilities. In A. Rogawski (Ed.), *Mental health consultation in community settings*. San Francisco: Jossey-Bass, 1979.

Pipes, R. Consulting in organizations. The entry problem. In J. C. Conoley (Ed.), *Consultation in schools*. New York: Academic Press, 1981.

Plovnick, M., Fry, R., & Rubin, I. New developments in OD technology. *Training and Development Journal*, April 1975.

Rinn, R., Turner, A., & Markle, A. Evaluation of consultation and education services in a CMHC. In G. Landsberg, W. Neigher, R. Hammer, C. Windle, & J. Woy (Eds.), *Evaluation in practice: A sourcebook of program evaluation studies from mental health care systems in the United States*. Washington, D.C.: U.S. DHEW, 1979.

Rogawski, A. (Ed.) *Mental health consultation in community settings*. San Francisco: Jossey-Bass, 1979.

Sandoval, J., Lambert, N., & Davis, J. Consultation *from the consultee's perspective. Journal of School Psychology*, 1977, **15**, 334–342.

Schowengerdt, R., Fine, M., & Poggio, J. An examination of some bases of teacher satisfaction with school psychological services. *Psychology in the Schools*, 1976, **13**, 264–275.

Stollack, G. Graduate education for early childhood consultation. *Professional Psychology*, 1978, **9**, 185–192.

Swenson, C. A symposium on evaluation of training for consultation. *Professional Psychology*, 1978, **9**, 185–192.

Taylor, E., & Vineberg, R. Evaluation of indirect services to schools. In C. Attkisson, W. Hargreaves, M. Horowitz, & J. Sorensen (Eds.), *Evaluation of human service programs*. New York: Academic Press, 1978.

Tombari, M., & Bergan, J. Consultant cues and teacher verbalizations, judgments, and expectancies concerning children's adjustment problems. *Journal of School Psychology*, 1978, **16**, 212–219.

Weisbrod, M. *Organizational diagnosis: A workbook of theory and practice*. Reading Mass.: Addison-Wesley, 1978.

White, M. Identifying a school's real agenda: Nine steps. *Journal of School Psychology*, 1978, **16**, 292–300.

Windle, C., & Flaherty, F. Indirect services: Consultation, education, and interagency relationships. In G. Landsberg, W. Neigher, R. Hammer, C. Windle, & J. Woy (Eds.). *Evaluation in practice: A sourcebook of program evaluation studies from mental health care systems in the United States*. Washington, D.C.: U.S. DHEW, 1979.

Woolfolk, R., & Woolfolk, A. Modifying the effect of the behavior modification label. *Behavior Therapy*, 1979, **10**, 575–578.

AUTHOR INDEX

SUBJECT INDEX

ABOUT THE EDITORS AND CONTRIBUTORS

The Editors

Michel Hersen (Ph.D., State University of New York at Buffalo, 1966) is Professor of Psychiatry and Psychology at the University of Pittsburgh. He is the Past President of the Association for Advancement of Behavior Therapy. He has co-authored, edited, and co-edited 26 books including: *Single-case experimental designs: Strategies for studying behavior change, Behavior therapy in the psychiatric setting, Behavior modification: An introductory textbook, Introduction to clinical psychology, The clinical psychology handbook,* and *The practice of outpatient behavior therapy.* With Bellack, he is editor and founder of *Behavior Modification* and *Clinical Psychology Review.* He is Associate Editor of *Addictive Behaviors* and Editor of *Progress in behavior modification.* Dr. Hersen is the recipient of several NIMH research and training grants.

Alan E. Kazdin (Ph.D., Northwestern University) is Professor of Child Psychiatry and Psychology and Research Director of the Child Psychiatric Treatment Service in the Department of Psychiatry, Western Psychiatric Institute and Clinic, University of Pittsburgh School of Medicine. He has been a past President of the Association for Advancement of Behavior Therapy, a Fellow of the Center for Advanced Study in the Behavioral Sciences, and Editor of *Behavior Therapy.* His books include: *Research Design in Clinical Psychology, Single-Case Research Designs, Behavior Modification in Applied Settings,* and the *History of Behavior Modification.* Dr. Kazdin's current research focuses on the assessment and treatment of childhood psychopathology, particularly depression and conduct disorder.

Alan S. Bellack (Ph.D., Pennsylvania State University, 1970) is Professor of Psychiatry at the Medical College of Pennsylvania and was formerly Professor of Psychology and Psychiatry and Director of Clinical Psychology Training at the University of Pittsburgh. He is co-author and co-editor of seven books including: *Behavior Modification: An Introductory Textbook, Research and Practice in Social Skills Training,* and *Introduction to Clinical Psychology.* He has published numerous journal articles and has received several NIMH research grants on social skills, behavioral assessment, and weight control. With Hersen, he is editor and founder of the journals *Behavior Modification* and

Clinical Psychology Review. He has served on the editorial boards of numerous journals and has been a consultant to a number of publishing companies and mental health facilities as well as NIMH.

The Contributors

Geary S. Alford, Ph.D. is Associate Professor of Psychiatry and Psychology, Assistant Professor of Pharmacology and Toxicology, and Clinical Assistant Professor of Family Medicine at the University of Mississippi Medical Center. A former recipient of a Career Medical Teacher Fellowship from the National Institute of Drug Abuse and the National Institute of Alcoholism and Alcohol Abuse, he has published articles and book chapters on a wide range of behavioral disorders and therapies. He is on the editorial board of *Behavior Modification* and serves as editorial consultant for a number of other journals.

Christopher R. Barbrack, Ph.D., is Assistant Professor at the Graduate School of Applied and Professional Psychology, Rutgers University. His major interests are in behavioral consultation, group behavior therapy, and evaluation of psychological interventions.

Kelly M. Bemis is a Doctoral Candidate of Clinical Psychology at the University of Minnesota. She has published in major journals including a major review of anorexia nervosa and the cognitive approach to its treatment. She is Coordinator of Notes and Announcements for the *Journal of Cognitive Therapy and Research.*

Roger Blashfield, Ph.D. is an Associate Professor of Psychology in the Department of Psychiatry at the University of Florida. His major area of interest is psychiatric classification.

Sidney J. Blatt, Ph.D., is a Professor of Psychology and Psychiatry at Yale University. He is Chief of the Psychology Section in the Department of Psychiatry and a member of the faculty of the Western New England Institute for Psychoanalysis. He has published extensively on topics in psychopathology, personality assessment and has recently been integrating cognitive developmental and psychoanalytic theory in the investigation of the development of mental representation and its impairment in different forms of psychopathology,

especially schizophrenia, depression, and the neuroses.

Theodore H. Blau received his Ph.D. from Pennsylvania State University in 1951. He has been in independent practice in Tampa, Florida since 1953. His major areas of research include neuropsychology, quality of life, and forensic issues. In 1977 he was President of the American Psychological Association.

Meg A. Bond is a Research Associate at the Institute for the Study of Developmental Disabilities, University of Illinois at Chicago. She recently completed her clinical internship at the University of Colorado Health Sciences Center in Denver and expects her degree in clinical/community psychology from the University of Oregon in 1983. Her major interests revolve around the development and evaluation of treatment and prevention programs for women, adolescents and families.

William S. Brasted, M.A., is currently completing an internship in clinical psychology and behavioral medicine at the Medical University of South Carolina and the Veterans Administration Hospital in Charleston, South Carolina. He is a fifth year graduate student in clinical psychology at West Virginia University. He has published articles in the area of behavioral medicine and several chapters related to enhancement of medical care and physician/patient interface.

Nicole Bussod received her B. S. at the University of Washington, Seattle, Washington, where she worked with Dr. Neil S. Jacobson in marital interaction and marital therapy research. She is now a graduate student in Clinical psychology at the University of California, Los Angeles. Her major area of interest is marital and family therapy.

James N. Butcher (Ph.D. 1964 University of North Carolina) is a Professor of Psychology and Director of Graduate Education in Clinical Psychology at the University of Minnesota. His research interests are in objective personality assessment, computerized personality assessment, research in cross-cultural aspects of personality; brief psychotherapy and abnormal psychology. He has published a number of books in the area of abnormal psychology and personality assessment and has contributed numerous articles to journals in psychology and psychiatry. He also serves as editorial consultant to several journals including *Journal of Consulting and Clinical Psychology* and *Journal of Behavioral Assessment.*

Nelson Butters (Ph.D.) is a Research Career Scientist at the Boston VA Medical Center and a Professor of Neurology (Neuropsychology) at the Boston University School of Medicine. After receiving his Ph.D. in Psychology from Clark University in 1964, Dr. Butters spent three years as a Postdoctoral Fellow at the Laboratory of Neuropsychology of the NIMH in Bethesda, Md. Dr. Butters is a Fellow of the American Psychological Association and is currently President of Division 40 of the APA. His present research focuses upon the memory disorders of amnesic and demented patients. He is co-author (with L. S. Cermak) of the book *Alcoholic Korsakoff's Syndrome: An Information Processing Approach to Amnesia.*

Timothy P. Carmody is Assistant Professor of Medical Psychology at the Oregon Health Sciences University. He obtained his Ph.D. in clinical psychology in 1977 from the University of Montana. His primary interest is in the area of health psychology with a major emphasis on coronary heart disease prevention and rehabilitation.

Robert C. Carson is Professor of Psychology and Medical Psychology and Chairman of the Department of Psychology at Duke University. He formerly served as Associate Editor of the *Journal of Consulting and Clinical Psychology*. He is author of *Interaction Concepts of Personality* and co-author of *Abnormal Psychology and Modern Life.* His long-term research interests center on interfaces between social and clinical psychology.

Harry Cole completed his Ph.D. at The Pennsylvania State University and is currently an intern in the Department of Psychiatry, Division of Medical Psychology, at the Duke University Medical Center. His current research consists of evaluating assessment and intervention techniques from a psychophysiological perspective.

Richard A. Depue is Professor of Psychology at the University of Minnesota. He is currently a Consulting Editor to the *Journal of Abnormal Psychology*. His research consists of identifying persons at risk for manic depressive disorder, and of studying predisposition to this disorder in these vulnerable individuals.

Barry A. Edelstein, Ph.D. is Associate Professor of Psychology and Director of Graduate and Clinical Training at West Virginia University. He is also Clinical Associate Professor of Behavioral Medicine and Psychiatry at West Virginia University School of Medicine, Director of Psychology at Spencer Hospital, and President of the West Virginia Psychological Association. He has been a member of the editorial board of *Behavior Modification* and is currently a member of the editorial board of *Clinical Neuropsychology.* His research is in the areas of social competence, clinical interviewing, and behavioral assessment.

Jean M. Edwards is a Research Associate in the Department of Psychology, York University and a psychometrist at Toronto East General Hospital. She received her M.A. degreee from York University in 1973. Her major research interest is in the area of an interactional model of personality.

Norman S. Endler is a professor of psychology, York University. He received his Ph.D. from the University of Illinois in 1958. Dr. Endler has co-edited two books on interactional psychology (N. S. Endler & D. Magnusson (Eds.), *Interactional Psychology and Personality.* Washington, D.C.: Hemiphere Publishing Corporation (Wiley), 1976, and D. Magnusson and N. S. Endler (Eds.), *Personality at the Crossroads: Current Issues in Interactional Psychology.* Hillsdale, N.J.: Lawrence Erlbaum Associates, 1977, as well as written numerous articles on personality, anxiety and social influence. Dr. Endler is a former Chairman, and currently Acting Chairman, of the Psychology Department, York University.

Stephen Finn is a Ph.D. candidate in clinical psychology at the University of Minnesota. His current research interests are in the areas of personality assessment and psychodiagnosis.

Constance T. Fischer is Professor of Psychology at Duquesne University. She is co-editor of *Client Participation in Human Services* (with S. L. Brodsky) and of *Duquesne Studies in Phenomenological Psychology*, Volume 2 (with A. Giorgi & E. Murray), and she is author of the textbook, *Individual-*

izing Psychological Assessment (in press). She is a consulting editor of the *Journal of Phenomenological Psychology*. Her pursuits include part-time private practice of psychotherapy and assessment, development of human-science assessment principles and practices, and applied qualitative research.

William F. Fischer, Ph.D. is a Professor of Psychology at Duquesne University in Pittsburgh, Pa. His phenomenological approach to psychological research is articulated primarily in the areas of anxiety, psychopathology, and self-deception.

Donald G. Forgays is Professor of Psychology at the University of Vermont. He obtained the Ph.D. degree in 1950 from McGill University. His principal research interests concern the influence of the environment on cognitive development and psychopathology.

Cyril M. Franks has been Professor of Psychology at the Graduate School of Applied and Professional Psychology, Rutgers University, since 1970. Prior to this, he was at the New Jersey Neuropsychiatric Institute, Princeton and the University of London Institute of Psychiatry, from whence he obtained his Ph.D. Co-founder and First President of the Association for Advancement of Behavior Therapy, he served as founding editor of the Association's journal, *Behavior Therapy*, for some nine years. Three decades of past research focused upon the laboratory parameters of conditioning. Current concerns stress the conceptual and empirical foundations of behavior therapy and its ongoing status.

Rohan Ganguli, M.D., received his medical degree from the Christian Medical College, Vellore, India. He completed a psychiatric residency at Memorial University in Newfoundland, Canada and is a Fellow of The Royal College of Physicians and Surgeons of Canada. Since 1978 he has been in Pittsburgh as Assistant Professor of Psychiatry at Western Psychiatric Institute and Clinic. His clinical work and research have been mainly with schizophrenic patients.

Linda R. Gonzales is a doctoral candidate at the clinical-community psychology training program at University of Oregon. Her major interests are in the areas of community psychology and geropsychology.

Robert L. Hale is currently an assistant professor in the Division of Counseling and Educational Psychology (Program in School Psychology) at the Pennsylvania State University. He obtained his Ph.D. from the University of Nebraska in 1979. His major interest is in the assessment of childhood learning disorders.

Sandra L. Harris, Ph.D. is Professor of Psychology in the Department of Psychology and Graduate School of Applied and Professional Psychology at Rutgers, The State University. A graduate of the State University of New York at Buffalo she has worked extensively in the area of developmental disabilities. She is the author of several books including *Families of the Developmentally Disabled: A Guide to Behavioral Intervention*. Her current area of primary research interest is the family of the handicapped child.

Dr. Steven C. Hayes in an Assistant Professor of Psychology at the University of North Carolina at Greensboro. He is an associate editor of the *Journal of Applied Behavior Analysis*, and is on the editorial boards of the *Journal of Consulting and Clinical Psychology, Behavior Modification*, and *Behavioral Assessment*. His research has been in self-control, cognitive therapy, single case designs, behavioral assessment, sexual behavior, and environmental problems.

Stephen N. Haynes is Professor of Psychology at Southern Illinois University at Carbondale. He has published several books and research artricles on behavioral assessment, psychosomatic disorders, and marital distress.

Robert Hays received his doctorate in social psychology from the University of Oregon in 1982 and is now a post-doctoral fellow at the University of Utah. His research interests include interpersonal processes and applications of social psychology to mental health issues.

Knoxice C. Hunter is a master's level clinical psychology graduate student currently on internship at the Charleston Veterans Administration Hospital. She has published articles in the areas of emergency care and social anxiety. Her areas of interest include post-traumatic stress disorders of Vietnam veterans and obesity.

Neil S. Jacobson, Ph.D. is a faculty member in the Department of Psychology, University of Washington, Seattle, Washington. He is coauthor (along with Gayla Margolin) of the book *Marital therapy: Strategies based on social learning and behavior exchange principles.* He has also published a number of articles and book chapters in the areas of marital interaction and therapy from a behavioral perspective, depression, and design considerations in behavior modification research. In addition to his position as the associate editor of *the American Journal of Family Therapy,* he serves as an editorial board member and editorial consultant for a number of other journals.

Jeanette M. Jerrell, Ph.D. is Assistant Professor of Psychiatry and Psychology at Western Psychiatric Institute and Clinic, University of Pittsburgh School of Medicine. She is the author of several articles and chapters on the practice of consultation and the evaluation of consultative interventions in mental health, educational and industrial settings.

Jack O. Jenkins is an associate professor of Psychology of the University of Georgia. He has published articles in the area of social skills and Black Psychology. He received his Masters and Doctoral degrees at the University of Georgia.

Barbara Pendleton Jones, Ph.D., is Assistant Clinical Professor of Psychiatry and Behavioral Sciences at George Washington University School of Medicine and Health Sciences in Washington, D.C. Her research interests include cognitive impairment in psychiatric patients and sensory deficits associated with cerebral lesions.

Alan E. Kazdin (Ph.D., Northwestern University) is Professor of Child Psychiatry and Psychology and Research Director of the Child Psychiatric Treatment Service in the Department of Psychiatry, Western Psychiatric Institute and Clinic, University of Pittsburgh School of Medicine. He has been a past President of the Association for Advancement of Behavior Therapy, a Fellow of the Center for Advanced Study in the Behavioral Sciences, and Editor of *Behavior Therapy.* His books include: *Research Design in Clinical Psychology, Single-Case Research Designs, Behavior Modification in Applied Settings,* and the *History of Behavior Modification.* Dr. Kazdin's current re-

search focuses on the assessment and treatment of childhood psychopathology, particularly depression and conduct disorder.

Philip C. Kendall, Ph.D. is Professor of Psychology at the University of Minnesota, Minneapolis, Minnesota. He currently is Associate Editor of *Cognitive Therapy and Research* and has been Associate Editor of *Behavior Therapy.* He is coauthor (with Julian Norton-Ford) of *Clinical Psychology: Scientific and Professional Dimensions* and (with Cyril Franks, G. Terence Wilson and Kelly Brownell) *Annual Review of Behavior Therapy* (Vol. 8) and coeditor (with Steven Hollon) of *Cognitive-Behavioral Interventions: Theory, Research, and Procedures* and *Assessment Strategies for Cognitive-Behavioral Interventions.* Dr. Kendall has been a Fellow at the Center for Advanced Study in the Behavioral Sciences and, presently, is engaged in research evaluating cognitive disorders and deficits in child psychopathology.

James G. Kelly, Ph.D. is Professor of Psychology and Public Health, University of Illinois, Chicago. He is an Associate Editor of the *American Journal of Community Psychology* and Consulting Editor for the *Journal of Applied Psychology* and *Journal of Primary Prevention.* He is a former President of Division 27 and Division 18 of APA, and a recipient of the Division 27 award for Distinguished Contributions to Community Psychology and Community Mental Health. His research interests are related to the design of preventive interventions, and the influence of social structure upon coping, efficacy and empowerment skills.

Charles A. Kiesler is Bingham Professor and Head of the Department of Psychology at Carnegie-Mellon University. He was formerly Executive Officer of the American Psychological Association. An experimental social psychologist by training, his recent research interests have been in mental health and public policy.

Robert H. Klein, Ph.D., is Associate Professor of Psychology in Psychiatry at Yale University School of Medicine, and is Director of Education and Training at the Yale Psychiatric Institute. He serves on the editorial board of the *International Journal of Group Psychotherapy* and is an editorial consultant for several other journals. His current research involves evaluating the process and outcome of intensive, long-term psychiatric treatment for severely disturbed patients.

Sheldon J. Korchin is Professor of Psychology at the University of California, Berkeley. He is the author of *Modern Clinical Psychology* and coauthor (with Basowitz, Persky, and Grinker) of *Anxiety and Stress* and (with E.E. Jones) of *University Mental Health.* He is a diplomate of the American Board of Professional Psychology, has served on various APA Boards, NIMH Research Review Committees, and Editorial Boards of scientific journals. He has twice held Fulbright Awards, is a member of the National Academy of Practice and, in 1978, was awarded the APA Division of Clinical Psychology's "Award for Distinguished Contribution to the Service and Practice of Clinical Psychology."

Thomas R. Kratochwill is Professor of Educational Psychology in the School Psychology Program at The University of Arizona. He currently is an associate editor of *Behavior Therapy* and serves on the editorial boards of several journals. He has written in the area of behavioral assessment and treatment of childhood disorders. His research interests include behavioral assessment, consultation, and research methodology in behavior therapy.

Anna C. Lee, Ph.D., is currently a psychologist at Hospital for Special Surgery and a faculty member in the Division of Psychology, Department of Psychiatry, Cornell University Medical Center, New York. She is also Vice-President of the Association for Play Therapy and author of a chapter on sex-role development to appear in the *Implications of Non-Clinical Research for Clinical Practice.* She is a candidate in Analytic Training at the New York University, Post-Doctoral Program in Psychotherapy and Psychoanalysis. Dr. Lee maintains a private practice in New York City.

Howard D. Lerner, Ph.D. is Assistant Professor of Psychiatry, University of Michigan Medical Center. He is co-editor of the book *Borderline Phenomena and the Rorschach Test.* His present research consists of assessing patterns of object relations among psychiatrically disturbed children, adolescents and adults.

Leon H. Levy, Professor of Psychology and Chairperson at the University of Maryland Baltimore County, received his Ph.D. in 1954 from the Ohio State University. He is author of *Psychological In-*

terpretation and *Conceptions of Personality: Theories and Research* and has published numerous articles and book chapters on topics in personality and clinical psychology, most recently focusing on self-help groups.

A. W. Logue is an Assistant Professor of Psychology at the State University of New York at Stony Brook. She has published a number of articles and chapters on the experimental analysis of self-control, choice, illness-induced food aversion learning, and the history of behaviorism.

F. Charles Mace is a pre-doctoral fellow at the John F. Kennedy Institute and the Johns Hopkins University School of Medicine. His research interests include applied behavior analysis with children, developmental disabilities, treatment of aggression, behavioral assessment methods and applied research methodology.

Joseph D. Matarazzo is Professor of Medical Psychology and Chairman of the Department of Medical Psychology in the School of Medicine, Oregon Health Sciences University. He is the author or co-author of textbooks in the areas of intelligence, the interview, and nonverbal communication and is Editor-in-Chief of the soon to be published *Behavioral Health: A Handbook of Health Enhancement and Disease Prevention.*

Richard K. Mcgee, Ph.D., is Chief of the Health Counseling & Rehabilitation Branch, Division of Medical Services, of the Tennessee Valley Authority. He was formerly Professor, Department of Clinical Psychology at the University of Florida, where he organized and managed the Suicide and Crisis Intervention Service, and directed the Center for Crisis Intervention Research. He has been an editorial board member for the *Journal of Community Psychology and Suicide and Life-Threatening Behavior.*

Scott M. Monroe is Assistant Professor of Psychology at the University of Pittsburgh. He obtained his Doctorate at the State University of New York at Buffalo in 1979. His major interest is in the implications of psychosocial stress for psychological and physical disorders.

Kevin J. O'Connor, Ph.D., is a staff psychologist at Blythedale Children's Hospital in Valhalla, New York. Dr. O'Connor maintains a private practice in Katonah, New York. He is President of the Association for Play Therapy and co-editor of the *Handbook of Play Therapy*. His major interest is in conducting psychotherapy outcome research with children.

Howard Rachlin received his B.E. in mechanical engineering from Cooper Union in 1956, his M.A. in psychology from The New School for Social Research in 1962, and his Ph.D. in psychology from Harvard University in 1965. He taught at Harvard from 1965 until 1969. He is Professor of Psychology at the State University of New York at Stony Brook where he has been teaching since 1969. His interests include self-control, the interaction of economics and psychology, the matching law, the psychology of eating and drinking, and the philosophy of psychology.

James M. Raczynski received his Ph.D. from the Pennsylvania State University and is presently at the University of Alabama at Birmingham. He is a co-author of *Evaluation of Clinical Biofeedback*. His research interests include psychophysiology and behavioral medicine.

William J. Ray is an Associate Professor of Psychology at The Pennsylvania State University. His research interest involves the interface between clinical psychology and psychophysiology/neuropsychology. Recent books include *Biofeedback: Potential and Limits* (with R. M. Stern); *Psychophysiological Recording* (with R. M. Stern & C. M. Davis): *Evaluation of Clinical Biofeedback* (with Raczynski, T. Rogers, & W. Kimball): and *Methods Toward a Science of Behavior and Experience* (with R. Ravizza).

Charles E. Schaefer, Ph.D. is Associate Director of Psychological Services at The Children's Village, Dobbs Ferry, New York. He has published a number of articles and books relating to childrearing, child psychotherapy, and creative thinking. He is co-founder and Chairman of the Board of the Association for Play Therapy (APT). APT is an international society dedicated to the development of play therapy as a therapeutic modality.

Herbert C. Schulberg, Ph.D. is Professor of Psychiatry and Psychology at the University of Pittsburgh School of Medicine, and Director, Social and Community Psychiatry Program, Western Psychiatric Institute and Clinic. He serves as Vice-President of the American College of Mental Health Administration and his interests are in the planning and evaluation of mental health service delivery systems.

June Sprock, M. S. is a graduate student in clinical psychology at the University of Florida. She obtained her M.S. in 1980 from San Diego State University. Her major areas of interest are psychopathology, especially the affective disorders, and classification.

Hans H. Strupp is Distinguished Professor of Psychology, Vanderbilt University, Nashville, Tennessee. He has been President of the Society for Psychotherapy Research and the Division of Clinical Psychology of the American Psychological Association. He has been engaged in psychotherapy research for thirty years.

Hugh B. Urban has been associated with The Pennsylvania State University throughout most of his career, earning both his M.S. and Ph.D. degrees in Clinical Psychology at that institution and subsequently returning to join its faculty. He has maintained an interest in personality theory, particularly as it applies to treatment and intervention. He has co-authored (with D. H. Ford) the book *Systems of psychotherapy: A comparative approach,* and has contributed a number of chapters in edited compendia dealing with psychotherapy and behavior change. He is presently serving as Professor of Human Development and Psychology, with the focus of his work devoted to the analysis of human functioning from a systems perspective, and the use of systems engineering approaches to the design, development, and evaluation of treatment.

Irving B. Weiner is a Vice Chancellor for Academic Affairs and Professor of Psychology at the University of Denver. He previously served as Dean of the School of Graduate Studies and as Chairman of the Department of Psychology at Case Western Reserve University. He is the author of *Psychodiagnosis in Schizophrenia, Psychological Disturbance in Adolescence, Principles of Psychotherapy,* and *Child and Adolescent Psychopathology;* co-author of *Rorschach Handbook of Clinical and Research Applications, Child Development: A Core Approach, Development of the Child,* and *The Rorschach Comprehensive System,* Volume 3, *Assessment of Children and Ado-*

lescents; and editor of *Readings in Child Development* and *Clinical Methods in Psychology.*

Arthur N. Wiens is Professor of Medical Psychology at the Oregon Health Sciences University. His interests include professional education and credentialing and he is a past president of the American Association of State Psychology Boards. He has published in the area of nonverbal communication. His present research is on assessment and psychotherapeutic interviewing, treatment outcome and clinical health psychology.

Pergamon General Psychology Series

Editors: Arnold P. Goldstein, Syracuse University
Leonard Krasner, SUNY at Stony Brook